The Handbook of
Organizational
Economics

The Handbook of Organizational Economics

Edited by

ROBERT GIBBONS and **JOHN ROBERTS**

PRINCETON UNIVERSITY PRESS

Princeton and Oxford

Library of Congress Cataloging-in-Publication Data

The handbook of organizational economics / edited by Robert Gibbons and John Roberts.
    p.   cm.
  Includes bibliographical references and indexes.
  ISBN 978-0-691-13279-2 (hbk. : alk. paper)
  1. Industrial organization (Economic theory)   2. Organizational sociology—Economic aspects.
3. Organizational behavior—Economic aspects. I. Gibbons, Robert, 1958– II. Roberts, John, 1945 Feb. 11–
HD2326.H285   2013
338.5—dc23   2012033072

British Library Cataloging-in-Publication Data is available

This book has been composed in Adobe Garamond Premier Pro with Officina Sans display using ZzTEX
by Princeton Editorial Associates Inc., Scottsdale, Arizona.

Printed on acid-free paper. ∞

Printed in the United States of America

10 9 8 7 6 5 4 3 2 1

CONTENTS

PART VI   BEYOND FIRMS

CONTRIBUTORS

Pierre Azoulay
Massachusetts Institute of Technology, Sloan
   School of Management
National Bureau of Economic Research

George P. Baker
Harvard University, Graduate School of
   Business Administration
National Bureau of Economic Research

Abhijit Banerjee
Massachusetts Institute of Technology,
   Department of Economics
National Bureau of Economic Research

James N. Baron
Yale University, School of Management

Patrick Bolton
Columbia University, Department of
   Economics and Graduate School of
   Business

Timothy Bresnahan
Stanford University, Department of
   Economics
Stanford Institute for Economic Policy
   Research
National Bureau of Economic Research

Erik Brynjolfsson
Massachusetts Institute of Technology, Sloan
   School of Management
National Bureau of Economic Research

Colin F. Camerer
California Institute of Technology, Division
   of Humanities and Social Sciences

Mathias Dewatripont
Université Libre de Bruxelles, Department of
   Economics

Luis Garicano
London School of Economics, Departments
   of Economics and Management

Robert Gertner
University of Chicago, Booth School of
   Business

Robert Gibbons
Massachusetts Institute of Technology, Sloan
   School of Management and Department
   of Economics
National Bureau of Economic Research

Ricard Gil
Johns Hopkins University, Carey Business
   School

Rema Hanna
Harvard University, Kennedy School of
  Government
National Bureau of Economic Research

Henry Hansmann
Yale University, School of Law

Rebecca Henderson
Harvard University, Graduate School of
  Business Administration
National Bureau of Economic Research

Benjamin E. Hermalin
University of California, Berkeley,
  Department of Economics and Haas
  School of Business

Casey Ichniowski
Columbia University, Graduate School of
  Business
National Bureau of Economic Research

Lewis A. Kornhauser
New York University, School of Law

David M. Kreps
Stanford University, Graduate School of
  Business

Francine Lafontaine
University of Michigan, Ross School of
  Business

Edward P. Lazear
Stanford University, Graduate School of
  Business
Hoover Institution
Stanford Institute for Economic Policy
  Research
National Bureau of Economic Research

Josh Lerner
Harvard University, Graduate School of
  Business Administration
National Bureau of Economic Research

Jonathan Levin
Stanford University, Department of
  Economics
Stanford Institute for Economic Policy
  Research
National Bureau of Economic Research

W. Bentley MacLeod
Columbia University, Department of
  Economics and School of Public Policy
  and International Affairs
National Bureau of Economic Research
IZA

James M. Malcomson
University of Oxford, Department of
  Economics and All Souls College

Niko Matouschek
Northwestern University, Kellogg School of
  Management

Claude Ménard
University of Paris Panthéon-Sorbonne,
  Department of Economics and Centre
  d'Économie de la Sorbonne

Paul Milgrom
Stanford University, Department of
  Economics
Stanford Institute for Economic Policy
  Research

Terry M. Moe
Stanford University, Department of Political Science
Hoover Institution

Dilip Mookherjee
Boston University, Department of Economics

Sendhil Mullainathan
Harvard University, Department of
  Economics
National Bureau of Economic Research

Paul Oyer
Stanford University, Graduate School of Business
National Bureau of Economic Research

John Roberts
Stanford University, Graduate School of Business
Stanford Institute for Economic Policy Research

Garth Saloner
Stanford University, Graduate School of Business

David Scharfstein
Harvard University, Graduate School of Business Administration
National Bureau of Economic Research

Ilya Segal
Stanford University, Department of Economics

Kathryn Shaw
Stanford University, Graduate School of Business
National Bureau of Economic Research

Margaret E. Slade
University of British Columbia, Department of Economics

Steven Tadelis
University of California, Berkeley, Haas School of Business

Timothy Van Zandt
INSEAD, Department of Economics

Michael Waldman
Cornell University, Johnson Graduate School of Management and Department of Economics

Roberto A. Weber
University of Zurich, Department of Economics

Michael D. Whinston
Northwestern University, Department of Economics

Oliver E. Williamson
University of California, Berkeley, Haas School of Business, Department of Economics, and School of Law

The Handbook of Organizational Economics

Introduction

Robert Gibbons and John Roberts

Organizational economics involves the use of economic logic and methods to understand the existence, nature, design, and performance of organizations, especially managed ones. As this handbook documents, economists working on organizational issues have now generated a large volume of exciting research, both theoretical and empirical. However, organizational economics is not yet a fully recognized field in economics—for example, it has no *Journal of Economic Literature* classification number, and few doctoral programs offer courses in it. The intent of this handbook is to make the existing research in organizational economics more accessible to economists and thereby to promote further research and teaching in the field.

The Origins of Organizational Economics

As Kenneth Arrow (1974: 33) put it, "organizations are a means of achieving the benefits of collective action in situations where the price system fails," thus including not only business firms but also consortia, unions, legislatures, agencies, schools, churches, social movements, and beyond. All organizations, Arrow (1974: 26) argued, share "the need for collective action and the allocation of resources through nonmarket methods," suggesting a range of possible structures and processes for decisionmaking in organizations, including dictatorship, coalitions, committees, and much more.

Within Arrow's broad view of the possible purposes and designs of organizations, many distinguished economists can be seen as having addressed organizational issues during the first two centuries of the discipline. For example, Adam Smith (1977) famously was concerned about moral hazard and free riding by directors of joint-stock companies, and his pin factory is a discussion of job design. A century after the initial publication of Smith's volume, in the first volume of the *Quarterly Journal of Economics*, the founding president of the American Economic Association, Francis Walker (1887), argued that differences in the quality of management account for persistent intra-industry differences in productivity and profitability. Frank Knight (1921) discussed entrepreneurship and the nature of the firm, which he saw as an institution in which the more uncertainty-averse worked for fixed wages, whereas the entrepreneur bore the risk but had authority over the employees. Berle and Means (1932) described conflicts of interest arising from the separation of corporate ownership by shareholders from corporate control by top managers. Ronald Coase (1937) raised the question of the boundaries of the firm, arguing that economizing on the costs of transacting would determine what was done in the market versus under hierarchic control.

Herbert Simon (1951) offered perhaps the first formal model in organizational economics, treating the employment relationship as the use of authority rather than as contracting in response to uncertainty and the need for adaptation. Edith Penrose (1959) studied managerial activities and decisionmaking, organizational routines, and knowledge creation in firms and argued that these are critical determinants of the success and growth of the firm. Alfred Chandler (1962, 1977) documented the historical emergence of the modern corporation and professional management.

At the edges of economics, there was related work in organizational theory. Chester Barnard (1938) was one of the earliest contributors, seeing organizations as systems of collaborative activity and discussing the roles of incentives and authority in the formal and informal aspects of organization. Building on Barnard, the Carnegie School then focused on two major issues: bounded rationality and conflict of interests. Simon (1947) and March and Simon (1958) asked how the organization can orchestrate the acquisition and communication of information and the allocation of decisionmaking so as to produce a tolerable outcome for the organization when its members are boundedly rational. Cyert and March (1963: 30) argued that "people (i.e., individuals) have goals; collectivities of people do not" and that "since the existence of unresolved conflict is a conspicuous feature of organizations, it is exceedingly difficult to construct a useful positive theory of organizational decision making if we insist on internal goal consistency." Instead, March (1962) described "The Business Firm as a Political Coalition."

Reflecting on these early developments, Arrow (1964: 397–398) noted that "the large organization, so prominent on our contemporary social landscape, is of great antiquity. . . . But it is perhaps only in our era, and even then haltingly, that the rational design of organization has become a subject of inquiry." Around 1970, however, the field began to take off.

Many important contributions in the 1970s concerned the nature and boundaries of the firm. Oliver Williamson (1971, 1975) proposed a theory of the replacement of market dealings by authority in the firm, based on the potential for inefficient haggling when unplanned adaptations are required. In contrast, Armen Alchian and Harold Demsetz (1972) argued against the idea that the firm is a manifestation of authority, proposing instead that the firm was best viewed as a collection of contracts. George Richardson (1972) undercut the simple firm-versus-market dichotomy by accentuating the great variety of organizational forms and relationships between firms that actually populate the economy, and he wrote convincingly of the role of capabilities—information, knowledge, and skills—in determining the effectiveness of activities in and between firms. And Benjamin Klein et al. (1978) and Williamson (1979) explored the consequences of specific assets and hold-up for firms' make-or-buy decisions and contracting between firms.

Other important contributions were focused within organizations. Arrow's (1974) beautiful little book addressed topics ranging from authority and codes to responsibility, trust, and values. Richard Nelson and Sydney Winter (1982) wrote in evolutionary terms about organizational routines that enable the organization to do what it does (and hence may convey competitive advantage or its opposite). And Michael Jensen and William Meckling (1976) provided the first treatment of agency costs as a necessary consequence of the separation of ownership from control.

In formal modeling, Jacob Marschak and Roy Radner (1972) modeled optimal communication and decisionmaking processes in uncertain environments with dispersed information but shared objectives. Leonid Hurwicz (1973) introduced the concept of incentive compatibility and initiated mechanism-design theory, where the institutions used to allocate resources become a choice variable, thereby setting the stage for economic analysis of organizational design. And James Mirrlees (1975/1999) and Bengt Holmström (1979) introduced formal models of moral hazard, launching a literature that would have tremendous influence on organizational economics.

What Are the Questions Addressed by Organizational Economics?

These early contributions laid the foundations for the work that has emerged in the past 30 years, which is the focus of this handbook. Extrapolating from this early work suggests a wide range of issues for organizational economics, including the following.[1] What are the vertical boundaries of the organization? How are relations with suppliers and customers organized? Who owns which assets, and how are the activities of the organization financed? How is governance defined and exercised, both internally, within the organization, and by external parties with ownership claims? What are the horizontal boundaries of the firm (i.e., what businesses is it in)? How are departments and divisions defined? How are resources of different types allocated? What is the role of hierarchy, how many levels are there, and what are the spans of control? Is the organization an expression of authority or a nexus of contracts? What are the roles of formal versus relational contracts in the organization? Where does decisionmaking occur in the organization? How is power achieved and exercised, and what role does politics play in organizations? What information is collected, by whom, to whom is it communicated, and how is it used? How are people recruited, trained, and assigned to jobs? How is performance measured? How are people rewarded? What effects do rewards have on behavior? What norms exist regarding behavior toward others in the organization, as well as outsiders, and how do these norms affect behavior and organizational performance? How do other aspects of corporate culture manifest themselves and affect behavior? What is the nature and role of leadership in organizations? And, finally, how do the answers to these questions depend on the markets in which the organization operates; the strategies it adopts to compete; and the social, legal, regulatory, and technological environment in which it is embedded; and how do all these choices interact and affect performance?

Related Fields

Given this agenda, it is clear that organizational economics overlaps with many other fields in economics, as well as with a variety of other disciplines in the social sciences and management.

In economics, there is a large intersection with personnel economics, which studies the relationship between employer and employee and the economics of managing human resources

---

1. We phrase these questions in positive terms, but their normative versions are equally important.

in firms. Industrial organization also has significant overlaps, sharing interest in the vertical and horizontal scope of the firm, supplier relations, and other contracts between firms, and the impact of compensation on firm behavior. More recently, international economics has begun investigating outsourcing and offshoring, as well as the multinational corporation, all of which raise organizational issues. In addition, development economics is studying the role of firms in economic growth, including the effects on their productivity of improving their organization and management and relaxing financial constraints. And researchers studying different economic systems and the transition from one to another—both historically and today—also share interests with organizational economics.

There are also important connections with disciplines beyond economics. The law literature has central interests in contracts and in governance. Social psychology is concerned with motivation, decisionmaking, and culture. Organizational sociology (and, more recently, economic sociology) studies the sociology of economic institutions, including firms, markets, and networks. And political science studies decision processes in government agencies, legislatures, communities, and more. However, this handbook focuses more on making organizational economics accessible to economists and hence less on forging the connections to other disciplines that ultimately could and should be made; see the Smelser and Swedberg (2005) *Handbook of Economic Sociology* for surveys of work in one social science and Ostrom (1990) for a leading example of work from another.

In business schools, scholars in organizational behavior have not only harnessed the insights of psychology and sociology to understand firms, they have also developed large bodies of research on issues ranging from compensation and job design to leadership and organizational change. And the overlaps between organizational economics and other areas of management are also significant. Corporate finance is concerned with the allocation of resources within the firm, the effects of the financing of the firm on managerial behavior, and issues of corporate governance. Managerial accounting is also concerned with resource allocation inside firms and with internal governance, as well as with acquiring and communicating information and with performance measurement and pay. Marketing addresses relations with suppliers and customers and also the management of sales forces. And strategy studies organizational capabilities (as a source of competitive advantage) and the vertical and horizontal boundaries of the firm (as a problem of corporate strategy). As with social sciences beyond economics, this handbook barely begins to explore the current and potential connections with management fields; see Baum's (2002) *Companion to Organizations* for surveys of work in organizational behavior and related fields.

Outline of the Handbook

Beyond this introduction, the handbook consists of six parts. Part I contains foundational material. Erik Brynjolfsson and Paul Milgrom survey the theory and econometrics of complementarity, seen as an alternative to the usual assumptions of microeconomics (concavity, divisibility, etc.) that allows modeling organizational questions with great richness and still permits drawing strong conclusions. Ilya Segal and Michael Whinston organize a broad literature on property rights and break new ground on this central issue in organizational economics. Steven Tadelis and Oliver Williamson discuss the theoretical and empirical literatures on transaction cost economics and develop a formal model that yields new insights. In addition, we offer an exposition of the means of motivating people in organizations, focusing on agency and performance contracting, but also mentioning nonfinancial means of motivating behavior.

Part II describes three empirical methods that loom large in organizational economics but may not be completely familiar to those not involved in the field. George Baker and Ricard Gil examine the role of clinical or case studies in organizational economics, arguing that (ever since the discussion of Fisher Body in Klein et al. [1978]) case studies can and do play a vital role in the process of scientific investigation and suggesting what characteristics of such studies make them particularly valuable. Colin Camerer and Roberto Weber discuss the role of experiments in studying organizational issues, describing a number of such studies and again explicating what makes for a good experimental study. Finally, Casey Ichniowski and Kathryn Shaw discuss insider econometrics, which involves careful econometric analysis of data whose collection inside organizations is guided by detailed knowledge of the phenomena gained both from insiders (managers and other employees) and from personal observation.

Each part in the remainder of the handbook then focuses on a specific set of organizational issues. Part III studies individuals and groups in organizations. It involves three contributions on employment by James Baron and David Kreps, by Edward Lazear and Paul Oyer, and by Michael Waldman; two chapters on authority, power, politics, and influence by Patrick Bolton and Mathias Dewatripont and by Niko Matouschek and ourselves; and an essay on culture and leadership by Benjamin Hermalin. The three chapters on employment illustrate the significant intersection between organizational economics and personnel economics, as well as connections to economic sociology and human resource management. The other three chapters in Part III can be seen as discussing different aspects of decisionmaking in organizations, often echoing Barnard (1938) and the Carnegie School's view of "the organization as a decision-making process" (Cyert and March 1963: 202), in which individuals compete for resources, power, and influence, and information is a strategic tool.

Part IV studies structures and processes in organizations, with two chapters on hierarchy by Luis Garicano and Timothy Van Zandt and by Dilip Mookherjee, and individual chapters on innovation and organization by Pierre Azoulay and Josh Lerner, on corporate governance by Benjamin Hermalin, on strategy and organization by John Roberts and Garth Saloner, on resource allocation by Robert Gertner and David Scharfstein, and on organizational capability by Robert Gibbons and Rebecca Henderson. The two chapters on hierarchy are complements, in that Garicano–Van Zandt follows the emphasis in Simon (1947), March and Simon (1958), and Marschak and Radner (1972) on the acquisition and communication of information, to the exclusion of incentive issues, whereas Mookherjee focuses entirely on the ways in which hierarchy may either ameliorate or exacerbate incentive issues (especially when Hurwicz's [1973] mechanism-design approach seems to offer a centralized method for all organizational communication and decisionmaking). The Azoulay-Lerner and Hermalin chapters—on innovation and corporate governance—connect to other fields in economics, such as growth on the one hand and law and economics on the other, with Azoulay-Lerner building on themes from Knight (1921) and Penrose (1959), and Hermalin on themes from Smith (1977) and Jensen and Meckling (1976). And the Roberts-Saloner, Gertner-Scharfstein, and Gibbons-Henderson chapters—on strategy, resource allocation, and capabilities—connect to management research on strategy, corporate finance, and managerial practices, echoing Walker (1887), Penrose (1959), Chandler (1962, 1977), and Nelson and Winter (1982).

Part V considers the boundary of the firm, contracts between firms, and multifirm governance structures, with chapters by Timothy Bresnahan and Jonathan Levin on vertical integration, Francine Lafontaine and Margaret Slade on the empirics of contracting between firms, Claude Ménard on hybrid organizations, James Malcomson on relational incentive contracts, Lewis Kornhauser and Bentley MacLeod on contract law and contract economics, and Henry Hansmann on legal forms of organization. The Bresnahan-Levin and Lafontaine-Slade chapters—on vertical integration and contracting—illustrate connections between organizational economics and industrial organization (building on Coase [1937], Williamson [1971, 1975, 1979], and Klein et al. [1978]). And Ménard's chapter on hybrids—such as alliances, joint ventures, and consortia—illustrates the rich middle ground between integration and simple contracting (building on Richardson [1972]). Malcomson's chapter on relational incentive contracts is cast in terms of buyer-supplier relations but applies as well within firms and so complements our chapter on motivation (building on Mirrlees [1975/1999] and Holmström [1979]). And the Kornhauser-MacLeod and Hansmann chapters illustrate connections with the legal literatures on contracts and organizations (connecting to Alchian and Demsetz [1972]).

Finally, although much of the foregoing could be applied to organizations other than firms, Part VI explicitly adopts this focus, with chapters by Abhijit Banerjee, Rema Hanna, and Sendhil Mullainathan on corruption and by Terry Moe on government agencies. The Banerjee et al. chapter applies a mechanism-design approach to understanding both the endogeneity and the net costs and benefits of corruption, illustrating connections to economic development. In contrast, Moe's chapter informally applies ideas about organizational design and performance to understand the complexity (and, at times, seeming perversity) of government agencies, illustrating connections to political science.

What Have We Left Out?

Despite the rich set of studies contained in this volume, there are other issues and areas of research that we see as potentially (and sometimes currently) important to organizational economics but that we could not include here for various reasons.

One of the most exciting of these is econometric investigation of management practices and managers and their impact on productivity and growth in organizations (e.g., Bertrand and Schoar 2003; Bloom and Van Reenen 2007). Closely related to this are field experiments in organizational economics (e.g., Paarsch and Shearer 1999; Bandiera et al. 2011). A very large fraction of the experimental work going on in firms concerns randomized controlled experiments in enterprises in emerging markets. The vast bulk of these studies is in micro and small enterprises (e.g., Bruhn et al. [2012] or the extensive references in Banerjee and Duflo [2011]), although there is also recent work in large companies in these markets (Bloom et al. 2012). More generally, it would be interesting to have more work on the connections between economic organizations and economic development. In addition, more work relating organizations and international economics (including trade, investment, and location choices and the choice of organizational form for multinationals) would be welcome.

Another class of subjects in which we would like to promote more research involves different organizational forms. Legislatures, government bureaus and departments, the courts, political parties, clubs, cooperatives, mutuals, family firms, state-owned enterprises, charities and not-for-profits, hospitals, universities, and schools—all raise interesting organizational issues and deserve more attention than they have received. Particularly prominent in current business school research (largely in operations) is the organization and management of supply chains (e.g., Lee et al. 1997). Finally, we are only too aware that the vast bulk of the work discussed here is rooted implicitly in the institutional context of the English-speaking economies. We would very much like to see this imbalance righted.

Hopes for the Future

To reiterate, our goal in assembling this handbook is to make existing research in organizational economics more accessible to economists. We hope that several things might then follow. First, we see the prospect of a coherent field here—with topics that relate to one another and methods that cut across topics. We hope this handbook's sketch of the field will inspire discussion and elaboration of what organizational economics is and could be. Second, we see exceptional potential for several dialogues—between theoretical and empirical researchers; between research and practice; and between organizational economics, other fields of economics, and other social sciences and management disciplines. We hope this handbook will facilitate those dialogues. Finally, turning from research to teaching, we think it is possible and desirable to teach doctoral courses in organizational economics, thereby preparing new generations of organizational economists who can build on and surpass the exciting developments of the past three decades. We hope the chapters in this handbook will appear in many syllabi—as central elements of courses on organizational economics and as complements to courses on industrial organization, labor, trade, development, and economic history.

REFERENCES

Alchian, Armen, and Harold Demsetz. 1972. "Production, Information Costs, and Economic Organization." *American Economic Review* 62: 316–325.
Arrow, Kenneth. 1964. "Control in Large Organizations." *Management Science* 10: 397–408.
———. 1974. *The Limits of Organization.* New York: W. W. Norton.
Bandiera, Oriana, Iwan Barankay, and Imran Rasul. 2011. "Field Experiments with Firms," *Journal of Economic Perspectives* 25(3): 63–82.
Banerjee, Abhijit, and Esther Duflo. 2011. *Poor Economics: A Radical Rethinking of the Way to Fight Global Poverty.* Philadelphia: Public Affairs.
Barnard, Chester. 1938. *The Functions of the Executive.* Cambridge, MA: Harvard University Press.
Baum, Joel. 2002. *Companion to Organizations.* Oxford: Blackwell.
Berle, Adolf, and Gardiner Means. 1932. *The Modern Corporation and Private Property.* New York: Harcourt, Brace and World.
Bertrand, Marianne, and Antoinette Schoar. 2003. "Managing with Style: The Effect of Managers on Firm Policies." *Quarterly Journal of Economics* 118: 1169–1208.
Bloom, Nicholas, and John Van Reenen. 2007. "Measuring and Explaining Management Practices across Firms and Countries." *Quarterly Journal of Economics* 122: 1351–1408.
Bloom, Nicholas, Benn Eifert, David McKenzie, Aprajit Mahajan, and John Roberts. 2012. "Does Management Matter? Evidence from India." Research Paper 2074 (revised), Stanford University Graduate School of Management, Stanford, CA.

Bruhn, Miriam, Dean Karlan, and Antoinette Schoar. 2012. "The Impact of Consulting Services on Small and Medium Enterprises: Evidence from a Randomized Trial in Mexico." Mimeo, Yale University Department of Economics, New Haven, CT.

Chandler, Alfred. 1962. *Strategy and Structure.* Cambridge, MA: MIT Press.

———. 1977. *The Visible Hand.* Cambridge, MA: Harvard University Press.

Coase, Ronald. 1937. "The Nature of the Firm." *Economica* 4: 386–405.

Cyert, Richard, and James March. 1963. *A Behavioral Theory of the Firm.* Englewood Cliffs, NJ: Prentice-Hall.

Holmström, Bengt. 1979. "Moral Hazard and Observability," *Bell Journal of Economics* 10: 74–91.

Hurwicz, Leonid. 1973. "The Design of Mechanisms for Resource Allocation." *American Economic Review* 63: 1–30.

Jensen, Michael, and William Meckling. 1976. "Theory of the Firm: Managerial Behavior, Agency Costs and Ownership Structure." *Journal of Financial Economics* 3: 305–360.

Klein, Benjamin, Robert Crawford, and Armen Alchian. 1978. "Vertical Integration, Appropriable Rents and the Competitive Contracting Process." *Journal of Law and Economics* 21: 297–326.

Knight, Frank. 1921. *Risk, Uncertainty and Profit.* Boston: Hart, Schaffner and Marx.

Lee, Hau, V. Padmanabhan, and Seungjin Whang. 1997. "Information Distortion in a Supply Chain: The Bullwhip Effect." *Management Science* 43: 546–558.

March, James. 1962. "The Business Firm as a Political Coalition." *Journal of Politics* 24: 662–678.

March, James, and Herbert Simon. 1958. *Organizations.* New York: John Wiley and Sons.

Marschak, Jacob, and Roy Radner. 1972. *Economic Theory of Teams.* New Haven, CT: Yale University Press.

Mirrlees, James. 1975/1999. "The Theory of Moral Hazard and Unobservable Behaviour: Part I." Mimeo, Oxford University. Published in *Review of Economic Studies* 66: 3–21.

Nelson, Richard, and Sidney Winter. 1982. *An Evolutionary Theory of Economic Change.* Cambridge, MA: Harvard University Press.

Ostrom, Elinor. 1990. *Governing the Commons: The Evolution of Institutions for Collective Action.* Cambridge: Cambridge University Press.

Paarsch, Harry, and Bruce Shearer. 1999. "The Response of Worker Effort to Piece Rates: Evidence from the British Columbia Tree-Planting Industry." *Journal of Human Resources* 34: 643–667.

Penrose, Edith. 1959. *The Theory of the Growth of the Firm.* New York: Wiley.

Richardson, George. 1972. "The Organisation of Industry." *Economic Journal* 82: 883–896.

Simon, Herbert. 1947. *Administrative Behavior.* New York: Free Press.

———. 1951. "A Formal Theory of the Employment Relationship." *Econometrica* 19: 293–305.

Smelser, Neil, and Richard Swedberg. 2005. *The Handbook of Economic Sociology,* second edition. Princeton, NJ: Princeton University Press.

Smith, Adam. 1977. *An Inquiry into the Nature and Causes of the Wealth of Nations.* Chicago: University of Chicago Press.

Walker, Francis. 1887. "The Source of Business Profits." *Quarterly Journal of Economics* 1: 265–288.

Williamson, Oliver. 1971. "The Vertical Integration of Production: Market Failure Considerations." *American Economic Review* 61: 112–123.

———. 1975. *Markets and Hierarchies: Analysis and Antitrust Implications.* New York: Free Press.

———. 1979. "Transaction Cost Economics: The Governance of Contractual Relations." *Journal of Law and Economics* 22: 233–261.

PART I

Foundations

1

Complementarity in Organizations

Erik Brynjolfsson and Paul Milgrom

1. Introduction

According to the *American Heritage* dictionary, a *synergy* is "the interaction of two or more agents or forces so that their combined effect is greater than the sum of their individual effects" or "cooperative interaction among groups, especially among the acquired subsidiaries or merged parts of a corporation, that creates an enhanced combined effect." *Complementarity,* as we use the term, is a near synonym for "synergy," but it is set in a decisionmaking context and defined in Section 1.2 with mathematical precision.

Complementarity is an important concept in organizational analysis, because it offers an approach to explaining patterns of organizational practices, how they fit with particular business strategies, and why different organizations choose different patterns and strategies. The formal analysis of complementarity is based on studying the interactions among pairs of interrelated decisions. For example, consider a company that is evaluating a triple of decisions: (i) whether to adopt a strategy that requires implementing frequent changes in its technology, (ii) whether to invest in a flexibly trained workforce, and (iii) whether to give workers more discretion in the organization of their work. Suppose that more-flexibly trained workers can make better use of discretion and that more-flexibly trained and autonomous workers make it easier to implement new technologies effectively, because workers are more likely to know what to do and how to solve problems. Then, there is a complementarity between several pairs of decisions, which is characteristic of a system of complements. The theory of complementarities predicts that these practices will tend to cluster. An organization with one of the practices is more likely to have the others as well. Suppose an organization employs these three practices. Should this organization now adopt job protections, incentive pay, or both? The answer depends in part on the presence or absence of complementarities: if these new practices enhance worker

We thank Josh Mollner, Shachar Reichman, and Adam Saunders for providing useful research assistance; Bob Gibbons and John Roberts for helpful comments; and the National Science Foundation (IIS-0085725 and ITR-0427770) and the Massachusetts Institute of Technology Center for Digital Business for research support.

Table 1. Interactions in a system of complements

Practice	(1)	(2)	(3)	(4)
(1) Make frequent technical changes	■	+	+	+
(2) Train workers flexibly	■	■	+	
(3) Give workers discretion	■	■	■	+
(4) Protect workers' jobs	■	■	■	■
(*) Frequent opportunities to upgrade technology	+			

Notes: The double rule separates the environmental variable from the practices being analyzed. An entry containing a plus symbol indicates a complementary practice to the one listed in the row containing the entry. Entries that do not need to be evaluated are shaded in gray.

cooperation with management in periods of technical change, then they, too, should be part of the same system.

Often there is a related environmental variable that drives an entire system. In our example, suppose the organization operates in an environment that contains frequent, substantial opportunities to upgrade technology to save costs or improve products. Then it would be natural for the organization to favor the first practice—making frequent technical changes. Because of complementarities, this would in turn favor adopting the whole group of practices described above. The clustering of practices, the way choices depend on the environment, and the influence of each practice on the profitability of the others are all empirical propositions that we summarize with our example in Table 1.

Table 1 is a prototype for portraying and discussing the interactions in a system of complements. Each decision about a particular practice is labeled and appears in both a row and a column. We put the environmental variables in the rows below the double rule. In this case, there is just one: the frequency of valuable opportunities to upgrade technologies. To verify the system of complements, it suffices to check just the upper half of the table, because the complementarity relation is symmetric. Also, we can omit checking the diagonal entries, because complementarity is defined in terms of interactions among different decisions. The plus symbols in cells (1, 2) and (1, 3) of the table represent the complementarities that we have hypothesized as present between frequent technical changes and two other labor practices, while the plus in cell (2, 3) represents our hypothesis that flexibly trained workers use discretion more effectively than other workers do. Worker protection aligns workers' long-term interests more closely with the firm's interest, reducing resistance to change and enlisting workers in implementation. That accounts for the plus symbols in cells (1, 4) and (3, 4).

The plus in the last row indicates that the environmental variable directly favors one of the choices and, through the system of complements, indirectly favors all the others. We leave the cells blank when a priori we do not believe there to be a direct interaction. A version of this tool, called the "Matrix of Change," has been used by managers and MBA students to analyze complementarities and thereby assess the feasibility, pace, scope, and location of organizational change efforts (Brynjolfsson et al. 1997).

1.1. Some Applications and Implications

Complementarity ideas can be usefully combined with ideas about the limits to coordination among separate firms to explore the scope of the firm. For example, in the early twentieth century, General Electric (GE) produced a wide array of products based on electric motors. Its intensive research into designing and producing electric motors complemented its strategy of producing a broad range of products using those motors. Improvements in the costs or capabilities of electric motors for one product line increased the probability of improvements for other product lines. Coordinating such variety in a single firm was favored by the concurrent development of a multidivisional organizational architecture.[1]

In addition, the analysis of complementarities can provide insights into organizational dynamics. For example, even when senior executives have a clear vision of a new strategy for a company, managing the change can be difficult or impossible (e.g., Argyris 1982; Siggelkow 2002b; Schein 2004).

Why is organizational change so difficult? Complementarities can provide part of the answer (Milgrom and Roberts 1990, 1992, 1995; Brynjolfsson et al. 1997). When many complementarities among practices exist in an established system, but practices from the established system and those from the new one conflict, then it is likely that the transition will be difficult, especially when decisions are decentralized. Because of the complementarities, changing only one practice, or a small set of them, is likely to reduce overall performance.[2] The natural conclusion is that the organization should change all the practices in the new system simultaneously. However, making these changes all at once can be difficult or infeasible for at least three reasons.

First, there is a basic coordination problem. Actors who control different business practices, assets, markets, and strategies, including some that may be outside the direct control of the firm, need to coordinate on the scope, time, and content of the change. Furthermore, because the exact outcomes and optimal levels of each factor are likely to be at least partially unpredictable, these actors need to continue to agree to and coordinate on any additional adjustments and rent reallocations. All this effort requires accurate communication and an alignment of incentives.

Second, organizations inevitably consist not only of numerous explicit well-defined practices and choices but also many that are implicit or poorly defined. These factors may include the "culture" of the organization and rules of thumb that employees use in completing their tasks. Employees and business partners are likely to continue to act with the same implicit mental

---

1. There can be several explanations for why coordination is often easier within a firm than across firm boundaries. One possibility based in contract theory is that contracting on knowledge inputs is especially difficult. A second possibility based on differences in beliefs (rather than differences in information) is that GE management may have been more confident about the potential of the electric motors technology than managers in similar firms. For each of these explanations, one is led to the conclusion that GE's role as the center for research in electric motors created a complementarity that favored its making a broader range of products.

2. Performance will suffer in absolute terms when adopting practices one at a time for a particular type of complementarity: the case where the benefit from adopting a practice in isolation is negative, even when the benefit from adopting the whole bundle of practices is positive. More generally, performance will increase less than proportionately whenever the sum of the benefits of adopting isolated practices is less than the benefit from adopting them as a bundle—in other words, whenever complementarities are present.

models, assumptions, and heuristics, despite changes in the explicit practices. Even if changes of all known practices are coordinated, the organization may end up worse off if the implicit practices are unchanged.

Third, even if a sufficient set of the relevant changes can be identified and defined, and all the relevant actors agree on an action plan (or the decision rights are re-assigned to a group that is in agreement), the timing of change can present difficulties. Because some variables (e.g., building a new plant, hiring and training new employees, or developing a new brand or reputation) take time, it will be difficult to synchronize all the changes. Some will need to start earlier than others (Jovanovic and Stolyarov 2000). Furthermore, when resources are limited and changes are costly, a firm may not have the capacity to do everything at once but must instead phase in the changes.

Each of these types of difficulties has distinct implications for firm and industry dynamics, favoring different subpopulations of organizational types and predicting different trajectories for technical and organizational change. For instance, if firms evolve more complex interdependent structures over time (e.g., Baron et al. 1999), then one might expect older firms to have more difficulty in adapting to rapid unpredictable changes in the environment insofar as this would require changing more complementary practices. If other conditions are right, start-ups might thrive in dynamic or volatile industries.

Thus, the complementarities framework is suitable for modeling situations where combinations of practices can lead to multiple local maxima, such as when the payoff function is discontinuous or the practices are discrete variables that cannot be adjusted continuously. These situations are characteristic of the "rugged landscapes" described by Levinthal (1997) and Rivkin (2000), where adaption and imitation can be difficult. In contrast, as noted by Roberts (2004), much of the standard economic treatment of firms assumes that performance is a concave function of a set of infinitely divisible design choices, and the constraint set is convex. Under these conditions, decisionmakers can experiment incrementally to gradually identify an optimal combination of practices.

The transition difficulties identified with complementarities also imply distinct managerial approaches. In some cases, it may make sense to reassign responsibilities and modularize activities. In other cases, change may be so difficult that it is best to start fresh at a greenfield site or an isolated skunkworks (i.e., a separate subsidiary or new spin-off). Some changes may simply be too costly to pursue for an organization starting with a given set of practices.

The insights into organizational change provided by complementarities also illuminate the difficulties firms have in imitating successful competitors. Such firms as Lincoln Electric, Walmart, or Toyota enjoyed sustained periods of high performance. As a result, they were intensively studied by competitors, consultants, and researchers, and many of their methods were documented in great detail. Nonetheless, even when competitors aggressively sought to imitate these methods, they did not have the same degree of success as these market leaders. Complementarities in organizations can help explain why. As noted by Rivkin (2000), it can be exceedingly difficult to search through a space of strategies with numerous elements that are complementary, and imitators may suffer large penalties from even small errors in attempting to match a particular combination of practices. Subtle complementarities can make imitation difficult even across plants in the same firm, where the participants are working to facilitate knowledge transfer, let alone across firm boundaries. Intel now follows a "copy-exactly" policy when new chip fabs are built. Previously, when the company copied only those elements of a previous fab that managers thought were important, the new fabs experienced much lower yields for several months. Rather than try to identify and implement each of the missing complementary elements of the coherent system, the copy-exactly approach replicates every element of the old fab, down to the choice of paint color and orientation of windows, regardless of whether it has any known relationship to the chip fabrication process.

Yet another related issue is mergers and acquisitions. When two organizations are combined, each brings with it a set of explicit and implicit business methods. Complementarities within and between these systems will influence how successful such a merger is likely to be, and whether one or the other organization will need to make significant changes to avoid a decline in performance. For example, Cisco Systems, a company that engages in frequent acquisitions, has implemented an explicit process for changing all acquired firms' processes to match Cisco's. The company has employed a director of culture, who issues "culture badges" to all employees in recognition of the complementarity of culture to the functioning of the rest of their systems.

1.2. Using Theory and Data to Study Complementarities

To define complementarity mathematically, we focus initially on the decision of a profit-maximizing firm that is considering changing one or both of two practices. The first assumption is that if it is possible to make the changes separately, it must be possible to make them together.

Definition *Let Δ_1 and Δ_2 be the increase in profits that would result from changing either alone, and let Δ_B be the increase that results from doing both together. Any Δ can be positive or negative and can depend on the other choices that the firm makes. The two changes are (weakly) complementary if $\Delta_B \geq \Delta_1 + \Delta_2$, regardless of the firm's other choices.*

If one or both changes involves setting the level of a variable, such as the number of workers or the amount of capital to be employed, then the relevant change is understood to be an increase in that level. For example, in the neoclassical theory of the firm, capital and labor inputs to production are complementary if the increase in output from raising both inputs together exceeds the sum from increasing either separately.[3]

The notion of complementarity can be extended to evaluate a larger set of practices or changes. If all combinations of changes are possible, then a set of changes is complementary if each pair in the set is complementary. In practice, this definition means that checking complementarity involves checking the entries of a table like Table 1. The full formal definition in which only some combinations are possible is postponed to the next section.

The formal definitions lead to a set of ten theorems about systems of complements (see Section 2). Importantly for the applications we have in mind, the theorems depend on complementarity alone; none depends on such additional assumptions as convexity of the feasible set or

---

3. For a firm choosing levels of two inputs, the textbook economic definition of complements is a property of the demand function. It holds that the two inputs are complements if an increase in the price of one leads to a decrease in the demand for the other. If the firm's technology is strictly convex, so that the firm's demand at any price vector is unique and the demand function is continuous, then inputs are complements in our sense if and only if they are demand-theoretic complements.

concavity of the objective. Two of these theorems are characterizations that tell us what needs to be checked to verify the complementarity relationship. One is about common mathematical structures that give rise to complementarity. The example of shared knowledge described above is an important example. Another theorem describes how the static optimum changes with parameters, yielding predictions about clustering and comparative statics. There are also dynamical implications about how such systems evolve over time, creating momentum for a series of changes. Accordingly, long-run changes in the maximum for such a system are always larger than short-run changes. There is a result characterizing the global maximum in a system of complements as a point from which no set of coherent complementary changes is an improvement. More strongly, starting from any position in a system of complements, at least half of the maximum improvement by changing decisions in any arbitrary way can be achieved by restricting attention to coherent complementary changes.

The empirical analysis of complementarities can take several forms. Examining or reexamining case studies through the lens of complementarities can often clarify outcomes and behavior that would otherwise resist explanation. More formal econometric techniques can also be used to explore complementarities. One approach examines firms' choices to assess theories of complementarity. Assuming that firms do maximize profits and that prices or other conditions facing the firm change, the goal is to test whether practices that are predicted to be complementary are shown to be so in the choice data. One may also ask about other implications of the theory and whether those are consistent with the data.

A second form of econometric analysis focuses on performance differences. Suppose that organizations sometimes make mistakes that lead to variation in the sets of choices observed by seemingly similar firms. The challenge then is to infer from the differences in performance across organizations whether the supposedly complementary practices actually lead to higher performance when adopted together than they do when adopted separately.

Complementarities theory promises answers to some of the most interesting questions about firms' practices and characteristics. For example, focusing on the different practices adopted for employees and independent contractors, one might ask:

- Why do employees usually work with assets owned by the firm, whereas independent contractors usually work with their own assets?

- Why do employees work exclusively for their employer during their work hours, whereas independent contractors more often have multiple clients and control their own work hours?

- Why are employees paid by the hour, whereas independent contractors are more often paid based on performance or deliverables?

- Why is training typically more extensive for employees than for independent contractors?

Such clusters of practices may reflect a simple complementarity: each change from an independent contracting practice to an employment practice makes the other changes of that sort more valuable, creating a tendency for practices to be grouped in a particular way. The complementarity relation is symmetric, so the logic can also be applied in the reverse direction:

each change from an employment practice to an independent contracting practice makes other changes of that sort more valuable.

Such complementarities make it risky for a manager to pick and choose best practices from various organizations or systems. For instance, an incentive system that leads to high performance in one context may be highly dysfunctional in a different one that lacks the supporting complementarities. Thus, complementarities can complicate learning and increase inertia, especially if they are not well understood.

2. Theory

For a precise mathematical treatment of complementarities, it is convenient to treat all choices as numeric. Some variables we study are inherently numeric, such as levels of inventory, years of training, or commission rates for salespeople. Others are qualitative binary choices, such as the decision to make or buy, to use an employee or a contractor, or to scrap or retain a line of business. For the qualitive choices, we represent the choice as being from the set $\{0, 1\}$, with 0 denoting what we call the "baseline" decision and 1 denoting the "alternative." When the variable is inherently numeric, the relevant change can be an increase or decrease, for example, a switch to higher or lower levels of inventories. For the mathematical development, we assume that the baseline refers to the lower level of the variable.

With n binary choices to make, the decisionmaker's payoff can be denoted by $f(x)$, $x \in \{0, 1\}^n$, which we may also write as $f(x_i, x_j, x_{-ij})$. The ith and jth choices are (weakly) complementary if for all x,

$$
\begin{aligned}
f(1, 1, x_{-ij}) - f(0, 0, x_{-ij}) \geq & \left(f(1, 0, x_{-ij}) - f(0, 0, x_{-ij}) \right) \\
& + \left(f(0, 1, x_{-ij}) - f(0, 0, x_{-ij}) \right)
\end{aligned}
\tag{1}
$$

To treat groups of coordinated changes, it is helpful to introduce some notation. Given profiles of decisions $x, y \in \{0, 1\}^n$, let $x \vee y$ be the profile that specifies the union of the changes in x and y. Mathematically, $x \vee y$ is the componentwise maximum of x and y. Similarly, let $x \wedge y$ be the profile that specifies the intersection of the changes in x and y. Mathematically, $x \wedge y$ is the componentwise minimum of x and y.

Using this notation, complementarity entails two mathematical conditions on the decisionmaker's optimization problem. The first condition restricts the constraint set: when x and y are both feasible decision profiles, then so are $x \vee y$ and $x \wedge y$. If $x \vee y$ were not included, then implementing some changes could preclude other changes, blocking the tendency for the changed practices to appear together. If $x \wedge y$ were not included, then failing to implement some changes could require implementing others, blocking the tendency for the unchanged practices to appear together. A set that satisfies this first restriction is a *sublattice* and is defined formally as follows.

Definition   *A set $S \subseteq \mathbb{R}^n$ is a sublattice if*

$$
(\forall x, y)(x, y \in S) \Rightarrow (x \vee y, x \wedge y \in S).
$$

The second condition is a payoff property similar to that identified by (1). The property can be written as $f(x \vee y) - f(x \wedge y) \geq (f(x) - f(x \wedge y)) + (f(y) - f(x \wedge y))$. This inequality asserts that starting from a point where all practices described by $x \wedge y$ are sure to be implemented, the additional return to implementing all remaining practices, which is $f(x \vee y) - f(x \wedge y)$, is at least as great as the sum of the returns from implementing each separately. A function with this property is said to be *supermodular*. For the definition, we rewrite this inequality in a more symmetrical form.

Definition   *A function $f: S \to \mathbb{R}$ is supermodular if $(\forall x, y \in S) f(x \vee y) + f(x \wedge y) \geq f(x) + f(y)$.*

The decision problems we evaluate are ones in which there may be some separate costs of returns $C_i(x_i)$ associated with each decision, but all payoff interactions are described by the function f. We impose no restrictions on the cost functions, except that each takes a single argument: $C_i : \mathbb{R} \to \mathbb{R}$. These choices lead us to the following formulation.

Definition   *The decision problem*

$$\max_{x \in S} f(x) - \sum_{i=1}^{n} C_i(x_i) \tag{2}$$

has complementarities if S is a sublattice and f is supermodular.

2.1. Example: Producer Theory

One example to illustrate complementarity arises in the neoclassical theory of a competitive firm. With two inputs x_1 and x_2 and a Cobb-Douglas production function, the firm solves the problem $\max_{x \geq 0} \lambda x_1^\alpha x_2^\beta - w \cdot x$, where $\lambda > 0$ and w is a vector of input prices. We may check the two complementarity conditions for this problem. First, the constraint set $S = \mathbb{R}_+^2$ is a sublattice, because for any $x, y \in \mathbb{R}_+^2$ and for $i = 1, 2$, $(x \wedge y)_i = \min(x_i, y_i) \geq 0$ and $(x \vee y)_i = \max(x_i, y_i) \geq 0$, so $x \vee y, x \wedge y \in \mathbb{R}_+^2$. Also, the incremental return to any increase from, say, x_1 to $\hat{x}_1 > x_1$ is $\lambda(\hat{x}_1^\alpha - x_1^\alpha) x_2^\beta - w_1(\hat{x}_1 - x_1)$, which is increasing in x_2 if $\alpha, \beta > 0$. With continuous choice variables, a convenient way to make the same point is to observe that the marginal return to x_1, $\lambda \alpha x_1^{\alpha-1} x_2^\beta - w_1$, is increasing in x_2.

2.2. Theorems about Decision Problems with Complementarities

The core of the theory comprises ten mathematical statements about decision problems with complementarities. The sections below report theorems that depend only on the complementarity conditions—sublattices and supermodularity—and not on any other common economic structure, such as divisibility (commonly assumed to justify the use of first-order conditions) or convexity (commonly assumed to imply the existence of supporting prices). These theorems are about decision problems with complementarities, and their scope is not limited, for example, to problems in price theory.

2.2.1. Complementarity Is a Pairwise Relationship

Theorems 1a and 1b explain the claim in Section 1 that complementarity is, essentially, a pairwise relationship among decisions. Theorem 1a is about sublattices. It asserts that a subset of $\mathbb{R}^n$ is a sublattice exactly when it can be expressed as the conjunction of a set of sublattice restrictions for each pair of decision variables separately. Theorem 1b concerns supermodularity. It asserts that a function on a product set (e.g., $\mathbb{R}^n$) is supermodular exactly when it is supermodular in each pair of variables separately.

Theorem 1a (Topkis 1978). *The set $S \subseteq \mathbb{R}^n$ is a sublattice if and only for each $1 \leq i < j \leq n$, there exist sublattices $S_{ij} \subseteq \mathbb{R}^2$ such that $S = \cap_{i,j=1, i<j}^n \{x | (x_j, x_j) \in S_{ij}\}$.*

Theorem 1b (Topkis 1978). *Suppose that $f : S \to \mathbb{R}$, where S is a product set $S = \times_{i=1}^n S_i$, and each $S_i \subseteq \mathbb{R}$. Then f is supermodular if and only if for all $1 \leq i < j \leq n$ and all $x \in S$, the function $g(z_i, z_j) \equiv f(z_i, z_j, x_{-ij})$ is supermodular.*

2.2.2. The Set of Optimizers Is a Sublattice

Theorem 2 is about the structure of the set of optimizers in a decision problem with complementarities, claiming that such a set is a sublattice. Thus in practice, when searching for an optimum, if we find an optimal profile at which certain optimal changes are made, then there is also an optimal profile at which all such optimal changes are made. Symmetrically, if there is an optimal decision profile in which certain changes are not made, then there is an optimal profile in which none of those changes are made. At an optimum, the individual decisions cluster at least weakly: they are adopted together or not at all.

Theorem 2 (Topkis 1978). *Suppose that (2) is a decision problem with complementarities. Then the set of optimal solutions $\arg\max_{x \in S} f(x) + \sum_{i=1}^n C_i(x_i)$ is a sublattice.*

2.2.3. "Coherent" Searches Can Find and Verify the Optimum

The message of Theorem 2 is further reinforced by considering how to locate and verify an optimum. Suppose that, in a decision problem with complementarities, we start our search for an optimum at some point z. Because z is arbitrary, the optimum might be in any direction, perhaps at some point with higher values of some components and lower values of others. We have made no convexity assumptions, so even if z is optimal in some local neighborhood, it may still fail to be a global optimum. As noted by Levinthal (1997) and Rivkin (2000), it can be particularly difficult if the landscape is "rugged," with numerous local optima, and the general problem may even be intractable in the sense of NP-completeness. Is there some way to restrict the search?

   If the decision problem has complementarities, then two important statements can be made. First, more than half of the gain from moving from decision profile z to the optimum can be realized just by optimizing over the sets with coherent changes, that is, with all choices weakly increased or all weakly reduced. Second, as a corollary, if there are no gains to be had in those coherent directions, then z is actually an optimal choice. To make these statements precise, we define $x \geq y$ to mean $x_i \geq y_i$ for $i = 1, \ldots, n$.

Theorem 3 (Milgrom and Roberts 1995).   *Suppose that (2) is a decision problem with complementarities. Then*

$$\left(\max_{\{x\in S|x\geq z\}\cup\{x\in S|x\leq z\}} f(x) - \sum_{i=1}^{n} C_i(x_i)\right) - \left(f(z) - \sum_{i=1}^{n} C_i(z_i)\right)$$

$$\geq \tfrac{1}{2}\left(\max_{x\in S}\left(f(x) - \sum_{i=1}^{n} C_i(x_i)\right) - \left(f(z) - \sum_{i=1}^{n} C_i(z_i)\right)\right).$$

Corollary 3   *Suppose that (2) is a decision problem with complementarities. Then*

$$z \in \arg\max_{x\in S} f(x) + \sum_{i=1}^{n} C_i(x_i)$$

if and only if

$$z \in \arg\max_{x\in S \text{ and } (x\geq z \text{ or } x\leq z)} f(x) + \sum_{i=1}^{n} C_i(x_i).$$

Thus, an understanding of complementarities may simplify the process of finding an optimum.

2.2.4. Comparative Statics Are Like Those of Demand Theory

The fourth theorem is about *comparative statics,* that is, about how the solution changes when a parameter changes. To motivate the discussion, suppose there is an exogenous change affecting just one of the variables, such as a price change, that makes increasing x_1 more profitable. If that change is enough to change the optimal decision, then the complementarity of choices would tend to favor the other choices as well, leading to increased levels of those decisions, too. Indeed, this is the very definition of complementarity in demand theory: reducing the price of an input raises the demand for complementary inputs. So, a comparative statics theorem of this sort is both useful for applications and verifies that the new definition of complements is consistent with earlier uses in demand theory.

For our formulation, we do not limit attention to changing prices, because many of the relevant decisions are not input quantities. Instead, we specify the payoff to consist of a joint part that depends on the parameter θ and individual costs $C_i(x_i)$ that may remain incompletely specified. We rewrite the choice problem with $x \in \mathbb{R}^n$ and $S \subseteq \mathbb{R}^{n+1}$ as follows:

$$X(\theta) = \arg\max_{\{x|(x,\theta)\in S\}} f(x,\theta) - \sum_{i=1}^{n} C_i(x_i) \tag{3}$$

Here, $X(\theta)$ is the set of optimizers, which we discuss as if it were a singleton. Formally, the next theorem applies even when the set has multiple elements or is empty (has no elements). The parameter θ in (3) enables us to capture changes in the constraint set or in the objective.

If we limit attention to parameters for which $X(\theta)$ is a singleton, it is clear what it means for the optimal solution to be nondecreasing in θ, but we cannot guarantee in general that the optimal solution will be unique. To treat the general case, we need a word and a definition that agrees with "nondecreasing" for the well-understood case but also describes a useful corresponding concept for the general case. The word is "isotone," and the definition is the following one.

Definition   *The set-valued function $X(\cdot)$ is isotone if for all $\theta > \theta'$, if $x \in X(\theta)$ and $x' \in X(\theta')$, then $x \vee x' \in X(\theta)$ and $x \wedge x' \in X(\theta')$.*

Theorem 4 (Topkis 1978).   *In (3), suppose that S is a sublattice and f is supermodular. Then $X(\cdot)$ is isotone.*

If we limit attention to parameters for which $X(\theta)$ is a singleton, then the theorem asserts that, on that domain, all components of the decision profile are nondecreasing functions of θ. So this theorem states that the new notion of complementarity coincides with the demand theory notion in such cases. Moreover, if we think of θ as a random variable and assume that $X(\theta)$ is almost always a singleton, then if what is observed are optimal choices, the choices will be positively correlated. This happens because they are all nondecreasing functions of the same one-dimensional random variable.

2.2.5. Complementarity Conditions Are Necessary for Some Comparative Statics . . .

The comparative statics implications of complementarity are interesting, but one might wonder whether similar results can be derived from alternative conditions. They cannot. Both the sublattice condition and the supermodularity condition are essential. We assert this with two theorems that treat the two conditions separately. We limit attention to finite feasible sets to avoid certain technical complications.

Theorem 5a (Milgrom and Shannon 1994).   *Suppose that the constraint set S is finite but is not a sublattice. Then for some cost functions C_i, $i = 1, \ldots, n$, and some $j \in \{1, \ldots, n\}$, the function*

$$X(\theta) = \arg \max_{\{x \mid (x,\theta) \in S\}} f(x) - \sum_{i=1}^{n} C_i(x_i) + \theta x_j$$

is not isotone.

Theorem 5b (Milgrom and Shannon 1994).   *Suppose that constraint set S is $\{0, 1\}^n$ and the function f is not supermodular. Then for some cost functions C_i, $i = 1, \ldots, n$, and some $j \in \{1, \ldots, n\}$, the function*

$$X(\theta) = \arg \max_{x \in S} f(x) - \sum_{i=1}^{n} C_i(x_i) + \theta x_j$$

is not isotone.

2.2.6. . . . But Limited Results Extend to Some Related Systems

Sometimes we study decision problems that can be broken into modules in which decisions about the modules, denoted by x, are complementary, but a set of more specialized decisions in each module has a more complicated structure. To study such cases, let y_i denote the decisions in module i, which may interact with x_i or with other decisions in the module but not with decisions in any other modules. Formally, the optimization problem is:

$$(X(\theta), Y(\theta)) = \arg \max_{\{x \mid (x, \theta) \in S\}, y_1 \in Y_1, \ldots, y_n \in Y_n} f(x, \theta) - \sum_{i=1}^{n} C_i(x_i, y_i). \quad (4)$$

Theorem 6   *In (4), suppose that S is a sublattice and f is supermodular. Then $X(\theta)$ is isotone.*

The theorem asserts that we can still make assertions about the complementary variables, even if their interaction with other related variables outside the cluster is arbitrarily complicated. The important condition for this conclusion is that these other variables do not interact with variables outside their own modules.

2.2.7. Long-Run Changes Are Larger Than Short-Run Changes

Another important idea that we borrow from demand theory is that, in certain circumstances, long-run adaptations are larger in magnitude than short-run adaptations. As is standard in economics, "short run" refers to a period over which some decisions are fixed, whereas "long run" refers to a period over which all decisions can change. Let x denote the group of decisions that are free (i.e., not fixed) in the short run and y the decisions that are free only in the long run.

For simplicity of our statement, we limit attention to values of the parameter for which the optimal long- and short-run decisions are unique. Thus, let $x^*(\theta, y)$ denote the short-run optimum for any given values of the parameter and the long-run decision y:

$$x^*(\theta, y) \in \arg \max_{\{x \mid (x, y, \theta) \in S\}} f(x, y, \theta) - \sum_{i=1}^{n} C_i(x_i) - \sum_{j=1}^{m} K_j(y_j), \quad (5)$$

where K_j is any cost function associated with decision y_j. We use $y^*(\theta)$ to denote the long-run optimal value of y for any fixed value of the parameter θ:

$$y^*(\theta) \in \arg \max \left(f(x^*(\theta, y), y, \theta) - \sum_{i=1}^{n} C_i(x_i^*(\theta, y)) - \sum_{j=1}^{m} K_j(y_j) \right) \quad (6)$$

Notice that the long-run optimal value of x is just $x^*(\theta, y^*(\theta))$.

When the parameter changes (e.g., by increasing from θ' to θ), the short-run reaction is for x to increase in response to the parameter change. In the long run, y also increases, and that acts like a parameter change to lead to a further increase in x. So x changes more in the long run than in the short run. A symmetric argument applies when the parameter change is a decrease. These relations are summarized by the following theorem.

Theorem 7 (Milgrom and Roberts 1996).   *If S is a sublattice and f is supermodular, then x^* and y^* are both nondecreasing. In particular, if $\theta > \theta'$, then*

$$x^*(\theta, y^*(\theta)) \geq x^*(\theta', y^*(\theta)) \geq x^*(\theta', y^*(\theta'))$$

and

$$x^*(\theta, y^*(\theta)) \geq x^*(\theta, y^*(\theta')) \geq x^*(\theta', y^*(\theta')).$$

2.2.8. Dynamical Systems of Complements Exhibit Momentum

A related conclusion applies not merely to long- and short-run equilibrium changes but also to explicitly dynamical systems in which frictions may limit the rate of adjustment. The system starts in a state x_0 and moves, by optimization, through a series of states x_1, x_2, and so on. The states may, for example, include levels of assets and associated employment, where an overly rapid adjustment of assets is impossible or costly. For example, building a structure in half the usual time typically entails significant additional costs, while attempting to complete a large software project in half the time may be impossible at any price. The conclusion is that there is momentum in a system of complementary choices: once the system variables begin moving in a given direction (up or down), they will tend to continue in that direction.

The assumption that adjustments are impossible or costly is quite naturally modeled by the idea that there are restrictions on successive choices, that is, $(x_{t-1}, x_t) \in S$, and that today's payoffs depend on choices from yesterday as well as today: $f(x_{t-1}, x_t)$. We study both myopic and far-sighted optimizations, as represented by the following two problems:

$$\max_{(x_{t-1}, x_t) \in S} f(x_{t-1}, x_t) - C(x_t), \tag{7}$$

$$\max_x \sum_{t=1}^{\infty} \delta^t \left(f(x_{t-1}, x_t) - C(x_t) \right) \text{ subject to } (x_{t-1}, x_t) \in S \text{ for all } t \geq 1, \tag{8}$$

where δ is the time discount factor.

Theorem 8 (Milgrom et al. 1991).   *If S is a sublattice and f is supermodular, then for both (7) and (8), if $x_1^* \geq x_0^*$, then for all $t \geq 1$, $x_t^* \geq x_{t-1}^*$.*

2.2.9. Complementarities Create a Value to Simple Coordination

Finally, we look at the implications of complementarities for coordination. Any decision system can entail errors, but in a system of complements, it is especially important that any errors be coherent (i.e., coordinated). Going too far in some direction is less costly if the other choices are exaggerated in the same direction.

Theorem 9   *Let $\varepsilon_1, \ldots, \varepsilon_n$ be independent identically distributed random variables. If f is supermodular, then, for every x and every vector $\alpha \in \mathbb{R}^n_+$,*

$$E\left[f(x_1 + \alpha_1\varepsilon_1, \ldots, x_n + \alpha_n\varepsilon_n)\right] \leq E\left[f(x_1 + \alpha_1\varepsilon_1, \ldots, x_n + \alpha_n\varepsilon_1)\right], \qquad (9)$$

where E is the expectations operator.

The point of Theorem 9 is that, regardless of the starting point x, if there are to be random errors in all choices, then regardless of their magnitudes (which are governed by α), it is better that all errors are perfectly correlated rather than being independent. In a system with complementarities, even if choices cannot be optimized, coordination remains important. Thus, having a single, decisive leader in an organization may be better than distributing decision rights, even if the central decisionmaker is imperfectly informed.

2.2.10. Returns to Scale and/or Scope Can Create Complementarities

One of the most common ways for complementarities to arise is from increasing returns to scale. A simple example is the function $f(x_1, x_2) = g(x_1 + x_2)$. It is easy to check that if g is convex, then f is supermodular. Indeed, the marginal return to x_1 is $f_1(x_1, x_2) = g'(x_1 + x_2)$, which is nondecreasing in x_2 if and only if g is convex.

A related example comes from the use of shared inputs for which there are economies of scale. Suppose that research that reduces the costs of chip manufacturing can be used both for memory chips and for microprocessors. Let k denote the expenditures on knowledge—research—and suppose the costs of production for goods $i = 1, 2$ are $c_i(x_i, k)$, where $\partial c_i/\partial x_i$ is decreasing in k. Then the firm's total profit

$$f(x_1, x_2, k) = R_1(x_1) + R_2(x_2) - c_1(x_1, k) - c_2(x_2, k) - k$$

is supermodular, regardless of the revenue functions $R_i(x_i)$. The shared input, which reduces the marginal cost of both kinds of manufacturing, makes the two complements.

Formally, this analysis relies on explicitly including the choice variable k in the formulation. If it is convenient, k can be legitimately pushed into the background by applying the following result.

Theorem 10 (Topkis 1978).   *Suppose that $f(x, k): \mathbb{R}^n \times \mathbb{R}^m \to \mathbb{R}$ is supermodular and $S \subseteq \mathbb{R}^n \times \mathbb{R}^m$ is a sublattice. Then the function $g(x) = \max_{\{k|(x,k)\in S\}} f(x, k)$ is supermodular and the set $S_x = \{x|(\exists k)(x, k) \in S\}$ is a sublattice.*

The theorem tells us that if the original decision problem exhibits complementarity and if some variables k are optimized away to allow us to focus just on the variables x, then the decision problem for these remaining variables also exhibits complementarity.

3. Empirical Evidence

Much of the first evidence on the relevance of organizational complementarities has come from case studies of individual firms. Cases often provide the richest insight into the nature of complementarities and can be very powerful for shaping our intuition about the underlying mechanisms at work. Conclusions drawn from case studies, however, can be misleading, because the observer may identify relationships that are idiosyncratic and not generalizable. To address these failings, econometric techniques have increasingly been used over the past decade to test theories of complementarities using sets of firms or establishments, rather than just a single case. Recently, some economists have argued that international differences in business practices and performance can be traced back to complementarities in organizations. Here we review this literature[4] with a more formal discussion of empirical techniques in Section 4.

3.1. Case Studies

A Harvard Business School case (Berg and Fast 1975) detailing Lincoln Electric's unique business methods and compensation scheme is among the school's best-selling cases ever, and it is still widely taught today. Lincoln Electric, an arc-welding company that began operations in 1895, has not laid off a worker in the United States since 1948[5] and has average earnings for hourly workers that are double those of their closest competitors (Milgrom and Roberts 1995: 200). The company uses piece rates as its main form of compensation, where workers are paid by the amount of output they produce, rather than a fixed salary. Once the piece rates are set, the company commits to that rate forever, unless new machinery or production methods are introduced. In addition, the company pays individual annual performance bonuses based on its profits that typically amount to 60–90% of the regular annual earnings for an average employee. If the company's methods are so widely studied, why has the remarkable success of Lincoln Electric not been copied by other firms? Rather than looking for the answer in the piece rates alone, Milgrom and Roberts (1995) hypothesize that it is the complementarities inherent in the workplace that make Lincoln Electric so difficult to copy. To copy piece rates may be easy enough, but all the other distinctive features of the company, such as internal ownership, promoting from within, high bonuses, flexible work rules, and credible commitments, are part of a reinforcing system. A system is much more difficult to reproduce than just one or two parts, especially when one considers that many of the important complements, such as corporate culture, may be difficult to accurately observe and even harder to translate to other contexts.

More recently, longitudinal case studies by Siggelkow (2001, 2002a,b) have found that complementarities can explain the evolution of the Liz Claiborne cosmetics company and Vanguard Group in financial services. For instance, Siggelkow found that complementarities at Liz Claiborne can limit managers' options when responding to environmental changes. This restriction leads them to favor "fit-conserving" change, even when it decreases the appropriateness of the overall choice set.

Holmes (2001) develops a model of complementarities relating to the use of technology in the retail sector in an attempt to explain the emergence of big-box retailers. The author explores

---

4. Appendix A provides a list of empirical studies of complementarities. Inevitably, our review will be incomplete. Ennen and Richter (2010) conducted a computerized search of the literature and found that between 1988 and 2008, 1,398 papers in management, economics, marketing, research and development (R&D), and information systems journals contain the word stem "complement." They review 73 of these papers, an overlapping set with those discussed below. See also useful discussions by Ichniowski and Shaw (2003) and Porter and Siggelkow (2008).

5. See http://web.archive.org/web/20090523223033/http://www.lincolnelectric.com/corporate/career/default.asp.

the complementarities between the use of bar codes and computer tracking of inventory. His model shows that "new technology induces stores to increase delivery frequency" (Holmes 2001: 708). This result leads to his second finding, that with more frequent deliveries, it is more efficient for stores to be larger. He points out that if the store remained the same size but received twice as many deliveries as before, then the trucks would only be half as full for each delivery (Holmes 2001: 708).

Barley (1986) explores the introduction of identical computed tomography (CT) scanners in two different hospitals in the same metropolitan area and finds that identical technology led to very different organizational outcomes, depending on what other practices were also in place. The CT scanners disrupted the existing power structure between the radiologists and technicians and led to different forms of organization around the technology. He concludes that

> Technologies do influence organizational structures in orderly ways, but their influence depends on the specific historical process in which they are embedded. To predict a technology's ramifications for an organization's structure therefore requires a methodology and a conception of technical change open to the construction of grounded, population-specific theories. [Barley 1986: 107]

Autor et al. (2002) study the effect of introducing check imaging and optical character recognition technologies on the reorganization of two floors of a bank branch. In the downstairs deposit-processing department, image processing led to computers substituting for high-school educated labor. In the upstairs exceptions-processing department, image processing led to the integration of tasks, with "fewer people doing more work in more interesting jobs" (Autor et al. 2002: 442). The authors conclude that the same technology can have radically different effects on workplace reorganization, depending on the level of human capital and other nontechnology-related factors, even within one building of a single company.

In some cases, the complementarities among practices are subtle and not well understood even by the participants themselves. Brynjolfsson et al. (1997) write about the business process reengineering efforts at one of Johnson & Johnson's manufacturing plants. The company sought to make almost exactly the sort of transition that Milgrom and Roberts (1990) describe from traditional manufacturing practices, similar to those used by Ford Motor Company in the early years of the twentieth century, to "modern manufacturing."[6] Despite a clear plan and an explicit written description by senior management of many of the specific complementarities inherent in both the old and the new systems,[7] the initial reengineering efforts were unsuccessful. After spending millions of dollars on new, highly flexible production equipment, key performance

---

6. Milgrom and Roberts (1990) trace a broad set of organizational practices to improvements in information technology. One extended example they explore involves the use of computer-aided design/computer-aided manufacturing (CAD/CAM) engineering software in manufacturing. This software promotes the use of programmable manufacturing equipment, which makes it possible to offer a broader product line and more frequent production runs. This in turn affects marketing and organization. Shorter production runs lower inventory costs, which lower prices. Buyers also value shorter delivery times. Thus, the firm now has a substantial incentive to reduce other forms of production delays and invest in computerized ordering systems. The example illustrates how important it is to think in terms of systems of activities, rather than trying to adopt one particular practice.

7. See Appendix B for an example of reengineering efforts at Merrill Lynch.

metrics were largely unchanged. An interview with a 30-year veteran line supervisor revealed a potential explanation. He was sincerely intent on making the transition a success and he explained, "I've been here a long time and I know that the key to productivity is avoiding change-overs [the transition from one product to another using the same equipment]. You get killed in the change-overs." Accordingly, he and his team were using the new flexible production equipment to produce long, unchanging product runs. This is precisely the opposite of what management had intended and what Milgrom and Roberts (1990: 524) predicted in their paper. However, the supervisor and his team had built up numerous such heuristics as part of their decades-old investment in work practices. In other words, their organizational capital, much of it implicit, turned out to be a poor fit for the new physical capital. Ultimately, the company canceled the change effort at the existing site and restarted it at a new site, with a hand-picked set of new, mostly very young, workers. The new effort was such a success that the windows were painted black to make it more difficult for competitors to learn about the new system of technology and practices.

This kind of difficulty in managing transitions appears to be common. For instance, McAfee (2002) quantitatively examines an enterprise resource planning (ERP) system implementation over a period of several months in one firm. The ERP system was introduced without any other business process changes at first. McAfee finds a significant dip in company performance after it adopted the system, which he attributed to this lack of business process redesign. After several months, however, the firm adapted, and post-ERP performance was better than pre-ERP adoption, reflecting the successful adjustment of complementarity practices.

In many other cases, change efforts remain unsuccessful when the complementarity organizational practices are not revised along with the introduction of new technologies. For instance, General Motors (GM) spent $650 million on new technology at one plant in the 1980s but did not make any important changes to its labor practices. The new technology at GM did not result in any significant quality or productivity improvements (Osterman 1991).

3.2. Econometric Studies of Complementarities

3.2.1. United States

One of the clearest analyses of complementarities and productivity comes from Ichniowski et al. (1997). They use data from 36 steel finishing lines in 17 different companies and measure the impact of different clusters of workplace practices on productivity and product quality. By focusing on a single production process, they are able to use a narrow productivity metric (uptime of the production line) and avoid many potential sources of unobserved heterogeneity. One important difference that remained was the choice of work practices adopted at the line, which varied across lines, as well as across time at the same line in about 14% of the cases. Ichniowski et al. (1997) looked at both correlations as well as productivity regressions and found evidence that work practices that include incentive pay, teams, flexible job assignments, employment security, and training were mutually complementary, compared to a more traditional set of work practices. Their two key conclusions are that (i) workplace practices tend to cluster more than random chance would predict, and (ii) clusters of workplace practices have significant and positive effects on productivity, but isolated changes in individual work practices have little effect on productivity.

Bresnahan et al. (2002) run an analysis at the firm level and reach similar conclusions. The authors examine 300 large firms using data for 1987–1994 from both manufacturing and service industries in the United States. They study the organizational complements to technology and their impacts on productivity, and find that "increased use of IT [information technology], changes in organizational practices, and changes in products and services *taken together* are the skill-biased technical change that calls for a higher skilled-labor mix" (Bresnahan et al. 2002: 341). Furthermore, the interaction of IT, workplace organization, and human capital are good predictors of productivity. Because organizational changes take time, this can help explain the finding that the largest productivity increases often come several years after major IT investments (Brynjolfsson and Hitt 2003).[8]

Using plant-level data on almost 800 establishments for 1993–1996, Black and Lynch (2004) find that productivity is positively correlated with the proportion of nonmanagers using computers, teams, profit sharing, employee voice, and reengineering. They assert that "workplace organization, including re-engineering, teams, incentive pay and employee voice, have been a significant component of the turnaround in productivity growth in the US during the 1990s" (Black and Lynch 2004: F97). In a related 2001 paper, Black and Lynch examine the impact of a total quality management (TQM) system on productivity. Using data from 600 manufacturing plants for 1987–1993, they find that adopting a TQM system alone does not meaningfully affect productivity. However, they do find that giving employees greater voice or profit-sharing programs alongside a TQM program has significantly positive effects on productivity.

Autor et al. (2003) conduct a study the impact of computerization on job tasks. They use job and occupation data from the U.S. Department of Labor's Dictionary of Occupational Titles from 1960 to 1998. In line with the other studies we examined, the authors derive two main conclusions. First, computers substitute for routine tasks, and second, computers complement workers doing complex or problem-solving tasks.

More recently, Garicano and Heaton (2010) find support for complementarities in a public sector context. They use information from a panel of police departments in the United States that contains detailed information on IT usage and organizational practices between 1989 and 2003. The productivity variables in this context are local crime clearance rates and crime rates, controlling for local demographics. They find that IT by itself has little positive impact on either of those performance metrics—that is, departments that invested more in IT did not see larger drops in crime or better arrest rates. However, when IT was introduced together with a new system of organizational practices, IT had significant effects on police performance. The successful system of practices in this context is the CompStat system, which combines real-time geographic information on crime with strong accountability by middle managers in the form of daily group meetings, geographic resource allocation, and data-intensive police techniques. The CompStat practices were associated with crime clearance rates an average of 2.2 percentage points higher in agencies implementing this integrated set of practices; the individual practices

---

8. Using data from about 500 large firms for 1987–1994, Brynjolfsson and Hitt (2003) find that the returns to IT are no different than those of ordinary capital when looking only at the short-term, 1-year impact. However, when they look at 5- or 7-year time horizons, the productivity and output contributions of the same technology investments are five times as large. For a broader review of related findings, see Brynjolfsson and Hitt (2000).

composing CompStat had no independent ameliorative impact on crime levels or clearance rates.

Complementarities have also been explored in the strategy literature, often as part of the resource-based view of the firm. For instance, Tanriverdi and Venkatraman (2005) analyze 303 multibusiness firms and find evidence of complementarities in the performace benefits of combining customer knowledge, product knowledge, and managerial knowledge. In contrast, both market-based and accounting-based performance metrics are not significantly improved from any of these types of knowledge in isolation.

Researchers in the R&D literature have identified complementarities in interfirm relationships. For instance, Belderbos et al. (2006) found evidence of complementarity relationships when measuring the productivity effects of R&D cooperation strategies among competitors, customers, and universities. Similarly, Colombo et al. (2006) found that complementarity assets, including technologies and commercial assets, could explain the success of alliances for high-tech start-ups.

3.2.2. International Comparisons

There has been much debate about why productivity growth has been higher in the United States than in Europe (for a review of the literature, see O'Mahony and van Ark 2003). One class of possible explanations focuses on various country-specific factors that are external to the organization of the firm, such as taxes, regulation, and culture. However, another promising line of research studies the differences in the ways that firms organize themselves from country to country.

Recent research suggests that differences in productivity between the United Kingdom and the United States may indeed be due to organizational differences and, more specifically, to the firm-specific IT-related intangible assets that are often excluded in accounts of macroeconomic growth. The research compares differences between U.S.- and British-owned firms operating in the United Kingdom. With this data, the authors hope to discover whether there is something unique about American ownership versus being located on U.S. soil (with less regulation or stronger product market competition) that drives higher productivity growth.

Bloom et al. (2007) conduct a study on a panel of about 8,000 establishments across all industries in the United Kingdom from 1995 to 2003. They found that U.S.-owned establishments were both more IT-intensive and more productive than British- or other foreign-owned companies operating in the United Kingdom. They specifically attribute this difference to complementarities between IT and the types of organizational capital that are more common in American firms.

Crespi et al. (2007) present similar evidence that American firms operating in the United Kingdom are more productive and implement more related organizational capital than do their British counterparts. Their study, based on a dataset including approximately 6,000 British firms from 1998 to 2000 across all industries, introduces a variable as a proxy for organizational capital. The authors find that IT has high returns regardless of organizational factors. However, when they control for an organizational proxy variable, the measured returns attributed to IT are lower, which suggests that some of the measured IT-related boost in productivity actually came from organizational factors. In contrast to the evidence of complementarity between IT and organization, the authors find that there is "no additional impact on productivity growth from the interaction of organizational capital and non-IT investment" (Crespi et al. 2007: 2). The authors' new findings are that organizational change is affected by ownership and market competition, and that U.S.-owned firms operating in the United Kingdom are more likely to introduce organizational change than non-U.S.-owned firms. In turn, non-American multinationals are more likely to introduce organizational change than domestically owned (British) firms.

Bugamelli and Pagano (2004) work with a dataset for about 1,700 Italian manufacturing firms and conclude that Italian firms have a 7-year technological gap compared to similar American firms. They reject the notion that the gap is due to sectoral specialization of the Italian economy into such industries as textiles, clothing, and food, which are not IT intensive. Rather, they argue that it is the missing complementary business reorganization that has been the barrier to investment in IT in Italy.

Caroli and Van Reenen (2001) generate three major findings with British and French establishment data from 1984 and 1990 (Great Britain) and 1992 (France). First, organizational change is associated with a decline in demand for unskilled workers. Second, higher cost of skills leads to a lower probability of organizational change. Third, organizational changes are associated with greater productivity in establishments with more skilled workers. All three findings are consistent with complementarities between workplace reorganization and skilled labor.

4. Testing for Complementarities: Theory and Practice

When the costs and benefits of organizational practices can be accurately measured, complementarities theory provides clear empirical predictions. In this section, we consider two types of statistical tests for complementarities: performance differences and correlations. For each test, we discuss the assumptions that are necessary to make them effective ways to reveal the existence and magnitude of complementarities. In many cases, the conditions that make it difficult to identify complementarities by examining performance differences will actually make it more likely that they can be identified via correlations, and vice versa. We then analyze the role of unobserved heterogeneity in the costs or benefits of changing organizational practices. Such differences can bias tests for complementarities. Finally, we discuss various empirical approaches for overcoming these problems.

4.1. Performance Equations

Consider a case where potential complements y_1 and y_2 each vary independently and exogenously. For instance, a new computer system, y_1, is implemented randomly across offices based on a lottery, while employee training, y_2, is deployed randomly across employees based on the last digits of their social security numbers. Each choice is binary, so $(y_1, y_2) \in \{0, 1\}^2$. Thus, given the independence of the design choice, we will have a random sample in each of the four ordered pairs $(0, 0)$, $(0, 1)$, $(1, 0)$, and $(1, 1)$. If the practices are complements, then by (1) in Section 2, the change in total output is greater when both practices are implemented together than the sum of the changes when each practice is implemented separately:[9]

$$f(1, 1) - f(0, 0) \geq f(1, 0) - f(0, 0) + f(0, 1) - f(0, 0).$$

9. To simplify notation, we omit reference to other choices of the decisionmaker x_{ij} or to exogenous variables.

This suggests an obvious test statistic for complementarities using performance differences:

$$\kappa_p \equiv f(1, 1) + f(0, 0) - f(1, 0) - f(0, 1). \tag{10}$$

Of course, f may be measured with error and other exogenous factors may affect performance, either directly or in combination with one of the complements. Thus, a typical approach is to estimate performance with a multivariate regression, which accounts for these other factors and their interactions, holding them fixed and thereby allowing the researcher to focus on the potential complementary practices themselves. When κ_p is significantly greater than zero, we can reject the null hypothesis of no complementarities.

Many authors have implemented this approach. For instance, as noted in Section 3.2.1, Ichniowski et al. (1997) compared steel finishing lines and, using ordinary least squares and fixed effects regressions, found that those implementing certain human resources practices together were significantly more productive than implementing the same practices separately. More recently, Bloom et al. (2009a) gathered data on IT and organizational practices for a sample of American and European firms. In each case, the predicted pattern of complementarities was evident.

Of course, in many cases the variables will naturally be continuous, such as the quantity of IT capital stock or hours spent on training, so information would be lost if they were discretized into two categories. Instead, the continuous versions of the variables can be included in a performance regression along with an interaction term that multiplies two of the choice variables together. If the variables are normalized with their means set equal to zero, then it is easy to interpret the coefficient of the interaction term, assuming that the choices were made independently and exogenously. A value greater than zero at a chosen significance level (such as 5%) is evidence of complementarity. Brynjolfsson et al. (2002) provide a plot that shows market value as a continuous function of both IT and an index of organizational practices (Figure 1).

The performance tests can be generalized to the case of three or more complements. For instance, Aral et al. (2012) and Tambe et al. (2012) each model different three-way systems of complements. The theory suggests four performance tests of complementarities, which can readily be seen with a cube diagram. For instance, Tambe et al. test for complementarities in the triple (x, y, z), where x represents IT investments, y is decentralized work organization, and z is external orientation (meaning information systems are focused on customers, competitors, and suppliers, instead of on primarily internal data). There are eight potential systems, and the theory of complementarities predicts that they will be related to one another by the four inequalities depicted in Figure 2.[10]

4.2. Correlations and Demand Equations

The assumption that the adoption decisions are exogenous and uncorrelated is a strong one. In particular, managers usually will be consciously trying to maximize, or at least increase, performance, so when two practices are actually complementary, managers will seek to adopt them together. If the managers have perfect foresight and full control over both choice variables,

---

10. Additional inequalities may be inferred by comparing the performance of intermediate systems with the performance of the two fully complementary systems at $(0, 0, 0)$ and $(1, 1, 1)$.

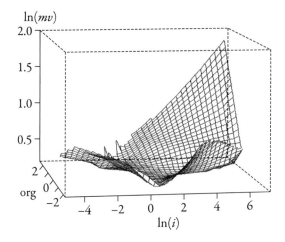

Figure 1. Normalized market value $\ln(mv)$ as a function of information technology investment $\ln(i)$ and an index of organizational practices *org* for a sample of 372 firms. From Brynjolfsson et al. (2002).

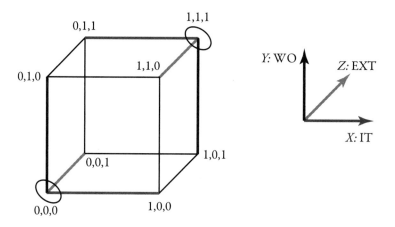

Four tests of complementarities:

1. IT: $F(1,1,1) - F(0,1,1) > F(1,0,0) - F(0,0,0)$ Fail $p = 0.333$
2. WO: $F(1,1,1) - F(1,0,1) > F(0,1,0) - F(0,0,0)$ ✓ $p = 0.043$
3. EXT: $F(1,1,1) - F(1,1,0) > F(0,0,1) - F(0,0,0)$ ✓ $p = 0.007$
4. The system: ✓ $p = 0.008$
   $[F(1,1,1) - F(0,1,1)] + [F(1,1,1) - F(1,0,1)] + [F(1,1,1) - F(1,1,0)] - [F(1,0,0) - F(0,0,0)] + [F(0,1,0) - F(0,0,0)] + [F(0,0,1) - F(0,0,0)] > 0$

Figure 2. Cube view of three-way complementarities. EXT, external orientation; IT, information technology; WO, decentralized work organization. From Tambe et al. (2012).

then in the absence of other exogenous forces, the complementary variables will always be adopted together. In this case, all observations (y_1, y_2) will be either $(0, 0)$ or $(1, 1)$; there will be no off-diagonal observations in the data. As a result, it will be impossible to identify values for $f(1, 0)$ or $f(0, 1)$, and we cannot estimate κ_p econometrically.

Similarly, market competition might reduce or eliminate the population of firms that attempts to implement inefficient combinations of practices. As with conscious choice by managers, this effect will reduce the share of off-diagonal observations and weaken the power of the performance test. Of course, in either of these cases, the very fact that the practices are correlated provides evidence of complementarities. This suggests a second test for complementarities using the correlation of practices:

$$\kappa_c \equiv \text{correlation}(y_1, y_2).$$

A larger value of κ_c provides more evidence against the null hypothesis of no complementarities. If other exogenous factors affect the choices, then this correlation should be made conditional on those factors.

In many cases, it can be useful to think of this test as estimating a factor demand equation: the demand for one practice, y_1, will be higher when the levels of the other practice, y_2, are higher, conditional on other observable characteristics. If y_2 is determined exogenously, then a multivariate regression will provide an estimate of κ_c. When y_2 is endogenous, then it may be possible to identify exogenous instrumental variables and use two-stage least squares.

Measuring the correlation, or clustering, of practices is perhaps the most common approach to testing for complementarities. It has the virtue that it does not require performance metrics, only observability of the practices themselves. Arora and Gambardella (1990) were the first to explicitly use this fact as a test for complementarities, and it was further analyzed by Holmström and Milgrom (1994). See also Arora (1996).

4.3. Boundedly Rational Decisionmaking: Random Error

Although the extreme cases of random and independent assignment of practices on one hand or perfectly correlated choices on the other hand are useful brackets, most real-world cases are likely to fall somewhere in between. In part, this is because decisionmakers may have imperfect information or bounded capabilities to assess the optimal levels of each practice. Furthermore, they may not be optimizing the same performance metric that the econometrician is measuring. If the choice of practices reflects both some degree of random error and of conscious choice, then both tests may be useful.

The correlation test $\kappa_c > 0$ has the most power when managers know about the relevant complementarities and are able to act effectively on that knowledge, so that errors in choosing practices are small. Conversely, the performance-based test $\kappa_p > 0$ is most powerful when the practices are randomly determined.

In practice, both tests are often useful. For instance, the Ichniowski et al. (1997) analysis presents data on both the clustering of practices and the performance effects of certain clusters. Similarly, the Bresnahan et al. (2002) analysis of IT and organizational practices included a series of 2×2 charts. The productivity differences relative to the base case of low IT and low

Table 2. Productivity differences for four combinations of information technology (IT) and new organizational practices (ORG)

Adoption of ORG	Adoption of IT	
	Low	High
High	.0258	.0643
	(.0188)	(.0174)
	[N = 67]	[N = 97]
Low	0	.0130
	(n.a.)	(.0178)
	[N = 97]	[N = 68]

Source: Adapted from Bresnahan et al. (2002).
Notes: n.a., not applicable. Standard errors are in parentheses. The number of observations is in brackets. The diagonal mentioned in the text runs from the lower left to the top right.

adoption of new organizational practices are consistent with complementarities as measured by the performance test ($\kappa_p \equiv f(1, 1) + f(0, 0) - f(1, 0) - f(0, 1) = 0.0255 > 0$), but the magnitude is not statistically significant (Table 2).[11] At the same time, the disproportionate share of observations on the diagonal (low-low, or high-high) cells is consistent with correlation test of complementarities and is statistically significant (Pearson chi-square test for association: $\chi^2 = 10.58$; $p < 0.001$).

Table 2 matches the organizational data to 1994 IT spending by the same firms. In contrast, when 1987 data are used, the performance test is significantly greater than zero, whereas the correlation test is positive but not statistically significant. One interpretation is that managers learned and adjusted their IT investments over the intervening 7 years, which is consistent with optimizing behavior and would affect the two complementarities tests as predicted.

4.4. Unobserved Heterogeneity

Problems created by unobserved heterogeneity are particularly salient when examining complementarities in organizations.

The adoption of practices will be a function of their costs and benefits, just as decisions about physical inputs are. However, although the prices of physical capital or labor are often observable, the costs of adopting organizational practices usually are not.

In general, the firm, but not the econometrician, may observe a broad set of exogenous variables. These might be, for example, managerial talent, worker attitudes, or beliefs about market conditions. When these cannot be explained by observables but still affect the marginal returns to adoption, then the econometric estimates of complementarities can be biased. The

11. Note that in Table 2, the output increase for the high-org/high-IT quadrant (.0643) is significantly greater than in the low-org/low-IT quadrant and is also greater than any of the other strategies. However, this does not by itself indicate complementarity, unless the output changes exceed the sum of changes in the off-diagonal quadrants.

standard econometrics of production functions and demand equations (e.g., see Berndt 1991) can provide useful guidance on potential biases, as can the broader literature on the effects of unobserved heterogeneity and endogeneity in regression estimates.

In particular, Athey and Stern (1998), drawing in part on the work on discrete choice and switching regressions (e.g., Heckman and MaCurdy 1986; Heckman and Honoré 1990) carefully analyze how unobserved heterogeneity can bias the performance and correlation tests for complementarities we described above. Here, we closely follow their approach to replicate key insights from their model and summarize some of their important results. We refer the interested reader to their very thorough paper for further detail.

For simplicity, assume firm t makes a discrete 0-or-1 choice for each practice, and the practices are endogenously determined by the firms' managers. As above, let y_1 and y_2 represent Practice 1 and Practice 2, respectively, for example,

y_1 represents a new computer system, and

y_2 is a training course.

Let $\mathbf{X}$ represent the practice-specific exogenous variables that, regardless of the other practices that the firm adopts, will affect the returns to that practice. For example, worker familiarity with computers will affect the returns to investing in the new computer system. An important assumption is that, regardless of what other practices the firm has in place, these practice-specific variables will affect the returns to adopting that practice.

In particular, the practice-specific return for each practice is

$\beta_1\mathbf{X}_1$ if the firm adopts Practice 1, and

$\beta_2\mathbf{X}_2$ if the firm adopts Practice 2.

Now we have described $\mathbf{X}$, the variables that affect the returns to the practices.

In addition, there also may be factors that affect adoption but not productivity. For example, training subsidies will make it more likely that the firm adopts training programs, but the subsidies themselves do not directly affect productivity. Let $\mathbf{W}$ represent these practice-specific exogenous variables that will affect adoption. Similar to the case for $\mathbf{X}$, an important assumption is that these are practice-specific variables, and they affect the adoption choice for the practice irrespective of what other elements are adopted.

4.4.1. Observability and Bias

Consider the case where the firm is aware of benefits or costs of adopting practices that the econometrician cannot observe. Thus, following Athey and Stern (1998), we further parse the elements of exogenous variation $(\mathbf{X}, \mathbf{W})$ each into an observed component and an unobserved component:

let $\mathbf{X}_j = (\mathbf{x}_j, \chi_j)$ for Practice j ($j = 1, 2$), and

let $\mathbf{W}_j = (\mathbf{w}_j, \omega_j)$ for Practice j ($j = 1, 2$).

Table 3. Examples of observable and unobservable exogenous variations in the adoption of computers

Variable	Observable	Unobservable
X	$\mathbf{X}_j$ (e.g., years of experience, education)	χ_j (e.g., home use of computers, whether software is user friendly)
W	$\mathbf{w}_j$ (e.g., state or federal tax laws to subsidize technology investment, regulation requiring use of a particular technology)	ω_j (e.g., beliefs about whether computer system will be adopted by other firms [if network effects are present], manager inclination to adopt fads)

Table 3 is an example of the observed components $(\mathbf{x}, \mathbf{w})$ and unobserved components (χ, ω) of exogenous variation for adopting Practice 1, a computer system.

The observable factors can be incorporated into the estimating equations. However, depending on the nature of the unobserved heterogeneity, econometric approaches may be biased to either overestimate or underestimate complementarity. Consider an estimate of a complementarity parameter from interaction effects using an ordinary least squares or two-stage least squares estimation of the organizational design production function. Assume that the interaction effects θ_{ij} are constant across firms,[12] where the first subscript indexes the level of the first practice (0 or 1), and the second subscript indexes the level of the second practice (also 0 or 1).

The total payoff for each of the four systems will now consist of three components:

1. the direct effect of Practice 1, if it is present;
2. the direct effect of Practice 2, if it is present; and
3. the pure interaction effect θ_{ij} for the relevant system.

Thus we have the following estimating equation:

$$f^t(i, j) = \beta_{1t}x_{1t}y_{1t} + \beta_{2t}x_{2t}y_{2t} + \theta_{ij} + \xi_t, \qquad (11)$$

where x represents the observables, y is a dummy variable that is equal to 1 if the firm adopts the practice, and θ_{ij} is the pure interaction effect. We use t to index the firm, and ξ is a firm-specific error term. Equation (11) is similar to the approach of Ichniowski et al. (1997).

As Athey and Stern (1998) point out, we can further break up the error into the following terms:

$$\xi_t = \chi_{1t}y_{1t} + \chi_{2t}y_{2t} + \varepsilon_t, \qquad (12)$$

---

12. In other words, assume that there is no systematic variation across firms in the performance effects of interactions. We discuss implications of relaxing this assumption in Section 4.4.4.

so that

$$f^t(0, 0) = \theta_{00} + \varepsilon_t, \text{ if the system} = (0, 0)$$

$$f^t(0, 1) = \theta_{01} + \beta_{2t}x_{2t} + \chi_2 + \varepsilon_t, \text{ if the system} = (0, 1)$$

$$f^t(1, 0) = \theta_{10} + \beta_{1t}x_{1t} + \chi_1 + \varepsilon_t, \text{ if the system} = (1, 0)$$

$$f^t(1, 1) = \theta_{11} + \beta_{1t}x_{1t} + \beta_{2t}x_{2t} = \chi_1 + \chi_2 + \varepsilon_t, \text{ if the system} = (1, 1).$$

The problem is that χ_1 and χ_2 are unobservable. For example, the ordinary least squares estimate of the payoff from adopting both practices together, $\hat{\theta}_{11}^{OLS}$, will have two bias terms (one each from χ_1 and χ_2).

Now recall the complementarity test discussed in Section 4.1:

$$\kappa_p \equiv f(1, 1) + f(0, 0) - f(1, 0) - f(0, 1).$$

The expected value of the test statistic will be

$$E[\hat{\kappa}^{OLS}] = \kappa + E[\chi_1 | ij = (1, 1)] + E[\chi_2 | ij = (1, 1)]$$
$$- E[\chi_1 | ij = (1, 0)] - E[\chi_2 | ij = (0, 1)].$$

The last four terms add up to zero only if $\kappa_p = 0$ and χ_1 and χ_2 are uncorrelated or are equal to zero. Otherwise, there is bias, which we explore next.

4.4.2. Biases in the Performance Test

Under reasonable assumptions, the performance tests may reject the existence of complementarities even when they actually exist. Consider the following assumptions (Athey and Stern 1998: 18):

1. There are no unobserved exogenous drivers of adoption for the practices: $\omega_1 = \omega_2 = 0$.

2. χ_1 and χ_2 are uncorrelated.

3. The practices are truly complements: $\kappa_p > 0$.

Then we have $E[\hat{\kappa}_p^{OLS}] < \kappa_p$ and $E[\hat{\kappa}_p^{2SLS}] < \kappa_p$.

This result may seem a bit counterintuitive. Why should the existence of uncorrelated χ_1 and χ_2 bias the statistic downward, leading us to possibly reject complementarities when in actuality they exist?

To see the problem, write the test statistic as follows:

$$E[\hat{\kappa}_p^{OLS}] = \kappa_p + E[\chi_1 | ij = (1, 1)] - E[\chi_1 | ij = (1, 0)]$$
$$+ E[\chi_2 | ij = (1, 1)] - E[\chi_2 | ij = (0, 1)].$$

Consider the first term after κ_p. When a firm has adopted both practices, and the practices are truly complementary, then a manager is more likely to find it beneficial to adopt the new computer system, even if there is not much of an unobserved shock χ_1. Now examine the second term. If there is no training, and the practices are complementary, then the manager is less likely to adopt the computer system unless there is a beneficial unobserved productivity shock χ_1. Take an extreme case and suppose that, unless there is training, the econometrician has good reason to believe from the observed variables that the firm is worse off adopting computers than not adopting. Therefore, assuming that the manager is optimizing, if the firm adopts computers but not training, there must have been a large source of unobserved benefits to adopting computers that the manager was aware of, but the econometrician did not see. Therefore, $E[\chi_1|ij = (1, 0)] > E[\chi_1|ij = (1, 1)]$, and so $E[\chi_1|ij = (1, 1)] - E[\chi_1|ij = (1, 0)] < 0$. Using similar reasoning, $E[\chi_2|ij = (1, 0)] > E[\chi_2|ij = (1, 1)]$, and so $E[\chi_2|ij = (1, 1)] - E[\chi_2|ij = (0, 1)] < 0$.

Thus, when the manager is optimizing and faces practice-specific productivity shocks that are unobserved by the econometrician, then the sum of the four last terms is always negative, biasing down the test statistic.

As a practical example, this might be the case if spare computer capacity can be leased out at some firms, generating additional profits from computer purchases for those firms but not for others. Then some firms (those with leasing opportunities) will choose to purchase computers even when the complementary practice (training) is not present. In contrast, firms that already have a training system in place are more likely to find it profitable to purchase computers, even when they do not obtain any additional profits from leasing opportunities. If the econometrician does not observe these leasing opportunities, then the test statistic can be biased downward.

4.4.3. Biases in the Correlation Test
Now assume the following:

1. There are no unobserved exogenous drivers of adoption for the practices: $\omega_1 = \omega_2 = 0$.

2. χ_1 and χ_2 are positively correlated (not uncorrelated, as in Section 4.4.2).

3. The practices are truly independent: $\kappa_p = 0$.

Then we have

$$E[\hat{\kappa}_c^{OLS}] > 0 \quad \text{and} \quad E[\hat{\kappa}_c^{2SLS}] > \kappa.$$

That is, the researcher would find that there is a correlation between the practices, even though there are no complementarities between them.

With these assumptions, the unobserved returns to the new computer system could be high when the unobserved returns to training are also high. For example, it might be that firms in information-intensive industries have higher returns to computer investments than other firms have. Similarly, they might also experience greater benefits from training their workers. Then computer purchases would disproportionately occur if χ_1 is high, which is exactly when χ_2 is high as well, leading to greater training.

This example can be thought of as a basic case of bias stemming from omitted variables. Obviously, if the potential for such variables exists, the econometrician should make every effort to measure them (i.e., convert them from χ to $\mathbf{x}$) and explicitly include them in the regression.

4.4.4. Systems of Equations and Instruments

Organizational practices can be thought of as inputs to production, much like labor, capital, and materials. They have costs and generate output, when combined with the right set of matching practices. Accordingly, the potential biases in estimating equations for the effects of organizational practices have direct analogues in production functions and factor demand equations. Thus, we can look to those theories for tools to address these biases.

For instance, the bias in the performance equation, as discussed above, arises because the choice of practices is endogenously determined. Higher levels of one practice will lead to higher levels of a complementary practice. However, if all exogenous drivers $\mathbf{W}$ can be identified for the practices, then these drivers can be used as instruments, and a two-stage regression can be estimated. In essence, the econometrician first estimates a demand equation for $\mathbf{X}$, which includes all exogenous determinants of the practice level. If the instruments are valid, then this approach may eliminate the endogeneity problem and thereby eliminate the resulting bias from these particular unobservables in the performance equation.

If the econometrician has insight into the specific structure of the production function and the relationships among the variables, then a more structural model can be estimated. In particular, the performance and the demand equations can be simultaneously estimated as a system of equations with appropriate cross-equation restrictions (for a general discussion of this approach, see, e.g., Berndt 1991: 449–509).

4.4.5. System-Specific Variables

Just as there may be unobservables that are correlated with specific practices, there may also be unobservables that are correlated with specific systems of practices, even if they are not correlated with the practices themselves. Unfortunately, by positing a set of unobserved productivity shocks with a suitable pattern of correlations, one can derive any type of bias at all.

For instance, suppose firms that allocate budgets based on a centralized rule gain no benefit from investing in training when they also buy computers—then there is no true complementarity. However, suppose that they tend to invest in both practices or in neither one proportionately (because of the standardized budgeting rule, e.g., spending a fixed percentage of last year's sales on each new practice). In that case, one can see that if having the centralized rule happens to be correlated with greater output, for reasons having nothing to do with complementarities, then both complementarities test statistics will be biased toward finding complementarities. Firms will be more likely to adopt one practice when they adopt the other, and firms with higher performance will be more likely to adopt the practices together than separately.[13] Of course,

---

13. In some cases, it may make sense to expand the system of practices that are considered potential complements to include such a third factor. For instance, it may be plausible that the correlation between a decisionmaking rule and certain clusters of practices is not due to chance, but rather reflects some complementarity between the practices and this type of decisionmaking itself. In that case, the interesting question may not be whether the complementarities exist, but rather what the mechanism is through which they work.

the opposite bias is equally easy to imagine. If the centralized budgeting rule is correlated with lower performance, then firms that adopt the practices together will have a negative productivity shock, biasing the performance test against finding complementarities even while the correlation test is biased toward finding them.

In most settings, with a little creativity and effort, one can imagine all manner of unobserved variables that add or subtract performance to certain clusters of practices or that create correlations among certain practices and yet are unrelated to direct complementarities. This fact underscores the importance of the econometrician having genuine domain knowledge of the particular set of practices being studied. In the abstract, with zero knowledge, any pattern of unobservable productivity shocks is theoretically possible, and thus, any type of bias is possible. Insofar as unobservables cannot, by definition, be measured, there cannot be a purely econometric solution to this concern. Instead, the researcher needs to gain sufficient expertise regarding the setting to be confident that all relevant variables are included in the model and that specific, plausible alternative explanations are duly considered and assessed. A convincing analysis will rarely, if ever, rely solely on econometric evidence.

4.5. Mitigating Unobserved Heterogeneity

Because unobserved heterogeneity can seriously undermine estimates of complementarities, it is important to address it. There are four principal approaches to mitigating the effects of unobserved heterogeneity: homogeneous populations, panel data, natural experiments, and designed experiments.

4.5.1. Homogeneous Populations

The researcher can remove as much unobserved variation as possible ex ante by focusing on homogeneous populations. This approach makes it possible to specify narrow production functions and performance metrics that are tightly linked to the underlying factor changes.

For example, Ichniowski et al. (1997) deliberately limited their analysis to organizations with nearly identical production processes and outputs to eliminate most sources of heterogeneity even before beginning their analysis. Bartel et al. (2004) and Ichniowski and Shaw (2003) provide good reviews of "insider econometrics," which often employs this approach.

An important benefit of this approach is that it makes it possible to specify a narrow performance metric that is specifically adapted to the production process being studied. In this case, rather than look at overall market value, profits, or sales, each of which could be affected by a variety of outside, and often unobservable, factors, Ichniowski et al. (1997) measure the "uptime" of the production line. Based on visits and interviews at the production sites, they determined that the proportion of time that a line was actually running, as opposed to being down for some reason, almost uniquely determined its performance. Accordingly, focusing on this particular metric provided a sufficient statistic for performance without contamination from other factors. Subsequently, Bartel et al. (2007) took a similar approach in a longitudinal study of 212 plants in the valve manufacturing industry. They looked at several distinct performance metrics, each one matched to a predicted effect of a specific type of IT. They found evidence that IT increased productivity via its complementarities with certain business strategies (more customization and smaller batches), human capital, and new human resource practices.

Although this approach is very powerful, it is not without its weaknesses. First, it requires a suitably homogeneous population. Second, the very narrowness of the production function implies that the results may not be readily applicable to other settings. Finally, unobservables may still play a critical role. For instance, the choices of different work practices at different minimills may have reflected differential (perceived) costs of adoption, differential (perceived) benefits, or random error. Without knowing exactly what factors drove adoption, it is difficult to assess the strength of the evidence for complementarities. Furthermore, although the homogeneous population may reduce the unobserved heterogeneity, it is also likely to reduce the observed variation that drives the regressions of interest, so the signal-to-noise ratio may not be improved as much as hoped. As the late Zvi Griliches once remarked, when one slices the data more and more finely, one often discovers a fractal-like self-symmetry on smaller scales, leaving the ratio of observable and unobservable economic phenomena relatively unaffected.

4.5.2. Panel Data

Even though focusing on narrow production functions comes at the cost of generalizability, in some cases one can get the best of both worlds. One way to look at multiple industries while still controlling for heterogeneity to some extent is to use panel data. In particular, including fixed effects or taking long differences can remove potential biases from unobserved heterogeneity when the effects of the unobserved variables do not change over time. In this way, a much larger and more diverse sample can be studied.

An example of this strategy is the quantification of IT-related organizational capital for 272 American firms by Brynjolfsson et al. (2002). The firms were in a variety of industries, and each began with its own idiosyncratic combination of observable and unobservable characteristics. To address the unobservables, the authors estimated a specification with firm fixed effects. Thus, a firm with unusually high market value stemming from any unobservables that were invariant over time would not be credited with this high value when assessing the interaction of observable organizational practices and IT. A similar argument applied to their analysis of long differences. This specification subtracted out the historical levels of each of the variables and only examined changes in these variables.

A benefit of this approach is that it is possible to detect patterns that show up across numerous industries. This possibility increases the likelihood that similar patterns will hold outside the sample, and it makes it easier to make fairly general statements about characteristics of the economy as a whole. It also can make it easier to gather larger samples, because the units of observation are not constrained to be as similar ex ante.

However, there are also some important weaknesses. First, the fixed effects or long differences will not control for unobservables that change over time. Obviously, a change in one or more of these unobservables can bias the results if (i) it is correlated with the observed variables being studied and (ii) it has an effect on either the levels of the other potential complements (creating a spurious correlation or spurious lack thereof) or performance (affecting the productivity regressions). In particular, the same issue of unknown drivers recurs, as it did when using homogeneous populations.

Second, the production functions themselves remain heterogeneous. As a result, the same shock may affect the observed variables in different ways across different firms. For instance, suppose that there is strong complementarity among certain inputs in some firms, while those same inputs are substitutes in other firms that have different production functions. The net result may be that, when the data are aggregated, none of the tests show evidence of complementarity.

The researcher can never eliminate either of these potential problems but can mitigate them by (i) including as many relevant drivers of performance and input demand in the set of observed variables as possible and (ii) explicitly identifying the shocks or drivers that lead to changes in their levels and distinguishing their effects in relevant subsamples of the data. The more sharply defined these exogenous shocks are, the less likely it is that they are coincident with an unobservable.

4.5.3. Natural Experiments

If the researcher can clearly identify an exogenous source of variation in the observable factors, then the potential role of unobserved drivers can be greatly reduced. The importance of explicitly identifying the sources of changes in the factors is often overlooked, but it should be an indispensable component of empirical research on complementarities.

There are several categories of change that can provide the requisite drivers of variation. For instance, legal and institutional changes are often ideal candidates to consider, because a change in a law or government policy can provide a precise date and specific geographic area or jurisdiction for which the change occurs. Given the power of the state, the costs of noncompliance can be extremely high, which also creates a sharp contrast before and after the change. The Athey and Stern (2002) study of the introduction of Enhanced 911 service is an excellent example of this type of exogenous variation. Advances in IT made it possible to identify the location of emergency callers. However, by government edict, the adoption was phased in county by county across the state of Pennsylvania, making it possible to identify the changes in complementary activities and several specific outcome measures before and after the adoption of the technology. Given the known government policy change, endogeneity and unobservables could be virtually ruled out as causing the adoption of the technology, making it much easier to make causal inferences about its effects. Each year, cities, states, nations, and other government entities introduce, modify, or repeal thousands of regulations and laws that can affect the relative costs and benefits of different organizational practices. Many such changes are promising candidates for exogenous drivers, although researchers must be cognizant that some legal changes themselves are endogenous to the organizational changes. For instance, differences in minimum wage laws may, in part, be influenced by the differences in the industry mix or organizational practices across state lines, or even changes in the relative importance—and political power—of different industries over time.

The introduction of management practices across plants by a multinational corporation can also provide a source of exogenous variation. For instance, the Bloom et al. (2007) study, as described earlier, uses data from a set of establishments in the United Kingdom and traces ownership of the parent company to the country where it is based. Because the plants in the study were from the same locality, the institutional differences, derived from the nationalities of their owners, provided a valuable source of identification for the observed differences in technology use and performance.

Technology and resource price shocks are particularly promising candidates. As noted in Section 2.2.4, the definition of complementarity in demand theory is that increasing the price of an input reduces the demand for complementary inputs. For example, an increase in the price of oil would be expected to decrease the demand for complements to oil, which might include energy-intensive methods of production and organizational practices. For instance, commuting by car and traveling by jet might be replaced by telecommuting and videoconferencing. In turn, such substitutions might affect the attractiveness of other organizational complements, such as the types of incentive systems used, the way tasks are allocated across jobs, and the criteria for hiring and training. A technology shock that reduced the costs of electronic interactions might have similar effects on telecommuting and videoconferencing and thereby on the associated complements. Accordingly, shocks to the price of oil or sudden innovations in technology are likely to be useful for identifying the reasons for changes in the other complements, especially if the shocks vary cross-sectionally in an observable way. For instance, a multibusiness firm that rolls out a new technology across the firm over a period of months or years can create a natural experiment, particularly if the rollout is randomized or at least uncorrelated with the variables of interest. The larger, more precisely timed, and more numerous the exogenous shocks are, the better, because they are then more likely to overwhelm other unobservable drivers of adoption.

In each of these cases, an exogenous shock can address the identification issue. Of course, the econometrician needs to make the case that the shock is truly exogenous.

4.5.4. Designed Experiments

Last but not least of the mitigations of unobserved heterogeneity are the increasing opportunities for economists to participate in designed experiments. Such experiments are, of course, the gold standard for research in the natural sciences. However, given that economists typically study organizations with large numbers of humans and millions or billions of dollars of assets, it has historically been beyond their power, or budgets, to run controlled experiments to test organizational hypotheses. However, the opportunities for such experiments are growing, and they are underexploited. In particular, more and more managers today have analytical backgrounds, springing from more formal training in quantitative methods in MBA and other educational programs. As a result, they are already carrying out controlled experiments to assess alternative policies in the course of their decisionmaking. This trend is especially prevalent in direct marketing and Internet retailing policies, but it also occurs in work practices and technology adoption. For instance, Gary Loveman, CEO of Harrah's, who has a doctorate in economics, regularly experiments with alternative incentive and promotion programs for employees and customers. Harrah's gathers copious data from these tests and uses them to design and implement new policies. Similarly, Amazon continuously experiments in both subtle and radical ways with its web design, pricing, delivery options, product selection, recommendation tools, and new features—individually and in combination with one another. At both companies, the richness and complexity of the choice set provide ample opportunities for identifying potential complementarities. Although these two firms are unusual in their commitment to experimentation, they are far from unique.

Historically, the costs of large-scale field experiments have discouraged economists from relying on them for data gathering. However, by using data from experiments already conducted by business managers, or better yet, coordinating with them in advance to design more careful experiments, the cost issue can be overcome. When the manager is genuinely uncertain about the optimal policy combination, a well-designed experiment can pay for itself many times over, because the better-informed decisions following the experiment are more likely to be profitable than uninformed choice. Hence, managers can benefit as much, or more, from joint work with academic researchers as the academics can.

For example, Bhansali and Brynjolfsson (2007) worked with a large insurance firm to analyze the effects of a new electronic document management system on work practices, time use, and performance. The company had employees in locations across the country engaged in largely identical claims-processing work. They phased in the technology at different offices over time and allowed the researchers to gather data pre- and post-implementation, as well granting them access to historical data. The resulting quasi-experiment not only addressed many causality issues, but also made it possible to compare practices and productivity both across time and across different locations. As a result, the correlation of technology use with decreased routine work, increased cognitive work, and higher performance on several performance measures was much easier to interpret.

More recently, Bloom et al. (2009b, 2011) have conducted randomized control trials in textile firms in India. The treatment was to offer organizational consulting advice to a random sample of the firms. They found that the treated firms became more computerized and more decentralized in their decisionmaking, consistent with earlier findings about the complementarity of these practices. In turn, average productivity increased by about 10% after the treatment, reflecting improved quality and reduced inventories.

The growing success of the experimental approach in addressing issues of causality is underscored by the large number of field experiments reviewed in Lazear and Oyer (this volume).

5. Conclusion

5.1. Implications for Managers

Complementarities in organizations can be analyzed rigorously using theory and data, but they also have important practical relevance for managers and those who educate or advise them. For instance, the frameworks and approaches we review in this chapter can provide insights into

- choices about organizational practice,
- change management,
- competitive strategy,
- mergers and acquisitions, and
- leadership and culture.

Managers are deluged with examples of "best practice," yet when they implement these same practices at their own firms, they rarely have as much success as the exemplar that they seek to imitate. Complementarities can help explain why. The success of a practice almost always depends on the system of complementary practices in which it is embedded. Thus, the concept of "best practice," devoid of context, can be misleading. The same piece rate pay rules that work so well at Lincoln Electric may end up undermining performance if implemented à la carte in another organization. Thus, before implementing a new incentive system, hiring practice, training program, or technology, managers should explicitly consider the existence or absence of the relevant complements. Of course, specifically identifying the relevant complements will often be nontrivial, but merely being aware of their relevance is a necessary first step.

A fruitful application of the theory of complementarities has been to change management. In particular, taking advantage of new technologies or other innovations typically requires substantial changes in a broad set of related business practices. Insights into the optimal pace, sequence, location, and even feasibility of change efforts can be provided by analyzing the situation from the perspective of complementarities. Although the mathematics of complementarities can be daunting, the underlying concepts are not hard for managers to grasp and manipulate. For instance, the Matrix of Change tool (Brynjolfsson et al. 1997) mentioned in Section 1 has been used by thousands of managers to make explicit organizational complementarities that might otherwise remain hidden. Appendix B provides a simple illustration.

Complementarities can also affect competitive strategy by creating lasting entry barriers and accompanying rents. As the Lincoln Electric case (Berg and Fast 1975) illustrates, best practices can be difficult to imitate if they rely on a web of interactions with other practices for success. As Milgrom and Roberts (1990) point out, this gives economic content and rigor to the concept of "core competence." Ironically, as noted by Roberts (2004), organizations that succeed in implementing tightly coupled systems of highly complementary practices may have the greatest difficulty adopting new combination of practices when external factors warrant a change.

Complementarities among organizational practices create risks in mergers and acquisitions. The real value of many, perhaps most, businesses lies not in their tangible assets but in their intangible organizational capital. But this organizational capital can be fragile; the practices that are successful in one setting may not be so after being meshed with different practices in a merger or acquisition. Understanding the role of complementarities in organizations can make this management task less mysterious and more manageable.

Finally, leadership and culture might be thought of as far removed from quantitative analysis, and in many ways they are. However, an understanding of complementarities can illustrate why and when a clear leadership vision and strong organizational culture can be most beneficial. When practices are complementary, there are multiple equilibria. Coordinating on one of these equilibria, even if it is not the global optimum, will often be more successful than choosing practices in a decentralized and uncoordinated way. In contrast, optimizing individual practices on their own does not necessarily maximize total firm performance. This line of thinking suggests a clear role for leadership and culture. The task becomes even more important when conditions call for moving from one equilibrium to another one. Just as complementarities can create inertia to prevent change, they can also create momentum for a virtuous cycle of change— if the right set of practices is changed first.

Historically, the theory and analytical tools developed in economics and related disciplines have provided clear guidelines for managers who wish to use quantitative analysis instead of just heuristics and instincts to manage and price physical assets and technologies. The formal analysis of organizational complementarities promises to do the same for a much broader set of management challenges facing companies today.

5.2. An Agenda for Economists

There are at least three major frontiers for economic research on complementarities in organizations that overlap with one another: applications of existing theory, empirical assessments of complementarities, and extensions of the basic theory.

5.2.1. Applications of Existing Theory

In some ways, the agenda for economists seeking to advance the frontiers of complementarities research parallels the implications for managers. By identifying specific sets of complementary practices, we may shed light on a remarkably broad range of economic questions. For example:

- Can organizational complements to new technologies explain changes in productivity growth across geography, time, and industry?[14]

- Can such complements explain the growth in income inequality and the demand for certain types of labor or skills?

- Why are firms exiting certain industries and what do they have in common? What about entrants, including those with operations in other industries, as well as start-ups?

- To what extent do patterns of exports and imports, or regional trade, match the geographic distributions of complementary factors?

- How well can complementarities explain the specific set of activities retained in house and those outsourced or spun off? When can they explain mergers and acquisitions?

In addition, there may be some general implications of complementarities beyond those linked to specific practices. If one thinks of organizations as large clusters of complements, including many that are intangible or subtle, then the theory has several implications. For instance, when combined with game theory, complementarities can be a part of a theory of organizational inertia (e.g., Baron et al. 1996), explaining why and when change can be difficult. It can be very difficult to coordinate change on multiple practices when decisionmaking is decentralized, communication is imperfect, incentives do not match output, or all of the above.

A closely related question is the existence of persistent performance differences among seemingly similar firms (Gibbons 2006). Subtle complementarities can explain why apparently similar competitors do not obtain the same benefits from activities. If the complements are long lived, then the systematic performance differences can also be persistent.

Complementarities literally mean that the whole is greater than the sum of its parts, which suggests a role in valuing the organizational capital and other intangible assets of firms. Although neoclassical theory tends to model firms as production functions that simply combine various inputs to produce output, complementarities provide an explanation for why a going concern may be much more valuable than the same components à la carte. Similarly, by identifying and exploiting complementarities, the overall output of an economy can consistently exceed the weighted sum of its factor growth rates. In addition, the more heterogeneity there is among inputs, the more combinations are possible, and the greater the potential there is for complementarities.

14. For example, see Bresnahan and Trajtenberg (1995) and Basu et al. (2003).

Finally, the interplay of practices in sustaining a system of complements may shed light on corporate culture. Because of the multiplicity of equilibria that arise when systems have large numbers of potentially complementary practices, a general coordinating device, such as culture, can play an important role. For instance, it might be possible to extend the Kreps (1990) model of corporate culture by incorporating a more explicit role for complementarities.

5.2.2. Empirical Assessments of Complementarities

Most, if not all, applications discussed above lend themselves to empirical work. Embedding econometric work in a complementarities framework can make it easier to develop testable hypotheses.

Thus far, most empirical work on complementarities has relied on cross-sectional studies or relatively short panels. However, some of the most interesting issues raised by the theory pertain to changes in organizations over time. Thus, there is an opportunity for more work using longer panels and longitudinal data, with attention to entrants, exits, and persistence of performance differences.

Methodologically, some of the current frontiers for empirical work on complementarities include:

- panel data on relatively homogeneous populations and clear, exogenous drivers of variation in practices, or preferably changes in those practices;

- novel metrics of activity and performance, such as fine-grained, practice-specific inputs and outputs;

- structural modeling of systems of both the performance and demand equations, drawing on significant domain-specific knowledge of the setting, relevant practices, and likely interactions; and

- exploitation and even design of controlled field experiments to isolate the role of changing specific practices.

There has been significant progress in all these areas. However, the last one, controlled field experiments, may be the most important for eliminating the biases discussed in Section 4 and clearly quantifying complementarities. There are significant limits to how much can be learned solely by more sophisticated modeling. Fortunately, managers are increasingly receptive to the experimental approach. They are designing and implementing controlled experiments on their own and in cooperation with researchers. Part of this trend reflects the more academic and often quantitative training that managers have today and part reflects the relative flexibility of some new technologies, making controlled rollouts and careful monitoring of results easier. The success of the experimental approach in interactive marketing has made it more attractive as a way to improve organizational design choices as well.

5.2.3. Extensions of the Basic Theory

There are several ways the theory of complementarities can be extended. One interesting tack is to explore the dynamics of learning and growth in larger systems of complements. As the number of potential organizational complements increases, the number of potentially profitable systems to explore explodes combinatorially. This brings to the fore the issue of efficient search and learning. Learning need not occur primarily or even at all on the level of an individual through conscious deliberation. It is also possible that learning occurs at the organizational level, perhaps through a quasi-evolutionary process. For instance, the influential paper by Cohen et al. (1972) argued that managerial decisions should not be thought of as being made rationally, but rather through the random matching of problems and solutions, as if being jostled about in a garbage can (see also Levinthal and March 1981).

In practice, innovative combinations of business practices are sometimes achieved by extensive trial and error. If the production process is complex, with many potentially relevant variables and interactions, it can be very difficult to identify the optimal combinations. Strong complementarities can significantly retard such a process by reducing the value of local experimentation, especially if the choices are indivisible and nonconcave. At the same time, the theory can provide guidance about ways to simplify the search process.

If this mechanism of tinkering is important, then except in environments that have been very stable for a long time, the population of firms will exhibit a variety of different strategies, including both successful and unsuccessful ones. As argued by Nelson and Winter (1982), successful systems may increase their share of the population of firms if they survive longer or attract more imitation. However, the most profitable combinations will not necessarily be the ones that dominate the population (e.g., see Cowperthwaite et al. 2008). There is recent evidence that design modularity can affect the nature and speed of this evolution by bundling together complementary components (MacCormack et al. 2007), and complementarities can create momentum as well as inertia (Milgrom et al. 1991), but a comprehensive theory remains to be developed.

In conclusion, there is a plethora of opportunities for further research using the tools and insights of complementarities in organizations. Such research may shed light on some of the longstanding puzzles and challenges that have confronted economists and others who study organizations.

Appendix A: Empirical Papers

| Type of study | Focus of study | | | |
	Firm	Plant or establishment	Production line or business unit	Individual
Complementarities between human resource management and workplace variables	Huselid (1995) Whittington et al. (1999) Kato and Morishima (2002) Graff et al. (2003) Bertschek and Kaiser (2004) Janod and Saint-Martin (2004)		Dunlop and Weil (1996) Ichniowski et al. (1997) Ichniowski and Shaw (1999) Boning et al. (2007)	Gant et al. (2002)

Type of study	Focus of study			
	Firm	Plant or establishment	Production line or business unit	Individual
Complementarities between information technology and human resource management/workplace variables	Bresnahan et al. (2002) Brynjolfsson et al. (2002) Brynjolfsson and Hitt (2003) Bugamelli and Pagano (2004) Crespi et al. (2006) Bloom et al. (2008)	Lynch and Black (1998) Black and Lynch (2001, 2004) Caroli and Van Reenen (2001) Bartel et al. (2007) Bloom et al. (2007)		Athey and Stern (2002) Autor et al. (2003)
Complementarities and innovation	Laursen (2002) Scott Morton (2002) Laursen and Foss (2003) Mohnen and Roller (2005)	Bresnahan and Greenstein (1996) Zoghi et al. (2007)	MacCormack et al. (2007)	
Case studies	Berg and Fast (1975) Enright (1995) Brynjolfsson et al. (1997) Siggelkow (2001, 2002a) Autor et al. (2002) McAfee (2002) Brynjolfsson (2005) Bhansali and Brynjolfsson (2007)	Barley (1986) Krafcik (1988) Womack et al. (1991)		
Complementarities of decision rights		Arruñada et al. (2001)		

Appendix B: Example of the Matrix of Change

When Merrill Lynch's brokerage business was confronted with competition from online brokers, the company contemplated changing over to an all-electronic approach. Although the technology itself was relatively straightforward, it was clear that the associated complementary changes that would also need to be made would be traumatic. In addition to physical stores, the existing brokerage business had several other important characteristics: assignment of a personal broker to each client; relatively high fees; use of the human broker to mediate trades; provision of investment recommendations; heavy investment in an in-house research staff; and focus on a

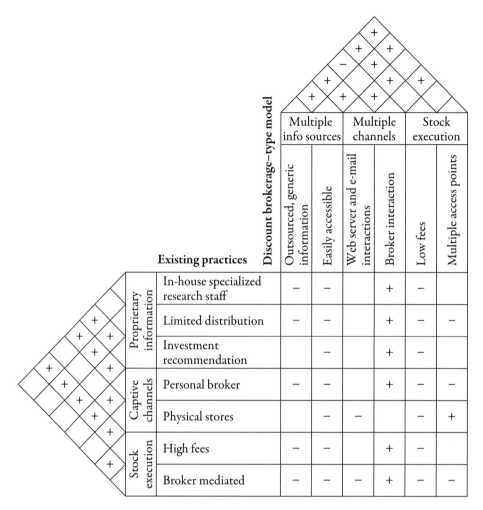

Existing practices		Discount brokerage–type model	Multiple info sources		Multiple channels		Stock execution	
			Outsourced, generic information	Easily accessible	Web server and e-mail interactions	Broker interaction	Low fees	Multiple access points
Proprietary information	In-house specialized research staff		−	−		+	−	
	Limited distribution		−	−		+	−	−
	Investment recommendation				−	+	−	
Captive channels	Personal broker		−	−		+	−	−
	Physical stores			−	−		−	+
Stock execution	High fees			−	−	+	−	
	Broker mediated		−	−	−	+	−	−

Figure B1. Matrix of Change analysis for the transition from traditional brokerage to online brokerage.

relatively limited, high net worth client base. Every one of these characteristics was eliminated in the reigning approach to electronic trading, and a new set of practices was implemented.

The Matrix of Change analysis showed that the old practices formed a coherent system of mutual complements. The new system also was dominated by complementary interactions. However, interactions between the old and new practices were rarely complementary and more often conflicted with one another. The Matrix of Change tool illustrated these effects by denoting complementary interactions with "+", and conflicts with "−" as described in Figure B1.

The complementarities in the old system suggest it would have a great deal of inertia, and the conflicts in the transition matrix suggest that an organization that tried to run with a mixture of old and new practices would be relatively inefficient. Hence, the change effort would likely be difficult, and there were relatively few synergies between the old and new systems. Finally, it was clear that the new system was itself fairly coherent, but perhaps not quite as much so as the old system. These insights, while drawing on complementarities theory, can be visualized easily in the Matrix of Change without a formal economic or mathematical analysis.

REFERENCES

Aral, Sinan, Erik Brynjolfsson, and Lynn Wu. 2012. "Assessing Three-Way Complementarities: Performance Pay, Monitoring and Information Technology." *Management Science* 58: 913–931.

Argyris, Chris. 1982. "The Executive Mind and Double-Loop Learning." *Organizational Dynamics* 11: 5–22.

Arora, Ashish. 1996. "Testing for Complementarities in Reduced-Form Regressions: A Note." *Economics Letters* 50: 51–55.

Arora, Ashish, and Alfonso Gambardella. 1990. "Complementarity and External Linkages: The Strategies of the Large Firms in Biotechnology." *Journal of Industrial Economics* 38: 362–379.

Arruñada, Benito, Luis Garicano, and Luis Vazquez. 2001. "Contractual Allocation of Decision Rights and Incentives: The Case of Automobile Distribution." *Journal of Law, Economics, and Organization* 17: 257–284.

Athey, Susan, and Scott Stern. 1998. "An Empirical Framework for Testing Theories about Complementarity in Organizational Design." Working Paper 6600, National Bureau of Economic Research, Cambridge, MA.

———. 2002. "The Impact of Information Technology on Emergency Health Care Outcomes." *RAND Journal of Economics* 33: 399–432.

Autor, David H., Frank Levy, and Richard J. Murnane. 2002. "Upstairs, Downstairs: Computers and Skills on Two Floors of a Large Bank." *Industrial and Labor Relations Review* 55: 432–447.

———. 2003. "The Skill Content of Recent Technological Change: An Empirical Exploration." *Quarterly Journal of Economics* 118: 1279–1333.

Barley, Steven R. 1986. "Technology as an Occasion for Structuring: Evidence from Observations of CT Scanners and the Social Order of Radiology Departments." *Administrative Science Quarterly* 31: 78–108.

Baron, James N., M. Diane Burton, and Michael T. Hannan. 1996. "Inertia and Change in the Early Years: Employment Relations in Young, High-Technology Firms." *Industrial and Corporate Change* 5: 503–536.

———. 1999. "Engineering Bureaucracy: The Genesis of Formal Policies, Positions, and Structures in High-Technology Firms." *Journal of Law, Economics, and Organization* 15: 1–41.

Bartel, Ann, Casey Ichniowski, and Kathryn Shaw. 2004. "Using 'Insider Econometrics' to Study Productivity." *American Economic Review* 94: 217–223.

———. 2007. "How Does Information Technology Affect Productivity? Plant-Level Comparisons of Product Innovation, Process Improvement, and Worker Skills." *Quarterly Journal of Economics* 122: 1721–1758.

Basu, Susanto, John G. Fernald, Nicholas Oulton, and Sylaja Srinivasan. 2003. "The Case of the Missing Productivity Growth, or Does Information Technology Explain Why Productivity Accelerated in the United States but Not in the United Kingdom?" *NBER/Macroeconomics Annual* 18: 9–71.

Belderbos, René, Martin Carree, and Boris Lokshin. 2006. "Complementarity in R&D Cooperation Strategies." *Review of Industrial Organization* 28: 401–426.

Berg, Norman A., and Norman D. Fast. 1975. "The Lincoln Electric Company." Harvard Business School Case 376-028. Cambridge, MA: Harvard Business School.

Berndt, Ernst. 1991. *The Practice of Econometrics: Classic and Contemporary.* Reading, MA: Addison-Wesley.

Bertschek, Irene, and Ulrich Kaiser. 2004. "Productivity Effects of Organizational Change: Micro-econometric Evidence." *Management Science* 50: 394–404.

Bhansali, Sumit, and Erik Brynjolfsson. 2007. "Digitizing Work: Measuring Changes in Information Worker Time Use and Performance with a Quasi-Experiment." Cambridge, MA: Center for Digital Business, Massachusetts Institute of Technology.

Black, Sandra E., and Lisa M. Lynch. 2001. "How to Compete: The Impact of Workplace Practices and Information Technology on Productivity." *Review of Economics and Statistics* 83: 434–445.

———. 2004. "What's Driving the New Economy? The Benefits of Workplace Innovation." *Economic Journal* 114: F97–F116.

Bloom, Nicholas, Raffaella Sadun, and John Van Reenen. 2007. "Americans Do I.T. Better: US Multinationals and the Productivity Miracle." Working Paper 13085, National Bureau of Economic Research, Cambridge, MA.

Bloom, Nicholas, Luis Garicano, Raffaella Sadun, and John Van Reenen. 2009a. "The Distinct Effects of Information Technologies and Communication Technologies on Firm Organization." Working Paper 14975, National Bureau of Economic Research, Cambridge, MA.

Bloom, Nicholas, Benn Eifert, Aprajit Mahajan, David McKenzie, and John Roberts. 2009b. "Management Matters: Evidence from India." Available at: http://www.stanford.edu/~nbloom/MM.pdf.

Bloom, Nicholas, Christos Genakos, Raffaella Sadun, and John Van Reenen. 2011. "Management Practices across Firms and Countries." Working Paper 12-052, Harvard Business School, Cambridge, MA.

Boning, Brent, Casey Ichniowski, and Kathryn Shaw. 2007. "Opportunity Counts: Teams and the Effectiveness of Production Incentives." *Journal of Labor Economics* 25: 613–650.

Bresnahan, Timothy, and Shane Greenstein. 1996. "Technical Progress and Co-Invention in Computing and in the Uses of Computers." *Brookings Papers on Economic Activity* 1996: 1–77.

Bresnahan, Timothy F., and Manuel Trajtenberg. 1995. "General Purpose Technologies 'Engines of Growth'?" *Journal of Econometrics* 65: 83–108.

Bresnahan, Timothy F., Erik Brynjolfsson, and Lorin M. Hitt. 2002. "Information Technology, Workplace Organization, and the Demand for Skilled Labor: Firm-Level Evidence." *Quarterly Journal of Economics* 117: 339–376.

Brynjolfsson, Erik. 2005. "VII Pillars of IT Productivity." *Optimize* 4(5): 6.

Brynjolfsson, Erik, and Lorin M. Hitt. 2000. "Beyond Computation: Information Technology, Organizational Transformation and Business Performance." *Journal of Economic Perspectives* 14(4): 23–48.

———. 2003. "Computing Productivity: Firm-Level Evidence." *Review of Economics and Statistics* 85: 793–808.

Brynjolfsson, Erik, Amy Austin Renshaw, and Marshall van Alstyne. 1997. "The Matrix of Change." *Sloan Management Review* 38(2): 37–54.

Brynjolfsson, Erik, Lorin M. Hitt, and Shinkyu Yang. 2002. "Intangible Assets: Computers and Organizational Capital." *Brookings Papers on Economic Activity* 2002: 137–198.

Bugamelli, Matteo, and Patrizio Pagano. 2004. "Barriers to Investment in ICT." *Applied Economics* 36: 2275–2286.

Caroli, Eve, and John Van Reenen. 2001. "Skill-Biased Organizational Change? Evidence from a Panel of British and French Establishments." *Quarterly Journal of Economics* 116: 1449–1492.

Cohen, Michael, James March, and Johan Olsen. 1972. "A Garbage Can Model of Organizational Choice." *Administrative Science Quarterly* 17: 1–25.

Colombo, Massimo G., Luca Grilli, and Evila Piva. 2006. "In Search of Complementary Assets: The Determinants of Alliance Formation of High-Tech Start-Ups." *Research Policy* 35: 1166–1199.

Cowperthwaite, Matthew C., Evan P. Economo, William R. Harcombe, Eric L. Miller, and Lauren Ancel Meyers. 2008. "The Ascent of the Abundant: How Mutational Networks Constrain Evolution." *PLoS Computational Biology* 4(7): e1000110. DOI: 10.1371/journal.pcbi.100011.

Crespi, Gustavo, Chiara Criscuolo, and Jonathan Haskel. 2007. "Information Technology, Organisational Change and Productivity Growth: Evidence from UK Firms." CEPDP 783, Centre for Economic Performance, London School of Economics and Political Science, London.

Dunlop, John T., and David Weil. 1996. "Diffusion and Performance of Modular Production in the U.S. Apparel Industry." *Industrial Relations* 35: 334–355.

Ennen, Edgar, and Ansgar Richter. 2010. "The Whole Is More Than the Sum of Its Parts—Or Is It? A Review of the Empirical Literature on Complementarities in Organizations." *Journal of Management* 36: 207–233.

Enright, Michael J. 1995. "Organization and Coordination in Geographically Concentrated Industries," in Naomi R. Lamoreaux and Daniel M. G. Raff (eds.), *Coordination and Information: Historical Perspectives on the Organization of Enterprise.* Chicago and London: University of Chicago Press, pp. 103–142.

Gant, Jon, Casey Ichniowski, and Kathryn Shaw. 2002. "Social Capital and Organizational Change in High-Involvement and Traditional Work Organizations." *Journal of Economics and Management Strategy* 11: 289–328.

Garicano, Luis, and Paul Heaton. 2010. "Information Technology, Organization, and Productivity in the Public Sector: Evidence from Police Departments." *Journal of Labor Economics* 28: 167–201.

Gibbons, Robert. 2006. "What the Folk Theorem Doesn't Tell Us." *Industrial and Corporate Change* 15: 381–386.

Graff, Gregory D., Gordon C. Rausser, and Arthur A. Small. 2003. "Agricultural Biotechnology's Complementary Intellectual Assets." *Review of Economics and Statistics* 85: 349–363.

Heckman, James J., and Bo E. Honoré. 1990. "The Empirical Content of the Roy Model." *Econometrica* 58: 1128–1149.

Heckman, James J., and Thomas E. MaCurdy. 1986. "Labor Econometrics," in Zvi Griliches and Michael Intriligator (eds.), *Handbook of Econometrics,* volume III. New York: Elsevier/North-Holland, pp. 1917–1977.

Holmes, Thomas J. 2001. "Bar Codes Lead to Frequent Deliveries and Superstores." *RAND Journal of Economics* 32: 708–725.

Holmström, Bengt, and Paul Milgrom. 1994. "The Firm as an Incentive System." *American Economic Review* 84: 972–991.

Huselid, Mark A. 1995. "The Impact of Human Resource Management Practices on Turnover, Productivity, and Corporate Financial Performance." *Academy of Management Journal* 38: 635–672.

Ichniowski, Casey, and Kathryn Shaw. 1999. "The Effects of Human Resource Management Systems on Economic Performance." *Management Science* 45: 704–721.

———. 2003. "Beyond Incentive Pay: Insiders' Estimates of the Value of Complementary Human Resource Management Practices." *Journal of Economic Perspectives* 17(1): 155–180.

Ichniowski, Casey, Kathryn Shaw, and Giovanna Prennushi. 1997. "The Effects of Human Resource Management Practices on Productivity: A Study of Steel Finishing Lines." *American Economic Review* 87: 291–313.

Janod, Veronique, and Anne Saint-Martin. 2004. "Measuring the Impact of Work Reorganization on Firm Performance: Evidence from French Manufacturing, 1995–1999." *Labour Economics* 11: 785–798.

Jovanovic, Boyan, and Dmitriy Stolyarov. 2000. "Optimal Adoption of Complementary Technologies." *American Economic Review* 90: 15–29.

Kato, Takao, and Motohiro Morishima. 2002. "The Productivity Effects of Participatory Employment Practices: Evidence from New Japanese Panel Data." *Industrial Relations* 41: 487–520.

Krafcik, John F. 1988. "Triumph of the Lean Production System." *Sloan Management Review* 30(1): 41–52.

Kreps, David M. 1990. "Corporate Culture and Economic Theory," in James E. Alt and Kenneth A. Shepsle (eds.), *Perspectives on Positive Political Economy.* Cambridge: University Press, pp. 90–143.

Laursen, Keld. 2002. "The Importance of Sectoral Differences in the Application of Complementary HRM Practices for Innovation Performance." *International Journal of the Economics of Business* 9: 139–156.

Laursen, Keld, and Nicolai J. Foss. 2003. "New Human Resource Management Practices, Complementarities and the Impact on Innovation Performance." *Cambridge Journal of Economics* 27: 243–263.

Levinthal, Daniel A. 1997. "Adaptation on Rugged Landscapes." *Management Science* 43: 934–950.

Levinthal, Daniel A., and James G. March. 1981. "A Model of Adaptive Organizational Search." *Journal of Economic Behavior and Organization* 2: 307–333.

Lynch, Lisa M., and Sandra E. Black. 1998. "Beyond the Incidence of Employer-Provided Training." *Industrial and Labor Relations Review* 52: 64–81.

MacCormack, Alan, John Rusnak, and Carliss Y. Baldwin. 2007. "The Impact of Component Modularity on Design Evolution: Evidence from the Software Industry." Research Paper 08-038, Harvard Business School Technology and Operations Management Unit, Cambridge, MA.

McAfee, Andrew. 2002. "The Impact of Enterprise Information Technology Adoption on Operational Performance: An Empirical Investigation." *Production and Operations Management* 11: 33–53.

Milgrom, Paul, and John Roberts. 1990. "The Economics of Modern Manufacturing: Technology." *American Economic Review* 80: 511–528.

———. 1992. *Economics, Organization and Management.* Upper Saddle River, NJ: Prentice Hall.

———. 1995. "Complementarities and Fit: Strategy, Structure, and Organizational Change in Manufacturing." *Journal of Accounting and Economics* 19: 179–208.

———. 1996. "The LeChatelier Principle." *American Economic Review* 86: 173–179.

Milgrom, Paul, and Chris Shannon. 1994. "Monotone Comparative Statics." *Econometrica* 62: 157–180.

Milgrom, Paul, Yingyi Qian, and John Roberts. 1991. "Complementarities, Momentum, and the Evolution of Modern Manufacturing." *American Economic Review* 81: 84–88.

Mohnen, Pierre, and Lars-Hendrik Roller. 2005. "Complementarities in Innovation Policy." *European Economic Review* 49: 1431–1450.

Nelson, Richard R., and Sidney G. Winter. 1982. *An Evolutionary Theory of Economic Change.* Boston: Harvard University Press.

O'Mahony, Mary, and Bart van Ark (eds.). 2003. *EU Productivity and Competitiveness: An Industry Perspective. Can Europe Resume the Catching-up Process?* Luxembourg: European Commission.

Osterman, Paul. 1991. "Impact of IT on Jobs and Skills," in Michael S. Scott Morton (ed.), *The Corporation of the 1990s—Information Technology and Organizational Transformation.* Oxford: Oxford University Press, pp. 220–243.

Porter, Michael, and Nicolaj Siggelkow. 2008. "Contextuality within Activity Systems and Sustainability of Competitive Advantage." *Academy of Management Perspectives* 22(2): 34–56.

Rivkin, Jan W. 2000. "Imitation of Complex Strategies." *Management Science* 46: 824–844.

Roberts, John. 2004. *The Modern Firm: Organizational Design for Performance and Growth.* Oxford: Oxford University Press.

Schein, Edgar H. 2004. *Organizational Culture and Leadership.* San Francisco: Jossey-Bass.

Scott Morton, Fiona M. 2002. "Horizontal Integration between Brand and Generic Firms in the Pharmaceutical Industry." *Journal of Economics and Management Strategy* 11: 135–168.

Siggelkow, Nicolaj. 2001. "Change in the Presence of Fit: The Rise, the Fall, and the Renaissance of Liz Claiborne." *Academy of Management Journal* 44: 838–857.

———. 2002a. "Evolution toward Fit." *Administrative Science Quarterly* 47: 125–159.

———. 2002b. "Misperceiving Interactions among Complements and Substitutes: Organizational Consequences." *Management Science* 48: 900–916.

Tambe, Prasanna, Lorin Hitt, and Erik Brynjolfsson. 2012. "The Extroverted Firm: How External Information Practices Affect Productivity." *Management Science* 58: 843–859.

Tanriverdi, Huseyin, and Venkat N. Venkatraman. 2005. "Knowledge Relatedness and the Performance of Multibusiness Firms." *Strategic Management Journal* 26: 97–119.

Topkis, Donald M. 1978. "Minimizing a Submodular Function on a Lattice." *Operations Research* 26: 305–321.

Whittington, Richard, Andrew Pettigrew, Simon Peck, Evelyn Fenton, and Martin Conyon. 1999. "Change and Complementarities in the New Competitive Landscape: A European Panel Study, 1992–1996." *Organization Science* 10: 583–600.

Womack, James P., Daniel T. Jones, and Daniel Roos. 1991. *The Machine That Changed the World: The Story of Lean Production.* New York: HarperPerennial.

Zoghi, Cindy, Robert D. Mohr, and Peter B. Meyer. 2007. "Workplace Organization and Innovation." Working Paper 405, Bureau of Labor Statistics, Washington, DC.

2

Economic Theories of Incentives in Organizations

Robert Gibbons and John Roberts

1. Motivation in Organizations

Managed organizations serve both to coordinate the decisions and actions of individuals and groups and to motivate these people to perform the needed activities. This chapter considers the nature of motivation problems in organizations and summarizes theories of the means to address these problems, focusing on the literature in economics but drawing ideas and observations from such fields as economic sociology and accounting where possible.

Both in well-functioning competitive markets and under efficient Coasian bargaining, the motivation problem is fully solved. But familiar sources of contracting problems—precontractual private information leading to adverse selection, observability problems leading to moral hazard, or contractual incompleteness from whatever cause—mean that neither the market nor bargaining always works perfectly. In these circumstances, other ways to solve the coordination and motivation problems should be considered (Arrow 1974; see also Roberts 2004). Managed organizations are a prominent alternative.

Motivation can be an issue in organizations because self-interested behavior by the organization's members may not produce a Pareto-efficient outcome for the group as a whole. The problem is one of externalities: the members of an organization typically do not bear all the costs and benefits of the actions they take and the decisions they make in the organization.

Of course, the distribution of costs and benefits within an organization is not exogenous. For example, it can be altered by contracts. More generally, managed organizations have many means to affect incentives and behavior—every aspect of the organization's design can in principle be used (Roberts 2004). First, attracting, engaging, and retaining the right set of people can be important. People who enjoy their work and are skilled at it or who believe in what the organization is trying to accomplish are likely to be more highly motivated. Giving individuals appropriate training can also help motivation, because well-trained employees are more confident that they will succeed and that their efforts will be rewarded. The formal organizational

The authors thank Dan Barron, Florian Ederer, and Heikki Rantakari for their very helpful comments and the Massachusetts Institute of Technology Sloan School's Program on Innovation in Markets and Organizations for financial support.

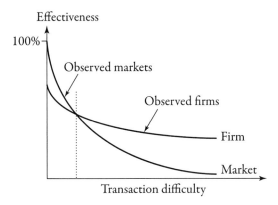

Figure 1. Coase (1937) meets Heckman (1979).
Reprinted from *Journal of Economic Behavior and Organization,* vol. 58, no. 2, Robert Gibbons, "Four Formal(izable) Theories of the Firm?" pp. 200–245, copyright © 2005, with permission from Elsevier.

architecture, including such matters as the allocation of decision rights, the definition of sub-units, the financing and governance structure, and the boundaries of the organization, can have a strong effect on behavior. So too can the routines, processes, and procedures through which information is gathered and shared, people and resources are allocated, performance is monitored and rewarded, and work is done. Additionally, the culture of the organization is perhaps particularly important. In particular, the shared values in the organization and the social norms that guide behavior are both important sources of motivation. Finally, the firm's strategy can be an element of motivation (Roberts and Saloner, this volume).

As generations of sociologists and management scholars have documented, however, organizations often—perhaps typically—do a pretty bad job of motivating their members. Workers shirk. Mid-level employees, seeking advancement, manipulate information and practice politics at the expense of performance. Cautious bureaucrats avoid taking risks that are clearly worthwhile for the organization. Managers sacrifice long-term performance in the pursuit of short-term results. Top executives pursue personal gain at the cost of wrecking the organizations they head. Why is this? Why do managed organizations perform so poorly?

The answer comes from recognizing that firms will not be immune to forces that wreck markets. As Williamson put it, for example, "substantially the same factors that are ultimately responsible for market failures also explain failures of internal organization" (1973: 316) and, hence, "distortion-free internal exchange is a fiction and is not to be regarded as the relevant organizational alternative in circumstances where market exchange predictably experiences non-trivial frictions" (1975: 125).

In short, markets work well (and perhaps better than managed organizations) in circumstances where contracting is not particularly problematic. But as contracting difficulties increase, the performance of market solutions falls, *as does that of managed organizations.* But the latter, with the broad array of levers they have to affect motivation, are less disadvantaged than markets are when contracting is beset by great difficulties. Thus, managed organizations are observed precisely when there are significant contracting problems, and these cannot be easily overcome. Gibbons (2005) summarizes this argument with Figure 1.

The figure illustrates not only Coase's (1937) hypothesis (that firms exist only where they perform better than markets would, which is to the right of the dotted vertical line in this figure), but also its unremarked corollary: that the firms we then observe will be less efficient than the markets we observe, even though the observed firms will be more efficient than markets would be, so the former comparison is biased by sample-selection issues like those addressed in Heckman (1979).

From the perspective of organizational design, the solution to motivation problems is to shape the organization to bring a closer alignment of interests between the organization and its members and thereby increase the efficiency of the choices they make. In this task, the designer in a firm can have access to all the elements of organizational design, and in many contexts all these elements should be used. In particular, motivation is not just a matter of monetary incentives, as important as these are in some cases. Rewards can be dollars, but they can also be other sorts of resources, as well as personal satisfaction or social approval and status. Furthermore, although the motivation problem arises fundamentally at the level of the individual, it may be attacked at more aggregated levels, such as teams, departments, or divisions.

This chapter connects to many others in this volume that treat related issues, often in greater depth. For example, chapters in this volume by Baron and Kreps, Camerer and Weber, Hermalin ("Leadership and Corporate Culture"), Ichniowski and Shaw, Lazear and Oyer, Malcomson, and Waldman all address people aspects of organization relative to incentive and motivation issues. In addition, chapters by Bresnahan and Levin, Garicano and Van Zandt, Hansmann, Mookherjee, Roberts and Saloner, and Segal and Whinston address architectural issues, some of which are driven by motivation concerns. Issues relevant to organizational routines, processes, and procedures are addressed in chapters by Bolton and Dewatripont, Gertner and Scharfstein, Gibbons and Henderson, Gibbons et al., and Roberts and Saloner, as well as in the chapters already cited in connection with the people part of organization. Finally, Hermalin's chapter ("Leadership and Corporate Culture") addresses some issues connected to culture as a motivation and control device.

Despite our conviction that motivation is a lot more than contracts and money, given the coverage of these other chapters, this chapter will largely focus on the use of monetary incentives. Further, it is concerned almost exclusively with the economic theories behind these incentives. The logic is that other chapters deal with different aspects of motivation and discuss the managerial implications and economic evidence.

We begin with a primer on basic agency theory: we develop in some detail the models of single-person, static agency contracts designed to induce "effort," even though much of this material will be familiar to many or most readers of this volume. We then examine contracts with multiple agents and dynamic contracting. Next we consider relational contracts and then situations with no contracts, where career concerns are paramount. We then move to more recent work, particularly the use of other aspects of organization as tools for motivation, motivating actions other than "effort," and economic (optimizing) models of various behavioral phenomena related to motivation in organizations.

2. Formal Performance Contracts

Most economic research on incentives has focused on pay for performance. Here we start with static models of performance contracts between a principal and a single agent. We then move to multiperson contracts and dynamic issues in contracting.

2.1. Static Principal-Agent Models

Much of the economic analysis of motivating people in organizations is couched in terms of principal-agent models, where explicit formal contracts link financial rewards to contractible signals that give information about the agent's unobservable behavior. (If the agent's behavior is contractible, there is no real problem: specify what you want done, and pay if and only if it is done.) Although we reiterate that motivation in organizations is in fact a much broader and more complex phenomenon, we start our discussion with this sort of agency model, with cash compensation used to motivate a behavior that can be labeled "effort."

The basic setup is that there are two actors, a principal (conventionally female) and an agent (conventionally male). The agent may take some action a that affects the welfare of both parties. Often this action is called "effort," but it might be any of a variety of things, including making investments, evaluating options, or abjuring theft of the principal's wealth. The action has a private, convex cost $C(a)$ for the agent,[1] and it generates benefits y for the principal (these may be random). Higher values of a lead (probabilistically) to higher levels of y. There are also contractible signals x carrying information about the chosen level of a, so pay could depend on the signal.[2] The principal decides whether to use the agent and designs a contract promising payments $w = w(x)$ to the agent. This contract is then accepted or rejected, depending on how it compares to the options the agent faces if he rejects the contract. If the contract is accepted, then the agent chooses his action to maximize his expected utility under the contract, recognizing how his choice will affect his pay. Then the signals x are observed, the benefits y are realized, and the principal pays $w(x)$ to the agent in accordance with the contract. The principal thus receives $y - w(x)$, the realized payoff less the payment to the agent, and the agent receives $w(x) - C(a)$, the payment less the cost of action.

There are three main approaches to creating an incentive problem in this context: (1) risk aversion for the agent combined with noisy signals, (2) manipulable signals of the agent's effort, and (3) exogenous limits on the amounts that the agent can be paid. We focus on the first two; the third raises fewer fundamental issues than the first two, so we only sketch the basic idea.

2.1.1. Risk Aversion and Noisy Measures

The workhorse model during the 1980s and early 1990s assumed that the agent is risk averse and the signals about behavior are noisy. For example, the signals might be imperfect observations of the agent's actual choices, or they could be the outcomes of his efforts, where these are also affected by unobserved random factors. In this case, rewarding the agent based on the signals puts randomness into his income. In particular, making the rewards vary more with the signals, which would normally occur if the incentives were made stronger, increases the amount of risk the agent bears. The optimal contract then trades off the cost of inefficient risk-bearing against the benefits of inducing the desired behavior less its cost to the agent. The result is

---

1. Note that it is not necessary to assume that costs are always strictly increasing. There may be some level of effort that the Agent would supply without explicit incentives, because the job was enjoyable or important to him. But if effort is productive at the margin in creating value, efficiency would argue for inducing more than this level of effort that comes for free.

2. In the early models in the agency literature, the signal and the benefit are not distinguished from one another, so $y = x$.

typically that the agent bears excessive risk and delivers too little effort relative to the first best that would be achieved were it not for the contractibility problems. However, obtaining clear predictions about the shape of the performance contract beyond this basic one proved very difficult without putting strong assumptions on the preferences and the information structures, although important results were obtained regarding the information structure. For example, Holmström's sufficient-statistic condition (Holmström 1979; see also Shavell 1979) states that if we have a signal x of the agent's effort and another signal z becomes available, then z should enter the performance contract if and only if x is not a sufficient statistic for (x, z). And, as another result about the information structure, Milgrom (1981) showed that, for the case where the signal x is identical to the benefit y, the contract $w(y)$ is monotone if the conditional distribution $f(y|a)$ has the monotone likelihood ratio property.

Given the difficulties of working with a general model, the highly tractable linear-exponential-normal (LEN) specification of the agency model has become widely used. (As we discuss below, Holmström and Milgrom (1987) provided microfoundations for this model, but here we simply assume that contracts are linear.) Suppose the agent's utility for income w and effort a is

$$U(w, a) = -\exp(-r[w - C(a)]),$$

where r is the agent's coefficient of absolute risk aversion. The expected benefit to the principal is $P(a)$, and the observed signal (performance measure) is $x = a + \varepsilon$ where ε is a normally distributed noise term with zero mean and variance σ^2. The contract is assumed to take the form $w = s + bx$. Because the principal is risk neutral, her problem is to optimize her expected payoff, $P(a) - (s + ba)$, with respect to s, b, and a, subject to the agent being willing to select the indicated value of a when faced with the corresponding values of s and b and to his weakly preferring to enter the relationship than pursue his outside options.

In this context, the agent's choice can be determined from maximizing his certainty equivalent, which is $E(s + bx) - C(a) - \frac{1}{2}r\,\text{Var}(s + bx)$, where Var denotes the variance. Substituting gives $s + ba - C(a) - \frac{1}{2}rb^2\sigma^2$. Thus, his choice satisfies $b = C'(a^*)$, whence $da/db = 1/C''(a^*)$. These results and the fact that the agent can be held to the value of his outside option by the choice of s without affecting his effort choice lead to an expression for the principal's payoff in terms of b. Then maximizing leads to the key conclusion of this model: the optimal value of b is given by[3]

$$b^* = \frac{P'}{1 + r\sigma^2 C''}.$$

This result makes intuitive sense. Because P', r, σ^2, and C'' are positive, b^* is between zero (full insurance) and P' (full incentives). Furthermore, b^* is smaller if the marginal productivity of effort is lower (P' is lower), the agent is more risk averse (r is higher), there is more noise in the performance measure (σ^2 is higher), or the agent's effort choice is less responsive to increased incentives (C'' is higher). If the agent is risk neutral or if there is no noise in the signal, then the optimal incentive payment is equal to the marginal productivity of effort in creating benefits. If

---

3. For a full derivation of these results, see Milgrom and Roberts (1992).

y and x were the same, then the expected benefit would be $P(a) = a$, and the optimal value of b would be $1/(1 + r\sigma^2 C'')$.

Simple extensions of the basic LEN model generate versions of some of the classic results of agency theory. For example, allowing a second noisy signal z that is unrelated to a but may be correlated with x permits deriving a particular version of Holmström's Informativeness Criterion (1979) in a clean and revealing form: The optimal value of b_z in the contract $w = s + b_x x + b_z z$ is $b_z = -\rho b_x/\sigma_z^2$, where ρ is the correlation between z and x. Thus, if x and z are uncorrelated, so z gives no information about the value of ε and thus about the choice of a, then z should not be used in the optimal incentive contract. If there is information in z about a, then it should be used. Further, if x and z are positively (negatively) correlated, then a high (low) z suggests that ε was high (low). Thus, a given level of x is less (more) favorable information about the agent's choice, and so his reward is reduced (increased). The weight put on z is inversely related to its variance, so that a poor measure does not get much weight. And the greater the weight put on x, the more that z is used to offset the increased variance in the pay. Similarly, allowing the variance of the measurement error in x to be decreased at a cost leads to a conclusion that the intensity of incentives b and the precision of the performance measure $1/\sigma^2$ are complements, so anything favoring increasing one favors increasing the other too.

A key extension of the basic model allows for multiple kinds of effort, say a_1 and a_2. In the case where these compete for the agent's time and attention—for example, $C(a_1, a_2) = \frac{1}{2}(a_1 + a_2)^2$—each sort of activity must be compensated equally at the margin if it is to be provided at all. Yet if noise in the measures on the two differ, then the formula above cannot yield $b_1 = b_2$. So if the principal desires the agent to undertake positive levels of both actions (multitasking), then the choice of the incentive intensities is constrained. The result is that muted incentives are optimally offered even for well-measured actions when multitasking is desired. In fact, the optimal common b may be lower than that which would be given to motivate only the worse-measured action in isolation. These arguments have been used to explain why activities that it might seem could be rewarded with strong incentives are in fact not, for fear of driving out other desired activities. They also have been used to investigate elements of job design (see Section 5.2).

This model has been widely used in applied work, but in fact its fit with the empirical evidence is mixed. In particular, the model suggests that strong (respectively, weak) incentives should be observed where there is little (much) noise in the performance measures, yet this is not obviously the case. For example, Prendergast (2002) documented that it is not uncommon to use stronger incentives when there is more uncertainty—at least for certain industries and occupations.

One explanation for this observation is that there might be a second form of noise that is omitted from the formal model but is important in real contracting environments. In particular, in addition to the noise in the performance measure, the marginal productivity of effort might be random (Zábojník 1996; Raith 2008; Rantankari 2008b). In this context Rantakari (2008b) identified four distinct mechanisms through which this production uncertainty could affect the optimal intensity of incentives by affecting the value of effort to the principal and the agent's choice. Any of these could generate a positive relationship between the aggregate amount of uncertainty and the intensity of incentives.

2.1.2. Manipulable Performance Measures

A second approach to capturing conflicts of interest in an agency framework is based on the available performance measures' being manipulable by the agent through actions that do not benefit the principal.[4] The first models in this spirit were Holmström and Milgrom (1991) and Baker (1992). The tractable framework we present here was developed by Feltham and Xie (1994); see Datar et al. (2001) and Baker (2002) for enrichments and applications. This approach is becoming increasingly influential, for several reasons: it captures the idea that one might get what one pays for, it avoids the necessity of assuming risk aversion and uncertainty (which are important in some real-world environments but absent in others), and it is tractable (like the LEN model discussed above) and so lends itself to further applications.

The basic idea is that the benefits to the principal, y, may differ systematically from the signal, x, in how they respond to the agent's choices, and that it may be possible to contract only on x and not on y. Then the problem would be that paying on x would motivate the agent to produce x, and that may be very different from what the principal values, namely, higher levels of y: you get what you pay for. Yet it may still be worthwhile to offer a contract on x, so long as she gets some extra y in return.

For example, if the benefit y were simply an invertible function of the performance measure x, then there would be no problem: simply calculate the optimal contract to induce y and then translate into a contract stated in terms of x. But even in more complicated cases, where x and y are not so aligned, there can be value in contracts on x. The agent will respond to the incentives to affect x, but these can be designed to provide useful incentives for y. For example, suppose that $y = a + \varepsilon$ and $x = a + \phi$. Note that the two different noise terms mean that the benefits and the performance measure are not in a one-to-one relation. Still, a contract based on x creates incentives to increase x, and the induced action increases y.

More generally, as long as effort is one dimensional and the noise is additive (as in the LEN model), the performance measure x and the benefit to the principal y are essentially aligned, because the principal can induce any choice of a she might want. Thus there are essentially two ways to create an incentive problem. The first was identified by Baker (1992): if the marginal products of a in creating x and in creating y are not perfectly correlated (e.g., when the noise is multiplicative), it may be impossible to induce some levels of effort that the principal might want. The second, to which we now turn, involves multidimensional effort.

So now suppose that there are two kinds of actions that the agent can take, a_1 and a_2. To keep things simple, assume that costs are separable:

$$C\left(a_1, a_2\right) = \frac{1}{2}\left(a_1^2 + a_2^2\right).$$

In this multitask environment, if $y = a_1 + a_2 + \varepsilon$ and $x = a_1 + \phi$, then a contract based on x creates incentives for a_1 but cannot create incentives for a_2. Yet increasing a_2 from zero is costless to a first approximation and has a first-order positive effect in increasing y. Alternatively, if $y = a_1 + \varepsilon$ and $x = a_1 + a_2 + \phi$, then a contract based on x creates an incentive for the agent

---

4. Parts of this section draw on Gibbons (2010) with permission from the *Annual Review of Economics,* Volume 2, © 2010 by Annual Reviews, http://www.annualreviews.org.

to take action a_2, even though a_2 is irrelevant to the principal's return, y. This action is pure social waste, and if the agent is being held to his outside option, the cost will be borne entirely by the principal. Finally, in an extreme case, such as $y = a_1 + \varepsilon$ and $x = a_2 + \varepsilon$, a contract based on x will create no value at all. (Note that, in this example, y and x will be perfectly correlated because of the common noise term ε. However, in line with Baker (1992), the marginal products are completely uncorrelated.)

Generalizing these examples, suppose that the technology of production is $y = f_1 a_1 + f_2 a_2 + \varepsilon$, the technology of performance measurement is $x = g_1 a_1 + g_2 a_2 + \phi$, the contract is $w = s + bx$, and the payoffs are $y - w$ to the principal and $w - C(a_1, a_2)$ to the agent.[5] The first-best actions, which maximize $E(y) - C(a_1, a_2)$, are thus $a_1^{FB} = f_1$ and $a_2^{FB} = f_2$. With contracts based on only x, however, we will see that the agent typically cannot be induced to take these first-best actions.

The timing is as before. The principal offers the agent a compensation contract, $w = s + bx$.[6] The agent accepts the contract or rejects it in favor of an alternative opportunity with payoff U_0. The agent chooses his actions (a_1, a_2). These are not observed by the principal. Unobserved random events (ε, ϕ) that are beyond the agent's control occur. Measured performance (x) is observed by the principal and the agent (and by a court, if necessary). The agent receives the compensation specified by the contract, and the principal realizes her return net of the payment.

The risk-neutral agent chooses a_1 and a_2 to maximize $E(w) - c(a_1, a_2)$, so the chosen actions under the contract are $a_1^*(b) = g_1 b$ and $a_2^*(b) = g_2 b$. Thus, to induce the first-best actions $a_1^{FB} = f_1$ and $a_2^{FB} = f_2$, the principal would like to choose b to satisfy $g_1 b = f_1$ and $g_2 b = f_2$. However, this is impossible unless $f_1 g_2 = f_2 g_1$ (in which case, in expectation, x and y are just multiples of each other, and the optimal contract is the first-best one adjusted for the multiplicative effect). When $f_1 g_2 \neq f_2 g_1$, the optimal contract for the principal is given by setting s to hold the agent to utility U_0 and setting

$$b^* = \frac{f_1 g_1 + f_2 g_2}{g_1^2 + g_2^2} = \frac{\|f\|}{\|g\|} \cos(\theta),$$

where θ is the angle between the vectors $f = (f_1, f_2)$ and $g = (g_1, g_2)$.

There are two important features of b^*: scaling and alignment, reflected by $\|f\|/\|g\|$ and $\cos(\theta)$, respectively. Scaling is intuitive but not very interesting. For example, if $f_i = \lambda g_i$, $i = 1, 2$, so that the two vectors are just multiples of each other, then the first best is achieved by $b^* = 1/\lambda$, which scales the rewards to reflect the actual value of effort in generating y. More generally, if g_1 and g_2 are both much larger (smaller) than f_1 and f_2, then the efficient contract puts a small (large) bonus rate on x, as shown by $\|f\|/\|g\|$. Alignment, however, is the key to the model. As one example, if the f and g vectors lie almost on top of each other (regardless of their lengths), then the incentives created by paying on x are quite valuable for increasing y, and b^* is relatively large. In contrast, if the f and g vectors are almost orthogonal to each other, then the incentives created by paying on x are almost useless for increasing y, and b^* is near zero.

---

5. As noted earlier, there is no need to assume risk aversion as there was in the classic setup.

6. To motivate the assumption of linear contracts, imagine that $x \in \{0, 1\}$ and $Pr(x = 1) = g_1 a_1 + g_2 a_2$, where f_1, f_2, g_1, and g_2 are sufficiently small. In general, however, linear contracts are not optimal.

More generally, the efficient contract has a larger bonus rate b when f and g are more closely aligned, as measured by $\cos(\theta)$.

One further example may be illuminating in this regard. Suppose $f = (1, 1)$, and consider different possible values for g where $\|f\| = \|g\| = 2^{1/2}$. Then, from the formula above, $b^* = (g_1 + g_2)/2$. Consequently the agent maximizes $[(g_1 + g_2)(g_1a_1 + g_2a_2) - a_1^2 - a_2^2]/2$, yielding $a_i = g_i(g_1 + g_2)/2$, $i = 1, 2$. Now consider how the effort choices change as g_1 increases and g_2 decreases to keep $\|g\| = 2^{1/2}$. Let $g_1 = \lambda g_2$, where we vary λ. Then one can calculate that $a_1 = \lambda(1 + \lambda)/(1 + \lambda^2)$ and $a^2 = (1 + \lambda)/(1 + \lambda^2)$. At $\lambda = 1$, $a_1 = a_2 = 1$. As λ increases from unity, a_2 falls, while a_1 initially rises and then falls. As λ goes to infinity, so (g_1, g_2) approaches $(2^{1/2}, 0)$, a_1 decreases to 1, and a_2 goes to zero.

Examples of such misaligned measures abound. Often, rewards within firms are based on accounting numbers, even though the firm's owners care not about these, but instead about long-run profitability. The latter, however, is difficult to measure and thus is problematic for contracting, while the accounting measures are only loosely connected to profitability (particularly as they are not forward looking) and can be manipulated in a variety of ways (the timing of revenue recognition, choosing different financing options, etc.). Similarly, sales people are often compensated for revenues, not profitability, and this leads them to focus their efforts on revenue maximization, not profits. Likewise, teachers are measured against student achievement on standardized tests in a few subjects rather than on overall learning, and this motivates them to teach to these tests at the expense of other important aspects of their job. In each case, the agent's behavior is twisted away from generating what the principal actually values.

2.1.3. Wealth Constraints

If there is a minimum amount that the agent has to be paid in any circumstance (say, $w \geq 0$), then this alone may create a contracting problem, even when both parties are risk neutral. For example, suppose $y \in \{0, 1\}$ and $Pr(y = 1) = a$, where $C(a) = a^2$ and $a \leq 1$. First best involves $a^{FB} = \frac{1}{2}$, yielding total utility $\frac{1}{4}$. The first-best effort can be induced by setting $b_1 = b_0 + 1$ in a contract that pays b_1 if $y = 1$ and b_0 if $y = 0$.[7] In this case, the agent's expected utility is $b_0 + \frac{1}{4}$. Now suppose the agent must receive a nonnegative payment in any event, so that $b_0 \geq 0$. This means he must receive an expected utility of $\frac{1}{4}$ if the first best is to be induced, leaving nothing for the principal. As a consequence, the principal will find it optimal to induce less than first best effort.

More generally, motivation here ideally involves both carrot and stick (positive and negative payments, depending on results). The stick is used to ensure that the agent does not earn any rents, so the principal will seek to maximize the total surplus. If negative payments are not available, then motivating efficient effort takes a big carrot, because there must be a large enough difference in pay across possible outcomes to provide motivation. Then, unless the agent's outside options are very attractive, he will earn rents. Thus, the principal will look to maximize her share of the surplus, rather than the total surplus, and this leads her to induce less effort than would be efficient.

---

7. The contract could also include a payment that is independent of the level of y without affecting the conclusion.

Sappington (1983) combined wealth constraints with postcontractual private information in an interesting fashion. He supposes that the risk-neutral agent becomes privately informed about a productivity parameter after the contract has been agreed. Higher values of the parameter correspond to lower values of the agent's total and marginal costs of achieving any expected level of output. Sappington shows in this context that the optimal contract induces efficient effort choice only in the highest productivity states. In all others, the amount of effort elicited is less than efficient in order to reduce the rents that the agent receives.

Wealth constraints also play a role in efficiency-wage models (e.g., Shapiro and Stiglitz 1984; Akerlof and Yellen 1986). In these, the principal pays the agent enough that he enjoys returns on the job in excess of the value of his outside option. Thus, if he loses his job, he will suffer a discrete utility loss, and the threat of being fired if caught shirking in a random inspection motivates him to work. More frequent or more accurate tests increase the probability of catching slackers and reduce the amount that the agent must lose if fired in order to motivate him.

If the agent were not wealth constrained, he could be charged for the job up front, and the excess returns would be reduced to being quasi-rents, with no rents being earned by the agent. However, if he is wealth constrained, then the returns are actual rents—returns in excess of his opportunity costs. Consequently, the cost to the principal of motivating effort is increased, as it was above, and again this may reduce the amount of effort demanded to inefficient levels.

2.1.4. Choosing the Principal

In many settings, the roles of principal and agent are not a matter of choice, in one or both of two senses: who does the work and who gets the returns?[8] Regarding the former, sometimes only the agent has the skills or knowledge needed to carry out the productive activity. In other settings, however, it is possible to allocate at least some of the tasks to either the principal or the agent. Because several other chapters in this volume—including Bolton and Dewatripont, Garicano and Van Zandt, Gibbons et al., Mookherjee, and Roberts and Saloner—discuss various aspects of this delegation problem, we sidestep it here.

Even when it is preordained who does what work, however, there is still the question of who gets the returns (and then contracts with the other, if useful). As with who does the work, sometimes who receives the returns from an activity is preordained (e.g., in the relation of a patient and surgeon). In other cases, however, the returns could be alienated from one party and transferred to the other, so we can then analyze which party should receive the returns. We now briefly discuss this issue, both to address a loose end from Section 2.1.2 and to illustrate the larger "incentive system" approach we describe in Section 5, where multiple instruments are available and are used in combination to address a given incentive problem.

In the classic case of the risk-aversion model of Section 2.1.1, where $y = x$, an incentive contract $w = s + by$, where $b = 1$ (and $s < 0$), transfers the full returns of his effort to the agent. This contract would create first-best effort incentives, but the agent would also bear all the risk in y. This would involve inefficient distribution of the risk, because the agent is risk averse while the principal's risk-bearing ability is wastefully unused. In particular, because this

---

8. Parts of this section draw on Gibbons (2010) with permission from the *Annual Review of Economics,* Volume 2, © 2010 by Annual Reviews, http://www.annualreviews.org.

contract was feasible but not optimal in Section 2.1.1, we know that this method of selling the agent the firm is not optimal.

We could also imagine situations in which it is possible to transfer the right to receive the payoff y, even if y itself is not contractible. For example, perhaps this return accrues automatically to whomever owns a particular asset, and transfer of the asset would transfer the return. In the classic model, this runs into the same problem: it is optimal to share the risk in y. Thus, once the transfer of title has been made, the resulting allocation of the risky return is inefficient. If possible, the parties would benefit by signing a risk-sharing contract. This is not possible if y is not contractible, so the inefficiency remains. If it were possible to share the risk, however, doing so would reduce the effort incentives facing the former agent. Accounting for this would result in contract terms that reproduce the distribution of returns (and effort) under the original optimal agency contract.

We next consider these issues in the manipulable-measures model from Section 2.1.2. A core aspect of this model is that y is not directly contractible and $x \neq y$, so it is not possible to sell the agent the firm in the first sense discussed above, by means of an incentive contract $w = s + by$ with $b = 1$ and $s < 0$. However, the agent is risk neutral, so literally selling the agent the right to receive the benefits y (the second approach above) would now create first-best incentives for the agent, because there would be no reason to write any contract with the (former) principal. To prevent this argument from eliminating the applicability of the manipulable-measures model, we now enrich that model to explain why the principal should not sell the agent the right to receive y. Simply put, the reason will be that, in a richer setting where both the principal and the agent take actions to increase firm value, the agent should be the actor whose performance measure is less easily manipulable (so that the principal can contract with the agent without too much loss from the "get what you pay for" problem).

Formally, suppose there are two actors ($i = 1, 2$), each of whom can take both a productive action (a^i) and a manipulative action (m^i). The actors' collective contribution to firm value is $y = a^1 + a^2$, the available performance measures are $x^i = a^i + g_2^i m^i$, and each actor's cost function is $C(a^i, m^i) = ((a^i)^2 + (m^i)^2)/2$. Thus, each $f^i = (1, 0)$, while $g^i = (1, g_2^i)$. Suppose actor i is the principal and signs the incentive contract $w = s + b^j x^j$ with actor j. An optimal contract can then be derived from the logic of the manipulable-measures model:

$$b^{j*} = \frac{1}{1 + \left(g_2^j\right)^2} = \frac{\|f\|}{\|g^j\|}\cos(\theta^j).$$

Because the principal receives y (and the actors' productive actions are additively separable in producing y), the principal has first-best incentives. Higher values of g_2^j (equivalently, lower values of $\cos(\theta^j)$) reduce the optimal b^j, the corresponding induced effort, and the final payoff. The expected payoff to the two parties is therefore maximized by avoiding having to contract with the actor whose performance measure is more manipulable: actor j should be the principal if $g_2^i < g_2^j$.

Finally, in the wealth-constraints model, the agent simply lacks the resources to buy the firm. Further, if negative values of y are possible, then even loans from the original owner will not work, because bankruptcy provisions shield the agent from having to repay the loan.

2.2. Contracting with Multiple Agents

Of course, it is rare that a principal would be dealing with a single agent if we think about a firm. What difference does it make when there are multiple agents?

The multi-agent problem perhaps closest to the single-agent analyses in Section 2.1 is Holmström's (1982) model of relative performance evaluation. Imagine that each agent's effort affects only that agent's output (e.g., $y_i = a_i + \varepsilon_i$), but the agents' noise terms are subject to common shocks (e.g., $\varepsilon_i = \theta + \mu_i$). Holmström's Informativeness Principle (1979) then implies that, because there is statistical information in one agent's results about other agents' noise terms, the pay of the latter should depend on the former's performance. For example, the performance of other firms facing similar market conditions ought to be informative about the extent to which a CEO's good performance was a matter of effort or instead due to luck in that market conditions were good.

The evidence on the extent of such use of relative performance evaluation for CEOs is mixed (Murphy 1999). To the extent that it is not used, it may be because of multitasking concerns: for example, relative performance evaluation might encourage collusion among CEOs to keep effort and performance low. In other contexts, beyond CEOs, concerns with sabotage of others' efforts, collusion among the workers, shopping for a "good" reference group, and mismanagement of positive spillovers among different agents' work could all discourage the use of relative performance evaluation (Gibbons and Murphy 1990). Still, some forms of relative performance evaluation seem widespread in various contexts. A prominent example is tournaments.

In a tournament, the performances of multiple agents are ranked, and higher rewards are given to those with higher ranks. For example, with two agents, the principal prespecifies wages w_H and $w_L < w_H$, and the agent with the higher output receives w_H; see Lazear and Rosen (1981) for an early treatment. The relative-performance aspect of a tournament filters out common shocks, such as if $y_i = a_i + \theta + \mu_i$, but tournaments also provide incentives in the absence of common shocks, such as if $y_i = a_i + \mu_i$. Furthermore, tournaments can provide incentives when only ordinal rather than cardinal performance information is available. Finally, the fact that a tournament's wages can be not only prespecified but also prepaid (into, e.g., an escrow account, awaiting distribution to the appropriate agents) is one way to address a possible commitment problem where the principal is tempted not to pay high wages resulting from high output under a contract, such as $w = s + by$; see Malcomson (1984). Lazear and Oyer (this volume) and Waldman (this volume) describe more recent work on tournaments. See also the use of tournament models in the dynamic settings discussed in Section 2.3 and in the context of promotions in Section 5.4.

Other analyses of multi-agent incentive problems place greater emphasis on team production, free riding, and one agent helping another. As a first step in this direction, Holmström and Milgrom (1990) assumed that a team works together for a boss but then decides how to share the rewards paid to them. An example might be a fruit-picking team in California agriculture. The key insight here is that if the team shares output optimally (as in Wilson's (1968) theory of syndicates) and the team can avoid the free-rider problem, then it is as if the boss were contracting with a single individual whose risk tolerance is the sum of the risk tolerances of the team. This means stronger incentives than under individual contracting.

Rather than assuming that a team can avoid the free-rider problem, other papers have asked whether and when this might occur. The first results are due to Holmström (1982), who analyzed an N-person partnership with individual actions x_i, where all that can be observed is total output $y = f(x_1, \ldots, x_N)$ and so payments must be $s_i(y)$. Note that here there is not (yet) a principal; there are just the N partners. Holmström showed it is impossible for the partnership to achieve Pareto-optimal output as a Nash equilibrium of the game where all the agents choose their input levels simultaneously if we insist that all the output be distributed: for all y, $\sum s_i(y) = y$. The essential logic is the free-rider problem. On average, an agent can get only y/N, so on average, individuals will each equate their marginal productivity divided by N to their marginal cost of input. But y is, in essence, a public good, so optimality requires that each individual's marginal cost be equated to the full marginal productivity.

In Holmström's model, one way to restore the possibility of achieving optimality in Nash equilibrium is by agreeing to throw away output if the Pareto-optimal level is not achieved, but the team may have difficulty committing to throwing away resources in this way. To avoid this commitment problem, one could introduce an $N + 1$st party who absorbs the team output if it differs from the Pareto-optimal level, but labeling this $N + 1$st party (who plays only this budget-breaking role) the principal does not easily match common conceptions of the roles of a boss. In particular, she does well only when the others fail.

More optimistically, Che and Yoo (2001) analyzed when and how a pair of workers might overcome the free-rider problem by mutual monitoring in a repeated game if each can observe the other's performance. Assume that the workers' production functions are independent, so that independent pay-for-performance rather than a group bonus would be optimal in a static model. Che and Yoo showed, however, that in a repeated game, the principal optimally chooses a group bonus for the pair of workers, exactly because the free-rider problem then threatens to make the workers' continuing relationship inefficient if cooperation between them breaks down. See Section 3 for more on such relational contracts, often constructed vertically between principal and agent, rather than horizontally between workers as here.

Continuing to consider horizontal effects between workers, it may be that formal contracts other than a group bonus may also support cooperation between workers (either by reducing the reneging temptation today or, as in Che and Yoo, by increasing the punishment if reneging were to occur). In particular, the observed practice of allocating a fraction of ownership of the firm to the workers might function this way. And, moving from instrumental to behavioral theories, allocating a fraction of the firm's ownership to workers may also change "mindsets," so agents "think like owners," although it is hard to see why they would think like more than $1/N$th owners absent some peer pressure. See Section 7.2 for more on peer pressure.

There are also analyses of one worker's incentive to help other workers. For example, Itoh (1991) modeled a situation in which workers decide both how much effort to devote to their own responsibilities and how much to help co-workers and thereby increase co-workers' measured performance. If the principal wants the agents to focus on their own jobs, she offers pay based only on individual performance, which induces the agents to choose not to help one another. However, if she pays each agent on both his and the other's output, she will induce team production. Itoh shows that either may be optimal. In particular, team pay is optimal if the two sorts of effort are strategic complements, so getting more help from the other induces an agent to work harder at his own job.

Finally, there are a class of problems involving a multilevel hierarchy with a third party (the supervisor) between the principal and agent. For a wide-ranging discussion of models of incentives in hierarchies, see Mookherjee (this volume).

2.3. Dynamics

The preceding sections were largely concerned with one-shot contracting situations. However, many relationships extend over time, especially in organizations, and incentive contracts can have intertemporal aspects. For example, in a single contract, there may be opportunities to respond to new information as it arrives—including but not limited to interim performance evaluation. Also, over time, there can be either a sequence of short-term contracts or a long-term contract. We now discuss these issues in turn.

2.3.1. Responding to New Information

One of the strong assumptions in a one-shot model, including those discussed above, is that no-body learns anything until the end of the transaction. At the other extreme, there are continuous-time models in which the principal and agent are constantly observing how things are going (see Section 2.3.3 for more on this). As a first step between these two extremes, in this section we consider some of the issues that arise when new information becomes available during the course of the contract. Sometimes such information may be valuable. At other times, the additional information may be harmful. This is especially likely if the parties lack commitment power, but it can also arise in other contexts.

A prominent example involves interim performance evaluation in a context where the agent takes repeated actions and the principal gets information before the second action is taken. Here, feedback may or may not be useful. To see this, consider two different models where the agent acts repeatedly and the principal, but not the agent, observes the results of each action before the next is taken. On the one hand is the model in Fuchs (2007), which is discussed in more detail in Section 3. In this model, the principal wants the agent to take the same action in every period. Given that the desired behavior is unchanging, there is no value to providing the agent with performance information. In fact, providing such information just increases the number of incentive constraints that must be met, and so makes the principal worse off (without benefiting the agent). On the other hand, in Manso (2011), which is discussed further in Section 6.2, the principal sometimes wants the agent to change his action, depending on the results of early actions. In this case, feedback is necessary.

Ederer (2010) explored the costs and benefits of providing feedback and finds that several competing effects can arise. Specifically, in a sequence of two tournaments, if effort and ability are complements, feedback can inform workers about their relative position in the tournament (evaluation effect) as well as their relative productivity (motivation effect), and it can also create signal-jamming incentives to exert effort prior to the performance evaluation. These effects suggest a trade-off in giving feedback between evaluation and motivation. Ederer suggests that this finding is in accordance with behavioral research and actual practices.

In addition to providing the information, the principal might also act on it. We mention two papers in this vein. First, Crémer (1995) showed that it can be costly for the principal if she cannot commit not to gather information. In his model, the principal can find out whether a bad outcome was the result of low effort or bad luck. This possibility makes it infeasible to carry out threats, such as "I will fire you if output is low." This weakens the incentives that can be provided, and in fact the principal would be better off if she did not have access to the information. In Meyer (1992) the principal's reaction to new information can be contractually specified. She showed that, in a sequence of two tournaments where the principal's goal is to maximize the sum of the agents' efforts over time, it is efficient to commit ex ante to biasing the second-round tournament in favor of the first-round winner. Such a bias reduces second-round effort, but it also increases first-round effort. Furthermore, these effects are second and first order, respectively, so the optimal incentive scheme produces a fast track (i.e., those who win early are more likely to win later as well).

2.3.2. The Ratchet Effect

Although it is sometimes feasible for the parties to specify in advance how they will respond to new information, it seems at least as common for such responses to be noncontractible.[9] This is either because the response is never contractible (e.g., the agent's action, in a setting with repeated actions), or because the response is not yet contractible (e.g., the contract the principal will offer next period, in a setting where the principal can commit within but not between periods).

A classic example of the latter is the ratchet effect, where the firm reduces its piece rate if it learns that a job can be done more easily than was thought at first. Anticipating such a reduction, workers restrict output, working slowly to prevent the firm from discerning the true pace at which the job could be done. Mathewson (1931) and Roy (1952) offered rich descriptions of both the ratchet effect and output restriction.

To explore these qualitative accounts analytically, it seems natural to consider an environment in which the workers have private information about the job's difficulty and a worker's effort cannot be monitored. Gibbons (1987) showed that, in this environment, if the firm cannot commit to maintain the piece rate and the worker cannot commit to remain with the firm, then both the ratchet effect and output restriction are unavoidable: there is no equilibrium compensation scheme that induces efficient effort.

Lazear (1986) analyzed a similar model but assumed that the worker is bound to the firm. In this case, a sufficiently steep slope in the initial incentive contract induces the worker to put forth efficient effort today (i.e., there is no output restriction), even though the worker understands that the rate will ratchet tomorrow. Under Gibbons's assumption that the worker is not bound to the firm, in contrast, such a steep slope would cause the worker to "bust the rate" (i.e., maximize earnings, producing more than is efficient) today and quit tomorrow.

Kanemoto and MacLeod (1991) and Carmichael and MacLeod (2000) studied mechanisms that allow firms to avoid the ratchet effect (and so avoid output restriction as well). Kanemoto and MacLeod analyzed the case where the worker's output conveys information about the worker's ability, rather than about the job's difficulty, as in Lazear (1986) and Gibbons (1987). In the Kanemoto-MacLeod model, competition for the worker's services from the market of prospective employers effectively allows the firm to commit. Carmichael and MacLeod explored repeated-game models in which the future value of the ongoing relationship may allow the firm to commit. For example, they described mutual-monitoring arrangements among British cotton spinners in the nineteenth century, in which piece rates were publicly posted and sanctions were administered (by other firms!) against firms that cut rates.

---

9. Parts of this section are reprinted with permission from Gibbons (1997), © 1997 Cambridge University Press.

2.3.3. Long-Term Contracts

The ratchet effect (and its associated output restriction) arises because firms are assumed to be able commit to only short-term contracts. In such situations, the ability to commit to future piece rates by means of a multiperiod contract could be very valuable. However, the world changes over time (e.g., new techniques of production may warrant new piece rates), sometimes in ways that cannot be included in a contract ex ante, so long-term contracts may at least need to be renegotiated and might not even be feasible.

In a sufficiently stationary setting, however, long-term contracts may be feasible but not necessary, in the sense that a sequence of short-term contracts may be just as efficient as the optimal long-term contract. Holmström and Milgrom (1987) provided the first result in this spirit, by reinterpreting the classic model from Section 2.1.1: instead of assuming that the agent takes a single action a that influences a single output y, Holmström and Milgrom assumed that the agent takes a sequence of actions a_t, each of which produces its own output y_t, where all past outputs are observed before the next action is taken. For the case where $y_t \in \{0, 1\}$, we can interpret output in the classic model as the sum of the individual outputs here, $y = \sum y_t$. For example, the actions and outputs a_t and y_t might happen every day, and y in the classic model might refer to aggregate output during one year (with, say, T days in the year).

One of Holmström and Milgrom's insights is that if a contract based on aggregate output, $w(y)$, is nonlinear in y, then the agent will face different incentives for a_t depending on what prior outputs have been realized (y_τ for $\tau < t$). But if there is no reason for the agent's incentives to vary (or, more strongly, if the principal would like the agent to take the same action in each period), then there are two equivalent ways to proceed. First, the parties could sign a contract $w(y) = S + By$ that is linear in aggregate output. Second, the parties could sign a sequence of single-period contracts $w_t(y_t) = s + by_t$, with the same values of s and b in each period. Given such assumptions as exponential utility (so that there are no income effects), each of these approaches creates constant incentives for the agent. Moreover, the two approaches create the same constant incentive if $B = b$, and they deliver the same certainty equivalent to the agent if $S = Ts$.

In fact, we take three points from Holmström and Milgrom (1987). The first is the one we started this section with: in a sufficiently stationary setting, a sequence of short-term contracts may be just as efficient as the optimal long-term contract. Fudenberg et al. (1990) explored the domain over which this result holds. They showed that if the following conditions all hold, then a sequence of short-term contracts can achieve everything a long-term contract could: (1) all public information can be used in contracting, (2) the agent can save and borrow on the same terms as the principal, (3) technology and preferences are common knowledge between the agent and principal at each time of contracting, and (4) the utility possibility frontier generated by the set of all incentive-compatible contracts is always downward sloping. Condition (1) means insurance opportunities are not lost, (2) means the agent can do any consumption smoothing on his own and does not need to use the principal to do it by means of the contract, (3) avoids adverse selection when contracting (including private information about unobserved actions), and (4) ensures that an efficient contract can achieve any utility level for the agent that is relevant. These conditions seem quite restrictive, suggesting that long-term contracts should often be valuable. It is therefore important to think about why long-term contracts are not more common (or, where they exist, are often simple rather than detailed).

The second point we take from Holmström and Milgrom (1987) is that, given several assumptions, the optimal contract for the year not only is linear in aggregate output but also has exactly the optimal slope b^* from the LEN model in Section 2.1.1. This is the sense in which Holmström and Milgrom (1987) provided microfoundations for the LEN model. This interpretation of the linear contracts in the LEN model has been offered in many subsequent static models, perhaps beginning with Holmström and Milgrom (1991).

Finally, the third point we take from Holmström and Milgrom (1987) is that long-term contracts may fruitfully be modeled in continuous time. That is, in models with discrete time periods, optimal multiperiod performance contracts tend to be very complicated, and it is typically hard to get clean results, let alone explicit solutions (for an early contribution, see Rogerson 1985). However, in recent years, continuous-time models of agency have been developed and have proven to be remarkably tractable, and Holmström and Milgrom (1987) initiated this approach. Informally, one can think of the agent acting more and more frequently, so that each period is very small. Formally, the agent selects at each instant over a finite horizon the drift $\mu(t)$ of a one-dimensional Brownian motion. He has exponential utility for income less the cost of effort and consumes only at date T, the end of the relationship. It turns out that the best the principal can do is to induce a constant drift (effort) over time and to pay the agent a linear function of final profits. Even if the agent controls a multidimensional process, the result holds if the principal can observe only a one-dimensional function of the outcomes.

More recently, some papers have explored other continuous time formulations (for references, see Edmans et al. 2012). For example, Sannikov (2008) offered an infinite-horizon, continuous-time agency model where the agent again controls the drift of a Brownian motion by his efforts, but in contrast to Holmström and Milgrom (1987), his supply of effort is subject to income effects, and consumption occurs at each instant. Sannikov is able to obtain a closed-form solution for this problem. DeMarzo and Sannikov (2006) used the techniques of Sannikov (2008) to study an agency problem where the agent may divert corporate resources to his private use. As well, Edmans et al. (2012) analyzed a very rich model, allowing not just for effort provision by the agent (thought of as a CEO), but also manipulation of earnings that shifts returns across periods at a cost to the firm (e.g., inflating current returns at a real long-run cost) and private, unobserved borrowing and saving by the agent that could undo the contract's terms. There can be stochastic linkages across periods as well. Again, the authors obtain an explicit expression for the optimal contract. Further, they are able to show that it can in fact be implemented in a simple manner using a cash and equity compensation whose mix is altered over time in a "dynamic incentive account" in which the agent's expected pay is escrowed.

3. Relational Incentive Contracts: Informal Instruments

In Section 2 we examined formal performance contracts—those that can rely on court enforcement. We turn now to relational contracts—those that use performance measures that cannot be verified by third parties.[10] Because they use such performance measures, relational contracts

---

10. Parts of this section draw on Gibbons (2010) with permission from the *Annual Review of Economics,* Volume 2, © 2010 by Annual Reviews, http://www.annualreviews.org.

must be self-enforcing: the parties need to find it in their interest to adhere to the mutually understood terms.

A classic example involves Lincoln Electric (Fast and Berg 1975), where a piece-rate formula ties part of a worker's pay to objective measures of the worker's output, but typically about half of a worker's pay is a bonus based on the supervisor's subjective assessment of the worker's cooperation, innovation, dependability, and so on. Workers expect supervisors to judge them fairly and the firm to pay the bonus earned because they are in a long-term relationship, which allows misbehavior today to be punished in future dealings.

Our treatment of relational contracts is short. See Malcomson (this volume) for an entire chapter on such models, Baron and Kreps (this volume) for a nuanced application of these ideas to employment relationships, and Gibbons and Henderson (this volume) for some of the difficulties in reaching mutually understood terms. Also, it is important to note that relational contracts may not always be efficiency enhancing. For example, recall Roy's (1952) description of output restriction in response to the ratchet effect, where the firm's ability to collect information and implement change was limited by an informal agreement among the workers that was enforced by ostracism and physical punishment.

To formalize the idea of relational incentive contracts, we sketch Bull's (1987) model, as interpreted by Baker et al. (1994), in which the relational contract is an equilibrium of a repeated game between a principal and an agent. In each period, the agent chooses an unobservable action, a, that stochastically determines the agent's total contribution, y. For simplicity, suppose that y is either High ($y = H$) or Low ($y = L < H$), and that $\text{Prob}(y = H | a) = a$, where $a \in [0, 1]$. If total compensation is w, the principal's payoff is $y - w$, and the agent's is $w - C(a)$, where $C(0) = 0$ and $C' \to \infty$ as $a \to 1$.

Now suppose y cannot be objectively measured in a way that is verifiable in a court of law, but that it can be assessed by both parties. Further, assume for now that their assessments are identical. In particular, let the compensation consist of a base salary, s, whose payment can be court enforced, and a bonus, B, which the principal promises to pay if the parties' common assessment is $y = H$. Note that the bonus is in fact discretionary, because no court can enforce the promise. The timing of events in each period is as follows. First, the principal offers the agent a compensation package. Second, the agent either accepts the compensation package (in which case s is paid) or rejects it in favor of an alternative employment opportunity with payoff U_0. Third, if the agent accepts, then the agent chooses an action at cost $C(a)$, but the principal does not observe the agent's action. Fourth, the principal and the agent observe the realization of y (but a court cannot). Finally, if $y = H$, then the principal chooses whether to pay the agent the bonus B specified in the relational contract.

In a single-period employment relationship, the principal would choose not to pay a bonus, so the agent (anticipating the principal's decision) would choose not to supply effort, and so the agent's contribution would be $y = L$. Anticipating this, the most the principal would offer is a salary $s = L$. Then, if $L < U_0$, the agent would choose not to work for the principal.

But things can be different in an ongoing relationship. Formally, consider an infinitely repeated game in which both parties discount future payoffs at rate r. We focus on equilibria in which the principal and the agent play trigger strategies (roughly speaking, the parties begin by cooperating and then continue to cooperate unless one side defects, in which case they refuse to cooperate forever after).

If the agent believes the principal will pay the bonus B, then the agent's optimal action, $a^*(B)$, satisfies $C'(a) = B$. If the principal offers the minimum salary that the agent will accept, then the principal's expected profit per period is

$$L + a^*(B) \cdot (H - L) - C(a^*(B)) - U_0 \equiv V(B) - U_0,$$

where $V(B)$ is the expected gross surplus (output minus cost) from the effort induced by the bonus B.

But should the agent believe that the principal will pay the bonus B if the outcome is H, as she is supposed to? If the principal does not pay the bonus, then her payoff is $H - s$ this period but zero thereafter, whereas if the principal does pay the bonus, then her payoff is $H - s - B$ this period but equal to the expected profit from the relationship thereafter. Thus, the principal should pay the bonus if and only if

$$(H - s - B) + \frac{1}{r}[V(B) - U_0] \geq (H - s) + \frac{1}{r} \cdot 0,$$

or $B \leq [V(B) - U_0]/r$. In words, the reneging temptation must be smaller than the present value of the net surplus from the relationship. If enough value is created in the relationship, then incentives for positive effort can be provided.

This basic model of relational incentive contracts has been enriched by MacLeod and Malcomson (1989) and Levin (2003), who established a number of key features of the set of optimal contracts and characterized the range of economic outcomes consistent with equilibrium. It has also been used as an ingredient in models of the combined use of formal and relational contracting (see the beginning of Section 5) and to study empowerment (Baker et al. 1999), partnerships (Doornik 2006), job design (Schöttner 2008), supervision (Thiele 2012), and other incentive issues in organizations. In addition, there has been some progress in relaxing the strong information assumptions in this basic model (where everything is commonly known or observed except the agent's effort), with interesting implications for the dynamics of relational contracts, some of which we now discuss.

One natural change in this basic model is to move from *discretionary* bonuses (where the parties both see the agent's output, but the court does not, so the principal can decide whether to pay a bonus after the agent produces high output) to *subjective* bonuses (where only the principal sees the agent's output, so the principal can claim that output was low and no bonus should be paid). Levin (2003), MacLeod (2003), and Fuchs (2007) have analyzed such subjective bonuses.

In a static model, MacLeod (2003) noted that truth telling by the principal requires that the principal's payment be independent of her report about the agent's output. From this, it follows that with a budget-balanced contract (i.e., one where everything paid by the principal is received by the agent), the agent's pay is independent of the principal's report, and so he cannot be induced to supply any effort. MacLeod characterized the optimal contract, and he interpreted the necessary instances of "money burning" (i.e., states of the world in which the principal pays more than the agent receives) as inefficient conflict that occurs on the equilibrium path (specifically, after the principal reports low output by the agent). MacLeod's static model simply allows any amount of money burning (say, as though a third party were available to receive the difference between what the principal pays and the agent receives).

In contrast, in a repeated-game model, Levin (2003) endogenized the upper bound on how much expected future inefficiency the parties can tolerate and still maintain their relationship today. Under the "full-review" assumption that the principal gives the agent a performance review (i.e., truthfully reveals the agent's output) each period, Levin shows that the optimal relational contract takes a threshold form: for sufficiently high output, the agent receives a bonus and the relationship continues; for output below the threshold, there is no bonus and the relationship ends.

Finally, Fuchs (2007) shows that, by releasing more information to the agent, the full-review policy cannot help and might hurt in implementing the optimal relational contract. This is because releasing more information about past performance gives the agent more histories on which he can condition his effort decision this period and thus increases the number of incentive constraints the contract must meet. A superior approach is to keep the agent in the dark for blocks of 7 periods, after which the principal provides performance information. Even better, the principal could withhold performance information for the entire relationship, meaning that the optimal contract is a termination contract: the agent receives a constant wage each period until the principal decides to fire him.[11]

A second natural way to enrich the basic model of relational incentive contracting is to add private information not about outcomes but instead about payoffs—such as the agent's cost function or the principal's discount factor. MacLeod and Malcomson (1988) and Halac (2012a) have analyzed such models where the party's type is permanent, and Li and Matouschek (2012) and Halac (2012b) have analyzed models with a transient type. We discuss each of these now.

In MacLeod and Malcomson's (1988) model, workers know their own abilities (but firms do not), and it is efficient for higher ability workers to exert more effort. The result is akin to heats in a track meet. In the first round, only the least-able workers fail to qualify for the second round (i.e., fail to get promoted); all other workers work just hard enough to qualify. Of those promoted, the least able fail to qualify for the third round (i.e., a second promotion), and the others work just hard enough to qualify. Eventually, the workers' ability distribution is broken into intervals, corresponding to the groups of workers who have chosen to stop on each rung of this endogenous promotion ladder. Having reached its steady-state rung on the ladder, each such group then works hard enough to avoid demotion but finds it not worthwhile to work hard enough to induce further promotion. This gradual learning, in which different types settle into different steady states for the remainder of the repeated game, is a prominent theme in the literature. See Gibbons and Henderson (this volume) for descriptions of how Chassang (2010) and Halac (2012a) also fit this description. In Li and Matouschek (2012) and Halac (2012b), where types are transitory, it is not surprising that learning does not cause different types to settle into different steady states for the remainder of the game, but even one-period types can nonetheless cause longer run inefficiencies. Again, see Gibbons and Henderson (this volume) for details.

---

11. Fong and Li (2010) build on Fuchs's logic to show that an intermediary who can induce intertemporal garbling of performance information (producing a garbled public signal instead of either the principal or the agent observing true output) can improve relational contracting compared to the full information about performance in the basic model.

4. No Contracts: Career Concerns

The models in Sections 2 and 3 analyzed formal and then relational contracts. In this section, we take the next step and analyze situations with no contracts.[12] Workers can still have incentives, now from career concerns: the worker's current performance affects the market's belief about the worker's ability, and hence the worker's future compensation. Fama (1980) argued informally that such career concerns might make incentive contracts unnecessary. In line with Fama's intuition, career concerns may have a positive effect when the issue is motivating effort (although, even in this case, effort may be too high or too low), but career concerns can also have a very bad effect when trying to motivate other forms of behavior, such as risk taking (see Section 6.2).

The first formal investigation of Fama's idea is Holmström's (1982/1999) model, in which an agent's output in any period depends not only on the agent's effort but also on his ability plus random noise: $y_t = a_t + \eta + \varepsilon_t$. Both ability η, which is persistent, and the noise in each period, ε_t, are normally distributed random variables. Firms and the agent are initially uncertain about the agent's ability and so use observed performance y_t to update their beliefs. As in the relational-contracting model in Section 3, the agent's output here is observable but not verifiable. Nonetheless, competition among prospective employers (all of whom see the agent's output) makes the agent's future wages depend on firms' updated beliefs about his ability, so he has an incentive to perform well today to try to influence these beliefs.

Holmström showed that, in the absence of incentive contracts, career concerns do provide incentives but produce an inefficient (but intuitive) pattern of effort over time: agents typically work too hard (relative to the efficient first best) in early years (while the market is still assessing the agent's ability and he has a long time to reap the rewards of improving the market's belief) and not hard enough in later years (when the market's belief is hard to budge and the agent has little time to go). The idea is that by working harder than might be optimal under full information, the agent can hope to make employers believe he is more productive than he actually is. However, in equilibrium the employers recognize this incentive and account for it in their inferences. Yet the agent is stuck trying too hard, because if he does not, his low output will be seen as evidence that he is especially untalented.

With its additive production function and normal uncertainty, Holmström's model is tractable enough to allow analyses of short, long, and infinite horizons (as well as of the case where the agent's ability changes as a random walk over time). Dewatripont et al. (1999a) took a complementary approach, allowing both for multidimensional actions (multitasking) and signals and for different distributions relating signals, actions, ability, and noise. Given these generalizations, their analysis allows only two periods. Their focus is on how information structures familiar from standard agency theory (e.g., Holmström's (1979) sufficient statistic result) influence equilibrium effort in this context. In Dewatripont et al. (1999b), they applied a career-concerns model to governmental agencies, where budgetary and political limitations may curtail the use of explicit performance pay, and career concerns may consequently be more

---

12. Parts of this section draw on Gibbons, "Incentives between Firms (and Within)," *Management Science* 51(1), 2005, pp. 2–17, by permission from the Institute for Operations Research and the Management Sciences, 7240 Parkway Drive, Suite 300, Hanover, MD 21076, USA.

salient, but observers may be less able to interpret output signals than in some private sector contexts.

MacLeod and Malcomson (1988) analyzed something like career concerns in a model where workers now know their own abilities (but firms still do not) and it is efficient for higher ability workers to exert more effort (unlike the additive production function above). The result is akin to heats in a track meet. In the first round, only the least-able workers fail to qualify for the second round (i.e., fail to get promoted); all other workers work just hard enough to qualify. Of those in the second round, the least able fail to qualify for the third, and the others work just hard enough to qualify. Eventually, the ability distribution is broken into intervals, corresponding to the groups of workers who failed to qualify for each round. Having reached its steady-state level, each such group then works hard enough to avoid demotion but finds it not worthwhile to work hard enough to induce further promotion.

5. Beyond Contracts: Incentive Systems

Having discussed (and seen the limitations of) formal contracts, relational contracts, and no contracts in providing incentives, we now consider other ways to improve incentives when each of these is of only limited use by employing several motivating devices at once.

One approach is to mix formal contracts with relational contracts and/or career concerns. For example, Baker et al. (1994) examined the interplay between formal and relational contracts, showing that they could be complements in providing incentives (if the formal contract alone would be quite ineffective) but more typically are substitutes. Indeed, if the formal contracts are imperfect but nonetheless too effective, they can make relational contracts impossible, even where relational contracts alone would be more effective than these imperfect formal contracts. Other models in this vein have been explored by Pearce and Stacchetti (1998), Che and Yoo (2001), Kvaløy and Olsen (2006), Rayo (2007), and Battigalli and Maggi (2008); see Malcomson (this volume) for a discussion. The common theme of these models is that formal and relational contracts not only co-exist but also interact. Roughly speaking, the idea is to choose the formal contract to minimize the reneging temptation created by the relational contract (which typically means choosing a different formal contract than would be optimal if the parties had access to formal contracts only).

Similarly, Gibbons and Murphy (1992) added single-period formal contracts to Holmström's (1982/1999) career-concerns model. Because career-concern incentives decline as the agent approaches retirement, the slope of the optimal incentive contract increases, keeping total incentives (roughly) constant. Gibbons and Murphy presented evidence on CEO compensation consistent with this prediction, and Gompers and Lerner (1999) did likewise for venture capitalists. Meyer and Vickers (1997) also allowed single-period formal contracts in addition to career concerns, but they added the possibility of relative performance evaluation in a model where the principal employs one agent but can observe the output of another. Formal contracts depend only on the agent's own output, but the career-concerns mechanism (updating beliefs about the agent's ability) is allowed to depend on past performances by both agents and hence can involve relative performance evaluation. Meyer and Vickers showed that relative performance evaluation in the career-concerns mechanism can help or hurt welfare—unlike in the classic agency model, where relative performance evaluation always improves incentives (see

Section 2.2). They suggest that their result may help interpret the mixed evidence on relative performance evaluation noted above.

Our focus in this section, however, is on using other features of the organizational design (besides pay for performance) to affect incentives, rather than merely blending the three approaches from Sections 2–4. By using these new instruments appropriately, the principal and agent may be able to create an improved solution to their incentive problem. In particular, the features of organizational design we consider sometimes have their own effect on the agent's incentives, but often also function by allowing the parties to utilize formal or relational contracts differently, thereby improving the overall results. In short, the overarching theme of this section is that no single instrument is likely to create perfect (or perhaps even tolerable) incentives, so multiple instruments are likely to be used in combination as an incentive system (Holmström and Milgrom 1994). Indeed, although we break this section's discussion into several parts, the spirit of the argument is not only that each of these can be combined with formal or relational contracts, but also that some or even all of these organizational features often can be usefully combined with one another. The organizational features we discuss are employees versus independent contractors; job design; empowerment; promotion; selection; and strategy, vision, and leadership.

5.1. The Agent as Employee or Contractor

If the identity of the principal has been established along the lines discussed in Section 2.1.4, it remains to determine whether the agent should be an employee or an independent contractor for the principal.[13] Inspired by Holmström and Milgrom (1991), we now enrich the manipulable-measures model from Section 2.1.2 by assuming that there is a machine that the agent uses in producing y. The resale value of the machine (after it is used in production) is $v = h_1 a_1 + h_2 a_2 + \xi$. As with y, we assume that v is not contractible, so contracts continue to depend on only x. If the principal owns the machine (so the agent is an employee), then the principal's payoff is $y + v - w$ and the agent's is $w - c$. Alternatively, if the agent owns the machine (so the agent is a contractor), then the principal's payoff is $y - w$ and the agent's is $w + v - c$. In short, the parties now have two instruments to influence the agent's incentives—the formal incentive contract and ownership of the asset—and they need not use these instruments independently; to the contrary, we expect different formal contracts to be optimal depending on who owns the asset.

As stark illustrations of this incentive-system model, consider the following pair of examples.

Example 1: $y = a_1$, $v = a_2$, and $x = a_1$.

Example 2: $y = a_1$, $v = a_2$, and $x = a_1 + a_2$.

In Example 1, the parties are better off having the agent own the machine, because if the principal owns it, there is no way to provide incentives for the agent to enhance the machine's resale value (through action a_2). In Example 2, the reverse is true. In fact, in these simple examples, with the wrong choice of asset ownership the parties create a "get what you pay for" problem, but with the right choice the parties can then write incentive contracts that induce the first-best actions.

---

13. Parts of this section draw on Gibbons (2010) with permission from the *Annual Review of Economics*, Volume 2, © 2010 by Annual Reviews, http://www.annualreviews.org.

5.2. Job Design

Next, we return to the suggestion from the end of Section 2.1.1, that there may be better and worse ways to group tasks, for purposes of performance measurement and formal incentive contracting. Consider a multitask LEN model where there are four different tasks and the cost of effort for either of two agents is

$$C(a_1, a_2, a_3, a_4) = \frac{1}{2}(a_1 + a_2 + a_3 + a_4)^2$$

if at most two of the a_i variables are positive and infinity otherwise. Thus, each agent can undertake at most two tasks and the marginal cost of effort on any task is increasing in the amount of effort that the agent devotes to other tasks. Assume contracts are of the form

$$w = s + \sum_1^4 b_i x_i,$$

where $x_i = a_i + \varepsilon_i$. Because of the cost function, if the b_i values differ for any tasks the agent is asked to perform, only the most highly rewarded type of effort will be provided.

Now suppose the variances on the measures differ, with $\sigma_1 > \sigma_2 > \sigma_3 > \sigma_4$, and suppose that each agent can do only two tasks and all four tasks are desired by the principal. How should the tasks be allocated? The answer is that one agent should take tasks 1 and 2, the poorly measured ones, and the other should take 3 and 4. The agent taking the poorly measured tasks will receive quite muted incentives (small b), and the other agent will receive stronger incentives. This choice is better than mixing the tasks and having both agents necessarily receive the weak incentives that would then be optimal. Thus, as with the decision to make the agent an employee or a contractor, the decision about bundling tasks into jobs affects the formal incentive contracts that are then optimal.

Using a model based on Meyer and Vickers (1997), Meyer et al. (1996) asked whether this lesson about job design in a static model continues to hold in a dynamic model with limited commitment. Parallel to the Meyer and Vickers finding that relative performance evaluation (which has an unambiguously positive effect in a static model) can help or hurt welfare in a dynamic model with limited commitment, here Meyer et al. found that the optimal bundling of tasks may no longer be high versus low variance. Corts (2007) considered the job-design problem with two tasks, two customers for which these must be carried out, and two agents. He showed that it may be better to make both agents accountable for both tasks for both customers. The reason is that the team arrangement gives two measures on each agent, and this can be advantageous if the multitasking problem is severe and the risk costs are low. Even so, the basic incentive-systems point continues to hold: choosing the bundling of tasks appropriately allows the parties to choose a different formal incentive contract and improve their overall results.

5.3. Empowerment

The allocation of decision authority can have strong motivational effects. For example, in the early 1990s, large amounts of authority were delegated to front-line managers at BP, the energy company. They spoke of how motivating having this authority was, to feel that they had control and were responsible for a piece of business (Roberts 2004).

Usually, economic models aimed at this phenomenon assume that there are private benefits that the agent can enjoy if he is in charge (e.g., Aghion and Tirole 1997). As in Van den Steen (2010), an alternative modeling allows that the principal and agent may fundamentally disagree about which decision will lead to a good outcome, but that both principal and agent may gain if a good outcome occurs. If the agent believes the decision is more likely to be right if he makes it than if the principal does, then the agent will be more motivated to work hard (to develop decision-relevant information or to implement the chosen course of action successfully) if he can choose the decision.

If empowerment creates incentives (as did ownership of the machine when the agent is a contractor in Section 5.1), then one would expect different formal incentive contracts to be optimal, depending on whether decision rights were or were not delegated to the agent. As noted in Section 2.1, Prendergast (2002) developed a model in this spirit. See Bolton and Dewatripont (this volume), Gibbons et al. (this volume), and Mookherjee (this volume) for more on these and other aspects of delegation and empowerment.

5.4. Promotion

The up-or-out systems used in law firms, consultancies, and other professional service firms can induce exceptional levels of effort among junior members of the firms. See Kahn and Huberman (1988) and Waldman (1990) on the incentives created by such up-or-out contracts.

The tournament model sketched in Section 2.2 is another way to analyze the incentives created by the prospect of promotion. One drawback of using the tournament model (or up-or-out contracts) to study promotions is that, taken literally, the model implies that there are no incentives after being promoted. Of course, the model could be enriched to allow, say, formal incentive contracts, which could indeed be used to create incentives for agents who have been promoted. But in this enriched model, one should also ask why incentives before promotion are created by the prospect of promotion rather than by formal incentive contracts. See Baker et al. (1988) for an early exploration of these issues.

Another way to analyze incentives after a first promotion is to suppose that a second promotion is then possible. If there are fewer jobs at each successive level of the hierarchy, and pay rises with hierarchical level, then competition for promotion creates a tournament at each level. See Rosen (1986) for a first model of such elimination tournaments.

Finally, as we discuss in Section 6.1, Prendergast (1993) has shown how promotion policies can affect incentives for other desired behaviors (besides effort), such as the acquisition of firm-specific human capital. See Lazear and Oyer (this volume) and Waldman (this volume) for more on these and other aspects of promotions.

5.5. Selection

Offering performance pay can attract some agents while encouraging others to look elsewhere. In this sense, incentive pay may cause selection, and the productivity effects of this selection could be as important as the productivity effects of the incentives themselves. See Lazear (1986) for theory and Lazear (2000) for evidence.

Of course, the argument can also work in the other direction: having caused a narrow group of workers to select into the firm, the parties may then be able to use different formal or relational contracts than would have been optimal for a broader population of workers. For example, in Sappington's (1983) model with limited liability and private information from Section 2.1.3, different contracts would be optimal if selection led to different supports of the agent's private information (and the same would be true in Laffont and Tirole (1986) and the models that followed).

5.6. Strategy, Vision, and Leadership

Various papers have suggested ways in which a firm's commitment to a strategy (or a vision or leadership style) can motivate employees. For example, defining a strategy as a specification of the lines of business in which the firm will operate, Rotemberg and Saloner (1994) developed a model in which a narrower portfolio of businesses makes it easier to execute useful incentive contracts. In this model, the agent supplies effort toward generating new projects, and the principal commits to a payment to the agent if a new project is implemented, but the principal retains control over whether projects are implemented (and so makes this decision based on the net benefits from implementing the project less compensating the agent). Tension arises if the agent generates a new project with value less than the compensation promised if a project is implemented, because the principal then prefers not to implement the project; anticipating this, the agent's incentives for effort then fall. If a narrow portfolio of businesses is more likely to generate "home-run" innovations or nothing (i.e., a broader portfolio generates more projects of intermediate value, perhaps because a given project has weaker synergies across a broader portfolio of businesses), then this tension arises less often if the firm pursues a narrow strategy. (See the discussion of Prendergast (1993) in Section 6.1 for a similar mechanism applied to workers' investments in firm-specific human capital and firms' subsequent decisions about whether to promote workers to higher paying jobs.)

Other approaches are similar in spirit but operate through other mechanisms, more along the lines of the differing beliefs mentioned in Section 5.3 on empowerment. For example, Rotemberg and Saloner (2000) called a top manager "visionary" if she is known to be biased toward a particular course of action. Knowing that a manager is visionary gives workers stronger incentives to invest in projects that are consistent with the manager's vision, because the workers are confident that such projects will indeed be implemented; see Van den Steen (2005) for more along this line.

Finally, Hermalin (1998) explored a signaling model of leading by example, where a leader has private information about the productivity of her own and followers' efforts, and observing high effort by the leader causes the followers to conclude that their productivity is high and so to work hard. See Camerer and Weber (this volume), Hermalin ("Leadership and Corporate Culture," this volume), and Roberts and Saloner (this volume) for more on strategy, vision, and leadership.

5.7. The Organizational Architecture

Sections 2–4 discussed performance incentives created by formal, relational, and no contracts, whereas this section has shifted attention to instruments besides pay-for-performance for creating incentives. Having discussed various instruments internal to the firm—such as job design, empowerment, promotions, selection, and leadership—we now conclude this section by considering one last instrument: the formal architecture of the firm itself. Although we briefly mention a variety of aspects of the architecture that can affect effort incentives, most of our attention is on the boundaries of the firm.

Many aspects of organizational architecture are discussed in other chapters of this volume. These include the horizontal and vertical boundaries of the firm (Bresnahan and Levin; Ménard; Roberts and Saloner), its ownership structure (Hansmann), its corporate governance system (Hermalin, "Corporate Governance"), its internal structure of hierarchy and authority (Bolton and Dewatripont; Gibbons et al.; Mookherjee; Roberts and Saloner), and its decisionmaking systems (Gertner and Scharfstein; Gibbons et al.). As argued in Roberts (2004), each of these can have implications for incentives.

For example, the owners of a traditional partnership facing unlimited liability might be expected to exert quite different efforts toward mutual monitoring than they would if they were owner-managers of a limited liability corporation. The make-up of the board of directors and its compensation can certainly affect their incentives for oversight of the executives and thus the latter's behavior. We have already considered an example of the effect of the internal structure and allocation of decision rights in Section 5.3. And, as noted in Jensen (1986), the choice of debt or equity financing can significantly affect managerial behavior.

In Section 5.1's analysis of whether the agent should be an employee or an independent contractor, we have already touched on the idea that the boundary of the firm (there construed as the payoff right attached to asset ownership) might be a useful complement to formal incentive contracting. Here we sketch further applications of this idea, motivated by Holmström's (1999) view that the firm is a "subeconomy" in which the principal can set the rules. For example, the principal can allow the agent to contract with outside parties at will, within limits, or not at all.

The following simple model shows that the boundary of the firm can matter for creating incentives even in the absence of formal incentive contracts. This model follows Grossman and Hart (1986) in emphasizing the role of property rights in creating hold-up, but it incorporates a multitask aspect from Holmström and Milgrom (1991) to produce an intuitive trade-off. Our discussion is informal; see Aghion and Tirole (1994), Holmström (1999), and Baker et al. (2002) for related formal models.

Consider an upstream biotech unit that can produce drug candidates for two downstream pharmaceutical firms—say, Merck and Pfizer. If one of the pharmas (say, Merck) owns the biotech, then Merck can forbid the unit to sell drug candidates to Pfizer. In addition, suppose that when Merck owns the biotech unit, the unit also cannot bargain with Merck, in the sense that Merck owns any drug candidates that the unit produces. In these circumstances, Merck may seek to create incentives for the biotech unit, perhaps through a formal contract, but we have seen that this can be exceedingly difficult to do well.

An alternative is to spin off the biotech unit as its own separate firm. The downside (from Merck's perspective) is that the biotech is now free to bargain with and sell to Pfizer. The upside, however, is that the biotech's opportunity to hold up Merck (i.e., to present a competing offer from Pfizer for a given drug candidate) may create useful incentives for the biotech (again, from Merck's perspective). For example, suppose that the actions the biotech can take to create a drug candidate that is valuable to Pfizer also make that candidate valuable to Merck. In this case, the prospect of holding up Merck creates strong and useful incentives for the biotech during the creation of the drug candidate. As an opposite example, however, suppose that actions that make the candidate more valuable to Pfizer instead reduce its value to Merck. In this case, the prospect of holding up Merck may create equally strong incentives for the biotech, but now these incentives are destructive rather than useful from Merck's perspective. In the former case, hold-up may be Merck's friend, and spinning off the biotech may be optimal; in the latter case, hold-up is disastrous for Merck, and they might be better advised to retain the biotech unit inside Merck, in spite of difficulties in then creating incentives for the unit.

This argument is another application of the fundamental insight from Grossman and Hart (1986): a benefit of nonintegration is that it creates strong incentives. Holmström's (1999) complementary insight is that when these high-powered incentives from nonintegration are misdirected, the low-powered incentives from integration may be preferred.

6. Beyond Effort

Most of the preceding discussion has focused on the problem of inducing the agent to supply what we have called "effort": an action that is costly for the agent, benefits the principal, and cannot be directly stipulated by contract. But there are many other actions, besides effort, that may have these three attributes, and there are still other noncontractible actions that may be beneficial to the agent and costly to the principal.

In this section we briefly discuss several such actions: investing in firm-specific skill; risk taking; information acquisition, communication, and decisionmaking; obedience; and influence activities. Similar to the organizational instruments discussed in Section 5, the contexts discussed here place less weight on formal or relational contracting than do the traditional agency models described in Sections 2 and 3. The distinction we draw between this section and the previous one, however, is that here we focus on models with enough context to make clear that the problems (and organizational responses) are not as simple as inducing effort from the agent to create output for the principal.

6.1. Investing in Firm-Specific Skill

Becker (1962) analyzed investment in firm-specific human capital in a world with complete contracting.[14] In this world, workers' investments are verifiable by a court, so it is easy to induce efficient investment: simply have the firm reimburse the agent for the costs of his time and effort if he has acquired the requisite skills. Suppose, however, that a court cannot verify whether the investments have been made properly. The incentive problem is then two-sided: the parties need incentives that both induce the workers to invest and induce the firm to pay workers once they have invested. Put differently, the problem is that the firm will hold up the workers, refusing to pay once the investment cost is sunk, and the workers, foreseeing this, will not invest.

---

14. Parts of this section draw on Gibbons, "Incentives between Firms (and Within)," *Management Science* 51(1), 2005, pp. 2–17, by permission from the Institute for Operations Research and the Management Sciences, 7240 Parkway Drive, Suite 300, Hanover, MD 21076, USA.

Prendergast (1993) has shown that a firm's promise to promote skilled workers can some-times overcome this two-sided incentive problem.[15] Formally, let the agent's skill level be L if he has not invested in the requisite skills and $H > L$ if he has invested. The agent incurs an opportunity cost of c to improve his skill from L to H.

Having now described dozens of models above in which the agent's output is at best imper-fectly contractible (if at all), we note here that the agent's skill is likely to be at least as difficult to contract on as his output is, because skill is a determinant of future output. For simplicity, Prendergast assumes that the agent's skill level is not contractible, even imperfectly so. How-ever, imagine that the principal has two tasks to which the agent could be assigned. Call these tasks "easy" and "difficult," meaning that the agent's skills are more important in the production process for the difficult (D) task than for the easy (E) one. More specifically, suppose that an agent with skill s ($= L$ or H) assigned to task p ($= E$ or D) has productivity v_{sp} satisfying: (1) an agent who has not invested is more productive when assigned to task E ($v_{LE} > v_{LD}$); (2) one who has invested is more productive when assigned to the difficult task ($v_{HD} > v_{HE}$); and (3) training is efficient, because the productivity difference with optimal job assignments exceeds the investment cost ($v_{HD} - v_{LE} > c$).

Suppose that job assignments are verifiable by the court, so the principal can commit to paying a high wage (w_D) to the agent if the agent is assigned to the difficult task and a low wage ($w_E < w_D$) if the agent is assigned to the easy task. If the agent believes that investing will lead to assignment to the difficult task, then he will invest if $w_D - w_E > c$. The principal, for her part, will choose to assign a skilled agent to the difficult task if $v_{HD} - w_D > v_{HE} - w_E$. Unfortunately, these two conditions may be incompatible, even if investment is efficient: the agent's and principal's incentive conditions require $v_{HD} - v_{HE} > w_D - w_E > c$, but the assumption that investment is efficient guarantees only that $v_{HD} - v_{LE} > c$, not that $v_{HD} - v_{HE} > c$.

In short, the firm's promise to promote skilled workers creates a tension between needing a large enough difference in wages to induce the agent to invest, but a small enough difference to induce the principal to assign a skilled agent to the difficult task. If the change in value created from assigning a skilled agent efficiently is sufficiently large ($v_{HD} - v_{HE} > c$), then there exists a difference in wages that meets both these constraints. But if the two tasks satisfy $v_{HD} - v_{HE} < c$, then the promise of promotion cannot simultaneously provide an incentive for the agent to invest and an incentive for the principal to reward investment.[16]

The promise of promotion in Prendergast's (1993) model illustrates a contract different from the formal contracts analyzed in Section 2. Here, the agent's compensation is based on the principal's decision (the job assignment) rather than on the outcome that the agent's action produces (the skill level). Incentives for the agent then arise from how the principal's

---

15. See Lazear and Oyer (this volume) and Waldman (this volume) for more on skill development and promotions.

16. Recall from Section 5.6 that the Rotemberg and Saloner (1994) model of narrow business strategies has an analogous tension. Following Rotemberg and Saloner's idea that the firm might choose (at an opportunity cost) a narrow instead of a broad business strategy, where the former resolves the tension in their model but the latter does not, one could imagine by analogy in Prendergast's model that the firm might choose (at an opportunity cost) job technologies where $v_{HD} - v_{HE} > c$ instead of not.

decision (d) depends on the outcome the agent produces (v). If the principal's decision and the agent's outcome create value $y(d, v)$ for the principal, and the agent's compensation contract is $w(d)$, then the principal's optimal decision $d^*(v)$ maximizes $y(d, v) - w(d)$. In Prendergast's model, the agent chooses v directly, so one can express the agent's problem as choosing v to maximize $w(d^*(v)) - c(v)$; in a richer model, the agent might choose an action a that generates a stochastic outcome with distribution $f(v|a)$.

Obviously, this indirect approach to creating incentives for the agent would fail if $d^*(v)$ were a constant (e.g., if the principal never promoted the agent). This is one way that incentives for effort differ from incentives for developing skill: if "effort" means that the agent's total contribution is already realized (e.g., $y(d, v) = v - d$), then the principal has no incentive to make a decision that depends on the agent's outcome, whereas if "skill" means that (at least some of) the agent's total contribution depends on the principal's decision (e.g., $y(d, v) = dv$), then $d^*(v)$ may create useful incentives for the agent.[17]

6.2. Risk Taking and Experimentation

Agents are frequently asked to make choices among risky alternatives. This can be problematic if the agent is risk averse, his compensation depends on the results of his choice, and his risk attitudes differ from those of the principal. The obvious solution—disconnect his pay from the results of his choice—would work if he could demonstrate to the principal the basis for his choice. But such a demonstration is not possible, and if the principal wants to motivate the agent to exert unobservable effort to learn about the choice, then an agency problem arises of getting the agent to exert effort on research and then make a choice the principal would like.

Lambert (1986) studied this problem. A risk-averse agent is charged with selecting between a safe investment yielding y_0 for sure or a risky investment yielding either y_L or y_H, where $y_H > y_0 > y_L$. The prior probability that the risky investment yields y_H is 0.5, but at a cost c the agent can learn the actual probability p of success, which is distributed uniformly on $[0, 1]$. The risk-neutral principal would like the risky investment chosen if $py_H + (1 - p)y_L > y_0$. However, she does not observe p, and Lambert assumes that if the agent does observe p, he cannot communicate it credibly to the principal.

Given payments $w_i, i = L, 0, H$, from the principal in each of the three possible outcomes that yield U_L, U_0, and U_H, respectively, the agent will select the risky investment if either he has not learned p and $(U_H + U_L)/2 > U_0$ or he has learned p and $pU_H + (1 - p)U_L > U_0$. In the latter case, this leads him to adopt a cutoff value r such that he chooses the risky investment only if $p > r$. Thus, if he learns p, his expected utility is $rU_0 + [(1 - r^2)U_H + (1 - r)^2U_L]/2$, so he will invest in learning p if this expected utility, evaluated at the optimal value of r (which depends on the utility levels) exceeds $\max\{U_0, (U_H + U_L)/2\}$ by at least his cost of effort, c. This in turn requires $U_H > U_0 > U_L$: risk is imposed on the agent to get him to work, as in

---

17. The implementation literature in contract theory has asked whether there exists a contract $w(d)$ that induces the principal to implement a desired decision rule $d^*(v)$ in a world where v is uncertain, exogenous, and noncontractible; see Moore and Repullo (1988), for example. Prendergast's (1993) model can be seen as endogenizing v, by introducing the agent and allowing him to choose v to maximize $w(d) - c(v)$. See Aghion et al. (1994) for more abstract progress along Prendergast's line.

the standard models. However, unlike the standard models, increasing the amount of risk the agent faces does not necessarily increase his incentives, because at some point the risk he faces is so great that he becomes better off not working and always selecting the safe investment.

In Lambert's (1986) model, at the optimal contract, the agent does not always choose the principal's preferred project. Note that this conflict of interest involves which project should be selected after the agent observes the value of p. But the compensation contract not only seeks to align interest in this regard but also to motivate the agent to invest in learning p. Consequently, the contract trades off the costs of motivating the agent to work against the benefits of having him adopt a project-selection strategy that the principal likes.

Manso (2011) offered a different take on motivating appropriate risk taking. He considered a problem where the risk-averse agent has three choices in each period: shirk; try the established way of carrying out his responsibilities, which has a known probability of success; or try a new way, which has an unknown probability of success. Each option carries a positive probability of success and of failure, but the new way is, in expectation, inferior to the old. Further, both yield more value, net of the agent's cost of effort, than does shirking. In a single period, therefore, the principal would want to motivate the agent not to shirk and to follow the standard procedure. However, suppose that if the new way is tried and it succeeds, then the updated posterior on its probability of further success exceeds the known probability of success of the established way. In this case, in a two-period setting, the principal may want the agent to experiment with the new way, with the intention of adopting it in the second period if it is a success and otherwise reverting to using the old way.

Motivating the agent to adopt the established way involves a contract design that is absolutely standard from the literature on unobservable costly effort. In contrast, motivating experimentation necessitates muted first-period incentives, because success is more likely if the agent adopts the established way, and so observing success is bad news about the choice he made. In fact, it may even be necessary to reward first-period failure if the agent finds it easier to do things the old way. However, second-period rewards have to be quite large to deter shirking.

6.3. Information Acquisition, Communication, and Decisionmaking

The Lambert (1986) and Manso (2011) papers on risk taking begin to illustrate three larger issues that are related to incentives in organizations but often are quite different from the idea in the classic agency model that the goal is to induce something like effort from the agent: information acquisition, communication, and decisionmaking. These topics are discussed in detail in Bolton and Dewatripont (this volume) and Gibbons et al. (this volume), so we treat them only briefly here.

Information acquisition can be like effort in that it is costly to the agent. This cost is direct in Lambert (1986) and somewhat indirect in Manso (2011), where it is subsumed in the cost of effort. However, unlike effort, information itself does not typically produce a benefit for the principal. Instead, a decision is taken on the basis of the information, and then the principal receives the benefits.

In some contexts, information may be "hard," in that the agent cannot distort it. For example, Athey and Roberts (2001) made such an assumption in modeling whether to give control of investment decisions to a third party rather than leave them with the parties that originated the opportunities. There are few interesting incentive issues in communicating hard information of this sort. However, one could also imagine that, even though the information cannot be distorted, it can be withheld, with the agent falsely claiming that he is uninformed. This gives rise to richer strategic communication possibilities. And moving to "soft" information that can be directly misrepresented raises especially rich opportunities for strategic communication.

The baseline model of strategic communication of soft information is the Crawford and Sobel (1982) analysis of cheap talk. The agent is informed (for free) about a state of the world. The principal wants to make her decision match the state, but the agent wants the decision to differ systematically from the actual value of the state by a constant amount, b. The rewards to both parties depend only on how the decision is tailored to the state. Crawford and Sobel showed that it is impossible to induce complete revelation of the agent's information.

It is also possible that the decisions might be delegated to the agent, as can happen in Dessein (2002). Recent papers by Alonso et al. (2008) and Rantakari (2008a) have built models of adaptation and coordination of decisions in multiproduct firms based on cheap talk. The issue is whether decisions should be taken centrally or in a delegated fashion by the agents, where in either case there is strategic communication. Friebel and Raith (2010) have generated a theory of the multiproduct firm based on the possibility of resource reallocations within the firm where communication is strategic and productive effort must be induced.

Finally, an important line of work embeds career concerns in models of project development and selection—see, for example, Holmström and Ricart i Costa (1986), Scharfstein and Stein (1990), and Zwiebel (1995). In these papers, career concerns, which were shown to be good for inducing effort, have a very negative impact. The idea is basically Mark Twain's: "Better to keep your mouth shut and appear stupid than to open it and remove all doubt." In Holmström and Ricart i Costa (in the case without incentive contracts), for example, a manager forgoes a profitable investment, because the result of the investment would reveal information about his ability to choose investments. Similarly, Scharfstein and Stein (1990) and Zwiebel (1995) show that managers will exhibit "herd behavior," choosing the investment chosen by others even when their own information shows that another investment has a higher expected return.

6.4. Obedience

Superiors' giving orders and subordinates' deciding whether to obey is a characteristic of most organizations. The basic agency model can be thought of in these terms, with the principal telling the agent to exert the amount of effort that he finds optimal under the contract, given that the principal cannot directly see whether the agent has obeyed her instructions. Yet this model does not seem to be all there is to the matter (or even much of it). In particular, there is no actual need (or value) in those models to issue an order: the agent can work out what he wants to do, and if the principal designed the contract correctly, he will do what the principal intended.

A few recent papers have addressed the obedience issue directly. For example, Van den Steen (2010) considered situations where the principal and agent differ fundamentally in their beliefs about how the agent should carry out a task or address a problem (i.e., they have differing prior beliefs about the best way to do whatever it is that the agent is supposed to do). In such a context, rewarding the agent for success will motivate him to do things the way he thinks is best, which may well be counter to what the principal wants and believes is best. Because the principal thinks the best course of action is to follow her beliefs, she should not reward the agent much for success. This phenomenon leads to a hierarchic, superior-and-subordinate relationship. The principal hires the agent and tells him what to do. If he obeys, which may mean making a choice contrary to what he thinks is most likely to succeed, he receives an efficiency wage that does not vary with the results of his effort and that makes him strictly better off than had he refused the offer to work for the principal. If he disobeys, he is fired. To improve the incentives of each party, the principal should own any assets being used in the relationship, because then the agent, if fired, has a weaker position, while the principal may more easily replace him. This improves the agent's incentives to obey and the principal's to carry through with the termination threat. Thus, several characteristic features of firms emerge endogenously: authority of one party over the other, minimal explicit incentives, and ownership of assets by the hierarchic superior. If moral hazard on effort is an issue, then there is performance pay, but it is muted.

Marino et al. (2010) considered a private-benefit model of authority and disobedience based on the model of Aghion and Tirole (1997).[18] They studied a two-period problem. As usual in models derived from Aghion and Tirole, the principal and agent may have differing benefits from particular decisions. In Marino et al., the agent receives information for free, whereas the principal's efforts to become informed about the returns to different decisions are costly and uncertain. The payoffs to different decisions are such that the principal will want to leave decisions to the agent unless she has become informed. The principal may choose to direct the agent to make a particular choice, but she will do so only if she is informed. Nevertheless, he may choose to disobey and take his preferred option. Following disobedience in the first period, the principal may fire the agent and hire another to complete the project.

In the model by Marino et. al., the agent will disobey if his returns from making the choice he prefers are high enough and the cost of being fired is low enough. If the principal expects her orders to be ignored, she will not invest in becoming informed, and the decision is effectively delegated. In contrast, an agent whose preferred choice is different from the principal's may obey in the first period if the costs of doing so are low and the costs of being fired are high. (Then he disobeys for sure in the second period, because the principal has no recourse.) Expecting at least partial obedience, the principal may invest in becoming informed and so may hold the authority herself. Thus, external labor-market conditions and the ease of firing affect the functioning of the firm and the allocation of authority (whether the principal decides to become informed). For example, because it is easy to fire in the private sector, harder in the public sector, and virtually impossible under tenure schemes, orders are common in business and typically obeyed, they are given but often ignored in government, and nobody orders tenured faculty to do anything.[19] Moreover, disobedience may occur in equilibrium (unlike in Van den Steen 2010).

18. The Aghion-Tirole model is discussed in Bolton and Dewatripont (this volume) and Gibbons et al. (this volume).

19. This observation is credited to George Shultz, former CEO of Bechtel, U.S. secretary of state, and dean of the Chicago Business School.

6.5. Influence Activities

Most of the preceding discussion has focused on the problem of inducing the agent to take actions that are costly for the agent, beneficial for the principal, and cannot be directly stipulated by contract. But there are other actions that may be almost the reverse: beneficial to the agent and costly to the principal, but still noncontractible.

Milgrom and Roberts (1988) suggested that organizational decisions often have distributional effects that are separate from their efficiency effects. For example, someone must be assigned to Paris, Texas, and someone to Paris, France. It may not matter at all to overall performance who is assigned where, but the candidates may care a lot. Each then may seek to influence the decision in his preferred direction. This effort may involve all sorts of politicking, including misrepresentation, sabotage, or side payments of various sorts. Milgrom and Roberts argued that these influence activities can be costly in several ways: resources are expended that bring no corresponding social benefits, decisions are potentially twisted, and the organization may alter its routines and processes to discourage attempts at influence.

Meyer et al. (1992) developed a model of how organizational design can reduce the incentives for influence activities. In their setting, lobbying occurs from the prospect of organizational decline. To reduce wasteful lobbying, it may be more efficient to spin off declining units.

Powell (2012) offered another formal model of these ideas, in the spirit of Holmström's (1982/1999) career-concerns model. In Powell's framework, there are two parties and two decisions. Before these decisions can be made, the parties decide who will be empowered to make each decision, but once this allocation of decision authority is set, contracting difficulties prevent renegotiation. If the other party is to make a decision, then the disempowered party may have incentives to try to affect the decision by undertaking (unobserved) influence activities that are in the spirit of signal jamming.

Given an arbitrary allocation of decision rights, Powell solved for the equilibrium level of influence. In equilibrium, the party making a decision will correctly anticipate the amount of influence the other party is undertaking and, using that correct estimate, will back out the effect of the influence and make the decision that is best for him. So the influence does not distort decisions, but it does occur and impose costs.

The optimal allocation of decision rights maximizes the sum of utilities given that the parties will choose their levels of influence in the equilibrium fashion. This may be either divided control, with each controlling one decision (which involves lower costs, because the costs of influence are convex and so it is better to have the total amount of influence split between the two parties) or unified control, with both decisions being made by the party who cares more about the outcome.

Powell then examined some suggestions made by Milgrom and Roberts (1988) for limiting influence activities and mitigating influence costs. In particular, a "closed-door" policy is modeled as unified control, with no public signal being observed (because the parties agreed not to hire the needed staff, loaded their calendars so they were too busy, and limited their meetings). This policy eliminates the disempowered party's incentive to attempt influence, but it also deprives the party in control of useful information. However, if the initial uncertainty was not great, then not a lot has been lost, and the closed-door policy may be preferred to the alternative of playing the game as originally specified.

Also, if there is a lot of disagreement about how to tailor decisions to the state of the world, then again it may become worthwhile to adopt the closed-door policy. Then a selection story like that in Figure 1 (from Section 1) applies: as disagreement increases, both the open- and closed-door policies do worse, but the closed door does relatively better at high levels of disagreement. Thus, the rigid, apparently bad management practice of limiting communication obtains when circumstances are bad, and observed firms with these practices are worse performers than those that are observed adhering to open-door policies. However, the closed-door firms perform better in the environments they inhabit than would firms with apparently "better" management practices.

7. Behavioral Economic Theories of Incentives

Most of the preceding discussion focused on egoists who find their work burdensome (at least at the margin). However, such phenomena as intrinsic motivation, altruism, reciprocity, gift exchange, status, self-image, and self-justification have figured prominently in discussions of incentives in sociology, psychology, and management. Partly in response to these ideas, an active intersection between organizational economics and behavioral economics has arisen in what might be called "behavioral incentive theory." As an introduction to evidence on this issue, see Fehr and Falk (2002) and Bandiera et al. (2005, 2007). Recently, there is an emerging theoretical literature, including Bénabou and Tirole (2003, 2006), Besley and Ghatak (2005), Prendergast (2007), Sliwka (2007), and Ellingsen and Johannesson (2008). Here we briefly mention some highlights of this literature. See also Baron and Kreps (this volume) for discussion and references to the literatures in sociology and psychology.

7.1. Intrinsic Motivation

One of the most striking differences between standard economics and more behavioral fields involves the phenomenon of intrinsic motivation—the idea that people are inherently motivated to do a good job—and the possibility that providing explicit incentives for something may reduce intrinsic motivation enough to be counterproductive, actually reducing overall motivation. There is evidence that extrinsic incentives can reduce intrinsic motivation (see, e.g., the summary in Bénabou and Tirole 2003), but at the same time, there is also evidence on the economists' side that extrinsic incentives can be productive (Lazear 2000). The issue is how to reconcile these observations.

The paper by Bénabou and Tirole (2003) is a notable first attempt to do so while sticking to the usual economic assumptions of rational egoistic behavior. The analysis here relies on the principal being privately informed about the difficulty of the task being set for the agent, on his productivity at the task, or the match of the two. Explicit rewards may lead the agent to infer that the principal's information is negative. This inference may then result in reduced effort, but need not, and may have differing short- and long-run effects.

Bénabou and Tirole (2006) departed from standard models of preferences in attempting both to understand the interplay of intrinsic and extrinsic motivation and also the fact that people often appear to be motivated by how others will view them or by how their self-image will be affected. Bénabou and Tirole offered a theory that combines heterogeneity in the extent of individuals' altruism and greed with a concern for social reputation or self-respect to investigate decisionmaking with pro- or antisocial effects. Much of their analysis is aimed at a wider social context than motivation in organizations, but parts of it are directly relevant to our concerns.

The heart of the model is that parties' actual behavior is driven by three separate motives, which Bénabou and Tirole labeled intrinsic, extrinsic, and reputational incentives. Decisionmakers and others may both care about the actual mix of motives behind any decision, but the drivers of decisions are not observable, so motivation must be inferred from choices and the context.

In this framework, offering extrinsic incentives clouds inferences about the motives behind apparent good deeds: Did the good behavior arises because the party is well intentioned or even altruistic, or was it motivated by the explicit rewards? This signal-extraction problem can result in fewer good deeds when there are explicit rewards for them, and, in particular, it may be that discretely more are supplied when there is no outside reward at all. So if the culture of an organization places value on those who are motivated to act in the common good, the provision of explicit incentives may be counterproductive.

In addition, Bénabou and Tirole noted that there is a trade-off regarding making contributions memorable, as through "employee of the month" programs. Public recognition of good behavior increases the incentives for signaling by acting nicely, but it also clouds the inference because of the possibility that the action was motivated by the hope of recognition. They also note that the inferences that are drawn from a person's actions depend on others' actions, which creates spillovers and multiple equilibria corresponding to different norms of behavior, and they investigate the nature and determinants of these spillovers.

7.2. Peer Effects

That people work together, rather than as isolated individuals, potentially affects the motivation problem. For example, peer pressure, mutual monitoring, and group norms are often suggested as important determinants of behavior.

Kandel and Lazear (1992) presented a simple model of these phenomena. Output is a function F of the efforts e_i of N identical individuals, who share the output equally. Thus, for $N > 1$, there is the free-rider problem discussed in Section 2.2, because each individual gets only $1/N$ of the extra output F_i generated by extra effort but bears the entire additional costs, $C'(e_i)$. Kandel and Lazear then introduced a peer pressure function $P(e_i; e_{-i}, a_1, \ldots, a_N)$, where e_{-i} is the effort level of the parties other than i, and the a_j are other actions that may effect the pressure. The payoff to i is now $F/N - C - P$. If P is decreasing in its first argument (working harder leads to less peer pressure), then the level of effort will increase, improving efficiency.

Kandel and Lazear then investigated the P function, discussing how it might arise; the roles of norms and guilt if efforts are not observable; those of mutual monitoring, shame, and social punishment if the parties can observe one another's choices; and the problems of motivating the group's members to carry out punishments if these are costly.

Recent empirical work has pointed to several other peer effects. Ichino and Maggi (2000) studied regional differences in shirking in a large Italian bank and found that these are related to peer effects: otherwise similar individuals shirk more in work environments where others are shirking more. Hamilton et al. (2003) found that some workers apparently like working in teams, even when doing so lowers their incomes, because in the team they are linked to less-productive workers. Mas and Moretti (2009) found that supermarket workers' productivity is higher if they can be seen at work by high-productivity co-workers. Card et al. (2011) reported that learning of co-workers' pay has asymmetric effects on those above and below the group median. Lower paid workers reported lowered satisfaction with their pay and jobs and an increased likelihood of seeking a new employer, but there was no effect among those paid more than the median. Modeling such effects, particularly in a unified fashion, would be interesting.

7.3. Altruism, Fairness, Reciprocity, and Gift Exchange

Some people sometimes seem to care about the welfare of some others. People also sometimes care about whether outcomes are fair or just. The norm of reciprocity—do unto others as they have done to you—is widely documented and manifests itself, in particular, in the exchange of gifts. Here we briefly discuss some of the economic research relating to these ideas.

Rotemberg (1994) studied what might cause workers to become altruistic toward one another and whether the firm can benefit from such feelings. Rotemberg assumes that individuals are initially entirely selfish but can choose to become altruistic toward specific individuals. He argued that if different individuals' actions are strategic complements, then becoming known to be an altruist will be advantageous, because it will affect others' expectations about one's future behavior and thereby make their future behavior more favorable. Rotemberg then suggested that altruism should be expected to arise when employees work as a team and are rewarded on aggregate team output. In addition, when a group leader is charged with setting the pace of work, it is advantageous for her to be altruistic toward the workers, because they will be more trusting of her.

Building on Rotemberg (1994), Dur and Sol (2010) have explored how workers' altruistic feelings toward one another might interact with the compensation contracts optimally offered. Suppose workers care about their incomes; the costs of effort and of the time they devote to being nice to one another; and the others' welfare, provided the others have been nice to them. If pay is not purely on individual output but involves some element of either relative performance evaluation or group pay, then workers will be better off if they induce altruism toward themselves in their colleagues by being nice. When the contract has team incentives, an agent's provision of attention induces the other agent to exert more effort, which benefits the agent. Likewise, when the contract has relative incentives, the agent's provision of attention induces the other agents to exert less effort, which again benefits the first agent.

Akerlof (1982) brought economists' attention to the idea from the behavioral sciences that the employment relationship could involve a gift exchange. In particular, the firm in this context offers pay in excess of market levels, and in return the employees work at a level above that which the firm demands. Akerlof suggested this behavior arises because workers come to care for the firm as an institution, so the norm of reciprocity is activated. Presumably the same behavior would obtain if they care about their boss as an individual.

Experimental evidence lends some support to this approach. For example. Fehr et al. (1997) ran an experiment where one party, the firm, offers a wage to several potential workers, who each accept or reject it. Then one acceptor is chosen at random, and the chosen one makes a choice of costly effort from an internal $[e_L, e_H]$, where $C(e_L) = C'(e_L) = 0$, and C is strictly increasing and convex above e_L. Assume the value of effort is such that e_H maximizes the returns to effort less its cost. The predictions of standard economic theory would be that the worker will always choose e_L, the cost minimizing effort level. Then the firm will offer a wage of zero, and all the gains from trade accrue to the firm. What happens in the laboratory, however, is that firms offer significantly positive wages, and workers respond with effort levels well above e_L. Further, wage offers and effort choices are positively correlated. More recent field observation has produced rather mixed results on gift exchange, however (see Englemaier and Leider 2011). Some of these observations can be reconciled through a field experiment conducted by Englemaier and Leider, where they observed that the worker's choice to provide more than perfunctory effort depended on whether the boss's reward was responsive to the worker's efforts. If the worker could not return the favor, then the gift wage was not offered.

Fehr and Schmidt (1999) suggested a theory of fairness that generates, inter alia, gift-exchange behavior. The essence of their theory is that the utility to an individual of an amount x when others are getting $x_n, n = 1, \ldots, N$, is

$$Nx - \alpha \sum_{n=1}^{N} \max[x_n - x, 0] - \beta \sum_{n=1}^{N} \max[x - x_n, 0],$$

where $\alpha \geq \beta \geq 0$ and $0 \leq \beta \leq 1$. Thus, the individual suffers a loss of utility of α for each dollar of income anyone has in excess of what he has, and a smaller loss of β for every dollar he has more than any other person. So the individual cares about inequality, but only relative to himself.

Fehr and Schmidt (1999) then argued that a firm that offers a low wage to a person with these sorts of preferences will induce low effort, because by reducing effort, the worker can reduce the inequality between the firm's returns and his own. Note that this is not a factor in final goods markets, where buyers typically have no such recourse. Fehr and Schmidt also showed that their theory explains a variety of other findings. A notable one is why fairness seems to be a force in "divide the dollar," ultimatum games, where (contrary to the predictions of standard theory) players reject offers that they deem too low, even though they (and the player making the offer) then get zero, and yet fairness is not an issue in competitive market games where several parties compete to sell an item to a single party and the play very closely matches the competitive equilibrium where the buyer gets all the gains from trade.

8. Conclusion

We have surveyed economic theories of the basic incentive problem of getting an agent to take an unobserved, costly action from which the principal benefits. Much of this is well known among economists, but there are pieces that may be less familiar. Our intent was to provide a common source to which those reading the other chapters of this volume could refer, for the ideas in this chapter reappear throughout this volume.

REFERENCES

Aghion, Philippe, and Jean Tirole. 1994. "On the Management of Innovation." *Quarterly Journal of Economics* 109: 1185–1207.

———. 1997. "Formal and Real Authority in Organizations." *Journal of Political Economy* 105: 1–29.

Aghion, Philippe, Mathias Dewatripont, and Patrick Rey. 1994. "Renegotiation Design with Unverifiable Information," *Econometrica* 62: 257–282.

Akerlof, George. 1982. "Labor Contracts as Partial Gift Exchange." *Quarterly Journal of Economics* 97: 543–569.

Akerlof, George, and Janet Yellen. 1986. *Efficiency Wage Models of the Labor Market.* Cambridge: Cambridge University Press.

Alonso, Ricardo, Wouter Dessein, and Niko Matouschek. 2008. "When Does Coordination Require Centralization?" *American Economic Review* 98: 145–179.

Arrow, Kenneth. 1974. *The Limits of Organization.* New York: W. W. Norton and Co.

Athey, Susan, and John Roberts. 2001. "Organizational Design: Decision Rights and Incentive Contracts." *American Economic Review* 91: 200–205.

Baker, George. 1992. "Incentive Contracts and Performance Measurement." *Journal of Political Economy* 100: 598–614.

———. 2002. "Distortion and Risk in Optimal Incentive Contracts." *Journal of Human Resources* 37: 728–751.

Baker, George, Michael Jensen, and Kevin J. Murphy. 1988. "Compensation and Incentives: Practice vs. Theory." *Journal of Finance* 43: 593–616.

Baker, George, Robert Gibbons, and Kevin J. Murphy. 1994. "Subjective Performance Measures in Optimal Incentive Contracts." *Quarterly Journal of Economics* 109: 1125–1156.

Baker, George, Robert Gibbons, and Kevin J. Murphy. 1999. "Informal Authority in Organizations." *Journal of Law, Economics, and Organization* 15: 56–73.

Baker, George, Robert Gibbons, and Kevin J. Murphy. 2002. "Relational Contracts and the Theory of the Firm." *Quarterly Journal of Economics* 117: 39–83.

Bandiera, Oriana, Iwan Barankay, and Imran Rasul. 2005. "Social Preferences and the Response to Incentives: Evidence from Personnel Data." *Quarterly Journal of Economics* 120: 917–962.

———. 2007. "Incentives for Managers and Inequality among Workers: Evidence from a Firm-Level Experiment." *Quarterly Journal of Economics* 122: 729–773.

Battigalli, Pierpaolo, and Giovanni Maggi. 2008. "Costly Contracting in a Long-Term Relationship." *RAND Journal of Economics* 39: 352–377.

Becker, Gary. 1962. "Investment in Human Capital: A Theoretical Analysis." *Journal of Political Economy* 70: 9–49.

Bénabou, Roland, and Jean Tirole. 2003. "Intrinsic and Extrinsic Motivation." *Review of Economic Studies* 70: 489–520.

———. 2006. "Incentives and Prosocial Behavior." *American Economic Review* 96: 1652–1678.

Besley, Timothy, and Maitreesh Ghatak. 2005. "Competition and Incentives with Motivated Agents." *American Economic Review* 95: 616–636.

Bull, Clive. 1987. "The Existence of Self-Enforcing Implicit Contracts." *Quarterly Journal of Economics* 102: 147–159.

Card, David, Alexandre Mas, Enrico Moretti, and Emmanuel Saez. 2011. "Inequality at Work: The Effect of Peer Salaries on Job Satisfaction." *American Economic Review,* forthcoming.

Carmichael, Lorne, and Bentley MacLeod. 2000. "Worker Cooperation and the Ratchet Effect." *Journal of Labor Economics* 18: 1–19.

Chassang, Sylvain. 2010. "Building Routines: Learning, Cooperation, and the Dynamics of Incomplete Relational Contracts." *American Economic Review* 100: 448–465.

Che, Yeon-Koo, and Seung-Weon Yoo. 2001. "Optimal Incentives for Teams." *American Economic Review* 91: 525–541.

Coase, Ronald. 1937. "The Nature of the Firm." *Economica* New Series 4: 386–405.

Corts, Kenneth. 2007. "Teams versus Individual Accountability: Solving Multitask Problems through Job Design." *RAND Journal of Economics* 38: 467–479.

Crawford, Vincent, and Joel Sobel. 1982. "Strategic Information Transmission." *Econometrica* 50: 1431–1451.

Crémer, Jacques. 1995. "Arm's Length Relationships." *Quarterly Journal of Economics* 110: 275–295.

Datar, Srikant, Susan Kulp, and Richard Lambert. 2001. "Balancing Performance Measures." *Journal of Accounting Research* 39: 75–92.

DeMarzo, Peter, and Yuliy Sannikov. 2006. "Optimal Security Design and Dynamic Capital Structure in a Continuous-Time Agency Model." *Journal of Finance* 61: 2681–2724.

Dessein, Wouter. 2002. "Authority and Communication in Organizations." *Review of Economic Studies* 69: 811–838.

Dewatripont, Mathias, Ian Jewitt, and Jean Tirole. 1999a. "The Economics of Career Concerns, Part I: Comparing Information Structures." *Review of Economic Studies* 66: 183–198.

———. 1999b. "The Economics of Career Concerns, Part II: Application to Missions and Accountability of Government Agencies." *Review of Economic Studies* 66: 199–217.

Doornik, Katherine. 2006. "Relational Contracting in Partnerships." *Journal of Economics and Management Strategy* 15: 517–548.

Dur, Robert, and Joeri Sol. 2010. "Social Interaction, Co-Worker Altruism, and Incentives." *Games and Economic Behavior* 69: 293–301.

Ederer, Florian. 2010. "Feedback and Motivation in Dynamic Tournaments." *Journal of Economics and Management Strategy* 19: 545–562.

Edmans, Alex, Xavier Gabaix, Tomasz Sadzik, and Yuliy Sannikov. 2012. "Dynamic CEO Compensation." *Journal of Finance,* forthcoming.

Ellingsen, Tore, and Magnus Johannesson. 2008. "Pride and Prejudice: The Human Side of Incentive Theory." *American Economic Review* 98: 990–1008.

Englemaier, Florian, and Stephen Leider. 2011. "Managerial Payoff and Gift Exchange in the Field." CESifo Working Paper 3707, Ifo Institute, Center for Economic Studies, Munich.

Fama, Eugene. 1980. "Agency Problems and the Theory of the Firm." *Journal of Political Economy* 88: 288–307.

Fast, Norman, and Norman Berg. 1975. "The Lincoln Electric Company." Harvard Business School Case 376-028. Boston: Harvard Business School Press.

Fehr, Ernst, and Armin Falk. 2002. "Psychological Foundations of Incentives." *European Economic Review* 46: 687–724.

Fehr, Ernst, and Klaus Schmidt. 1999. "A Theory of Fairness, Competition, and Cooperation." *Quarterly Journal of Economics* 114: 816–868.

Fehr, Ernst, Simon Gächter, and Georg Kirschsteiger. 1997. "Reciprocity as a Contract Enforcement Device: Experimental Evidence." *Econometrica* 65: 844–860.

Feltham, Gerald, and Jim Xie. 1994. "Performance Measure Congruity and Diversity in Multi-Task Principal/Agent Relations." *Accounting Review* 69: 429–453.

Fong, Yuk-Fai, and Jin Li. 2010. "Information Revelation in Relational Contracts." Mimeo. Northwestern University Kellogg School of Management, Evanston, IL.

Friebel, Guido, and Michael Raith. 2010. "Resource Allocation and Organizational Form." *American Economic Journal: Microeconomics* 2(2): 1–33.

Fuchs, William. 2007. "Contracting with Repeated Moral Hazard and Private Evaluations." *American Economic Review* 97: 1432–1448.

Fudenberg, Drew, Bengt Holmström, and Paul Milgrom. 1990. "Short-Term Contracts and Long-Term Agency Relationships." *Journal of Economic Theory* 51: 1–31.

Gibbons, Robert. 1987. "Piece-Rate Incentive Schemes." *Journal of Labor Economics* 5: 413–429.

Gibbons, Robert. 1997. "Incentives and Careers in Organizations," in David Kreps and Kenneth Wallis (eds.), *Advances in Economics and Econometrics: Theory and Applications,* volume 2. Cambridge: Cambridge University Press, pp. 1–37.

———. 2005. "Four Formal(izable) Theories of the Firm?" *Journal of Economic Behavior and Organization* 58: 200–245.

———. 2010. "Inside Organizations: Pricing, Politics, and Path-Dependence." *Annual Review of Economics* 2: 337–365.

Gibbons, Robert, and Kevin J. Murphy. 1990. "Relative Performance Evaluation for Chief Executive Officers." *Industrial and Labor Relations Review* 43: 30S–51S.

———. 1992. "Optimal Incentive Contracts in the Presence of Career Concerns: Theory and Evidence." *Journal of Political Economy* 100: 468–505.

Gompers, Paul, and Josh Lerner. 1999. "An Analysis of Compensation in the US Venture Capital Partnership." *Journal of Financial Economics* 51: 3–44.

Grossman, Sanford, and Oliver Hart. 1986. "The Costs and Benefits of Ownership: A Theory of Vertical and Lateral Integration." *Journal of Political Economy* 94: 691–719.

Halac, Marina. 2012a. "Relational Contracts and the Value of Relationships." *American Economic Review* 102: 750–779.

———. 2012b. "Relationship Building: Conflict and Project Choice over Time." Working Paper, Columbia University Graduate School of Business, New York.

Hamilton, Barton, Jack Nickerson, and Hideo Owan. 2003. "Team Incentives and Worker Heterogeneity: An Empirical Analysis of the Impact of Teams on Productivity and Participation." *Journal of Political Economy* 111: 465–497.

Heckman, James. 1979. "Sample Selection Bias as a Specification Error." *Econometrica* 47: 153–161.

Hermalin, Benjamin. 1998. "Toward an Economic Theory of Leadership: Leading by Example." *American Economic Review* 88: 1188–1206.

Holmström, Bengt. 1979. "Moral Hazard and Observability," *Bell Journal of Economics* 10: 74–91.

———. 1982. "Moral Hazard in Teams." *Bell Journal of Economics* 13: 324–340.

———. 1982/1999. "Managerial Incentive Problems—A Dynamic Perspective," in Björn Walroos, Bo-Göran Ekholm, Alf-Erik Lerviks, and Hendrik Meyer (eds.), *Essays in Economics and Management in Honor of Lars Wahlbeck.* Helsinki: Swedish School of Economics and Business Administration, pp. 209–230. Republished in *Review of Economic Studies* 66: 169–182.

———. 1999. "The Firm as a Subeconomy." *Journal of Law, Economics, and Organization* 15: 74–102.

Holmström, Bengt, and Paul Milgrom. 1987. "Aggregation and Linearity in the Provision of Incentives." *Econometrica* 55: 303–328.

———. 1990. "Regulating Trade among Agents." *Journal of Institutional and Theoretical Economics* 146: 85–105.

———. 1991. "Multitask Principal-Agent Analyses: Incentive Contracts, Asset Ownership, and Job Design." *Journal of Law, Economics, and Organization* 7: 24–52.

———. 1994. "The Firm as an Incentive System." *American Economic Review* 84: 972–991.

Holmström, Bengt, and Joan Ricart i Costa. 1986. "Managerial Incentives and Capital Management." *Quarterly Journal of Economics* 101: 835–860.

Ichino, Andrea, and Giovanni Maggi. 2000. "Work Environment and Individual Background: Explaining Regional Shirking Differentials in a Large Italian Firm." *Quarterly Journal of Economics* 115: 1057–1090.

Itoh, Hideshi. 1991. "Incentives to Help in Multi-Agent Situations." *Econometrica* 59: 611–636.

Jensen, Michael. 1986. "The Agency Costs of Free Cash Flow, Corporate Finance and Takeovers." *American Economic Review* 76: 323–329.

Kahn, Charles, and Gur Huberman. 1988. "Two-Sided Uncertainty and 'Up-or-Out' Contracts." *Journal of Labor Economics* 6: 423–444.

Kandel, Eugene, and Edward Lazear. 1992. "Peer Pressure and Partnership." *Journal of Political Economy* 100: 801–817.

Kanemoto, Yoshitsugu, and Bentley MacLeod. 1991. "The Ratchet Effect and the Market for Second-hand Workers." *Journal of Labor Economics* 10: 85–98.

Kvaløy, Ola, and Trond Olsen. 2006. "Team Incentives in Relational Employment Contracts." *Journal of Labor Economics* 24: 139–169.

Laffont, Jean-Jacques, and Jean Tirole. 1986. "The Use of Cost Observations to Regulate Firms." *Journal of Political Economy* 94: 614–641.

Lambert, Richard. 1986. "Executive Effort and Selection of Risky Projects." *RAND Journal of Economics* 17: 77–88.

Lazear, Edward. 1986. "Salaries and Piece Rates." *Journal of Business* 59: 405–431.

———. 2000. "Performance Pay and Productivity." *American Economic Review* 90: 1346–1361.

Lazear, Edward, and Sherwin Rosen. 1981. "Rank Order Tournaments as Optimal Labor Contracts." *Journal of Political Economy* 89: 841–864.

Levin, Jonathan. 2003. "Relational Incentive Contracts." *American Economic Review* 93: 835–857.

Li, Jin, and Niko Matouschek. 2012. "Managing Conflicts in Relational Contracts." Working paper, Northwestern University Kellogg School of Management, Evanston, IL.

MacLeod, Bentley. 2003. "Optimal Contracting with Subjective Evaluation." *American Economic Review* 93: 216–240.

MacLeod, Bentley, and James Malcomson. 1988. "Reputation and Hierarchy in Dynamic Models of Employment." *Journal of Political Economy* 96: 832–854.

———. 1989. "Implicit Contracts, Incentive Compatibility, and Involuntary Unemployment." *Econometrica* 57: 447–480.

Malcomson, James. 1984. "Work Incentives, Hierarchy, and Internal Labor Markets." *Journal of Political Economy* 92: 486–507.

Manso, Gustavo. 2011. "Motivating Innovation." *Journal of Finance* 66: 1823–1860.

Marino, Anthony, John Matsusaka, and Ján Zábojník. 2010. "Disobedience and Authority." *Journal of Law, Economics, and Organization* 28: 427–459.

Mas, Alex, and Enrico Moretti. 2009. "Peers at Work." *American Economic Review* 99: 112–145.

Mathewson, Stanley. 1931. *Restriction of Output among Unorganized Workers.* Carbondale, IL: Southern Illinois University Press.

Meyer, Margaret. 1992. "Biased Contests and Moral Hazard: Implications for Career Profiles." *Annales d'Économie et de Statistique* 25/26: 165–187.

Meyer, Margaret, and John Vickers. 1997. "Performance Comparisons and Dynamic Incentives." *Journal of Political Economy* 105: 547–581.

Meyer, Margaret, Paul Milgrom, and John Roberts. 1992. "Organizational Prospects, Influence Costs, and Ownership Changes." *Journal of Economics and Management Strategy* 1: 9–35.

Meyer, Margaret, Trond Olsen, and Gaute Torsvik. 1996. "Limited Intertemporal Commitment and Job Design." *Journal of Economic Behavior and Organization* 31: 401–417.

Milgrom, Paul. 1981. "Good News and Bad News: Representation Theorems and Applications." *Bell Journal of Economics* 12: 380–391.

Milgrom, Paul, and John Roberts. 1988. "An Economic Approach to Influence Activities in Organizations." *American Journal of Sociology* 94: S154–S179.

Milgrom, Paul, and John Roberts. 1992. *Economics, Organization and Management.* Englewood Cliffs, NJ: Prentice Hall.

Moore, John, and Rafael Repullo. 1988. "Subgame Perfect Implementation." *Econometrica* 56: 1191–1220.

Murphy, Kevin J. 1999. "Executive Compensation," in Orley Ashenfelter and David Card (eds.), *Handbook of Labor Economics,* volume 3b. Elsevier Science/North-Holland, pp. 2485–2563.

Pearce, David, and Ennio Stacchetti. 1998. "The Interaction of Implicit and Explicit Contracts in Repeated Agency." *Games and Economic Behavior* 23(1): 75–96.

Powell, Michael. 2012. "Influence Cost Models of Firms' Boundaries and Control Structures." Mimeo, Northwestern University Kellogg School of Management, Evanston, IL.

Prendergast, Canice. 1993. "The Role of Promotion in Inducing Specific Human Capital Acquisition." *Quarterly Journal of Economics* 108: 523–534.

———. 2002. "The Tenuous Trade-off between Risk and Incentives." *Journal of Political Economy* 110: 1071–1102.

———. 2007. "The Motivation and Bias of Bureaucrats." *American Economic Review* 97: 180–196.

Raith, Michael. 2008. "Specific Knowledge and Performance Management." *RAND Journal of Economics* 39: 1059–1079.

Rantakari, Heikki. 2008a. "Governing Adaptation." *Review of Economic Studies* 75: 1257–1285.

———. 2008b. "On the Role of Uncertainty in the Risk-Incentives Tradeoff." *B.E. Journal of Theoretical Economics (Topics)* 8. DOI: 10.2202/1935-1704.1407.

Ray, Korok. 2007. "Performance Evaluations and Efficient Sorting." *Journal of Accounting Research* 45: 839–882.

Rayo, Luis. 2007. "Relational Incentives and Moral Hazard in Teams." *Review of Economic Studies* 74: 937–963.

Roberts, John. 2004. *The Modern Firm: Organizational Design for Performance and Growth.* Oxford: Oxford University Press.

Rogerson, William. 1985. "Repeated Moral Hazard." *Econometrica* 53: 69–76.

Rosen, Sherwin. 1986. "Prizes and Incentives in Elimination Tournaments." *American Economic Review* 76: 701–715.

Rotemberg, Julio. 1994. "Human Relations in the Workplace." *Journal of Political Economy* 102: 684–717.

Rotemberg, Julio, and Garth Saloner. 1994. "Benefits of Narrow Business Strategies." *American Economic Review* 84: 1330–1349.

———. 2000. "Visionaries, Managers, and Strategic Direction." *RAND Journal of Economics* 31: 693–716.

Roy, Donald. 1952. "Quota Restriction and Goldbricking in a Machine Shop." *American Journal of Sociology* 57: 427–442.

Sannikov, Yuliy. 2008. "A Continuous-Time Version of the Principal-Agent Problem." *Review of Economic Studies* 75: 957–984.

Sappington, David. 1983. "Limited Liability Contracts between Principal and Agent." *Journal of Economic Theory* 29: 1–21.

Scharfstein, David, and Jeremy Stein. 1990. "Herd Behavior and Investment." *American Economic Review* 80: 465–479.

Schöttner, Anja. 2008. "Relational Contracts, Multitasking, and Job Design." *Journal of Law, Economics, and Organization* 24: 138–162.

Shapiro, Carl, and Joseph Stiglitz. 1984. "Equilibrium Unemployment as a Worker Discipline Device." *American Economic Review* 74: 433–444.

Shavell, Steven. 1979. "Risk Sharing and Incentives in the Principal Agent Relationship." *Bell Journal of Economics* 10: 55–73.

Sliwka, Dirk. 2007. "Trust as a Signal of a Social Norm and the Hidden Costs of Incentive Schemes." *American Economic Review* 98: 999–1012.

Thiele, Veikko. 2012. "Subjective Performance Evaluations, Collusion, and Organizational Design." *Journal of Law, Economics, and Organization,* forthcoming.

Van den Steen, Eric. 2005. "Organizational Beliefs and Managerial Vision." *Journal of Law, Economics, and Organization* 21: 256–283.

———. 2010. "Interpersonal Authority in a Theory of the Firm." *American Economic Review* 100: 466–490.

Waldman, Michael. 1990. "Up-or-Out Contracts: A Signaling Perspective." *Journal of Labor Economics* 8: 230–250.

Williamson, Oliver. 1973. "Markets and Hierarchies: Some Elementary Considerations." *American Economic Review* 63: 316–325.

———. 1975. *Markets and Hierarchies: Analysis and Antitrust Implications.* New York: Free Press.

Wilson, Robert. 1968. "The Theory of Syndicates." *Econometrica* 36: 119–132.

Zábojník, Ján. 1996. "Pay-Performance Sensitivity and Production Uncertainty." *Economics Letters* 53: 291–296.

Zwiebel, Jeffrey. 1995. "Corporate Conservatism and Relative Compensation." *Journal of Political Economy* 103: 1–25.

3

Property Rights

Ilya Segal and Michael D. Whinston

1. Introduction

Every organization, whether a firm, a nonprofit organization, or a society, must confront two basic problems. The first is the creation of incentives for efficient behavior among its members. The second is the efficient allocation among those members of the resources available to and produced by the organization. These problems are closely related, because the rule for allocating resources generally affects individuals' incentives.

Organizations have many ways of trying to achieve these goals. Sometimes they use contracts. These may explicitly specify behavior or attempt to indirectly encourage desirable behavior through incentive pay. At other times they allocate decision rights to parties and leave them considerable discretion. In this chapter, we focus on one particular instrument: the allocation of property rights over assets.

The basic concept of a property right is relatively simple: A property right gives the owner of an asset the right to the use and benefits of the asset, and the right to exclude others from them. It also, typically, gives the owner the freedom to transfer these rights to others. Roman law referred to these elements as *usus* (the right to use), *abusus* (the right to encumber or transfer), and *fructus* (the right to the fruits). The American jurist Oliver Wendell Holmes put it this way:

> But what are the rights of ownership? They are substantially the same as those incident to possession. Within the limits prescribed by policy, the owner is allowed to exercise his natural

We thank Robert Gibbons and John Roberts, the volume editors; Bengt Holmström; and seminar participants at Arizona State, Cambridge, Institut D'Economie Industrielle, London School of Economics, Northwestern, Oxford, University College London, a meeting of the NBER Working Group in Organizational Economics devoted to reviewing early drafts of chapters from this handbook, and the Boston University conference on "New Directions in Organization Theory" for helpful comments. Segal thanks the Toulouse Network for Information Technology and the National Science Foundation for financial support. Whinston thanks the Toulouse Network for Information Technology, the Leverhulme Trust, and the National Science Foundation for financial support as well as Nuffield College and Oxford University's Department of Economics for their hospitality.

powers over the subject matter uninterfered with, and is more or less protected in excluding other people from such interference. The owner is allowed to exclude all, and is accountable to no one but him. [Holmes 1881: 246; quoted in Grossman and Hart 1986: 694]

Thus, property rights over an asset can be defined as a bundle of decision rights involving the asset (also called "entitlements" in the legal literature), which provide rights to take certain actions ("rights of access") and to prevent others from taking certain actions ("rights of exclusion"), including the right to take the profit generated by use of the asset and to prevent others from doing so (often called "profit rights" or "cash flow rights" in the literature).[1]

This chapter surveys some theories of the optimal allocation of property rights. The problem of optimal allocation of property rights differs from the classical economic problem of optimal allocation of goods in an important way. As suggested by the above definitions, a central feature of property rights is that although they may influence economic allocations, many of the details of the allocation are left for future specification by the agents, either unilaterally or by negotiation with one another. For example, *usus* leaves it up to the owner to decide how exactly the asset should be used. *Abusus* leaves it to the owner in negotiation with other agents to decide who the asset should be transferred to and on what terms. In this sense, property rights are simple (or "incomplete") contracts that specify some aspects of the status quo but leave discretion for economic agents to fill in the gaps. This incompleteness is, of course, inevitable in the real world, because it may be difficult to list all possible deployments of an asset in advance or all relevant variables on which the deployment should be contingent, and specifying such a contingent rule would be very costly. As a result, as Grossman and Hart (1986) note, property rights confer *residual rights of control* to the owner of an asset: the owner is entitled to the use and fruits of the asset except insofar as she has contractually agreed to limits on those rights (say, by transferring them to others).

To fix ideas and foreshadow the models discussed in this chapter, consider the following framework in which property rights may influence subsequent economic outcomes:

Stage 1. An allocation of property rights $\hat{x} \in \hat{X}$ is chosen.

Stage 2. Agents individually choose some noncontractible actions $a \in A$.

Stage 3. Uncertainty $\theta \in \Theta$ is realized.

Stage 4. Agents can renegotiate the initial property rights allocation, specifying a new outcome $x \in X$, where $\hat{X} \subseteq X$ (outcomes that are in X but not in $\hat{X}$ cannot be specified contractually ex ante, but they are contractible ex post). Should the agents not reach an

---

1. In practice, however, complications can arise in the notion of a property right. First, these rights of ownership are not always bundled together. Consider the following examples: (i) some stockholders of a firm may own a share of its profits but may not have the right to vote on the use of the firm's assets; (ii) an individual may possess the right to use an asset but may not have the right to exclude others from using this asset (e.g., a community garden or lake); and (iii) an owner may not possess the right to transfer ownership rights to others, as with the prohibition against slavery. In addition, property rights are in practice often held collectively. For example, no single shareholder in a firm may be able to use the firm's assets as he sees fit. Yet a majority of the shareholders, should they reach an agreement, can do so.

Table 1. Alternative assumptions about bargaining and actions

Bargaining efficiency	Noncontractible actions?	
	No	Yes
Efficient bargaining	Coasian benchmark	Section 3 (hold-up models)
No bargaining	Simple allocation benchmark	Section 2 (Tragedy of the Commons, adaptation, and incentives models)
Imperfect bargaining	Section 4 (asymmetric information or bilateral contracting)	

agreement, the initial property rights remain unchanged, so that $x = \hat{x}$.[2] Each agent i's utility is $v_i(x, a, \theta) + t_i$, where t_i is a monetary transfer.[3]

The framework encompasses many models of property rights in the literature. These differ in which of the variables are actually present (Are there noncontractible actions a? Are there decisions that are noncontractible ex ante but contractible ex post?) and the nature of the ex post negotiation process (Is bargaining perfectly efficient? Is it imperfect due to asymmetric information about θ or due to agreements involving only subsets of the agents?). They also differ in how property rights matter. In some models, property rights are rights to asset returns (*fructus*) that directly affect payoffs $v_i(\cdot)$ and are possibly valued differently by different agents. In others, property rights are "control rights" that determine who takes noncontractible actions (*usus*) but leave payoffs as a function of the chosen actions unchanged (e.g., all payoffs may be inalienable private benefits). To formally capture the latter case in the above framework, we can allow each agent to take the action in question but have only the action choice of the asset's owner (as determined by $\hat{x}$) matter for payoffs (see Remark 1 in Section 2.2).

Table 1 organizes these various possibilities according to whether noncontractible actions are present and to the efficiency of ex post bargaining. In the simplest settings, the effect of property rights $\hat{x}$ is simply to allocate assets to agents, who derive a direct private benefit from them, and there are neither noncontractible actions a nor ex post negotiations. In this case, an optimal property rights allocation is very simple: it gives assets to the agents who value them most in expectation. That is, $\hat{x}$ is set to maximize $E\left[\sum_i v_i(\hat{x}, \theta)\right]$. Thus, setting optimal property rights in this case is just like choosing an optimal allocation of goods in an exchange economy. (Of course, if externalities are present, so agents care about others' possession of assets in addition to their own, then this must be taken account of in determining the optimal allocation.) We call these settings cases of "simple allocation."

The case of simple allocation, however, fails to capture property rights' role as an incomplete contract, because it does not envision any activities after the initial property rights allocation is

---

2. As an example, suppose the only ex ante contractible decision is the ownership of assets, denoted $z \in Z$, while ex post the parties also can contract on decisions $q \in Q$ (e.g., cooperation in the use of the assets). Then, letting $q^\circ \in Q$ denote the default that arises when no ex post agreement is reached, we have $\hat{X} = Z \times \{q^\circ\}$, while $X = Z \times Q$.

3. This framework could be enriched in many respects without altering the fundamental conclusions. For example, after stage 4 the agents may be able to choose noncontractible noncooperative actions, in which case the functions $v_i(x, a, \theta)$ incorporate Nash equilibrium choices of such actions.

specified. Of greater interest for the study of organizations are settings in which agents engage in such activities.

One simple benchmark of this type arises when all decisions can be efficiently bargained over and contractually specified ex post. That is, no noncontractible actions a exist, and ex post bargaining yields a surplus-maximizing outcome in X for every state θ. In this case, as the celebrated Coase Theorem (Coase 1960) points out, the initial specification of property rights $\hat{x}$ is irrelevant for efficiency of the final outcome, which is always first best, and affects only the distribution of the first-best surplus among the agents.[4]

In this chapter, we focus on models in which, in contrast to the Coase Theorem, the initial allocation of property rights matters, but their optimal allocation amounts to more than a case of simple allocation. In these cases, depicted in the remaining entries of Table 1, either the agents choose noncontractible actions a, or ex post bargaining occurs but is imperfect.

We begin in Section 2 by examining settings in which agents choose noncontractible actions a, but no bargaining occurs (see Table 1). Thus, the setting is essentially static, and an optimal property rights allocation must take account of the effect of the property rights allocation on agents' choices of noncontractible actions. Discussions of property rights in such static settings—in the guise of the famous tragedy of the commons—were the first writings in the economics literature to consider how property rights can improve economic efficiency. Static settings appear in the more recent literature in what Gibbons (2005) has called "adaptation models" of the firm (e.g., Hart and Holmström 2010; Baker et al. 2011), as well as in incentive models, such as Holmström and Milgrom (1991, 1994).[5] We examine when (and how) the first best can be achieved in such settings, as well as the nature of distortions and second-best property rights when the first best cannot be achieved. Throughout, we emphasize the role of property rights in ameliorating inefficiencies caused by externalities.

In Section 3, we extend Section 2's model of noncontractible actions by introducing perfect ex post renegotiation (although some results also hold with imperfect renegotiation). In this context, the noncontractible actions are typically interpreted as long-term investments that are subject to hold-up in the subsequent bargaining. These hold-up models, whose use for examining the optimal allocation of property rights began with the seminal contribution of Grossman and Hart (1986), have been a workhorse of much of organizational economics over the past 25 years.[6] We discuss the nature of optimal property rights in these settings, including how they depend on the nature of agents' investments, the characteristics of assets, and the form of bargaining. We show how the analysis of hold-up models can make use of the insights from

---

4. Note, however, that when utilities are not quasi-linear (there are wealth effects), final outcomes will typically depend on the property rights specified in stage 1. Still, the final outcome will be on the ex post Pareto frontier. In this chapter, we ignore wealth effects. For the role of property rights in the presence of wealth effects or credit constraints, see, for example, Legros and Newman (1996) and Segal and Whinston (2012a). Note also that in this case, initial property rights may have ex ante efficiency consequences due to risk-sharing considerations.

5. Gibbons uses the term "adaptation" in reference to Simon (1951), in which authority is granted ex ante to one individual (the "boss") to make a decision following the resolution of some uncertainty. This fits into our framework in Section 2 by viewing that individual's action a as the choice of a decision rule describing his ex post action as a function of the state θ.

6. They have also been used extensively in other fields, such as industrial organization and corporate finance.

Section 2 by applying them to a new form of externalities—bargaining externalities. We also discuss the use of more complicated mechanisms than simple property rights, which relates to discussions of the foundations of incomplete contracts.

In Section 4, we suppose instead that renegotiation does occur but is imperfect. We examine two reasons for imperfect renegotiation and their implications for optimal property rights. We first suppose that θ is not public information—pieces of it are observed privately by different agents. With such asymmetric information, renegotiation may be hindered by agents' incentives to misrepresent θ, incentives that can depend on the initial property rights. We then suppose that the impediment to bargaining is that the agents cannot all get together and write a grand contract. Rather, contracting is bilateral, which can create externalities on other parties. These models can be viewed as possible formalizations of Williamson's (1971) focus on integration as a means of affecting ex post haggling costs.[7]

Our discussion of optimal property rights that follows can be viewed either as prescriptive (normative) or descriptive (positive). If perfect (coasian) bargaining regarding property rights occurs at the ex ante stage 1 (even if bargaining is imperfect at the ex post stage 4), then the parties will arrive at an optimal initial property rights allocation.[8] However, the same factors that may cause imperfections in negotiation at the ex post stage (e.g., private information or the inability to write grand contracts) may also be present at the ex ante stage, in which case the parties may fail to achieve an optimal allocation of property rights on their own.[9] In such cases, legal rules can improve efficiency by setting the optimal property rights allocation as the default.

Even though our chapter focuses on property rights, the variable $\hat{x}$ in our framework could in principle represent not only an allocation of property rights but also any other kind of ex ante contractible choices facing the organization. These could include, for example, the allocation of decision rights that are not linked to assets, as in Aghion et al. (2004) or Baker et al. (2008). It could also include compensation schemes, as in Holmström and Milgrom (1991, 1994). That said, the results we discuss here depend on the assumed properties of $v_i(\cdot)$, which depend on the interpretation of $\hat{x}$. For example, in the literature on hold-up models, which we discuss in Section 3, Hart and Moore (1990) assume that increases in $\hat{x}$ (greater ownership of assets) increase the marginal returns to a (investments), which is motivated by their interpretation of $\hat{x}$ as asset ownership and a as an investment in asset-specific human capital.

Finally, the scope of our discussion is limited by space considerations, and we omit a number of topics that could naturally fall within a survey of the effects of property rights on organizations. For example, in Section 2's discussion of static settings, we do not consider a set of interesting recent papers in which agents' actions include communication, and this communication affects how the holders of property or decision rights choose to exercise their rights based

---

7. Gibbons (2005) instead formalizes ex post haggling costs as arising from influence costs. Influence cost models are closest to the static models we consider in Section 2, although with the presence of learning and the addition of signal jamming as a noncontractible action.

8. Although, unlike in the Coase Theorem, the outcome need not be first best—it may be second best, given subsequent contracting imperfections.

9. An additional reason ex ante bargaining may be imperfect is that agents may not know who all the relevant parties are at the ex ante stage.

on their information (e.g., Aghion and Tirole 1997; Alonso et al. 2008; Rantakari 2008). We also discuss in only a limited way the interaction between property rights and other incentive instruments (e.g., Holmström and Milgrom 1991, 1994). The effects of property rights with relational contracts (as in Baker et al. 2002) are also not considered. We also do not discuss the extensive, but less formal, literature on transaction cost economics. However, these topics are covered in chapters in this volume by Bolton and Dewatripont, Gertner and Scharfstein, Gibbons and Henderson, Malcolmson, and Tadelis and Williamson.

2. Static Models of Property Rights, Externalities, and Efficiency

The importance of property rights for incentives has been recognized since at least Aristotle:

> That which is common to the greatest number has the least care bestowed upon it. Everyone thinks chiefly of his own, hardly at all of the common interest; and only when he is himself concerned as an individual. [Aristotle (1885 translation), *Politics*, Book II, Chapter III, 1261b]

A popular nineteenth-century text conveyed the point as follows:

> Suppose that the earth yielded spontaneously all that is now produced by cultivation; still without the institution of property it could not be enjoyed; the fruit would be gathered before it was ripe, animals killed before they came to maturity; for who would protect what was not his own . . . ? [Marcet 1819: 60–61; quoted in Baumol and Oates 1988: 28]

As these quotes suggest, the incentives created by property rights are important when behavior can generate externalities (for a more recent discussion of this point, see Demsetz 1967). When this is so, efficiency may call for allocating an asset to an individual or individuals who do not derive the greatest benefit from it, to induce desirable behavior. In this section, we explore this trade-off in a simple static setting. We first illustrate these effects in a classic model of property rights, the tragedy of the commons, and then derive some more general results about the efficiency effects of property rights. These results turn out to apply as well to a variety of dynamic settings, as we will see in Section 3.

2.1. An Example: The Tragedy of the Commons

We begin by considering the classic tragedy of the commons, updated with a modern organizational spin. Suppose there are two managers, denoted $i = 1, 2$, who each try to meet their clients' consulting needs. There is a single asset, a data center. Access to the data center enables a manager to better serve his clients. Each manager i can exert some effort to meeting client needs, denoted by $a_i \in [0, \bar{a}_i] \subseteq \mathbb{R}$. Access to the data center, determined by the specification of property rights, is captured by the variables $(\hat{x}_1, \hat{x}_2) \in \{0, 1\}^2$. Manager i has access to the data center if $\hat{x}_i = 1$, and does not if $\hat{x}_i = 0$. Private ownership gives the owner access to the data center and the ability to exclude all others from access to it, and given the negative externalities we assume below, the owner always exercises this right of exclusion. So private ownership by manager 1 results in $(\hat{x}_1, \hat{x}_2) = (1, 0)$; private ownership by manager 2 leads to $(\hat{x}_1, \hat{x}_2) = (0, 1)$. In contrast, with common ownership, both managers have the right to use the data center and neither has a right to exclude the other, so $(\hat{x}_1, \hat{x}_2) = (1, 1)$.

Given access $(\hat{x}_1, \hat{x}_2)$ and efforts (a_1, a_2), manager i's payoff is given by the function

$$\hat{x}_i V_i(a_i, \hat{x}_{-i}a_{-i}) - C_i(a_i),$$

where $V_i(\cdot) \geq 0$ is the gross benefit that manager i receives if he has access to the data center, and $C_i(\cdot)$ is his cost of effort, normalized so that $C_i(0) = 0$. The function $V_i(\cdot)$ is nonincreasing in its second argument, reflecting the fact that when manager $-i$ has access to the data center (so $\hat{x}_{-i} = 1$), her increased use may lower manager i's payoff.[10] We assume that these benefits are private, so that they cannot be transferred through a contract and that each manager's effort is noncontractible. Thus, ownership is the only thing that is contractible. Finally, because of the urgency of the clients' needs, access to the data center cannot be renegotiated.[11]

Because a manager generates an externality only if he exerts effort, there is always a first-best outcome in which both managers have access to the data center. Indeed, if $V_i(0, a_{-i}) > 0$ for all a_{-i} and $i = 1, 2$, using the data center without effort generates a strictly positive payoff for a manager regardless of the other manager's level of effort, which implies that all first-best outcomes involve giving both managers access. When benefits and costs are differentiable, (interior) efficient effort levels (a_1^*, a_2^*) then satisfy $\partial V_i(a_i^*, a_{-i}^*)/\partial a_i + \partial V_{-i}(a_{-i}^*, a_i^*)/\partial a_i = C_i'(a_i^*)$ for $i = 1, 2$. In contrast, (interior) equilibrium effort levels with common ownership (a_1°, a_2°) satisfy $\partial V_i(a_i^\circ, a_{-i}^\circ)/\partial a_i = C_i'(a_i^\circ)$ for $i = 1, 2$, because the managers ignore the external effects of their actions. If $V_i(\cdot)$ is independent of a_{-i} for $i = 1, 2$, so that externalities are absent, the equilibrium is efficient. This would be the case if there were no congestion (e.g., a large enough data center). But if $\partial V_{-i}(\cdot)/\partial a_i < 0$, then any interior equilibrium is inefficient.

In some cases, there is also a first-best outcome in which only one manager has access to the data center. This occurs, for example, when $a_2^* = 0$ and $V_2(0, a_1) = 0$ for all a_1. This case can arise when manager 2's cost of effort is very high and she derives no benefits from the data center without exerting effort. Because there are no externalities under private ownership, private ownership by manager 1 then achieves the first best.

Which property rights allocation maximizes aggregate surplus when the first best requires giving access to both managers, but externalities are present? In that case, the optimal (second-best) property rights allocation involves a trade-off: common ownership allows both managers to benefit from the data center but introduces externalities, while private ownership denies the benefit to one manager but avoids externalities. As an illustration, consider a situation with symmetric managers, where $V_i(a_i, \hat{x}_{-i}a_{-i}) = v(a_i) - e(\hat{x}_{-i}a_{-i})$ with $e(0) = 0$, and

10. Note that $V_i(0, a_{-i})$ may be positive and that the externality arises in this example only from manager $-i$'s effort, not her access per se. We can imagine that certain low-urgency uses of the data center, such as billing, are not generated by managerial effort, create no externalities, and provide a benefit for serving clients that is independent of congestion effects. In contrast, urgent uses are generated by a manager's effort and both create and are subject to congestion externalities.

11. A manager's value of access could be uncertain ex ante. Because we assume that the urgency of the tasks precludes renegotiation of access ex post, we can think of V_i as manager i's expected payoff.

$C_i(a_i) = c(a_i)$ for $i = 1, 2$. In that case, common ownership is optimal if and only if $v(a^\circ) - c(a^\circ) \geq 2e(a^\circ)$, that is, if the direct benefit of granting a second manager access exceeds the externalities that this access creates.

2.2. A General Static Model

We now consider what can be said more generally about the optimal allocation of property rights in a static setting.[12] Suppose there is a set $\mathcal{N}$ of N agents, each of whom chooses an action $a_i \in A_i$. The profile of actions is $a = (a_1, \ldots, a_N) \in A = \Pi_i A_i$. Before actions are chosen, a property rights allocation $\hat{x} \in \hat{X}$ is specified (e.g., $\hat{x}$ may be a vector of zeros and ones, indicating, for each asset and individual, whether the individual has access to the asset). Agent i has quasi-linear utility of the form $U_i(\hat{x}, a) + t_i$.[13]

The aggregate surplus given property rights $\hat{x}$ and action profile a is therefore $S(\hat{x}, a) = \sum_i U_i(\hat{x}, a)$, and the first-best outcomes are denoted

$$O^* = \underset{\hat{x} \in \hat{X},\, a \in A}{\arg\max}\ S(\hat{x}, a) .$$

It is also useful to define the efficient actions given some fixed property rights $\hat{x} \in \hat{X}$ as $A^*(\hat{x}) = \arg\max_{a \in A} S(\hat{x}, a)$ and the efficient allocation of property rights given some fixed actions $a \in A$ as $\hat{X}^*(a) = \arg\max_{\hat{x} \in \hat{X}} S(\hat{x}, a)$. If actions were fixed at a, so that incentive effects were not an issue, the optimal property rights would be an element of $\hat{X}^*(a)$, reflecting the principle that the individual or individuals who most value access to an asset should have it. We also let $\hat{X}^* = \left\{ \hat{x} \in \hat{X} : (\hat{x}, a) \in O^* \text{ for some } a \in A \right\}$ be the property rights allocations that can arise in a first-best outcome.

Given an allocation of property rights $\hat{x}$, the agents choose their actions noncooperatively to maximize their individual payoffs. The resulting Nash equilibrium set is

$$A^\circ(\hat{x}) = \left\{ a \in A : a_i \in \underset{a_i' \in A_i}{\arg\max}\ U_i(\hat{x}, a_i', a_{-i}) \quad \text{for all } i \right\}. \tag{1}$$

We will be interested in studying the second-best optimal assignment of property rights, which takes into account not only the property rights' direct effect on payoffs but also their effect on agents' actions.

Remark 1 In some cases property rights specify control rights, which give agents the rights to take certain actions. As mentioned in Section 1, the model can formally capture these cases in the following way. Suppose there are K actions to be chosen: $\alpha = (\alpha_1, \ldots, \alpha_K)$, where

---

12. The model we examine here is a version of the model studied in Segal and Whinston (2012a), specialized to transferable utilities and (later) to one-dimensional actions.

13. In terms of the framework in Section 1, the important assumption here is that there is no bargaining in stage 4. Although, strictly speaking, the model introduced here has no uncertainty θ, we can think of the functions $U_i(\cdot)$ as specifying expected payoffs (averaging over realizations of θ).

$\alpha_k \in \mathcal{A}_k$ for each $k = 1, \ldots, K$, which result in payoffs $\mathcal{U}_i(\hat{x}, \alpha)$ to each agent i. A property rights allocation specifies $\hat{x}_{ik} \in \{0, 1\}$ for each agent i and each action k, with $\hat{x}_{ik} = 1$ when agent i has the right to choose action k, and $\sum_i \hat{x}_{ik} = 1$ for each k. To incorporate this setting in our general framework, we endow all agents i with the same action set $A_i = \Pi_{k \in K} \mathcal{A}_k$ and let $a_i = (a_{i1}, \ldots, a_{ik}) \in A_i$ describe the agent's plan for all the actions, with the actual implemented actions being $\alpha(\hat{x}, a) = (\sum_i \hat{x}_{ik} a_{ik})_{k=1}^{K}$. The resulting payoffs take the form $U_i(\hat{x}, a) = \mathcal{U}_i(\hat{x}, \alpha(\hat{x}, a))$. When property rights do not affect these payoffs directly but only through implemented actions α [i.e., when we can write $U_i(\hat{x}, a) = \mathcal{U}_i(\alpha(\hat{x}, a))$], we will call them "pure control rights."

The model includes the tragedy of the commons as a special case. The following two examples, drawn from the recent literature, also illustrate the model. In the first, property rights affect only payoffs. In the second, property rights affect not only payoffs but also who takes certain actions, as in Remark 1.

Example 1 (agency model)   Consider a principal-agent setting in which two individuals pursue a project. Individual P is the principal and takes no actions, while individual A is the agent and has a noncontractible action choice $a \in A$. As in Demski and Sappington (1991) and Holmström and Milgrom (1991), there is an indivisible asset that may be owned by either the principal or the agent, and we let $\hat{x} \in \{0, 1\}$ denote the agent's ownership share. We let $V_i(a)$ denote the asset's value to individual i, for $i = A, P$. The project also generates inalienable returns to the principal equal to $Y(a)$, while the agent's private cost of taking action a is $C(a)$. (This private "cost" may include private benefits as well as costs and so may be negative.) In some applications the agent's actions move Y and each V_i in the same direction (e.g., Y and V_i are the project's current and future profits, respectively, both of which are enhanced by greater agent effort); in other cases they move in opposite directions (e.g., increasing current project returns depletes the asset). Because these returns are private, ownership of the asset is the only thing that is contractible and is the only mechanism for providing incentives.[14] The principal's payoff is

$$U_P(\hat{x}, a) = Y(a) + (1 - \hat{x})V_P(a),$$

while the agent's is

$$U_A(\hat{x}, a) = \hat{x}V_A(a) - C(a).$$

In one well-studied case, the parties' different values for the asset are attributed entirely to their differing risk aversion and the randomness of the asset's returns. Namely, if individual i has constant absolute risk aversion with coefficient $r_i \geq 0$, and the asset's returns are normally

---

14. In Holmström and Milgrom (1991), returns $Y(a)$ are also verifiable, so incentive schemes can be based on them as well.

distributed with mean $\mu(a)$ and variance $\sigma^2(a)$, then her certainty equivalent asset value equals $V_i(a) = \mu(a) - \frac{1}{2}r_i\sigma^2(a)$.[15]

In this example, efficiency calls for the individual i with the higher value $V_i(a)$ to own the asset. However, note that incentive effects may call for a different asset ownership $\hat{x}$, because ownership may affect the agent's action: $A^{\circ}(\hat{x}) = \arg \max_{a \in A}\left[\hat{x}V_A(a) - C(a)\right]$.

Example 2 (coordination model of firm scope)   This example is based on Hart and Holmström (2010). In this setting, property rights allocate control rights as in Remark 1 but also affect payoffs directly. For each of two production units indexed by k an action in $\{0, 1\}$ is to be chosen, with action 1 being the "coordination" action and action 0 being the "noncoordination" action. There are three agents and two possible property rights considered: nonintegration, in which the action for each unit $k = 1, 2$ is chosen by agent $k = 1, 2$ (the unit's manager-owner), and integration, in which both actions are chosen by agent 3 (the owner of the integrated firm). If the coordination action is chosen for both units, the coordinated outcome $c = 1$ results, and otherwise the noncoordinated outcome $c = 0$ results.

To fit this setting into the general framework, as in Remark 1, we let the action set of manager 3 be $A_3 = \{0, 1\}^2$, where $a_{3k} \in \{0, 1\}$ is her planned action for unit $k = 1, 2$, and let the action set for each agent $i = 1, 2$ be $A_i = \{0, 1\}$, with $a_i \in \{0, 1\}$ being his planned action for his unit i. Letting $\hat{x} \in \{0, 1\}$, where $\hat{x} = 1$ stands for integration and $\hat{x} = 0$ for nonintegration, the resulting outcome is $c(\hat{x}, a) = (1 - \hat{x})\, a_1 a_2 + \hat{x} a_{31} a_{32}$.

Hart and Holmström (2010) assume that in addition to control rights over unit k, its owner receives its alienable profit flows $v_k(c)$. In addition, each unit manager $i = 1, 2$ receives private benefits $w_i(c)$ from his unit. Coordination is assumed to reduce the unit managers' private benefits, so $w_i(1) \leq w_i(0)$ for $i = 1, 2$. These assumptions yield the following payoffs:

$$U_i(\hat{x}, a) = (1 - \hat{x})\, v_i\big(c(\hat{x}, a)\big) + w_i\big(c(\hat{x}, a)\big) \quad \text{for } i = 1, 2,$$

$$U_3(\hat{x}, a) = \hat{x}\left[v_1\big(c(\hat{x}, a)\big) + v_2\big(c(\hat{x}, a)\big)\right].$$

The total surplus in this setting is

$$S(\hat{x}, a) = v_1\big(c(\hat{x}, a)\big) + v_2\big(c(\hat{x}, a)\big) + w_1\big(c(\hat{x}, a)\big) + w_2\big(c(\hat{x}, a)\big).$$

Note that because property rights here allocate control rights and cash rights that are valued equally by all agents, their effect on the total surplus is entirely through the implemented actions.[16]

---

15. Many papers study the case with risk aversion in which the asset is divisible, so that $\hat{x} \in [0, 1]$. Then fractional ownership is typically optimal, with $\hat{x}$ interpreted as the strength of the agent's incentives. Although our analysis extends straightforwardly to this case, for simplicity, we restrict attention to an indivisible asset.

16. Unlike in our discussion, Hart and Holmström (2010) assume that an agent i may feel "aggrieved" when he gets less than his maximal possible payoff, and that such aggrievement causes agent i to lower agent j's payoff through "shading," which induces a loss for agent j proportional to the level of aggrievement. Under nonintegration, for example, the payoff for each manager $i = 1, 2$ is then $\hat{U}_i(0, a) = U_i(0, a) - \theta[\max_{\hat{a}} U_{-i}(0, \hat{a}) - U_{-i}(0, a)] = U_i(0, a) + \theta U_{-i}(0, a) - \theta \max_{\hat{a}} U_{-i}(0, \hat{a})$ for some $\theta > 0$.

Examples 1 and 2 illustrate what might be called cases of "pure cash rights" and "pure control rights." Pure cash rights allocate the benefits of an asset valued identically by all agents. Pure control rights, as defined in Remark 1, alter who takes actions without changing agents' payoffs conditional on the implemented actions. In Example 1, property rights are pure cash rights when the two agents have equal values for the asset ($V_A(a) = V_P(a)$ for all a). In Example 2, property rights are a hybrid of pure cash rights and pure control rights. Note that in cases of pure cash rights and pure control rights, the first best can be achieved for any property rights allocation provided that the appropriate actions are implemented: formally, $\hat{X}^* = \hat{X}$. In fact, for pure cash rights, $\hat{X}^*(a) = \hat{X}$ for all $a \in A$, whereas for pure control rights, this is true for all $a \in A$ in which all agents specify the same plan for each action. These properties play a role in some of our characterizations of optimal property rights.

2.3. Achieving Efficiency

We begin with a result identifying conditions under which a first-best outcome can be achieved. The basic idea is that efficiency can be sustained in equilibrium if there is a first-best outcome without harmful externalities.

Definition 1   *There are no harmful externalities at $(\hat{x}, a) \in \hat{X} \times A$ if*

$$ U_i(\hat{x}, a) \le U_i\left(\hat{x}, a_i, a'_{-i}\right) \quad \text{for all } i \text{ and all } a'_{-i}. $$

Proposition 1   *If there are no harmful externalities at some first-best outcome $(\hat{x}^*, a^*) \in O^*$, then $a^* \in A^\circ(\hat{x}^*) \subseteq A^*(\hat{x}^*)$; that is, given property rights $\hat{x}^*$, action profile a^* is sustained in a Nash equilibrium, and every Nash equilibrium action profile a° is efficient (and thus $(\hat{x}^*, a^\circ) \in O^*$).*[17]

Proof   For all j and $a_j \in A_j$,

$$ U_j(\hat{x}^*, a^*) = S(\hat{x}^*, a^*) - \sum_{i \ne j} U_i(\hat{x}^*, a^*) $$

$$ \ge S\left(\hat{x}^*, a_j, a^*_{-j}\right) - \sum_{i \ne j} U_i\left(\hat{x}^*, a_j, a^*_{-j}\right) $$

$$ = U_j\left(\hat{x}^*, a_j, a^*_{-j}\right), $$

where the inequality holds because $a^* \in A^*(\hat{x}^*)$ and any externalities are nonharmful. Hence, $a^* \in A^\circ(\hat{x}^*)$.

---

17. It is clear from the proof that for the first result ($a^* \in A^\circ(\hat{x})$), the nonharmful externalities assumption can be weakened to requiring that for each j and a_j, $\sum_{i \ne j} U_i\left(\hat{x}^*, a_j, a^*_{-j}\right) \ge \sum_{i \ne j} U_i(\hat{x}^*, a^*)$ (i.e., that unilateral deviations have no harmful externalities on the aggregate payoff of the other agents).

Next, for any $a° \in A°(\hat{x}^*)$,

$$U_i(\hat{x}^*, a°) \geq U_i\left(\hat{x}^*, a_i^*, a_{-i}°\right) \geq U_i(\hat{x}^*, a^*) \quad \text{for each agent } i, \tag{2}$$

where the first inequality follows from Nash equilibrium and the second inequality from non-harmful externalities at $(\hat{x}^*, a^*)$. Summing over agents yields $\sum_i U_i(\hat{x}^*, a°) \geq S(\hat{x}^*, a^*)$. Because the reverse inequality also holds due to $(\hat{x}^*, a^*) \in O^*$, we have $\sum_i U_i(\hat{x}^*, a°) = S(\hat{x}^*, a^*)$, so $a° \in A^*(\hat{x}^*)$.

Consistent with this result, recall that in our tragedy of the commons example, common ownership is efficient if, because the data center capacity is large, congestion externalities are absent. Similarly, when there is a first-best outcome involving private ownership (so that only one manager has access to the data center), private ownership—which involves no externalities—leads to a first-best outcome.[18] In the agency model (Example 1) when $Y(a) = 0$ and $V_A(a) \geq V_P(a)$ for all a, there is a first-best outcome with no externalities in which the asset is owned by the agent. For example, this case applies to the classical incentive model when the agent is risk neutral, because selling the asset to her achieves optimal risk sharing and at the same time lets the agent internalize any externalities from her actions. Proposition 1 tells us that agent ownership sustains the first best in such cases.

Recall that when property rights consist of pure control rights and/or pure cash rights, we have $\hat{X}^* = \hat{X}$ (i.e., any property rights allocation can arise in the first best). (This property will also hold in dynamic settings considered in the next section in which any property rights allocation is renegotiated toward an ex post efficient allocation after actions are chosen.) For such cases, Proposition 1 establishes that any property rights allocation $\hat{x} \in \hat{X}$ such that there are no harmful externalities at $(\hat{x}, a^*)$ for some $a^* \in A^*(\hat{x})$ ensures that a first-best outcome results. For example, if property rights allocate pure cash flows and pure control rights, and their transfer to a single owner eliminates all externalities—as in the traditional view of vertical integration—it yields the first best. More generally, it suffices to eliminate only harmful externalities. For instance, in the coordination model of firm scope (Example 2), integration eliminates harmful externalities at coordinated actions, as the owner's deviation would raise the managers' private benefits. In contrast, nonintegration eliminates externalities at noncoordinated actions, as a change in just one manager's action then has no effect on the outcome. So, Proposition 1 tells us that the first best is sustained by integration when coordination is efficient and by nonintegration when noncoordination is efficient.

2.4. Externalities and Distortions

When harmful externalities are instead present at all first-best outcomes, efficiency typically cannot be achieved. As intuition suggests, equilibrium actions will be distorted in directions that generate harmful externalities. We now formalize this point, focusing for simplicity on the case in which each action space A_i is a subset of the real line $\mathbb{R}$. (A more general case, where

---

18. Note also that, according to Proposition 1, in both of these cases efficiency would be preserved if, in addition, the individuals could take actions (make "investments") that enhanced their own value from using the data center or reduced their cost of effort, as such actions generate no externalities.

action spaces could be multidimensional, is treated in Segal and Whinston 2012a.) For this purpose, consider the following definition.

Definition 2   *Actions generate positive (negative) externalities at $\hat{x}$ if, for all i, all $j \neq i$, and all $a_{-i} \in A_{-i}$, $U_j(\hat{x}, a)$ is nondecreasing (nonincreasing) in a_i.*

First we show that if a single agent has a one-dimensional action choice that generates positive (negative) externalities, in equilibrium he will choose an action that is too low (high) relative to the efficient level.

Proposition 2   *Suppose that only agent i takes actions, and his action generates positive (negative) externalities at $\hat{x}$. Then $A^{\circ}(\hat{x})$ is below (above) $A^*(\hat{x})$ in the strong set order.*[19]

Proof   Consider the case of positive externalities. Define the function

$$\Psi_i(\hat{x}, a, \lambda) = U_i(\hat{x}, a) + \lambda \sum_{j \neq i} U_j(\hat{x}, a) = (1 - \lambda)U_i(\hat{x}, a) + \lambda S(\hat{x}, a), \qquad (3)$$

where $\lambda \in [0, 1]$. Observe that $A^*(\hat{x}) = \arg\max_{a \in A} \Psi_i(\hat{x}, a, 1)$ and $A^{\circ}(\hat{x}) = \arg\max_{a \in A} \Psi_i(\hat{x}, a, 0)$. Positive externalities imply that the function $\Psi_i(\cdot)$ has increasing differences in (a, λ).[20] The result follows by Topkis's Monotonicity Theorem (see Milgrom and Roberts 1990). The result for negative externalities follows similarly.

As an illustration, in the agency model (Example 1), if both $Y(a)$ and $Y(a) + V_P(a)$ are nondecreasing in a (greater effort raises Y by more than any asset value deterioration for the principal), Proposition 2 tells us that the agent's choice of a will be weakly too low (in the strong set order) under any ownership structure.

The result also implies that when many agents choose actions, the equilibrium level of any action that generates positive (negative) externalities will be too low (high), holding fixed all other actions. To get a result comparing the entire equilibrium action profile with the first-best action profile, we need to make assumptions on the interactions among different actions, so that we can apply the theory of supermodular games (Milgrom and Roberts 1990).

Definition 3   *Actions are strategic complements at property rights allocation $\hat{x}$ if, for each i, A_i is a compact subset of $\mathbb{R}$, and $U_i(\hat{x}, a_i, a_{-i})$ is continuous in a and has increasing differences in (a_i, a_{-i}).*

19. For two sets $A, B \subseteq \mathbb{R}$, A is below B in the strong set order if for all $a \in A \setminus B$, $b \in B \setminus A$, and $c \in A \cap B$, we have $a \leq c \leq b$.

If we know that the action has strictly positive (negative) externalities at $\hat{x}$, in the sense that $U_j(\hat{x}, a)$ is strictly increasing (decreasing) in a_i for all $j \neq i$ and all $a_{-i} \in A_{-i}$, then we can obtain the stronger conclusion that every element of $A^{\circ}(\hat{x})$ is below (above) every element of $A^*(\hat{x})$ by using the Monotone Selection Theorem of Milgrom and Shannon 1994.

20. A function $f(x, y, z)$ has increasing differences in (x, y) if

$$f(x', y', z) - f(x, y', z) \geq f(x', y, z) - f(x, y, z)$$

for all $(x', y') \geq (x, y)$. See Milgrom and Roberts (1990).

Proposition 3 *Suppose that at a given property rights allocation $\hat{x} \in \hat{X}$, actions are strategic complements and generate positive (negative) externalities. Then $A^{\circ}(\hat{x})$ is below (above) $A^{*}(\hat{x})$ in the weak set order.*[21]

Remark 2 By Milgrom and Roberts (1990), the Nash equilibrium set $A^{\circ}(\hat{x})$ in a game with strategic complements is nonempty and contains the largest and smallest equilibria $\bar{a}^{\circ}(\hat{x})$ and $\underline{a}^{\circ}(\hat{x})$, respectively. Thus, the proposition's conclusion is equivalent to saying that with positive (negative) externalities, $\underline{a}^{\circ}(\hat{x}) \leq a^{*} \; (\bar{a}^{\circ}(\hat{x}) \geq a^{*})$ for all $a^{*} \in A^{*}(\hat{x})$ and $\bar{a}^{\circ}(\hat{x}) \leq a^{*}$ $(\underline{a}^{\circ}(\hat{x}) \geq a^{*})$ for some $a^{*} \in A^{*}(\hat{x})$.[22] In the special case in which $A^{*}(\hat{x})$ contains a unique action profile a^{*}, Proposition 3 establishes that a^{*} is above the largest Nash equilibrium $\bar{a}^{\circ}(\hat{x})$ (below the lowest Nash equilibrium $\underline{a}^{\circ}(\hat{x})$).

Proof Consider the case of positive externalities (the case of negative externalities is symmetric). Take any $a^{\circ} \in A^{\circ}(\hat{x})$ and any $a^{*} \in A^{*}(\hat{x})$. (Both $A^{\circ}(\hat{x})$ and $A^{*}(\hat{x})$ are nonempty under our assumptions.) For the weak set order comparison, we must establish that (i) there exists $\bar{a} \in A^{*}(\hat{x})$ such that $\bar{a} \geq a^{\circ}$, and (ii) there exists $\underline{a} \in A^{\circ}(\hat{x})$ such that $\underline{a} \leq a^{*}$.

For part (i), we take $\bar{a}_i = \max\{a_i^{*}, a_i^{\circ}\}$ for each i and show that $U_i(\hat{x}, \bar{a}) \geq U_i(\hat{x}, a^{*})$ for each agent i. We do this by moving from a^{*} to $\bar{a}$ in two steps and showing that agent i cannot become worse off at either step. In the first step, we hold agent i's action fixed at a_i^{*} and increase the other agents' actions from a_{-i}^{*} to $\bar{a}_{-i}$. This increase can only benefit agent i due to positive externalities. In the second step, if $a_i^{\circ} > a_i^{*}$, we increase agent i's action from a_i^{*} to $\bar{a}_i = a_i^{\circ}$ (otherwise, $\bar{a}_i = a_i^{*}$, and we do nothing). Note that this increase cannot harm agent i if all the others played a_{-i}° (because $a^{\circ} \in A^{\circ}(\hat{x})$), so by strategic complementarity it also cannot harm agent i if the others play $\bar{a}_{-i} \geq a_{-i}^{\circ}$. Formally, we have

$$U_i(\hat{x}, a_i^{\circ}, \bar{a}_{-i}) - U_i(\hat{x}, a_i^{*}, \bar{a}_{-i}) \geq U_i(\hat{x}, a_i^{\circ}, a_{-i}^{\circ}) - U_i(\hat{x}, a_i^{*}, a_{-i}^{\circ}) \geq 0. \qquad (4)$$

Thus, the second step does not reduce agent i's payoff either. Therefore, we have $U_i(\hat{x}, \bar{a}) \geq U_i(\hat{x}, a^{*})$ for all agents i, and therefore $S(\hat{x}, \bar{a}) \geq S(\hat{x}, a^{*})$. Because $a^{*} \in A^{*}(\hat{x})$, it follows that $\bar{a} \in A^{*}(\hat{x})$, which establishes (i), since $\bar{a} \geq a^{\circ}$.

To establish (ii), we observe that none of the inequalities in (4) can be strict, for otherwise we would obtain $S(\hat{x}, \bar{a}) > S(\hat{x}, a^{*})$, contradicting $a^{*} \in A^{*}(\hat{x})$. Thus, when $a_i^{\circ} > a_i^{*}$, strategy a_i^{*} must be (along with strategy a_i°) agent i's best response to a_{-i}° and is therefore a rationalizable strategy. Thus, the strategy $\hat{a}_i = \min\{a_i^{*}, a_i^{\circ}\}$ is rationalizable for each i, and by Milgrom and Roberts (1990: Theorem 5), the smallest Nash equilibrium $\underline{a}^{\circ}(\hat{x}) \in A^{\circ}(\hat{x})$ has $\underline{a}^{\circ}(\hat{x}) \leq \hat{a} \leq a^{*}$.

The result implies, for instance, that efforts are weakly too high (in the weak set order) under common ownership in the tragedy of the commons example when each function $V_i(\cdot)$

---

21. For nonempty sets $A, B \subseteq \mathbb{R}^N$, A is below B in the weak set order if for all $a \in A$ there exists $b \in B$ such that $a \leq b$, and for all $b \in B$ there exists $a \in A$ such that $a \leq b$.

22. Furthermore, with positive (negative) externalities, $\bar{a}^{\circ}(\hat{x})$ $(\underline{a}^{\circ}(\hat{x}))$ is the agents' Pareto optimal Nash equilibrium, and it is a unique Pareto optimal Nash equilibrium up to payoff equivalence.

has increasing differences in its two arguments. In the coordination model of firm scope example (Example 2), it implies that coordination is weakly too low under nonintegration when $v_i(1) + w_i(1) \geq v_i(0) + w_i(0)$ for $i = 1, 2$, so that externalities are positive (of course, this result is immediate in any case).

Finally, Propositions 2 and 3 do not rule out the possibility that an equilibrium action profile could be efficient. However, if payoff functions are differentiable and the marginal externalities are strict, using the approach of Edlin and Shannon (1998), it can be shown that there is necessarily inefficiency.

2.5. Second-Best Property Rights Allocations

When there are unavoidable externalities and therefore inefficiency, what can be said about the welfare effect of the property rights allocation, and about optimal (second-best) property rights allocations? We define second-best outcomes as optimal outcomes subject to the constraint that agents choose their actions noncooperatively:[23]

$$O^{**} = \arg \max_{\hat{x} \in \hat{X}, \, a \in A^\circ(\hat{x})} S(\hat{x}, a) .$$

We also let $\hat{X}^{**} = \left\{ \hat{x} \in \hat{X} : (\hat{x}, a) \in O^{**} \text{ for some } a \in A \right\}$ be the property rights allocations that can arise in a second-best outcome.

We first observe that because actions are too low (high) with positive (negative) externalities, any change in property rights that is both directly beneficial and encourages (discourages) those actions is welfare enhancing.

Lemma 1 *Consider two property rights allocations $\hat{x}$ and $\hat{x}'$ and a pair of Nash equilibria resulting from these property rights allocations, $a \in A^\circ(\hat{x})$ and $a' \in A^\circ(\hat{x}')$. If actions generate positive (negative) externalities at $\hat{x}'$, $S(\hat{x}', a) \geq S(\hat{x}, a)$, and $a' \geq a$ ($a' \leq a$), then $S(\hat{x}', a') \geq S(\hat{x}, a)$.*

Proof Note that

$$S(\hat{x}', a') - S(\hat{x}, a) \geq S(\hat{x}', a') - S(\hat{x}', a) \geq \sum_i \left[U_i\left(\hat{x}', a_i, a'_{-i}\right) - U_i(\hat{x}', a) \right] \geq 0,$$

where the first inequality is due to $S(\hat{x}', a) \geq S(\hat{x}, a)$, the second is due to $a' \in A^\circ(\hat{x}')$, and the third is due to positive (negative) externalities at $\hat{x}'$ and $a' \geq a$ ($a' \leq a$).

Lemma 1 considers property rights changes that increase the ex post surplus holding actions fixed, and also lead to surplus-enhancing behavioral changes. Such changes involve no trade-

---

23. This definition makes the optimistic assumption that if a property rights allocation induces multiple Nash equilibria, the agents coordinate on a surplus-maximizing Nash equilibrium. Note that if arbitrary equilibrium selections were allowed, agents may switch between equilibria arbitrarily, depending on property rights, even when property rights are not payoff relevant, which could alter the effects of property rights. However, Proposition 4 could be reformulated under the alternative assumption that the worst equilibrium is always selected—a case examined, for example, by Mookherjee (1984).

offs. In general, the optimal (second-best) property rights allocation will trade off these two effects. Our next result shows that a second-best property rights allocation is distorted away from what would be efficient ex post given the actions individuals take, and this distortion is in the direction that increases (reduces) incentives for actions with positive (negative) externalities. For simplicity, we formulate the result for the case in which the property rights allocation is one dimensional. This result will be applied later to cases with multidimensional property rights (e.g., specifying different agents' access to different assets) by varying one of these dimensions at a time.

Proposition 4 *Suppose that $\hat{X} \subseteq \mathbb{R}$, that $U_i(\hat{x}, a_i, a_{-i})$ has increasing differences in $(\hat{x}, a_i)$ for all i, and that actions are strategic complements at all property rights allocations. Take any second-best outcome $(\hat{x}^{**}, a^{**}) \in O^{**}$ and any ex post efficient allocation given actions $a^{**}, \hat{x}' \in \hat{X}^*(a^{**})$. If actions generate positive (negative) externalities at $\hat{x}'$, then either $\hat{x}^{**} > \hat{x}'$ ($\hat{x}^{**} < \hat{x}'$) or $\hat{x}' \in \hat{X}^{**}$.*

Remark 3 In the simple case in which there is a unique second-best outcome, that is, $O^{**} = \{(\hat{x}^{**}, a^{**})\}$, and actions generate positive (negative) externalities at all $\hat{x}$, Proposition 4 implies that $\hat{x}^{**}$ is weakly higher (lower) than any ex post efficient allocation $\hat{x}' \in \hat{X}^*(a^{**})$ given actions a^{**}.

Proof Suppose that actions generate positive externalities at $\hat{x}'$, and let $\hat{x}' > \hat{x}^{**}$ (with the reverse inequality, the conclusion is trivial since either $\hat{x}^{**} > \hat{x}'$ or $\hat{x}' = \hat{x}^{**} \in \hat{X}^{**}$). Under the hypotheses of the proposition, Theorems 5 and 6 in Milgrom and Roberts (1990) imply that given the property rights allocation $\hat{x}'$ there is a largest Nash equilibrium action profile $a' = \max A^\circ(\hat{x}')$, and $a' \geq a^{**}$. Because $\hat{x}' \in \hat{X}^*(a^{**})$ implies that $S(\hat{x}', a^{**}) \geq S(\hat{x}^{**}, a^{**})$, we can apply Lemma 1 to see that $S(\hat{x}', a') \geq S(\hat{x}^{**}, a^{**})$, so $\hat{x}' \in \hat{X}^{**}$. The proof for the case of negative externalities is similar.

As an illustration, consider again the agency model (Example 1) with $a \in \mathbb{R}$ and $Y(a)$, $Y(a) + V_P(a)$, and $V_A(a)$ all nondecreasing in a. Then externalities are positive for any ownership share $\hat{x}$, and the agent's payoff has increasing differences in $(\hat{x}, a)$. Proposition 4 tells us that the second-best property rights allocation in that case will be distorted toward agent ownership of the asset: in particular, she may be the optimal owner even if she values the asset less than the principal given her equilibrium action (e.g., due to being more risk averse than the principal).

An interesting special case arises when the maximal (minimal) property rights allocation is efficient for all investments. In this case, applying Proposition 4 to $\hat{x}' = \max \hat{X}$ ($\hat{x}' = \min \hat{X}$) yields the following.

Corollary 1 *Suppose that, in addition to the assumptions in the first sentence of Proposition 4, the maximal (minimal) property rights allocation is in $\hat{X}^*(a)$ for all $a \in A$, and actions generate positive (negative) externalities at this allocation. Then this allocation lies in the set $\hat{X}^{**}$ of second-best optimal property rights allocations, provided that the set is nonempty.*

For an illustration, take the agency model of Example 1 with $A \subseteq \mathbb{R}$ and $V_A'(a) > 0$ (so the increasing differences and strategic complementarity assumptions of Proposition 4 hold). Then, if agent ownership is optimal for any given action a (i.e., $V_A(a) \geq V_P(a)$ for any a), and we have positive externalities at that ownership allocation (i.e., $Y'(a) > 0$), by Corollary 1 agent ownership is a second-best optimal property rights allocation (provided that one exists). Similarly, if principal ownership is optimal for any action a (i.e., $V_A(a) \leq V_P(a)$ for all a), and we have negative externalities at that ownership allocation (i.e., $Y'(a) + V_P'(a) \leq 0$; e.g., agent effort may increase asset value but reduce the principal's current profit $Y(a)$ by more), then by Corollary 1 it is a second-best optimal property rights allocation (provided that one exists).

An important application of the Corollary is to the case in which the allocation of property rights has no direct efficiency consequences given the agents' actions, that is, $\hat{X}^*(a) = \hat{X}$ for all a. (Recall that this condition arises for pure cash flow rights. In the dynamic setting considered in the next section, this condition arises as a natural consequence of efficient renegotiation.) For this case, Corollary 1 says that the maximal (minimal) property rights allocation is optimal when the assumptions of Proposition 4 hold and actions generate positive (negative) externalities at this allocation.[24]

3. Property Rights and Investment Hold-Up

In the previous section, property rights affected efficiency directly as well as through incentives to take noncontractible actions. However, in a longer term context, after noncontractible actions are taken, the parties may be able to renegotiate property rights that are ex post inefficient. For example, although giving an agent property rights over an asset may be optimal to increase his incentives for noncontractible investment, if he is not the efficient ex post owner, he may resell the asset to whomever is. Such renegotiation improves ex post efficiency, but it also introduces a new source of externalities, which may distort investments. These "bargaining externalities" arise because an individual's noncontractible actions may affect the surplus created by renegotiation, which is shared in bargaining with other individuals.

Example 3   Consider again the agency model of Example 1. Now, however, assume that as in Demski and Sappington (1991) and Hermalin and Katz (1991), after the agent chooses action $a \in A \subseteq \mathbb{R}$ (interpreted now as an investment), the parties can renegotiate the allocation of the asset to some other allocation $x \in \hat{X}$ (here we assume that there are no ex ante noncontractible allocations, so $X = \hat{X}$). Suppose that renegotiation is always efficient and that it gives the agent share $\lambda \in [0, 1]$ of the renegotiation surplus. Consider the case in which the principal's inalienable return $Y(a)$ is independent of the agent's actions, and normalize $Y(a) = 0$. Assume that the agent's investment raises asset values ($V_P'(a) > 0$, $V_A'(a) > 0$), and that the principal is always the efficient owner ex post ($V_P(a) > V_A(a)$ for all a).

Because the agent's investment has a positive externality on the principal at the first-best allocation (since $V_P'(\cdot) > 0$), the first best cannot be achieved if renegotiation is impossible, and

---

24. Corollary 1 could also be extended to cases of pure control rights. In such cases, we have $\hat{X}^*(a) = \hat{X}$ only for those $a \in A$ in which all agents choose the same action plan, but we can always find a second-best outcome $(\hat{x}^{**}, a^{**}) \in O^{**}$ with this property and apply Proposition 4 to this outcome.

we then have underinvestment under principal ownership ($\hat{x} = 0$), according to Proposition 2. In that case, agent ownership ($\hat{x} = 1$), which eliminates this externality and increases the agent's incentives to invest, may be second-best optimal (by Proposition 4), even though the asset then ends up in the hands of the agent, who values it less than does the principal.

When perfect renegotiation is possible, however, agent ownership will always be renegotiated ex post to give the asset to the principal. In that case, it may be possible to achieve the first best. Given this renegotiation, when $\hat{x} = 1$, the post-renegotiation payoffs of the principal and the agent, $U_P(\hat{x}, a)$ and $U_A(\hat{x}, a)$, respectively, are

$$U_P(1, a) = (1 - \lambda)[V_P(a) - V_A(a)]$$

$$U_A(1, a) = V_A(a) + \lambda[V_P(a) - V_A(a)] - C(a).$$

Even though agent ownership eliminates the direct externality of the agent's investment on the principal, renegotiation may create a bargaining externality, because the principal gets a share $(1 - \lambda)$ of the renegotiation surplus $V_P(a) - V_A(a)$. When either the agent has all the bargaining power ($\lambda = 1$) or the investment is general in the sense that it raises the principal's and agent's values for the asset equally ($V'_P(a) = V'_A(a)$), there is no bargaining externality, and agent ownership attains the first best. But when the principal has some bargaining power ($\lambda < 1$) and the agent's investment affects the principal's and agent's values for the asset differently, the agent's investment creates a bargaining externality. For example, if $V'_P(a) > V'_A(a)$, so the investment increases the principal's value more than the agent's, the externality from investment is positive, leading to underinvestment by the agent.

The effects of property rights on noncontractible investments when renegotiation is possible after investments have been chosen has been examined in the so-called hold-up literature. This literature generalizes the idea from the above example: that agents' incentives to invest may be reduced when they expect others to "hold them up" and extract some of the gains from the investments in future bargaining. In this section, we survey the hold-up literature. Paralleling our discussion of the static model, we begin by considering when the parties can achieve the first best. We then examine settings in which harmful externalities cannot be eliminated, so that a first-best outcome cannot be achieved. We focus there on the Property Rights Theory of the Firm of Grossman and Hart (1986), Hart and Moore (1990), and Hart (1995). Then we discuss how the findings of that theory are modified when some of its assumptions are altered. Finally, we discuss the potential of designing property rights mechanisms and renegotiation procedures that reduce or eliminate investment inefficiencies.

3.1. A Model of Hold-Up

We consider a general hold-up model involving a set $\mathcal{N}$ of N agents whose interaction unfolds according to the stages described in Section 1 and depicted in Figure 1. In the ex ante stage, the parties specify property rights $\hat{x} \in \hat{X}$ and then choose actions a. Next, some uncertainty θ is realized. Both uncertainty θ and the chosen actions a are observed by all agents prior to bargaining but are not verifiable. Then, in the ex post stage, the parties can renegotiate to some other allocation $x \in X$ (recall that $X \backslash \hat{X}$ represents decisions that are contractible ex post but

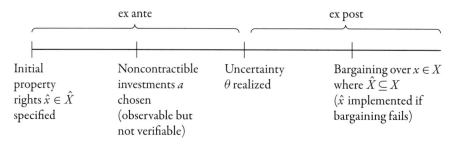

Figure 1. Timing of the hold-up model.

not ex ante). If bargaining fails, the property rights allocation $\hat{x}$ is unchanged (i.e., $x = \hat{x}$). Agent i's payoff given the final allocation x, noncontractible actions a, uncertainty θ, and transfer t_i is $v_i(x, a, \theta) + t_i$.

Let $x^*(a, \theta)$ be an efficient ex post decision given (a, θ), that is,

$$x^*(a, \theta) \in \arg\max_{x \in X} \sum_i v_i(x, a, \theta) \quad \text{for all } (a, \theta),$$

and denote the resulting maximal ex post surplus by

$$S(a, \theta) = \max_{x \in X} \sum_i v_i(x, a, \theta).$$

The set of first-best investment profiles is $A^* = \arg\max_{a \in A} E[S(a, \theta)]$.

To formulate results that apply to a variety of settings, we sometimes avoid a specific model of bargaining and instead make only two weak assumptions on the utilities that the parties obtain by bargaining. We denote by $u_i(\hat{x}, a, \theta)$ party i's *post-renegotiation utility*, given the initial property rights allocation $\hat{x}$, following investments a and uncertainty realization θ.[25] The first assumption is *feasibility*:

$$\sum_i u_i(\hat{x}, a, \theta) \leq S(a, \theta) \quad \text{for all } \hat{x}, a, \theta. \tag{5}$$

In particular, if bargaining is efficient, (5) holds with equality for all $(\hat{x}, a, \theta)$. The second is *individual rationality*:

$$u_i(\hat{x}, a, \theta) \geq v_i(\hat{x}, a, \theta) \quad \text{for all } i, \hat{x}, a, \theta. \tag{6}$$

---

25. Note that this reduced-form utility is assumed independent of any transfer t, because we think of t as a transfer made ex ante before bargaining. For some bargaining solutions (e.g., the Nash solution), a contractually stipulated ex post transfer is equivalent to an ex ante transfer, so it is irrelevant for bargaining. For other solutions—such as outside option bargaining considered in Section 3.6—a contractually stipulated ex post transfer may affect bargaining, unlike an ex ante transfer. In this case, the ex post transfer would need to be viewed as part of $\hat{x}$.

It says that each agent's payoff in bargaining is at least her payoff from the outcome that follows a bargaining breakdown. The two assumptions allow for a range of bargaining processes. At one extreme, we could have no renegotiation at all (bargaining always fails), in which case we are back in the static model of the last section, albeit with some uncertainty in payoffs due to θ. At the other extreme, we could have efficient bargaining, which could in principle take various forms.[26]

One specific model of individually rational and efficient renegotiation is given by the (generalized) Nash bargaining solution

$$u_i(\hat{x}, a, \theta) = v_i(\hat{x}, a, \theta) + \lambda_i R(\hat{x}, a, \theta), \tag{7}$$

where $\lambda_i \geq 0$, $\sum_i \lambda_i = 1$, and $R(\hat{x}, a, \theta) = S(a, \theta) - \sum_j v_j(\hat{x}, a, \theta)$ is the *renegotiation surplus*.

We say that there is "no renegotiation" at $(\hat{x}, a, \theta)$ if (6) holds with equality for each i, that is, if each party's payoff equals the continuation payoff he would get under the original property rights allocation $\hat{x}$. (Note that, strictly speaking, the parties might renegotiate their original contract in such a case, but this renegotiation would yield none of them any gain; their payoffs would be the same as if they did not renegotiate.)

We will apply the static analysis of Section 2 to this dynamic setup by defining the agents' reduced-form payoffs given a property rights allocation $\hat{x}$ and investments a as their expected post-renegotiation payoffs: $U_i(\hat{x}, a) = E_\theta[u_i(\hat{x}, a, \theta)]$. The set of equilibrium investments is then given by the Nash equilibrium set $A^\circ(\hat{x})$ of the induced static investment game, given by (1).

3.2. Achieving Efficiency

We begin by considering circumstances in which a first-best outcome can be achieved. We first observe that the first best can be achieved provided that it is possible to specify a first-best property rights allocation at which there are no harmful direct externalities at the efficient investments, that is, if there would be no harmful externalities in the absence of renegotiation.

Definition 4 *There are no harmful direct externalities at $(\hat{x}, a) \in \hat{X} \times A$ if $v_i(\hat{x}, a, \theta) \leq v_i\left(\hat{x}, a_i, a'_{-i}, \theta\right)$ for all i, a'_{-i}, and θ.*

Proposition 5 *Suppose that there exists an efficient investment profile $a^* \in A^*$ and a property rights allocation $\hat{x} \in \hat{X}$ such that (i) $\hat{x}$ is ex post efficient in all states θ given investments a^*, and (ii) there are no harmful direct externalities at $(\hat{x}, a^*)$. Then, for any bargaining process that satisfies feasibility (5) and individual rationality (6), $a^* \in A^\circ(\hat{x}) \subseteq A^*$. That is, given property rights $\hat{x}^*$, investment profile a^* is sustained in a Nash equilibrium, and every Nash equilibrium investment profile a° is efficient (and thus $(\hat{x}^*, a^\circ) \in O^*$).*

---

26. Note that (6) might not hold if $N > 2$, and without i's consent other parties can agree to changes in parts of x that have externalities on party i. We discuss such situations in Section 4.2.

Proof Individual rationality (6) and feasibility (5) of bargaining together with (i) imply that $u_i(\hat{x}, a^*, \theta) = v_i(\hat{x}, a^*, \theta)$ for all i and θ, so $U_i(\hat{x}, a^*) = E_\theta[u_i(\hat{x}, a^*, \theta)] = E_\theta[v_i(\hat{x}, a^*, \theta)]$ for all i. Using this fact, for all a_{-i} we have

$$U_i(\hat{x}, a_i^*, a_{-i}) \geq E_\theta[v_i(\hat{x}, a_i^*, a_{-i}, \theta)] \geq E_\theta[v_i(\hat{x}, a^*, \theta)] = U_i(\hat{x}, a^*),$$

where the first inequality is by individual rationality of bargaining and the second by nonharmful direct externalities at $(\hat{x}, a^*)$. Thus, the induced static investment game has nonharmful externalities at $(\hat{x}, a^*)$. Because $(\hat{x}, a^*)$ is a first-best outcome in the induced static game (since $\sum_i U_i(\hat{x}, a^*) = \sum_i E_\theta[v_i(\hat{x}, a^*, \theta)] = E_\theta[S(a^*, \theta)]$), applying Proposition 1 to this game yields the result.

The intuition behind Proposition 5 is that if a property rights allocation achieves efficiency without renegotiation following equilibrium investments, then any agent's investment deviation, by creating renegotiation surplus, could only have beneficial bargaining externalities on the others. If, in addition, investment deviations do not generate harmful direct externalities, then nobody will deviate from an efficient outcome.

A simple special case in which there are no harmful direct externalities occurs when direct externalities are completely absent.

Definition 5 *Agent i's investment a_i is a self-investment if agent j's disagreement payoff $v_j(\hat{x}, a, \theta)$ is independent of a_i for all $j \neq i$ for all $\hat{x}$, a_{-i}, and θ.*

This assumption applies, say, to agents' investment in their own human capital. It rules out both investments in physical capital that could benefit other agents and investments in other agents' human capital. If all agents' investments are self-investments, then each agent's disagreement payoff has the form $v_i(\hat{x}, a_i, \theta)$. If in addition there are no ex ante noncontractible decisions (i.e., $\hat{X} = X$) and no noncontractible uncertainty θ, then by Proposition 5, letting the property rights allocation be a first-best allocation given efficient investments (i.e., $\hat{x} = x^*(a^*)$) sustains first-best investments.[27]

Example 4 Consider again Example 3, but assume that $V_P(a)$ and $Y(a)$ are both independent of a, so the agent's investment is a self-investment, and that the efficient ex post owner may depend on the agent's investment a. In this case, whether renegotiation is possible or not, the first best can be obtained by giving the asset to its efficient owner given first-best investments a^*. If renegotiation is not possible, this would follow from Proposition 1. If renegotiation is possible, the agent's investment deviation may induce renegotiation when it changes the ex post optimal owner. But, as Proposition 5 shows, because such renegotiation could only bestow a positive bargaining externality on the principal, the agent would not want to deviate from the efficient investment a^*.

Consider now a richer application of Proposition 5, which allows for ex ante noncontractible decisions and uncertainty.

---

27. This conclusion extends to cases with uncertainty θ that is verifiable, so that a contingent property rights allocation $\hat{x}(\theta) = x^*(a^*, \theta)$ can be specified ex ante. Indeed, Proposition 5 extends to such cases.

Example 5 Grossman and Hart (1986) consider a setting in which two agents make self-investments. However, unlike in our basic model, the ex post disagreement point is given by the agents' noncooperative choices of ex ante noncontractible actions $q_1 \in Q_1$ and $q_2 \in Q_2$ resulting in payoffs $v_i(a_i, \theta, q_1, q_2)$ to each agent i. Furthermore, the role of the property rights allocation $\hat{x}$ is to define control rights over these actions: similarly to the setting in Remark 1, the agent who owns asset $k = 1, 2$ has the right to choose action $q_k \in Q_k$. As a result, the ex post Nash equilibrium choice of the noncontractible actions q yields a default noncooperative outcome $q^{\circ}(\hat{x}, a, \theta) \in Q_1 \times Q_2$. Thus, the disagreement payoffs can be defined as $v_i(\hat{x}, a, \theta) = v_i(a_i, \theta, q^{\circ}(\hat{x}, a, \theta))$. The assumptions of Proposition 5 are satisfied in this setting for any property rights allocation $\hat{x}$ such that (i) $q^{\circ}(\hat{x}, a, \theta)$ is efficient for all (a, θ) and (ii) $v_i(\hat{x}, a, \theta) = v_i(a_i, \theta, q^{\circ}(\hat{x}, a, \theta))$ is independent of a_{-i} for $i = 1, 2$. Note that both conditions are satisfied when property rights $\hat{x}$ eliminate all externalities from ex ante noncontractible actions q. Grossman and Hart's (1986) Proposition 1 identifies some such cases. First, if both decisions q_1, q_2 affect the payoff of only one agent i, giving this agent control over both actions ("agent i integration" in Grossman and Hart's terminology) eliminates all the externalities from q and achieves the first best. Similarly, if the payoff of each agent $i = 1, 2$ depends only on action q_i, then giving each agent i control over action q_i ("nonintegration") achieves the first best.[28]

The first-best result of Proposition 5 relies on the ability to eliminate renegotiation in equilibrium by specifying a property rights allocation $\hat{x}$ that is ex post efficient in all states θ following first-best investments a^*. Specifying such an allocation will be impossible when the efficient ex post outcome depends on noncontractible uncertainty and/or when ex post efficient allocations following a^* are not contractible ex ante (i.e., are outside $\hat{X}$). Fortunately, the first best may still be implementable in some such cases, provided that there is efficient renegotiation, so that initial property rights have no direct effect on efficiency. For this case, according to Proposition 1, we can sustain efficient investments a^* using any property rights $\hat{x}$ that eliminate harmful externalities at $(\hat{x}, a^*)$. However, unlike in the static setting, investments now have two sources of externalities: direct externalities and bargaining externalities through renegotiation surplus, and we now need to ensure that both kinds of externalities are nonharmful.

One example of this approach is provided by Edlin and Reichelstein (1996). In their model, all agents' investments are self-investments; hence, there are no direct externalities. As for bargaining externalities, it turns out that in some cases there is a property rights allocation that makes them nonharmful.

Proposition 6 (*Edlin-Reichelstein 1996*) *Suppose all agents make self-investments, bargaining is given by the Nash bargaining solution, $X \subseteq \mathbb{R}^m$, and payoffs satisfy the following separability condition:*[29]

---

28. Note that some of the assumptions of Grossman and Hart are unnecessary for these results: namely, the absence of uncertainty, the separability of payoffs that ensures that noncooperative equilibrium values $q^{\circ}(\hat{x}, a)$ are independent of a, and the restriction to the Nash bargaining solution (instead, any bargaining process satisfying (5) and (6) would work).

29. Edlin and Reichelstein (1996) assume that property rights and investments are one dimensional (X, $A_i \subset \mathbb{R}$), assumptions that we relax here by allowing arbitrary action sets A_i and multidimensional property rights.

$$v_i(x, a_i, \theta) = \bar{v}_i(a_i) \cdot x + \hat{v}_i(x, \theta) + \tilde{v}_i(a_i, \theta) \quad \text{for all } i. \tag{8}$$

Then for property rights allocation $\hat{x} = E_\theta[x^*(a^*, \theta)] \in \hat{X}$ (the expected efficient allocation given first-best investments $a^* \in A^*$), we have $a^* \in A^\circ(\hat{x}) \subseteq A^*$. That is, given property rights $\hat{x}$, investment profile a^* is sustained in a Nash equilibrium, and every Nash equilibrium investment profile a° is efficient.

Proof   Agent i's payoff in the induced static investment game is

$$U_i(\hat{x}, a) = E_\theta[u_i(\hat{x}, a, \theta)] = E_\theta[v_i(\hat{x}, a_i, \theta)] + \lambda_i E_\theta[R(\hat{x}, a, \theta)].$$

Due to efficient renegotiation, $\hat{X}^*(a) = \hat{X}$ for all a. We now show that there are no harmful externalities at $(\hat{x}, a^*)$, when $\hat{x} = E_\theta[x^*(a^*, \theta)]$, which yields the result by Proposition 1. Given self-investments, it suffices to show that the expected renegotiation surplus $E_\theta[R(\hat{x}, a, \theta)]$ is minimized at $a = a^*$. To see this, observe that for any $a \in A$ and any $\theta \in \Theta$, $S(a, \theta) \geq \sum_i v_i(x^*(a^*, \theta), a_i, \theta)$, and the inequality holds with equality when $a = a^*$. Therefore,

$$E_\theta[R(\hat{x}, a, \theta)] \geq E_\theta\left[\sum_i [v_i(x^*(a^*, \theta), a_i, \theta) - v_i(\hat{x}, a_i, \theta)]\right]$$

$$= \sum_i E_\theta[\hat{v}_i(x^*(a^*, \theta), \theta) - \hat{v}_i(\hat{x}, \theta)],$$

and the inequality holds with equality at $a = a^*$, which implies the result.

Note that the presence of noncontractible uncertainty θ typically requires equilibrium renegotiation to achieve efficient allocations. However, under the assumptions of Proposition 6, specifying the expected efficient allocation $\hat{x} = E_\theta[x^*(a^*, \theta)]$ ensures that the expected renegotiation surplus is minimized at first-best investments a^* and thus eliminates harmful bargaining externalities at $(\hat{x}, a^*)$.

Another way to ensure efficiency is by ruling out bargaining externalities at all property rights allocations $\hat{x}$ and finding a property rights allocation at which direct externalities are nonharmful. In particular, bargaining externalities are always absent when one agent invests and she has all the bargaining power; hence, other agents do not capture any of the renegotiation surplus.

Proposition 7   *Suppose that only agent i invests, that renegotiation is efficient and gives agent i all the bargaining power (i.e., it is the Nash bargaining solution with $\lambda_i = 1$), and that there is an efficient investment $a^* \in A^*$ and a property rights allocation $\hat{x} \in \hat{X}$ such that there are no harmful direct externalities at $(\hat{x}, a^*)$. Then $a^* \in A^\circ(\hat{x}) \subseteq A^*$. That is, given property rights $\hat{x}$, investment a^* is optimal for the agent, and every optimal investment profile a° is efficient.*

Proof   The assumptions imply that there are no harmful externalities at $(\hat{x}, a^*)$, and $\hat{X}^*(a^*) = \hat{X}$ due to efficient renegotiation, so Proposition 1 yields the result.

For an illustration of this result, recall that in Example 3, the first best can be achieved with agent ownership if the agent has all the bargaining power ($\lambda = 1$); the agent then sells the asset ex post to the principal at price $V_P(a)$ and captures the entire social surplus $V_P(a) - C(a)$, which gives him an incentive to invest efficiently.

Proposition 7 can be extended to settings with many investing agents. Of course, in such settings it is impossible to give more than one agent the full renegotiation surplus. However, if renegotiation is governed by coalitional bargaining (formally defined in Section 3.5), there may be a set $T \subseteq \mathcal{N}$ of agents, each of whom receives her marginal contribution to the total surplus. If only agents from T make investments, we can sustain an efficient investment profile a^*, provided that property rights $\hat{x}$ eliminate any harmful direct externalities at $(a^*, \hat{x})$ (e.g., if each agent has the right to exclude all others from profiting from her investment). Indeed, because each agent $i \in T$ appropriates her full marginal contribution, she has no aggregate bargaining externality on the others, so her total externality on their aggregate post-renegotiation payoff $\sum_{j \neq i} u_j(\hat{x}, a, \theta)$ is then nonharmful as well. A part of Proposition 1 applies to this case, implying that investment profile a^* can arise as a Nash equilibrium (see footnote 17).[30] However, some inefficient investment equilibria ("coordination failures") may exist as well. (Coordination failures could be ruled out with a no complementarities condition, but it is a rather strong condition; see, e.g., Brandenburger and Stuart 2007a,b.)

Makowski and Ostroy (1995, 2001) note that when each agent has very close substitutes, it may be in fact possible to give each agent his marginal contribution. For example, this happens in classical economies when the competitive equilibrium is unique and the core shrinks to this equilibrium as the number of agents grows large. Indeed, when the core is single valued, it must give each agent his marginal contribution.[31] In such "competitive" settings, first-best incentives are sustained when each agent is given full property rights to the fruits of his labor, so that he has no direct externality on others.

3.3. Externalities and Distortions

We now shift attention to settings in which the first best cannot be achieved with a property rights allocation. We focus here on cases studied in the Property Rights Theory of Hart and Moore (1990) and Hart (1995). This theory examines situations in which parties make self-investments (e.g., investments in their own human assets), so that there are no direct externalities. Inefficiencies in this theory are entirely due to harmful bargaining externalities, which arise because investing agents do not fully appropriate their contributions to renegotiation surplus (in contrast to the setting of Proposition 7). In contrast to the settings of Propositions 5 and 6, these bargaining externalities cannot be avoided because of the presence of decisions that are contractible ex post but not ex ante.

---

30. For examples of two-sided markets in which all the agents on one side receive their marginal contributions so that their efficient self-investments can be sustained, see Felli and Roberts (2001) and Kranton and Minehart (2001).

31. Examples of two-sided markets in which this occurs, so that efficient self-investments by all agents can be sustained, are given by Cole et al. (2001a,b).

Example 6   Consider the setting of Example 4, in which $V_P(a)$ and $Y(a)$ are both independent of a, so that direct externalities are absent. However, suppose that ex ante the parties can only contract on property rights $\hat{x} \in \hat{X} = \{0, \gamma\}$, where $\gamma \in (0, 1)$, while the ex post available outcomes are $X = \{0, \gamma, 1\}$. We can interpret $x = 1$ as the agent's utilization of the asset with cooperation by the principal, which is not contractible ex ante, while $x = \gamma$ (which is contractible ex ante) corresponds to the agent's ownership without the principal's cooperation. (Only share γ of the asset can be effectively used by the agent without the principal's cooperation.) The payoffs continue to be described as in Example 3.

Suppose that $V_A(a) > V_P$ for all a, which means that agent utilization with full cooperation is always ex post optimal. The parties always renegotiate to this allocation using the Nash bargaining solution, which gives them the following payoffs:

$$U_A(\hat{x}, a) = \hat{x} V_A(a) + \lambda (1 - \hat{x}) [V_A(a) - V_P] - C(a),$$

$$U_P(\hat{x}, a) = (1 - \hat{x}) V_P + (1 - \lambda)(1 - \hat{x}) [V_A(a) - V_P] + Y.$$

Thus, when $\lambda < 1$ and $V_A'(a) > 0$, under both ex ante contractible property rights allocations $\hat{x} \in \{0, \gamma\}$ the agent's investment creates a positive bargaining externality, so underinvestment results. Note that if the parties were able to specify agent ownership with full cooperation ($\hat{x} = 1$), the externality would be eliminated and optimal investment would be sustained (according to Proposition 5). The inability to specify cooperation ex ante ($\gamma < 1$) and the agent's lack of full bargaining power ex post ($\lambda < 1$) allow the principal to hold up the agent ex post in return for cooperation, reducing the agent's investment incentives.

Hart and Moore (1990) examine a model of optimal property rights based on the assumption of positive bargaining externalities. Here we discuss their model, focusing for simplicity on the case with $N = 2$ agents, where renegotiation is governed by the Nash bargaining solution (7).[32] As in Hart and Moore (1990), we assume one-dimensional self-investments, so that for each agent i, $A_i \subseteq \mathbb{R}$, and we can write her disagreement payoff as $v_i(\hat{x}, a_i, \theta)$.[33] Thus, any externalities from investments come through the renegotiation surplus $R(\hat{x}, a, \theta)$. We have positive externalities when the renegotiation surplus is increasing in investments, that is, when the incremental impact of investment on the total surplus $S(a, \theta)$ is greater than on the parties' disagreement payoffs, as was true in Example 6. This condition is defined as follows.

Definition 6   *Investments are relationship specific at $\hat{x}$ if the renegotiation surplus $R(\hat{x}, a, \theta) = [S(a, \theta) - \sum_i v_i(\hat{x}, a, \theta)]$ is nondecreasing in a for all θ. Investments are relationship specific if they are relationship specific at all $\hat{x}$.*

Note that self-investments are relationship specific when each agent i's disagreement payoff $v_i(\hat{x}, a, \theta)$ increases less with his investment than does the efficient surplus $S(a, \theta)$. A simple set of sufficient conditions ensuring this is the following.

---

32. This analysis applies to $N > 2$ agents provided that any renegotiation requires unanimous agreement. We discuss the extension to $N > 2$ agents with coalitional bargaining in Section 3.5.

33. Hart and Moore (1990) do not explicitly model uncertainty θ, but one can view their payoff functions as expected payoffs over the realizations of some uncertainty.

Lemma 2 *Suppose that we have self-investments, that $X \subseteq \mathbb{R}^m$, and that $v_i(x, a_i, \theta)$ has increasing differences in (x, a_i) for all i. Then all investments are relationship specific at any property rights allocation $\hat{x}$ such that $\hat{x} \leq x^*(a, \theta)$ for all (a, θ).*

Proof Given the assumptions, we obtain, for any $a_i' > a_i$,

$$S(a_i', a_{-i}, \theta) - S(a, \theta) \geq v_i(x^*(a, \theta), a_i', \theta) - v_i(x^*(a, \theta), a_i, \theta)$$

$$\geq v_i(\hat{x}, a_i', \theta) - v_i(\hat{x}, a_i, \theta),$$

which implies that investments are relationship specific at $\hat{x}$.

Lemma 2 shows that investments are relationship specific if they are complementary to allocations x and if the allocations contracted ex ante are always below their ex post efficient levels. For example, these assumptions are satisfied for any property rights allocation $\hat{x} \in \{0, \gamma\}$ in Example 6 (because ex post efficiency always requires $x^* = 1 \geq \gamma$), but not for the expected-efficient allocation in Proposition 6 (the model of Edlin and Reichelstein 1996), which in some states ends up below and in others above the ex post efficient level.

Because relationship-specific investments generate positive bargaining externalities, by Proposition 2 this implies underinvestment when one agent makes an investment. This conclusion extends to multiagent investments, provided that the investments are strategic complements (i.e., reduced-form payoffs $U_i(x, a) = E_\theta[u_i(x, a, \theta)]$ satisfy Definition 3), in which case Proposition 3 implies the following.

Proposition 8 *Suppose that there is Nash bargaining, and at property rights allocation $\hat{x}$ all agents' investments are relationship specific and are strategic complements.[34] Then $A^\circ(\hat{x})$ is below $A^*(\hat{x})$ in the weak set order.*

When there is a unique efficient investment profile a^*, Proposition 8 implies that any equilibrium investment profile is (weakly) below a^*.

One way to understand this underinvestment problem is by thinking of the parties' split of the renegotiation surplus $R(\hat{x}, a, \theta)$ in proportion to their fixed bargaining powers as an output-sharing scheme. Holmström (1982) showed that when output is an increasing function of efforts (as relationship specificity postulates), then any such output-sharing scheme yields free riding in effort provision.

3.4. Second-Best Property Rights Allocations

3.4.1. The Hart-Moore Theory

In the models of Hart and Moore (1990) and Hart (1995), the ex ante contractible decision $\hat{x} \in \hat{X}$ is a "control structure" over a set K of assets. In contrast to our treatment of the tragedy of the commons in Section 2.1, Hart and Moore's control structures rule out situations in

---

34. Sufficient conditions for strategic complementarity of relationship-specific investments in the induced static investment game are that for each agent i, $A_i \subseteq \mathbb{R}$, the functions $v_i(\hat{x}, a_i, \theta)$ are equicontinuous in a_i, and the function $S(a, \theta)$ is supermodular.

which more than one agent can independently access an asset. Thus, letting $\hat{x}_{ik} \in \{0, 1\}$ denote whether agent i has access to asset k, the set of feasible control structures is defined as

$$\hat{X} = \left\{ \hat{x} \in \{0, 1\}^{NK} : \sum_i \hat{x}_{ik} \leq 1 \quad \text{for all } k \in K \right\}. \tag{9}$$

Hart and Moore refer to the case in which no agent has control of an asset k (so that $\hat{x}_{ik} = 0$ for all i) as "joint ownership" of the asset. (This is the opposite of common ownership in the tragedy of the commons, in the sense that each agent can exclude the others without himself having the right to access the asset.) Hart and Moore also assume that there are no externalities from access in the following sense.

Definition 7   *There are no externalities from access to assets if, for all agents i, $v_i(\hat{x}, a, \theta)$ does not depend on $\hat{x}_{-i}$.*

When there are no externalities from access to assets, each agent i's disagreement payoff depends on his access to assets, but not on other agents' access, and so can be written as $v_i(\hat{x}_i, a, \theta)$. (Note that this assumption would not be natural if common access, as in the tragedy of the commons, were allowed.) An important implication of this assumption is that, with self-investments and Nash bargaining, it makes each agent's post-renegotiation utility $u_i(\hat{x}, a, \theta)$ additively separable between a_i and $\hat{x}_{-i}$:

$$u_i(\hat{x}, a, \theta) = (1 - \lambda_i) v_i(\hat{x}_i, a_i, \theta) + \lambda_i S(a, \theta) - \lambda_i \sum_{j \neq i} v_j(\hat{x}_j, a_j, \theta). \tag{10}$$

Hence, an agent's investment incentives are affected only by his own asset ownership.

To study second-best optimal control structures, Hart and Moore also assume that access to assets increases agents' marginal incentives to invest.

Definition 8   *Investments are asset specific if, for each agent i, $v_i(\hat{x}_i, a, \theta)$ has increasing differences in $(\hat{x}_i, a_i)$.*

This property implies that the agent's post-renegotiation utility (10) has increasing differences in $(\hat{x}_i, a_i)$, so that her investment incentives are increased by shifting assets to her.

It is instructive to compare the predictions of Hart and Moore's Property Rights Theory (Hart and Moore 1990; Hart 1995) to those of the simple allocation benchmark described in Section 1. In that benchmark, there are no investments and no renegotiation, and the optimal property rights allocation simply maximizes the expected surplus $E[\sum_i v_i(\hat{x}, \theta)]$. Thus, in the absence of externalities, it is optimal simply to give assets to agents who value them the most.

In contrast, in Hart and Moore's theory, what determines efficiency is not the expected surplus at the disagreement point per se (because it is renegotiated toward full efficiency) but the sensitivity of this surplus to investments. Thus, instead of allocating assets to the highest-value agents, Hart and Moore's theory allocates assets to agents for whom they create the most beneficial investment incentives.

In particular, when only one agent invests, only her incentives matter, so she should optimally own all the assets.

Proposition 9 *(Hart and Moore 1990: proposition 2)* *If only agent i invests (i.e., A_{-i} is a singleton), $A_i \subseteq \mathbb{R}$, the investment is an asset-specific relationship-specific self-investment, there are no externalities from access to assets, and the set $\hat{X}^{**}$ of second-best optimal property rights is nonempty, then it is optimal for agent i to own all the assets (i.e., $(\hat{x}_i, \hat{x}_{-i}) = ((1, \ldots, 1), (0, \ldots, 0)) \in \hat{X}^{**})$.*

Proof Note first that because agent i's investment is determined by $\hat{x}_i$, we can set $\hat{x}_{-i} = 0$ without affecting equilibrium investments or the resulting total surplus, which makes the constraint in (9) nonbinding. Next, under the assumptions of the proposition, $U_i(\hat{x}, a_i) = E_\theta[u_i(\hat{x}, a_i, \theta)]$ has increasing differences in $(\hat{x}_i, a_i)$. Relationship-specific investment a_i generates positive externalities. Moreover, because ex post bargaining is efficient, the aggregate surplus $\sum_i U_i(\hat{x}, a_i)$ is independent of $\hat{x}$, or in terms of the notation of Section 2, $\hat{X}^*(a_i) = \hat{X}$ for all a_i. Then applying Corollary 1 sequentially to $\hat{x}_{ik}$ for each $k \in K$ implies that it is optimal to set $\hat{x}_i = (1, \ldots, 1)$.

To illustrate this result, consider again Example 6, which satisfies all the assumptions of Proposition 9. In this example, the agent underinvests for any ownership structure, since the benefit of his relationship-specific investment is partially captured by the principal through the renegotiation surplus. Because this investment is asset specific, agent ownership maximizes this investment and the resulting total surplus.

If more than one agent invests, then optimal asset allocation generally involves trade-offs, because moving an asset from agent i to agent j has the direct effect of raising i's asset-specific investment incentives (i.e., his best-response curve) and lowering j's. In some special cases, however, agent j's incentives may not be affected, in which case, if agents' investments are strategic complements, we may be able to conclude that all agents' equilibrium investments increase, and welfare unambiguously goes up. Hart and Moore (1990) identified a number of such cases, and here we present a few of these results as an illustration. To do so, we first need to state two definitions.

Definition 9 Agent i *is indispensable to asset $k \in K$ if, for each agent $j \neq i$ and all a', a, θ, $v_j(\hat{x}_j, a', \theta) - v_j(\hat{x}_j, a, \theta)$ does not depend on $\hat{x}_{jk}$.*

Intuitively, indispensability of agent i to asset k means that the marginal product of other agents' investments on their disagreement payoffs is unaffected by whether they own asset k.

Definition 10 *Assets l and m are perfectly complementary if, for each agent i, $v_i(\hat{x}_i, a', \theta) - v_i(\hat{x}_i, a, \theta)$ depends on $(\hat{x}_{il}, \hat{x}_{im}) \in \{0, 1\}^2$ only through the product $\hat{x}_{il}\hat{x}_{im}$.*

Intuitively, when two assets are perfectly complementary, the marginal product of each agent's investment when he has only one of the two assets equals the marginal product when he has neither.

Proposition 10 *(Hart and Moore 1990: propositions 4, 6, and 8)   If investments are asset-specific relationship-specific self-investments that are strategic complements, there are no externalities from access to assets, and the set $\hat{X}^{**}$ of second-best property rights is nonempty, then the following statements hold:*

(i). *Joint ownership is unnecessary in an optimal control structure; that is, there exists a second-best ownership structure $\hat{x} \in \hat{X}^{**}$ such that $\sum_i \hat{x}_{ik} = 1$ for all $k \in K$.*

(ii). *If agent i is indispensable to asset k, then agent i optimally owns asset k; that is, there exists $\hat{x} \in \hat{X}^{**}$ such that $\hat{x}_{ik} = 1$.*

(iii). *It is optimal for perfectly complementary assets l and m to be owned together; that is, there exists $\hat{x} \in \hat{X}^{**}$ such that $\hat{x}_{il} = \hat{x}_{im} = 1$ for some i.*

Proof   Take any $\hat{x} \in \hat{X}^{**}$. For result (i), if $\sum_{ik} \hat{x}_{ik} = 0$ for some $k \in K$, then (because $U_i(\hat{x}, a) = E_\theta[u_i(\hat{x}, a, \theta)]$ has increasing differences in $(\hat{x}_i, a_i)$ and positive externalities from a_{-i} for each agent i), by Corollary 1, changing to $\hat{x}'_{ik} = 1$ for any given i holding the other dimensions of $\hat{x}$ fixed yields another allocation in $\hat{X}^{**}$. For result (ii), if $\hat{x}_{jk} = 1$ for some $j \neq i$, then (because $v_j(\hat{x}_j, a_j, \theta)$, and hence $U_j(\hat{x}, a)$, has (weakly) increasing differences in $(-\hat{x}_{jk}, a_j)$) Corollary 1 implies that changing the property rights over asset k to joint ownership $[(\hat{x}'_{ik}, \hat{x}'_{jk}) = (0, 0)]$ while holding fixed the ownership of the other assets yields another allocation in $\hat{X}^{**}$. By the argument used to show result (i), changing the property rights over asset k to agent i ownership $[(\hat{x}'_{ik}, \hat{x}'_{jk}) = (1, 0)]$ while holding fixed the ownership of the other assets must yield another allocation in $\hat{X}^{**}$. For result (iii), if $\hat{x}_{il} = \hat{x}_{jm} = 1$ for some agents $i \neq j$, then (because $v_j(\hat{x}_j, a_j, \theta)$, and hence $U_j(\hat{x}, a)$, has (weakly) increasing differences in $(-\hat{x}_{jm}, a_j)$) Corollary 1 implies that changing the ownership of asset m to joint ownership $[(\hat{x}'_{im}, \hat{x}'_{jm}) = (0, 0)]$ while holding fixed the ownership of the other assets yields another allocation in $\hat{X}^{**}$. Finally, by the argument used to show result (i), changing the ownership of asset m to agent i ownership $[(\hat{x}'_{im}, \hat{x}'_{jm}) = (1, 0)]$, making agent i the owner of both assets, must yield another allocation in $\hat{X}^{**}$.

Note that while Hart and Moore's concepts of indispensable agents and perfectly complementary assets are formulated in terms of the marginal returns to investments, $v_i(\hat{x}_i, a'_i, \theta) - v_i(\hat{x}_i, a_i, \theta)$ with $a' > a$, it seems natural for the same properties to also be satisfied by the absolute payoffs $v_i(\hat{x}_i, a_i, \theta)$. In that case, the simple allocation benchmark makes exactly the same asset ownership recommendations as Proposition 10, because the proposed asset reallocations (weakly) increase the payoff of each agent (and not just the sensitivity of this payoff to investment). The same argument applies to the proposition's recommendation of no joint ownership. Thus, Proposition 10's recommendations also hold in settings without investments in which renegotiation is either impossible or breaks down with an exogenous probability. (When the probability of bargaining breakdown is affected by property rights, the conclusion may change, as we analyze in Section 4.) Thus, although some of Hart and Moore's predictions (e.g., Proposition 9) are distinct from those of the simple allocation benchmark, others are similar, which can make it difficult to distinguish their theory empirically from alternative theories. Another difficulty in testing the theory stems from the sensitivity of its predictions to alternative assumptions about the nature of investments, which we now examine.[35]

3.4.2. Violation of Self-Investments: Cooperative Investment

We now relax the assumption of self-investments to allow so-called cooperative investments, which directly affect other agents' disagreement payoffs. Examples include an agent's training of other agents (i.e., investments in others' human capital) and investments in physical capital owned by others. For simplicity, we assume that these cooperative effects are positive.

Definition 11 *Agent i's investment is cooperative at $\hat{x}$ if $v_j(\hat{x}, a, \theta)$ is nondecreasing in a_i for $j \neq i$ and all θ. It is cooperative if it is cooperative at every $\hat{x}$.*

Consider again Example 3, and allow $Y(a)$ to depend on the agent's investment a. Then the agent's investment is cooperative at agent ownership ($\hat{x} = 0$) when $Y'(a) \geq 0$, it is cooperative at principal ownership ($\hat{x} = 1$) when $Y'(a) + V_P'(a) \geq 0$, and it is cooperative when both inequalities hold. Optimal property rights when investments have cooperative components have been examined by Demski and Sappington (1991), MacLeod and Malcomson (1993), Hart et al. (1997), Che and Hausch (1999), Edlin and Hermalin (2000), Segal and Whinston (2000: 24–28), Guriev (2003), and Roider (2004).

Cooperative investments introduce a direct route by which an agent's investment can generate positive externalities in addition to the bargaining externalities present in Hart and Moore's Property Rights Theory (Hart and Moore 1990; Hart 1996). As a result, the one-sided underinvestment result generalizes to the following.[36]

Proposition 11 *If only agent i invests, $A_i \subseteq \mathbb{R}$, her investment is a cooperative relationship-specific investment, and there is Nash bargaining, then there is underinvestment for all ownership structures: $A^\circ(\hat{x})$ is below $A^*(\hat{x})$ in the strong set order for all $\hat{x} \in \hat{X}$.*

Proof The payoff of agent $j \neq i$ in the induced static game is $U_j(\hat{x}, a) = E_\theta[v_j(\hat{x}, a_i, \theta) + \lambda_j R(a_i, \theta)]$, which is nondecreasing in a_i. Applying Proposition 2 then yields the desired result.

How does asset ownership affect cooperative investment? To look at this issue in the cleanest possible way, we examine the special case of purely cooperative investments, which can be interpreted as investments in the other agents' human capital (e.g., training).

Definition 12 *Cooperative investments are purely cooperative if $v_i(\hat{x}, a, \theta) = \bar{v}_i(\hat{x}, a_{-i}, \theta) + \psi_i(a_i)$ for all i.*

---

35. See Whinston (2003) for a discussion of issues involved in testing Hart and Moore's theory against the transaction cost economics theory of integration (Williamson 1975, 1979, 1985; Klein et al. 1978), and of the sensitivity of Hart and Moore's theory to the nature of investments.

36. The underinvestment result also extends to bilateral cooperative investment when investments are strategic complements. However, strategic complementarity is harder to ensure when agents' disagreement payoffs depend on both their own and others' investments.

With purely cooperative investments, each agent i's payoff in the induced static game when there are no externalities from access to assets takes the form:

$$U_i(\hat{x}, a) = E_\theta \big[(1 - \lambda_i) \, \bar{v}_i(\hat{x}_i, a_{-i}, \theta) - \lambda_i \bar{v}_{-i}(\hat{x}_{-i}, a_i, \theta) + \lambda_i S(a, \theta) \big]$$

$$+ (1 - \lambda_i) \, \psi_i(a_i) - \lambda_i \psi_i(a_i) \, .$$

Thus, with purely cooperative investments, agent i's investment incentives are affected only by the other agent's property rights $\hat{x}_{-i}$, not his own. Moreover, when agent i's investment is asset specific, so that $v_{-i}(\hat{x}_{-i}, a_i, \theta)$ has increasing differences in $(\hat{x}_{-i}, a_i)$, his investment incentives are increased by taking assets away from agent $-i$. Therefore, with purely cooperative investments, all agents' investment incentives are maximized at once with joint ownership, and we have the following proposition.[37]

Proposition 12   *If investments are asset-specific, relationship-specific, purely cooperative, and strategic complements; there are no externalities from access to assets; and the set $\hat{X}^{**}$ of second-best property rights is nonempty, then joint ownership is an optimal control structure, that is, $0 \in \hat{X}^{**}$.*

Intuitively, as first shown by Che and Hausch (1999), an agent's incentive to make a purely cooperative investment is enhanced rather than reduced by bargaining, because the bargaining surplus is sensitive to her investment, whereas her own disagreement payoff is not. Minimizing externalities at the disagreement payoffs now often corresponds to minimizing the disagreement payoffs and maximizing the renegotiation surplus, in contrast to the findings of Propositions 5 and 10. For instance, in Example 3 when $V_P'(a) > V_A'(a) = 0$ for all a, it is optimal to specify agent ownership and induce renegotiation, rather than specifying the ex post efficient principal ownership. (One way to think about this is that the investment's direct externality under principal ownership exceeds its bargaining externality under agent ownership.) Note also that the principal does not optimally own the asset in this example, even though she is indispensable to it.[38]

3.4.3. Violation of Relationship-Specific Investments: Overinvestment in External Investments

Next, consider the assumption of relationship specificity. Recall that relationship-specific self-investment by agent i increases the efficient surplus $S(a, \theta)$ by more than it increases the

---

37. Note, however, that if only one agent invests, the same optimal outcome as under joint ownership is sustained by making him the owner of all the assets, because this takes access away from the other agents. Thus, Proposition 9 does extend to purely cooperative investments. It also extends to cooperative investments that are not purely cooperative: in that case agent i's investment incentives increase both when assets are taken away from agent $-i$ and when assets are given to agent i.

Joint ownership also proves to be optimal in some settings in which investments are cooperative but not purely cooperative—see the example in Hart (1995: 68).

38. Even when there is no physical asset, an exclusive right can sometimes be created to enhance efficiency with cooperative investments. For instance, in Example 3, agent ownership could just be the agent's right to exclude the principal from collecting $V_P(a)$ (so the agent may have no direct benefit from the asset: $V_A(a) \equiv 0$). When given this right to exclude, the agent is able to capture some share of her investment return through bargaining, which enhances her investment incentives. Marvel (1982) offers this motive as a justification for exclusive dealing contracts between manufacturers and retailers. See also Segal and Whinston (2000).

agent's disagreement payoff $v_i(\hat{x}, a_i, \theta)$. For an investment that violates this property, take Example 4 (in which $V_P(a)$ and $Y(a)$ are independent of a, so the agent's investment is a self-investment) and suppose that principal ownership is always ex post optimal and that $V_A'(a) > 0$. Then under agent ownership the agent's investment increases his disagreement payoff but does not increase the efficient surplus, leading to a negative, rather than positive, bargaining externality and inducing overinvestment. Because the investment is asset specific, it is reduced by taking the asset away from the agent, the only investing party, in contrast to Proposition 9. In fact, in this example principal ownership induces efficient investment by the agent.

As other examples of this point, Holmström and Tirole (1991) consider negotiated transfer pricing and show that it may be optimal to ban trade outside the firm to reduce rent-seeking investment. Bolton and Whinston (1993) show that vertical integration can result in overinvestment in an integrated downstream division. This motivation can also lead to exclusive dealing contracts being adopted to induce retailers not to allocate effort or investment to other manufacturers (see e.g., Areeda and Kaplow 1988; and Segal and Whinston 2000).[39]

3.4.4. Violation of Asset-Specific Investments: Ownership Reduces Investment Incentives

In contrast to the examples considered previously, we can also have examples in which the marginal benefit of investment is higher when an agent does not own an asset than when he does. For instance, in Example 4, we may have $V_A'(a) < 0$ if the investment reduces the agent's need for the asset. In such cases, investment is increased by taking the asset away from the agent, that is, by specifying principal ownership ($\hat{x} = 0$). (Recall also that principal ownership sustains efficient investment if it is ex post efficient given this investment.)

3.5. Property Rights with Coalitional Bargaining

Here we enrich the model to include coalitional bargaining with more than two agents, as in the model of Hart and Moore (1990). Now, what each coalition $T \subseteq \mathcal{N}$ can achieve matters, not just individual agents' disagreement payoffs and the total surplus achievable by the grand coalition $\mathcal{N}$, as we have assumed until now.[40] Our exposition generalizes Hart and Moore's framework in several dimensions.

We begin by defining the value of each coalition T, that is, how much joint surplus it can achieve through efficient negotiation by itself, without outsiders. This value is denoted by $S_T(\hat{x}, a, \theta)$, and we assume that $S_{\mathcal{N}}(\hat{x}, a, \theta) = S(a, \theta)$ and $S_{\varnothing}(\hat{x}, a, \theta) = 0$.[41] Under standard cooperative game theory, these values are assumed to be independent of what agents outside of T choose to do. For example, this assumption rules out common ownership in the

---

39. Other examples of overinvestment in external investments and the resulting optimality of taking assets away from investing parties can be found in Rajan and Zingales (1998) and Cai (2003). Schmitz (2006) makes a related point, except that the investment is in information about the outside option, and the resulting renegotiation proceeds under asymmetric information and yields inefficiencies (as in the model studied in Section 4.1).

40. We note that in Hart and Moore (1990), x are investments and a are assets, the reverse of our notation here. To maintain comparability to the rest of the chapter, we maintain our earlier notation.

41. For example, these coalitional values could be derived as follows: letting $X_T(\hat{x}) \subseteq X$ denote the set of allocations that can be attained with cooperation of members of coalition T under property rights $\hat{x}$, the cooperative value of this coalition is $S_T(\hat{x}, a, \theta) = \sup_{x \in X_T(\hat{x})} \sum_{i \in T} v_i(x, a, \theta)$.

tragedy of the commons, where the agents' actions have externalities on each other, but it permits joint ownership in which neither agent can access the asset without the other's permission.[42]

Hart and Moore suppose that coalitional bargaining yields Shapley value payoffs. Here we extend their results to general random-order bargaining payoffs. To do so, we define $M_T^i(\hat{x}, a, \theta) = S_{T \cup \{i\}}(\hat{x}, a, \theta) - S_T(\hat{x}, a, \theta)$ to be agent i's marginal contribution when added to coalition T. Let Π denote the set of orderings of $\mathcal{N}$ and, for each ordering $\pi \in \Pi$ and each agent i, let π^i denote the set of agents who come before agent i in ordering π. Agent i's bargaining payoff is assumed to be a weighted average of her marginal contributions to the preceding agents in different orderings, with the weights given by a probability distribution $\alpha \in \Delta(\Pi)$ over orderings:[43]

$$U_i(\hat{x}, a) = E_\theta \left[\sum_{\pi \in \Pi} \alpha(\pi) \, M_{\pi^i}^i(\hat{x}, a, \theta) \right].$$

The Shapley value, for example, corresponds to the uniform distribution over orderings: $\alpha(\pi) = 1/N!$ for all π.

We next generalize the notion of relationship-specific investments to the coalitional setting.

Definition 13   *Investments are relationship specific if, for each i, $j \neq i$, and coalition $T \subseteq \mathcal{N}$, the marginal contribution $M_T^i(\hat{x}, a, \theta)$ is nondecreasing in a_j.*

This definition states that an agent's investments increase other agents' marginal contributions. For example, when specialized to the case of self-investments and $N = 2$, an agent's investment increases surplus more than it increases her disagreement payoff, as in our earlier definition. Definition 13 allows, however, for cooperative investments (e.g., it allows agent j's investment to increase agent i's marginal contributions to coalitions that do not include j). We can now state a result on underinvestment.[44]

Proposition 13   *Suppose investments are relationship specific and are strategic complements.[45] Then $A^\circ(\hat{x})$ is below $A^*(\hat{x})$ in the weak set order.*

42. For examples of bargaining with externalities, see Section 4.2.

43. This bargaining solution can be characterized either axiomatically (Weber 1988) or with a noncooperative bargaining process, in which, for each realized random ordering, agent i makes a take-it-or-leave-it offer to the group of players π^i that precede her.

Brandenburger and Stuart (2007a,b) study a similar model in which each agent instead expects to receive a weighted average of her highest and lowest payoffs in the core of the cooperative bargaining game (which is nonempty in their settings). Their examples of underinvestment are similar to those of Hart and Moore (1990), but they do not study the effects of property rights.

44. Hart and Moore (1990) also prove uniqueness of equilibrium investments given any property rights allocation. This follows if the coalitional values are concave in investments and bargaining is given by the Shapley value.

45. Sufficient conditions for investments to be strategic complements in the induced static game are that for each i, A_i is a compact subset of $\mathbb{R}$, and for each $j \neq i$ and each coalition $T \subseteq \mathcal{N}$, the marginal contribution $M_T^i(\hat{x}, a, \theta)$ is equicontinuous in a and has increasing differences in (a_i, a_j). This assumption generalizes Hart and Moore's (1990) assumption A4.

Proof   The relationship-specificity assumption implies positive externalities in the induced static investment game, so the result obtains by Proposition 3.

Note that Proposition 13 generalizes Hart and Moore's (1990) underinvestment result by not restricting to self-investments (their assumption A3). In particular, the proposition incorporates the underinvestment result we discussed for cooperative investments in Section 3.4.2.

Now consider optimal asset ownership. Following Hart and Moore (1990), we define the set of feasible property rights, which Hart and Moore call "control structures":

Definition 14   *A control structure over K assets is a vector $\hat{x} \in \{0, 1\}^{2^N \times K}$ having the following properties:*

(i). *$\hat{x}_{Tk}$ is nondecreasing in the size of coalition T,*

(ii). *$\hat{x}_{Tk} + \hat{x}_{(N \setminus T)k} \leq 1$, and*

(iii). *$\hat{x}_{Nk} = 1$ for all k.*

The interpretation of $\hat{x}_{Tk} = 1$ is that coalition T has access to asset k. Restriction (ii) means that an asset cannot be accessed by both a coalition and its complement, which rules out access externalities. Property (iii) means that the grand coalition can access anything. Note that, in general, $\hat{x}$ assigns coalitional rights as well as individual rights. As a special case, we can have $\hat{x}_T^k = \max_{i \in T} \hat{x}_{\{i\}}^k$ for all T; that is, a coalition can only access assets that could be accessed by one of its individual members. However, we can also have $\hat{x}_T^k > \max_{i \in T} \hat{x}_{\{i\}}^k$ (the reverse strict inequality cannot hold by property (i)). For example, with majority voting, a coalition of more than $N/2$ members can access an asset even when no individual member could do so.

The next three definitions generalize concepts introduced earlier to the coalitional setting.

Definition 15   *There are no externalities from access to assets if, for all coalitions $T \subseteq N$, $S_T(\hat{x}, a, \theta)$ does not depend on $\hat{x}_{-T}$.*

Definition 16   *Investments are self-investments if, for all coalitions $T \subseteq N$, $S_T(\hat{x}, a, \theta)$ does not depend on a_{-T}.*

Definition 17   *Investments are asset specific if, for all coalitions $T \subseteq N$, $S_T(\hat{x}, a, \theta)$ has increasing differences in $(\hat{x}_T, a)$.*

We can now state the following proposition.

Proposition 14   *If only agent i makes an investment, $A_i \subseteq \mathbb{R}$, his investment is an asset- and relationship-specific self-investment, there are no externalities from access to assets, and $\hat{X}^{**} \neq \varnothing$, then it is optimal for agent i to own all of the assets, that is, to set $\hat{x}_T^{**} = 1$ if and only if $i \in T$.*

We omit the proof, which is similar to that of Proposition 9. We could likewise generalize Proposition 10. Note that in deriving these results, Hart and Moore's (1990) concavity assumptions, A1 and A2, are not needed.

3.6. Property Mechanisms

Property rights are simple (i.e., incomplete) contracts, which are often not sufficient to attain the first best. This raises the following natural question: is it possible to achieve an improvement with more complicated contracts? As one example, instead of a simple (noncontingent) property right, the parties might specify an option-to-own contract that gives one party the right to buy an asset ex post at a specified price. One could imagine even more complicated contracts, in which all parties have contractual choices. Formally, a contract then defines a message game in which the parties send messages and the outcome is determined by these messages. Can an improvement be achieved with such message games? In cases in which the answer is "no," this offers a foundation for incomplete contracts.

3.6.1. Mechanism Design without Renegotiation

The hold-up model assumes that investments a and uncertainty θ are observable but not verifiable, so a contract cannot condition upon them. In particular, it is impossible to stipulate efficient investments in the contract. However, in a contractual message game, the equilibrium outcome can indirectly depend on nonverifiable information, such as investments, through messages sent in the game. This dependence in turn can improve investment incentives and perhaps even sustain first-best investments.

For the simplest possible example, consider the game in which the agents must report all information (a, θ) and are severely penalized when the reports do not agree. Truthful reporting constitutes a Nash equilibrium of this game. However, this game has two obvious problems. One is that the penalties may be renegotiated by the agents. For now we abstract from this problem, assuming that renegotiation outside the contractual framework is impossible (but see Section 3.6.2 for a discussion of renegotiation). The other problem is that the game has "bad" equilibria in which the agents coordinate on reporting a false state. This problem, however, can be avoided. To eliminate bad equilibria, the agents can be made to play a somewhat more sophisticated game, and we can use an equilibrium refinement. In particular, by asking the parties to play an extensive-form game and using the refinement of subgame-perfect equilibrium as proposed by Moore and Repullo (1988), it is possible to sustain efficient investments in the unique subgame-perfect equilibrium.

For a simple example of such subgame-perfect implementation, consider any setting in which only agent 1 invests and his investment has no harmful direct externalities at $(\hat{x}, a^*)$ for some property rights allocation $\hat{x}$ and some first-best investment $a^* \in A^*$ (e.g., it could just be self-investment). Suppose the initial contract specifies that the agents play the following two-stage **ultimatum game** ex post, and that renegotiation of this mechanism is impossible:

Stage 1. Agent 1 names an outcome (x, t).

Stage 2. Agent 2 accepts or rejects.

If agent 2 accepts, the outcome named by agent 1 is implemented; otherwise, property right allocation $\hat{x}$ is implemented.

In the unique subgame-perfect equilibrium of this game, a surplus-maximizing outcome results, and agent 2 receives his reservation payoff. In effect, this game introduces a contract-specified renegotiation that gives agent 1 all the bargaining power. Thus, according to Proposition 7, agent 1 will invest efficiently ex ante.[46]

A common informal justification of incomplete contracts appeals to the parties' inability to foresee future allocations x or contingencies θ ex ante. However, at the same time parties are still assumed to be rational, foreseeing their future payoffs and choosing investments optimally. One way to reconcile these assumptions, proposed by Maskin and Tirole (1999), is that the parties foresee their payoffs from all possible future contingencies and actions but cannot describe them in an ex ante contract due to not yet having the "names" for them. In this light, note that the ultimatum game can be described ex ante without naming any specific ex post decisions or contingencies. Maskin and Tirole generalize this observation, showing that any mechanism can be described ex ante without naming actions or contingencies, letting the agents fill in these names in the ex post message game. Thus, the parties' inability to describe future actions or contingencies ex ante does not impose any additional restrictions on what can be implemented in a contractual message game.[47]

In sum, even if unable to describe future contingencies and actions ex ante, parties who can foresee future payoffs can quite generally achieve efficiency with a sufficiently complicated contract, provided that renegotiation can be prevented.

3.6.2. Mechanism Design with Renegotiation

In reality, the parties may be able to renegotiate the contractual outcome when it is inefficient. This possibility can have dramatic effects on what can be achieved with complicated contracts. As an illustration, note that the ultimatum game prescribes an inefficient outcome $\hat{x}$ after agent 2 rejects the offer. Suppose that this outcome is always renegotiated to an efficient outcome, with agent 2 receiving share λ_2 of the renegotiation surplus. Anticipating such renegotiation, agent 2 will reject any stage-1 offer leaving him a smaller share of renegotiation surplus than λ_2. Thus, the ultimatum game followed by renegotiation yields exactly the same outcome as does a noncontingent contract specifying property right $\hat{x}$ followed by renegotiation.

Segal and Whinston (2002) examine the power of general two-sided mechanisms (message games) under the assumption of Maskin and Moore (1999) that any inefficient outcome prescribed by the mechanism will be followed by efficient renegotiation. The role of the mechanism is thus to affect the division of surplus between the agents, which in turn affects the parties' ex ante investments. In particular, Segal and Whinston (2002) identify conditions under which a mechanism cannot improve upon simple (noncontingent) property rights followed by exogenous renegotiation.

Segal and Whinston's analysis can be explained heuristically as follows. Suppose that there is no uncertainty θ and that only one agent i chooses an investment $a \in A = [\underline{a}, \bar{a}] \subseteq \mathbb{R}$.

---

46. More generally, with quasi-linear utilities, using the three-stage mechanism of Moore and Repullo (1988), the agents' payoffs can be made to depend in any manner on the state (a, θ), provided that agents' preferences vary across states. For example, with self-investments, the parties can always sustain the first best.

47. However, Segal (1999a: 68–72, 2012) identifies some settings in which an optimal mechanism requires filling in the names of a large number of possible ex post actions (unlike in the ultimatum game). In such settings, with a constraint on the length of ex post communication, the inability to name actions ex ante may indeed constrain contractual mechanisms and prevent any improvement upon an incomplete contract, such as the null contract or an authority contract in which one agent describes the outcome.

Following the investment, the two agents can send messages, and the mechanism prescribes an outcome (x, t_1, t_2) conditional on the messages, but it is always renegotiated according to the Nash bargaining solution. Let $V_i(a)$ denote agent i's equilibrium utility in the mechanism following any investment choice a. (It is uniquely defined by the Minimax Theorem, because the mechanism defines a constant-sum game due to efficient renegotiation.) Segal and Whinston (2002) show that, provided that the agents' utilities satisfy some smoothness conditions and the space $\hat{X}$ of property rights is connected, $V_i(a)$ is differentiable almost everywhere, and its derivative takes the form

$$V_i'(a) = \frac{\partial u_i(x(a), a)}{\partial a} \tag{11}$$

for some allocation rule $x(\cdot) : A \to \hat{X}$. For mechanisms in which only one party sends a message (i.e., option mechanisms), this result follows from Mirrlees's (1971) classical Envelope-Theorem characterization of incentive compatibility (see also Milgrom and Segal 2002), and in addition, the allocation rule $x(\cdot)$ must then be nondecreasing if $u_i(\cdot)$ has increasing differences. Segal and Whinston (2002) show that the same formula must still hold for two-sided mechanisms, although the allocation rule can now be arbitrary.[48]

To see how (11) implies the optimality of simple contracts, note that if a mechanism sustains investment $a^\circ \in (\underline{a}, \bar{a})$, agent i's utility must satisfy the first-order condition $V_i'(a^\circ) = 0$. By (11), this first-order condition is preserved if we replace the mechanism with the noncontingent property rights allocation $\hat{x} = x(a^\circ)$. Thus, provided that agent i's payoff is sufficiently concave in a, this noncontingent property rights allocation also sustains investment a°. Segal and Whinston (2002) show that the optimality of simple (noncontingent) property rights extends to a number of cases with uncertainty θ and multidimensional and/or two-sided investments, provided that the investments affect post-renegotiation payoffs through a one-dimensional state. They also identify additional settings in which noncontingent contracts can be improved upon by more complex contracts.

3.6.3. Irreversible Options and Renegotiation Design

Segal and Whinston's (2002) analysis of when mechanisms cannot strengthen incentives over noncontingent property rights hinges on the assumption that renegotiation can always occur after the mechanism is played. Noldeke and Schmidt (1995), Watson (2007), and Buzard and Watson (2012) instead consider cases in which one of the parties faces a technologically irreversible verifiable choice, and they show that this irreversibility can often be exploited to sustain first-best investments. For example, in the ultimatum game, suppose that agent 2's acceptance or rejection involves an irreversible choice of allocation x (e.g., there may be a deadline after which the asset is worthless). In that case, effective renegotiation is possible only

---

48. For continuous mechanisms, $x(a)$ is the allocation prescribed by the mechanism in equilibrium in state a. In general, however, $x(a)$ is a limit of off-equilibrium decisions prescribed by the mechanism when agents disagree but send reports close to a.

before agent 2's choice but not after. But note that renegotiation before agent 2's choice has no power, because her equilibrium choice is efficient.[49]

Some other papers assume that while each agent has an irreversible option, she also has the choice to postpone exercising her option and continue bargaining (i.e., her option can be viewed as an "American" rather than "European" option). Such postponable irreversible options can be used to shift the division of bargaining surplus, mimicking the outcome of the ultimatum game. To understand the effect of such options, consider the following noncooperative infinite-horizon bargaining game, which is played ex post following the choice of investments a and the realization of uncertainty θ. Let $\bar{S} = S\,(a, \theta)$ denote the maximum available ex post surplus, and suppose that the parties have so-called outside option payoffs (o_1, o_2) and so-called disagreement payoffs (d_1, d_2), such that $\max\,\{o_1 + o_2, d_1 + d_2\} \leq \bar{S}$.

> **Outside option bargaining game:** In odd periods, agent 1 is the proposer and agent 2 the responder. In even periods, agent 2 is the proposer and agent 1 the responder. In each period, there are two stages:
>
> Stage 1. The proposer offers a new contract, describing payoffs (s_1, s_2) to the two parties, with $s_1 + s_2 \leq \bar{S}$.
>
> Stage 2. The responder accepts, rejects, or exercises her outside option. If the responder accepts, the game ends, and the agents receive payoffs (s_1, s_2). If the responder exercises her outside option, the game ends, and the agents receive payoffs (o_1, o_2). Otherwise, with probability $\delta \in (0,\ 1)$ the game proceeds to the next period, and with the complementary probability the game terminates, and the agents receive payoffs (d_1, d_2).[50]

Sutton (1986) shows that the unique subgame-perfect equilibrium expected payoffs of this game are

$$(u_1, u_2) =$$

$$\begin{cases} (e_1, e_2) = \left(d_1 + \frac{1}{1+\delta}[\bar{S} - d_1 - d_2]\,,\, d_2 + \frac{\delta}{1+\delta}[\bar{S} - d_1 - d_2]\right), & \text{if } (o_1, o_2) \leq (e_1, e_2)\,, \\ (o_1, \bar{S} - o_1)\,, & \text{if } o_1 > e_1, \\ (\bar{S} - o_2, o_2)\,, & \text{if } o_2 > e_2. \end{cases}$$

---

49. Rubinstein and Wolinsky (1992) study a model of message games that proceed concurrently with renegotiation and find that if renegotiation occurs only after a one-period delay, then the same outcomes can be implemented as when renegotiation can only precede the game.

50. Equivalently, we can imagine that the game never terminates, but the agents are impatient and discount their future payoffs with discount factor δ, and that they receive flow payoffs $((1 - \delta)\,d_1, (1 - \delta)\,d_2)$ in every period before an agreement is reached or an outside option is exercised.

Allowing the proposer to exercise her outside option before proposing would not affect the game's equilibrium outcome (the option would not bind). Allowing the proposer to exercise her outside option after her proposal is rejected would give rise to multiplicity of subgame-perfect equilibria. In that case, by switching between equilibria to punish investment deviations, first-best investments can be sustained, as noted by Evans (2008). Note, however, that this finding relies on the parties being able to coordinate on the right continuation equilibrium, much as the Nash equilibrium considered at the start of Section 3.6.1 did.

In words, the parties split the renegotiation surplus over the disagreement point in proportion $\left(\frac{1}{1+\delta}, \frac{\delta}{1+\delta}\right)$ if neither agent's outside option binds. If one agent's outside option binds, he receives his outside option payoff, and the other agent receives the rest of the surplus (both parties' outside options cannot bind at once, because $e_1 + e_2 = \bar{S} \geq o_1 + o_2$). This conclusion is known as the *outside option principle*. As $\delta \to 1$, the first-mover advantage disappears, and the renegotiation surplus is split equally when the outside options do not bind.

Different papers make different assumptions about the nature of the agents' outside options and disagreement payoffs. First note that if both the outside options and the disagreement payoffs are given by the initial property rights, so that $(o_1, o_2) = (d_1, d_2)$, then outside options do not bind, and each agent i's equilibrium payoff is $u_i = \bar{v}_i + \frac{1}{2}(\bar{S} - d_1 - d_2)$ as $\delta \to 1$. This is the standard noncooperative foundation for the Nash bargaining solution used in our previous model of renegotiation (Stahl 1972; Rubinstein 1982).

In contrast, Hart and Moore (1988), MacLeod and Malcomson (1993) and Aghion et al. (1994) examine situations in which the initial contract can have distinct effects on the parties' disagreement outcome and their outside options.[51] One common feature of these papers is that it is possible to make one agent's—say, agent 2's—outside option very attractive relative to his disagreement payoff by entitling him to a large payment for exercising this option.[52] As a result, agent 2's outside option binds, and letting x^o and p^o denote the resulting allocation and payment, respectively, outside option bargaining gives agent 1 the payoff $S(a, \theta) - v_2(x^o, a, \theta) - p^o$, mimicking the outcome of the ultimatum game with property rights allocation x^o. By Proposition 7, this outcome induces agent 1 to invest efficiently, provided that his investment has no direct externalities at x^o. This is true, in particular, in the case of self-investments. Furthermore, in Aghion et al. (1994), the outside option allocation x^o can be stipulated in the initial contract in a way that also provides agent 2 with the incentive to make an efficient self-investment, resulting in a first-best outcome.[53] In contrast, in Hart and Moore (1988) and MacLeod and Malcomson (1993), achieving the first best is generally impossible, because the contract cannot affect the outside-option allocation x^o (which represents either no trade or trade with outsiders) and can only affect the associated monetary payment.

Chiu (1998) and De Meza and Lockwood (1998) apply the same approach to examine the role of asset ownership under outside-option bargaining. They assume that asset ownership gives the owner an irreversible outside option to use her assets. Furthermore, they assume that asset use is not verifiable, so the exercise of outside options cannot be influenced by monetary rewards, such as financial hostages or breach penalties. In this case, one agent's outside option can still be made to bind by giving her the ownership of a sufficiently valuable asset, which

51. MacLeod and Malcomson (1993) postulate the outside option principle, whereas Hart and Moore (1988) postulate a noncooperative renegotiation game that differs from the one described above but yields the same outcome.

52. In Aghion and et al. (1994), the payment is interpreted as a financial hostage that agent 2 is entitled to receive back from agent 1; in Hart and Moore (1988) and MacLeod and Malcomson (1993), the payment is a breach penalty imposed on agent 1 by a court that cannot observe which party exercised its outside option.

53. The same result is obtained by Chung (1991), who allows the contract to shift bargaining power to one party rather than deriving this shift from the outside option principle.

induces the other agent to make an efficient self-investment, in contrast to the underinvestment that obtains when her outside option does not bind. This conclusion reverses the key finding of Hart and Moore (1990) that an agent's investment incentives are raised by asset ownership (see our Proposition 9). Also, in contrast to Hart and Moore (1990), the conclusion does not depend on whether the investment is asset specific. For example, the asset could be fully general (e.g., equivalent to a financial hostage). What is important is that its ownership gives an attractive unilateral option that forestalls any subsequent renegotiation.

The applicability of these theories depends on the availability of irreversible unilateral decisions. For example, if the use of an asset requires some irreversible modifications that rule out any alternative uses, we can think of this use as an outside option. If, instead, an agent can use the asset without modifying it while continuing to bargain with others regarding its alternative uses, then asset ownership defines the disagreement point, as in Hart and Moore's (1990) theory. In that case, option contracts are of limited benefit and often cannot improve upon simple property rights.

4. Property Rights and Bargaining Inefficiencies

The allocation of property rights can matter, even in the absence of noncontractible actions or investments, when these rights affect the efficiency of agreements reached by the parties. As noted in Section 1, in the simple allocation benchmark in which renegotiation is impossible, optimal property rights simply allocate assets to agents who value them the most in expectation. The same conclusion obtains if bargaining completely breaks down with an exogenous probability and is perfectly efficient with the complementary probability. However, a richer model of property rights emerges when property rights affect the probability and the extent of bargaining inefficiencies.

In this section we discuss the impact of property rights with two sources of bargaining imperfections—asymmetric information and contracting externalities. We can think of the parties bargaining either over a final allocation (as in stage 4 of the model described in Section 1) or over initial property rights (as in stage 1). In the latter interpretation, the parties' payoffs should be viewed as reduced-form payoffs that account for the effects of property rights on future noncontractible investments and/or bargaining. The analysis then shows how bargaining outcomes may differ from the optimal property rights identified in Sections 2 and 3. In such cases, legal rules defining ex ante property rights (prior to stage 1) and/or restricting the parties' abilities to strike bargains may affect efficiency, in contrast to the assertion of the Coase Theorem.

4.1. Asymmetric Information

One important reason negotiations may break down is asymmetric information (for another discussion of this issue, see Farrell 1987).

Example 7 Two agents may each use an asset for production. Ex post efficiency requires that the asset be owned by the agent who can use it most productively. Each agent i's value from use θ_i is uncertain initially, is independently drawn from a uniform distribution on $[0, 1]$, and is known only by agent i.

The celebrated Myerson-Satterthwaite Theorem (Myerson and Satterthwaite 1983) states that efficient bargaining is impossible if the asset is initially owned by one agent.[54] Formally, their result follows from the finding that no efficient, incentive-compatible, interim individually rational, and budget-balanced mechanism exists in this setting, because any efficient (voluntary) bargaining procedure must have these four properties. Intuitively, efficient revelation of information requires that each agent appropriate the whole gains from trade, which is impossible. When each agent must instead share the gains from trade with the other agent, he has an incentive to understate these gains. Thus, the initial owner—the potential seller of the asset—has an incentive to overstate his valuation in negotiations, while the potential buyer of the asset has an incentive to understate his valuation. These incentives for misrepresentation inevitably lead to breakdowns in bargaining, where the asset remains in the hands of the agent with the lower value.

In contrast, efficient bargaining may be possible in this example for other property rights allocations. Cramton et al. (1987) consider the case in which property rights are divisible: for example, either the asset is perfectly divisible (with agent i's property right providing him with payoff $\theta_i x_i$ when he owns fraction $x_i \in [0, 1]$) or randomized ownership is possible (where x_i is the probability of agent i owning the asset (with $x_1 + x_2 = 1$)).[55] They show that efficient bargaining is possible (i.e., there is an efficient, incentive-compatible, individually rational, and budget-balanced mechanism) provided that the agents start from an allocation of property rights (x_1, x_2) that is close enough to the equal allocation (1/2, 1/2). Intuitively, intermediate ownership levels reduce the incentives for misrepresentation, because each agent does not know whether he will ultimately end up as a seller or a buyer of the asset.

4.1.1. A Characterization of When Efficient Bargaining Is Possible

We now formulate a model to investigate more generally which property rights permit efficient bargaining (generalizing the insight of Cramton et al. 1987) and which do not (generalizing the insight of Myerson and Satterthwaite 1983). The model covers as special cases a large number of settings considered in the literature.

Consider a set $\mathcal{N}$ of N of expected-utility maximizing agents whose utilities are quasi-linear in money. The agents' privately observed types are independently distributed random variables $\tilde{\theta}_1, \ldots, \tilde{\theta}_N$ with values in the sets $\Theta_1, \ldots, \Theta_N$.[56] The state space is thus $\Theta = \Pi_i \Theta_i$. The utility of each agent i is given by $u_i(x, \theta_i) + t_i$, where $t_i \in \mathbb{R}$ is the payment to the agent, $x \in X$ is the final allocation, and $\theta_i \in \Theta_i$ is the agent's type.[57] The total surplus given allocation x and state θ is $s(x, \theta) = \sum_i u_i(x, \theta_i)$, and the maximal available surplus in state θ is

---

54. The result holds more generally: efficient bargaining is impossible when each agent i's value is drawn from a strictly increasing distribution function F_i on some set $[\underline{\theta}_i, \overline{\theta}_i]$ and $(\underline{\theta}_1, \overline{\theta}_1) \cap (\underline{\theta}_2, \overline{\theta}_2) \neq \varnothing$.

55. The agents must be able to bargain with each other before learning the outcome of the randomization.

56. Riordan (1990) and Schmidt (1996) assume that property rights directly affect the information structure, but here we assume that this structure is independent of property rights. In a hybrid model, Schmitz (2006) endogenizes the effect of property rights on noncontractible efforts to acquire private information.

57. Formally, we assume that the spaces $X, \Theta_1, \ldots, \Theta_N$ are measurable, that X is a subset of a convex topological space, and that the functions $u_i : X \times \Theta_i \to \mathbb{R}$ are measurable and uniformly bounded (i.e., $\sup_{i, x \in X, \theta_i \in \Theta_i} |u_i(x, \theta_i)| < \infty$). The last two assumptions ensure that expectations exist and that the infima below are finite.

$S(\theta) = \max_{x \in X} s(x, \theta)$. An allocation rule $x^* : \Theta \to X$ is *efficient* if $s\left(x^*(\theta), \theta\right) = S(\theta)$ for all $\theta \in \Theta$. Throughout we shall assume that an efficient allocation rule $x^*(\cdot)$ exists.

Following Myerson and Satterthwaite (1983), the literature has adopted the following definition.

Definition 18 *The property rights allocation $\hat{x} \in X$ permits efficient bargaining if there exists a Bayesian incentive-compatible and interim individually rational mechanism implementing an efficient allocation rule in which the total payment to the agents is zero in all states.*

By the revelation principle, to see whether efficient bargaining is possible given an initial property rights allocation $\hat{x}$, we can focus on direct revelation mechanisms $\langle x^*, \tau \rangle$ with an efficient allocation rule $x^*(\cdot)$ and a payment rule $\tau : \Theta \to \mathbb{R}^N$. The Bayesian incentive compatibility and interim individual rationality constraints can be written as

$$E_{\tilde{\theta}_{-i}}\left[u_i(x^*(\theta_i, \tilde{\theta}_{-i}), \theta_i) + \tau_i(\theta_i, \tilde{\theta}_{-i})\right] \geq E_{\tilde{\theta}_{-i}}\left[u_i(x^*(\theta_i', \tilde{\theta}_{-i}), \theta_i) + \tau_i(\theta_i', \tilde{\theta}_{-i})\right] \quad \text{(IC)}$$

$$\text{for all } \theta_i, \theta_i' \in \Theta_i$$

$$E_{\tilde{\theta}_{-i}}\left[u_i(x^*(\theta_i, \tilde{\theta}_{-i}), \theta_i) + \tau_i(\theta_i, \tilde{\theta}_{-i})\right] \geq u_i(\hat{x}, \theta_i) \quad \text{for all } \theta_i \in \Theta_i. \quad \text{(IR)}$$

Note that the property rights allocation $\hat{x}$ enters the IR constraints, determining agents' payoffs if bargaining breaks down (by an agent opting out of the mechanism).

It will prove convenient to focus on mechanisms with payments of the following form:

$$\tau_i(\theta | \hat{x}, \hat{\theta}_i) = \sum_{j \neq i} u_j\left(x^*(\theta), \theta_j\right) - K_i(\hat{x}, \hat{\theta}_i), \quad (12)$$

where $\hat{\theta}_i$ is some fixed type of agent i, and

$$K_i(\hat{x}, \hat{\theta}_i) = E_{\tilde{\theta}_{-i}}[S(\hat{\theta}_i, \tilde{\theta}_{-i})] - u_i(\hat{x}, \hat{\theta}_i). \quad (13)$$

Note that these payments describe a Vickey-Clarke-Groves mechanism (see Mas-Colell et al. 1995; 876–882). The variable portion of the payment, $\sum_{j \neq i} u_j\left(x^*(\theta), \theta_j\right)$, causes each agent i to fully internalize her effect on aggregate surplus, thereby inducing her to announce her true type and implementing the efficient allocation rule $x^*(\cdot)$. The fixed participation fee K_i equals type $\hat{\theta}_i$'s expected gain from participating in the mechanism absent the fixed charge, so it causes that type's IR constraint to hold with equality. If we imagine that there is an intermediary in

---

For analyses in which types are interdependent, see Fieseler et al. (2003), Jehiel and Pauzner (2006), and Segal and Whinston (2011). See Rahman (2010) for a model with correlated types.

charge of this trading process, her expected profit with this mechanism is given by

$$\pi(\hat{x}, \hat{\theta}) = -E\left[\sum_i \tau_i(\tilde{\theta}|\hat{x}, \hat{\theta}_i)\right]$$

$$= \sum_i \{E_{\tilde{\theta}_{-i}}[S(\hat{\theta}_i, \tilde{\theta}_{-i})] - u_i(\hat{x}, \hat{\theta}_i)\} - (N - 1)\, E[S(\tilde{\theta})] \tag{14}$$

$$= \sum_i E_{\tilde{\theta}_{-i}}[S(\hat{\theta}_i, \tilde{\theta}_{-i})] - s(\hat{x}, \hat{\theta}) - (N - 1)\, E[S(\tilde{\theta})]. \tag{15}$$

To ensure that all types participate, the participation fee for each agent i can be at most $\inf_{\hat{\theta}_i \in \Theta} K_i(\hat{x}, \hat{\theta}_i)$, resulting in an expected profit for the intermediary of

$$\overline{\pi}(\hat{x}) = \inf_{\hat{\theta} \in \Theta} \pi(\hat{x}, \hat{\theta}). \tag{16}$$

The sign of this expected profit determines whether property rights allocation $\hat{x}$ permits efficient bargaining.[58]

Lemma 3   *(i) Any property rights allocation $\hat{x} \in X$ at which $\overline{\pi}(\hat{x}) \geq 0$ permits efficient bargaining. (ii) If, moreover, for each agent i, Θ_i is a smoothly connected subset of a Euclidean space, and $u_i(x, \theta_i)$ is differentiable in θ_i with a bounded gradient in θ_i on $X \times \Theta$, then property rights allocation $\hat{x} \in X$ permits efficient bargaining only if $\overline{\pi}(\hat{x}) \geq 0$.*

4.1.2. Impossibility Results
Part (ii) of Lemma 3 can be used to show that efficient bargaining is impossible in some cases. For instance, consider Example 7 when one agent i initially owns the asset. Taking $\hat{\theta} = (\hat{\theta}_i, \hat{\theta}_{-i}) = (1, 0)$—the types who never find it efficient to trade—we have $S(\hat{\theta}_i, \theta_{-i}) = s(\hat{x}, \hat{\theta}) = 1$ for all θ_{-i} and $S(\theta_i, \hat{\theta}_{-i}) = \theta_i$ for all θ_i. Thus, $\overline{\pi}(\hat{x}) \leq \pi(\hat{x}, \hat{\theta}) = E[\tilde{\theta}_i - S(\tilde{\theta})] < 0$ when trade is efficient with a positive probability.

This impossibility argument can be extended to a number of settings where each agent has an "opt-out type," for which it is efficient to keep the agent at his initial property rights allocation regardless of other agents' types (if $N > 2$, it may still be efficient for the others to trade among themselves). Our exposition here draws on and extends unpublished work by Makowski and Ostroy (1989).

Let $X \subseteq \Pi_i X_i$, where $x_i \in X_i$ represents the property rights allocation of agent i, and assume that there are no externalities at property rights $\hat{x}$ (i.e., that $u_i(\hat{x}_i, x_{-i}, \theta_i)$ does not depend on x_{-i}). As in Section 3.5, define the cooperative value of each coalition $T \subseteq \mathcal{N}$ given $\hat{x}$ when

---

58. Versions of this result appear, for example, in Makowski and Mezzetti (1994), Krishna and Perry (1998), Neeman (1999), Williams (1999), Che (2006), Schweizer (2006), Figueroa and Skreta (2008), and Segal and Whinston (2011, 2012b). Part (i) of Lemma 3 can be proven by building a budget-balanced mechanism as suggested by Arrow (1979) and d'Aspremont and Gérard-Varet (1979), and satisfying all agents' participation constraints with appropriate lump-sum transfers. Part (ii) follows from the classical Revenue Equivalence Theorem.

its members' types are θ_T as the maximum joint surplus it can attain while holding outsiders at their status quos:

$$S_T\big(\hat{x}, \theta_T\big) = \sup_{x \in X:\, x_{-T}=\hat{x}_{-T}} \sum_{i \in T} u_i\big(x, \theta_i\big).$$

Definition 19   *Given property rights $\hat{x} \in X$, type $\theta_i^\circ \in \Theta_i$ of agent i is an opt-out type if there is an efficient allocation rule $x^*(\cdot)$ such that $x_i^*\big(\theta_i^\circ, \theta_{-i}\big) = \hat{x}_i$ for all $\theta_{-i} \in \Theta_{-i}$.*

In words, given property rights $\hat{x} = (\hat{x}_i, \hat{x}_{-i})$, agent i's type θ_i° is an opt-out type if regardless of θ_{-i} it is efficient for agent i to get his initial ownership allocation $\hat{x}_i$. Note that when an opt-out type θ_i° exists, this is always the type with the smallest participation surplus $E_{\tilde{\theta}_{-i}}[S(\hat{\theta}_i, \tilde{\theta}_{-i})] - u_i(\hat{x}, \hat{\theta}_i)$ in the above mechanism, often called the agent's "critical type."

Lemma 4   *For a given property rights allocation $\hat{x} \in X$, if type $\theta_i^\circ \in \Theta_i$ is an opt-out type for agent i, then it is also agent i's critical type in any Vickey-Clarke-Groves mechanism.*

Proof   Because θ_i° is an opt-out type, we can write $S\big(\theta_i^\circ, \theta_{-i}\big) = S_{\mathcal{N}\setminus\{i\}}\big(\hat{x}, \theta_{-i}\big) + u_i\big(\hat{x}, \theta_i^\circ\big)$. Thus,

$$S\big(\theta_i^\circ, \theta_{-i}\big) - u_i\big(\hat{x}, \theta_i^\circ\big) = S_{\mathcal{N}\setminus\{i\}}\big(\hat{x}, \theta_{-i}\big) \le S\big(\theta_i, \theta_{-i}\big) - u_i\big(\hat{x}, \theta_i\big) \quad \text{for all } \theta_i,$$

where the inequality follows from the definitions of $S\big(\theta_i, \theta_{-i}\big)$ and $S_{\mathcal{N}\setminus\{i\}}\big(\hat{x}, \theta_{-i}\big)$.[59]

When every agent has an opt-out type $\hat{\theta}_i^\circ$, the profile of these critical types achieves the infimum in (16) (as an examination of (14) shows). In this case, the participation fee for each agent i is $K_i(\hat{x}, \hat{\theta}_i^\circ) = E_{\tilde{\theta}_{-i}}[S(\hat{\theta}_i^\circ, \tilde{\theta}_{-i})] - u_i(\hat{x}, \hat{\theta}_i^\circ) = S_{\mathcal{N}\setminus\{i\}}\big(\hat{x}, \theta_{-i}\big)$. Substituting into (14), we see that when all agents have opt-out types, the expected profits (16) can be written as

$$\overline{\pi}(\hat{x}) = E\left[S(\tilde{\theta}) - \sum_i \big(S(\tilde{\theta}) - S_{\mathcal{N}\setminus\{i\}}(\hat{x}, \tilde{\theta}_{-i})\big) \right]. \tag{17}$$

Thus, each agent i receives a payoff equal to his marginal contribution to the total surplus, $S(\theta) - S_{\mathcal{N}\setminus\{i\}}(\hat{x}, \theta_{-i})$, and the intermediary collects the total surplus net of these marginal contributions. This profit can be shown to be negative, and efficient bargaining impossible, in a number of economic settings in which the core is nonempty.[60]

59. Another way to understand why the opt-out type θ_i° is agent i's critical type is by observing that any other type of agent i could get the opt-out type's expected participation surplus $E_{\tilde{\theta}_{-i}}[\tau_i(\theta_i^\circ, \tilde{\theta}_{-i})]$ by reporting θ_i° and receiving allocation $\hat{x}_i$.

60. Recall that, given an initial property rights allocation $\hat{x}$, $w \in \mathbb{R}^N$ is a core payoff vector in state θ if the payoff of every coalition of players is at least as large as what they can receive on their own; that is, $\sum_{i \in T} w_i \ge S_T(\hat{x}, \theta_T)$ for all $T \subseteq \mathcal{N}$, with equality when $T = \mathcal{N}$.

Proposition 15 *If at property rights allocation $\hat{x} \in X$ there are no externalities, each agent has an opt-out type, and the core is nonempty in all states and contains multiple payoffs with a positive probability, then property rights allocation $\hat{x}$ does not permit efficient bargaining.*

Proof If w is a core payoff vector in state θ, then using the core conditions for $T = \mathcal{N}$ and $T = \mathcal{N}\setminus\{i\}$ for all i, we have

$$\sum_i \left(S(\theta) - S_{\mathcal{N}\setminus\{i\}}(\hat{x}, \theta_{-i}) \right) \geq \sum_i \left(\sum_j w_j - \sum_{j \neq i} w_j \right) = \sum_i w_i = S(\theta) \, .$$

Furthermore, if there exist two distinct core payoff vectors in state θ, then in at least one of them the core inequality holds strictly for $T = \mathcal{N}\setminus\{i\}$ for some i, so the inequality in the above display is strict. Hence, under the assumptions of the proposition, the expected profit in (17) is negative.

The assumptions of Proposition 15 cover many classical economic settings. For one example, consider the double-auction setting of Williams (1999), in which there are N_s sellers with values drawn from a distribution on $[\underline{\theta}_s, \overline{\theta}_s]$ and N_b buyers with values drawn from a distribution on $[\underline{\theta}_b, \overline{\theta}_b]$ with $(\underline{\theta}_b, \overline{\theta}_b) \cap (\underline{\theta}_s, \overline{\theta}_s) \neq \varnothing$. Note that (i) a buyer of type $\underline{\theta}_b$ is an opt-out type if either $\underline{\theta}_b \leq \underline{\theta}_s$ or $N_b > N_s$, and (ii) a seller of type $\overline{\theta}_s$ is an opt-out type if either $\overline{\theta}_s \geq \overline{\theta}_b$ or $N_s > N_b$. Moreover, a competitive equilibrium exists in every state and is not unique with a positive probability. Because a competitive equilibrium is always in the core, Proposition 15 applies when both (i) and (ii) hold.[61]

Proposition 15 also applies to the public good setting of Mailaith and Postlewaite (1990), in which each of N consumers' values is drawn from a distribution on $[0, \overline{\theta}]$, the cost of provision is $c > 0$, and the status quo property right is no provision ($\hat{x}_i = 0$ for all i). Letting $x_i \in \{0, 1\}$ denote whether agent i is given access to the public good and assuming a default of equal cost-sharing among the agents who have access to it, we have $u_i(x, \theta_i) = \theta_i - c/\sum_j x_j$ if $x_i = 1$, and $= 0$ otherwise. Thus, when $\hat{x} = 0$ we have no externalities, and each agent's type 0 is an opt-out type. Note that a Lindahl equilibrium exists in every state and is not unique with a positive probability. Because a Lindahl equilibrium is in the core, Proposition 15 applies.[62]

---

61. The argument can also be extended to show impossibility when $N_b = N_s$. In this case, note that in an efficient allocation, any agent of type below $\underline{\theta} \equiv \max\{\underline{\theta}_s, \underline{\theta}_b\}$ receives an object with probability zero, so she is therefore indistinguishable from type $\underline{\theta}$, and any agent of type above $\overline{\theta} \equiv \min\{\overline{\theta}_s, \overline{\theta}_b\}$ receives an object with probability one, so she is therefore indistinguishable from type $\overline{\theta}$. Therefore, the profit in the mechanism must be the same as if all agents' types were instead distributed on the same interval $[\underline{\theta}, \overline{\theta}]$ (with possible atoms at its endpoints), in which case efficient bargaining is impossible by the argument given in the text.

62. Proposition 15 does not address the extent of bargaining inefficiencies or the form they take. These questions have been studied in a number of papers. Myerson and Satterthwaite (1983) and McKelvey and Page (2002) find that in certain settings, the inefficiencies exhibit a status quo bias: the final allocation lies between the initial and efficient allocations. Other papers examine the dependence of inefficiency on the number of agents. In the double-auction setting, Gresik and Satterthwaite (1989) find that the inefficiency in an ex ante optimal mechanism shrinks to zero as $N_b, N_s \to \infty$. Intuitively, this finding relates to the fact that the core converges (in

4.1.3. Efficiency-Permitting Property Rights Allocations

We now use Lemma 3 to investigate when efficiency is possible and which property rights allocations permit efficient bargaining. Segal and Whinston (2011) establish the following result.

Proposition 16 *Suppose that the total surplus $s(x, \theta)$ is convex in x for all $\theta \in \Theta$ and that $x^* : \Theta \to X$ is an efficient allocation rule. Then the initial property rights allocation $\hat{x} = E[x^*(\tilde{\theta})] \in \hat{X}$, equal to the expected efficient allocation, permits efficient bargaining.*

For example, in the Cramton et al. (1987) model, in which all agents' valuations are drawn from the same distribution and their utilities are linear in the allocation x, the expected efficient allocation involves giving each agent an equal ownership share. But the result applies to cases with asymmetric valuations and to much more general allocation problems. Indeed, the result generalizes several previous results in the literature that establish the existence of an efficiency-permitting property rights allocation (Cramton et al. 1987; Schmitz 2002; Che 2006; Schweizer 2006; Gershkov and Schweinzer 2010; Yenmez 2012) and also points to a natural property rights allocation that achieves this goal: the expected efficient allocation.[63]

To understand the result, recall that—ignoring IR—an efficient ex post allocation can be achieved with a Vickey-Clarke-Groves mechanism. Furthermore, as noted by Arrow (1979) and d'Aspremont and Gérard-Varet (1979), the transfers in this mechanism can be modified to yield a balanced-budget mechanism (the expected externality mechanism) while preserving agents' incentives for truth telling (IC). Observe, however, that one way agent i could lie is by announcing randomly each of his possible types with their true probabilities. Doing so results in a random allocation with the same distribution as the efficient allocation. Because the agent never has an incentive to lie, this random outcome must be worse for every type of agent i than what he gets in the mechanism. Now, if agent i's payoff is convex in the allocation, the expected efficient allocation must be even worse for him than this random outcome, ensuring that IR is satisfied when the initial property rights allocation is the expected efficient allocation. Using part (i) of Lemma 3, this conclusion can be extended to cases in which only the sum of the agents' payoffs, the surplus $s(x, \theta)$, is convex in the allocation x.

Of course, as originally seen in the Cramton et al. (1987) model, when efficient bargaining is possible, there are typically many property rights allocations that allow it.[64] For example, the expected efficient allocation typically differs from the property rights allocation that maximizes

---

probability) to the unique competitive equilibrium of the continuous limit economy; hence, in the limit the agents can fully appropriate their marginal contributions (as in Makowski and Ostroy 1989, 1995, 2001). In contrast, in the public good setting of Mailaith and Postlewaite (1990), the core grows in relative size as $N \to \infty$, and inefficiency is exacerbated (in fact, the probability of providing the public good in any mechanism goes to zero).

63. In some cases, efficient noncontractible actions can also be sustained with this property rights allocation; see the discussion in Segal and Whinston (2011), which extends an insight of Rogerson (1992).

64. Indeed, this multiplicity typically obtains when $\overline{\pi}(E[x^*(\tilde{\theta})]) > 0$, because $\overline{\pi}(\hat{x})$ is continuous in $\hat{x}$ as long as each $u_i(\cdot)$ is equicontinuous in x. Moreover, when the convexity assumptions of Proposition 16 hold, the intermediary's expected profit function $\overline{\pi}(\hat{x})$ is concave in $\hat{x}$, implying that the set $\hat{X}^*$ of property rights allocations permitting efficient bargaining is a nonempty convex set.

the intermediary's profit, $\hat{x}^* = \arg\max_{\hat{x}\in X}\overline{\pi}(\hat{x})$. The latter allocation is studied by Schmitz (2002: proof of proposition 3), Che (2006), Schweizer (2006), and Figueroa and Skreta (2008).

Note, however, that when the space of feasible property rights X is not convex, it may not contain an expected efficient allocation $E[x^*(\tilde{\theta})]$, in which case Proposition 16 does not apply and there may be no feasible property rights allocation permitting efficient bargaining. For example, in the setting of Example 7, when only extreme property rights allocations are feasible (agent 1 ownership or agent 2 ownership), neither permits efficient bargaining.[65] Even with a convex allocation space X, the assumption of convexity of the total surplus $s(x, \theta)$ in the allocation x is also crucial. Neeman (1999: 685) offers an example of bargaining over pollution, in which the convexity assumption fails and there is no efficiency-permitting property rights allocation.[66] In contrast, Segal and Whinston (2011) offer examples with concave payoffs in which efficient bargaining is still permitted by some property rights allocations (which may or may not include the expected efficient allocation).

Applying the Envelope Theorem to (16) using (15), we can see that $\nabla\overline{\pi}(\hat{x}) = -\nabla_x s(\hat{x}, \hat{\theta})$, so changes in property rights that reduce surplus at the critical types make efficient negotiation (which requires $\overline{\pi}(\hat{x}) \geq 0$) more likely. This result highlights an important difference between the role of property rights when we are concerned with bargaining efficiency under asymmetric information and their role when we are concerned with noncontractible investments. In the Hart and Moore (1990) model with noncontractible investments, increased ownership is good in that it encourages investments, which are in general below efficient levels. With asymmetric information bargaining, however, ownership is an impediment (as it was with cooperative investments in Section 3.4.2): efficiency is easiest to achieve when the parties have no claims at all to useful assets. Thus, for example, splitting up the ownership of complementary assets, so that no one can use them in the event of a disagreement, can enable efficient bargaining.[67]

One can also ask which property rights are optimal when efficiency cannot be achieved, perhaps because the set of feasible property rights allocations is constrained in some way (e.g., in Example 7, the asset might have to be owned by a single agent, and we might ask which one should own it). The answer to this question may depend on the setting. When an outside agency will subsidize bargaining to achieve efficiency, the appropriate criterion would be maximization of the profit $\overline{\pi}(\hat{x})$. When no such agency exists, we may instead want property rights that maximize the expected surplus that can be achieved in a second-best (balanced-budget) mechanism. And if bargaining is impossible, it is instead best simply to maximize the expected disagreement surplus, as in the simple allocation benchmark. Matouschek (2004), in the first paper to consider second-best optimal property rights under asymmetric information bargaining, studies a model in which one agent is initially the owner of an asset x and there are later trade decisions q.

---

65. For other examples with a nonconvex decision space X in which there is no property rights allocation permitting efficient bargaining, see Ornelas and Turner (2007) and Turner (2008).

66. When simple property rights allocations cannot lead to efficiency, more complicated property rights mechanisms might be optimal. The legal literature, for example, has discussed the benefits of liability rules—which can be interpreted as options to own—relative to simple property rights (Ayres and Talley 1995; Kaplow and Shavell 1995–1996; Ayres 2005). For a formal analysis of liability rules, see Che (2006) and Segal and Whinston (2012b).

67. The benefit of having a default outcome for which the total surplus is low also arises in self-enforcing contracts, where the default is used as an off-equilibrium punishment, as discussed in Malcomson (this volume).

(There are no noncontractible actions a.) Trade decisions q cannot be specified ex ante, while ownership of the asset x cannot be renegotiated ex post. He analyzes how ownership of the asset should be allocated ex ante to maximize the expected surplus achieved in the best budget-balanced mechanism at the ex post bargaining stage. He finds that, depending on the parameters, the optimal property rights x will either maximize the total surplus at the disagreement point (as if no renegotiation were possible) or minimize it (as if renegotiation were possible over both x and q). In more recent work, Segal and Whinston (2012b) study second-best optimal property rights when the set of ex ante and ex post contractible decisions are the same (so $\hat{X} = X$), comparing the optimal property rights for settings with no ex post bargaining (the simple allocation benchmark of Section 1), bargaining subsidized by an outside agency, and second-best (budget-balanced) bargaining.

Finally, we note that the mechanism-design approaches taken in the above work may well adopt too optimistic a view of bargaining procedures. One response to this concern would be to study optimal property rights for specific suboptimal bargaining processes. Another would be to incorporate additional constraints in the mechanism-design approach.[68]

4.2. Bilateral Contracting with Externalities

Even if bargaining over the ex post allocation of property rights occurs under symmetric information, inefficiency may nonetheless arise if there are more than two parties bargaining and they cannot write a single "grand" contract. When agents can write only bilateral contracts (i.e., make bilateral trades), they may fail to internalize externalities from their trades on others, yielding inefficient outcomes. In this section, we examine how the initial allocation of property rights affects their final allocation in such settings. The following example shows one situation in which such externalities can arise.

Example 8 (common agency model) Consider an extension of the agency model (Example 1) to the case of $N \geq 2$ principals. Suppose that the asset is divisible, and let $x_i \in [0, 1]$ denote the share of the asset held by each principal $i = 1, \ldots, N$, with the remaining share $1 - \sum_{i=1}^{N} x_i$ held by the agent. Suppose that the asset's values to the principals and the agent, $V_P\left(1 - \sum_{i=1}^{N} x_i\right)$ and $V_A\left(1 - \sum_{i=1}^{N} x_i\right)$, respectively, depend on the agent's share. This dependence captures in reduced form the effects of the agent's ownership on her noncontractible actions affecting the asset's value. For instance, as in Example 1, holding a larger share of the asset may better incentivize the agent to enhance its value. Alternatively, the agent's control rights stemming from her higher share may enable her to engage in value-reducing activities (e.g., looting, empire-building, or resisting value-enhancing takeovers). The agent's resulting inalienable costs (or negative benefits) from these activities are represented by $C\left(1 - \sum_{i=1}^{N} x_i\right)$. As for the

---

68. One sense in which the approach described here may be too optimistic is in the IR and IC constraints it assumes. Because an agent may be able to walk away from a deal at the last moment, an ex post IR constraint may make more sense. Galavotti et al. (2011) identifies some cases in which efficiency can be achieved when ex post IR is required. For example, in the setting of Example 7, he shows that equal ownership permits efficient bargaining in this stronger (ex post IR) sense. Compte and Jehiel (2007) suggest that an even stronger constraint might be appropriate if agents can lie and then quit.

principals' inalienable benefits (Y), we assume them to be zero. Therefore, the parties' payoffs exclusive of transfers take the form

$$U_A(x_1, \ldots, x_N) = \left(1 - \sum_{i=1}^{N} x_i\right) V_A\left(1 - \sum_{i=1}^{N} x_i\right) - C\left(1 - \sum_{i=1}^{N} x_i\right)$$

$$U_i(x_1, \ldots, x_N) = x_i V_P\left(1 - \sum_{i=1}^{N} x_i\right) \quad \text{for } i = 1, \ldots, N.$$

These payoffs exhibit externalities from asset ownership when the asset's public value V_P depends on the agent's ownership share. By selling or buying shares from a principal, the agent imposes externalities on every other principal i for whom $x_i > 0$.

Externalities from bilateral contracts may arise from many underlying forces other than those identified in the example. For example, they may arise when the parties subsequently bargain and the initial bilateral contracts affect the division of subsequent bargaining surplus (see, e.g., Segal 2003a; Gans 2005; Elliott 2009). Many other examples of externalities are discussed in Segal (1999b). Here, we incorporate the externalities in reduced-form payoffs, subsuming any noncontractible actions or bargaining that generate these externalities.

Many possible bargaining procedures could arise in these settings. Here we focus on the very simple contracting game considered in Segal (1999b), in which one agent makes simultaneous take-it-or-leave-it bilateral contracting offers to $N \geq 2$ other agents. This game illustrates the role of property rights in these environments, although it lacks some of the richness of outcomes that arise in more dynamic processes of bargaining with externalities that have been studied (e.g., Jehiel and Moldovanu 1999; Bloch and Gomes 2006; Gomes and Jehiel 2005).[69]

A key feature of this contracting game turns out to be whether commitment to a set of publicly observed contract offers is possible—that is, whether the offers are publicly or privately made.

4.2.1. Public Offers

Suppose that one party, agent 0 (the proposer), can contract with N other agents labeled $i = 1, \ldots, N$ (the responders). Each responder i's final property rights allocation is denoted by $x_i \in X_i$, and the overall allocation $x = (x_1, \ldots x_N) \in X = \prod_{i=1}^{N} X_i$ determines each agent's nonmonetary utility $U_i(x)$ for $i = 0, 1, \ldots, N$ (the proposer's property rights are the residual available given those of the responders). The initial allocation of property rights, the status quo, is $\hat{x} \in X$. Let X^* denote the set of allocations maximizing the total surplus of the $N + 1$ parties, $\sum_{i=0}^{N} U_i(x)$.

In this section we analyze the following two-stage game: In the first stage, agent 0 publicly proposes a pair (x_i, t_i) to each other agent i, naming the responder's final property rights allocation x_i and a transfer t_i. In the second stage, those agents simultaneously respond, either

---

69. A distinct literature on bargaining inefficiencies under full information takes a coalitional approach—see Ray (2007) for a survey. This approach allows each agent to enter into one contract (coalition) at a time, whereas in Example 8 and the model of this section, one of the agents could simultaneously write separate contracts with different agents.

accepting or rejecting their respective offers. We study the proposer's preferred subgame-perfect Nash equilibrium (SPNE) of the game.[70]

Because the proposer can always make the status quo offer $(x_i, t_i) = (\hat{x}_i, 0)$ to agent i, without loss of generality we can restrict attention to equilibria in which all offers are accepted, which occurs if and only if

$$U_i(x) + t_i \geq U_i(\hat{x}_i, x_{-i}) \quad \text{for all } i \in 1, \ldots, N. \tag{18}$$

The right-hand side of (18) is the reservation utility of responder i, that is, the utility he gets by rejecting his offer, provided that everyone else accepts. In the proposer's preferred SPNE, all responders' participation constraints must bind (otherwise she could reduce some payments while preserving the constraints). Expressing transfers from the binding constraints and substituting them in the proposer's objective function, her profit-maximizing property rights offers given the initial property rights allocation $\hat{x}$ can be defined as

$$X^\circ_{pub}(\hat{x}) = \arg\max_{x \in X} \sum_{i=0}^{N} U_i(x) - \sum_{i=1}^{N} U_i(\hat{x}_i, x_{-i}). \tag{19}$$

Note that the proposer's objective function differs from the total surplus by its last term, the sum of the responders' reservation utilities, which depends on the initial property rights allocation. As a result, the proposer's incentive to deviate from efficiency arises precisely when she can harm the other agents at their status quos. This observation leads to the following definition and result.[71]

Definition 20   *There are no harmful externalities on agent* $i = 1, \ldots, N$ *at allocation* $x \in X$ *if* $U_i(x) \leq U_i(x_i, x'_{-i})$ *for all* $x'_{-i} \in X_{-i}$; *these externalities are absent if* $U_i(x_i, x'_{-i})$ *does not depend on* $x'_{-i} \in X_{-i}$.

Proposition 17   *If* $x^* \in X^*$ *and there are no harmful externalities on each agent* $i \geq 1$ *at allocation* $(\hat{x}_i, x^*_{-i})$, *then* $x^* \in X^\circ_{pub}(\hat{x}) \subseteq X^*$.[72] *If externalities on all agents are absent at the status quo* $\hat{x}$, *then* $X^\circ_{pub}(\hat{x}) = X^*$.

Proof   For each $x^\circ \in X^\circ_{pub}(\hat{x})$, condition (19) implies that

$$\sum_{i=0}^{N} U_i(x^\circ) - \sum_{i=1}^{N} U_i\left(\hat{x}_i, x^\circ_{-i}\right) \geq \sum_{i=0}^{N} U_i(x^*) - \sum_{i=1}^{N} U_i\left(\hat{x}_i, x^*_{-i}\right). \tag{20}$$

70. Under some conditions, the game may have more than one SPNE, and the equilibrium preferred by the responders may differ from that preferred by the proposer. See Segal (2003b) for conditions in which multiple equilibria arise and an analysis of equilibria preferred by the responders.

71. Propositions 17 and 19 generalize results from Segal (1999b) to the case of nonharmful externalities.

72. It is enough for this result to assume that $\sum_{i=1}^{N} U_i(\hat{x}_i, x_{-i})$ is minimized at $x = x^*$.

By nonharmful externalities, we have $U_i\left(\hat{x}_i, x^\circ_{-i}\right) \geq U_i\left(\hat{x}_i, x^*_{-i}\right)$ for all $i \geq 1$; hence, (20) implies that $x^\circ \in X^*$. Moreover, for any such $x^* \in X^*$, nonharmful externalities imply that

$$\sum_{i=0}^{N} U_i(x^*) - \sum_{i=1}^{N} U_i\left(\hat{x}_i, x^*_{-i}\right) \geq \sum_{i=0}^{N} U_i(x') - \sum_{i=1}^{N} U_i\left(\hat{x}_i, x'_{-i}\right) \quad \text{for all } x' \in X,$$

so $x^* \in X^\circ_{pub}(\hat{x})$. Finally, if externalities are absent at $\hat{x}$, then they are nonharmful at $(\hat{x}_i, x^*_{-i})$ for any $x^* \in X^*$, which implies that $X^* \subseteq X^\circ_{pub}(\hat{x}) \subseteq X^*$.

The result states that when, given initial property rights $\hat{x}$, the proposer can maximize the total surplus while at the same time minimizing the agents' reservation utilities, this is optimal for her, and any equilibrium outcome must do so. For instance, in the common agency model (Example 8), externalities are absent when the agent is the proposer and initially owns the entire asset ($\hat{x} = 0$). In contrast, when externalities are present at any status quo, efficiency cannot be attained, because the proposer has an incentive to distort the allocation to reduce the sum of agents' reservation utilities. Segal (1999b) shows that the effect of this rent-seeking motivation on the contracting outcome x depends on the sign of these externalities: when efficiency depends only on the aggregate allocation $\sum_i x_i$ as in Example 8 (and a domain restriction holds), positive (negative) externalities on reservation utilities imply that the allocation is too low (high).[73] Note in particular that if the status quo is efficient but has externalities, the final allocation may be inefficient, so bargaining may actually reduce aggregate welfare.

4.2.2. Private Offers

Now consider what happens when the proposer cannot publicly commit. Various contracting games in which the proposer does not have commitment power have been considered in the literature. Here we simply modify the observability in the two-stage game to make the offers private. Each responder $i = 1, \ldots, N$ observes the offer (x_i, t_i) made to him but not the offers made to the other responders. (Note that because an equilibrium outcome must still satisfy participation constraints (18), this private observability can only hurt the proposer, agent 0.)

Each responder's acceptance decision in this game depends on his beliefs about offers extended to other agents. In a perfect Bayesian equilibrium, arbitrary beliefs can be assigned following the proposer's out-of-equilibrium offers, which gives rise to enormous multiplicity of equilibria. To make a more precise prediction, Segal (1999b) follows Crémer and Riordan (1987), Hart and Tirole (1990), and McAfee and Schwartz (1994) in assuming so-called passive beliefs: even after observing an unexpected offer from the proposer, a responder continues to believe that other responders have received their equilibrium offers.

---

73. For example, note that increasing the status quo in Example 8 from $\hat{x} = 0$ to $\hat{x} > 0$ will increase or decrease the final allocation, depending on the sign of externalities at $\hat{x}$.

This inefficiency is eliminated if the principal can make an offer conditional on the acceptance of all agents, while implementing maximal punishment following anyone's rejection (as with conditional tender offers in takeovers). However, Segal (1999b) shows that when the number of agents is large and their acceptances are subject to noise, the power of such conditional offers to make individual agents pivotal vanishes, and the same inefficiencies obtain as with bilateral contracting.

Consider the proposer's incentive to deviate from an equilibrium allocation x°. Because she can always make agent i the offer $(x_i, t_i) = (\hat{x}_i, 0)$, without loss of generality, we can restrict attention to deviations in which all responders accept their offers. When responder i holds passive beliefs, he accepts an offer (x_i, t_i) if and only if $U_i(x_i, x^\circ_{-i}) + t_i \geq U_i(\hat{x}_i, x^\circ_{-i})$. The proposer's optimal deviation maximizes her payoff subject to these participation constraints, which always bind at her optimal offers. Expressing transfers from the binding constraints and substituting them into the objective function, we find that x° is an equilibrium allocation if and only if[74]

$$x^\circ \in \arg\max_{x \in X} U_0(x) + \sum_{i=1}^{N} U_i(x_i, x^\circ_{-i}). \tag{21}$$

Letting X°_{pr} denote the set of property rights x° satisfying (21), our first observation is the following.

Proposition 18   *The set X°_{pr} of equilibrium property rights allocations with private offers does not depend on the initial property rights allocation $\hat{x}$.*

Although this irrelevance of initial property rights is reminiscent of the Coase Theorem, the contracting outcome with externalities may be inefficient. This inefficiency can be traced to externalities at efficient allocations. When externalities at an efficient allocation are nonharmful, private contracting yields efficient outcomes, regardless of any externalities at other allocations.

Proposition 19   *If there exists $x^* \in X^*$ at which externalities are nonharmful, then $X^\circ_{pr} \subseteq X^*$.*

Proof   For any $x^\circ \in X^\circ_{pr}$, condition (21) and nonharmful externalities at x^* imply that

$$\sum_{i=0}^{N} U_i(x^\circ) \geq U_0(x^*) + \sum_{i=1}^{N} U_i(x^*_i, x^\circ_{-i}) \geq \sum_{i=0}^{N} U_i(x^*).$$

Therefore, $x^\circ \in X^*$.

For an application, consider the common agency model (Example 8) under the assumption that it is efficient to have $x = 0$ (full agent ownership). Then any contracting outcome with private offers must be efficient, regardless of the property rights allocation. Contrast this to the public offers setting, where the bargaining outcome may be inefficient due to externalities at the initial property rights allocation when $\hat{x} \neq 0$.

---

74. The condition implies (but is stronger than) the condition

$$x^\circ_i \in \arg\max_{x_i \in X_i} \left[U_0(x_i, x^\circ_{-i}) + U_i(x_i, x^\circ_{-i}) \right] \quad \text{for all } i \geq 1,$$

which is called "contract equilibrium" by Crémer and Riordan (1987) and "pairwise proofness" by McAfee and Schwartz (1994). The nonemptiness of X°_{pr} is only ensured under additional assumptions (see Segal 1999b: 384–386), and all subsequent results will be vacuous (but formally correct) when X°_{pr} is empty.

When externalities are present at all efficient allocations, they must distort the contracting outcome. Segal (1999b) shows that when efficiency depends only on the aggregate allocation $\sum_i x_i$ (and a domain restriction holds), this aggregate allocation is too low (high) when there are positive (negative) externalities at any efficient allocation. To compare this outcome to that under public offers, note that, with private offers and passive beliefs, the proposer can no longer influence the responders' reservation utilities, but she also ceases to internalize the externalities on responders' equilibrium payoffs from changes in the proposed allocation. So the noninternalized externalities are now those at equilibrium allocations rather than the status quo allocation. Depending on the comparison of these externalities, one contracting regime may be more or less efficient than the other.

Although we have focused on a simple two-stage contracting game, similar results on bargaining inefficiencies have been obtained for infinite-horizon games with frequent recontracting. Thus, in Jehiel and Moldovanu (1999) and Gomes and Jehiel (2005), any allocation can be renegotiated very soon, and because of this lack of commitment, the game's equilibrium outcomes are similar to those of the two-stage game with private offers (in particular, they obtain results similar to Propositions 18 and 19).[75] In contrast, Bloch and Gomes (2006) consider a game in which agents can exercise irreversible outside options during bargaining (as in Section 3.6.3), and the inefficiencies are due to externalities on these outside options, as in the two-stage public-offers game.

5. Conclusion

The importance of property rights for reducing externalities, improving incentives, and achieving more efficient outcomes has been noted for centuries. However, the subject of property rights received renewed attention following the suggestion of Grossman and Hart (1986) and Hart and Moore (1990) that property rights over assets can be used to define boundaries of firms. Since then, much progress has been made in applying game-theoretic tools to study property rights. Still, much remains to be learned.

One area where more work would be useful is the examination of optimal property rights when the first best cannot be achieved, both in hold-up models and in models of inefficient bargaining (as well as in hybrid models that include both features). In addition, work that examines the determinants of optimal property rights in models with more structure on the actual decisions being made (e.g., in Alonso et al. 2008; Rantakari 2008) would be welcome.

A better understanding of the reasons property rights are used instead of more complete contracts is of great importance. In most existing models of property rights, they can be improved on by more complicated contracts. The literature on "foundations of incomplete contracts" (discussed in Section 3.6) identified some assumptions under which more complicated mechanisms cannot improve on simple property rights. However, this literature also finds that the optimal arrangement is sensitive to very fine technological details, such as the degree to which choices

---

75. Segal and Whinston (2003) examine the set of equilibrium outcomes in a class of bargaining games without commitment, allowing for arbitrary beliefs. In their model, the proposer may be able to benefit from offering more complicated mechanisms (specifically, menus from which the proposer will later choose) because of their ability to influence responders' beliefs. They show that in many cases in which externalities are present at the efficient property rights allocation, inefficiencies must arise in all equilibria when such menus can be used.

are irrevocable or which mechanisms would be enforced by courts. In reality, these details may not be known with great precision by market participants.[76] One advantage of simple contracts, such as property rights, over more complicated contracts may be that their performance could be more robust to features of the environment. This robustness is particularly important for complex environments. On the one hand, in complex environments the agents may have many ways to game a complicated contract, so simple contracts can emerge as being optimal (e.g., Segal 1999a). On the other hand, complicated contracts in complex environments may be prohibitively costly to write or execute because of contracting or communication costs (e.g., Segal 2012) or cognitive limitations.

Another issue is that property rights over assets are only one of many ways incentives are provided in large firms or other organizations. Other incentive instruments include decision rights that are not tied to assets, for example, authority over people (see Bolton and Dewatripont, this volume), compensation schemes (Mookherjee, this volume), relational incentives (Gibbons and Henderson, this volume; Malcomson, this volume), and promotions (Waldman, this volume). One view is that in large firms, property rights do not play a central role. For example, shareholders hold property rights, but effective rights of control seem to reside with top management. One reason for this may be that managers' superior information gives them "real authority" over the decisions (Aghion and Tirole 1997). Yet, changes in the boundaries of large firms—that is, changes in property rights—often seem to lead to changes in many of these other instruments. For example, when one firm acquires another, which firm is the acquirer does appear to matter (e.g., the CEO of the acquired firm, while often given a top job at the time of acquisition, often seems to leave unhappily not long after, and the business of the acquired firm often withers). So property rights may indeed matter, but they are filtered through the decision rights that are conveyed to management. (Alternatively, the identity of the acquirer may matter simply because its managers are in control.)

Finally, it is important to understand how the predictions of the theories outlined here match facts with regard to both the effects of property rights on incentives and the determination of property rights. Different theories do give rise to distinct predictions, but the distinctions often hinge on such features as the relative importance of various kinds of investments, which can be difficult to assess empirically (see, e.g., the discussion in Whinston 2003). In particular, even though there exists a substantial literature testing the predictions of transactions cost economics (see Tadelis and Williamson, this volume), only recently have papers been published that try to test some theories surveyed in this chapter (e.g., Baker and Hubbard 2003, 2004; Elfenbein and Lerner 2003). Much more work on this front is needed.

REFERENCES

Aghion, P., and J. Tirole. 1997. "Formal and Real Authority in Organizations." *Journal of Political Economy* 105: 1–29.
Aghion, P., M. Dewatripont, and P. Rey. 1994. "Renegotiation Design with Unverifiable Information." *Econometrica* 62: 257–282.
———. 2004. "Transferable Control." *Journal of the European Economic Association* 2: 115–138.
Alonso, R., W. Dessein, and N. Matouschek. 2008. "When Does Coordination Require Centralization?" *American Economic Review* 98: 145–179.

76. They are even less likely to be known to economists, which would make testing these theories difficult.

Areeda, P., and L. Kaplow. 1988. *Antitrust Analysis, Problems, Texts, Cases,* fourth edition. Boston: Little, Brown.

Aristotle. 1885. *The Politics of Aristotle: Translated into English with Introduction, Marginal Analysis, Essays, Notes, and Indices.* Translated by B. Jowett. Oxford: Clarendon Press.

Arrow, K. 1979. "The Property Rights Doctrine and Demand Revelation under Incomplete Information," in M. Boskin (ed.), *Economics and Human Welfare.* New York: Academic Press, pp. 23–29.

Ayres, I. 2005. *Optional Law: The Structure of Legal Entitlements.* Chicago: University of Chicago Press.

Ayres, I., and E. Talley. 1995. "Solomonic Bargaining: Dividing a Legal Entitlement to Facilitate Coasean Trade." *Yale Law Journal* 104: 1027–1117.

Baker, G., and T. Hubbard. 2003. "Make versus Buy in Trucking: Asset Ownership, Job Design, and Information." *American Economic Review* 3: 551–572.

———. 2004. "Contractibility and Asset Ownership: On-Board Computers and Governance in U.S. Trucking." *Quarterly Journal of Economics* 4: 1443–1480.

Baker, G., R. Gibbons, and K. J. Murphy. 2002. "Relational Contracts and the Theory of the Firm." *Quarterly Journal of Economics* 117: 39–84.

———. 2008. "Strategic Alliances: Bridges between 'Islands of Conscious Power'." *Journal of the Japanese and International Economies* 22: 146–163.

———. 2011. "Relational Adaptation." Massachusetts Institute of Technology Sloan School working paper, Cambridge, MA.

Baumol, W. J., and W. E. Oates. 1988. *The Theory of Environmental Policy,* second edition. Cambridge: Cambridge University Press.

Bloch, F., and A. Gomes. 2006. "Contracting with Externalities and Outside Options." *Journal of Economic Theory* 127: 172–201.

Bolton, P., and M. D. Whinston. 1993. "Incomplete Contracts, Vertical Integration, and Supply Assurance." *Review of Economic Studies* 60: 121–148.

Brandenburger, A., and H. Stuart. 2007a. "Biform Games." *Management Science* 53: 537–549.

———. 2007b. "Creating Monopoly Power." *International Journal of Industrial Organization* 25: 1011–1125.

Buzard, K., and J. Watson. 2012. "Contract, Renegotiation, and Hold Up: Results on the Technology of Trade and Investment." *Theoretical Economics* 7: 283–322.

Cai, H. 2003. "A Theory of Joint Asset Ownership." *RAND Journal of Economics* 34: 63–77.

Che, Y.-K. 2006. "Beyond the Coasian Irrelevance: Asymmetric Information." Unpublished notes, Columbia University.

Che, Y.-K., and D. Hausch. 1999. "Cooperative Investments and the Value of Contracting." *American Economic Review* 89: 125–147.

Chiu, Y. S. 1998. "Noncooperative Bargaining, Hostages, and Optimal Asset Ownership." *American Economic Review* 88: 882–901.

Chung, T.-Y. 1991. "Incomplete Contracts, Specific Investments, and Risk-Sharing." *Review of Economic Studies* 58: 1031–1042.

Coase, R. H. 1960. "The Problem of Social Cost." *Journal of Law and Economics* 3: 1–69.

Cole, H. L., G. Mailaith, and A. Postlewaite. 2001a. "Efficient Non-Contractable Investments in Large Economies." *Journal of Economic Theory* 101: 333–373.

———. 2001b. "Efficient Non-Contractible Investments in Finite Economies." *Advances in Theoretical Economics* 1: article 2. Available at: http://www.bepress.com/bejte/advances/vol1/iss1/art2.

Compte, O., and P. Jehiel. 2007. "On Quitting Rights in Mechanism Design." *American Economic Review* 97: 137–141.

Cramton, P., R. Gibbons, and P. Klemperer. 1987. "Dissolving a Partnership Efficiently." *Econometrica* 55: 615–632.

Crémer, J., and M. H. Riordan. 1987. "On Governing Multilateral Transactions with Bilateral Contracts." *RAND Journal of Economics* 18: 436–451.

d'Aspremont, C., and L. A. Gérard-Varet. 1979. "Incentives and Incomplete Information." *Journal of Public Economics* 11: 25–45.

De Meza, D., and B. Lockwood. 1998. "Does Asset Ownership Always Motivate Managers? Outside Options and the Property Rights Theory of the Firm." *Quarterly Journal of Economics* 113: 361–386.

Demsetz, H. 1967. "Toward a Theory of Property Rights." *American Economic Review* 57: 347–359.

Demski, J. S., and D. A. Sappington. 1991. "Resolving Double Moral Hazard Problems with Buyout Agreements." *RAND Journal of Economics* 22: 232–240.

Edlin, A., and B. Hermalin. 2000. "Contract Renegotiation and Options in Agency Problems." *Journal of Law, Economics, and Organization* 16: 395–423.

Edlin, A., and S. Reichelstein. 1996. "Holdups, Standard Breach Remedies, and Optimal Investments." *American Economic Review* 86: 478–501.

Edlin, A., and C. Shannon. 1998. "Strict Monotonicity in Comparative Statics." *Journal of Economic Theory* 81: 201–219.

Elfenbein, D., and J. Lerner. 2003. "Ownership and Control Rights in Internet Portal Alliances, 1995–1999." *RAND Journal of Economics* 34: 356–369.

Elliott, M. 2009. "Inefficiencies in Networked Markets." Working paper, Stanford University, Stanford, CA.

Evans, R. 2008. "Simple Efficient Contracts in Complex Environments." *Econometrica* 76: 459–491.

Farrell, J. 1987. "Information and the Coase Theorem." *Journal of Economic Perspectives* 1: 113–129.

Felli, L., and K. Roberts. 2001. "Does Competition Solve the Hold-Up Problem?" SSRN Working Paper 171920. Available at Social Science Research Network: http:/ssrn.com/abstract=171920.

Fieseler, K., T. Kittsteiner, and B. Moldovanu. 2003. "Partnerships, Lemons, and Efficient Trade." *Journal of Economic Theory* 113: 223–234.

Figueroa, N., and V. Skreta. 2008. "What to Put on the Table." SSRN Working Paper 1120987. Available at Social Science Research Network: http:/ssrn.com/abstract=1281903.

Galavotti, S., N. Muto, and D. Oyama. 2011. "On Efficient Partnership Dissolution under ex post Individual Rationality." *Economic Theory* 48: 87–123.

Gans, J. S. 2005. "Markets for Ownership." *RAND Journal of Economics* 36: 433–455.

Gershkov, A., and P. Schweinzer. 2010. "When Queueing Is Better Than Push and Shove." *International Journal of Game Theory* 39: 409–430.

Gibbons, R. 2005. "Four Formal(izable) Theories of the Firm." *Journal of Economic Behavior and Organization* 2: 200–245.

Gomes, A., and P. Jehiel. 2005. "Dynamic Processes of Social and Economic Interactions: On the Persistence of Inefficiencies." *Journal of Political Economy* 113: 626–667.

Gresik, T., and M. Satterthwaite. 1989. "The Rate at Which a Simple Market Converges to Efficiency as the Number of Traders Increases: An Asymptotic Result for Optimal Trading Mechanisms." *Journal of Economic Theory* 48: 304–332.

Grossman, S. J., and O. D. Hart. 1986. "The Costs and Benefits of Ownership: A Theory of Vertical and Lateral Integration." *Journal of Political Economy* 94: 691–719.

Guriev, S. 2003. "Incomplete Contracts with Cross-Investments." *Contributions to Theoretical Economics* 3: Article 5. Available at: http://works.bepress.com/sergei_guriev/2.

Hart, O. 1995. *Firms, Contracts, and Financial Structure*. Oxford: Oxford University Press.

Hart, O., and B. Holmström. 2010. "A Theory of Firm Scope." *Quarterly Journal of Economics* 125: 483–513.

Hart, O., and J. Moore. 1988. "Incomplete Contracts and Renegotiation." *Econometrica* 56: 755–785.

———. 1990. "Property Rights and the Nature of the Firm." *Journal of Political Economy* 98: 1119–1158.

Hart, O., and J. Tirole. 1990. "Vertical Integration and Market Foreclosure." *Brookings Papers on Economic Activity* (special issue) 205–276.

Hart, O., A. Shleifer, and R. Vishny. 1997. "The Proper Scope of Government: Theory and an Application to Prisons." *Quarterly Journal of Economics* 112: 127–161.

Hermalin, B. E., and M. L. Katz. 1991. "Moral Hazard and Verifiability: The Effects of Renegotiation in Agency." *Econometrica* 59: 1735–1753.

Holmes, O. W. 1881. *The Common Law*. Boston: Little, Brown and Company. (Reprinted 1946.)

Holmström, B. 1982. "Moral Hazard in Teams." *Bell Journal of Economics* 13: 324–340.

Holmström, B., and P. Milgrom. 1991. "Multitask Principal-Agent Analyses: Incentive Contracts, Asset Ownership, and Job Design." *Journal of Law, Economics, and Organization* 7: 24–52.

———. 1994. "The Firm as an Incentive System." *American Economic Review* 84: 972–991.

Holmström, B., and J. Tirole. 1991. "Transfer Pricing and Organizational Form." *Journal of Law, Economics, and Organization* 2: 201–228.

Jehiel, P., and B. Moldovanu. 1999. "Resale Markets and the Assignment of Property Rights." *Review of Economic Studies* 66: 971–991.

Jehiel, P., and A. Pauzner. 2006. "Partnership Dissolution with Interdependent Values." *Rand Journal of Economics* 37: 1–22.

Kaplow, L. and S. Shavell. 1995–1996. "Do Liability Rules Facilitate Bargaining: A Reply to Ayres and Talley." *Yale Law Journal* 105: 221–233.

Klein, B., R. G. Crawford, and A. A. Alchian. 1978. "Vertical Integration, Appropriable Rents, and the Competitive Contracting Process." *Journal of Law and Economics* 21: 297–326.

Kranton, R., and D. Minehart. 2001. "A Theory of Buyer-Seller Networks." *American Economic Review* 91: 485–508.

Krishna, V., and M. Perry. 1998. "Efficient Mechanism Design." SSRN Working Paper 64934. Available at Social Science Research Network: http://ssrn.com/abstract=64934.

Legros, P., and A. F. Newman. 1996. "Wealth Effects, Distribution, and the Theory of Organizations." *Journal of Economic Theory* 70: 312–341.

MacLeod, W. B., and J. M. Malcomson. 1993. "Investments, Holdup, and the Form of Market Contracts." *American Economic Review* 83: 811–837.

Mailaith, G., and A. Postlewaite. 1990. "Asymmetric Information Bargaining Procedures with Many Agents." *Review of Economic Studies* 57: 351–367.

Makowski, L., and C. Mezzetti. 1994. "Bayesian and Weakly Robust First Best Mechanisms: Characterizations." *Journal of Economic Theory* 64: 500–519.

Makowski, L., and J. M. Ostroy. 1989. "Efficient and Individually Rational Bayesian Mechanisms Only Exist in Perfectly Competitive Environments." Working Paper 566, Department of Economics, University of California, Los Angeles.

———. 1995. "Appropriation and Efficiency: A Revision of the First Theorem of Welfare Economics." *American Economic Review* 85: 808–827.

———. 2001. "Perfect Competition and the Creativity of the Market." *Journal of Economic Literature* 39: 479–535.

Marcet, J. H. 1819. *Conversations in Political Economy*, third edition. London.

Marvel, H. P. 1982. "Exclusive Dealing." *Journal of Law and Economics* 25: 1–26.

Mas-Colell, A., M. D. Whinston, and J. R. Green. 1995. *Microeconomic Theory*. New York: Oxford University Press.

Maskin, E., and J. Moore. 1999. "Implementation and Renegotiation." *Review of Economic Studies* 66: 39–56.

Maskin, E. and J. Tirole. 1999. "Unforeseen Contingencies and Incomplete Contracts." *Review of Economic Studies* 66: 83–114.

Matouschek, N. 2004. "Ex post Inefficiencies in a Property Rights Theory of the Firm." *Journal of Law, Economics, and Organization* 20: 125–147.

McAfee, P., and M. Schwartz. 1994. "Opportunism in Multilateral Vertical Contracting: Nondiscrimination, Exclusivity, and Uniformity." *American Economic Review* 84: 210–230.

McKelvey, R. D., and T. Page. 2002. "Status quo Bias in Bargaining: An Extension of the Myerson–Satterthwaite Theorem with an Application to the Coase Theorem." *Journal of Economic Theory* 2: 336–355.

Milgrom, P., and J. Roberts. 1990. "Rationalizability and Learning in Games with Strategic Complementarities." *Econometrica* 58: 1255–1278.

Milgrom, P., and C. Shannon. 1994. "Monotone Comparative Statics." *Econometrica* 62: 157–180.

Milgrom, P., and I. Segal. 2002. "Envelope Theorems for Arbitrary Choice Sets." *Econometrica* 70: 583–601.

Mirrlees, J. 1971. "An Exploration in the Theory of Optimal Income Taxation." *Review of Economic Studies* 38: 175–208.

Mookherjee, D. 1984. "Optimal Incentive Schemes with Many Agents." *Review of Economic Studies* 51: 433–446.

Moore, J., and R. Repullo. 1988. "Subgame Perfect Implementation." *Econometrica* 56: 1191–1220.

Myerson, R., and M. Satterthwaite. 1983. "Efficient Mechanisms for Bilateral Trading." *Journal of Economic Theory* 29: 265–281.

Neeman, Z. 1999. "Property Rights and Efficiency of Voluntary Bargaining under Asymmetric Information." *Review of Economic Studies* 66: 679–691.

Noldeke, G., and K. Schmidt. 1995. "Option Contracts and Renegotiation: A Solution to the Hold-Up Problem." *RAND Journal of Economics* 26: 163–179.

Ornelas, E., and J. L. Turner. 2007. "Efficient Dissolution of Partnerships and the Structure of Control." *Games and Economic Behavior* 60: 187–199.

Rahman, D. 2010. "Detecting Profitable Deviations." Working paper, University of Minnesota, St. Paul.

Rajan, R. G., and L. Zingales. 1998. "Power in a Theory of Firm." *Quarterly Journal of Economics* 113: 387–432.

Rantakari, H. 2008. "Governing Adaptation." *Review of Economic Studies* 75: 1257–1285.

Ray, D. 2007. *A Game-Theoretic Perspective on Coalition Formation*. Oxford: Oxford University Press.

Riordan, M. 1990. "What Is Vertical Integration?" in M. Aoki, B. Gustafsson, and O. Williamson (eds.), *The Firm as a Nexus of Treaties*. London: Sage, pp. 94–111.

Rogerson, W. 1992. "Contractual Solutions to the Hold-Up Problem." *Review of Economic Studies* 59: 774–794.

Roider, A. 2004. "Asset Ownership and Contractibility of Interaction." *RAND Journal of Economics* 35: 787–802.

Rubinstein, A. 1982. "Perfect Equilibrium in a Bargaining Model." *Econometrica* 50: 97–109.

Rubinstein, A., and A. Wolinsky. 1992. "Renegotiation-Proof Implementation and Time Preferences." *American Economic Review* 82: 600–614.

Schmidt, K. M. 1996. "The Costs and Benefits of Privatization: An Incomplete Contracts Approach." *Journal of Law, Economics, and Organization* 12: 1–24.

Schmitz, P. 2002. "Simple Contracts, Renegotiation under Asymmetric Information, and the Hold-Up Problem." *European Economic Review* 46: 169–188.

———. 2006. "Information Gathering, Transaction Costs, and the Property Rights Approach." *American Economic Review* 96: 422–434.

Schweizer, U. 2006. "Universal Possibility and Impossibility Results." *Games and Economic Behavior* 57: 73–85.

Segal, I. 1999a. "Complexity and Renegotiation: A Foundation for Incomplete Contracts." *Review of Economic Studies* 66: 57–82.

———. 1999b. "Contracting with Externalities." *Quarterly Journal of Economics* 114: 337–388.

———. 2003a. "Collusion, Exclusion, and Inclusion in Random-Order Bargaining." *Review of Economic Studies* 70: 439–460.

———. 2003b. "Coordination and Discrimination in Contracting with Externalities: Divide and Conquer?" *Journal of Economic Theory* 113: 147–181.

———. 2012. "Communication Complexity and Coordination by Authority." *Advances in Theoretical Economics,* forthcoming.

Segal, I., and M. D. Whinston. 2000. "Exclusive Contracts and Protection of Investments." *RAND Journal of Economics* 31: 603–633.

———. 2002. "The Mirrlees Approach to Mechanism Design with Renegotiation (with Applications to Hold-Up and Risk Sharing." *Econometrica* 70: 1–45.

———. 2003. "Robust Predictions for Bilateral Contracting with Externalities." *Econometrica* 71: 757–791.

———. 2011. "A Simple Status Quo that Ensures Participation (with Application to Efficient Bargaining)." *Theoretical Economics* 6: 109–125.

———. 2012a. "Equilibrium, Externalities, and Efficiency in Games." Working paper, Stanford University, Stanford, CA.

———. 2012b. "Property Rights and the Efficiency of Bargaining." Working paper, Stanford University, Stanford, CA.

Simon, H. 1951. "A Formal Theory of the Employment Relation." *Econometrica* 19: 293–305.

Stahl, I. 1972. "Bargaining Theory." Stockholm School of Economics, Stockholm.

Sutton, J. 1986. "Non-Cooperative Bargaining Theory: An Introduction." *Review of Economic Studies* 53: 709–724.

Turner, J. L. 2012. "Dissolving (In)effective Partnerships." *Social Choice and Welfare,* forthcoming.

Watson, J. C. 2007. "Contract, Mechanism Design, and Technological Detail." *Econometrica* 75: 55–81.

Weber, R. 1988. "Probabilistic Values for Games." in A. Roth (ed.), *The Shapley Value*. Cambridge: Cambridge University Press.

Whinston, M. D. 2003. "On the Transaction Cost Determinants of Vertical Integration." *Journal of Law, Economics, and Organization* 19: 1–23.

Williams, S. R. 1999. "A Characterization of Efficient Bayesian Incentive Compatible Mechanisms." *Economic Theory* 14: 155–180.

Williamson, O. E. 1971. "The Vertical Integration of Production: Market Failure Considerations." *American Economic Review* 61: 112–123.

———. 1975. *Markets and Hierarchies: Analysis and Antitrust Implications*. New York: Free Press.

———. 1979. "Transaction Costs Economics: The Governance of Contractual Relations." *Journal of Law and Economics* 22: 233–262.

———. 1985. *The Economic Institutions of Capitalism*. New York: Free Press.

Yenmez, M. B. 2012. "Dissolving Multi-Partnerships Efficiently." *Journal of Mathematical Economics* 48: 77–82.

4

Transaction Cost Economics

Steven Tadelis and Oliver E. Williamson

1. Introduction

The study of the governance of economic organization has become a lively and diverse field of research over the past four decades. This chapter describes the fundamental ideas of transaction cost economics (TCE) as these evolved in the 1970s and since to offer a methodology through which to analyze how the governance of economic organization has economizing consequences. Our view, as well as the general outlook of TCE, is that organization matters for economists if and as organization is made susceptible to analysis by the application of economic reasoning.

As such, TCE is part of a broader effort to study the economics of organization, which includes agency and/or mechanism-design theory, team theory, property rights theory, and resource-based and/or competency theories. Many of these are explored in this handbook and, as appropriate, we make references to the similarities and difference between them and TCE. Lest we be misunderstood, we do not regard TCE as an all-purpose theory of firm and market organization. Instead, we subscribe to pluralism—on the conditions that all candidate theories (1) name the phenomena to which they apply and (2) derive refutable implications that lend themselves to empirical testing. Subject to these provisos, we are certain that a richer, deeper, better understanding of complex economic organization is well served by the spirit of pluralism.

We begin in Section 2 by sketching early contributions on which TCE builds, and we describe how TCE differs from the orthodoxy of the 1960s in three crucial respects: moving from the *lens of choice* to the *lens of contract;* taking *adaptation* to be the main problem of economic organization; and taking *transaction cost economizing* to be the main case for deriving refutable implications.

In Section 3 we lay out the working parts by which TCE was transformed into an operational methodology by taking the make-or-buy decision to be the focal transaction. We thereafter introduce the proposition that transactions, which differ in their attributes, will be implemented

We thank Bob Gibbons, Jon Levin, and John Roberts for helpful comments on previous drafts, as well as Tarek Ghani for providing excellent research assistance. Financial support from National Science Foundation grant SES-0239844 is gratefully acknowledged.

by different modes of governance, which differ in their adaptive strengths and weaknesses. Section 4 presents a simple formal model of TCE that parallels the less formal arguments of Section 3, with emphasis on how the choice of governance elicits different contractual incentives. Extensions and applications—including hybrid contracting, reality testing, variations on a theme, empirical TCE, and ramifications for public policy—are sketched in Section 5. Section 6 relates TCE to other economic theories of organization. Section 7 concludes.

2. Background and Essential Ideas

TCE traces its origins to a series of developments between 1930 and 1970 in economics (Commons 1932; Coase 1937, 1960; Hayek 1945; Simon 1951; Arrow 1969), organization theory (Barnard 1938; Simon 1947; Selznick 1949), contract law (Llewellyn 1931; Summers 1969), and business history (Chandler 1962). Because this chapter is mainly directed to an economics audience and organization theory, contract law, and business history are addressed elsewhere,[1] we focus in this section, as well as in this chapter, mainly on the economic arguments.

2.1. Transactions and Transaction Costs

Albeit largely ignored in textbook microeconomic theory, John R. Commons early perceived the need to move beyond simple market exchange (e.g., exchanging nuts for berries on the edge of the forest or buying a can of coke at a vending machine) to include transactions for which the continuity of an exchange relationship was often important. He furthermore described the fundamental problem of economic organization as follows: "the ultimate unit of activity . . . must contain in itself the three principles of conflict, mutuality, and order. This unit is a transaction" (Commons 1932: 4). As developed in Section 3, TCE concurs that the transaction is the basic unit of analysis and treats governance as the means by which to infuse order, thereby to mitigate conflict and realize mutual gain.[2]

Ronald Coase, in his classic 1937 paper "The Nature of the Firm," both introduced the concept of transaction costs to the study of firm and market organization[3] and uncovered a serious lapse in the accepted textbook theory of firm and market organization. Upon viewing firm and market as "alternative methods of coordinating production" (Coase 1937: 388), Coase observed that the decision to use one mode rather than the other should not be taken as given (as was the prevailing practice) but should be derived. Accordingly, economists were advised

> to bridge what appears to be a gap in [standard] economic theory between the assumption (made for some purposes) that resources are allocated by means of the price mechanism

1. On organization theory, contract law, and business history, see Williamson (1993, 2005a, and 1985: 273–297, respectively).

2. Whereas Commons viewed organization and the continuity of contractual relations as important, the economic paradigm of resource allocation, which dominated the field all through the 1970s, made negligible provision for either. Instead, it focused on prices and output, supply and demand. The institutional economics of the 1930s was mainly relegated to the history of thought because it failed to advance a positive research agenda that was replete with predictions and empirical testing.

3. Though Coase did not use the term "transaction costs" in his 1937 article, he did suggest that employment relations were especially susceptible to transaction costs.

and the assumption (made for other purposes) that that allocation is dependent on the entrepreneur-coordinator. We have to explain the basis on which, in practice, this choice between alternatives is effected. [Coase 1937: 389]

Although this challenge was ignored over the next 20 years, two important articles in the 1960s would upset this dismissive state of affairs. Upon pushing the logic of zero transaction costs to completion, the unforeseen and disconcerting implications of the standard assumption of zero transaction cost were displayed for all to see.

Coase's 1960 article "The Problem of Social Cost" reformulated the externality problem in contractual terms and pushed the logic of zero transaction cost reasoning to completion, with an astonishing result: "Pigou's conclusion (and that of most economists of that era) that some kind of government action (usually the imposition of taxes) was required to restrain those whose actions had harmful effects on others (often termed negative externalities)" was incorrect (Coase 1992: 717). That is because with zero transaction costs, parties will costlessly bargain to an efficient result whichever way property rights are assigned at the outset. In that event, externalities and frictions of other kinds would vanish. But the real message was this: hereafter, "study the world of positive transaction costs" (Coase 1992: 717). Kenneth Arrow's 1969 examination "The Organization of Economic Activity: Issues Pertinent to the Choice of Market versus Nonmarket Allocation" likewise revealed a need to make a place for positive transaction costs, both with respect to market failures and in conjunction with intermediate product market contracting: "the existence of vertical integration may suggest that the costs of operating competitive markets are not zero, as is usually assumed in our theoretical analysis" (Arrow 1969: 48).

Introducing positive transaction costs, however, posed three problems. First, upon opening the "black box" of firm and market organization and looking inside, the black box turned out to be Pandora's Box: positive transaction costs were perceived to be everywhere. Because some form of transaction cost could be invoked to explain any condition whatsoever after the fact, the appeal to transaction costs acquired a "well deserved bad name" (Fischer 1977: 322). Second, transaction costs take on comparative institutional significance only as they can be shown to differ among modes of governance (say, as between markets and hierarchies). Third, transaction costs that pass the test of comparative contractual significance need to be embedded in a conceptual framework from which predictions can be derived and empirically tested. The unmet need was to focus attention on key features and provide operational content for the intriguing concept of positive transaction costs.

2.2. Governance and the Lens of Contract

James Buchanan (1975: 225) distinguished between the lens of choice and lens of contract approaches to economic organization and argued that economics as a discipline went "wrong" in its preoccupation with the science of choice and the optimization apparatus associated therewith. If "mutuality of advantage from voluntary exchange is . . . the most fundamental of all understandings in economics" (Buchanan 2001: 29), then the lens of contract approach is an underused perspective. Thus, to analyze the inner working of such institutions as markets and hierarchies, the orthodox lens of choice (the resource allocation paradigm, with emphasis on prices and output, supply and demand) would need to give way to the evolving lens of contract. This position was implicit in Commons (1932) and Coase (1937) and was explicit in Coase (1960) and Arrow (1969). Upon examining governance and organization through the lens of contract, the firm was no longer a black box for transforming inputs into outputs according to the laws of technology but was interpreted instead as an alternative mode of contracting.

Indeed, this shift to the lens of contract was adopted not only by TCE but also more generally—in mechanism design, agency theory, information economics, and formal property rights theory. But there were also differences (described in more detail in Section 6). Whereas the aforementioned theories located the analytical action in the ex ante incentive alignment stage of contract, TCE concentrated the main action in the ex post governance of contractual relations. This emphasis on ex post governance is congruent with TCE's taking adaptation to be the main problem of economic organization.

2.3. Adaptation as the Central Problem

Hayek (1945) suggested that "economic problems arise always and only in consequence of change" (1945: 523), whereupon "rapid adaptation to changes in the particular circumstances of time and place" was taken to be the main problem of economic organization (1945: 524). Interestingly, Chester Barnard (1938), who was an organization theorist rather than an economist, likewise regarded adaptation as the central problem of organization. But while Barnard and Hayek were in agreement on the importance of adaptation, each had reference to different types of adaptation.

Hayek focused on the adaptations of autonomous economic actors who adjusted spontaneously to changes in the market, mainly as signaled by changes in relative prices. An illustrative recent example is the increase in the demand for fossil fuels that caused gasoline prices to rise sharply in 2008. As a result, automobile firms adapted their strategies to invest in alternative-energy vehicles and create new products, which in turn will affect the demand for fuel. Prices will shift to equilibrate the new choices, and consumers and producers will adapt their consumption and production behavior as part of the equilibrium. The marvel of the market thus resides in "how little the individual participants need to know to be able to take the right action" (Hayek 1945: 526–527).

In contrast, Barnard featured coordinated adaptation among economic actors working through administration. In his view, the marvel of hierarchy is that coordinated adaptation is accomplished not spontaneously but in a "conscious, deliberate, purposeful" way through administration (Barnard 1938: 4). As an illustration, Boeing experienced major malcoordination problems in 2007, because its outside suppliers were preoccupied and sometimes overwhelmed with their own problems to the neglect of Boeing's systems concerns. Serious delays in the production of their most important future aircraft, the 787 Dreamliner, resulted. Boeing, in effect, bet on the efficacy of outsourcing on a scale that they had never previously attempted, to the neglect of the benefits of ongoing coordinated adaptation to which Barnard ascribed to hierarchy. The problem was relieved when Boeing acquired the fuselage supplier in the summer of 2009.

TCE takes adaptation to be the central problem of economic organization and makes provision for both autonomous and coordinated adaptations. The "marvel of the market" (Hayek) and the "marvel of hierarchy" (Barnard) are now therefore joined. The upshot is that the old ideological divide of markets or hierarchies now gives way to the combined use of markets and hierarchies.

2.4. Efficiency

TCE holds that adaptations of both kinds are undertaken principally in the service of efficiency. Specifically, the choice among alternative modes of governance mainly has the purpose of economizing on transaction costs.

However, although TCE claims that nonstandard and unfamiliar contracting practices mainly operate in the service of efficiency, other purposes, of which market dominance (monopoly) is one, are sometimes responsible for nonstandard practices. Making allowance for monopoly is very different, however, than presuming that monopoly is mainly responsible for nonstandard and unfamiliar contracting practices and modes of organization. As discussed in Section 5.5, this preoccupation with monopoly was wrongheaded and gave rise to convoluted antitrust enforcement, which in the 1960s sometimes spun out of control.

3. Making TCE Operational: Vertical Integration

As developed elsewhere (Williamson 1971, 1975, 1985, 1991), and as described in this section, TCE was made operational by taking three basic steps. First, it took the transaction to be the basic unit of analysis and named the key attributes across which transactions differ. Second, it described the properties of alternative modes of governance. Third, these two were joined by applying the discriminating alignment hypothesis: different kinds of transactions are more efficiently governed by different modes of governance (see Section 3.3).

Conceivably, these ideas could be implemented in the abstract. But rather than develop a general theory from the outset, TCE was built from the ground up by examining the particulars. Taking vertical integration (more generally, the intermediate product market transaction—the make-or-buy decision) to be the focal transaction led quickly and easily to an interpretation of many other phenomena as variations on a theme.

The other obvious candidate to serve as a focal transaction was the employment relation (as in Coase 1937; Simon 1951). Although both of these papers were influential, the employment relation never led to a theory of firm and market organization where other transactions were interpreted as variations on a theme. One possible reason is that the employment contract possessed "peculiarities . . . that distinguish it from other types of contracts" (Simon, 1951: 293). Indeed Coase, in the first of his lectures at the conference organized in 1987 to celebrate the fiftieth anniversary of his 1937 paper, identified a "weakness in my [1937] exposition . . . that hampered further developments" (1988: 37). Specifically, "the main weakness of my article stems from use of the employer-employee relationship . . . [in that it both] gives an incomplete picture of the nature of the firm . . . [and] more important . . . it misdirects attention" (Coase 1988: 37).[4]

4. Coase appealed to labor law to support the primacy of labor: because "the fact of direction is the essence of the legal concept of 'employer and employee' just as it was in the economic concept which was developed above . . . [we can] conclude that the definition we have given is one which approximates closely to the firm as it is considered in the real world" (1937: 404).

Once a focal transaction has been decided, the three key operational moves are to (1) name the attributes of the unit of analysis, (2) do the same for modes of governance, and (3) advance the efficient alignment hypothesis.

3.1. Unit of Analysis: Classifying Transaction Attributes

The obvious place to start is with the ideal transaction of simple market exchange where identity does not matter and the terms of trade are completely specified. Competition and market-mediated exchange can be presumed to prevail in such circumstances. A simple example would be the market for standard thread screws, but any well-defined, standardized commodity that is readily and competitively supplied through anonymous spot market transactions will do.

Whereas simple market exchange works well for transactions where identity does not matter, transactions where identity does matter pose complications for which added governance might be warranted. Longer term contracts for which the parties value continuity come under scrutiny in this way.

3.1.1. Asset Specificity and the Fundamental Transformation

TCE gave early prominence to the relatively neglected condition of *asset specificity,* which became a crucial defining attribute of transactions. Asset specificity describes the condition where the identity of the parties matters for the continuity of a relationship. It can take a variety of forms—physical, human, site specific, dedicated, brand name capital, and episodic (sometimes described as temporal specificity)—the optimal response to which varies somewhat but involves greater reliance on "administration." Whatever the form, these assets cannot be redeployed to alternative uses or users without loss of productive value (Williamson 1971, 1975, 1976, 1985; Klein et al. 1978). Although asset specificity is often purposeful, it can also arise spontaneously, without conscious and costly investments, as with knowledge and skills that are incidentally acquired by the parties while working together.

By transaction-specific assets we mean ones for which a *bilateral dependency relationship develops between the parties.* Even though a large number of qualified suppliers could compete for the initial contract, investments in transaction-specific assets made by the initial winning bidder, either at the outset or during contact implementation, effectively transforms this large numbers bidding competition into a small numbers supply relationship thereafter. A *fundamental transformation* in the contractual relation thus sets in as bilateral dependency builds up.[5] Identity thereafter matters.

3.1.2. Uncertainty, Complexity, and Incomplete Contracts

Asset specificity, in any of its forms, does not by itself pose contractual hazards that require nonmarket governance. In principle, a long-term contract could stipulate how future contingent decisions will be made and proper compensation accomplished. In fact, contractual hazards arise if and as long-term contracts *are incomplete* (by reason of the prohibitive cost [Dye 1985; Bajari and Tadelis 2001] or the impossibility of contractual completeness) and are subject

---

5. Note that because asset specificity is a design variable, the good or service to be delivered could be redesigned by reducing asset-specific features, albeit at a sacrifice in performance of the good or service in question (Riordan and Williamson 1995).

to (1) disturbances (or contingencies) during the contract implementation phase for which (2) defection from the spirit of cooperation to insist on the letter of the contract can be projected for outliers (where the stakes are great), and (3) inability of the courts to fill gaps and settle disputes in a timely, knowledgeable, and efficient fashion.

Accordingly, in addition to a condition of bilateral dependency (a consequence of asset specificity), factors that contribute to contractual hazards for which added governance measures can sometimes provide relief include (1) uncertainty and contractual incompleteness,[6] (2) strategic defection (when the stakes are large), and (3) the serious limits of court ordering. On the assumption that contractual incompleteness, strategic propensities, and the limits of court ordering are all consequential, *asset specificity and disturbances for which unprogrammed adaptations are needed* are the key attributes of transactions for understanding the governance of contractual relations.[7]

3.2. Governance Structures

Problems with outsourcing become more severe as assets become more specific and contracts more incomplete. An obvious solution is to introduce governance safeguards that mitigate these contractual hazards. This poses the challenge of naming and describing alternative modes of governance and explaining the strengths and weaknesses that are associated with each. Following our discussion in Section 2, we focus principally on the two conventional polar modes of governance—markets ("buy") and hierarchies ("make").

TCE maintains that each polar mode of governance—market and hierarchy—is described as an internally consistent pattern of attributes that describe its core adaptive competence. Although Williamson (1985, 1991, 2010) makes provision for three main attributes by which to describe each mode of governance—(1) *incentive intensity* (which is measured by the extent to which a technologically separable stage of economic activity appropriates its net profits), (2) *administrative authority and control* (which has a bearing on the autonomy of a stage in both operating and investment respects as well as on procedural controls [routines, accounting procedures]), and (3) *contract law regime*—our focus in this chapter, especially in the formal model of Section 4, is on the first two attributes: incentive intensity and administrative control.[8]

---

6. Incompleteness becomes more severe as the number of features of transactions (precision, linkages, compatibility) across which adaptations are needed increases and as the number of consequential disturbances that impinge on these features increases. These features can be thought of as a measure of complexity (see Section 4.1.2).

7. A related factor, which we pass over here because of its ambiguous implications, is the frequency with which transactions recur. On the one hand, if a transaction seldom recurs, it may not be cost effective to develop a specialized internal structure. If instead it recurs frequently, then recovering the costs of creating a specialized management infrastructure is possible. On the other hand, recurrent contracting implies that future business is at stake, for which a good reputation figures in. Market contracting, if supported by good-reputation effects, thus becomes part of the comparative contractual calculus.

8. The important consideration of supporting legal regimes is set aside due to the challenge of modeling this aspect of governance. By and large the formal literature—be it mechanism design or the property rights approach—assumes that whatever is contractually verifiable will be enforced by some unmodeled third party. In this regard one can view this chapter as a bit schizophrenic: we recognize here that contract law regime can and will vary along with the choice of governance, yet in Section 4 we follow the standard modeling approach and focus only on incentive intensity and administrative control.

Assuming that incentive intensity and administrative control can take on either of two values, strong or weak, we describe the market mode (independent ownership) as having strong incentive intensity within each stage and weak administrative controls at the contractual interface, whereas hierarchy (unified ownership) has weak incentives within each stage and strong administrative control at the interface. Recall, moreover, that TCE takes the main problem of economic organization to be that of adaptation, of which autonomous and coordinated adaptation are distinguished. The decision of which transactions are organized by which mode of governance thus turns on how the attributes of different transactions pose different adaptation needs, on the one hand, and how alternative modes of governance are, by reason of their attribute differences, well or poorly qualified to respond to different adaptation needs, on the other.

Getting this balance "right" is what efficient alignment is all about. Specifically, the market mode is superior for dealing with transactions of the generic kind for which autonomous adaptations suffice (the so-called marvel of the market; Hayek 1945), whereas transactions where the parties are bilaterally dependent benefit from coordinated adaptation (the "marvel of hierarchy"; Barnard 1938).

With respect to this last point, note that low-powered incentives in firms are not to be thought of as a cost of hierarchy (bureaucracy burdens aside, see Section 5.2) but as a purposeful attribute of hierarchy without which coordinated adaptation would be compromised. To repeat, low-powered incentives in combination with administrative control at the interface (as implemented by the interface coordinator, as shown in Figure 1) are what hierarchy is all about. There is a place for each generic mode, and each should be kept in its place.

Note that two other configurations can be described. Strong incentives at each stage and strong administrative control at the interface is an inconsistent combination that leads to conflict. Strong incentives are accomplished if each stage has claims on its own net receipts. Strong administrative control accomplishes cooperative adaptation at the interface, provided that compliance by each stage can be presumed—which entails the sacrifice by each stage of claims on its own net receipts.

Weak incentives at each stage and weak administrative control at the interface lead to what is more akin to noncommercial organization. It is approximated among commercial firms by cost-plus outside procurement where, within some bounds, the supplier does what the buyer asks because it is assured of reimbursement, although some auditing by the buyer will usually attend such relations.[9] Table 1 summarizes the four implied governance modes.[10]

As stated above, market-mediated exchange takes place between independently owned and operated stages, whereas hierarchy-mediated exchange is accomplished by unified ownership and coordinated interface mediation. These operating differences are truly consequential and warrant elaboration.

---

9. For a formal treatment of relative benefit of cost-plus contracts over fixed price contracts with respect to adaptation, see Bajari and Tadelis (2001).

10. To briefly relate legal rules to the choices of incentives and administrative control, a contract law regime must be supportive of the attribute that is strong (incentive intensity or administrative control). For strong incentives to be effective, parties should have control over their processes and the letter of the contract should be expected to be enforced (strong legal rules). In contrast, the forbearance law contract regime (private ordering with weak legal rules) is supportive of strong administrative control, because interference by courts would undermine the efficacy of control by fiat. For more, see Williamson (1991).

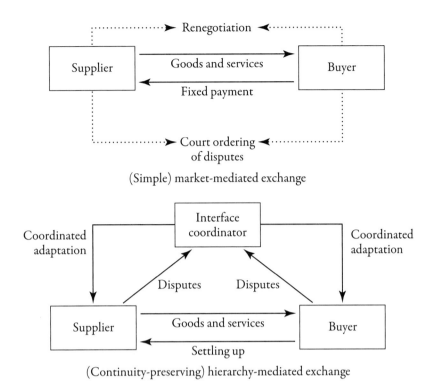

Figure 1. Interface mediation: market versus hierarchy.

Table 1. Alternative modes of governance

Administrative	Incentive intensity	
Control	Strong	Weak
Weak	Market (buy)	Cost-plus contracts (less common)
Strong	Recipe for conflict (empty)	Hierarchy (make)

The upper and lower panels of Figure 1 illustrate how market and hierarchy differ in mediating the exchange between successive stages of production with respect to trading, adaptation, and dispute settlement. The upper panel corresponds to market-mediated exchange where the supplier receives a fixed payment for delivery of the prescribed goods and services, changes require renegotiation, and disputes are dealt with by courts, which apply the appropriate legal rule to award monetary damages. The parties to simple market exchange play hard ball.

In contrast, coordinated adaptation under hierarchy, as shown in the lower panel of Figure 1, is promoted by unified ownership of the two stages coupled with the creation of a new actor, *the interface coordinator*, to whom each stage reports and receives administrative direction and control. Consequential disturbances that would give rise to poor coordination are dealt with by the interface coordinator, who has ultimate responsibility for coordinated responses; internal disputes between stages are likewise settled by the interface coordinator with reference to mutual gain (private ordering).[11]

3.3. Efficient Alignment

The *discriminating alignment hypothesis* to which TCE owes much of its predictive content is this: transactions, which differ in their attributes, are aligned with governance structures, which differ in their adaptive capacities, so as to realize an efficient result. Note that (1) markets enjoy the advantage of autonomous adaptation for transactions that are supported by generic assets, (2) the importance of coordinated adaptation increases as the supporting assets become more specific, and (3) the loss of incentive intensity and the bureaucratic costs of hierarchy are a deterrent to integration except when coordinated adaptation benefits are more than offsetting.

Figure 2 further illustrates the trade-offs using σ as an index of asset specificity. Efficient alignment is accomplished by assigning transactions for which asset specificity is low to markets and transactions for which asset specificity is high to hierarchy.[12]

The previously discussed adaptation differences that distinguish market and hierarchy (where the market has the advantage for autonomous adaptations and hierarchy has the advantage for coordinated adaptations) are implicit in Figure 2.

Thus, the market enjoys the advantage when asset specificity is negligible (σ close to 0), because the disturbances for which adaptations are needed are signaled by changes in relative prices to which buyers and sellers respond autonomously (the "marvel of the market"). The use of hierarchy in these circumstances would entail a loss of incentive intensity, and the added costs of mediating the interface with a coordinator (as shown in Figure 1) would be quite without purpose.

The affirmative case for unified ownership of successive stages builds up as bilateral dependency progressively increases due to asset specificity (increases in σ). Because the need for coordinated adaptations now presents itself, unified ownership becomes the governance structure of choice for values of σ that exceed σ^*.

Note, moreover, that the associated lowering of incentives is not an unwanted consequence of unified ownership but is purposeful—it predisposes each stage to respond cooperatively to a succession of adaptive needs as perceived by the interface coordinator. This lowering of internal incentives nevertheless incurs added bureaucratic costs and reduces productive efficiency. For one thing, because the pecuniary rewards that attend autonomous adaptation are absent, the

---

11. To tie this discussion briefly to legal rules and regimes, the efficacy of internal dispute resolution and of coordinated adaptations, as decided by the interface coordinator, would be severely compromised if disgruntled managers could go over the coordinators' heads and appeal to the courts. In effect, the firm is its own court of ultimate appeal.

12. In this binary setup, transactions for which asset specificity is in the neighborhood of σ^* can go either way, because it does not matter very much; but see the discussion of hybrids in Section 5.1.

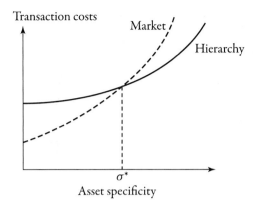

Transaction costs

Market

Hierarchy

σ^*

Asset specificity

Figure 2. Efficient governance.

individual stages have less incentive to be diligent. And there are system consequences as well. As additional stages are integrated, the oversight and control of the operating units by the top management is compromised. Sometimes this can be mitigated by organizational innovations, of which the move from a unitary to a multidivisional structure—as discussed by Chandler (1962) and interpreted by TCE in efficiency terms (Williamson 1981)—is an example.

Note, however, that whereas TCE can help to interpret the efficiency benefits that accrue to major changes in the structure of bureaucracy in large corporations, organization form differences are not matters that TCE can address as variations on the basic contractual theme of which vertical integration is the paradigmatic case. As this *Handbook* demonstrates, economic organization is a big house—to which TCE relates but is not an all-purpose construction.

3.4. The Impossibility of Combining Replication with Selective Intervention

Sections 3.1–3.3 outline the main logic of TCE as applied to the make-or-buy problem. We discuss here a related but different puzzle posed by Frank Knight (1921) and Ronald Coase (1937): Why can't a large firm do everything that a collection of smaller firms can do and more? Tracy Lewis (1983: 1092) argues that an established firm can always realize greater value because it can "utilize the input exactly as the entrant would have used it . . . [and can furthermore] improve on this by coordinating production from his new and existing inputs." TCE takes exception with this argument by examining the efficacy of the two mechanisms on which Lewis's formulation implicitly relies: *replication* and *selective intervention*.

Imagine, without loss, that the buyer stage acquires the supplier stage with the understanding that (1) the supplier will operate in the same autonomous way post-acquisition as in the pre-acquisition status (by replication) except when (2) the buyer intervenes selectively, because expected net gains can be achieved through coordinated adaptations. The combined firm can then never do worse (by replication) and will sometimes do better (by selective intervention). Therefore, more integration is always better than less, and repeating this logic implies that everything will be organized in one large firm.

This logic breaks down upon examining four implicit assumptions on which the implementation of replication and selective intervention rely: (1) the buyer (owner) promises the acquired supplier its net receipts in all state realizations, thereby preserving strong incentives; (2) the supplier promises to use the supply-stage assets that the buyer now owns with due care; (3) the buyer promises to exercise authority (fiat) only when expected net gains can be ascribed to selective intervention; and (4) the buyer promises to reveal and divide the net gains from selective intervention as stipulated in the original agreement. The problem is that none of these promises is self-enforcing. To the contrary, in the absence of perfect information (to include a costless arbiter), each condition will be compromised. An elaboration on why each of the four conditions above fails is reported elsewhere (Williamson 1985: 135–139).[13]

Note the recurrent theme: the action resides in the application of a focused lens to identify and examine the mechanisms of alternative modes of economic organization in a comparative institutional way—which reveals that markets and hierarchies differ in discrete structural respects, each with its strengths and weaknesses.

4. A Simple Model of Governance

Building on Tadelis (2002), we construct a model of contractual choice that parallels the arguments in Section 3. Despite its extreme reduced form, the model relies on microfoundations developed by Grossman and Hart (1986), Holmström and Milgrom (1991), and Bajari and Tadelis (2001).[14] The model contributes by exposing complementarities between cost incentives and governance that help clarify the underpinnings of the TCE framework outlined in Section 3.

The model parallels Section 3 in that (1) exchange takes place between successive (technologically separable) stages of production; (2) spot markets aside, all contracts are incomplete to varying degrees; (3) the critical attributes of transactions are asset specificity and contractual incompleteness (disturbances), where the former is responsible for bilateral dependency and the latter creates the adaptive need; (4) if the parties are independent and if a disturbance occurs for which the contract is not adequate, adaptation is accomplished by renegotiation and/or court ordering; and (5) efficiency is served by aligning transactions with governance structures in a way that economizes on transaction costs.

To simplify, however, there are two differences between the formal model and Section 3 that are worth noting, and more discussion will follow. First, adaptation costs are incurred only by the buyer. (The efficient alignment result does not depend on this asymmetry.) Second, asset specificity is treated as a probability of finding an alternative seller without incurring adaptation costs, rather than as an actual loss in surplus if the seller is replaced. This is done for simplicity purposes.

---

13. Contributing factors include (1) the owner (buyer) controls the accounting system and, within limits, can declare depreciation, transfer prices, and benefits so as to shift net receipts to its advantage; (2) failures of due care become known only with delay and are difficult to prove; (3) the buyer can also falsely declare state realizations to favor its own stream of net receipts; and (4) in consideration of the foregoing, the division of benefits under selective intervention can be compromised. Also, (5) the political game is now played in a larger firm that is more susceptible to bureaucratic ploys and political positioning than in smaller firms. Suffice it to observe that the breakdowns to which we refer are not beyond the grasp of intelligent businessmen and their lawyers, who recognize the trade-offs and factor them into the integration calculus.

14. An early step in formalizing TCE can be found in Riordan and Williamson (1985).

4.1. Transactions and Governance

Consider a transaction where a buyer achieves value $v > 0$ if it procures a good (or service) from a supplier and successfully incorporates it into its own output. The transaction is characterized by the degrees of asset specificity and contractual incompleteness.

4.1.1. Asset Specificity

Recall from Section 3.1.1 that asset specificity can manifest itself in several ways: physical, human, site, dedicated assets, and brand name capital. Asset specificity can arise from both purposeful investments and spontaneously, where the latter takes the form of knowledge and skills that are incidentally acquired by the parties while working together. Whatever the form, these assets cannot be redeployed to alternative uses and users without some loss of productive value.

Asset specificity is modeled by $\sigma \in [0, 1]$, where higher values of σ represent higher degrees of asset specificity. It will be technically convenient to interpret σ as the probability that the supplier cannot be replaced by a competitor when disturbances occur, and adaptation costs will be incurred. With probability $(1 - \sigma)$, however, there exists an alternative supplier who will compete to perform any adaptations that are needed, and adaptation costs will be avoided.

Though we believe that more asset specificity does imply that more value is lost when an alternative supplier is used, from an ex ante perspective the probabilistic nature of our measure of asset specificity is equivalent: when σ is higher, the expected loss from having to switch suppliers will be larger, making the fundamental transformation more severe.

4.1.2. Complexity and Incomplete Contracts

Let $\rho \in [0, 1]$ be the probability that the contract will need to be renegotiated due to a significant disturbance, at which point the contract's ex ante design will fail to achieve the value v. In this event, ex post adaptation at some extra cost will be needed to achieve v.[15] Bajari and Tadelis (2001) consider a model where it is possible to invest more or fewer resources in design ex ante, making design (i.e., contractual incompleteness) an endogenous variable that responds to project complexity. They show that transactions characterized by higher degrees of exogenous complexity result in endogenously chosen contracts that are more incomplete. We thus treat ρ as exogenous and interpret it as the *contractual incompleteness* of the transaction, a characteristic discussed in Section 3.1.2, where higher values of ρ correspond to transactions with higher degrees of contractual incompleteness.[16]

4.1.3. Markets and Hierarchies

Two modes of governance are considered: market and hierarchy. Recall from Section 3.2 that TCE identifies markets with two features: high-powered cost incentives and retention of administrative control by each party. In contrast, hierarchy is identified with low-powered cost incentives and the parties relinquishing administrative control to an interface coordinator. We

---

15. For simplicity we keep v constant, so that any loss from adaptation is captured by adaptation costs, to be defined precisely later.

16. In addition to design costs there are also costs of measuring whether performance was met as planned, which are another form of transaction costs (see Barzel 1982).

proceed to formally define market versus hierarchy using only one of these attributes: the assignment of administrative control over production and adaptation processes. The strength of incentives will be endogenously derived.[17]

Define market governance M to be the choice in which each party retains autonomy over its own production process decisions, and the supplier is expected to deliver a product that meets the contractual specifications. Any adaptation to adjust the ex ante design due to disturbances needs to be renegotiated by the autonomous parties. For simplicity, we assume that adaptation will be required only for the supplier's production process. Our asymmetric treatment of disturbances simplifies the analysis and offers a first step in formalizing the ideas described in Section 3. Naturally, the buyer may have to adapt its process to accommodate some disturbances as well. Symmetric disturbances on both sides of the transaction will result in a more cumbersome analysis, obscuring the main insights.

Define hierarchy H to be the choice in which the parties relinquish administrative control to a third party, the interface coordinator. Thus, routine tasks are followed as planned, but when disturbances arise, the decisions are made by the interface coordinator, who possesses unified ownership and control over production and adaptation for both stages of buyer and supplier.

It is important to note that our notion of hierarchy as unified control and coordinated adaptation differs from a directional integration argument of whether the buyer integrates the supplier into its business and becomes the interface coordinator, or the reverse, which is a novel and central feature of the Property Rights Theory (PRT) that is presented in Segal and Whinston (this volume). In contrast, our notion of integration assigns responsibility for implementing routines to the managers at each stage, whereas disturbances for which coordinated adaptations are required are done at the direction of the interface coordinator (see Figure 1). TCE identifies this interface coordinator as often being a third party whose incentives are aligned with total profit maximization. That is, instead of a preexisting buyer and supplier, the transaction is a de novo investment whose governance needs to be determined. Efficiency considerations will determine whether the transaction is integrated (controlled by an interface coordinator) or not integrated (controlled by the contract and mutually agreed-upon adaptations). PRT, in contrast, identifies integration with the situation in which one of the two parties becomes the owner of all productive assets and controls the decisions related to their use. The predictions of PRT are as much about which of the two parties maintains control as about when unified ownership is called for.

Aside from the allocation of administrative control, a compensation scheme that the buyer (or interface coordinator) uses to compensate the supplier must also be chosen as part of the interfirm contract (or intrafirm compensation scheme). This scheme will influence the supplier's incentives to reduce costs. Denote the supplier's production costs by c, which includes material and other expenses (lost opportunities, possibly the wages of laborers under its direction, etc.). We restrict attention to linear compensation schemes that have a fixed component F and a share of production costs $(1 - z) \in [0, 1]$. A supplier that incurs cost c is paid $F + (1 - z)c$, where $z \in [0, 1]$ is the share of production costs that are borne by the supplier, often referred to as the

---

17. The model ignores conflict resolution law and follows the common approach in contract theory that the courts will enforce whatever the contract stipulates. This approach is also taken by Grossman and Hart (1986). It is important to note, however, that current business law, which is very much commensurate with the brief description in Section 3.3, would further strengthen the conclusions of our theoretical modeling exercise.

"strength" of cost incentives that the supplier faces. For example, if $z = 1$ and $F > 0$, then the supplier receives a fixed-price payment of F and bears all the production costs, which seems to be the norm for almost all market transactions. The supplier will have strong incentives to reduce production costs. In contrast, if $z = 0$ and $F > 0$, then a cost-plus contract is in place where the supplier receives some fixed compensation F and bears none of the production costs c, which seems to be the case for most hierarchical structures (of course, in this case the chosen level of F will be different from the case in which $z = 1$). The supplier has no gain from engaging in activities that reduce production costs. Both F and z will be endogenously chosen in our analysis.

4.2. Production Costs

The supplier's production costs are given by the function $c(e, G) = \bar{c} - Ge$, where $e \geq 0$ is the effort intensity that the supplier puts into the project, and $G \in \{M, H\}$ denotes the mode of governance, where $M > H > 0$. Effort is the extra time and attention that the supplier puts into directing production of other employees, into choosing production alternatives that reduce costs, and so forth. The (opportunity) cost to the supplier of effort e is equal to $y(e)$, where $y'(e) > 0$, $y''(e) > 0$, and $y'''(e) \leq 0$.[18] To guarantee an interior solution to the seller's optimization problem we assume that $y'(0) = 0$. We also impose the standard agency assumption that contracting on effort is impossible.

As is apparent, we assume that more effort reduces production costs, and effort is more effective in reducing production costs when market governance is chosen. This assumption seems intuitive because decisions about how to produce or adapt the production process are an input into this process. If the supplier has complete control of its production process, then the ability to control all the inputs, including effort and decisions, should make the supplier more effective at cutting costs. If, however, decisions are in the hands of the interface coordinator, then the supplier's lack of autonomy will make its effort less effective.[19]

In addition to its intuitive appeal, the assumption that effort is more effective when the supplier maintains control has some established microfoundations.[20] Note also that this assumption

18. As shown in the proof of our main proposition, this last condition is sufficient but not necessary for monotone comparative statics.

19. Expanding the model to have buyer effort and a role for buyer incentives is easy, with each stage's effort being more effective for that stage when the stage has control over all aspects of production. Our asymmetric simplification relates this to the supplier stage alone.

20. First, Grossman and Hart (1986) model ex post decisions that need to be made after a state of nature is realized, yet contingent contracts cannot be written ex ante. The state of nature is very much like our ex post disturbances that are not contracted for. If the decisions themselves affect the way in which effort reduces production costs, then when the supplier controls both decisions and effort, it is better able to reduce its costs. Ownership of productive assets—as defined by PRT—gives the supplier control over the allocation of productive assets ex post, and this makes its cost-reducing effort more effective. Indeed, this assumption is our parallel of assumption 6 in Hart and Moore (1990). Second, our assumption is also consistent with the models of Holmström and Milgrom (1991, 1994). They show that the supplier's effort may be misdirected when it does not own the productive assets, where ownership is associated with having control over the use and sale of assets. If the productive assets are not owned by the supplier, then it will not necessarily take the asset's long run value into account, imposing additional long-run costs on production. (This idea is discussed explicitly in Williamson 1985: 137–138.)

is about a marginal reaction, namely, the effect of the allocation of administrative control on the slope of the cost function with respect to effort, which is a common assumption in the PRT literature.[21]

4.3. Adaptation Costs

If a disturbance occurs, then additional costly adaptations must be made to obtain the value v. Adaptation costs can have at least two sources. The first involves activities that were wasted and redone, or modifying initially planned production processes that fit the original design. These adaptation costs stem from contractual incompleteness and could have been spared if a complete contract and accurate design were in place. The second source of adaptation costs results from haggling, rent seeking, and other renegotiation costs that parties expend to get a better deal, which are a pure dead-weight loss.[22] We are agnostic as to which of these two sources of adaptation costs dominates, and we aggregate them together as total adaptation costs, denoted by $k(z, G) > 0$.

Adaptation costs are incurred if and only if two events happen. First, a disturbance must happen, which occurs with probability ρ, the incompleteness of the contract. Second, a new supplier from the competitive market cannot do the work, which occurs with probability σ, our measure of specificity. Indeed, if the required adaptation is not specific, then other suppliers can compete to perform the adaptation, and no loss from haggling will occur.

We simplify and assume that adaptation costs are borne only by the buyer. We can easily have the supplier also bear some adaptation costs, which would add symmetry to the problem of adaptation without changing the qualitative results.[23] We also assume that $v - k(z, G) > 0$, implying that adaptation costs are worth incurring ex post to achieve v. Hence, the expected gross benefit from the transaction is given by $v - \rho\sigma k(z, G) > 0$, and expected adaptation costs are increasing in both contractual incompleteness ρ and asset specificity σ.[24]

---

21. Thus, we make use of the method developed by Grossman and Hart (1986) to model the effect of administrative control. They modeled changes in the ownership of assets as changing the marginal effect of effort. Even though the driving forces and economic insights that we derive are different than those in PRT, the PRT modeling method will prove useful in formalizing the original ideas developed by TCE.

22. These haggling costs can be generated from a rent seeking game in the spirit of Tullock (1980) or Skaperdas (1992). As a simple example, imagine that the surplus to be split is 10 and that without hiring lawyers, a court (or arbitrator) would direct the parties to split the surplus equally. Assume that if a party hires a lawyer to argue in court, then it would get 3/4 of the surplus if the other party has no lawyer, but symmetrically, would get 1/2 of the surplus if the other party has a lawyer. If the lawyer costs are $k < 2.5$, then this game is a prisoner's dilemma in which hiring a lawyer is a dominant strategy, the parties split the 10 equally, but each pays k and is left with $5 - k$. Hence, as far as the relationship is considered, rents were dissipated. This idea is explored in Ashenfelter and Bloom (1993), who show that parties to disputes indeed have an incentive to engage in legal representation, which suggests that some excessive legal expenses are incurred.

23. For instance, if ex ante competition pushes expected rents ex ante to zero, then any adaptation costs (or renegotiation income) that the supplier expects to spend (or gain) will be incorporated into his bid and will fall back on the buyer (see, e.g., Bajari et al. 2012).

24. One can model the effects of adaptation as lowering the payoff v to some $v' < v$, above and beyond any additional adaptation costs of k, as in Tadelis (2002). This is redundant, because the expected gross benefit (ignoring production costs) to the buyer would be $(1 - \rho)v + \rho[(1 - \sigma)v + \sigma(v' - k)] = v - \rho\sigma(v - v' + k)$,

We assume further that the choice of governance affects adaptation costs.[25] Bilateral dependence causes a conflict of interest between the buyer (or the interface coordinator) and the supplier when adaptation is required. With autonomy (market), the supplier is in a stronger position to hold up the buyer and direct activities in its interest. Furthermore, if the supplier controls the adaptation process, then it has more power to choose actions that direct rents toward it, which would impose added costs on the buyer even at the expense of total surplus. In a hierarchy, however, the interface coordinator has control over the adaptation process. This reduces the adaptation costs that the supplier can impose.[26] The following assumption summarizes this discussion.

Assumption 1 *Adaptation costs are lower in hierarchy: $k(z, M) > k(z, H)$ for all z.*

The intuitive justification of Assumption 2 is further supported by the microfoundations of the hold-up problem. The more specific assets of any kind are concentrated under an independent supply stage, the worse is the fundamental transformation. When the supplier owns the dedicated assets, then the *temporal lock-in* is stronger, because the aggregate degree of bilateral dependency has increased.[27]

The choice of incentives will also affect adaptation costs. Williamson proposed that "low powered incentives have well known adaptability advantages. That, after all, is what commends cost plus contracting." (1985: 140). Indeed, if the supplier bears less of the production costs, then it has less to gain from haggling with the buyer (or interface coordinator) over the adaptation.

Assumption 2 *Adaptation costs are lower when cost incentives are weaker: $\frac{\partial k(z, G)}{\partial z} > 0$.*

The microfoundations for Assumption 3 are explored in Bajari and Tadelis (2001). In a buyer-supplier contracting model with bilateral dependency they show that if the supplier's incentives are stronger, then the rents dissipated during adaptation are larger. Intuitively, when the supplier incurs more of the costs, then the conflict of interest between buyer and supplier is intensified: the buyer wants a change that maximizes its net benefit, while the supplier will be motivated to reduce its costs.[28] This insight should carry over to an integrated setting where

---

and because $v - v' > 0$, this is just part of the adaptation costs as we define them above. Also, it is without loss of generality that we assume that adaptation is always efficient. It is easy to incorporate a more involved setting where adaptation costs are random and may sometimes be inefficient, in that projects are sometimes terminated (see, e.g., Bajari and Tadelis 2001).

25. This general idea appears already in Williamson (1985: 131–147) and is also related to the work of Milgrom and Roberts (1988).

26. In a symmetric model where the buyer can impose adaptation costs on the supplier (or interface coordinator), then with autonomy, the buyer can impose adaptation costs to redirect rents toward itself. Adaptation costs imposed by both sides would be reduced under hierarchy.

27. Furthermore, consistent with the assumptions of PRT, giving the supplier ownership over assets (or simply control over adaptation decisions) will strengthen its bargaining position (outside option) and increase its renegotiations rents.

28. Bajari and Tadelis (2001) show that ex ante competition between potential suppliers will cause any adaptation costs borne by the supplier to be passed on to the buyer. This idea is used by Bajari et al. (2012) to measure adaptation costs in highway procurement.

an interface coordinator directs adaptation: if the interface coordinator mediates both stages of production and seeks to maximize combined surplus, then both supplier and buyer will impose more resistance if they face stronger cost incentives.

Bajari and Tadelis (2001) do not include governance in their analysis of contracts, so we need to consider ways in which changes in governance will change the marginal effect of incentives on adaptation costs. To fix ideas, begin with a fixed-price contract, $z = 1$, where adaptation costs are highest, and consider a reduction in incentives (a decrease in z) that will in turn reduce adaptation costs. From Assumption 2, adaptation costs in a hierarchy are lower than in market governance. From Assumption 3, a decrease in supplier incentives will reduce adaptation costs. We add a third assumption that the marginal reductions in adaptation costs are higher when hierarchy is chosen.

Assumption 3   *Reducing adaptation costs by weakening incentives is more effective under hierarchy:* $\frac{\partial k(z, H)}{\partial z} > \frac{\partial k(z, M)}{\partial z} > 0.$

This assumption lacks microfoundations, but it seems reasonable in light of the argument that hierarchy promotes coordinated adaptations. To keep things simple, we assume that when adaptation happens, we are not affecting the utility of the supplier (it is exactly compensated for any extra costs that adaptation imposes on it). As such, adaptation causes extra costs and inefficiencies that are imposed on the buyer or the interface coordinator, but no extra rents are gained or lost by the supplier. This assumption is not important, but it conveniently simplifies the analysis.[29]

4.4. Selective Intervention

Assumptions 1–3 imply that supplier autonomy defined by market governance reduces production costs but increases adaptation costs, while hierarchy does the opposite. There is, perhaps, an obvious solution: let the supplier retain control of production decisions related to the original design, and let the interface coordinator (or possibly the buyer) retain control over adaptation decisions. This, however, is ruled out by the assumption that *selective intervention* is severely limited.

Assumption 4   *Administrative control is allocated over both production and adaptation, and the two processes cannot be separated to allow for selective intervention.*

This assumption is in line with the discussion in Section 3.4 where it was argued that it is impossible to combine replication and selective intervention (Williamson 1985: 135–140). The model takes an extreme position on the inability to have selective intervention, but clearly what matters is that at the margin some selective intervention is impossible. Realistically, a contract may specify some domains of control that each party may have. As long as contracts are incomplete, however, the impossibility of perfect selective intervention will persist.

29. In Bajari and Tadelis (2001), when adaptation occurs, there are some expected rents to the supplier due to lock-in, and they are competed away ex ante. This could be included here with a more sophisticated focus on ex post adaptation with asymmetric information, but it would not shed light on the forces we wish to illuminate.

4.5. Markets versus Hierarchies

We proceed with the analysis of endogenously choosing governance and incentives. First consider the objective of the supplier,

$$\max_{e \geq 0} \ u_S(e; z, G) = F - z(\overline{c} - Ge) - y(e).$$

Lemma 1   *Given the pair (z, G), the supplier's optimal choice $e^G(z)$ is increasing in z, $e^G(0) = 0$ for $G \in \{M, H\}$, and $e^M(z) > e^H(z) > 0$ for any $z \in (0, 1]$. Furthermore, $\frac{de^M(z)}{dz} > \frac{de^H(z)}{dz}$ for any $z \in [0, 1]$.*

This result is derived in the Appendix and follows from the rather standard assumptions made in Section 4.2. It says that stronger incentives increase effort, which is expected, and that given a fixed strength of incentives, effort is higher under market governance. This is a consequence of the assumption that the supplier's effort is more effective when it maintains control over decisions. Finally, the marginal response of the supplier to incentives is stronger under market governance.

Given the optimal response of the supplier, surplus maximization is given by the following program:[30]

$$\max_{\substack{G \in H, M \\ z \in [0, 1]}} S(z, G; \rho, \sigma) = v - \overbrace{\underbrace{(\overline{c} - Ge^G(z))}_{\text{Production costs}} - \underbrace{y(e^G(z))}_{\text{Compensation}} - \underbrace{\sigma \rho k(z, G)}_{\text{Expected adaptation costs}}}^{\text{Total transaction costs}}.$$

The components of this program are easy to see. The benefit is the value to the buyer, and the costs have three components. The first is the production cost, the second is the compensation needed to cover the seller's opportunity costs of effort, and the third is the expected adaptation cost. Solving this program leads to the central result of this section.

Proposition 1   *When asset specificity increases (higher σ), or when contracts are more incomplete (higher ρ), the relative benefits of hierarchy over markets increase. Furthermore, optimal incentives become weaker.*

In the Appendix we show that the program exhibits increasing differences in all of its arguments, resulting in monotone comparative statics (see, e.g., Milgrom and Shannon 1994). The intuition for this result is quite straightforward. Strong cost-reducing incentives reduce production costs at the expense of raising adaptation costs (Assumption 2). Market governance makes cost-reducing incentives more effective at the expense of raising adaptation costs (Assumption 1). Hence, more asset specificity and more contractual incompleteness, which increase

---

30. We substitute $e^G(z)$ in place of e in the objective function to take account of the supplier's incentive compatibility constraint. We assume that the participation constraint does not impose a problem, which in itself is innocuous. The buyer's expected utility is $u_B(z, G; \rho) = v - F - (1 - z)c(e^G(z), G) - \sigma \rho k(z, G)$, and total surplus is just $S(\cdot) = u_B(\cdot) + u_S(\cdot)$.

the expected costs of adaptations, favor the use of hierarchies with weak cost-reducing incentives. Because at the margin, controlling adaptation costs through incentives is more effective under hierarchy (Assumption 3), incentives and governance choices are *complements* in the organizational design. This result is not transparent in the less formal arguments of TCE. Finally, the entire argument rests on the impossibility of selective intervention (Assumption 4). Without it, one can assign control of different processes selectively to the agent who is most impacted, reducing adaptation costs dramatically without the sacrifice of lower productivity. Illuminating the complementarity between governance and incentives is a useful contribution of the formal model with respect to the semi-formal arguments in Section 3.[31]

It is useful to illustrate the result through a simple numerical example. Let $k(z, G) = G + 4z$ and $y(e) = e^2/2$, where $G = 1$ represents hierarchy, and $G = 2$ represents market. Given an incentive scheme $F + (1 - z)c$, the supplier chooses $e^G(z)$ to maximize $F - z(2 - Ge) - e^2/2$, resulting in the optimal choice $e^G(z) = zG$. Substituting this into the objective function of surplus maximization yields

$$\max_{\substack{z \in [0, 1] \\ G \in \{1, 2\}}} S = v - (\bar{c} - G^2 z) - \sigma \rho (G + 4z) - \frac{z^2 G^2}{2}.$$

Because $G \in \{1, 2\}$ corresponds to $\{H, M\}$, we can separately solve for $z_H^*(\sigma, \rho) = \max\{0, 1 - 4\sigma\rho\}$ and $z_M^*(\sigma, \rho) = 1 - \sigma\rho$. The resulting optimal surplus for market is $S_M^*(\sigma, \rho) = v - \bar{c} - 6\sigma\rho + 2(\sigma\rho)^2 + 2$ and for hierarchy is

$$S_H^*(\sigma, \tau) = \begin{cases} v - \bar{c} - 5\sigma\rho + 8(\sigma\rho^2 + \frac{1}{2}) & \text{if } 0 \le \sigma\rho \le \frac{1}{4} \\ v - \bar{c} - \sigma\rho & \text{if } \frac{1}{4} \le \sigma\rho \le 1. \end{cases}$$

Comparing the expressions for total surplus, we obtain $S_H^*(\sigma, \rho) > S_M^*(\sigma, \rho)$ if and only if $\sigma\rho > 0.5$. For example, if the contract is not too incomplete ($\rho < 0.5$) or if the transaction is not too specific ($\sigma < 0.5$), then markets are always optimal. If, however, the contract is totally incomplete ($\rho = 1$), then for $\sigma > 0.5$ hierarchy will dominate the market, because it has lower total transaction costs. This case corresponds exactly to Figure 2 with $\sigma^* = 0.5$.

In reference to Figure 2, as contractual incompleteness increases, total transaction costs increase for both markets and hierarchies, causing both functions to rise. However, market transactions costs increase faster, making hierarchies better for a larger range of specificity σ. This is a point that the model illuminates. Because σ and ρ are multiplied, contractual incompleteness and asset specificity are complementary. Thus, the negative effects that incompleteness has on

---

31. The appropriate legal rules would strengthen our result. Namely, if the contract stipulates that the supplier retains control of supply processes, then the courts will enforce the letter of the contract that defines performance (design) and payments. This gives the supplier more bargaining power when adaptation is requested—it can use the original contract as a threat, which imposes extra costs due to haggling during the renegotiation process. If, however, the contract stipulates that both stages implement adaptations at the direction of the interface coordinator, then the courts will not enforce the performance measures under the doctrine that if the interface coordinator maintains control and can direct the parties as it wishes, then the supplier (or buyer) cannot be made accountable for detailed design-based performance. In this situation the courts will defer to the power of fiat, as is common in employment relationships. As such, adaptation is further facilitated when hierarchy is selected.

adaptation costs are exacerbated when asset specificity is higher. One can consider other speci-fications where this would not be the case, yet interestingly, this specification is consistent with the empirical results of Masten (1984).

5. Extensions and Applications

5.1. Hybrids

The advantages of the two polar modes, simple market exchange and hierarchy, are pronounced for transactions that deviate significantly from the crossover value σ^*, as shown in Figure 2. Hybrid contracting arrangements, however, that are located between hierarchy and simple spot market transactions, appear to be common and thus warrant brief consideration. We interpret the hybrid as an intermediate mode of organization that uses credible commitments to support exchange for transactions that pose an intermediate range of hazards (close to the value σ^*).

In some instances credible commitments are contractually agreed on by the parties to help provide additional assurances, of which the 32-year coal supply agreement between the Nevada Power Company and the Northwest Trading Company is illustrative (Williamson 1991: 272–273).[32] These assurances may include additional supports, such as formal auditing and informa-tion disclosure procedures, as well as reliance on private ordering dispute resolution mechanisms that are outside the formal courts (Llewellyn 1931; Macaulay 1963; Summers 1969; Macneil 1974; Galanter 1981). The use of hostages to support exchange (Williamson 1983) is both an ancient and contemporary example that can be interpreted in credible contracting terms, in that defection from cooperation is deterred by reciprocal exposure of specific assets that experience positively correlated disturbances.

5.2. Reality Testing

TCE addresses itself to issues of scaling up, remediableness, and bureaucracy, and recommends that other theories of firm and market organization consider doing likewise.

5.2.1. Scaling up

The object of a simple model is to capture the essence, thereby to explain puzzling practices and make predictions that are subjected to empirical testing. But that is not the only relevant test. Simple models can also be tested with respect to scaling up. Does repeated application of the simple model's basic mechanism yield a result that recognizably describes the phenomenon in question?

The test of scaling up is often ignored, possibly out of awareness that scaling up of the model in question is very demanding. Sometimes it is recognized but deferred,[33] possibly in the belief that scaling up can be accomplished easily. We advise that claims of real world relevance,

32. In other instances credible commitments come into place spontaneously, which is the case when a supplier's good (poor) history becomes a reputational asset (liability). See, for example, Bar-Isaac and Tadelis (2008).

33. Michael Jensen and William Meckling expressly recognized the importance of scaling up from a single owner-manager to a multitude of owners in a modern corporation and stated that this was an issue that they planned to deal with it in a later paper (1976: 356). That paper never materialized, presumably because of the difficulties. (Their 1976 paper has nonetheless been influential.)

including public policy relevance, of any candidate theory of the firm that cannot be shown to scale up from toy model status to approximate the phenomenon of interest (usually, the modern corporation) should be regarded with caution.

With reference to the theory of the firm as governance structure, the question is this: Does successive application of the make-or-buy decision, as it is applied to individual transactions in the TCE setup, scale up to describe something that approximates a multistage firm? Note that, as described previously, TCE assumes that the transactions of principal interest are those that take place *at the interface between* (rather than within) technologically separable stages, which is the "boundary of the firm" issue as described elsewhere (Williamson 1985: 96–98). Upon taking the technological core as given, attention is focused on a series of separable make-or-buy decisions— backward, forward, and lateral—to ascertain which should be outsourced and which should be incorporated within the ownership boundary of the firm. So described, the firm is the inclusive set of transactions for which the decision is to make rather than buy—which does implement scaling up, or at least is an approximation thereto (Williamson 1985: 96–98).[34]

Indeed, whereas examining whether to make or buy a series of technologically separable components is a relatively straightforward process where stages, if acquired, are all under unified ownership, it is not at all obvious how scaling up applies to the employment relationship (where successive employees have different propensities, e.g., for risk aversion) or to directional integration (as opposed to unified ownership) in the modern property rights setup.

5.2.2. Remediableness

Public policy analysts have often assumed that transaction costs in the public sector are zero. That is unrealistic, yet standard public policy proceeded in an asymmetric way: private sector contracting experienced market failures, by reason of positive transaction costs, but there was no corresponding concept for public sector failures.[35] Little surprise, then, that convoluted public policy prescriptions were often (unwittingly) anchored in the asymmetric application of zero transaction cost reasoning, of which public policy on regulation was an example: only private sector supply was burdened with positive transaction costs; regulation was a zero transaction cost alternative (Coase 1964).

The remediableness criterion is an effort to deal symmetrically with real world institutions, both public and private. The criterion is this: an existing mode of organization for which no superior feasible form of organization can be described and implemented with expected net gains is presumed to be efficient (Williamson 1996: 195–213). In other words, a "revealed preference" approach is applied to the choice of governance.

Because all feasible modes of organization are flawed, the feasibility stipulation precludes all appeals to the fiction of zero transaction costs (in any sector whatsoever—public, private, nonprofit, etc.) from the very outset. The implementation stipulation requires that the costs

34. In the context of a multidivisional firm (Chandler 1962), the scaling up to which we refer corresponds more nearly to that of an operating division (which could be a freestanding firm that has been acquired by a diversified enterprise) than to the entire multidivisional enterprise—where the general office provides an additional level of strategic participation.

35. Albeit a caricature, "normative public policy analysis began by supposing that . . . policy was made by an omnipotent, omniscient, and benevolent dictator" (Dixit 1996: 8)—which, in transaction cost terms, assumes the absence of implementation obstacles, bounds on rationality, and opportunism, respectively.

of implementing a proposed feasible alternative (one that is judged to be superior to an extant mode in a de novo side-by-side comparison) be included in the net gain calculus.[36]

The upshot is that the remediableness criterion is an effort to disallow asymmetric efficiency reasoning of a zero transaction cost kind, thereby to force the relevant efficiency issues for the making of public policy (Dixit 1996) to the surface.

5.2.3. Burdens of Bureaucracy

The impossibility of implementing either replication or selective intervention is partly attributable to the incentive distortions that arise when successive stages of production that had previously been independent are placed under unified ownership (to include the control over accounting practices that accrues thereto). But there is more to it than that.

Reaching beyond the scope of the analysis in Sections 3 and 4, some of the more insidious burdens of bureaucracy arise because "integration affects the internal politics of the corporation with systematic performance consequences" (Williamson 1985: 145). These effects include tilting the managerial promotion game away from merit in favor of politics (subgoal pursuit), the increased propensity to intervene (overmanage and overcontrol), limits on internal incentives due to internal equity considerations, and the distortion of operating and investment decisions (Williamson 1985: 147–152). The appearance of what Paul Milgrom and John Roberts (1988) refer to as "influence costs" are also in the spirit of bureaucratic burdens.

Understanding of the strengths and weaknesses of bureaucracy is very underdeveloped compared with understanding of the strengths and weaknesses of markets—mainly because bureaucracy is both a comparatively neglected and a formidably difficult subject. Robert Michels nevertheless taught us how to proceed. Rather than end his study with the finding that "who says organization, says oligarchy" (1962 [1911]: 365), Michels advises instead that, upon recognition of this prospect, we take the next step and push the logic to completion: "nothing but a serene and frank examination of the oligarchical dangers of [organization] will enable us to [mitigate] these dangers" (1962 [1911]: 370). The corresponding lesson for our purposes here is this: a more informed assessment of markets and hierarchies will result as we uncover the basic regularities and work out the ramifications for economic organization in a candid, disciplined, and microanalytic way.

5.3. Variations on a Theme

Many regularities that are associated with the intermediate product market transaction recur, in variable degree, as variations on a theme. TCE not only has many applications in the field of industrial organization but also in most applied fields of economics as well, including labor, public finance, comparative economic systems, and economic development and reform. Applications to business—to the fields of strategy, organizational behavior, marketing, finance, operations management, and accounting—are likewise numerous. Many applications to the contiguous social sciences (especially sociology, political science, social psychology, and aspects of the law;

---

36. The presumption that a chosen mode is efficient if the expected net gain is negative is nevertheless rebuttable: it can be challenged by showing that the obstacles to implementing an otherwise superior feasible alternative are unfair. See Williamson (1996: 195–213) for a discussion.

Williamson 2005b) have also been made. More generally, TCE has broad reach because any problem that arises as or can be reformulated as a contracting problem can be examined to advantage in TCE terms. (See Macher and Richman (2008) for a discussion of the applications with references to the relevant literature.)

5.4. Empirical Evidence

Shortly after the main ideas of TCE were laid out, several seminal empirical papers confirmed the main prediction of the theory, including Monteverde and Teece (1982), Masten (1984), Joskow (1985); also see Shelanski and Klein (1995), and Lafontaine and Slade (2007). Macher and Richman (2008) report that there were more than 900 published empirical papers on TCE during 1980–2004, with more in progress. Indeed, "despite what almost 30 years ago may have appeared to be insurmountable obstacles to acquiring the relevant data [which are often primary data of a microanalytic kind], today transaction cost economics stands on a remarkably broad empirical foundation" (Geyskens et al. 2006: 531). As Michael Whinston puts it: TCE has been "one of the great [empirical] success stories in industrial organization over the past [30] years" (Whinston 2001: 185). There is no gainsaying that TCE has been much more influential because of its broad and varied applications and the empirical work that it has engendered. Most recently, new empirical studies have focused attention on the importance of adaptation to empirically validate the central themes of TCE (e.g., Forbes and Lederman 2009, 2010; Costinot et al. 2011).

5.5. Antitrust and Regulation

TCE was stimulated in part by the disarray in antitrust enforcement and regulation during the 1960s. As Coase observed,

> If an economist finds something—a business practice of one sort or another that he does not understand, he looks for a monopoly explanation. And as in this field we are very ignorant, the number of ununderstandable practices tends to be very large, and the reliance on a monopoly explanation, frequent. [Coase 1972: 67]

The possibility that complex contract and organization had beneficial governance purposes was ignored. The implausibility of such monopoly reasoning coupled with a small but growing interest in transaction cost economizing would eventually help to bring relief from such excesses.[37]

---

37. Interestingly, Timothy Muris, during his term as chair of the Federal Trade Commission, held that much of the new institutional economics "literature has significant potential to improve antitrust analysis and policy. In particular, . . . [the transaction cost branch has] focused on demystifying the 'black box' firm and on clarifying important determinants of vertical relationships" (2003: 15). Opening the black box and acquiring an understanding of the mechanisms inside has had an impact, moreover, on practice:

> The most impressive recent competition policy work I have seen reflects the NIE's teachings about the appropriate approach to antitrust analysis. Much of the FTC's best work follows the tenets of the NIE and reflects careful, fact-based analyses that properly account for institutions and *all* the relevant theories, not just market structure and [monopoly] power theories. [Muris 2003: 11; emphasis in original]

As applied to regulation and deregulation, more attention to the details and to strategic behavior on the part of participants in regulated or deregulated sectors needs to be factored in.[38] As Paul Joskow observes of efforts to deregulate electricity in California, too much deference was given to the (assumed) efficacy of smoothly functioning markets and insufficient attention to potential investment and contractual hazards and appropriate governance responses thereto:

> Many policy makers and fellow travelers have been surprised by how difficult it has been to create wholesale electricity markets . . . . Had policy makers viewed the restructuring challenge using a TCE framework, these potential problems are more likely to have been identified and mechanisms adopted ex ante to fix them. [Joskow 2000: 51]

6. Some Challenges

As Williamson (2010) observes, TCE, like many other theories, has undergone a natural progression from informal (1930–1970), to pre-formal (1970s), to semi-formal (1980s and beyond), of which full formalization is the last step.

The pathbreaking paper by Sanford Grossman and Oliver Hart (1986) and the follow-on paper by Hart and John Moore (1990), which founded the PRT literature, have been very influential. They have established the modeling apparatus used in Section 4, in which governance choices affect the incentives of parties to a transaction. That said, there are three fundamental differences between the PRT and TCE approaches.

First, TCE emphasizes ex post adaptation as the main problem of organization, whereas the PRT has focused more on the problem of ex ante alignment of incentives to invest in specific assets, mainly of the intangible (human asset) kind. This same focus on ex ante incentives is also at the core of most agency-based theories.

Second, PRT and agency-based theories are silent about how transactions differ with respect to complexity, uncertainty, and contractual incompleteness. Instead, agency theory and PRT explore the consequences of incomplete information in that some aspects of the transaction have zero costs of contracting, while others have infinite costs. Namely, in standard agency models, output measures of the transaction (e.g., the component's functionality, quality, or a signal of these) can be specified at no cost, while the effort and actions of people who work toward achieving the desired goals cannot be specified at any cost. The PRT paradigm assumes that contingent decisions related to how to do the job or how to respond to changes in the environment cannot be specified at any cost, whereas it is costless to decide who has the rights to make decisions and execute them, and it is costless to enforce these rights. TCE, in contrast, focuses on measurable dimensions over which transactions differ, with emphasis on identifying how different kinds

---

38. Interestingly, the first "empirical" application of TCE was to regulation. The issue was the purported efficacy of franchise bidding for natural monopoly, as advanced by Demsetz (1968) and applied to the cable television industry by Posner (1972). Missing from both of these sanguine assessments of the efficacy of franchise bidding were (1) an examination of the details by which franchise bidding would be implemented and (2) an awareness that the nonredeployability of asset-specific investments would pose serious (but unexamined) problems (Williamson 1976).

of transactions are discriminately allocated to different governance structures. This emphasis accounts for much of its predictive content and empirical success described in Section 5.4.[39]

Third, PRT identifies ownership of assets as the critical variable and takes the view that ownership determines who has the residual right to decide how to use the productive assets. As such, changes in ownership of assets from one party to another will change the incentives of the parties to invest in the specific relationship, implying a unified framework for the costs and benefits of integration. The implications are that separable, well-defined assets ought to be owned by the individuals whose incentives are most affected by ownership. But there is more: *directional* ownership is predicted. PRT asserts that either buyer or seller should own the assets, and it matters who the owner is. In fact, however, bundles of assets are owned by firms, not by individuals. Holmström (1999), who raises this important critique, argues that owning bundles of assets allows the firm to internalize many of the externalities that are associated with incentive designs in a world characterized by informational imperfections, which are responsible for contractual incompleteness. By associating the decisionmaker with more assets under his control, his administrative control is expanded, and he possesses more levers through which to implement coordinated adaptation. This observation is very much in line with our notion of the interface coordinator as the executive who has the authority to coordinate adaptation as needed, even though she as an individual need not own the assets.

Still, the Grossman-Hart methodology is an instrumental contribution. Building on their methods and the insights in Bajari and Tadelis (2001), Tadelis (2002) makes a step toward formalizing some of the central ideas of TCE. Additional efforts have been made by Gibbons (2005). The model we offer in Section 4 is an attempt to push the full formalization of TCE yet another modest step forward. More work, however, still needs to be done, and a full incorporation of the role of law in formal models is indeed very challenging.

7. Conclusion

Compared with the top-down neoclassical theory of the firm as production function, the theory of the firm as governance structure is a bottom-up construction in the following respects: (1) rather than work through the price-theoretic lens of choice, TCE examines economic activity through the lens of contract; (2) rather than focus on composite goods and services (supply and demand, prices and output), TCE focuses on transactions and the organization thereof; (3) rather than take the boundary of the firm as given by technology, TCE derives the boundary in comparative contractual terms; (4) the resulting contractual strategy for examining

---

39. Despite TCE being an empirical success story, there is an interesting challenge in making more progress on the empirical front. As discussed in Section 5.2, a complete understanding of the pros and cons of bureaucracy is still underdeveloped. Indeed, "distortion-free internal exchange is a fiction and is not to be regarded as the relevant organizational alternative in circumstances where market exchange predictably experiences nontrivial frictions" (Williamson 1975: 124–125). Most empirical studies of TCE show that relative to internal organization, market transactions do worse when there is either more asset specificity or more transaction complexity (which leads to contractual incompleteness). What these studies cannot usually measure is by how much do the costs of each mode of governance change with changes in a transaction's attributes. A first step in this direction was made by Masten et al. (1991), who use a censored regression approach to study the procurement of components and services by a large naval shipbuilder.

economic organization in terms of the microanalytics of transactions and governance structures has broad reach, in that a large number of contractual phenomena turn out to be variations on a few key contractual themes to which the discriminating alignment hypothesis applies; (5) transaction-level analysis opens up a whole new range of activities to which empirical analysis can be applied; and (6) public policy analysis is more nuanced and more objectively comparative in the process. Also, although fully formal TCE analysis is a work in progress, headway has been made, and more is in prospect.

Indeed, headway in the future will be realized as it has in the past—not by the creation of a general theory but by proceeding in a modest, slow, molecular, definitive way, placing block upon block until the value added cannot be denied. It is both noteworthy and encouraging that so many young scholars have found productive ways to relate. More generally, the economics of organization has benefited from rival and complementary perspectives, especially those that subscribe to the four precepts of pragmatic methodology. Such pluralism brings energy to the elusive ambition of realizing the "science of organization" to which Chester Barnard (1938) made reference 75 years ago and to which this *Handbook of Organizational Economics* speaks.

Appendix

Here we prove the Lemma and Proposition stated in Section 4.5.

Proof of Lemma: It follows from $y(e)$ being convex with $y'(0) = 0$ that there is a unique solution $e^G(z)$ to the first-order condition, $zG - y'(e^G(z)) = 0$, with $e^G(0) = 0$. Because $M > H > 0$, it immediately follows that $e^M(z) > e^H(z) > 0$ for all $z \in (0, 1]$. Now consider the derivative of the first-order condition with respect to z:

$$G - y''(e^G(z))\frac{de^G(z)}{dz} = 0,$$

or

$$\frac{de^G(z)}{dz} = \frac{G}{y''(e^G(z))}.$$

Because $M > G > 0$ and $e^M(z) \geq e^H(z)$, the assumption that $y'''(e) \leq 0$ is a sufficient condition for $\frac{de^M(z)}{dz} > \frac{de^H(z)}{dz}$.

Proof of Proposition: The proposition states that as σ or ρ increase, both solutions $z^*(\sigma, \rho)$ and $G^*(\sigma, \rho)$ will (weakly) decrease. It therefore suffices to prove that the objective function of maximizing total surplus exhibits increasing differences (Milgrom and Shannon 1994). In particular, we need to show that $\frac{\partial^2 S}{\partial z \partial \rho} < 0$ and $\frac{\partial^2 S}{\partial z \partial \sigma} < 0$, that $\frac{\partial S}{\partial \rho}$ and $\frac{\partial S}{\partial \sigma}$ are decreasing in G, and that $\frac{\partial S}{\partial z}$ is increasing in G. Observe that

$$\frac{\partial S}{\partial z} = G\frac{\partial e^G(z)}{\partial z} - y'(e^G(z))\frac{\partial e^G(z)}{\partial z} - \sigma\rho\frac{\partial k(z, G)}{\partial z}, \tag{1}$$

and in turn,

$$\frac{\partial^2 S}{\partial z \partial \rho} = -\sigma \frac{\partial k(z, G)}{\partial z} < 0,$$

and

$$\frac{\partial^2 S}{\partial z \partial \sigma} = -\rho \frac{\partial k(z, G)}{\partial z} < 0,$$

which both follow from $\frac{\partial k(z,G)}{\partial z} > 0$ (Assumption 2). To show that $\frac{\partial S}{\partial \rho}$ is decreasing in G, we need to show that

$$\left.\frac{\partial S}{\partial \rho}\right|_{G=M} - \left.\frac{\partial S}{\partial \rho}\right|_{G=H} < 0.$$

Observe that $\frac{\partial S}{\partial \rho} = -\sigma k(z, G)$, so that

$$\left.\frac{\partial S}{\partial \rho}\right|_{G=M} - \left.\frac{\partial S}{\partial \rho}\right|_{G=H} = -\sigma k(z, M) + \sigma k(z, H) < 0,$$

which follows from Assumption 1. Showing that $\frac{\partial S}{\partial \sigma}$ is decreasing in G follows the same steps (where σ is replaced with ρ). We are left to show that $\frac{\partial S}{\partial z}$ is increasing in G. That is, we need to show that $\left.\frac{\partial S}{\partial z}\right|_{G=M} - \left.\frac{\partial S}{\partial z}\right|_{G=H} > 0$ or, using (1),

$$[M - y'(e^M(z))]\frac{\partial e^M(z)}{\partial z} - [H - y'(e^H(z))]\frac{\partial e^H(z)}{\partial z}$$

$$+ \sigma\rho \left(\frac{\partial k(z, M)}{\partial z} - \frac{\partial k(z, M)}{\partial z}\right) > 0.$$

Assumption 2 implies that $\sigma\rho \left(\frac{\partial k(z, M)}{\partial z} - \frac{\partial k(z, M)}{\partial z}\right) > 0$, so it suffices to show that

$$[M - y'(e^M(z))]\frac{\partial e^M(z)}{\partial z} - [H - y'(e^H(z))]\frac{\partial e^H(z)}{\partial z} > 0. \tag{2}$$

From the supplier's first-order condition, we can substitute $y'(e^G(z)) = zG$ into the left-hand side of (2) to obtain

$$(1 - z)M\frac{\partial e^M(z)}{\partial z} - (1 - z)H\frac{\partial e^H(z)}{\partial z} > 0,$$

which is satisfied because $M > H$ and from Lemma 1, $\frac{\partial e^M(z)}{\partial z} > \frac{\partial e^H(z)}{\partial z}$.

REFERENCES

Arrow, Kenneth J. 1969. "The Organization of Economic Activity: Issues Pertinent to the Choice of Market versus Nonmarket Allocation," in *The Analysis and Evaluation of Public Expenditure: The PPB System,* volume 1, U.S. Joint Economic Committee, 91st Congress, 1st session. Washington, DC: U.S. Government Printing Office, pp. 39–73.

Ashenfelter, Orley, and David Bloom. 1993. "Lawyers as Agents of the Devil in a Prisoner's Dilemma Game." Working Paper 4447, National Bureau of Economic Research, Washington, DC.

Bajari, Patrick, and Steven Tadelis. 2001. "Incentives versus Transaction Costs: A Theory of Procurement Contracts." *Rand Journal of Economics* 32: 387–407.

Bajari, Patrick, Stephanie Houghton, and Steven Tadelis. 2012. "Bidding for Incomplete Contracts: An Empirical Analysis of Adaptation Costs." *American Economic Review,* forthcoming.

Bar-Isaac, Heski, and Steven Tadelis. 2008. "Seller Reputation." *Foundations and Trends in Microeconomics* 4: 273–351.

Barnard, Chester. 1938. *The Functions of the Executive.* Cambridge: Harvard University Press (fifteenth printing, 1962).

Barzel, Yoram. 1982. "Measurement Cost and the Organization of Markets." *Journal of Law and Economics* 25: 27–48.

Buchanan, James. 1975. "A Contractarian Paradigm for Applying Economic Theory." *American Economic Review* 65: 225–230.

———. 2001. "Game Theory, Mathematics, and Economics." *Journal of Economic Methodology* 8(March): 27–32.

Chandler, Alfred D. 1962. *Strategy and Structure.* New York: Doubleday and Co.

Coase, Ronald H. 1937. "The Nature of the Firm." *Economica* 4: 386–405. Reprinted in Oliver E. Williamson and Sidney Winter (eds.) 1991. *The Nature of the Firm: Origins, Evolution, Development.* New York: Oxford University Press, pp. 18–33.

———. 1960. "The Problem of Social Cost." *Journal of Law and Economics* 3: 1–44.

———. 1964. "The Regulated Industries: Discussion." *American Economic Review* 54: 194–197.

———. 1972. "Industrial Organization: A Proposal for Research," in Victor R. Fuchs (ed.), *Policy Issues and Research Opportunities in Industrial Organization.* New York: National Bureau of Economic Research, pp. 59–73.

———. 1988. "The Nature of the Firm: Influence." *Journal of Law, Economics, and Organization* 3: 33–47.

———. 1992. "The Institutional Structure of Production." *American Economic Review* 82: 713–719.

Commons, John R. 1932. "The Problem of Correlating Law, Economics, and Ethics." *Wisconsin Law Review* 8: 3–26.

Costinot, Arnaud, Lindsay Oldenski, and James Rauch. 2011. "Adaptation and the Boundary of Multinational Firms." *Review of Economics and Statistics* 93: 298–308.

Demsetz, Harold. 1968. "Why Regulate Utilities?" *Journal of Law and Economics* 11: 55–66.

Dixit, Avinash. 1996. *The Making of Economic Policy: A Transaction Cost Politics Perspective.* Cambridge, MA: MIT Press.

Dye, Ronald A. 1985. "Disclosure of Nonproprietary Information." *Journal of Accounting Research* 23: 123–145.

Fischer, Stanley. 1977. "Long-Term Contracting, Sticky Prices, and Monetary Policy: Comment." *Journal of Monetary Economics* 3: 317–324.

Forbes, Silke Januszewski, and Mara Lederman. 2009. "Adaptation and Vertical Integration in the Airline Industry." *American Economic Review* 99: 1831–1849.

———. 2010. "Does Vertical Integration Affect Firm Performance? Evidence from the Airline Industry." *RAND Journal of Economics* 41: 765–790.

Galanter, Marc. 1981. "Justice in Many Rooms: Courts, Private Ordering, and Indigenous Law." *Journal of Legal Pluralism* 19: 1–47.

Geyskens, Inge, Jan-Benedict E. M. Steenkamp, and Nirmalya Kumar. 2006. "Make, Buy, or Ally: A Meta-Analysis of Transaction Cost Theory." *Academy of Management Journal* 49: 519–543.

Gibbons, Rober. 2005. "Four Formal(izable) Theories of the Firm." *Journal of Economic Behavior and Organization* 58: 202–247.

Grossman, Sanford J., and Oliver D. Hart. 1986. "The Costs and Benefits of Ownership: A Theory of Vertical and Lateral Integration." *Journal of Political Economy* 94: 691–719.

Hart, Oliver D., and John Moore. 1990. "Property Rights and the Nature of the Firm." *Journal of Political Economy* 98: 1119–1158.

Hayek, Friedrich. 1945. "The Use of Knowledge in Society." *American Economic Review* 35: 519–530.

Holmström, Bengt. 1999. "The Firm as a Subeconomy." *Journal of Law, Economics, and Organization* 15: 74–102.

Holmström, Bengt, and Paul Milgrom. 1991. "Multi-Task Principal-Agent Analysis." *Journal of Law, Economics, and Organization* 7(special issue): 24–52.

———. 1994. "The Firm as an Incentive System." *American Economic Review* 84: 972–991

Jensen, Michael, and William Meckling. 1976. "Theory of the Firm: Managerial Behavior, Agency Costs, and Capital Structure." *Journal of Financial Economics* 3: 305–360.

Joskow, Paul L. 1985. "Vertical Integration and Long-Term Contracts." *Journal of Law, Economics, and Organization* 1: 33–80.

———. 2000. "Transaction Cost Economics and Competition Policy." Mimeo, Massachusetts Institute of Technology, Cambridge, MA.

Klein, Benjamin, Robert G. Crawford, and Armen A. Alchian. 1978. "Vertical Integration, Appropriable Rents, and the Competitive Contracting Process." *Journal of Law and Economics* 21: 297–326.

Knight, Frank H. 1921. *Risk, Uncertainty and Profit.* Boston, New York: Houghton Mifflin.

Lafontaine, Francine, and Margaret Slade. 2007. "Vertical Integration and Firm Boundaries: The Evidence." *Journal of Economic Literature* 45: 629–685.

Lewis, Tracy. 1983. "Preemption, Divestiture, and Forward Contracting in a Market Dominated by a Single Firm." *American Economic Review* 73: 1092–1101.

Llewellyn, Karl N. 1931. "What Price Contract? An Essay in Perspective." *Yale Law Journal* 40: 704–751.

Macaulay, Stewart. 1963. "Non-Contractual Relations in Business." *American Sociological Review* 28: 55–70.

Macher, Jeffrey T., and Barak D. Richman. 2008. "Transaction Cost Economics: An Assessment of Empirical Research in the Social Sciences." *Business and Politics* 10: 1–63.

Macneil, Ian R. 1974. "The Many Futures of Contracts." *Southern California Law Review* 47: 691–816.

Masten, Scott. 1984. "The Organization of Production: Evidence from the Aerospace Industry." *Journal of Law and Economics* 27: 403–418.

Masten, Scott, James W. Meehan, and Edward A. Snyder. 1991. "The Costs of Organization." *Journal of Law, Economics, and Organization* 7: 1–25.

Michels, Robert. 1962. [1911] *Political Parties.* Glenco, IL: Free Press.

Milgrom, Paul, and John Roberts. 1988. "An Economic Approach to Influence Activities in Organizations." *American Journal of Sociology* 94(supplement): S154–S179.

Milgrom, Paul, and Chris Shannon. 1994. "Monotone Comparative Statics." *Econometrica* 62: 157–180.

Monteverde, Kirk, and David Teece. 1982. "Supplier Switching Costs and Vertical Integration in the Automobile Industry." *Bell Journal of Economics* 13: 206–213.

Muris, Timothy J. 2003. "Improving the Economic Foundations of Competition Policy." *George Mason Law Review* 12: 1–30.

Posner, Richard A. 1972. "The Appropriate Scope of Regulation in the Cable Television Industry." *Bell Journal of Economics and Management Science* 3: 98–129.

Riordan, Michael, and Oliver E. Williamson. 1985. "Asset Specificity and Economic Organization." *International Journal of Industrial Organization* 3: 365–378.

Selznick, Philip. 1949. *TVA and the Grass Roots.* Berkeley: University of California Press.

Shelanski, Howard, and Peter Klein. 1995. "Empirical Research in Transaction Cost Economics: A Review and Assessment." *Journal of Law, Economics, and Organization* 11: 335–361.

Simon, Herbert. 1947. *Administrative Behavior.* New York: Macmillan.

———. 1951. "A Formal Theory of the Employment Relation." *Econometrica* 19: 293–305.

Skaperdas, Stergios. 1992. "Cooperation, Conflict and Power in the Absence of Property Rights." *American Economic Review* 82: 720–739.

Summers, Clyde. 1969. "Collective Agreements and the Law of Contracts." *Yale Law Journal* 78: 537–575.

Tadelis, Steven. 2002. "Complexity, Flexibility and the Make-or-Buy Decision." *American Economic Review* 92(papers and proceedings): 433–437.

Tullock, Gordon. 1980. "Efficient Rent Seeking," in James M. Buchanan, Robert D. Tollison, and Gordon Tullock (eds.), *Toward a Theory of the Rent-Seeking Society.* College Station: Texas A&M University Press, pp. 97–112.

Whinston, Michael. 2001. "Assessing Property Rights and Transaction-Cost Theories of the Firm." *American Economic Review* 91: 184–199.

Williamson, Oliver E. 1971. "The Vertical Integration of Production: Market Failure Considerations." *American Economic Review* 61: 112–123.

———. 1975. *Markets and Hierarchies: Analysis and Antitrust Implications.* New York: Free Press.

———. 1976. "Franchise Bidding for Natural Monopolies—In General and with Respect to CATV." *Bell Journal of Economics* 7: 73–104.

———. 1981. "The Modern Corporation: Origins, Evolution, Attributes." *Journal of Economic Literature* 19: 1537–1568.

———. 1983. "Credible Commitments: Using Hostages to Support Exchange." *American Economic Review* 73: 519–540.

———. 1985. *The Economic Institutions of Capitalism.* New York: Free Press.

———. 1991. "Comparative Economic Organization: The Analysis of Discrete Structural Alternatives." *Administrative Science Quarterly* 36: 269–296.

———. 1993. "Transaction Cost Economics and Organization Theory." *Institutional and Corporate Change* 2: 107–156.

———. 1996. *The Mechanisms of Governance.* New York: Oxford University Press.

———. 2005a. "The Economics of Governance." *American Economic Review* 95: 1–18.

———. 2005b. "Why Law, Economics and Organization?" *Annual Review of Law and Social Science* 1: 369–396.

———. 2010. "Transaction Cost Economics: The Natural Progression." *American Economic Review* 100: 673–690.

PART II

Methods

5

Clinical Papers in Organizational Economics

George P. Baker and Ricard Gil

1. Introduction

1.1. The Legacy of Fisher Body

The story of General Motors' acquisition of the Fisher Body company in 1926 constitutes one of the more influential anecdotes in economics. Along with Adam Smith's pin factory, Ronald Coase's lighthouse, and George Akerlof's used-car market, the story of how General Motors first contracted with, then got held up by, and finally bought out Fisher Body has influenced the way economists have thought of agency problems, transactions costs, and make-or-buy decisions for more than 30 years. The paper that first told this story—Klein et al. (1978) in the *Journal of Law and Economics*—stands as the fourth most highly cited paper in that journal, with the number of citations in the thousands. It has inspired many other articles, motivated much theory, and generated a considerable amount of controversy. To refresh the memory of the reader, we provide the famous paragraph in its entirety here:

> [I]t is interesting to study in some detail the vertical merger that occurred in 1926 of General Motors with Fisher Body. The original production process for automobiles consisted of individually constructed open, largely wooden, bodies. By 1919 the production process began to shift towards largely metal closed body construction for which specific stamping machines became important. Therefore in 1919 General Motors entered a ten-year contractual agreement with Fisher Body for the supply of closed auto bodies. In order to encourage Fisher Body to make the required specific investment, this contract had an exclusive dealing clause whereby General Motors agreed to buy substantially all its closed bodies from Fisher. This exclusive dealing arrangement significantly reduced the possibility of General Motors acting opportunistically by demanding a lower price for the bodies after Fisher made the specific investment in production capacity. Since exclusive dealing contractual conditions are relatively cheap to effectively specify and enforce, General Motor's post-contractual threat to purchase bodies elsewhere was effectively eliminated. But large opportunities were created by this exclusive dealing clause for Fisher to take advantage of General Motors, namely to

demand a monopoly price for the bodies. Therefore, the contract attempted to fix the price which Fisher could charge for the bodies supplied to General Motors. However, contractually setting in advance a "reasonable" price in the face of possible future changes in demand and production conditions is somewhat more difficult to effectively accomplish than merely "fixing" required suppliers. The price was set on a cost plus 17.6 per cent basis (where cost was defined exclusive of interest on invested capital). In addition, the contract included provisions that the price charged General Motors could not be greater than that charged other automobile manufacturers by Fisher for similar bodies nor greater than the average market price of similar bodies produced by companies other than Fisher and also included provisions for compulsory arbitration in the event of any disputes regarding price. Unfortunately, however, these complex contractual pricing provisions did not work out in practice. The demand conditions facing General Motors and Fisher Body changed dramatically over the next few years. There was a large increase in the demand for automobiles and a significant shift away from open bodies to the closed body styles supplied by Fisher. Meanwhile General Motors was very unhappy with the price it was being charged by its now very important supplier, Fisher. General Motors believed the price was too high because of a substantial increase in body output per unit of capital employed. This was an understandable development given the absence of a capital cost pass-through in the original contract. In addition, Fisher refused to locate their body plants adjacent to General Motors assembly plants, a move General Motors claimed was necessary for production efficiency (but which required a large very specific and hence possibly appropriable investment on the part of Fisher). By 1924, General Motors had found the Fisher contractual relationship intolerable and began negotiations for purchase of the remaining stock in Fisher Body, culminating in a final merger agreement in 1926. [Klein et al. 1978: 308–310]

Note how this story touches on many relevant aspects of hold-up, appropriable quasi-rents, and vertical integration decisions. The complex and interrelated roles of specific investments, unforeseen contingencies, and contractual incompleteness are all highlighted. Fisher Body serves as an example of the role that stories play in economic research and organizational economics in particular.

1.2. Why Are Stories So Powerful?

Stories hold a privileged position in the human mind. They are more interesting, more memorable, and more powerful (to most people) than facts or theories.

> The story—from Rumplestiltskin to *War and Peace*—is one of the basic tools invented by the human mind, for the purpose of gaining understanding. There have been great societies that did not use the wheel, but there have been no societies that did not tell stories. [Ursula K. Le Guin, *The Language of the Night*, 1979]

Throughout human history, stories have been used to create and diffuse knowledge. McCloskey (1990) argues that there are only two ways of understanding things: metaphor (read "model") and story. The story as a cognitive tool has been widely used in the social sciences, the humanities, and even in the "hard" sciences (Einstein's man in a rocket and Schrödinger's cat are well-known examples). McCloskey postulates that even when we are trying to fit complex reality through highly stylized models, we are storytellers who focus on the very important details of each specific case under study and fill the sketch with unmodelable features that are better explained by narrative.

The Fisher Body story related by Klein et al. (1978) has many of the ingredients to which Le Guin and McCloskey refer. The paragraph cited in Section 1 presents a situation rich in detail, yet provides a very simple and elegant explanation that allows us to gain understanding of the forces involved in setting firm boundaries. We believe that the story of Fisher Body has been so influential largely because of this combination of the particular and the general: the specifics of the story are relevant and important, yet the generality of the situation is obvious. The theory that explains the set of facts and actions presented in this story can be used, and has been used, to provide a very general explanation that can be applied to many other settings.

1.3. What Are Clinical Studies?

This chapter discusses clinical studies in organizational economics. Most clinical studies are stories, and we argue in this chapter that clinical studies (stories) can and should play an essential role in the development of theories in organizational economics, as well as in the design and implementation of empirical research. Like the Fisher Body story, they combine the specific and the general to guide theorists and empiricists in what to model, how to model it, and how to tell whether their results are valid and sensible.

A clinical study is essentially a detailed account, often involving a combination of qualitative data, anecdotal evidence, and sometimes quantitative data of a specific situation or phenomenon. Several things may distinguish a clinical study from a more standard empirical investigation. Clinical studies often contain qualitative information that is not amenable to statistical analysis. They also make no strong claim to representativeness; indeed, it is often the case that the best clinical studies are about situations that are clearly outliers or extreme cases. Although this trait would be considered a significant drawback for a standard empirical investigation, it is often a very important characteristic of a clinical study: if the purpose is to better uncover the causal mechanisms behind some phenomenon, then finding an extreme situation may be the best place to look.

Clinical studies also frequently contain data—qualitative or quantitative—that may or may not be relevant to understanding the situation. This is what distinguishes a clinical study from an *example*. An example is generally used to illustrate some theoretical insight or result. Clinical studies are most useful when they describe situations for which the existing theory is inadequate or nonexistent. This is the reason that clinical studies often contain (what will turn out to be) irrelevant data: without good theory, one does not know which data are relevant and which are not.

What purpose do clinical studies serve? As mentioned above, clinical studies are most useful when they examine phenomena for which we do not have adequate theory. In this chapter we argue that clinical studies serve four important functions in the development of the field:

(1) telling theorists what to model, (2) providing guidance on how to model these things, (3) assessing "possibility theorems," and (4) providing evidence of a certain type for testing theory.

1.4. Types of Clinical Studies

Before discussing the role of clinical studies in the development of organizational economics, we begin with a simple classification of types of studies and short discussions of numerous papers that fit into these classifications. We come back to discuss some of these papers in more detail in later sections. All share the characteristics of in-depth description of one or a small number of situations, questionable (or at least difficult to prove) representativeness, and the likely inclusion of irrelevant detail.

The most common type of clinical study is the *teaching case.* The Harvard Business School case library alone contains more than 10,000 case titles. Teaching cases range from the prosaic (e.g., *Butler Lumber,* a small lumber yard, which, though profitable, needs to borrow money to grow) to the bizarre (e.g., *Optical Distortion* [Clarke and Wise 1975], a case about a company trying to market contact lenses for chickens to keep them from pecking each other to death in captivity). Some teaching cases are very well known: Lincoln Electric (Berg and Fast 1975), the best-selling case in the business school's history, describes an aggressive incentive system in an American arc-welding company. The case details not only the ingredients of the tremendously successful incentive system but also all the other organizational features that surround the incentive program. Reading through the text, it is hard to miss that there may be other, softer, factors at work than simply a high-powered incentive scheme. Indeed, there is so much about culture and leadership in the case that by the end the reader wonders whether the main purpose of the text was to highlight the importance of incentives or underline the relevance of leadership and culture in organizations.

Aside from the entertainment and education about the world provided to students by teaching cases, we might ask whether they also provide value to scholars outside the classroom, in their writing and research. One may worry that the style encountered in teaching cases, mostly narrative and descriptive, resembles too much the journalistic style of the business press. At the same time, teaching cases present scholars with facts about organizations, industries, and markets, and they often highlight interesting and important issues faced by economic agents. Teaching cases, like newspaper articles, highlight the key trade-offs necessary to understand how a firm or industry works. In the same way that economists turn to newspapers and magazines to collect institutional knowledge necessary for their research, they can also use information from teaching cases. In that sense, teaching cases help economists highlight the important features in their models despite their journalistic style.

A second type of study, and the central focus of this chapter, is the *in-depth clinical paper.* As we describe below, this work ranges from relatively qualitative narratives to relatively quantitative investigations. For the most part, however, all these papers stop short of explicitly testing hypotheses.

Some of the earliest papers that we describe here were published as a result of an initiative by the *Journal of Financial Economics.* Beginning in 1989, this journal began to publish papers about individual firms or a small number of them. Among the first of these to appear was by Baker and Wruck (1989) on the leveraged buyout (LBO) of the O. M. Scott & Sons grass seed company. In this study Baker and Wruck document in detail the divisional LBO of the O. M. Scott & Sons company by Clayton & Dubilier from giant conglomerate ITT, while identifying the organizational changes that took place within O. M. Scott & Sons that led the firm to increase performance after the buyout. We discuss this paper in greater detail in Section 2.2.

Another of this genre is the excellent series of articles by Kaplan (1989, 1990, 1994) on the acquisition of Federated department stores by the Canadian financier Robert Campeau in 1988 and its ultimate bankruptcy in 1990. This series of clinical studies does a remarkable job of clarifying the value creation potential of LBOs, even when the ultimate fate of the company is bankruptcy. Campeau bought Federated for $7.6 billion, which represented a $3.4 billion premium over the pre-buyout value of the company. Ninety-seven percent of the buyout price was financed with debt. The main contribution of the papers is Kaplan's painstaking and detailed reconstruction of the value of Federated post-bankruptcy and his demonstration of the value that was actually created by the buyout. This analysis shows that Federated's bankruptcy was not a consequence of value destruction in the post-LBO company but rather of overoptimism at the time of the buyout and the contractual "locking in" of this optimism through very high leverage. In fact, Campeau increased the value of Federated by $1.8 billion (43%) through the LBO, but because this was not enough to cover the money borrowed for the deal, he still went bankrupt. Through this clinical study and the rich detail provided in it, Kaplan differentiates the economic concept of value creation (through a more efficient allocation of resources) from the contractual concept of bankruptcy.

Another *Journal of Financial Economics* clinical paper, by Dial and Murphy (1995), explores the issue of value creation in a dying industry. They describe the trajectory of General Dynamics (GD) between 1991 and 1994 under the leadership of CEO William Anders. GD was the third largest defense contractor in the world but was suffering from serious declines in profitability and market value after the fall of the Berlin Wall. This paper, which is discussed in more detail in Section 2.1, tells the story of how Anders and others at GD adopted a strategy of downsizing, consolidation, and exit at the end of the Cold-War era as long-term demand and profitability in the weapons manufacturing industry suffered what appeared to be a permanent negative shock. Through the rich detail offered in this story, Dial and Murphy clarify two important concepts. First, value-creating actions in a booming industry are likely to have the opposite effect in a shrinking one. Second, they show that even in a shrinking business it is possible to create value effectively (if somewhat more painfully) through the efficient allocation of resources.

Baker's (1992) paper on the growth by acquisition and death by divestiture of the conglomerate Beatrice takes a broad historical look at a single firm. It attempts to answer the questions: How does a strategy of acquisition—Beatrice was the most acquisitive firm in America during the 1950s and 1960s—create value? And then how can a strategy of divestiture—Beatrice did more divestitures in the 1980s than any other firm—also create value? Baker uses data from company documents, press accounts, personal remembrances of managers, and accounting and market data to reconstruct the strategic direction of the firm throughout its 80-year history, noting the shifts in corporate strategy associated with different CEOs and attempting to account for value creation and value loss stemming from these changes in firm policies and strategy.

In addition to these early clinical studies in the *Journal of Financial Economics,* there are similar contributions ranging from the mostly qualitative to more quantitative. One example of in-depth clinical studies at the qualitative end of the spectrum is the study of the Danish hearing-aid company Oticon by Foss (2003). In this paper, Foss provides an intimate account of how Oticon's CEO Lars Kolind reorganized the Danish hearing-aid firm to delegate as much authority and decision power as possible to employees. To do so, Kolind engineered a "market for ideas" within the firm in which employees were allowed to start on their own projects, recruit teams within the firm, and even set their own wages. All this occurred under very little oversight or control from top management. As a result, the average time to project completion was cut by half, and the rate of innovation improved drastically in the 3 years after the reorganization. As time went on, however, the management began to "selectively intervene" in several projects that appeared unprofitable, discouraging workers from pursuing their own initiatives. Foss, through the story of Oticon, sheds light on the debate among theorists about how to model delegation. This story shows that managers are unable to formally delegate decision rights to their subordinates; in fact, decision rights are only loaned to subordinates even when (ex-ante) managers want to commit to do otherwise.

Two other papers are not close examinations of a particular firm or firms, but rather careful descriptions and analyses of phenomena of interest. One is the Milgrom and Roberts (1990) paper on modern manufacturing systems. These authors describe how manufacturing industries have evolved from the times of Ford's Model T car factory to the present. The evidence collected on how such firms as General Motors and Caterpillar organize factory work pushes Milgrom and Roberts to hypothesize that optimally changes in the production chain must take place not in isolation but in groups. They use this anecdotal evidence to guide the development of a theory of complementarities between inputs, outputs, and methods of production.

The other paper is Asanuma (1989). Asanuma documents a large amount of informal interaction taking place between auto makers, electric component makers, and their input suppliers in the Japanese auto and electric component industries. Moreover, Asanuma describes in detail how ex post contractual changes and contractual renegotiation are resolved. The evidence in Asanuma's paper is some of the earliest on the impact of relations on business practices and economic outcomes. As the Fisher Body and General Motors story did with make-or-buy theories, Asanuma's study inspired many to pursue theory on the nature and consequences of relational contracting.

We also note that there were many social scientists outside economics undertaking in-depth clinical studies decades before economists started contributing to this type of research methodology. For example, there are the classic sociology works by Philip Selznick (1957) and Michel Crozier (1964) that studied organizations and Alfred Chandler's (1962, 1977) books in business history. To illustrate work in this tradition, we include one example of an in-depth clinical study from outside the economics literature—the early and influential paper in the sociology literature by Donald Roy (1952).

Roy's detailed account of piece-rate workers in a machine shop on the south side of Chicago in the 1950s provides tremendous insight into the inner workings of a shop floor. Roy was a graduate student in the Sociology Department of the University of Chicago, and he spent 11 months as a (clandestine) participant-observer in a machine shop near the university. This gave him access to worker "inside talk and activity" and allowed Roy to document the motivations of individual workers, the social interactions among workers, and their coordinated efforts to get the most out of the compensation scheme implemented in the plant. We discuss this paper more fully in Section 2.3.

Complementing the studies just discussed, we also find in-depth clinical studies roughly in the middle of the qualitative-quantitative spectrum, such as Blanchard et al. (1994). Motivated by existing theories of asymmetric information and agency, they ask: what do firms do with cash windfalls? They use a narrow selection criterion to choose 11 firms that received significant amounts of cash, for reasons (winning lawsuits) that should not affect their rate of return on future investment. By examining what firms actually do with this money, they can look at (test?) whether managers are acting in the best interests of shareholders or in their own best interest.

The paper bristles with tables, virtually all with 11 rows. Blanchard et al. (1994) show tables that reveal the characteristics of the firms, the characteristics of the cash windfalls, the historical investment behavior and returns of the firms, and the performance of the firms after they received the money. The text is sprinkled with stories about individual firms, but the real story is in the tables, which show the remarkable consistency with which the firms' managers waste the windfall to ensure the survival of the firms under their command. Although the quantitative result could be consistent with managerial information asymmetry theories, the detailed (and colorful) descriptions of the waste of the windfalls, especially on dividend payments and executive compensation, leave little doubt about the accuracy of the agency-theoretic explanation.

Another example of a similarly quantitative in-depth clinical study is by Cutler and Summers (1988). In this paper, the authors examine the costs of financial distress and look to see whether these costs have an effect on firm productivity. They do so by comparing the losses in market value suffered by Texaco and Pennzoil with the actual legal and administrative costs of the litigation in their fight over the Getty Oil takeover. They show that the loss of total value during litigation was much higher than even the most generous estimate of litigation costs. Their evidence suggests that the soft costs of financial distress—diversion of managerial time, loss of strategic focus and direction—appear to be real, at least in this case, and that financial markets take these costs into account. The meticulous recollection of events and information in this paper shed light on how economists ought to model financial distress episodes and their implications for firm performance.

The industrial organization literature has also provided several works that fall into this category of in-depth clinical papers, for instance, Joskow's (1985) paper on the contractual and institutional arrangements between coal-fired power plants and coal mines. Joskow documents coal supply arrangements between electric utilities and coal suppliers, focusing on the structure of vertical relationships for mine-mouth generating plants. He compares the characteristics of transactions for mine-mouth plants to those of plants located farther from coal supplies. Although the sample sizes are small by the standards of traditional empirical work, the richness of the descriptive results (the actual contracts are analyzed in detail) provides real insight into the importance of asset and locational specificity for organizational form and contract type. Paradoxically, it is the overwhelming amount of detail in this paper that allows the reader to understand the foundations of contracting costs in this industry and to apply this understanding to other settings facing the same economic trade-offs.

This paper shows the value of deep institutional knowledge when studying contracting arrangements between firms since the examination of data may not tell the whole story. As Joskow (1985: 34) put it:

Detailed knowledge of a variety of characteristics of buyers and sellers seems essential for applying and testing transactions cost theory empirically. . . . Furthermore, in part because they are regulated, there is a lot of information available about particular utilities, their power plants, and their coal supply arrangements. It is even possible to obtain a large set of actual coal supply contracts and related documents. The opportunity to analyze data at this level of microeconomic detail is extremely rare.

Finally, and farther toward the quantitative end of the spectrum, there are clinical studies that look like large-sample empirical work but use data from a single (or very small number of) firms. The first of two such studies that we discuss uses large proprietary panel datasets with no apparent exogenous variation in the data. These papers are not trying to test, or even really explore, any particular causal mechanism or hypothesis. Rather, they allow the authors to establish a set of facts for which economists may not previously have had a good grasp or understanding. The two studies—Baker et al. (1994) and Lazear (1992)—both follow individuals across different jobs within the same firm over a large number of years. By doing so, they are able to study the empirical cross-sectional relationships among jobs, job levels, wages, and changes in each of these. We come back to these papers in Section 2.1.

Two other studies in roughly this style are the analyses of peer effects by Ichino and Maggi (2000) and Mas and Moretti (2009). Ichino and Maggi explore the causes behind regional disparities in shirking behavior in a large Italian bank. By focusing on movers within the bank across offices in different regions, they were able to assert that cross-regional differences in shirking behavior were mainly due to individual taste for shirking, peer effects, and workers sorting into branches with similar shirking habits.

Mas and Moretti (2009) study cashier productivity at a large supermarket chain. They find that high-productivity checkout clerks have a positive impact on the productivity of other clerks working at the same time, through some type of peer effect, and that this effect on worker productivity is stronger in the presence of high-productivity co-workers with whom workers interact often. More interestingly, Mas and Moretti are able to exploit precise information about the physical arrangement of the cash registers to show that this productivity effect only occurs if the high-productivity clerks can see the lower productivity ones: when the more productive clerks are located in front of the less productive cashiers, and therefore the former cannot see the latter, there is no peer effect.

A second type of large-sample clinical studies consists of those that study events or changes that occurred inside firms or industries. In these papers, the authors attempt to show the consequences of such changes for the inner workings of the organization under study. An example of this type of paper is Lazear (2000), which is an event study of the change in compensation system at a large auto glass company, Safelite Glass Corporation. Between 1994 and 1995 the company changed its compensation system from hourly wages to piece rates.[1] Lazear calculates that this change in compensation system was associated with a 44% gain in productivity at the firm. He further documents that this productivity gain has two sources: increase in the

---

1. Lazear (2000) never mentions, and seems unconcerned with, the possible endogeneity of this change. However, the results are sufficiently striking and abrupt that the possible explanations involving endogeneity seem implausible.

productivity of individual workers who stay through the change and a selection effect (the more productive workers stay with the firm and the less productive ones leave). Lazear also documents that both average pay and firm profits increase after the change in compensation system.

Two papers along similar lines by Paarsch and Shearer (1999, 2000) examine the response of workers to piece rates using personnel records of a British Columbia tree-planting company. Their careful examination of changes in worker productivity stemming from changes in compensation allows Paarsch and Shearer to show that more aggressive piece-rate systems are associated with larger output yield per worker, but that the gain in output comes at the expense of quality. They also highlight the potential gains of sorting workers by productivity type but provide evidence suggesting that workers strategically choose how much effort to exert to prevent revealing their type, which reduces the productivity effect of sorting.

Knez and Simester (2001) offer another example of an event study, one that explores the role of social relations within firms. They examine the impact of firmwide bonus compensation system at Continental Airlines established in 1995. Conventional economic logic would predict that the scheme, which paid all workers a bonus based on firmwide profitability, ought to be plagued by a serious free-rider problem, because each worker has an indistinguishable impact on overall profits. Surprisingly they find that this bonus system increases firmwide productivity despite free-riding concerns. After carefully considering a number of alternative sources of individual incentives that could be spurring productivity, Knez and Simester attribute their result to the organization of workers into distinct autonomous work groups that enabled mutual monitoring among employees. Similarly to other clinical studies described in this section, it is this paper's attention to the detail and internal organization (carefully exploiting what is not in the quantitative data) that provides an understanding of the source of the increase in productivity and the lack of free riding.

2. What Purposes Do Clinical Papers Serve?

The traditional model of the scientific method describes a process that begins with observation and proceeds through hypothesis generation, formal modeling, and hypothesis testing. The third and fourth of these steps are well-trodden grounds in economic research; the first two rarely appear in journals. But observation and hypothesis generation are no less important parts of the process of understanding and testing the world: they just do not generate published papers very often. Clinical papers represent the tangible product of observation and hypothesis generation. It teaches us what to model, how to model things, and whether the models that we build are sensible. Each of these purposes of clinical studies is explored in this chapter.

2.1. Knowing What to Model

A clinical study can provide a highly detailed set of facts that may cry out for a more formal and general explanation (or a more thorough empirical analysis) than exists in the current literature. The story of Fisher Body proved very useful in providing enough detail about hold-up to allow theorists like Oliver E. Williamson, Sanford J. Grossman, and Oliver D. Hart to construct models, of varying degrees of formality, of this phenomenon.

The two papers on personnel economics mentioned in Section 1.4—Baker et al. (1994) and Lazear (1992)—have had a similar type of effect. These papers differ from others mentioned in this chapter in that they lack narrative structure, and therefore they cannot be classified as stories in the traditional sense. Yet these papers describe facts that are informative to organizational researchers about the inner workings of internal labor markets unclear to economists (not so much to other social scientists) up to that moment. By revealing the workings of two large firms, these authors prompted numerous theoretical papers on wages, learning, and careers within firms. Gibbons and Waldman (1999) pose the puzzle that they are trying to solve based on the observations of Baker et al. (1994).

The still-unidentified (despite the best efforts of several of the authors' colleagues) firm studied by Baker et al. (1994) was no mom-and-pop operation: it was a large and established firm in the financial services industry. This fact, combined with many others in the paper that "rang true" to those familiar with personnel systems in large firms, leads to the conclusion that these facts were important enough to model, and that these models would prove useful in predicting human resources practices in other firms.

The Baker et al. (1994) dataset contained data on 7,000 employees over 20 years. The data that the authors studied included information for each employee-year observation on the employee's salary, job title, and other demographic information. The paper documented some previously explored facts and found some (at the time) puzzling results that organizational economists had no solid explanations for. In particular, they found that wage changes at promotion are much smaller than cross-sectional differences in wages across levels. In addition, real wage declines were common, but nominal wage declines and demotions were rare. Baker et al. also found evidence for "fast tracks" in promotion and showed serial correlation between wage increases and promotions. They found that wage changes are a good predictor of promotions. The results in Baker et al. (1994) are still prompting theorists and empiricists to study the nature and robustness of their findings. In fact, these authors added dimensionality to an existing literature in internal labor markets (wage variation in organizations) and linked different literatures pertaining to different fields in the social sciences when relating wages (labor economics) to sequence of jobs in careers (sociology). Some examples of recent papers in economics referencing the work in Baker et al. (1994) are another by Gibbons and Waldman (2006) (explaining the presence of cohort effects in firms through the introduction of task-specific human capital) and Moldovanu et al. (2007), who explore why firms tend to have ports of entry primarily at low levels in their hierarchy.

The description and analysis provided in the Dial and Murphy (1995) account of GD provides similar grist for the theorist's (and empiricist's) mill. They show that tremendous value can be created, even in industries characterized by excess capacity and shrinking demand. This account of how the new CEO of GD (William Anders) developed and implemented a strategy to downsize and liquidate the defense contracting giant uncovers some important insights about the nature of organizational change and value creation. What was clear to Anders after the fall of the Berlin Wall was that there was far too much capacity in the defense industry. Most industry participants developed a strategy of expansion, trying to build up their capabilities so that they would weather the inevitable shake-out. Anders led GD on a totally different path, recognizing that efficiently liquidating the firm was the best thing to do from society's (and his shareholders') perspective.

Implementing Anders's strategy would prove to be difficult, however. The firm would need a management team with experience and knowledge of the firm and industry, who were committed to create value for GD's shareholders and were willing to make difficult and painful choices to shrink the firm. And Anders would have to recruit and retain this management team to a task that was virtually guaranteed to put them out of a job. His solution—a highly leveraged compensation plan that awarded very large bonuses and stock options to management based on the firm's market value—worked from the standpoint of motivation and results, but it proved to be a public relations nightmare. Every time the firm announced a move that reduced capacity from the industry, through either the sale of a division or the closing of a plant, GD's stock price would rise, and the managers who caused this pain and dislocation to workers would receive huge bonus payments! In spite of the firm's public relations problems (Anders was featured on *60 Minutes* as an example of outrageous executive pay—he was accused of graduating from the Marie Antoinette School of Management), GD was the best-performing company on the New York Stock Exchange for the 3 years from January 1991 to January 1994.

The insights from the GD clinical study are both obvious and profound. At one level, the story demonstrates nothing more than the tautology that moving resources to their highest valued use creates value—value that can be captured by the agents who develop and implement the strategy to do so. The GD story is enlightening in showing how this tautology holds even in situations that look like recipes for value loss and destruction.

2.2. Showing How to Model Things

A second important role that clinical studies play in the development of theory is to uncover and clarify the mechanisms at work in complex and poorly understood situations, so that theorists and empiricists can model them better. The authors of such studies do so by getting closer to the phenomenon and collecting qualitative data and anecdotal evidence. This often implies investing in such time-intensive activities as interviewing firm managers and employees, industry observers, and consumers. The object of these interviews is to understand the motivation and thoughts as well as the opportunities and constraints of economic agents and therefore to better understand how they make decisions.

It is important to recognize that a good understanding of the phenomenon under study is just as important to empirical research as it is to theory building. An incorrect empirical model can lead to specification errors that result in drastically misleading empirical results. An obvious example of such misspecifications occurs when empiricists leave out important variables from a regression, either because they do not understand that such variables are important or because collecting this variable is too difficult or costly. The problem is that variables that have no relevance whatsoever for the research question, but are coincidentally correlated with the relevant omitted variable, will have great statistical significance in this misspecified regression. An empirical investigator who understands what the important variables are would never even run this regression, recognizing that she has to either abandon the project or bear the costs of collecting the data to allow her to model the situation correctly. Qualitative detail in a clinical study will often guide empirical researchers to what the "right" regression model is.

An early example of this type of clinical paper is the Baker and Wruck (1989) study of the LBO of O. M. Scott & Sons. This paper followed several large-sample studies (DeAngelo and

DeAngelo 1987; Kaplan 1989) about the nature and consequences of LBOs. In their study Baker and Wruck take as a starting point the conclusions of Kaplan (1989) and DeAngelo and DeAngelo (1987) that LBOs create substantial value. Their task is to understand why. Baker and Wruck identify in detail the organizational changes that took place in O. M. Scott & Sons that led the firm to increase performance after the buyout: changes in organizational structure and governance, creation of new performance metrics, and implementation of new incentive plans. Whereas the literature previously hypothesized that changes in governance and incentives lead to the observed value increases, Baker and Wruck both document these changes and show (in this one case) how the changes lead to an increase in firm performance and value.

2.3. Assessing "Possibility Theorems"

In the editorial note introducing the clinical papers section in the *Journal of Financial Economics*, Jensen et al. (1989) lobby for the growing importance and role of clinical studies in the effort to improve existing and future theoretical and empirical research. Jensen et al. (1989: 3–4) warn us about the danger of "possibility theorems" in finance:

> The unique and well-defined perfect market theory provides a useful standard of comparison as the limit toward which unencumbered markets move. There are, however, an infinite number of imperfect market theories corresponding to the limitless combinations of alternative assumptions. Unfortunately, most of these theories are irrelevant to understanding the world. In this sense they are "possibility theorems"—propositions that, while logically correct, have little or no probability of explaining any real phenomenon. The imperfect market theories that interest us are those that have a reasonable probability of explaining reality.

Possibility theorems start from a fact and then develop a model that explains this fact. The problem is: how does one assess the validity of this new model? To simply "check the math" to be sure that the model is solved correctly, and to make sure that it does indeed predict the initial fact, seems less than a thorough validity check. The chemist Manfred Eigen (1973: 618) states the problem succinctly: "A theory has only the alternative of being right or wrong. A model has a third possibility—it may be right but irrelevant."

The standard method for assessing models that "predict" known facts is to demand that they make *new* predictions—perhaps with greater precision, or in realms outside those of the original fact. Thus, when Isaac Newton delivered the theory of gravity after sitting under the (proverbial) apple tree, that prediction that apples fall from trees does little to substantiate Newton's theory of gravity. It is the fact that Newton's theory of gravity, derived from observing apples falling, accurately predicts the movement of celestial bodies that validates this theory.

But a second method exists for validating possibility theorems: we can consider whether the model is sensible. To do this, we must understand the phenomenon with enough richness and detail to be able to say whether the model captures the trade-offs that agents and organizations face when making decisions. It is as part of this second method that clinical studies play a very important role. Clinical studies should provide this type of richness and detail and therefore help theorists produce better, more accurate, and more sensible models.[2] As discussed above,

---

2. This idea—that models in economics should reflect the underlying thoughts, motivations, and capabilities that agents have—is not universally accepted. Milton Friedman, using his famous analogy to billiard players, argued

the same goes for empirical models and empirical analyses that build on a well-known set of stylized facts.

There is an excellent historical example of how an in-depth study of a particular situation "tested" the sensibility of a perfectly plausible theory in the realm of incentives and motivation. Despite the widely accepted belief among economists that employee incentives raise productivity, there is much evidence that piece rates lead to shirking and restrictions in output by workers. Much of the early evidence on this phenomenon comes from the famous experiments, conducted by Elton Mayo and Fritz Rothlisberger, at the Hawthorne Works of the Western Electric Company.

Mayo (1946: 120) offers a theory in his book *The Human Problems of an Industrial Civilization* to explain how piece rates lead to shirking and output restriction:

> Human collaboration in work . . . has always depended for its perpetuation upon the evolution of a non-logical social code which regulates the relations between persons and their attitudes to one another. Insistence upon a merely economic logic of production . . . interferes with the development of such a code and consequently gives rise in the group to a sense of human defeat. This . . . results in the formation of a social code at a lower level and in opposition to the economic logic. One of its symptoms is "restriction."

Mayo had stated that workers were not obeying the will of their employers, because they were unable to process the set of incentives presented to them. He (and others) went a step further and claimed that the economic "logic" imposed on the workers made them feel disoriented, discouraged, and distracted from achieving their true potential, and therefore, they attained a new "lower social code" as described in his book.

Roy's (1952) observations at the machine shop in Chicago suggest a very different theory. He notes that when the workers on the floor exceeded a specific "bogey" for a particular part, management (using classic ratchet logic) would conclude that the piece rate for this part was too high and would instruct the time-study department to retime the work and reset the piece rate. Thus, exceeding the bogey led to a short-run gain for the worker who worked hard, but a significant reduction in welfare for himself and all of his co-workers in the future. Not surprisingly, workers developed social norms that discouraged co-workers from exceeding the bogey.

Based in his observations, Roy discusses Mayo's theory of human motivation regarding "quota restriction." Roy (1952: 430) refers in the following way to Mayo's conclusions regarding the observation in the Hawthorne studies, and to his own results:

> Mayo thus joins those who consider the economic man a fallacious conception. Now the operators in my shop made noises like economic men. Their talk indicated that they were canny calculators and that the dollar sign fluttered at the masthead of every machine. Their actions were not always consistent with their words; and such inconsistency calls for further

---

that all we ask for in economic models is that they make good predictions. It does not matter whether the billiard player is actually an expert in trigonometry. The model that assumes that he is will make good predictions about his shots; however, models of this sort tend to be fragile. The billiard-trigonometrist would have little trouble with a billiard table that was a parallelogram; one would expect that the real-world billiard player would have a very hard time.

probing. But it could be precisely because they were alert to their economic interests . . . that the operators did not exceed their quotas.

Roy's observation casts doubt on the empirical relevance of Mayo's hypotheses. By developing a careful understanding of the motivations of his co-workers (at least as he understood them), Roy is able to conclude that Mayo's theory, while in principle correct, is not a sensible one to explain the behavior of his co-workers, given his (and, one suspects, many others') understanding of the behavior of piece-rate workers. It is not that his co-workers did not understand the motivation of their employer in setting and resetting piece rates. They did: far better than their employers would have liked them to. As rational individuals, they were maximizing their own well-being and therefore obtaining the higher pay with lower effort.

Similar to the controversy over Mayo's (1946) hypotheses, Roy's (1952) careful observations may also allow us to reject some economic theories regarding the consequences of the ratchet effect. Take, for example, Lazear (1986), where he models the presence of the ratchet effect in a two-period model in which workers understand the consequences of showing high productivity in the first period on their pay for the second period. Under the assumption that workers do not contemplate employment in another firm, Lazear finds that workers actually operate at first-best effort through both periods, resulting in no loss of efficiency. The accounts in Roy's passages, however, suggest that workers very much take into account their outside opportunities and therefore consider outcomes, such as being fired, laid off, or changing jobs. Following Roy's accounts accurately, Gibbons (1987) shows that the ratchet effect does indeed create inefficiency and that workers may not be producing the first-best effort when strategically responding to ratchetlike incentive schemes.

This particular set of cases makes clear the usefulness of clinical studies. Clinical studies allow outsiders to put themselves in the shoes of the agents and organizations involved in the decisionmaking process under study, and to discard improbable explanations that may yield the same set of observed well-established facts.

2.4. Clinical Studies as Evidence

In assessing the validity of a theory and the role that clinical studies play, we must ask the question of what can confirm and what can disconfirm a theory. Strict adherence to the scientific method would suggest that a single case can be used to declare a theory invalid. In practice, of course, such a strict interpretation rarely holds sway. Nonetheless, clinical studies can be useful as evidence to support or weaken theoretical conclusions.

Several excellent examples of this sort of insight from clinical studies have already been mentioned. Lazear's (2000) study of incentives and sorting at Safelite Glass Corporation provides a compelling example of the potential for piece-rate incentives to increase productivity. The Knez and Simester (2001) study of group incentives at Continental Airlines provides a similar benchmark for the use of group-based incentives. Both these papers not only provide evidence on the sign of the impact on productivity of the implementation of an incentive system but can also measure the magnitude of the impact. The Blanchard et al. (1995) paper on cash windfalls provides insight of a similar nature, as does the Cutler and Summers (1988) estimate of the total wealth loss stemming from litigation between Texaco and Pennzoil.

3. Should Economists Write Clinical Studies?

Clinical studies in economics are still a rare form, which means that few of us are doing them. We can think of three reasons that scholars can, and should, write clinical studies. The first is, of course, to aid in teaching. Teaching with cases generally enriches the pedagogy and makes concrete concepts that may otherwise be sterile or overly theoretical. Of course, the standards for what makes a good teaching case may differ from those for publishable clinical studies: more on this below.

A second reason to carry out clinical studies is to enrich one's own research. Most authors of clinical studies are also producers of standard economics research. From their perspective, beginning a research stream with something akin to a clinical study is a preliminary step to devising better models and conducting more sensible and relevant empirical analysis (even if the clinical study and consequent analysis appear in the same study). Take, for example, research by Arruñada et al. (2001) on allocation of decision rights across firm boundaries in the Spanish car retailing industry, or Baker et al. (2008) on strategic alliances in the biotech industry. These are examples of papers that detail patterns in organizations and then use that institutional knowledge to inform subsequent empirical and theoretical work.

Similarly, Gil's (2013) work studying contractual practices in the Spanish film industry documents the interplay of formal and relational contracting between Spanish movie distributors and a large exhibitor. Interviews with industry managers and practitioners revealed that contractual renegotiation of each one of the weekly revenue-sharing terms takes place after the movie is pulled from the theater. This is a fact impossible to identify from just looking at the data, and yet it is key for understanding the nature and source of renegotiation in this industry. The exhibitor (theater owner) is not holding up the movie distributor to get the latter to show the movie an extra week. Instead, the distributor is compensating the exhibitor for keeping the movie on screen even in weeks for which it would not be profitable for the theater alone to do so, but it is jointly profitable for both exhibitor and distributor to do so. Knowledge of this institutional detail drives not only the understanding of contracting in this industry but also the way to approach the data and the empirical analysis.

A third reason is to provide information and data for others. As we commented before, clinical studies may be the spark for further research by providing a thorough description of a poorly understood phenomenon. Helper (2000) argues that clinical studies are beneficial to everyone when paraphrasing the New York Yankees philosopher Yogi Berra: "You can observe a lot by just watching." The benefits of "observing" are highest when focusing attention on areas with little data or theory and when paying attention to the motivations and constraints of the economic agents. She also points to the value of providing vivid images that aid the reader by developing economic intuition.

Even if we accept that clinical studies should be carried out, and that we all benefit from them, we can ask the question of whether we *economists* should spend time and resources on writing clinical studies. The answer is ambiguous. Economists may not have a comparative advantage in doing this kind of work. Although economists are not trained to do this kind of intense and time-demanding data collection, some sociologists and psychologists do have the training. Perhaps economists should leave the writing of clinical studies to other social scientists.

Letting others do this job for us comes with its own set of advantages and disadvantages. One advantage is that other social scientists, by virtue of their different training and theoretical approaches, will tend to observe and report facts that economists might have missed entirely. An excellent example of this is sociologist Robert Eccles's book *The Transfer Pricing Problem* (1985). Although economists (up to that time) believed that the purpose of transfer pricing was to allocate resources within firms, Eccles points out that few transfer pricing systems employed in firms actually do so. Eccles instead focuses on the conflict and political wrangling that transfer pricing systems cause in organizations.

However, this same strength—that clinical studies conducted by other social scientists may provide observation on things that economists would miss—may also be a weakness. When we borrow studies from other disciplines, the studies may fail to report on or even observe phenomena that are critically important to an economic theory. For example, a clinical study of almost any phenomenon inside an organization that fails to report on the incentives presented to the agents by the compensation system is likely to frustrate an economist's thorough analysis of the situation.

4. Standards for Clinical Studies

Good clinical studies ought to be interesting and compelling. Obviously, these two properties are especially important if clinical studies are intended for teaching purposes: less so if they are targeting a research audience. What other characteristics would we expect clinical studies to have to be effective in communicating those details and institutions that will enable economists to do better research?

Generally, good clinical studies will contain a detailed and rich description of the situation. Clinical studies without this detail are more like examples: useful for illustrating existing theory, but much less valuable as a tool for generating new theory. In addition, a good study ought to be generalizable, in the sense that insight derived from a particular situation is useful elsewhere. Without this characteristic, it is hard to see the point and relevance, other than pure entertainment.

In a similar vein, a clinical study should also address a topic that is, or eventually will be, modelable. This does not mean that the topic can be modeled with current technology: a good example is the description of the ratchet effect of piece rates in Donald Roy's machine shop. This phenomenon was not adequately modeled for 35 years until Gibbons's (1987) dissertation.

In this regard, we observe that many clinical studies and teaching cases about organizations, especially those by noneconomists, highlight the importance and relevance of corporate culture and leadership to corporate success. These are concepts that economists either failed to notice, or at least found too difficult to model, for decades. The Kreps (1990) paper—"Corporate Culture and Economic Theory"—was among the first to attempt this. Since that time, some economists have taken on the challenge of modeling these concepts (see Hermalin [1998] on leadership or Van den Steen [2006] on corporate culture).

One final standards question still looms: accuracy. It would seem that accuracy is a key ingredient of high-quality clinical studies. But is this really true? The legacy of Fisher Body again is relevant. Although this story has been central to theory development for more than 30 years now, the actual chain of events that led to the acquisition of Fisher Body by General Motors is very much in dispute. Papers by Casadesus-Masanell and Spulber (2000), Coase (2000), Freeland (2000), and Helper et al. (2000) dispute most, if not all, of the central factors playing a role in the Klein et al. (1978) version of the story. However, controversy over the facts notwithstanding, no one can dispute the usefulness of the story of Fisher Body to the field of organizational economics and the generation of theory in the field. Given the usefulness of the case as related by in Klein et al., should we care about any lack of accuracy and discount the scholarly contribution of the work?[3]

4.1. Areas of Concern

Several criteria that are standards for empirical research in economics are problematic for clinical studies. These include representativeness, bias, and replicability.

4.1.1. Representativeness and Bias

There is, and we believe there should be, real concern that the body of knowledge that results from a set of clinical studies will not be representative of any set of real-world settings that scholars might choose. This is because one of the main impediments to clinical studies, at least inside organizations, is access. Scholars must get permission from organizations to go inside them, talk to people, look at potentially sensitive information, and report what they believe is a complete picture of the phenomenon under study. This problem introduces a kind of sample selection bias that is very difficult to get a handle on, but it is surely important. We can speculate on the types of organizations that are likely to allow this type of work: those that care about knowledge generation, those that seek publicity, those that are successful, and those that use academics as consultants.

Perhaps the most troubling of these biases is that favoring success. Clinical studies and business teaching cases tend to be about successful organizations and their strategies rather than about failed organizations and the factors that led them to failure. Why is this the case? A first reason is that the reigning teaching philosophy in business school, law school, and other professional and graduate schools is more about the "Dos" than it is about the "Do Nots." A second reason is that firms going through failures that are worth writing about are also more likely to cease to exist. Finally, given that organizations must generally give their consent to allow a clinical study to be performed, it is human nature that those involved in success are more likely to agree to be the subject of a clinical paper than are those involved in failure.

4.1.2. Replicability

Another source of concern when evaluating the validity of clinical studies is the lack of replicability. Replicating most clinical studies is extremely costly, if not impossible, mainly because clinical studies often cover scenarios that are unusual and generally involve permissions and access that are hard to obtain. Later scholars' likelihood of finding additional sites and circumstances that replicate the original setting is low. However, there is a serious question of whether replicability is necessary for a study to be acceptable. Because the situations described in clinical studies are often helpful precisely because they are unusual, and because much of the value is in

---

3. Along these lines, it is interesting to note the disclaimer printed on the first page of every Harvard Business School case: "HBS cases are developed solely as the basis for class discussion. Cases are not intended to serve as endorsements, *sources of primary data*, or illustrations of effective or ineffective management" (emphasis added).

the high content of institutional and situational detail, replicability is probably not a criterion that we may want to apply to clinical studies, even though we may want to apply it to all other empirical studies.

5. Conclusion

Although this chapter has focused on clinical studies in organizational economics, many of the arguments for (and against) the usefulness of clinical papers are relevant to all of economics. However, we believe that clinical studies are particularly useful and important to building good theories and designing sensible tests of these theories in the field of organizations.

It is easy to forget that the neoclassical theory of the firm was all we had as recently as 30 years ago. Indeed, in many introductory and even intermediate microeconomics classes, the firm is still treated as a black box that transforms inputs into outputs through some monotone mechanical relation called the production function. Thanks in part to the work of psychologists and sociologists, economists now recognize that organizations are complex in their workings and that many aspects of organizational design and function are still beyond the scope of our modeling technology.

Because organizations are such rich and complex systems, understanding this complexity as completely as possible is important to building good models of how organizations work. In addition, much probably depends on the subtle and "soft" mechanisms that are best understood by the direct and careful observations provided by clinical studies. Understanding how relationships are managed both within and between firms, the role of corporate culture that mediates these relationships, and the role of leadership and personalities are best understood, we believe, by the slow and meticulous work involved in performing clinical studies.

Indeed, it is difficult to imagine how we could make much real progress on the issues that are central to the study of organizations without clinical studies to help and guide us. Even considering their costs in terms of time and money, clinical studies seem a necessary, though certainly not sufficient, condition for progress in this field. We hope that they will become more common, and more valued.

REFERENCES

Arruñada, B., L. Garicano, and L. Vazquez. 2001. "Contractual Allocation of Decision Rights and Incentives: The Case of Automobile Distribution." *Journal of Law, Economics, and Organization* 17: 257–284.

Asanuma, B. 1989. "Manufacturer-Supplier Relationships in Japan and the Concept of Relation-Specific Skill." *Journal of the Japanese and International Economies* 3: 1–30.

Baker, G. 1992. "Beatrice: A Study in the Creation and Destruction of Value." *Journal of Finance* 47: 1081–1119.

Baker, G., and K. Wruck. 1989. "Organizational Changes and Value Creation in Leveraged Buyouts: The Case of O.M. Scott & Sons Company." *Journal of Financial Economics* 25: 163–190.

Baker, G., M. Gibbs, and B. Holmström. 1994. "The Internal Economics of the Firm: Evidence from Personnel Data." *Quarterly Journal of Economics* 109: 881–919.

Baker, G., R. Gibbons, and K. J. Murphy. 2008. "Strategic Alliances: Bridges between 'Islands of Conscious Power.'" *Journal of the Japanese and International Economies* 22: 146–163.

Berg, N., and N. Fast. 1975. "Lincoln Electric Co." HBS Premier Case Collection, Product 376028-PDF-ENG.

Blanchard, O., F. Lopez-de-Silanes, and A. Shleifer. 1994. "What Do Firms Do with Cash Windfalls?" *Journal of Financial Economics* 36: 337–360.

Casadesus-Masanell, R., and D. Spulber. 2000. "The Fable of Fisher Body." *Journal of Law and Economics* 43: 67–104.

Chandler, A. 1962. *Strategy and Structure: Chapters in the History of the American Industrial Enterprise.* Cambridge, MA: MIT Press.

———. 1977. *The Visible Hand: The Managerial Revolution in American Business.* Cambridge, MA: Belknap Press of Harvard University Press.

Clarke, D., and R. Wise. 1975. "Optical Distortion, Inc. (A)." HBS Premier Case Collection, Product 575072-PDF-ENG.

Coase, R. 2000. "The Acquisition of Fisher Body by General Motors." *Journal of Law and Economics* 43: 15–31.

Crozier, M. 1964. *The Bureaucratic Phenomenon.* Chicago: University of Chicago Press.

Cutler, D., and L. Summers. 1988. "The Costs of Conflict Resolution and Financial Distress: Evidence from the Texaco-Pennzoil Litigation." *RAND Journal of Economics* 19: 157–172.

DeAngelo, H., and L. DeAngelo. 1987. "Management Buyouts of Publicly Traded Corporations." *Financial Analysts Journal* 43(3): 38–49.

Dial, J., and K. Murphy. 1995. "Incentives, Downsizing, and Value Creation at General Dynamics." *Journal of Financial Economics* 37: 261–314.

Eccles, R. G. 1985. "The Transfer Pricing Problem: A Theory for Practice." Lexington, MA: Lexington Books.

Eigen, M. 1973. *The Physicist's Conception of Nature,* J. Mehra (ed.). New York: Springer-Verlag.

Foss, N. 2003. "Selective Intervention and Internal Hybrids: Interpreting and Learning from the Rise and Decline of the Oticon Spaghetti Organization." *Organization Science* 14: 331–349.

Freeland, R. 2000. "Creating Holdup through Vertical Integration: Fisher Body Revisited." *Journal of Law and Economics* 43: 33–66.

Gibbons, R. 1987. "Piece-Rate Incentive Schemes." *Journal of Labor Economics* 5: 413–429.

Gibbons, R., and M. Waldman. 1999. "A Theory of Wage and Promotion Dynamics inside Firms" *Quarterly Journal of Economics* 114: 1321–1358.

———. 2006. "Enriching a Theory of Wage and Promotion Dynamics inside Firms." *Journal of Labor Economics* 24: 59–107.

Gil, R. 2013. "The Interplay of Formal and Relational Contracts: Evidence from Movies." *Journal of Law, Economics, and Organization* 29, forthcoming.

Helper, S. 2000. "Economists and Field Research: 'You Can Observe a Lot Just by Watching.'" *American Economic Review* 90: 228–232.

Helper, S., J. P. MacDuffie, and C. Sabel. 2000. "Pragmatic Collaborations: Advancing Knowledge While Controlling Opportunism." *Industrial and Corporate Change* 9: 443–483.

Hermalin, B. 1998. "Toward an Economic Theory of Leadership: Leading by Example." *American Economic Review* 88: 1188–1206.

Ichino, A., and G. Maggi. 2000. "Work Environment and Individual Background: Explaining Regional Shirking Differentials in a Large Italian Firm." *Quarterly Journal of Economics* 115: 1057–1090.

Jensen, M., E. Fama, J. Long, R. Ruback, W. Schwert, C. Smith, and J. Warner. 1989. "Clinical Papers and Their Role in the Development of Financial Economics." *Journal of Financial Economics* 24: 3–6.

Joskow, P. 1985. "Vertical Integration and Long-Term Contracts: The Case of Coal-Burning Electric Generating Plants." *Journal of Law, Economics, and Organization* 1: 33–80.

Kaplan, S. 1989. "Management Buyouts: Evidence on Taxes as a Source of Value." *Journal of Finance* 44(papers and proceedings): 611–632.

———. 1990. "Campeau's Acquisition of Federated: Value Created or Value Destroyed?" *Journal of Financial Economics* 25: 191–212.

———. 1994. "Campeau's Acquisition of Federated: Post-Bankruptcy Results." *Journal of Financial Economics* 35: 123–136.

Klein, B., R. Crawford, and A. Alchian. 1978. "Vertical Integration, Appropriable Rents, and the Competitive Contracting Process." *Journal of Law and Economics* 21: 297–326.

Knez, M., and D. Simester. 2001. "Firm-Wide Incentives and Mutual Monitoring at Continental Airlines." *Journal of Labor Economics* 19: 743–772.

Kreps, D. 1990. "Corporate Culture and Economic Theory," in J. Alt and K. Shepsle (eds.), *Perspectives on Positive Political Economy.* New York: Cambridge University Press, pp. 90–143.

Lazear, E. 1986. "Salaries and Piece Rates." *Journal of Business* 59: 405–431.

———. 1992. "The Job as a Concept," in W. J. Bruns, Jr. (ed.), *Performance Measurement, Evaluation, and Incentives.* Boston: Harvard Business School Press, pp. 183–215.

———. 2000. "Performance Pay and Productivity." *American Economic Review* 90: 1346–1361.

Mas, A., and E. Moretti. 2009. "Peers at Work." *American Economic Review* 99: 112–145.

Mayo, E. 1946. *The Human Problems of an Industrial Civilization,* second edition. Boston: Division of Research, Graduate School of Business Administration, Harvard University.

McCloskey, D. 1990. "Storytelling in Economics," in C. Nash and M. Warner (eds.), *Narrative in Culture.* London: Routledge, pp. 5–22.

Milgrom, P., and J. Roberts. 1990. "The Economics of Modern Manufacturing: Technology, Strategy, and Organization." *American Economic Review* 80: 511–528.

Moldovanu, B., A. Sela, and X. Shi. 2007. "Contests for Status." *Journal of Political Economy* 115: 338–363.

Paarsch, H., and B. Shearer. 1999. "The Response of Worker Effort to Piece Rates: Evidence from the British Columbia Tree-Planting Industry." *Journal of Human Resources* 34: 643–667.

———. 2000. "Piece Rates, Fixed Wages, and Incentive Effects: Statistical Evidence from Payroll Records." *International Economic Review* 41: 59–92.

Roy, D. 1952. "Quota Restriction and Goldbricking in a Machine Shop." *American Journal of Sociology* 57: 427–442.

Selznick, P. 1957. *Leadership in Administration: A Sociological Interpretation.* Berkeley: University of California Press.

Van den Steen, E. 2006. "On the Origin of Shared Beliefs (and Corporate Culture)." Working Paper 4553-05, Sloan School of Business, Massachusetts Institute of Technology, Cambridge, MA.

6

Experimental Organizational Economics

Colin F. Camerer and Roberto A. Weber

1. Introduction

This chapter is about experiments that study aspects of organizational structure and economic performance. Relative to field studies using empirical data, experiments often have obvious advantages, especially that of control and randomized assignment to implement theoretical assumptions that can only be imperfectly measured or controlled econometrically when using field data. Despite these advantages, the range of organizational hypotheses studied in experiments is small, although it is growing rapidly.

What makes an experiment organizational? The working definition we use to define the scope of this chapter is the following.

Definition   *In an organizational experiment, two or more subjects engage in a productive enterprise (usually a highly reduced-form model of a more complex organization) where the impact of the structure of the organization and incentives on productivity, through the characteristics and choices of subjects, are the variables of central interest.*

This definition is crafted to exclude (for brevity) consideration of many experiments relevant to organizations but not unique to them and those that do not vary structural variables of most interest in the economic study of organizations. One prominent class of such experiments is those that aim to use simple interactions to estimate the prevalence, characteristics, or consequences of social preferences on behavior (e.g., dictator, ultimatum, and trust games). Although valuable, this research is not unique to organizations, because the games also apply to market bargaining, groups, households, and other contexts (for reviews, see Camerer 2003: 336–407; Cooper and Kagel, in press). Another prominent class consists of experiments on negotiations studied by scientists interested in organizational behavior. We exclude these important experiments, because they do not typically alter incentives or hierarchical structure to test particular

We thank Scott Rick for very active collaboration on the first draft.

ideas in organizational economics, and their results are well reviewed elsewhere (e.g., Bazerman et al. 2000). Finally, we also exclude a considerable number of relevant research studies due to the sheer volume of experiments that one could consider "organizational"—even using our definition.[1]

An obvious concern about using experiments to study organizations is that the organizations that are the typical focus of theorizing—such as large firms—are complicated. Experiments are necessarily much simpler and are usually constrained in the numbers of agents and length of time that can be studied in a way that is both inexpensive and well controlled. This mismatch in scope naturally leads to heightened concerns about generalizability (which we discuss in Section 2.1).

The chapter is organized in seven sections. Section 2 presents an introduction to experimental principles and some early history of organizational experiments in psychology and sociology. The central sections discuss experimental research in four important organizational areas: basic theories of incentives and worker effort (Section 3), voluntary effort and reciprocity (Section 4), coordination (Section 5), and leadership and hierarchy (Section 6). Section 7 concludes and discusses some types of organizational experiments that could potentially provide valuable insights into organizational economics.

2. Experimental Principles and Some History

2.1. Basic Principles of Experimentation in Economics

Experiments are useful in all sciences. The experimental environment is one carefully designed and controlled by the researcher to provide the cleanest possible test of a theory or hypotheses. For instance, an experiment can allow researchers to measure the outcomes of both an event and its counterfactual (e.g., an institutional change or a merger), when the counterfactual is typically not observed outside the lab. An experiment also allows a researcher to avoid the endogeneity biases present in much empirical field research, by providing the researcher control over what is exogenous. Experiments also allow the researcher to distinguish among and test different explanations for an observed phenomenon (by controlling for transactions costs, risk aversion, beliefs, etc.) that are hard to separate parametrically in field data. Thus, the key feature of any experiment, and the central quality that makes experiments valuable, is control—over factors that are important in the theory being tested and over those that need to be excluded from the environment to properly test theory.

Good experiments typically satisfy four basic criteria: control over all relevant factors in the experimental environment, internal validity (the treatments work as intended and for the reasons claimed by the researcher), statistical integrity (using standards applicable to other empirical work),[2] and likely generalizability to naturally occurring settings with similar

---

1. We direct the reader interested in a more comprehensive review to other reviews that overlap considerably with ours in focus (Camerer and Malmendier 2007; Charness and Kuhn 2011; Kriss and Weber, in press).

2. In economics experiments with interacting groups and repeated behavior, it is generally inappropriate to treat individual observations as independent identically distributed (iid) draws. Instead, the appropriate tools

features.[3] It is usually easy to evaluate these criteria. But even when it is not, the threat of direct replication (and actual replication) disciplines researchers and gradually weeds out unreliable effects that might result from weaknesses in the basic criteria.

Really good experiments have other properties that are more difficult to define than the basic ones but are just as important. For example, an "interesting" experiment grabs attention by producing a result that is both surprising—Davis (1971: 327) calls it "denying assumptions of the audience"—and comprehensible after the surprise wears off. A "fruitful" experiment creates a paradigm (and sometimes tools, like software) and a result that piques curiosity and leads to natural extensions of the paradigm. One component of fruitfulness is the capacity of an experiment that rejects a theory to suggest an alternative theory and new experiments worth doing.

2.2. Organizational Experiments and Generalizability

The canonical organizations of most interest in economics—large firms—consist of agents who are both self-selected and selected by organizational promotion tracks, highly motivated by financial incentives, often highly experienced in their roles, and familiar with other organizational members. The typical laboratory experiment uses random assignment of inexperienced subjects (often college students), who are unfamiliar with one another, to simple organizational settings (often a single, abstract task, e.g., a number choice representing effort) with relatively modest incentives. Despite the obvious challenge of generalizing from such simple experiments, there are three arguments in favor of doing simple laboratory experiments on organization.

First, in science it is usually surprisingly useful to start with the simplest cases and then generalize (much as in producing formal theory). Basic genetics were first understood by studying fruit flies, which are much simpler than humans. Earthquakes are understood by using slider block models that study wooden blocks connected by metal springs (representing tectonic plates). Such simple experiments can produce an understanding of basic phenomena of significant importance. At this point, organizational experiments are similar in complexity to fruit fly studies of genetics and slider block models of earthquakes. Fortunately, there is plenty of future opportunity to create experimental organizations that are larger in scale, complexity, and temporal scope than the simple ones we describe.

---

are those used for time-series panel data with some specification of interaction effects among agents and over time. Controlling for various levels of clustering is one approach (see Frechette, in press). In practice, researchers often report tests using both incorrect iid assumptions and overly conservative assumptions (e.g., treating behavior averaged across an entire session as a single data point and testing across sessions).

3. However, it is important to note that generalizability is simply one criterion on which many experiments can be evaluated and is not a litmus test that must be applied to determine the usefulness of every experiment. Testing theories often requires creating environments that are different from what we typically observe in the natural world but contain all the key elements of a theory (Falk and Heckman 2009; Camerer 2011). In the physical sciences theoretically motivated experiments similarly often use environments that are atypical, dissimilar from where the theory is usually applied, and do not exist naturally (e.g., in particle accelerators, zero gravity, or a vacuum). Camerer (2011) also carefully reviews data from the closest matches of lab and field settings and finds that in only one of several cases does lab data provide a different answer than field data. Thus, generalizability is quite good, despite concerns voiced by Levitt and List (2007).

Second, some organizations are simple, so simple experiments are good analogies. A start-up with a few inexperienced employees or a project team in a firm that involves a small group of strangers who interact in an unfamiliar production task for a limited period might be well modeled by simple experiments like those described in this chapter.

Third, the presumption in economic theory is that basic principles apply widely unless the theory explicitly contains variables that parameterize boundaries of likely empirical applicability. Nothing in principal-agent theory, for example, says the theory should apply to CEO compensation but not to a three-person law firm with one lawyer and two paralegals, or to a three-person lab experiment with the economic structure of the law firm. If obvious distinctions between large firms and small experiments—like incentives or experience and selection of agents—are expected to make a difference in behavior, then the way in which those distinctions matter should be part of the theory. If they are not, experimental findings can suggest how those distinctions should be included.

When judging the generalizability of organizational experiments, it is also important to distinguish the power of the experimental method with the progress made from experiments thus far. If there are doubts about whether worker reciprocity persists over long periods, for example, this is a criticism about the generalizability of specific short-run experiments to particular long-term settings, but it is not a criticism of the experimental method—because, in principle, experiments can be conducted over the long run. Moreover, field experiments in markets and firms, with some degree of control, can be powerful complements to laboratory experiments. Thus, where there is a doubt that a particular experimental finding will generalize, those doubts are most useful if expressed as a conjecture about how extending the criticized experiment in some feasible way would change the results, an endeavor we fully encourage that is compatible with the experimental approach.

2.3. Early (Noneconomic) Organizational Experiments

The earliest organizational experiments, as we define them, were simple social psychological experiments aimed at understanding how performance and productivity change in the presence of others. Early experiments on "social facilitation" (Triplett 1898) measured how the presence of other individuals can lead to increased effort and performance in simple tasks (e.g., pedaling a bicycle). Later experiments by management researchers and industrial psychologists (Taylor 1911; Mayo 1933) studied factors that influence productivity and performance. Most of this research took place in real firms. Researchers exogenously varied factors, such as incentives, task design, and environmental influences, and then measured performance under these varying factors. This early research demonstrated the value of experimentation for understanding organizations and influenced the development of management and organizations as areas of scholarly inquiry (March and Simon 1958).

Starting in the 1950s, organizational psychologists began using simple laboratory experiments to study social factors that might influence efficiency and productivity in organizations. For example, several experiments explored the impact of group structure or "communication nets" on productivity in simple tasks (e.g., Bavelas and Barrett 1951; Leavitt 1951; Guetzkow and Simon 1955). These experiments provided valuable insights into how communication and authority structures in organizations might influence performance, and they also demonstrated the potential value of simple laboratory experiments for understanding organizational phenomena.

In subsequent decades, managerial and organizational researchers—usually trained as psychologists—continued to use experiments to understand organizations. In 1969, a special issue of a leading management journal was dedicated to experiments on organizations (see Weick 1969). This special issue addressed such topics as performance in hierarchical versus flat organizations (Carzo and Yanouzas 1969), internal resource allocation (Pondy and Birnberg 1969), and employee performance in response to varying levels of payment (Evan and Simmons 1969)—an experiment similar to recent "gift exchange" experiments in economics (see Section 4.1). The experiments varied in whether they took place in a laboratory or in the field, and as with many subsequent noneconomic organizational experiments, they also frequently involved deception of subjects by the researchers (a practice frowned on by experimental economists; see Ortmann and Hertwig 2002).

Following the abovementioned research, organizational and managerial researchers have since continued to rely on laboratory and field experiments to address similar questions (e.g., Argote et al. 1989; Greenberg 1990; Bottom et al. 2006). Although we omit this research to focus on experiments in organizational economics, this work frequently explores similar questions to those addressed in the work we review below.[4]

We now review experimental research in four areas of interest to organizational economists: (1) theories of incentives and worker effort, (2) voluntary effort and reciprocity, (3) coordination, and (4) leadership and hierarchy. Each of the next four sections reviews experimental research on one of these topics, focusing on a few key studies and cumulating regularity across studies.

3. Incentives and Worker Effort

The first wave of experiments we describe study the most basic propositions of incentive theory. The relationships among different kinds of incentives, effort, and productivity are central to organizational economics. Many of these experiments exploit the sharp precision of predictions that can be derived when cost of effort is induced experimentally and comparative statics make clear predictions about which types of contracts will work well or poorly.

3.1. Basic Incentives

Nalbantian and Schotter (1997) studied a variety of incentive schemes in simple lab experiments. In their setup, teams of six agents choose efforts e_i in the interval [0, 100]. Group output is a simple sum of effort plus a random term, $Y = 1.5(\Sigma_i e_i + \varepsilon)$, where ε is uniform in $[-40, +40]$. Revenue is equal to group output times a constant ($R = 1.5Y$). Agents' effort costs are $(e_i)^2/100$.

Optimal net revenue for the group (less effort costs) occurs at $e_i^* = 75$. Nalbantian and Schotter (1997) consider a variety of contracts that either induce this effort (in theory) or that

---

4. For example, the recent paper by Bottom et al. (2006) examines how employees respond to both financial and social incentives. This similar in focus to the work reviewed in Section 3.1.

Table 1. Equilibrium and actual effort in various incentive schemes

Contract	Individual payoff to i	Equilibrium effort e^*	Equilibrium group profit	Mean effort
Revenue sharing	$Y/6 - c(e_i)$	$e^* = 12.5$	103.1	19
Forcing contract (75)	$Y/6 - c(e_i)$ if $Y \geq R^* = 450$; $B = 1.125$ otherwise	$e^* = 75$	337.5	16
Profit sharing	$(Y - Y^*)/6 - c(e_i)$ if $Y \geq Y^* = 75$; $B = 0$ otherwise	$e^* = 19.1$	150.0	22
Team competition	$(Y_1 + T)/6 - c(e_i)$ if $Y_1 > Y_2$; $(Y_1 - T)/6 - c(e_i)$ if $Y_1 < Y_2$; $T = 360$	$e^* = 75$	337.5	35 [a]
Monitoring ($p = 0.7$)	Earn $W = 112.5$ if $e_i = 75$, $W = 18.75$ if $e_i < 75$	$e^* = 75$	337.5	68
Monitoring ($p = 0.3$)	Earn $W = 112.5$ if $e_i = 75$, $W = 18.75$ if $e_i < 75$	$e^* = 0$	-506.25	4

Source: Data are from Nalbantian and Schotter (1997).
Notes: Mean effort is from the last 5 periods (out of 25) in phase I only. Means are estimated from plots.
a. Mean is from phase II, estimated from Nalbantian and Schotter (1997: figure 10) (corresponding mean for forcing contract with $e^* = 75$ is effort of 19).

theoretically induce lower effort due to shirking. These contracts and some basic results are summarized in Table 1.

Phase I experimental sessions begin with a 25-period revenue-sharing segment, followed by a switch to another scheme. Phase II experiments used the opposite order. Two experimental sessions used monitoring schemes, reversing the order of two different probabilities ($p = 0.3$ and 0.7) of being monitored.

The baseline contract is simple revenue sharing, in which players earn $R/6$ and pay their own effort costs.[5] This contract should induce shirking and does so reliably; mean efforts start at about 35 and drift down to 18, toward the equilibrium of 12.5. A related contract, profit sharing, involves players sharing revenue only if average output exceeds the equilibrium quantity. This treatment also works roughly as predicted and generates little effort.

In a Holmström-type (1982) forcing contract, players share revenue only if total revenue is above the efficient level of 675 (corresponding to $e_i^* = 75$); otherwise, all players earn a low penalty wage $B \leq 1.125$. This forcing contract does badly because it is so fragile: mean efforts start at about 45, but all groups fall below the threshold output requirement, everyone earns the penalty wage, and efforts then fall. A forcing contract that is inefficient, inducing effort of

5. Revenue-sharing contracts are interesting because many firms use variants of group-based performance schemes (e.g., employee stock ownership plans). In theory, these schemes should not work well, because in large teams, workers should free ride if their shirking cannot be monitored and punished. Yet group-based performance schemes often work surprisingly well in practice (Nalbantian 1987; Blinder 1990), which motivates an interest in understanding when teams do not fail as badly as they should in theory.

40 in theory rather than 75, actually works much better in practice than the efficient forcing contract, as it is more easily met.

The contracts that work best, both at producing high effort and in the accuracy of theoretical predictions, involve team competition and monitoring. In the competitive teams treatment, firms consist of two six-person teams, and efforts create team output and revenue as in the revenue-sharing treatment. However, the lower output team in each pair of teams pays a transfer of $T = 360$ (shared equally among team members) to the team with higher output. In theory this contract should induce equilibrium effort of 75. Actual mean efforts are about half that level (with low variance across subjects).

Monitoring contracts works best of all. Players choose effort and are monitored with probability p. If they are monitored and chose effort of 75 or more, or are not monitored, they earn a high wage $W = 112.5$. If they are monitored and chose $e < 75$, they earn 18.75. When the monitoring probability is $p = 0.7$, they should choose $e^* = 75$, and monitoring indeed works incredibly well—median effort is 75 in about 90% of the experimental periods. When $p = 0.3$, they should shirk and choose $e^* = 0$, and median efforts are indeed very low.

More recent research studies how worker self-selection between different incentive schemes can affect firm productivity. For example, Dohmen and Falk (2011) use a real-effort task, in which subjects multiply one-digit numbers by two-digit numbers, and correctly entered answers constitute the worker's output. Subjects initially performed the task under no incentives and piece rate incentives, to provide measures of baseline productivity. They were then given the option to continue the task for 10 minutes under either a fixed-pay contract or one with pay dependent on performance. The variable-pay schemes varied by treatment and included piece rate, tournament, and revenue-sharing incentives. Across treatments, between 50% and 60% of subjects opted for variable pay. The main finding in the experiment is that output is higher under variable pay, with subjects completing roughly twice as many problems (about 60) under the variable-pay schemes than with fixed pay. Moreover, this result is driven mainly by more productive subjects opting for the variable-pay schemes. For example, when the variable-pay incentive was a piece rate, subjects who chose this option had completed, on average, 27.3 correct problems in the first part of the experiment, while those who opted for the fixed payment had completed only 13.8. Thus, different pay schemes not only affect productivity because of the effort they induce but also because of the different kinds of people they attract.

3.2. Tournaments and Sabotage

Lazear and Rosen (1981) note that many labor markets, particularly internal competition for promotion in firms, are organized as tournaments. In the simplest tournament model, individual workers exert costly effort e_i, their individual output (y_i) is a combination of (unobserved) effort and a measurement error term θ_i, and workers are ranked by total output $y_i = e_i + \theta_i$. Workers with rank r earn a pre-announced prize $M(r)$. Ranking workers is often cognitively easier than measuring their absolute outputs. Lazear and Rosen show conditions under which tournaments elicit maximum effort and are better incentive schemes than piece rates and other individual-specific wage packages.

Explicit tournaments are often used in sports (e.g., Ehrenberg and Bognanno 1990) and some areas of the economy (e.g., Knoeber 1989; Lambert et al. 1993). Generally, however, it is difficult

Table 2. Predicted and actual behavior in two-player tournaments

Treatment	Equilibrium prediction	Effort in rounds 7–12	
		Mean	Variance
Piece rate	37	38.91	87
Baseline	37	38.75	499
High effort equilibrium	74	69.91	892
Wide random number ($a = 80$)	37	33.41	286
Asymmetric costs	70, 35	73.60, 56.91	708, 905
Medium information (output)	37	48.91	442
High information (output, e_i)	37	33.48	552
Automaton opponent	37	44.62	276
Twenty-five-round experiment	37	48.00 [a]	362 [a]

Source: Data are from Bull et al. (1987).
a. Data are from the last half of the experiment (rounds 13–25).

to test the sharpest predictions of tournament theory with field data, because it is difficult to measure or influence key variables, making the laboratory a valuable testing ground.

Bull et al. (1987) did the first such tournament experiment. Subjects chose effort $e_i \in [0, 100]$ in two-player tournaments, with output $y_i = e_i + \theta_i$ determined by effort and an iid stochastic term θ_i drawn from the uniform interval $[-a, +a]$, with $a = 40$, and convex effort costs $c(e_i) = e_i^2/K$, where K varied from 10,000 to 25,000. The winning prize $M(1)$ varied from \$1.02 to \$1.45, while the second (losing) prize $M(2)$ varied from \$0.43 to \$0.86.

Table 2 gives results from the last half of the 12-period experimental session. The piece rate incentive produced outcomes very close to the theoretical prediction under risk neutrality. Although aggregate behavior in the first three tournament sessions (baseline, high-effort, and wide random number) converges toward the respective theoretical predictions, the variance in effort is quite large (much higher than for the piece rate) and does not decline across the session.

The results of providing additional information are a little puzzling. Providing ranks (baseline), or ranks and opponent effort (high information) produce efforts close to the equilibrium prediction, but supplying only rank and outputs (medium information) produces efforts that are much higher. Subjects appear to overreact to learning that their opponent's output is high, even though they realize that high output could be due to luck.

Sessions with automated opponents choosing Nash effort levels generally produce efforts close to equilibrium and lower variance than sessions with human opponents, which shows that strategic uncertainty when playing other subjects may increase variance.

Bull et al. (1987) also conducted one session with asymmetric costs, in which one player's cost function was twice that of the other player. Both players chose effort levels above equilibrium, which is important, because most naturally occurring tournaments do have cost asymmetries.

Schotter and Weigelt (1992) studied asymmetric two-player tournaments with two kinds of handicaps for player 2. In uneven tournaments the disadvantaged player has effort costs that are $\alpha > 1$ times larger than the advantaged player. In unfair tournaments the disadvantaged player must have output that is $k > 0$ units higher than the advantaged player in order to win.

Table 3. Predicted efforts and actual efforts (periods 11–20) in asymmetric two-player tournaments

Type of tournament	Cost handicap α	Effort advantage k	Advantaged player effort		Disadvantaged player effort	
			Equilibrium	Mean (standard deviation)	Equilibrium	Mean (standard deviation)
Baseline	None	None	73.8	77.9 (24.8)	n.a.	n.a.
Unfair	None	25	58.4	74.5 (19.9)	58.4	58.7 (37.9)
Uneven	2	None	74.5	78.8 (21.8)	37.3	37.1 (28.9)
Affirmative action	2	25	59.0	64.2 (32.3)	29.5	36.4 (27.7)
Affirmative action	4	25	60.2	85.8 (19.6)	15.1	32.4 (25.7)

Source: Data are from Schotter and Weigelt (1992).
Note: n.a., not applicable.

With a cost handicap α and the evaluation bias k, the equilibrium efforts for players 1 and 2 are $e_1^* = \alpha e_2^*$ and

$$e_2^* = \frac{[(1/2a) - (k/4a^2)]\,c(M-m)/2\alpha}{1 + [(1-\alpha)/4a^2]\,c(M-m)/2\alpha}.$$

These tournaments have interesting properties. If there is no cost handicap ($\alpha = 1$), then even when there is a bias k, both players should exert the same effort ($e_1^* = e_2^*$). When there is a bias k, both players' efforts are decreasing in k. Intuitively, when there is a bias, the advantaged agent does not have to work too hard (because the marginal impact of effort on winning probability is lower) and the disadvantaged agent should not bother to work too hard (because extra effort probably will not overcome the bias). In addition, in the presence of a cost handicap α, a bias k in evaluation can raise total effort. This provides a possible rationale for affirmative action, adding a handicap to even a tournament where one player has a cost advantage.

Table 3 summarizes predicted efforts and mean efforts in the last 10 periods of Schotter and Weigelt's 20-period sessions. With no asymmetry ($\alpha = 1$, $k = 0$), average efforts of 77.9 are close to the predicted effort of 73.8, replicating the Bull et al. (1987) result. When asymmetries are introduced, all the comparative statics move in the right direction. However, both a cost handicap and evaluation bias lead to more effort by both advantaged and disadvantaged players than is predicted by theory.

The experiments described above all use two-player tournaments. However, organizational tournaments typically involve more than two workers. More recent experiments study multi-person ($n > 2$) tournaments.

Orrison et al. (2004) used the paradigm and parameter values in the experiments above. They varied the size of the tournament ($k = 2$, 4, or 6 players), the proportion of players to be awarded the high prize, and the symmetry of the competition (by varying the handicap k between 0 and 25).

In their symmetric treatments, predicted effort is always the same (73.75). As predicted, Orrison et al. (2004) find that behavior is insensitive to tournament size when half the players win the high prize. However, the proportion of large prizes influences behavior in a way that is not predicted by theory. In six-player tournaments, when two or three of the players earn the highest prize, effort is close to that predicted, but when the large prize is awarded to four players, mean effort drops to 59. In the asymmetric treatments, predicted effort is higher in six-person groups than in four-person groups, as predicted. But contrary to the theoretical predictions, two-person groups do not produce lower effort—and often even have higher effort than the larger groups.

Müller and Schotter (2010) study a more complicated tournament in which four workers have private costs parameters and there are two prizes V_1 and V_2, with a fixed total $V_1 + V_2 = 1$ (based on Moldovanu and Sela 2001). Theoretical predictions are sharply confirmed with two interesting exceptions. Low-cost workers should win all the time, but the predicted winners win only about half the time. And when costs are low, subjects typically exert too much effort ("workaholics"); when costs are high, subjects often drop out and choose $e_i = 0$.[6]

Although tournaments have many advantages—chiefly, they require only relative comparisons of output—they have a major drawback: workers may have an incentive to spend effort sabotaging perceptions of the output of other workers. If sabotage is cheap and effective, heightened incentives to work hard from tournament bonuses may be undermined by both the diversion of effort into sabotage and by the withdrawal of effort in anticipation of sabotage (see Milgrom and Roberts 1988).

Carpenter et al. (2010) conducted a clever experiment on sabotage with actual effort. Groups of eight subjects privately filled out forms and hand-addressed envelopes for 30 minutes. This simple activity permits differentiation of the quality of output, because envelopes can be either clearly or sloppily addressed. The quality of each envelope was rated on a 0–1 scale of deliverability by an actual letter carrier from the U.S. Postal Service. Measured output is the sum of these quality ratings across all the addressed letters. In addition, after finishing the task, all the workers looked at the output of other workers, selected one envelope at random to inspect, and rated its quality.

There are three experimental conditions: piece rate ($1 times output), tournament ($25 bonus for highest output), and tournament with sabotage. In the tournament with sabotage, the quality-adjusted output of a worker is determined by the average of the other worker's quality ratings (like a "360-degree evaluation" system). Opportunistic workers should work hard, but they should also sabotage their peers by underrating the quality of the latter's work. Hiring the postal carrier to rate objective quality provides a clear way in which to address whether peer-rated quality is lower than objective quality (i.e., whether there is sabotage).

Table 4 summarizes raw and quality-adjusted output in the three experimental treatments. In the piece rate treatment, workers addressed 12.8 envelopes, but both peers and the expert adjusted the output downward by about 20% for quality of handwritten envelope addresses. In the tournament with no sabotage (where peer ratings do not matter for payoffs), output goes up in raw terms and as judged by the expert, compared to the piece rate, but peers still rate quality as lower (even though underrating their peers does not benefit them). Carpenter et al. (2010) interpret this result as an automatic affective response to competition. In the sabotage treatment, where workers might benefit from underrating peer quality, peer-rated quality is about 40% lower than in the piece rate baseline—there is strong sabotage—and expert-rated quality falls as well. That is, when workers can have a direct influence on how their peers' work is perceived, there is both substantial sabotage of high-achieving peers and a drop in effort (judged by expert

---

6. These deviations could be explored with newer models of stochastic response (McKelvey and Palfrey 1998) or limited strategic thinking (Camerer et al. 2004); see Camerer (2003) for a review of these theories and others that incorporate players' regard for the payoffs of others.

Table 4. Average raw output and quality-adjusted output (peer and expert ratings) in piece rate and tournament conditions

| Quality adjustment | Piece rate | Tournament output minus piece rate output | |
		No sabotage	Sabotage
None (total letters)	12.8	+1.4	−1.3
Peer rated	11.0	−0.6	−5.3
Expert rated	10.5	+1.3	−1.4

Source: Data are from Carpenter et al. (2010).
Note: Outputs are envelopes stuffed and addressed. Quality adjustment is output times a 0–1 measure assessed by peer ratings or expert (letter-carrier) ratings.

quality ratings) in anticipation of sabotage. The drop in effort is so strong that output is higher in the piece rate condition than in the tournament with sabotage.

3.3. Anomalous Response to Incentives

Several experiments show responses to incentives that are theoretically surprising and counter-intuitive. These studies are important for understanding when incentives in organizations are likely to have unintended effects.

3.3.1. Incentives Do Not Necessarily Produce More Effort (Crowding Out)

One of the simplest predictions of labor economics is that the supply of labor should increase in response to a transitory increase in wage. Studies of temporary wage increases (e.g., Mulligan 1995) suggest this law of supply is often true. However, using field data on cab driver hours, Camerer et al. (1997) found that labor supply of inexperienced drivers slopes downward, because inexperienced drivers act as if they establish a daily income target and quit when they reach the target.[7] In a field experiment with bicycle messengers, Fehr and Goette (2007) found that hourly effort of messengers decreased with temporary wage increases (though they also worked more hours, which led to an increase in the amount of labor supplied under the wage increase). These studies suggest that labor supply and effort are sometimes sensitive to a point of reference in income.

This sensitivity is more directly tested in a laboratory experiment by Abeler et al. (2011), which studies how productivity varies in a real-effort task. In the task, subjects counted the number of zeros in tables consisting of 150 ones and zeros, with each completed table counting as output. They could quit the task and leave the experiment whenever they wanted and were paid either a piece rate for their performance or a fixed wage, but they did not know which of the two payment mechanisms would apply until the end of the experiment. The key treatment variable manipulated the size of the possible fixed payment. Consistent with effort provision being influenced by reference levels, subjects worked harder when the fixed payment was higher, and they often worked until their earnings from the piece rate equaled the possible fixed earnings.

---

7. Farber (2005) finds a stronger effect of hours than of cumulative daily income but does find evidence consistent with targeting in three of six drivers for which he has many days of data. Using a different approach, Farber (2008) finds clearer evidence of targeting, although inferred targets are statistically imprecise.

This experiment nicely demonstrates how the control afforded by the laboratory can allow researchers the ability to conduct carefully specified tests of a theory while controlling for myriad possible confounds that are difficult to rule out in the field.

Another kind of reference point is a standard for a fair or reasonable wage. Gneezy and Rustichini (2000a) investigated effort in response to no incentive, very low incentives, and higher incentives, in performance on a 50-question IQ test. When pay is only 0.1 new Israeli shekels (at the time of the experiment, about $0.03) per correct answer, the average number of questions answered correctly is lower than when there is no pay, mostly because several subjects quit and did poorly on the test (like a labor strike; see also Frey and Jegen 2001; Heyman and Ariely 2004).

Such crowding out of intrinsic incentives can also occur when people exert effort out of moral obligation, and pay drives out moral obligation. Gneezy and Rustichini (2000b) studied this effect in a field experiment at 10 private daycare centers in Israel. Before the experiment, parents were told to pick up their children on time. During the experiment, a modest fine was instituted for late pickups and was then rescinded. When the fine was introduced, late pickups actually increased (compared to control groups with no new fine). When the fine was rescinded, late pickups dropped but settled down to about twice the rate of late pickups before the fine. Gneezy and Rustichini (2000b) suggest the fine is a price—the moral obligation of picking up your children on time is driven out by a new low price you can comfortably pay for being late; and when the price is removed, the moral obligation is not restored (e.g., Lepper et al. 1973).

3.3.2. Higher Effort Does Not Necessarily Improve Performance

The standard incentive model assumes that higher incentives lead to higher effort, which improves performance. Psychologists, however, have long suspected that at very high levels of arousal, performance can suffer because of arousal and distraction (e.g., "choking"). Yerkes and Dodson (1908) initially demonstrated this effect by testing the ability of rats to discriminate between safe and dangerous (i.e., shock-inducing) areas in a cage. The rats learned to do so most quickly when the shocks were at an intermediate level of intensity and actually learned more slowly when shocks were stronger. Camerer (1998) noted this effect and reported data from NBA playoff free-throw shooting. Players make significantly fewer shots in the playoffs than in the regular season (about 75% versus 73%), presumably because of the heightened pressure during the playoffs.

Ariely et al. (2009) demonstrated the Yerkes-Dodson pattern with a high-stakes experiment in a poor town in India, using six games that require concentration and physical skill. The highest performance level in each game earned 400 Indian rupees, about a month's worth of consumer spending. Subjects reached the highest performance in only 6% of games with high stakes, compared to 22% and 26% for low and medium stakes. The highest stakes seem to create nervousness, or choking, which actually lowers short-run performance.

3.4. Field Experiments on Incentives and Monitoring

Some interesting experiments on the effect of incentives on employee effort and productivity have been conducted in the field. These studies serve as a valuable complement to laboratory experiments.

Nagin et al. (2002) report an interesting field experiment that tests the effect of monitoring on employee moral hazard. Their experiment was conducted by a company that hires people to solicit donations to nonprofit organizations over the phone. The experiment varies the likelihood of detecting low effort on the part of employees (as in the monitoring treatments of Nalbantian and Schotter 1997).

The workers earn a piece rate wage that increases with the number of successful solicitations. As a result, there is a moral hazard incentive to claim that people who were called had pledged donations over the phone, when those people actually had not. The employer tried to limit moral hazard by independently calling back a fraction of the people who had allegedly pledged to give money and identifying "suspicious bad calls" (SBCs), or cases indicative of misrepresentation by the employees. SBCs were deducted from the original piece rate pay but were not directly linked to firing or other sanctions.

Because the callbacks are expensive, the company was interested in whether lowering the rate of calling back would lead to many more SBCs. They designed an experiment in which the monitoring (callback) rates were varied across 16 separate call centers and across time, from 0 to 25%. At four sites, the actual rate of calling back was 25% during the experimental period, but only a fraction of those monitored call results were reported to the employees. For example, at one site, 25% of the successful calls were called back, but only 8% of those results were reported back to the employees, so the employees were getting feedback as if they faced a 2% callback rate. This design enabled the firm to measure whether employees who were actually making a lot of SBCs but thinking that they were "getting away with it" most of the time would increase their SBC moral hazard in the future. (The design was double-blind, so that both supervisors and employees did not know the percentage of monitored calls.)

Table 5 shows the marginal effect on the number of per-week SBCs for week t, based on the monitoring percentage observed by employees in the previous week $t - 1$. For example, employees who were subjected to no reported monitoring in the previous week had 0.031 SBCs (per employee, per week) more than the baseline category (25% monitoring). Very low rates of monitoring (0–5%) produced substantial jumps in SBCs, although the numbers are still rather low. Most of the aggregate effect is due to a jump in later SBCs among employees who had earlier made an SBC that was not reported back to them. For example, in the four 0–10% groups, about a third of employees made an SBC in week 61 that was not reported back to them. The SBC rate for those employees in the subsequent week 62, across the four experimental sites, was 5.29, 1.33, 2.73, and 0.47.

There is a remarkable amount of heterogeneity in moral hazard. In the weeks when reported monitoring was 0, the median number of SBCs per employee is 0.25. The 80th, 90th, and 95th percentiles of the cross-employee distribution, however, are 1.99, 3.80, and 6.45, respectively. The top tenth of cheaters are cheating 15 times higher than the median. In a distribution with such a long right tail, the basic managerial challenge is to prevent moral hazard among that minority who are inclined to cheat a lot, if they can.[8]

8. Nagin et al. (2002) also used surveys to compare the influence of psychological and economic factors on generating SBCs. Measures of difficulty of finding a comparable job and expected tenure with the firm (typical economic variables) were not correlated with SBCs, but employee attitudes toward their employer did have a significant effect, consistent with pure reciprocity.

Table 5. Effect of frequency of call monitoring in week $t - 1$ on suspicious bad calls (SBCs) in week t

Monitoring in previous week $t - 1$ (%)	Change in SBCs per week, week t	
	Coefficient	t-statistic
0 (no monitoring)	.031	2.69
2	.006	2.81
5	.019	6.29
10	.002	1.36
15 (high monitoring)	.002	1.20
25 (constant term)	.002	0.44

Source: Data are from "OLS" column 1 in Nagin et al. (2002: table 2).
Note: Constant additional hours and call center fixed effects are included in the regression but omitted from this table.

Several other field experiments have studied the effects of simple changes in incentives on worker productivity. For example, Bandiera et al. (2007) report the results of a natural field experiment on incentive change on a British farm where workers either pick fruit or do other tasks. Increasing bonus pay for managers who supervise workers increased fruit-picking productivity of workers, due to both closer monitoring and managerial selection of more productive workers to pick fruit and less productive workers to do other tasks.

3.5. Summary

The experiments on basic incentives described above are mostly supportive of basic theory, with interesting exceptions.[9] Effort in piece rate and experimental tournaments are close to those predicted. However, when there is a deliberate tournament bias, all workers work too hard, and when workers can sabotage others (through peer-rating of quality), they do so. Field experiments that increase high-powered incentives among managers increase productivity, due to more work effort and selection of harder workers by managers. In experimental team production (with no communication), forcing contracts—which penalize all workers if a team goal is not reached—work very poorly, and team competition does not work much better. The most robust experimental institution is the threat of monitoring. A field experiment with phone callers also shows that when monitoring drops to zero, shirking rises sharply, but mostly among a small number of workers; the effect is smaller if employees like their employer.

4. Voluntary Effort and Reciprocity in Organizations

Employment contracts typically have some degree of contractual incompleteness. Incompleteness raises the prospect of moral hazard (hidden action)—that is, when workers are expected to

---

9. For further discussion of theoretical approaches to employee motivation, and particularly how these have evolved to reflect "nonstandard" preferences demonstrated in some of the experiments we review, see Rebitzer and Taylor (2011).

exert effort that is costly for them, but valuable to the firm, firms should not expect much effort (absent reputational concerns and contractual requirements or penalties). Several experiments explore the conditions under which organizational members voluntarily exert effort absent any extrinsic incentives for doing so.

4.1. Simple Worker-Firm Gift Exchange

A potential constraint on moral hazard is reciprocity: if A feels B treated her well (badly), then A may sacrifice to help (hurt) B. Moral hazard by reciprocity-minded employees may be limited, leading employees to exert costly effort that is valuable to firms if employees feel firms have treated them well. Akerlof (1982) called this phenomenon "gift-exchange" and used it to explain the persistence of above-market wages and associated unemployment.

Gift-exchange is an ideal topic to explore in experiments, because the crucial economic variable that is typically unobservable in field data—worker effort—can be observed by the experimenter, even if subjects acting as employers cannot contract on effort. It is hard to imagine how one could possibly collect these data in a typical firm, because any component of effort that cannot be measured (and contracted upon) by firms would typically also be unmeasurable by an economist.

The gift-exchange labor market paradigm was pioneered by Fehr et al. (1993). Their study was modified and expanded by Fehr et al. (1998). Because the Fehr et al. (1998) design became standard in many subsequent studies, we will describe it in detail.

In their paradigm, firms offer a wage w. Workers who accept a wage then choose an effort in increments of 0.1 ($e \in \{0.1, 0.2, \ldots, 0.9, 1.0\}$). Firms earn $(120 - w)e$, and workers earn $w - 20 - c(e)$, where $c(e)$ is a cost-of-effort function that is convex (with $c(0.1) = 0$ and $c(1) = 18$). Note that the gains from gift-exchange are large. In markets where effort is low ($e = 0.1$), the market-clearing wage is 21, so firms earn 9.9 and workers earn 1.0, a total surplus of 10.9. But if $e = 1$ could be achieved, firms would earn $120 - w$ and workers would earn $w - 20 - 18$, for a total surplus of 118. The gains from obtaining high effort are therefore very large.

Fehr et al. (1998) use explicit labor market language to describe the experiment.[10] They compare three market institutions. One institution is one-sided oral bidding by firms with an excess supply of labor (a gift-exchange market), another is a bilateral market (workers and firms are matched individually, firms offer a wage to their worker, and their worker takes it or leaves it). The third institution is a complete contract condition in which effort is fixed at $e^* = 1$ and workers' cost at $c(e) = 0$.

In the standard gift-exchange markets and bilateral matching markets, wages and efforts are persistently above the competitive level and do not decline over time, and efforts are strongly correlated with wages. Under the complete contract condition, at the mandated effort $e^* = 1$, firms earn $120 - w$ and workers earn w, so a wage offer is essentially an ultimatum offer of how the surplus of 120 is to be divided. In simple ultimatum games, average offers are about 40%, which would predict a wage offer of 48. Wages in these experiments are close to that figure

---

10. In Fehr et al. (1993) the labor market is described in plain buyer-seller language. Switching to explicit labor market language does not seem to make much difference.

although clearly lower. In this complete contract condition, wage offers of military subjects are higher (average 44) than those of students (average 32), and the student offers decline over time more strongly than do those of the soldiers.

Fehr and Falk (1999) ran experiments with double-auction institutions, in which firms and workers both offer wages (subject to an improvement rule: firms must outbid, and workers must underbid, standing offers on their respective sides of the market). There is a large amount of underbidding by workers, but firms often take the highest wage bids and reject lower ones (as occurs in the field, too; see Agell and Lundborg 1995). This strategy turns out to be profitable for firms—profits increase in higher wages, because higher wages elicit greater effort from most subjects.

4.2. Replication and Robustness of Simple Gift Exchange

The apparent strength of gift exchange surprised experimental economists and inspired many replications and extensions designed to establish the boundaries and robustness of the phenomenon. Several of these studies are summarized in Table 6. Three questions that immediately arise concern the effects of experimental procedures and subject demographics, the influence of trading institutions and other components of economic structure, and the persistence over time of reciprocity. Estimates with individual fixed effects show that there certainly is heterogeneity, although most individual workers' efforts respond positively to higher accepted wages.

Charness et al. (2004) find that when the possible payoffs from various (w, e) combinations are presented in a table form, wages and efforts are lower, although the effort-wage relation is still strong. Hannan et al. (2002) explored differences in subject pools, using University of Pittsburgh undergraduates and MBA students.[11] The mean wages and efforts of MBAs are close to those observed in Fehr et al. (1998), but the undergraduate wages and efforts are substantially lower. However, the effort response to wages is comparable in magnitude and significance across both groups.

Hannan et al. (2002) also conducted sessions in which firms both offer wages and request effort levels; this change seems to raise effort. Interestingly, regressions of actual effort choices that include both wages and effort requests show that MBAs respond to requests but not to wages, and undergraduates respond to wages but not to requests. This difference may reflect some socialization in workplace norms (or other differences in MBA and undergraduate groups).

Fehr et al. (2002) did experiments in Russia with very high stakes (about one week's income per trade) and found similar results to Fehr et al. (1998).

Brandts and Charness (2004) experimented with four changes in structure. First, they varied the degree of excess labor supply from four extra workers to four extra firms. Wages and efforts are lower, but insignificantly so, when there is excess labor, which suggests that excess labor supply is not that important. Second, they had sessions with one-shot matches in the bilateral market institution; in these sessions, wages and effort are substantially lower, which shows a role for repeated-market effects (even though matches are anonymous). Third, in one treatment, they

---

11. Hannan et al. (2002) also varied the value of effort to firms, comparing profit functions $(120 - w)e$ with $(90 - w)e$. There are not large differences, except that the low-value firms pay lower wages in the MBA sessions and request higher effort levels.

Table 6. Results of several worker-firm gift-exchange experiments

Reference	Experimental treatment	Number of firms, workers	Wage range	Worker utility	Firm profit	Mean wage	Mean effort	Effort-wage coefficient (value of t)	Comments
Fehr et al. (1998)	Bilateral (BGE)	10, 10	0–120	$w - c(e) - 20$	$(120 - w)e$	57.7[a]	.34[a]	.0057 (8.0)	Study subjects are soldiers
	Competitive (GEM)	6, 9				56.4[b]	.395[b]	.0088 (8.8)	
	Complete contract			$c(e) = 0$	$120 - w$	44.3	$e^* = 1$ (fixed)	—	Soldiers, students differ
Fehr and Falk (1999)	GEM double auction	7, 11	FWKG	FWKG	FWKG	62.5	.348	.0064 (6.4)	
Charness et al. (2004)	BGE	10, 10	0–100	$w - c(e)$	$(100 - w)e$	39.8	.315	.014 (10.0)	
	With payoff table					33.5	.227	.011 (10.7)	
Hannan et al. (2002)	Posted offer GEM MBAs	10, 12	FWKG	FWKG	FWKG	59.4	.34[c]	.0214 (2.6)	High productivity firms ($v = 120$) only
	Undergraduates					45.0	.21[c]	.0280 (3.9)	

Continued

Table 6. *Continued*

Reference	Experimental treatment	Number of firms, workers	Wage range	Worker utility	Firm profit	Mean wage	Mean effort	Effort-wage coefficient (value of t)	Comments
Brandts and Charness (2004)	Excess labor	12, 8	0–10	$5w - e$	$5e - w$	74.5[d]	.384[d]	.384 (10.4)	
	Excess demand	8, 12				83.6	.440	.354	
	BGE one-shot	16, 16				48.5	.242	—	Incentive higher
	Minimum wage	12, 8	$w \geq 5$			78.2	.293	.451	
Charness (2004)	BGE firms choose wages	10, 10	FWKG	FWKG	FWKG	54.9	.313	.0120 (11.2)	Workers must take offer
	Random wages					Same	.331	.0088 (14.4)	
Hennig-Schmidt et al. (2003)	Baseline BGE	10, 10	FWKG	FWKG	$(120 - w)ef,$ $f = 0.5$ or 1.5	59.9	.32[c]	.0054	
	Unknown f					55.5	.27	—	
	Firm knows f					46.1	.27	—	

Table 6. *Continued*

Reference	Experimental treatment	Number of firms, workers	Wage range	Worker utility	Firm profit	Mean wage	Mean effort	Effort-wage coefficient (value of t)	Comments
Rigdon (2002)	Linear $v(e)$, double-blind	6, 8	10–35	$w - (2e - 2)$	$27 + 8e - w$	17.0	.129[f]	—	$p(\text{pay}) = 0.5$ for last period
Engelmann and Ortmann (2009)	Interior high $m = 80$	6, 6	0–200	$w*\min(1.5.5 + 0.5e) - c(e)$	$em - w*\min(1.5, 0.5 + 0.5e)$	44.4	1.77	.007[g] (5.6)	e in [1–3], equilibrium $w* = 20, e* = 1.8$
	Interior low $m = 50$		0–100			31.8	1.75		
	Corner low $m = 50$			$wn - c(e)$	$50e - wn$	22.9	1.33		Equilibrium $w* = 2 - 3$, $e* = 1.2$

$$n = 1 \text{ for } e = 1, n = 1.5 \text{ for } e > 1$$

Notes: Empty cell entries are the same as the entries in the cell just above. BGE, bilateral market; FWKG, Fehr et al. (1998); GEM, gift-exchange market; —, not available.

a. Figures are reported in Charness et al. (2004).

b. Figure is estimated from binned histogram (Fehr et al. 1998: figure 1).

c. Mean effort is estimated from effort at mean wage in Hannan et al. (2002: figure 1).

d. Figures are normalized to 0–1 for effort, 0–100 for wages.

e. Mean efforts are estimated by multiplying average wage and period in effort-wage regression in Hennig-Schmidt et al. (2003: table 4).

f. Effort is normalized by subtracting minimum (1) and dividing by range $(6 - 1) = 5$. Unnormalized mean effort is 1.64.

g. Correlation is between wages and effort minus best reply effort (Engelmann and Ortmann 2009: table 9), excluding corner-equilibrium treatment.

required a minimum wage equal to the midpoint between the highest and lowest wage. Accepted wages are very similar when the minimum wage is instituted, and efforts are a little lower. There is also a sharp downturn in wages, a drop of about half, in the final (tenth) period (except for the minimum wage condition).

The reciprocity account of these patterns depends on workers knowing that firms intentionally shared surplus with them. Charness (2004) explored this aspect by comparing three treatments: firms intentionally choose wages; or wages were either clearly drawn randomly from a bingo cage or were "preselected by an experimenter." In the latter two treatments, wages were actually drawn from a distribution matched to the wages chosen by firms in the first condition (although subjects did not know this). The hypothesis is that effort response to wages will be higher when firms intentionally choose wages. Overall effort is slightly lower in the intentional-wage condition, but the response of efforts to wages is significantly higher (0.0120 versus 0.0088).

Hennig-Schmidt et al. (2010) explored the effect of incomplete information on the profitability of worker effort for firms. Incomplete information could undermine reciprocity, because it limits workers' confidence that firms are sharing surplus generously. The authors used a firm profit function $(120 - w)ef$, where f is equally likely to be 0.5 or 1.5. In one condition, neither side knows the value of f; in the more interesting condition, firms know f, but workers do not (and the asymmetry is commonly known). In the firm-knows-f condition, wages are about 15 points lower but do respond to the profitability factor f (increasing f from 0.5 to 1.5 raises average wages by 6.67), as if firms were willingly sharing surplus. Efforts are modestly lower when f is unknown. Overall, the information asymmetry has a small corrosive effect on wages and effort (and hence, on efficiency).

Healy (2007) explores the possibility that even with random rematching and excess labor supply, reputational considerations might generate cooperative behavior. He derives conditions for a "full reputational equilibrium," in which firms pay the highest wage and workers reciprocate with the highest effort (until the last period, when workers shirk by giving low effort). He derives a threshold probability that workers are reciprocal that supports full reputational equilibrium. Parametrically, this probability is often rather low when the marginal profit from hiring shirking workers is low relative to the gain to firms from high effort at high wages. Importantly, Healy notes that if workers believe that firms think reciprocal types are correlated, then workers are more inclined to reciprocate. Intuitively, when types are uncorrelated, then a worker who is lucky enough to get a high wage in one period can shirk and not suffer direct consequences from low wages in the future. But when types are correlated, the worker's shirking affects the firm's perceptions of all workers, which may affect the shirking worker's wages in the future. Incorporating stereotyping of this sort expands the range of beliefs about the proportion of reciprocal workers that supports full reputational equilibrium.

Healy (2007) then conducts experiments in which the threshold is low—replicating the original Fehr et al. (1993) design (Healy treatment; LA) and then changing the design so that worker ID numbers are known to everyone, so that firms can keep track of who shirks and who works hard (LP). In these designs there is substantial gift exchange and a strong correlation between wages and effort until a sharp dropoff in the last period. In another treatment (HP), firm profits are quasi-linear in effort, approximately $0.275 + 0.0725e$, rather than the multiplicative function $(v - w)e$ used in earlier designs. Healy shows that the threshold probability of reciprocal workers necessary to sustain full reputational equilibrium with these parameters is much higher, which implies that unless firms are very sure many workers are reciprocal, gift exchange will not emerge. Indeed, wages and efforts are much lower in this treatment, where the value of effort to firms has much lower marginal product, although there is still a strong effort-wage relation.

Rigdon's (2002) parameters and design provide a boundary case in which gift exchange is likely to disappear and does. She uses linear effort costs (efforts 1–6 have cost $c(e) = 2e − 2$) and firm profit is linear in effort, $v(e) = 27 + 8e − w$ (with a minimum wage of 10). Because $v(e)$ is linear in effort, the gains from gift exchange are much smaller than in other designs (25 at the self-interest equilibrium versus a maximum of 65). She also uses a double-blind procedure (subjects receive keys to a box in which their payoffs are deposited). There are $T = 16$ periods, and only one is chosen for payment. The probability that the last period is chosen for payment is 0.5 (all earlier periods are equally likely), so there is a strong economic emphasis on the last period. The trading institution is a sealed-bid offer market, and employers request effort levels. Employers request 3.5 units of effort and receive 1.64 on average (see Table 6). Wages and efforts decline over time until they are very close to the competitive equilibrium in the last period. This example shows that gift exchange does not survive a combination of procedural factors (double blindness) and design parameters that make the gains from gift exchange small and the economic value of the last period large.

Engelmann and Ortmann (2009) varied the efficiency gains from gift exchange and implemented a design with an interior wage-effort equilibrium (assuming self-interest). Creating an interior equilibrium is important, because when a predicted equilibrium is at the boundary (like zero effort), any confusion or deviations from equilibrium create positive effort, which could look like reciprocity. (This concern is allayed, because every study reports that wage-effort relations show a strong response of effort to wages, which suggests high-effort choices are typically deliberate.) To create an interior equilibrium, Engelmann and Ortmann (2009) used efforts in the interval [1, 3] and a worker utility function of $1.5w − c(e)$ for $e \leq 2$ and $(e + 1)w/2 − c(e)$ for $e \geq 2$. Profit functions are $em − 1.5w$ for $e \leq 2$ and $em − (e + 1)w/2 − c(e)$ for $e \geq 2$. Values of $m = 50$ and $m = 80$ create high and low efficiency gains from effort with an equilibrium of $w^* = 21$ and $e^* = 1.8$. The authors also compare abstract and worker-firm experimental framing (which has only a small positive effect when $m = 80$ and the efficiency gains are large). Efforts are close to those predicted under self-interest, although wages are above the equilibrium level, and there is a relationship between effort and wages.

4.3. A Second Wave of Gift-Exchange Experiments

Other experiments explore how institutional changes designed to enhance the power of reciprocity affect behavior. Fehr et al. (1997) study the influence of types of reciprocity on wages and effort. In their weak reciprocity treatment, firms offer a wage w, a requested effort $\tilde{e}$, and a fine f. A worker who accepts the offer chooses a costly effort e. If $e < \tilde{e}$, the worker is fined with probability s, and earns $w − f − c(e)$ rather than $w − c(e)$. In a strong reciprocity treatment, the firm can also punish a worker who shirks and is fined, at a cost $k(p)$, by multiplying the worker's total payoff b a shrinkage factor $p < 1$. The firm can also reward a worker who chooses effort $e \geq \tilde{e}$, at cost $k(p)$, by multiplying the worker's payoffs by a multiple $1 \leq p \leq 2$.

The results are simple. In the weak treatment, efforts are low (about 0.1), even though firms offer substantial job rents $w - c(\tilde{e})$ and efforts do respond to offered rents. However, strong reciprocity works very well. Efforts are about 0.8, and workers only shirk about 20% of the time. Shirkers are typically punished by the firm, and workers who choose the requested effort are rewarded about half the time.

Brown et al. (2004) examined the effect of allowing implicit long-term contracting by announcing ID numbers of workers and allowing firms to offer contracts to specific (identified) workers. Their session had $L = 7$ firms, $N = 10$ employees, and $T = 15$ periods.

Firms pay wages $w \in \{1, 2, \ldots, 100\}$ and workers choose efforts $e \in \{1, 2, \ldots, 10\}$. Firms earn $10e - w$, and workers earn $w - c(e)$, where $c(e)$ is convex (as in Fehr et al. (1998) and other studies). In the specific-contract condition, about two-thirds of the offers are earmarked for a specific employee, wages are higher, and wage offers depend on previous effort. For example, if the worker provided the maximum effort in period $t - 1$, the probability of getting a new contract in t is close to 1. However, the probability of renewal falls to 0.2 for effort levels below 7. As a result, efforts are generally higher when offers are specified for particular workers than when worker IDs are not provided. Both employees and firms in the specified-offer condition earn more per round the longer they have been in a relationship. Firms initiate long-term relationships by initially paying relatively high wages, and employees can signal their trustworthiness by meeting or exceeding the firm's effort expectations. These results have been replicated and appear to be robust to change in excess worker supply (Brown et al. 2010) and to random worker layoffs (Linardi and Camerer 2011).

4.4. Field Experiments

Four field experiments on gift exchange shed light on how long reciprocity persists. Gneezy and List (2006) recruited a small sample of 19 undergraduate students (who were unaware they were participating in an experiment) for a one-time 6-hour job entering information from library books into a computer. Ten of the subjects were paid the $12/hour wage offered during recruitment ("no gift" condition) and nine were paid $20/hour instead ("gift" condition), with no explanation given for the increased wage.

Figure 1 presents the mean number of books catalogued by subjects in the gift and no gift treatments averaged over 90-minute intervals. There is a significant difference in output in the first 90-minute period, consistent with the gift exchange hypothesis, but the difference decreases over time. A second field experiment used 23 participants in a door-to-door fundraising task. In that study, the effect of the gift wage is sensitive to how effort and output are measured, and to whether demographic subject controls are included (which are known to have a large effect on output).

Kube et al. (in press a) ran a close replication of the Gneezy and List (2006) field experiment on cataloging books. Their study consisted of 68 participants in three conditions who all expected initially to earn €15/hour: neutral (paid €15), kind (paid €20), and unkind (paid €10). The results are also shown in Figure 1. There is a little (insignificant) evidence of positive gift exchange from the kind wage increase (compared to a baseline), and the effect does not decline with time as in the Gneezy and List (2006) experiment. Pooling the two datasets, there is little

Mean number of books logged

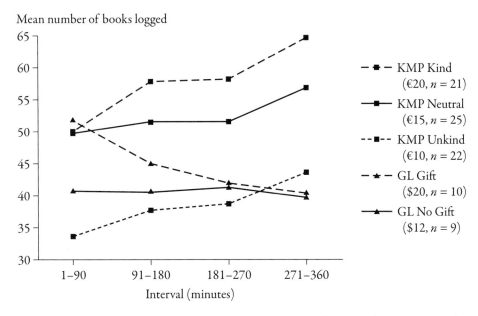

Figure 1. Mean output (books catalogued) in Gneezy and List (2006; GL) and Kube et al. (in press a; KMP) experiments. The GL "gift" and "no gift" conditions correspond to the KMP "kind" and "neutral" labels, respectively.

clear evidence of a persistent positive gift-exchange in several hours in the field, compared to shorter (2-hour) laboratory experiments, at least when it comes to cataloging books.

In the unkind treatment of Kube et al. (in press a), however, participants produced significantly lower output throughout the 6 hours, and this difference was always statistically significant. Therefore, this experiment presents clear evidence of persistent reciprocity in worker output, with a stronger negative reaction to a below-expected (unkind) wage than the positive reaction to the kind wage. Taken together, the experiments show little evidence of positive reciprocity but strong evidence of negative reciprocity. (Of course, the fact that subjects worked at all could be thought of as evidence in support of the gift-exchange hypothesis, because nothing prevents them from shirking completely.) The field experiments therefore demonstrate at least one way in which the main laboratory phenomenon extends to the field, but they also raise questions about when and precisely why they do so.

Bellemare and Shearer (2009) describe a gift-exchange experiment in which British Columbian tree planters were awarded a 1-day bonus, which was said to result from unpaid wages negotiated for a different purpose. Workers plant about 1,000 trees/day and usually earn a piece rate of $0.20/tree (about $200/day). The work is hard and varies with terrain and weather. The 1-day bonus raises productivity by about 100 trees/worker-day and is highly significant. The effect is also stronger for longer tenured workers, and long-tenured workers showed a productivity boost in the Monday after the week in which there was a 1-day gift.

The results from these three field experiments do not all agree. In one book-cataloguing study the effect of the wage gift appears to wear off after 90 minutes. The other book-cataloguing study finds the opposite: there is no difference initially, but those workers receiving a gift learn more quickly. A 1-day bonus for tree planters has a day-long effect.[12] In all cases there is at least some effect of the gift wage.

Reciprocity is probably most strongly activated if workers feel that employers are sharing surplus with them voluntarily (the book-cataloguing experiments said nothing to the study subjects about why the wage was higher than originally offered). The type of gift provided by the employer also appears to affect worker performance. A recent study, also by Kube et al. (in press b), demonstrates this by varying the type of gift. Workers again catalogued books for an hourly wage. The gifts, which varied by treatment, included an unexpected additional payment (€7, on top of an expected €12 wage) and a thermos worth the same amount as the monetary gift. Although the monetary gift has little effect, confirming the null or weak findings in the abovementioned studies on book cataloguing, the nonmonetary gift increases effort by approximately 25 percent. This result holds even when workers are made aware of the gift's monetary value. Moreover, when workers are given the choice between money and the thermos, most choose the former but work harder, as if they had received the nonmonetary gift. Finally, a €7 monetary gift that is arranged—with effort—in the form of an origami figure similarly elicits high effort. Thus, the experiment reveals that the thought and effort that an employer puts into a gift determine its effectiveness.

The notion that how an employer treats employees can affect their effort and cooperativeness is also addressed in a large literature on procedural justice and its effect on organizational outcomes (e.g., Lind and Tyler 1992). One of the best early studies was done in two aerospace/car parts plants by Greenberg (1990). The company determined that it needed to cut wages for 10 weeks by 15% to avoid laying off workers. It randomly assigned to each plant one of two methods of explaining the pay cuts to workers. In one plant the company's president spent 90 minutes explaining the decision and expressing remorse; he then answered questions for 60 minutes. In the other plant a vice-president spent 15 minutes explaining the decision and wrapped up the meeting by saying "I'll answer one or two questions, but then I have to catch a plane for another meeting." Compared to the short speech, the longer and more remorseful explanation lowered the number of resignations in the subsequent paycut period from 27% to 2%, and it lowered employee theft from 8.7% to 5.7% (though both theft rates were higher than the rate of 3% before and much after the pay cuts).

4.5. Compositional and Sorting Effects on Voluntary Effort and Reciprocity

The research discussed above shows that the social and financial incentives presented to a particular set of employees can be a powerful determinant of the effort they exert. However, employees are often free to select between organizations with different incentives and composed of different kinds of people. Experimental research also studies how the process by which groups are formed can impact cooperative behavior and productivity. This research studies how group formation and individuals sorting among environments (organizations) can help produce groups that are more or less cooperative and likely to exert voluntary effort. We have already

12. Field data from police union arbitration (Mas 2006) and a long tire company strike (Krueger and Mas 2004) also suggest very long-term effects linked to perceptions of fairness and reciprocity.

reviewed one paper (Dohmen and Falk 2011) showing that sorting by employees between incentive contracts can affect productivity. Here, however, we particularly focus on how it can affect cooperative behaviors, such as voluntary effort.[13]

4.5.1. Voluntary Cooperation and Endogenous Group Formation

Public goods experiments and n-person prisoner's dilemmas are a useful model for some kinds of organizational processes, such as voluntary effort for production with group incentives or revenue sharing. Experiments using the voluntary contribution mechanism, in which individuals contribute linearly to a public good, show that contributions typically begin at about 50% and steadily decline to close to the inefficient Nash equilibrium level, with a small percentage of "moral exemplars," who always contribute regardless of what others do (see Ledyard 1995). When the game is unexpectedly or randomly restarted, contributions tend to jump back up to high levels and then decline again over further periods (Andreoni 1988; Ambrus and Pathak 2011).

Although these experiments typically assign individuals to groups randomly, organizations and groups within them are usually formed endogenously, based on individuals' preferences, past behaviors, and what they know about the past behaviors of other potential group members. A handful of recent studies explores how contributions vary by allowing such endogenous group formation. Page et al. (2005) explore the influence of endogenous selection of group members on cooperation in a linear public goods game with a voluntary contribution mechanism. In one treatment, group members are allowed to rank others in all groups according to their match desirability every three periods, but ranking is costly. Most subjects (80%) choose to rank others and generally rank others who contributed most highly. Subjects are then regrouped in an assortative-matching scheme, creating groups of players who matched one another most closely. Regrouping based on costly ranking has a huge effect (compared to a no-rank, no-regrouping baseline), doubling overall contributions (70% versus 38%). In the most "selective" groups (i.e., among those who were most frequently chosen), contributions approach the maximum.

Ahn et al. (2008, 2009) show similar effects of endogenous grouping in public goods games. Allowing subjects to determine who enters their group increases contribution rates (though only by about 10%). Thus, the ability of people to sort endogenously into groups—a key feature of organizations—can help mitigate free rider and incentive problems.

4.5.2. Endogeneous Sorting among Organizations

A central question in organizational economics is how workers sort (or self-select) themselves into different economic environments. Lab experiments typically assign subjects to roles and environments, whereas most firms use various kinds of nonrandom sorting (including self-selection). However, it is easy to study sorting experimentally (e.g., Orbell and Dawes 1993). Indeed, the ideal way to study sorting is to assemble a pool of people, measure their characteristics and expectations, and then allow them to sort into economic environments and see what

---

13. Several experiments have studied endogenous sorting in market entry games (see Camerer and Lovallo 1999; Rapoport et al. 2002; Duffy and Hopkins 2005), but those experiments are of limited interest in the study of organizations. Our focus here is on the kind of sorting that occurs within organizational contexts and deals with voluntary effort and reciprocity.

types of people sort into what opportunities (see Dohmen and Falk 2011). It is very difficult to infer this type of sorting from field data and extremely easy to do so in experiments. For example, Lazear et al. (2012) show the effects of sorting on the expression of social preferences. Subjects who can take a certain amount of money, or play a dictator game, often prefer to take the certain money rather than play.

An experiment on sorting that is central to organizational outcomes was conducted by Eriksson and Villeval (2008). Incentive theory predicts that higher performance-based incentives will raise the effort of all workers and also induce sorting of higher productivity workers into such a scheme, if workers could choose those incentives over a fixed wage (as in Bandiera et al. 2007; see also Lazear 2000). It is also conceivable that when reciprocity plays a strong role, even highly productive employees might prefer high-fixed-wage contracts to performance-based incentives if the high wages indicate an employers' trust in the workers' willingness to work hard even without extrinsic incentive. It is therefore helpful to understand how sorting into different incentive systems works, and the lab provides a good measure of control.

In the Eriksson and Villeval (2008) experiment, there are eight firms and eight workers. Effort is less costly for some (high-skilled) workers and more costly for other (low-skilled) workers. Firms either post contract offers to all employees each period (a market condition) or offer contracts to the same employee each period (a matching condition). In the first eight periods, firms can only offer a fixed wage and stipulate a desired (but noncontractible) level of effort. Employees either agree to a contract or reject all contracts (earning nothing in that period); those who agree to a contract then choose their level of effort. In the last eight periods, each firm offers a fixed wage and offers a piece rate wage, specifying a marginal wage for each unit of effort. In these periods, employees who agree to work with a particular firm also choose among the two offered fixed-wage and piece rate contracts, and they also choose an effort level.

In the market condition, firms initially offer wages above the minimum, but workers do not reciprocate with high effort, so wages and efforts rapidly disintegrate to a low-wage/ low-effort equilibrium. However, when piece rate contracts are allowed, average effort increases substantially, because high-skilled (i.e., low-effort-cost) workers sort into the piece rate contracts and low-skilled workers choose fixed wages. This sorting parallels a field study in which an autoglass installation firm switched to piece rates, increasing effort by all employees and also causing less-productive workers to leave the firm (Lazear 2000).

In the matching condition, firms offer higher fixed wages than firms in the market condition, and employees reciprocate with high effort. When piece rates are allowed, high-skilled workers are more inclined to continue working for fixed wages than are high-skilled employees in the market condition.

Together, these results show that high-productivity workers often sort into piece rate work environments in a market condition. However, when repeated matching is possible, as with relational contracting, sorting is less important, because the long-term contract generates effective reciprocity and high effort even when wages are fixed. Sorting across piece rates, and long-term contracting, are therefore substitutes in creating high worker effort.

4.6. Summary

Many experiments explore conditions under which reciprocity and voluntary worker effort occur or do not occur. The existence of such reciprocity, in the context of labor relationships, seems to be robust to trading institutions and to variables that should matter in theory (e.g., excess supply of labor and time horizon), but results are sensitive to other procedural details of experiments.

The clearest result is that when the gain to gift exchange is largest, with multiplicative productivity $(v - w)e$, gift exchange is substantial and robust across time, but when productivity is linear in effort, $ve - w$, or has an interior equilibrium, there is much less gift exchange. However, every study reports a strong response of efforts to wages, even when wages and efforts are low (e.g., see Section 4.2, HP treatment). Moreover, nonpecuniary factors, such as how wages are communicated and the kind of gift provided by an employer, appear to be important as well. Field experiments involving temporary wage increases that last a day yield mixed results.

Finally, sorting and voluntary association can be important determinants of voluntary effort and cooperativeness. Sorting can work very well in creating cooperative groups. In a labor-market experiment, allowing workers to sort into high- or low-incentive contracts (piece rates or fixed wages) does create strong sorting, but sorting is much weaker when there is long-term contracting (even with fixed wages) because of reciprocity.

5. Coordination

The need for coordination arises when interdependence among organizational agents requires them to act consistently with one another but there is strategic uncertainty about what others are likely to do (see March and Simon 1958; Schelling 1960; Thompson 1967). Coordination is central in games with multiple equilibria, creating strategic uncertainty about which equilibrium will be played (Mehta et al. 1994; Bacharach and Bernasconi 1997; Cooper 1999).

From an organizational perspective, coordination problems are important, because they create the possibility of inefficiencies when agents' behaviors are mismatched or when an organization is stuck in an inefficient set of practices that a small group of workers cannot change on their own. Heath and Staudenmayer (2000) highlight the importance and difficulty of solving coordination problems in organizations. They note that organizations often neglect the importance of coordination and tend to focus excessively on partitioning tasks into specialized subtasks, without paying proper attention to the need to eventually integrate the specialized output in a coordinated manner.[14] As a result, they argue, coordination failure is ubiquitous in organizations and is often quite hard to overcome.

The research below seeks to understand mechanisms and interventions that might help organizations overcome coordination problems. For an alternative review and discussion, see Devetag and Ortmann (2007).

---

14. Heath and Staudenmayer (2000) describe an experiment in which groups of MBA students have to assemble a "Lego man" consisting of arms, legs, and a torso. A long period of untimed planning is followed by a timed period of assembly. The goal is to assemble the Lego man properly in the fastest assembly time. Planning time spent on partitioning (dividing up tasks) and time spent on integration (discussing how to assemble the parts later) are equally valuable in speeding up assembly time, but groups tend to do more partitioning and less integration.

Table 7. Payoffs for weak-link coordination game

		Minimum choice of all players						
		7	6	5	4	3	2	1
	7	130	110	90	70	50	30	10
	6		120	100	80	60	40	20
Player's	5			110	90	70	50	30
choice	4				100	80	60	40
	3					90	70	50
	2						80	60
	1							70

5.1. Minimum-Effort (Weak-Link) Coordination

The coordination game applied most frequently to study organizational phenomena is the minimum-effort (or weak-link) coordination game (see Van Huyck et al. 1990).[15] In this game, $n \geq 2$ players simultaneously choose numbers $a_i \in \{1, 2, \ldots, K\}$ and earn $\alpha + \beta \min_{j \neq i}(a_i, a_j) - \gamma a_i$, with $\beta > \gamma$ (so that each player would prefer to choose a higher number only if it increases the minimum). The payoff is increasing in the minimum and decreasing in the player's own choice. A payoff function of this form used in many experiments is shown in Table 7 (corresponding to $\alpha = 60$, $\beta = 20$, $\gamma = 10$).

In this game, all outcomes in which players select the same number are pure-strategy Nash equilibria. The equilibria are Pareto-ranked, because equilibria in which all players choose higher numbers are better for everyone.

The game is appealing for organizational research because it captures situations in which strategic uncertainty creates a conflict between efficiency and security. Players would all prefer to coordinate on the equilibrium corresponding to a choice of 7, but uncertainty about what others are likely to do also creates an incentive to choose lower numbers. Situations like this arise frequently in organizations when the quality of a good depends on the lowest quality input or when the completion of a joint activity is determined by the slowest completion of any component activity (see Camerer and Knez 1997).

Initial experiments on weak-link games demonstrated that when players choose simultaneously without the ability to communicate before playing, coordination near the efficient equilibrium (in which everyone chooses the maximum payoff of 7) is almost impossible for groups larger than three (Van Huyck et al. 1991; see also Weber 2006). However, groups of two often coordinate on the efficient equilibrium if one player chooses 7 and patiently teaches the other player to learn to choose 7. Thus, coordination failure in groups larger than two raises an

---

15. See Hirshleifer (1983) for an early discussion of this game and Becker and Murphy (1992) for applications to economic growth and firm output. This game falls into a more general class of games known as order-statistic games, in which each player's payoff is a function of her own choice and some order statistic (e.g., the minimum or median) of all players' choices (see Van Huyck et al. 1991; Crawford 1995).

important issue for organizational research: given the prevalence of similar kinds of problems in real firms, how can we solve such coordination failure?

5.2. Incentives

A natural candidate for improving coordination is incentives. If adding incentives for coordinating efficiently works for the game in Table 7, then similar incentives might produce efficient coordination in real organizations. Of particular interest is the possibility that a temporary incentive increase might have long-term positive effects on efficiency by coordinating players on better equilibria, which are subsequently self-reinforcing, even after the incentive has been removed.

Goeree and Holt (2005) studied two-player versions of the game with continuous strategy choices. Their experiment varied the cost of selecting high choices (i.e., analogous to varying γ in the payoffs in Section 5.1), keeping the equilibria unchanged. They find that this parameter has a strong effect on behavior. Subjects' choices are significantly lower when the cost of choosing high effort increases.

Bornstein et al. (2002) created team competition. Players in two seven-person teams earn their own outcome and a bonus if their group's minimum is higher than the other group's minimum. This manipulation produces a slight improvement, raising the average minimum by about 1.5.

Perhaps the most dramatic demonstration that incentives can improve coordination in a setting mimicking organizational production is by Brandts and Cooper (2006). They use a five-action turnaround game (with strategies {0, 10, 20, 30, 40}), in which coordination failure occurs reliably in the first 10 periods. The reward for efficient coordination (β) is then increased for 10 periods to induce a change to an efficient equilibrium. The solid line in Figure 2 shows the effect of increasing the bonus during periods 11–20 (for 37 groups) and then reducing the bonus back to the original level (for 9 groups). The graph presents the average minima for groups in their experiment and also in a follow-up experiment by Hamman et al. (2007) that used a slightly different kind of incentive. Both lines report only groups that experienced coordination failure in the initial 10-period block.

In the Brandts and Cooper (2006) data, the increase in incentive improves coordination reliably: 70% of the groups move to a higher equilibrium and more than a third coordinated on the efficient equilibrium. When the increased incentives were removed, half the groups were able to maintain coordination above the minimum. This finding suggests that even temporary incentive increases can permanently draw firms away from inefficient equilibria.

Hamman et al. (2007) provide an interesting contrast to the Brandts and Cooper (2006) results. Their experiment used a very similar design to the latter, in which groups are first induced to fall to the lowest minimum. Then flat (all-or-none) incentives of the kind regularly used in real organizations are introduced: subjects receive a fixed bonus (or avoid a fixed penalty) if their group minimum reaches a certain threshold. Figure 2 shows that this flat bonus produces a large immediate improvement in group effort choices, as in the Brandts and Cooper design, but the long-term improvement is significantly smaller, by about half. One interpretation of the difference in the two designs is that the all-or-nothing incentive either works immediately or does not work at all, but the Brandts and Cooper linear bonus from increasing β allows groups

Average minimum effort

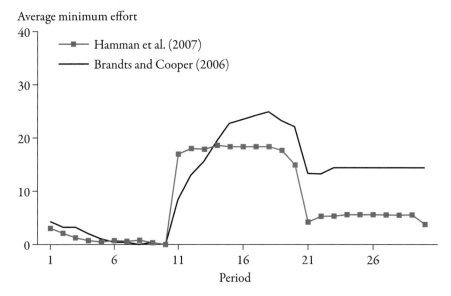

Figure 2. Average minima across periods in weak-link games: Hamman et al. (2007) versus Brandts and Cooper (2006) (initial failure only). For both experiments, periods 1–10 involved baseline incentives, periods 11–20 used increased incentives, and periods 21–30 returned to baseline incentives. Data from Hamman et al. (2007).

to slowly climb out of the bad equilibrium and obtain more efficient coordination. Thus, the latter kind of incentive is more effective at aiding long-run turnaround in firms coordinated on inefficient equilibria.

5.3. Communication

A natural candidate for increasing coordination is pre-play communication about strategies. Cooper et al. (1992) investigated one- and two-way communication in a two-player version of the weak-link game with strategies 1 and 2, and payoffs $\alpha = 600$, $\beta = 1000$, and $\gamma = 800$ (this two-player, two-action version of the game is frequently referred to as a "stag hunt," or "assurance game"). Subjects playing without communication overwhelmingly choose strategy 1—the inefficient but safe strategy. With one-way communication, however, 87% of subjects say they will choose 2, and, conditional on receiving a message indicating action 2, the other subject chooses 2 76% of the time. The efficient $(2, 2)$ equilibrium results roughly half the time. With two-way communication, subjects always indicate the intention to play action 2, and the efficient equilibrium results in 91% of groups.

Blume and Ortmann (2007) measured the effect of communication in nine-person weak-link games with the payoffs given in Table 7. In the baseline, subjects play eight times without any communication. Choices begin at about 6–7 and drop to 1–2 within five periods (as is typical in many studies). In the pre-play communication treatment, every subject also sends a message (1, 2, . . . , 7) before playing and observes the distribution of messages sent by others. Pre-play communication has a very strong positive effect on choices: the median message is 7 (the maximum choice), and the post-message choices have a median of 7 and an average of about 6.

However, Kriss et al. (2011) present a caveat to the Blume and Ortmann (2007) results by modifying the communication in two ways that are likely to apply to many organizational contexts. First, their experiment makes sending messages optional, meaning that players can choose not to send a pre-play message. Second, they make sending messages costly, with the costs equal to either 1 or 5 cents. They find that both levels of cost significantly decrease message use and lead to fewer groups coordinating on action 7 than in Blume and Ortmann's experiment. Thus, an employee's ability to forgo communication, coupled with very small costs for communication, can dramatically decrease the frequency with which people in an organization use communication to solve coordination problems and can therefore reduce its effectiveness as a mechanism for solving coordination problems.

Aside from pre-play messages, other forms of communication are generally less successful for inducing efficient coordination. For example, players' willingness to pay to play a coordination game should signal intentions to choose high numbers, through a forward induction-like argument: Players who pay a lot to play the game can only benefit by doing so if the profits from the game are also high. So, for example, someone indicating a willingness to pay 125 to play the game in Table 7 is signaling an expectation that the payoff from the game will be at least this amount. Cachon and Camerer (1996) find that although players opting to pay a fixed amount to play the game coordinate on higher (more efficient) equilibria, they do not converge to the efficient equilibrium in which all players select 7.[16]

Chaudhuri et al. (2009) also find many kinds of intergenerational communication ineffective. In their experiment, players in one generation provide advice on which strategies to play to members of a subsequent generation, as when members of a firm train their successors. Players earn payoffs from their own play and from that of their successor. Advice rarely improves the efficiency of coordination and often makes it worse. Advice only improves efficiency when it is public and commonly known (i.e., when the advice of all members of the preceding generation is read publicly to all members of the subsequent generation), a rather extreme form of intergenerational communication.

Taken together, the above results suggest that communication can help solve even the most difficult coordination problems—those with relatively large numbers of players and where the minimum effort determines the entire group's output. However, the most success occurs with very extreme forms of communication, in which players must all send messages and observe the messages sent by all others. Such communication is unlikely in many organizational contexts.

5.4. Managed Growth

Organizations might also achieve efficient coordination by obtaining it when they are small—when coordination is easier among a small number of members—and then maintaining it by growing slowly and ensuring that new entrants are aware of the group's history of success. Weber (2006) studied how a group's ability to maintain efficient coordination is influenced by the

---

16. Van Huyck et al. (1993) find that pre-play bidding works extremely well in coordinating activity efficiently in a game where the group payoff depends on the median choice rather than on the minimum, a version of the game with weaker interdependence between players. However, the kind of communication that occurs through other kinds of markets can decrease choices and efficiency by reinforcing pessimistic expectations (Kogan et al. 2011).

group's growth process and by the kind of entrants the group brings in. The experiment uses a 7-action game very similar to that in Table 7 (except that $\alpha = 20$).

The experiment compares groups that start off large (12 players) with those that grow to that size by starting small (2 players) and adding new entrants slowly. Replicating previous research (e.g., Van Huyck et al. 1990), groups that start off large converge to the inefficient outcome—all five 12-person groups converge to a minimum of 1. Also replicating previous work, 2-person groups all coordinate at higher levels of efficiency (minima of 6 or 7) than do large groups.

The two-person groups then grow slowly—usually by adding only one person at a time. Two treatments differ in the information provided to new entrants. In a history condition, new entrants observe the full history of outcomes (minima) obtained by the group, and this history is common knowledge. In a no-history condition, however, entrants are completely unaware of the minima obtained by the group prior to entry.

Groups without history all converge to the lowest minimum. However, although several groups in the history condition also fall to the lowest minimum as they grow, several groups do not. In fact, more than half of the groups maintain coordination on minima greater than 1, and two of nine groups remain coordinated on the efficient equilibrium (minimum = 7) throughout the entire growth process. This result presents one reason we might observe large efficiently coordinated organizations—they start off at a small size, when coordination problems are easier to solve, and then maintain efficiency by growing slowly and exposing new entrants to the group's history.

5.5. Coordination and Organizational Culture

Organizational economists have noted organizational culture as a potentially important concept for understanding behavior in firms. Much of their work focuses on the relationship between culture and equilibrium selection in coordination games (see, e.g., Kreps 1990; Crémer 1993; Hermalin 2001; see also Arrow 1974). Culture can serve as a means for resolving strategic uncertainty or selecting among equilibrium behaviors by individual members of a firm. Thus, a strong organizational culture might be one way to prevent coordination problems. (One way to interpret the above results on firm growth is that the efficient coordination obtained in small groups is similar to the strong culture that might develop in a small firm, and that such strong culture helps maintain efficient coordination as the firm grows.)

An important property of organizational culture is that it is sensitive to changes to the organization's size and boundaries, such as during a merger. Given the difficulty in identifying organizational culture and its effects on performance in real firms, the laboratory presents a useful domain for isolating the effects of changes to an organization on its culture.

An experiment providing insights into what happens when firms with different cultures merge was conducted by Knez and Camerer (1994). They studied what happens when two groups playing the weak-link coordination game are combined into a single larger group. In their experiment three-person groups play the weak-link game in Table 7 for five periods. Three-person groups playing this game exhibit a large degree of heterogeneity in outcomes—some coordinate efficiently (4 of 20 groups obtain a minimum of 7 in the fifth period), others fall to the inefficient outcome (6 of 20 groups have a minimum of 1), and several end up in between (minima of 2, 3, or 4). Two three-person groups were then combined into six-person groups for another five-period block. The minimum in the larger combined group usually fell to that of its component three-person groups (or lower), and eventually to the global minimum of 1 in 80% of the cases. Thus, maintaining efficient coordination (or a successful culture) while merging small laboratory groups into larger ones appears to be difficult.

Weber and Camerer (2003) further studied difficulties in merging firms with distinct cultures and how such difficulties might be underestimated by firm members. Their paper introduced a paradigm for studying organizational culture using simple laboratory experiments. In the paradigm, groups of subjects develop a code to jointly identify sets of complex pictures as quickly as possible. More precisely, in every period a manager receives some information regarding an exogenous state of the world (some subset of a batch of pictures that the group must identify during that period) and must verbally communicate this information to get employees to respond appropriately by selecting the correct pictures. To do so, the manager and employees must develop a shared understanding of what words or phrases will be used to identify each picture (i.e., a code). This code is a shared understanding that allows firm members to solve coordination problems while minimizing the need for costly communication. As Crémer (1993) notes, such code shares many features with organizational culture. Much as with organizational culture, each firm's code is likely to be idiosyncratic, history dependent, and reflect the firm members' jointly developed shared perspective. Moreover, each code is likely to be well suited for that firm's performance, but different firms are likely to have codes that differ.

In each experimental session, two two-person firms develop code/culture independently over the first 20 periods. As the left part of Figure 3 indicates, firms initially lack a shared understanding, and it takes them a long time to complete the picture identification task. However, with repetition, both two-person firms develop a code/culture that allows them to perform the task efficiently.

Following period 20, the two firms in each session merge, with one firm taking over the other and eliminating the redundant manager. The new firm therefore comprises one manager, one familiar employee (who previously worked with the manager), and one new employee. The merged firm performs the same task as before (using the same set of pictures) for 10 additional periods. Prior to merging, members of both firms forecast the performance of the merged firm (with an incentive for accuracy).

As the right side of Figure 3 reveals, the merger has a detrimental effect on the performance of both employees. The manager and new employee find it very difficult to integrate their distinct codes/cultures, and this miscoordination negatively affects the performance of the familiar employee. Therefore, integrating two distinct codes/cultures—which had been equally efficient at solving the coordination problem before the merger—proves quite difficult. Moreover, subjects significantly overestimate postmerger performance, indicating unawareness of the difficulty of integrating the two firms' codes. Finally, questionnaires in which subjects rate the ability and competence of other subjects in the experiment reveal that the postmerger integration difficulties are attributed to perceived incompetence on the part of the individual(s) from the other pre-merger firm. Taken together, this study provides an illustration of the pitfalls present in real-world mergers that are often discussed anecdotally after a highly touted merger ends in failure but that are difficult to demonstrate conclusively using nonlaboratory data.

Feiler and Camerer (2009) replicated the Weber and Camerer (2003) experiment using a computerized interface and endogenous mergers. Subjects in the separate groups (students from

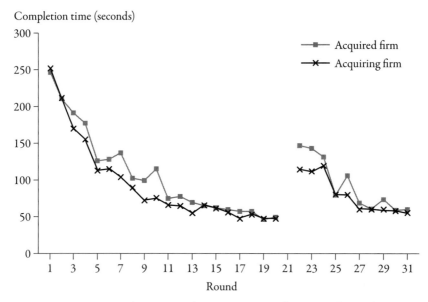

Figure 3. Average completion times (11 merger sessions). From Weber and Camerer (2003). Reprinted by permission. Copyright © 2003 the Institute for Operations Research and the Management Sciences, 7240 Parkway Drive, Suite 300, Hanover, MD 21076 USA.

the University of California, Los Angeles, and the California Institute of Technology identifying pictures of their own campuses) bid for payments demanded to join a mixed-picture (cross-campus) group (rather than staying in a same-campus group) in a first and a second "merger." The central question is whether bids to join a merged group correctly price the economic loss from the merger (similarly to the pre-merger estimates in Weber and Camerer). In the first merger into mixed groups, the average bids to join the mixed groups are too low by $0.32/period (using Vickrey auctions, which in theory are demand revealing).[17] There seems to be an organizational winner's curse, in which the successful bidders do not recognize how relatively optimistic they are about the profit that can be produced in the merger.

5.6. Summary

The experiments discussed above analyze different ways in which activity in firms might be effectively coordinated. The results show that the process of coordinating choices, even when there is a clearly payoff-dominant equilibrium that everyone in the organization prefers, is not straightforward. The degree of coordination success can depend critically on such factors as incentives, communication, and how the organization undergoes transitions. For example, the experiments show that some kinds of communication are effective for coordinating employee

17. Feiler and Camerer (2009) also conducted regular auctions in which successful bidders pay their bids (in this case, because bids are demands for payment, successful bidders are paid what they demanded). As these bids are not, in theory, the same as actual valuations, an inferential procedure is used to estimate from bids the true willingness to accept. Both raw bids and inferred valuations suggest that winning bidders are too optimistic about the merger.

effort, while others are not. Similarly, a growing organization needs to be aware of the need for managed growth that brings in entrants slowly and exposes them to the firm's history, to maintain efficient coordination. The studies on merging groups reveal that coordination among newly integrated units might be difficult, and the difficulty is underestimated.

6. Leadership and Hierarchy

Organizations of almost any scale have some hierarchical structure in which authority relations substitute for price mechanisms and contracts. Hierarchical superiors typically have residual control rights and authority over what subordinates do. A special aspect of hierarchy is leadership, in which values and broad strategic direction are espoused by a leader in an implicit contract. These topics are also a natural meeting ground for rational theories (based on information and contracting) and behavioral theories (in which leaders inspire and serve symbolic functions).

The experiments discussed below explore how hierarchy and leadership affect organizational behavior and productivity. Experimental control has a special power in these studies, because experimenters can randomly assign firms to be either flat or hierarchical, can assign subjects to leadership roles, and can also allow self-selection to estimate the power of sorting and selection.

6.1. Hierarchy and Incentives

Alchian and Demsetz (1972) were among the first to recognize the advantage of an organization's members hiring a supervisor to monitor them. In an experimental analogue of this process, van der Heijden et al. (2009) studied the effect of supervisory power in a simple public goods game with predicted free riding. Subjects in groups of four choose simultaneously to either shirk or work (a binary choice, $e_i \in \{0, 1\}$). Shirking enables a worker to keep his endowment of 120; working means he loses the endowment but contributes to group output, determined by $Q = 60(\sum_i e_i)^2$, which is shared equally. If all four work, the net total payoff is $60(4)^2 = 960$, which is higher than the net total payoff when all shirk (480).

In a baseline (revenue-sharing) condition, group output is shared equally. As is typical in repeated public goods experiments—and in the experiments by Nalbantian and Schotter (1997) reviewed above—total effort begins at a high level (three workers chose to work) and shrinks to an average total group effort of 0.5 in 15 periods. There is substantial variation across groups, showing that local cooperative norms can emerge.

In a hierarchical (leader-determined sharing) condition, one person is randomly chosen to both choose effort as a worker in the group and also to assign output to individual subjects after each round however she likes. Although this hierarchy could backfire (the manager can grab all the output), the manager typically divides output evenly among those who exert effort and gives nothing to those who shirked. Subjects learn this pattern and work, because free riding will earn them nothing. As a result, the mean group effort is about three until the last round, when there is a sharp endgame drop in effort.

This experiment nicely shows that cooperation is sensitive to institutional rules and to the willingness of some players to punish defectors, as in many experiments in which costly punishment reliably raises contributions in public goods games (e.g., Fehr and Gächter 2000).

Having a worker-manager who can allocate output to all workers coordinates punishment of all free riders, because of her ability to allocate group output to each worker, and leaders do not grab too much output (presumably because they know it would lower future effort). As a result, leadership works well enough to produce sustained cooperation close to full efficiency.

Hierarchy is also studied in a recent experiment by Fehr et al. (2010), who consider a manager's decision of whether to delegate a decision right to a subordinate. Following from a model by Aghion and Tirole (1997), their experiment includes situations in which it may be optimal for a manager to delegate, because of the incentive this creates for the subordinate to acquire costly information concerning the best action to take. The key finding in their experiment is that managers delegate less often than they should, appearing to value authority inherently. Moreover, the extent to which they underdelegate is related to the degree of loss aversion they exhibit. Thus, managers in an organization may hold on to power excessively, even when it benefits them to let it go, because of some inherent value they place on possessing authority.

6.2. Leadership and Public Goods

An important aspect of leadership in organizations is signaling (e.g., Hermalin 1998). Leaders signal private information about desirable collective outcomes through observable announcements or through their behavior, or by changing economic incentives. Recent experiments explore this phenomenon in public goods.

Güth et al. (2007) explored the effectiveness of leadership for improving cooperation in public goods games. In their experiment, groups of $k = 4$ subjects play a public goods game under the voluntary contribution mechanism. Endowments are 25 tokens, which have a private return of 1 and a public return of 1.6 (so the marginal per capita return is 0.4).

In the baseline condition, contributions begin at about half of the 25 tokens and decline to about 6 after $T = 16$ periods, a typical pattern (e.g., Ledyard 1995). In the weak-leader condition, one player moves first, and her contribution is visible to others. In this condition, average contributions are about 3 units higher and exhibit the same typical decline over time. In the strong-leader condition, the leader can also penalize free riders by excluding one player from the group in the following round (the excluded player earns nothing). In this condition, average contributions start at 18 tokens and rise slightly (until a sharp drop in the final period). The strong and weak leader conditions together show that the ability of one player to establish a norm by moving first has a small effect, but combining that with the ability to "lay off" a free rider increases contributions substantially.[18]

Potters et al. (2007) examined contributions to a public good when the value of the good is only known by an early-moving leader. In this case, the leader's action can signal information about the value of the public good. In their experiment, subjects play a public goods game in pairs, composed of players 1 and 2. Each player can choose one of two options: A or B. Choosing A gives the individual a private return of 0.4 (in £). Choosing B gives each of the players a return

18. In a second part of the experiment (periods 17–24), groups voted on whether to have a leader (with unanimity required). Only 40 percent of the subjects voted to have leaders, but groups with leaders obtained significantly higher contributions and earnings. This raises the interesting question of why a structural change that benefits the group as a whole is not more popular. Subjects might not like ceding authority to a leader, or they may underestimate the leader's economic impact, which helps everyone.

of 0.0, 0.3, or 0.6. The exact return from choosing B was randomly determined. For the small return (0.0), choosing A maximizes both individual and collective payoffs. The medium return (0.3) is a prisoner's dilemma (A is privately better but two choices of B are best for both). For the highest return (0.6), choosing B is both individually and collectively better.

The design is fixed-role, random rematching with $T = 18$ periods. Choices are either made simultaneously or sequentially. Additionally, either both players observe the return rate prior to making a choice (full information) or only player 1 is able to do so (asymmetric information). Under full information, the order of play should not matter, and leadership should have no effect. However, under asymmetric information (when the leader observes private information), sequential play should implement efficient behavior (B choices by both players) when the return rate is 0.3 or 0.6, which is not predicted under simultaneous play. The interesting case that might show an effect of leadership is that of the sequential leader information with a return of 0.3. Suppose the leader knows the return is 0.3. If she chooses the cooperative B in those cases, a follower should infer that the leader's observed B choice either means the return is 0.3 or 0.6; the mean inferred return is therefore 0.45, which makes the marginal public return above the private return, so the follower should contribute. A leader contributing when she observes a return of 0.3 therefore coaxes followers, in theory, into contributing, which is mutually beneficial.

As predicted, under full information, both subjects rarely contribute when the return is 0.0 (less than 5%) and almost always contribute when the return is 0.6 (more than 90%). When the return is 0.3, leaders contribute a little more when playing sequentially (27%) than when playing simultaneously (16%). However, followers in the sequential treatment mimic leaders only a third of the time (and therefore contribute 9% of the time).

In the asymmetric information treatment, when the return is 0.3, player 1 does lead by choosing B 75% of the time when choosing sequentially, as theory predicts, compared to only 15% in the simultaneous condition. Followers contribute 81% of the time when leaders contribute, so the efficient outcome occurs more than half of the time.

These experiments highlight the significance of leadership in organizational settings when obtaining cooperation and voluntary effort is important. In both cases, leadership has beneficial effects, inducing higher contributions and generating greater earnings for the group as a whole (see also Moxnes and van der Heijden 2004; Gächter et al., in press). However, experiments of this kind also shed light on when leadership is likely to work and what characteristics make it effective.

6.3. Leadership in Coordination

Another way in which leadership might be valuable for organizations is in coordinating members' activity. When interdependent agents are faced with the problems of strategic uncertainty and equilibrium selection that we described in Section 5, having a leader direct behavior toward an efficient equilibrium through public statements might help produce efficient coordination (Foss 2001). Understanding when statements by a manager can induce a change in behavior to a new (more efficient) equilibrium is important for understanding the role of leadership in organizations.

Van Huyck et al. (1992) studied the effectiveness of public statements directing players toward one equilibrium in coordination games (see also Brandts and MacLeod 1995). In their experiment, pairs of subjects play three-action games with multiple equilibria, as in the game

Table 8. Coordination-game payoffs and influence of recommendations

		Column's choice		
		A	B	C
	A	$5+X, 5+X$	0, 0	0, 0
Row's choice	B	0, 0	5, 5	0, 0
	C	0, 0	0, 0	$5-X, 5-X$

	($X = 4$)		
Recommendation	Players' choice of option (%)		
	A	B	C
None	97	2	1
A	99	1	0
B	51	48	1
C	62	0	38

	($X = 1$)		
None	100	0	0
B (from experimenter)	50	50	0

	($X = 1$) [a]		
None	39	61	0
B (from interested third subject)	37	63	0
B (from disinterested third party)	19	81	0

Sources: Data for the second panel from the top are from Van Huyck et al. (1992); data for the bottom two panels are from Kuang et al. (2007).
a. The third subject received $5 for successful coordination on option B by the other players.

in the top panel of Table 8, which, for numerical values of X satisfying $0 < X < 5$, has three pure-strategy equilibria (the outcomes along the diagonal). In the Van Huyck et al. (1992) experiment, in which $X = 4$, most subjects (97 percent) select the action that corresponds to the efficient equilibrium (A) when there is no advice (see the second panel from the top in Table 8).

The experimental treatments vary whether there is a recommendation from the experimenter to play a particular strategy. As the row "A" indicates, advice is strongly followed (99 percent of the time) when it coincides with efficiency. Recommendations to play the Pareto-inferior equilibrium strategies B and C produce mixed behavior, and are followed 48 and 38 percent of the time, respectively. Thus, public statements by leaders in settings involving coordination can change behavior, even toward actions that are inefficient from the players' perspectives. For example, a manager who wants employees to adopt and use a new communication technology or bookkeeping system may produce an impact through public statements, even when employees do not prefer the change.

Kuang et al. (2007) used payoffs similar to those of Van Huyck et al. (1992), with $X = 1$, and compared the effectiveness of recommendations from the experimenter, from an disinterested third party, and from a self-serving third "player" who earns $5 if the two players in the coordination game follow her recommendation to play B (although the third player does not play). As the bottom panel in Table 8 reveals, the mere presence of the third party, who receives a payoff of $5 if the players coordinate on action B, makes B the modal choice even when there is no recommendation. (That is, concerns for equity and the third party's payoff appear to be important for equilibrium selection in this modified game.) However, when the interested third subject makes a recommendation of B, it is largely ineffective, and increases the frequency of B play by 2% (from 61% to 63%) relative to when there is no recommendation. But the recommendation of a disinterested third party—who does not benefit from the recommendation being followed—produces a significant increase. Thus, recommendations are more likely to be followed when they are impartial.

In Section 5, we discussed weak-link coordination problems (see Table 7). Given the difficulty of obtaining efficient coordination in such games, understanding the effectiveness of leaders' recommendations to play the efficient equilibrium is important. Can a leader urging players to move away from the secure but inefficient equilibrium toward the efficient but risky equilibrium convince them to do so?

Brandts and Cooper (2007) explored this question. In their experiment, firms of four subjects play a weak-link coordination game. Worker subjects choose among five possible effort levels $e_i \in \{0, 10, 20, 30, 40\}$. Worker i's payoff $u_i(e_i)$ is $200 - 5e_i + (B \min_{j=1-4}(e_j))$; that is, each unit of effort privately costs 5 units, and the group payoff is B times the lowest effort, where $B \in \{6, 7, 8, \ldots, 15\}$. Each firm also has a fifth subject, who plays the role of manager. In the first 10 periods, the manager is a passive observer (B is fixed at 6). In these first 10 periods, firms typically sink to the inefficient equilibrium in which efforts are close to zero.

In the remaining periods of the experiment (11–20), the manager takes control of the firm and attempts to induce coordination on the efficient equilibrium. The manager sets the bonus and receives the payoff: $100 + (60 - 4B) \min_{j=1-4}(e_j)$. This payoff function means managers benefit if the firm coordinates on higher minimum effort, but they also prefer to pay the lowest B that increases effort. In different treatments, managers had the ability to send natural language messages to employees (one-way communication) and receive messages back from employees (two-way communication).

Figure 4 shows the average minimum effort across the manager-run periods, using only those firms that experience initial coordination failure (i.e., firms in which the manager could "turn things around"). "Computer manager" refers to a treatment in which the role of manager is played by a computer who always selects $B = 10$. (This bonus is very close to the average bonus set by human managers across all treatments.)

Managers who are unable to communicate (but who set the bonus) produce very little improvement in efficiency, as do computer managers. However, communication improves the firm's performance, and two-way communication produces the greatest improvement. Thus, allowing better channels of communication between managers and employees improves the efficiency of coordination, suggesting a critical motivational role for managers when coordination is important in organizational settings.

Brandts and Cooper (2007) also explored the content of messages from managers to employees. Managers who ask employees for greater effort, who draw their attention to the bonus, and who describe a long-term plan for improving efficiency obtain the greatest improvements in efficiency. Communication is a complement to incentive change.

Average minimum effort

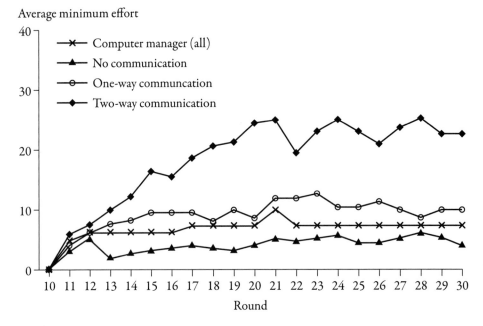

Figure 4. Average minimum effort (group output) in different conditions, for firms with initial coordination failure. From Brandts and Cooper (2007).

In a follow-up paper, Cooper (2006) used the one-way communication treatment described above to explore differences in the effectiveness of student subjects and actual managers (executive MBA students). Actual managers are slightly more effective than student managers, particularly at obtaining a rapid improvement in group outcomes, because they are more likely to employ the communication strategies found to be effective by Brandts and Cooper (2007).

6.4. The Illusion of Leadership

The abovementioned studies show that leaders, by recommending particular equilibria to organizational members, can improve the efficiency of coordination. Another study, however, highlights that such leadership may have limits to its effectiveness, and that such limits may be detrimental to the followers' perceptions of the leader's ability.

Weber et al. (2001) examined the ability of large and small groups to coordinate efficiently in the weak-link coordination game under a simple form of leadership. As mentioned in Section 5, previous studies using this game show a consistent group-size effect: small groups almost always coordinate successfully, while large groups never do (Van Huyck et al. 1990). Weber et al. (2001) examined whether simple leadership in the form of one subject addressing the group and urging them to coordinate efficiently would improve the ability of large groups to coordinate.

Each session consists of nine or ten subjects playing in one of two conditions. In the large-group condition, all nine or ten subjects play a four-action version of the weak-link game together. In the pairs condition, subjects are randomly and anonymously paired with one of the other nine people in the room and play the same game with this person only. The game is played eight times.

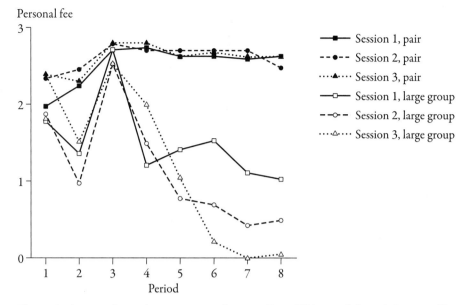

Personal fee

Figure 5. Average choices by treatment and session. From Weber et al. (2001). Reprinted by permission. Copyright © 2001 the Institute for Operations Research and the Management Sciences, 7240 Parkway Drive, Suite 300, Hanover, MD 21076 USA.

Prior to the first round, a leader is randomly selected and told that she will, after the second round, address the entire group (or all pairs, in the pairs condition) to organize and prepare the players for the remaining rounds. Leaders are given a simple message to guide their statements, highlighting the efficient equilibrium and the mutual gains from selecting it

Figure 5 shows the average effort choices (which were framed in the context of a "fee" voluntarily contributed to the group) for three sessions each of large groups and pairs. As expected, the pairs coordinate efficiently in the first two periods, but the large groups begin to fall toward the inefficient equilibrium.

After period 2, the leaders address the groups. The effectiveness of leaders' statements can be seen in period 3: in both treatments, average choices are close to the maximum. However, for the large groups this is not enough to overcome coordination failure, and these groups subsequently begin to converge again toward the lowest choice. Thus, even though Brandts and Cooper (2007) showed that simple leadership in the form of public statements is effective at inducing turnarounds in groups of four individuals, this is not the case here for larger groups (of nine or ten) and when the leader only has one chance to speak.

Weber et al. (2001) were primarily concerned with what effect the different situations have on followers' perceptions of the leaders' abilities. Immediately after leaders speak, subjects in both treatments rate the leaders' speeches and leadership ability equally highly (means ratings of 5.8 (pairs) and 5.9 (large groups), on a 9-point scale). However, when the same questions are asked again at the end of the experiment, subjects in the large-group condition rate leaders as significantly less able (4.5) than do subjects playing in pairs (6.2). Thus, even though the situation in which subjects were placed (i.e., the size of the group they were leading) determines their outcomes—and subjects even recognize that leading small groups is easier than leading large ones in separate questionnaire responses—followers mistakenly attribute good outcomes to good leadership and poor outcomes to poor leadership. An additional experiment replicated these results and showed that subjects are even willing to act on their perceptions of leadership quality by casting a costly vote to replace the leader.

6.5. Summary

The experiments discussed in Section 6 all study the extent to which hierarchy and leadership yield efficient organizational outcomes. In each case, there is some inefficiency that obtains in flat organizations—because of either moral hazard or coordination failure. The experiments explore the extent to which efficiency is improved by assigning differential roles and giving some roles greater information, power, or prominence. In most cases, there is some beneficial effect of hierarchy and leadership on efficiency. However, the success of these treatments is not always perfect, even when theory predicts it should be. They may even produce perverse effects, as in the misattributions of leadership ability in weak-link games with small and large groups.

7. Conclusion

Laboratory and field experiments are a useful method for addressing important organizational questions, such as how worker effort will respond to different kinds of monetary and social incentives and how hierarchy and communication can help improve the efficiency of firm outcomes. In each of these cases, laboratory experiments provide very high degrees of control, which is helpful for testing theoretical predictions and comparing institutions and which is typically difficult to obtain in the field.

The results vary in what they tell us about organizations. In some cases, the results are highly supportive of theory. For example, worker efforts are close to those predicted in tournaments, and workers do respond to piece rates and monitoring. However, sabotage in tournaments with peer rating of quality is strong, and team-forcing contracts do not work.

Many of the results do not refute or confirm theory per se but instead illustrate empirical effects of variables that have ambiguous theoretical effects. For example, communication typically expands the set of equilibria, so data are helpful in determining whether communication leads to better outcomes. It appears that large-group coordination is difficult, but extensive types of communication and leadership can solve coordination problems, though the extent to which they actually do so in more practical situations remains an opportunity for further study.

An advantage of the lab is that it is often possible to clearly measure heterogeneity in responses and its influence. For example, the field experiment on monitoring by Nagin et al. (2002) showed that reducing monitoring increases moral hazard but usually only among a small set of workers (and the effect is moderated by workers' attitudes toward their employer). Heterogeneity is also evident in experiments on gift exchange: even though a minority of subjects are self-interested and shirk if they can, a majority of subjects' efforts reliably respond to wages (indicating positive reciprocity), although procedural details and economic structure matter, too.

When some results are surprisingly consistent with theory, and others are not, one hopes for a generalization of standard theory that could explain both kinds of evidence. In game theory, models that assume equilibrium beliefs but relax best response or assume a hierarchy of cognitive sophistication have proved useful in explaining when standard theory works well and when it does not (e.g., McKelvey and Palfrey 1998; Camerer et al. 2004). Models like these, along with specifications of reciprocal or altruistic preferences (Fehr and Schmidt 1999) or of employees motivated by concerns for image or esteem (Bénabou and Tirole 2006; Ellingsen and Johannesson 2008), might be able to unify many disparate results and make interesting new predictions.

In reviewing this research, we were struck by how many interesting topics have been understudied or completely unstudied. Most of what is discussed in a modern doctoral-level course has never been studied experimentally. Employment contracts are usually surprisingly simple and incomplete (and relative performance evaluation is rare for executives), job design is crucial when multitasking makes it difficult to incentivize the optimal mix of activity, and sorting is presumably important. But all these topics are rarely studied, even though it is arguably even easier to study them in a lab experiment than with naturally occurring data. And in many cases, there is a clear complementarity of theory and experimentation, because an obvious experimental design walks right off the pages of a theory paper into the lab (particularly in game theory).

There are also many opportunities for entirely new experimental directions. Web-based software and the reasonable availability of funds for subject payments (and the capacity to do experiments with highly literate subjects in low-income countries) mean that experiments that are much more elaborate than most of those described in this chapter are feasible. Such experiments could explore how results scale up to larger groups and longer spans of time. Some topics that are ripe for additional and more thorough experimentation include the following.

Multitasking. When workers perform multiple activities, it is generally impossible to find contracts in which performance-based incentives induce agents to provide the mix of activity levels across tasks that firms would like. This fact shifts attention from single-activity contracts trading off risk and incentive to an incentive system including job design and monitoring (Holmström and Milgrom 1994). But there are only a handful of experimental studies of multitasking (e.g., Fehr and Schmidt 2004). This paucity of research presents a ripe empirical opportunity, because it is conceivable that studies would find that heterogeneity, sorting, and reciprocity could limit problems that appear to arise in theoretical multitasking models, or they could guide job design in an unexpected direction.

Social networks. Recently, economists have caught up to sociologists, who have been taking empirical snapshots of networks and studying their properties and influence on behavior (e.g., Jackson 2010). Networks are clearly important inside organizations. And because naturally occurring networks are both created by and influence behavior, experiments that assign networks exogenously are scientifically useful to establish causality. Experiments have been used to study the influence of network structure on solving combinatorially explosive operations research problems (Kearns et al. 2006), financial contagions (Corbae and Duffy 2008), and other topics (see Kosfeld 2004), but none of these experiments deals with the central questions in organizational economics.

Virtual worlds. Commercial firms have developed online gaming virtual worlds, in which players inhabit personal roles, interact socially, and develop economic exchange for scarce resources that enable players to succeed (e.g., SimCity and Second Life). These games represent a mouthwatering empirical opportunity, because they attract large numbers of players who spend hours playing. Experimental control could either come from collaborations with designers or from running true experiments inside the virtual world (see Bloomfield 2007).

More broadly, we advocate richer, more complex—and therefore often more informative and realistic—experiments on organizations.

REFERENCES

Abeler, J., A. Falk, L. Goette, and D. Huffman. 2011. "Reference Points and Effort Provision." *American Economic Review* 101: 470–492.

Agell, J., and P. Lundborg. 1995. "Theories of Pay and Unemployment: Survey Evidence from Swedish Manufacturing Firms." *Scandinavian Journal of Economics* 97: 295–307.

Aghion, P., and J. Tirole. 1997. "Formal and Real Authority in Organizations." *Journal of Political Economy* 105: 1–29.

Ahn, T. K., M. Isaac, and T. C. Salmon. 2008. "Endogenous Group Formation." *Journal of Public Economic Theory* 10: 171–194.

———. 2009. "Coming and Going: Experiments on Endogenous Group Sizes for Excludable Public Goods." *Journal of Public Economics* 93: 336–351.

Akerlof, G. A. 1982. "Labor Contracts as Partial Gift Exchange." *Quarterly Journal of Economics* 97: 543–569.

Alchian, A. A., and H. Demsetz. 1972. "Production, Information Costs, and Economic Organization." *American Economic Review* 62: 777–795.

Ambrus, A., and P. Pathak. 2011. "Cooperation over Finite Horizons: Theory and Experiments." *Journal of Public Economics* 95: 500–512.

Andreoni, J. 1988. "Why Free Ride? Strategies and Learning in Public Goods Experiments." *Journal of Public Economics* 37: 291–304.

Argote, L., M. E. Turner, and M. Fichman. 1989. "To Centralize or Not to Centralize: The Effects of Uncertainty and Threat on Group Structure and Performance." *Organizational Behavior and Human Decision Processes* 43: 58–74.

Ariely, D., U. Gneezy, G. Loewenstein, and N. Mazar. 2009. "Large Stakes and Big Mistakes." *Review of Economic Studies* 76: 451–469.

Arrow, K. J. 1974. *The Limits of Organization.* New York: Norton.

Bacharach, M., and M. Bernasconi. 1997. "The Variable Frame Theory of Focal Points: An Experimental Study." *Games and Economic Behavior* 19(1): 1–45.

Bandiera, O., I. Barankay, and I. Rasul. 2007. "Incentives for Managers and Inequality among Workers: Evidence from a Firm-Level Experiment." *Quarterly Journal of Economics* 122: 729–773.

Bavelas, A., and D. Barrett. 1951. "An Experimental Approach to Organizational Communication." *Personnel* 27: 367–371.

Bazerman, M., J. R. Curhan, D. A. Moore, and K. L. Valley. 2000. "Negotiation." *Annual Review of Psychology* 51: 279–314.

Becker, G. S., and K. M. Murphy. 1992. "The Division of Labor, Coordination Costs, and Knowledge." *Quarterly Journal of Economics* 107: 1137–1160.

Bellemare, C., and B. Shearer. 2009. "Gift Giving and Worker Productivity: Evidence from a Firm-Level Experiment." *Games and Economic Behavior* 67(1): 233–244.

Bénabou, R., and J. Tirole. 2006. "Incentives and Prosocial Behavior." *American Economic Review* 96: 1652–1678.

Blinder, A. 1990. *Paying for Productivity: A Look at the Evidence.* Washington, DC: Brookings Institution Press.

Bloomfield, R. 2007. "Worlds for Study: Invitation—Virtual Worlds for Studying Real-World Business (and Law, and Politics, and Sociology, and . . .)." Available at Social Science Research Network: http://ssrn.com/abstract=988984 or doi:10.2139/ssrn.988984.

Blume, A., and A. Ortmann. 2007. "The Effects of Costless Pre-Play Communication: Experimental Evidence from Games with Pareto-Ranked Equilibria." *Journal of Economic Theory* 132: 274–290.

Bornstein, G., U. Gneezy, and R. Nagel. 2002. "The Effect of Intergroup Competition on Group Coordination: An Experimental Study." *Games and Economic Behavior* 41(1): 1–25.

Bottom, W. P., J. Holloway, G. J. Miller, A. Mislin, and A. Whitford. 2006. "Building a Pathway to Cooperation: Negotiation and Social Exchange between Principal and Agent." *Administrative Science Quarterly* 51: 29–58.

Brandts, J., and G. Charness. 2004. "Do Labour Market Conditions Affect Gift Exchange? Some Experimental Evidence." *Economic Journal* 114: 684–708.

Brandts, J., and D. Cooper. 2006. "A Change Would Do You Good . . . An Experimental Study on How to Overcome Coordination Failure in Organizations." *American Economic Review* 96: 669–693.

———. 2007. "It's What You Say, Not What You Pay: An Experimental Study of Manager-Employee Relationships in Overcoming Coordination Failure." *Journal of the European Economic Association* 5: 1223–1268.

Brandts, J., and W. B. MacLeod. 1995. "Equilibrium Selection in Experimental Games with Recommended Play." *Games and Economic Behavior* 11(10): 36–63.

Brown, M., A. Falk, and E. Fehr. 2004. "Relational Contracts and the Nature of Market Interactions." *Econometrica* 72: 747–780.

———. 2010. "Competition and Relational Contracts—The Role of Unemployment as a Disciplinary Device." IZA Discussion Paper 3345. Available at: http://ftp.iza.org/dp3345.pdf.

Bull, C., A. Schotter, and K. Weigelt. 1987. "Tournaments and Piece Rates: An Experimental Study." *Journal of Political Economy* 95: 1–33.

Cachon, G. P., and C. Camerer. 1996. "Loss-Avoidance and Forward Induction in Experimental Coordination Games." *Quarterly Journal of Economics* 111: 165–194.

Camerer, C. F. 1998. "Behavioral Economics and Nonrational Organizational Decision Making," in J. Halpern and R. Stern (eds.), *Debating Rationality: Nonrational Aspects of Organizational Decision Making.* Ithaca, NY: ILR Press, pp. 53–77.

———. 2003. *Behavioral Game Theory: Experiments in Strategic Interaction.* Princeton, NJ: Princeton University Press.

———. 2011. "The Promise and Success of Lab-Field Generalizability in Experimental Economics: A Critical Reply to Levitt and List." Available at Social Science Research Network: http://papers.ssrn.com/sol3/papers.cfm?abstract_id=1977749.

Camerer, C. F., and M. Knez. 1997. "Coordination in Organizations: A Game-Theoretic Perspective," in Z. Shapira (ed.), *Organizational Decision Making.* Cambridge: Cambridge University Press, pp. 158–187.

Camerer, C. F., and D. Lovallo. 1999. "Overconfidence and Excess Entry: An Experimental Approach." *American Economic Review* 89: 306–318.

Camerer, C. F., and U. Malmendier. 2007. "Behavioral Economics of Organizations," in P. Diamond and H. Vartiainen (eds.), *Behavioral Economics and Its Applications.* Princeton, NJ: Princeton University Press, pp. 235–280.

Camerer, C. F., L. Babcock, G. Loewenstein, and R. Thaler. 1997. "Labor Supply of New York City Cab Drivers: One Day at a Time." *Quarterly Journal of Economics* 111: 408–441.

Camerer, C. F., T.-H. Ho, and J.-K. Chong. 2004. "A Cognitive Hierarchy Model of Games." *Quarterly Journal of Economics* 119: 861–898.

Carpenter, J., P. H. Matthews, and J. Schirm. 2010. "Tournaments and Office Politics: Evidence from a Real Effort Experiment." *American Economic Review* 100: 504–517.

Carzo, R., Jr., and J. N. Yanouzas. 1969. "Effects of Flat and Tall Organization Structure." *Administrative Science Quarterly* 14: 178–191.

Charness, G. 2004. "Attribution and Reciprocity in an Experimental Labor Market." *Journal of Labor Economics* 22: 665–688.

Charness, G., and P. Kuhn. 2011. "Lab Labor: What Can Labor Economics Learn from the Lab?" in O. Ashenfelter and D. Card (eds.), *Handbook of Labor Economics,* volume 4(A). Amsterdam: Elsevier, pp. 229–330.

Charness, G., G. R. Frechette, and J. Kagel. 2004. "How Robust Is Laboratory Gift Exchange?" *Experimental Economics* 7: 189–205.

Chaudhuri, A., A. Schotter, and B. Sopher. 2009. "Talking Ourselves to Efficiency: Coordination in Inter-Generational Minimum Games with Private, Almost Common and Common Knowledge of Advice." *Economic Journal* 119: 91–122.

Cooper, D. J. 2006. "Are Experienced Managers Experts at Overcoming Coordination Failure?" *Advances in Economic Analysis and Policy* 6(2): 1–50.

Cooper, D. J., and J. Kagel. In press. "Other Regarding Preferences: A Selective Survey of Experimental Results," in J. Kagel and A. Roth (eds.), *Handbook of Experimental Economics,* volume II. Princeton, NJ: Princeton University Press.

Cooper, R. W. 1999. *Coordination Games: Complementarities and Macroeconomics.* Cambridge: Cambridge University Press.

Cooper, R. W., D. V. DeJong, R. Forsythe, and T. W. Ross. 1992. "Communication in Coordination Games." *Quarterly Journal of Economics* 107: 739–771.

Corbae, D., and J. Duffy. 2008. "Experiments with Network Formation." *Games and Economic Behavior* 64(1): 81–120.

Crawford, V. P. 1995. "Adaptive Dynamics in Coordination Games." *Econometrica* 63: 103–143.

Crémer, J. 1993. "Corporate Culture and Shared Knowledge." *Industrial and Corporate Change* 2: 351–386.

Davis, M. 1971. "That's Interesting!" *Philosophy and Social Science* 1: 309–344.

Devetag, G., and A. Ortmann. 2007. "When and Why? A Critical Survey on Coordination Failure in the Laboratory." *Experimental Economics* 10: 331–344.

Dohmen, T., and A. Falk. 2011. "Performance Pay and Multidimensional Sorting: Productivity, Preferences and Gender." *American Economic Review* 101: 556–590.

Duffy, J., and E. Hopkins. 2005. "Learning, Information and Sorting in Market Entry Games: Theory and Evidence." *Games and Economic Behavior* 51(1): 31–62.

Ehrenberg, R. G., and M. L. Bognanno. 1990. "The Incentive Effects of Tournaments Revisited: Evidence from the European PGA Tour." *Industrial and Labor Relations Review* 43: S74–S88.

Ellingsen, T., and M. Johannesson. 2008. "Pride and Prejudice: The Human Side of Incentive Theory." *American Economic Review* 98: 990–1008.

Engelmann, D., and A. Ortmann. 2009. "The Robustness of Laboratory Gift Exchange: A Reconsideration." Working paper, University of Mannheim, Baden-Württemberg. Germany. Available at: http://engelmann.vwl.uni-mannheim.de/fileadmin/user_upload/engelmann/Working_Papers/RobustGXExpEcon.pdf.

Eriksson, T., and M.-C. Villeval. 2008. "Other-Regarding Preferences and Performance Pay: An Experiment on Incentives and Sorting." *Journal of Economic Behavior and Organization* 68: 412–421.

Evan, W. M., and R. G. Simmons. 1969. "Organizational Effects of Inequitable Rewards: Two Experiments in Status Inconsistency." *Administrative Science Quarterly* 14: 224–237.

Falk, A., and J. Heckman. 2009. "Lab Experiments Are a Major Source of Knowledge in the Social Sciences." *Science* 326: 535–538.

Farber, H. S. 2005. "Is Tomorrow Another Day? The Labor Supply of New York City Cab Drivers." *Journal of Political Economy* 113: 46–82.

———. 2008. "Reference-Dependent Preferences and Labor Supply: The Case of New York City Taxi Drivers." *American Economic Review* 98: 1069–1082.

Fehr, E., and A. Falk. 1999. "Wage Rigidity in a Competitive Incomplete Contract Market." *Journal of Political Economy* 107: 106–134.

Fehr, E., and S. Gächter. 2000. "Cooperation and Punishment in Public Goods Experiments." *American Economic Review* 90: 980–994.

Fehr, E., and L. Goette. 2007. "Do Workers Work More If Wages Are High? Evidence from a Randomized Field Experiment." *American Economic Review* 97: 298–317.

Fehr, E., and K. Schmidt. 1999. "A Theory of Fairness, Competition and Cooperation." *Quarterly Journal of Economics* 114: 817–868.

———. 2004: "Fairness and Incentives in a Multi-Task Principal-Agent Model." *Scandinavian Journal of Economics* 106: 453–474.

Fehr, E., G. Kirchsteiger, and A. Riedl. 1993. "Does Fairness Prevent Market Clearing? An Experimental Investigation." *Quarterly Journal of Economics* 108: 437–459.

Fehr, E., S. Gächter, and G. Kirchsteiger. 1997. "Reciprocity as a Contract Enforcement Device: Experimental Evidence." *Econometrica* 65: 833–860.

Fehr, E., R. Kirchler, A. Weichbold, and S. Gächter. 1998. "When Social Norms Overpower Competition: Gift Exchange in Experimental Labor Markets." *Journal of Labor Economics* 16: 324–351.

Fehr, E., U. Fischbacher, and E. Tougareva. 2002. "Do High Stakes and Competition Undermine Fairness? Evidence from Russia." Working Paper 120, Institute for Empirical Research in Economics, University of Zurich.

Fehr, E., H. Herz, and T. Wilkening. 2010. "The Lure of Authority: Motivation and Incentive Effects of Power." Working Paper 1115, Department of Economics, University of Melbourne.

Feiler, L., and C. F. Camerer. 2009. "Code Creation in Endogenous Merger Experiments." *Economic Inquiry* 48: 337–352.

Foss, N. J. 2001. "Leadership, Beliefs and Coordination: An Explorative Discussion." *Industrial and Corporate Change* 10: 357–358.

Frechette, G. In press. "Session Effects in the Laboratory." *Experimental Economics.* Available at: http://dx.doi.org/10.1007/s10683-011-9309-1.

Frey, B. S., and R. Jegen. 2001. "Motivation Crowding Theory." *Journal of Economic Surveys* 15: 589–612.

Gächter, S., D. Nosenzo, E. Renner, and M. Sefton. In press. "Who Makes a Good Leader? Cooperativeness, Optimism, and Leading-by-Example." *Economic Inquiry.* Available at: http://dx.doi.org/10.1111/j.1465-7295.2010.00295.x.

Gneezy, U., and J. A. List. 2006. "Putting Behavioral Economics to Work: Testing for Gift Exchange in Labor Markets Using Field Experiments." *Econometrica* 74: 1365–1384.

Gneezy, U., and A. Rustichini. 2000a. "Pay Enough or Don't Pay at All." *Quarterly Journal of Economics* 115: 791–810.

———. 2000b. "A Fine Is a Price." *Journal of Legal Studies* 29: 1–18.

Goeree, J. K., and C. A. Holt. 2005. "An Experimental Study of Costly Coordination." *Games and Economic Behavior* 51(2): 349–364.

Greenberg, J. 1990. "Employee Theft as a Reaction to Underpayment Inequity: The Hidden Cost of Pay Cuts." *Journal of Applied Psychology* 75: 561–568.

Guetzkow, H., and H. A. Simon. 1955. "The Impact of Certain Nets upon Organization and Performance in Task-Oriented Groups." *Management Science* 1: 233–250.

Güth, W., M. V. Levati, M. Sutter, and E. van der Heijden. 2007. "Leading by Example with and without Exclusion Power in Voluntary Contribution Experiments." *Journal of Public Economics* 91: 1023–1042.

Hamman, J., S. Rick, and R. A. Weber. 2007. "Solving Coordination Failure with 'All-or-None' Group-Level Incentives." *Experimental Economics* 10: 285–303.

Hannan, L., J. H. Kagel, and D. V. Moser. 2002. "Partial Gift Exchange in an Experimental Labor Market, Impact of Subject Population Differences, and Effort Requests on Behavior." *Journal of Labor Economics* 20: 923–951.

Healy, P. J. 2007. "Group Reputations, Stereotypes, and Cooperation in a Repeated Labor Market." *American Economic Review* 97: 1751–1773.

Heath, C., and N. Staudenmayer. 2000. "Coordination Neglect: How Lay Theories of Organizing Complicated Coordination in Organizations." *Research in Organizational Behavior* 22: 155–193.

Hennig-Schmidt, H., B. Rockenbach, and A. Sadrieh. 2010. "In Search of Workers' Real Effort Reciprocity—A Field and a Laboratory Experiment." *Journal of the European Economic Association* 8: 817–837.

Hermalin, B. E. 1998. "Toward an Economic Theory of Leadership: Leading by Example." *American Economic Review* 88: 1188–1206.

———. 2001. "Economics and Corporate Culture" in C. Cooper, S. Cartwright, and C. Earley (eds.), *The International Handbook of Organizational Culture and Climate*. Chichester, UK: John Wiley and Sons, pp. 217–262.

Heyman, J., and D. Ariely. 2004. "Effort for Payment: A Tale of Two Markets." *Psychological Science* 15: 787–793.

Hirshleifer, J. 1983. "From Weakest-Link to Best-Shot: The Voluntary Provision of Public Goods." *Public Choice* 41: 371–386.

Holmström, B. 1982. "Moral Hazard in Teams." *Bell Journal of Economics* 13: 324–340.

Holmström, B., and P. Milgrom. 1994. "The Firm as an Incentive System." *American Economic Review* 84: 972–991.

Jackson, M. O. 2010. *Social and Economic Networks*. Princeton, NJ: Princeton University Press.

Kearns, M., S. Suri, and N. Montfort. 2006. "An Experimental Study of the Coloring Problem on Human Subject Networks." *Science* 313: 824–826.

Knez, M., and C. F. Camerer. 1994. "Creating Expectational Assets in the Laboratory: Coordination in 'Weakest-Link' Games." *Strategic Management Journal* 15: 101–119.

Knoeber, C. R. 1989. "A Real Game of Chicken: Contracts, Tournaments, and the Production of Broilers." *Journal of Law, Economics, and Organization* 5: 271–292.

Kogan, S., A. Kwasnica, and R. A. Weber. 2011. "Coordination in the Presence of Asset Markets." *American Economic Review* 101: 927–947.

Kosfeld, M. 2004. "Economic Networks in the Laboratory: A Survey." *Review of Network Economics* 3: 20–41.

Kreps, D. M. 1990. "Corporate Culture and Economic Theory," in J. Alt and K. Shepsle (eds.), *Perspectives on Positive Political Economy*. Cambridge: Cambridge University Press, pp. 90–143.

Kriss, P. H., and R. A. Weber. In press. "Economic Laboratory Experiments on Organizational Formation and Change," in Anna Grandori (ed.), *Handbook of Economic Organization*. London: Edward Elgar.

Kriss, P. H., A. Blume, and R. A. Weber. 2011. "Coordination, Efficiency and Pre-Play Communication with Forgone Costly Messages." Working Paper econwp034, University of Zurich, Department of Economics.

Krueger, A. B., and A. Mas. 2004. "Strikes, Scabs, and Tread Separations: Labor Strife and the Production of Defective Bridgestone/Firestone Tires." *Journal of Political Economy* 112: 253–289.

Kuang, X. (J.), R. A. Weber, and J. Dana. 2007. "How Effective Is Advice from Interested Parties? An Experimental Test Using a Pure Coordination Game." *Journal of Economic Behavior and Organization* 62: 591–604.

Kube, S., M. Marechal, and C. Puppe. In press a. "Do Wage Cuts Damage Work Morale? Evidence from a Natural Field Experiment." *Journal of the European Economic Association.*

———. In press b. "The Currency of Reciprocity—Gift-Exchange in the Workplace." *American Economic Review.*

Lambert, R. A., D. F. Larcker, and K. Weigelt. 1993. "The Structure of Organizational Incentives." *Administrative Science Quarterly* 38: 438–461.

Lazear, E. P. 2000. "Performance Pay and Productivity." *American Economic Review* 90: 1346–1361.

Lazear, E. P., and S. Rosen. 1981. "Rank-Order Tournaments as Optimum Labor Contracts." *Journal of Political Economy* 89: 841–864.

Lazear, E. P., U. Malmendier, and R. A. Weber. 2012. "Sorting in Experiments with Application to Social Preferences." *American Economic Journal: Applied Economics* 4: 136–163.

Leavitt, H. J. 1951. "Some Effects of Certain Communication Patterns on Group Performance." *Journal of Abnormal Psychology* 46:38–50.

Ledyard, J. O. 1995. "Public Goods: A Survey of Experimental Research," in J. Kagel and A. Roth (eds.), *Handbook of Experimental Economics.* Princeton, NJ: Princeton University Press, pp. 111–194.

Lepper, M. R., D. Greene, and R. E. Nisbett. 1973. "Undermining Children's Intrinsic Interest with Extrinsic Reward: A Test of the 'Overjustification' Hypothesis." *Journal of Personality and Social Psychology* 28: 129–137.

Levitt, S. D., and J. A. List. 2007. "What Do Laboratory Experiments Measuring Social Preferences Tell Us about the Real World?" *Journal of Economic Perspectives* 21(2): 153–174.

Linardi, S., and C. F. Camerer. 2011. "Can Relational Contracts Survive Stochastic Interruptions? Experimental Evidence." Working paper, University of Pittsburgh.

Lind, E. A., and T. R. Tyler. 1992. *The Social Psychology of Procedural Justice.* New York: Plenum.

March, J. G., and H. A. Simon. 1958. *Organizations.* New York: Wiley.

Mas, A. 2006. "Pay, Reference Points and Police Performance." *Quarterly Journal of Economics* 121: 783–821.

Mayo, E. 1933. *The Human Problems of an Industrial Civilization.* Manchester, NH: Ayer.

McKelvey, R., and T. Palfrey. 1998. "Quantal Response Equilibria for Extensive Form Games." *Experimental Economics* 1: 9–41.

Mehta, J., C. Starmer, and R. Sugden. 1994. "The Nature of Salience: An Experimental Investigation of Pure Coordination Games." *American Economic Review* 84: 658–673.

Milgrom, P., and J. Roberts. 1988. "An Economic Approach to Influence Activities in Organizations." *American Journal of Sociology (supplement: Organizations and Institutions: Sociological and Economic Approaches to the Analysis of Social Structure)* 94: S154–S179.

Moldovanu, B., and A. Sela. 2001. "The Optimal Allocation of Prizes in Contests." *American Economic Review* 91: 542–558.

Moxnes, E., and E. van der Heijden. 2004. "The Effect of Leadership in a Public Bad Experiment." *Journal of Conflict Resolution* 47: 773–795.

Müller, W., and A. Schotter. 2010. "Workaholics and Drop Outs in Optimal Organizations." *Journal of the European Economic Association* 8: 717–743.

Mulligan, C. 1995. "The Intertemporal Substitution of Work—What Does the Evidence Say?" Population Research Center working paper, University of Chicago.

Nagin, D. S., J. B. Rebitzer, S. Sanders, and L. Taylor. 2002. "Monitoring, Motivation and Management: The Determinants of Opportunistic Behavior in a Field Experiment." *American Economic Review* 92: 850–873.

Nalbantian, H. R. (ed.). 1987. *Incentives, Cooperation, and Risk Sharing.* Totowa, NJ: Rowman and Littlefield.

Nalbantian, H. R., and A. Schotter. 1997. "Productivity under Group Incentives: An Experimental Study." *American Economic Review* 87: 314–341.

Orbell, J. M., and R. M. Dawes. 1993. "Social Welfare, Cooperators' Advantage, and the Option of Not Playing the Game." *American Sociological Review* 58: 787–800.

Orrison, A., A. Schotter, and K. Weigelt. 2004. "Multiperson Tournaments: An Experimental Examination." *Management Science* 50: 268–279.

Ortmann, A., and R. Hertwig. 2002. "The Costs of Deception: Evidence from Psychology." *Experimental Economics* 5(2): 111–131.

Page, T., L. Putterman, and B. Unel. 2005. "Voluntary Association in Public Goods Experiments: Reciprocity, Mimicry and Efficiency." *Economic Journal* 115: 1032–1053.

Pondy, L. R., and J. G. Birnberg. 1969. "An Experimental Study of the Allocation of Financial Resources within Small, Hierarchical Task Groups." *Administrative Science Quarterly* 14: 192–201.

Potters, J., M. Sefton, and L. Versterlund. 2007. "Leading-by-Example and Signaling in Voluntary Contribution Games: An Experimental Study." *Economic Theory* 33: 169–182.

Rapoport, A., D. Seale, and Y. Winter. 2002. "Coordination and Learning Behavior in Large Groups with Asymmetric Players." *Games and Economic Behavior* 39(1): 111–136.

Rebitzer, J., and L. Taylor. 2011. "Extrinsic Rewards and Intrinsic Motives: Standard and Behavioral Approaches to Agency and Labor Markets," in O. Ashenfelter and D. Card (eds.), *Handbook of Labor Economics,* volume 4A. Amsterdam: Elsevier, pp. 701–772.

Rigdon, M. 2002. "Efficiency Wages in an Experimental Labor Market." *Proceedings of the National Academy of Sciences* 99: 13348–13351.

Schelling, T. C. 1960. *The Strategy of Conflict.* Cambridge, MA: Harvard University Press.

Schotter, A., and K. Weigelt. 1992. "Asymmetric Tournaments, Equal Opportunity Laws, and Affirmative Action: Some Experimental Results." *Quarterly Journal of Economics* 107: 511–539.

Taylor, F. W. 1911. *Principles of Scientific Management.* New York: Harper and Brothers.

Thompson, J. D. 1967. *Organizations in Action: Social Science Administration Theory.* New York: McGraw-Hill.

Triplett, N. 1898. "The Dynamogenic Factors in Pacemaking and Competition." *American Journal of Psychology* 9: 507–533.

van der Heijden, E., J. Potters, and M. Sefton. 2009. "Hierarchy and Opportunism in Teams." *Journal of Economic Behavior and Organization* 69: 39–50.

Van Huyck, J. B., R. C. Battalio, and R. O. Beil. 1990. "Tacit Coordination Games, Strategic Uncertainty, and Coordination Failure." *American Economic Review* 80: 234–248.

———. 1991. "Strategic Uncertainty, Equilibrium Selection, and Coordination Failure in Average Opinion Games." *Quarterly Journal of Economics* 106: 885–910.

Van Huyck, J. B., A. B. Gillette, and R. C. Battalio. 1992. "Credible Assignments in Coordination Games." *Games and Economic Behavior* 4(4): 606–626.

Van Huyck, J. B., R. C. Battalio, and R. O. Beil 1993. "Asset Markets as an Equilibrium Selection Mechanism." *Games and Economic Behavior* 5(3): 485–504.

Weber, R. A. 2006. "Managing Growth to Achieve Efficient Coordination in Large Groups." *American Economic Review* 96: 114–126.

Weber, R. A., and C. F. Camerer. 2003. "Cultural Conflict and Merger Failure: An Experimental Approach." *Management Science* 49: 400–415.

Weber, R. A., Y. Rottenstreich, C. F. Camerer, and M. Knez. 2001. "The Illusion of Leadership: Misattribution of Cause in Coordination Games." *Organization Science* 12: 582–598.

Weick, K. E. 1969. "Laboratory Organizations and Unnoticed Causes." *Administrative Science Quarterly* 14: 294–303.

Yerkes, R. M., and J. Dodson. 1908. "The Relation of Strength of Stimulus to Rapidity of Habit Formation." *Journal of Comparative Neurology and Psychology* 18: 459–482.

7

Insider Econometrics
Empirical Studies of How Management Matters
Casey Ichniowski and Kathryn Shaw

1. Introduction

Survey data and casual observation suggest that there are striking differences in management practices among firms and establishments that operate within the same industry. Human resource management (HRM) practices—such as types of compensation, teamwork, job design, or training activities—vary across firms. Decisions about the scope of the firm, such as the extent of outsourcing or vertical integration and about adopting new technologies, are among the many management policies that vary across firms.[1] Industries are not populated by homogeneous firms having a single set of optimal management practices. Why do some firms within the same industry look so different from one another? Are some management practices more productive than others?[2] Do differences in management practices help explain large differences in productivity that exist among firms and establishments within the same industry?[3] Can one set of management practices be the right choice for some firms, while a different set of practices is appropriate for other firms that compete with them?

Researchers are now going inside firms and industries to answer these questions. With firms increasing their use of new software to track the productivity of their employees and operations, managers in these firms are looking for new ways of using these data to elevate the performance of their firms. As economists obtain access to these data, they can identify more detailed determinants of productivity and test richer theories of the firm than was previously possible.

In this chapter, we describe an empirical research strategy for investigating these questions about the effects of management practices on productivity and the determinants of the choice of

---

1. See Osterman (1994, 2000), Ledford et al. (1995), and Lawler and Mohrman (2003) for surveys on HRM practices. See Bresnahan et al. (2002) for data on computer technologies and other management practices.

2. For survey articles on personnel economics topics, see Lazear (1999), Ichniowski and Shaw (2003), Lazear and Shaw (2007), Oyer and Schaefer (2011), Rebitzer and Taylor (2011), and Lazear and Oyer (this volume).

3. Haltiwanger (2008) documents very large differences in productivity across establishments within narrowly defined industry categories.

management practices. We refer to this research strategy as "insider econometrics." The term "insider" refers to the use of rich micro-level data on workers or work groups inside firms that share a common production function. "Insider" also refers to the use of insights from insiders—from managers and employees—that inform almost every facet of the research. The term "econometrics" refers to the use of rigorous statistical tests of the effects of management practices on workers' performance, or tests of why some firms adopt one set of management practices rather than an alternative set. In sum, insider econometric research combines insiders' insights with econometric techniques applied to the right data to reveal when and why management practices matter.

2. The Distinctive Characteristics of Insider Econometric Research

Five characteristics are common in insider econometric studies. We first list these features and then describe them in more detail. Insider econometric studies

1. estimate a productivity regression in which productivity is a function of some management practice;

2. identify why management practices raise productivity and where the practice has larger and smaller effects on productivity;

3. model the adoption of the management practices;

4. analyze micro-level data on production units (e.g., individual employees or teams of employees) or larger work groups (e.g., establishments) that share a common production process; and

5. use field research and interviews from industry insiders to formulate testable hypotheses, interpret results, and provide additional evidence of the mechanisms behind the econometric results.

The first three features identify the objectives of insider research—what questions do insider econometric studies try to answer? The last two features are two defining methodological features of insider econometric research—asking what are the main methods used to answer insider questions?

The first question insider econometric research tries to answer is: does a new management practice raise productivity? Thus, the first step is the estimation of the treatment effect in a productivity regression. While the treatment effect literature in economics has often been concerned with estimating the effects of changes in public policies, such as that of an increase in unemployment compensation on labor supply,[4] insider econometric studies analyze the effects of management policies. Therefore, the *treatment is the adoption of a new management practice,* and the *treatment effect is the effect of the new practice on workers' performance.*

What are examples of the management treatments in insider studies? Because insider studies focus on a single production process, treatments are often changes in how workers are managed. Treatments therefore include changes in personnel and HRM practices; changes in interactions

---

4. For a discussion of the evolution of treatment effect research in economics, see Levitt and List (2009).

among co-workers, such as new shift assignments; changes in employees' social networks; and many other people management practices implemented in firms. Other insider studies examine differences in technological features in a given production process, such as the adoption of new computer technologies. Treatments also include changes in the scope of the firm's activities, and thus in the boundary of the firm itself.

Throughout this chapter, we refer to the treatment effects as the effects of the new management practice on productivity, but the term "productivity" is really shorthand for different measures of performance that are relevant for the given production process. The performance outcome is more accurately defined as any variable that the firm monitors and the worker controls that affects the firm's profits. Examples of productivity outcomes in insider studies include product quality, production line downtime, number of customers processed per hour, patents granted to research teams, speed of order fulfilment, worker absenteeism, or worker turnover. The performance variable is rarely profits, because profits are measured at the level of the firm, and insider studies use samples below that level. Management practices are typically not the same across all workers in a firm. Production workers are not covered by the same practices as managers, and employees in one site may be covered by different practices than those at another site.

The second question addressed by insider econometric research is a natural extension of the first. Why does the new management practice raise productivity? To build richer theories of the firm, researchers must find out why a management practice is or is not effective. One way insider studies address this question is by identifying reasons why the treatment effect of a management practice varies across workers, work groups, or establishments in the same industry. Productivity may increase considerably after a new practice is adopted among some workers or work groups in the study, while for others, the productivity effect is negligible. This variation can help identify the mechanisms and behaviors that explain the productivity increases. Insider studies allow workers and work groups to respond differently to a management practice; therefore, these studies almost always estimate the production function with heterogeneity in the management treatment effect.

The third question that insider econometric research addresses is why and where is the new management practice adopted? Insider studies document systematic answers to the questions about why management practices change and why management practices are not universally adopted for all workers and plants, even among seeming competitors. First, best management practices evolve over time. For example, new information technologies are invented. New technologies may also call for the adoption of new management practices. Second, the profitability of practices varies across firms. For example, the expected productivity gains depend on subtle differences in the production functions of competing firms. They may also depend on other management practices in the firms. The expected profitability of a new practice also depends on the costs of adoption, which can vary across firms because of differences in managers' and workers' resistance to change or differences in managerial knowledge about the existence or effects of new practices. The expected profitability can also depend on the firm's strategy.[5]

---

5. See Section 6 for a systematic discussion of causes of adoption.

Even if the researcher does not have the data to estimate the full adoption equation, reports on managers' views of the reasons for adoption can be very helpful in interpreting results from the productivity equations.[6] These three questions—about the effects of management practices on productivity, the mechanisms behind the estimated productivity effects, and the reasons for adopting different management practices—are the focus of insider econometric research.

The fourth feature of insider econometric research is the analysis of micro-level data from one narrowly defined production process. The observations that form the dataset should be the natural production units for the single production process being studied. These production units can be individual workers (if employees work alone), small groups of employees (e.g., problem-solving or project-development teams), or relatively large groups of employees (e.g., retail stores or production lines in manufacturing plants). The focus on one specific production process helps isolate the productivity effects of new management practices, reduces concerns about omitted variable bias in the productivity regression, and allows the researcher to build and estimate an accurate production function. For example, by modeling one specific production process, the researcher can choose a logical dependent variable for that process, leading to the many different variables that insider studies use to measure productivity—sales volume for salespeople, calls for call center workers, flight delays for airline carriers, downtime for a production line, or student achievement in a classroom. The focus on a single production process also allows the researcher to identify the determinants of that specific measure of performance.

The last feature in the list is perhaps the defining feature of insider econometric research: consultation with industry insiders who have direct experience in the production process. These insider insights help identify practices and policies that are relevant to managers in the industry, the most appropriate measures of productivity, other determinants of productivity that might be correlated with the management treatment, reasons a management practice was adopted for one work group or plant but not another, how employees responded to the new management policy, examples of actual workers and plants that illustrate the productivity effects, and more. Insiders therefore are instrumental in identifying meaningful hypotheses about the effects of practices on productivity outcomes and on worker behaviors, and about the determinants of adoption of the practices. They also can help identify what factors need to be included in an accurate model of productivity or adoption and therefore what kinds of data are needed to estimate those models.

Insider studies usually cover four of the five features listed above. Specifically, insider datasets often do not permit the researcher to estimate both the productivity regression and the adoption regression (in features 1 and 3). As the examples below show, researchers often estimate the production function but carefully describe the likely conditions for adoption based on interview evidence. Other examples below show that researchers estimate the adoption regression and use interviews to describe the production function underlying the adoption decisions. Overall, all

---

6. However, many insider studies reviewed in this chapter do try to add up the broader economic and welfare effects of a given management practice beyond its effects on productivity outcomes, such as the effects on overall firm profitability or the prospects for future growth.

insider studies aim to marshal micro-level data and insights from industry insiders to study the effects of management practices on workers' performance; changes in worker behavior when new practices are adopted; the costs of the practices; and ultimately, the reasons for the adoption of the practices.

3. Illustrating the Challenges and Advantages of Insider Econometric Research

Researchers face analytical challenges and unique opportunities in undertaking insider studies. We illustrate both.

The key challenge is that firms are making optimizing decisions when they choose management practices, and therefore, the adoption of the treatment is not random.[7] Therefore, our models of the effects of these practices on productivity face all the traditional problems of using nonexperimental data. There is likely selection bias and endogeneity in the choices of workers and managers. There is omitted variable bias in the production function. We cannot know the unobserved counterfactuals about what would have happened if nonadopting firms had adopted some new management practice or if adopting firms had not adopted.

There are advantages to modeling treatment effects in insider studies. The quality of the data, the information from industry insiders who adopt the practice or work under it, and the types of comparisons the researcher can make with the data all add more information than is typically available in traditional treatment effects research. Perhaps most important, access to knowledgeable insiders and to rich data on the operations of the actual production process can potentially address all the key challenges by providing insights into the decisions of workers and managers, by reducing the extent of omitted variable bias (by modeling a specific production process with real operating data), and through insiders' views about how a process would work without the given management practice.

To illustrate the challenges that selectivity in the adoption of a new management treatment poses and the opportunities to address those challenges through insider econometric research, we display the production functions and patterns of adoption for a hypothetical insider study in Figure 1. Figure 1 shows two age-productivity profiles. For convenience, we refer to these productivity profiles as the profiles for two groups of establishments, such as plants in a manufacturing industry or stores in a retail industry. However, insider datasets focus on a single production function, and thus the data can also be observations on workers, work teams, or parts of an establishment. Many of our examples are insider studies with worker-level datasets from a single firm, and so Figure 1 could also represent the age-productivity profiles of different types of workers in the firm.

The two hypothetical productivity profiles in Figure 1 reflect several assumptions that are made or tested in insider econometric studies. First, despite being in the same industry and

---

7. The case of random adoption is relevant for some insider applications, such as those studying personnel records for a single firm that adopts a new work practice for all employees, because universally applied practices are not applied selectively (for that firm's population). Also, field experiments in developing countries can impose random assignment—see Bloom et al. (2011b) for a random treatment in textile firms in India. Doyle et al. (2010) examine the performance of different kinds of physicians through random assignment of patients.

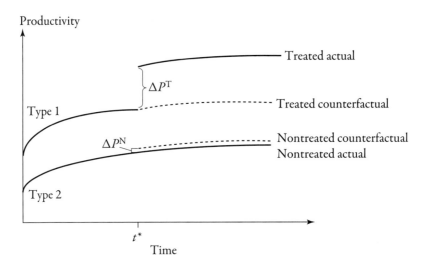

Figure 1. Productivity effects of adopting a new management practice: a hypothetical age-productivity profile for treated and nontreated groups. Note that t^* is the time that the treatment, such as an organizational change, occurs.

even having the same basic production process, differences still exist between the two sets of plants; the Type 1 group has a higher level of productivity than the Type 2 group. Second, both productivity profiles are upward sloping, reflecting factors like learning-by-doing and experience. In this illustration, we let the basic growth rate in productivity be the same for the two types of establishments. Third, at t^*, management in the high-productivity Type 1 establishments adopts some new practice, for example, a new work practice or technological enhancement in their operations. Management in the low-productivity Type 2 establishments does not adopt. The new management practice causes a one-time increase in productivity by an amount equal to ΔP^T. Finally, productivity continues to grow in both types of establishments after t^* due to continued effects of experience and learning.

Figure 1 also displays assumptions about two unobserved counterfactuals. First, we assume that the change in productivity among Type 2 nonadopting establishments had they adopted (ΔP^N) would be positive but smaller than what was observed for the Type 1 adopters. Though the productivity gains for nonadopters, ΔP^N, are shown to be positive, these establishments still do not adopt, because the gains are insufficient to overcome the costs of adopting. Second, the post-t^* profile for the adopters would have continued along the same pre-t^* trajectory but without the one-time increase.

The hypothetical example in Figure 1 highlights the basic empirical challenges. Consider two types of data that could be used to estimate the treatment effect of the new management practice on productivity. First, consider the case where the researcher obtains true experimental data—data from a sample of organizations with random adoption of the new practice at time t^*. Figure 1 does not depict this case but rather the case of nonrandom adoption: organizations that would experience bigger productivity gains are the adopters in Figure 1.

If adoption of the management practice were randomly assigned across both Type 1 and Type 2 establishments as part of an experiment, the estimated gain in productivity from the new practice will be an average of ΔP^{T} and ΔP^{N}, because the group of adopters in an experimental design would include both types of establishments. As with any experiment, this estimated gain is an unbiased estimate of the average effect of the practice on productivity across all plants in this industry. However, in the real world, this estimate of the change in productivity due to the management practice will never be observed in any single establishment: a firm will never randomly adopt a new management practice. From the perspective of a manager in any of the organizations in the dataset, the experimental estimate of the productivity gain due to the adoption of the practice will not answer his exact question: what happens to productivity in my business if I adopt this new management practice?

Therefore, random assignment of the treatment does not offer all the methodological advantages one desires for studying productivity effects of new management practices. The manager wants to know what the expected productivity gain is for his operations. He would like to know the "treatment of the treated" and the "treatment of the nontreated" effects displayed by the Type 1 and Type 2 groups, respectively, and he wants to know whether his workers and plants are in the Type 1 or Type 2 group. Researchers want to know the same things. Insider studies—with good data and knowledge—test theoretical models of why and how Type 1 establishments benefit, while Type 2 establishments do not.

In what follows we use Figure 1 to frame our discussion of the insider econometric methodology. The examples provided illustrate the two distinctive methodological features of insider studies—analysis of rich micro-level data about one specific production process and access to insiders who are knowledgeable about their management practices and operations—that are instrumental in constructing convincing empirical tests of the effects of management practices on productivity.

4. Examples Illustrating the Methods of Insider Econometric Research

In this section, we review eight examples of insider econometric research to illustrate the common features of this research and to give the new researcher a true feel for both the methods and results from this body of work. After reading these examples, it is much easier for the researcher to understand the econometric methods, which we describe in Section 5, and the key decisions about more specific elements of the research design of an insider study (beyond the use of micro-level data on a single production process), which we describe in Section 7.

The review of each example follows a pattern: we describe the sample and the production process; the nature of the management practices; the basic empirical findings about adoption of the practice and its effects on productivity; and the results on why productivity does or does not rise due to management practices. Variants of the Figure 1 profiles are used to summarize the studies. These examples also illustrate a range of management treatments that insider studies investigate, from the adoption of a single new compensation practice, to the adoption of sets of HRM practices, to changes in the scope of the firm's work tasks and activities. We conclude the section with a broader review of insider studies, where we categorize a large number of insider studies according to the type of management practices analyzed.

4.1. Two Single-Firm Worker-Level Studies on the Productivity Effects of Incentive Pay

The first two studies use worker-level observations from a single firm. In both, the new practice adopted by management is an incentive pay practice that covers all employees in the firm. Despite these similarities, both confront their own unique methodological issues and each shows the importance of different insider insights.

4.1.1. Incentive Pay at Safelite Glass

Lazear (2000) studies the productivity of workers in one firm before and after the introduction of a new incentive pay plan. Lazear's study models automobile windshield installation for the Safelite Company. In this company, each employee drives a truck to the homes of people who need a new car windshield. The production function is worker-specific and measurable: employees work alone, installing about two or three windshields a day. The production unit is the worker. The data are monthly productivity data for some 3,000 workers for 19 months. During this period, the firm shifts from hourly pay to incentive piece rate pay, where pay is a function of the number of windshields the worker installs that day. After the move to piece rate pay, the average productivity of the Safelite workforce rises by 44%. Workers are highly sensitive to monetary incentives.

Why is this study interesting? The specific production setting is not important: the reader does not have to be interested in windshield installation per se. The management practice—piece rate pay—is of interest, because many firms use some form of individual performance incentive, even if incentive pay rarely takes the form of simple piece rates. Therefore, the evidence that monetary incentives raise workers' productivity is in itself valuable, though perhaps not surprising.[8] What makes the result valuable is that the study identifies why productivity goes up. First, as expected, some of the overall productivity increase is due to the same worker increasing his or her effort and output. Second, about half of the increase in the mean productivity of all workers comes from self-sorting by workers: those workers who have low productivity levels leave the firm (or are not hired by the firm) after incentive pay is adopted. The most interesting result of the paper is that the firm's choice of its incentive pay practice induces sorting by workers, and the sorting itself has a big productivity impact.

Figure 2 illustrates these results. The productivity response to the incentive pay is heterogeneous across workers. Analogous to Figure 1, the Safelite workers are classified as types—in this case three types. The pay plan is changed at time t^*. The response to the treatment is heterogeneous across the three types. Type 1 workers are employed before and after the new pay plan, and these workers raise their productivity (by 22%, according to the actual estimates in this study). Type 2 workers quit in response to the new incentive pay. Type 3 workers are hired after t^*. They have higher productivity and earn more under incentives than those who

---

8. Of course, the adoption of the incentive plan cannot be considered exogenous. Safelite adopts the practice because it expects productivity to increase. In Section 6, we consider the question of why optimal management practices can change over time.

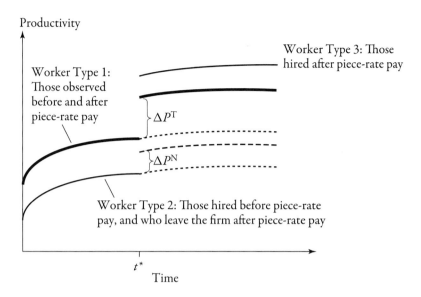

Productivity

Worker Type 3: Those
hired after piece-rate pay

Worker Type 1:
Those observed
before and after
piece-rate pay

ΔP^{T}

ΔP^{N}

Worker Type 2: Those hired before piece-rate
pay, and who leave the firm after piece-rate pay

t^*

Time

Figure 2. Incentive pay introduced in one firm (Safelite; Lazear 2000). Note
that t^* is the time of the treatment: the introduction of piece-rate pay. The solid
lines represent the observed productivity profiles for workers of Type 1, Type 2,
and Type 3. The dashed lines represent unobserved productivity profiles for the
different worker types.

left would have earned had they stayed. Together, productivity rises by an additional 22% from
the selection effects of losing Type 2 workers and the hiring of Type 3 workers.[9]

Obviously, not all firms would achieve this exact productivity gain. This is just one firm
that chose the practice, probably expecting it to be effective.[10] Although one cannot expect
the estimated productivity gains of this incentive pay plan to apply to other firms and production processes, the design of this study has several advantages that make the estimates of this
particular treatment effect especially convincing. Because the production function is very simple with workers working alone, the unobserved counterfactual productivity paths are easy to
model (based on the observed productivity paths, as shown in Figure 2). There is little likelihood of omitted variable bias, and thus, typical selection bias and endogeneity bias are not
relevant to the study. In studies of the effects of management practices on performance using
more heterogeneous samples of production units, one would be much more concerned that

9. The figure is not drawn to scale to capture this size of gain. Shaw and Lazear (2008) display this figure using
the actual Safelite data and offer more detail on differences between employees who leave and join this firm after
introduction of the new pay plan.

10. Note that the reason that the firm chose to adopt incentive pay at this time is that the firm had introduced
new information technology software that kept computerized records of each employee's productivity. Thus,
Lazear (2000) is estimating the joint impact of a change in the HRM practice and a change in information
technology infrastructure. Other firms that introduce piece rate pay may have lower performance gains and may
not find the use of piece rate pay optimal (for evidence from shoe manufacturing, see Freeman and Kleiner 2005).

unmeasured factors cause a selection bias, with some firms choosing the practice while others do not.

At the same time, in this study, there is still a different source of selection bias in the estimated treatment effects—workers decide whether to work at the firm or not, and that optimizing decision by workers affects the size of the productivity gain from incentive pay for the firm. But the study identifies and measures this self-selection, leading to the key theoretical point of the paper. An overall change in productivity can be decomposed into two components that are analogous to the intrinsic and extrinsic margins of each employee's labor supply decision. Some workers respond to the new incentive pay at the *intrinsic margin* by increasing the amount of labor (in this case, effort rather than hours) they supply. Other workers respond at the *extrinsic margin* by leaving their jobs, with different workers taking their place. The broader point for economic theory applies beyond the scope of the single firm in this study. When the firm selects its overall management practices, it must consider not only their effects as a motivation device but also their effects as a signaling device to sort specific kinds of workers into and out of the firm.

4.1.2. Incentive Pay among Fruit Pickers

Bandiera et al. (2005) analyze productivity of employees who pick fruit. The workforce in this study is hired only during the summer harvest season. The firm undertakes a series of experiments that change the payment schemes for these employees.[11] In one experiment, the firm introduces new piece rate pay, as in the Lazear (2000) paper discussed in the previous example. However, in Lazear (2000), the move was from hourly pay to piece rate pay; here the move is from a performance pay plan based on workers' relative performance to piece rate pay. In the relative output pay plan, the firm fixes the average pay for the field ex ante but pays each worker based on how much he or she does relative to other workers in his or her group (but keeping the mean pay fixed). In the second half of the picking season, the farm switches to simple piece rates: pay per unit of output is fixed ex ante and does not vary as a function of how co-workers perform. The panel data in this study cover 142 workers for 108 days spanning the periods in which different compensation plans are in place. After the switch to simple piece rates, the average productivity of workers rises by 58%. Nearly all workers increase their effort, and the variance of output also rises markedly with a jump in the number of high performers.

Figure 3 illustrates the unique results of this study. The productivity response to the incentive pay is heterogeneous across workers. Analogous to Figure 1, there are Type 1 and Type 2 workers, with a new incentive policy adopted at t^*. Unlike Figure 1, both types of workers are covered by the new incentive pay. Type 1 workers exhibit a bigger productivity jump after t^* than do Type 2 workers. The study identifies who the Type 1 workers are—employees who had been working with their friends under the initial relative pay plan. Prior to the piece rate pay plan, these workers probably withheld effort, because they knew that if they worked hard, they would

---

11. The experiment here does not randomly assign different workers at one point in time, but the timing of the change in compensation is exogenously determined by the analysts. For papers on their other experiments on managerial pay or on teamwork, see Bandiera et al. (2007, 2009).

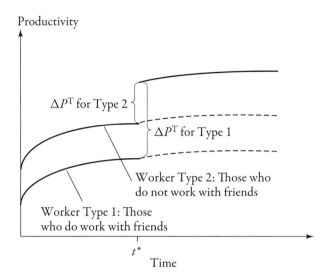

Figure 3. Incentive pay introduced in one firm (fruit pickers; Bandiera et al. 2005). Note that t^* is the time of the treatment: incentive pay plan changes from a relative pay plan before t^* to a per unit piece-rate plan after t^*. Insider information identifies Type 1 workers as those with friends as co-workers; Type 2 are workers without friends as co-workers. The solid lines represent the actual productivity profiles for workers of Type 1 and Type 2; the dashed lines represent the unobserved counterfactuals for these worker types. After the move to piece-rate pay at t^*, productivity rises, and there is no difference in the performance of those with and without friends. (The variance in performance goes up after piece rates are introduced, but that is a function of effort, not friendship, so that increase is not displayed here.)

lower their friends' pay. The Type 2 workers have lower productivity gains, because they were not working with their friends and thus were more productive than the Type 1 workers when they were working under the initial relative pay plan. The researchers reach this conclusion about why productivity increases, because they gathered additional data on friendships among workers.

What makes this study interesting? The readers of this paper do not have to be intrigued by either the occupation of fruit picking or even this specific case of piece rate pay. Unlike the setting for Lazear (2000), where workers came and went, all workers in this study stay for the short fruit picking season covered in the data. Thus, we are looking only at workers who are employed before and after the change in pay policy (in the Figure 2 illustration of the Safelite study, these would all be Type 1 workers). Here, however, we are examining the heterogeneity in productivity responses among these workers. The more fundamental economic insight in this study of fruit pickers is that workers with certain characteristics internalize an externality—the externality that their effort harms others—during the relative payment scheme. Thus, social relationships determine productivity. More broadly, this example identifies the importance of peer effects and social networks in the determination of worker productivity. Other insider style studies make related points about peer and network effects, including Ichino and Maggi (2000) for banking, Mas and Moretti (2009) for grocery stores, De Giorgi et al. (2009) for classrooms in education, Bartel et al. (2009a) for nursing, and Ingram and Roberts (2000) for hotels.

In the econometric treatment effects literature, it is widely acknowledged that treatment effects should vary across people.[12] But the design of this study is illuminating, because it solves other econometric problems associated with estimating treatment effects. In managing a firm, managers know that not all workers respond equally to a treatment. Often, a study would conclude that the variance in the treatment effects is from some unobserved abilities of the workers, but here the authors go inside the company and gather the data on friendships to identify the source of variance displayed across Type 1 and Type 2 workers. Even though the data pertain to the limited setting of one firm in one industry, the logic of the economic model applies more broadly. In settings where workers might withhold their effort because that effort can harm their co-workers, managers need to consider these peer effects in the design of compensation plans.

4.2. Two Cross-Company within-Industry Studies of the Productivity Effects of Innovative HRM Practices

In the next two examples, we contrast studies that examine the productivity effects of new HRM practices inside the steel industry. In both examples, the production process is a production line involving multiple employees. Despite these similarities, these studies analyze different segments of the steel industry and reach different conclusions about why these HRM treatments are or are not adopted.

4.2.1. Human Resource Systems in Integrated Steel Mills
In our third example of insider econometric research, two companion studies by Ichniowski et al. (1997) and Gant et al. (2002) analyze the productivity of finishing lines in integrated steel mills. The management innovation is the adoption of entire sets of new HRM practices in integrated steel mills, where the new HRM practices cover recruiting and selection policies, compensation, teamwork, communication, and employee training. The authors model production of one specific type of production line that finishes steel. These steel lines take a coil of very thin steel sheet, unwind it, and then chemically treat and coat the steel for use in products like auto bodies. In the 1997 study, the authors collect panel data on productivity outcomes for the finishing lines. The monthly productivity data for the rolling mill work groups in 36 steel mills cover several

---

12. In this study, there is no selectivity within the firm in the adoption of the practice, because all employees are covered by the change in pay policy at t^*. As in Lazear (2000), the treatment effects estimated are effects conditional on being employed in this firm. Even though the management policy change covers all employees in the dataset, there are still important unobserved counterfactuals; but in this case, these are outside the scope of the study's data. The workers' productivity profiles in Figure 3 come from only a subset of farms. As in the case of Figure 1, there are other farms, not in this particular study's dataset, that did not introduce incentive pay; these farms are analogous to the nontreated establishments in the bottom half of Figure 1. The fruit-pickers study shows us what would happen to the farming fields that adopt; we do not know anything about the nonadopters that are not covered in this study's data.

years for each line. The researchers identify four "systems" of HRM practices, ranging from the most innovative HRM system to the most traditional system with no such innovations.

Ichniowski et al. (1997) show that the mills with all the highly innovative HRM practices have the highest productivity levels. Yet some mills adopt the system of all the innovative practices and some do not. What accounts for the difference in adoption among a set of finishing lines that are competitors in a very narrowly defined industry and that are making very homogeneous products using the same machinery? Site visits to the finishing lines did not reveal any differences in product attributes, technologies, or demographic characteristics of the workers. Site visits did reveal that, even though older and newer vintage lines adopted the innovative practices, the only kind of older lines that adopted the innovative practices were old reconstituted lines—those that had been temporarily shut down and restarted by new owners. Based on this subtle distinction, the authors hypothesize that the difference in the adoption of innovative HRM systems is due to transition costs. Older continuously operating lines had higher transition costs; newer lines and those older mills that were restarted after a purchase by new owners did not have transition costs associated with changing their HRM systems (Ichniowski and Shaw 1995). All would have equal productivity gains, but older lines did not make the transition. Since the time of the study, more mills have adopted new HRM practices, but only after becoming reconstituted mills. One example is the private equity buyout by Wilbur Ross of multiple U.S. steel mills in 2002, which was followed by the introduction of new HRM practices in these mills, and then by the resale of the mills to Arcelor-Mittal in 2004 (Bose and Shaw 2008).

What makes this insider study interesting? Once again, readers of the paper do not have to be interested in the specific setting of steel finishing lines in this study. The authors not only show that HRM practices matter—that innovations in HRM practices produce tangible performance gains—they also show how such practices matter and why productivity goes up. Productivity increases only when a firm adopts a set of complementary HRM practices that together reinforce productive worker behaviors. Insider insights about why HRM practices are complementary lead the researchers to measure the management treatment as a set of practices rather than as a single HRM practice.

Moreover, research inside the finishing lines revealed why these bundles of HRM practices improve productivity. Gant et al. (2002) collect and analyze data on the communications patterns of workers in these lines and show that workers interact much more with one another as part of problem-solving activities in the high-productivity lines with innovative HRM practices. The lines with innovative HRM practices have much denser social networks and worker interactions, or higher levels of "connective capital" in the firm (Ichniowski and Shaw 2009). This difference in worker behavior provides another type of evidence—evidence on the work behavior of the employees in these lines—that helps explain why the treatment effect due to innovative HRM systems exists.

The evidence on the interactions among workers in Gant et al. (2002) also helps answer the question about why many lines do not adopt sets of new HRM practices that raise the productivity of other lines. Ichniowski et al. (1997) suggest that the productivity gains would be the same if nonadopters instituted the new HRM practices, but that nonadoption is explained by differences in the transition costs of adopting new HRM practices in older, continuously operating lines.[13] The evidence in Gant et al. (2002) suggests that changing the pattern of social relationships among workers could be a very costly process for any steel finishing line, and thus could be precisely the kind of transition cost that prevents older lines from adopting the new HRM practices.

4.2.2. Problem-Solving Teams in Steel Minimills

Boning et al. (2007) return to the steel industry but move to production lines in the minimill sector that use electric arc furnaces. Minimill lines produce steel bar products, like rebar used in construction and highways or large beams used in the construction of buildings. The mills melt steel scrap and cast it into the bar products. As in Ichniowski et al. (1997), the data here also come from one type of rolling line in these mills and thus pertain to very homogeneous production processes. The management innovation in this study is the adoption of problem-solving teams. Workers use problem-solving skills to increase the quality of the bars coming out of the mill by watching the production process as the bars roll through the mills and correcting problems as they arise. The authors collect panel data: monthly productivity data for the rolling mill work groups in 34 steel mills for about 5 years. In the beginning of the data, about 10% of the rolling mills had problem-solving teams; by the end, about half of the mills had teams.

Productivity regressions reveal significant productivity gains after problem-solving teams are adopted in minimills. However, some mills adopt teams and some do not. Once inside the mills, the reason for the difference was apparent. Some lines producing basic commodity bar products, like rebar steel, have fewer problems to solve compared to other lines making more complex products, such as thin steel wire or steel with intricate shapes. Using measures of product complexity, the authors show that 100% of the lines producing the most complex products adopt teams, and 23% of the lines producing the least complex products adopt teams.[14]

What makes this insider study interesting is that it identifies two broad economic principles. First, the study shows that product strategy decisions dictate the appropriate HRM or organizational design decisions. A strategy of making customized complex products requires HRM practices that foster more problem solving than does a strategy of making standardized products. The firm's product strategy determines its management practices. Second, firms do not benefit equally from teamwork. Here, it is complex production lines that gain the most; lines making simpler commodity products do not benefit from problem solving.[15] Economic theory suggests that teams will not be adopted by all firms. The insider insights revealed that the team effect observed among complex production lines does not apply to commodity lines.

---

13. See Ichniowski and Shaw (1995) for evidence on the transition costs of nonadopters.

14. The productivity regression results reinforce this conclusion: the productivity impact of teams is greater in the complex lines than it is among commodity lines (where teams are rarely adopted).

15. The conclusion that complex production processes value teamwork is also generalizable to some other settings. Recent researchers emphasize that firms in developed countries have a comparative advantage at producing sophisticated products, rather than commodities, so organizational innovations like teamwork are more likely to be adopted in the United States than in other countries across all firms (Bloom and Van Reenen 2007; Bloom et al. 2011a). Bartel et al. (2009b) document a similar conclusion in the U.S. and British valve-making industries.

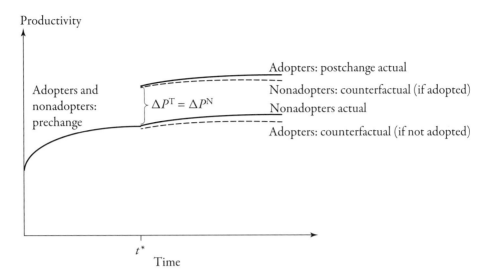

Figure 4. Innovative human resource management (HRM) systems introduced in steel finishing lines (Ichniowski et al. 1997). Note that t^* is the time of the treatment: introduction of the new HRM systems. Some steel mills are "adopters," and others are "nonadopters." The adopters and nonadopters are identical in their underlying production processes prior to t^*: there is one learning curve for both types. The one-time jump in productivity after adoption of new HRM systems at t^* is equal for these lines. For convenience in illustrating productivity profiles for different counterfactiuals by line type, the nonadopters have lower learning than the adopters after t^*, but our model would state that they are identical.

We contrast the findings of these two establishment-level studies of the effects of similar HRM practices in the same industry in Figures 4 and 5. Figure 4 summarizes the conclusions reached by Ichniowski et al. (1997) that the adoption of innovative HRM systems at t^* raises productivity in integrated steel mills. Figure 4 assumes that productivity gains of the non-adopters would be the same as those experienced by adopters. Nonadoption is instead explained by higher transition costs of adopting the new practices in older, continuously operating lines.

Despite studying similar HRM practices in a different part of the same industry, the minimill study of Boning et al. (2007) reaches different conclusions than does the study of integrated mills by Ichniowski et al. (1997). Figure 5 illustrates these differences. This figure shows selection bias in the adoption of teams at t^* with complex lines (the Type 2 adopters in Figure 5) having larger productivity gains from teams than do the commodity lines (the Type 1 nonadopters in Figure 5). In both steel studies, an understanding of selectivity in adoption of the management treatment is critical.

4.3. Two Studies with Experimental Interventions in Management Practices across Multiple Worksites

Our discussion in Section 3 emphasizes studies in plants and firms where decisions by the firms or their workers lead to nonrandom assignment of the new management practices. Recent

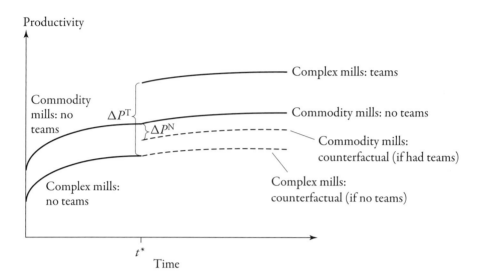

Figure 5. Problem-solving teams introduced in steel minimills (Boning et al. 2007). Note that t^* is the time of the treatment: the adoption of teams. The complex mills make more complex products and therefore have lower levels of productivity pre-t^* relative to commodity mills, which make simpler products. Complex mills are more likely to adopt teams, because they experience large gains from teamwork and problem solving.

studies in the economic development literature measure the impacts of new management practices that have been randomly assigned to work sites or workers. We review two such studies.

4.3.1. The Effects of Monitoring and Incentive Pay in Rural Indian Schools

Duflo et al. (2012) examine the effects of the introduction of new practices to monitor and reward teachers in informal education centers in remote rural areas of India. The sample includes teachers in 56 control centers and 57 treatment centers. In the controls, teachers received a fixed monthly salary of Indian rupees (Rs) 1,000 and were reminded of the importance of regular attendance at work and possible consequences of not attending regularly, such as termination. In the treatment centers, teacher attendance was monitored using cameras to provide photographic evidence. Teachers were also paid according to an incentive pay plan in which they received Rs500 if they attended 10 days or fewer per month and an additional Rs50 per day for each day beyond 10 days. Performance effects were dramatic. Attendance rates were 21 percentage points higher in the treatment centers. Moreover, according to subsequent testing, student achievement increased by 0.17 standard deviations under the new monitoring and incentive pay practices.

The study and its results are interesting for a number of reasons beyond the implied social impacts of increased teacher attendance and improvements in student achievement in rural regions of India. The study's design overcomes concerns about selectivity in the adoption of the new management practices because of the random assignment and sample sizes. Therefore, this study estimates an average treatment effect of these management practices. The implications of this particular point are worth emphasizing, given the overall themes of this review.

First, the average treatment effect can be expected to apply to the nontreated informal education centers, if the monitoring and incentive pay are instituted in the controls.[16] The well-understood advantage of an experimental design with random assignment is that it allows the researcher to make strong causal interpretations about the changes in performance that followed the adoption of the new management practices. Second, consistent with the examples illustrated in Figure 1, there is also a limitation of studies in which the new practices are randomly assigned to workers or work sites—we cannot directly examine the factors that explain the adoption and nonadoption of the practices. This does not mean that studies using random assignment cannot provide insights about adoption of management practices. In particular, if experimental studies have large enough samples to identify differences in the size of the observed treatment effects among the treated observations, then we know that the adoption of treatment should vary across those subgroups.

4.3.2. Modern Management Practices in Indian Textile Plants

Bloom et al. (2011b) study the impact of implementing modern management practices in textile plants in Mumbai. Modern management methods refer to practices that have largely been adopted in manufacturing in developed countries. The steel industry studies in Section 4.2 focused on innovative HRM practices, but in India, much of the challenge is to adopt modern methods for operating the factory, including methods of lean production and total quality management. Specifically, the authors consider the productivity effects of detailed changes in the operations of these textile plants, such as cleaning the shop floor, conducting preventative maintenance for machines, monitoring quality defects, and meeting to shut down production when quality is poor.

The researchers employ an experimental design in a sample of textile plants. In particular, they use a management consulting firm working with 17 textile firms with 20 plants to measure and evaluate the management practices in the plants. The 20 plants are then randomly assigned to two different treatments: 6 receive a 1-month treatment involving a diagnosis of what kinds of practices they have and what additional practices might make sense to adopt; 14 plants receive the same 1-month diagnosis plus an added 4-month treatment in which the consultants continue to assist with the implementation of new practices. Management changes are measured by an index of the percentage of 38 modern management practices present in any month in the various plants. The researchers track changes in this index of management practices and in three performance indicators on quality defects, fabric output, and inventories.

Productivity rises sharply, as do other performance measures, in plants that implement the new management practices with consultants. Adopting innovative management practices matters. Performance does not improve in plants that only received the diagnosis of their management practices, even though the adoption of new management practices increased

---

16. In fact, Duflo et al. (2012) estimate a structural model of the effects of the new practices and changes in pay for different numbers of days the teacher attended using just the data from the treatment centers. They find that the model predicts well the attendance of teachers in the controls when it is evaluated for zero incentives.

considerably in these plants as well. The study considers several different models to explain the timing, magnitude, and incidence of the effects of these new management practices on the performance outcomes.

The empirical results of this study also highlight the question of why these innovative lean manufacturing practices are not adopted earlier in these plants. The researchers cite several possible reasons. First, many of the practices were not common in this industry, and so a lack of knowledge about them plays some role. Second, top managers of the plant work very long hours, and so without the help of consultants, investing in changes in management methods seems less important than meeting immediate requirements of managing daily operations. Finally, consistent with the discussion of Figure 1, performance effects of the same management practices may vary, as in the case of management practices adopted in plants with 1-month versus 5-month interventions. Managers' uncertainty about whether the performance effects would occur in their plants is therefore another barrier to adoption.

4.4. Two Within-Industry Studies of the Adoption of Management Practices That Affect Productivity

In the previous examples, the production processes were relatively well understood. The examples of fruit pickers and windshield installers were individual-level production processes, and the manufacturing processes in steel, although highly technical, are relatively well understood by engineers. In some sense, these settings were the laboratories in which to study the effects of incentive pay, problem-solving teams, or new HRM systems on productivity outcomes. In other settings, such as the productivity of research and development (R&D) activities, the outcomes from the production process are much less predictable, even by the expert insiders. Yet innovations from R&D are fundamental to economic growth. The next two examples of insider econometric research are studies that shed light on determinants of productivity in research activity in the pharmaceutical industry. These papers examine fundamental issues in industrial organization economics related to the size and boundaries of the firm—managerial decisions about the number of projects to pursue and about contracting out work versus doing the tasks in-house.[17]

4.4.1. The Effects of Scale and Scope on Productivity in Pharmaceuticals
Henderson and Cockburn (1996) study productivity of early-stage research activity in the pharmaceutical industry. Research personnel in this phase try to find a chemical compound

---

17. Industrial organization research offers many other examples of empirical studies that follow an insider econometric approach of going deeply inside firms in one industry. For other discussions using micro-level data to model industrial organizational issues, see Bresnahan and Levin (this volume) and Lafontaine and Slade (this volume). In this chapter, we define insider econometrics by its focus on the internal management practices of the firm in the context of a single production process. Some empirical industrial organizational research that examines firms in a single industry would not fit this description, for example, studies of a change in firms' pricing policies (Chu et al. 2011) or in how information is revealed to customers (Leslie 2004; Bollinger et al. 2011), or studies using data on products rather than on production processes. Other examples of empirical industrial organizational research would also fit this chapter's description of insider econometrics, for example, whether the internal management practices of stores in an industry look different if the store is run by a franchisee versus an owner-operator (Lafontaine and Shaw 1999, 2005).

that has a desirable effect by mimicking aspects of a human disease. In this study, productivity is measured by the number of patents awarded, and the management treatments are changes in the scale of the firm's research activity (expenditures per project, per firm, etc.) and scope of research (extent of other research projects in similar classes of compounds in the firm, in other firms, etc.). The authors analyze 5,000 observations on annual research projects. The data come from ten firms with up to 38 projects per year and up to 30 annual observations on any one project. The authors describe the dataset assembly as an extensive iterative process with knowledgeable scientists identifying accurate detailed measures of research outputs and inputs in firms.

Henderson and Cockburn (1996) find that a wider scope of the firm, as measured by the number of large research projects, improves the chances of success in a research project. More specifically, knowledge spillovers across research on similar classes of drugs within a single firm and spillovers among firms working on the same drug class both raise research productivity. Also, there is a positive effect of the scale of the research project on research productivity, where the scale is measured by research expenditures on a given project.[18]

What makes this insider study interesting? The authors document how firm size matters for productivity. Henderson and Cockburn (1996) aggregate their project-level data up to the level of the firm and replicate a common result in prior firm-level pharmaceutical studies—that measures of firm size have little impact on patenting. When they subsequently analyze the project-level dataset they had constructed after extensive field investigations, they show just how misleading the conclusion based on firm-level analysis is. New insights surface by modeling a specific research production function at the level of individual projects. Insider insights allow them to identify why firm size matters. In addition, this study puts the micro-level productivity results into the larger public policy discussion of regulation of the industry. Allowing larger firms in the industry may in fact lead to concerns about monopoly power, but these concerns must be balanced with efficiency gains from knowledge spillovers within large firms.[19]

4.4.2. Vertical Integration Decisions in the Pharmaceutical Industry

After basic research, several stages of clinical trials take place prior to the U.S. Food and Drug Administration's approval of a new drug. Azoulay (2004) offers insider econometric research about management policy decisions in this phase of drug research.

In this study, the treatment is the drug company's decision on whether to outsource clinical trials to contract research organizations. The hypothesis is that clinical trials that are very data intensive are likely to be outsourced, whereas those that are knowledge-intensive stay in-house.

---

18. In this study, Henderson and Cockburn (1996) do not model why the treatment varies—that is, why the firms have different numbers of projects or different expenditures per project. However, they do use detailed insider insights about the causal nature of the link between the scale and scope measures and research productivity. Although their panel data document increased patent productivity when measures of scope change, they acknowledge that the question of what is the optimal research portfolio for any single firm in the dataset is beyond the scope of their analysis.

19. Other insider studies cited in Table 1 in Section 4.5 provide insights into the determinants of productivity in other knowledge-based or research-intensive industries, such as biotechnology, education, health care, law, and financial services and venture capital.

In-house trials are hypothesized to involve more subjective performance evaluations, whereas the outsourced trials involve a narrower set of more easily monitored tasks that can be covered by explicit pay-for-performance contracts. The data are project-level data from 6,826 projects spanning all pharmaceutical firms from 1991 to 1999. Coupling these rich micro-level data with insider insights from extensive field work, Azoulay (2004) models outsourcing decisions. Outsourcing is the better decision when the testing tasks can be reduced to standardized data collection tasks; testing that involves the generation of new findings and knowledge are more likely to be kept in-house.

Why is this paper interesting? First, the results of the Azoulay (2004) study deepen our understanding of a basic economic question: what determines the boundaries of the firm's activities? Furthermore, the evidence from this industry-specific example is consistent with broader economic models in which multitask jobs (e.g., jobs involving both knowledge generation and data generation) can be better managed with low-powered incentives and more intensive monitoring. Conversely, when the work involves only data-generation tasks that are easier to monitor, explicit high-powered incentive arrangements (that can be outsourced) may be more appropriate. This vertical integration decision in pharmaceuticals is therefore similar to franchising: the in-house contractors will have more subjective performance evaluations and less sensitive pay for performance, whereas the outside contractor will have more explicit pay for performance (or high-powered incentives) based on a narrow set of easy-to-monitor tasks.

In this insider study, data are not available on the success, or productivity, of drug testing; the empirical analysis focuses exclusively on the adoption of the management practice—the decision to outsource or not. The conclusion that knowledge-generating tests would be less successful were they to be outsourced to firms using high-powered incentive contracts is not tested.

These studies highlight that aggregating data up to the level of the firm produces misleading results (Henderson and Cockburn 1996: 35). Insider insights suggested that productivity in this part of the pharmaceutical industry could best be studied at the level of individual projects, so that cross-project productivity could be identified. Azoulay's (2004) study then goes on to reveal important sources of heterogeneity even within the drug testing activities in this industry: some testing should be kept in-house, while other testing should be outsourced. Thus, one reason for heterogeneity in practices within a single industry is the fact that firms are managing many different production processes at the same time.

4.5. Additional Insider Studies

The previous eight examples include some of the early research papers that use insider methods to model management treatments effects. To illustrate a broader range of topics, practices, and data analyzed with this kind of methodology, we present a longer list of studies in Table 1. This table summarizes the management practices studied, the nature of the dataset, and a short description of conclusions about the economic mechanisms that explain why productivity changes when the practice is adopted. The studies reviewed in Table 1 suggest that the methods in the examples above are representative. We refer to details of the studies mentioned in Table 1 when discussing emerging themes from insider econometric research (Section 8) and sources of data (Section 9).

Table 1. Additional insider econometric studies, by management practices analyzed

Type of study/reference/data	Performance outcome	Reason for outcome
Sets of complementary management practices		
Ichniowski et al. (1997) Data: team monthly productivity, 5 years, 36 steel production lines (17 companies)	Productivity rises by 10% due to combined use of incentives, teamwork, careful hiring, and other practices.	When firms implement multiple HRM practices, the complementarities between the practices raises performance.
Bloom et al. (2011b) Data: 20 textile plants, 1 year, in India	Productivity rises by 18% due to modern management practices in textile firms.	Managers did not have the information to adopt modern practices before experiment.
Duflo et al. (2009) Data: 70 schools in Kenya, 35 randomly treated with school-based management initiative	Student performance improves when schools adopt a set of practices, such as greater parental involvement and new hiring methods for teachers.	Performance improves for a set of management practices and curriculum and does not increase with added funding.
Griffith and Neely (2009) Data: retail stores, monthly sales, 72 months, one company	Productivity rises when the multidimensional Balanced Scorecard performance evaluation is introduced.	When Balanced Scorecard incentive pay is adopted, productivity rises only if managers are experienced.
Chan et al. (2009) Data: daily sales for 85 cosmetics sales workers, 791 days, 11 companies	Individual incentive pay raises individual productivity, but lowers within-team cooperation and lowers group productivity.	Individual incentive pay raises personal productivity, but it reduces cooperation and overall productivity. Team-based incentive pay increases cooperation within teams and increases competition across teams (or firms).
Baron and Hannan (2002) Data: 200 technology start-up companies in Silicon Valley, annual data, 1995 and 1997	Sets of innovative "star" HRM practices raise growth by 140% and reduce the probability of firm failure by 210%, relative to autocratic HRM practices.	The initial set of HRM practices that the start-up firm chooses has a large effect on all measures of firm success: "star" firms recruit only top talent, pay them top wages, and give them resources and autonomy. In autocratic firms, "you work, you get paid."
MacDuffie (1995) Data: 62 auto assembly plants	Productivity and quality outcomes are higher in plants that have systems of innovative HRM practices. Effects are larger if the plant also uses management practices for flexible production systems.	The organizational logic of lean manufacturing production processes is not supported by individual HRM practices but by multiple such practices that are elements of a system.

Continued

Table 1. *Continued*

Type of study/reference/data	Performance outcome	Reason for outcome
Sets of complementary management practices		
Dunlop and Weil (2000) Data: 42 business units in the men's suit, shirt, and pants sector and in the women's jeans and undergarment sectors of the apparel making industry	Lead times are substantially shorter when team-based systems of HRM practices in modular assembly production processes are used.	The adoption of team-based HRM systems in modular production processes is driven by the adoption of new complementary sales-tracking information technologies by large retailers who require apparel makers to fill smaller orders more rapidly. The effects of new HRM practices on performance outcomes are dependent on the effects of the use of new information technologies.
Berg et al. (1996) Data: production records and worker surveys from more than 100 workers in four plants of two apparel-making companies	Systems of HRM practices associated with the module system of manufacturing exhibit lower production costs, reduced throughput production times, reduced work-in-process inventories, and increased variety of clothing styles than seen in firms using HRM practices under the bundle system.	Team-based HRM practices under module production allow greater coordination of workers' activities that eliminates production bottlenecks and solves production problems.
Incentive pay		
Lazear (2000) Data: monthly measures of average daily output for 3,000 workers who install car windshields, 19 months, one company	Productivity of individual workers rises 44% due to a switch from hourly pay to piece rate pay.	Higher efforts by workers stemming from incentive pay raises productivity by 22%. Better sorting or selection of workers to the job raises productivity by an additional 22%.
Bandiera et al. (2005) Data: daily output for 142 workers, 108 days, picking fruit, one company	Productivity of workers increases by 58% when wages are switched to piece rate pay from a relative pay scheme.	Efforts of workers increase due to piece rate pay, because workers were withholding effort when friends were on their work teams.
Nagin et al. (2002) Data: daily data, 16 call centers, one company	Daily productivity of workers rises by about 3% when pay is tied to call monitoring.	Monitoring reduces instances of workers reporting unsuccessful sales calls as successes. Perceptions of a fair work culture also reduce this unproductive behavior.

Table 1. *Continued*

Type of study/reference/data	Performance outcome	Reason for outcome
Incentive pay		
Misra and Nair (2011) Data: monthly sales, 87 sales agents for contractors for 38 months, one company	Total revenues rose 9% following the introduction of an incentive pay plan that has a linear incentive (no quotas) and pays out more frequently.	A pay plan that is highly nonlinear and pays out over long intervals (quarters rather than months) results in gaming the system and in lower productivity for current employees.
Lavy (2002, 2008) Data: student test scores, 1 year, 629 teachers in the Israeli school system	Productivity of students rose 3% after the introduction of tournament bonus pay for teachers; it rose 1–6% in other similar plans.	Students' test scores in English and math improved due to a change in teaching methods and an increase in teachers' efforts in response to incentives.
Lerner and Wulf (2007) Data: 140 firms, 700 firm-years, compensation for R&D heads matched to patent data	R&D group productivity increased by 26%, as measured by citations or patents, when long-term incentives (measured as a percentage of pay) rose by 50%.	Use of long-term incentives for corporate heads of R&D departments rose 50% from 1988 to 1998 and is likely to have improved R&D project selection.
Peer effects		
Ichino and Maggi (2000) Data: 28,642 retail bank employees, 442 branches, 20 years, one company	Productivity (measured by absenteeism) rises by more than 15% when employees are located with peer employees who work harder.	Worker productivity is strongly influenced by personal background and culture, but these influences are reduced when workers are paired with more productive peers.
Mas and Moretti (2009) Data: all supermarket transactions, six stores, 2003–2006, one company, checkout clerks	Within a 10-minute work interval, personal productivity rises 1.7% when working near a peer who is 10% more productive than average.	The productivity gains from peer effects show that low-productivity workers work harder when a high-productivity worker watches them work.
Teamwork		
Hamilton et al. (2003) Data: weekly productivity, 132 workers, 156 weeks, apparel sewing, one company	Team-based pay increased productivity 14% compared to individual piece rate pay.	Team-based pay increases team output through collaboration among workers with complementary skills. Highly productive workers raise team productivity even more.

Continued

Table 1. *Continued*

Type of study/reference/data	Performance outcome	Reason for outcome
Teamwork		
Bartel et al. (2009a) Data: 431 hospital intensive care units, monthly productivity, 48 months, one company	Hospital units with more "unit-specific" human capital have a 1.5% reduction in patients' length of stay.	Teamwork in nurses' work area combines nurses' human capital, which raises productivity.
Boning et al. (2007) Data: 2,355 monthly productivity team-level observations for 34 steel minimills, 5 years, 19 companies	There is a 11–20% reduction in defective output when mills move to team-based problem solving.	Team-based problem solving is more valuable to the firm when the steel mill produces complex products than when it produces commodities.
Bandiera et al. (2009) Data: 407 fruit picking teams, 15 fields, 109 days	Productivity rises 24% when a team-based tournament reward system is introduced.	Workers of similar ability form teams in response to incentives; teams are not formed on the basis of friendship.
Social networks and information sharing		
Kalnins and Chung (2006) Data: 2,800 hotels, annual data for 1991–1999 on revenues, exit, and entry	Close social ties from same demographic group lowers the failure rate of hotels.	Employees from the same demographic group (Gujarati immigrants) share more information about management practices that work.
Bandiera et al. (2007) Data: daily worker output, 94 days, picking fruit, one company	Productivity increases by about 9% when workers are socially connected to managers who are paid incentives.	When the firm switches to incentive pay for managers, overall firm productivity rises, as managers allocate jobs to the most efficient workers rather than to their friends.
Gant et al. (2002) Data: daily communication ties among workers, 642 workers, 7 steel production lines	Direct communications for problem-solving is five times greater for workers on production lines with a set of innovative management practices.	Problem-solving activity, as measured by the amount of direct communications on operational issues, rises when workers are employed by firms using a set of management practices, such as teamwork, incentive pay, and careful hiring.

Table 1. *Continued*

Type of study/reference/data	Performance outcome	Reason for outcome
Hiring practices		
Autor (2001) Data: workers employed by 1,033 temporary help firms in 1994	The match quality of workers and firms is higher when workers self-sort in response to the firms' offers of general training.	Providing general human capital training induces workers to self-sort, so the most able are hired by firms offering the greatest amount of general training. (The temporary help firms then sell this worker-quality information to firms.)
Autor and Scarborough (2008) Data: 1,363 retail stores, one company	Productivity rises due to the switch from informal screening to test-based screening.	Testing yields more productive hires, resulting in a 10% increase in workers' average tenure.
Goldin and Rouse (2000) Data: orchestra auditions for 7,065 individuals, 508 audition rounds, 14,121 person-rounds	Promotion of women at each round of auditions increases by 50% when auditions are blind, and hiring of women increases substantially.	Better hiring techniques, such as reviewing orchestral auditions with a blind shield, substantially raises the percentage of women employed.
Lazear (2000) Data: monthly measures of average daily output for 3,000 workers who install car windshields, 19 months, one company	Productivity rises 22% when the most productive workers are hired and stay at the auto windshield installation firm.	Such HRM practices as incentive pay cause workers to self-select to the firms at which those workers are most productive.
Boundaries of the firm		
Forbes and Lederman (2010) Data: 2 million flights from 72 U.S. airports over 260 days	Flight delays at the same airport on the same day are significantly shorter for airlines that are vertically integrated (those with an owned, rather than independent, regional connecting partner).	Direct ownership of partner airlines promotes more efficient decisionmaking when airlines need to adapt to nonroutine conditions.

Note: HRM, human resource management.

5. Estimation of Treatment Effects and the Econometrics of Insider Studies

The kinds of productivity profiles shown in Figures 1–5 are typically estimated by analyzing panel data on workers or work teams. In this section, we consider issues that arise in applying econometric methods to obtain accurate estimates of treatment effects. Start with the simplest possible regression for estimating the impact of some management policy on productivity:

$$Y_{it} = \alpha D_{it} + \beta x_{it} + \eta_i + \epsilon_{it} \tag{1}$$

where i and t are subscripts for the worker- or work-group-specific observations and for time, respectively; Y_{it} is productivity;[20] x_{it} is a set of production function control variables; D_{it} is a dummy variable equal to 1 for the presence of the management practice; η_i is the worker-specific (or work-group) fixed effect; θ_t is the common time period effect; and ϵ_{it} is the transitory worker-specific effect. How should the insider econometrician elaborate on this simple model to estimate treatment effects of management practices on productivity?

A hallmark of insider econometric research is that it models the heterogeneity in workers' responses to the managerial practice. Even for workers within one occupation, there is heterogeneity in workers' responses to managerial treatments; for example, not all workers respond the same to incentive pay. This differential response is the reason management practices may not be effective. Translating this heterogeneity into the productivity regression, rewrite (1) to allow the treatment effect to vary across observations:

$$Y_{it} = \alpha_i D_{it} + \beta x_{it} + \eta_i + \theta_t + \epsilon_{it}. \tag{2}$$

The adoption of the management treatment D_t at time t^* is determined by its profitability:

$$D_{it} = \begin{cases} 1 & \text{if } \pi_{it} > 0 \text{ and } t > t^* \\ 0 & \text{otherwise} \end{cases} \tag{3}$$

$$\pi_{it} = \Gamma Z_{it} + v_{it}, \tag{4}$$

where the index π_{it} measures the expected profits from adopting the new practice; it is a function of observables Z_{it} and an error term.

Equations (3) and (4) imply that at time t^*, the treatment, some new management policy, is introduced. The treated group adopts ($D = 1$) when expected profits from adoption exceed zero. The nontreated group ($D = 0$) does not adopt, because expected profits after adoption are not sufficiently high. The treated group either has a different underlying production function or different underlying transition costs than the nontreated group. Because the adoption of the treatment is not random, selection bias arises.

---

20. Note we refer to Y_{it} as productivity, but the specific dependent variable used in any insider study is a measure of performance relevant to the setting of the specific study.

5.1. Estimating Treatment Effects

Insider econometricians typically estimate productivity regression (2)—a panel data regression with worker and time fixed effects. But what are the properties of the treatment effect estimated in this regression? To answer this question, rewrite the production function in a more general functional form in a switching regression framework.[21] The treated group has production function (5a), with superscript 1 to indicate $D = 1$ for treatment. The nontreated group has production function (5b), with superscript 0 to indicate $D = 0$ for nontreatment.

$$Y_{it}^1 = g_t^1(x_i) + u_{it}^1 \tag{5a}$$

$$Y_{it}^0 = g_t^0(x_i) + u_{it}^0, \tag{5b}$$

where x_i are basic production function variables that are not affected by the treatment and are uncorrelated with error term u_{it}.

Define the treatment effect as the productivity gain due to treatment, given by $\alpha_{it} = Y_{it}^1 - Y_u^0$. Given the productivity functions (5a) and (5b), the treatment effect is defined as

$$\alpha_{it}(x_i) \equiv g_t^1(x_i) - g_t^0(x_i) + \left(u_{it}^1 - u_{it}^0\right) \quad \text{for } t > t^*. \tag{6}$$

Intuitively, the treatment effect is the shift up in the production function after adoption. The estimated treatment effect, given real world data with nonrandom adoption of the treatment, is biased if the difference in the residual in (6) is not zero.

Now, rewrite the productivity equations to identify types of selection biases in the treatment effect. To form one productivity equation across the treated and nontreated groups, combine (5a) and (5b) by weighting them by the treatment dummy D_{it} to obtain

$$Y_{it} = D_{it}Y_{it}^1 + (1 - D_{it})Y_{it}^0.$$

Then, substitute into this equation the definition of the treatment effect from (6) with $\alpha_t = \bar{t}(\alpha_{it}) = g_t^1(x_i) - g_t^0(\bar{x}_i)$ to obtain

$$Y_{it} = g_t^0(x_i) + \alpha_t D_{it} + \left[u_{it}^0 + D_{it}\left(u_{it}^1 - u_{it}^0\right)\right]. \tag{7}$$

Equation (7) identifies the potential selection biases in the estimated treatment effect. The expected value of the treatment is

$$E(\hat{\alpha}_t) = \alpha_t + E(u_t^1 \mid x_t, D_t = 1) - E(u_t^0 \mid x_t, D_t = 0), \quad \text{with } t > t^*. \tag{8}$$

The two expected error terms are nonzero due to selection bias in the treatment—only those firms that gain the most from treatment will adopt.

21. This structure for the specification of treatment effects follows Blundell and Dias (2002). For further discussions of treatment effects and their estimation, see Meyer (1995), Heckman et al. (1999), Imbens (2004), List et al. (2010), and citations therein.

Equation (8) and Figure 1 can be combined to easily picture the three types of treatment effects that the insider econometrician might want to estimate with insider data:

1. The *treatment of the treated effect* (TTE) is the expected treatment effect among treated observations, that is, the mean value of the observation-specific treatment effects across all observations conditional on treatment occurring (i.e., $D_t = 1$) and on the production function control variables x_{it}:

$$\alpha^{\text{TTE}} \equiv E(\alpha_{it} \mid x = x_{it}, D_{it} = 1), \quad \text{with } t > t^*. \qquad (9)$$

    In Figure 1, this hypothetical treatment effect is $\alpha^{\text{TTE}} = \Delta P^{\text{T}}$.

2. The *treatment of the nontreated effect* (NTE) is the expected value for those groups who are never treated:

$$\alpha^{\text{NTE}} \equiv E(\alpha_{it} \mid x = x_{it}, D_{it} = 0), \quad \text{with } t > t^*. \qquad (10)$$

    In Figure 1, this hypothetical treatment effect is represented by $\alpha^{\text{NTE}} = \Delta P^{\text{N}}$. To illustrate potential selection bias, we assumed in Figure 1 that the treated group has bigger expected gains than the nontreated group would have.

3. The *average treatment effect* (ATE) is the average gain in productivity if the treatment were applied randomly across all i.

$$\alpha^{\text{ATE}} \equiv E(\alpha_{it} \mid x = x_{it}). \qquad (11)$$

    In Figure 1, it is the weighted average (with weights equal to the percentages of treated and nontreated subjects) of α^{TTE} and α^{NTE}.

Thus, TTE, NTE, and ATE are mean effects among the always treated observations, never treated observations, or randomly treated observations, respectively.

5.2. Estimation of Treatment Effects with Panel Data in Insider Studies

How do insider studies typically estimate the alternative treatment effects using panel data? First, we describe the estimation methods for alternative treatment effects and then provide examples from the literature for research using these alternative estimators.

Rewrite the production function (7) as

$$Y_{it} = g^0(x_{it}) + \alpha_{it} D_{it} + \eta_i + \theta_t + \epsilon_{it}, \qquad (12)$$

where η_i is the worker-specific fixed effect, θ_i is the common time period effect, and ϵ_{it} is the transitory worker-specific effect. Equation (12) matches the typical panel data regression presented in (2).

Depending on the exact nature of the panel dataset and the specific details of the treatment effect the researcher wants to estimate, there are four common options for estimating treatment effects in panel data.

5.2.1. First Differences

For this option, the researcher estimates the treatment of the treated, α^{TTE}, using data on only the treated group, before and after the treatment when the treatment is not randomly applied to workers or plants (i.e., the top productivity profiles in Figure 1). Estimate the production function (12) with first differences by introducing controls for the worker- or establishment-fixed effects and using only the before-after data for the treated group. The resultant α^{TTE} (for the Type 1 observations in Figure 1) is then equal to

$$\hat{\alpha}^{\mathrm{TTE}} = \left[\bar{Y}^1_{\mathrm{post}\text{-}t^*} - \bar{Y}^1_{\mathrm{pre}\text{-}t^*} \right], \tag{13}$$

which states that the treatment of the treated effect is the difference in the conditional means of the treated group before (the pre-t^* period) and after (the post-t^* period) the treatment. Assuming we know the right functional form and specification of $g^0(x_i)$, the unobserved counterfactual for the treated group in the post-t^* period can be estimated. Avoiding the use of the nontreated sample eliminates the need to make assumptions about that subsample—about why it was not treated and about its unobserved counterfactuals. An obvious drawback is that there are fewer observations when the nontreated sample is omitted, and we assume that time effects θ_t are uncorrelated with treatment D_{it}.

5.2.2. Difference-in-Differences Estimator

Researchers estimate the α^{ATE} effect using the difference-in-differences option when the treatment is randomly applied to a subpopulation of workers, plants, or stores, or when one can assume that the only difference between the control group and the treated group lies in the fixed effect η_i.[22] Given this assumption, the researcher has data on both the treated group, before and after the treatment, and on the nontreated group in Figure 1. Equation (12) is estimated with both the treated and nontreated samples, over time, so this option is double differencing, or "difference-in-differences," because we difference over time (before-after treatment) and cross-sectionally (for the treated and nontreated groups). This double differencing amends the estimated treatment effect (13) to be

$$\hat{\alpha}^{\mathrm{ATE}}(x) = \left[\bar{Y}^1_{\mathrm{post}\text{-}t^*} - \bar{Y}^1_{\mathrm{pre}\text{-}t^*} \right] - \left[\bar{Y}^0_{\mathrm{post}\text{-}t^*} - \bar{Y}^0_{\mathrm{pre}\text{-}t^*} \right], \tag{14}$$

which states that the average treatment effect is the difference in the conditional means of the treated group before (the pre-t^* period) and after (the post-t^* period) the treatment, relative to that difference for the nontreated group. The estimation method is the same as for first differences: we are differencing out the fixed effect η_i and then differencing out the effect θ_t, but here the second differencing occurs over treated and nontreated workers as well.

The basic advantage of double differencing compared to the first differencing is that we now have a control group, the nontreated group. Including the control group adds information in two ways. First, if we can assume that the time shocks θ_t are common between the two samples, then the nontreated control group lets us control for any time effects that altered productivity

---

22. Examples of this treatment can be found in Ichniowski et al. (1997), Lazear (2000), and Griffith and Neely (2009).

after t^* but are not due to the treatment. In contrast, first-difference models include no data on nontreated observations in the post-t^* period. Second, the control group gives us more information on which to estimate the underlying production function $g_t^0(x_i)$.[23]

5.2.3. Difference-in-Differences with Matching Estimator
For this option, the analyst again uses a difference-in-differences estimator and has the same data as in Figure 1 for difference-in-differences, but the matching estimator is estimating the production function nonparametrically. Each treated outcome $g_t^1(x_i)$ is paired with a nontreated outcome $g_t^0(x_i)$, and the difference is the treatment effect. Given the extra data needed for nonparametric estimation, few insider econometric studies use this approach.

5.2.4. Instrumental Variables or Semi-Parametric Methods
If there are nonrandom (selection bias) differences between control and treatment—between the Type 1 and Type 2 panels in Figure 1—then the researcher must address these differences. If there is selection bias, then ϵ_{it} is correlated with D_{it}, and we need to add instrumental variable (or matching) estimator techniques that model the selection of the treatment. We do not review these methods here.

The type of treatment effect that is estimated depends on both the type of data available and the reason why the management practice was adopted. For example, some field experiments are now being done within firms.[24] In those experiments with random assignment of new management treatments, the estimator is an average treatment effect conditional on being in the firm (Imbens 2004). It is an average treatment effect, because assignment of the treatment is random, but it is also conditional, because it depends on the reasons the firm agreed to adopt the practice. The estimated average treatment effect would not apply to other firms.

When data are gathered across work groups or plants, where some are adopters and others are not, the estimator is a treatment of the treated effect. The estimated treatment effect applies to those who adopt the treatment, not a random group or firm (e.g., Ichniowski et al. 1997; Boning et al. 2007). In these studies, the researcher tries to provide evidence on the adoption equation (3). Increasingly, studies in developing countries are imposing management treatments randomly across a set of firms in the education or health sector.

Table 1 gives many more examples, classified according to the management practices being studied. The table also describes the type of data and thus implies the likely type of estimator

---

23. A disadvantage of difference-in-differences estimation is that if the treated and nontreated groups should in fact have different coefficients on the control variables, then the estimators from the difference-in-differences models will be biased relative to first differences.

24. Bloom et al. (2011b) are randomly imposing lean manufacturing practices on a random set of small manufacturing firms in India that had not been using those practices. Thus, they are estimating the average treatment effect of lean manufacturing but cannot study the reasons some firms adopt and others do not. Duflo et al. (2012) introduce incentive pay for teachers randomly across a set of teachers and a control group. Presumably, in studies using random assignment of a management practice across workers or plants, identifying observations that enjoy relatively large and small treatment effects could offer clues about where adoption makes more economic sense. See Levitt and List (2009) for a review of the new field experiment literature.

of the treatment effect. For example, Griffith and Neely (2009) have data on an incentive pay treatment for treated and control groups of retail stores, so they use a difference-in-differences estimator with a matching estimator for the TTE.

5.3. Estimating Heterogeneous Treatment Effects in Insider Studies

Central to insider studies is that researchers are modeling variations across workers in their responses to a new management policy; that is, (2) allows heterogeneity in the response to the treatment. Management policies never should have a single treatment effect; people differ and technologies differ. Therefore, researchers increasingly gather additional data aimed at capturing this heterogeneity in responses to the treatment. Examples illustrating this point include:

- Bandiera et al. (2005) gather data on friendships among the work crew members, showing that those with friends respond more to piece rate pay.

- Mas and Moretti (2009) gather data on the physical location of workers in the grocery store, showing that when a checkout clerk is watched by a productive co-worker, she works harder.

- Gant et al. (2002) collect detailed data on workers' communications networks in steel production lines, showing that production lines with denser social networks are more likely to have innovative management practices and higher levels of productivity.[25]

6. Why Do Firms Adopt New Management Practices?

This question is crucial. To execute and interpret insider studies of the effects of management practices, we must know not only why the management practices were adopted by some establishments and not others but also why the adopters instituted the practices when they did. Economists believe that firms make optimal decisions about compensation plans, teamwork and related HRM practices, the scope and size of research projects, and whether to outsource certain work. So, why didn't Safelite adopt incentive pay for their windshield installers, or minimills put in problem solving teams, sooner than they did? Shouldn't these firms have always had these optimal practices? Fortunately, there are some clear reasons firms adopt new management policy treatments rather than having one set of optimal management practices from their inceptions.

There are several sources of time-series shocks to optimal management practices. First, there are shocks to the prices of capital inputs. If management practices are complements with capital inputs, then these practices change. Rapidly declining prices of new information technologies are an obvious recent shock. Several studies illustrate how, as information technology and

---

25. Of course, even great new datasets have their limits: we cannot extrapolate beyond the subgroups of workers who are employed by the firms. In econometric terms, we cannot extrapolate beyond the *common support*, which is the subspace of worker characteristics that are in the treated and nontreated samples.

processing become cheaper in firms, management practices also change.[26] New information technology in one industry also causes changes in management practices in related industries.[27] Furthermore, competitors in an industry are constantly changing, and new competitors can have modern management practices that force existing companies to change their practices.

There can also be technology shocks to management knowledge itself; best practices in management may improve over time. For example, the success of a distinctive set of management practices—including problem-solving teams, other innovative HRM practices, and lean manufacturing practices—among large Japanese manufacturers were slowly imported to other developed countries in the 1980s and 1990s.[28] Developing countries are still very slowly introducing these kinds of management practices to raise quality and productivity (see Bloom and Van Reenen 2007; Bloom et al. 2011b).

There are time series shocks to firms' external and internal labor markets. In a firm's internal labor market, stock options may become too diluted, or an aging workforce may need different incentive pay. External labor market shocks include immigration, which can increase the supply of workers with higher or lower levels of human capital than the existing workforce.

Cross-sectional within-industry shocks also exist. When firms enter an industry with new entrepreneurial ideas about the industry's products or processes, existing firms need to change product market strategies or processes. For example, as imports from Chinese firms enter U.S. markets, the U.S. firms move from the production of commodity-like products to customized products.[29] The production of customized products can change the demand for different types of workers, and as the skill or education levels of a workforce change, new management practices may be required.[30]

7. A Practical Roadmap for Designing Insider Econometric Studies

The insider econometrician is, in many ways, designing an empirical experiment. Even though the insider econometrician does not often conduct an experiment that can assign the management treatment, the researcher in insider studies is choosing the right firm to study, the questions to ask, hypotheses to test, the type of data and the variables to collect, and then the specific econometric methods to test the hypotheses. We identify five key design factors for insider econometric research.

26. For evidence, see Bresnahan et al. (2002) and Lemieux et al. (2009). Oliner and Sichel (2000) present macro-level evidence that productivity has increased over time in industries that use computers.

27. When large retailers adopted information technologies that tracked product sales and sent those sales data directly to suppliers, the suppliers adopted new team-based HRM practices that allowed them to restock the retailer with smaller batches on shorter notice (Dunlop and Weil 2000).

28. For more on the notion of HRM technology shocks, see Lazear and Shaw (2007) and Bloom and Van Reenen (2007). For more on the transfer of Japanese HRM practices to U.S. firms and the effects of these practices on productivity among manufacturers in the two countries, see Ichniowski and Shaw (1999).

29. In India, Bloom et al. (2011a) offer empirical evidence that reduced trade barriers increased the adoption of new HRM practices.

30. Product market strategies that favor customized versus commodity products are shown to affect the choice of management practices in the minimill industry (Boning et al. 2007) and in the valve manufacturing industry (Bartel et al. 2007).

7.1. Five Key Research Design Decisions

In this section, we provide advice about how to answer some of the more specific methodological questions that naturally arise when designing and executing an insider econometric study. In Section 2, we offered a list of five features that characterize insider econometric studies. These features tell us that insider studies use micro-level data on individual workers or groups of workers to study the productivity effects of a new management practice and the reasons for the adoption of the practice. Still, many more decisions must be made about specific features of an insider study. What management practices should I study? What should be the structure of the dataset? What can I do to address the concern that the data are specific to only one particular production process? Here we describe the features of studies that will produce the most convincing insider econometric results.

7.1.1. Key Design Decision 1: Identify a Treatment and Measure It Accurately

In most studies, the researcher must first identify a treatment variable that changes. Most firms that have interesting management practices never change them, and thus there is no variation for the treatment to test its effects. The treatment must also address an interesting theory that would predict that the treatment affects performance. The researcher may have a theory in mind and have been searching for data to test it, or she may be offered access to interesting data and have explored possible hypotheses by talking to insiders. Discussions with insiders always spark ideas; insiders know much more than the researcher knows about why they adopted the practice and the expected effects of the new practice.

How does the researcher obtain the treatment data? Many datasets have information on the productivity of workers or work groups, but they do not contain information on management practices. However, as in most examples of insider studies considered in Table 1, new management practices are discrete events that change infrequently in firms. The researcher can interview insiders and build a dataset on the time path of management practices in or across firms.

The treatment needs to be specified accurately. First, insider studies have several advantages over traditional surveys, and one is that the researcher can use interviews to measure exactly what the management practices are. In contrast, respondents to a survey question that asks "do you have teamwork?" may interpret the meaning of the question in many different ways. Insiders' insights help measure treatments accurately.

Second, the researcher needs to measure all dimensions of the management treatment. An important contribution of existing insider studies is that management treatments often involve the simultaneous adoption of a cluster of complementary management practices. The managers that researchers interview inside the firms will know that their new management initiative involved the adoption of multiple practices.[31]

---

31. MacDuffie (1995) finds that productivity is higher in auto plants that adopt several new HRM practices together with lean manufacturing methods and just-in-time inventory policies. Ichniowski et al. (1997) document improvements in productivity only when lines adopt entire systems of innovative HRM practices. Bartel et al. (2007) find that new computer-aided production equipment that raises productivity among customized valve manufacturers coincides with the adoption of complementary HRM practices. Azoulay (2004) identifies how the management decision to outsource drug trials always means the firm is putting the trial under a different compensation policy. See Milgrom and Roberts (1995) for discussions of complementarity.

Finally, the treatment need not always be a change in a formal management policy. Clever researchers are finding natural experiments in firms involving other kinds of treatments. For example, Mas and Moretti (2009) model the importance of peer effects on productivity. They identify the peer effects not from a change in management practices surrounding peer groups but instead from the movement of employees among different peer groups. That is, because workers are assigned randomly to different shifts, the authors can test whether working with different peers influences productivity. In another example, Lazear et al. (2011) model boss effects on workers' productivity. A good boss implements more effective training.

7.1.2. Key Design Decision 2: Test a Generalizable Principle by Modeling Economic Behavior

An important goal of insider econometric research is to test a more general economic principle that will enhance our understanding of the theory of the firm. In our review of eight insider studies in Section 4, we asked the question "why is this study interesting?" for each study. The answer was always that the results test a model of some fundamental economic principle. Even though only one firm or industry is studied, the testable hypothesis and results appear to be applicable to a wider set of workers or firms, because the paper models fundamental optimizing behavior.

Put differently, without insider datasets with rich details about the workers and production processes in a specific industry setting, convincing econometric tests of these fundamental models about worker and firm behavior would not be possible. The insider studies reveal factors that are routinely neglected in standard specifications of a firm's production function: friendship among co-workers, co-worker monitoring, complementarities among multiple HRM practices, interactions of HRM practices and product attributes, knowledge spillovers across workers and projects, and many more. Insider datasets that describe rich details about the context for a single production process are precisely the kind of data one needs to construct a convincing test of these novel hypotheses.[32] Insider studies are helping to develop a much more accurate picture of the economics of real production functions.

7.1.3. Key Design Decision 3: Balance Homogeneity and Heterogeneity in the Sample

Prior to insider studies, production functions were estimated with aggregate industry-level, firm-level, or establishment-level data in broad cross-industry samples. Although these data might be appropriate for estimating the effects of such factors as capital-labor ratios on productivity, they will be less helpful for identifying the effects of management practices on productivity and for isolating why similar organizations or workers are covered by different practices (see the discussion in Syverson 2011). With more aggregate data, there is not one common production process that generates the data. Therefore, the number of variables that might be correlated with the management treatment variable is exceptionally large.[33]

---

32. Consider the paper of Bandiera et al. (2005), in which friendships influence a worker's response to incentive pay (see Section 4.1.2). Their conclusion is not simply that friends influence people's behavior, but that when economists write a model of incentive pay, that model should include an externality—when maximizing utility in response to incentive pay, workers' responses internalize the externality of their friends' feelings. Economic theorists have introduced peer pressure and social norms into their theories of the firm (Kandel and Lazear 1992; Akerlof and Kranton 2000, 2005).

33. Differences in production equipment, worker and manager quality, occupational mix, and many other factors all could be correlated with differences in management practices and thus confound any attempts to use such industry-level data to generate a convincing estimate of a treatment effect due to any management practices. Of course, the methodological issues in generating a persuasive estimate of the effect of some management practice on

To mitigate the issues of unmeasured heterogeneity, insider studies seek data from production units—whether workers or work groups—that are very homogeneous. These workers all share one common production function that the researcher can model empirically—on-site car windshield installation, fruit picking in an orchard, finishing lines or rolling lines in steelmaking, and research projects or clinical testing processes in pharmaceuticals.

Although a homogeneous production function is important in insider studies, the insider dataset still needs heterogeneity to test hypotheses. Estimation of a treatment of the treated effect requires variance in the adoption of the management practice. Therefore, there must be subtle differences in the workers or organizations that lead to heterogeneity in the adoption of the treatment or in the response to a common treatment. The goal of sample design decisions in insider studies is to strike a purposeful balance between homogeneity in the production function and heterogeneity in either the adoption of the treatments or the magnitudes of the treatment effects.[34]

7.1.4. Key Design Decision 4: Collect Information on Why the Treatment Was Adopted

Once the researcher identifies a management innovation that varies across observations, she must understand why the treatment was adopted. Because the management treatments are rarely natural experiments, the researcher needs to collect information about the determinants of the adoption of the management practice being studied. Although this point is perhaps obvious, unless it is fully appreciated prior to data collection efforts, the researcher may focus only on data related to the production function and management practices and may miss opportunities to obtain data on the factors that cause adoption of the practices. When there is no systematic data available on adoption, a description of the reasons for adoption from industry insiders can still provide important insights about differences between adopters and nonadopters.

Some insider studies have concluded that, even though the data come from firms choosing optimal management practices, the treatment appears to be exogenous to the productivity regression. For example, when data describe worker-level productivity outcomes in a single firm, the management innovation is likely to be exogenous with respect to productivity outcomes. In these cases, the new management treatment is imposed by the firm on all its workers or establishments.[35] The management innovation can also be exogenous with respect to productivity

---

productivity extend well beyond issues of unmeasured heterogeneity and omitted variables. Measurement error in the dependent variable does not have to introduce bias in the estimated treatment effect in a production function. But production functions estimated with more aggregate data typically must rely on value-added data for the dependent variable, even though value added contains product mix changes that are not part of production per se and thus can differ dramatically from the variable the researcher hopes to be measuring. See Syverson et al. (2008) for a discussion of this point.

34. List et al. (2010) make this point about the trade-off between homogeneity and heterogeneity when designing optimal field experiments.

35. In the Safelite (Lazear 2000) and fruit picker (Bandiera et al. 2005) studies, the productivity data are on workers, and adoption is clearly exogenous to the worker. This is true for other studies of retail stores in a single firm (Lafontaine and Sivadasan 2009; Griffith and Neely 2009) or for teams of workers in an apparel firm (Hamilton et al. 2003). At the same time, as described in Section 4, there are still potential sources of selectivity in the application of the exogenous management practice: workers can leave or join the firm (and enter or leave the sample) after the firm imposes the practice (as in Lazear 2000); or workers might be the ones who decide to opt in or out of the new practice (as in the study of work teams by Hamilton et al. 2003).

outcomes across plants. In their integrated steel mills study, Ichniowski et al. (1997) conclude that expected productivity gains for nonadopters would be the same as those observed for adopters, but nonadopters are not willing to pay the transition costs of management changes.[36]

When the adoption is endogenous to productivity outcomes, researchers seek data to estimate the adoption regression. In minimills, mills adopting teamwork produce more complex products (Boning et al. 2007). In valve making, plants that adopt new information technologies produce more customized products (Bartel et al. 2007).

Researchers always want to know why firms do or do not adopt. Even in true experiments that impose new management practices randomly across firms, researchers ask: why don't firms adopt these practices on their own? For example, Bloom et al. (2011b) find that lean manufacturing practices raise productivity after these practices were randomly assigned in a sample of textile plants. A natural question to consider in light of these findings is why more of these plants do not use lean manufacturing and why the plants that were adopters in this study did not institute these practices on their own.

7.1.5. Key Design Decision 5: Collect Information on How Behavior Changes and Why the Treatment Was Successful

Even though insider econometric researchers use many different types of datasets and methodologies, all insider econometric studies document why the treatment was effective. In the broader treatment effects literature, this is typically not the case. When researchers study the effects of tax cuts on labor supply, researchers rarely collect data to explain why people increase their labor supply. However, in working with workers or establishments of firms, evidence on why the management practice is or is not effective is both available and essential. Models of the effects of management practices on productivity routinely model the reasons a practice is effective. Insiders can obtain the data to test these more detailed mechanisms and provide additional tests of the underlying model.

Consider some examples of the data researchers gather to test why management practices are effective. Bandiera et al. (2005) gather data on friendships among employees to show that a large gain in productivity after the firm switches from relative pay to piece rate pay is concentrated among employees who worked with friends and who were holding back their efforts under the old pay plan. Mas and Moretti (2009) gather data on where checkout clerks stand (relative to one another in the store) to document a large gain in the speed of grocery checkout clerks when a high-performing clerk joins a work shift. Gant et al. (2002) gather data on the communications social networks of all employees to show that interworker communication and problem-solving activities are much more pronounced among steel production lines with new HRM practices and higher productivity than they are in other lines. Many recent studies in behavioral economics are aimed precisely at showing how people behave in response to incentives or other HRM practices, and some of the most convincing evidence in insider econometric research describes the behavior of workers in treated and nontreated conditions.

36. With detailed insider data, it is possible to examine other reasons that could account for differences in the adoption of new practices. In the study of steel lines, for example, explanations related to differences in managerial quality, plant age, and prior productivity are tested and rejected, thus lending greater support to the conclusion that differences in transition costs explain nonadoption.

In sum, one advantage of doing insider research is that data are often available on why the treatment is effective, and these data allow the researcher to identify specific behavioral mechanisms that explain the connection between the management policy and the productivity outcomes. Insider studies are more convincing if they go beyond the estimation of a treatment effect. If additional data are collected about why the treatment is effective, the empirical work is more persuasive.

7.2. Detailed Steps to Take When Faced with Data

When faced with potential data from one or more firms, what should the researcher do? The following list offers some guidance:

1. Interview managers, workers, and others to learn about the mode of production and the management issues faced and addressed by the firm. Ask them to tell you what determines productivity. Learn the production process.

2. Identify a research question based on these interviews. Most researchers would not know the questions or potential hypotheses without the plant visits. Rule out some potential hypotheses.

3. Identify why this firm (or firms) has adopted these management practices and other firms have not.

4. Gather additional data needed for better tests of the hypotheses. Determine your econometric methods and how you will identify the appropriate treatment effect. If the data are on one new treatment in a single firm, can you collect data on factors that explain heterogeneity in observed treatment effects? If the data describe the adoption of the treatment across multiple firms or locations, can you collect data on the reasons for adoption versus nonadoption? Decide what is endogenous versus exogenous and where there might be measurement error or omitted variable bias.

5. Evaluate and interpret your results. Empirical researchers typically test the robustness of their models by introducing functional form changes. Insider econometric studies go a step further by asking the insider informants if the results make sense.

6. Collect additional data for more comprehensive and convincing tests. For example, though the primary model is a production function, it could be very persuasive to interview workers to gather other evidence to interpret or retest the results.

Insider studies identify factors that affect productivity, and they also identify what factors can be ruled out as determinants of productivity. Ruling out potential hypotheses can be as important as formulating new testable hypotheses. In cross-industry studies using firm-level data, the list of possible productivity determinants is endless. In insider studies, many possible reasons for productivity growth can be ruled out (or controlled for in the regressions) because of the narrow focus on a single production process, so the researcher can focus on testing the hypotheses that are most relevant to that firm, industry, or theoretical model.

Initial discussions with experienced insiders about how the production operations work can lead naturally to other steps. For example, the researcher may end up exploring managers' opinions about why some workers, work groups, or establishments are covered by the management treatment, whereas elsewhere the treatment is absent.

Ultimately, the researcher uses the real world experience of the industry insiders to inform their studies of the fundamental questions listed in Section 2. Why do some employees or organizations that appear to be competing in the same narrowly defined industry work under one set of managerial practices while others work under another set? When new practices are adopted, does productivity change, and do the changes in productivity vary across workers or establishments? Are there any changes in employee behavior that can help explain the changes in productivity?

8. Economic Lessons Learned from Insider Econometric Research

Many empirical findings across studies echo common themes. These broad economic themes emerging from insider studies can, we believe, provide guidance about the most promising avenues for developing richer theories of competing firms and their employees. In this section, we review several of these broad themes emerging from multiple insider studies.

1. Management matters. Effects of management practices on productivity can be big.

    The fundamental conclusion emerging from insider econometric research reviewed in this chapter is that management matters, and that it matters in several ways. First, insider studies routinely document substantial productivity effects from the adoption of new management practices. As examples, the magnitudes of the overall productivity gains among windshield installers in Lazear (2000) or fruit harvesters in Bandiera et al. (2005) are substantial—44% and 58%, respectively. Studies in many other industry settings reviewed above also show dramatic productivity increases after adoption of other new practices.

    Second, a wide array of management practices impact the productivity of workers, work groups, and plants in different industries. The two abovementioned examples focus on the productivity effects of incentive pay, but many other management practices are modeled in insider studies and are also shown to have big impacts (see Table 1).[37] Thus, managers must evaluate a very wide range of policy areas when deciding what practices would be optimal for their workers, their technologies, and their industries.

    Third, the large productivity gains arising from new management practice vary across firms in a given industry. Insider studies routinely document heterogeneity in the magnitude of performance gains across workers and plants that use similar production pro-

---

37. Even in the area of compensation policies, there are many other types of compensation plans that we have not reviewed. For example, tournaments are readily modeled in laboratory experiments, so there is extensive experimental evidence showing that tournaments can motivate individuals better than other kinds of incentive pay can in some settings (see Bull et al. 1987). See the insider studies of Knoeber and Thurman (1994) for producers of broiler chickens; Drago and Garvey (1998) for Australian firms, and Ehrenberg and Bognanno (1990) for professional golfers. Different methods for determining CEO or other top executive pay would be yet another set of management practices that impact firm performance.

cesses. Managers need to understand subtle within-industry differences in production or product mix to decide whether a new management practice will increase profits for their specific operations.

2. The productivity of an individual worker is determined by her work group.

   Several insider studies demonstrate that work groups matter. An individual's productivity is a function of her co-workers' productivity. Two work group effects stand out. First, productivity spillovers due to peer effects matter. When an employee is working next to a high performer, the employee works harder. We discussed this above regarding the Mas and Moretti (2009) paper showing that when a faster checkout clerk replaces a slower one on a shift, the shift becomes more productive not simply because the new clerk is faster than the old one, but because the other clerks also become faster.

   Second, employees are complements in production when they work as teams, and teams can be much more productive than individuals. Teamwork implies that workers do not have identical skills and thus can complement one another. In a team-based production function, output is not the sum of individual outputs but instead is a function of the multiplicative interaction among employees. Several insider papers reviewed above delve into the details of what makes work teams productive.[38]

   Third, a good boss makes his work team more productive by training more (Lazear et al. 2011). The quality of managers matters for work team productivity.

3. Employees respond to management practices at both the extensive margin of whether to work for the firm and the intensive margin in deciding how hard to work at their jobs.

   When firms introduce a new incentive pay plan, we expect workers to work harder and to target their efforts toward the output that is rewarded. This increase in effort operates on the worker's intensive margin (effort within the firm). Other management practices, such as teamwork or innovative job design, also aim to increase effort at the intensive margin. Management practices also have a big effect on workers at the extensive margin—on workers' decision to join the firm or the work group that offers the particular practice. Workers who do not like incentive pay avoid firms that pay for performance (Lazear 2000). In other cases, management can introduce teamwork into the firm but then leave it to the employees to join teams. There is selectivity in who joins which team (Hamilton et al. 2003). The key result is that when a firm chooses its management practice, it will cause worker sorting. Thus, the productivity gains that firms experience from management practices result from a combination of effort (the intensive margin) and optimal sorting (the extensive margin).

---

38. In steel finishing lines, problem-solving teams raise productivity because worker interactions become richer and more frequent. Problem solving requires interaction among co-workers (Gant et al. 2002). In apparel manufacturing, the productivity of work teams depends on the mix of skills and productivity levels of the team's members (Hamilton et al. 2003). In insider studies of orchards, the existence or absence of friendships among co-workers determines the extent to which efforts of the fruit pickers change after various kinds of incentive pay plans are adopted (Bandiera et al. 2005). In pharmaceuticals, the productivity of research on one project depends on knowledge spillovers from other related projects (Henderson and Cockburn 1996). Thus, in many settings, the true production function specifies not just an aggregate number of workers but also must capture the interactions among these individuals.

4. Firms compete using different product market strategies, and these different strategies require internal organizational structures to match the strategies.

   Two general reasons exist for the adoption of management practices. First, there are innovations in the best practices of management: much like the technology innovations of computers, there are technology innovations in how firms are managed. New ways of improving productivity are discovered. For example, innovations in modern methods of lean manufacturing and total quality management were introduced by large Japanese firms in the 1960s and 1970s and spread to manufacturers in other parts of the developed world in the decades that followed. When there are innovations in best practices, and some new management practices would raise productivity in all plants in an industry, only differences in adjustment and adoption costs prevent such adoption. This is the message of Ichniowski et al. (1997) and Bloom et al. (2011b).

   However, there is a second reason for the adoption of innovative practices: firms should adopt only the set of management practices that suits their strategy. Even though best practices are evolving over time, at any point in time, there are cross-sectional differences in the optimal adoption of practices. The business strategy literature has long recognized that firms in one industry compete in different product niches and therefore need different management practices. Low-cost mass producers coexist in industries alongside other businesses that serve customers who prefer higher cost specialty versions of the products. Several insider econometric studies document this link between product market strategy and internal management practices.[39] This link is an important result. It explains, in part, why some firms in an industry adopt certain management practices and other similar firms do not. It also explains why traditional output-per-personhour productivity measures will be higher for some firms than others in the same industry.

5. Management innovations often require the adoption of multiple practices that are complements of one another.

   Complementarities among management practices are pervasive. That is, the productivity gains from one management practice, such as problem-solving teams, interact with the gains from other practices, such as training, hiring, or compensation practices. Therefore, managers who are considering adopting one new management innovation cannot calculate the marginal gain from that practice independently of the set of other practices (Milgrom and Roberts 1990). There is extensive evidence from insider papers that choosing the right system of complementary practices increases productivity more than choosing individual practices in isolation.[40]

---

39. Minimills that make complex steel products adopt problem-solving teams more often than do minimills making commodity products (Boning et al. 2007). Valve manufacturers making more customized valve products adopt more innovative information technologies, training, and teamwork (Bartel et al. 2007). Software companies operating in market segments that have big upside gains to innovative software development pay higher wages and offer more performance pay than do software companies operating in more traditional product market niches (Andersson et al. 2009). Southwest Airlines, targeting bargain-hunting airline customers, uses different hiring and training and pay plans than does Singapore Airlines, which targets quality-conscious customers.

40. Ichniowski et al. (1997) document this result in the steel industry. In auto assembly plants, innovative HRM systems are typically adopted along with lean manufacturing methods and just-in-time inventory procedures

This review of broader themes emerging from the empirical findings of insider econometric research highlights how diverse and complex the determinants of productivity really are. Managers who want to achieve high levels of productivity from their workforces must consider a wide array of factors. Which employees are working together? What are the skill differences among co-workers, and what are their personal relationships like? When I adopt a new policy, am I likely to attract the kind of employee I really want, or will the better performers leave my firm? Is the new practice I am considering consistent with others I have in place, or do I need to change multiple practices? If I change my competitive business strategy, will I need to reconfigure how I manage my workforce? Insider econometric research paints a picture of the manager's job as one that is extremely challenging. As the first theme discussed in this section states, management certainly matters.

9. Data Sources for Insider Econometric Studies

In the insider studies reviewed above, researchers worked with firms to obtain data. That is not always necessary. As described in this section, researchers can use publicly available data and augment it with that from other sources or from their own surveys. Datasets may contain information on productivity or on management practices, but not both: researchers must combine data from several sources to obtain both. Many insider studies are now being conducted in education and health care, and in firms in developing economies. As researchers obtain data in these or other sectors, new insider studies will be possible. In the following list of possible data sources, we include lengthy footnotes with references to papers that have used data from these kinds of sources. However, the authors of these papers have also been creative in their use of data that spans these categories:

1. *Insider data from within one firm.* The firm provides the data.[41]
2. *Insider data from multiple firms in the same industry.* Researchers obtain data from the firms (through visits) or conduct surveys of the firms to measure management practices.[42] For surveys, the researchers use insider guidance to develop and administer their own

---

(MacDuffie 1995). In apparel manufacturing, new HRM systems are adopted when new information technologies that tie the manufacturer directly to large retailers are adopted (Appelbaum et al. 2000; Dunlop and Weil 2000). Decisions to adopt new information technologies are also linked with decisions to adopt a series of new HRM policies in valve manufacturing (Bartel et al. 2007) and in banking (Autor et al. 2002). Bresnahan et al. (2002) also find that HRM practices and new information technologies are complementary.

41. Studies in this category include Knoeber and Thurman (1994), Batt (1999), Lazear (2000), Autor et al. (2003), Hamilton et al. (2003), Bartel (2004), Gaynor et al. (2004), Bandiera et al. (2005, 2007, 2009), Bhattacherjee (2005), Freeman and Kleiner (2005), Encinosa et al. (2007), Kalmi and Kauhanen (2008), Griffith and Neely (2009), Jones and Kato (2011), and Lo et al. (2011).

42. Studies include Kruse (1993), Ichniowski and Shaw (1995, 2003), MacDuffie (1995), Berg et al. (1996), Huselid and Becker (1996), Oyer (1998), Dunlop and Weil (2000), Fernie and Metcalf (2003), Van Biesebroeck (2006), Bartel et al. (2007), Bloom and Van Reenen (2007), Boning et al. (2007), Kruse et al. (2008), and Bloom et al. (2011b, in press).

surveys, and the challenge is to obtain productivity data from the survey (or match it from a different dataset, e.g., census data).

3. *Insider analysis using data from public or regulated industries, such as education.*[43] The availability of data on teachers and students and keen interest in policy are resulting in much more insider work in education. Other regulated and government-funded industries—such as health care, trucking, and electricity generation—often have data available. The researcher may need to conduct surveys or visit firms to obtain information on HRM practices to link to the productivity data.

4. *Insider analysis using census data or datasets from consulting firms or industry associations.*[44] Some industries are followed by the U.S. Census Department, such as trucking, retail trade, and manufacturing industries. Some industries have consulting firms that follow the industry, as for venture capital. And some industries have industry associations or the desire to publicize their firm's attributes, as for franchising and law.

5. *Insider analysis using employer-employee matched datasets that are available for entire countries.* In Europe, the United States, and some developing countries, national census departments are matching data on individual workers to data from the firms where they work. These datasets span all workers in all industries. But it may be wise to take subsets of these datasets for certain industries or occupations and delve deeper into the production function. Though the datasets do not contain measures of management practices, researchers can use the wages and mobility of all workers in the firm to infer the sorts of HRM practices that firms are adopting.[45]

6. *Insider analysis using data from developing countries.* There are increasing numbers of papers with randomized treatments of management practices on performance: Two papers were reviewed in Section 4.3 (see Duflo et al. 2009, 2011, 2012). Such studies that measure average treatment effects offer some unique opportunities to identify observations that enjoy relatively large or small productivity impacts, which in turn could help identify the causes for any observed heterogeneity in the treatment effects.

To obtain data on both productivity outcomes and management practices, the researcher will often need to merge several datasets. Helper (2000) discusses additional issues and ideas on working with firms and their data. When working with firms, it is important for researchers to show what they can do for the firm, while acknowledging the importance of the firm's generosity in these efforts aimed at furthering our knowledge of how businesses really operate.

---

43. For education, see Kreuger (1999), Eberts et al. (2000), Hoxby (2002), Lavy (2002, 2008), Jacob and Levitt (2003), Rivkin et al. (2005), and Duflo et al. (in press). For other sectors, see Asch (1990), Baker and Hubbard (2003), Dranove et al. (2003), Dee and Keys (2004), Rosenthal et al. (2004), Kalnins and Chung (2006), Garicano and Heaton (2010), Propper and Van Reenen (2010), and Imberman et al. (2012).

44. See Clark (1980), Landers et al. (1996), Lafontaine and Shaw (1999, 2005), Hubbard (2000), Black and Lynch (2001, 2004), Baker and Hubbard (2003), Oyer and Schaefer (2007), Autor and Scarborough (2008), and Garicano and Hubbard (2009).

45. See Andersson et al. (2009) for work using employer-employee matched data for the software industry. See Lazear and Shaw (2007) for examples of other papers and the range of possible datasets.

10. Conclusion

Insider econometric research has two goals. First, combine information from inside the firm with sound econometric methods to estimate the impact of management practices on productivity. Second, use these results to enrich our theories of the firm.

Insider econometric studies focus on three basic questions:

1. Does a new management practice raise productivity?
2. Why does the new management practice raise productivity?
3. Why is the new management practice adopted?

Ultimately, designing and executing a study that answers these questions is part art and part science. Decisions about which management practices to study and how to measure them, about how to balance homogeneity and heterogeneity in the design of the sample and dataset, and about the many aspects of modeling the determinants of performance require careful judgment. This chapter offers guidance on the many decisions involved in conducting insider studies.

In many ways, the insider econometrician must be an expert translator. The researcher must translate the real world experience of the industry insiders into a dataset and research design that persuasively models fundamental questions about worker and firm behavior. The research designs of insider econometric research rely on rich micro-level data on workers or work groups from a single industry and production process. Although the empirical tests pertain to one industry setting, it is precisely this kind of detailed information about new management practices, worker characteristics, the production process, product characteristics, and other aspects of the industry setting that allows the researcher to test new theories about what makes workers productive and firms productive and profitable.

Why do we need more insider econometric studies? These studies address three needs. First, the science of economics evolves, and we are improving and updating our models. Empirical work on real workers and work sites will give us further guidance on this path, providing new insights while testing and refining old models. Second, we wish to better understand the causes of economic growth, and the impacts of management practices on productivity growth is one component of this larger topic. Third, models that incorporate more of the realism of contemporary firms will improve the advice we offer managers.

Why do we expect there to be more insider econometric studies? Management practices are constantly being updated, markets are changing, and data about these changes are becoming more prevalent in firms. Firms are experimenting more. Firms will need more guidance from researchers who are trained in analyzing these newly available data as managers move toward data-driven management decisions. Therefore, more researchers will seek to understand why, when, and how much management practices matter.

REFERENCES

Akerlof, George A., and Rachel Kranton. 2000. "Economics and Identity." *Quarterly Journal of Economics* 15: 715–753.

———. 2005. "Identity and the Economics of Organizations." *Journal of Economic Perspectives* 19(1): 9–32.

Andersson, Fredrik, Matthew Freedman, John C. Haltiwanger, Julia Lane, and Kathryn L. Shaw. 2009. "Reaching for the Stars: Who Pays for Talent in Innovative Industries?" *Economic Journal* 119: F308–F332.

Appelbaum, Eileen, Thomas Bailey, Peter Berg, and Arne Kalleberg. 2000. *Manufacturing Advantage: Why High-Performance Work Systems Pay Off.* Ithaca, NY: Cornell University Press.

Asch, Beth J. 1990. "Do Incentives Matter?—The Case of Navy Recruiters." *Industrial and Labor Relations Review* 43: 89–106.

Autor, David H., and David Scarborough. 2008. "Does Job Testing Harm Minority Workers? Evidence from Retail Establishments." *Quarterly Journal of Economics* 123: 219–277.

Autor, David H., Frank Levy, and Richard Murname. 2002. "Upstairs Downstairs: Computers and Skills in Two Floors of a Large Bank." *Industrial and Labor Relations Review* 55: 432–447.

———. 2003. "The Skill Content of Recent Technological Change: An Empirical Investigation." *Quarterly Journal of Economics* 118: 1279–1333.

Azoulay, Pierre. 2004. "Capturing Knowledge within and across Firm Boundaries: Evidence from Clinical Development." *American Economic Review* 94: 1591–1612.

Baker, George P., and Thomas N. Hubbard. 2003. "Make versus Buy in Trucking: Asset Ownership, Job Design, and Information." *American Economic Review* 93: 551–572.

Bandiera, Oriana, Iwan Barankay, and Imran Rasul. 2005. "Social Preferences and the Response to Incentives: Evidence from Personnel Data." *Quarterly Journal of Economics* 120: 917–962.

———. 2007. "Incentives for Managers and Inequality among Workers: Evidence from a Firm-Level Experiment." *Quarterly Journal of Economics* 122: 729–773.

———. 2009. "Social Connections and Incentives in the Workplace: Evidence from Personnel Data." *Econometrica* 77: 1047–1094.

Baron, James, and Michael Hannan. 2002. "Organizational Blueprints for Success in High-Tech Start-Ups: Lessons from the Stanford Project on Emerging Companies." *California Management Review* 44(3): 8–36.

Bartel, Ann. 2004. "Human Resource Management and Organizational Performance: Evidence from Retail Banking." *Industrial and Labor Relations Review* 57: 181–203.

Bartel, Ann, Casey Ichniowski, and Kathryn Shaw. 2007. "How Does Information Technology Affect Productivity? Plant-Level Comparisons of Product Innovation, Process Improvement, and Worker Skills." *Quarterly Journal of Economics* 122: 1721–1758.

Bartel, Ann, Ciaran Phibbs, Nancy Beaulieu, and Patricia Stone. 2009a. "Human Capital and Productivity: The Case of Nursing Teams." Working paper, Columbia University Graduate School of Business, New York.

Bartel, Ann, Casey Ichniowski, Kathryn Shaw, and Ricardo Correa. 2009b. "International Differences in the Adoption and Impact of New Information Technologies and New HR Practices: The Valve Making Industry in the U.S. and U.K.," in Richard Freeman and Kathryn Shaw (eds.), *International Differences in the Business Practices and Productivity of Multinational Firms.* Chicago and Cambridge, MA: University of Chicago and National Bureau of Economic Research.

Batt, Rosemary. 1999. "Work Organization, Technology, and Performance in Customer Services and Sales." *Industrial and Labor Relations Review* 52: 539–564.

Berg, Peter, Eileen Appelbaum, Thomas Bailey, and Arne L. Kalleberg. 1996. "The Performance Effects of Modular Production in the Apparel Industry." *Industrial Relations* 35: 356–374.

Bhattacherjee, Debashish. 2005. "The Effects of Group Incentives in an Indian Firm: Evidence from Payroll Data." *Labour* 19: 147–173.

Black, Sandra, and Lisa Lynch. 2001. "How to Compete: The Impact of Workplace Practices and Information Technology on Productivity." *Review of Economics and Statistics* 83:434–445.

———. 2004. "What's Driving the New Economy? The Benefits of Workplace Innovation." *Economic Journal* 114: 97–116.

Bloom, Nick, and John Van Reenen. 2007. "Measuring and Explaining Management Practices across Firms and Countries." *Quarterly Journal of Economics* 122: 1351–1408.

Bloom, Nick, Mirko Draca, and John Van Reenen. 2011a. "Trade Induced Technical Change? The Impact of Chinese Imports on IT and Productivity." NBER Working Paper 16717, National Bureau of Economic Research, Cambridge, MA.

Bloom, Nick, Benn Eifert, Aprajit Mahajan, David McKenzie, and John Roberts. 2011b. "Management as a Technology: Evidence from Indian Firms." NBER Working Paper 16658, National Bureau of Economic Research, Cambridge, MA.

Bloom, Nick, Christos Genakos, Raffaella Sadun, and John Van Reenen. In press. "Management Practices across Firms and Countries." *Academy of Management Perspectives.*

Blundell, Richard, and Monica Costa Dias. 2002. "Alternative Approaches to Evaluation in Empirical Microeconomics." *Portuguese Economic Journal* 1: 91–115.

Bollinger, Bryan, Phillip Leslie, and Alan Sorensen. 2011. "Calorie Posting in Chain Restaurants." *American Economic Journal: Economic Policy* 3: 91–128.

Boning, Brent, Casey Ichniowski, and Kathryn Shaw. 2007. "Opportunity Counts: Teams and the Effectiveness of Production Incentives." *Journal of Labor Economics* 25: 613–650.

Bose, Katherine, and Kathryn Shaw. 2008. "Shiny and New: The Evolution of ISG and Arcelor-Mittal Steel." Case E-285, Stanford University Graduate School of Business, Stanford, CA.

Bresnahan, Timothy, Erik Brynjolfsson, and Loren Hitt. 2002. "Information Technology, Work Organization and the Demand for Skilled Labor: Firm-Level Evidence." *Quarterly Journal of Economics* 117: 339–376.

Bull, Clive, Andrew Schotter, and Keith Weigelt. 1987. "Tournaments and Piece Rates: An Experimental Study." *Journal of Political Economy* 95: 1–33.

Chan, Tat, Jia Li, and Lamar Pierce. 2009. "Compensation and Peer Effects in Competing Sales Teams." Working paper, Washington University, St. Louis, MO.

Chu, Sean, Phillip Leslie, and Alan Sorensen. 2011. "Bundle-Size Pricing as an Approximation to Mixed Bundling." *American Economic Review* 101: 263–303.

Clark, Kim B. 1980. "The Impact of Unionization on Productivity: A Case Study." *Industrial and Labor Relations Review* 33: 451–469.

Dee, Thomas, and Benjamin Keys. 2004. "Does Merit Pay Reward Good Teachers? Evidence from a Randomized Experiment." *Journal of Policy Analysis and Management* 23: 471–488.

De Giorgi, Giacomo, Michele Pellizzari, and William Gui Woolston. 2009. "Class Size and Class Heterogeneity." IZA Discussion Paper 4443, Institute for the Study of Labor, Bonn, Germany.

Doyle, Joseph J., Steven Ewer, and Todd Wagner. 2010. "Returns to Physician Human Capital: Analyzing Patients Randomized to Physician Teams." *Journal of Health Economics* 29: 866–882.

Drago, Robert, and Gerald T. Garvey. 1998. "Incentives for Helping on the Job: Theory and Evidence." *Journal of Labor Economics* 16: 1–24.

Dranove, David, Daniel Kessler, Mark McClellan, and Mark Satterthwaite. 2003. "Is More Information Better? The Effects of 'Report Cards' on Health Care Providers." *Journal of Political Economy* 111: 555–588.

Duflo, Esther, Pascaline Dupas, and Michael Kremer. 2009. "Additional Resources versus Organizational Changes in Education: Experimental Evidence from Kenya." Working paper, Massachusetts Institute of Technology, Cambridge, MA.

———. 2011. "Peer Effects, Teacher Incentives, and the Impact of Tracking: Evidence from a Randomized Evaluation in Kenya." *American Economic Review* 101: 1739–1774.

Duflo, Esther, Rema Hanna, and Stephen Ryan. 2012. "Incentives Work: Getting Teachers to Come to School." *American Economic Review* 102: 1241–1278.

Dunlop, John T., and David Weil. 2000. "Diffusion and Performance of Modular Production in the U.S. Apparel Industry," in Casey Ichniowski, David Levine, Craig Olson, and George Strauss (eds.), *The American Workplace: Skills, Compensation and Employee Involvement*. Cambridge: Cambridge University Press, pp. 38–61.

Eberts, Randall, Kevin Hollenbeck, and Joe Stone. 2000. "Teacher Performance Incentives and Student Outcomes." *Journal of Human Resources* 37: 913–927.

Ehrenberg, Ronald G., and Michael L. Bognanno. 1990. "The Incentive Effects of Tournaments Revisited: Evidence from the European PGA Tour." *Industrial and Labor Relations Review* 43: 74–88.

Encinosa, William E. III, Martin Gaynor, and James B. Rebitzer. 2007. "The Sociology of Groups and the Economics of Incentives: Theory and Evidence on Compensation Systems." *Journal of Economic Behavior and Organization* 62: 187–214.

Fernie, Sue, and David Metcalf. 2003. "It's Not What You Pay It's the Way That You Pay It and That's What Gets Results: Jockeys' Pay and Performance." *Review of Labour Economics and Industrial Relations* 13: 385–411.

Forbes, Silke J., and Mara Lederman. 2010. "Does Vertical Integration Affect Firm Performance? Evidence from the Airline Industry." *RAND Journal of Economics* 41: 765–790.

Freeman, Richard B., and Morris M. Kleiner. 2005. "The Last American Shoe Manufacturers: Decreasing Productivity and Increasing Profits in the Shift from Piece Rates to Continuous Flow Production." *Industrial Relations* 44: 307–330.

Gant, Jon, Casey Ichniowski, and Kathryn Shaw. 2002. "Social Capital and Organizational Change in High-Involvement and Traditional Work Organizations." *Journal of Economics and Management Strategy* 11: 289–328.

Garicano, Luis, and Paul Heaton. 2010. "Information Technology, Organization, and Productivity in the Public Sector: Evidence from Police Departments." *Journal of Labor Economics* 28: 167–201.

Garicano, Luis, and Tom Hubbard. 2009. "Specialization, Firms and Markets: The Division of Labor within and between Law Firms." *Journal of Law, Economics, and Organization* 25: 311–338.

Gaynor, Martin, James B. Rebitzer, and Lowell J. Taylor. 2004. "Physician Incentives in HMOs." *Journal of Political Economy* 112: 915–931.

Goldin, Claudia, and Cecilia Rouse. 2000. "Orchestrating Impartiality: The Impact of Blind Auditions on the Sex Composition of Orchestras." *American Economic Review* 90: 715–741.

Griffith, Rachel, and Andy D. Neely. 2009. "Incentives and Managerial Experience in Multi-Task Teams: Evidence from within a Firm." *Journal of Labor Economics* 27: 48–82.

Haltiwanger, John. 2008. "Top Ten Questions for Understanding Firm Dynamics and Productivity Growth." Keynote address at the "Comparative Analysis of Enterprise Data Conference," May 24, Budapest, Hungary.

Hamilton, Barton, Jack Nickerson, and Hideo Owan. 2003. "Team Incentives and Worker Heterogeneity: An Empirical Analysis of the Impact of Teams on Productivity and Participation." *Journal of Political Economy* 111: 465–497.

Heckman, James J., Robert Lalonde, and J. Smith. 1999. "The Economics and Econometrics of Active Labor Market Programs," in Orley Ashenfelter and David Card (eds.), *Handbook of Labor Economics,* volume 3. Amsterdam: Elsevier Science, pp. 1865–2097.

Helper, Susan. 2000. "Economists and Field Research: 'You Can Observe a Lot by Just Watching.'" *American Economic Review* 90: 228–232.

Henderson, Rebecca, and Iain Cockburn. 1996. "Scale, Scope, and Spillovers: Determinants of Research Productivity in the Pharmaceutical Industry." *RAND Journal of Economics* 27: 32–59.

Hoxby, Caroline. 2002. "Would School Choice Change the Teaching Profession?" *Journal of Human Resources* 37: 846–891.

Hubbard, Thomas N. 2000. "The Demand for Monitoring Technologies: The Case of Trucking." *Quarterly Journal of Economics* 115: 533–560.

Huselid, Mark, and Brian Becker. 1996. "High Performance Work Systems and Firm Performance: Cross-Sectional versus Panel Estimates." *Industrial Relations* 35: 635–672.

Ichino, Andrea, and Giovanni Maggi. 2000. "Work Environment and Individual Background: Explaining Regional Shirking Differentials in a Large Italian Firm." *Quarterly Journal of Economics* 115: 1057–1090.

Ichniowski, Casey, and Kathryn Shaw. 1995. "Old Dogs and New Tricks: Determinants of the Adoption of Productivity-Enhancing Work Practices." *Brookings Papers on Economic Activity: Microeconomics:* 1–65.

———. 1999. "The Effects of Human Resource Systems on Productivity: An International Comparison of U.S. and Japanese Plants." *Management Science* 45: 704–722.

———. 2003. "Beyond Incentive Pay: Insiders' Estimates of the Value of Complementary Human Resource Management Practices." *Journal of Economic Perspectives* 17(1): 155–180.

———. 2009. "Connective Capital as Social Capital: The Value of Problem-Solving Networks for Team Players in Firms." NBER Working Paper 15619, National Bureau of Economic Research, Cambridge, MA.

Ichniowski, Casey, Kathryn Shaw, and Giovanna Prennushi. 1997. "The Effects of Human Resource Management Practices on Productivity: A Study of Steel Finishing Lines." *American Economic Review* 86: 291–313.

Imbens, Guido. 2004. "Nonparametric Estimation of Average Treatment Effects under Exogeneity: A Review." *Review of Economics and Statistics* 86: 4–29.

Imberman, Scott, Adriana Kugler, and Bruce Sacerdote. 2012. "Katrina's Children: A Natural Experiment in Peer Effects from Hurricane Evacuees." *American Economic Review,* forthcoming.

Ingram, Paul, and Peter Roberts. 2000. "Friendships among Competitors in the Sydney Hotel Industry." *American Journal of Sociology* 106: 387–423.

Jacob, Brian, and Steven Levitt. 2003. "Rotten Apples: An Investigation of the Prevalence and Predictors of Teacher Cheating." *Quarterly Journal of Economics* 118: 843–877.

Jones, Derek C., and Takao Kato. 2011. "The Impact of Teams on Output, Quality and Downtime: An Empirical Analysis Using Individual Panel Data." *Industrial and Labor Relations Review* 64: 215–240.

Kalmi, Panu, and Antti Kauhanen. 2008. "Workplace Innovations and Employee Outcomes: Evidence from Finland." *Industrial Relations* 47: 430–459.

Kalnins, Arturs, and Wilbur Chung. 2006. "Social Capital, Geography, and Survival: Gujarati Immigrant Entrepreneurs in the U.S. Lodging Industry." *Management Science* 52: 233–247.

Kandel, Eugene, and Edward Lazear. 1992. "Peer Pressure and Partnerships." *Journal of Political Economy* 100: 801–817.

Knoeber, Charles R., and Walter N. Thurman. 1994. "Testing the Theory of Tournaments: An Empirical Analysis of Broiler Production." *Journal of Labor Economics* 12: 155–179.

Kreuger, Alan. 1999. "Experimental Estimates of Education Production Functions." *Quarterly Journal of Economics* 114: 497–532.

Kruse, Douglas. 1993. *Profit Sharing: Does It Make a Difference?* Kalamazoo, MI: W. E. Upjohn Institute for Employment Research.

Kruse, Douglas, Joseph Blasi, and Rhokeum Park. 2008. "Shared Capitalism in the U.S. Economy: Prevalence, Characteristics, and Employee Views of Financial Participation in Enterprises." NBER Working Paper 14225, National Bureau of Economic Research, Cambridge, MA.

Lafontaine, Francine, and Kathryn Shaw. 1999. "The Dynamics of Franchise Contracting: Evidence from Panel Data." *Journal of Political Economy* 107: 1041–1080.

———. 2005. "Targeting Managerial Control: Evidence from Franchising." *RAND Journal of Economics* 36: 131–150.

Lafontaine, Francine, and Jagadeesh Sivadasan. 2009. "Within-Firm Labor Productivity across Countries: A Case Study," in Richard Freeman and Kathryn Shaw (eds.), *International Differences in the Business Practices and Productivity of Multinational Firms.* Chicago and Cambridge, MA: University of Chicago Press and National Bureau of Economic Research.

Landers, Renee M., James B. Rebitzer, and Lowell J. Taylor. 1996. "Rat Race Redux: Adverse Selection in the Determination of Work Hours in Law Firms." *American Economic Review* 86: 329–348.

Lavy, Victor. 2002. "Evaluating the Effect of Teachers' Group Performance Incentives on Students Achievements." *Journal of Political Economy* 110: 1286–1317.

———. 2008. "Gender Differences in Market Competitiveness in a Real Workplace: Evidence from Performance Based Pay Tournaments among Teachers." NBER Working Paper 14338, National Bureau of Economic Research, Cambridge, MA.

Lawler, Edward, and Susan Mohrman. 2003. *Creating a Strategic Human Resource Organization.* Stanford University Press, Stanford, CA.

Lazear, Edward. 1999. "Personnel Economics: Past Lessons and Future Directions." *Journal of Labor Economics* 17: 199–236.

———. 2000. "Performance Pay and Productivity." *American Economic Review* 90: 1346–1361.

Lazear, Edward, and Kathryn Shaw. 2007. "Personnel Economics: The Economist's View of Human Resources." *Journal of Economic Perspectives* 21(4): 91–114.

Lazear, Edward, Kathryn Shaw, and Christopher Stanton, 2011. "The Value of Bosses." Working paper, Stanford University Graduate School of Business, Stanford, CA.

Ledford, G. E. Jr., Edward Lawler III, and Susan Mohrman. 1995. "Reward Innovation in Fortune 1000 Companies." *Compensation and Benefits Review* 27: 76–80.

Lemieux, Thomas, Bentley MacLeod, and Daniel Parent. 2009. "Performance Pay and Wage Inequality." *Quarterly Journal of Economics* 124: 1–49.

Lerner, Josh, and Julie Wulf. 2007. "Innovation and Incentives: Evidence from Corporate R&D." *Review of Economics and Statistics* 89: 634–644.

Leslie, Phillip. 2004. "Price Discrimination in Broadway Theatre." *RAND Journal of Economics* 35: 520–541.

Levitt, Steven D., and John List. 2009. "Field Experiments in Economics: The Past, the Present, and the Future." *European Economic Review* 53: 1–18.

List, John, Sally Sadoff, and Mathis Wagner. 2010. "So You Want to Run an Experiment, Now What? An Introduction to Optimal Sample Arrangements." NBER Working Paper 15701, National Bureau of Economic Research, Cambridge, MA.

Lo, Desmond, Mrinal Ghosh, and Francine Lafontaine. 2011. "The Incentive and Selection Roles of Salesforce Compensation Contracts." *Journal of Marketing Research* 48: 781–798.

MacDuffie, John Paul. 1995. "Human Resource Bundles and Manufacturing Performance: Organizational Logic and Flexible Production Systems in the World Auto Industry." *Industrial and Labor Relations Review* 48: 197–221.

Mas, Alexandre, and Enrico Moretti. 2009. "Peers at Work." *American Economic Review* 99: 112–145.

Meyer, Bruce. 1995. "Natural and Quasi-Experiments in Economics." *Journal of Business and Economic Statistics* 13: 151–161.

Milgrom, Paul, and John Roberts. 1990. "The Efficiency of Equity in Organizational Decision Processes." *American Economic Review* 80: 154–159.

———. 1995. "Complementarities and Fit: Strategy, Structure and Organizational Change in Manu-facturing." *Journal of Accounting and Economics* 19: 179–208.

Misra, Sanjog, and Harikesh Nair. 2011. "A Structural Model of Sales-Force Compensation: Dynamics Estimation and Field Implementation." *Quantitative Marketing and Economics* 9: 211–225.

Nagin, Daniel S., James B. Rebitzer, Seth Sanders, and Lowell J. Taylor. 2002. "Monitoring, Motivation, and Management: The Determinants of Opportunistic Behavior in a Field Experiment." *American Economic Review* 92: 850–873.

Oliner, Stephen D., and Daniel E. Sichel. 2000. "The Resurgence of Growth in the Late 1990s: Is Information Technology the Story?" *Journal of Economic Perspectives* 14(4): 3–22.

Osterman, Paul. 1994. "How Common Is Workplace Transformation and Who Adopts It?" *Industrial and Labor Relations Review* 47: 173–188.

———. 2000. "Work Reorganization in an Era of Restructuring: Trends in Diffusion and Effects on Employee Welfare." *Industrial and Labor Relations Review* 53: 179–196.

Oyer, Paul. 1998. "Fiscal Year Ends and Non-Linear Incentive Contracts: The Effect on Business Seasonality." *Quarterly Journal of Economics* 113: 149–185.

Oyer, Paul, and Scott Schaefer. 2007. "Personnel-Economic Geography: Evidence from Large US Law Firms." Paper presented at the "2nd Annual Conference on Empirical Legal Studies," June 29, New York.

———. 2011. "Personnel Economics: Hiring and Incentives," in Orley Ashenfelter and David Card (eds.), *Handbook of Labor Economics,* volume 4b. Amsterdam: North-Holland, pp. 1769–1823.

Propper, Carol, and John Van Reenen. 2010. "Can Pay Regulation Kill? Panel Data Evidence on the Effect of Labor Markets on Hospital Performance." *Journal of Political Economy* 118: 222–273.

Rebitzer, James, and Lowell Taylor. 2011. "Extrinsic Rewards and Intrinsic Motives: Standard and Behavioral Approaches to Agency and Labor Markets," in Orley Ashenfelter and David Card (eds.), *Handbook of Labor Economics,* volume 4a. Amsterdam: North-Holland, pp. 701–772.

Rivkin, Steven, Eric Hanushek, and John Kain. 2005. "Teachers, Schools, and Academic Achievement." *Econometrica* 73: 417–458.

Rosenthal, Meredith, Rushika Fernandopulle, Hyun Sook Ryu Song, and Bruce Landon. 2004. "Paying for Quality: Providers' Incentive for Quality Improvement." *Health Affairs* 23: 127–141.

Shaw, Kathryn, and Edward Lazear. 2008. "Tenure and Output." *Labour Economics* 15: 710–724.

Syverson, Chad. 2011. "What Determines Productivity?" *Journal of Economic Literature* 49: 326–365.

Syverson, Chad, Lucia Foster, and John Haltiwanger. 2008. "Reallocation, Firm Turnover, and Effi-ciency: Selection on Productivity or Profitability?" *American Economic Review* 98: 394–425.

Van Biesebroeck, Johannes. 2006. "Complementarities in Automobile Production." *Journal of Applied Econometrics* 22: 1315–1345.

PART III

Within Firms:
Individuals and Groups

8

Employment as an Economic and a Social Relationship

James N. Baron and David M. Kreps

1. Introduction

Because employment is simultaneously an economic and a social relationship, one cannot profitably study it as one or the other in isolation. To understand employment relationships requires taking into account both economic and social-psychological dimensions of their content and context and, especially, how economic and social forces interact. This is true of many economic exchanges, but particularly of employment: Fraught with the complexities of time, uncertainty, and ambiguity, employment contracts are often massively incomplete. "Market discipline" is likely to become less and less acute the longer an employment relationship endures. Although supply-equals-demand may be informative in the aggregate, at the level of the relationships between an organization and its employees—the level of greatest interest to practitioners and of increasing interest to scholars—more nuanced and, to some extent, quite different ways of thinking should be employed. In particular, insights from social psychology and sociology about what drives employee behavior—about what employees value, what they expect, and how they assess their situations—are essential to a full and useful understanding of employment relationships. Economics by itself is far from sufficient.

Economic reasoning should not be abandoned in favor of these other disciplines. Instead, economics should be blended with social psychology and sociology. We have found it particularly helpful to use an economic skeleton derived from the theory of relational contracting within the broader framework of transaction cost economics and then to flesh out the skeleton with ideas from the other disciplines.

Economists are customarily schooled in the crisp, concise tradition of supply-equals-demand, in which sparse hypotheses generate broad conclusions. Accordingly, economists may be troubled by the complex animals we construct. If the skeletal structure is simple, the variety of muscle and flesh—and their complex dependence on the broader social environment—leaves one with an incredibly rich menagerie of employment relationships. This is not to say that useful

Authorship (and blame) is shared equally.

predictions are impossible. But they are more nuanced than might emerge from a purely economic perspective. And, in at least some cases, social forces can turn predictions derived from economics alone on their head.

We begin by describing the skeleton. Readers versed in the theory of relational contracts will find this description to be very familiar territory. Then, more by examples than anything else, we show how concepts from social psychology and sociology flesh out the skeleton in ways that a mainstream economist might not anticipate.

2. Employment as a Relational Contract

The economic skeleton for employment relationships is a standard version of relational contracting within the framework of transaction cost economics, mixing bilateral, hierarchical, and, in some cases, trilateral governance, and with more than a nod toward more mathematical theories of repeated games and reputation. We expect that this story is well known to most readers of this chapter, so we outline it succinctly.

We focus for the moment on the relationship between employer and employee:

1. The relationship endures for some length of time. This is not a theory of spot labor transactions.

2. Because it is too costly (or, more likely, impossible) to specify all contingencies in advance, the contract between employer and employee is massively incomplete, both at the outset and as it evolves. Among the many terms of the exchange that are specified only as time passes are: the precise tasks to be performed by the employee and how to assess performance; training that might be provided; decisions about reassignment, promotion, and changes in compensation; and the identities of co-workers, subordinates, and immediate hierarchical superiors.

3. Market forces working on both employer and employee might be acute at the start of the relationship (although institutional factors, such as "company towns" and collective bargaining, may work against even this). As time passes, however, both parties build relation-specific assets, which relax the discipline of the market. Each side gains the ability to hold up the other, albeit their powers may grow quite asymmetrically.

4. The relationship, and how it evolves in the face of contingencies that arise, is often best characterized by its terms of governance: who makes which decisions.

5. The precise design of the contractual relationship will tend to optimize the net benefits of the relationship, net (in particular) of the transaction costs of forming, (re-)negotiating, adapting, and enforcing the contract. (But see, in particular, our discussion below of reputation concerns and effects.)

How should decision rights be assigned? Efficiency considerations point us in two directions: decision rights should vest (1) in the party with superior information and ability to make a particular decision; and (2) in the party in whom greater trust can be reposed that the decision rights will not be abused.

In his classic article on the subject, Simon (1951) proposes that employment is typically a hierarchical relationship, with the employer or hierarchical superior making the vast majority of decisions. In Simon's model, the employee retains (only) the privilege of quitting, if the employer's demands become too onerous or distasteful. One can see both considerations at work here:

1. The employer, in many cases, acts to coordinate the activities of a number of employees. Being a specialist in coordinating the actions of others, the employer has greater access to information vital to decisions about what must be done when.

2. Trust is more naturally reposed in the party who has more at stake reputationally if the relationship is sundered. In employment, both employer and employee have assets at risk, because both have developed relation-specific assets. The employee expends time and energy acquiring knowledge and skills useful only for this employer, builds up a network of friends on the job, puts down roots in the community which she might lose if forced to seek employment elsewhere, and so on.[1] A list of the employer's assets at risk include: the employee, through time, learns on the job and through training provided by the employer, all of which must be repeated when turnover occurs; employees form networks within the employer's organization that are useful; and so forth. And each party has the substantial ability to diminish the value of the other party's assets. Absent slavery and indenture, the employee always retains the right to quit (although she may be bound to some extent by contractual non-compete clauses). The employer retains the ability to fire the employee, within the constraints that may be imposed by employment law and collective bargaining.

   Because both parties have assets at risk, either can conceivably be trusted by the other, based on a threat by the other to destroy those assets. Indeed, measured as a percentage of the party's overall assets, the employee probably has more at risk in the employment relationship than the employer does with any individual employee. This observation might argue, on reputational grounds, for assigning decision rights to the employee who, having relatively more at stake, is potentially more trustworthy and at the same time, less likely to resist a hold-up. (Bargaining theory does not provide us with absolutely firm grounds for this conclusion, but still it seems reasonable.) The information advantage of the employer could be sufficient to overcome this trustworthiness advantage, but another general force works to increase the potential trustworthiness of the employer: Because employers typically deal with more than one employee, they develop reputations among all employees and prospective hires for how they behave as employers. In the usual virtuous-cycle fashion of reputation constructions, a reputation that—if credible—would elicit desirable behavior from trading partners can become self-enforcing. A desire to protect the value of reputation makes the reputation credible; this credibility enhances the value of the reputation, making it worthy of protection through adherence. Therefore, to the extent that an employer deals with multiple employees, *if* maltreatment of

---

1. Even in a pure transaction cost economics account, social forces are clearly at work here. Many of the job- or relation-specific assets an employee develops on the job are social in character, such as friendships made. The employer can influence the extent to which these assets develop—for instance, by promoting social exchange on the job, encouraging after-work fraternization, or (in the other direction) by a policy of frequently breaking up teams, moving people from one location to another, and so forth. In general, the more assets the employee has at risk, the stronger is the employer's bargaining position, and so actions that promote the formation of these social assets, at this level, are good for the employer. But as we discuss later, social comparison processes and group dynamics can present nontrivial trade-offs along this dimension.

a single employee would harm the employer's reputation with other employees, the reputational cost of such maltreatment increases enormously, which dramatically increases the employer's trustworthiness. This gives a further rationale for assigning to employers the bulk of the decision rights.

To be clear, specific decision rights are in many cases vested in employees. (More rarely, the two parties resort to trilateral governance, utilizing third-party arbitrators.) Employers probably have superior information about the coordination of activities among different employees; with highly interdependent jobs, they may also have an advantage in deciding what is done and how. But, to take a contrary example, academic deans may often have an advantage in scheduling when certain courses will be taught and even what general material should be covered; yet individual professors are nonetheless typically left with substantial—if not total—discretion about the specifics of how the material will be taught.

It is also worth noting that worker collectives—work councils, labor unions, and the like—can turn this picture on its side, if not its head. Worker collectives provide employees with representatives who can specialize in collecting and processing information valuable for coordinating activities, as well as a collective reputation stake in the relationship between employer(s) and the collectivized employees. Political considerations (e.g., American traditions of bread-and-butter unionism) aside, worker collectives can render it quite efficient to reassign decision rights to employees collectively or, at least, to require in the governance structure a measure of consensus before a decision is made.

3. Behavior: Beliefs and Tastes?

To flesh out this skeleton, we have to specify how the parties involved will behave in various situations in which they find themselves.

For a formal and mathematically inclined economist, behavior is purposeful, driven to achieve specific aims as encoded by the individual's unchanging and unchangable utility function. That same economist views purposeful behavior as reflecting two distinct influences: *tastes* or *utility*, the primitives of value to the individual; and *beliefs*, predictions concerning how others will behave, particularly in response to one's own actions. But after acknowledging the importance of tastes and beliefs, economists do not have a lot more to say about either:

- Economists, by and large, forswear any competence in specifying tastes: *De gustibus non disputandum est* is perhaps economists' second favorite bit of Latin (after *ceteris paribus*). Having disavowed any competence to specify tastes, economists do so anyway, traditionally populating their models with individuals whose tastes are a function solely of their own consumption. Nothing in economic theory precludes *homo economicus* from having in her utility function a taste for justice, a competitive streak, a masochistic bent, or a desire to see her friends prosper and her rivals suffer. But one rarely finds these traits in economic models.[2]

---

2. For a recent attempt to infuse agency theory with more behavioral realism by invoking social and psychological forces, see Rebitzer and Taylor (2011).

- Beliefs are a more complex matter. In the repeated interaction and reputation stories that form the basic architecture of the skeleton we have proposed, equilibria are manifestly a matter of each party's beliefs. In more mathematical renditions of these stories, the Folk Theorem tells us that many equilibria are possible, depending on the equilibrium beliefs held by the parties. The importance of specific beliefs is clearly recognized, but little is said about where those beliefs come from, how they evolve, and so forth.

Our thesis is that social psychology and sociology provide substantial insight regarding individual tastes and beliefs in employment settings, especially the social nature of those tastes and beliefs. Accordingly, those disciplines may help illuminate which particular equilibria we might expect to see among the many possible options. But the insights provided by social psychology and organizational sociology generate a stronger challenge to the economists' way of thinking, sometimes blurring the line between beliefs and tastes and calling into question the economist's standard assumption that tastes are unchanging and unchangeable. A more accurate rendition of our thesis is that social psychology and sociology teach us much about individual behavior in employment settings, with special emphasis on social factors that affect behavior. In the next few sections, we provide some specific examples.

4. Agency and Consummate Effort

More attention in the economics literature on organizations is paid to problems of agency and incentives than perhaps to any other issue. Designing robust and well-functioning tangible incentives can be particularly difficult where (1) employees must tend to multiple tasks; (2) tasks are dynamic, interdependent among employees, and ambiguous (the links between employee inputs and observable outputs are noisy or, worse, subject to unforeseen contingencies); and (3) employees' levels of risk and effort aversion are not well known by employers.

Non-economics-based approaches sometimes "solve" the problem of agency in a manner that economists tend to regard as cheating; they appeal to social and psychological processes that lead employees to choose to act in the best interests of employers or some other constituency. Using the terminology of economics to express these social-psychological processes, they include:

- an appeal to motivation on the part of employees to do a good job because the task is inherently interesting, out of pride in the task itself, or because doing a good job is a general social norm;

- an appeal to the employee's sense of obligation (gift exchange); or

- an appeal to the employee internalizing (perhaps endogenously) the welfare of the employer or some other constituency.

All three of these work at the level of employee tastes; the idea is that, contrary to the assumptions of simple agency models, employees are not motivated solely by income received and the desire to avoid effort. Because one can incorporate these additional motivations in an employee's utility function, they are easily accommodated in the standard utility-maximization models of economists (but see the discussion in Section 4.4). Social psychology provides us with a number of interesting and even provocative hypotheses in this regard.

4.1. Explicit Extrinsic Rewards or Control Mechanisms Can Drive Out Intrinsic Motivation

When workers are intrinsically motivated to do a good job, emphasizing "supporting" explicit extrinsic rewards can dull or even reverse intrinsic motivation (see, e.g., Deci 1971, 1975; Lepper et al. 1973; Lepper and Greene 1975; Deci et al. 1999). Several psychological accounts are offered for this effect. Deci and colleagues associate intrinsic motivation with feelings of autonomy; imposing extrinsic rewards or external control mechanisms, such as surveillance, tends to increase the employee's sense of being controlled, diminishing the level of intrinsic motivation. (Why are individual faculty members given autonomy over what they teach and how? A partial explanation may lie in this direction: The freedom enhances the intrinsic motivation of the faculty member, which is an essential piece of motivation for this complex task.) A different psychological account involves self-perception theory (Bem 1967): An employee who works hard at some task, without explicit extrinsic rewards, is insufficiently justified cognitively and will tend to rationalize to herself that her efforts at doing a good job must stem from her own pride in or love of the job itself. Having so rationalized her prior efforts, she subsequently acts in accordance with these values; her pride in doing a good job or intrinsic interest in the task rises. When extrinsic rewards or explicit controls are made salient, the individual may become over-sufficiently justified: Now she can attribute effort to a desire to earn the specific reward or avoid punishment. If she comes to believe that that is what motivates her, then she may do what is required, but only just what is required. She is less likely to attribute her effort to pride or love and, the story goes, is less likely to provide consummate effort subsequently.[3]

This is not to say that, by reducing the salary of an intrinsically motivated employee, an employer would perforce intensify that intrinsic motivation. These effects have more to do with the extent to which extrinsic rationales are made cognitively salient than with the provision of extrinsic rewards per se. Moreover, demotivation may ensue if compensation levels are not fair and equitable, especially based on social comparisons, or are inconsistent with status (see Section 5). The point is, instead, that highlighting explicit extrinsic incentives—emphasizing an explicit quid pro quo—can dull intrinsic motivation, which in turn may either lower performance or raise the cost to the employer of achieving the optimal level of performance.

This is also not to say that focusing on extrinsic incentives is always a bad idea. In some settings, intrinsic motivation to perform is scarce and of limited relevance to individual or organizational performance. But intrinsic motivation can be a very powerful and inexpensive control mechanism in a wide variety of settings: where work has social meaning, such as nursing; where it involves the use of a skill or craft acquired through a process involving strong normative socialization, such as a crafts union or professional school; where the individual employee is better equipped than the employer to make real-time judgments about what actions to take and in what sequence; where the difference between adequate and superlative performance is highly valuable to the enterprise; and where individuals work interdependently, so that spillovers in attitudes and outputs are possible among members of the employee group.

---

3. A somewhat different account of the self-fulfilling nature of extrinsic controls emphasizes the dynamics of performance sampling or what psychologists term "asymmetric disconfirmation." Employers who underestimate the extent of employee opportunism will observe their errors and restructure jobs accordingly, producing a self-fulfilling cycle; in contrast, employers who overestimate the extent of employee opportunism are unlikely to structure jobs in such a way as to allow their priors to be disconfirmed (e.g., Denrell 2003; Larrick and Wu 2007).

4.2. Process (Language and Symbolism) Affects Gift Exchange

In a competitive labor market, profit-maximizing employers are meant to pay employees their market wages. Nonetheless, one sometimes observes employees being treated better—in terms of wages, benefits, or other perquisites—than their market alternatives. The typical economic explanation is that these are so-called "efficiency wages" (see, e.g., Campbell 1993): By paying above the market, the employer reduces the chances of the employee leaving the job for another opportunity or for personal concerns (e.g., one's spouse has found a better job elsewhere). This, the story goes, economizes on turnover, supervision, and training costs. Moreover, above-market compensation induces employees to take particular care not to be fired. To protect their privileged job (in an environment where they might be terminated unexpectedly), employees reciprocate with above-market diligence, they forbear from dysfunctional rent seeking, and so forth. These considerations suggest that efficiency wages are expected when it is difficult or costly to exercise direct managerial oversight; tasks are interdependent among employees; turnover, monitoring, and training are costly; and hold-up problems are intensified by virtue of scale, technology, worker organization, or skill monopolies among star employees with external opportunities. And empirical evidence is at least partially supportive; in particular, premium wages are often associated in a given labor market with larger firms, which complement premium wages with premium benefits.

An alternative and somewhat noneconomic view is that above-market wages and benefits actuate a reciprocal pattern of gift exchange. The employer is providing gifts to employees; employees are then motivated to reciprocate with gifts of consummate effort. Employees do not precisely calculate the monetary value of the gifts they are given or what it would cost them monetarily to lose the gifts by losing the job. Instead, employees feel a more basic social obligation to reciprocate gift for gift. In this story, the character of the gift from employer to employee can powerfully affect how the employee responds. Gifts are more likely to engender reciprocation the more personal the gift is, the more it seems to have been personally costly to the gift giver, and the more it seems to be a gift and not simply extra compensation. To reduce this idea to something of a caricature, a gift basket of books or music CDs at the holidays, particularly if the composition of the basket reflects the individual tastes of the recipient, is more effective than is the equivalent amount of cash, especially if the cash amount is determined by a specific formula that depends objectively on the employee's base salary. (Compare with the standard economic point of view: Except for their tax-favored status or economies due to large-scale purchases or the solution of adverse selection problems, specific benefits are less valuable to employees than is the equivalent amount of cash.)

A gift is more clearly and obviously a gift—and therefore more likely to trigger reciprocal gifts—the more clearly it is "unnecessary." Efficiency wage stories imply that employers should utilize efficiency wage regimes to mollify employees having the highest expectations, the most abundant external opportunities, and the greatest ability to impose costs on the employer. Yet these may well be the employees among whom it is most difficult to cultivate feelings of obligation by providing treatment that exceeds what is customary in a given occupation, industry, or locale. The relative affluence and clout of these employees makes it more likely that they will frame the above-market compensation simply as their due. In contrast, above-market rewards paid to those lower in the employment pecking order are, for that reason alone, more likely to be framed as gifts. It may be employees with lower expectations regarding compensation and treatment who are affected most profoundly by receiving a gift of a specific value.[4]

This insight has been leveraged to great effect by George Zimmer, founder of Men's Wearhouse, a retailer selling low-priced menswear in conveniently located establishments that minimize the travel and shopping time men must spend when purchasing clothing. In an industry characterized by astronomical turnover rates, low wages, minimal benefits, and reliance on technological surveillance and controls to deter employee misconduct, Zimmer has adopted a contrarian approach. He invests heavily in employee training and development, in providing short- and long-term benefits, and in making the workplace fun (O'Reilly and Pfeffer 2000). Many individuals he hires are passed over by competitors who do not see in the resume the indicia of trustworthiness and business acumen. For Zimmer, a lack of experience or a string of past travails creates opportunities to engender more intense feelings of obligation and gratitude. Zimmer offers these disadvantaged individuals not simply a job and a paycheck but also a chance for self-esteem and a new life.

There is evidence in support of the economic benefits realized through this regime. According to the *2005 National Retail Security Survey* (NRSS) of 156 retail chains (Hollinger and Langton 2006), shrinkage in retail averaged 1.59% of total annual sales in 2005, slightly higher (1.62%) in the men's and women's apparel sector.[5] A Stanford Business School case on Men's Wearhouse reports a shrink rate of "roughly 0.5%" (Pfeffer 1997). At the time of the NRSS survey (2005), the company reported revenues of $1.725 billion. If its shrinkage rate was 1.62% − 0.50% = 1.12% lower than its competitors, this represents a savings of about $19.3 million. According to the 2005 NRSS, on average 5% of theft was due to vendors, 15% to administrative and paperwork errors, 33% reflected shoplifting, and 47% was due to employee theft. Even if one assumes that Men's Wearhouse human resource (HR) practices only affect shrinkage from employee theft and shoplifting (80% of the total), the savings still add up to about $15.5 million for the year or about $1,120 per employee. And these rough estimates may well understate the savings from reduced shrinkage: the NRSS reports considerably higher shrinkage rates in retail establishments with high turnover and heavy reliance on part-time personnel (Hollinger and Langton 2006: figures 25 and 26), and Men's Wearhouse is far below the industry average on both dimensions.

On the expenditure side, it is difficult to calculate the magnitude of the efficiency wages being paid, but the Stanford case reports that training expenses (which include many social activities having team-building effects) average roughly 2% of payroll. In FY2005, selling, general, and administrative expenses for the entire company totaled $531.8 million, so an upper bound on the entire training tab is 2% of that amount or $10,637,000, which works out to $771 per employee. In short, the goodwill Zimmer creates by investing in a workforce whom others have shunned pays for itself handsomely simply due to reduced employee theft and increased employee attention to customer theft. This estimate ignores any benefits obtained through greater sales productivity, less turnover, or lower administrative overhead.

---

4. For some field-based and experimental evidence consistent with this speculation, see Baron (2011).

5. More recent annual versions of the NRSS yield very fairly similar estimates but warrant less confidence due to much lower response rates among firms in men's apparel.

		A	B	C		D
			Whining			
			Index			
		2009–10	(5 = non-stop			
		Performance	complainer	Probability		Recommended
Last	First	(1 = horrible	1 = like	Quit in		Turkey Size
Name	Name	4 = star)	a kitten)	Next Year	Comments	(lbs)***
Anise	Al	3	1	0.05	Caring for sick parent	25.5
Basil	Brian	2	5	0.50	Engaged to army officer	19
Caraway	Carl	4	4	0.10	Takes night classes at Tech	23
Dill	Dave	1	5	0.10	Let's hope his wife gets that job in Europe she's applied for!	12
Elder-Berry	Ellen	1	3	0.10	No talk of leaving lately	16
Fennel	Fiona	2	3	0.01	Joint custody of kids	18.1
Garlic	Greta	3	5	0.20	Always threatening to leave, but …	19
Herbes	Finis	4	2	0.80	Recently won lottery	28
Juniper-Berry	Jill	3	1	0.75	Two close friends just quit	27.5
Kaffir	Kris	2	3	0.50	Applied to grad school	23
Licorice	Linda	1	1	0.10	Coaches local youth sports	20
Marjoram	Marjorie	4	3	0.20	All her family members live locally	26
	Average	2.5	3	0.28		21.425

I. M. SPICE CORPORATION
Confidential (for Herb Spice only)

***Note: D = 8 + (3.0 * A) + {2.5 * (5 − B)} + [10 * {0.5 − |C − 0.5|}].

Figure 1. Proposed Thanksgiving gifts for employees of the I. M. Spice Corporation.

Interestingly, Zimmer apparently resists appeals from his management team to quantify the return on investment for expenditures such as the annual companywide retreat at the beach in Pajaro Dunes, California, to which all employees are invited. In a videotaped conversation with a class of Stanford students about the company, Zimmer says that this is "the best money we spend" and that the expenses will only be curtailed "over my dead body, even if it is hard to quantify from a cost-benefit point of view" (Pfeffer, personal communication, 1998). Given the apparent magnitude of the return and Zimmer's shrewdness, one cannot help but wonder whether this posture is intended to preserve the gift-exchange properties of the company's training investments by not emphasizing any calculative logic involved in having made them.

Conversely, opportunities to leverage gift exchange can be squandered through words or actions that emphasize the calculative underpinnings of employers' actions. For an (admittedly fowl) example, imagine employees of the fictional I. M. Spice Company discovering the spreadsheet shown in Figure 1 on their boss's desk just before Thanksgiving. It is hard to imagine Spice's employees responding to their proposed Thanksgiving perk with unbridled displays of loyalty and corporate citizenship.

Cultural and social factors largely outside the firm's control can also affect if and how employer largesse triggers reciprocity, by affecting how the recipients frame the gift. These cultural and social factors may pertain to the recipients. For instance, it is not a great overstatement to suggest that the educational experiences at elite business schools reduce mightily opportunities for engendering feelings of reciprocity and obligation among newly minted MBAs vis-à-vis the organizations that employ them. Throughout the business school experience, students are described and treated as the "best and brightest" and indoctrinated with the principles of neoclassical economics, a cocktail that encourages many students to presume (if not assert boldly) that they are worth whatever they are able to extract in the labor market. This, in turn, suggests that MBAs, especially those from elite programs, might be relatively more sought after by organizations that eschew gift-exchange processes in favor of greater reliance on extrinsic incentives.

Cultural and social factors may also relate to the gift itself. For instance, a gift that runs counter to the dominant local culture may be dysfunctional: Think of a very early provider of health benefits for same-sex domestic partners. This offering was more likely to have the desired effect in, say, San Francisco, than it might have in, say, Utah or the deep South. Moreover, the power of this gift was probably strongest in San Francisco for the early adopters: Whereas a gift that is utterly unusual or unprecedented may be misunderstood or misperceived, one that is utterly commonplace or has become an industry norm provides relatively little luster. The impact of a given HR system is likely to depend on the distribution of alternative systems being utilized within the relevant sphere(s) to which employees attend. Zimmer would presumably derive considerably less benefit if his approach to employment relationships were the norm in apparel retailing.

Evidence of similar effects is found in the high-tech sector. The Stanford Project on Emerging Companies examined how founders' early blueprints or mental maps regarding employment relations affected the evolution and performance of a large sample of Silicon Valley start-ups. The researchers found that companies founded with high-commitment HR systems displayed higher rates of survival and success from 1994 to 2001 than did most otherwise-comparable companies, even those founded with "star" models of the sort generally thought to promote technological excellence (see Baron and Hannan 2002). This was true in a locale (Silicon Valley) and time period (the Internet boom) in which "commitment" was generally regarded by the mid-1990s as an outmoded construct that impaired organizations from being flexible and fast. The point here is that if the significance of an employer's offer to employees depends on the benchmark in terms of which it is assessed, then the returns to building a high-commitment culture may be greatest precisely when such cultures are uncommon and somewhat suspect: the significance of investing in employees and committing to their long-term development is greater when few rivals are doing so and when it is relatively more constraining or costly for employers to do so.

4.3. Internalizing the Welfare of Others

Sections 4.1 and 4.2 considered situations in which one party, the employee, takes actions that benefit a second party, the employer, without any apparent extrinsic incentive to do so and, presumably, at some personal cost in time or effort. By the principle of revealed preference, the observation of such behavior is explained by supposing that this behavior is, on net, utility enhancing: The benefits to the first party exceed the cost of the time or effort required. One possible explanation—what we mean to suggest in Section 4.1—is that the party finds the act inherently enjoyable, takes pride in the act itself, or feels that the action per se is compelled by norms of proper behavior. We could test this idea by seeing whether the first party would take a similar action that benefits no one in particular or that benefits only unknown third parties. A second explanation—suggested by the language of gift exchange—is that the first party is discharging some perceived obligation to the second party; the action would not be taken for anonymous third parties, nor would it be taken on behalf of the specific second party once the original gift was adequately reciprocated. (This behavior can be rationalized as conformance to the norm of reciprocity, but it is reciprocation that is normative and not the specific behavior itself.) A third possibility, where the action would be taken for a specific second party (and not for an anonymous third party), is that the first party has (positively) internalized the welfare of the second party; roughly put, the first party's utility depends positively on the welfare of the second party.

It is probably difficult to separate the second and third explanations of this pattern of behavior empirically, especially where the two parties interact repeatedly: Unrequited love notwithstanding, any persistence in my internalizing your welfare is likely to require that you demonstrably reciprocate. One might simply view a sequence of back-and-forth gift exchanges as a device, especially on the employer's part, for increasing how much the employee internalizes the employer's welfare, thereby efficiently solving agency problems. However, in the spirit of escalating commitment (Staw 1981), which psychologists have examined primarily in the context of ill-fated decisions, we suggest that virtuous cycles of internalization can occur. The two parties might begin by exchanging small and inexpensive gifts, but as time passes and the relationship matures, if it matures positively, the extent to which each side internalizes the other's welfare will escalate.

Psychologists and others have documented a number of mechanisms by which this internalization occurs, aside from a generalized social norm of reciprocity. Studies of commitment in a variety of contexts (corporations, unions, voluntary associations, and long-term relationships) have documented that the time and effort associated with investment in a relationship itself tends to foster and deepen internalization of the other's welfare (e.g., Sheldon 1971). Moreover, the diminution of alternatives that often accompanies investment in building long-term alliances can strengthen the tendency for each party to internalize the welfare of its other exchange partners. And numerous studies of escalating commitment to ill-fated courses of action have highlighted the role of self-justification in sustaining prior commitments, lest the decision-maker appear unwise in the eyes of others (Brockner 1992). Similar processes of self-justification, self-perception (Bem 1967), or cognitive consistency (Festinger 1957) are presumably activated by taking actions that benefit another individual or entity without sufficient extrinsic rationale. In Section 4.1, we imagine an employee who exerts herself without the prospect of a contingent, extrinsic reward as rationalizing this effort, ex post, with "since I worked so hard on it, it must be because it was fun," or "because it is important to me personally to do a good job." In the right social environment—such as in an organizational culture that emphasizes cooperation and loyalty—she might justify her efforts with "I did it because I want my co-worker [or team, boss, department, organization] to succeed" and, having so justified her past efforts, might adopt this attitude when choosing her subsequent levels of effort.

Such justifications are not merely attempts to rationalize or justify one's actions to oneself or others. Behavioral scientists have documented an important moral dimension of commitment, which seems distinct from other facets of commitment. For instance, studies of marital commitment and duration have identified personal, moral, and structural dimensions of commitment, corresponding (respectively) to a person's responses when asked how much he or she wants to stay married, should stay married, and has to stay married due to irretrievable investments, limited alternatives, or social approval (Johnson 1991; Johnson et al. 1999). Moreover, research in a variety of contexts suggests that the persistence of all sorts of relationships depends on the individual internalizing the welfare of specific parties. For instance, commitment to one's spouse as a person, and changes in that commitment, predict the level of self-reported love and marital discord experienced in Norwegian marriages (Swensen and Trauhaug 1985).

In sum, prior investments, structural constraints, social and moral prescriptions, cognitive consistency and self-justification motives, and the familiarity that develops over time can all drive individuals to internalize the welfare of those with whom they transact, in ways that go far beyond straightforward self-interest. The rub, however, is that researchers have found this blissful state of affairs to be very difficult to sustain over long periods of time. Consider, for example, how the authors of the just-mentioned Norwegian marriage study summarized their research findings:

> Those [who developed] increased commitment to the spouse as a person over the course of marriage expressed significantly more love to their spouses and had significantly fewer marriage problems. *However, commitment to the spouse as a person declined for most couples over the course of marriage.* [Swensen and Trauhaug 1985: 939, emphasis added]

In a similar vein, Sheldon (1971) documented that the commitment of PhD scientists to their employer (a private laboratory) increased with their investments, captured by measures of age, length of service, and position level in the enterprise. But commitment to their profession also increased powerfully with work experience, beginning to undercut commitment to the organization after a moderate length of service. Sheldon found that social involvements—a high degree of involvement and identification with co-workers, on and off the job—mitigated the negative effects of professional commitment on organizational commitment. Put differently, as the scientists' commitments to the firm per se began to wane relative to their identification with the broader professional community, personal involvement and identification with their colleagues, on and off the job, became the focal mechanism for binding the scientists to the laboratory.[6]

In Section 4.1, we cited work that showed how (over)emphasizing extrinsic incentives can diminish intrinsic incentives. One explanation for this phenomenon is that emphasizing extrinsic rewards provides another rationale for the effort provided; an individual who is over-sufficiently justified (to use the language of social psychologists) need not resort to ex post rationalizations of how interesting the tasks are, or how important it was to her to do a good job. The same process, presumably, would dull the development of positive internalization; if I can rationalize help that I give you as being driven by extrinsic rewards, I am less likely to adopt the position that I do it because I care for you.

---

6. One cannot help but note an analogous pattern that sometimes occurs in long-term marriages, in which commitment to the spouse as a person wanes as a basis of marital attachment and is overtaken by a more vibrant commitment to the shared products of the marriage: the kids.

It is worth noting in this context that in all but the simplest of work technologies, employees must interact repeatedly with parties other than the "employer" (put in scare quotes because the employer is rarely a single individual but rather a conglomerate of hierarchical superiors, managers, etc.). In some work technologies, it is crucial that employees help one another. In some instances, strong and cooperative relationships between employees and clients are crucial to success. Our point is that internalizing others' welfare—which would induce helping efforts or strong and cooperative relationships with clients—is a possibility in virtually any long-term relationship. Moreover, employers have levers with which to control the extent and nature of this internalization, such as job rotation policies, workplace architecture, workforce demographics, and job titles. Of course, before an employer can employ these levers, she must first analyze where internalization is desirable and where it might work against her own interests. An appreciation of this social psychological process, of both its impact on economic outcomes and on the ways and means of controlling it, can be very informative in the study of particular job designs.

4.4. These Phenomena in the Economics Literature—and the Issue of Changing Tastes

A few economists have written papers concerning the psychological phenomena described above, although this work is not always cast in the employment context. Three important streams in the literature are:

- Frey (see, e.g., 2008) stresses the sorts of explanations given by Deci; i.e., the importance of autonomy to intrinsic motivation.

- Fehr and his associates present a series of experimental papers that put particular emphasis on the norm of reciprocity and the role of gift exchange. A survey of this work is provided in Fehr and Falk (2002).

- Gneezy and Rustichini (2000) provide some field data that they interpret as an example of extrinsic incentives driving out intrinsic motivation in the context of picking up children at the end of the day from daycare.

In addition, two papers by Bénabou and Tirole (2003, 2007) concern these phenomena and, in particular, an important methodological issue. At the start of Section 4, we said that accommodating these phenomena was "simply" a matter of introducing into the utility function of employees such arguments as the enjoyment of a specific task (i.e., performing the task raises utility directly); a primitive desire to do a good job or to conform to a particular norm; a propensity to reciprocate, especially to reciprocate a gift; or the welfare of another party. But, in fact, things are a bit more complex than simply putting those arguments into the utility function, because the phenomena we have described involve interactions between those arguments and things like the degree and salience of extrinsic, contingent rewards; the degree to which the individual perceives herself to be autonomous; and the degree to which a reward is perceived to be a gift. To develop formal models of the phenomena described, one requires either a utility function with complex interactions among its many arguments or—more simply, but more controversially—a model of endogenously changing tastes, where what the employee wants today concerning her efforts tomorrow is not what she will want tomorrow concerning those efforts. Behavioral models along these lines, particularly models of economic behavior with changing tastes, have become increasingly fashionable. But such forays into behavioral economics are still regarded with considerable suspicion by many mainstream economists.

Bénabou and Tirole, then, seek to explain the phenomena within a standard model, in which the economic actors have the standard sort of preferences. In Bénabou and Tirole (2003), a principal has private information about how onerous a particular task is for the agent. When and if the principal puts in place extrinsic rewards for good results, the agent (correctly) infers that the principal knows this task to be onerous, and she (the agent) is less intrinsically motivated to perform. In Bénabou and Tirole (2007), the agent has private information about how intrinsically motivated she is in general. Even if she is not intrinsically motivated, it is good for her to pretend to be, because of the treatment she will then receive from this principal or in other engagements, and she will therefore act as if she were intrinsically motivated, as long as doing so sends the "right" signal. But when and if the principal puts in place extrinsic rewards, consummate performance by the agent is no longer as powerful a signal; the agent might be responding (only) to the extrinsic incentives. The signal she wanted to send is jammed, and she acts as if she were less intrinsically motivated (closer to her true preferences) as a consequence.

These are very clever models, and Bénabou and Tirole argue that they fit well with specific phenomena observed in the field. Nonetheless, they involve a degree of calculativeness (each involves a complex signaling equilibrium) that we find somewhat implausible, especially in light of some of the experimental evidence, and they are not in accord with the psychological accounts of what is happening. So we continue to hold that understanding the psychological and sociological underpinnings of behavior is crucial to understanding incentives and motivation in employment, even at the cost of models in which utility functions sport arguments with which economists are largely unfamiliar and in which those utility functions—viewed as they should be, as modeling artifacts of revealed preference—may change according to the individual's experiences and environment.

5. "How Am I Doing?": Social Comparison, Procedural and Distributive Justice, and Status Consistency

In an ongoing employment relationship, participants continually must answer the question, Am I being treated appropriately? In a game-theoretic equilibrium, an objective, absolute standard must be met, but in real life, matters are not so simple. A host of social, psychological, and sociological factors play a pivotal role here.

For one thing, employees mix absolute standards with relative ones: They ask how they are being treated relative to others in the organization. These social comparisons can be with hierarchical subordinates or superiors, but perhaps most often they involve peers who are socially and/or demographically similar. Moreover, the social comparisons that are made are manipulable. Cognitive and social psychologists have demonstrated convincingly that the nature and extent of social comparisons can be influenced by such factors as formal categorical distinctions (e.g., job titles and subunit distinctions), physical propinquity, frequency and intensity of contact among group members, group demography (how similar members are), and the purpose or motive being served. Organizations have control over all these factors, in some cases at little or no incremental cost.

Theories of procedural and distributive justice offer a somewhat more specific formulation of how comparisons and equity judgments are made and assessed. Having identified a referent that (by virtue of functional role, social standing, or demographic traits) is viewed as comparable, person A compares the perceived ratio between rewards and output or performance for himself to the equivalent ratio for the referent.[7] Experimental and field research in a host of organizational settings has demonstrated that the process by which rewards are determined and distributed is also highly influential (Lind and Tyler 1988; Tyler 2010). One should not put too much weight on the prescriptions of simple agency theory, but it is easy to construct toy agency-theoretic models offering prescriptions that are utterly contraindicated by these social psychological considerations. Imagine, for instance, an agency problem in which persons A and B must each independently take an action. Independent outcomes for A and B are observed. If X is the desired action, agency theory says to reward A most highly when the observed outcome has a relatively high likelihood if X is taken, relative to the likelihood of X under other actions.[8] If B operates independently, and the connection between B's actions and outcomes are independent of those of A, then B faces similar incentives. And, without the appropriate monotone likelihood ratio properties (and more), this could result in a situation where A receives a greater reward, even if B's outcome is "better" for the firm. This result is fine if A and B don't engage in social comparisons or look for distributive justice. But, in real life, they often do, which complicates the agency problems facing the employer or, in some cases, even turns them on their head.

Status consistency can also play a role in these judgments. The idea underlying the notion of status consistency is quite simple: when an individual occupies multiple positions that differ markedly in their typical expectations and entitlements, he or she experiences a set of psychological stresses associated with this inconsistency. Some research (e.g., Jackson 1962; Hornung 1977; Bacharach et al. 1993) has documented emotional, psychosocial, and even physical strains associated with occupying multiple roles that vary markedly in their status or prestige (e.g., the CEO who is 20 years younger than everyone else on her leadership team or the London cabbie who received his doctorate in Classics from Oxford). However, the empirical results are far from conclusive or consistent, and this simple idea has proved astoundingly difficult to pin down theoretically or empirically. It raises all sorts of niggling questions about the referent against which to compare those in inconsistent situations; how to disentangle "inconsistency" effects from the main effects of the respective statuses; how to deal with change over the life course (if a person experiences upward mobility on one dimension but not on the others, does that have the same effect as experiencing "cross-sectional" inconsistency?); and so on.[9]

Notwithstanding these difficulties and ambiguities, there is considerable intuitive appeal to the notion that the utility employees derive from a particular allocative regime at work may depend on their relative standing in status hierarchies outside the workplace. For example, numerous quantitative and ethnographic accounts of the feminization of occupations document

---

7. The literature has identified a multiplicity of ways in which individuals respond to perceived equity, such as altering perceptions of rewards or performance for themselves or for the referent, altering their choice of referent, seeking to transform the allocative regime, or disinvesting psychologically in the activity or role at issue.

8. We are being very rough here, but readers versed in agency theory will know what this statement means.

9. For a trenchant overview, see Smith (1996).

the resentment and anger men often display, stemming from a perceived loss of status as their roles become "women's work." Conventional measures of males' satisfaction and organizational commitment decline as occupations become more gender integrated (Wharton and Baron 1987). Interestingly, however, there is some evidence that males working in integrated work settings are not particularly dissatisfied if they have a nonworking wife at home (Kessler and McRae 1982; Wharton and Baron 1987: 583–584). This finding suggests that among men working in previously male-dominated settings, those who retain the traditional role of sole breadwinner within their households are least troubled by the devaluation that occurs when the workplace becomes more gender integrated. Most economic models of employment and labor markets assume, explicitly or implicitly, that employers and employees compare the gains to trade against either their next-best alternative in the market or a no-trade state of affairs. But if employees are keenly attuned to their social standing relative to others and relative to how they rank in other social roles and settings, then two employees with observationally equivalent "next-best alternatives" might react very differently to identical offers or treatment from the same employer.

6. History Matters

In judgments made to answer the question "how am I doing?" and in the answers given by employees (and their employers) to such questions, history matters. There is now a massive literature documenting how anchoring and expectations mold judgments and decisionmaking, suggesting that early experiences are particularly important in determining what referents workers employ and what norms they invoke in responding to their workplace experiences. Some recent empirical studies corroborate this point. For instance, analyses based on the Stanford Project on Emerging Companies have documented a menu of five basic HR blueprints from which most entrepreneurial founders seemed to choose (commitment, star, engineering, bureaucracy, and autocracy), with the initial choice having profound and enduring consequences for the enterprises they created. Attempts to alter the initial employment model or blueprint generally had deleterious consequences for organizational survival and performance and heightened employee turnover, especially when the firm sought to change from one of these five relatively "pure" or clearly understood blueprints to one that was less coherent or internally consistent (Baron et al. 2001).

Social psychologists have also documented a widespread preference for increasing consumption and reward levels over time, even when other sequences (such as declining wages coupled with savings) would produce superior returns over time (Loewenstein and Prelec 1991, 1992). In the employment context, such a preference is consistent with the notion that initial treatment of employees establishes anchors and expectations that govern how subsequent allocations are assessed (also see Baron 2011).

History can matter in other ways. Sørensen (2000) has demonstrated that employees' turnover propensities are affected not simply by current organizational demography—which presumably captures patterns of communication, cohesion, and the like—but also by the entire demographic history individuals have experienced while employed at their current place of work. In other words, it is not simply how well one fits in demographically with one's co-workers today that determines "fit" or what economists might be inclined to call "match quality": It is the entire demographic history an individual has experienced in the work setting that influences present-day propensities to stay or remain. One cannot think of a career simply as a succession of job titles, responsibilities, and assignments. It also involves a series of relationships and interpersonal experiences at work, which may have persistent effects long after the relationships themselves have withered.

7. Reputation

For organizations scholars whose background is game theoretic, the concept of reputation is often enlisted as a magic bullet when it comes to employer credibility. For instance, an employer can credibly promise to reward employees later for something done today because, if she fails to carry out her promise, she will damage her reputation for doing so, and employees in the future will disbelieve her promises. If the ongoing value of keeping her promises so that employees trust her exceeds what the employer could earn (in present-value terms) from defaulting once on her promise, it is an equilibrium for her to make and keep the promises, and for the promises to be believed.

The magic in this magic bullet comes from the Folk Theorem (and similar results). Many things are equilibria, in theory, and the model builder gets to pick the equilibrium and corresponding reputation that best suits the point to be made. More specifically:

1. The employer seemingly selects whichever equilibrium makes her best off.
2. Having selected her preferred reputation and/or equilibrium, it is in fact attained.

It is a nice story. It even makes some sense within the confines of the typical model, where actions are simple and discrete and neither the population of employees nor the set of contingencies to be met varies much. Reputations are for things like "don't abuse employees" in a context where in each round the employer chooses between "abuse" and "don't abuse." In such a simple context, it makes sense that prospective employees will conclude that this is a valuable reputation for the employer, so she has instant credibility upon adopting it.

But this story does not match the complexities of the real world. Actions are not always discrete, and when they are, more than two or three options are usually available. Employees vary in their tastes and personal circumstances, and the employer must deal with a host of employees who vary along demographic, educational, and cultural lines, to say nothing of the types of work they do. The contingencies that must be met in specific situations vary enormously.

In real-world applications of this idea, reputations must be acquired, not announced. Assuming that the reputation inheres in the employer, it must be comprehensible to present and prospective employees. This is not simply a matter of learning what the reputation is. The core of a reputation construction is that the parties whose actions the reputation influences must be able, ex post, to verify that the reputation bearer acted in conformance with her reputation. Otherwise, the reputation exerts no constraint on the actions of the reputation bearer ex ante and has no particular value (as far as endowing credibility is concerned). So comprehensibility here entails a measure of ex post verifiability.

All these considerations point to several conclusions that bring us into the domain of sociological and psychological concerns:

1. Reputations must be relatively easily understood, communicated, and verified. They should reflect relatively few clear, simple precepts that are psychologically powerful and inexpensive to communicate.

2. To aid in understanding, it is helpful if reputations (bearing on workplace relations) mimic or are consistent with norms and roles routinely encountered elsewhere in the society. "They treat you like family at that firm" or "that's entirely a 'best athlete' culture" or "it's 'dog eat dog' when you work there" are the sorts of themes we have in mind. The Stanford Project on Emerging Companies research mentioned earlier found that there was not one efficient design or blueprint for the HR management policies of a high-tech Silicon Valley start-up; rather, there were five, each reflecting a relative clear and consistent pattern that could be communicated parsimoniously (e.g., "autocracy" versus "star" culture). Moreover, altering the HR blueprint resulted in dislocation and diminished organizational performance, as employees struggled to understand the new pattern of expectations. But the disruptions were less severe when firms shifted from an aberrant or incoherent blueprint (i.e., one not fitting into any of the five basic types) to one of the more prevalent and consistent types.[10]

3. Efficiency is enhanced by hiring individuals who commence employment with a superior understanding of the firm's informal practices and culture and whose background enhances their prospects for understanding those practices and internalizing the culture. For instance, notwithstanding its pernicious aspects, hiring through alumni networks or on the basis of internal referrals not only enables employers to get more and richer information on applicants, it also increases the likelihood that those hired will have expectations that are closely aligned with those of their superiors. Firms that mimic the military in management practices are inclined to hire from the military, and so forth.

7.1. Consistency of Practice in an Organization

Reputation comprehensibility and credibility require that "similar" employees in an organization must be treated with sufficient uniformity that a coherent picture of how the organization does business emerges. This requirement can limit the activities of the firm or specific subunits in the firm. For instance, a firm claiming to "treat employees like family" might expect to confront more difficulty and cost in outsourcing some of its activities, unless those outsourced activities involve employees who are conspicuously different socially from core employees. And, in such cases, it helps to minimize contact between the outsourced labor and the core employees—the

---

10. The exception to this pattern involved shifts to pure bureaucracy or pure autocracy. These invariably were destabilizing (inducing high turnover), irrespective of the initial HR blueprint being supplanted. Bureaucratic and autocratic cultures are universally reviled among scientific, technical, and engineering talent in Silicon Valley; hence, even when companies replaced an incoherent employment blueprint with a coherent bureaucratic or autocratic one, employees responded negatively. Put somewhat differently, when diners hate the dish, calling attention to it, making it easier to recognize, or serving larger portions only makes things worse.

archetypal example here is the custodial crew, which (only) comes in at night after core employees have left. But this family-culture firm is likely to find outsourcing menial tasks superior to insourcing them, if the employees performing these tasks are going to be treated menially.

To be sure, developing a consistent reputation does not require that all employees be treated the same in all respects. Almost every enterprise of any scale and complexity is vexed by the issue of how much uniformity to impose across subunits and localities in rewards, organizational structures and practices, and workplace cultures. It is self-evident that uniformity will be most problematic when the tasks involved are highly disparate among subunits or localities and when the labor markets in which tasks are carried out vary markedly. But we can offer some other conjectures and guidance by drawing on relevant psychological and sociological scholarship. Intra-organizational variation in HR practices across subunits and locales is likely to be most problematic when it is imposed

- on organizational units or locales whose employees share strong social connections,
- in organizations whose business strategy necessitates significant cooperative effort across units or locales,
- across geographical locales with similar regional or national cultures (Hofstede 2001), and
- across units or locales whose employees are in frequent contact and/or share abundant information.

Because of what might be thought of as psychological and sociological complementarities, differentiation among units or locales is also likely to be most contentious for organizations that knowingly or unknowingly foster uniformity among their employees in other ways. Examples might include extensive reliance on companywide jargon and centrally issued corporate communications, mandated stints at corporate headquarters by field personnel to soak up "HQ culture," or frequently rotating personnel geographically. Organizations may also foster uniformity of thought and behavior among employees by virtue of their linkages with particular sources of personnel, such as hiring heavily from the military, American schools worldwide, or religious schools, all institutions that themselves foster a certain degree of uniformity. And uniformity is likely to emerge when Organization X faces the same key supplier(s) or customer(s) across its divisions or locales, and those partner organizations themselves have very distinctive and uniform cultures and practices. The exigencies of collaborating with such partners will mandate a degree of cultural and behavioral uniformity across X's different divisions or locales, which complicates efforts to diversify local compensation systems, organizational practices, or cultural edicts.

7.2. Dynamics: Acquisition and Change

To maintain a reputation for behaving in some manner, it is manifestly important to behave in that manner. But to *acquire* a specific reputation, one must convince the intended audience that one *will* behave in that way. In some situations, the opportunity to demonstrate the desired behavior occurs naturally. For instance, a party seeking to dissuade others from challenging it—in the fashion of the chain-store paradox—fights when challenged and, it is hoped, slowly dissuades challenges. In cases where the reputation is specific behavior that elicits trust from others, bootstrapping the reputation is harder to imagine. In the simple situations of game-theoretic models, no one will trust someone who lacks a reputation for being trustworthy, and if no one trusts that party, the party never gets the opportunity to verify its trustworthiness. Either a leap of faith is made at the outset or, seemingly, it is not.

Bootstrapping this sort of reputation and equilibrium may be informed by social-psychological considerations. One might induce one party to make the necessary leap of faith and then, by treating that party well, slowly convince others to do likewise. One might begin with members of one's family or social acquaintances, individuals with a predisposition to trust. Trustworthiness might be "borrowed"—for example, by forging an alliance with a central, highly respected member of the local union or professional association, convincing that individual of your good intentions, and enlisting that individual to recruit others. Or a reputation for trustworthiness might be built in small steps: a party induces others to trust her in little things, again perhaps relying on related social exchanges, and then moves to bigger, and then even bigger, items. Whatever the means, it is clear how important founding circumstances and conditions are when it comes to establishing a reputation. Initial impressions are powerful anchors for subsequent expectations; stories about "the early days" can be used as vivid tools of acculturation, and changing a reputation, once it is established, can be a very difficult endeavor.

There is clear evidence that this sort of change in premises and expectations—and reputation in general—is regarded by managers as being of the utmost importance. For example, a study of 765 CEOs by IBM Global Business Services (2006) found that chief executives across diverse firms, industries, and nations were increasingly seeking innovation by transforming their organizations' underlying business model, rather than focusing simply on changes in operations or products and markets. The most frequent focus of such change initiatives was organizational structure, mentioned by roughly two-thirds of CEOs who were seeking to transform the business model for their enterprises. And when asked to identify the main obstacles to innovation they confront, "unsupportive culture and climate" topped the list, with "workforce issues" also represented among the most frequent responses.[11] A survey of leaders in 365 companies in Europe, Asia, and North America by Bain & Company highlights the difficulty of transforming organizational cultures: 68% of leaders responded that culture provides the greatest source of competitive advantage; 81% stated that an organization lacking a "high-performance culture" is doomed to mediocrity; 75% said that culture can be changed; and 65% admitted that cultural change was necessary in their own organization (Rogers et al. 2006). Yet, according to the study, fewer than 10% of firms actually succeed at achieving this cultural transformation.

The fact that cultures and HR systems are difficult to change should come as no surprise. Organizational cultures, reward systems, and control structures would have little value were they not difficult and costly to change. Or, to put it more in the language of competitive strategy, they would confer little competitive advantage if the currently most efficient system were easily imitated. But why is this so? If one accepts the game-theoretic constructions of reputation, it

---

11. Among internal obstacles, roughly 35% of CEOs mentioned unsupportive culture; 34% cited "limited funding for investment," and about 27% cited workforce issues. Only one external obstacle was cited by more than a fifth of the CEOs: "government and other legal restrictions," cited by about 31% of chief executives.

ought to be possible, when a superior alternative comes along, to tear up the old (implicit) agreements and initiate the new ones.[12]

We believe that an important sociological and psychological effect is at work here, having to do with the almost unconscious legitimacy of a given system in the minds of the employees and employer. To give a (psychological) analogy, people have internalized norms about interpersonal distance and turn-taking in conversations, which vary in rather subtle ways across contexts. We do not pay conscious attention to these norms unless or until we happen to observe them being substantially violated (e.g., you "can't get a word in edgewise" or someone is literally "in your face"). And the lack of conscious attention can promote efficient interpersonal interactions. Of course, individuals do pay some conscious attention to these things—for instance, by asking whether they themselves are talking too much.[13] But it is in the most relaxed and "natural" social settings that the least conscious attention is paid to them.

Similarly, we believe that much of the force and value of organizational control systems stems from their tacit and taken-for-granted character. Making controls explicit and salient generally entails costs—not only the costs of formulating and implementing explicit rules and controls, but also the costs of monitoring adherence to them. As we have argued, intense, formal, and explicit controls can also undermine intrinsic motivation and commitment processes, which often can provide more powerful and less expensive means for aligning employees' perceived interests with those of the enterprise. And, as Baker et al. (1994) have noted with regard to subjective performance criteria, tacit rules and controls may be more difficult for employees to circumvent; they also have the potential to broaden and generalize, subsuming a wide variety of contingencies for which no explicit provisions have been made.

It should be clear how all these considerations relate to changing a firm's reputation or organizational culture: Attempts to make changes will raise the level of salience of matters that have heretofore been tacit and implicit. This calls into question longstanding norms and expectations, often altering the categorizations and social comparisons to which employees have become accustomed and acclimated. And by opening up one set of issues, it raises the possibility that everything should be put on the table. Having started this chapter by recounting standard transaction cost economics, we cannot resist the opportunity to cast our argument in those terms: Attempts to change a piece of a firm's reputation will raise enormously the costs of adaptation and renegotiation, because it potentially takes a very efficient adaptation or renegotiation mechanism that resides somewhere beneath the full calculative consciousness

---

12. Mathematical economic and game-theoretic analyses are at a disadvantage on this point, because their agents are never so surprised by evolving circumstances that it makes sense to abrogate an old implicit contract and initiate a new one. In all but a handful of formal analyses, the economic actors anticipate the possibility of the specific contingency arising that would call for the new implicit arrangement, and the original arrangement includes an understanding of what will happen when and if the contingency arises. Formal and explicit contracts may be renegotiated, and old formal contracts may be important points of departure for the new agreements that are reached. But at the outset, everyone understands that if the specific contingency arises, this is what will happen next. So essentially, the old equilibrium, in the full sense of the term, is never modified. In that sense, the question being asked here is entirely outside the realm of economics or, at least, of standard economics.

13. Though it is seldom those who are talking too much who ask the question.

of employees and replaces it with some very conscious calculations about the overall legitimacy of the firm's employment transactions.

7.3. The Economizing Principle

These considerations bring us full circle to one of the basic premises of transaction cost economics, at least as presented by Williamson (1985). Williamson argues that the basic unit of analysis should be the individual transaction and, further, that one should expect that transaction to adopt whatever form of governance maximizes benefits from the transaction, net of transaction costs. The social and psychological effects we have discussed in this chapter suggest that his argument should be amended to some extent. First, individual transactions are important, but transactions are embedded in a social environment that cannot be disregarded. Furthermore, transactions are linked together—how firm A transacts with employee X powerfully constrains and is powerfully constrained by firm A's dealings with employees Y and Z. The individual transaction is, of course, important. But, especially in the intense social environment of employment, the constellation of transactions firm A has with all its (diverse) employees, situated within the particular society in which those transactions take place, may be the more appropriate unit of analysis.

And although a firm's constellation of transactions may tend toward the structures that maximize efficiency net of transaction costs, history—particularly the history of a firm's past management practices and relations with its employees—makes this only a tendency, not an indomitable economizing force. When confronted with secular changes in market conditions, we should expect to see firms, especially larger and more established ones, trapped in employment practices that no longer appear as fit as they once did. If employment were only an economic relationship, this might not be so. But employment's social character means that any economizing has to take into account the costs arising from the social and psychological processes we have discussed, as well as the economics of the situation.

8. Conclusion

In after-dinner remarks celebrating Oliver Williamson and his book *Markets and Hierarchies,* Jim March developed the simile that economists were well-regulated and orderly Methodists, who crave order and simplicity and know very well to stay away from what March termed "the saloons of sociology." Economists reading this chapter may be forgiven for thinking they have been touring one such saloon. Thinking of employment relationships as both economic and social relationships and, in particular, culling useful insights from social psychology and sociology, is not especially edifying if one craves the order and simplicity of Debreu's (1959) *Theory of Value.* For at least one of the two authors (Kreps), who masquerades as an economist and who has those cravings, writing this chapter was a frustrating exercise in trying to impose neat and tidy order on a messy collection of important ideas.

Yet when it comes to employment—and probably other forms of long-term economic exchange—that is the nature of the beast. It may not be pretty, at least to an economist's aesthetic sense, but incorporating psychological and sociological influences into economic models of employment relationships is useful for scholarship and managerial practice. And although these influences may not be as neat and tidy as economists like, they present important specific and generalizable insights:

- Knowledge about the psychological and sociological factors that foster commitment, promote organizational citizenship behaviors, build and maintain cohesive groups, and sustain adherence to norms (especially the norm of reciprocity) can be marshaled to identify where and when solutions inspired by agency theory are inefficient and even dysfunctional. The need for incentives or controls diminishes when employees are intrinsically motivated, can be motivated to reciprocate what they perceive as gifts, or internalize the welfare of co-workers and the firm generally. Especially when explicit incentives and controls are most difficult to get right—when employees must work innovatively, autonomously, and interdependently, and when they must deal with ambiguous and unanticipated contingencies without explicit control or oversight—high-powered incentives and controls may not only be less efficient; they may become dysfunctional, if they dull the more efficient motivations employees already have to "do the right thing."

- The processes by which individuals perceive and judge their own situations are rarely as straightforward and objective as is assumed in economic models. Anchoring and recency effects, social comparisons, and status consistency all play their roles, and perceptions and judgments can be profoundly influenced by what (to many economists) seem to be irrelevant facets of the social environment beyond the workplace.

- History powerfully shapes the behavior of individuals and organizations; to understand current patterns, one does well to study the course of past experiences. Reputation concerns can powerfully shape what a firm can and cannot do with its employment practices. Indeed, they can lead firms to decide not to alter their cultures or HR policies, even in the face of powerful environmental pressures.[14]

- Attending to differences in the psychological and sociological resonance of different incentive and control systems is also likely to prompt a reranking of various alternatives for rewards and organizational designs, relative to an ordering based solely on the direct and transactional costs and benefits associated with the production process. Approaches

14. An example that comes to mind concerns AES Corporation, a global power company founded in 1980 by two former government energy officials with strong moral and religious convictions, convinced that an energy company free from the bureaucratic constraints, functional specialization, and disempowering practices commonplace in the industry could produce extraordinary results. They built their culture around four core values: integrity, fairness, social responsibility, and having fun. In mid-June 1992, nine technicians at a new AES plant in Oklahoma conspired to falsify water test data required by state and federal regulators. Following these revelations, the firm's share price dropped by nearly 40%. The plant management, under intense pressure from lawyers, abandoned most of the company's distinctive HR practices. According to one of the firm's founders:

I mean, they just went for a total control kind of mentality, because they were scared to death . . . They basically fired me. They said "Please do not come back to the plant." . . . [It] was a real test of whether we were going backwards toward centralization . . . And we went along with it. I wouldn't go there for a whole year, and they finally called back and said, "We'd like you to come back again, we'd like to rejoin the company." . . . [It] illustrated a couple of things. One was that we did mean it when we were talking about decentralization and autonomy. And second, it proved . . . [that] support for AES principles was surprisingly strong." [Pfeffer 2004: 15–16; also see Bakke 2005]

that mimic or leverage values, attitudes, and behaviors that employees embrace frequently and fervently outside the workplace are likely to be easier and less costly to implement and sustain. This is true as well for approaches that leverage personal bonds and reputational concerns among employees outside the workplace, which is why firms and labor unions have sometimes embraced nepotistic practices. It is also one reason firms often take steps to get their employees deeply engaged in activities and institutions in their local communities.

Stated simply, what traditional models of economic exchange miss in the employment context is that many of the tasks for which employees are being compensated involve interaction with other human beings, inside and outside the organization. Those interactions occur in a social and cultural context from which employees cannot escape, and they manifest cognitive and social psychological processes that employees cannot put on hold (at least entirely) simply because the exchange is work related.

Having preached this message to incredulous economists over the years, we know that there will be objections. A standard rejoinder is that behavior is not as complex as we have claimed. And those making this rejoinder will point to organizations run according to a basic design right out of an agency theory primer, in which employees act just as agency theory predicts they will.

We do not doubt that such organizations can be found; they are part of the organizational menagerie. But they are only part, and their existence is entirely consistent with our view of things. One of our messages, after all, is that the style of on-the-job interactions can have a profound impact on their content. For the principals of agency theory to be able to carry out their prescribed role effectively would seem to require considerable detachment from the agents, lest a clever and cohesive band of agents manage to co-opt a vulnerable principal and play him or her against the remaining principals. (There are strict rules in prisons limiting fraternization between inmates and the guards whose job is to control them.) Yet a firm in which owners and managers adopt such a stance toward employees is a very different kind of firm simply by virtue of that stance, particularly in the employment context, where the inmates often have some role in determining who becomes their guard. Certainly, an HR blueprint will tend to attract and retain employees who are comfortable in enterprises run in that fashion. But the blueprint chosen for the firm will influence much more than that: the kinds of productive activities at which the firm's employees are likely to have an advantage; the intensity of social bonds that are likely to form among the labor force; and, perhaps most importantly, how both agents and principals come to think about their own and one another's roles. This endogeneity can produce among employees precisely the attitudes and orientations that the principals initially believed justified the incentives and controls put in place (e.g., effort aversion, lack of trustworthiness, lack of loyalty), creating a self-fulfilling prophecy.

Let us put it this way. Economists are sometimes demonized for creating their own (demonic, self-interested) reality. Much has been made of the fact that in a variety of experimental situations, economists and economics majors pursue more self-interested strategies than their counterparts in other professions or academic majors. They also contribute less to charities and public television than equally wealthy individuals in other occupations. And longitudinal studies indicate that these propensities increase with exposure to microeconomic theory (see Frank et al. 1993). Regardless of how one feels about economists' self-interest, it is precisely this sort of effect that we assert will take place in the context of employment. Different approaches to pay and control systems foster different ways of thinking, believing, and acting, which in turn shape the way that principals and agents think about the roles of each.

Economic models of employment should be tested not simply by asking, "do employees at firms that are run the way economic orthodoxy says firms should be run behave the way orthodoxy would expect them to?" One should also ask, "do employees at firms run on wholly different principles and blueprints behave in different ways? And when it comes to performance (the measurement of which is likely to become the next point of contention), is one way of managing human resources superior?"

Our answer is clear. Looking at a broad spectrum of employment situations, blending social insights into economics will increase the R^2 in analyses of organizational designs and incentive systems. But we believe it will do much more than that. It will illuminate the diversity of management regimes that can flourish in a given setting. It will clarify the complexity and fragility of those regimes and the challenges of trying to optimize employment relationships dynamically. And, in the process, it will produce insights that not only invigorate the scholarly study of organizational economics but also prove managerially useful.

REFERENCES

Bacharach, Samuel B., Peter Bamberger, and Bryan Mundell. 1993. "Status Inconsistency in Organizations: From Social Hierarchy to Stress." *Journal of Organizational Behavior* 14: 21–36.

Baker, George, Robert Gibbons, and Kevin J. Murphy. 1994. "Subjective Performance Measures in Optimal Incentive Contracts." *Quarterly Journal of Economics* 109: 1125–1156.

Bakke, Dennis W. 2005. *Joy at Work: A Revolutionary Approach to Fun on the Job.* Seattle: PVG.

Baron, James N. 2011. "Gratitude and Gift Exchange in Employment Relationships." Unpublished manuscript, Yale School of Management, Yale University, New Haven, CT.

Baron, James N., and Michael T. Hannan. 2002. "Organizational Blueprints for Success in High-Tech Start-Ups: Lessons from the Stanford Project on Emerging Companies." *California Management Review* 44: 8–36.

Baron, James N., Michael T. Hannan, and Diane M. Burton. 2001. "Labor Pains: Change in Organizational Models and Employee Turnover in Young, High-Tech Firms." *American Journal of Sociology* 106: 960–1012.

Bem, Darrell J. 1967. "Self-Perception: An Alternative Interpretation of Cognitive Dissonance Phenomena." *Psychology Review* 74: 183–200.

Bénabou, Roland, and Jean Tirole. 2003. "Intrinsic and Extrinsic Motivation." *Review of Economic Studies* 70: 489–520.

———. 2007. "Incentives and Prosocial Behavior." *American Economic Review* 96: 1652–1678.

Brockner, Joel. 1992. "The Escalation of Commitment to a Failing Course of Action: Toward Theoretical Progress." *Academy of Management Review* 17: 39–61.

Campbell, Carl M. 1993. "Do Firms Pay Efficiency Wages? Evidence with Data at the Firm Level." *Journal of Labor Economics* 11: 442–470.

Debreu, Gerard. 1959. *Theory of Value.* New Haven and London: Yale University Press.

Deci, Edward L. 1971. "The Effects of Externally Mediated Rewards on Intrinsic Motivation." *Journal of Personality and Social Psychology* 18: 105–115.

———. 1975. *Intrinsic Motivation.* New York: Plenum.

Deci, Edward L., Richard Koestner, and Richard M. Ryan. 1999. "A Meta-Analytic Review of Experiments Examining the Effects of Extrinsic Rewards on Intrinsic Motivation." *Psychological Bulletin* 125: 627–668.

Denrell, Jerker. 2003. "Vicarious Learning, Undersampling of Failure, and the Myths of Management." *Organization Science* 14: 227–243.

Fehr, Ernst, and Armin Falk. 2002. "Psychological Foundations of Incentives." *European Economic Review* 46: 687–724.

Festinger, Leon. 1957. *A Theory of Cognitive Dissonance*. Stanford, CA: Stanford University Press.

Frank, Robert H., Thomas Gilovich, and Dennis T. Regan, 1993. "Does Studying Economics Inhibit Cooperation?" *Journal of Economic Perspectives* 7: 159–171.

Frey, Bruno. 2008. "Motivation Crowding Theory—A New Approach to Behavior," in *Behavioural Economics and Public Policy*. Canberra: Australian Government Productivity Commission, pp. 27–54.

Gneezy, Uri, and Aldo Rustichini. 2000. "A Fine Is a Price." *Journal of Legal Studies* 29: 1–17.

Hofstede, Geert. 2001. *Culture's Consequences: Comparing Values, Behaviors, Institutions and Organizations across Nations,* second edition. Thousand Oaks, CA: Sage Publications.

Hollinger, Richard C., and Lynn Langton. 2006. *2005 National Retail Security Survey*. Gainesville, FL: Center for Studies in Criminology and Law, University of Florida.

Hornung, Carlton. 1977. "Social Status, Status Inconsistency and Psychological Stress." *American Sociological Review* 42: 623–638.

IBM Global Business Services. 2006. *Expanding the Innovation Horizon: The Global CEO Study—2006.* Somers, NY: IBM Corporation.

Jackson, Elton F. 1962. "Status Inconsistency and Psychological Stress." *American Sociological Review* 27: 469–480.

Johnson, Michael P. 1991. "Commitment to Personal Relationships," in W. H. Jones and D. W. Perlman (eds.), *Advances in Personal Relationships,* volume 3. London: Jessica Kingsley, pp. 117–143.

Johnson, Michael P., John P. Caughlin, and Ted L. Huston. 1999. "The Tripartite Nature of Marital Commitment: Personal, Moral, and Structural Reasons to Stay Married." *Journal of Marriage and the Family* 61: 160–177.

Kessler, Ronald C., and James A. McRae, Jr. 1982. "The Effect of Wives' Employment on the Mental Health of Married Men and Women." *American Sociological Review* 47: 216–227.

Larrick, Richard P., and George Wu. 2007. "Claiming a Large Slice of a Small Pie: Asymmetric Disconfirmation in Negotiation." *Journal of Personality and Social Psychology* 92: 212–233.

Lepper, Mark, and D. Greene. 1975. "Turning Play into Work: Effects of Adult Surveillance and Extrinsic Rewards on Children's Intrinsic Motivation." *Journal of Personality and Social Psychology* 30: 822–838.

Lepper, Mark, D. Greene, and Richard E. Nisbett. 1973. "Undermining Children's Intrinsic Interest with Extrinsic Rewards: A Test of the 'Over Justification' Hypothesis." *Journal of Personality and Social Psychology* 28: 129–137.

Lind, E. Allan, and Tom R. Tyler. 1988. *The Social Psychology of Procedural Justice*. New York: Plenum.

Loewenstein, George, and Drazen Prelec. 1991. "Negative Time Preference." *American Economic Review* 81(papers and proceedings): 347–352.

———. 1992. "Anomalies in Intertemporal Choice: Evidence and an Interpretation." *Quarterly Journal of Economics* 107: 573–597.

O'Reilly, Charles A., and Jeffrey Pfeffer. 2000. *Hidden Value: How Great Companies Achieve Extraordinary Results with Ordinary People*. Boston: Harvard Business School Press.

Pfeffer, Jeffrey. 1997. *The Men's Wearhouse: Success in a Declining Industry*. Stanford Business School Case Study HR5. Stanford, CA: Stanford University.

———. 2004. *Human Resources at the AES Corporation: The Case of the Missing Department.* Revised edition. Stanford Business School Case Study HR3. Stanford, CA: Stanford University.

Rebitzer, James B., and Lowell J. Taylor. 2011. "Extrinsic Rewards and Intrinsic Motives: Standard and Behavioral Approaches to Agency and Labor Markets," in Orley Ashenfelter and David Card (eds.), *Handbook of Labor Economics,* volume 4A. Amsterdam: Elsevier Science, pp. 701–772.

Rogers, Paul, Paul Meehan, and Scott Tanner. 2006. "Building a Winning Culture." Bain & Company. Available at: http://www.bain.com/bainweb/PDFs/cms/Marketing/Final draft-Building a winning culture.pdf.

Sheldon, Mary E. 1971. "Investments and Involvements as Mechanisms Producing Commitment to the Organization." *Administrative Science Quarterly* 16: 143–150.

Simon, Herbert A. 1951. "A Formal Theory of the Employment Relation." *Econometrica* 19: 293–305.

Smith, R. David. 1996. "The Career of Status Crystallization: A Sociological Odyssey." *Sociological Research Online* 1(3). Available at: http://www.socresonline.org.uk/1/3/3.html.

Sørensen, Jesper B. 2000. "The Longitudinal Effects of Group Tenure Composition on Turnover." *American Sociological Review* 65: 298–310.

Staw, Barry M. 1981. "The Escalation of Commitment to a Course of Action." *Academy of Management Review* 6: 577–587.

Swensen, Clifford D., and Geir Trauhaug. 1985. "Commitment and the Long-Term Marriage Relationship." *Journal of Marriage and the Family* 47: 939–945.

Tyler, Tom R. 2010. *Why People Cooperate: The Role of Social Motivations.* Princeton, NJ: Princeton University Press.

Wharton, Amy S., and James N. Baron. 1987. "So Happy Together? The Impact of Gender Segregation on Men at Work." *American Sociological Review* 52: 574–587.

Williamson, Oliver E. 1975. *Markets and Hierarchies: Analysis and Antitrust Implications.* New York: Free Press.

———. 1985. *The Economic Institutions of Capitalism: Firms, Markets, Relational Contracting.* New York: Free Press.

9

Authority in Organizations
A Survey
Patrick Bolton and Mathias Dewatripont

1. Introduction

Much of the theory of the firm has been concerned with what determines the boundaries of firms. When does a firm reach its efficient size? When does a merger between two separate entities improve efficiency of production? Which core activities should a firm focus on, and which should it outsource? A central achievement of the property rights theory of the firm (Grossman-Hart-Moore) is that these questions can all be framed in terms of an allocation problem of control rights or property rights over productive assets. That is, all questions relating to the boundaries of the firm can be phrased in terms of who should own which productive asset.

As powerful as this framework is for analyzing the boundaries of firms, it has little to say about what actually goes on inside firms and how firms should be organized internally. When it comes to understanding what managers do it is not very helpful to reduce firms to just a collection of productive assets and a set of owners. One needs to step back from this extreme abstraction and introduce elements from Coase (1937), Simon (1951), and Williamson's (1975, 1979, 1985) transactions-cost theory of the firm. In his foundational article Coase (1937) envisions firms with internal transactions processes that are different from market processes. He describes firms as relying on authority procedures in completing production and distribution of goods rather than on negotiation and exchange as in a market: "the operation of a market costs something and by forming an organisation and allowing some authority (an 'entrepreneur') to direct the resources, certain marketing costs are saved" (Coase 1937: 392).

Thus, what is special about internal transactions in firms is that they are based on a different mechanism, which we shall refer to in general terms as *authority*. This mechanism is a central and integral part of the process of production and distribution of goods. The exercise of authority broadly defined is what managers do. As we detail in the definition below, managers' day-to-day job is to execute the broad mandate that is handed to their teams by their superiors, to coordinate the execution of this mandate by their subordinates, and to keep tabs on what their subordinates

We are grateful to the volume editors, Robert Gibbons and John Roberts, for their comments.

are doing. Although the notion of authority is quite broad and complex, it is interesting to observe that almost all of its multiple facets are relevant to firms, how they are organized, and how they are run. Following Fama and Jensen (1983), let us define four main different aspects of authority:

1. Authority is a supervisor's power to initiate projects and direct subordinates to take certain actions.

2. Authority also involves the concomitant power to exact obedience. For if the supervisor was unable to get his subordinates to execute the directed actions and had to coax a negotiated agreement from the subordinate each time an action is required, there would not be much point in granting a manager the power to direct subordinates.

3. Authority is the power to ratify and approve actions in a predetermined area of competency. Formal authority in a firm rests with the firm's owners, who have the ultimate right to make decisions and to delegate authority to managers. In owner-managed firms there is full centralization of decisionmaking authority with the owner(s). In larger firms authority is delegated to a board of directors, and in turn to a professional management team and managerial hierarchy. However, this delegation of authority only stands if managers' power to ratify and approve action has been previously delineated.

4. Finally, authority also involves the manager's duty to monitor subordinates and her ability to reward them for good performance.

A central question for the theory of the internal organization of firms is the allocation of authority among its members. How to define lines of authority? How to circumscribe the authority, of any given agent? How to credibly delegate authority, and how to ensure that the exercise of authority is respected? A fundamental theme uniting all contributions surveyed in this chapter is that the role of authority and its separation from ownership rights arises from the presence of information processing and communication costs. The firm owner's inability to attend to all decisions involving the operation of the firm, his inability to master all relevant information to make decisions, and his limited capacity to communicate with all employees are the main reasons authority is separated from ownership. The same reasons are also the source of Coase's marketing costs, which authority procedures inside firms seek to economize.

In this chapter we survey the recent economics literature on the internal organization of firms that deals with authority inside firms. The literature surveyed in this chapter builds on the foundational works of Max Weber, Herbert Simon, Alfred Chandler, Anthony Downs, and Oliver Williamson, among others, but seeks to frame some of the core ideas of this literature in the language and formalism of modern contract theory. In the process, this literature offers new perspectives and sharper intuitions on the delegation of authority in organizations. Our goal in this survey is to provide a unified presentation of this contracting literature. A central question this literature is concerned with is how the ultimate holders of formal authority, the owners of the firm, are able to credibly delegate authority to managers further down the organization. A related question is how authority is optimally allocated inside the firm. To address these questions, it is helpful to begin with a taxonomy of contract-theoretic models, which will allow us to discuss the outline of this survey.

2. A Taxonomy of Contract Models

As a way of organizing the literature, it is helpful to distinguish between three different categories of contract models that differ in the degree of enforceability of contractual agreements. The first, classical, category assumes that essentially every transaction, service, or trade that is observable is enforceable. In particular, in the classical contract theory paradigm it is assumed that agreements on both ex ante and ex post action choices are enforceable. Under these broad enforceability assumptions the contracting parties are able to write an optimal comprehensive contract that fully determines how the game between the parties is played. There is then no role for an authority mode, as—so to speak—the contracting parties are then simply executing the prescribed actions by the mechanism designer under the optimal contract.

A second category of contract models allows for weaker enforceability assumptions, whereby some ex ante agreements on future action choices are not enforceable. Ex post agreements on ex post action choices, however, continue to be enforceable. The justification for these assumptions that is commonly given is that although agreements on action choices are easy to describe ex post, they are impossible to describe ex ante. The incomplete contracts literature following Grossman and Hart (1986) and Hart and Moore (1990) is the prime example of this category of models. It involves only partial contracting—to use the terminology of Aghion et al. (2002)—in the sense that the contracts that are superimposed on the underlying game between the contracting parties do not fully determine how the game is played. Some actions typically remain to be determined ex post. This category of contract models introduces the notion of ownership as residual rights of control, by defining a right of the owner to determine ex post all actions left unspecified in the ex ante contract. This is an important advance toward a formalization of authority, but as we shall argue, the assumptions about contractual enforcement must still be further weakened to be able to fully formalize the notion of authority. This framework (where only agreements on future action choices are not enforceable) opens the way for a theory of the optimal allocation of ex post bargaining power. However, it does not lead to a theory of authority over actions.

To be able to model the concept of authority, the assumptions about contractual enforcement must be weakened still further to allow for the nonenforceability of both ex ante and ex post agreements on action choice. This third category of contract models can be subdivided further into two subcategories: models where allocations of control are enforceable even though agreements over action choice are not, and models where neither agreements over action choice nor allocations of control rights are enforceable.

The category of models assuming contractible control focuses on the decision rights facets of authority (parts 1 and 3 in our definition) and allows for the formalization of three different notions of authority, which we refer to as *horizontal, vertical,* and *contingent authority.* Section 3 addresses horizontal authority, which deals with issues relating to the delineation and assignment of tasks or missions to individual agents; Section 4 focuses on vertical authority, which is concerned with the definition of lines of authority, precedence, and responsibility; and Section 5 deals with contingent authority, which addresses the rationale for and merits of temporary assignments of authority over specific issues or projects.

After reviewing these contractible control models, we turn in Section 6 to models with noncontractible control, which focus on the interpersonal facets of authority (parts 2 and 4 in our definition). In these models the agent has effective control over actions (because of the principal's limited attention) but the principal will still want to align the agent's objectives through some incentive scheme. He may still attempt to "get his way" by incentivizing agents to do what he wants (as in classical moral hazard models), by partially monitoring agent's actions (as in efficiency wage models), and through relational contracts, or persuasion. We follow Van den Steen's (2007, 2010) terminology and refer to these models as models of interpersonal authority.

Finally, Section 7 offers concluding comments and suggestions for future research.

3. Horizontal Allocation of Authority: Multitask Perspectives

While the early contracts literature on the economics of organization based on the principal-agent framework by and large simplified the agency problem by assuming that agents are only responsible for a single task ("hidden effort"), contributions of the past decade have recognized the need for a broader perspective. Managers, workers, and bureaucrats not only need to be motivated to work but also must be incentivized to optimally allocate their attention among several different activities they are responsible for. Their allocation of attention to the different tasks is determined both by the relative (intrinsic or financial) benefits they derive from the various tasks and by the technological complementarity or substitutability across tasks. This section discusses how the multitask principal-agent framework can shed light on the organizational problem of horizontal allocation of authority.[1]

3.1. A Framework

Consider the following multitask incentive problem, where π_i denotes the level of output on task $i = 1, \ldots, m$. The distribution of output can be altered through the agent's allocation of effort (or attention) across tasks. The principal has access to a population of identical agents who can exert effort on the various tasks. The principal is interested in maximizing the expectation of an output function ψ, which depends on the vector of statistics π minus the wage costs of the agents he hires. A special case that we shall refer to for most of the discussion below is the functional form $\psi(\pi) = \sum_{i=1}^{n} \pi_i$. In reduced form, we can define $\Psi(a) = E\left[\psi(\pi) \mid a\right]$, where a is the constellation of the agents' effort vectors. For an individual agent, an effort vector $a = (a_1, a_2, \ldots, a_n)$ has utility cost $c(a)$. An individual agent's objective function is a (linear or concave) separable function U of her wage w minus her effort cost $c(a)$.

The first-best efficient outcome is achieved if effort a is directly contractible. It is obtained by maximizing the principal's gross payoff $\Psi(a)$ minus the agents' wage bill, which is just sufficient to induce them to accept the employment contract of the principal (participation constraint). The first-best cost of obtaining effort a from an agent is given by the function $U^{-1}(U^* + c(a))$, where U^* is the agents' reservation payoff. Whether it is optimal to rely on one or several agents depends on the shape of this function, which is affected by the level of the reservation utility and the curvature and economies of scale and scope of the cost of effort function $c(\cdot)$.

Noncontractibility of effort, however, means adding to the maximization problem of the principal an incentive constraint on top of the participation constraint. This incentive

1. See Dewatripont et al. (2000) for additional details.

constraint takes into account the impact of agents' efforts on the level of the contractible variables and on wage levels. What can be contracted on is only the outcome $F(\pi_1, \pi_2, \ldots, \pi_m)$, which can be a scalar or a vector. In general, the dimensionality of the contracting problem an organization faces depends on both the number of tasks m and the number of outputs m. The traditional single-task principal-agent problem with output as the only performance measure involves $n = 1$ and $F(\pi_1) = \pi_1$. In this section we survey a number of approaches on horizontal allocation of authority for the multitask case ($m > 1$). The constrained optimization problem for the multitask case then takes the following form:

$$\max_{a,\, w(F(\pi_1, \pi_2, \ldots, \pi_m))} \quad \Psi(a) - E(w(F(\pi_1, \pi_2, \ldots, \pi_m)) \mid a)$$

subject to

$$E(U(w(F(\pi_1, \pi_2, \ldots, \pi_m))) \mid a) - c(a) \geq U^*$$

and

$$a \in \arg \max_{\tilde{a}} \; E(U(w(F(\pi_1, \pi_2, \ldots, \pi_m))) \mid \tilde{a}) - c(\tilde{a}).$$

3.2. Multiple Tasks and Effort Substitution

Focusing on the two-task case for simplicity, the mainstream multitask problem is based on the observation that encouraging effort on one task may crowd out effort on the other task when the cross-partial derivative of the effort cost function is strictly positive ($\partial^2 c / \partial a_1 \partial a_2 > 0$). A major theme from this literature is that when a single agent has authority over multiple tasks, then the incentive scheme must be designed to balance incentives across tasks. In a moral hazard context, if, for example, the performance on task 1 were measured more precisely than that on task 2 ($\pi_1 = a_1 + \varepsilon_1$ and $\pi_2 = a_2 + \varepsilon_2$, where ε_2 is noisier than ε_1), it would seem natural that the incentives be more high-powered on the first task (i.e., $dw/d\pi_1 > dw/d\pi_2$), for which the agent is exposed to low compensation risk. Yet if $c(a_1, a_2) = c(a_1 + a_2)$, for example, the incentive powers on the two tasks cannot differ without the agent neglecting completely the less-rewarded task.[2]

The cost of balancing incentives across tasks is thus that overall, the agent is given low-powered incentives even on tasks with well-measured outputs (Holmström and Milgrom 1991).[3] This will lead the organization to either (1) go for a job design that gives authority to agents for tasks that are equally easy or hard to measure (with high-powered incentive schemes given only when a precise measurement is possible) or (2) assign authority over the two tasks to two different agents. Indeed, just as a profit-maximizing multiproduct firm must take into account possible cannibalizing effects of a reduction in price of one product on the sales of other

---

2. That is, $dw/d\pi_1 > dw/d\pi_2$ will imply $a_2 = 0$.

3. Holmström and Milgrom (1991) also discuss incentive pay for teachers: since only a subset of the skills taught to pupils can be measured (e.g., standardized math or language scores), a cost from introducing explicit incentive pay for teachers is that it can lead them to neglect general education to train pupils exclusively for the purpose of doing well on tests.

products, a principal must factor in the fact that offering stronger performance incentives along some dimension, while inducing the agent to spend more time on the corresponding task, may also divert attention from the other tasks.[4]

3.3. Conflicts between Tasks

The optimality of task separation is even clearer in the presence of direct conflicts between tasks. Conflicts between two tasks arise, for example, when $F(\pi_1, \pi_2)$ is single dimensional and depends positively on π_1 but negatively on π_2. In this case, it is clearly hard to induce the agent to increase both π_1 and π_2 simply by providing wage incentives on the basis of $F(\pi_1, \pi_2)$. This situation arises in the following circumstances:

- Assume (e.g., Dewatripont and Tirole 1999) that π_1 and π_2 represent the amount of verifiable evidence obtained, respectively, on the pros and cons of a given decision. Efforts spent looking for pros and cons increase, respectively, π_1 and π_2. The decision $F(\pi_1, \pi_2)$ will then depend positively on π_1 and negatively on π_2, while ex ante the principal cares about obtaining the best possible evidence on both sides, so $\Psi(a_1, a_2)$ is increasing. Such an adverserial setup is to be expected in any situation where the firm faces a major decision that is not clear cut, such as a merger with another firm or the launch of a new product, and where the decision is improved if it is based on the best available information for or against the decision. As Dewatripont and Tirole (1999) have shown, the principal may then benefit by deliberating with two managers, each with an opposing stake in the decision.

- Managers who have to perform both ex ante and ex post monitoring of agents in the organization will face a dilemma: uncovering shirking or a faulty product only ex post reveals that the manager has failed to spot the problem ex ante. The manager may then be conflicted ex post in revealing the problem. Separation of ex ante and ex post monitoring can then help avoid cover ups (see, e.g., Boot et al. 1993; Dewatripont and Tirole 1994).[5] Interestingly, such a separation has been implemented in the area of banking regulation in the United States: the Office of the Comptroller of the Currency (OCC) is in charge of the ex-ante monitoring of banks, while the Federal Deposit Insurance Corporation (FDIC) is in charge of ex post intervention in case the bank is in trouble.

4. Other interesting implications of this framework in terms of job design include the following topics:

   1. *Helping coworkers in organizations* (Itoh 1991; Auriol et al. 2002): Managers facing high-powered incentives on their own performance will probably spend less time helping their fellow managers. In academia, individual research incentives may lead to reduced effort in teaching and/or interaction with students and colleagues.

   2. *Multiple principals and exclusivity* (see, e.g., Martimort 1996): Effort substitution induces principals to compete for the agent's attention. This leads to incentive schemes that are too high powered and may justify exclusivity (the agent being forced to deal with a single principal).

5. Of course, separation of tasks also involves duplication of effort and moral hazard in teams à la Holmström (1982a).

3.4. Implicit Incentives and Missions

Multitask problems giving rise to a horizontal authority allocation problem are also present when there are no (or not only) explicit incentives in place to motivate managers, such as when managers are mainly motivated by career concerns or their reputations, as in Holmström (1982b). In the standard career concerns model the managerial labor market tries to infer a manager's talent from his past performance. The manager's incentives to expend effort on one task then depend on how the market infers the manager's talent based on his performance on that task. Such career concerns can be captured in our framework by assuming that $F(\pi_1, \pi_2, \ldots, \pi_m) = (\pi_1, \pi_2, \ldots, \pi_m)$, and that the strength of the reward connecting $F(\pi_1, \pi_2, \ldots, \pi_m)$ to wages for an agent is not contractually chosen but is determined by the labor market. The agent's effort level in a rational-expectation equilibrium is then determined by

$$a \in \arg\max_{\tilde{a}} E(U(w_0 + w(F(\pi_1, \pi_2, \ldots, \pi_m), a^*)) \mid \tilde{a}) - c(\tilde{a}) \quad \text{and} \quad a = a^*.$$

In the simplest version of this problem, π_i depends positively on the agent's effort a_i on task i, her talent θ (which neither the agent nor the market knows a priori), and noise. On observing the vector of performances $(\pi_1, \pi_2, \ldots, \pi_m)$, the market tries to infer the talent parameter θ given the expectation of effort a^*, which is assumed to be correct in equilibrium. In a later period, the agent is then rewarded (through promotion, new job offers, etc.) according to her perceived talent, which is embodied in the formulation $w(F(\pi_1, \pi_2, \ldots, \pi_m), a^*)$. Note that the agent's incentive to work here is driven solely by her desire to influence the market's perception of her talent, and her current-period wage w_0 is, by assumption, constant. In equilibrium, she does not succeed in fooling the market; however, she is still driven to perform to avoid disappointing the market: she expends effort ex post because the market expects it. Whether she ex ante benefits from this incentive depends on whether the initial wage w_0 reflects the market's expectations about equilibrium effort.

Dewatripont et al. (1999) study how equilibrium effort depends on the number of tasks the agent has authority over. For example, they establish conditions under which reducing the number of tasks n the agent has authority over increases her total effort $(a_1 + a_2 + \cdots + a_n)$ and the principal's total profit. The reduction in tasks tends to increase overall performance when the link between performance and perceived talent is enhanced with fewer tasks, due to less-noisy performance measures (higher signal-to-noise ratio). Note that lowering n has more drastic consequences here than in the standard multitask problem with explicit incentives: it is not a matter of less effort substitution but of an increase in total effort!

This benefit from focus is consistent with Wilson's (1989) celebrated study of bureaucracy, where he argues that successful government agencies are the ones that manage to concentrate on reasonably focused missions. Focus means that accountability improves, because performance is easier to evaluate. The agency in the end benefits from this situation if better accountability translates into enhanced autonomy.

Wilson's book is replete with examples of processes by which bureaucracies have transformed their grand-but-vague objectives into more specific and more operational missions. For example, the Department of Agriculture's mission of feeding the nation has been transformed into mainly helping farmers, and the Department of Transportation's mission of improving the safety of transportation has traditionally been confined to improving car safety.

The three approaches detailed above all point to the cost of multiple tasks and the advantage of splitting them among several agents. They also imply predictions concerning optimal task clustering when each agent has to be allocated several tasks. First, the traditional multitask approach suggests that agents have to be given authority over tasks that have similar degrees of measurability. Agents allocated easily measurable tasks can be given more powerful financial incentives, while others must find less powerful incentives. Second, the conflicting-task approach argues for avoiding conflicts of interest in job design. This will lead to specialization of management in pursuing narrow goals and reliance on competition among specialized managers to ensure overall balance. Finally, the focused-mission approach pleads for functional specialization. That is, it calls for specializing agents in tasks that require similar talents, so as to keep the inference process between overall performance and talent strong.

4. Vertical Allocation of Authority

As Alfred Chandler (1962) has emphasized, most large firms are run by professional managers, and shareholders—the ultimate owners of the firm—have relatively little say in firms' day-to-day operations or strategic decisions. In other words, in most larger firms the owners delegate authority to the CEO and the management team. The CEO in turn delegates authority further down the hierarchy to divisional managers, product managers, and so on. A central question for the theory of organizations is: How can owners credibly delegate authority to managers? How can owners transfer residual rights of control to nonowners? Can they formally transfer authority without transferring ownership rights?

One basic difficulty for owners in delegating authority to managers is that it is very hard to formally describe the manager's area of competency and duties to shareholders. Thus, it is tricky for owners to commit to delegating discretion to the CEO over some decisions, such as the firm's marketing strategy, outsourcing policy, or product design. A dominant owner who has board representation can always meddle in the managerial decision process, and it is difficult for the CEO to ignore such a shareholder if she has the power to fire the manager. Thus, for example, when there is a transfer of ownership of a newspaper or a television channel, to what extent can the new owner credibly delegate editorial policy to the managing editor? This question is always critical when there is a change in ownership of a media company.

One answer to this question is that the transfer of authority can be made more credible if there are higher costs for the owner of firing the manager. There is then a trade-off for the principal between more effective (or credible) delegation of authority and better incentives for the agent. One extreme way of delegating authority—as in academia or in the judiciary—is to grant tenure to the agent. Although there are undoubtedly incentive reasons for the tenure system, as Carmichael (1988), Waldman (1990), and Friebel and Raith (2004) have notably argued, another important reason for the system is surely to be able to credibly delegate hiring decisions to departments and to guarantee academic freedom or the independence of the judiciary.

Another answer, which has received more attention in the literature, is that the credibility of delegated authority rests on the superior knowledge or information of the agent. In other words, if shareholders of large firms do not have the skills or knowledge to run a firm efficiently—which is likely to be the case when ownership is dispersed and no single owner has a strong incentive to become more knowledgeable about the firm's business—then the delegation of authority to a team of professional managers is credible.

In this section we first review and discuss the fundamental contribution of Aghion and Tirole (1997), which has spawned a large literature. This article directly addresses the question of how a principal can use an agent's informational advantage to credibly commit to an arm's-length incentive scheme or credibly delegate authority to an agent. As we detail in Section 4.1, Aghion and Tirole show how real decisionmaking depends on individual costs of information acquisition, the degree of congruence of the parties involved in the relationship, and the allocation of formal authority. We also discuss the credibility of the allocation of formal authority, with special emphasis on the case of academic contracts.

Aghion and Tirole explain how, in some cases, parties not endowed with formal authority can, when they enjoy an informational advantage, "have their way" by communicating to the other party what to do. In settings more general than theirs, this leads to the question of strategic information transmission as in Crawford and Sobel (1982). The desirability of delegation in such a context has been studied by Dessein (2002), and we discuss this work in Section 4.2 as well as extensions of it in Section 4.3, which focuses on the interplay between delegation and adaptation to an uncertain environment.

4.1. Formal and Real Authority

4.1.1. *The Aghion-Tirole Model*

Aghion and Tirole (1997) focus on a noncontractible action, which in their setup amounts to choosing one project that the agent has to work on. There are initially $N \geq 3$ potential projects. Project $k \in \{1, 2, \ldots, N\}$ gives the principal a private benefit B_k and the agent a private benefit b_k. Initially, these various projects are indistinguishable from one another. At least one of them is sufficiently bad that choosing one project at random is worse for both parties than undertaking no project (with associated payoff normalized to zero in this case). In contrast, the parties know in advance that the best project for the principal gives him $B > 0$, while it gives the agent $\beta b > 0$, and that the best project for the agent gives her $b > 0$, while it gives the principal $\alpha B > 0$. Call α and β the "congruence parameters," and assume that they are positive but smaller than one. The higher these parameters are, the more congruent the preferences of the two parties will be. Note that partial congruence is built into the setup in any case, because one has assumed that (1) the two parties agree that choosing a project at random is worse than undertaking no project and (2) they each prefer to allow the other party to choose his/her favorite project rather than undertaking no project (since α and β are assumed to be positive).

These assumptions about congruence are crucial given the information acquisition technology: although both parties are initially uninformed about the private benefits associated with individual projects, they can each exert effort to improve their information. Specifically, the principal can at cost $\psi_P(E)$ (increasing and convex in E) become fully informed with probability E about project benefits, while he remains fully uninformed with probability $1 - E$. Similarly, the agent can at cost $\psi_A(e)$ (increasing and convex in e) become fully informed with probability e about project benefits, while she remains fully uninformed with probability $1 - e$.

The timing of the game is as follows. In stage 1, the parties contract; in stage 2, they exert effort to acquire information about individual project payoffs; finally, in stage 3, a decision can be taken on which project to undertake, if any. Assuming that efforts are privately chosen and that parties only care about their private benefits,[6] the contract only consists of an allocation of authority for stage 3. As Aghion and Tirole (1997) stress, what can be contractually allocated is solely formal authority, that is, who has the right to make the decision. This differs from real authority, that is, who actually makes the decision. Indeed, given the partial congruence built into the model, a party endowed with formal authority chooses to undertake a project only if she is informed about project benefits; otherwise, she transfers authority to the other party (or equivalently, asks the other party for a recommendation and follows it). In turn, this other party chooses a project/makes a recommendation only if he is informed about project benefits. Otherwise no project is undertaken.

Given this continuation equilibrium in stage 3, if the contract allocates formal authority to the principal, the payoffs for the principal and the agent (U_P and u_A, respectively) upon choosing their effort levels are

$$U_P = EB + (1 - E)e\alpha B - \psi_P(E)$$

$$u_A = E\beta b + (1 - E)eb - \psi_A(e).$$

These conditions reflect the fact that the principal chooses his favorite action whenever he is informed about individual project payoffs, while the agent's information matters only when the principal is uninformed. In stage 2, simultaneous effort choice leads to the following first-order conditions:

$$(1 - \alpha e)B = \psi'_P(E)$$

$$(1 - E)b = \psi'_A(e).$$

As indicated by the second first-order condition, higher effort E by the principal crowds out effort e by the agent, who understands that her effort matters with a lower probability. There may therefore be a gain for the principal to commit to exerting lower effort, for example, by choosing an agent who is more congruent with him (that is, an agent with a higher α).[7] In this case, indeed, the principal exerts less effort, as indicated by the first first-order condition. He is less worried about being uninformed, because the project chosen by the agent when she is the only one informed leads to a lower relative loss for the principal.

Another way for the principal to induce the agent to work harder is to delegate her formal authority on project choice. In this case, given the continuation equilibrium in stage 3, the payoffs for the principal and the agent upon choosing their effort levels are

$$U_P = e\alpha B + (1 - e)EB - \psi_P(E)$$

$$u_A = eb + (1 - e)E\beta b - \psi_A(e).$$

6. This is assumed for the sake of presentation and can be generalized (see Aghion and Tirole 1997).

7. Aghion and Tirole (1997) also look at increases in the span of control of the principal as a way for him to commit to spend less effort per agent, because he then has more projects to acquire information about.

The agent now chooses her preferred action whenever she is informed, while the principal's information matters only when the agent is uninformed. Simultaneous effort choice now leads to the following first-order conditions:

$$(1 - e)B = \psi'_P(E)$$

$$(1 - \beta E)b = \psi'_A(e).$$

A comparison of these first-order conditions with those in which the principal has formal authority indicates that the agent exerts more effort and the principal exerts less effort under delegation. Indeed, the two effort levels are strategic substitutes, which reinforces the fact that the individual endowed with formal authority has more incentives to exert effort, ceteris paribus, since he can have the first go at choosing the action.

Using a very simple model, Aghion and Tirole are able to generate interesting predictions about the allocation of authority in organizations (e.g., as Burkart et al. 1997 argue, that shareholder dispersion acts as a commitment device to empower management). These predictions are in line with some prominent cases of internal organization described by Roberts (2004), such as BP's (or Johnson & Johnson's and ABB's) organizational strategy to empower front-line managers by lightly staffing its corporate headquarters. Using a similar model, Rotemberg and Saloner (1993) have also been able to generate simple predictions on what traits a CEO should have to be an effective leader in motivating agents under her authority. They show that a more empathic CEO (i.e., a CEO who puts more weight on maximizing her subordinate's utility) may be able to induce greater incentives for subordinates to exert effort to come up with new ideas, even if this comes at the cost of implementing too many bad ideas ex post. In general, Rotemberg and Saloner show that a somewhat empathic CEO is optimal for the firm: she provides the agent with some incentive to exert effort but also rejects the worst ideas he proposes.

4.1.2. Credible Delegation?

Although the key innovation behind the Aghion-Tirole model concerns the concept of real authority, it has also generated debate about formal authority. At some level, one can interpret delegating formal authority simply as the equivalent, in the Grossman-Hart-Moore approach, of selling the underlying asset necessary to get the project going. This interpretation is straightforward, but it is not that interesting if one focuses on authority within organizations. In such a case, delegation of formal authority is problematic because, at least in the United States, the business judgment rule typically leads courts not to enforce contracts written between parties within a single firm. It thus seems that, as far as authority within organizations is concerned (e.g., between the firm and one of its divisions), one can choose the allocation of real authority but not of formal authority. In the end there is no credible way for the boss to commit not to take back formal authority when it is in his interest to do so. This can be circumvented in a repeated-game setting, where allocation of formal authority does matter for efficiency, as has been analyzed by Baker et al. (1999; see also Section 6.2), but these arguments do not work in a one-shot setting.

Note, however, that there are exceptions to this business judgment rule. First of all, it does not apply to financial investors: as has been discussed in the financial contracting field, there are enforceable allocations of formal authority among the various investors who have put money in the firm. Another exception, already mentioned in the introduction of this section, concerns some employment contracts: as academics, we are well aware of contracts that grant us not only tenure but also academic freedom. Aghion et al. (2008) have built on this observation to discuss the relative merits of academia and the private sector in the innovation process. In fact, as a modeling strategy, they keep at a minimum the differences between academia and private sector profit-maximizing firms, focusing solely on the allocation of formal authority between the researcher and the organization.

They consider an economically viable product (e.g., a new drug), which starts with an idea I_0, that can be built on by researchers, leading to idea I_1, I_2, . . ., until idea I_k, which generates economic value V. Assume that, for each of the k stages, one researcher can work on the idea (this can be generalized to more than one researcher). In academia, the researcher is free to pursue his own strategy. He can therefore choose the practical strategy, which yields a probability p of being successful, that is, of moving to the next stage. However, he can also choose the alternative strategy, which yields a probability 0 of moving to the next stage.

Why would the researcher go for the alternative strategy? There are several reasons. First, (and this makes it hard for academia to emerge as an efficient organization) one assumes that financial incentives are not possible, and only fixed wages are possible. Second, although the alternative strategy involves zero disutility for the researcher, the same is not true for the practical strategy: with probability α, it does generate zero disutility, but with probability $1 - \alpha$, the researcher will have a disutility z from the practical strategy. Moreover, at the time of being hired, the researcher does not know what his preferences will be.

Consequently, when the researcher is protected by academic freedom, that is, can choose his research strategy, he will only pursue the practical strategy with probability α (this also makes it hard for academia to emerge as an efficient organization: in reality, the alternative strategy will not have zero value). Instead, in the private sector, the researcher's boss can direct her research, that is, impose the practical strategy. This raises the probability of success, from αp to p, which is the benefit of private research. However, there is also a cost. Having a boss imposes an ex ante disutility of $(1 - \alpha)z$ on researchers, and if researchers have an outside option whose value is R, equilibrium academic wages will be R and private-research wages will be $R + (1 - \alpha)z$. This is in fact consistent with evidence presented by Stern (2004) on academic versus private sector wage offers given to the same individuals.

The cost and benefit of academia are intuitive, but they generate an interesting prediction in the context of a sequential innovation process. Indeed, in the last stage of research, that is, when one already has idea I_{k-1}, the private sector is the more efficient way of organizing research if and only if

$$\pi(k) = pV - R - (1 - \alpha)z > \alpha pV - R.$$

Assume this first condition is satisfied. Then, in the next-to-last stage, the private sector is the more efficient way of organizing research if and only if

$$p\pi(k) - R - (1 - \alpha)z > \alpha p\pi(k) - R.$$

Interestingly, because $\pi(k) < V$, this second condition is harder to satisfy than the first one. Intuitively, the idea is that, if as assumed, the wage difference between academia and the private sector is (roughly) constant across stages, then academia looks worse and worse when one moves downstream in the innovation process, because the cost of a lower probability of moving to the next stage represents a bigger and bigger financial stake. As the two conditions above indicate, in the last stage the stake is V, but in the next-to-last stage, the stake is only $\pi(k)$, the value of moving to the last stage. Indeed, the main result is that the efficient sequence will have academia perform the earlier stages and the private sector the later stages of the innovation process. And the efficient transition from academia to the private sector occurs earlier the lower the level of α or z is and the higher that of V is. The model therefore generates academia as an endogenously efficient institution, even if the assumptions make academic freedom costly, by not allowing (explicit or implicit) incentive schemes and by assuming away any value for the alternative strategy except in terms of the researcher's disutility.

As shown by Aghion et al. (2008), real authority can also be brought into the picture: if to exert her authority, the boss of a private firm needs to expend effort to be informed about the specifics of the practical strategy, it is easy to see that the return to such effort, and therefore its intensity, will grow as research progresses. The model therefore generates the prediction that the private firm becomes "bossier," and pays higher wages, the closer one gets to the final product.

4.2. Strategic Information Transmission and Delegation

The Aghion-Tirole model stresses the importance of information as the source of real authority and casts the problem of optimal allocation of formal authority in terms of an incentive problem to obtain information. An extension of this model by Dessein (2005) shows that relinquishing formal authority may be a way for the principal to signal congruence with the agent and therefore to increase his real authority. This can make sense in the setting considered by Dessein, where there is a probability that the principal, even when keeping formal authority and being informed about his favorite project, cannot "get his way," because his control over the agent is imperfect. In such a case, the agent's behavior when uninformed will depend on her belief about the congruence between the two parties. Relinquishing formal authority can then be a credible way for the principal to signal such congruence, because it is less costly for him to do so if the parties are actually more congruent. Dessein argues that this setting can help explain how venture-capital contracts are structured and how formal authority is allocated between the venture capitalist and entrepreneur. In a somewhat similar vein, Aghion at al. (2004) discuss a model where a principal also faces an agent over which he has only partial control, and may initially want to relinquish partial (formal) authority to learn about her type—in this case, her degree of trustworthiness.

A key assumption of the Aghion-Tirole model is that communication between the parties takes an extreme form: when uninformed, a principal with formal authority blindly follows the instructions of the agent. In general, one would expect that the principal would, in such cases, try to elicit information from the agent and then make the best decision from his point of view, as in the "cheap-talk" model of Crawford and Sobel (1982). Of course, the informed agent may then respond by attempting to manipulate the principal. As shown by Crawford and Sobel, equilibrium communication will then inevitably be noisy communication, with a higher level of noise when the principal's and agent's objectives are less congruent. Dessein (2002) builds on the Crawford-Sobel model by adding the possibility for the principal to delegate the decision altogether to the agent (and giving up on communication). In Dessein's expanded problem, the principal has to decide between informed-but-biased decisions (under delegation) and noisy-but-unbiased decisions (under no delegation).

For the sake of brevity, let us focus here only on a very simple example, where one project $k \in \{1, 2, 3, 4, \ldots\}$ has to be chosen, and where the loss function of the principal is $(s - k)^2$, while the loss function of the agent is $(s + b - k)^2$. The variable s is the value of the profit-maximizing project. It can take values 1, 2, or 3, with respective probabilities p_i, $i = 1, 2, 3$. The agent has a bias $b > 0$ in favor of bigger projects. This would be the case, for example, if the agent were an empire builder.

Dessein compares two organization structures: delegation and no delegation. Under delegation, of course, the higher the bias b is, the worse the outcome for the principal becomes. For $b < 1/2$, the agent always chooses the project the principal prefers, leading to a loss of 0 for him; for $1/2 < b < 3/2$, the agent always chooses a project one unit higher than what the principal prefers, leading to a loss of 1 for him; for $3/2 < b < 5/2$, the agent always chooses a project two units higher than what the principal prefers, leading to a loss of 4 for him; and so on.

Without delegation, we are in the Crawford-Sobel setting, where communication involves the agent sending (costless) messages to the principal about s. Without loss of generality, given rational expectations, we can assume that these messages are truthful (with noise), but obviously the amount of information they reveal will depend on parameter values. Just as with delegation, the principal will be worse off when the bias rises, because communication will become less revealing. But here, since the principal can always choose the best outcome from his point of view (conditional on the information he has), the loss is bounded. At worst, he can disregard any information sent by the agent and choose the loss-minimizing project, that is, choose the k which minimizes $\sum_k p_i (s - k)^2$. For example, if the principal chooses $k = 2$, his loss is limited to $p_1 + p_3$, which is less than 1. Clearly, delegation is therefore dominated in this example when $b > 1/2$.

The next question is: how well can the principal do without delegation?

1. For $b > 3/2$, he can do no better than disregard information sent by the agent. Because the agent knows that the principal will never choose any project greater than 3, the principal cannot hope to receive information leading him to choose a project lower than 3. Indeed, in this case, even if $s = 1$, the agent prefers the principal to choose $k = 3$, so that the only equilibrium involves full pooling (i.e., no meaningful communication).

2. The principal can hope to obtain some information for lower levels of the bias b. In fact, for $b < 1/2$, full revelation is possible, because the agent prefers the principal to choose $k = s$ rather than a higher k. Here we have equivalence between delegation and no delegation (zero loss for the principal) even if, in the absence of delegation, less than full communication is also an equilibrium. As is well known, cheap-talk games also admit "babbling equilibria" with coordination failures; namely, the agent sends an uninformative message because she expects the principal not to pay attention, and this expectation is self-fulfilling.

3. Finally, for $1/2 \leq b \leq 3/2$, the possibility of partial communication depends on parameter values. Because the principal will never choose $k > 3$, the principal cannot hope to distinguish between $s = 2$ and $s = 3$. Similarly, if $p_2 > p_3$, it will be impossible for the principal to distinguish between $s = 1$ and $s > 1$: indeed, the latter case would imply $k = 2$, which is then attractive for the agent if she knows $s = 1$. In this case, we are back to no information revelation. In contrast, if $p_2 < p_3$, it becomes possible for the principal to distinguish between $s = 1$ and $s > 1$: indeed, the latter case would now imply $k = 3$, which is unattractive for the agent if she knows $s = 1$, because she prefers $k = 1$ to $k = 3$. In this case, the loss for the principal is only p_2, and he does strictly better than under delegation.

This example delivers a number of general lessons. First, it illustrates the general trade-off for the principal between informed-but-biased decisions and noisy-but-unbiased decisions. Second, it shows that an increase in the bias hurts the principal both under delegation (because the decision becomes more and more biased) and under no delegation (because it becomes noisier and noisier). Third, it shows that delegation becomes worse when the bias is high enough, because without delegation the loss for the principal is bounded.

One dimension for which the answer delivered by the example is special concerns the potential optimality of delegation when the bias b is low (so much so that communication is possible under no delegation). In the original Crawford-Sobel example (which allows for continuous values for k and s and assumes a uniform distribution for s on a bounded interval), Dessein shows that delegation dominates no delegation for all parameter values for which communication becomes possible under no delegation, which is quite a striking result. Dessein shows, moreover, that his result does depend on the uniform-distribution assumption. And indeed, here, there exists an equilibrium where no delegation strictly dominates delegation while involving communication when $1/2 \leq b \leq 3/2$ and $p_2 < p_3$. However (and in keeping with the Crawford-Sobel setting), when $p_2 > p_3$, delegation does as well as no delegation when communication is possible under no delegation, and one can argue that it is safer to delegate in this case, because this guarantees that a babbling equilibrium is avoided.

4.3. Coordination, Adaptation, Costly Communication, and Decentralization

We now turn to another rationale for delegation or decentralization inside an organization: economizing on the costly communication, red tape, and costly bureaucracy that coordination of multiple agents' actions entails under a centralized command. We discuss this theme in the context of the Dessein and Santos (2006) model of an organization, where the benefit of multiple agents working together in an organization arises from individual agents' abilities to increase their productivity through specialization.[8] To reap the benefits of specialization, however, requires coordination. In particular, in a changing environment the organization must be able to

---

8. The notion that gains from specialization are the source of value added of an organization is, of course, not new to Dessein and Santos (2006). This idea can be traced back at least to Adam Smith and also underlies recent models of optimal team organization following Radner (1993). See, for example, Garicano and Van Zandt (this volume).

adapt to new circumstances, which means that individual agents' tasks must be continuously redefined and coordinated to achieve maximum productivity. This coordination may involve more-or-less high communication costs, depending on how centralized the organization is. Dessein and Santos assume away incentive problems in their model for simplicity (in this respect following the team theory literature), whereas we continue our discussion by exploring how incentives may be introduced in their setting and the implications for delegation that follow from such an extension, using an approach developed by Dewatripont (2006) (itself based on Dewatripont and Tirole 2005).

4.3.1. The Dessein-Santos Model

In their model, Dessein and Santos (2006; hereafter DS) endogenize the degrees of centralization and adaptiveness of an organization with an arbitrary number N of agents as well as the quality of its internal communication. For consistency and simplicity, we shall only consider a simplified version of their model, with only two agents and two actions: a primary action a and a complementary action b. Action a should ideally be as close as possible to local information θ, a random variable with mean θ_0 and variance σ_θ^2. One can interpret θ_0 as the status quo and the realized θ as the change in the organization's environment. Also, action b should ideally be as close as possible to action a (think of b as an input that must fit with a). The expected misadaptation and miscoordination cost to the organization is given by $E\left[\phi(a-\theta)^2 + \beta(b-a)^2\right]$, where ϕ is the weight given to misadaptation and β the weight given to miscoordination. With two agents there can only be two possible organizational forms: decentralization (or delegation), where each agent is assigned decision rights over one action, and centralization, where a single agent (the boss) has authority to command both actions (and the other agent simply executes what he is told to do). Under delegation each agent is more specialized and therefore more productive, but the organization faces greater coordination and adaptation problems. Centralization allows better coordination and adaptation, but there are lower returns to specialization.

4.3.1.1. Decentralized Organization. Decentralization means that two individuals are hired and each controls one and only one action. We assume that the individual who chooses a is able to first observe θ but that the individual who chooses b observes neither θ nor a. Let the individual who chooses a be called the "sender" (S, "she"), because she must send a message about a to the other individual, called the "receiver" (R, "he"). Communication is assumed to be imperfect: S's message is received by R only with probability p, while R learns nothing with probability $1 - p$.

The timing of the game is assumed to be as follows. In stage 1, S observes θ, chooses a, and communicates it to R; in stage 2, R receives S's message with probability p and sets b. Given that we take a team-theoretic perspective, both parties want to minimize miscoordination and misadaptation costs $E\left[\phi(a-\theta)^2 + \beta(b-a)^2\right]$, and so R sets $b = a$ when he learns the value of a and sets $b = \theta_0$ otherwise. Consequently, S chooses a to minimize $\phi(a-\theta)^2 + \beta(1-p)(\theta_0-a)^2$ for each realization of θ:

$$a = \theta_0 + \frac{\phi}{\phi + \beta(1-p)}(\theta - \theta_0).$$

The ratio $\phi/[\phi + \beta(1 - p)]$ can be interpreted as the degree of adaptiveness of the organization and also as the level of discretion enjoyed by S. It grows with ϕ and p and goes down with β. Substituting for the value of the optimal action a into $E\left[\phi(a - \theta)^2 + \beta(b - a)^2\right]$ yields the equilibrium expected cost for the decentralized organization:

$$\frac{\phi\beta(1 - p)}{\phi + \beta(1 - p)}\sigma_\theta^2.$$

As is intuitive, equilibrium costs are increasing with the variance σ_θ^2 (the change in the environment), the importance of misadaptation measured by ϕ, and the importance of miscoordination measured by β; and they are decreasing with the quality of communication measured by p. If the quality of communication can be improved at a cost (i.e., if the firm can invest in better internal communication), DS ask what determines the optimal choice of p. They allow for a continuous p and a continuous convex cost function, but here, for simplicity, we shall only allow for two levels: $p_L = 0$ and $p_M > 0$, where p_M is obtained at a cost F to the organization. With an endogenous p, the expected cost to the organization under decentralization is then

$$EDC = \min\left\{\frac{\phi\beta}{\phi + \beta}\sigma_\theta^2, \frac{\phi\beta(1 - p_M)}{\phi + \beta(1 - p_M)}\sigma_\theta^2 + F\right\}.$$

4.3.1.2. Centralized Organization. Miscoordination costs can be reduced under centralization, as a single individual commands which actions all agents in the organization must take. However, centralization comes at the cost of more costly communication, red tape, and less individual discretion (or initiative), which lowers the beneficial scope of specialization. In our simple two-agent version of the DS model, we can only crudely represent centralization and the benefits and costs it entails.

We shall assume that centralization is essentially a more extreme form of decentralization, with higher quality and costs of communication. That is, under centralization the quality of communication p_H and cost K is such that $1 \geq p_H > p_M$ and $K > F$. Moreover, under centralization a single individual commands both actions a and b when communication is effective (with probability p_H). When communication is ineffective, the second agent does not receive her order from the boss and makes a best effort to coordinate by choosing $b = \theta_0$. Under centralization, the expected cost of the organization is then

$$ECC = \frac{\phi\beta(1 - p_H)}{\phi + \beta(1 - p_H)}\sigma_\theta^2 + K.$$

The choice of centralization or decentralization for the firm then reduces to a comparison of EDC with ECC. When is decentralization likely to be better than centralization?

4.3.1.3. Results. The comparison of ECC and EDC illustrates the following results derived in a more general setting by DS:

- Higher uncertainty σ_θ^2 or higher misadaptation costs ϕ raise the benefits of adaptiveness, which in turn raises the benefits of communication and centralization. Thus, in highly volatile environments it is best not to decentralize. A decentralized organization would either incur high costs of miscoordination or high costs of misadaptation, as the agent who observes the realization of θ would choose to be less responsive to improve coordination. The DS model thus captures in a simple way why disaster relief is best done by highly centralized organizations.[9]

- Higher miscoordination costs β have ambiguous effects: for β close to 0 or ∞, decentralization with $p = 0$ is optimal, but for intermediate values of β this is not necessarily the case. Indeed, a rise in β from a very low level raises the value of communication to keep achieving ex post coordination. But when β is very large, the best solution is to have $a \to \theta_0$ and thus avoid miscoordination costs. In this case the organization relies on ex ante coordination, with very little communication and responsiveness to local information. Decentralization is then optimal to reap the smithian returns from specialization.

- Lower communication costs F under decentralization may result in (1) a move away from centralization (with a move from p_H to p_M) and therefore lead to decreased adaptiveness or (2) a rise in adaptiveness (with a move from $p_L = 0$ to p_M) while the organization remains decentralized. In a symmetric multitask setting DS also show that lower communication costs—by raising the attractiveness of adaptiveness—may at times imply more (partial) centralization with more task bundling and less specialization.

The DS model offers a rich setting, which our two-agent illustration cannot fully do justice to. It sheds light on the recent moves toward higher adaptiveness as well as increased communication and task bundling in organizations. In particular, their analysis helps explain the empirical findings of the simultaneous shift toward more communication and more decentralization in organizations of Caroli (2001), Caroli and Van Reenen (2001), and Bresnahan et al. (2002).

The DS model (at least in our two-agent formulation) is also a good starting point to introduce incentive considerations. Assuming away internal incentive problems is a useful first step in the study of organization design, but it is only a first step. To better capture the internal organization design problems firms face in practice, it is important to also allow for the incentive problems associated with hidden information and/or hidden actions. As far as communication is concerned, incentive problems can hinder efficient communication in two main respects. First, a lack of congruence of objectives can arise between the sender and the receiver with respect to the decision to be taken. Second, the problem of moral hazard in communication can arise. This is really a form of moral hazard in teams problem, because (1) the sender must spend time, attention, and other resources to communicate her knowledge effectively; and (2) the receiver must spend time by paying attention, decoding, understanding, and rehearsing the acquired knowledge. In a nutshell, when it comes to communication, it takes two to tango.

---

9. A related but somewhat orthogonal explanation by Bolton and Farrell (1990) is that a centralized organization can respond more quickly to a change in the environment (there is no delay) and can achieve better coordination (there is no duplication of actions). However, this comes at the cost of worse adaptation (decentralization is better at using local information).

4.3.2. Cheap Talk versus Costly Communication

Imperfect communication with incentives is largely an unexplored topic.[10] One exception is Dewatripont and Tirole (2005; hereafter DT), who discuss a model that considers both imperfect congruence and moral hazard in teams. It distinguishes in particular between costless but soft communication—cheap talk, where the receiver must decide whether to trust the sender's message or not—and hard-but-costly communication—which the receiver knows he can trust but which entails a cost for both parties.

To introduce communication incentives in the DS framework, suppose first that achieving hard-but-costly communication (with probability p_M) requires the principal and agent to expend one unit of effort at cost $F/2$. That is, any single effort is wasted if the other party does not also expend effort. Second, to make the problem interesting, suppose also that the two parties have different objectives. Indeed, if they had the same objective then there is no role for costly communication, because soft communication about the value of a can occur at no cost.

Specifically, assume that (as in DS) S has payoff $U_S \equiv -sE(\phi(a - \theta)^2 + \beta(b - a)^2)$, but that R has payoff $U_R \equiv -r(\alpha E |b - a| + (1 - \alpha)E |b - \theta_0|)$. With probability α it is then in R's interest to align his action with that of S by picking $b = a$, and with probability $(1 - \alpha)$ it is in R's interest to instead stay with the status quo ($b = \theta_0$). Thus, α is a measure of the degree of congruence between the two parties. Assume, finally, that neither S nor R know the realization of R's objective function, but that α is common knowledge.

The timing of the game is then as follows. In stage 0, each party privately decides whether to expend one unit of effort, at an individual cost of $F/2$. In stage 1, S observes θ, chooses a, and—if she has expended effort—can at no further cost try to engage in hard-but-costly communication. In stage 2, if both parties have expended effort, then R learns the outcome of hard-but-costly communication. Cheap talk is also always possible, independently of communication efforts. Finally, in stage 3, R sets b.

What is the difference between cheap talk and hard-but-costly communication in this setting? We assume that hard-but-costly communication enables R to learn his objective function. In contrast, under cheap talk, R has to trust S about a and cannot learn his objective function (which S does not know and therefore cannot convey).[11] For simplicity, we further assume that cheap talk conveys the value of a to R with probability 1.

Under these assumptions, it is easy to see that one of two outcomes will obtain:

- Under high congruence (which occurs when $\alpha > 1/2$), S has real authority in the sense of Aghion and Tirole (1997): she can pick $a = \theta$ and announce it to R using cheap talk while not expending effort on costly communication, because faced with the impossibility of learning about his objective function, R cannot do better than choosing $b = a$.

- Under low congruence (which occurs when $\alpha < 1/2$), R will not select $b = a$ unless he becomes convinced that his objective function is $-rE |b - a|$. In this case, cheap talk is useless and the only way to induce R not to pick $b = \theta_0$ is to have successful

---

10. There is a literature on costly state verification (starting with Townsend 1979), which considers costly audits. This literature concerns unilateral information acquisition and thus differs from the model presented here, where communication is costly for both parties.

11. Note, however, that S has an incentive to tell the truth about a.

costly communication.[12] For a given α, an equilibrium of costly communication (with probability p_M) exists when the cost of communication F is low enough and when both parties' stakes in the relation are high enough (i.e., when min $\{s, r\}$ is sufficiently high).

An increase in the congruence parameter α between S and R therefore leads at some point to the breakdown of costly communication when S can start counting on R to rubber-stamp her (costless) recommendation. This breakdown leads to an upward (respectively, downward) jump in S's (respectively, R's) expected payoff. When this point is reached, centralization is of course not attractive for the sender. In contrast, centralization might be attractive for $\alpha < 1/2$, provided its cost is not too high.

While the DT model allows for costly communication as an alternative to cheap talk, Kartik et al. (2007) and Kartik (2009) have more recently generalized the Crawford-Sobel cheap-talk paradigm (Crawford and Sobel 1982) to allow for endogenously costly soft information communication by introducing intrinsic lying costs for the sender. Kartik et al. (2007) show that even with low costs of lying, it is possible for the sender to truthfully communicate her information (without noise) in a separating (signaling) equilibrium when the sender's type space is unbounded. In a more general model with convex lying costs Kartik (2009) also shows that signaling equilibria involve language inflation in the sense that equilibrium messages overstate the truth in the direction of the sender's bias. Moreover, when lying costs decrease, the equilibria with language inflation involve more inflation and become less informative. A natural question worth exploring in such a model is when delegation of authority from the receiver to the sender is a superior outcome to centralization with inflated and distorted (costly) communication.

5. Contingent Allocation of Authority

Another common form of authority allocation in organizations is a temporary contingent allocation in response to major changes in the environment, unexpected events, or the advent of special problems. There may be several reasons control needs to be shifted in this way.

A first reason may be the limited attention of the party in control. When major new changes occur the controlling party may not have the time to deal with these new problems or opportunities. As is often the case in government, one response is to delegate decisionmaking authority over these new tasks to a new agent or committee. Even if the original party retains formal control rights, the committee gains real authority, because it is able to make better informed decisions, as Aghion and Tirole (1997) have stressed.

A second reason control needs to be allocated to a new party (typically appointed from outside the organization) is that the existing holder of authority may no longer be best placed to deal with the new situation. Thus, a common practice in many corporations is to replace managers of underperforming units and to temporarily appoint so called "turnaround managers," who are specialized in restructuring failing businesses. These managerial services are often provided by major consulting firms, or by buy-out firms, who then also acquire the unit and run it until it is turned around and resold. In addition, large distressed corporations

---

12. Even then R picks $b = a$ only with probability α.

entering chapter 11 often appoint a specialized crisis manager referred to as "chief restructuring officer" to provide expertise in reorganizing the firm while it operates under bankruptcy protection.

A third reason control is removed from the agent in charge when there is significant underperformance is to protect other agents in the organization against decisions that may go against the interests of the organization. The manager in charge of the failing unit may, for example, be tempted to gamble for resurrection by taking excessively risky actions that could restore her reputation and further her career in the event of a good outcome.

Although the contracting literature has not analyzed the turnaround management problem per se, there are at least two closely related literatures that can shed light on this problem. One is the literature on referrals in hierarchies initiated by Garicano (2000), and the other is the literature on state-contingent allocations of control following Aghion and Bolton (1992). We shall discuss the main themes of these two strands of literature in turn and explain how they shed light on the turnaround management problem.

Taking the referral, or management-by-exception, perspective of Garicano (2000), the management turnaround intervention can be seen as an optimal institutional arrangement designed to address unusual problems requiring extraordinary skills. Thus, according to Garicano, it would be too costly to train all managers to be able to rectify the operations of their divisions when they seriously underperform, because in normal circumstances divisions are expected to perform properly and turnaround of operations requires more involved and costly training. In an effort to minimize managerial training costs it may be more desirable to let a few talented managers specialize in turnaround skills (the management consultants and private equity shops) and let them take over control of a division or the entire firm in the event of major underperformance. It is worth noting that this is an efficient organizational arrangement even in situations considered by Garicano, where all managers' objectives are aligned.

In contrast, when managers' objectives cannot be perfectly aligned with the firm's overall objectives, the choice between an internal or external turnaround manager may no longer be a matter of indifference. When the divisional manager has private information on when it is optimal to allocate authority to a turnaround manager, he may choose to delay the reporting of damaging information to hold off the change in control. In such situations it may be optimal to give the divisional manager either a stake in the success of the turnaround or some alternative job protection or career path. Although these incentives have the negative effect of dulling the divisional manager's incentives to run the divisions' day-to-day operations, they have the advantage of avoiding the worst underperformance and of permitting more timely interventions. However, as suggested by Garicano and Santos (2004) in their analysis of optimal referrals under asymmetric information, to make way for such incentive adjustments, a more inconspicuous internal turnaround procedure may be desirable than the very visible outsourcing to an external turnaround expert.

Related to the Garicano (2000) analysis of ad hoc efficient interventions is the analysis of ex ante contingent allocation of authority or control in Aghion and Bolton (1992) and the subsequent literature on financial contracting. However, unlike in the literature on hierarchies and referrals, the basic reason a change of management may be desirable in response to underperformance is not so much to appoint a turnaround manager with special skills as to ensure that divisional managers' objectives are best aligned with the firm's objectives.

To see why an ex ante commitment to replace a divisional manager in only some contingencies helps align managerial and firm objectives, consider the following stylized example of a division in a firm. The division's lifecycle can be divided into three key dates: date 1, when the division's investment of I is undertaken; date 2, when a new event or state of nature occurs, which calls for new actions on how to run the division (e.g., whether to let it continue or close down its poorly performing operations); and date 3, when the final returns from the division's operations are realized. In our simple example we normalize the returns to 0 in the event of failure of the division's investment and 1 in the event of success. We shall also take it that the probability of success or failure of the investment depends both on the (verifiable) realization at date 2 of a state of nature θ and on a managerial decision to be taken following the realization of the state. There are only three equally likely states of nature in our example, denoted by θ_1, θ_2, and θ_3.

As in the previous sections, the role for managerial authority arises from a basic limitation of contract enforceability: the inability to specify a complete state-contingent enforceable action plan to be carried out by the divisional manager. All the contract with the manager can specify is that he is in charge of running a division and that he is ultimately responsible for its performance. The contract can also specify an incentive scheme that is based on the division's final performance and, if the division is a wholly owned subsidiary, in what states of nature θ the holding company can remove the divisional manager.

We shall also simplify the managerial decision problem to the extreme and assume that in each state of nature the divisional manager only needs to decide whether to restructure the division or to continue operating as usual. In our example, expected payoffs in each state and for each action choice are then given as follows:

1. Returns. In any given state θ the probability of success of the investment is π_R when the manager chooses to restructure. In contrast, when the manager chooses to continue operations as usual, the probability of success is π_i in state θ_i, with $\pi_1 < \pi_2 < \pi_3$.

2. Payoffs. Company headquarters' objectives for the division are to obtain the highest possible financial return. The divisional manager, however, also derives on-the-job, private, benefits (in the form of perquisites, prestige, reputation, power, etc.) as long as the division is not restructured. We denote these benefits by $B > 0$. These payoffs capture the idea that divisional managers often don't like to rock the boat or are reluctant to fire their employees in a restructuring out of loyalty to them.

3. Optimal decision. Assume restructuring is desirable in a first-best world only in state θ_1, that is, $\pi_1 + B < \pi_R < \min\{\pi_2, \pi_3\} + B$. But from the point of view of company headquarters alone, we assume it would be best to restructure in both states θ_1 and θ_2, because $\pi_2 < \pi_R < \pi_3$.

4. Participation constraint. The new investment is worth undertaking as long as the division is restructured in at least state θ_1, because we assume that $(\pi_R + \pi_2 + \pi_3)/3 > I$. However, the new investment is unprofitable if the divisional manager has to be compensated for the loss of private benefits in state θ_1, that is, $((\pi_R - B) + \pi_2 + \pi_3)/3 < I$.

In this example the first-best outcome can be achieved if headquarters can commit to only leaving the divisional manager in charge in states θ_2 and θ_3. If the divisional manager could not be dismissed in any state without cause, he would only agree to restructure the division in state θ_1 if he is fully compensated for the loss of private benefits B. But then the divisional manager would be too entrenched and would make the division unprofitable.

Unfortunately, letting headquarters decide on management changes and on appointments of turnaround managers ex post would also be inefficient. Indeed, because $\pi_2 < \pi_R < \pi_3$, headquarters would choose to appoint a turnaround manager in both states θ_1 and θ_2, thus rendering the divisional manager's job too precarious. This is why there is generally a benefit of committing ex ante to precise and objective conditions that can lead to a managerial turnover or a change in control.

In mature and stable organizations, it may be possible to achieve such a credible ex ante commitment informally by developing a reputation for predictable human resource management policies. However, for younger and smaller firms the choice is often only between full entrenchment of divisional management or complete discretion of headquarters. An intermediate solution is to set up the division as a wholly owned subsidiary and to write an enforceable management contract, with contingent control change clauses, between the subsidiary and the holding company.

6. Interpersonal Authority

In this section we review models of organizations where contractual enforcement is extremely limited. Ex ante agreements on action choices between a principal and an agent are not enforceable, and formal agreements on transfers of authority (absent transfers of ownership titles) are also not enforceable. The key question these models are concerned with is how the principal—who does not have formal control rights or who has to rely on the agent taking a desired action—can nevertheless exercise authority. When can she rely on her superior knowledge—her intellectual authority—to induce the agent to implement her recommendations? When does she need to give a more formal order, how can she get the agent to follow her orders, and, finally, what is the role of financial incentives in helping induce the agent do what the principal wants?

The first model we discuss builds on the Aghion and Tirole 1997 model (AT). Unlike in their model, the principal cannot formally appropriate authority from the agent. The principal may, however, rely on her intellectual authority to get the agent to do what she wants. She has intellectual authority over the agent when she is informed but the agent is not. In that case a simple recommendation will be sufficient to induce the agent to do what she wants. The principal may also exercise her authority by giving the agent an order. This is a more effective way of getting things done, as the agent then has to do what he is told, even when he prefers some other action. However, to make sure that the agent executes the order, the principal then has to rely on a costly enforcement technology.

6.1. A Simple Model of Hard and Soft Authority

The model outlined in this section is concerned with the question of how to best exercise authority. Three main modes of authority are considered and compared. First, hard authority takes the form of the principal ordering the agent to take a specific action. Second, the strong form of soft authority involves the principal making recommendations rather than issuing orders. Third, discretion (or the weak form of soft authority) consists of the principal giving discretion to the agent to decide what to do.

As the focus of the analysis is on the relative benefits of soft and hard authority, we simplify the model by assuming that the principal is always well-informed about project returns. As in AT, we reduce the authority problem to a one-shot relation, where the principal cannot take the action himself and has to rely on the agent to get things done. The principal's options are:

- **Hard authority.** The principal can at some cost K make his orders *verifiable*, and thus force the agent to follow them.

- **Soft authority.** The principal makes a recommendation or gives advice at some cost $k \in (0, K)$, but ultimately the agent is free to ignore the advice and to take whatever action she prefers.

- **Discretion.** The principal gives the agent *carte blanche* and lets her decide what the best action is.

More formally, as in AT, assume the two parties face $N > 3$ mutually exclusive (ex ante identical) actions (or projects). Ex post, all but two of these projects produce losses for both parties. Of the two remaining projects, one gives the principal a private benefit $B > 0$ and the agent a private benefit βb (with $1 > \beta > 0$). The other project gives the principal a lower private benefit of αB (with $1 > \alpha > 0$) and the agent a higher private benefit of $b > 0$. Finally, inaction is also an option and gives both parties a payoff of zero.

Although the principal always knows the true payoffs of all the projects, the agent only obtains this information with probability $p \in (0, 1)$. Ex ante expected payoffs are then as follows under the different modes of authority:

- Hard authority. The principal is sure to be able to enforce her preferred action and obtains $B - K$, while the agent obtains βb.

- Soft authority. When the principal makes a recommendation it will be followed by the agent if and only if he is uninformed. Thus, the principal can expect to get $(1 - p)B + p\alpha B - k$, while the agent expects $(1 - p)\beta b + pb$.

- Discretion. The agent chooses his preferred action when informed and otherwise chooses inaction. Thus, the principal expects to get $p\beta B$ and the agent pb.

Although this is a highly stylized model of interpersonal authority it still produces some striking insights. First, if p is small enough, the principal does not need to rely on hard authority, where the agent is required to follow specific orders: all she needs to do is recommend an action (provided k is small enough), and the agent will follow the recommendation with high probability. Second, if p is high, the principal may want to rely on hard authority (provided K is not too large), as otherwise the agent will, with high probability, not follow her recommendations. In other words, the principal may be worse off hiring an agent who knows too much or is overqualified (the principal's payoff is not monotonic in p). This may be one simple explanation for the observed difficulty highly qualified unemployed workers have of finding employment in jobs requiring lesser skills or experience. Third, when principal and agent objectives are highly congruent (α and β are close to one) then the principal may prefer to give full discretion to agents with a high p.

The insights gained from this simple model can be applied to two important aspects of job design. First, if the amount of discretion granted to the agent can be contracted on, how much discretion should the agent be given? Second, if the principal can give financial incentives to the agent, to what extent should the agent's compensation be based on output performance?

6.1.1. Partial Contracting over Authority

Suppose that the probability p that the agent learns the true payoffs of all the projects is a function of some prior effort of the agent. That is, the agent could choose to learn more, gain more skills, and thus be able to raise p. As we have seen, to the extent that a higher value of p may force the principal to switch from a soft to a hard authority mode, the principal could be made worse off by such an increase in p. In such a situation, the principal could benefit from contractually limiting the agent's discretion, either by reducing the number of actions in her action set, or by committing to a hard authority mode. By only granting partial control to the agent, the principal could discourage the agent from learning too much and thus make the agent more compliant.

As an illustration, suppose that a contract can be written giving the agent only partial authority over projects $j = \xi, \ldots, N$, where $\xi \geq 1$. Suppose in addition that if the agent puts in effort e, she becomes informed with probability $p(e) = e$, and that her effort cost is $\psi_A(e) = \frac{1}{2}e^2$. Then, given that projects are ex ante identical, under a mode of soft authority, the agent chooses e to maximize her expected payoff:

$$\frac{N - \xi + 1}{N}eb + (1 - e)\beta b - \frac{1}{2}e^2.$$

The probability $p(e^*) = e^*$ that the agent becomes informed is then given by $e^* = ((N - \xi + 1)/N - \beta)b$, so that the agent can be induced to become more and more compliant by limiting her authority by means of increasing ξ.

6.1.2. Authority and Financial Incentives

Except for the very top managers in a firm, it is rare to see other employees' compensation be based mainly on firm performance.[13] As Van den Steen (2007) argues, one reason may be that, although high-powered output-based incentives boost employees' effort incentives, they may also exacerbate differences of opinion and conflicts over the optimal choice of projects. He argues that output-based incentive schemes may therefore be dominated by input-based incentive schemes.

To illustrate this point in our simple model, suppose that the monetary payoff of any project q_j can take two possible values $q_j \in \{0, X\}$, where $X > 0$. The principal and agent's "private benefits," B and b, respectively, now stand for the principal's and agent's respective beliefs of success: $B = \Pr_P(q_j = X) \in [0, 1]$ and $b = \Pr_A(q_j = X) \in [0, 1]$. Each project costs $\kappa > 0$ to undertake, and as always, we assume that only two actions generate positive net payoffs, given the

---

13. Two notable exceptions, in which output-based incentive schemes are more common, are high-technology start-ups and investment banking.

principal's and agent's respective beliefs: $\alpha BX - \kappa > 0$ and $\beta bX - \kappa > 0$ (where, as before, $\alpha \in (0, 1]$ and $\beta \in (0, 1]$). In addition, when uninformed, all projects look alike to the principal and the agent and have a negative net expected value: $E_0[q_j] - \kappa < 0$.

Suppose that the principal learns the payoffs associated with each project with fixed probability $E \in (0, 1)$. The principal could offer the agent an output-based incentive scheme to induce her to invest in knowledge and discover the payoffs associated with each project. The benefit to the principal is that a positive net present-value project is then more likely to be selected. Let $\theta \in (0, 1)$ denote the share of profits the agent receives under an output-based incentive scheme, and suppose that θ maps into a probability $e = \upsilon\theta$ of the agent learning the payoffs of each project, where $\upsilon \in (0, 1)$ is a parameter measuring the incentive efficiency of the performance-based compensation contract.

The agent's knowledge about projects is only valuable in states of nature where the principal is uninformed. In those states the net benefit to the principal is $\alpha B(1 - \theta)X - \kappa$, because (1) the agent chooses her preferred project and thus generates an expected payoff αB given the principal's beliefs, and (2) the principal only receives a share $(1 - \theta)$ of the financial returns and pays the setup cost κ. From an ex ante perspective, the expected value to the principal of giving the agent a performance-based incentive contract θ under a soft authority mode is then

$$E([(1 - \upsilon\theta)B + \upsilon\theta\alpha B](1 - \theta)X - \kappa - k) + (1 - E)\upsilon\theta(\alpha B(1 - \theta)X - \kappa - k),$$

where, recall, $k \in (0, K)$ is the cost to the principal of making a recommendation. Indeed, when the agent is informed, she ignores the principal's recommendation and just picks her favorite action. Therefore, with probability $\upsilon\theta$ the principal only obtains $\alpha B(1 - \theta)X$. The marginal benefit of raising θ is then

$$(1 - E)\upsilon(\alpha BX(1 - 2\theta) - \kappa - k),$$

and the marginal cost is

$$EBX(1 + \upsilon(1 - \alpha)(1 - 2\theta)).$$

Therefore, when

$$EBX(1 + \upsilon(1 - \alpha)) > (1 - E)\upsilon(BX\alpha - \kappa - k),$$

it is optimal for the principal not to put the agent under a high-powered output-based incentive scheme. Note, in particular, that this condition is more likely to hold the lower is α. In other words, the more the principal and agent's beliefs differ, the less the principal will want to reward the agent based on output performance:[14] he would rather protect his real authority over the agent.

---

14. Similarly, the less effective is the incentive scheme (the lower υ), the more likely it is that this condition will hold.

6.1.3. Abuse of Authority

So far we have only considered situations where both the principal and agent benefit from an action choice. Moreover, we have assumed that the congruence of the principal's and agent's objectives is commonly known to both parties. As a result, an uninformed agent is happy to follow the principal's recommendation, as she knows that she would also benefit from taking the recommended course of action.

But suppose now that the principal's recommended actions do not always benefit the agent, and that the principal may have better information than the agent on the two parties' objectives. Specifically, suppose that the degree of congruence can be either (α_H, β_H) or (α_L, β_L), where $1 > \alpha_H > \alpha_L > 0$ and $1 > \beta_H > 0 > \beta_L$. And assume that the principal knows the true value of α and β, but the agent's prior beliefs put equal probability weight on high and low congruence. Under these parameter values, the principal may want to take an action under low congruence, even though the agent is made worse off by that action choice. Thus, the agent now worries that with a 50% probability, the principal's favorite project is worse than doing no project at all.

Under these circumstances the preferred mode of authority may vary, depending on the realization of (α, β), so that the principal's chosen mode of authority may itself be a signal of congruence. For example, the principal may choose soft authority when congruence is high and hard authority when it is low. This is the case when the following conditions hold:

$$p\alpha_L B + (1 - p)B - k \leq B - K - \beta_L b$$

$$p\alpha_H B + (1 - p)B - k \geq B - K.$$

This simple example illustrates the effect first highlighted in Dessein (2005) and mentioned at the beginning of Section 4.2: when congruence is high but unknown to the agent, the principal may prefer to give her more discretion. The principal's recommendation then carries more weight, as the agent always chooses to follow the principal's recommendation when she is uninformed herself.

The example above illustrates a situation of benign potential abuse of authority, which can be overcome through an appropriate choice of mode of authority. In the next section, however, we explore a situation with more severe abuse of authority, which cannot be overcome in a simple one-shot interaction between the principal and agent. In this situation the principal always has an informational advantage over the agent ($p = 0$) and may prefer actions that make the agent strictly worse off. For example, the principal may have an action in his choice set with payoffs $(\theta B, \lambda b)$, where $\theta > 1$ and $\lambda < 0$, but where $\theta B + \lambda b < B + \beta b$. Clearly, in a one-shot contracting relation the agent will not be able to stop the principal from recommending the abusive or exploitative action. But as we illustrate in the next section, in a repeated long-term employment relation similar to relational contracting situations studied in Bull (1987), MacLeod and Malcomson (1989), Baker et al. (1999), and Levin (2003), among others, it is possible for the principal to gain authority over the agent by developing a reputation for treating employees fairly.

6.2. Authority as an Optimal Relational Contract

This final section also discusses a form of authority that has to do with issuing orders that are expected to be followed by subordinates because of an informational advantage of the principal, and that is sustained by an ongoing relation built on trust, as Bolton and Rajan (2001) have argued (see also Bolton and Dewatripont 2005: 585–594). The central questions concerning this form of authority are why it exists in the first place, and why this mode of transaction is preferred over a spot-contracting mode.

Bolton and Rajan (2001) assume that giving orders requires in the first place superior information by the principal (the issuer of orders). The principal must have superior information on which action by the agent is best for the agent. Second, an ongoing authority relationship based on trust is fundamentally more flexible than a spot-market negotiation-based transaction. However, such a relation is not always sustainable if the agent suspects that the principal will exploit the agent in the authority relation.

As in Simon (1951), Bolton and Rajan compare two modes of transacting, a *negotiation/ contracting mode* in anonymous markets and an *authority mode* built on long-term personal relations. In the contracting mode, the services or goods to be provided by an agent (the seller) as well as the terms of trade are spelled out in detail in a spot contract. In the authority mode, the principal (the buyer) writes a long-term employment contract with the agent (seller), specifying only the terms of employment, leaving the details of which service to provide in any given period unspecified. In this mode, the buyer gives orders or directs the seller to perform a specific service in each period. The seller only has the choice of executing the order or quitting. There are no ongoing negotiations about which service to provide or at what terms.

As the authority mode is based on a long-term contract and an ongoing relationship, the timing of the seller's payments can be made more flexible. The principal can now compensate the agent with a bonus after the latter has carried out a particularly costly service. The principal's incentive to voluntarily pay such a bonus, which is purely discretionary, is supported by the agent's threat to dissolve the relationship should the principal not compensate him adequately. When the principal is expected to always fully cover the agent's costs ex post, the agent is also willing to execute the order. Moreover, since the principal always ends up paying the true cost of services ordered under the authority relation, she has an incentive to always demand the value-maximizing services. In other words, the principal chooses the first-best action in the authority mode and thus generates an efficiency gain, which will be lost should the agent (employee) decide to quit. It is the prospect of losing this efficiency rent that preserves the principal's incentives to adequately compensate the employee's costs and induce him to stay. Thus, as long as the principal and agent transact sufficiently frequently and do not discount the future too much, they will be better off in a long-term employment relationship than by trading anonymously in a spot market.

A related analysis of authority as an optimal relational contract has been proposed by Wernerfelt (1997). He considers an employment relationship as an efficient relational contract to economize on explicit contract negotiation costs. The main benefit of the employment relation in his model is that fewer contractual terms have to be bargained over before trade can take place.

7. Conclusion

As the literature discussed in this chapter highlights, approaching the analysis of the internal organization of firms from the perspective of allocation of authority to managers is a fruitful avenue of research. This approach emphasizes the dilemmas managers face in exercising authority and thereby sheds new light on the importance of (formal and informal) internal communication protocols, as well as institutional commitments to preserve managerial discretion. The rational contracting perspective of most articles reviewed in this chapter, however, paints an excessively hopeful picture of the efficiency of firms' internal organizations. In reality, the sheer complexity of the problem of dynamic organizational design is likely to overwhelm even the most persistent efforts at rationalizing the firm's internal hierarchy. What is more, power struggles and office politics, forces this chapter has entirely ignored, substantially complicate the implementation of a rational internal order.

REFERENCES

Aghion, P., and P. Bolton. 1992. "An Incomplete Contracts Approach to Financial Contracting." *Review of Economics Studies* 59: 473–494.

Aghion, P., and J. Tirole. 1997. "Formal and Real Authority in Organizations." *Journal of Political Economy* 105: 1–29.

Aghion, P., M. Dewatripont, and P. Rey. 2002. "On Partial Contracting." *European Economic Review* 46: 745–753.

———. 2004. "Transferable Control." *Journal of the European Economic Association* 2: 115–138.

Aghion, P., M. Dewatripont, and J. Stein. 2008. "Academic Freedom, Private-Sector Focus and the Process of Innovation." *RAND Journal of Economics* 39: 617–635.

Auriol, E., G. Friebel, and L. Pechlivanos. 2002. "Career Concerns in Teams." *Journal of Labor Economics* 20: 289–307.

Baker, G., R. Gibbons, and K. Murphy. 1999. "Informal Authority in Organizations." *Journal of Law, Economics, and Organization* 15: 56–73.

Bolton, P., and M. Dewatripont. 2005. *Contract Theory.* Cambridge, MA: MIT Press.

Bolton, P., and J. Farrell. 1990. "Decentralization, Duplication, and Delay." *Journal of Political Economy* 98: 803–826.

Bolton, P., and A. Rajan. 2001. "The Employment Relation and the Theory of the Firm: Arm's Length Contracting versus Authority." Working paper, Princeton University, Princeton, NJ. Available at: http://www0.gsb.columbia.edu/faculty/pbolton/research.html.

Boot, A. W., S. I. Greenbaum, and A. V. Thakor. 1993. "Reputation and Discretion in Financial Contracting." *American Economic Review* 83: 1165–1183.

Bresnahan, T., E. Brynjolffson, and L. M. Hitt. 2002. "Information Technology, Workplace Organization, and the Demand for Skilled Labor: Firm-Level Evidence." *Quarterly Journal of Economics* 117: 339–376.

Bull, C. 1987. "The Existence of Self-Enforcing Implicit Contracts." *Quarterly Journal of Economics* 102: 147–160.

Burkart, M., D. Gromb, and F. Panunzi. 1997. "Large Shareholders, Monitoring, and the Value of the Firm." *Quarterly Journal of Economics* 112: 693–728.

Carmichael, L. H. 1988. "Incentives in Academia: Why Is There Tenure?" *Journal of Political Economy* 96: 453–472.

Caroli, E. 2001. "New Technologies, Organizational Change, and the Skill Bias: What Do We Know?" in P. Petit and L. Soete (eds.), *Technology and the Future Employment of Europe*. London: Edward Elgar, pp. 259–292.

Caroli, E., and J. Van Reenen. 2001. "Skill Biased Organizational Change? Evidence from a Panel of British and French Establishments." *Quarterly Journal of Economics* 116: 1449–1492.

Chandler, Alfred D., Jr. 1962. *Strategy and Structure: Chapters in the History of the American Industrial Enterprise*. Cambridge, MA: MIT Press.

Coase, R. H. 1937. "The Nature of the Firm." *Economica* 4: 386–405.

Crawford, V., and J. Sobel. 1982. "Strategic Information Transmission." *Econometrica* 50: 1431–1452.

Dessein, W. 2002. "Authority and Communication in Organizations." *Review of Economic Studies* 69: 811–838.

———. 2005. "Information and Control in Ventures and Alliances." *Journal of Finance* 60: 2513–2550.

Dessein, W., and T. Santos. 2006. "Adaptive Organizations." *Journal of Political Economy* 114: 956–995.

Dewatripont, M. 2006. "Costly Communication and Incentives." *Journal of the European Economic Association* 4 (papers and proceedings): 253–268.

Dewatripont, M., and J. Tirole. 1994. *The Prudential Regulation of Banks*. Cambridge, MA: MIT Press.

———. 1999. "Advocates." *Journal of Political Economy* 107: 1–39.

———. 2005. "Modes of Communication." *Journal of Political Economy* 113: 1217–1238.

Dewatripont, M., I. Jewitt, and J. Tirole. 1999. "The Economics of Career Concerns, Part I: Comparing Information Structures; and Part II: Application to Missions and Accountability of Government Agencies." *Review of Economic Studies* 66: 183–217.

———. 2000. "Multitask Agency Problems: Task Separation and Clustering." *European Economic Review* 44: 869–877.

Fama, E. F., and M. C. Jensen. 1983. "Separation of Ownership and Control." *Journal of Law and Economics* 26: 327–349.

Friebel, G., and M. Raith. 2004. "Abuse of Authority and Hierarchical Communication." *RAND Journal of Economics* 35: 224–244.

Garicano, L. 2000. "Hierarchies and the Organization of Knowledge in Production." *Journal of Political Economy* 108: 874–904.

Garicano, L., and T. Santos. 2004. "Referrals." *American Economic Review* 94: 499–525.

Grossman, S., and O. Hart. 1986. "The Costs and Benefits of Ownership: A Theory of Vertical and Lateral Integration." *Journal of Political Economy* 94: 691–719.

Hart, O., and J. Moore. 1990. "Property Rights and the Nature of the Firm." *Journal of Political Economy* 98: 1119–1158.

Holmström, B. 1982a. "Moral Hazard in Teams." *Bell Journal of Economics* 13: 324–340.

———. 1982b. "Managerial Incentive Problems: A Dynamic Perspective," in *Essays in Economics and Management in Honor of Lars Wahlbeck*. Helsinki: Swedish School of Economics. (Reprinted in 1999 in the *Review of Economic Studies* 66: 169–182.)

Holmström, B., and P. Milgrom. 1991. "Multi-Task Principal Agent Analyses." *Journal of Law, Economics, and Organization* 7 (special issue): 24–52.

Itoh, H. 1991. "Incentives to Help in Multi-Agent Situations." *Econometrica* 59: 611–636.

Kartik, N. 2009. "Strategic Communication with Lying Costs." *Review of Economic Studies* 76: 1359–1395.

Kartik, N., M. Ottaviani, and F. Squintani. 2007. "Credulity, Lies, and Costly Talk." *Journal of Economic Theory* 134: 93–116.

Levin, J. 2003. "Relational Incentive Contracts." *American Economic Review* 93: 835–857.

MacLeod, B., and J. Malcomson. 1989. "Implicit Contracts, Incentive Compatibility, and Involuntary Unemployment." *Econometrica* 57: 447–480.

Martimort, D. 1996. "Exclusive Dealing, Common Agency and Multiprincipals Incentive Theory." *RAND Journal of Economics* 27: 1–31.

Radner, R. 1993. "The Organization of Decentralized Information Processing." *Econometrica* 61: 1109–1146.

Roberts, J. 2004. *The Modern Firm: Organizational Design for Performance and Growth.* Oxford: Oxford University Press.

Rotemberg, J., and G. Saloner. 1993. "Leadership Styles and Incentives." *Management Science* 39: 1299–1318.

Simon, H. 1951. "A Formal Theory of the Employment Relationship." *Econometrica* 19: 293–305.

Stern, S. 2004. "Do Scientists Pay to Be Scientists?" *Management Science* 50: 835–853.

Townsend, R. 1979. "Optimal Contracts and Competitive Markets with Costly State Verification." *Journal of Economic Theory* 21: 265–293.

Van den Steen, E. 2007. "The Cost of Incentives under Disagreement (Can an Employee Be Too Motivated?)." Working paper, Massachusetts Institute of Technology, Cambridge, MA.

———. 2010. "Interpersonal Authority in a Theory of the Firm." *American Economic Review* 100: 466–490.

Waldman, M. 1990. "Up-or-Out Contracts: A Signaling Perspective." *Journal of Labor Economics* 8: 230–250.

Wernerfelt, B. 1997. "On the Nature and Scope of the Firm: An Adjustment-Cost Theory." *Journal of Business* 70: 489–514.

Williamson, O. 1975. *Markets and Hierarchies: Analysis and Antitrust Implications.* New York: Free Press.

———. 1979. "Transaction-Cost Economics: The Governance of Contractual Relations." *Journal of Law and Economics* 22: 3–61.

———. 1985. *The Economic Institutions of Capitalism.* New York: Free Press.

Wilson, J. Q. 1989. *Bureaucracy: What Government Agencies Do And Why They Do It.* New York: Basic Books.

10

Decisions in Organizations

Robert Gibbons, Niko Matouschek, and John Roberts

1. Introduction

Organizations exist largely to get things done. Determining what should be done, by whom, how, when, and where (and then actually getting it done) requires decisions, and making good decisions depends on the decisionmaker's having the relevant information. However, as emphasized by Hayek (1945), the relevant information is typically dispersed (and may need to be developed). Thus, communication is necessary if decisionmakers are to become informed. If those communicating the information recognize how what they transmit will affect decisions, then they may be led to communicate strategically, withholding information or misrepresenting it. Then the decisionmaker will need to take account of this behavior when making decisions. This chapter investigates these issues and how the negative consequences of strategic behavior can be limited and the quality of decisionmaking improved through design of the decision process and the reward structure of the organization.

Jacob Marschak initiated the formal study of the value of information in decision problems under uncertainty during the 1950s, culminating in Marschak (1971). In parallel, Hurwicz (1960) began exploring the problem of designing communication and decision systems to achieve allocative and informational efficiency. Especially notable in this vein of research is the Marschak and Radner (1972) theory of teams, which analyzed systematically the problems of information acquisition, communication, and decisionmaking in organizations. Notably, this work and the large literature that follows from it assume that all parties share a common objective, such as maximizing the firm's profit. There is thus no shirking, free riding, lying, lobbying, collusion, or politics in these models.[1]

We are very grateful for help from Ricardo Alonso, Dan Barron, Nancy Beaulieu, Leshui He, Anton Kolotilin, Hongyi Li, Meg Meyer, Mike Powell, Michael Raith, Heikki Rantakari, Eric Van den Steen, Tommy Wang, Julie Wulf, Luis Zermeño, and seminar participants at Oxford. We also gratefully acknowledge research support from the Massachusetts Institute of Technology Sloan School's Program on Innovation in Markets and Organizations.

1. See Garicano and Van Zandt (this volume) for a thorough treatment of common-interests models of organizations.

The formal analysis of such incentive issues in decision and allocation mechanisms began with Hurwicz (1972, 1973), who introduced explicit game-theoretic treatments of strategic communication and first investigated the possibility of designing mechanisms to minimize the effects of strategic behavior induced by the mechanism. Essentially all the literature we discuss in this chapter builds on the foundations that Hurwicz laid.[2]

The other key element in developing the literature we examine here is contractual incompleteness.[3] The parties not only cannot bind themselves to be fully honest in their reports, they also cannot necessarily commit to particular decision rules or future reward schemes. This moves the analysis from the domain of "mechanism design" that has flourished in the wake of Hurwicz's initial contributions to one where shirking, free riding, lying, lobbying, collusion, or politics are central.

Informal arguments that conflicting interests in organizations are widespread and important for the design and functioning of the organization go back a long way in economics. For example, Knight (1921/1964: 254) observed that the "internal problems of the corporation, the protection of its various types of members and adherents against each other's predatory propensities, are quite as vital as the external problem of safeguarding the public interests against exploitation by the corporation as a unit."

Consistent with the importance of these issues, outside economics, the political approach to organizational behavior also has a long pedigree. For example, March (1962/1988: 110–112) described "the business firm as a political coalition" in which "the executive . . . is a political broker" who cannot "solve the problem of conflict by simple payments to the participants and agreement on a superordinate goal." In a similar spirit, Zald and Berger (1978) described organizational conflict and change in terms of social movements, finding inside corporations analogues of coups d'etat, bureaucratic insurgencies, and mass movements.

As Gibbons (2010: 347) suggests, some of this early work outside economics is close in spirit to current economic modeling. For example, Cyert and March (1963: 30, 32) constructed strategic accounts of organizational behaviors in terms of individuals' decisionmaking, beginning from the assertions that "people (i.e., individuals) have goals; collectivities of people do not" and "the existence of unresolved conflict is a conspicuous feature of organizations." More specifically, Cyert and March (1963: 79) anticipated the application of information economics to the study of organizations, arguing first that "where different parts of the organization have responsibility for different pieces of information relevant to a decision, we would expect . . . attempts to manipulate information as a device for manipulating the decision." They also saw that such strategic behavior would generate attempts by the decisionmaker to undo the attempted manipulation: "We cannot reasonably introduce the concept of communication bias without introducing its obvious corollary—'interpretive adjustment' " (Cyert and March 1963: 85). In short, compared to the traditional description of an organization in terms of an organization

---

2. See Maskin (1977/1999) and Myerson (1981) for seminal contributions to mechanism design; see Mookherjee (this volume) for applications of these ideas to organizational issues.

3. Williamson (1975) was a leader in insisting on the importance of contractual incompleteness in organizational problems, although, for example, Simon (1951) also depends on incomplete contracting. Grossman and Hart (1986) introduced formal models of incomplete contracts.

chart, Cyert and March (1963: 202) suggested that "the kinds of models presented in this book describe the organization as a decision-making process"—and a strategic one, at that.

This chapter surveys the theoretical literature in organizational economics on decisions in organizations, focusing on models where parties' interests are imperfectly aligned. This literature is mostly recent but is growing quickly. Our overarching perspective is that this literature is very much in the spirit of the approach initiated by March (1962/1988) and Cyert and March (1963).

More specifically, we break our discussion into two parts. In the first half of the chapter (Sections 2 and 3), we study game-theoretic models of communication and decisionmaking under fixed decision processes (e.g., fixed specifications of who controls which decisions). These models categorize various ways in which strategic considerations with respect to information transmission can impose costs on organizations. In the second half (Sections 4 and 5), we then endogenize the decision process (e.g., we ask what allocation of decision rights the parties should choose). More generally, in these sections we explore the tools that organizations have to mitigate the costs identified in Sections 2 and 3.

2. Fixed Decision Processes

This section is the first of two on decisionmaking under fixed decision processes. Here we describe and analyze a basic model that is on one hand quite simple but on the other surprisingly flexible, in that it encompasses a wide range of models from the literature. We use this basic model mostly to introduce ideas. Section 3 then discusses richer analyses.

One of the motivations for our basic model comes from Milgrom and Roberts (1988), who discussed the incentives for people in organizations to distort information collection and transmission to influence decisions to their advantage. They recognized a variety of possible costs of such "influence activity," including the opportunity costs of time and other resources spent on trying to affect the distribution of costs and benefits without improving efficiency, the possibility of decisions being distorted by the influence, and the costs of altering the organizational design and decision processes to limit influence.

Another motivation comes from Mintzberg (1979), who described a decision process as moving from information to advice to choice to execution, as shown in Figure 1.[4] We begin by defining our basic model based upon what we see as the influence link in Mintzberg's schema, from advice to choice. While a surprising array of models can be captured this way, in Section 3 we discuss both a reinterpretation of our basic model as being from choice to execution and an enrichment of the model to being from information to advice to choice.

After describing the basic model in Section 2.1, in Sections 2.2–2.6 we analyze five illustrations of the basic model, motivated by the cheap-talk model in Crawford and Sobel (1982), the signal-jamming models in Holmström (1982/1999) and Gibbons (2005), the signaling models in Austen-Smith and Banks (2000) and Kartik (2007), the verifiable-information models in Grossman (1981) and Milgrom (1981), and the strategic management of public information

---

4. Fama and Jensen (1983) proposed a related process running from initiation to ratification to implementation to monitoring. This process does not so directly involve communication, so we favor Mintzberg's for present purposes.

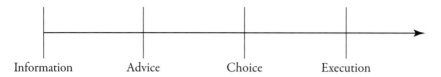

Figure 1. The decision process, adapted from Mintzberg (1979).

models in Rayo and Segal (2010) and Kamenica and Gentzkow (2011).[5] These five illustrations show how even this basic model, although simple, also can generate quite rich examples of strategic political behavior in communication and decisionmaking. We illustrate how different environments for communication and decisionmaking produce different strategic behaviors that impose different costs on the organization.

In Sections 2.2–2.6 we present just the core results that arise from these five illustrations of the basic model. In Section 2.7 we compare, contrast, and interpret these five models and relate their results to prominent claims and observations in the noneconomic literature.

2.1. A Basic Model

Our basic model has only two players, each of whom moves once in the following simple sequence:

1. The state of the world $s \in S$ is drawn from the distribution $f(s)$.
2. Player 1 privately observes the signal θ drawn from the distribution $g(\theta|s)$.
3. Player 1 chooses an *influence action* $a \in A$.
4. Player 2 privately observes the signal σ drawn from the distribution $h(\sigma|s, a)$.
5. Player 2 chooses a *decision* $d \in D$.
6. The players receive payoffs $U_i(s, a, d)$ for $i = 1, 2$.

Note that we assume that payoffs $U_i(s, a, d)$ are independent of the signals θ and σ, capturing the idea that it is really the state $s \in S$ and the players' choices that matter.

For simplicity (and, to some extent, for realism regarding the environments we attempt to capture), we assume that nothing in this model is contractible. For example, player 1's influence action $a \in A$ is not contractible, nor is player 2's decision $d \in D$, nor are the players' payoffs $U_i(s, a, d)$. Thus, there cannot be bargaining over either player's move, nor can there be mechanisms designed to elicit either player's private signal, nor can there be outcome-contingent incentive contracting.

---

5. Although the terms "signaling," "cheap talk," and perhaps "signal jamming" are well established, the models in Sections 2.5 and 2.6 go by various names, some of which apply to most or all models in this section, such as "persuasion" or "information disclosure." We have therefore chosen names for the models in these two sections that illustrate their core assumption or interpretation: "verifiable information" and "strategic management of public information," respectively.

For definiteness, we take player 1 to be male and player 2 female. As appropriate below, we also refer to the players as "sender" and "receiver," "employee" and "owner," or "leader" and "follower," respectively.[6]

2.2. Cheap Talk

Perhaps the most direct application of our basic model is the seminal theory of "cheap talk" by Crawford and Sobel (1982), in which messages are costless (so talk is not just cheap but actually free). In particular, player 1 learns the state of the world (i.e., $\theta = s$), player 1's action is to send a message to player 2 (i.e., $\sigma = a$), and this message is payoff irrelevant (i.e., payoffs are $U_i(s, d)$). The major result in such models is that the misalignment of preferences typically prevents full revelation of information.

As an informal example of a cheap-talk sender-receiver game, consider a biased local manager advising a CEO about capital allocation to the manager. The manager can say anything he wants to the CEO, at no cost. The CEO wants to gear her decision to the local information that only the manager has, but the manager is known to want the decision to differ systematically from what the CEO would want in any particular state, for instance because of empire building or career concerns. Although the manager is biased, suppose he also has an interest in the CEO's decision being geared to the environment. Then the manager's interest in the CEO's decision being geared to the environment may limit, but not eliminate, his incentive to misrepresent his information. Put differently, in a cheap-talk setting, the CEO cannot accept at face value any claim the manager makes (lest the manager make an inflated claim that would then cause the CEO to take the decision the manager wants), nor can the manager tell the CEO the full truth (lest the CEO then ignore the manager's preferences and impose the decision she prefers). In equilibrium, however, if the manager is not too biased, then partial communication can occur, as follows.

Suppose that the state s is uniformly distributed on $[0, 1]$ and the parties have quadratic payoffs $U_2(s, a, d) = -(d - s)^2$ and $U_1(s, a, d) = -(d - [s + b])^2$, where the imperfect alignment of the parties' interests is captured by the parameter b, which we take to be positive for definiteness. In this setting, the sender's message rule $a(s)$ cannot perfectly reveal the state. Loosely, if the sender's message did reveal the state, then the receiver would choose the decision $d = s$, so the sender would want to send a message that induced the receiver to choose $d = s + b$.

Instead of full revelation of the sender's information, what does happen is that all perfect Bayesian equilibria are economically equivalent to partition equilibria: the state space is partitioned into N intervals $0 = s_0 \leq s_1 \leq \ldots \leq s_{N-1} \leq s_N = 1$ and the sender's message reveals which interval $[s_{i-1}, s_i)$ contains the state. For any value of b, there is an uninformative equilibrium in which $N = 1$ (i.e., the sender's message is equivalent to saying that $s \in [0, 1]$, which reveals nothing about the state, so the receiver retains her prior belief that s is uniform on $[0, 1]$

---

6. Although all examples that follow exhibit some degree of conflict of interest between the players, this framework can also be used to explore team-theoretic models, which assume common interests. For example, see Section 4.3 of Bolton and Dewatripont (this volume) for a simplified version of Dessein and Santos (2006) that fits our basic framework.

and hence chooses $d = \frac{1}{2}$). For sufficiently small values of b, however, there are also other equilibria with more intervals. For example, if $b < \frac{1}{4}$, then there exists a two-interval equilibrium in which $s_1 = (1 - 4b)/2$. In this equilibrium the sender's message reveals whether $s \in [0, s_1)$ or $s \in [s_1, 1]$, and the receiver's decision is then $d = s_1/2$ or $d = (1 + s_1)/2$, accordingly. Note that the ideal decision for sender type $s = s_1$ is $d = s_1 + b$, so sender type $s = s_1$ is indifferent between the receiver's two decisions in this equilibrium, $d = s_1/2$ or $d = (1 + s_1)/2$, and this indifference is what makes all sender types $s < s_1$ prefer to say $s \in [0, s_1)$ and all those $s > s_1$ prefer to say $s \in [s_1, 1]$.

For sufficiently small values of b, there are more equilibria—one for each number of intervals from $N = 1$ to $N = N(b)$, where $N(b)$ weakly increases as b falls toward zero. In each such equilibrium, the sender type on the boundary between two intervals, $s = s_i$ between $s \in [s_{i-1}, s_i)$ and $s \in [s_i, s_{i+1})$, is again indifferent between the receiver's equilibrium decisions following these messages, and this indifference is again what makes other sender types strictly prefer to send their equilibrium messages. When b falls, the necessary distance between these two decisions decreases, so it becomes possible to have more interval messages in equilibrium (i.e., $N(b)$ increases).

Interestingly, although Crawford and Sobel's original motivation was from bargaining with asymmetric information, their model has recently become a workhorse in the organizations literature. See Sections 3.1, 3.2, 3.3, and parts of Section 5 for the next steps and Sobel (2012) for a comprehensive survey.

2.3. Signal Jamming

One of the central ideas in the Milgrom and Roberts (1988) work on influence activities is the observation that those in control get lobbied.[7] This idea also fits naturally in our basic model, such as when an owner controls a decision and would like to have the decision tailored to the state of the world but does not know the state, and an employee has an opportunity to influence the signal about the state that the owner observes (and hence to influence the owner's belief about the state and thus influence the owner's decision). The major result of such models is that resources are spent on lobbying even though, in equilibrium, lobbying does not affect the decision.

More formally, consider the following model from Gibbons (2005), which adapts Holmström's (1982/1999) model of career concerns in labor markets to consider influence activities in organizations. A key point is that these models analyze *signal jamming*. That is, in a departure from both the cheap-talk model in Section 2.2 and the signaling model in Section 2.4, here there is symmetric uncertainty about the state s (i.e., player 1's signal θ in stage 2 of the basic model is uninformative). Nonetheless, the employee (player 1) does have an opportunity to influence the signal that the owner (player 2) observes about the state (σ in stage 4 of the basic model). In particular, $\sigma = s + a + \varepsilon$, where $a \geq 0$ at cost $k(a)$ is the employee's choice of "lobbying" activities in stage 3 of the basic model. We assume that s is normally distributed with mean m and variance $1/h$ (i.e., precision h) and ε is normally distributed with mean zero and precision h_ε.

7. Parts of this section draw on Gibbons (2010), with permission from the *Annual Review of Economics*, Volume 2, © 2010 by Annual Reviews, http://www.annualreviews.org.

Because the state s is normal, assume that the owner's decision space is $D = \Re$. Finally, let the cost function satisfy $k'(0) = 0$, $k'(\infty) = \infty$, and $k'' > 0$, and suppose that the parties again have quadratic loss functions. The parties' payoffs are then $U_1(s, a, d) = -(d - [s + b])^2 - k(a)$ and $U_2(s, a, d) = -(d - s)^2$, where again $b > 0$ for definiteness.

The signal σ is the crux of the model: even though neither party knows the true state, both parties care about how the eventual decision will relate to the state, so the owner will try to extract from the signal whatever information σ might contain about the state, prompting the employee to try to move the realization of σ upward. In equilibrium, however, the owner correctly anticipates the employee's attempts to influence σ and so correctly accounts for those attempts when interpreting σ as a signal about s. Nevertheless, the employee has an incentive to increase σ. In particular, even though the owner is not fooled, the equilibrium level of lobbying cannot be zero, because if the owner believed the employee to be doing no lobbying, then the employee would have a strong incentive to lobby.

To analyze the model, we work backward. The owner will choose d to solve

$$\max_{d \in D} E_s \left[U_2(s, d) | \sigma \right],$$

so the solution is $E_s[s | \sigma]$. If the owner's conjecture about the employee's lobbying is a, then DeGroot (1970: 155–189) shows that

$$E_s[s | \sigma] = \frac{hm + h_\varepsilon(\sigma - \hat{a})}{h + h_\varepsilon}.$$

The employee therefore chooses a to solve

$$\max_{a \geq 0} - E_{s,\varepsilon} \left[\left(\frac{hm + h_\varepsilon(\sigma - \hat{a})}{h + h_\varepsilon} - (s + b) \right)^2 \right].$$

The first-order condition for a is then

$$-2 \left(\frac{h_\varepsilon}{h + h_\varepsilon} \right) \left\{ \frac{h_\varepsilon}{h + h_\varepsilon}(a - \hat{a}) - b \right\} = k'(a),$$

which implicitly defines $a^*(\hat{a})$, the employee's best response to the owner's conjecture.

In equilibrium, the owner's conjecture must be correct, so imposing $a^*(\hat{a}) = \hat{a}$ yields the first-order condition for the equilibrium level of the employee's lobbying activity. Denoting this equilibrium level of lobbying by a^*, we have

$$2 \frac{h_\varepsilon}{h + h_\varepsilon} b = k'(a^*).$$

In words, the equilibrium level of lobbying is positive, even though in equilibrium the owner is not fooled (so the lobbying costs are a deadweight loss). Furthermore, a^* increases with the employee's bias b (because the employee cares more about moving the owner's decision), with the precision of the public signal h_ε (because the owner will put more weight on the signal, so it is more useful to the employee to influence the signal), and with the prior variance of the state $1/h$ (because the owner will again put more weight on the signal, now for lack of useful prior information about the state).

2.4. Signaling

To complement the foregoing cheap-talk and signal-jamming models illustrating the basic model, we turn next to a third category of games, again familiar from information economics: signaling. (See Fudenberg and Tirole (1991: 324–336) for the basic game theory.) As in a cheap-talk game, player 1 has private information (i.e., $\theta = s$ in stage 2 of the basic model), and player 2 observes player 1's action (i.e., $\sigma = a$ in stage 4), so the sender's choice of a may change the receiver's belief about s and hence change the receiver's choice of d in stage 5. As in the signal-jamming game, but unlike the cheap-talk game, player 1's action (a in stage 3) incurs cost. The major result in the models that follow Spence (1973) is that some actions may convey information because only certain types would be willing to take those actions (and they are willing only because these actions will indeed convey information). This may happen either because the costs of the action to the sender or the sender's benefit from the receiver's response are related to the state in such a way that, on one hand, it is worthwhile expending the costs to have the decisionmaker infer the state correctly for some realizations of the state, and on the other, it is not worthwhile for senders in other states to try to fool the decisionmaker.[8]

Hermalin (1998) uses a signaling model to study leadership. He begins from the view that "a defining feature of leadership . . . [is that a] leader is someone with followers" (Hermalin: 1188), from which it follows that "a central question in understanding leadership is how does a leader induce others to follow?" In his model of "leading by example," the leader (here, player 1) observes the state of the world and takes an observable action; the follower (player 2) then draws an inference about the state and subsequently makes a decision. In "good" states, where having the followers actually follow is more important, the leader will take a more costly action to signal that his private information really does indicate that following is particularly valuable. Hermalin (this volume) discusses several models in this vein.

When there are benefits to revealing player 1's information about the state, signaling can occur simply by expending resources in an otherwise useless fashion. Such wasting of resources has come to be called "money burning," but in an organizational context it might be fighting through red tape and bureaucratic sclerosis: being willing to spend one's time on such activities signals one's conviction. For expositional simplicity, we describe a signaling model of money burning adapted from Austen-Smith and Banks (2000) and Kartik (2007); see Kartik et al. (2007) and Kartik (2009) for similar models with lying costs instead of money burning. As in the cheap-talk model, suppose the state is uniformly distributed on $[0, 1]$. As in the signal-jamming model, the parties' payoffs are again $U_1(s, a, d) = -(d - [s + b])^2 - k(a)$ and $U_2(s, a, d) = -(d - s)^2$, with $b > 0$ for definiteness. To capture the idea that player 1's action is burning money, however, assume that $k(a) = a$ for $a \geq 0$. Unlike the cheap-talk model, where

---

8. This is essentially a matter of the sign of the cross partial derivative of the sender's payoff with respect to the receiver's inference about the state and the sender's action.

the sender's action could not perfectly reveal the state, here a separating equilibrium can exist, as follows.

If the sender's action perfectly reveals the state, then the receiver's optimal decision is equal to the state that the sender's action revealed, so the sender of type s could choose to induce any decision $d' = s'$ by taking the action intended to be taken by sender type s'. To deter such deviations, the sender's action rule $a^*(s)$ must satisfy

$$-b^2 - a^*(s) \geq - \left(s' - [s + b]\right)^2 - a^*(s')$$

for all s'. It is straightforward to check that $a^*(s) = 2bs$ satisfies the above incentive-compatibility condition for the sender and thus can be the basis for a separating perfect Bayesian equilibrium in this signaling game. Compared to the signal-jamming game (which has symmetric uncertainty about s and, as a result, the cost of influence activities is $k(a^*)$, regardless of the state), here the cost of money burning increases with the state, because, in a separating equilibrium, each sender of type s needs to distinguish himself from those just below.

2.5. Verifiable Information

Grossman (1981) and Milgrom (1981) introduced the possibility that the sender can withhold information but cannot otherwise misrepresent his information. As opposed to the cheap-talk game (where the sender can say anything) and the signal-jamming and signaling games (where the sender's action is not a direct report about the state of the world), here we call any information the sender presents "hard" or "verifiable." Some such models lead to efficient decisions and outcomes, because the incentives for the sender not to be thought to have very negative information lead to full revelation of the state. Thus, a major result in such models is that strategic considerations may carry no cost in communication and decisionmaking.

Formally, as in the cheap-talk game, player 1 learns the state of the world (i.e., $\theta = s$), player 1's action is to send a message to player 2 (i.e., $\sigma = a$), and this message is payoff irrelevant (i.e., payoffs are $U_i(s, d)$). The question is then how to model the idea that player 1 can withhold but not misrepresent information. The simplest approach is to enrich the basic model slightly, by allowing the feasible set A to depend on the state and to assume that $A = \{s, \phi\}$, meaning that player 1's options are to reveal the state ($a = s$) or say nothing ($a = \phi$).[9]

After receiving the signal σ, player 2 then chooses a decision d, and the parties receive their payoffs. Player 1's payoff is increasing in d and independent of s, whereas player 2's is such that, if player 2 knew s, then her optimal choice of d would be strictly increasing and continuous in s. For now, assume $U_1(s, a, d) = d$ and $U_2(s, a, d) = -(d - s)^2$. As a result, player 1 wants to persuade player 2 that the state is high. For simplicity, suppose that s is distributed on $[0, 1]$.

The first (and striking) result in this model is that any equilibrium has full revelation. The key to this revelation result is an "unraveling" argument. Suppose first that the sender announces $a = \phi$ for all s. Then the receiver will optimize given her prior distribution on the state space, choosing $d = E(s)$. However, when $s = 1$ (and actually for any s close to 1), the sender would

---

9. The same basic results hold if one assumes instead that A is all the subsets of the state space S and player 1 of type s can send any message as long as it contains s.

gain from deviating from announcing the actual state, because this would lead to a higher decision. In fact, if there are any two different states s' and s'', with $s' > s''$, that both send the same message, then the receiver's decision will be higher if s' reveals itself rather than sending that message, so unraveling will occur. So the equilibrium must have correct revelation (except perhaps at $s = 0$, but this case is immaterial).

Milgrom and Roberts (1986) and Okuno-Fujiwara et al. (1990) extended the basic analysis in a number of directions, such as competition among senders and general Bayesian games (i.e., many players with private types, each taking their own actions). Seidmann and Winter (1997) provide general conditions (on the preferences of players 1 and 2) for existence and uniqueness of a fully revealing equilibrium; in particular, they show that the quadratic-loss, constant-bias payoffs $U_1(s, a, d) = -(d - [s + b])^2$ and $U_2(s, a, d) = -(d - s)^2$ also necessitate full revelation in equilibrium (for overviews, see Milgrom 2008; Sobel 2012).

Finally, although full revelation necessarily occurs in the equilibrium of the basic verifiable-information game above, this result depends on it being common knowledge that the sender is informed (see, for instance, Dye 1985). Suppose instead that in stage 2 there is probability q that $\theta = s$ and probability $1 - q$ that $\theta = \phi$ (i.e., the sender receives no information at all). Straightforward calculations then show that in equilibrium there is a critical value $s^*(q)$ such that

1. if $\theta = s$ and $s > s^*(q)$, then the sender reveals s;
2. if $\theta = s$ and $s < s^*(q)$, then the sender reports $a = \phi$; and
3. if $\theta = \phi$, then the sender reports $a = \phi$.

To compute $s^*(q)$, suppose that s is uniformly distributed on $[0, 1]$, $U_1(s, a, d) = d$ and $U_2(s, a, d) = -(d - s)^2$. If the sender reveals s, then the receiver chooses $d = s$, whereas if the sender reports $a = \phi$, then the receiver chooses $d = q \times s^*(q)/2 + (1 - q) \times \frac{1}{2}$, so $s^*(q) = (1 - q)/(2 - q)$. Naturally, for $q = 1$, we recover full revelation, whereas for $q = 0$, only the upper half of the type space reveals itself.

2.6. Strategic Management of Public Information

The final illustration of our basic model concerns the strategic management of public information. A major contribution of this emerging literature is to shed light on the conditions under which the ability to manage public information strategically leads to a loss of information.

To introduce this final illustration of our basic model, consider the issue of agenda control. In some settings, for instance, information acquisition and deliberation are followed by voting, but one or more actors can call the question, meaning that the vote must occur immediately, which prevents further information acquisition. For a simple model motivated by Brocas and Carrillo (2007), suppose player 1 has no private information, but he can attempt to influence player 2's belief by affecting what public information she observes. Formally, the state is uniformly distributed on $[\underline{s}, \bar{s}]$, where $\underline{s} < 0 < \bar{s}$, player 1's signal θ is uninformative, player 1's influence action is $a \in A = \{0, 1\}$, and player 2's signal is $\sigma = sa$.

Now suppose that player 2's decision d is binary: either she implements a new project with payoff s for her or she preserves the status quo with payoff 0 for her. Player 1, however, benefits when the new project is implemented and not otherwise, and player 1's action a is costless. Formally, $D = \{0, 1\}$, $U_1(s, a, d) = d$, and $U_2(s, a, d) = ds$.

In this setting, player 1 has two choices: $a = 0$, in which case player 2 chooses $d = 1$ if and only if $E(s) > 0$, or $a = 1$, in which case player 2 observes $\sigma = s$ and then chooses $d = 1$ if and only if $s > 0$. Clearly, if $E(s) > 0$, then player 1 should choose $a = 0$, and otherwise he should roll the dice by choosing $a = 1$. In a richer model, instead of being uninformative, player 1's signal θ could be publicly observed, in which case analogous reasoning begins by assessing whether $E(s|\theta) > 0$.

Beyond agenda control, now consider a pharmaceutical company designing a clinical trial to influence a regulator. Alternatively, to give an example from inside an organization, imagine a boss, who, as part of rolling out a new program, can commission a study in the hope that its public results will motivate employees to implement the program well. What kind of trial/study should player 1 design?

Formally, the model is as above, except now suppose that player 1's influence action is to choose a critical value $s^* \in [\underline{s}, \bar{s}]$ such that player 2's signal will be $\sigma = (s^*, x)$, where x is a binary random variable: $x = L$ if $s < s^*$, and $x = H$ if $s > s^*$. To keep things interesting, suppose that $E(s) < 0$ (i.e., $|\underline{s}| > \bar{s}$), in which case player 1's optimal influence action is to choose $s^* = -\bar{s}$, maximizing the probability that player 2 will choose $d = 1$.

Kamenica and Gentzkow (2011) study a general version of this model, which can be interpreted as strategic management of public information by an interested party. This final illustration of our basic model is closer to the signal-jamming than to the cheap-talk, signaling, or verifiable-information illustrations, because we assume that player 1 has no private information and his influence activity is an attempt to change player 2's belief by changing the design of a public signal. Formally, player 1's influence action a is to choose a realization space X and a family of likelihood functions $\{\lambda(x|s)\}_{s \in S}$. Player 2's signal σ is then the family of likelihood functions and a realization $x \in X$. In the clinical trial/corporate study example above, the critical value s^* was all player 2 needed to know to understand the family of likelihood functions $\{\lambda(x|s)\}_{s \in S}$.

Kamenica and Gentzkow (2011) provide necessary and sufficient conditions for player 1's optimal influence action to be uninformative (e.g., X has only one element), and they derive other properties of player 1's optimal influence action, including the case of quadratic loss functions (which we discuss further in Section 2.7). Kolotilin (2012a) analyzes the special case above, where D is binary and player 1's payoff is $U_1(s, a, d) = d$, for which he fully characterizes player 1's optimal influence action. Finally, Rayo and Segal (2010) and Kolotilin (2012b) analyze the case where player 2 has private information, separate from the realization of player 1's likelihood functions. This case is important, both because a single player 2 may indeed have private information and because there may instead be a group of player 2s with known but heterogeneous preferences.

2.7. Summary

We now summarize and assess the models in this section, noting both their similarities and their differences, as well as some of their existing and potential connections to past and future literatures. To emphasize some important similarities, we begin with the special case of our basic model in which the parties have quadratic loss functions. To encompass the signal-jamming and signaling models, we also include the cost $k(a)$ in player 1's payoff, so the payoff functions are $U_1(s, a, d) = -(d - [s + b])^2 - k(a)$ and $U_2(s, a, d) = -(d - s)^2$.

Under full information about s, the action $a = 0$ and the decision $d = s + (b/2)$ would maximize the parties' total payoff

$$U_1(s, a, d) + U_2(s, a, d) = -\left(d - [s + b]\right)^2 - k(a) - (d - s)^2,$$

producing a total payoff of $-\frac{1}{2}b^2$. Because d is not contractible, however, in all five models in this section—cheap talk, signal jamming, signaling, verifiable information, and strategic management of public information—player 2's equilibrium decision is $d^*(\sigma) = E_{s|\sigma}(s|\sigma)$. We therefore can write the parties' equilibrium expected total payoff as

$$E[U_1(s, a, d) + U_2(s, a, d)] = E_s\left[-\left(d - [s + b]\right)^2 - k(a(s)) - (d - s)^2\right]$$

$$= E_\sigma\left\{E_{s|\sigma}\left[-\left(d - [s + b]\right)^2 - (d - s)^2\right]|\sigma\right\} - E_s[k(a(s))]$$

$$= -b^2 - 2E_\sigma[Var(s|\sigma)] - E_s[k(a(s))].$$

Thus, regardless of the model, the loss the parties suffer between their optimized total payoff under full information, $-\frac{1}{2}b^2$, and their equilibrium expected total payoff in any of our models, $-b^2 - 2E_\sigma[Var(s|\sigma)] - E_s[k(a(s))]$, is

$$\tfrac{1}{2}b^2 + 2E_\sigma[Var(s|\sigma)] + E_s[k(a(s))].$$

This expression measures the total expected equilibrium loss from strategic communication and decisionmaking in all five models. The first term, $\frac{1}{2}b^2$, captures the loss in total payoff from the noncontractibility of d, so player 2's equilibrium decision is $d^*(\sigma) = E_{s|\sigma}(s|\sigma)$ rather than $E_{s|\sigma}(s|\sigma) + \frac{1}{2}b$. In this sense, the average decision is not optimal, regardless of the state. The parties incur this loss in all five models.

The second term, $2E_\sigma[Var(s|\sigma)]$, measures the loss $E_\sigma[Var(s|\sigma)]$ that each party incurs because the decision is not perfectly adapted to the state, as it would be if the decision were $d = s + (b/2)$ or any other function $d = s + z$ for some constant z. This loss is not about the average decision, but instead about how the decision varies with the state. Because different models produce different equilibrium signals σ, the size of this loss varies across models. For example, the coarse communication in the cheap-talk model does not reduce this term to zero, whereas the full revelation that may occur in the signaling, verifiable-information, and public-information models does, and the way the receiver accounts for the sender's influence activity in the signal-jamming model reduces this term not to zero but at least to as low as it can be, given the noise ε in the signal $\sigma = s + a + \varepsilon$.

Finally, the third term, $E_s[k(a(s))]$, reflects player 1's expected costs of influence activities, so it is zero in the cheap-talk, verifiable-information, and public-information models, but positive in the signal-jamming and signaling models. As we formulated both of the latter models, this cost is a pure waste, undertaken by the sender in equilibrium only to influence the receiver's beliefs and hence her decision. In alternative formulations of both models, however, the sender's influence activity could also be productive (e.g., in Holmström's (1982/1999) signal-jamming model of wage determination or Hermalin's (1998) signaling model of leadership), but the inefficiency we capture in pure form here would not disappear.

We think the similarities across these models do a nice job formalizing the quotations from Cyert and March (1963) in Section 1 about "attempts to manipulate information as a device for manipulating the decision" and "interpretive adjustment" being an "obvious corollary" of communication bias. Almost two decades later, March (1981: 217) summarized subsequent work (outside economics) by asserting that

> information is an instrument of consciously strategic actors. Information may be false; it is always serving a purpose. . . . Thus information itself is a game. Except insofar as the structure of the game dictates honesty as a necessary tactic, all information is self-serving.

Again, this section's models seem consistent with this summary. For example, the full-revelation result in the verifiable-information game could be an example where "the structure of the game dictates honesty as a necessary tactic." Ironically, the models and techniques we have surveyed began to appear in about 1981, whereas this was about the end of this literature outside economics.

Naturally, one of the reasons to build models is to explore the many different environments in which strategic communication and decisionmaking can play out and the many different behaviors and inefficiencies that can then result, so we see the differences among this section's models as useful in that regard. For example, Feldman and March (1981) describe various organizational activities not too distant from money burning in the signaling model: wasteful ways that organization members need to jump through hoops to establish credibility.

More generally, beyond money burning, after presenting several case studies and alluding to many others on information gathering, communication, and decisionmaking in organizations, Feldman and March (1981: 174) summarize these studies with six observations:

1. Much of the information that is gathered and communicated by individuals and organizations has little decision relevance.

2. Much of the information that is used to justify a decision is collected and interpreted after the decision has been made, or substantially made.

3. Much of the information gathered in response to requests for information is not considered in the making of decisions for which it was requested.

4. Regardless of the information available at the time a decision is first considered, more information is requested.

5. Complaints that an organization does not have enough information to make a decision occur while available information is ignored.

6. The relevance of the information provided in the decisionmaking process to the decision being made is less conspicuous than is the insistence on information.

Without taking these small-sample observations as gospel, they fit sufficiently well with our experiences that we suspect there would be steep returns to integrating the kinds of theoretical approaches sketched here with both qualitative and quantitative empirical work on information gathering, communication, and decisionmaking in organizations. To do so, we need to move beyond the relatively simple models described in this section to address more complex and realistic issues in organizational design and performance. In the next section, we begin to undertake this task.

3. Richer Analyses

Having introduced our basic model and its five illustrations, we turn next to several richer analyses. Specifically, we consider

Section 3.1: multidimensional cheap talk;

Section 3.2: more parties (senders, receivers, or both);

Section 3.3: more periods;

Section 3.4: a reinterpretation of the basic model as the choice-to-execution stages of Mintzberg's (1979) timing;

Section 3.5: an enrichment of the basic model to include the information-to-advice-to-choice stages;

Section 3.6: enrichments where some aspect of the model is contractible; and

Section 3.7: models of contests for control, where the right to make decision d cannot be allocated ex ante to player 2 but instead must be secured by one of the parties before d can be chosen in stage 5 of the basic model.

Although one of our main purposes in Section 2 was to specify models clearly enough to analyze and compare them, here we shift gears somewhat, focusing more on sketching applications than on formulating models or deriving results. One exception, however, is Section 3.1, because the recent models of multidimensional cheap talk importantly enrich the basic intuition from Section 2.2.

3.1. Multidimensional Cheap Talk

The cheap-talk model by Crawford and Sobel (1982) captures the fundamental insight that costless communication is less effective when the parties' interests are less aligned. Even our basic model in Section 2.1, however, placed no restrictions on the state space S or the decision space D, and hence allowed the possibility of multidimensional cheap talk. And, interestingly, recent work has shown that multidimensional cheap talk creates new ways for the parties' interests to be aligned and hence costless communication to be effective. Sobel (2012) discusses several papers in this vein; we therefore complement his discussion by giving three additional examples.

Chakraborty and Harbaugh (2007) provide a direct example of how multidimensional cheap talk creates new ways for the parties' interests to be aligned: they show that comparative cheap talk, across dimensions of the state space, can be credible, even if cheap talk about any one dimension would not be. As a simple example, suppose that the state space is $S = S_1 \times S_2$, and the decision space is $D = D_1 \times D_2$, where the state is uniformly distributed on the unit square, each decision is from the real line, and the parties' payoffs are $U_2(s, d) = -(d_1 - s_1)^2 - (d_2 - s_2)^2$ and $U_1(s, d) = -(d_1 - (s_1 + b))^2 - (d_2 - (s_2 + b))^2$. That is, the sender's bias is b on both dimensions, and suppose $b > \frac{1}{4}$, so that cheap talk cannot be effective on one dimension alone.

Chakraborty and Harbaugh (2007) show, however, that comparative cheap talk can be effective. For example, consider the messages "$s_1 > s_2$" and "$s_2 > s_1$" (where we ignore equality, because it has zero probability). Because $E[\max\{s_1, s_2\}] = \frac{2}{3}$ and $E[\min\{s_1, s_2\}] = \frac{1}{3}$, in equilibrium, if the sender says "$s_1 > s_2$," then the receiver chooses $(d_1, d_2) = (\frac{2}{3}, \frac{1}{3})$, whereas if he says "$s_2 > s_1$," then she chooses $(d_1, d_2) = (\frac{1}{3}, \frac{2}{3})$. For a given state (s_1, s_2), the sender's gain from inducing $(d_1, d_2) = (\frac{2}{3}, \frac{1}{3})$ instead of $(d_1, d_2) = (\frac{1}{3}, \frac{2}{3})$ is $\frac{2}{3}(s_1 - s_2)$, so such comparative cheap talk is indeed an equilibrium, and the expression for the sender's gain reveals why: $\frac{2}{3}(s_1 - s_2)$ is independent of the one-dimensional bias b.

Che et al. (2012) also consider comparative cheap talk. For example, suppose the receiver can choose either of two new projects, d_1 or d_2, or the status quo, d_0, so $D = \{d_0, d_1, d_2\}$. The parties' payoffs from the new projects depend on the state, but their payoffs from the status quo do not. Unlike in the other models we have discussed, the parties' payoffs are identical for either new project: $U_1(s, d_i) = U_2(s, d_i) > 0$ for $i = 1, 2$, which bodes well for communication. There is a difference in their payoffs from the status quo, however: the sender receives zero from the status quo, but the receiver receives a positive payoff, $0 = U_1(s, d_0) = U_{10} < U_2(s, d_0) = U_{20}$, which complicates communication. In particular, the sender would like to persuade the receiver to choose the superior new project (or, failing that, even the inferior new project), but the receiver might prefer the status quo.

As a numerical example, suppose that the payoff from d_1 is either 1 or 7, the payoff from d_2 is either 4 or 6, and all four payoff combinations are equally likely. In a full-revelation equilibrium, if the sender says "d_1 is better than d_2," then the receiver compares $E[U_2(s, d_1)|U_2(s, d_1) > U_2(s, d_2)] = 7$ to U_{20}, whereas if the sender says "d_2 is better than d_1," then the receiver compares $E[U_2(s, d_2)|U_2(s, d_2) > U_2(s, d_1)] = 5$ to U_{20}. For full revelation, where the sender's recommendation is always accepted, the receiver's payoff from the status quo must be sufficiently small: $U_{20} \leq 5$. For somewhat larger values of U_{20}, the sender panders to project 1, sometimes recommending it when it is the inferior new project. For example, if $U_{20} = 5.25$, then there is a mixed-strategy equilibrium where the sender recommends the superior new project unless the payoffs are $(1, 4)$, in which case he recommends project 1 with probability $\frac{2}{5}$ (even though it is the inferior project). This strategy by the sender strengthens the receiver's belief about project 2 when it is recommended, so that the expected payoff from project 2 can compete with U_{20}. In response, the receiver always accepts project 1 but rejects project 2 in favor of the status quo with probability $\frac{3}{4}$.

Finally, in an intriguing model of the development and exercise of expertise, Callander (2008b) imagines that one dimension of the state is simple (e.g., what project to adopt), but another is potentially quite complex (e.g., expertise about the probability distribution over outcomes from adopting a project). Callander assumes that an expert can talk about the first dimension but not the second, and he finds that equilibrium communication depends importantly on the correlation between the two. As we discuss in Section 5.2.1, these ideas have important implications for the feasibility and desirability of delegation. For now, however, we simply provide a third example of multidimensional cheap talk, inspired by Callander's (2008b: 124) critique of existing models in which "a single recommendation by an expert can render an intelligent layperson an expert."

Our setting is more abstract than Callander's. Here, the state space S consists of pairs $s = (s_1, s_2)$. The probability distribution over S puts zero weight on pairs (A, A), (B, B), and (C, C), but puts positive weight on each realization of s_2: $\Pr(s_2 = X) > 0$, $X = A, B, C$. Player 1 observes $\theta = s_1$, and his cheap-talk message a is an element of $\{A, B, C\}$. Think of it as his claim as to the value of s_1. (For simplicity, we depart from Callander (2008b) by assuming that player 1 does not observe s_2.) Player 2 then observes $\sigma = a$ and selects d, an element of $\{A, B, C\}$.

The sender wants the decision d to match the first element of the state, but the receiver wants to match the second. Because the two elements of the state are always different, the parties' interests are always conflicting in this respect. However, neither wants the decision to differ from both s_1 and s_2, because both would then receive negative payoffs. Formally, if $d = s_1$, then $U_1 = b_1 > 0$ and $U_2 = 0$. Symmetrically, if $d = s_2$, then $U_1 = 0$ and $U_2 = b_2 > 0$. In addition, if d is not equal to either s_1 or s_2, then both parties receive $K < 0$.

Depending on the probability distribution over states, it may be possible for the receiver to invert the sender's message if he reports honestly, as in Crawford and Sobel (1982). For example, suppose that, conditional on s_1, the probability distributions over s_2 are degenerate, in each case placing probability zero not just on $s_2 = s_1$ but also on one of the two remaining options. For example, $\Pr(A|A) = \Pr(B|A) = 0$, $\Pr(B|B) = \Pr(C|B) = 0$, and $\Pr(C|C) = \Pr(A|C) = 0$, so that if the first element of the state is A, then the second is C; if B, then A; and if C, then B. If the sender announced truthfully, $a = s_1$, then the receiver could immediately determine the value of s_2 and choose accordingly, $d = s_2$. The sender would then have a profitable deviation from the action that induces $d = s_1$, so the equilibrium cannot involve full revelation by the sender.

Alternatively, suppose each of the alternatives to $s_2 = s_1$ is equally likely—for example, $\Pr(B|A) = \Pr(C|A) = \frac{1}{2}$. If the sender is presumed to report honestly, then the receiver faces a choice between accepting the sender's "recommendation" (setting $d = a$, which by hypothesis is equal to s_1) or picking one of the remaining two options, each of which is equally likely to be the receiver's preferred decision. The first alternative yields $U_2 = 0$, whereas the second gives expected value $EU_2 = (b_2 + K)/2$. If K is sufficiently negative, then the first alternative is more attractive, and the receiver simply rubber-stamps the sender's choice, knowing it is surely not the option she would prefer. In this case, a single recommendation by the sender does not render the receiver an expert.

3.2. More Parties

Many organizational settings involve more than the two parties envisioned in the basic model in Section 2.1. Here we briefly discuss three such settings: more senders, more receivers, and more of both (e.g., because each party is both sending and receiving).

3.2.1. More Senders

In a cheap-talk setting, when two senders share the same information but different preferences about how the decision should be tailored to the state, there is an opportunity for their separate reports to discipline each other, together providing more information to the receiver than had either sender reported alone. In applied models, Gibbons (1988) and Gilligan and Krehbiel (1989) study arbitration and legislative committees, respectively. Krishna and Morgan (2001) and Battaglini (2002) analyze more abstract cheap-talk models, and Milgrom and Roberts (1986) analyze competition among senders in a verifiable-information game. See Sobel (2012) for a review of these and subsequent papers.

3.2.2. More Receivers

Complementing the idea that two senders might discipline each other's reports in a cheap-talk game, one can also imagine how two receivers with different preferences about how the decision should be tailored to the state could discipline the report sent by a single sender. In addition, with two receivers, one can analyze whether communication should be in public, in private, or both. Farrell and Gibbons (1989) offer a simple first analysis of these issues; Goltsman and Pavlov (2011) provide a considerable generalization.

Switching from cheap talk to verifiable information, Caillaud and Tirole (2007) develop another model with multiple receivers, asking how a project's sponsor, who is known to benefit if the project is implemented, can recruit necessary support from potentially skeptical group members. Potential applications include flat organizations—such as a partnership, committee, or consortium—as well as such settings as a matrix organization, where an employee has multiple bosses.

In the Caillaud and Tirole model, implementing the project may or may not be in the interest of a given group member. To attempt to gain a member's support, the sponsor can supply partial but verifiable information to the member, who can then further investigate the project at a cost. A member with a sufficiently strong prior that the project is in her interest does not find it worthwhile to investigate (because the resulting information is too unlikely to sway the member's decision), whereas a member with an intermediate prior does find it worthwhile to investigate, and a member with a sufficiently weak prior again does not find it worthwhile to investigate (because the resulting information again is too unlikely to sway the member's decision).

Members potentially differ in the payoffs they would receive if the project were implemented, but they know that their payoffs are correlated, so learning about another member's payoff would be useful. As a result, the sponsor may attempt to induce a "persuasion cascade." For example, the sponsor may supply information to a slightly skeptical first member, in the hope that this member's endorsement may then persuade a more skeptical second member, even if the sponsor herself could not have persuaded this second member directly. Such persuasion by the first member may result in the second member either investigating when she would originally have rejected the proposal outright or supporting the proposal without investigation when she would originally have insisted on investigating. Alternatively, sometimes the optimal cascade for the sponsor is to supply information to the more skeptical member first, because her approval may then convince the less skeptical member to support the proposal without investigation.

3.2.3. More of Both

A third setting may be especially natural and interesting, where some or all parties both have information and control a decision, so they have both sender and receiver roles. Because this literature is fairly new, we start by noting recent contributions from team theory, where the parties share common interests, such as Dessein and Santos (2006) and Calvó-Armengol et al. (2011). This work serves as a benchmark for models that introduce strategic considerations.

Okuno-Fujiwara et al. (1990) analyze communication of verifiable information in a Bayesian game, where different players have private information and control their own actions in the game. Hagenbach and Koessler (2010) and Galeotti et al. (2011) explore related settings with cheap-talk communication. In the latter papers an interesting issue arises because, building on the multisender case, the effectiveness of one party's cheap-talk communication with a second party now depends not only on the divergence in these parties' preferences but also on how communication from a third party may already have changed the second party's beliefs and hence in effect her preferences. This logic has implications for the equilibrium level of communication in a network, for example.

3.3. More Periods

Another stark limitation of our basic model is that it has only one period, thereby eliminating reputation effects and other consequences of learning.

In a two-period model with a unique (or, at least, specified) second-period continuation equilibrium as a function of first-period outcomes, one can substitute the second-period equilibrium payoffs into the first-period analysis, thereby hinting at a dynamic analysis in a one-period model (albeit one with possibly unusual payoff functions). Ottaviani and Sorensen (2006a,b) take this kind of reduced-form approach to analyzing how first-period cheap talk by a professional advisor can affect the advisor's second-period reputation. Prendergast (1993) uses a similar reduced-form modeling strategy to analyze "yes men"—that is, workers whose incentives are to distort their reports in the direction of what they believe their manager wants to hear.

Sobel (1985), Bénabou and Laroque (1992), and Morris (2001) take the next step, building dynamic models that repeat our basic model but also include a permanent type for the sender. Their models analyze cheap talk; more could be done by building on the other approaches discussed in Section 2.

3.4. Reinterpretation: From Choice to Execution

Van den Steen (2010b) makes a fundamental observation about the large literatures on authority and delegation—surveyed, respectively, by Bolton and Dewatripont (this volume) and in Section 5: almost without exception, these models do not involve a principal giving an agent an order. Rather, these literatures focus on what should be called "decision" authority, to distinguish it from what Van den Steen calls "interpersonal" authority, where the former analyzes who should control a decision right and the latter analyzes when orders will be given and whether they will be followed.

As Barnard (1938) emphasizes, orders are not simple—either to enforce or, therefore, to model:

A most significant fact of general observation relative to authority is the extent to which it is ineffective in specific instances. [Barnard 1938: 161]

The decision as to whether an order has authority or not lies with the persons to whom it is addressed, and does not reside in "persons of authority" or those who issue these orders. [Barnard 1938: 163]

I suppose all experienced executives know that when it is necessary to issue orders that will appear to the recipients to be contrary to the main purpose, especially as exemplified in prior habitual practice, it is usually necessary and always advisable, if practicable, to explain or demonstrate why the appearance of conflicts is an illusion. . . . Otherwise the orders are likely not to be executed, or to be executed inadequately. [Barnard 1938: 166]

Motivated by these cautionary tales, we now reinterpret the basic model from Section 2.1 as describing the choice and execution stages of Mintzberg's decision process in Figure 1. Our main purpose in doing so, however, is to surface these issues for further modeling, not to propose this simple model as anything beyond a first attempt.

Although most of our interpretations of the models in Section 2 have so far been that player 1 (who seeks to influence a decision) is the agent and player 2 (who controls the decision) is the principal, we now reverse the roles: player 1 is the principal, whose influence action a is an order (in the suggestive sense of the term emphasized by Barnard), and player 2 is the agent, whose decision d concerns whether or how well to execute the order. In addition to reinterpreting the players, we also impose new structure on the payoffs. For example, it seems important to distinguish between orders and advice (even if the advice comes from the principal), so we interpret the cheap-talk model in Section 2.2, where the principal's action a does not affect the parties' payoffs, as more the latter than the former. Also, the typical order does not seem to be directly costly to the principal, in the sense in which signal jamming and signaling involved a cost $k(a)$ in Sections 2.3 and 2.4, so we do not directly use those models, either.

We therefore imagine a setting where neither the principal's order (a) nor the agent's execution of that order (d) has much impact on the parties' payoffs on its own. Instead, the best payoffs arise when the order and the execution are well matched—to each other and also to the state s. There are of course many ways to formalize ideas like these, including not only Van den Steen (2010b) but also Landier et al. (2009) and Marino et al. (2010). The approach described below is inspired by Blanes i Vidal and Möller (2007). The resulting model does not focus on an order by the principal but instead explores another aspect of the choice and execution stages of Mintzberg's (1979) decision process, where the principal's action is a project choice, and the agent's decision is execution effort.

To keep things simple, suppose that there are only two states, $s = A$ or B. There are also two projects, but the parties can achieve positive payoffs only if the project is appropriate for the state. In addition, the parties are more likely to realize these positive payoffs if the agent's execution effort is high.

The principal's signal θ consists of two parts, public and private, both of which are noisy measures of the state. That is, $\theta = (\theta_{\text{pub}}, \theta_{\text{pvt}})$, where $\theta_i \in \{A, B\}$, and θ_{pub} and θ_{pvt} are conditionally independent given the state. To keep things interesting, suppose that the principal's private signal is more accurate: $\text{Prob}(\theta_i = s|s) = p_i$ and $p_{\text{pvt}} > p_{\text{pub}} > \frac{1}{2}$.

The principal's action is a project choice, $a = A$ or B, and the agent's signal then consists of the public signal and the principal's project choice, $\sigma = (\theta_{\text{pub}}, a)$. After receiving her signal, the agent chooses execution effort $d \in [0, 1]$ at convex cost $c(d)$. Finally, the project's output is $y = L$ or H, where $y = L$ if $a \neq s$ but $y = H$ with probability d if $a = s$. For simplicity, the parties split the project's output, so the payoffs are $U_1 = \frac{1}{2}y$ and $U_2 = \frac{1}{2}y - c(d)$.

Because the principal's private signal is more accurate, the first-best project choice is for the principal to follow his private signal, $a = \theta_{\text{pvt}}$. Because the public and private signals are conditionally independent, the first-best execution effort by the agent then depends on both signals. In particular, first-best effort is higher when the signals agree with each other and with the principal's project choice.

In equilibrium, however, the principal may not follow his private signal in choosing the project, exactly because the agent's execution effort is higher when she thinks that the project and both signals all agree. Instead, if the private signal is not too much more accurate than the public one, in equilibrium the principal may choose the project indicated by the public signal when the public and private signals disagree. Of course, the agent understands this and chooses her effort based on a correct belief about whether the project matches the private signal. Such a model thus takes a first step toward Barnard's (1938: 166) observation that contrary "orders are likely not to be executed, or to be executed inadequately."

3.5. Enrichment: From Information to Advice to Choice

Casual observations suggest that shareholders often rubber-stamp the board's decisions, the board rubber-stamps the CEO's decisions, the CEO rubber-stamps the division managers' decisions, and so on. Aghion and Tirole (1997) model such outcomes by distinguishing between formal authority held by an owner versus real authority held by an employee. Their model expands the basic model from Section 2.1 to include information acquisition as well as advice and choice.[10]

Suppose there are three possible projects, indexed by $k = 1, 2, 3$. Project k delivers benefits B_k to the owner and b_k to the employee. One project is terrible for both parties: $B_k = b_k = -\infty$. The other two projects deliver benefits of 0 and $B > 0$ to the owner and 0 and $b > 0$ to the employee. With probability α, the payoffs from the latter two projects are (B, b) and $(0, 0)$; with probability $1 - \alpha$, the payoffs from these projects are $(B, 0)$ and $(0, b)$. Thus, a higher value of α means that the owner's and the employee's interests are more likely to be aligned.

The problem is that, initially, neither the owner nor the employee knows which project is which. That is, each party can see the three possible projects, but neither party knows which project is the terrible one or which is the good one for him or her. Because of this uncertainty (and the severity of the terrible project), if no information is collected about which project is which, neither party will want any project to be chosen.

Both the owner and the employee can try to collect information about which project is which, but at a cost. If the owner incurs the cost $c_B(E)$, then the owner learns her own payoff on each project with probability E but learns nothing with probability $1 - E$. Similarly, if the employee

---

10. Parts of this section draw on Gibbons (2010), with permission from the *Annual Review of Economics*, Volume 2, © 2010 by Annual Reviews, http://www.annualreviews.org.

incurs the cost $c_s(e)$, then the employee learns his own payoff on each project with probability e but learns nothing with probability $1 - e$ (where these events for the employee are independent of those just described for the owner).

To analyze the parties' incentives to collect information, consider what happens in the following three situations. First, if the owner becomes informed about her payoffs on the three projects, then she will choose the project that pays her B. Second, if the owner remains uninformed but the employee becomes informed, then the employee will recommend the project that pays him b; even though the owner cannot observe the projects' payoffs (and, by assumption, the employee cannot communicate them), the owner will accept the employee's proposed project, because its expected payoff to the owner is $\alpha B + (1 - \alpha) \times 0 = \alpha B > 0$. Finally, if neither the owner nor the employee becomes informed, then neither party will want any project to be chosen, as described above.

From these three situations, we can write the expected payoffs to the owner and the employee if the owner incurs the cost $c_B(E)$ and the employee incurs the cost $c_s(e)$:

$$U_B = EB + (1 - E)e\alpha B - c_B(E)$$

and

$$U_s = E\alpha b + (1 - E)eb - c_s(e),$$

respectively. From these expected payoffs, we can compute the Nash equilibrium choices of E and e. Assuming that the cost functions have the usual properties (namely, convexity, zero slope at zero, and infinite slope at one), the Nash equilibrium (E^*, e^*) satisfies:

$$B(1 - e\alpha) = c'_B(E)$$

and

$$b(1 - E) = c'_s(e).$$

In our view, the Aghion and Tirole (1997) model is an elegant and insightful explanation of equilibrium rubber-stamping: with probability E^*, the owner becomes informed and chooses the project; but with probability $(1 - E^*)e^*$, only the employee becomes informed, in which case he proposes a project, and the owner rubber-stamps the proposal. This rubber-stamping can be seen as the difference between formal and real authority: the owner does not cede formal authority, but rather cedes real authority when the employee has superior information and sufficiently similar preferences. (To see the role of similar preferences, imagine revising the model to allow projects with payoffs $B_k = -\infty$ and $b_k = b$: now the owner would not dare to cede real authority.) For further approaches to this section's information-acquisition issue, see the discussions of Che and Kartik (2009) and Rantakari (2012) in Section 5.1.4.1.

3.6. Enrichments: Contractibility

We emphasized in Section 2.1 that nothing in our basic model was contractible: not player 1's action, player 2's decision, or the parties' payoffs, so there cannot be bargaining over either player's move, mechanisms to elicit their signals, or outcome-contingent incentive contracts. As we explained, we made this assumption not only for simplicity but also to some extent for realism, given that our focus is on organizations. That is, if everything were contractible, then any governance structure would suffice, as argued by Coase (1960). And, loosely considering settings somewhat shy of that extreme, if contracts were only slightly imperfect, then markets might do fine at inspiring and implementing the acquisition and dissemination of information, as argued by Hayek (1945). As Arrow (1974: 33) puts it, however, "organizations are a means of achieving the benefits of collective action in situations where the price system fails." And recall from Section 1 March's (1962/1988: 110–112) view of "the business firm as a political coalition" in which "the executive . . . is a political broker" who cannot "solve the problem of conflict by simple payments to the participants and agreement on a superordinate goal."

In this section, therefore, we begin to relax our stark assumption in Section 2.1 that nothing is contractible, but we hasten to add that this must be done with care. That is, if too much is contractible, then the transaction should probably be conducted in a market rather than in an organization. Analyzing this macro-level choice of governance structure, between organization and market, is of course both important and well beyond the scope of this chapter; see Bresnahan and Levin (this volume) and Tadelis and Williamson (this volume).

As a first exploration of contracting issues, we return to the information-acquisition problem of Section 3.5. Lambert (1986) and Demski and Sappington (1987) were the first to analyze models in which player 1 does not have a direct interest in player 2's decision (i.e., player 1's payoff is independent of d) but can exert effort to improve the quality of his information. To induce such effort, the parties can write contracts that specify payment schemes for the expert that are contingent on the outcome of the decision. As in the standard agency framework, the only source of friction in these models is that the expert must be induced to exert effort. In contrast to the standard framework, however, here effort generates information rather than output. As Dewatripont and Tirole (1999) show, when effort is about acquiring information, the Monotone Likelihood Ratio Property is lost. A major insight of this literature is that, to provide better incentives for information acquisition, a contract may have to create an endogenous conflict of interest regarding the decision to be made; see, for example, Inderst and Klein (2007), Malcomson (2009, 2011), and Zermeño (2012).

Another organizational literature that assumes some contractibility studies committees. Indeed, such models are close to those described in Section 3.2, where more parties are added to our basic model. For example, each committee member might receive private information, then engage in cheap talk, and finally vote; see Feddersen and Pesendorfer (1998), Persico (2004), Levy (2007), and Visser and Swank (2007) for related models. A key assumption in such models, however, is that the eventual decision is a predictable consequence of the votes, such as by majority rule, thus raising the question of whether the parties might instead use direct-revelation mechanisms, mapping type reports into decisions, rather than use voting schemes. See Mookherjee (this volume) for more on this approach.

Another approach is to assume that, although the state s and the decision d are non-contractible, messages are. For example, in a cheap talk equilibrium with a finite number of messages, one could imagine payments to the sender to be contingent on the message he sends. Krishna and Morgan (2008) examine such a model, assuming that the sender has limited liability (i.e., cannot be forced to pay money to the receiver). They then show that full revelation is always feasible but never optimal. Instead, for the standard example with uniform state s, quadratic loss functions, and sender bias $b > 0$, they show that, because of the standard argument that integrates the local incentive-compatibility constraints, inducing revelation by high types requires large payments to lower types if they are to reveal themselves. As a result, the optimal payment and communication scheme has positive payments and full revelation for low states but no payment and no communication for high states. We see this kind of analysis, where limited contractibility relaxes the stark assumption in Section 2.1 that nothing is contractible, as a productive vein for further work.

3.7. Contested Control

As a transition to our discussion in Sections 4 and 5 of decision architectures that are designed ex ante, here we consider situations where decision rights are not allocated ex ante but are contested ex post. Tullock (1980) provided an elemental model of rent seeking in such an environment. Two contestants (A and B) purchase lottery tickets in amounts x_A and x_B, respectively, each hoping to win a prize of \$100. Contestant i's expected payoff is then $x_i/(x_i + x_j) \times 100 - x_i$, so the symmetric Nash equilibrium has positive expenditures on lottery tickets, but in this equilibrium the contestants have the same probabilities of winning as if neither had spent anything—namely, one-half. Skaperdas (1992) and Rajan and Zingales (2000) used similar models to analyze battles for control (in organizations and other settings).

As a simple version of some of Skaperdas's ideas, suppose that each of two parties ($i = 1, 2$) is endowed with resources r_i that can be spent either on producing output (y_i) or on developing "arms" (a_i) that can be used in a later conflict over dividing the aggregate output. Specifically, let $y_i = y(r_{yi})$ and $a_i = a(r_{ai})$, where $r_{yi} + r_{ai} = r_i$, and suppose that the payoff to party i is $p(a_i, a_j)[y_i + y_j]$, where $p(a_i, a_j)$ can be interpreted as the probability that party i wins the conflict and so receives the aggregate output. Skaperdas derives conditions under which the equilibrium allocations of the parties' resources into outputs and arms are efficient (i.e., both parties put all their resources into output) or partially so (one party puts all its resources into output). More often, however, as in Tullock's model, the equilibrium is inefficient and sometimes dramatically so.

Rajan and Zingales analyze a two-period model that can be seen as having fully contractible trade in the first period and Skaperdas's model in the second. Trade in the first period endogenizes heterogeneous resource endowments (r_i) and heterogeneous production functions (now $y_i(r_{yi})$) for the second period. The second-period consequences of this heterogeneity can be so severe that the parties forgo a contractible and seemingly Pareto-improving trade in the first period. For example, consider two divisions in a company (or two adjacent countries). Suppose that party i has a machine that it could sell to party j, and suppose that party j is already more productive than party i and so could make better use of the machine ($y_j' > y_i'$). Selling the machine increases i's endowment for the second period (r_i increases) but reduces its productivity (y_i' falls), and the reverse holds for j. What then happens to the equilibrium allocations of the parties' resources into outputs and arms? Loosely, reducing i's productivity increases i's incentive to invest in arms, and increasing j's productivity (more precisely, j's output) also increases i's incentive to invest in arms, but an increase in a_i then increases j's incentive to invest in arms, and so on. In equilibrium, these increases in arms (and reductions in output) can be severe enough to overwhelm the supposed efficiency advantages from allocating the machine to the more productive party j, so no trade occurs in the first period.

In all these rent seeking models, control is valuable, because it allows one party to consume the prize in question—$100 in Tullock's (1980) model and aggregate output in those of Skaperdas (1992) and Rajan and Zingales (2000). As a slight variant on this approach, suppose instead that control allows one party to take a decision (e.g., about the organization's strategy). The argument is then similar, with the new feature that different parties may place different values on being able to take the decision in question, thus creating different incentives for gaining control.

As a concrete example, consider the following game (which is intended to illustrate some of the central governance challenges in decision architectures involving shared control, e.g., joint ventures, consortia, and matrices): (1) the parties publicly observe the state of the world, $s \in S$; (2) the parties engage in a battle for control (specifically, to keep things simple, we follow Tullock—each party expends x_i for probability $x_i/(x_i + x_j)$ of winning control); (3) the party who wins control then chooses a decision $d \in D$; and (4) the parties receive payoffs $U_i(s, d)$, gross of their expenditures in stage 2. Now the prize to party i for winning control is not $100 but rather $U_i(s, d_i^*(s)) - U_i(s, d_j^*(s))$, where $d_i^*(s)$ maximizes $U_i(s, d)$ over $d \in D$. Because the prizes are asymmetric, so are the equilibrium expenditures in the battle for control: the party with the larger prize fights harder. This example is of course extremely stark, but it nonetheless captures some of the tensions that commonly arise under shared control.

4. Endogenous Architectures: Fixed Decision Allocations

In the previous sections we explored the inefficiencies that can arise in organizations from strategic communication under fixed decision processes and (except for Section 3.7) a fixed allocation of decision rights among the interested parties. One reason to have done so was to focus on situations where the decision rights are inalienable. For instance, the right to appoint a CEO in a corporation is vested in the board of directors. The board can seek advice on its choice, and it may even sometimes rubber-stamp the advisors' recommendation, but it cannot formally delegate the actual decision. One can also view our discussion in the previous sections as having been about the second stage of a two-stage game in which the owner of the organization allocates decision rights in the first stage and the different members of the organization take their actions in the second.

In this section we turn to actions that the owner can take in the first stage to mitigate the inefficiencies of organizational communication and decisionmaking in the second stage. In particular, in Section 4.1 we explore three suggestions put forward by Milgrom and Roberts (1988) aimed at controlling influence activities:

1. the owner could close communication channels, at least for some decisions;

2. she could commit not to respond to information provided by others; or

3. she could try to align incentives through compensation, promotion, and similar policies, including altering the decision processes and even the boundaries of the firm itself.

In Section 4.2, we move away from the rich organizational descriptions that characterize the discussion in Section 4.1 to a more abstract formulation, based on our model from Section 2, that allows us to explore just what responses may be feasible and effective.

Alternatively, of course, the owner could simply delegate the decision directly to the employee. Although delegation might be considered an instance of the Milgrom-Roberts's third option (change the organizational design), it has been the focus of most of the recent formal literature on responses to inefficiency in decisionmaking. Thus we make it the focus of Section 5.

4.1. Organizational Responses in the Case of Fixed Decision Rights

The first published work on influence costs is Milgrom (1988). A simplified version of the model he considered is the following. There are a manager and an employee, both risk neutral, and the former contracts with the latter to deliver unobservable effort. The employee can allocate a fixed amount T of effort between productive activities t and influence x. (Effort is thus not directly costly to him.) The manager may be able to make a change decision that gives benefits k to the employee that are, in effect, a transfer from another (unmodeled) employee. Thus, k enters the employee's utility function but not the aggregate welfare. Implementing the change brings benefits $r(x)I$ to the manager.

If the manager is allowed discretion over adopting the change, then the probability that she does adopt it is a function $q(x)$ that is assumed to be increasing. The employee's productive effort, $t = T - x$, produces a benefit π with a probability $p(t)$ that is increasing in t, with $p(0) = 0$. The problem is to determine a wage for the agent as a function of whether the benefit π was realized and whether the change was implemented, with the objective to maximize total surplus, namely, $p(t)\pi + q(x)r(x)I$, subject to t and x maximizing $p(t)q(x)w_{11} + p(t)(1 - q(x))w_{10} + (1 - p(t))q(x)w_{01} + (1 - p(t))(1 - q(x))w_{00} + q(x)k$ given $t + x = T$. Meanwhile, if the manager does not have discretion, then the payoff is simply $p(T)\pi$, because the agent has no incentive to exert influence and so can be assumed to devote all his time to production.

The key result is that it may be optimal to deny the decisionmaker discretion over implementing the change: there are values of I and k such that eliminating discretion (i.e., fixing $q(x)$ at zero rather than using pay to deter influence) is optimal, and this is true for all higher values of k (when redistribution effects are greater) and lower values of I (when the change is less valuable). This is an example of Milgrom and Roberts's (1988) second suggestion: limiting discretion can be valuable.

The logic behind the q and r functions is not explored in Milgrom (1988). Note, however, that delegation might be an attractive alternative here, especially if $r(x)$ is not increasing. In this case, if the implementation decision could be and were delegated, then the first best would be achieved.

Milgrom and Roberts (1988, 1999) considered a problem with two employees, each of whom has to allocate a fixed amount of time between influence activity and productive effort, with the principal unable to observe their choices. The principal values the output that results (probabilistically) from their efforts, but she also wants to promote one of the two workers to another job, where his underlying, unknown ability will be valuable. (Ability does not influence productivity in the current job.)

The new job is desirable to the workers in that it must, for competitive reasons, carry a wage that exceeds the outside option of the person appointed to it. There is symmetric information about the workers' abilities, which are identically distributed. The impact of influence activity and determination of its equilibrium level are not modeled in detail. Instead, the influence activity is assumed to "build credentials," making the worker's ability appear greater but also providing information about ability. One possibility that Milgrom and Roberts (1999) suggest is a test on which promotion might be based, with the employees' influence activities consisting of diverting time to prepare for the test. Simply taking the test generates information, but once the test is scheduled and its results will be used in the promotion decision, there will be incentives to try to increase one's performance on the test.

In this context, the principal has to decide on wage payments for the current period, wages to pay to each employee once the promotion decision is made, and the criteria to use in promotion.

Milgrom and Roberts (1988) consider only a limited class of possible decision rules, to any of which the employer can commit. Even so, a full solution to this design problem has not been obtained. However, several points can be established. First, if the importance of assigning the better person to the new job is sufficiently low and the productivity of effort is high, then the employer will choose not to use apparent qualifications at all in the promotion decision. In this case, both employees will devote full time to work. Further, no incentive pay will be needed (because the work is not itself costly, and there is no reward to diverting time to influence). Promotion will be random. This can be interpreted as an instance of option 1, cutting communication.

If the marginal impact of employee quality on performance in the new job is sufficiently high, however, then the employer will want to use apparent qualifications in the promotion choice. The danger is now that, unless there is a reward to productive effort, the employees will concentrate solely on building credentials. This in turn results in several possible adjustments. One is to pay a bonus for individual output, even though there is no inherent cost of effort. A second is to raise the wage of the employee who is not promoted closer to the level paid the promoted employee. This adjustment reduces the return to being promoted and thus the incentives to exert influence to get a raise (this works only once there is pay for performance). Finally, it may be worthwhile to promote partially on current performance, even though it is not informative about the candidate's actual ability, because this lowers the amount of performance pay necessary to induce productive effort. Thus, all aspects of the organizational design can be altered to limit the cost of influence activities, in line with the third suggestion of Milgrom and Roberts (1988).[11]

An important organizational decision that has been much studied, both theoretically and empirically, is the allocation of capital inside firms. In particular, Meyer et al. (1992) modeled a situation in which failing businesses in a multidivisional firm exert influence to try to obtain more corporate resources to keep themselves alive. In equilibrium, the top decisionmaker is not fooled by these attempts, so the allocation of capital is not distorted. As in the signal-jamming model in Section 2.3, however, resources are wasted on attempts at influence. The solution Meyer et al. suggested is to spin off units that are prone to attempt influence.

More recently, several papers, beginning with Rajan et al. (2000), Scharfstein and Stein (2000), and Wulf (2002), have examined in more detail situations where lower level managers seek to use strategic communication so that more capital is allocated to them than is optimal for the firm. In these models, the allocation rules are distorted to reduce the costs of such strategic behavior. The resulting misallocation is costly. In addition, Wulf (2002, 2007) investigated the

---

11. Note that delegation is not a real option in this model.

interplay between the design of capital budgeting processes and the basis for and extent of performance pay in light of influence activities, and in Wulf (2009) she documents patterns in these variables consistent with limiting the costs of influence. For a discussion of this literature, including newer contributions, see Gertner and Scharfstein (this volume).

Finally, Powell (2012) analyzed a rich formal model of influence, building on the signal-jamming models in Holmström (1982/1999) and Gibbons (2005) discussed in Section 2.3. In Powell's framework, there are two parties and two decisions. Before these decisions can be made, the parties decide who will be empowered to make each decision, but once this allocation of decision authority is set, contracting difficulties prevent renegotiation. If the other party is to make a decision, then the disempowered party may have incentives to try to affect the decision by undertaking (unobserved) influence activities.

Given an arbitrary allocation of decision rights, Powell solves for the equilibrium level of influence. In equilibrium the party making a decision will correctly anticipate the amount of influence the other party is undertaking and, using that correct estimate, will back out the effect of the influence and make the decision that is best for him. So, again, the influence does not distort decisions, but it does occur and it imposes costs.

The optimal allocation of decision rights maximizes the sum of utilities, given that the parties will choose their levels of influence in the equilibrium fashion. This allocation may consist of either divided control, with each controlling one decision (which is advantageous, because the costs of influence are convex, and so it is better to have the total amount of influence split between the two parties), or unified control under the party who cares more about the outcome.

Powell then examined some suggestions made by Milgrom and Roberts (1988) for limiting influence activities and mitigating influence costs. A "closed-door" policy of limiting communication is modeled as no public signal being observed (because the parties agreed not to hire the needed staff, loaded their calendars so they were too busy, and limited their meetings). This policy eliminates the disempowered party's incentive to attempt influence, but it also deprives the party in control of useful information. However, if the initial uncertainty was not great, then not much is lost, and the closed-door policy may be preferred to the alternative of playing the game as originally specified.

Also, if there is a lot of disagreement about how to tailor decisions to the state of the world, then again it may become worthwhile to adopt the closed-door policy. Then a selection story applies: as disagreement increases, both the open- and closed-door policies do worse, but the closed door does relatively better at high levels of disagreement. Thus, the rigid, apparently bad management practice of limiting communication obtains when circumstances are bad, and observed firms with these practices are worse performers than those that are observed adhering to open-door policies. However, the closed-door firms perform better in the environments they inhabit than would firms with apparently "better" management practices. See the right-hand side of Figure 1 in Gibbons and Roberts ("Economic Theories of Incentives in Organizations," this volume) for a graphical representation of this selection argument.

4.2. An Abstract Approach

Having analyzed potential inefficiencies in communication and decisionmaking under fixed decision processes in Sections 2 and 3, our focus here in Section 4 has been on ways the parties might design their environment ex ante so as to ameliorate some of these inefficiencies. Similar to the way that the Milgrom and Roberts (1988) focus on the costs of influence activities animated many models we discussed in Section 2, their suggestions of strategies for reducing influence inefficiencies motivated the organizational responses described in Section 4.1.

Consistent with Milgrom and Roberts (1988), the models in Section 4.1 are detailed enough to suggest and analyze concrete organizational responses to influence costs. But each considers a separate organizational environment, making it hard to assess whether the full range of possible interventions has been considered. In this section, therefore, we pursue an abstract approach that we see as complementary to the more grounded analyses in Section 4.1. This abstract approach allows us, for a simple environment, to characterize a set of responses to influence inefficiencies that are collectively exhaustive and, in a sense, mutually exclusive.

The environment we consider in this section is the basic model from Section 2.1. For this model we follow Kolotilin et al. (2012) by describing five ways that the parties might respond to influence activities by reshaping their environment ex ante. (Kolotilin et al. do this for a cheap-talk model, but we apply their ideas to our basic model, thus covering not only cheap talk but also the other four illustrations discussed in Section 2.) As we discuss below, these five potential responses to influence inefficiencies overlap partially with both the three Milgrom-Roberts approaches described in Section 4.1 and the delegation models described in Section 5, but they also include other options, so we discuss all five here, as well as note papers that investigate these five options.

Imagine enriching our basic model to add a nonstrategic player who accepts an informational input and returns a (possibly stochastic) output according to some prespecified mapping. This nonstrategic player can be seen as a machine, which could be designed by the parties ex ante and then inserted into various moments of our basic model. Proceeding sequentially through the timing of our basic model, there could then be the following five interventions (after each of which the timing of the basic model resumes):

a. "information control," where the new player, instead of the sender, observes the sender's signal θ in stage 2 of the model in Section 2.1 and delivers a signal θ' to the sender in stage 2.5, according to the distribution $\gamma(\theta'|\theta)$, after which the sender chooses the influence action a in stage 3;

b. "influence control," where the new player replaces the sender, receiving the signal θ in stage 2 and choosing the action $a \in A$ in stage 3 according to the distribution $q(a|\theta)$, after which the receiver receives the signal σ in stage 4;

c. "communication control," where the new player, instead of the receiver, observes the receiver's signal σ in stage 4 and then delivers a signal σ' to the receiver in stage 4.5 according to the distribution $\eta(\sigma'|\sigma)$, after which the receiver chooses a decision $d \in D$ in stage 5;

d. "decision control," where the new player replaces the receiver, receiving the signal σ in stage 4 and choosing a decision $d \in D$ in stage 5 according to the distribution $r(d|\sigma)$, after which the parties receive their payoffs; and

e. "execution control," where the receiver observes the signal σ in stage 4 and then in stage 5 recommends a decision $d \in D$ to the new player, who then chooses a decision $d' \in D$ in stage 5.5 according to the distribution $\rho(d'|d)$, after which the parties receive their payoffs.

To interpret just one of these five interventions, "execution control" includes the case where the parties agree ex ante that the receiver can choose from only a specified set of decisions ex post. In this abstract approach, there are no natural limits on the size or composition of such a decision set; deriving such limits is one of the complementary benefits one can get from the more grounded models in Section 4.1.

We note that although these five interventions are collectively exhaustive (in that there are no other moments in the timing of our basic model at which one could intervene), they are in some sense not mutually exclusive, because influence control and decision control, where the new player replaces the sender or receiver, weakly dominate the other options, where the new player is injected into the information flow of the model. In particular, influence control weakly dominates information control, and decision control weakly dominates both communication control and execution control.[12] However, it may be impossible to replace a player in intervention b or d, but it may still be possible to intervene as envisioned in a, c, or e, so we present all five interventions here.

Compared with the approaches that Milgrom and Roberts (1988) consider, communication control encompasses their first approach (reducing communication channels), and execution control encompasses their second (limiting the receiver's discretion to respond), but their third approach (changing the alignment of interests by changing organizational policies) does not fit easily in this framework.

One way to interpret their third approach is as changing the parties' payoff functions, such as modifying the bias b in the quadratic-loss functions illustrated throughout Section 2. Although literally changing utility functions is perhaps outside the standard toolkit of economics, their third approach can instead be interpreted in more standard terms by imagining that there are multiple periods, as described in Section 3.3, and the parties' payoff functions at the end of this basic model reflect the continuation equilibrium for the remainder of the game. Under this interpretation, the Milgrom-Roberts ideas of changing organizational policies for the remainder of the game could well be represented in our basic model as changing the bias b. Absent a grounded model like those in Section 4.1, however, it is unclear what changes in b can be accomplished and at what costs, so we sidestep this question for the remainder of this section.

In addition to the three Milgrom-Roberts approaches discussed in Section 4.1, we also discuss delegation as a response to influence inefficiencies in Section 5, which relates to decision control, and influence control is akin to the strategic management of public information model described in Section 2.6. Finally, there is information control, which is related to our discussion in Section 3.5 of the information-to-advice-to-choice parts of Mintzberg's (1979) decision process. In particular, whereas Aghion and Tirole (1997) envision keeping the receiver busy, so as to increase her marginal cost of becoming informed and thus empower the sender, here one can imagine keeping the sender busy, so as to increase his marginal cost of becoming informed and then being motivated to engage in influence activities.

There are several papers that analyze some of interventions a–e for cheap-talk games, including Green and Stokey (2007) and Ivanov (2010) on information control; Krishna and Morgan (2004), Blume et al. (2007), and Goltsman et al. (2009) on communication control;

---

12. For example, to see that delegation weakly dominates limited authority, note that if the receiver's strategy under limited authority is $d(\sigma)$, then delegation can mimic limited authority by choosing the rule $r(d'|\sigma) = \rho(d'|(\sigma))$.

and Kolotilin et al. (2012) on execution control, as well as many of the papers on delegation discussed in Section 5. It would be interesting to explore some of these interventions in the other settings illustrated in Section 2, beyond cheap talk. Regardless of the setting, we see this framework as complementing Section 4.1 in two ways: it exhaustively categorizes what interventions are possible, and it allows analysis of the maximum reduction in influence inefficiencies that any one of these interventions can achieve.

5. Endogenous Architectures: Delegation

In Sections 2 and 3 we explored the inefficiencies that can arise in organizations from strategic communication under fixed decision processes. In Section 4 we then discussed possible organizational responses that attempt to reduce these inefficiencies. One such response—which was ignored in Section 4 but is prominent in the literature—is delegation of the decision right to the employee. In this section we survey this literature on delegation.

We start by looking at an organization that consists of an owner and an employee. As in the previous section, the organization has to make a decision that is both ex ante and ex post noncontractible. The parties, however, can now contract over the right to make the decision. At the beginning of the game, the owner offers the employee a contract that specifies a wage and an allocation of the decision right. If the employee rejects the offer, both parties realize a zero outside option. For the time being, we assume that neither the wage nor the decision right can be made contingent on any information that is revealed during the game. Moreover, we assume that if the employee accepts the contract, it cannot be renegotiated at any point.

In the next section we discuss some of the main reasons for delegation that have been examined in the literature. The models that we discuss in that section focus on the choice between centralization and delegation, and they abstract from some factors that complicate delegation in real organizations. The models, for instance, assume that the owner is able to delegate decision rights formally and irrevocably to her employee. In practice, however, legal barriers make full delegation in organizations impossible. The models also abstract from actions the owner can take to control the employee, such as constraining the decisions he can make or aligning his incentives through incentive contracts. We discuss these additional issues in Sections 5.2 and 5.3.

Throughout, we focus on the economics literature on delegation in firms. We therefore do not discuss the related political science literature on the delegation of public policymaking from elected politicians to bureaucrats (see, e.g., Epstein and O'Halloran 1999; Huber and Shipan 2006) and from legislatures to standing committees (e.g., Gilligan and Krehbiel 1987, 1989; Krishna and Morgan 2001).

5.1. Why Delegate?

In this section we discuss some of the main reasons for delegation that have been examined in the literature.

5.1.1. To Economize on Limited Resources
Probably the most common reasons for assigning a task to another person that one could do oneself are to add capacity to carry out the task and to tap into comparative advantage. In the

context of delegated decisionmaking, both factors can be at work. Gathering information and analyzing it to support good decisions is a time-consuming activity. Sharing the load allows decisions to be made more quickly. This in turn may be desirable because "time is money" or because, in a dynamic context, decisions are made on the basis of more up-to-date information. At the same time, there may be efficiency gains from using someone who is especially efficient in developing information, analyzing it, and making the needed choices. This efficiency could come from experience or ability. In addition, as Jensen and Meckling (1992) accentuated, delegation of decisions might be driven by the difficulties of communication that limit the possibility of informing the original decisionmaker, a phenomenon they referred to as "specific information." We discuss this motivation for delegation in Section 5.1.3.

The most prominent model of delegation of decision rights to increase capacity is Geanakoplos and Milgrom (1991). They consider the problem of allocating a target output among n production facilities whose costs are random. The amount of information a manager can obtain about these costs is an increasing function of the time he spends and his ability. Geanakoplos and Milgrom show that a hierarchical structure, in which targets tumble down to the next level, where new targets for the succeeding level are calculated, is an efficient approach to the problem. However, the model is formulated as a team problem, so there are none of the incentive issues that are the focus of this chapter. Moreover, this model is analyzed in detail in Garicano and Van Zandt (this volume). Thus we will not develop it further here.

The models of organization based on distributed computing of an associative operation that begin with Mount and Reiter (1990) can also be thought of as delegation to increase the speed of arriving at a solution. And although the interpretation of the knowledge-based hierarchy in Garicano (2000) as delegation seems a stretch, his model does feature the use of multiple agents to add processing power. Again, incentive issues are ignored in these literatures, so we simply refer the reader to the extensive discussions in Garicano and Van Zandt (this volume).

One literature in which incentive issues are central that can be interpreted as involving delegation to increase capacity (although it is not usually formulated this way) concerns using an agent to select a risky investment. This literature begins with Lambert (1986), who posed the problem of motivating a risk-averse agent to gather information about the returns to a risky investment and then choose between this investment and a safe alternative. To think of this as a delegation problem, we could imagine that the principal could make the choice herself, and perhaps even develop the information, but assume that the agent is more efficient at doing so. Lambert (1986) noted an interesting nonmonotonicity: increasing the sensitivity of the agent's pay to the performance of the investment does not always increase his effort, because at some point he bears too much risk and switches to choosing the safe investment. Even under the optimal contract, the agent does not always choose the investment the principal would prefer. For details of this model, see Gibbons and Roberts ("Economic Theories of Incentives in Organizations," this volume).

A second literature that can be interpreted in the same way as involving delegation to a more efficient agent concerns delegated portfolio management. The models here, beginning with Bhattacharya and Pfleiderer (1985) and Admati and Pfleiderer (1997), have assumed that the manager to whom selection of a portfolio of safe and risky assets is delegated knows ex ante if he is good or bad at his task. In addition, there is a moral hazard problem in inducing him to invest in information about the risky assets. Clean, positive results in these models are difficult to obtain (see Stracca 2006 for a survey).

A third context involves "referrals" (Garicano and Santos 2004), where a party must decide whether to delegate a task to another party who may be better suited to doing it. Referring the task means, however, that the referring party will not get the rents that attach to carrying it out. Garicano and Santos (2004) analyze the complex incentives that arise when the original party is privately informed about the returns to the task and effort exerted in carrying it out is unobservable. They suggest that ex ante sharing arrangements (partnerships) may arise.

Finally, Athey et al. (1994) investigate a model of management by exception, where managers delegate decisions to lower level employees to preserve managerial time, even if the managers might make better decisions than the employees. Which level is better equipped to make a decision depends on the state of the world. As the probability distribution over states shifts to increase the likelihood of decisions where the manager is the better decisionmaker, the range of decisions delegated to the employees increases to free up managerial bandwidth.

5.1.2. To Pay the Employee Less

Many employees value the right to make decisions. Employees may, for instance, believe that being in charge allows them to make decisions that are better for them personally. Or they may believe that being in charge is good for their careers, for instance, because it allows them to signal their abilities or develop their human capital. And, of course, they may simply value the right to make decisions per se, even if they end up making the same decisions that their superiors would have made. Whatever their reasons, if employees value the right to make decisions, firms may be able to charge them for this right by cutting wages. Delegation is then optimal if the reduction in wages is larger than any adverse effect that delegated decisionmaking may have on gross profits. This basic motivation for delegation has been explored in several papers, including (the first part of) Aghion and Tirole (1997) and Bester (2009). Our discussion below is based on the first part of Bester (2009).

To explore this motivation for delegation, recall the cheap-talk model discussed in Section 2.2, but suppose now that both parties can observe the state. Also, payoffs are now given by

$$U_1(d, w) = K - k_1(d - s - b)^2 + w \tag{1}$$

and

$$U_2(d, w) = K - k_2(d - s)^2 - w, \tag{2}$$

where w is the wage, K is a constant, and k_1 and k_2 are parameters that measure the importance of the decisions to the employee and the owner, respectively. We assume throughout that K is sufficiently large for joint surplus to be positive. Moreover, we now assume that the state is drawn from a uniform distribution with support $[-L, L]$.

If the owner has the right to make the decision, she will always make her preferred decision $d^C = s$, where C stands for centralization. To ensure participation, she then has to offer the employee a wage $w^C = -(K - k_1 b^2)$. If, instead, the owner delegates the decision right to the employee, the employee will always make his preferred decision $d^D = s + b$, where D stands for delegation. The owner then has to offer the employee only $w^D = -K$ to ensure participation. On one hand, delegation therefore reduces gross profits by $k_2 b^2$. On the other hand, it also allows the owner to cut wages by $k_1 b^2$.

In the case of quadratic preferences, delegation is therefore optimal if the employee's payoff is more sensitive to the decision than is the owner's, that is, if $k_1 \geq k_2$. More generally, delegation is optimal if the decision is more important to the employee than to the owner, in the sense that his willingness to pay for the right to make the decision $E[U_1(d^D, w) - U_1(d^C, w)]$ is larger than the owner's willingness to pay $E[U_2(d^C, w) - U_2(d^D, w)]$. Notice that this is equivalent to saying that delegation is optimal if the expected surplus $S(d) \equiv E[U_1(d, w) + U_2(d, w)]$ is larger when the employee makes the decision than when the owner makes it herself. In the next few sections we explore different reasons this may be the case.

Before we do so, it is worth making two observations. First, our focus on the efficient allocation of decision rights is different from some papers in the literature that instead focus on the allocation that maximizes expected profits gross of wages. This difference does not affect the main insights from these papers, but it does affect some of the comparative statics.

Second, the prediction that organizations allocate decision rights to whomever values them the most is not uncontroversial. Rotemberg (1993), in particular, argues that firms instead allocate decision rights to those employees they most want to retain. To explain why this may be so, he points to a difference between paying with cash and paying with control that we abstracted from above. In particular, he observes that some benefits of being allowed to make a decision today accrue to an employee only if he is still with the firm tomorrow. Rotemberg therefore views control as a form of deferred compensation. He then shows that if the manager cannot commit to future wages, and the determination of future wages is hindered by asymmetric information, the owner may find it optimal to give decision rights to the employees she most wants to retain rather than to the ones who value decision rights the most.

5.1.3. To Make Better Use of the Employee's Information

A common argument for delegation is that it allows the owner to make better use of her employee's information. Two early papers that explore this argument are Holmström (1977, 1984) and Jensen and Meckling (1992). Both papers focus on the trade-off between the benefit of making better use of the employee's information and the costs that arise because the employee's decisionmaking is biased toward decisions that are good for him but not necessarily good for the organization as a whole. The papers differ, however, in their explanation for why the owner cannot retain the decision right and simply have the employee communicate his information to her. In particular, whereas Jensen and Meckling (1992) focus on communication costs that arise because of bounded rationality, in Holmström (1977, 1984) communication is costly because of the employee's incentives to use his information strategically.

Below we start by discussing Dessein (2002), who provides a more recent exploration of these issues. Similar to Holmström (1977, 1984), Dessein focuses on communication costs that arise because of the employee's incentives to use his information strategically. In contrast to both Holmström (1977, 1984) and Jensen and Meckling (1992), however, Dessein does not allow the owner to constrain the employee's decision or align his preferences through incentive contracts. Dessein's focus on the choice between centralization and unconstrained delegation is in line with the other models that we discuss in this section. As mentioned above, we discuss models that allow the owner to control the employee by constraining his decisions or by using incentive contracts in Section 5.3.

A feature of Dessein (2002) is that there is a single decision, and all information that is relevant for this decision is concentrated in a single employee. We first discuss this case. We then turn to an extension of Dessein (2002) in which information is vertically dispersed, in the sense that the employee knows more about some factors that are relevant for the decision and the owner knows more about others. Finally, we discuss recent work by Alonso et al. (2008) and Rantakari (2008), in which there are multiple decisions that have to be coordinated and relevant information is dispersed horizontally among multiple employees.

5.1.3.1. Concentrated Information. For an illustration of the main arguments in Dessein (2002), recall the model we described in the previous section, but suppose now that the owner cannot observe the state of the world s. Suppose also that the decision is more important to the owner than to the employee, that is, $k_2 > k_1$. It follows from our discussion in the previous section that if this were not the case, delegation would always be optimal.

If the owner delegates the decision right to the employee, the employee will make his preferred decision, just as in the previous section. The difference between first-best expected surplus and expected surplus under delegation is then given by

$$S(d^{FB}) - S(d^D) = \frac{k_2^2}{k_1 + k_2} b^2, \tag{3}$$

where the right-hand side is the inefficiency that arises because the employee's preferences are different from first best.

If the owner does not delegate the decision right to the employee, the employee sends the owner a cheap-talk message, after which the owner makes her preferred decision. Under centralization, the model is therefore the same as the cheap-talk model we examined in Section 2.2, except that the owner now has to pay the employee a wage to ensure participation. In Section 2.2 we saw that if $b > 0$, communication is imperfect. Moreover, the quality of communication is measured by the residual variance

$$V(b) = \frac{Var(s)}{N(b)^2} + \frac{N(b)^2 - 1}{3} b^2, \tag{4}$$

where $Var(s)$ is the variance of s, and $N(b)$ is the maximum number of partitions given by the smallest integer larger than or equal to

$$-\frac{1}{2} + \frac{1}{2}\sqrt{1 + \frac{4L}{b}}, \tag{5}$$

where $2L$ is the length of the support. The difference between first-best expected surplus and expected surplus under centralization is then given by

$$S(d^{FB}) - S(d^C) = \frac{k_1^2}{k_1 + k_2} b^2 + (k_1 + k_2) V(b). \tag{6}$$

where the first term on the right-hand side is the distortion that arises because the owner's preferences are different from first best, and the second term is the distortion that arises because the owner is imperfectly informed about the state.

It follows from (3) and (6) that the owner will delegate to the employee if and only if

$$\left(k_2 - k_1\right) b^2 \leq \left(k_1 + k_2\right) V(b). \tag{7}$$

One implication of this expression is that delegation can be optimal even though the decision is more important to the owner than to the employee. The reason, of course, is that delegation now has the additional benefit of allowing the owner to make more efficient use of the employee's information. Another implication of the above expression is that the optimal allocation of the decision right depends on the quality of communication between the employee and the owner. To understand the effect of changes in the environment on the efficient allocation of decision rights, one therefore has to understand how such changes affect the flow of information in organizations.

In particular, consider a reduction in the divergence parameter b. On one hand, such a reduction leads to more efficient decisionmaking under delegation. On the other hand, it also improves communication under centralization. A reduction in b therefore favors delegation only if it has a more beneficial effect on decisionmaking under delegation than on communication under centralization. To see that this is indeed the case, consider (4), (5), and (7). It follows from these expressions that delegation is optimal if and only if

$$\left(k_2 - k_1\right) b^2 \leq \left(k_1 + k_2\right) Var(s), \tag{8}$$

where we are using the fact that delegation is always optimal when informative communication is feasible. Delegation is therefore optimal if the divergence in preferences is small relative to both the employee's informational advantage and the importance of the decision to the owner. Moreover, more congruent preferences can lead to a switch from centralization to delegation but not the reverse.

5.1.3.2. Vertically Dispersed Information. A key implication of Dessein (2002) is that the efficient allocation of decision rights depends on the endogenous flow of information. Extending the model by allowing for dispersed information further highlights the importance of taking into account the endogenous flow of information. Our discussion of this case is based on Harris and Raviv (2005).

For an illustration of their main arguments, suppose that there is another state $\hat{s}$, which is independently drawn from a uniform distribution with support $[-\hat{L}, \hat{L}]$ and variance $Var(\hat{s}) = \hat{L}^2/3$. The state $\hat{s}$ is observed by the owner but not by the employee. Under either organizational structure, the party without the decision right sends a single cheap-talk message to the decisionmaker, after which the decisionmaker makes his or her preferred decision. Finally, the owner's and the employee's payoffs are now given by

$$U_1(d, w) = K - k_1(d - s - \hat{s} - b)^2 + w \tag{9}$$

and

$$U_2(d, w) = K - k_2(d - s - \hat{s})^2 - w. \tag{10}$$

Proceeding as we did above, one can show that delegation is now optimal if and only if

$$\left(k_2 - k_1\right) b^2 \le (k_1 + k_2)(V(b) - \hat{V}(b)), \tag{11}$$

where the residual variance $\hat{V}(b)$ characterizes the quality of communication under delegation and can be obtained by replacing $\mathrm{Var}(s)$ with $\mathrm{Var}(\hat{s})$ in (4) and L with $\hat{L}$ in (5). As in the model with concentrated information, a reduction in the divergence parameter improves both decisionmaking under delegation and communication under centralization. In addition, however, a reduction in b now improves communication under delegation. As a result, such a reduction can actually lead to a switch from delegation to centralization. Although this result contradicts the prediction of the model with concentrated information, it underlines that model's central insight that the efficient allocation of decision rights depends on the endogenous flow of information.

5.1.3.3. Horizontally Dispersed Information. So far we have focused on a setting with a single decision. Additional issues arise when there are multiple decisions that have to be coordinated and the information that is relevant for the decisions is dispersed among multiple employees. Coordinated decisionmaking then requires aggregation of the dispersed information. Some recent papers explore the allocation of decision rights in such a setting (Alonso et al. 2008; Rantakari 2008; Dessein et al. 2010; Friebel and Raith 2010). In line with the models we just discussed, these papers focus on communication costs that arise because of the employees' incentives to use their information strategically, which is why we concentrate on this branch of the literature below. For related models in which communication is not strategic, see, in particular, Aoki (1986), Hart and Moore (2005), Dessein and Santos (2006), and Crémer et al. (2007).

To illustrate the main insights in Alonso et al. (2008), suppose now that there are two employees. We think of the owner as the CEO of a multidivisional firm and the employees as the division managers.

Profits depend on two decisions, one of which is associated with Division 1 and the other with Division 2. For each decision, the firm faces a trade-off between coordination and adaptation. On one hand, each decision should be adapted to the business environment faced by the relevant division; on the other hand, decisions should also be coordinated with each other. Suppose, for instance, that the firm is a car manufacturer and that each division serves a particular country. Moreover, the firm has to decide what car it should produce for, and sell in, each country. The firm then faces a trade-off between tailoring the car types to the local tastes in each market—and thus increasing revenue—and coordinating the car types across markets—and thus reducing costs. This trade-off is captured in the profit functions

$$\pi_1 = K - \left(d_1 - s_1\right)^2 - \delta \left(d_1 - d_2\right)^2 \tag{12}$$

and

$$\pi_2 = K - \left(d_2 - s_2\right)^2 - \delta \left(d_1 - d_2\right)^2, \tag{13}$$

where K is a constant and $\delta \ge 0$ is the parameter that measures the relative importance of adapting each decision to the state and setting them equal to each other. Consistent with the notation in the previous sections, d_1 and d_2 are the two decisions, and s_1 and s_2 are the states that summarize the business environment faced by each division.

All managers are risk neutral and thus care about expected profits. They differ, however, in how much weight they put on the expected profits of the different divisions. In particular, although the CEO cares about the firm's overall profits, each division manager puts weight λ on the profits of his own division and only $1 - \lambda$ on that of the other division. The parameter $\lambda \in (1/2, 1]$ therefore measures each division manager's own-division bias.

In line with the models in Section 5.1, we are interested in comparing the efficiency of two organizational structures, centralization (in which case both decisions are made by the CEO) and decentralization (in which case each division manager makes his decision without knowing what decision the other division manager has made). Under centralization the division managers communicate vertically with the CEO, and under decentralization they communicate horizontally with each other. In either case, communication takes the form of a single cheap-talk message that each division manager sends to either the CEO (in the case of centralization) or to his counterpart (in the case of decentralization). These messages are always sent simultaneously.

The endogenous quality of communication is crucial for the main result of the model. To see this, suppose first that the quality of communication is exogenously given. This would be the case, for instance, if communication were imperfect because of physical constraints rather than because of the division managers' strategic incentives to manipulate their information. And to keep things simple, suppose also that the exogenously given quality of communication is the same across organizational structures.

In such a setting, it is not immediately obvious whether the firm should centralize or decentralize. On one hand, the division managers know more about the states of the world than the CEO; on the other, their incentives to make the right decisions are distorted. If the quality of communication were perfect, centralization would therefore be optimal. If communication were entirely uninformative, however, decentralization would always be optimal. And in between these two extremes, the choice between the two organizational structures is determined by the need for coordination δ: whatever value λ takes, centralization is always optimal provided that the need for coordination is sufficiently strong. This conclusion is also illustrated in Figure 2. In the limit, however, in which δ goes to ∞, expected profits under the two organizational structures converge to the same level. The reason is that as coordination becomes all important, the division managers understand that setting decisions equal to each other is all important, and they act accordingly. In spite of this convergence, however, it is still the case that for any large but finite δ, centralization is optimal. And this result, of course, is in line with the received wisdom that if coordination is important, centralization outperforms decentralization.

The main insight of the model is that this intuitive result depends crucially on the assumption that communication is exogenous. To see this, we need to understand the division managers' incentives to misrepresent their information under the two organizational structures. Consider, then, the incentives of one of the division managers, say, Manager 1, the division manager in charge of Division 1. From his perspective, when the CEO makes decision d_1, she puts too little weight on adapting it to s_1 and too much on coordinating it with d_2. Thus if Manager 1 would truthfully communicate his state, he would expect the CEO's choice of d_1 to be too close to zero. To induce the CEO to make a more extreme decision, Manager 1 therefore exaggerates his state and reports that its absolute value is larger than it actually is. Crucially, the more important is coordination, the more weight the CEO will put on setting d_1 equal to d_2 and

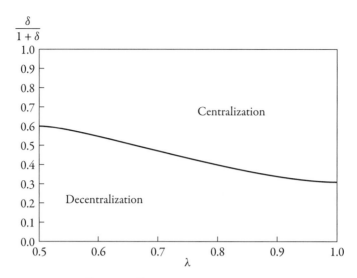

Figure 2. Exogenous communication.

the less weight she will put on setting d_1 equal to s_1. Under centralization, therefore, the more important is coordination, the more the division managers will exaggerate their states, and the less information will be communicated in equilibrium.

This comparative static is the exact opposite under decentralization. To see this, consider Manager 1's incentives to misrepresent his information under decentralization. From his perspective, Manager 2 puts too little weight on coordinating d_2 with d_1 and too much weight on adapting d_2 to s_2. Thus if Manager 1 truthfully communicated his state, he would expect Manager 2's choice of d_2 to be too close to zero. To induce Manager 2 to make a more extreme decision, Manager 1 will therefore once again exaggerate his state. In contrast to the centralized structure, however, Manager 1's incentive to exaggerate his state is weaker, the more important coordination is. Essentially, the more important is coordination, the more weight Manager 2 will put on coordinating d_2 with d_1 and the less weight he will put on adapting d_2 to s_2. Under decentralization, therefore, the more important coordination, the less the division managers will exaggerate their states, and thus the more information will be communicated in equilibrium.

This difference between horizontal and vertical communication has important implications for the choice between the two organizational structures. In particular, with endogenous communication it is no longer the case that centralization is optimal when coordination is sufficiently important. This is illustrated in Figure 3. As with exogenous communication, decentralization is optimal if coordination is sufficiently unimportant. If λ is small, however, decentralization now remains optimal even if coordination becomes arbitrarily important. This model therefore once again highlights the importance of taking into account the endogenous nature of communication when predicting how changes in the environment affect the optimal allocation of decision rights.

5.1.4. To Motivate the Employee
Another common argument for delegation is that it motivates employees to provide more effort (Aghion and Tirole 1997). In line with our discussion in Section 3.5, it is useful to

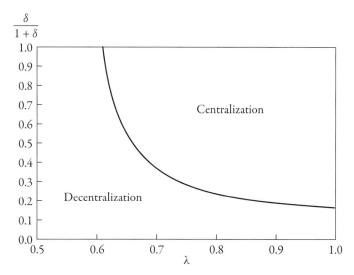

Figure 3. Endogenous communication.

distinguish between motivating the employee to put more effort into information acquisition and motivating him to put more effort into execution.

5.1.4.1. Motivating Information Acquisition. Delegation not only allows the owner to make more efficient use of the employee's information, as we saw in the previous section. It may also allow the employee to use his information more effectively in pursuing his own goals. One would therefore expect delegation to increase the value of information to the employee and thus increase his incentives to become informed. In this section we first explore this motivational effect of delegation in the context of Aghion and Tirole (1997). We then return to Che and Kartik (2009), who show that in some cases delegation may actually reduce the value of information to the employee and thus weaken his incentives to become informed.

To explore the motivational effect of delegation, we make three changes to the version of Aghion and Tirole (1997) described in Section 3.5. First, at the beginning of the game, the owner now offers the employee a contract that specifies a wage and an allocation of the decision right. Second, we assume that the decision is more important to the owner than to the employee, that is, $B > b$. If this were not the case, delegation would be optimal even if both parties were perfectly informed. Third, to focus on the employee's incentives, we assume for now that the probability E with which the owner becomes informed is fixed. This would be the case, for instance, if her expertise were based on past experience rather than on current efforts to acquire information.

In Section 3.5 we saw that if the owner retains the right to make the decision, the employee benefits from becoming informed only if the owner is uninformed. Specifically, the employee's marginal benefit of getting informed is given by $(1 - E)b$.

If, instead, the owner delegates the decision right to the employee, the employee benefits from becoming informed even if the owner is informed too, because he can then insist on his preferred decision being made rather than having to accept the owner's. As a result, under delegation, the employee's marginal benefit of becoming informed is given by $(1 - E)b_E + E(1 - \alpha)b = b(1 - \alpha E)$.

Delegation therefore increases the employee's marginal benefit of becoming informed, which in turn induces him to provide more effort. Delegation is then optimal if this motivational effect is sufficiently large relative to the cost of having decisions made by someone whose preferences are further from first best. In particular, delegation is optimal if

$$S^D - S^C = \left[(1 - E)\left(e^D - e^C\right)(\alpha B + b) - \left(c\left(d^D\right) - c\left(d^C\right)\right) \right]$$
$$- Ee^D(1 - \alpha)(B - b) > 0, \tag{14}$$

where the first term on the right-hand side captures the benefit of a more motivated employee, and the second term captures the loss of control.

So far we have taken the owner's effort as exogenous. If effort is endogenous, delegation discourages information acquisition by the owner, for the same reason that it encourages information acquisition by the employee. As in Grossmann and Hart (1986) and Hart and Moore (1990), a change in residual control rights therefore leads to changes in the equilibrium levels of effort or investment.

The observation that delegation may involve a trade-off between losing control and motivating the employee is a central insight of Aghion and Tirole (1997). Although this trade-off is intuitive, some papers have explored conditions under which delegation may actually discourage the employee. The model in Rantakari (2012), for instance, can be viewed as a multitasking version of Aghion and Tirole (1997) in which the employee can choose both how much effort he puts into information acquisition and the type of decisions that he investigates. In such a setting, delegation motivates the employee to put effort into finding decisions that are good for him personally, but it discourages him from finding decisions that are good for the owner.

Another model in which delegation can discourage the employee is Che and Kartik (2009). They consider a model in which the owner and the employee have the same preferences over decisions but different priors about the state of the world and thus about what decision to make. One motive for the employee to acquire information is then to persuade the owner of his own opinion (see also Van den Steen 2002). Under delegation, the employee no longer needs to persuade the owner and may thus be less motivated to acquire information. This complacency effect of delegation can arise even if the employee and the owner have the same priors. To see this, notice that in Aghion and Tirole (1997) the allocation of the decision right does not matter if both parties are uninformed, because they then agree to make the default decision. Suppose in contrast that there are two default decisions, one that gives the owner zero but costs the employee $c > 0$ and another that gives the employee zero and costs the owner c. Under centralization, the employee's marginal benefit of becoming informed is then given by $(1 - E)(b + c)$, whereas under delegation it is still given by $b(1 - \alpha E)$. Delegation then discourages the employee, provided that c is sufficiently large. In the terminology of Che and Kartik (2009), delegation makes the employee "complacent," because it makes it less costly for him to be uninformed.

5.1.4.2. Motivating Execution.
Delegation might motivate the employee to put more effort not only into information acquisition but also into implementing and executing decisions. The employee may, for instance, believe that his preferred decision has a higher chance of

succeeding than that of the owner (Zábojník 2002; Van den Steen 2006). Or he may simply receive a larger private benefit from successfully implementing his preferred decision (Bester and Krähmer 2008).

Delegation can motivate execution; however, the need to motivate execution may actually make delegation less efficient relative to centralization (Bester and Krähmer 2008). The reason is that if the owner has to motivate execution, she needs to take the employee's preferences into account when she makes a decision. The need to motivate execution therefore acts as a disciplinary device on the owner that makes centralized decisionmaking more efficient relative to delegated decisionmaking.

To see this more clearly, consider a simplified version of the model in Bester and Krähmer (2008). In particular, recall the model in Section 5.1.2, but suppose now that after a decision has been made, the employee has to choose his implementation effort $e \in \{0, 1\}$. The decision succeeds if and only if the employee provides effort and success is not contractible. The parties' payoffs are then given by

$$U_1(d, e) = e\left[K - k_1(d - \theta - b)^2\right] - ce + w \tag{15}$$

and

$$U_2(d, e) = e\left[K - k_2(d - \theta)^2\right] - w, \tag{16}$$

where c is the employee's cost of effort. Suppose also that effort costs satisfy

$$K - k_1 b^2 < c < K - k_1 E\left[\left(d^{FB} - \theta - b\right)^2\right], \tag{17}$$

where d^{FB} is the first-best decision if the employee does provide effort. Finally, suppose that $k_1 > k_2$, so that the decision is more important to the employee than to the owner.

If effort is contractible, motivating execution is not a concern. As in the model in Section 5.1.2, it is then efficient to give the decision right to the party that values this right more highly, which in this case is the employee. If effort is not contractible, however, motivating execution does become a concern. Under centralization, the owner then cannot simply make her preferred decisions, because if she did, the employee would not put any effort into execution. To motivate execution, the owner therefore has to bias her decision toward the employee's preferred decision, which makes her decision more efficient. In contrast, if the owner delegates, the employee will still make his preferred decision. The need to motivate execution therefore makes centralized decisionmaking more efficient relative to delegation. As a result, the owner may find it optimal to centralize when she has to motivate execution, even though she would delegate if motivation were not a concern.

5.1.5. To Learn More about the Employee

Delegation can also be a tool to test the employee and to learn more about his ability or preferences. For instance, a CEO may delegate control over a division to a senior executive to test the executive's ability to run his own business. Or she may delegate to the executive to find out more about his preferences, such as whether he is an empire builder or is focused on generating profits. Aghion et al. (2002, 2004) explore this second possibility. In doing so, they also challenge the assumption in most of the literature that the allocation of decision rights is deterministic. In this section we first discuss the use of delegation as a means to learn more about the employee's preferences and then discuss contingent allocations of decision rights.

5.1.5.1. Learning about the Employee's Preferences.   To see some of the insights in Aghion et al. (2002, 2004), consider the following two-period model. In the first period an organization has to decide on the type of project it wants to design, and in the second it has to decide on whether to implement the project. In the first period Aghion et al. make three changes to the model in Aghion and Tirole (1997), which we described in the previous section. First, wages are fixed at zero. Second, the owner and the employee both know the payoffs of all the projects, that is, $E = e = 1$. Third, the employee is privately informed about his type, either bad (which happens with probability $\mu < \frac{1}{2}$) or good (which happens with probability $1 - \mu$). If the employee is a good type, the congruence parameter α is equal to one, and if he is a bad type, it is equal to zero. For reasons that will become apparent, we assume that $b > 1$.

In the second period, the owner decides whether to implement the project that was designed in the first. If the owner does not implement the project, both parties receive a zero payoff, regardless of whether the employee is a good or a bad type. But if the owner does implement the project, she gets $+1$ if the employee is a good type and -1 if he is a bad type, while the employee obtains $+1$ in either case. Implementing the project is therefore in the owner's interest only if the employee is a good type.

In this setting, if the owner does not delegate the design decision, she will choose her preferred design in the first period and then implement it in the second period. In this case, the owner's expected payoff is therefore given by $E\left[U_2^C\right] = B + 1 - 2\mu$. If, instead, the owner does delegate the design decision, the employee will always choose his preferred design and thus reveal his type. In the second period, the owner then implements the design if and only if the employee is a good type. In this case, the owner's expected payoff is therefore given by $E\left[U_2^D\right] = (1 - \mu)(B + 1)$.

The gain from delegation is then given by $E\left[U_2^D - U_2^C\right] = \mu - \mu B$, which is positive if $B < 1$. In this setting, delegation is therefore a tool that allows the owner to learn more about the employee's preferences. For the owner to make use of this tool, however, her future benefit of knowing the employee's preferences must outweigh current costs of learning them, that is, $B < 1$. At the same time, the employee's current benefit of using authority in his favor must outweigh the future costs of a ruined reputation, that is, $b > 1$.

5.1.5.2. Contingent Allocations of Decision Rights.   The models we have examined so far assume that, although decision rights are contractible, their allocation cannot be made contingent on any information that is revealed after the initial contract is signed. This assumption is typically justified informally by arguing that the reallocation of decision rights in organizations takes too long relative to the time frame in which most decisions have to be made. In practice, reallocations certainly appear to be rare relative to the frequency with which decisions are made.

In the confines of the models that we have examined so far, however, there is no reason the owner should not be able to commit to contingent allocations of the decision rights. And as shown in Aghion et al. (2002, 2004) and Krähmer (2006), doing so can indeed make the owner better off.

To see why contingent allocations can make the owner better off, consider the setting we sketched above, and suppose that the allocation of the first-period decision right is made contingent on a message sent by the employee. In particular, if the employee admits to being a bad type, he is rewarded by receiving the decision right with probability $1/b$; if, however, he claims to be a good type, the owner retains the decision right for sure. The probability $1/b$ with which the decision right is delegated to the employee ensures that a bad employee is just indifferent between revealing his type (in which case he expects to make $(1/b)b$ today and zero tomorrow) and claiming to be a good type (in which case he makes zero today and $+1$ tomorrow). In this setting, contingent delegation therefore allows the owner to learn the employee's type at a lower cost and thus makes her better off.

If contingent delegation can make the owner better off, why would she ever delegate to the employee unconditionally? One reason is that the contingent allocation requires the owner to delegate to the employee when she has learned that the employee is a bad type. One can imagine situations in which the owner is unable to commit herself to such an ex post inefficient action, even if it is ex ante efficient to do so.

Notice also that in a slightly more general setting than the one we examined above, the optimal revelation mechanism may call for the unconditional transfer of the decision right to the employee. In particular, suppose that the good employee does not have the same preferences as the owner. Aghion et al. (2002, 2004) show that if the owner's preferences are sufficiently different from those of both types of employees, it is no longer possible to induce the employee to reveal his type. The owner can then no longer be made better off by making delegation contingent on the employee's messages.

Finally, as we discuss in Section 5.2, legal barriers prevent organizations from committing to contracts that transfer decision rights from the top to others in the organization. Below we argue that organizations may still be able to implement deterministic allocations through other means that do not require formal contracts. It is unclear, however, whether these other mechanisms would also allow for the implementation of contingent allocations of decision rights. For these reasons, in the remainder of this chapter we return to the assumption that the allocation of decision rights is deterministic.

5.1.6. Anything Else?

Alfred Sloan, the longtime President and CEO of General Motors, is widely regarded as one of the inventors of the multidivisional organization that is now common in large corporations. A major theme in his autobiography is the importance for corporate performance of properly allocating decision rights between headquarters and the divisions. As he puts it in the last chapter of his autobiography:

> It has been a thesis of this book that good management rests on the reconciliation of centralization and decentralization, or "decentralization with coordinated control." . . . From decentralization we get initiative, responsibility, development of personnel, decisions close to the facts, flexibility—in short, all the qualities necessary for an organization to adapt to new conditions. From coordination we get efficiencies and economies. It must be apparent

that co-ordinated decentralization is not an easy concept to apply. There is no hard and fast rule for sorting out the various responsibilities and the best way to assign them. The balance which is struck between corporate and divisional responsibility varies according to what is being decided, the circumstances of the time, past experience, and the temperaments and skills of the executives involved. [Sloan 1964: 429]

Much of what Sloan says in this quotation is reflected in the literature on delegation that we have discussed so far. Just like Sloan, for instance, the literature has focused on "initiative," "flexibility," and "decisions close to the facts" as primary benefits of a decentralized structure. And the trade-off between adaptation and coordination that Sloan describes has been at the center of much recent work. The quotation, however, also points to some issues that we have not yet addressed.

For instance, Sloan is not the only practitioner who believes in the importance of delegation for the "development of personnel." Nevertheless, little, if any, work has been done on the role of delegation in the development of managerial human capital. More generally, the literature has so far focused largely on static models of delegation. The dynamics of delegation is an important and potentially fruitful area of future research.

The models that we have discussed so far are also quite stark in that they force the owner to choose between centralization and unconstrained delegation and do not allow her to control the employee through different means. As such, these models do not capture Sloan's policy of "decentralization with coordinated control."

In the rest of this chapter we explore some of these additional issues. In particular, in the next section we discuss the issues that arise if the owner cannot commit to contracts that transfer decision rights to the employee. This is one area of the literature in which dynamic models of delegation do play a prominent role. In Section 5.3 we then discuss models that allow the owner to better control the employee by either constraining the decisions he can make or by using incentive contracts to align his preferences.

5.2. How to Delegate

The models we have discussed so far ask *why* the owner may find it optimal to delegate decision rights, but they do not examine *how* the owner may do so. This is potentially problematic, because, by law, formal authority resides at the top of organizations and the "business judgment rule" makes it impossible to write legal contracts that transfer formal authority to other parties in the organization (see Kornhauser and MacLeod, this volume).

One way for the owner to transfer formal authority to an employee is to sell him the assets that are necessary to make the decision and thus turn him into an independent subcontractor (Grossman and Hart 1986; Hart and Moore 1990). Given our focus on internal organization, however, we are interested in how the owner can delegate formal authority to an employee without changing the boundaries of the organization.

In this section we review some papers that show that even if the owner cannot write legal contracts delegating formal authority to another party in her organization, she may be able to commit to behaving as if formal authority had been delegated. We first discuss how the owner may be able to do so by committing to an information structure in which it is optimal for her to rubber-stamp any recommendation that the employee might make. We then discuss models in which reputational concerns induce the owner to rubber-stamp the employee's recommendations, even if it is not in her short-term interest to do so.

5.2.1. Delegation through Ignorance

The old saying that knowledge is power suggests that information can lead to the separation of real and formal authority, which is a central observation in Aghion and Tirole (1997). We saw above that in their model an uninformed owner finds it optimal to rubber-stamp her employee's recommendation, even if she knows that the employee is selfishly recommending his own preferred decision. This suggests that an owner who cannot commit to delegation contractually may still be able to do so by committing to an appropriate information structure.

For an owner to delegate by committing to an appropriate information structure, two conditions have to hold. First, it must be the case that even if the owner knows that the employee is simply recommending his preferred decision, she cannot invert the recommendation and thus infer his information. Second, there must be an underlying congruence in the two parties' preferences: the owner must prefer the employee's preferred decision to her either doing nothing or making a decision at random.

Both conditions are satisfied in Aghion and Tirole (1997). First, if the employee recommends a decision, the owner cannot infer the payoffs associated with the other decisions. Second, because the owner expects a positive payoff from the employee's preferred decision, she prefers that decision to her either doing nothing, in which case she gets zero, or making a decision at random, in which case she expects to be wiped out. In this setting, the owner can therefore transfer real authority to the employee by committing to not becoming informed. Aghion and Tirole (1997) suggest that the owner may be able to do so, for instance, by becoming overloaded with other decisions.

In Aghion and Tirole (1997) the employee's recommendation is entirely noninvertible. Callander (2008b) instead develops a model in which an employee's recommendations are partially invertible. To see a simple version of his model, suppose that an owner and an employee have quadratic preferences over an outcome $x \in \mathfrak{R}$, with the employee preferring a larger outcome than does the owner. An outcome function maps the decision d into the outcome. The crucial feature of the model is that the outcome function is generated by Brownian motion. Both parties know the drift and variance of the Brownian motion, and they know the outcome associated with a default decision. However, only the employee knows the full realization of the Brownian motion.

In this setting, if the employee recommends the decision that leads to his preferred outcome, and the owner is aware of this, the owner can infer some information about the outcomes associated with other decisions. Callander (2008b) shows that the owner finds it optimal to rubber-stamp the employee's selfish recommendations if the variance of the Brownian motion is above a threshold, in which case the owner is very uncertain about the outcomes associated with the other decision. If the variance is below the threshold, however, the owner may find it optimal to use the information that she can infer from the employee's recommendation to overrule the employee and make another decision. This model suggests that the owner's ability to delegate through ignorance depends on the complexity of the decision, where the complexity is captured by the variance of the Brownian motion.

5.2.2. Informal Delegation

We now turn to papers that explore the feasibility and optimality of informal delegation. The first section examines the conditions under which an owner is able to maintain a reputation for rubber-stamping her employee's recommendations, even if it is not in her short-term interest to do so. In the second section we then ask whether an owner who is able to maintain such a reputation finds it optimal to do so. The reason she may not is that if she can implement delegation, she may be able to implement other decision processes that do even better than either centralization or delegation.

5.2.2.1. Feasibility of Informal Delegation. We first examine the conditions under which an owner is able to resist the short-term temptation of overruling her employee and thus is able to engage in informal delegation. Baker et al. (1999) show that these conditions can be different from, and sometimes the opposite of, the conditions under which the owner would want to delegate to the employee in the first place.

To capture some of their insights, we make four changes to the version of Aghion and Tirole (1997) that we discussed in Section 5.1.4. First, we now assume that the owner is never informed about the decisions, that is, $E = 0$. Second, the employee's cost of effort is now given by $c(e) = ce^2$. Third, if the employee recommends a decision, the owner learns the payoffs from that decision. Information is therefore now assumed to be hard. Finally, we continue to assume that with probability α one of the decisions pays the owner B and the employee b, whereas the other pays each party zero. With probability $1 - \alpha$, however, one of the decisions now pays the owner B and the employee zero, whereas the other pays the owner and the employee $-B$ and b, respectively. In this case, the owner therefore prefers the default decision to the employee's preferred decision.

Before we turn to the infinitely repeated version of this game, consider a once-off interaction in which the owner is able to commit to delegation contractually. If the owner does delegate to the employee, the employee will always make his preferred decision. Effort and expected surplus will then be given by

$$e^D = \arg \max_e w + eb - ce^2 \tag{18}$$

and

$$S^D = e^D[\alpha(B + b) + (1 - \alpha)(-B + b)] - c(e^D)^2. \tag{19}$$

Suppose now that the owner does not delegate to the employee. If the employee becomes informed, he will then recommend his preferred decision if it coincides with the owner's preferred decision, but he will recommend the default decision if their preferred decisions do not coincide. Effort and expected surplus will then be given by

$$e^C = \arg \max_e w + e\alpha b - ce^2 \tag{20}$$

and

$$S^C = e^C \alpha(B + b) - c(e^C)^2. \tag{21}$$

We are interested in the case in which delegation is more efficient than centralization, but the owner is not able to commit to delegation contractually. For the rest of this section, we therefore suppose that $S^D > S^C$, which will be the case if the congruence parameter α is sufficiently large.

Consider then an infinitely repeated version of the game in which a long-lived owner faces a series of short-lived employees, each of whom she interacts with only once.[13] We focus on trigger strategies in which the owner promises to rubber-stamp any recommendation an employee might make and in which the parties revert to the best static equilibrium if the owner breaks her promise.

Standard arguments then show that the owner can implement delegation informally if and only if

$$S^D - S^C \geq rB, \tag{22}$$

where r is the discount rate. As one would expect, the owner is therefore able to replicate delegation informally, provided that she is sufficiently patient. More interestingly, the model predicts that the feasibility of informal delegation depends on the owner's reneging temptation, which, in turn, depends on both the average and the extreme realizations of payoffs. Suppose, for instance, that we increase B but also adjust b and α in such a way that $S^D - S^C$ stays constant. Even though such a change does not affect the efficiency of delegation, it makes it more difficult to implement it, because the change increases the owner's reneging temptation. Finally, notice that when preferences are highly congruent, delegation is efficient but cannot be implemented informally, because the owner's fallback option is then too attractive. This result is in stark contrast to models with contractible control, many of which predict that the owner will engage in delegation when preferences are highly congruent (e.g., see Dessein 2002; Alonso et al. 2008).

5.2.2.2. Optimality of Informal Delegation. We now turn to whether a long-lived owner who is able to replicate delegation informally finds it optimal to do so. Baker et al. (1999) and Alonso and Matouschek (2007) show that she may not, even if delegation is more efficient than centralization. As mentioned above, the reason is that if the owner is able to engage in informal delegation, she may also be able to commit to other, more efficient decision processes.

To understand the argument in Alonso and Matouschek (2007), consider an infinite repetition of the version of Dessein (2002) model that we described in Section 5.1.3. In line with the model in the previous section, suppose that the owner is long-lived and that she faces a series of short-lived employees. Delegation can then be implemented informally if and only if

$$S^D - S^C \geq rb^2, \tag{23}$$

where S^D and S^C are given by (18) and (20), and we are again assuming that if the owner reneges on her promise, the parties revert to centralization. Notice that the maximum reneging temptation is given by b^2, because when an employee truthfully reveals the state, the owner can always implement her preferred decision rather than that of the employee.

---

13. The main insights of the model would be unchanged if the long-lived owner interacted with a single, long-lived employee. The above formulation highlights that we are focusing on the owner's reputational concerns rather than those of the employees.

The key observation now is that if the owner is patient enough to engage in delegation, she is also patient enough to engage in threshold delegation. Under this scheme, the owner makes the employees' preferred decision if they report a state below the threshold $s^* = L - 2bk_2/(k_1 + k_2)$, and she implements $d = s^* + b$ otherwise. Threshold delegation involves the same maximum reneging temptation as delegation, but it is more efficient.

If an owner is sufficiently patient to replicate delegation informally, she may therefore also be able to commit to decision processes that perform better than either centralization or delegation. On one hand, this provides a challenge to our analysis, because it requires us to consider many more decision processes than the two that we have focused on so far. On the other hand, it also brings the analysis closer to the real world, because firms clearly do use many different types of decision processes. In the next section we go beyond the simple example in this section and examine optimal decision processes in more general environments.

5.3. How to Control the Employee

The models we have discussed so far focus on the choice between centralization and delegation and mostly abstract from any actions that the owner might be able take to control the employee. The ability of the owner to take actions to control the employee in many settings has been noted by Holmström (1977, 1984) and Jensen and Meckling (1992), among others. For instance, the owner may be able to constrain the decisions the employee can make. Or she may be able to use incentive contracts to align the employee's incentives. In this section we discuss these two options in turn.

5.3.1. Optimal Decision Processes

In the previous section we saw that even if decisions are ex ante and ex post noncontractible, a sufficiently patient owner can implement decision processes other than just centralization and delegation. This raises the question of what is the optimal process among all deterministic decision processes. A related question is what the owner should do if she is able to constrain the decisions the employee can make. It turns out that these two questions are actually the same, at least if one restricts attention to deterministic decision rules. In particular, Holmström (1977, 1984) observes that searching for the optimal deterministic decision rule is equivalent to figuring out how to optimally constrain the set of decisions from which the employee is allowed to choose. In this section we discuss Holmström (1977, 1984) and the literature built on his contributions.

Holmström (1977, 1984) starts by posing a general class of problems in which an owner needs to make a decision that affects her payoff and that of her employee. The employee privately observes the state of the world that determines each party's preferred decision. In contrast to the models we have examined so far, Holmström allows the owner to commit to any deterministic outcome function that maps the employee's recommendations to decisions. He does, however, continue to rule out contingent payments between the two parties.

In this setting, the Revelation Principle implies that one can restrict attention to direct mechanisms in which the employee truthfully reveals the state. Any deterministic direct mechanism in turn can be implemented through a constrained delegation scheme in which the owner offers the employee a set of decisions from which the employee can then choose. The contracting problem therefore reduces to finding the optimal delegation set. However, the optimal delegation set can take essentially any form, the only requirement being that the employee's choice is well defined.

In practice, constrained delegation of this type is very common. Alfred Sloan, for instance, delegated the pricing decisions of the different types of cars to his division managers but allowed them to choose only prices between certain thresholds (Sloan 1964).

However, notice that although constrained delegation is weakly optimal in this setting, there may be other decision processes that might perform equally well. Mylovanov (2008), for instance, shows that when the optimal delegation set takes the form of a single interval, and the owner's and employee's preferred decision functions intersect at most once, the optimal delegation set can be implemented through veto delegation.

After posing the general problem and showing that a solution exists, Holmström (1977, 1984) shows that in the standard uniform-quadratic–constant-bias case the optimal delegation set takes the form of a single interval. As mentioned above, some papers have built on Holmström's work. For instance, Melumad and Shibano (1991), Martimort and Semenov (2006), Alonso and Matouschek (2008), and Amador and Bagwell (2011) characterize the optimal delegation set for more general settings. Koessler and Martimort (2012) and Frankel (2012) extend the standard setting by allowing for multidimensional decisions. Szalay (2005) endogenizes information acquisition by the employee. And Ambrus and Egorov (2009) allow for the owner to impose decision-contingent costs on the employee. All these papers focus on deterministic mechanisms. In contrast, Kovac and Mylovanov (2009) allow for stochastic mechanisms and provide sufficient conditions under which the optimal mechanism is in fact deterministic.

One insight from this literature is that even if the owner is able to commit to essentially any decision process, delegation can arise as the optimal one. And if delegation is not optimal, other commonly observed decision processes often do arise. For instance, Alonso and Matouschek (2008) and Amador and Bagwell (2011) provide necessary and sufficient conditions for the optimal delegation set to consist of a single interval. Even though commonly observed decision processes can arise as optimal, however, some of the widely held beliefs about how changes in the environment affect decisionmaking may no longer hold. For instance, Alonso and Matouschek (2008) show that if one allows for any decision process, the owner may give less discretion to an employee whose preferences are more aligned with the owner's or to one with a greater informational advantage.

To illustrate an application of this literature, albeit in a different context, consider the classic problem of regulating a monopolist who is privately informed about his costs (Baron and Myerson 1982). But in contrast to Baron and Myerson, suppose that transfers between the regulator and the monopolist are ruled out by law, as is often the case in practice. In particular, suppose that the monopolist can produce $q \geq 0$ units of a good at costs θq and faces a linear demand curve $d = A - Bq$, where d is the price, and A and B are both strictly positive parameters. Marginal costs s are drawn from a unimodal distribution with support $[0, 1]$. The monopolist's preferred price is then given by $d_S(s) = (A + s)/2$, whereas the regulator would like to set the price equal to marginal costs. Finally, suppose that the maximum willingness to pay A is larger than the largest marginal cost, that is, $A > 1$. Our discussion of this example follows Alonso and Matouschek (2008).

A first question is whether the regulator should give the firm any discretion over pricing. The answer is that the regulator should do so if and only if $A/2 < E(s)$. This condition is more likely to be satisfied the smaller is A, which is intuitive, because a reduction in A reduces the firm's preferred price. However, notice that the condition depends only on the mean of the cost distribution and not on any measure of its dispersion. The magnitude of the firm's informational advantage therefore has no affect on whether the regulator should give it any discretion over pricing.

The second question is then what prices the firm should be allowed to choose from, if the above condition is indeed satisfied. The answer turns out to be very simple: for any unimodal cost distribution, the regulator cannot do better than to let the firm choose any price below a threshold. This result is consistent with the widespread use of price-cap regulation in the United Kingdom and the United States (Armstrong and Sappington 2007). Finally, it can be shown that the price cap is decreasing in A and that the effect of a change in the firm's informational advantage is in general ambiguous. Even though this example deals with the organization of a regulatory system, it does suggest that the results from this literature can be fruitfully applied to similar issues that arise in firms, such as the design of capital budgeting rules and the design of transfer pricing schemes.

The general problem that this literature examines has been further explored in the context of various economic problems. For instance, Athey et al. (2005) study the optimal degree of discretion for a monetary authority. Amador et al. (2006) explore how an agent may want to restrict his future decisions in a setting where the agent expects to receive relevant information in the future but also knows that he suffers from self-control problems. Martimort and Semenov (2006) examine a delegation problem with multiple employees to analyze the organization of lobbying by interest groups. And in a setting with a different information structure than the one shared by the models that we have described so far, Armstrong and Vickers (2010) develop a model of delegated project choice and apply it to the optimal design of competition policy.

5.3.2. Endogenous Incentives

In addition to constraining the decisions the employee can make, the owner might be able to control the employee through the use of incentive contracts. Most of the literature on delegation assumes that the owner cannot rely on incentive contracts to align the employee's incentives, just as most of the literature on incentive contracts assumes that the owner cannot contract on the allocation of decision rights. One reason for ruling out incentive contracts is that they can be difficult to reconcile with the assumption that contracts are highly incomplete (see, for instance, Mookherjee, this volume), which is central to all the models of delegation discussed in this chapter. As observed by Jensen and Meckling (1992) and others, however, in practice the design of incentive contracts and the allocation of decision rights are interdependent. Indeed, there is a strong sense that the use of incentive contracts and delegation are not only interdependent but also complementary. For instance, Milgrom and Roberts (1992: 17) observe that "incentives and delegated authority are complements: each makes the other more valuable." In this section we discuss papers that explore this interdependence. In line with our discussion above, we distinguish between models in which there is only one employee and one decision and others in which there multiple employees and decisions.

5.3.2.1. Incentive Contracts for a Single Employee. The trade-off between risk and incentives is a central insight of the literature on incentive schemes. But as Prendergast (2002) observes, there is only weak empirical support for this trade-off. Indeed, if anything, firms appear to be using steeper incentives in more, rather than less, uncertain environments. To provide an explanation for this empirical pattern, Prendergast develops a model in which incentives and the allocation of decision rights are jointly determined. In the model, the more uncertain is the environment, the more discretion an owner gives her employee over what he can do on the job. And the more discretion the employee has over what he can do on the job, the more important it is that his pay be closely tied to his performance. In line with the observation above, incentives and discretion are therefore complements.[14] And because incentives and discretion are complements, an increase in uncertainty that leads to more discretion also leads to steeper incentives.[15]

Krishna and Morgan (2008) also allow for endogenous incentives in a setting with a single employee. In their model, however, incentives and delegation are substitutes. Specifically, they consider a version of the model in Dessein (2002) in which the owner can make wages contingent on messages sent by the employee. They then show that even if wages cannot be negative, contingent wages improve communication under centralization. Because message-contingent wages do not improve decisionmaking under delegation, the owner's ability to commit to incentive contracts then makes centralization more likely. In this setting, incentives contracts and delegation are therefore substitute tools that the owner can use to make decisions more sensitive to the state.

A key difference between Prendergast (2002) and Krishna and Morgan (2008) is that in Prendergast's model incentive contracts improve decisionmaking under delegation, whereas in Krishna and Morgan's model they improve communication under centralization. In practice, incentive contracts may improve both decisionmaking and communication. For incentive contracts and delegation to be complements, as is often argued, incentive contracts must more effectively improve decisionmaking under delegation than they do communication under centralization. This observation once again highlights the importance of taking into account the endogenous nature of communication for the analysis of efficient organization.

5.3.2.2. Incentive Contracts for Multiple Employees. Some papers also explore the joint determination of incentives and the allocation of decision rights in a setting with multiple employees, who are typically thought of as division managers.

In Athey and Roberts (2001) there are two division managers who have two tasks: to put effort into increasing their divisions' profits and to select a project. A central insight of the paper is that there is a trade-off between motivating effort provision and project selection. In particular, effort provision is best motivated through relative pay, which filters out shocks that are common to both divisions; however, relative pay distorts project selection, because it gives

---

14. The literature has identified additional reasons for why incentives and delegation may be complements. For instance, Van den Steen (2010a) explores a setting in which the owner and the employee have different priors about what decision is most likely to lead to the successful conclusion of a project. In his setting, income and decision rights should be concentrated in the same party, because the party with the income right cares the most about the decision being correct, and the party with the decision right has the highest valuation of the project.

15. For a further discussion on why more uncertainty may lead to steeper incentives, see Raith (2008).

the division managers poor incentives to internalize externalities. Instead of letting the division managers decide on projects, it may then be better to move this decision to a third employee who gets paid a small fraction of overall profits. The model therefore provides a rationale for the incentives that are assumed in Alonso et al. (2008), Rantakari (2008), and other papers. As discussed in Section 5.1.3, these models assume that the CEO cares about overall profits, whereas division managers are biased toward their divisions.

In a related paper, Dessein et al. (2010) develop a model in which it is optimal to bias functional managers toward standardization and division managers toward local adaptation. They then explore the interdependence between the endogenously created incentive conflict and the allocation of decision rights. Friebel and Raith (2010) also explore the joint determination of incentives and the allocation of decision rights in a multidivisional firm. However, they focus on the boundary of the firm, which they allow to be endogenously determined. Rantakari (2011) takes the boundary of the firm as given but endogenizes the degree of operational integration, in addition to incentives and the allocation of decision rights. He argues that stable environments give rise to tightly integrated and centralized organizations with firm-wide incentives for division managers, whereas volatile environments induce firms to adopt more loosely integrated and decentralized organizational structures with division-level incentives for division managers.

6. Conclusion

A number of the first scholars to examine organizations (both within and outside the field of economics) identified both the crucial role of decisionmaking and the inherently strategic nature of communication. In the intervening years, a large volume of economic research has explored these ideas (although often without being aware of their origins). In this chapter we have surveyed this work.

It should be clear that there remain many open theoretical questions. For example, each individual line of inquiry could be deepened, as we described the cheap-talk literature moving from its origins in Section 2.2 to recent work in Section 3.1. Furthermore, there are likely to be advances from combining some of the approaches described here, such as by adding limited opportunities for contracting to several of the existing research streams, as we began to describe in Section 3.6. Finally, the question of what an organization might do to ameliorate some of the inefficiencies we describe has only just begun to be analyzed, so there is much work to do in continuing that described in Sections 4 and 5.

Probably more important than all these opportunities for more theory, however, we believe that—as is true throughout most of organizational economics—the greatest need is for empirical work in this area. We hope this need will begin to be met soon.

REFERENCES

Admati, Anat, and Paul Pfleiderer. 1997. "Does It All Add Up? Benchmarks and the Compensation of Active Portfolio Managers." *Journal of Business* 70: 323–350.

Aghion, Philippe, and Jean Tirole. 1997. "Formal and Real Authority in Organizations." *Journal of Political Economy* 105:1–29.

Aghion, Philippe, Mathias Dewatripont, and Patrick Rey. 2002. "On Partial Contracting." *European Economic Review* 46(papers and proceedings): 745–753.

———. 2004. "Transferable Control." *Journal of the European Economic Association* 2: 115–138.

Alonso, Ricardo, and Niko Matouschek. 2007. "Relational Delegation." *RAND Journal of Economics* 38: 1070–1089.

———. 2008. "Optimal Delegation." *Review of Economic Studies* 75: 259–293.

Alonso, Ricardo, Wouter Dessein, and Niko Matouschek. 2008. "When Does Coordination Require Centralization?" *American Economic Review* 98: 145–179.

Amador, Manuel, and Kyle Bagwell. 2011. "The Theory of Optimal Delegation with an Application to Tariff Caps." Working paper, Stanford University, Stanford, CA.

Amador, Manuel, Ivan Werning, and George-Marios Angeletos. 2006. "Commitment vs. Flexibility." *Econometrica* 74: 365–396.

Ambrus, Attila, and Georgy Egorov. 2009. "Delegation and Nonmonetary Incentives." Working paper, Harvard University, Cambridge, MA.

Aoki, Masahiko. 1986. "Horizontal vs. Vertical Information Structure of the Firm." *American Economic Review* 76: 971–983.

Armstrong, Mark, and David Sappington. 2007. "Recent Developments in the Theory of Regulation," in Mark Armstrong and Robert Porter (eds.), *Handbook of Industrial Organization,* volume 3. Amsterdam: North-Holland, pp. 1557–1700.

Armstrong, Mark, and John Vickers. 2010. "A Model of Delegated Project Choice." *Econometrica* 78: 213–244.

Arrow, Kenneth. 1974. *The Limits of Organization.* New York: W. W. Norton.

Athey, Susan, and John Roberts. 2001. "Organizational Design: Decision Rights and Incentive Contracts." *American Economic Review* 91: 200–205.

Athey, Susan, Joshua Gans, Scott Schaefer, and Scott Stern. 1994. "The Allocation of Decisions in Organizations." Stanford University Graduate School of Business Research Paper 1322, Stanford, CA.

Athey, Susan, Andrew Atkeson, and Patrick Kehoe. 2005. "The Optimal Degree of Discretion in Monetary Policy." *Econometrica* 73: 1431–1475.

Austen-Smith, David, and Jeffrey Banks. 2000. "Cheap Talk and Burned Money." *Journal of Economic Theory* 91: 1–16.

Baker, George, Robert Gibbons, and Kevin J. Murphy. 1999. "Informal Authority in Organizations." *Journal of Law, Economics, and Organization* 15: 56–73.

Barnard, Chester. 1938. *The Functions of the Executive.* Cambridge, MA: Harvard University Press.

Baron, David, and Roger Myerson, 1982. "Regulating a Monopolist with Unknown Costs." *Econometrica* 50: 911–930.

Battaglini, Marco. 2002. "Multiple Referrals and Multidimensional Cheap Talk." *Econometrica* 70: 1379–1401.

Bénabou, Roland, and Guy Laroque. 1992. "Using Privileged Information to Manipulate Markets: Insiders, Gurus, and Credibility." *Quarterly Journal of Economics* 107: 921–958.

Bester, Helmut. 2009. "Externalities, Communication and the Allocation of Decision Rights." *Economic Theory* 41: 269–296.

Bester, Helmut, and Daniel Krähmer. 2008. "Delegation and Incentives." *RAND Journal of Economics* 39: 664–682.

Bhattacharya, Sudipto, and Paul Pfleiderer. 1985. "Delegated Portfolio Management." *Journal of Economic Theory* 36: 1–25.

Blanes i Vidal, Jordi, and Marc Möller. 2007. "When Should Leaders Share Information with Their Subordinates?" *Journal of Economics and Management Strategy* 16: 251–283.

Blume, Andreas, Oliver J. Board, and Kohei Kawamura. 2007. "Noisy Talk." *Theoretical Economics* 2: 395–440.

Brocas, Isabelle, and Juan Carrillo. 2007. "Influence through Ignorance." *RAND Journal of Economics* 38: 931–947.

Caillaud, Bernard, and Jean Tirole. 2007. "Consensus Building: How to Persuade a Group." *American Economic Review* 97: 1877–1900.

Callander, Steven. 2008a. "Political Motivations." *Review of Economic Studies* 75: 671–697.

———. 2008b. "A Theory of Policy Expertise." *Quarterly Journal of Political Science* 3(2): 123–140.

Calvó-Armengol, Antoni, Joan de Martí, and Andrea Prat. 2011. "Communication and Influence." Working Paper 1-60, London School of Economics, London.

Chakraborty, Archishman, and Rick Harbaugh. 2007. "Comparative Cheap Talk." *Journal of Economic Theory* 132: 70–94.

Che, Yeon-Koo, and Navin Kartik. 2009. "Opinions as Incentives." *Journal of Political Economy* 117: 815–860.

Che, Yeon-Koo, Wouter Dessein, and Navin Kartik. 2012. "Pandering to Persuade." *American Economic Review,* forthcoming.

Coase, Ronald. 1960. "The Problem of Social Cost." *Journal of Law and Economics* 3: 1–44.

Crawford, Vincent, and Joel Sobel. 1982. "Strategic Information Transmission." *Econometrica* 50: 1431–1451.

Crémer, Jacques, Luis Garicano, and Andrea Prat. 2007. "Language and the Theory of the Firm." *Quarterly Journal of Economics* 122: 373–407.

Cyert, Richard, and James March. 1963. *A Behavioral Theory of the Firm.* Englewood Cliffs, NJ: Prentice-Hall.

DeGroot, Morris H. 1970. *Optimal Statistical Decisions.* New York: McGraw-Hill.

Demski, Joel, and David Sappington. 1987. "Delegated Expertise." *Journal of Accounting Research* 25: 68–89.

Dessein, Wouter. 2002. "Authority and Communication in Organizations." *Review of Economic Studies* 69: 811–838.

Dessein, Wouter, and Tano Santos. 2006. "Adaptive Organizations." *Journal of Political Economy* 114: 956–995.

Dessein, Wouter, Luis Garicano, and Robert Gertner. 2010. "Organizing for Synergies." *American Economic Journal: Microeconomics* 2(4): 77–114.

Dewatripont, Mathias, and Jean Tirole. 1999. "Advocates." *Journal of Political Economy* 107: 1–39.

Dye, Ronald. 1985. "Disclosure of Nonproprietary Information." *Journal of Accounting Research* 23: 123–145.

Epstein, David, and Sharyn O'Halloran. 1999. *Delegating Powers: A Transaction Cost Politics Approach to Policy Making under Separate Powers.* Cambridge: Cambridge University Press.

Fama, Eugene, and Michael Jensen. 1983. "Separation of Ownership and Control." *Journal of Law and Economics* 26: 301–325.

Farrell, Joseph, and Robert Gibbons. 1989. "Cheap Talk with Two Audiences." *American Economic Review* 79: 1214–1223.

Feddersen, Timothy, and Wolfgang Pesendorfer. 1998. "Convicting the Innocent: The Inferiority of Unanimous Jury Verdicts under Strategic Voting." *American Political Science Review* 92: 23–35.

Feldman, Martha, and James G. March. 1981. "Information in Organizations as Signal and Symbol." *Administrative Science Quarterly* 26: 171–186.

Frankel, Alex. 2012. "Delegating Multiple Decisions." Working paper, University of Chicago Booth School of Business.

Friebel, Guido, and Michael Raith. 2010. "Resource Allocation and Organizational Form." *American Economic Journal: Microeconomics* 2(2): 1–33.

Fudenberg, Drew, and Jean Tirole. 1991. *Game Theory*. Cambridge, MA: MIT Press.

Galeotti, Andrea, Christian Ghiglino, and Francesco Squintani. 2011. "Strategic Information Transmission in Networks." Economics Discussion Paper 668, University of Essex, UK.

Garicano, Luis. 2000. "Hierarchies and the Organization of Knowledge in Production." *Journal of Political Economy* 108: 874–904.

Garicano, Luis, and Tano Santos. 2004. "Referrals." *American Economic Review* 94: 499–525.

Geanakoplos, John, and Paul Milgrom. 1991. "A Theory of Hierarchy Based on Limited Managerial Attention." *Journal of the Japanese and International Economies* 5: 205–225.

Gibbons, Robert. 1988. "Learning in Equilibrium Models of Arbitration." *American Economic Review* 79: 896–912.

———. 2005. "Four Formal(izable) Theories of the Firm?" *Journal of Economic Behavior and Organization* 58: 200–245.

———. 2010. "Inside Organizations: Pricing, Politics, and Path Dependence." *Annual Review of Economics* 2: 337–365.

Gilligan, Thomas, and Keith Krehbiel. 1987. "Collective Decisionmaking and Standing Committees: An Informational Rationale for Restrictive Amendment Procedures." *Journal of Law, Economics, and Organization* 3: 287–335.

———. 1989. "Asymmetric Information and Legislative Rules with Heterogeneous Committees." *American Journal of Political Science* 33: 459–490.

Goltsman, Maria, and Gregory Pavlov. 2011. "How to Talk to Multiple Audiences." *Games and Economic Behavior* 72: 100–122.

Goltsman, Maria, Johannes Hörner, Gregory Pavlov, and Francesco Squintani. 2009. "Mediation, Arbitration and Negotiation." *Journal of Economic Theory* 144: 1397–1420.

Green, Jerry, and Nancy Stokey. 2007. "A Two-Person Game of Information Transmission." *Journal of Economic Theory* 135: 90–104.

Grossman, Sanford. 1981. "The Role of Warranties and Private Disclosure about Product Quality." *Journal of Law and Economics* 24: 461–483.

Grossman, Sanford, and Oliver Hart. 1986. "The Costs and Benefits of Ownership: A Theory of Vertical and Lateral Integration." *Journal of Political Economy* 94: 691–719.

Hagenbach, Jeanne, and Frédéric Koessler. 2010. "Strategic Communication Networks." *Review of Economic Studies* 77: 1072–1099.

Harris, Milton, and Artur Raviv. 2005. "Allocation of Decision-Making Authority." *Review of Finance* 9: 353–383.

Hart, Oliver, and John Moore. 1990. "Property Rights and the Nature of the Firm." *Journal of Political Economy* 98: 1119–1158.

———. 2005. "On the Design of Hierarchies: Coordination versus Specialization." *Journal of Political Economy* 113: 675–702.

Hayek, Friedrich. 1945. "The Use of Knowledge in Society." *American Economic Review* 35: 519–530.

Hermalin, Benjamin. 1998. "Toward an Economic Theory of Leadership: Leading by Example." *American Economic Review* 88: 1188–1206.

Holmström, Bengt. 1977. *On Incentives and Control in Organizations*. PhD thesis, Stanford University, Stanford, CA.

———. 1982/1999. "Managerial Incentive Problems: A Dynamic Perspective," in Björn Walroos, Bo-Göran Ekholm, Alf-Erik Lerviks, and Hendrik Meyer (eds.), *Essays in Economics and Management in Honor of Lars Wahlbeck*. Helsinki: Swedish School of Economic and Business Administration, pp. 209–230. Republished in *Review of Economic Studies* 66: 169–182.

Holmström, Bengt. 1984. "On the Theory of Delegation," in M. Boyer and R. Kihlstrom (eds.), *Bayesian Models in Economic Theory.* New York: North-Holland, pp. 115–141.

Huber, John, and Charles Shipan. 2006. "Politics, Delegation, and Bureaucracy," in Barry Weingast and Donald Wittman (eds.), *The Oxford Handbook of Political Economy.* Oxford: Oxford University Press.

Hurwicz, Leonid. 1960. "Optimality and Informational Efficiency in the Design of Resource Allocation Processes," in Kenneth Arrow, Samuel Karlin, and Patrick Suppes (eds.), *Mathematical Methods in the Social Sciences 1959.* Palo Alto: Stanford University Press, pp. 27–46.

———. 1972. "On Informationally Decentralized Systems," in Charles McGuire and Roy Radner (eds.), *Decision and Organization: A Volume in Honor of Jacob Marschak.* Amsterdam: North-Holland, pp. 279–336.

———. 1973. "The Design of Mechanisms for Resource Allocation." *American Economic Review* 63: 1–30.

Inderst, Roman, and Manuel Klein. 2007. "Innovation, Endogenous Overinvestment, and Incentive Pay." *RAND Journal of Economics* 38: 881–904.

Ivanov, Maxim. 2010. "Communication via a Strategic Mediator." *Journal of Economic Theory* 145: 869–884.

Jensen, Michael, and William Meckling. 1992. "Specific and General Knowledge and Organizational Structure," in Lars Werin and Hans Wijkander (eds.), *Contract Economics.* Oxford: Blackwell, pp. 251–274.

Kamenica, Emir, and Matthew Gentzkow. 2011. "Bayesian Persuasion." *American Economic Review* 101: 2590–2615.

Kartik, Navin. 2007. "A Note on Cheap Talk and Burned Money." *Journal of Economic Theory* 136: 749–758.

———. 2009. "Strategic Communication with Lying Costs." *Review of Economic Studies* 76: 1359–1395.

Kartik, Navin, Marco Ottaviani, and Francesco Squintani. 2007. "Credulity, Lies, and Costly Talk." *Journal of Economic Theory* 134: 93–116.

Knight, Frank. 1921/1964. *Risk, Uncertainty, and Profit.* New York: Hart, Schaffner, and Marx. Reprinted by New York: Harper and Row.

Koessler, Frederic, and David Martimort. 2012. "Optimal Delegation with Multi-Dimensional Decisions." *Journal of Economic Theory,* forthcoming.

Kolotilin, Anton. 2012a. "Experimental Design to Persuade." Working paper, Massachusetts Institute of Technology, Cambridge, MA.

———. 2012b. "Optimal Information Disclosure to an Informed Decision-Maker." Working paper, Massachusetts Institute of Technology, Cambridge, MA.

Kolotilin, Anton, Hao Li, and Wei Li. 2012. "Optimal Limited Authority for Principal." Working paper, Massachusetts Institute of Technology, Cambridge, MA.

Kovac, Eugen, and Tymofiy Mylovanov. 2009. "Stochastic Mechanisms in Settings without Monetary Transfers: The Regular Case." *Journal of Economic Theory* 144: 1373–1395.

Krähmer, Daniel. 2006. "Message-Contingent Delegation." *Journal of Economic Behavior and Organization* 60: 490–506.

Krishna, Vijay, and John Morgan. 2001. "Asymmetric Information and Legislative Rules: Some Amendments." *American Political Science Review* 95: 435–452.

———. 2004. "The Art of Conversation: Eliciting Information from Experts through Multi-Stage Communication." *Journal of Economic Theory* 117: 147–179.

———. 2008. "Contracting for Information under Imperfect Commitment." *RAND Journal of Economics* 39: 905–925.

Lambert, Richard. 1986. "Executive Effort and Selection of Risky Projects." *RAND Journal of Economics* 17: 77–88.

Landier, Augustin, David Sraer, and David Thesmar. 2009. "Optimal Dissent in Organizations." *Review of Economic Studies* 76: 761–794.

Levy, Gilat. 2007. "Decision Making in Committees: Transparency, Reputation, and Voting Rules." *American Economic Review* 97: 150–168.

Malcomson, James. 2009. "Principal and Expert Agent." *B.E. Journal of Theoretical Economics* 9(contributions): Article 17.

———. 2011. "Do Managers with Limited Liability Take More Risky Decisions? An Information Acquisition Model." *Journal of Economics and Management Strategy* 20: 83–120.

March, James. 1962/1988. "The Business Firm as a Political Coalition." *Journal of Politics* 24: 662–678. Reprinted in James March (ed.), *Decisions and Organizations.* Oxford: Basil Blackwell, pp. 101–115.

———. 1981. "Decisions in Organizations and Theories of Choice," in Andrew Van de Ven and William Joyce (eds.), *Perspectives on Organization Design and Behavior.* New York: Wiley Interscience, pp. 205–244.

Marino, Anthony, John Matsusaka, and Jan Zábojník. 2010. "Disobedience and Authority." *Journal of Law, Economics, and Organization* 26: 427–459.

Marschak, Jacob. 1971. "The Economics of Information Systems," in Michael Intriligator, (ed.), *Frontiers of Quantitative Economics.* Amsterdam: North-Holland, pp. 32–107.

Marschak, Jacob, and Roy Radner. 1972. *Economic Theory of Teams.* New Haven, CT: Yale University Press.

Martimort, David, and Aggey Semenov. 2006. "Continuity in Mechanism Design without Transfers." *Economics Letters* 93: 182–189.

Maskin, Eric. 1977/1999. "Nash Equilibrium and Welfare Optimality." Mimeo, Massachusetts Institute of Technology, Cambridge, MA. Reprinted in *Review of Economic Studies* 66: 23–38.

Melumad, Nahum, and Toshi Shibano. 1991. "Communication in Settings with No Transfers." *RAND Journal of Economics* 22: 173–190.

Meyer, Margaret, Paul Milgrom, and John Roberts. 1992. "Organizational Prospects, Influence Costs, and Ownership Changes." *Journal of Economics and Management Strategy* 1: 9–35.

Milgrom, Paul. 1981. "Good News and Bad News: Representation Theorems and Applications." *Bell Journal of Economics* 12: 380–391.

———. 1988. "Employment Contracts, Influence Activities, and Efficient Organization Design." *Journal Political Economy* 96: 42–60.

———. 2008. "What the Seller Won't Tell You: Persuasion and Disclosure in Markets." *Journal of Economic Perspectives* 22(2): 115–132.

Milgrom, Paul, and John Roberts. 1986. "Relying on the Information of Interested Parties." *RAND Journal of Economics* 17: 18–32.

———. 1988. "An Economic Approach to Influence Activities in Organizations." *American Journal of Sociology* 94: S154–S179.

———. 1992. *Economics, Organization and Management.* Englewood Cliffs, NJ: Prentice-Hall.

———. 1999. "The Internal Politics of the Firm," in Samuel Bowles, Maurizio Franzini, and Ugo Pagano (eds.), *The Politics and Economics of Power.* London: Routledge, pp. 46–62.

Mintzberg, Henry. 1979. *The Structuring of Organizations: A Synthesis of the Research.* Englewood Cliffs, NJ: Prentice-Hall.

Morris, Stephen. 2001. "Political Correctness." *Journal of Political Economy* 109: 231–265.

Mount, Kenneth, and Stanley Reiter. 1990. "A Model of Computing with Human Agents." Discussion Paper 890, Northwestern University Center for Mathematical Studies in Economics and Management Science, Evanston, IL.

Myerson, Roger. 1981. "Optimal Auction Design." *Mathematics of Operations Research* 6: 58–73.

Mylovanov, Tymofiy. 2008. "Veto-Based Delegation." *Journal of Economic Theory* 138: 297–307.

Okuno-Fujiwara, Masahiro, Andrew Postlewaite, and Kotaro Suzumura. 1990. "Strategic Information Revlation." *Review of Economic Studies* 57: 25–47.

Ottaviani, Marco, and Peter Sørensen. 2006a. "Reputational Cheap Talk." *RAND Journal of Economics* 37: 155–175.

———. 2006b. "The Strategy of Professional Forecasting." *Journal of Financial Economics* 81: 441–466.

Persico, Nicola. 2004. "Committee Design with Endogenous Information." *Review of Economic Studies* 71: 165–191.

Powell, Michael. 2012. "Influence Cost Models of Firm's Boundaries and Control Structures." Working paper, Northwestern University Kellogg School of Management, Evanston, IL.

Prendergast, Canice. 1993. "A Theory of 'Yes Men.'" *American Economic Review* 83: 757–770.

———. 2002. "The Tenuous Trade-off between Risk and Incentives." *Journal of Political Economy* 110: 1071–1102.

Raith, Michael. 2008. "Specific Knowledge and Performance Measurement." *RAND Journal of Economics* 39: 1059–1079.

Rajan, Raghuram, and Luigi Zingales. 2000. "The Tyranny of Inequality." *Journal of Public Economics* 76: 521–558.

Rajan, Raghuram, Henri Servaes, and Luigi Zingales. 2000. "The Cost of Diversity: The Diversification Discount and Inefficient Investment." *Journal of Finance* 55: 35–80.

Rantakari, Heikki. 2008. "Governing Adaptation." *Review of Economic Studies* 75: 1257–1285.

———. 2011. "Organizational Design and Environmental Volatility." *Journal of Law, Economics, and Organization,* forthcoming.

———. 2012. "Employee Initiative and Managerial Control." *American Economic Journal: Microeconomics* 4(3): 171–211.

Rayo, Luis, and Ilya Segal. 2010. "Optimal Information Disclosure." *Journal of Political Economy* 118: 949–987.

Rotemberg, Julio. 1993. "Power in Profit-Maximizing Organizations." *Journal of Economics and Management Strategy* 2:165–198.

Scharfstein, David, and Jeremy Stein, 2000. "The Dark Side of Internal Capital Markets: Divisional Rent-Seeking and Inefficient Investment." *Journal of Finance* 55: 2537–2564.

Seidmann, Daniel, and Eyal Winter. 1997. "Strategic Information Transmission with Verifiable Messages." *Econometrica* 65: 163–169.

Simon, Herbert. 1951. "A Formal Theory of the Employment Relationship." *Econometrica* 19: 293–305.

Skaperdas, Stergios. 1992. "Cooperation, Conflict, and Power in the Absence of Property Rights." *American Economic Review* 82: 720–739.

Sloan, Alfred P. 1964. *My Years with General Motors,* John McDonald (ed.). Garden City, NJ: Doubleday.

Sobel, Joel. 1985. "A Theory of Credibility." *Review of Economic Studies* 52: 556–573.

———. 2012. "Giving and Receiving Advice," in Daron Acemoglu, Manuel Arellano, and Eddie Dekel (eds.), *Advances in Economics and Econometrics.* Cambridge: Cambridge University Press, forthcoming.

Spence, Michael. 1973. "Job Market Signaling." *Quarterly Journal of Economics* 87: 355–374.

Stracca, Livio. 2006. "Delegated Portfolio Management: A Survey of the Theoretical Literature." *Journal of Economic Surveys* 20: 823–848.

Szalay, Dezso. 2005. "The Economics of Extreme Options and Clear Advice." *Review of Economic Studies* 72: 1173–1198.

Tullock, Gordon. 1980. "Efficient Rent Seeking," in James Buchanan, Robert Tollison, and Gordon Tullock (eds.), *Toward a Theory of the Rent-Seeking Society.* College Station: Texas A&M University Press, pp. 97–112.

Van den Steen, Eric. 2002. "Disagreement and Information Collection." Working paper, Massachusetts Institute of Technology, Cambridge, MA.

———. 2006. "Limits of Authority: Motivation versus Coordination." Working paper, Massachusetts Institute of Technology, Sloan School of Management, Cambridge, MA.

———. 2010a. "Disagreement and the Allocation of Control." *Journal of Law, Economics, and Organization* 26: 385–426.

———. 2010b. "Interpersonal Authority in a Theory of the Firm." *American Economic Review* 100: 466–490.

Visser, Bauke, and Otto Swank. 2007. "On Committees of Experts." *Quarterly Journal of Economics* 122: 337–372.

Williamson, Oliver. 1975. *Markets and Hierarchies: Analysis and Antitrust Implications.* New York: Free Press.

Wulf, Julie. 2002. "Internal Capital Markets and Firm-Level Compensation Incentives for Division Managers." *Journal of Labor Economics* 20: S219–S262.

———. 2007. "Authority, Risk and Performance Incentives: Evidence from Division Manager Positions inside Firms." *Journal of Industrial Economics* 55: 169–196.

———. 2009. "Influence and Inefficiency in the Internal Capital Market." *Journal of Economic Behavior and Organization* 72: 305–321.

Zábojník, Jan. 2002. "Centralized and Decentralized Decisions in Organizations." *Journal of Labor Economics* 20: 1–22.

Zald, Mayer, and Michael Berger. 1978. "Social Movements in Organizations: Coup d'Etat, Insurgency, and Mass Movements." *American Journal of Sociology* 83: 823–861.

Zermeño, Luis. 2012. "A Principal-Expert Model and the Value of Menus." Working paper, Instituto Tecnológico Autónomo de México, Mexico City.

11

Leadership and Corporate Culture

Benjamin E. Hermalin

1. Introduction

Much of the economics of organization deals with the formal rights and rules that govern organizations, both in normative and positive analyses. Who should have legal claim to what resources? Who should have authority over whom or what? What contracts should be utilized? But importantly, the operation of organizations is also determined by informal means. Two such means are *leadership,* a concept distinct from authority, and *corporate culture,* a broad concept covering the informal rules and expectations that affect operations. This chapter surveys the literature on these informal aspects of organization.[1]

1.1. What Is Leadership?

The word "leadership" has many meanings and connotations. Some pertain to roles assigned to certain offices. For instance, a prime minister is often the leader of her party and her nation. Yet leadership is also distinct from any office or formal authority. For although being prime minister might enhance a politician's capacity to serve as a leader, one presumes that she became prime minister in part because of her leadership abilities. Furthermore, in organizations and institutions, a person can be a leader without office or portfolio; a politician can, for instance, be a leader of her party (although perhaps not *the* leader) even if she holds no title in the party or the government. Leadership is, thus, distinct from formal authority.[2] Indeed, history is replete with examples of important leaders who held no official position (e.g., Jeanne d'Arc).

---

1. For other surveys of leadership from an economics perspective, see Bolton et al. (2010) and Zupan (2010). For another survey of corporate culture from an economics perspective, see Hermalin (2001). Langevoort (2006) offers a partial survey on corporate culture from a law and economics perspective.

2. Some authors, rather than distinguish leadership from (formal) authority, use leadership to refer to both formal authority (e.g., deriving from an office) and the less-formal idea of leadership adopted in this chapter. Typical means of referring to this distinction are, respectively, "formal leadership" and "emergent leadership" (House and Baetz 1979) or "de jure leadership" and "de facto leadership" (Peters 1967).

Leadership is, therefore, a phenomenon that exists independent of office or title. Without office or title, a leader's ability to influence the behavior of others is limited. Without office or title, she lacks authority to order others to undertake actions, and she lacks the right to provide them incentives via contract. Even when a leader possesses an office or title, the formal authority so provided could be limited; for instance, the president of a school's Parent-Teacher Association (PTA) cannot order its members (i.e., other parents) to show up for a school clean-up day. As Weber (Gerth and Mills 1946: 248–249) puts it:

> The [leader] does not deduce his authority from codes and statutes, as is the case with the jurisdiction of office; nor does he deduce his authority from traditional custom or feudal vows of faith, as in the case with patrimonial power.

As the PTA example suggests, one of the essences of leadership is the ability to induce others to follow absent the power to compel or to provide formal contractual incentives. This notion of leadership is perhaps most closely related to Weber's idea of *charismatic* leadership. Indeed, in this chapter, the operational definition of leadership is that a leader is someone with followers *who follow voluntarily*. The critical question then becomes how does a leader induce others to follow?[3]

Even when the leader has *formal authority*—the power to coerce (directly or indirectly through incentives)—such authority is rarely absolute. Certainly, sociology, political theory, and organizational behavior still see a need for leaders to encourage and motivate a following.[4]

1.2. What Is Corporate Culture?

"Culture," too, is a word with many meanings. With respect to organizations, the most relevant meaning in the dictionary would be "the distinctive customs, achievements, products, outlook, etc., of a society or group; the way of life of a society or group," a meaning that the word acquired in the late nineteenth century (Brown 1993: 568). Some definitions from the social sciences include:

> A pattern of shared basic assumptions that the group learned as it solved its problems of external adaptation and internal integration, that has worked well enough to be considered valid and, therefore, to be taught to new members as the correct way to perceive, think, and feel in relation to those problems. [Schein 1992: 12)

> [V]alues that are shared by the people in a group and that tend to persist over time even when group membership changes. [Kotter and Heskett 1992: 4]

---

3. Handy (1993: 97) describes answering this question as one of the "Holy Grails" of organization theory.

4. See, for example, chapter 19, "On Avoiding Being Despised and Hated," and chapter 21, "How a Prince Should Act to Acquire Esteem," of Niccolò Machiavelli's *The Prince* (Bondanella and Musa 1979); part III, chapter 9 of Max Weber's *Wirtschaft und Gesellschaft* (Gerth and Mills 1946: 245–252); part II of McGregor (1966: 49–80); chapter 4 of Handy (1993: 96–122); and chapter 2 of Wrong (1995: 21–34). Motivating a following is also a large part of "how-to" analyses of leadership, such as Kouzes and Posner (1987), Bennis (1989), Heifetz (1994), and Kotter (1996).

[C]orporate culture [is] partly . . . the interrelated principles that the organization employs and partly the means by which [its] principle[s are] communicated to hierarchical inferiors and hierarchical superiors. It says how things are done, and how they are meant to be done. . . . Because it will be designed through time to meet unforeseen contingencies as they arise, it will be the product of evolution inside the organization and will be influenced by the organization's history. [Kreps 1990: 224]

In economics, the modeling of corporate culture has taken a number of different paths. Kreps (1990), for instance, focuses on culture as a way of dealing with unforeseen contingencies. Others consider culture as convention (Young 1993, 1998) or as a means of equilibrium selection (Kreps 1990). Related to this idea, some model culture as an economizing device (Crémer 1993). Culture is sometimes seen as equivalent to organizational reputation (Crémer 1986; Kreps 1990). There is also the question of how culture arises; some have sought to model its transmission (Lazear 1998) or its emergence through forces that lead to homogeneity of beliefs (Van den Steen 2010c).

1.3. Culture and Leadership

There is some reason the volume editors chose to combine the discussion of corporate culture and leadership into one chapter (other than, perhaps, the convenient fact that I have written on both in the past). There are least five reasons the topics might profitably be linked:

1. *Leaders are proselytizers.* Leaders are the people who disseminate culture within an organization. For example, chapter 11 of Schein (1992: 211–227) deals with the role of leadership in building culture (consider, e.g., the role often attributed to Herb Kelleher at Southwest).[5] Chapter 12 of Schein (1992: 228–253) discusses how leaders embed and transmit culture.

2. *Leaders are judges.* Leaders are the people who determine whether behavior adheres to the organization's norms and set sanctions on those who violate those norms.

3. *Culture makes leaders trustworthy.* Being part of the corporate culture can serve to make leaders trustworthy. Followers follow because they trust the leader to share their concerns and interests (see, e.g., Rotemberg and Saloner 1993).

4. *Leaders are change agents.* Along the lines of the first point, but somewhat contrary to the previous one, leaders are those who can break from an existing culture and lead an organization to a new way of doing things; that is, leaders can be "change agents" (what Burns [1978] refers to as "transforming leaders"). "How-to" books often focus on this role (e.g., Kotter 1996).

5. *Asabīyah.* The effectiveness of the leader may depend on the strength of the corporate culture. One version of this idea was set forth by Ibn Khaldūn, the 14th century North African historian, who argued that a group's success depended on its *asabīyah* or "group

---

5. There are numerous business school cases on the role played by Mr. Kelleher in building Southwest's culture. See also the chapter on Mr. Kelleher in Pandya et al. (2004: 21–46).

feeling," and the leader who can best harness a group's *asabîyah* will be the most successful (Ibn Khaldūn 2004).

2. Leadership

Leadership should be seen as a phenomenon distinct from authority or the exercise of some office or title. The defining feature of leadership is that a leader is someone with *voluntary* followers. A central question is, therefore, why do they follow? What is it that leaders do that make followers want to follow? Before turning to these questions in Section 2.2, it is worth considering the notion of "voluntary" a bit further.

2.1. How Voluntary Is Voluntary?

2.1.1. Psychological Predispositions
It is possible that followers follow, at least in part, because of a psychological predisposition to be a follower. Such a predisposition could represent learned behavior. For instance, as children, we are taught to follow instructions, and we may consequently become predisposed to follow orders. An objective of military drilling and discipline is to impose a reflexive response to orders (see, e.g., Akerlof and Kranton [2005] on West Point).

Additionally, a psychological predisposition to be a follower could be innate. One of the few economic articles to take a behavioral approach to "followership" (Huck and Rey-Biel 2006) explicitly assumes that followers have a desire to conform; that is, they have an inherent distaste for choosing actions that are different from those of others.

One reason that following could, to an extent, be innate is that humans are primates and primate social groups typically possess dominance relations (de Waal 1998; McFarland 1999). To be sure, the alpha male of a chimpanzee tribe is not a leader in the sense meant here; such males coerce, rather than induce, a following through actual or threatened violence. Nevertheless, being able to assume subordinate status when necessary is a critical survival skill.[6] Therefore, it is possible that many of us are predisposed to take a subordinate status in social groupings even subconsciously.[7] Certainly, there is evidence that we respond to many nonverbal cues with respect to who we tend to follow as leaders (e.g., age, height, gender).[8]

2.1.2. Fear of Sanctions
In normal parlance, voluntary means without compulsion or duress; that is, freely decided. However, as members of a profession that has ruled out the free lunch, we know that there are trade-offs in most decisions, and presumably that applies to following the leader. If, for instance, I disregard the PTA president's request to participate in a school clean-up day, then there are

---

6. This skill is critical both because young males typically are not in a position to challenge for leadership (de Waal), so must bide their time, and because even subordinate males can find mating opportunities if they are crafty (Sapolsky 2005).

7. To be more accurate, we likely have a predisposition to grasp social structures and hierarchies and to slot ourselves into them accordingly. It has been argued that the relatively large and sophisticated brains of primates are the consequence of an evolutionary arms race to outsmart others in social settings (see, e.g., Sapolsky 2005).

8. See, for example, House and Baetz (1979) for a discussion of such leadership attributes.

likely some adverse consequences, such as having her speak poorly of me or having her be less responsive to my suggestions for PTA activities.

In other words, rarely, if ever, is a leader without recourse to sanctions against followers who fail to follow her lead. A distinction, however, exists between circumstances in which the power to sanction comes with the office (e.g., a military officer has the right to demand punishment for insubordination, a manager can dismiss a disobedient worker) and circumstances in which the power to sanction arises because other followers will carry out sanctions imposed by a leader (e.g., agree to treat a disloyal follower as an outcast). The power of, say, a PTA president to sanction me for not participating in a PTA activity arises not from her office but is granted her by her followers, who effectively agree they will apply a social stigma to me at her behest. Consequently, if they lose faith in her leadership—they conclude, for example, that she is acting like a martinet—then her power to impose sanctions is also lost. In contrast, the power of my commanding officer to sanction me is essentially independent of what my fellow subordinates think of her leadership.[9]

Some of the most dramatic examples of a leader being granted social-sanctioning power can be seen among teenaged girls, where cliques (sometimes called "posses") form around a leader, the "queen bee" (Wiseman 2003).[10] The queen bee's ability to sanction members of her posse is wholly a function of the power over them that the other girls grant the queen bee. Similar phenomena no doubt exist in gangs and other voluntary groupings. Queen bees also illustrate a particularly important dynamic by which a leader obtains power: The leader is bestowed by her followers with the power to determine who is in—that is, who obtains the benefits of membership—and who is out.

It is has long been known that the power to exclude (by labeling or outright ostracizing) is a strong form of control, particularly with regard to discipline within prestigious "in groups" (Becker 1963; Goffman 1963; Erikson 1966; Goode 1978; Sidanius and Pratto 1999). To an extent, this power has recently been recognized in economics (Kandel and Lazear 1992; Bowles and Gintis 2004; see also the survey articles Hermalin 2001; Akerlof and Kranton 2005), although it would also be fair to say this is an area where further work would be productive. Yet the question of why members of a group would bestow this power on a leader has, to the best of my knowledge, been largely ignored. Certainly in the economics literature, social sanctions have been modeled in a leaderless fashion (e.g., Kandel and Lazear 1992; Kandori 1992; Bowles and Gintis 2004).

2.2. What Do Leaders Do?

So what is it that leaders do? There are many ways that question can be answered, as, in part, evidenced by the large number of books on leadership that have been written over the years. For the purposes of this chapter, I divide what leaders do into three categories with, admittedly, considerable overlap:

9. Although perhaps not completely independent; in extreme circumstances (e.g., those depicted in the *Caine Mutiny;* Wouk 1951) the loss of faith by all subordinates can preclude an officer from sanctioning insubordination by any one.

10. See Lohéac (2005) for an economic study of this phenomenon.

1. Leaders serve as judges.
2. Leaders serve as experts.[11]
3. Leaders serve as coordinators.

This list is not exhaustive. Other leadership activities are not covered here:

4. Leaders are symbols. This has two meanings. First, the leader can be a living representation of the group, so that the honors she receives provide positive utility—basking in the glory—for followers and the dishonors she suffers harm followers (e.g., cause anger or shame). Second, the leader symbolizes the group's ideals with respect to beliefs and deportment. In essence, the leader exemplifies the norms of the group.[12] This second meaning overlaps with the idea of leaders as experts.

5. Leaders are shapers of preferences. In standard theory, preferences are fixed. Yet preferences must, ultimately, come from somewhere, and it seems logical that they derive in part from the actions of others (e.g., what we are fed as children, or the music our parents play). It is plausible, therefore, that a person with a strong personality—a charismatic leader—will influence the preferences of others.[13] But proving this idea, if true, is difficult: We observe behavior, not motives. So, for example, does seeing a hero do something make one inherently wish to do it? Or does it simply signal that one gains more status from doing so than previously thought?[14]

2.2.1. Leaders as Judges

Within an organization or group, a leader can serve as a judge; that is, she is the arbiter of disputes and the determiner of sanctions.[15] This is not to say all informal judges are leaders; nevertheless, there is a tendency to have a leader serve as the group's judge. For instance, in days gone by, Eastern European Jews would call on their local rabbi to settle disputes.[16]

There are a number of reasons a single individual would be selected to be the group's judge:

• Predictability. When the judge is known ex ante, there is less uncertainty and risk about how cases will be resolved than if the judge were to be chosen at random.

• Reputation building. A group presumably wants a judge who is impartial or incorruptible. Depending on the benefits of being a judge (leader), an individual might wish to establish

---

11. For an interesting—if perhaps limited—empirical assessment of leaders as experts, see Goodall et al. (2011).

12. Pfeffer (1981) makes a similar point.

13. To the extent that others teach us about our preferences (e.g., help us learn we like sushi by taking us to a Japanese restaurant), the shaping-of-preferences role overlaps with the expertise role.

14. In an earlier survey, Hermalin (2001: 258) referred to this as the "directive versus internalization issue." It is a debate to which I return later. See also Kreps (1997).

15. Interestingly, the section of the Bible that presents the history of the Israelites in the period between Exodus and the Davidic dynasty, a period when the Israelites had informal leaders, is called *Judges*.

16. Although the rabbi held an office and, thus, his judicial powers might, in part, be seen to come from that, it is also true that (1) the rabbi had no authority by which to enforce his decisions, and (2) the parties could, in some circumstances, have selected another arbiter, such as the secular courts.

a reputation for impartiality and incorruptibility. Reputation building, however, requires frequent repeat play, which is an argument for bestowing the judgeship on a single individual.

- Efficient division of labor. If there are economies of scale or scope in being the judge, then it could be most sensible to have only one individual make the relevant investments.

- Avoidance of free riding. If no one were responsible for monitoring behavior and passing judgment on it, then it would be the group's responsibility, which could lead to free-riding problems if group members shirked their responsibilities.

From the earlier discussion of queen bees, for instance, it is clear that leaders frequently play a role as a group or organization's judge. This judicial role is also an important way in which the organization's culture is transmitted, because followers infer the cultural norms from the leader-judge's decisions (see the discussion in Schein 1992: 228–253; this also relates to labeling theory: Becker 1963). Yet why a single leader is necessary or how followers empower her with this authority is less well studied. It is to be hoped that the four possibilities listed above will eventually be fleshed out by future research.

2.2.2. Leaders as Experts
One reason to follow a leader is that you believe the leader knows better than you what should be done. This is what I mean by the *leader as expert*. There are three ways in which a leader can be an expert: (i) she is endowed with the relevant expertise; (ii) she undertakes an activity to learn the relevant knowledge; and (iii) she defines what is the truth. The last of these refers to situations where the leader is a lawgiver (e.g., in a religious sense or by defining the corporate culture). One might argue that this third way is subsumed by the first two. A devout person would certainly argue that religious lawgivers were given their knowledge by a higher authority. Alternatively, lawgivers use their expertise to derive laws (customs, norms, etc.), where their expertise has been endowed previously or results from their actively acquiring the relevant knowledge. Yet, to the extent there is no clear rationale for a law (e.g., Deuteronomy 22:11, the prohibition on wearing wool and linen together), its purpose being only to divide adherents from nonadherents, this third category of expertise could be considered separate from the first two.[17]

2.2.3. Leaders as Coordinators
Many organizational issues can be modeled as games, and games often have multiple equilibria. A role, therefore, for the leader could be to select the equilibrium to be played. Consider, for instance, the game in Figure 1. It has three Nash equilibria: both players play A as pure strategies, both play B as pure strategies, and a mixed-strategy equilibrium. Total expected welfare is,

---

17. A law such as Deuteronomy 22:11 is known as a *chok*. *Chukim* (plural of *chok*) are rules that are seen by commentators on the Torah (e.g., Talmudic scholars) as having apparently no rational justification. A less religious example would be the requirement that once existed that IBM salesmen wear white shirts. Harris (1978) suggests that one justification is to maintain group integrity by brightening the line demarcating in-group from out-group. This interpretation is bolstered in the case of Deuteronomy 22:11, given that book was written in a time of conflict between two priestly castes (Friedman 1997). Such a *chok* could have served to distinguish one side from the other (and give one side a better claim to righteousness).

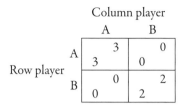

Figure 1. A coordination game.

respectively, 6, 4, and 12/5 across these equilibria. Clearly, it behooves the players to coordinate on the first. A leader could announce that players are to play A. Given that a Nash equilibrium is a self-enforcing contract—that is, the followers would have an incentive to voluntarily follow the leader's direction—this should be sufficient to ensure that the A-equilibrium is played.[18]

It is also conceivable that the leader can cause coordination when coordination is not necessarily warranted by starting an informational cascade or causing herding (Banerjee 1992; Bikhchandani et al. 1992; Smith and Sørensen 2000).[19] For instance, in network economies, the technology adopted in equilibrium will depend heavily on the behavior of early adopters (Katz and Shapiro 1986). In situations in which the leader is wrong or when more heads are better than one (i.e., private signals should be shared), the group can readily end up conforming to a standard or to actions that are not optimal. As an extreme example, suppose that members of an organization must choose between two options (e.g., a word-processing program, or how to treat customers), each of which is equally likely ex ante to be the correct option. Imagine the population is divided between those with information relevant to choosing the right option and those without. If the first person who chooses is known to be at least as knowledgeable as anyone else and his choice is more likely to be correct than wrong, then his choice will determine the organization's choice; that is, everyone will follow his lead.[20] The probability that the leader's information is correct thus becomes the probability the organization makes the correct choice. If, however, the organization could have polled people before choices were made, then the organization's probability of making the correct decision would be greater.[21]

18. Other arguments for why the A-equilibrium would be played include that a Pareto-optimal equilibrium is focal and the money-burning argument of Dekel and Ben-Porath (1992).

19. Chamley (2004) is a good introduction to this literature.

20. A given follower can believe, when it is his turn to choose, the common choice of those who went before is wrong with no more than probability 1/2 (and typically less). Even if it is 1/2, if there are network effects or he breaks ties by following the consensus, he will follow suit.

21. Assume $2M + 1 > 1$ informed individuals, each of whom gets a signal that is correct with probability p (assume the signals are independent draws conditional on the truth). Then, under majority rule, the probability the group would make the correct decision, assuming information could be pooled before any actions are taken, is

$$1 - \sum_{m=0}^{M} \binom{2M+1}{m} p^m (1-p)^{2M+1-m} > p,$$

where the right-hand side is the probability the correct decision is made absent pooling of information when the group follows the leader. For example, if $M = 20$ and $p = .6$, then collective decisionmaking implies a better than 90% chance of making the correct decision.

2.3. The Economic Analysis of Leadership

2.3.1. *Leading by Example and Sacrifice*

Hermalin (1998) recognizes that followers often face the danger that the leader is tempted to mislead them. Figure 2 illustrates this tension. Suppose the leader knows which state "nature" has chosen. If she would report honestly, the follower would adjust his effort based on her report, working hard if she says the state is good and working "easy" if she says the state is poor. The leader, however, always does better if the follower works hard; thus, she has an incentive to mislead the follower, always claiming the state is good regardless of what it truly is. A rational follower anticipates this, however, and disregards her announcement. If the probability of the good state is less than 1/2, then a rational follower will always work easy regardless of the leader's announcement.

The outcome that the follower disregards the leader's announcement is suboptimal. Welfare would be greater if the leader would announce the state truthfully and the follower could believe her announcement.

The leader gains 3 if she convinces the follower the state is good when it is truly good, but she gains only 1 when she misleads the follower into thinking the state is good when it is not. A convincing signal that the state is good is for the leader to destroy D units of her utility when the state is good, where $D \geq 1$.[22] Imposing the Cho and Kreps (1987) intuitive criterion as an equilibrium refinement, the unique equilibrium is the one in which the leader publicly destroys one unit of utility when the state is good, but not when it is bad. The follower responds to this signal by working hard when he sees a unit destroyed and by working easy when he does not. Hermalin (1998) calls this form of leadership *leading by sacrifice;* depending on the circumstances, it may be only one of the ways in which the leader can signal.[23]

2.3.1.1. Leading by Example. As noted earlier, leaders often serve as examples. Moreover, their example can be effective because it can serve as a signal that what the leader is advocating (e.g., working hard) is a true reflection of her knowledge. Historical examples include civil rights leaders (e.g., Martin Luther King, Jr. or César Chávez) being at the front of a march or Stalin's decision to remain in Moscow to lead resistance to the approaching *Wehrmacht*. Presumably these leaders would not have put themselves in danger if they did not truly believe the struggle could be won.

---

22. It is beyond the scope of this chapter to review signaling fully. Signaling games, first studied by Spence (1973), are games of asymmetric information in which the better-informed party can act so as to convey—"signal"—her information to the less-well-informed party. The classic example (Spence) is a worker who signals her ability to potential employers through the amount of education she gets. An equilibrium of a signaling game is *separating* if the equilibrium actions of the informed player vary with her information (e.g., talented workers acquire more education than less-talented workers). A *pooling* equilibrium is one in which the equilibrium actions of the informed player don't vary with her information (e.g., all workers get the same level of education). The multitude of equilibria can sometimes be reduced via a forward-induction refinement, such as the intuitive criterion (Cho and Kreps 1987).

23. In Hermalin (1998), the sacrifice went from the leader to the followers. While this affects the welfare analysis of the model, it is not essential to the signaling function of the sacrifice. A real-life example might be a PTA president who springs for simple refreshments for an event as a way of signaling the importance of the event (the refreshments are too simple to constitute a reasonable payment to the other parents; that is, it is the signal, not the desire for a free donut, that gets the parents to participate).

	Follower	
	Work hard	Work easy
Good state	4 5	3 2
Bad state	0 2	1 1

(Nature on the left axis for Good state / Bad state)

Figure 2. A leadership game. The leftmost number in each cell is the leader's (i.e., not nature's) payoff.

A model of this (Hermalin 1998) is the following: a team has N identical individuals indexed by n. Each simultaneously supplies effort. The value to the team of these efforts is $V = \theta \sum_{n=1}^{N} e_n$, where $\theta \in [0, 1]$ is a stochastic productivity factor realized after efforts, the e_ns, have been supplied. Individual n's utility is $w_n - e_n^2/2$, where w_n is his payment.[24]

Assume, keeping with Holmström (1982), that although contracts can be written contingent on V, they cannot be written contingent on the individual team members' efforts. Assume, too, that contracts cannot be contingent on θ directly. Credible contracts must be balanced (i.e., pay out exactly V in total to the team members). Given these conditions, there is no loss of generality in restricting attention to the following contracts: individual n is paid $s_n(\hat{\theta})V + t_n(\hat{\theta})$, where $\hat{\theta}$ is a possible announcement about the value of θ; $\sum_{n=1}^{N} s_n(\hat{\theta}) = 1$ for all $\hat{\theta} \in [0, 1]$; and $\sum_{n=1}^{N} t_n(\hat{\theta}) = 0$ for all $\hat{\theta} \in [0, 1]$. Ruling out negative shares (i.e., $s_n < 0$ for some n), it can further be shown that, if all team members hold the same belief about θ, then the optimal contract is an equal-shares contract: $s_n(\hat{\theta}) = 1/N$ for all n and $\hat{\theta}$.[25]

Let $\tilde{\theta}$ denote the expected value of θ given common beliefs. Then each team member maximizes

$$\frac{\tilde{\theta}}{N} \left(e_n + \sum_{j \neq n} e_j \right) + t(\hat{\theta}) - \frac{e_n^2}{2}. \tag{1}$$

The cross-partial derivative of (1) with respect to $\tilde{\theta}$ and e_n is positive; hence, an individual's effort is increasing in his expectation of θ under an equal-shares contract.

Make one of the team the leader, and suppose she is endowed with knowledge of what θ will be. This is her private information. Suppose, hypothetically, that she truthfully announces what θ will be. Then all team members would be symmetrically informed. The optimal contract would thus be equal shares, and the effort of a follower, $e(\hat{\theta})$, would be increasing in the leader's announcement of θ, $\hat{\theta}$ (because the followers are identical, the subscript n can be dispensed with). The only question, then, is would the leader announce truthfully? Her utility is

$$\frac{\theta}{N} \left((N - 1)e(\hat{\theta}) + e_L \right) + t_L(\hat{\theta}) - \frac{e_L^2}{2}, \tag{2}$$

---

24. Hermalin (1998) assumes a more general disutility of effort function than $e^2/2$.
25. See the discussion in Hermalin (1998) for why negative share contracts can be ruled out.

where L indexes the leader. Suppose that $t_L(\hat{\theta})$ is a constant. Then the leader does best to make $e(\hat{\theta})$ as large as possible regardless of the true value of θ. Hence, the leader would always announce the maximum value of θ. The hypothesis that she will tell the truth is false.

Of course, rational followers understand this. Hence, if $t_L(\hat{\theta})$ is a constant, then they will rationally disregard the leader's announcement and always choose effort $e(\bar{\theta})$, where $\bar{\theta} = E\{\theta\}$, where E is the expectation operator. Hermalin (1998) shows it is inefficient for the followers not to base their effort on the true value of θ; hence welfare would be improved if the leader could be given an incentive to tell the truth.

One way around this problem would be leading by sacrifice. From (2), this would require making $t_L(\hat{\theta})$ vary in such a way as to provide the leader an incentive to tell the truth. It can be shown that she will tell the truth if

$$t_L(\hat{\theta}) = T - \int_0^{\hat{\theta}} z \frac{N-1}{N} e'(z) dz, \tag{3}$$

where T is a constant and $e(\cdot)$ is a follower's optimal response function to a truthful revelation of θ (proposition 3 of Hermalin 1998).

The focus here, however, is on leading by example. To that end, set $t_n(\hat{\theta}) \equiv 0$ for all n and $\hat{\theta}$. Furthermore, suppose that the leader can choose her effort before the rest of the team in a way that is observable to them (but not verifiable). From (2), the leader has a greater incentive to raise her effort the greater is θ. Consequently, her choice of effort—her example—can serve as a signal to her followers. To begin, consider the contract

$$s_L = \frac{1}{1 + N(N-1)} \quad \text{and} \quad s_n = \frac{N}{1 + N(N-1)} \tag{4}$$

for $n \neq L$. It can be shown that under this contract, the equilibrium is for the followers to mimic the leader; that is, choose the same effort level that she does. Moreover, aggregate expected welfare is greater under this contract than under optimal leading by sacrifice or symmetric information.

The welfare gain from leading by example is a demonstration of the theory of the second best. Because the followers make inferences about θ based on the leader's effort, the leader's effort serves as a signal of the state. In particular, the harder the leader works, the harder the followers will work. This gives the leader an additional incentive beyond that generated by her share of the value created. In fact, her incentives are sufficiently increased that the team can reduce her share, thereby increasing the shares (incentives) for the other workers. Consequently, each member of the team works harder than under symmetric information. Because the free riding endemic to teams means too little effort to begin with, inducing harder work is welfare improving.[26]

As it turns out, (4) is not the welfare-maximizing contract. The general formula for the welfare-maximizing contract is lengthy and not worth repeating here. It can be shown that the

---

26. A related reasoning lies behind Zhou (2011), which explores how information should flow through an organization. If credible transmission of information can only be by example and the organization can control who sees whose actions, then the organization can boost all but one team member's effort by having each team member set an example for one follower, who then sets an example for the next follower, and so forth.

leader's share is decreasing in N but is bounded below by a positive constant. Consequently, in small teams ($N \leq 6$), the leader's share is less than that of any of her team members if the objective is to maximize welfare; but in large teams ($N \geq 7$), her share is greater.

If, for some reason, the team were required to have equal shares, it is still true that leading by example is welfare superior to symmetric information or leading by sacrifice (proposition 6 of Hermalin 1998). Again, this is because the need to set an example provides the leader extra incentives to supply effort.

2.3.2. More on Leaders Conveying Information: Extensions of the Hermalin Model

2.3.2.1. Repeated Leadership Games. A drawback to Hermalin (1998) is that it is a one-shot model, whereas leadership is often a repeated phenomenon; today's leader tends to be tomorrow's as well. As is well known from the theory of repeated games, behavior that is unsupportable in the equilibrium of a one-shot game can often be supported in a repeated setting. In particular, could a leader simply develop a reputation for truthful announcements in a repeated game?

Hermalin (2007) addresses some issues that arise when the one-shot game of Hermalin (1998) is infinitely repeated.[27] The same leader plays in all stage games, but the followers are new in each stage game. Each generation of followers knows, however, the history of the game prior to it; in particular, the time t generation knows the realizations of θ in the first $t - 1$ periods, and it knows the leader's announcements of θ in those periods.[28] There is no correlation in the productivity parameter, θ, across periods.

To begin, assume there is no scope for the leader to signal. Hence, if her reputation for making honest announcements about θ is ruined, play reverts to infinite repetition of the equilibrium of the one-shot announcement game. In that game, talk is cheap, so the equilibrium is a garbling one in which the followers ignore the leader's announcement. The threat of such reversion is most effective at keeping the leader honest when uncertainty about θ is greatest—an equilibrium with honest announcements exists for a wider range of parameters the greater is the uncertainty about θ. Intuitively, if there were little uncertainty about θ, then the leader's gain from honesty is relatively small—the followers essentially know what θ will be anyway. When, however, uncertainty is large, considerable surplus—some of which would go to the leader—is lost when the followers do not know θ and thus, their efforts tend to be highly inefficient.

Now suppose the leader can signal if she wishes. This changes the equilibrium of the one-shot stage game; it is now one in which the followers adjust their efforts to the state, but only because the leader has engaged in signaling that is costly to her. Because a distrusted leader needs to signal in the good state only, her loss from a tarnished reputation is increasing in the probability of the good state. Consequently, an equilibrium of the infinitely repeated game in which the leader is truthful (and does not signal) is sustainable for a wider range of parameters the greater is the probability of the good state.

The followers, as well as the leader, benefit if they know the true state. They have an incentive, therefore, to pay the leader for being truthful. Indeed, in real life, followers often bestow tribute

---

27. In Hermalin (2007), attention is limited to equal-share contracts, and the state space is the binary set $\{\theta_0, \theta_1\}, \theta_1 > \theta_0 > 0$.

28. The assumption of short-lived followers avoids issues of cooperation in the teams problem. Hermalin (2007) offers some economic justifications for this assumption.

on their leaders.[29] Tribute can be financial, in kind, or emotional. In a one-shot game (e.g., Hermalin 1998), tribute would never be paid, because there is no way to contract on the truthfulness of the announcements. But once the game is repeated, the followers can make future tribute contingent on past honesty and thus can effectively contract on truthfulness (for details, see Hermalin 2007).

Tribute is especially effective in supporting honest leadership when tribute costs the followers nothing (e.g., tribute is the prestige of office). In this case, the followers' incentive constraint to pay tribute is trivially met. A game with "free" tribute might be seen as corresponding closest to Weber's image of charismatic leadership.

2.3.2.2. Informational Issues. In Hermalin (1998), the leader's signaling action (i.e., amount of sacrifice or exemplary effort) fully reveals the state (i.e., θ). What would happen if the leader's action only partially revealed the state?

Komai et al. (2007) explores this issue.[30] Suppose $e \in \{0, 1\}$ and $\theta \in (0, 1)$. If the leader leads by example, then the followers know only that the state is in the subset of states in which the leader chooses e. Agent n's payoff is

$$\pi(\theta, e_n, \mathbf{e}_{-n}) = \frac{\theta}{N} \left(\sum_{j=1}^{N} e_j \right) - ce_n,$$

where $\mathbf{e}_{-n}$ is the vector of actions chosen by the other team members, and $c > 0$ is the cost of effort (participation). The sharing rule is equal shares.

If θ is common knowledge, then $e_n = 1$ if $\theta \geq Nc$ and $e_n = 0$ otherwise. Efficiency, however, requires that $e_n = 1$ if $\theta \geq c$. Full information does not, therefore, yield an efficient solution because of the teams problem.

Assume $\bar{\theta} \equiv E\{\theta\} < Nc$; absent any information, no team member would choose $e = 1$. Critically, assume

$$\frac{1}{1 - F(c)} \int_{c}^{1} tf(t)dt \geq Nc, \tag{5}$$

where $F(\cdot)$ is the distribution function over θ, and $f(\cdot)$ is the corresponding density. Suppose only the leader learns θ, and she publicly chooses her e first. Let θ^e be the followers' expectation of θ based on the leader's action, e. It is not an equilibrium strategy for the leader to play $e = 1$ if and only if $\theta \geq Nc$. If it were, then $\theta^1 > Nc > \theta^0$, and the followers would mimic the leader. Consider the state $\theta = Nc - \varepsilon$, where $\varepsilon > 0$ but small. If the leader deviated and chose $e = 1$ for such a θ, then her payoff would be

$$Nc - \varepsilon - c > 0.$$

---

29. Max Weber (Gerth and Mills 1946), for instance, considers tribute, either in material or emotional terms, as a principal reward for charismatic leaders.

30. A further exploration, in a somewhat richer model, can be found in Komai and Stegeman (2010).

Zero is her payoff were she to play $e = 0$; hence, for ε small enough, it is not an equilibrium for her to play the strategy $e = 1$ if and only if $\theta \geq Nc$.

In fact, (5) implies an equilibrium exists that achieves full efficiency. In this equilibrium, the leader plays $e = 1$ if $\theta \geq c$ and $e = 0$ otherwise, and the followers mimic her. This is an equilibrium because, if the followers will mimic her, the leader plays $e = 1$ if and only if $\theta - c \geq 0$. Given this rule, $\theta^0 < c$, and

$$\theta^1 = \frac{1}{1 - F(c)} \int_c^1 t f(t) dt \geq Nc.$$

Hence, mimicry is a best response for the followers. This illustrates that there exist scenarios in which it is better for the leader to signal limited rather than full information.[31]

If (5) does not hold, then an equilibrium exists in which the followers play a mixed strategy. Whether the mixed-strategy equilibrium (MSE) is superior to symmetric information depends on the parameter values. This reflects the following trade-off. In the MSE, there is a positive amount of effort for $\theta \in [\hat{\theta}, Nc)$, whereas there is none under symmetric information. But the amount of effort is less in the MSE when $\theta \in [Nc, 1)$ than under symmetric information.

In Hermalin (1998), the asymmetry of information has no impact ultimately on the teams problem with respect to the followers' effort.[32] In contrast, in Komai et al. (2007), by preventing full revelation of the state, the followers are induced to work harder than they would were the leader's action to reveal the state fully. In the Komai et al. setup, there is thus a benefit to keeping information from the followers; an organization could have a motive to limit the amount of information the leader can credibly communicate.

2.3.2.3. Sequential Provision of a Public Good. Hermalin (1998) provides insights about the private provision of a public good. Briefly, rather than efforts, imagine the team members are donating to a public good. One donor knows the marginal value of a donation. Having her make her donation first and publicly—leading by example—improves welfare both vis-à-vis the situation in which θ is unknown and vis-à-vis the situation in which it is known to all donors.

This observation suggests an explanation for the real-world phenomenon of fund raising campaigns being launched with a large public donation by a well-respected individual and then followed up by solicitations of others. Absent an information story, it is difficult to explain this pattern of sequential donation: theory predicts that, under symmetric information, sequential donating raises less than simultaneous donating (Varian 1994). The issue of informational signaling by lead donors has been further studied by Vesterlund (2003) and Andreoni (2006).

The private-provision-of-public-goods interpretation of Hermalin (1998) lends itself well to experiments. Experiments have generally found support (see Gächter and Renner 2003; Potters et al. 2005, 2007; Gächter et al. 2010) for the leading-by-example model, although some experimental work (Meidinger and Villeval 2002) suggests that it is not signaling that is being

---

31. In a very different modeling context, Blanes i Vidal and Möller (2007) reach a different conclusion, at least with respect to a self-confident leader. They argue that a self-confident leader fares better in a transparent organization.

32. Assuming the shares are not optimally adjusted; but even then, information creates no changes in the incentives of the followers given their shares.

observed but reciprocity (e.g., as suggested by Rabin 1993). Methodological issues in Meidinger and Villeval—specifically, the use of repeated interactions between leader and follower—make their analysis less than definitive insofar as they could be observing the truth-telling-with-no-signaling equilibrium of Hermalin (2007).

2.3.2.4. Choice of Leader. Recently, economists have turned to the question of which group member becomes the leader (Kobayashi and Suehiro 2005; Andreoni 2006; Huck and Rey-Biel 2006). The first two develop models based on Hermalin (1998). The third utilizes a different model and is discussed later.

Andreoni adds a stage prior to the beginning of the Hermalin (1998) game in which, by expending c, any team member can learn θ. Andreoni limits attention to the case of small c: not only is it socially optimal to expend c, but it is also privately optimal for any given individual to invest it if she knew the alternative was she invests or no one invests. The problem is that, absent any compensation mechanism, each team member would prefer that someone else make the investment. This is both because each team member wishes to avoid paying c and because, absent an adjustment in shares, the leader does worse than her followers under either leading by example or leading by sacrifice. For the public-goods problem in Andreoni, it makes sense to suppose that the other team members (the rest of society) can neither compensate an individual for expending c nor adjust shares so as not to be disadvantageous to the leader.

In Andreoni's (2006) model, the goal is a mechanism to coordinate on the leader. Absent such a coordination, the outcome will be inefficient with positive probability; either no one will invest or more than one person will invest.

Consider a simple model based on Andreoni's. The utility function is the same as (1) in Section 2.3.1. Assume there is a single moment in time at which anyone can buy the signal. Like Andreoni, limit attention to equal shares.

Assume, first, that if θ is learned by anyone, then it is honestly shared with all. That is, the problem is solely one of coordination. Absent coordination on who is to be leader, the team members play a mixed-strategy equilibrium. The equilibrium symmetric mixed strategy is to spend c with probability p and to not spend with probability $1 - p$. The total expected social loss vis-à-vis a situation in which there was coordination is $(N - 1)c$. Intuitively, relative to a situation of coordination, $N - 1$ team members are taking independent gambles with an expected loss of c, so the expected welfare loss must be $(N - 1)c$.[33]

This loss is increasing in N and equals the welfare loss (relative to coordination) that would result if everyone collected the information with probability 1.

Clearly, there is a social benefit to leadership, and it is increasing in the size of the group. Presumably, when feasible, the group will therefore wish to coordinate on a leader. Although each individual would, in this setting, prefer someone else be the leader (i.e., let someone else incur

---

33. An individual's expected loss if no information is obtained vis-à-vis if it were obtained is

$$\mathrm{Var}(\theta)\frac{2N-1}{2N^2}.$$

So an individual is willing to mix if

$$c = (1-p)^{N-1}\mathrm{Var}(\theta)\frac{2N-1}{2N^2}.$$

c), no individual would shirk leadership if appointed. If followers believe the appointed leader will collect the information, then they have no incentive to do so themselves. The appointed leader will, therefore, have a strict incentive to collect the information.

What if the information collected by the appointed leader cannot be honestly and freely transmitted to the followers, so she faces the problem in Hermalin (1998)? Would the leader have an incentive to save *c* by not collecting the information and simply playing as if she had collected it? The answer is no, at least if *c* is small enough. A leader who does not collect information when expected to by followers is in exactly the same situation as a leader who has observed the mean value, $\bar{\theta}$. Signaling is fully revealing, so the followers each expend effort $\tilde{\theta}/N$, where $\tilde{\theta}$ is their belief about θ. Let $\Pi(\theta, \tilde{\theta})$ be the leader's payoff if the true state is θ and everyone believes it to be $\tilde{\theta}$. Under signaling by sacrifice, the leader's payoff is then

$$\Pi(\theta, \bar{\theta}) = \frac{\theta}{N}\bar{\theta} - \int_0^{\bar{\theta}} \frac{z(N-1)}{N^2}dz - \frac{\bar{\theta}^2}{2N^2}$$

if she has not learned the state (but is expected to have) and

$$\Pi(\theta, \theta) = \frac{(2N-1)\theta^2}{2N^2} - \int_0^{\theta} \frac{z(N-1)}{N^2}dz$$

if she has learned the state. The leader, therefore, has an incentive to learn the information if and only if

$$c \leq E\left\{\Pi(\theta, \theta) - \Pi(\theta, \bar{\theta})\right\} = \frac{N}{2N^2}\text{Var}(\theta).$$

A similar result can be shown to hold when signaling is leading by example.

Although it is clear that the team should coordinate on a leader, it is worth returning to the question of who might arise endogenously as the leader. To study that, return to the assumption that the leader reveals what she learns truthfully and costlessly (i.e., she need not signal). If all group members are identical, then the analysis is not particularly illuminating, so assume that each team member *n* has a unique cost of information acquisition, c_n. Were the team able to coordinate on a leader, efficiency would dictate that the leader be the member with the lowest *c*. Assume, however, no ex ante coordination is possible, and consider the mixed-strategy equilibrium. A team member is willing to mix when his cost of obtaining the information equals his expected loss if he does not, namely, the probability that no one else obtains the information times the expected loss from not having the information:

$$c_n = \text{Var}(\theta)\frac{2N-1}{N^2} \times \prod_{j \neq n}(1 - p_j). \tag{6}$$

The solution to this system of equations can be expressed as

$$\log(1 - p_n) = \frac{1}{N-1}\sum_{j \neq n}\log\left(\frac{c_j N^2}{\text{Var}(\theta)(2N-1)}\right) - \frac{N-2}{N-1}\log\left(\frac{c_n N^2}{\text{Var}(\theta)(2N-1)}\right).$$

Surprisingly, the equilibrium probability that a given team member obtains the information is increasing in his own cost and decreasing in the other team members' costs. Intuitively, from (6), for a player to mix, he must be indifferent between the cost of obtaining the information and the expected cost of not doing so. If the former goes up, then the latter must also, if he is to remain willing to mix. The latter goes up if the probability that the others will not get the information goes up. To keep the others playing a mixed strategy, it follows that the team member in question must obtain the information with a greater probability.

If c_n is too large, then (6) does not have a solution in which all $p_j \in (0, 1)$; in this case, team member n plays the pure strategy of not obtaining the information. Consequently, the probability of becoming the leader is, first, increasing in the cost of obtaining the information, but then falls to zero. Although counterintuitive, this result is not necessarily at odds with reality. My informal observation of organizations with endogenous leadership (e.g., academic departments, PTAs) suggests that it is the people in the middle of the opportunity-cost-of-time distribution who are the most likely to take the lead on a given issue.[34]

Kobayashi and Suehiro (2005) consider a different variant of Hermalin (1998). Suppose, now, all team members are endowed with information, but the information is imperfect. Specifically, each team member gets a realization of a binary signal, $s \in \{B, G\}$, where G is good news about the productivity state and B is bad news. Conditional on the true state, each team member's signal is determined independently. Assume a team member can publicly (but not verifiably) expend effort in one of two periods, $t = 1$ or 2. If a team member knew that his teammates would expend effort at $t = 1$, he does better to wait until $t = 2$, because he then can base his effort on the inferences he draws from their efforts. However, if he knew that his teammates would wait until $t = 2$, then he may wish to expend effort at $t = 1$ if he can convey information that increases their efforts; that is, if he can lead by example.

Among the possible equilibria of the game is one in which a team member who observes $s = G$ expends effort at time $t = 1$ and a team member who observes $s = B$ expends effort at time $t = 2$. In this equilibrium, there is endogenous leadership, insofar as who leads by example (if anyone does) is not predetermined but arises as part of the equilibrium play of the game.

Kobayashi and Suehiro (2005) is a clever attempt to endogenize leadership, but it is not without problems. One is the possibility that both team members attempt to lead by example. Although leadership battles are by no means unheard of, they typically arise when would-be leaders hold different views; not, as in Kobayashi and Suehiro, when they hold the same view. Leadership battles, it should be noted, have not been explored in the economics literature, although they have certainly received considerable attention in other literatures (e.g., Machiavelli [Bondanella and Musa 1979]; Wrong 1995; de Waal 1998).

2.3.3. The Role of Conformism

Huck and Rey-Biel (2006) consider the endogenous emergence of leadership in a two-member team. Unlike earlier models, there is no uncertainty about the state of the world; it is commonly known that the value of the team's efforts are $V = 2(r_1 e_1 + r_2 e_2)$, where r_n is the commonly

---

34. This observation is consistent with one of my father's sayings: "If you want something done, ask a busy person."

known productivity of team member n. The sharing rule is equal shares.[35] Unlike earlier models, team members have a bias, $b_n \geq 0$, toward conformism: team member n's utility is

$$u_n = \frac{V}{2} - \frac{1}{2}e_n^2 - \frac{b_n}{2}(e_n - e_m)^2,$$

where e_m is his teammate's effort.

Team member n's best response to e_m is readily shown to be

$$e_n(e_m) = \frac{r_n + b_n e_m}{1 + b_n}. \tag{7}$$

If $b_n = 0$ (i.e., no conformity bias), then $e_n(e_m) = r_n$, the usual result for the teams problem.

Given simultaneous play, the equilibrium is the solution to the simultaneous equations (7):

$$e_n^{\text{SIM}} = \frac{r_n(1 + b_m) + r_m b_n}{1 + b_n + b_m}. \tag{8}$$

Observe that if the biases are the same and the marginal productivities are the same, then the standard solution to the teams problem results; that is, $e^{\text{SIM}} = r$. If the team members' conformity bias is the same, then the greater this common bias, the lower is output (unless bias is irrelevant because $r_1 = r_2$, so the team members naturally choose the same level of effort). Because teams produce an inefficiently low level of output and bias is directly taxing on the team members, it follows that an increase in bias lowers welfare.

Now consider sequential play. One team member leads by choosing her effort first, followed by the other, who chooses his effort after observing the leader's. The follower's response is given by (7). The leader's problem is thus

$$\max_e r_L e + r_f \frac{r_f + b_f e}{1 + b_f} - \frac{1}{2}e^2 - \frac{b_L}{2}\left(\frac{r_f - e}{1 + b_f}\right)^2,$$

where the subscripts L and f refer to the leader and follower, respectively. Algebra readily reveals that the resulting output is greater than the output under simultaneous play (if $b_f > 0$).

If $r_f = r_L = r$ and $b_f = b_L = b$, then welfare is increasing in bias. This result is not surprising: the follower's conformity bias increases the leader's incentives to work hard. Moreover, hard work by the leader increases, via the conformity bias, the follower's incentive to work hard. Given that the teams problem means too little effort, it follows that a conformity bias can increase welfare.

---

35. Equal shares are not an optimal contract under the usual teams problem if $r_1 \neq r_2$; in that case, optimal shares are

$$s_n = \frac{r_n^2}{r_n^2 + r_m^2}.$$

Because of how leading and following change incentives, the Huck and Rey-Biel (2006) model offers insights on who the leader should be. If the bias parameters are the same, but one worker is more productive than the other, then the leader should be the less-productive team member. If the productivity parameters are the same, but one worker has a greater bias toward conforming, then the less-biased worker should be the leader.

2.3.4. Leadership Styles

Rotemberg and Saloner (1993, 1998) focus not on what leaders do, but how they do it. Specifically, they seek to fit leadership style into models of organizations. The first article considers the effect of an empathetic or participatory leadership; the second deals with the effect of vision. In both, leadership style is taken to be an innate, immutable, and known characteristic of the leader. Because leadership style shapes the leader's behavior, it can serve as a commitment to certain behaviors. The organization can lever that commitment to compensate, at least partially, for an assumed inability to write complete contracts.

To illustrate their ideas, consider a model with a leader and a follower. The follower can incur private cost c to devise a project for the organization to undertake; if he does not spend c, there is no project. Prior to sinking c, the gross profit, π, from the to-be-devised project is uncertain; that it is distributed $F(\cdot)$ is commonly known. Assume $F(0) > 0$ and $E\{\pi\} > c$. Once devised (once c is sunk), the project's π is learned with certainty by the leader and follower. At this point, the leader has the authority to decide either to undertake the project, yielding the organization π, or to forgo the project, yielding it zero. Critically, neither whether the follower has devised a project nor the prospective or actual outcome of the project are verifiable (can serve as a contractual contingency). The leader's decision to undertake the project is, however, verifiable. Thus, a contract can stipulate a payment, w, should the project be implemented. The leader's utility is $\lambda w + (1 - \lambda)(\pi - w)$ if the project is undertaken and zero otherwise, where $\lambda \in [0, 1)$ is the extent to which she is empathetic with the follower (has a participatory leadership style).[36] A λ of zero is a pure profit-maximizing ("autocratic") leader. A follower devises a project if and only his expected payment, w times the probability he devises a project the leader implements, exceeds his cost.

In the first best,[37] a project is undertaken if and only if $\pi \geq 0$. In the first best, the expected payoff to devising a project is $\int_0^\infty \pi \, dF(\pi)$, which exceeds $E\{\pi\}$, which exceeds c; projects should be devised in the first best.

In the actual situation, the leader undertakes a project if and only if

$$\pi \geq \frac{1 - 2\lambda}{1 - \lambda} w. \tag{9}$$

36. The Rotemberg and Saloner (1993) identification of empathy with a participatory leadership style is motivated by studies that show a participatory leadership style exhibits empathetic behaviors (e.g., "solicit opinions, facts, and *feelings* from . . . participants"; House and Baetz 1979: 364 [emphasis added]). See also Gächter et al. (2010) for experimental evidence on the importance of leaders having cooperative dispositions.

37. To be precise, first-best actions are here defined as those that maximize the organization's expected net profit; that is, they maximize the expected value of the difference $\pi - c$. This is a standard welfare measure if $\lambda = 0$ and upfront noncontingent transfers can be made. When $\lambda > 0$, this definition is less obviously the right one.

If $\lambda = 1/2$, then this rule replicates the first-best rule; otherwise—including if the leader is a pure profit-maximizer—the decision is distorted. The follower's expected payment if he devises a project is

$$\bar{W} \equiv w \left(1 - F \left(\frac{1 - 2\lambda}{1 - \lambda} w \right) \right). \tag{10}$$

If $\bar{W} \geq c$, the follower will devise a project, but not otherwise. Depending on $F(\cdot)$ and λ, there may be no w such that the right-hand side of (10) exceeds c. For instance, if

$$F(\pi) = 1 - \exp \left(-\pi - \frac{1}{2} \right), \tag{11}$$

$c = 1/3$, and the leader is a pure profit-maximizer, then no solution exists ($E\{\pi\} = 1/2$ for this example). Welfare with a pure profit-maximizing leader would be zero in this example. Empathetic leadership can help: the first best is always achievable if $\lambda = 1/2$ by setting $w = c/(1 - F(0))$, so the follower has an incentive to invest, and because the right-hand side of (9) is 0, the implementation decision is efficient.

Even if the organization cannot optimize its leader's empathy level (i.e., set $\lambda = 1/2$), continuity implies that some levels of empathy are superior to no empathy. In some situations, even extreme empathy, $\lambda \to 1$, is superior to no empathy at all. A totally empathetic leader would always implement the project regardless of π or w. Setting $w = c$, the follower has the appropriate incentives to devise a project. For the example in which $F(\cdot)$ is defined by (11), expected net profit is $E\{\pi\} - c = 1/6 > 0$; the organization's expected net profit is greater with a totally empathetic leader than with a purely profit-maximizing leader.

Rotemberg and Saloner (1998) consider the importance of vision, particularly the extent to which an organization benefits from a leader with a contrarian vision.[38] Consider the following extension of the previous model.[39] Interpret π not as actual profits, but as a signal of expected profits if the project is undertaken. The objective (industry consensus) view is that the signal equals expected profits. The leader, however, is more optimistic and believes expected profits are $\pi + \Delta$, $\Delta \geq 0$. The leader is a risk-neutral profit-maximizer and undertakes the project if

$$\pi + \Delta - w \geq 0. \tag{12}$$

The follower will devise a project if and only if

$$w(1 - F(w - \Delta)) \geq c. \tag{13}$$

If $\Delta = c/(1 - F(0))$, then $w = \Delta$ makes (13) an equality. Moreover, when $w = \Delta$, (12) becomes the first-best rule for maximizing expected profit (objectively). Hence, a visionary

---

38. Van den Steen (2005) is a model in a similar vein. Van den Steen's work is discussed in Section 3.2.5.

39. Rotemberg and Saloner (1998) deal with how organizations choose among competing strategies and the value of managerial vision with respect to providing incentives to develop multiple strategies. The article's insights into leadership per se, however, are captured by the extension of Rotemberg and Saloner (1993) considered here.

leader with a Δ of $c/(1 - F(0))$ yields the first best (objectively). Continuity implies there is a range of Δs that do better than a "visionless" leader (i.e., whose $\Delta = 0$). Indeed, if $F(\cdot)$ is given by (11) and $c = 1/3$, then an infinitely optimistic leader ($\Delta \to \infty$), who yields an expected net profit of $1/6$, is superior to a visionless leader, who yields no profit at all.

From the literature on relational contracts, these outcomes can be sustained given repeated play if a rational autocratic and visionless leader can develop a reputation for playing *as if* she had a $\lambda = 1/2$ or a $\Delta = c/(1 - F(0))$.[40] From a game-theoretic perspective, a leader with "style" is replicable by a leader who has no style but knows how to play optimally in a repeated setting.

Consequently, examples of successful leadership could fail to prove leadership style matters, but examples of unsuccessful leadership suggest it does matter. Plenty of smart people, who presumably know how to be strategic, have been undone by their poor leadership style. A salient example for economists would be Larry Summers's effective ouster from the presidency of Harvard due to a problematic leadership style. Professor Summers's brilliance and ability to think strategically are undisputed. Nevertheless, it would appear in his case that style trumped strategy.[41] Bertrand and Schoar (2003) provide more systematic evidence that leadership style matters; specifically, they find significant and persistent differences in how different managers make decisions and that these differences correlate with individual attributes (e.g., age, education) that might influence managers' outlooks and beliefs.

2.3.5. Overconfident Leaders
In the variant of Rotemberg and Saloner (1998) presented above, the parameter Δ represented vision. It could, just as readily, represent the degree to which the leader suffers from the cognitive bias of overoptimism. Another well-researched cognitive bias is overconfidence—believing you know more than you really do. Camerer and Lovallo (1999) present experimental evidence and Malmendier and Tate (2005) statistical evidence on the prevalence of overconfidence. Given overconfidence is a prevalent bias among managers (Malmendier and Tate), the obvious question is: Why hasn't this bias been driven out by rationality? Could it, similar to the overoptimism bias in a Rotemberg and Saloner–like model, be organizationally useful?

Blanes i Vidal and Möller (2007) offer a model in which an overconfident leader can be superior to an unbiased one.[42] A simplified version of their model is as follows. Initially, nature decides which of two projects, A or B, is the correct project. Assume the projects are equally

---

40. For more on relational contracts, see MacLeod (2007) and cites therein.

In an infinitely repeated game or one with an uncertain end, such a reputation is worth establishing if

$$\delta \int_0^\infty \pi \, dF(\pi) - \delta c - \frac{c}{1 - F(0)} \geq \delta V,$$

where δ is the discount factor and

$$V = \begin{cases} \int_w^\infty (\pi - w) \, dF(\pi), & w \text{ the smallest solution to (10) for } \lambda = 0 \\ 0, & \text{if (10) has no solution for } \lambda = 0. \end{cases}$$

41. It is not my intention to comment positively or negatively on Professor Summers's tenure as Harvard's president. It is, however, objectively true that a significant number of Harvard faculty were upset by his leadership style and that this was a factor behind his having to resign as Harvard's president.

42. A recent working paper by Bolton et al. (2007) considers the advantage of an overconfident leader in a situation in which coordinating the followers' actions is important.

likely to be the correct one. A public signal, $s_{PUB} \in \{A, B\}$, is then realized. Denote the probability that the signal is accurate by p.[43] Assume $1/2 < p < 1$. The leader receives a private signal, $s_{PRI} \in \{A, B\}$, that she cannot share with her single follower. Denote the objective probability that the private signal is accurate by q. Assume $1/2 < q < p$. Note the private signal is less precise than the public one. Once both signals are realized, the leader chooses the project to be undertaken. If she chooses the correct project, then the team produces $2e$, where e is the follower's effort. If she chooses the wrong project, then the team produces 0 regardless of e. As previously, contracts cannot be based on e, and the follower's utility is $w - e^2/2$, where w is his portion of the output. Assume an equal sharing rule between leader and follower. If the follower believes the probability of the leader's having selected the correct project to be b, then he chooses his effort to solve

$$\max_{e} be - \frac{e^2}{2}. \tag{14}$$

The solution to (14) is $e = b$.

Consider, initially, an objective (unbiased) leader. Because $p > q$, she should choose the project solely on the basis of the public signal. If $s_{PUB} = s_{PRI}$ and the follower could learn s_{PRI}, then

$$b = \frac{pq}{1 - p - q + 2pq} > p;$$

so the follower would work harder than if he knew only the public signal. Given that the leader always does better in expectation the harder the follower works, she has, similar to Hermalin (1998), an incentive to always claim her private signal agrees with the public signal. The follower, understanding this incentive, rationally disregards such announcements. The leader's private signal does, however, represent valuable information vis-à-vis the optimal amount of effort for the follower to expend. The leader's inability to communicate her signal credibly thus leads to a loss in team welfare relative to the first best. In this scenario, expected welfare is $W^u \equiv 3p^2/2$.

Now suppose the leader is overconfident: she believes the probability that her private signal is correct is $\hat{q} > p > q$. One can interpret this as her believing that she is better able to assess the market/situation/environment than she truly is. The value of $\hat{q}$ is common knowledge. Because $\hat{q} > p$, she bases her choice of signal on her private information and not the public signal.[44] Knowing this, the follower assesses the probability of the leader's chosen project being the correct project as

$$b_+ \equiv \frac{pq}{1 - p - q + 2pq}$$

if the chosen project agrees with the public signal and

$$b_- \equiv \frac{q(1 - p)}{p + q - 2pq}$$

---

43. That is, $p = P\{s_{PUB} = X \mid X \text{ is the correct project}\}$.
44. If you are worried that I just pulled a fast one, don't; I tidy things up in the next paragraph.

if the chosen project disagrees with the public signal. Observe that an overconfident leader credibly communicates her private signal, albeit at the cost of potentially acting on the wrong signal. Expected team welfare (using objective probabilities) is

$$W^o \equiv 2pqb_+ - (1 - q - p + 2pq)\frac{b_+^2}{2} + 2(1-p)qb_- - (q + p - 2pq)\frac{b_-^2}{2}.$$

There exist values of p and q such that $W^o > W^u$; the team is better off with an overconfident leader than an objective leader for those values.[45]

The preceding analysis presumes naïveté on the part of the leader; specifically, she chooses the project on the basis of her private signal without regard for how the follower will respond. If q is also common knowledge,[46] then the leader realizes $b_+ > b_-$, and she may therefore have an incentive to deviate from relying solely on her private signal when it disagrees with the public one. This incentive exists only if

$$\frac{\hat{q}(1-p)}{p + \hat{q} - 2p\hat{q}} \, b_- < \left(1 - \frac{\hat{q}(1-p)}{p + \hat{q} - 2p\hat{q}}\right) b_+. \tag{15}$$

Hence, the above equilibrium exists if (15) does not hold, which is to say

$$\hat{q} \geq \frac{p^3 + p^2q - 2p^3q}{1 - 3p + 3p^2 - q + 4pq - 4p^2q} \tag{16}$$

(the right-hand side of (16) < 1 given $p < 1$). For example, if $p = 0.85$, $q = 0.82$, and $\hat{q} = 0.95$, then the leader would rely solely on her private signal in equilibrium, and this would yield greater expected welfare than having an objective leader.

Although overconfidence can be an asset, it can also be disastrous given different parameter values (expected welfare, e.g., is reduced if $p = 0.85$, $q = 0.75$, and $\hat{q} = 0.95$), a point also recognized by Blanes i Vidal and Möller (2007). From Sophocles's *Oedipus Rex* to the political fallout from the Iraq war, literature and history are replete with examples of leaders brought low by their overconfidence (hubris). Literature and history, of course, are also replete with examples of bold leaders who triumphed against the odds. It may well be that overconfidence is neither a virtue nor a vice, but simply increases the variance of outcomes vis-à-vis those achieved by objectively correct leaders.

This last point can be illustrated from some work of mine in progress. Consider the simultaneous-play game shown in Figure 3. Two leaders are squaring off in a variation of a hawk-dove game. Assume the payoffs in the bold-bold cell arise as follows: In any conflict, one side triumphs and gains 1, and the other is crushed and loses 5. The objective probability of

---

45. For example, if $p = 0.85$, then $W^o \geq W^u$ for all $q \in (0.817, 0.85)$. The shortness of that interval is, in part, a function of the production function used to illustrate the model; other production functions can yield larger intervals.

46. Subtle issues arise if we assume that both q and $\hat{q}$ are common knowledge, and these issues are somewhat contentious in economics; see, for example, Gul (1998) and the response of Aumann (1998). I will, however, pass over these subtleties here.

Column leader

	Bold	Timid
Bold	-2 / -2	0 / 1
Timid	1 / 0	0 / 0

Figure 3. A hawk-dove-like game.

Less able leader

	Bold	Timid
Bold	-3 / -1	0 / 1
Timid	1 / 0	0 / 0

Figure 4. The misperceived game.

being the triumphant side in such a conflict is 1/2. In a world of objective leaders (i.e., who know the probability of triumph is 1/2), the unique evolutionarily stable equilibrium is the mixed-strategy Nash equilibrium in which each leader is bold with probability 1/3 and timid with probability 2/3. Payoff variance is 2/3.

Now suppose a proportion μ of all leaders hold the following objectively incorrect beliefs: (i) some leaders are more able than others; (ii) they themselves are such leaders; and (iii) when equally able leaders are in conflict, the probability of triumphing is 1/2, but an abler leader against a less-able one triumphs with probability 2/3. Such an overconfident leader thus believes if he plays against an abler leader, then the game is as shown in Figure 3; but it is as shown in Figure 4 if he plays against a less-able leader. Assume that μ is common knowledge, as are the beliefs of overconfident leaders and objective (unbiased) leaders.[47] Assume that when leaders are paired off to play the game, they do not know whether their opponent is overconfident or objective.

Let p_t be the probability that a type t leader is bold, $t \in \{o, u\}$ (overconfident or unbiased, respectively). The unique symmetric (in leader type) Nash equilibria are

$$p_o = \frac{1}{3\mu} \quad \text{and} \quad p_u = 0 \quad \text{if } \mu \geq \frac{1}{3},$$

$$p_o = 1 \quad \text{and} \quad p_u = \frac{1-3\mu}{3(1-\mu)} \quad \text{if } \mu < \frac{1}{3}.$$

47. Again this assumption creates subtle issues. In this model they could be avoided when $\mu \geq 1/3$ by making the structure of the game common knowledge among the objective leaders, but having the overconfident leaders hold a fourth belief that less-able leaders are always timid.

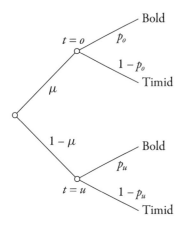

Figure 5. Compound lottery. Given equilibrium values of p_o and p_u, probability of playing bold is 1/3 and that of playing timid is 2/3.

It is worth noting the equivalence of this game to one in which all leaders are unbiased, but they execute their mixed strategies according to the compound lottery shown in Figure 5. It follows that each type of leader has an equilibrium expected payoff of 0, so a leader neither suffers nor gains from being overconfident. It further follows that these equilibria are evolutionarily stable. In particular, overconfidence is neither evolutionarily advantaged nor disadvantaged. If σ_t^2 is the payoff variance for type t, it follows that

$$\sigma_o^2 = \begin{cases} \frac{2}{3\mu}, & \text{if } \mu \geq 1/3 \\ 2, & \text{if } \mu < 1/3 \end{cases} \quad \text{and} \quad \sigma_u^2 = \begin{cases} 0, & \text{if } \mu \geq 1/3 \\ \frac{2-6\mu}{3(1-\mu)}, & \text{if } \mu < 1/3 \end{cases}.$$

Observe $\sigma_o^2 > \sigma_u^2$ in both equilibria—payoffs are more volatile with an overconfident leader than an unbiased one, consistent with the idea that overconfident leaders have the most dramatic successes and the most catastrophic failures.

2.3.6. Is Leadership Illusory?

Overoptimism and overconfidence are cognitive biases suffered by leaders. A potential cognitive bias suffered by followers is the *fundamental attribution bias*—the well-documented tendency of people to ascribe outcomes to the attributes of the individual actors rather than to the situation they faced; effectively, to underweight the base rates of success or failure at a task when updating beliefs about an actor's ability from his or her success or failure at the task. Organizational behavior scholars have long postulated that followers will, consequently, unduly attribute the group's success or failures to its leaders, the so-called "illusion of leadership" (for citations to some of this literature, see Weber et al., 2001).

Weber et al. test this idea experimentally. They consider a teams problem with a weakest-link technology:

$$\text{team member } n\text{'s payoff} \equiv \begin{cases} \frac{5}{4}(\min\{e_1, \ldots, e_N\} + 1) - e_n, & \text{if } \min\{e_1, \ldots, e_N\} > 0 \\ 1, & \text{if } \min\{e_1, \ldots, e_N\} = 0 \end{cases},$$

where, for each n, $e_n \in \{0, 1, 2, 3\}$. The game has four pure-strategy Nash equilibria, each characterized by all N team members playing the same e. The equilibria are Pareto ranked, with a higher-e equilibrium dominating a lower-e equilibrium. Earlier experimental evidence by Van Huyck et al. (1990) shows that large teams end up coordinating on the $e = 0$ equilibrium, while small teams can successfully coordinate on the $e = 3$ equilibrium.[48] In other words, cooperation is harder to sustain the larger the team. In Weber et al., one of the team members is made leader and the leader is allowed to make a speech exhorting her fellow team members to cooperate (i.e., play $e = 3$). Despite this, cooperation is far less common in large teams than in small teams, consistent with cooperation being harder to sustain in large teams. Through various methods, Weber et al. have team members indicate why their teams were successful (i.e., tended to cooperate) or unsuccessful. To a significant degree, team members ascribe the outcome to the ability of the leader; that is, they appear to be ignoring the effect of the situation (large versus small team) and overweighting the leader's leadership abilities.

Although insightful, this work is not without problems. First, in the Van Huyck et al. experiments, which had no leaders, large teams *never* coordinated. In the Weber et al. experiments, large teams are sometimes able to sustain coordination, suggesting that there is a role for leadership (or at least announcements). Second, the questionnaires given team members do not ask whether the size of the team contributed to success or failure. Hence, unless leadership ability were truly irrelevant to the outcome, it is not clear that one may conclude that the team members were assigning the wrong weights to the situation vis-à-vis leadership ability. Indeed, given the first point, it is not clear that team members were necessarily erring in attributing—at least in part—the outcome to the leader's ability.

To expound on these two points, consider a world in which ability, α, is drawn uniformly from $\{-1, 0, 1\}$. Assume there are two tasks, easy and difficult ($t \in \{E, D\}$). Let the probability of success conditional on task and ability be $p_t + \alpha \varepsilon$, where $0 < \varepsilon < p_D < p_E < 1 - \varepsilon$. Suppose people are surveyed after the task's outcome is realized and are asked what the most likely ability of the actor (leader) is. Bayes Rule requires $\hat{\alpha} = 1$ for success and $\hat{\alpha} = -1$ for failure. Given a large number M of such trials, approximately $M p_t$ successes should be observed for task t. If $p_E > 1/2 > p_D$, then the median rating of actors doing the easy task will be 1 and the median rating of those doing the difficult task will be -1. The averages will be approximately $2 p_E - 1 > 0$ and $2 p_D - 1 < 0$, respectively. These values would give results analogous to those in Weber et al., but these results are perfectly consistent with unbiased attribution.[49]

To be clear, however, this is not to say that the Weber et al. (2001) results can't be due to the fundamental attribution bias. The case for the fundamental attribution bias is strong in general, and there is no reason to think it, as well as biases like the hindsight bias, do not apply to followers' assessments of their leaders. The volatilities of established politicians' poll ratings

---

48. The actual game in Van Huyck et al. (1990) differs slightly in details, but that is immaterial for this discussion.

49. Weber et al. (2001) ask the team members to "rate the leader's overall leadership ability" on a nine-point scale, 1 = extremely poor; 9 = extremely good. (Note: in the reported tables, Weber et al. write "9 = average"; I believe, however, that must be a typographical error.) Medians for large teams are 3 or 4, depending on experimental design, and they are 5–7 for small teams. Means are similar but closer in value than medians, consistent with the hypothetical example in the text.

do not seem, for instance, readily reconcilable with rational Bayesian updating. However, as the above discussion shows, followers are not necessarily mistaken when they attribute at least some of the team's success or failure to their leader.

3. Corporate Culture

As the quotes in Section 1.2 demonstrate, corporate culture is not a precisely defined concept. It can be seen as encompassing the norms and customs of a firm, its informal and unwritten rules of behavior. As such, culture governs actions both in the firm and instructs members of the firm how to act with those outside the firm (e.g., suppliers or customers). Corporate culture is also defined to encompass the experiences, knowledge, and language shared by those belonging to the firm. Although shapeable by individuals, especially leaders, culture is more than an amalgam of current personalities in the firm; it is a property of the firm. Consequently, given normal personnel turnover, the culture will persist over time, evolving slowly if at all. Finally, although a firm's culture can be influenced by broader social mores and customs, it is nevertheless distinct from national or regional culture.[50]

3.1. Assessment and Measurement of Corporate Culture

Given that corporate "culture is not just a concept but a family of concepts" and "like a Rorschach [test] means different things to different people" (O'Reilly and Chatman 1996: 159), it is not surprising that corporate culture has proved difficult to assess and measure. These difficulties, in turn, can create problems for a quantitative science such as economics.

In assessing and measuring corporate culture, a researcher could conceivably wish to know some or all of the following:

- What is the strength of the culture? How committed to it are people? How uniform is commitment across the ranks of the hierarchy? Across employee cohorts?

- What is the impact of the culture? How does it aid or hinder the firm?[51]

- How stable is the culture? Is it prone to decay? If so, at what rate?

- What resources does management expend on the maintenance of the culture?

- What resources would management need to expend to change the culture? How would it accomplish that task?

As detailed in Payne (2001) and Sparrow (2001), the principal measurement tools are surveys. Some surveys are conducted throughout the organization, and others (e.g., Kotter and

---

50. There is, however, a literature that considers the link between social customs and corporate culture. The influence of the broader society has been invoked, for example, to explain systematic differences in the corporate cultures of American and Japanese firms. See, e.g., Ferris and Wagner (1985), Okuno-Fujiwara (1994), Morita (2001), and Tackney (2001).

51. A certain suspicion must apply to any prediction that a strong corporate culture is always advantageous. If that were true, then how would one explain variation in the strength of culture across firms? Why wouldn't all weak culture firms become strong culture firms (or die)? Hermalin (2001: 243–248) discusses this issue in greater depth.

Heskett 1992) are sent only to top management. Sometimes, as in Kotter and Heskett, managers of one firm are asked questions about the culture of other firms as well as their own. For instance, people could be asked to rate a firm on the extent to which it is managed according to long-standing policies and practices, to rate it on whether it has a style or way of doing things, and so forth (see Payne). Sometimes people are asked directly to rate the strength of a firm's culture.

An indirect means of measuring the strength of a culture is to ascertain the degree of consensus on various attitudinal questions. Sometimes (see Payne 2001: 113) people are explicitly surveyed about the degree of consensus among people in the firm. The rationale behind these approaches is that a strong culture should lead to strong consensus in beliefs and attitudes.

Another indirect approach is to measure an organization's investment in correlates of strong culture (O'Reilly and Chatman 1996). From studies of organizations with notoriously high levels of indoctrination, such as religious cults, certain practices are known to lead to indoctrination or at least correlate with it. For instance, table 1 of O'Reilly and Chatman offers a list of such practices, such as "use multiple recruiting steps requiring escalating commitment on the part of the recruit," a practice used in religious recruitment. The rationale is that firms that employ strong indoctrination techniques will wind up with strong cultures.

Purely ethnographic methods have also been employed. Although such research can serve to enrich our understanding of corporate culture, it does not lend itself to quantitative conclusions, limiting its usefulness for any kind of statistical analysis.

In economics, where survey and ethnographic methods are rarely used, other approaches have been taken to the empirical study of corporate culture. An example is the study by Cronqvist et al. (2007), which posits that if cultures are influential and persistent, then firms' investment, financial, and operational policies should also be persistent; moreover, spinoffs should follow policies similar to their parents. The empirical evidence presented by Cronqvist et al. is consistent with these hypotheses.

3.2. The Economic Analysis of Corporate Culture

3.2.1. Coordination, Reputation, and Unforeseen Contingencies

Consider Figure 6, a "battle of the sexes" game between a senior and a junior person. An issue with such games is how do the players determine which of the game's three Nash equilibria is to be played? Absent some institution for selecting the equilibrium, there is no clear prediction of what the players will do. Experiments indicate, however, that the players will frequently fail

Figure 6. Coordination game between junior and senior personnel.

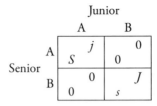

Figure 7. Family of coordination games between junior and senior personnel.

to coordinate (i.e., they will often get 0; see, e.g., Charness et al. 2007). It would therefore be welfare superior to have an institution that selected one of the two pure-strategy equilibria prior to play.

Kreps (1990) suggests that corporate culture is just such an institution. Suppose, for instance, it is understood, as matter of culture, that juniors are to defer to seniors. Consequently, juniors and seniors expect that the A-A equilibrium will be played, given it is best for the senior player.

3.2.1.1. Unforeseen Contingencies. Given that coordination on the A-A equilibrium could also be achieved by other means, including contractually, the usefulness of corporate culture is not immediately obvious. As Kreps (1990) suggests, its usefulness is more apparent if we imagine a world of unforeseen contingencies: Consider Figure 7. Provided $S > s > 0$ and $J > j > 0$, this figure generalizes the game of Figure 6. Imagine, now, that there are many such coordination games that junior and senior personnel will play. What A and B will be is not known ex ante, nor are the values of S, s, J, and j known. A player may not even know in advance if he will be the junior or senior player. In short, the details of all possible coordination games could be unforeseen contingencies. In such an environment, contracting could be impractical (although see the discussion at the end of Section 3.2.1.2).[52] A cultural norm of deferring to seniors could serve as an efficient substitute for explicit contracting, ensuring that a Pareto efficient outcome is reached.

3.2.1.2. Corporate Reputation. A prevalent view is that a corporation's culture belongs to the corporation in the sense that it is robust to turnover in personnel. Building on Kreps (1990), consider the game in Figure 8: This is a game between a boss and an underling. The boss can treat the underling fairly or exploit him. The underling can trust the boss or not. The latter strategy partially protects the underling against exploitation, but is harmful to him if the boss plays fairly. Observe that exploit is a dominant strategy for the boss. In a one-shot game, she can, therefore, be expected to exploit. The underling's best response to being exploited is not to trust. Hence, the one-shot equilibrium outcome is the bottom-right cell. Both players would, however, be better off in the top-left cell.

---

52. Contracting includes a corporation's written rules, policies, and procedures, as well as explicit contracts between employees and the corporation.

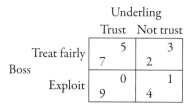

Figure 8. Trust game.

Suppose, conditional on survival to any given period, the game is repeated in (survives to) the next period with probability β.[53] For the moment, assume the boss and her underling live at least as long as the game is repeated. It is readily shown that if the per-period survival probability $\geq 40\%$ (i.e., $\beta \geq \frac{2}{5}$), then there is a subgame-perfect equilibrium in which the boss treats the underling fairly and he, in turn, trusts the boss to do so (for details, see Hermalin 2001).[54]

In this model, the underling need not be a long-lived player. Period by period, he simply plays his best response to what the boss is supposed to do given the history of the game; he could, thus, live only one period *provided he, like the member of each generation, knows the history of the game to that point*. The boss, in contrast, does need to care about the future. She need not, however, be infinitely lived.[55] Specifically, suppose the current-period boss's compensation is an increasing function of the value of the firm, the sum of current payout plus expected future value (e.g., she has stock-based compensation or is an owner who cashes out). Suppose that each generation's underling expects his boss to treat him fairly if every boss in the firm's history has done so, but otherwise he expects to be exploited. The firm's expected future value is

$$V_F = \frac{7\beta}{1 - \beta} \quad \text{or} \quad V_E = \frac{4\beta}{1 - \beta},$$

depending, respectively, on whether bosses have treated underlings fairly or a boss has ever exploited an employee. Consider a firm in which bosses have so far treated their underlings fairly. This generation's boss will continue this tradition, provided her compensation from doing so exceeds her compensation from exploiting; that is, provided $7 + V_F \geq 9 + V_E$. A little algebra reveals that inequality holds provided $\beta \geq 2/5$. Observe that the reputation for treating employees fairly resides with the firm, not an individual. The corporation's culture can, thus, sustain desirable outcomes.

"Fair treatment" and "exploitation" are fairly amorphous concepts. Typically, whether behavior is fair is specific to the situation. Treating an employee harshly could be seen as fair if

---

53. Equivalently, the game is infinitely repeated with certainty, and β is the common discount factor.

54. Rob and Zemsky (2002) use another approach to modeling how social capital might be built in an organization. Rather than relying on the logic of repeated play, the authors assume the organization's personnel are endowed with a reciprocity norm. See Rob and Zemsky (2002) for details.

55. Crémer (1986) defines a model with a similar flavor. In that article, there is a team with N individuals, each of a different age cohort. An individual lives N periods. Except for the last period of his life, an individual has some incentive to cooperate if failure to cooperate today destroys future cooperation. Under certain conditions, cooperation is sustainable among the younger cohorts.

he is performing poorly, but not if he is performing well. Ex ante, it is difficult to foresee all the possible treatments that could be judged fair or unfair and, likewise, to enumerate all the situations in which they are fair or unfair. Again, the environment is plagued by unforeseen contingencies. What is fair and what is exploitation cannot be defined in advance; yet, under the rules of a given culture, ex post behavior can be judged to be fair or not. This is analogous with pornography regulation in the United States—material is legally obscene if it violates community standards, and whether it does is judged ex post by the criterion that people know obscene material when they see it.[56] Corporate culture matters in two ways: as reputation or tradition, and as the means of defining compliance with the reputation or tradition when it is infeasible to define future circumstances ex ante.

A concrete example will prove useful. A company seeks to lure a top employee from a rival. Before moving, the employee attempts to reach firm agreements with his new boss about the details of his employment. But situations can arise, which he failed to anticipate, in which he would want his new boss to take actions beneficial to him but costly to her. For instance, imagine he does not foresee that his current daycare arrangement will fall apart and that the best alternative arrangement will require him to leave work early. Although he's willing to make up the work, regularly leaving early imposes a cost on the boss (e.g., meetings are harder to schedule). The boss can bear that cost, she can demand he not leave early—although this means a worse daycare arrangement for his child—or she can exploit the employee's problem to hold him up by, then, renegotiating aspects of his contract. In short, this is the game of Figure 8: The employee can "trust"—go to a new firm knowing that he will be vulnerable— or "not trust"—stay put; likewise, the boss can be accommodating—let him adjust his schedule without penalty—or "exploit" him—force him to stay until five or otherwise give something up. The key point, however, is the following: Whereas the employee can't anticipate that he will want accommodation, he should realize he will be relying on his new boss to treat him fairly. His decision to switch employers would depend, in part, on his assessment of the reputation (corporate culture) of his potential new employer.

From the perspective of economic theory, however, this analysis is not without problems. Although specific contingencies could well be unforeseen, general types of contingencies—will he be treated fairly or not—should be foreseeable. Why can't the parties write a contract that says that the boss will treat the employee fairly? The obvious—but seriously incomplete—answer is that it would be difficult for a judge (jury, arbitrator, etc.) to determine whether treatment was fair. That is, a judge's assessment of how the employee was actually treated is subject to error. However, as Hermalin and Katz (1991), Edlin and Hermalin (2001), and Hermalin (2008) demonstrate, imprecise assessments do not preclude efficient contracting. As long as the judge's assessment is correlated with what the boss actually did, the parties can rely on this assessment as follows. They write a contract calling for the boss to treat the employee fairly, and after the boss has acted, they renegotiate the contract in anticipation of what might happen should they go to court. Under fairly general conditions (see, e.g., Edlin and Hermalin 2001), the parties can construct a contract that duplicates the outcome they would have enjoyed were the boss's

56. To paraphrase the standard for pornography set down by Supreme Court Justice Potter Stewart. Personally, the standard I've favored—which is not original to me—is pornographic material is material read with one hand.

action verifiable without error. That is, as a matter of contract theory, there is no need to rely on culture at all—the parties can instead rely on formal contracts.

In reality, the costs associated with negotiating, monitoring, and enforcing these contracts could make them a less desirable means of inducing fair treatment—reputation can be equally effective and cost less.[57] Note, however, the transaction costs associated with contracting need to be substantial in the following sense: the possibility of formal contracting can destroy the possibility of using reputation when the two are close substitutes. Reputations are more sustainable the greater the difference between the cooperative and the noncooperative payoffs. If noncooperation results in switching to contracts and contracting is a close substitute for cooperation, then this difference is small, and consequently, reputation could be unsustainable (for more on this point, see Schmidt and Schnitzer 1995).[58]

3.2.2. Culture as Technology

One way to view culture is as a type of technology. That is, just as a firm may have certain processes by which it produces its goods or services, its culture could also play a role in the transformation of inputs into outputs. For instance, to the extent that understanding organizational norms avoids miscoordination and other mistakes, it could make the organization more productive, just as a superior production technology might.

One article that explores this view is Carillo and Gromb (1999). Consider the following, simplified version of their model. Workers are either productive in a culture or not. Whether they are or are not is an intrinsic characteristic, with a random worker's probability of being productive in any given culture equal to $p \in (0, 1)$ (and independent across cultures). Hence, over time, a firm is essentially trying to match workers to its culture (similar to some of the selection models discussed in Sections 3.2.4 and 3.2.5). Let R_t be what a worker productive under culture t produces. There are two cultures: A, which a firm is endowed with initially, and B, which it may subsequently have an opportunity to adopt. Culture B is superior insofar as

$$R_B > (2 - p)R_A; \tag{17}$$

however, its superiority is limited:

$$R_B < \frac{R_A}{p}. \tag{18}$$

In what follows, assume the firm's workforce is a continuum of measure one.

Just prior to the first period, when the firm has only culture A available (the possibility of B does not arrive until the next period), it affords workers who would otherwise not be productive under A an opportunity to possibly become productive. Specifically, it allows them to invest in human capital, so that the probability that such a worker is productive under A is a, where the value of a depends on how much is invested. The success of this investment is only known at the end of the first period (i.e., after observing a worker's output). Consequently, in the first

57. Although contracts (typically implicit or default) are not unheard of—there are plenty of employee lawsuits alleging unfair treatment.

58. See also Baker et al. (1994) and Kvaløy and Olsen (2009). Hermalin et al. (2012) make the point that sometimes reputations permit parties to write contracts that would be ineffectual in a one-shot setting.

period, the probability that a worker is productive is $p + (1 - p)a$. At the end of the first period, the firm fires all nonproductive workers. With probability $1 - s$, the firm has the opportunity to switch to culture B prior to the second period; if it does switch, then it tests its existing workers to see whether they will be productive under B, letting go those who will not be. It then hires replacements for any dismissed workers and produces in a second and final period under whichever culture it has. Workers at this stage cannot invest in human capital. Recall the probability that a worker is productive under B is p. Accounting for new hires, the probability that a random worker is productive under A is

$$p(2 - p) + a(1 - p)^2.$$

Given (17) and (18), a firm would rationally switch cultures if $a = 0$, but not if $a = 1$. Hence, there is a value of $a \in (0, 1)$ such that the firm is indifferent between switching or not; let $\hat{a}$ denote that value.

If a period-one worker anticipates no switch in culture, he chooses a to maximize

$$wa - c(a), \tag{19}$$

where w is the wage premium for working for the firm in period 2 and $c(\cdot)$ is the differentiable cost of making the necessary investment in human capital; for convenience, assume $c'(0) = 0$ and $c'(1) > w$. If he anticipates the firm will switch if given the opportunity, he chooses a to maximize

$$w((1 - s)p + sa) - c(a). \tag{20}$$

Let a^* maximize (19) and a^{**} maximize (20). Given $s < 1$, $a^{**} < a^*$. Moreover, it follows that $da^{**}/ds > 0$. The parameter s can be thought of as the strength of the initial culture, A.

If $a^* > \hat{a}$, then there is an equilibrium in which those workers who need to invest choose a^* and the firm maintains culture A even if B is available. This equilibrium relies on workers believing their colleagues will invest more than $\hat{a}$. Given that workers will never invest less than a^{**}, this equilibrium is unique if $a^{**} > \hat{a}$. Conversely, if $a^* < \hat{a}$, the only equilibrium is one in which workers invest a^{**}. If $a^* \geq \hat{a} \geq a^{**}$, then two symmetric pure-strategy equilibria exist: one in which a^* is played and another in which a^{**} is played.

This analysis makes clear that the stronger its culture (i.e., the greater is s), the weakly better off the firm is. It is strictly better off from a marginal increase in s if $a^* < \hat{a}$. Even if $a^* > \hat{a}$, the firm could be strictly better off from an increase in s, depending on equilibrium selection or if that increase eliminates the inferior equilibrium. Consequently, the model offers an explanation for why strong cultures can be valuable. It also suggests that a firm with a strong but intrinsically inferior culture could nevertheless do well—even outperforming a firm with a intrinsically superior culture (e.g., in an equilibrium in which workers play $a^* > \hat{a}$, an A-culture firm in its second period would outperform an otherwise identical firm with a B culture in its first period).

Although an intriguing model, it is not without its limitations. One is the assumption that some individuals are endowed with the ability to automatically be productive in a particular culture. If, instead, the parameter $p = 0$, then the assumed inability to learn culture B means that no firm would ever change from A; strength of culture would be irrelevant. Conversely, if B can be learned, then, with a long enough horizon, it would be hard to see why the firm wouldn't always switch to B given the opportunity. Another issue is the interpretation of s as a measure of cultural strength: although the inability to conceive—or implement even if desired—another culture could be a measure of the strength of the incumbent culture, it is not clear that this fully encompasses what is meant by strength of culture. Finally, it is not always clear that a strong culture is desirable. Prebankruptcy General Motors, for instance, had a strong culture but arguably quite a dysfunctional one.

3.2.3. Culture as Convention

The discussion of Figures 6 and 7—the "defer-to-seniors norm"—illustrates what could be called the "culture-as-convention" view. One question, left unexplored by Kreps (1990), is where these coordinating conventions come from. Young (1993, 1998) has taken an adaptive-learning approach to the issue: Players adapt their play as a function of past experiences. In adaptive play, players randomly draw (recall) k observations from the past m periods of play. For a two-player game, each player treats the frequency of his opponent's actions in his k-sized sample as the mixed strategy his opponent will play in the current period; he, thus, plays his best response to that mixed strategy. It is readily seen, given this rule, that if the same pure-strategy equilibrium is played for m periods running, then it will be played forever after—play has converged on a convention.

What is the probability of getting a run of m instances of the same pure-strategy equilibrium? Young (1993, theorem 1) proves that if m is sufficiently greater than k, then adaptive play will converge almost surely to a pure-strategy equilibrium. Drawing from the discussion in Fudenberg and Levine (1998: 115), this result can be illustrated as follows. Let $m = 3$ and $k = 1$. Suppose the A-A equilibrium is played at time t, in the subsequent period both players sample the play of period t, and in the period thereafter neither player samples period $t - 1$. Then, in periods t, $t + 1$, and $t + 2$, the A-A equilibrium is played and is established as a convention. The probability of this occurring is $4/81$. A similar argument applies to the B-B equilibrium. Provided A-A or B-B are played infinitely often, such a run of either A-A or B-B will almost surely occur. The only question left is whether A-A or B-B are played infinitely often. The answer is yes, because it is impossible to have a run of three or more occurrences of A-B or B-A, and therefore, over any sample period there is a positive probability of the players both sampling the same action (i.e., both sample an A or both a B), thereby resulting in an A-A or B-B outcome.

Although clever, this approach has a few drawbacks. First, it implies culture is all random evolution and no intelligent design. No doubt, random evolution is the best model for biology, but it is doubtful it is the best model for organizations. There is no role for leadership or other influences. Second, cultures that emerge this way seem more fragile than real corporate cultures. If, for instance, the A-A convention emerged, it could be set aside the next day if the head of the corporation announced that henceforth the B-B convention held in the corporation—provided people believed enough people would follow this diktat, playing B would be everyone's best response and, thus, B-B the new convention. In reality, changing corporate culture is frequently seen as a difficult task (see, e.g., Selznick 1984; Schein 1992; and Kotter 1996).

A partial response to the second point is that going from a state of no convention to one with a convention can be Pareto improving, whereas as switching from one convention to another can create winners and losers. In a more elaborate model, the losers could seek to block the change in convention. Concretely, for the game in Figure 6, let σ_i be the probability that player i plays A in the absence of a convention. If $1/5 < \sigma_i < 4/5$ for both i, then either convention is Pareto superior to no convention and presumably would be supported by both players. But given an A-A (defer to seniors) convention, a move to a B-B convention would be opposed by seniors. Hence a more elaborate model could serve to explain both why conventions form and why, once formed, they are difficult to change. Exploration of this issue is an interesting area for future work.

3.2.4. Artificial Selection

If pure natural selection—random evolution—is not the best description of how cultures arise, perhaps artificial selection is a better one. Consider the following model, which is drawn from Hermalin's (2001) version of Lazear (1998). Consider the games shown in Figures 6 and 7. Suppose that there are two possible preferences (beliefs, mindsets, etc.), A and B. Of these, A is the preference that top management wishes to promote. Assume the organization in question has a continuum of individuals of measure one, $p(t)$ of whom prefer A at time t. At each moment in time, individuals are randomly paired. Let $s \in (0, 1)$ denote top management's effort to promote the adoption of A. Suppose this works to cause a proportion s of B-preferrers paired with A-preferrers to become A-preferrers. Consequently, $dp(t)/dt = sp(t)(1 - p(t))$. Suppose $p(0) = 1/2$; then

$$p(t) = \frac{e^{st}}{1 + e^{st}}.$$

Clearly, $\lim_{t \to \infty} p(t) = 1$—given enough time, almost everyone will wish to play A.

Lazear (1998) posits that management seeks a homogeneous organization (e.g., all A-workers) and chooses (invests) s in such a way to maximize the returns from homogeneity less the cost of investing s. By what mechanisms does management set s? Lazear (1998: 105) offers two answers:

- Let s be the probability that a B-worker who plays against an A-worker is fired and replaced with an A-worker. Investments in human resources that aid in routing out B-workers and identifying A-workers among potential replacements determine s.

- When noncoordination occurs (i.e., an A-worker meets a B-worker), the B-worker thinks "something went wrong here." With probability s, he then recalls the training seminar, the distributed literature, or a motivational speech telling him this is an A organization, which leads him to become an A-worker. The effectiveness of the training seminar, the salience of the literature, and the frequency of speeches determine s.

A third possibility is sanctions: A proportion s of A-workers who play against B-workers feels free to sanction the B-workers they play against with sufficient vehemence that the B-workers switch to being A-workers. Under this interpretation, the encouragement management gives A-workers to sanction B-workers or the severity they permit them to employ determines s.

3.2.5. Culture as Self-Selection

The idea, noted in the previous section, that an organization might select like-minded individuals is an example of a more general view of corporate culture as the outcome of processes that lead to like-minded individuals joining or being selected for the same organization.[59] There is a long tradition in economics of models that predict that people will cluster into homogeneous groupings (e.g., Schelling 1971; Young 2001), and such modeling would seem readily applicable to organizations.

Van den Steen (2005, 2010c) offers one way homogeneous organizations could emerge. Individuals hold differing priors about what is the best technology, strategy, or course of action for a firm to adopt. When individual efforts are complementary and each individual is motivated, in part, by her private assessment of the likelihood of success, then individuals do better, in their expectation, to cluster into organizations of like-minded folks.

Van den Steen's ideas can be partially illustrated as follows. Each firm has two individuals. Firm profit, which is equally divided between the individuals, is $2\theta \min\{e_1, e_2\}$, where θ is a productivity parameter of uncertain value. Let $\hat{\theta}_n$ be individual n's expected value for θ, and assume that all such beliefs are common knowledge.[60] Individual n's expected utility given her beliefs is

$$\hat{\theta}_n \min\{e_n, e_{-n}\} - \frac{e_n^2}{2}.$$

Her best response function is, therefore,

$$BR_n(e_{-n}) = \begin{cases} e_{-n}, & \text{if } \hat{\theta}_n \geq e_{-n} \\ \hat{\theta}_n, & \text{if } \hat{\theta}_n < e_{-n} \end{cases}.$$

It follows that the second-best equilibrium is $e_1 = e_2 = \min\{\hat{\theta}_1, \hat{\theta}_2\}$. If $\hat{\theta}_2 > \hat{\theta}_1$, then individual 2 is unhappy insofar as she believes the firm is squandering $(\hat{\theta}_2 - \hat{\theta}_1)^2$ of potential surplus in expectation.

Suppose there are $K \geq 2$ technologies indexed by k. A k-individual is one who believes that if her firm adopts technology k, its expected θ is $\bar{\theta}$; but that if it adopts another technology, its expected θ is $\underline{\theta} < \bar{\theta}$. Given the previous paragraph's analysis, a k-individual prefers both to work for a firm using the k technology and to have a co-worker who is also a k-individual. Suppose, for simplicity, that there are the same even number of k- and k'-individuals for any k and k'. In equilibrium, each firm will be homogeneous with respect to beliefs about the correct technology to utilize. An outside observer, noting this homogeneity, might ascribe it to indoctrination by the firms, when, in fact, it simply reflects the desire of like-minded individuals to group with one another.

---

59. See Chatman (1991), O'Reilly and Chatman (1996), and Cronqvist et al. (2007) for empirical evidence supporting this view.

60. Again, this assumption raises subtle issues concerning the overall consistency of beliefs. See footnote 46.

Is this intrafirm homogeneity a good thing? To answer this, suppose that the probability that a k-individual is correct is, objectively, $1/K$. Per-firm expected surplus is, therefore,

$$\frac{1}{K}\bar{\theta}^2 + \frac{K-1}{K}(2\underline{\theta}\bar{\theta} - \bar{\theta}^2), \tag{21}$$

given firms with workers holding homogeneous beliefs, that is, in the self-selection equilibrium that would emerge absent any interference. In contrast, if firms were compelled to hire workers holding different beliefs, with equal numbers of firms adopting each of the K technologies, then per-firm expected surplus would be

$$\frac{1}{K}(2\underline{\theta}\bar{\theta} - \underline{\theta}^2) + \frac{K-1}{K}\underline{\theta}^2. \tag{22}$$

Expression (22) less (21) is

$$\frac{K-2}{K}(\bar{\theta} - \underline{\theta})^2 \geq 0. \tag{23}$$

Hence, unless $K = 2$, the population's expected surplus is greater with heterogeneous workplaces than with homogeneous ones.

What should be made of this result? Note, first, that by limiting attention to weakest-link production, the free-riding problem that is endemic to teams problems has been avoided. Were there a teams problem—workers undersupply effort vis-à-vis the first best—then devices that increase their incentives (e.g., working for a firm where they believe $\theta = \bar{\theta}$) could be welfare improving. However, this result is broadly consistent with empirical work on corporate culture (see, e.g., Sørensen 2002). This work suggests that strong culture—homogeneous—firms do less well when there is uncertainty about the environment (e.g., appropriate technology) than do heterogeneous firms. In other words, there is evidence to suggest that the greater is K—here, equivalent to a measure of environmental uncertainty—the worse strong culture firms will do.[61]

In addition, the analysis above presumes that there is no explicit coordination between the individuals. In particular, neither individual is the boss of the other. Most organizations are, however, hierarchical; hence, there is the prospect that one member of the pair has some authority over the other. Van den Steen (2010a,b) explores the effect of authority in settings similar to the one considered above. For instance, following somewhat in the lines of Van den Steen (2010a), suppose that one person in the pair (she) is the boss and can, at personal cost $c > 0$, compel the other person (he) to choose whatever effort she wishes. Suppose the boss believes $\hat{\theta}_B = \bar{\theta}$ and she knows the other person, the worker, believes $\hat{\theta}_W = \underline{\theta}$. From the above analysis, the boss will compel the worker to choose effort equal to $\bar{\theta}$ if

$$\frac{1}{2}(\bar{\theta} - \underline{\theta})^2 > c.$$

61. Another, quasi-biological, explanation for this finding could be that firms are like species. As in biology, the less intraspecies genetic variation (the greater the homogeneity of the employees in terms of knowledge, experience, world view, etc.), the greater a species' risk of decline or extinction should the environment change.

Assume that condition holds. Suppose the two individuals are equally likely to be right in their beliefs. It follows from (23) that there is no expected gain from compulsion, so the expenditure of c is a complete waste in expectation. Of course, if the organization were homogeneous in terms of beliefs, then the boss would have no reason to expend c. Hence, in this simple model, it follows that homogeneity is superior to heterogeneity when one takes into account control costs. More generally, heterogeneity leads to control costs, as those with authority seek to get underlings with different beliefs to line up behind what they believe. If these costs are large, then organizations with greater homogeneity of beliefs (stronger cultures) can outperform those with greater heterogeneity of beliefs (weaker cultures) even when there would otherwise be advantages to "genetic variation."

3.2.6. Shared Knowledge, Language, and Custom

The previous models effectively define corporate culture largely in terms of shared norms (e.g., play A) or shared beliefs. Another aspect of corporate culture is shared knowledge—knowledge of procedures, pertinent facts, goals and objectives, and social structure and personalities.[62] Such shared knowledge is beneficial to a firm insofar as it prevents people from working at cross-purposes, reinventing the wheel, and going up the same blind alleys. It also streamlines communications, because some knowledge can be presumed and not spoken. Of course, if the flip side of shared knowledge is shared ignorance, then there can be a downside, because such firms could be more vulnerable to changes in their environments.

Crémer (1993) and Crémer et al. (2007) consider an aspect of how shared knowledge streamlines communications. Specifically, they look at the value of jargons and technical language in an organization.[63] Organizations and trades tend to develop their own vocabularies, which are often impenetrable by outsiders. For example, The University of California at Berkeley faculty know the meaning of the "words" apee-em, beecee, elleness, and youcop, whereas outsiders typically do not. As an economist, your vocabulary includes ellem, emmar, Pigouvian, and Walrasian.

Crémer (1993) explains the value of language as a coding that saves on transmission costs. Sending a name requires fewer bits than sending a description of what is named. "Penguin," for instance, uses fewer bits than "flightless black-and-white aquatic bird from the southern hemisphere." Of course, at some point, people in an organization have to be taught the definition of names, which entails an upfront cost. If an organization needs to refer to something often enough, the savings on future transmissions makes it profitable to make the upfront expenditure on teaching its name. Infrequently referred-to things are left unnamed.

Crémer et al. (2007) consider efficient coding when there is a limit on how much can be learned. A simplified version of their model will serve to illustrate their main point. Suppose that people can learn only two words, w_1 and w_2. Suppose there are three possible states, x_1, x_2, and x_3, that people in an organization might wish to communicate. One word, say w_1, can be assigned one state and the other word can be assigned two states. Hence, the vocabulary

---

62. Note, though, the overlap with norms and reputations, ingredients of the previous models.

63. Some of their ideas build on Arrow (1974). Other work examining the role of language in economics is Lazear (1999), Rubinstein (2000), and Dewatripont and Tirole (2005). Garicano (2000) looks at the organization of knowledge within organizations.

could be $w_1 \Rightarrow x_1$ and $w_2 \Rightarrow x_2 \lor x_3$. An individual who hears w_2 needs to expend $c > 0$ to determine whether the sender means to refer to state x_2 or x_3. Is this an efficient coding? To answer, we need to know the frequency of the states. Let f_n be the relative frequency of x_n. If $f_1 > \max\{f_2, f_3\}$, then this vocabulary minimizes expected communication cost, which is $(1 - f_1)c$; otherwise, if $f_1 < \max\{f_2, f_3\}$, another vocabulary would be more efficient. In general, the precise term—the word that refers to one state—should refer to the most frequent state and the broader term—the word that refers to two states—should refer to the less-frequent states. As Crémer et al. show, this logic extends to more words and more states; in an optimal code, broader words describe less-frequent states.

As normative models of coding, the logic of this work is irrefutable. As positive models, however, they are less convincing. It is clear from any book on the subject (e.g., McWhorter 2001; Deutscher 2005) that languages evolve in an unplanned manner. One of the drivers of this evolution is a tendency of speakers (and, to an extent, writers) to economize for their private benefit (see Deutscher 2005: 73–114). That it is a private benefit is illustrated when 2nite u get txt msg from ur teen—she will spend less time typing it than if she were to spell out every word, but it will take you longer to decipher it than if she would. However, if u get enuf txt msgs, then you will become as adept at reading them as standard English, so total communication time (yours and your daughter's) will clearly fall. In this sense, then, Crémer (1993) reflects an aspect of reality: senders economize for private reasons; receivers, if they interact repeatedly with the same senders, as in an organization, become adept at understanding the senders' shorthand lingo and terse messaging. Total communication cost—in terms of time—is reduced.

An idea that has not received attention is how culture permits the creation of jargon. If the message sender believes she shares knowledge with the receiver, then she is more likely to believe her linguistic economizings will be understood by the receiver. For instance, consider the sentence, "The dean of 'elleness' is likely to be the new provost." Even if you do not immediately know what "elleness" means, your immersion in the culture of academia allows you to deduce its meaning: (i) deans head colleges; (ii) elleness must be a college; (iii) "elleness" resembles the abbreviation "L&S"; (iv) in academia, particularly in reference to colleges, "L" often abbreviates "letters" and "S" "science" or "sciences"; (v) therefore, the sentence means the dean of the College of Letters and Science(s) is expected to be the next provost. In other words, much of our vocabulary is learned through the context in which we hear new words, and thus, whether jargon or neologisms spread depends on whether listeners grasp the context of conversations (i.e., their level of acculturation).

Economizing is not the only force that influences the evolution of language. Another important influence is the tendency of people to employ metaphors and similes (Deutscher 2005: especially 144–170). Metaphors and similes rely on shared knowledge. Suppose, for example, that Robin is known to be forgetful. When another person forgets something, a third person might quip, "You're acting like Robin." As that quip becomes stale, it may evolve and be economized (Deutscher 2005: 115–143), becoming "that's a Robin" or "he Robined that meeting." Through this process, the in-house verb meaning to forget could end up "to Robin." There are two points to this example: (i) observe that in-house slang and jargon can often arise not to streamline communications—"you're forgetful" is shorter than "you're acting like Robin"—but out of the universal tendency to use metaphors and similes, and (ii) such slang and jargon are at least as much a product of the culture as they are definers of the culture. In fact, slang and jargon could arise from people's desire to prove they are plugged into the culture (e.g., know Robin's reputation).[64] A related point is that the use of slang and jargon could serve to maintain group integrity, to help distinguish in-group from out-group, and this could be its purpose as much as streamlining communication (on the use of customs to distinguish in-group from out-group see, e.g., Harris 1978).

Weber and Camerer (2003) present an experimental study of culture formation, specifically, of jargon. In the experiment, each subject privately views a fixed and common set of 16 pictures showing office environments. The pictures are distinct but share common elements. Pairs of subjects played together as "firms." In each round of the experiment, the subject serving as a firm's "manager" for that round had, through the descriptions she offered, to get her partner, the "employee," to select eight of the 16 pictures in an order specific to that round. For example, imagining the 16 pictures as being indexed in a fixed manner, the manager might be required in a given round to get her employee to pick, in order, 5, 2, 6, 4, 3, 1, 14, and 12. The subjects' payoff per round was a function of how fast they completed the task. Because they received more the faster they completed the task, the pressure to economize on language was especially strong.

Consistent with the ideas in Crémer (1993), subjects develop names for the pictures. An example of such evolution is the following:

> one pair of subjects began by referring to a particular picture as: "The one with three people: two men and one woman. The woman is sitting on the left. They're all looking at two computers that look like they have some PowerPoint graphs or charts. The two men are wearing ties and the woman has short, blond hair. . . . " After several rounds, this [pair's] description of this picture was condensed to simply "PowerPoint." [Weber and Camerer 2003: 408]

Also consistent with the idea that language becomes idiosyncratic to firms, another pair named this picture "guy hunching" and yet another "woman sitting, smiling." Note, however, in contrast to a model of fully rational language or coding, the names could have been shorter (e.g., "charts," "hunch(er)," "woman who sits, smiles," respectively). In addition, there is evidence of metaphors and similes: one pair named a picture "Uday Rao" because of the similarity between a figure in that picture and a well-known professor of that name.

3.3. The Directive versus Internalization Debate

One question in the study of corporate culture is whether individuals adhere to the prevalent culture because it is rational for them to do so (e.g., it is a Nash equilibrium; as in Kreps 1990) or because they truly believe in the culture and adherence is almost instinctual (e.g., somewhat as in Van den Steen 2010c). This is sometimes referred to as the "directive versus internalization debate."

---

64. Sometimes the jargon outlasts its cause: we use the "cc" line in our emails, even though no carbon paper is involved; a committee on which I serve makes much use of the red and burgundy books, although neither has been a physical book with a colored cover since well before any member of the committee began his or her service; and so forth.

Not surprisingly, given neoclassical economics' reliance on the rational-actor paradigm, most economic work on culture falls into the directive camp (e.g., Crémer 1986, 1993; Kreps 1990; Young 1993, 1998). Even when the actors are not fully rational, fail to foresee contingencies, or engage in adaptive learning, their motive to adhere to the culture is strategic rather than intrinsic.[65] The work of Van den Steen and, depending on interpretation, Lazear (1998) are exceptions: some beliefs and behavior are intrinsic.

One might imagine that evidence of adherence to norms that are irrational would provide the internalization side with compelling evidence. Fair play in dictator and ultimatum games (for discussions, see Rabin 1993, 1998) would suggest that people have internalized a fairness norm. Yet, as Sugden (1985) notes in his critique of Jones (1984), in real-life, nonexperimental settings, one often observes sanctioning mechanisms lurking in the background when there is conformism to norms. Evidence from biology is also less than clear-cut: on the one hand, chimpanzees seem to abide by hierarchical norms, yet on the other, they also scheme in various ways against them (de Waal 1998). As noted earlier, some view the evolutionary advantage of a large hominoid brain in terms of its usefulness for strategizing against your social group (Sapolsky 2005).

A personal experience may help convince you that witnessing norm violation can create a visceral reaction: In the early 1990s, Berkeley was plagued(?) by people walking about naked in public. The first time I saw a naked woman walking down the street toward me, the sense of shock was palpable—I felt as if I'd been hit in the chest.[66] A visceral reaction or acting in an emotionally hot state can lead to actions that the actor would consider irrational in an emotionally cool state.[67] Consequently, such reactions could lead people to carry out sanctions against norm violaters that are not in their rational self-interest, even in a repeated-game setting.

To be speculative, a possible synthesis of the directive versus internalization debate is that norm adherence or violation is directive (strategic), but sanctioning norm violaters is internalized. Evolutionarily, it would seem advantageous to be committed to punish those who harm you (i.e., violate norms), as this serves as an effective deterrent against others, but to be flexible yourself as to whether you adhere to norms, as this allows you an opportunity to gain advantage (e.g., seize a mating opportunity even if you aren't the dominant male). Like any reductionist argument, exceptions exist. It is difficult to explain tipping at restaurants we will never visit again or not stealing when detection is impossible without some sense that adherence to (some) norms is internalized. Conversely, long-term (strategic) considerations often allow us to calm ourselves and forgive norm transgressors.

4. Conclusion

Throughout this chapter, I have sought to flag areas that strike me as ripe for future work. In addition to those, let me conclude by listing a few more.

65. The same schism exists in the leadership literature: Hermalin (1998) and its extensions are rational-actor models, whereas Rotemberg and Saloner (1993, 1998), Huck and Rey-Biel (2006), and Blanes i Vidal and Möller (2007) presume some degree of norm internalization.

66. Although it may reflect poorly on me, the reaction was definitely shock and not arousal.

67. Some economic work on the role of emotions in decisionmaking includes Loewenstein (1996, 2000), MacLeod (1996), Loewenstein and O'Donaghue (2005), and Hermalin and Isen (2008).

- *The interaction between leadership and corporate culture.* In particular, how do leaders shape culture? Is a strong leader essential or detrimental to a strong culture? Does a strong culture make a leader more or less effective (does *asabîyah* apply in corporations)?

- *The time path of cultures.* What are the evolutionary forces that lead cultures to change? Are cultures self-sustaining? Do they erode absent intervention?

- *The emergence of leaders.* How do would-be leaders compete to become the leader? How do followers choose among competing leaders? When do leadership battles lead to organizational schisms?

- *The interaction between leaders and followers' affective states.* How, for instance, do leaders boost morale and affect the emotional states of their followers?

- *The role of emotions in organizations.* How do emotions govern norm adherence and the sanctioning of norm violation? To what extent do cultures rely on and exploit emotional needs?

Even if this chapter fails to inspire you to engage in such work, it should enrich your understanding of organizations by illustrating the power and importance of the informal aspects of organization, such as leadership and corporate culture. Leadership is critical if managers and officers are to be effective in their jobs. Corporate culture is a vital component in the control of organizations and with respect to organizational efficiency.

REFERENCES

Akerlof, George A., and Rachel E. Kranton. 2005. "Identity and the Economics of Organizations." *Journal of Economic Perspectives* 19(1): 9–32.

Andreoni, James. 2006. "Leadership Giving in Charitable Fund-Raising." *Journal of Public Economic Theory* 8: 1–22.

Arrow, Kenneth J. 1974. *The Limits of Organization.* New York: W. W. Norton and Co.

Aumann, Robert J. 1998. "Common Priors: A Reply to Gul." *Econometrica* 66: 929–938.

Baker, George, Robert Gibbons, and Kevin J. Murphy. 1994. "Subjective Performance Measures in Optimal Incentive Contracts." *Quarterly Journal of Economics* 109: 1125–1156.

Banerjee, Abhijit V. 1992. "A Simple Model of Herd Behavior." *Quarterly Journal of Economics* 108: 797–818.

Becker, Howard. 1963. *Outsiders: Studies in the Sociology of Deviance.* New York: Free Press.

Bennis, Warren G. 1989 *On Becoming a Leader.* Reading, MA: Addison-Wesley.

Bertrand, Marianne, and Antoinette Schoar. 2003. "Managing with Style: The Effect of Managers on Firm Policies." *Quarterly Journal of Economics* 118: 1169–1208.

Bikhchandani, Sushil, David Hirshleifer, and Ivo Welch. 1992. "A Theory of Fads, Fashion, Custom, and Cultural Changes as Informational Cascades." *Journal of Political Economy* 100: 992–1026.

Blanes i Vidal, Jordi, and Marc Möller. 2007. "When Should Leaders Share Information with Their Subordinates?" *Journal of Economics and Management Strategy* 16: 251–283.

Bolton, Patrick, Markus K. Brunnermeier, and Laura Veldkamp. 2007. "Leadership, Coordination, and Mission-Driven Management." Working paper, Columbia University, New York.

———. 2010. "Economists' Perspective on Leadership," in Nitin Nohria and Rakesh Khurana (eds.), *Handbook of Leadership Theory and Practice.* Boston: Harvard Business School Publishing, pp. 239–264.

Bondanella, Peter, and Mark Musa. 1979. *The Portable Machiavelli.* New York: Penguin.

Bowles, Samuel, and Herbert Gintis. 2004. "Persistent Parochialism: Trust and Exclusion in Ethnic Networks." *Journal of Economic Behavior and Organization* 55: 1–23.

Brown, Lesley (ed.). 1993. *The New Shorter Oxford English Dictionary*, Vol. 1. Oxford: Clarendon Press.

Burns, James MacGregor. 1978. *Leadership*. New York: Harper and Row.

Camerer, Colin, and Dan Lovallo. 1999. "Overconfidence and Excess Entry: An Experimental Approach." *American Economic Review* 89: 306–318.

Carillo, Juan D., and Denis Gromb. 1999. "On the Strength of Corporate Cultures." *European Economic Review* 43: 1021–1037.

Chamley, Christophe P. 2004. *Rational Herds: Economic Models of Social Learning*. Cambridge: Cambridge University Press.

Charness, Gary, Luca Rigotti, and Aldo Rustichini. 2007. "Individual Behavior and Group Membership." *American Economic Review* 97: 1340–1352.

Chatman, Jennifer A. 1991. "Matching People and Organizations: Selection and Socialization in Public Accounting Firms." *Administrative Science Quarterly* 36: 459–484.

Cho, In-Koo, and David Kreps. 1987. "Signaling Games and Stable Equilibria." *Quarterly Journal of Economics* 102: 179–222.

Crémer, Jacques. 1986. "Cooperation in Ongoing Organizations." *Quarterly Journal of Economics* 101: 33–50.

———. 1993. "Corporate Culture and Shared Knowledge." *Industrial and Corporate Change* 2: 351–386.

Crémer, Jacques, Luis Garicano, and Andrea Prat. 2007. "Language and the Theory of the Firm." *Quarterly Journal of Economics* 122: 373–407.

Cronqvist, Henrik, Angie Low, and Mattias Nilsson. 2007. "Does Corporate Culture Matter for Firm Policies?" Working paper, Ohio State University, Columbus.

de Waal, Frans. 1998. *Chimpanzee Politics: Power and Sex among Apes,* revised edition. Baltimore: Johns Hopkins University Press.

Dekel, Eddie, and Elchanan Ben-Porath. 1992. "Signaling Future Actions and the Potential for Sacrifice." *Journal of Economic Theory* 57: 36–51.

Deutscher, Guy. 2005. *The Unfolding of Language: An Evolutionary Tour of Mankind's Greatest Invention*. New York: Owl Books.

Dewatripont, Mathias, and Jean Tirole. 2005. "Modes of Communication." *Journal of Political Economy* 113: 1217–1238.

Edlin, Aaron S., and Benjamin E. Hermalin. 2001. "Implementing the First Best in an Agency Relationship with Renegotiation: A Corrigendum." *Econometrica* 69: 1391–1395.

Erikson, Kai T. 1966. *Wayward Puritans*. New York: John Wiley and Sons.

Ferris, Gerald R., and John A. Wagner. 1985. "Quality Circles in the United States: A Conceptual Reevaluation." *Journal of Applied Behavioral Science* 21: 155–167.

Friedman, Richard Elliott. 1997. *Who Wrote the Bible?* New York: Harper Collins.

Fudenberg, Drew, and David K. Levine. 1998. *The Theory of Learning in Games*. Cambridge, MA: MIT Press.

Gächter, Simon, and Elke Renner. 2003. "Leading by Example in the Presence of Free Rider Incentives." Working paper, Universität Erfurt, Erfurt, Germany.

Gächter, Simon, Daniele Nosenzo, Elke Renner, and Martin Sefton. 2010. "Who Makes a Good Leader? Cooperativeness, Optimism, and Leading-by-Example." *Economic Inquiry,* 2010. Published online.

Garicano, Luis. 2000. "Hierarchies and Organization of Knowledge in Production." *Journal of Political Economy* 108: 874–904.

Gerth, Hans H., and C. Wright Mills. 1946. *From Max Weber: Essays in Sociology*. New York: Oxford University Press.

Goffman, Erving. 1963. *Stigma: Notes on the Management of Spoiled Identity*. Englewood Cliffs, NJ: Prentice-Hall.

Goodall, Amanda H., Lawrence M. Kahn, and Andrew J. Oswald. 2011. "Why Do Leaders Matter? A Study of Expert Knowledge in a Superstar Setting." *Journal of Economic Behavior and Organization* 77: 265–284.

Goode, William J. 1978. *The Celebration of Heroes: Prestige as a Control System*. Berkeley: University of California Press.

Gul, Faruk. 1998. "A Comment on Aumann's Bayesian View." *Econometrica* 66: 923–927.

Handy, Charles. 1993. *Understanding Organizations*. Oxford: Oxford University Press.

Harris, Marvin. 1978. *Cows, Pigs, Wars, and Witches*. New York: Vintage.

Heifetz, Ronald A. 1994. *Leadership without Easy Answers*. Cambridge, MA: Belknap Press of Harvard University Press.

Hermalin, Benjamin E. 1998. "Toward an Economic Theory of Leadership: Leading by Example." *American Economic Review* 88: 1188–1206.

———. 2001. "Economics and Corporate Culture," in Cary L. Cooper, Sue Cartwright, and P. Christopher Earley (eds.), *The International Handbook of Organizational Culture and Climate*. Chichester, England: John Wiley and Sons, pp. 217–261.

———. 2007. "Leading for the Long Term." *Journal of Economic Behavior and Organization* 62: 1–19.

———. 2008. "Vague Terms: Contracting when Precision in Terms Is Infeasible." *Journal of Institutional and Theoretical Economics* 164: 76–94.

Hermalin, Benjamin E., and Alice M. Isen. 2008. "A Model of the Effect of Affect on Economic Decision Making." *Quantitative Marketing and Economics* 6: 17–40.

Hermalin, Benjamin E., and Michael L. Katz. 1991. "Moral Hazard and Verifiability: The Effects of Renegotiation in Agency." *Econometrica* 59: 1735–1753.

Hermalin, Benjamin E., Larry Li, and Tony Naughton. 2012. "The Welfare Consequences of Legal System Improvement." Working paper, University of California, Berkeley.

Holmström, Bengt. 1982. "Moral Hazard in Teams." *Bell Journal of Economics* 13: 324–340.

House, Robert J., and Mary L. Baetz. 1979. "Leadership: Some Empirical Generalizations and New Research Directions." in Barry M. Staw (ed.), *Research in Organizational Behavior,* Volume 1. Greenwich, CT: JAI Press.

Huck, Steffen, and Pedro Rey-Biel. 2006. "Endogenous Leadership in Teams." *Journal of Institutional and Theoretical Economics* 162: 253–261.

Ibn Khaldūn. 2004. *The Muqaddimah: An Introduction to History*. Translated and introduced by Franz Rosenthal. Edited and abridged by N. J. Dawood. Princeton, NJ: Princeton University Press.

Jones, Stephen R.G. 1984. *The Economics of Conformism*. Oxford: Basil Blackwell.

Kandel, Eugene, and Edward P. Lazear. 1992. "Peer Pressure and Partnerships." *Journal of Political Economy* 100: 801–817.

Kandori, Michihiro. 1992. "Social Norms and Community Enforcement." *Review of Economic Studies* 59: 63–80.

Katz, Michael L., and Carl Shapiro. 1986. "Technology Adoption in the Presence of Network Externalities." *Journal of Political Economy* 94: 822–841.

Kobayashi, Hajime, and Hideo Suehiro. 2005. "Emergence of Leadership in Teams." *Japanese Economic Review* 56: 295–316.

Komai, Mana, and Mark Stegeman. 2010. "Leadership Based on Asymmetric Information." *RAND Journal of Economics* 41: 35–63.

Komai, Mana, Mark Stegeman, and Benjamin E. Hermalin. 2007. "Leadership and Information." *American Economic Review* 97: 944–947.

Kotter, John P. 1996. *Leading Change*. Boston: Harvard Business School Press.

Kotter, John P., and James L. Heskett. 1992. *Corporate Culture and Performance*. New York: Free Press.

Kouzes, James M., and Barry Z. Posner. 1987. *The Leadership Challenge*. San Francisco: Jossey-Bass.

Kreps, David M. 1990. "Corporate Culture and Economic Theory," in James E. Alt and Kenneth A. Shepsle (eds.), *Perspectives on Positive Political Economy*. Cambridge: Cambridge University Press, pp. 90–143.

———. 1997. "Intrinsic Motivation and Extrinsic Incentives." *American Economic Review* 87: 359–364.

Kvaløy, Ola, and Trond E. Olsen. 2009. "Endogenous Verifiability and Relational Contracting." *American Economic Review* 99: 2193–2208.

Langevoort, Donald C. 2006. "Opening the Black Box of 'Corporate Culture' in Law and Economics." *Journal of Institutional and Theoretical Economics* 162: 80–96.

Lazear, Edward P. 1998. "Hiring Risky Workers," in Isao Ohashi and Toshiaki Tachibanaki (eds.), *Internal Labour Markets, Incentives, and Employment*. New York: St. Martin's Press.

———. 1999. "Culture and Language." *Journal of Political Economy* 107(Part 2: Symposium on the Economic Analysis of Social Behavior in Honor of Gary S. Becker): S95–S126.

Loewenstein, George. 1996. "Out of Control: Visceral Influences on Behavior." *Organizational Behavior and Human Decision Processes* 65: 272–292.

———. 2000. "Emotions in Economic Theory and Economic Behavior." *American Economic Review* 90: 426–432.

Loewenstein, George, and Ted O'Donaghue. 2005. "Animal Spirits: Affective and Deliberative Processes in Economic Behavior." Working paper, Cornell University, Ithaca, NY.

Lohéac, Youenn. 2005. "To Lead or to Follow? Popularity and Adolescents' Behaviors." Working paper, École Supérieure de Commerce Bretagne Brest, Brest, France.

MacLeod, W. Bentley. 1996. "Decision, Contract, and Emotion: Some Economics for a Complex and Confusing World." *Canadian Journal of Economics* 29: 788–810.

———. 2007. "Reputations, Relationships, and Contract Enforcement." *Journal of Economic Literature* 45: 595–628.

Malmendier, Ulrike, and Geoffrey Tate. 2005. "CEO Overconfidence and Corporate Investment." *Journal of Finance* 60: 2661–2700.

McFarland, David. 1999. *Animal Behaviour,* third edition. Harlow, England: Longman.

McGregor, Douglas. 1966. *Leadership and Motivation*. Cambridge, MA: MIT Press.

McWhorter, John. 2001. *The Power of Babel*. New York: Perennial.

Meidinger, Claude, and Marie-Claire Villeval. 2002. "Leadership in Teams: Signaling or Reciprocating?" Working paper, Université Lumière Lyon 2.

Morita, Hodaka. 2001. "Choice of Technology and Labour Market Consequences: An Explanation of U.S.-Japanese Differences." *Economic Journal* 111: 29–50.

Okuno-Fujiwara, Masahiro. 1994. "The Economic System of Contemporary Japan: Its Structure and Possibility of Change." *Japanese Economic Studies* 22: 76–98.

O'Reilly, Charles, and Jennifer A. Chatman. 1996. "Culture as Social Control: Corporations, Cults, and Commitment." in Barry M. Staw and L. L. Cummings (eds.), *Research in Organizational Behavior,* Volume 18. Greenwich, CT: JAI Press, pp. 157–200.

Pandya, Mukul, Robbie Shell, Susan Warner, Sandeep Junnarkar, and Jeffrey Brown. *Lasting Leadership: What You Can Learn from the Top 25 Business People of Our Times*. Philadelphia: Wharton School Publishing.

Payne, Roy L. 2001. "A Three Dimensional Framework for Analyzing and Assessing Culture/Climate and its Relevance to Cultural Change," in Cary L. Cooper, Sue Cartwright, and P. Christopher

Earley (eds.), *The International Handbook of Organizational Culture and Climate.* Chichester, England: John Wiley and Sons, pp. 107–122.

Peters, R. S. 1967. "Authority." in Anthony Quinton (ed.), *Political Philosophy.* Oxford Readings in Philosophy. Oxford: Oxford University Press, pp. 83–96.

Pfeffer, Jeffrey. 1981. "Management as Symbolic Action: The Creation and Maintenance of Organizational Paradigms," in L. L. Cummings and Barry M. Staw (eds.), *Research in Organizational Behavior,* Volume 3. Greenwich, CT: JAI Press, pp. 1–52.

Potters, Jan, Martin Sefton, and Lise Vesterlund. 2005. "After You—Endogenous Sequencing in Voluntary Contribution Games." *Journal of Public Economics* 89: 1399–1419.

———. 2007. "Leading-by-Example and Signaling in Voluntary Contribution Games: An Experimental Study." *Economic Theory* 33: 169–182.

Rabin, Matthew. 1993. "Incorporating Fairness into Game Theory and Economics." *American Economic Review* 83: 1281–1302.

———. 1998. "Psychology and Economics." *Journal of Economic Literature* 36: 11–46.

Rob, Rafael, and Peter Zemsky. 2002. "Social Capital, Corporate Culture, and Incentive Intensity." *RAND Journal of Economics* 33: 243–257.

Rotemberg, Julio J., and Garth Saloner. 1993. "Leadership Style and Incentives." *Management Science* 39: 1299–1318.

———. 1998. "Visionaries, Managers, and Strategic Direction." Working paper, Stanford Graduate School of Business, Stanford, CA.

Rubinstein, Ariel. 2000. *Economics and Language.* Cambridge: Cambridge University Press.

Sapolsky, Robert M. 2005. *Monkeyluv.* New York: Scribner.

Schein, Edgar H. 1992. *Organizational Culture and Leadership,* second edition. San Francisco: Jossey-Bass.

Schelling, Thomas C. 1971. "Dynamic Models of Segregation." *Journal of Mathematical Sociology* 1: 143–186.

Schmidt, Klaus M., and Monika Schnitzer. 1995. "The Interaction of Explicit and Implicit Contracts." *Economic Letters* 48: 193–199.

Selznick, Philip. 1984. *Leadership in Administration: A Sociological Interpretation.* Berkeley: University of California Press.

Sidanius, Jim, and Felicia Pratto. 1999. *Social Dominance.* Cambridge: Cambridge University Press.

Smith, Lones, and Peter Sørensen. 2000. "Pathological Outcomes of Observational Learning." *Econometrica* 68: 371–398.

Sørensen, Jesper. 2002. "The Strength of Corporate Culture and the Reliability of Firm Performance." *Administrative Science Quarterly* 47: 70–91.

Sparrow, Paul R. 2001. "Developing Diagnostics for High Performance Organization Cultures," in Cary L. Cooper, Sue Cartwright, and P. Christopher Earley (eds.), *The International Handbook of Organizational Culture and Climate.* Chichester, England: John Wiley and Sons, pp. 85–106.

Spence, A. Michael. 1973. "Job Market Signaling." *Quarterly Journal of Economics* 87: 355–374.

Sugden, Robert. 1985. " 'The Economics of Conformism' by Stephen R. G. Jones." *Economic Journal* 95: 502–504.

Tackney, Charles T. 2001. "The Modes of Social Relation in Japanese Management Practice," in Cary L. Cooper, Sue Cartwright, and P. Christopher Earley (eds.), *The International Handbook of Organizational Culture and Climate.* Chichester, England: John Wiley and Sons, pp. 377–390.

Van den Steen, Eric. 2005. "Organizational Beliefs and Managerial Vision." *Journal of Law, Economics, and Organization* 21: 256–283.

———. 2010a. "Culture Clash: The Costs and Benefits of Homogeneity." *Management Science* 56: 1718–1738.

Van den Steen, Eric. 2010b. "Interpersonal Authority in a Theory of the Firm." *American Economic Review* 100: 466–490.

———. 2010c. "On the Origin of Shared Beliefs (and Corporate Culture)." *RAND Journal of Economics* 41: 617–648.

Van Huyck, John B., Raymond C. Battalio, and Richard O. Beil. 1990. "Tacit Coordination Games, Strategic Uncertainty, and Coordination Failure." *American Economic Review* 80: 234–248.

Varian, Hal. R. 1994. "Sequential Contributions to Public Goods." *Journal of Public Economics* 53: 165–186.

Vesterlund, Lise. 2003. "The Informational Value of Sequential Fundraising." *Journal of Public Economics* 87: 627–657.

Weber, Roberto A., Colin F. Camerer, Yuval Rottenstreich, and Marc Knez. 2001. "The Illusion of Leadership: Misattribution of Cause in Coordination Games." *Organization Science* 12: 582–598.

Weber, Roberto A., and Colin F. Camerer. 2003. "Cultural Conflict and Merger Failure: An Experimental Approach." *Management Science* 49: 400–415.

Wiseman, Rosalind. 2003. *Queen Bees and Wannabees*. London: Piatkus Books.

Wouk, Herman. 1951. *The Caine Mutiny*. Garden City, NY: Doubleday.

Wrong, Dennis H. 1995. *Power: Its Forms, Bases, and Uses*. London: Transaction.

Young, H. Peyton. 1993. "The Evolution of Conventions." *Econometrica* 61: 57–84.

———. 1998. *Individual Strategy and Social Structure*. Princeton, NJ: Princeton University Press.

———. 2001. "The Dynamics of Conformity," in Steven N. Durlauf and H. Peyton Young (eds.), *Social Dynamics*. Cambridge, MA: MIT Press, pp. 133–153.

Zhou, Junjie. 2011. "Economics of Leadership and Hierarchy." Working paper, University of California, Berkeley.

Zupan, Mark. 2010. "An Economic Perspective on Leadership," in Nitin Nohria and Rakesh Khurana (eds.), *Handbook of Leadership Theory and Practice*. Boston: Harvard Business School Publishing, pp. 265–290.

12

Personnel Economics

Edward P. Lazear and Paul Oyer

1. Introduction

Personnel economics is the application of economic and mathematical approaches to traditional topics in the study of human resource management. This includes such topics as compensation, turnover, and incentives that are inherently economic, as well as those that do not at first appear to be economic topics (e.g., norms, teamwork, worker empowerment, and peer relationships). Using the tools from advances in game theory, information economics, econometrics, and other areas of economics, personnel economics has come a long way over the past few decades. It now produces a large share of the labor economics literature, has earned its own code in the *Journal of Economic Literature* classification system (M5), and has its own working group in the National Bureau of Economic Research. In this chapter, we review how this literature has developed and discuss some avenues for fruitful future research.

Personnel economics provides both positive and normative analyses of human resource practices and methods. On the positive (or descriptive) side, we study a range of questions. When do firms choose to use one form of compensation over another? When are teams important? How do firms find the right workers? When are certain benefits or stock grants given to workers? The list extends to any decision an employer has to make with respect to its dealings with employees. That is, personnel economics attempts to describe how human resource practices can best address an employer's goals, subject to the constraint that employee actions will be affected by those practices.

Perhaps because the subject was taken up by business school economists, whose job it is to teach managers what to do, personnel economics has not shied away from being somewhat prescriptive. Several MBA textbooks and numerous MBA classes that are either focused on personnel economics or cover it as part of a broader subject deliver research findings to current

We thank the editors of this volume, Robert Gibbons and John Roberts; James Malcomson; Bentley MacLeod; Scott Schaefer; Michael Waldman; Jan Zábojník; and participants in the *Handbook of Organizational Economics* 2006 conference for comments.

and future managers.[1] In many ways, the basic outlines and topics of this chapter are similar to the syllabi for the MBA classes we teach at Stanford (though the details are very different). Given the importance of human resources to many organizations' success and the fact that labor accounts for the majority of business costs, bringing research findings to managers can have an important effect.

In this review, we introduce the key topics of personnel economics. We also focus on some relatively new findings that have emerged since prior reviews of some or all of the personnel economics literature, such as Gibbons and Waldman (1999), Lazear (1999, 2000b), Malcomson (1999), Murphy (1999), and Prendergast (1999). Throughout the discussion and in the conclusion, we suggest open questions where future research can make valuable contributions to the literature.

Personnel economics research has focused on five aspects of employment relationships: incentives, matching firms with workers, compensation, skill development, and the organization of work. Though some research focuses on only one of these, much of the literature touches on multiple aspects of jobs. For example, incentives have an effect on which workers accept positions, and the organization of the workplace depends on the skills a firm develops (or selects for). Nonetheless, these five areas of employment relationships allow for a broad categorization of research in personnel economics. So we explore each of these in turn, reviewing the main theories, empirical tests of those theories, and the open questions in each area.

Before proceeding, it is worth briefly noting what personal economics is *not*. Personnel economics is a branch of labor economics, but there is a great deal of labor economics that is not personnel economics. Studies that do not consider interactions between a firm and its workers or that do not explicitly or implicitly consider a firm trying to maximize some objective (usually profits) are not personnel economics. Many findings in labor economics are important conceptual or empirical inputs to, but not part of, personnel economics. For example, labor economists estimate Mincer-ian earnings functions of the returns to experience and the return to schooling, and they estimate labor supply functions. Although these equilibrium outcomes are very important issues to firms designing personnel policies, they are not strategic choices of the firm. Similarly, most personnel economics is not policy oriented. Personnel economics models typically focus on welfare within a given employment relationship rather than on the overall social welfare function. In the absence of a market failure, firms' best interests will be the same as those of the economy as a whole. Although there are some exceptions (e.g., policy and personnel economics influence one another in the study of workplace discrimination), the main contributions of personnel economics to social welfare are in research advances and helping managers to run their businesses more efficiently rather than in influencing policymakers' decisions.

2. Incentives

Firms and employees naturally have opposing interests in that employee effort typically leads to benefits to the firm and costs to the employee. However, there can be gains from trade if the value to employers is enough to compensate workers for the cost of their effort. Encouraging employee effort is a central issue in personnel economics and, as with much of economics, has

---

1. A recent paper by Bloom and Van Reenen (2007) suggests that managers can benefit from using modern managerial practices, including some specific practices studied in personnel economics.

led to a large literature on incentives. When effort is contractible, providing efficient incentives is trivial. But in the more realistic case where there is hidden action (moral hazard), one of the keys to successful personnel practices is to design incentives for employees.

When effort is not contractible, one potential way (though not the only way) to obtain the socially efficient level of worker effort is to pay the worker the full value of output—that is, sell the firm to the worker. The firm could set a base salary to meet the worker's participation constraint and let the worker keep all the marginal fruits of his effort. The base salary will need to be negative—that is, the worker will pay the firm for the right to work there—for the firm to find the employment arrangement profitable. In other words, moral hazard problems can be solved by making employees the residual claimants on their effort. If individuals own all their output, they will efficiently match the marginal benefits of their effort to the marginal cost.

There are employment arrangements that involve selling the firm to the worker (e.g., taxi drivers who rent cabs for a shift and keep all fares), but these jobs are exceptions. Why does this simple model fail for the vast majority of workers who have positive base wages and piece rates of less than one (and usually zero)? There are many reasons, but they generally relate to the facts that worker output (i.e., measures of the worker's productivity) is imperfectly related to inputs (i.e., the worker's effort), that firms cannot always credibly commit to reward effort ex post, and that individuals are typically more risk averse than employers.

2.1. The Trade-off between Risk and Incentives

Most theoretical principal-agent models assume that output is an increasing function of effort and that it is also influenced by some unobservable random shock.[2] The employee's utility is decreasing and concave in effort (i.e., her disutility of effort is positive and convex). Because she is risk averse, utility is increasing and concave in income. The complication, which makes it impossible to simply pay the agent for her inputs, is that the principal can only observe the output measure, so this is the only variable on which compensation contracts can be based. If the two parties could write enforceable contracts based on effort, the problem would be simple. The risk-neutral firm would simply pay for effort, and the agent would be completely insured.

The problem for the principal is to set the compensation scheme to maximize profit subject to incentive compatibility and participation constraints. A key implication is that there is now a trade-off between insurance and incentives. Because workers do not like risk, the firm must dampen the relation of wages to output. If compensation is based largely on output, the firm may have to provide substantial risk compensation. But if compensation is not based on output, workers will put forth little effort. The second-best solution, though the "best" compromise, forces the worker to bear risk and provides the firm with an inefficient amount of effort.

This model has two key predictions. First, the stronger the incentives are, the harder the employee will work. As we discuss below, there is ample empirical evidence to suggest that this relationship holds in most employment relationships. Second, there is a trade-off between risk and incentives. Everything else equal, in settings where factors beyond the employee's control

---

2. See Prendergast (1999) for a somewhat more detailed description of moral hazard theory. See Johnson (1950) and Cheung (1969) for important early compensation analyses from the agricultural economics literature and Ross (1973), Mirrlees (1974), Stiglitz (1975), Bergson (1978), and Holmström (1979) for early modern treatments of the moral hazard problem.

have a relatively large effect on output, incentives will be weaker. As we also discuss below, the empirical evidence on this linkage is decidedly mixed (probably at least partially due to an inability to make "everything else equal").

2.1.1. Distortions in Performance Measures

Imperfections in performance measurement can lead firms to limit the use of incentives, even when employees are risk neutral. In addition to exogenous shocks to output measures, the usefulness of a performance measure may also be limited by employees having private information or by their ability to influence the measure without actually advancing the principal's goals.

Gibbons (1987) considers the case where only the worker knows the difficulty of the job and only the worker knows his true action. Under these circumstances, Gibbons shows that workers will restrict output (i.e., there will be a "ratchet effect") when the firm cannot commit not to use information it learns about the difficulty of the task. He argues that this effect contributed to the decline of piece rate systems, which were extensively used at the end of the nineteenth century.

Another class of models considers the implications of employees who can affect the output measure differently from their effect on actual output. Lazear (1986a) briefly discussed the implications for incentives and performance measurement when workers can increase quantity at the expense of quality. Baker (1992) provides a more general model of a firm that wants to maximize some noncontractible objective (call it V). The firm can write compensation contracts based on P, which is imperfectly correlated with V. The employee has private information about how her actions affect both P and V. The firm wants to provide incentives so that the employee will exert more effort, but it has to trade this off against the possibility that the employee may exert effort when that effort has a large effect on P but not on V. That is, the firm has to worry about the fact that incentives drive efficient effort and gaming at the same time.

Holmström and Milgrom (1991) explore the limits of measurement from a slightly different perspective. They derive a multitasking model where an employee engages in two tasks that affect actual output and measured output differently. Incentive contracts may drive the employee to underinvest or overinvest in one or both tasks. They discuss how this process may explain the limits of incentive pay for teachers. Although incentives may lead teachers to work harder, they may also focus their effort on teaching rote skills that are rewarded on standardized tests at the expense of teaching logical reasoning and other skills, where the payoff is not easily measured in the short term.[3] As we discuss below, these models are generally consistent with several empirical studies showing unintended responses to incentives.[4]

2.1.2. Subjective Measures of Performance

Given the limits of objective performance measures, what alternatives do firms have for motivating workers? The answer for most employees is various incentives based on subjective measures

---

3. Lazear (2006) lays out how the performance measures should be designed and how much information about them should be given to employees when employees engage in multiple tasks.

4. One case study that shows direct evidence of the importance of multitask issues is Brickley and Zimmerman (2001). They show that teacher ratings rose and research output fell at the University of Rochester's Simon School of Business, New York, after the administration increased the relative importance of teaching in its reward structure.

of performance. That is, the performance of most employees is monitored by some supervisor(s) who develops a reasonably accurate, but nonverifiable, signal of how good a job that employee does. Good performance can then be rewarded through a variety of mechanisms, including increases in base salary, subjectively determined bonus payments, or promotions.

Bull (1987), MacLeod and Malcomson (1989), and Baker et al. (1994) model the use of subjective performance evaluation. They analyze the optimal mix of incentives based on imperfect objective measures and perfect (but unverifiable) subjective measures. These models highlight the trade-off between strong incentives from well-designed subjective measures and the fact that employees have to trust firms to follow through on the inherently implicit contracts involved in any nonverifiable performance measure. For example, many Wall Street firms distribute year-end bonuses to employees based on largely subjective measures of the individuals' contributions. The shareholders of those firms would gain in the short term by announcing that nobody had earned any bonus in a given year, but the firm would find it hard to motivate employees in the future.

As the pioneering career concerns models of Fama (1980) and Holmström (1999) discuss, immediate pay for performance is not necessary if current performance affects an employee's reputation and future compensation.[5] Gibbons and Murphy (1992), building on these models, analyze employees that exert effort both in response to explicit incentives and in the hopes of improving employers' beliefs about their abilities. Firms do not need to provide strong current-period incentives for young workers, who have more reason to be motivated by future promotions and opportunities. They find some support for the model in the way CEO compensation varies with age and experience. Chevalier and Ellison (1999), who study mutual fund managers, find further support for age-based variation in the need for objective incentives.

In addition to the limits that stem from using implicit contracts for enforcement, subjective performance evaluation also is limited by differences between actual and measured performance. There are interesting models of at least three ways that subjective assessments can differ from actual productivity. First, employees can take actions that affect their supervisors' assessments. This issue has been studied in a series of papers on "influence activity," starting with Milgrom and Roberts (1988). The key idea is that employees will try to influence their bosses' decisions in their favor (and not necessarily in the interests of the firm) if their pay does not properly reflect their productivity. Firms face a trade-off between taking advantage of the manager's information and letting the manager manipulate decisions in her own best interests. For decisions that do not affect the distribution of benefits within the firm, this presents no problem. But when decisions have distributional implications, the firm may want to commit not to use information provided by agents. For example, the firm may commit to promote according to seniority rather than based on subjective assessments of performance. Meyer et al. (1992) and Schaefer (1998) show how the firm can benefit from a crisis (i.e., very bad alternatives for agents) to reduce influence activity and align the interests of employees and the firm.[6]

---

5. See Prendergast (1999) and Gibbons and Waldman (1999) for more detail on career concerns models.

6. Also see Fairburn and Malcomson (2001), who develop an integrated model of incentives and promotions when managers can engage in influence activity. They argue that managers with sufficient monetary incentives will be resistant to influence activity when making promotion decisions, which both makes promotion-based incentives stronger and more efficiently matches workers to appropriate jobs.

Second, Prendergast and Topel (1996) consider a manager who favors some workers over others. That is, the manager affects the payoffs of the employees, and the distribution of employee payoffs, in turn, affects the utility of the manager. The firm has to trade off the informational advantage of the manager regarding the employees' true performance, the taste for the manager to have more discretion, and the distortion to incentives caused by favoritism. In order to avoid the ill effects of favoritism, the firm reduces overall incentives and relies on imperfect (but noncorruptible) objective performance measures.

Finally, MacLeod (2003) considers the optimal contract when the manager and employee have different opinions about the employee's performance. He shows how the optimal implicit contract will vary with the degree of correlation between the manager's assessment of the employee's performance and the employee's self-assessment. The model predicts the tendency of managers to bunch or compress employee's ratings. MacLeod (2003) also studies the effects of favoritism, allowing for a more general set of contracts than Prendergast and Topel (1996) study. He shows that favoritism reduces the incentives of employees who are discriminated against, leading pay to suffer due to discrimination and lower effort. This result has the interesting implication that, holding performance constant, measured differences in wages will understate the importance of manager bias, because it will ignore the effect on the employees' incentives.

These models of subjective performance evaluation and implicit contracts have made important contributions to personnel economics and our understanding of compensation structure. However, even though these models are consistent with anecdotal examples and case studies, they have not been backed up by a great deal of rigorous empirical corroboration. Hayes and Schaefer (2000) provide compelling (though indirect) evidence on the importance of implicit contracts and subjective performance evaluation of executives. They argue that a board of directors that uses subjective evaluation will reward executives in the current period for actions that will affect objective measures of performance in future periods. They then show that there is an important empirical relationship between current pay and future performance and that this relationship is stronger at firms where they would expect subjective performance measures to be relatively advantageous for providing efficient incentives.

2.1.3. Relative Performance Evaluation

Some performance measures, whether objective or subjective, can be improved by making them depend on an employee's relative performance rather than on some absolute standard. Relative performance evaluation (RPE) can be used in two different ways. First, firms can use the performance of a peer group of competitors to filter out shocks that are common to the whole peer group. This helps the firm to lower the risk (and the associated compensation premium) imposed on individual employees. As Antle and Smith (1986) and Gibbons and Murphy (1990) discuss, this idea has the empirical implication that pay will be increasing in the employee's own performance but decreasing in the average performance of the reference group. As we discuss in Section 4.4, at least in the case of CEOs (whose performance and that of a peer group are easily observed), there is surprisingly little evidence that firms filter out common shocks of a peer group.

A second form of RPE is to use fixed rewards for a fixed group of people, where the distribution of rewards is based on the order of the participants' performance. This form of reward system, generally known as a tournament, can vary from a group of people competing for a single promotion (e.g., to CEO) to a large set of prizes that diminish in value as a person's relative performance diminishes (e.g., at a golf tournament or in the memorable real estate sales tournament in the film drama *Glengarry Glen Ross*).

Tournament theory, as modeled by Lazear and Rosen (1981), models promotions as a relative game. The compensation at one level of the firm, in addition to motivating individuals at that level, motivates those at lower levels. There are three basic principles of tournament theory. First, prizes are fixed in advance and depend on relative rather than absolute performance. Second, larger spreads in wages at different levels of the hierarchy motivate those at lower levels to put forth more effort. Third, there is an optimal spread. Although a greater spread increases effort, at some point the additional wages necessary to compensate workers for the increased effort are larger than the additional output generated.

An important variable in the Lazear and Rosen (1981) model is the amount of noise—that is, the degree to which luck affects the probability of winning. When there is more noise (so that luck becomes relatively more important and effort relatively less important), workers will try less hard to win, because effort has a reduced effect on whether they win. In production environments that are very uncertain, large raises must be given to offset the tendency by workers to reduce effort. Similarly, the number of slots available affects effort. If a firm has 100 vice presidents (VPs) and only one slot for president, most VPs will give up trying to become president, thinking that the chance of promotion is too slim. At the other extreme, if there were 100 VP slots and 95 president slots, so that each VP knew that she would almost surely be promoted to president, VPs would become complacent.

The firm can use the size of the spread between pay at various levels to manage effort. When luck is unimportant, the wage spread will be small. But when luck is important, the firm needs to increase the spread to boost effort. This may help explain differences in salary structure across countries or across industries. The model of Lazear and Rosen (1981) implies that riskier industries (where this is interpreted as risk that affects individual output) should have larger wage spreads than less risky industries to induce workers to put forth the appropriate amount of effort.[7]

These basic ideas of tournament theory have been extended in numerous ways. For example, while Lazear and Rosen (1981) focus on relative performance strictly as a means of generating incentives, Green and Stokey (1983) highlight the potential usefulness of tournaments in removing common shocks from risky performance measures. They show how individual incentive contracts compare to tournaments based on variation in how common the shocks to agent output are, how easily the firm can observe these shocks, and how many employees participate in the tournament. Nalebuff and Stiglitz (1983) allow for risk-averse employees, allow the number of participants in the contest to vary, and allow for both rewards and penalties. They derive a large set of results regarding when tournaments will be more efficient than incentive schemes that are not based on relative performance and how the optimal incentive system will vary with the number of participants, environmental uncertainty, and other factors. Rosen (1986b) extends basic tournament theory to a multiple-round elimination ladder and shows that, to keep incentives strong, prizes must be concentrated among a select few participants.

---

7. This prediction also comes from incentive models where agents are risk averse.

Dye (1984) and Lazear (1989) consider how the potential for collusion, sabotage, or other forms of noncooperative behavior in tournaments counter the incentive value of a large spread in rewards. Chan (1996) considers how firms should balance the incentive value of internal promotion tournaments against the value of retaining the option to hire an outsider when a senior opening occurs. He suggests that giving insiders a handicap in the tournament may help mitigate the possibility of influence activity or sabotage.

Patterns of pay and promotions in firms and in other contest contexts fit the predictions of tournament theory. DeVaro (2006) uses a sample of recent hires and their initial promotions to fit a structural model of tournaments. He shows the importance of relative, rather than absolute, performance in determining promotions. Knoeber and Thurman (1994) provide empirical evidence consistent with several specific predictions of tournament theory in the context of rewards for producers of broiler chickens. They show, for example, that spreads between prize values affect output. Drago and Garvey (1998), using a survey of Australian firms, show that individuals are less cooperative with other employees and work harder when promotion incentives are strong. Ehrenberg and Bognanno (1990) show that golfers are affected by prize spreads in tournaments. Finally, Bull et al. (1987) perform laboratory experiments (so that "effort" is chosen and stated rather than experienced) on how people respond to contests with piece rates and tournaments. The results of their experiments are generally supportive of tournament theory, though they find that less able people expend more effort than the theory would predict.

2.1.4. Alternative to Incentives I—Monitoring

An alternative to financial incentives is to simply monitor workers. If a supervisor can keep close watch over employees, she can ensure that the employee takes the best action. However, monitoring is typically imperfect, which led to the idea of efficiency wages. Shapiro and Stiglitz (1984) suggest that a firm will pay workers a wage premium when it cannot perfectly monitor effort. Workers, facing a choice between earning this wage premium if they work hard and facing a probabilistic chance of being caught and fired if they shirk, choose to work hard.

Efficiency wage theory implies a negative relationship between monitoring intensity and wages.[8] The empirical evidence in favor of this prediction is mixed at best.[9] This may be because the conditions that make efficiency wages optimal for individual employers may not exist at a large subset of firms in the economy. That is, there could well be many firms that can monitor very effectively or use output-based incentives, while other firms (such as the one studied by Cappelli and Chauvin 1991) use efficiency wages.

A recent study by Nagin et al. (2002), although not directly testing the relevance of efficiency wage theory, finds empirical support for the underlying relationship between employee productivity and the probability of catching employees that do not act in the firm's best inter-

---

8. The monitoring/pay relationship is the primary implication for the personnel economics literature. But Shapiro and Stiglitz (1984) actually focus on the fact that efficiency wages also lead to equilibrium unemployment. Bulow and Summers (1986) also model equilibrium efficiency wages and focus on equilibrium unemployment. They discuss how the reaction to Ford Motor Company's $5 day for assembly line workers, introduced in 1914, is consistent with efficiency wage theory.

9. See Malcomson (1999) and Gibbons and Waldman (1999) for further discussion of the empirical relevance of efficiency wage theory.

ests. They run a field experiment at a telephone solicitation company where employees spend their workdays calling people to ask for donations to charitable organizations. They find that the rate at which workers "cheat" by trying to get paid for donations people did not actually make varies inversely with the rate at which managers audit donations. When the probability of getting caught goes up, workers cheat less.[10] However, based on a survey of the telephone solicitors, Nagin et al. (2002) conclude there is little evidence to support another key idea in efficiency wage models—that those workers who value a job most will react most strongly to monitoring.

2.1.5. Alternative to Incentives II—Intrinsic Rewards

One way to save on both the costs of incentives and those of monitoring is to rely on the intrinsic value workers get from doing their jobs well. If firms pick workers carefully and create the right work environment, won't their employees be productive? In other words, standard moral hazard models assume that all productive effort is distasteful to the employee. But perhaps this assumption is not reasonable.

All else being equal, people who are intrinsically motivated to do certain types of jobs (or, put another way, those who simply enjoy certain jobs) will find work with firms that let them do those jobs.[11] If the labor market is reasonably competitive, then no matter how much workers enjoy the job, the firm will still have to pay them to do it, because employers will bid wages up to the person's marginal product of labor. But if people like their jobs enough, why would firms ever need to provide incentives or monitor workers?

The answer to this question, and the limit to intrinsic motivation, is not that people are not intrinsically motivated or that they do not like their jobs (though this is surely true in many cases). Rather, it is that the efficient outcome in most employment relationships is for the employee to dislike her job on the margin. Put another way, the key assumption in moral hazard models is not that all effort is distasteful. The key assumption is that the marginal disutility of effort is convex.

Many employees are intrinsically motivated to expend at least some effort at their jobs. However, at some point between zero and twenty-four hours of work in a given day, the marginal cost of an additional hour of work becomes positive. If a somewhat intrinsically motivated worker had no incentives or monitoring, she would do some work but would stop at some point. Assuming the person is still productive at the effort level where marginal work becomes costly, it is efficient to induce her to work more. It makes sense for her to work until the marginal disutility of her effort hits the marginal value to the firm.

This argument in no way implies that intrinsic motivation is not important. In fact, as our discussion of selection and matching below makes clear, firms should work hard to find workers who are motivated so as to decrease their own costs of compensation. But it does suggest that, on the margin, agency theory and other economic principles about motivation and incentives apply even when workers like their jobs.

---

10. Duflo et al. (2012) show that monitoring works in increasing teacher attendance in India. In their case, the employees do not have to infer the monitoring rate.

11. See Prendergast (2007) for a model of how different forms of intrinsic motivation should affect the matching of people to employers.

Although this very simple discussion of intrinsic motivation gets at the key economic issue regarding intrinsic motivation, it misses some potentially important and subtle effects having to do with the context of intrinsic motivation. Firms may affect employees' intrinsic rewards with the signals they send. Bénabou and Tirole (2003) formalize this idea and argue that a traditional economic model can be reconciled with many of the findings by psychologists about the demotivating effects of incentives.[12] They set up a model where both the employee and the firm have private information. The employee has better information about his abilities and his own interests, while the firm has better information about the attractiveness of the task. The contract offered by the firm affects the employee's beliefs about the task or the firm's beliefs regarding the employee. Under certain conditions, incentives can have negative effects on the employee.

2.2. Responses to Incentives—Empirical Studies

In a variety of situations where economists have been able to study the effects of incentives in relatively controlled settings, employees respond to incentives. However, although incentives work, several studies have shown some of the unintended consequences created by employee incentives. That is, the distortions predicted by some theoretical work appear to be important empirically. Some of these studies, because they focus on individual firms, could be capturing mistakes. Others, which show systematic and long-term costs of incentive schemes, suggest that incentives cannot be implemented perfectly but that the costs are worth bearing.

In this section, we review the empirical work on incentives. We first review several studies that establish that employees respond to incentives. We then discuss studies that show the importance of distortions in incentive schemes. There are several important empirical papers that consider how incentives operate in group settings. We defer the discussion of these studies to Section 6, where we discuss the organization of work.

Lazear's (2000a) study of the Safelite Glass Company provides a case study of the effect of incentives on both effort and worker selection. Safelite switched from paying windshield glass installers an hourly wage to paying them a piece rate per windshield installed. Because Safelite implemented the new pay scheme at different times at different locations, Lazear (2000a) could isolate the effect of the pay scheme while controlling for other companywide changes. In addition, because he was able to observe many new workers under both pay schemes and could control for on-the-job learning (i.e., tenure effects), he could separate the degree to which any change in productivity was due to changes in individual worker behavior and to changes in the types of workers that Safelite was able to attract. He finds that the piece rate system increased productivity at Safelite by about 44%. About half of this increase was the pure productivity effect. That is, the typical windshield installer that worked at Safelite under both pay schemes increased his productivity by about 22% upon the implementation of the piece rate scheme. The rest of the increase in productivity came about because the piece rate scheme led to self-selection of more-productive workers joining Safelite (and the self-selection of less-productive employees leaving the company).

---

12. For a review of many of these papers, see Deci et al. (1999). As we discuss below, in contrast to these suggestions of incentives demotivating workers, empirical studies by economists have generally found that explicit incentives increase productivity (though not always profits).

Shearer (2004) studies how piece rates affect the productivity of tree planters in British Columbia. Working in cooperation with the company that employs the tree planters, Shearer was able to implement a true experiment where a treatment group was randomly assigned to be paid a piece rate while a control group was paid an hourly wage. Thus, he cannot estimate a selection effect of piece rates but ensures the validity of a causal interpretation of the incentive effect that he measures. Shearer (2004) finds that workers paid through a piece rate are approximately 20% more productive than those paid by the hour, which is nearly identical to the effect in Lazear (2000a).

Bandiera et al. (2007) consider how the implementation of an incentive pay system affects the productivity of managers of fruit pickers on a U.K. farm. The pickers themselves are on a piece rate system at all times, but the farm made an unannounced switch to incentive pay for managers in the middle of one season. Bandiera et al. (2007) show that the average picker's productivity increased by 21% when his manager's pay was related to his productivity. They go on to show that much of this increase is due to the managers focusing their effort more carefully on those pickers for whom it will have the largest marginal effect on productivity, but that at least half is due to the managers being more discriminating about which workers they select.[13]

Freeman and Kleiner (2005) provide a useful reminder that while incentive pay generally increases productivity, it does not necessarily increase profits. They study a footwear manufacturer that switched from piece rate pay to an hourly wage as part of an attempt to cut costs and change its manufacturing processes. The firm implemented numerous other changes at the time of the change in compensation system, so it is difficult to isolate the exact effect of the change in pay scheme on productivity. But Freeman and Kleiner (2005) do find a significant reduction in productivity, and an increase in profits when piece rates were removed.[14]

These studies all show that incentives can be a powerful managerial tool for affecting individuals' behavior. Asch (1990) shows the same thing but highlights the more problematic side of incentives. She studies U.S. Navy recruiters who were measured, and in some cases paid, based on their ability to enlist sailors. To the extent that productivity affected compensation for the recruiters, it was based on whether they met annual quotas. Therefore, recruiter incentives were low if they either had already reached their quotas or if it became apparent that they would not reach them. In addition, due to discounting, the return to recruiter effort grew as the end of the measurement period approached. Asch (1990) shows that recruiting success was higher near the end of the year as the end of the measurement cycle approached. So even though incentives "worked," they did not work consistently. It is difficult to determine whether this inconsistency had any negative ramifications for the Navy.

Courty and Marschke (2004) examine the response of another set of government workers—managers of job training centers—to nonlinear incentives. However, in this case the incentives are indirect: performance affects the budget of the job training office and not the employees' compensation. Courty and Marschke (2004) show that managers act so as to increase the expected amount of incentive payouts near the end of each measurement period, but that their

---

13. Other studies showing evidence that incentives affect employee behavior but not allowing ready interpretation of the "incentive effect" include Groves et al. (1994), Fernie and Metcalf (1999), and Gaynor et al. (2004).

14. Note, however, that this profit effect could reverse in the long run if employees become more productive in the future due to current effort. See Friedman and Kelman (2008), who show that short-term financial incentives in British hospitals had long-run effects on productivity.

actions generate real costs in terms of lowering the quality of overall training. The incentives may lead to benefits in terms of overall quality, but it seems likely that these benefits could be captured without the costs imposed by the focus on year-end results.

The analyses by Asch (1990) and Courty and Marschke (2004) suggest that incentives can have a costly and inefficient side to them. However, because these studies are each based on a single institution (and one that is not subject to competition), it is feasible that they are simply studies of mistakes. Over time and facing competition, perhaps the Navy and the job training incentive systems would be changed or driven out of existence. However, there are broader (though less direct) studies of unintended consequences of incentives suggesting that firms choose to live with some of these consequences for the sake of capturing other benefits.

Oyer (1998), for example, analyzes the effects of the tendency of firms to plan their budgets and their incentive systems around a fiscal year. Executives and salespeople typically have contracts with a nonlinear relationship between pay and performance. Salespeople often have annual quotas, for example, and many executives receive certain bonus payments only if they surpass some target. This provides these employees with incentive to try to exert some discretion over when certain results are achieved. For example, a salesperson who is rushing to meet a quota near the end of the year may offer a customer a big (but unnecessary) price break if the customer orders immediately. He shows that, controlling for the calendar seasonality of a firm's industry, firms tend to sell more (and at lower margins) near the end of fiscal years than they do in the middle of the year. They also tend to sell less early in the year, suggesting that salespeople and/or executives "borrow" from the next year to meet the current year's quota.[15] Larkin (2007), using data from a large software company, finds that salespeople's reaction to their incentive contracts cost the firm 6–8% of potential revenue.

The specific example studied by Larkin (2007), as well as the broader pattern identified by Oyer (1998), raises the interesting question of why these nonlinear contracts are so prevalent, given that they create inconsistencies in the production process and cut profit margins at the end of the year. However, given that these fiscal-year effects have been so common for so long, it appears there must be some benefit from these contracts that outweighs the apparent costs.

Chevalier and Ellison (1997) show that nonlinearities also lead to persistent distortions for mutual fund managers, though these nonlinearities are not chosen by firms.[16] Specifically, they show that there is a nonlinear relationship between mutual fund investment returns over a calendar year and investment inflows into those funds. As a result, near the end of the year, some mutual fund managers have an incentive to change the level of risk in their funds. They show that such changes in risk do occur, suggesting that mutual fund managers choose their portfolios' risk with more than just maximizing return in mind. Again, given that this distortion has been taking place in a competitive market for a long time, it appears that the costs imposed by this behavior of mutual fund managers are outweighed by some benefits.[17]

15. See Healy (1985) and Murphy (2000) for further evidence that there is a relationship between executive contracts and timing of performance within fiscal years.

16. Also see Brown et al. (1996), who reach similar conclusions about mutual fund managers.

17. For other examples of problematic responses to incentives and measurement, see Dranove et al. (2003) and Jacob and Levitt (2003).

2.3. Empirical Relevance of the Risk/Incentive Trade-Off

In a series of papers over the past decade, Canice Prendergast has explored the trade-off between risk and incentives discussed above. First, in a review of the incentives literature at that time (Prendergast 1999), he argued that the empirical evidence was mixed on the risk/incentives trade-off.[18] Then, in a series of papers, Prendergast (2000, 2002a,b) more carefully lays out the evidence on the risk/incentive trade-off and offers several explanations for why the risk/incentive trade-off may be difficult to find in the data even if the underlying idea is correct.

In Prendergast (2002a), risky environments are likely to be those where a manager's private information is more valuable. A firm will be willing to pay the additional costs to compensate a manager for additional risk to make sure the manager uses his private information profitably. In other words, the marginal value of the manager's effort is increasing in environmental risk such that the natural trade-off between risk and the cost of incentives may be overwhelmed by a positive relationship between risk and the benefits of incentives.[19] Initial attempts to test Prendergast's model have been generally supportive (see Adams 2005; DeVaro and Kurtulus 2010), though they are limited by the difficulty of finding exogenous variation in the delegation of decision rights.

Prendergast (2002b) presents a model of subjective assessments and shows that either favoritism or costs to the manager of making assessments can lead firms to find incentives more valuable when risk is higher. Prendergast (2000) argues that if the costs of monitoring effort directly are correlated with risk, then firms may use more incentives in riskier environments, because the requisite risk premium is smaller than the cost of the additional resources that would be required to directly monitor the agent's actions.

Oyer (2004) offers an alternative reason risk and the value of incentive contracts can be positively correlated, even when the pay scheme is not meant to affect the agent's actions. He develops a model where the employee's reservation wage and the firm's value or profits are correlated with each other because they are both affected by macroeconomic shocks. The firm ties the employee's pay to the firm's success to lower contracting and renegotiation costs if a shock affects the employee's outside opportunities. In environments where shocks (and therefore, risk) are greater, the firm will tie more pay to firm performance to more closely match compensation to the employee's outside opportunities. However, if the environment gets too risky, the firm will abandon performance-based compensation and renegotiate wages when conditions change. This suggests that the incidence of "incentives" will be negatively related to risk but the amount of incentive will increase with rising risk.

Prendergast (1999: 21) summarized the research on the risk/incentive trade-off as of the time he wrote by stating, "there is some evidence that contracts are designed to optimally trade off risk against incentives" and "it would not appear that on the margin, the risk measures that have been considered are the true constraining factors on the provision of incentives." These conclusions

---

18. See Aggarwal and Samwick (1999a) and Jin (2002) for recent evidence that the trade-off holds for American CEOs.

19. Zábojník (1996) draws similar implications in a model where a portion of market risk is related to the manager's marginal product and is revealed to the manager before she chooses her effort, though Zábojník does not model the decision rights of the manager.

are still appropriate. But in the past several years, some of the extensions to the basic moral hazard model reviewed above have uncovered possible reasons empirical researchers find the risk/incentive trade-off to be so elusive. The challenge in the years ahead is to design empirical strategies and measures that can confirm or refute these newer models, as well as the basic moral hazard model.

3. Matching Firms and Workers

Matching firms with workers would be an easy process if labor were a commodity like some other inputs. However, labor is probably the most heterogeneous of all inputs in production functions. This is true on both sides of the market—the value of a given worker is likely to vary dramatically across potential employers, and the disutility of effort associated with work will vary for a typical worker across the firms she might work for. Matching the right firms to the right workers (as well as matching workers to the most appropriate jobs within the firms) creates economic value of a magnitude that few other economic processes can.

Given the importance of job market matching, it is not surprising that economists have been studying the selection process since well before there was a field known as personnel economics. Important theoretical contributions have come in two varieties—game-theoretic models of asymmetric information and models of efficient matching with symmetric learning about worker productivity.

3.1. Learning Models

Suppose individual i's output y in period t, if employed at firm j, can be written as

$$y_{ijt} = \alpha_i + \mu_{ij} + \epsilon_{ijt},$$

where α is the innate ability of worker i, μ is the "match" productivity of the worker i and firm j combination, and ϵ is a productivity shock. Suppose all three variables on the right-hand side of the equation are random variables with mean zero and variance σ_α, σ_μ, and σ_ϵ, respectively.

Consider the case where $\sigma_\alpha = \sigma_\mu = 0$. In this case, each individual is identical and labor is a commodity. Efficiency is independent of how workers are matched to firms. If this case were a reasonable representation of the world, then the field of personnel economics would not study selection of workers.

Now consider the somewhat more interesting example where $\sigma_\mu = 0$, but $\sigma_\alpha > 0$. In this case, workers differ in their productivity, but their productivity is independent of where they work. Again, selection is uninteresting in this environment as long as information about an individual's value of σ is symmetric between firms and the worker.[20]

Now consider the more interesting example where $\sigma_\mu > 0$. In this case, which is the core of the matching model in Jovanovic (1979), a worker's expected productivity in any given period

---

20. While selection issues are not important in models with symmetric learning about general ability (i.e., ability that is equally useful to all employers), these models have interesting implications for compensation. See Section 4.1.

depends on where she works. Then it is important, in terms of economic efficiency, to maximize the firm/worker match quality μ. Though exactly who captures the value of this match quality will differ, depending on the competitive environments in the labor and production markets, the total size of the economy will increase in average match quality. In the absence of any cost of changing jobs, workers would switch jobs several times early in their careers in search of the best match. But, given some search or other transaction cost in job switching, workers will switch jobs only if the expected gains to doing so are large enough.

There are two key empirical implications of matching models, both of which are also consistent with models of firm-specific human capital. First, turnover rates will decrease with job tenure (i.e., the longer a person stays in a job, the less likely she is to leave the job in any given period). Farber (1994) and others confirm that this pattern generally holds. Second, as long as it takes at least a little time for the worker and firm to learn the value of their match, wages will increase with job tenure. This implication holds in most specifications, but there has been some controversy as to whether it is true when the wage model to be estimated is properly specified. Abraham and Farber (1987), Altonji and Shakotko (1987), and Neal (1995) all argue that the wage/tenure relationship does not hold when properly controlling for other proxies of match quality. Topel (1991), using a different method, argues that the causal effect of tenure on wages is quite high, which is consistent with firm-specific human capital being important.

The relative importance of matching and firm-specific human capital is still somewhat of an open question. Although the patterns in the data sometimes appear consistent with both models, the managerial implications of these models are drastically different. If σ_μ is very high, so that match quality varies, employers should invest carefully in screening and selection. But if match quality does not vary and firm-specific human capital is an important driver of productivity, firms should focus on training and other human capital development.

Note that the matching literature is vague about what underlies the value μ of a match. Two recent models explore this. Lazear (2009) models a world where all skill is completely general, but employers value mixes of skills differently. Hayes et al. (2006) emphasize the value of co-worker specific match quality. Employees are more valuable at some firms than others, because they work more productively with the employees at some firms. Although both these ideas can help get to the root of matching, they do not help with distinguishing matching from firm-specific human capital. The mix of skills and/or relationships with co-workers can be developed after taking a job, which would make them a form of firm-specific human capital rather than ex ante match quality.[21]

Two recent papers that look more directly at the importance of matching are Woodcock (2008) and Andersson et al. (2009). Andersson et al. (2009) examine the matching of the most-talented software engineers to the firms with the highest returns to talent, while Woodcock (2008) analyzes the importance of individual skill, firm effects, and match-specific productivity on wages. Empirical research along these lines, which has become more feasible as rich employer-employee datasets have become available, could shed some light on how the matching process

---

21. Backes-Gellner et al. (2011) test Lazear's model using German data on employer-provided training. Their results suggest that the skills mix idea is enhanced by on-the-job training, though this conclusion does not exclude the possibility that employers select employees that already have (or show the ability to acquire) the range of skills the firms need.

takes place and how much value it creates.[22] In addition, research at single firms or small groups of firms that analyzes job applicants, those offered jobs who do not accept, and those who accept positions might inform research and practice in selection and matching.

3.2. Asymmetric Information Models

While matching models focus on firms and workers that are equally well informed, other models consider how employees match to firms when one party is better informed. An important example of how asymmetric information can be critical in the labor market is when a person knows her ability but a firm has only a noisy estimate. If all workers were honest, firms could simply ask job applicants about their ability and make hiring decisions based on what the applicants say. Less qualified applicants have considerable incentive to exaggerate their qualifications, so firms must find another way to extract this information.

Two solutions to this problem have been suggested. In the pioneering work of Spence (1973), employers use costly signals to infer the ability of applicants. The cost to an individual of obtaining an education is inversely related to her ability (and, therefore, her productivity as an employee). Signaling will only solve selection problems when acquiring the signal is sufficiently costly and when the cost of acquiring it is inversely related to the person's ability. However, signaling is an inefficient solution to the selection process, because the cost of acquiring the signal is a deadweight loss. Another way to separate people of differing skill is to use self-selection (see Salop and Salop 1976). If some portion of compensation or other parts of the employment relationship differ in their value to prospective employees, and if these differences in value are related to productivity, then more productive employees will self-select into an organization. Self-selection has the advantage of not wasting the resources involved in acquiring a signal, but it relies on employers being able to find a condition of employment that will separate people based on ability.

Lazear (1986a) models how incentive schemes can be useful for signaling and self-selection. Suppose that potential workers know their abilities but employers do not. If productivity differences cannot be measured on the job, then all employees will be paid the average workers' productivity. But suppose an employer can measure an individual's productivity at some cost. Lazear (1986a) assumes that all employers in the marketplace observe the person's productivity when one employer measures it, so the firm will only undertake this measurement if the employee pays for it (presumably through lower compensation). Once productivity is measured, employee wages are bid up to their individual productivity level. If measurement is costless, then the system fully unravels and everyone is paid exactly their productivity. But if measurement is costly enough, then those with relatively low productivity are not willing to pay to be separated from those with the lowest productivity. As a result, some firms pay a fixed salary for all workers and attract those of relatively low ability. Other firms set up compensation systems related to output and measure workers. This simple framework may explain why salespeople are paid commissions, which is output-based pay, whereas most high-level service workers are paid salaries.

---

22. Oyer and Schaefer (2010) also use a newly available data source—directories of employees from law firms' web sites—to study the match between firms and workers.

In the latter case, it is more costly to obtain a decent measure of output, so more pooling occurs and pay relies on proxies for input.

Now consider a different type of asymmetric information model that can lead to inefficiencies in the labor market. Suppose each employee has ability a_i as in the prior discussion and firms cannot observe an individual's ability before hiring her. However, suppose the firm obtains a precise estimate of the person's ability shortly after hiring her. Then, as Greenwald (1986) shows in an extension of the early work by Akerlof (1970), under certain conditions, employee mobility (especially among higher ability workers) will be impaired.[23] Firms use their informational advantage to retain high-ability workers when they receive outside offers while not responding to outside offers made to mediocre performers (known as "lemons" in the paper). Fearing this information disadvantage will lead them to the winner's curse and overpaid lemons, firms are reluctant to make offers and workers will not change firms.

In some labor markets, this may not be an issue. For example, the productivity of professional athletes (and academic economists) is readily observable to other teams (universities), and the markets for these professionals' services are quite liquid with significant volume of trade. However, in other markets, ability is not as easily observed by outsiders and this observability need not be completely exogenous. Several models have advanced Akerlof (1970) and Greenwald (1986) by analyzing how employers can best take advantage of their inside knowledge of their workers' abilities. For example, Waldman (1984) considers strategic assignment of employees to jobs within a firm when outside firms take these assignments as signals of employees' ability. He shows that employees may not be assigned to the jobs where they would be most productive and that pay will depend on job assignment rather than strictly on ability.

Milgrom and Oster (1987) extend this idea by considering two classes of workers—a regular group and a disadvantaged group. If it is easier to hide the disadvantaged group than the regular one, then firms will not promote or pay the skilled members of the disadvantaged group as much as they pay other skilled workers. This tendency leads to persistent discrimination (i.e., lower wages and underrepresentation in senior positions) against the disadvantaged workers and less investment in human capital by members of this group. Bernhardt (1995) also assumes that incumbent firms can exploit an informational advantage regarding employee ability and that this advantage may vary across certain classes of workers. He develops a model that is consistent with several stylized facts of some labor markets. The model also predicts the so-called "Peter Principle" where some managers are promoted to positions that are no longer appropriate for their skill levels.[24]

Although layoffs, or even voluntary turnover, may reveal a "lemons" problem in some cases, Gibbons and Katz (1991) point out that this will not be the case when a firm fails. They predict that, because of the inferences drawn by employers, the reemployment wages of a worker at a plant that closes will be higher than the wages of a worker who is laid off from a continuing operation. They find some empirical evidence to support this prediction, though follow-up

---

23. Lazear (1986c) also formalizes the adverse selection issue in the employment setting by putting the problem in the context of efficient turnover and auctions.

24. For alternative explanations of the Peter Principle, see Lazear (2004a), who shows that on average, early success is at least partially good luck and Fairburn and Malcomson (2001), who indicate that risk-averse managers may inefficiently promote underlings to provide them with more incentive.

studies have argued that their results are fragile (see Song 2007 and other work cited there). Nonetheless, the insight that there might be more stigma attached to losing a job at a downsizing firm than at one that is closing an operation has become widely used in the labor economics literature.[25]

The asymmetric information literature has been quite successful at developing realistic models that match some basic stylized facts. Until recently, the models have not been tested or estimated carefully because of a lack of empirical proxies for some key parameters in these models. However, several recent empirical papers have emerged, using a variety of strategies to test for asymmetric learning. DeVaro and Waldman (2012) find evidence consistent with asymmetric learning being an important factor in one large firm's pay and promotion practices. Zhang (2007) and Kahn (2008), using the National Longitudinal Survey of Youth, find evidence that asymmetric learning is important in the broader labor market, whereas Schonberg's (2007) analysis of the same data suggests this is only true for more skilled workers.

3.3. Firing and Displacement

In addition to selecting workers when they hire them, firms have the opportunity to change their selection of workers at any time by layoffs. If firms could freely adjust wages to an employee's marginal product, then worker displacement would not be an issue, because workers would make efficient voluntary decisions about when to leave. However, because of wage compression within firms, norms against nominal wage reductions, and other factors, workers often do not voluntarily quit when firms would like them to.

Most worker displacement is simply the result of some significant negative shock to a firm or its industry or is the result of an individual proving to be significantly less productive than the firm anticipated. This type of turnover does not generate particularly interesting insights into how firms manage their human resource systems, so we do not cover it in detail here. It is worth noting, however, that displacement typically has negative and economically significant consequences for workers stemming from loss of firm-specific human capital (or match-specific productivity), stigma of losing a job, or other factors. See Farber (2005) and Kletzer (1998) for reviews of the frequency and effects of job loss in the United States and Hallock (2006) for a discussion of the layoff process.

One way that displacement affects the way firms run their personnel systems is through limits that are placed on firm's ability to dismiss workers. A firm making decisions about who to hire and whether to hire may act differently if it loses the option of correcting bad hiring decisions through dismissal. Consider a firm weighing the possibility of taking on a particular candidate. The firm trades off the expected costs and benefits of hiring that person versus its next-best option (which may be an alternative candidate or it may be to not hire at all). The firm will typically have an imperfect estimate of the benefits an employee will bring the firm, because it does not know the person's ability (or match) exactly and the firm's business environment could change in a way that affects the potential employee's marginal product.

---

25. This stigma of some layoffs is similar to the signal sent by not getting outside offers discussed in Lazear (1986c).

Consider a firm that is choosing between candidates A and B. Normalize the person's expected marginal product of labor in a given period (and, therefore, their reservation wage) to 0. But suppose that candidate A produces 0 for sure, candidate B produces either z or $-z$ (each with 50% probability), and output-contingent contracts are not feasible. Assuming everyone is risk neutral and the person is hired for only one period, a firm would be indifferent between the two candidates. However, if the employment match can last multiple periods, then under certain conditions and all else being equal, the firm will prefer type-B workers for their option value. In equilibrium, type-B workers will earn a wage premium and only certain types of firms will want these workers. Lazear (1998) develops a model along these lines, where he explores the market equilibrium when workers have option value.[26] The option value of risky workers will be highest in contexts where workers are somehow tied to their firms and where it is relatively easy for employers to dispose of workers that turn out to be unproductive.

In many cases, firms face barriers to dismissing workers stemming from legal or other institutional (e.g., union) reasons. This makes the cost of employing workers higher, lowering labor demand, and it can lead to some combination of lower wages and lower employment.[27] In addition to lowering overall labor demand, firing costs can reverse the logic of preferring risky workers for their option value, because substantial negative realizations relative to expected productivity can be very costly. That is, a firm that cannot lower wages substantially will want to fire a type-B worker that turns out to have productivity of $-z$. If firing costs are substantial enough, then the costs of hiring an unproductive type-B worker can outweigh the option value of having a productive type-B worker. Oyer and Schaefer (2002) model how equilibrium wages and employment will change for different types of workers when these workers differ in the observability of their abilities or productivity. They argue that increases in firing costs that are constant across workers should increase the wage premium to seniority, because employers have more precise estimates of the ability of workers with more experience. They find support for this model empirically, using labor market and civil rights litigation data around the time of an increase in employer liability for discrimination in displacement.

In addition to affecting the riskiness of workers a firm would want to hire, firing costs also affect the types of workers that a firm will displace. If the costs of firing a worker increase, a firm will be willing to live with a less productive worker, because the benefits of firing the previously marginal worker will no longer outweigh the costs. Thus, those workers whom a firm fires when firing costs are high will be, on average, of lower ability than the ones it fires when firing costs are low. Empirical support for this idea has been found using variation in firing costs generated by three different institutional settings: U.S. Civil Rights legislation, institutional barriers to worker displacement in Europe, and firing restrictions imposed by state courts and legislatures. Oyer and Schaefer (2000) find evidence consistent with this idea by using variation in firing costs by race. Extending this logic one step, the stigma that Gibbons and Katz (1991) argue

---

26. See Bollinger and Hotchkiss (2003) for an analysis of risky hires in professional baseball. Lazear (1998) may also apply to academic labor markets, because moving costs tie professors to their institutions while the tenure system allows schools to displace less experienced workers relatively easily.

27. As Lazear (1990) points out, perfectly efficient labor markets could undo the negative consequences of firing costs. However, as Lazear (1990), Dertouzos and Karoly (1992), DeLeire (2000), Acemoglu and Angrist (2001), and Autor et al. (2006) show, there is substantial evidence that firing costs increase unemployment.

will go along with displacement should be greater when firing costs are greater. Canziani and Petrongolo (2001) formalize this idea and find empirical support using data from Spain around the time of easing of firing restrictions in the mid-1980s. Kugler and Saint-Paul (2004) develop a similar model, focusing on the choice of firms to hire workers who are unemployed or working at other firms. Using variations in firing restrictions across U.S. states, they find that the "lemons" effect increases with firing costs.

4. Compensation

4.1. The Level of Compensation

How much will firms pay their employees? In the absence of incentive issues and any firm-specific productivity, compensation will be just enough to keep employees from leaving the firm (as long as the firm does not lose money). In equilibrium, this amount will be equal to the expected marginal product of the employee's labor. But how do firms and employees determine an employee's marginal product? How do they know what is a reasonable amount to pay? For some employees with a lot of experience, firms and workers have a pretty good idea of what a reasonable wage is. But when an employee enters the labor market, firms have to rely on observable features, such as the person's education, performance during interviews, and performance on tests. Over time, firms and employees learn more about the employee's skill and tailor jobs and his pay accordingly.[28]

Farber and Gibbons (1996) model this learning process. Consider a person entering the labor market. The firm that hires him expects his productivity (y_{it}) to be

$$y_{it} = F(\alpha_i, X_{it}),$$

where α_i is the innate ability of worker i, and X is a set of characteristics that are observable to the firm (e.g., education). Because neither the firm nor the individual know the exact value of α, initial wages are based largely on X. However, over time, the firm observes a set of noisy signals about y_{it} and updates its estimate of α. Farber and Gibbons (1996) derive empirical implications of employer learning on the measured correlation between pay and X, as well as how pay is related to characteristics firms cannot observe at the time of hiring. Using data from the National Longitudinal Survey of Youth, they find empirical results that are broadly consistent with employer learning playing a large role in the development of wages over careers.[29] Altonji and Pierret (2001) develop this idea further and point out that, until the learning process is fairly developed, employers are statistically discriminating on the basis of the observable X characteristics. A key point in these models is that the level of pay will more closely approximate the worker's marginal product as the firm and worker learn about the worker's true ability.

Competitive labor markets do not require that workers earn their expected marginal products in any given period. Firms may set implicit contracts across multiple periods as a means of facilitating long-term relationships, providing incentives or more efficiently sharing risk. Lazear

---

28. See Waldman (2010) for a more detailed survey of careers in organizations.

29. Gibbons et al. (2005) and Lluis (2005) extend this learning model and the empirical analysis in Farber and Gibbons (1996) by noting that employees may have differing productivity in different ranks within a firm. Firms and workers learn about workers' innate skills, as well as which rank best fits their skills, over time.

(1979) focuses on the long-term relationship and incentives ideas. He notes that a firm can provide incentives through fixed wages if the firm pays the worker less than his marginal product early in his career and more than his marginal product later. After a person has been at the firm for a while, he has incentives to perform well and avoid being fired to enjoy the rents he has been promised later. Because this ties the worker to the firm, it may also encourage development of firm-specific human capital. Older workers are overpaid in this model and need to be induced to leave the firm either through a mandatory retirement policy or an appropriate pension scheme.

Harris and Holmström (1982) model wage dynamics over careers when employees are risk averse and when firms and workers learn symmetrically about workers' ability. In their model, workers are insured against negative shocks to their realizations on ability. In equilibrium, individuals never have wage decreases and wages increase faster than productivity. Frank (1984) offers an alternative explanation for why workers may not be paid their marginal products and why wages are generally thought to be more compressed than productivity. He argues that, if workers care about their pay relative to their peers within the firm, high-ability workers will be willing to take a wage discount for the value they get from being near the top of the pay scale.

A look inside firms shows that actual wage dynamics are driven largely by the jobs people hold. That is, individual jobs have a fairly narrow band of possible wages. The learning process that leads to people settling into the appropriate compensation scheme over time appears to be largely about finding the right job for the person rather than finding the right pay for different people doing similar jobs. This can be seen in the firms studied by Lazear (1992), Baker et al. (1994), and several more recent studies (see Waldman, this volume, for more details).

4.2. The Mix of Compensation

Money isn't everything, but everything can be expressed in terms of its monetary equivalent. That is, in most markets, consumers pay some amount of cash in return for a good or a service. In some labor markets, such as temporary help or "under-the-table" work, transactions take this form. But most people sell labor services in exchange for a range of cash and other compensations. Interpreted broadly, the other compensations can include standard noncash benefits, such as health care, retirement benefits, and employer-sponsored child care as well as amenities, such as a large or nicely decorated office, low risk of injury or death, or a job that consists of largely interesting tasks. If all firms had the same cost structure, all employees had the same preferences, and employees could buy any amenities or benefits from other sources for the same prices the employer would pay to procure them, then labor would be traded for money and individuals would buy their own basket of benefits to best suit their needs.

However, because of institutional features (e.g., tax incentives) or economies of scale, firms often have a comparative advantage in providing benefits or amenities relative to workers. In addition, some firms are better at providing benefits than other firms, and individuals vary in terms of how they value benefits. For example, a restaurant can more cost effectively provide meals to its employees than a firm that manufactures ball bearings, and some people place a higher value on food provided by their employers than do other people.[30]

---

30. For alternative justifications of certain benefits, see Rajan and Wulf (2006), Marino and Zábojník (2008), and Oyer (2008). They consider the relationship among benefits, employees' cost of effort, and productivity.

These forms of differentiation lead to two important conclusions. First, it is often efficient for firms to provide a compensation package that mixes cash with other things.[31] Second, the total economic value of employment relationships can be enhanced by matching workers who value a given benefit or amenity with firms that have a comparative advantage in providing that benefit. That is, one of the determinants of the match-specific surplus discussed in Section 3.1 is the degree to which a firm efficiently provides amenities valued by its employees.

The classic work by Rosen (1974) laid out the theoretical foundations for this job differentiation, and Rosen (1986a) provides an intuitive discussion of how this model leads to the theory of compensating differentials in labor markets. Rosen (1974) shows how market equilibrium prices allow inferences about the monetary value of some characteristic. For example, suppose that we want to determine the monetary equivalent value of interesting work in a firm. Define X as the proportion of tasks in a given job that are new to the employee. Suppose that data were available on wages and the proportion of tasks on a job that were new per day. Consider the following regression:

$$\text{Wage on job } j = a + bX.$$

The coefficient b reveals the value that the market places on having flexibility on the job. The coefficient reflects the market value and not necessarily the tastes of any one individual. Employees who value new tasks relatively highly can earn rents by taking jobs at firms that offer many new tasks, and firms that can provide new tasks to workers at relatively low cost can earn rents by providing a relatively high proportion of new tasks. Rosen (1974, 1986a) discusses the conditions under which the market price reflects individual tastes, firm technologies, or neither.

There is an empirical literature that attempts to examine the relation of wages to nonmonetary benefits and to determine the "price" of various benefits and amenities.[32] These analyses are very challenging, however, because of the effects of unobserved ability. Consider two people who are observationally equivalent (same age, education, etc.), but one has more skill that is observable to employers and unobservable to an econometrician. The more highly skilled employee will be able to command higher total compensation. However, because of regressive taxes on cash compensation and the fact that income effects will generally make the marginal utility of workplace amenities (relative to cash compensation) higher for more highly paid workers, such workers will take some of their additional compensation in the form of workplace amenities. As a result, Ehrenberg (1980) found that pensions and wages were positively correlated (when there should be a trade-off between the two), and numerous studies have shown that wages are positively related to benefits.[33] This does not mean that hedonic wage theory or the concept of

31. Employer-provided health care and pensions account for a large share of the cost of employee benefits, as well as of economics research on benefits. Gruber (2000) reviews the huge literature on employer health insurance. The large literature on pensions focuses on the various types of pensions offered and how they affect retirement behavior. See surveys by Lazear (1986b) and Lumsdaine and Mitchell (1999).

32. See Antos and Rosen (1975), Thaler and Rosen (1976), Brown (1980), and Woodbury (1983) for early examples of this literature.

33. Hamermesh (1999) and Pierce (2001) highlight an interesting implication of the income effects of benefits. They show that changes in wage inequality in the United States in recent decades understate the total increase in compensation inequality, as benefits have become relatively more generous for highly paid workers.

compensating wage differentials is wrong. It just means that measuring the market price of these differentials is difficult.

There are at least three potential ways that future research can get around the challenges presented by unobserved ability. First, if there are variables that are correlated with whether a person receives a benefit at work but not otherwise related to that person's earning potential, then instrumental variables can be used to identify the salary/benefit trade-off. Olson (2002) uses this approach to estimate that married women will accept a 20% salary reduction in return for health insurance, using their husbands' union status and firm size as an instrument for whether the women have employer-provided health insurance. Although this approach can be useful when looking at health insurance, the value of other benefits is unlikely to be high enough to allow for precise estimation of the salary/benefit trade-off. Second, detailed information on multiple job offers made to the same person can provide estimates of trade-offs, assuming the value of the employee is roughly equal to the various employers. Stern (2004) takes this approach by surveying scientists about the compensation and research components of their job offers. His estimates suggest scientists are willing to accept substantial wage decreases to engage in on-the-job research. However, highlighting a potential weakness of this approach, his estimates are imprecise, because his sample size is small and respondents' recall of job offer details is likely to include substantial measurement error. Third, given that benefits are such an important part of human resource policies, a large firm might be willing to work with economists to design experiments that randomize across workers by location. Large firms that have many locations and are known for providing generous benefits (e.g., Starbucks or Whole Foods Markets) are promising candidates. Laboratory experiments may also be helpful for learning about how people view benefits relative to cash, but the short-term and relatively low-stakes nature of that environment is likely to be an important limitation.

4.3. Equity Ownership

Over the past few decades, stock and stock options have grown as compensation tools. This trend probably reflects several factors, including attempts to increase worker incentives and the fact that, as economic growth has made workers wealthier, employee risk aversion may have gotten lower. Think about a middle manager at a large firm. If this person were truly risk neutral, he would be indifferent between taking his compensation in the form of cash or in terms of company stock. The stock would have the benefit of aligning his incentives with those of other shareholders. However, given that this manager's efforts have only a trivial value on stock holdings, it would be difficult to generate incentives unless the firm issued him huge amounts of stock (as in Holmström 1982). In this case, risk costs would certainly become important. So why do firms grant stock to employees?

One possible answer is to retain employees, as in the Oyer (2004) model we discuss below. Another possible answer is to attract the right employees. There may be several "sorting" benefits of making equity compensation part of the employment agreement, even in the absence of incentives. The manager who has many stock options and a low base salary does not earn much unless the company does well. Thus, a manager who is willing to take a job under these circumstances reveals that he believes in the company. This information may be valuable to investors, whose information about the true value of the company is not as good as that of managers. See Salop and Salop (1976) and Lazear (2004b).

Similarly, equity compensation, like any other noncash benefits, may be used when a firm can provide it at relatively low expense and the employees value it. That is, firms can use equity-based pay to lower compensation costs by attracting employees that are particularly optimistic about the firm's prospects. A slightly different, but closely related, idea is that if workers who are optimistic about a firm are also the most productive (perhaps because of enthusiasm or an understanding of the firm's environment), then equity-based pay would just lead to the type of self-selection in Salop and Salop (1976) that we discussed above. See Oyer and Schaefer (2005) and Bergman and Jenter (2007) for theoretical and empirical analyses of this idea in the context of broad-based stock option plans.

Although attraction and retention may be important reasons to grant equity to employees, perhaps the most important justification for equity-based pay is to generate incentives. This explanation is likely to apply in small firms or among very high-level managers at large firms. These employees can have an important impact on the firm's value, and the incentive effects of ownership can outweigh the inefficiency in asking these employees to bear the risk of factors beyond their control that affect firm value.

4.4. Executive Compensation

One set of workers that has been widely studied, with much of this work falling in the arena of personnel economists, is top executives. There are several reasons executives have received more than their share of attention in the personnel economics literature.[34] First, executives (and especially CEOs) receive a great deal of compensation. The average CEO of a large American company now makes several million dollars per year, and the growth rate over the past few decades has been much faster than for compensation more generally. Second, due to disclosure regulations, publicly traded firms have to provide information about both executive compensation and company performance. This information allows empirical economists to create large datasets of individuals' pay and "performance" (where performance is a firm's stock return or measures based on a firm's or division's accounting statements). For these reasons, CEOs and other executives have been widely studied.

Murphy (1999) documents the rise in executive-related academic work and provides a summary of this literature. We refer readers interested in details on the institutional features, the level and structure, and the politics of executive pay to Murphy's review.

However, we highlight a few stylized facts from the executive compensation literature that relate directly to personnel economics. First of all, as one might expect, given the large effect CEOs can have on firms' outcomes and the relatively easy availability of performance measures, CEOs have high levels of incentive-based pay. Much of it is based on explicit incentives, such as performance-contingent bonuses and equity ownership. A smaller, but important, amount of incentives comes in the form of subjective or implicit incentives, including adjustments to salary and bonuses not tied to objective metrics. These incentives vary in ways that most theories predict, with stronger incentives at firms where the marginal product of the CEO is likely to be higher (e.g., larger firms, those with more capital, and unregulated firms).

---

34. This is certainly true on a per-worker basis and is probably still true on a per-compensation-dollar basis.

Murphy (1999) also shows that executive turnover is somewhat based on firm performance, but that the relationship is not as strong as one might expect and, at least as of the time of his writing, had weakened over time. In addition, he shows that there is a surprising lack of RPE in executive pay. Executives are rewarded (penalized) for good (bad) macroeconomic conditions, though it would seem easy for firms to filter this uncontrollable risk out of pay/performance contracts.

Murphy's (1999) survey ends with suggestions for future research. He asked why RPE is rare.[35] Numerous explanations have been suggested since Murphy posed the question. First, in trying to justify the lack of RPE for executives, Garvey and Milbourn (2003, 2006) have provided both supply (i.e., executive-driven) and demand (firm-driven) explanations. They argue that there is RPE for some executives, but that the average effect is small, because there are many cases where RPE is not used. In Garvey and Milbourn (2003), they argue that RPE is unnecessary once an executive attains sufficient wealth. Once his assets that are not part of current compensation are large enough, he can completely undo any position in the firm's stock in his private portfolio such that the use of RPE is irrelevant. Consistent with this idea, they find that younger and less wealthy CEOs, who are less likely to have sufficient assets to unwind compensation contracts imposed by the firm, are more likely to be subject to RPE. Garvey and Milbourn (2006) suggest that CEOs will try to influence boards of directors to limit RPE when the market is performing well. They then show empirically that CEOs are more likely to have their pay indexed during bad times than during favorable markets.

Aggarwal and Samwick (1999b), influenced by an idea proposed in Fershtman and Judd (1987), suggest that RPE will be counterproductive when products are strategic substitutes (as in differentiated Bertrand markets) and when market competition is imperfect. Pay based on relative output will lead managers to be too aggressive in product market competition. They find empirical support for this idea by showing that the typical level of RPE is higher when product market competition is more intense.

Oyer (2004) models a case where adjusting compensation contracts is costly and employees' reservation wages are correlated with their firms' performance. Firms provide at least some compensation in the form of equity ownership, because this will give workers a raise when there is greater demand for their services and a pay cut when labor demand is lower. Options or shares in the firm's stock can therefore serve two purposes: providing incentives and adjusting pay to market rates. RPE is useful for incentive purposes, but firms would not want to insulate employees from marketwide conditions when equity compensation is used for the other purpose.

Yet another possible explanation for the lack of RPE is that the marginal return to effort may be correlated with the state of the market. Suppose the firm's value Π is an additively separable function of the CEO's effort e, macroeconomic conditions θ, and an idiosyncratic shock ϵ, so we can write $\Pi = v_1 e + v_2 \theta + \epsilon$. Then it is clearly optimal to filter out the macroeconomic effects. But if the marginal product of effort v_1 is correlated with the macroeconomic conditions θ, then the optimal contract will be an increasing function of θ.

---

35. See Bertrand and Mullainathan (2001) for details on the lack of RPE in executive compensation. Note that Murphy (1999) also posed the question of why executive pay has increased so much in recent decades. Several explanations have been put forward. However, because these explanations are largely a debate about corporate governance rather than personnel policies, we do not address that issue here.

Just as we might expect CEO pay to use RPE, we might also expect relative outcomes to affect CEO dismissals. Barro and Barro (1990), who focused on bank CEOs, found that pay is not related to relative outcomes but turnover is. Two more recent and broader studies, however, show that CEO turnover is affected by both overall market conditions and relative performance of individual firms. Jenter and Kanaan (2011) and Kaplan and Minton (2008) both show that CEO turnover is higher when the firm's industry performs poorly and when the firm underperforms the industry.

5. Skill Development

The analysis and discussion to this point have been naïve in assuming the person's ability and match-specific productivity as given. In reality, people develop skill over time both before and after joining a given firm, and this skill development affects productivity. As Becker (1964) laid out in his classic study of human capital, people can develop general skill that is equally useful to multiple employers (and, therefore, becomes part of what we called "ability," or α, in Section 3.1) or that is more useful to one employer than to any other (and, therefore, becomes part of the match-specific component μ in Section 3.1).[36]

Becker (1964) argued that the efficient way to divide the investment costs of skill is for firms to pay for firm-specific human capital acquisition of workers and for workers to pay for their own general human capital. Any other means of splitting human capital investments costs will lead to the potential for the firm or the worker to hold up the other party after sinking the cost of a relationship-specific investment.

This allocation of human capital investment clearly applies in most situations and, in particular, when the investment is large. For example, almost all people pay the cost of their own secondary, college, and graduate education. There are exceptions, such as firms that sponsor their employees earning MBAs, but these arrangements often come with a contractual commitment not to leave the firm for some set period. Similarly, firms generally pay employees the going wage during training periods and early in job tenure while the employee is largely acquiring the skill and knowledge necessary to be productive in a given firm.[37]

Recently, some papers have argued that Becker's optimal allocation of human capital investments does not appear to be applied in certain situations and have tried to explain why. There are situations that are fairly clear examples of firms paying for the acquisition of workers' general human capital. For example, Stanford University offers free computer training in a variety of programs to all employees, sometimes including programs not related to a person's current job. Employees who take advantage of this suffer no compensation ramifications and are allowed to attend training while being paid. A series of recent papers has attempted to explain

36. One important idea related to human capital is the extent to which incentives to acquire general and firm-specific human capital are related to promotions, careers within organizations, and even optimal organizational form. See Kahn and Huberman (1988) on firm-specific human capital and up-or-out contracts, Waldman (1990) on general human capital and up-or-out contracts, Prendergast (1993) on the relationship between promotion and firm-specific human capital, and Levin and Tadelis (2005) on partnerships in high-skill industries.

37. Note that it is often difficult to determine whether a firm or a worker have paid for the acquisition of skill, because generally we do not have complete information on both the compensation arrangements in a given job and what those arrangements would be in the absence of skill acquisition.

why situations may arise where firms find it in their best interest to pay for employees' acquisition of general human capital. Most of these papers focus on the same informational advantage of incumbent firms modeled by Greenwald (1986) and discussed above.

An example is Autor (2001), who focuses on a specific example that clearly violates Becker's model. Manpower Associates is a large U.S.-based temporary help services firm. This firm offers potential "temps" free computer training. The training provides skill in common computer programs, is completely free to the person, and is not coupled with any obligation to work for Manpower. A person can take this class and then go down the street to another temp agency or any other employer and use her new computer skills.

Why would Manpower offer such a program? Building on ideas in Katz and Ziderman (1990), Autor (2001) argues that the process of training gives the firm asymmetric information about the ability of the temporary worker. The firm then can use that information to match temps to assignments in a way that creates rents, at least until the person has been out on enough assignments that another temporary agency can infer her ability and where to assign her. He argues that this information advantage may be made even more valuable when free training helps a temporary help agency attract higher quality workers. He develops a model of the agency's acquisition and exploitation of private information, arguing that it will lead to particular relationships between market wages, training, and the degree of local temporary labor market competition. He then uses data from a Bureau of Labor Statistics survey of temporary service suppliers and finds evidence that is consistent with the model's predictions. For example, firms that offer free training offer slightly lower wages, but this gap gets smaller in more competitive markets.

Acemoglu and Pischke (1998) offer a related explanation for firms making investments in general human capital, based on the information structure in Greenwald (1986). In their model, firms have some level of monopsony power over workers and can capture some of the rents associated with acquisition of general human capital. Because workers do not capture the full value of general human capital investments, they will underinvest in these skills. Some firms may therefore find it profitable to sponsor this training. They find evidence consistent with the predictions of their model using a test, in the spirit of Gibbons and Katz (1991), that looks at the relative wages of German apprentices who stay at the firm that trains them, those who quit and move to another firm, and those who quit for an exogenous reason (random selection into the military).

In another study, Acemoglu and Pischke (1999) show that, even in the absence of information asymmetry, firms may sponsor general training if wages in the labor market are compressed relative to workers' marginal products. This compression, which they argue can arise from search costs or other transaction costs or from institutional factors (e.g., unions and minimum wages), may differ across labor market settings, leading firms in some markets to be relatively likely to sponsor human capital investments.

Another justification for firms making investments in worker general human capital is that it may provide incentives for the employee to stay at the firm while in training. Manchester (2008) analyzes data from a single nonprofit institution's training programs and from a cross-section of firms. She finds that training is related to increased employee retention.

The work by Autor, by Acemoglu and Pischke, and, to a lesser extent, by Manchester focuses on general training of relatively low-skilled workers. There are interesting examples of firm-provided general human capital for higher skilled workers, often including cases where the training is highly visible to outside employers. For example, both of us (the authors) previously held positions at business schools that offered part-time MBA programs for people with full-time jobs. Most of these students were sponsored by their employers and were not paid less than people doing similar jobs (though some firms required workers to partially repay these investments if they leave before a specified time). Future research focused on advanced training and degree programs might provide useful insights into optimal human capital investment for highly skilled workers.

6. Organization of Work

To this point, we have acted as though a firm picks a single worker to do a well-defined set of tasks. However, in reality, firms are made up of a group of diverse people doing different sets of tasks. In this section, we briefly look at how firms decide who does what, who works with whom, and who works for whom.

6.1. Job Design

Most firms beyond some minimum size set up organization charts that show individual jobs designed to do some set of tasks. Several studies of individual companies, including Lazear (1992), Baker et al. (1994), and Gibbs and Hendricks (2004), show how firms divide jobs into well-defined pay grades. Given this importance of jobs, how do firms divide tasks into jobs? There has been very little empirical analysis of this question because of the difficulty in measuring, categorizing, and describing the tasks workers perform in a day. In addition, the way tasks are combined into jobs is often driven by obvious cross-task complementarities (e.g., teaching and research for professors or sales and service for copy machine providers). However, there have been numerous theories emphasizing how incentives, an employer's desire to learn about employees, the firm's production function, and other factors may affect job design.

Prendergast (1995) models the interaction of human capital, incentives, and job design. If performing tasks provides human capital, managers will hoard tasks and overextend themselves. Prendergast's paper and related ones on incentives and job design consider who will determine what tasks should be performed, as well as how to bundle tasks into jobs. For example, Zábojník (2002) shows that firms may want to let workers decide what to do even when the manager has superior information, if worker liquidity constraints limit the available incentive contracts. Olsen and Torsvik (2000) add a dynamic element to this issue. They show that the ability of the firm to learn about the difficulty of the tasks workers engage in will induce the firm to give workers more discretion over tasks and weaker incentives. Specifically, this learning process will mute the positive correlation between discretion and incentives predicted by static models. Crémer (1986) also analyzes job design in a dynamic context. He focuses on the relationship between job design and career concerns when firms want to promote cooperation among employees.

Holmström and Milgrom (1991) note that firms may want to bundle tasks with similar degrees of measurability, so that workers do not ignore tasks that are difficult to measure. Itoh (1994) and Schöttner (2007) show that the implications of multitask considerations for task assignment differ depending on the circumstances. Itoh (1994) notes that, when individual task outcomes cannot be measured, firms will make workers generalists by bundling all tasks into one job, while Schöttner (2007) shows that the ability to write relational contracts will mitigate some of the potential concerns of assigning multiple tasks to a single job.

The models just discussed generally explain why firms may have different jobs even if workers are homogeneous. But, even if these are the reasons that firms differentiate jobs, an important consideration in jobs will be assigning heterogeneous workers to jobs that match their skills. Rosen (1978) focuses on worker heterogeneity in his model of matching firms and workers based on the tasks firms need done and the comparative advantage of workers in performing each of these tasks. (For a review of assignment models, see Sattinger 1993.) In many ways, this model matches firms to workers based on tasks the same way that Rosen (1986a) models the matching of firms and workers based on employee preferences. A similar model underlies the analysis in Gibbons et al. (2005), which highlights the importance of assigning workers to their most productive sectors. Gibbons and Waldman (2006), however, develop a model where workers develop task-specific human capital, so that a person's job assignment has important effects on how her career develops.[38] The lack of good empirical proxies for how firms assign tasks to jobs makes it difficult to assess the relative importance of these models that emphasize optimal matching of heterogeneous workers to tasks and the homogenous worker models discussed above, but it seems likely that these matching concerns are first-order determinants of job design.

6.2. Teams, Worker Interaction, and Human Resource Practices

Successful human resource management is not simply a matter of giving each individual proper incentive to engage in work in isolation. If it were, there would be no need for the firm. Perhaps the greatest value of the firm is that it provides a mechanism for people to work together and take advantage of complementarities in their skills and interests. The evidence that there can be gains from assembling workers into teams or groups has to be done at a firm-by-firm level because of the need for data on productivity and team structure. As a result, much of this work falls into the category of "insider econometrics." Ichniowski and Shaw (this volume) review this method. We briefly discuss a few papers related to the issue of group incentives.

Hamilton et al. (2003) study a garment manufacturer that switched from an individual piece rate system to group-based piece rates. Workers were given some discretion over when they made the switch. Though the most productive workers had the most to lose financially from the switch, they tended to be early adopters. Productivity went up (and stayed higher) overall, suggesting that collaboration was valuable at this company. The gains were greater for more heterogeneous teams, and abler team members had a bigger influence on others' productivity than did less able team members. Not all manufacturers get such positive results from the switch to teams, however. King (1998) provides anecdotal evidence of a much different (and much less successful) transition to teams at Levi's.

Boning et al. (2007) look at the effects of team production in the steel industry. Most firms in their sample pay some sort of group-based incentive, but only some organize their workers

38. Also see Garicano and Rossi-Hansberg (2006) on dividing tasks based on skill level, though they do not focus on within-firm task allocation.

into cooperative teams. They find that productivity is higher at firms that use teams and that this effect is especially large where the product and production process are more complicated. Incentive pay is also associated with higher productivity at these firms.[39]

What are the sources of these group-based productivity benefits? In some cases, groups allow people to solve problems better and to take advantage of different skills. Gant et al. (2002, 2003), again focusing on the steel industry, show that interactions among a larger set of workers are associated with higher levels of production.

Mas and Moretti (2009) show how supermarket clerks are affected by the productivity of other clerks working at the same time. They find that high-productivity clerks increase the productivity of peers. Like Hamilton et al. (2003), they find larger productivity gains when groups of workers are more diverse in skill. Mas and Moretti (2009) also find evidence suggesting social pressure is important, because productive checkers have larger effects on peers who can see them while they work. Similarly, Ichino and Maggi (2000) show that absenteeism and misconduct has an effect on peers in an Italian bank.

In addition to these field studies, Falk and Ichino (2006) find noteworthy peer effects in an experimental environment. Subjects were given a mundane task (stuffing envelopes) and no financial incentive. Average worker productivity was higher when each person worked in the same room as another person than when people worked in isolation. The least productive workers were the most affected by working in a group, so the increase in their output more than made up for the decrease in output of the most productive workers. The results of all these studies taken together suggest that, at least in many environments, people prefer working in groups to working in isolation, people working in groups feel some pressure to keep up with the efforts of those around them, and/or the most productive workers pressure others into working harder.

As the theoretical work of Milgrom and Roberts (1990) and Kandel and Lazear (1992) suggests, the effectiveness of team-based systems is likely to vary from firm to firm because of complementarities across human resource practices. That is, team-based productivity may be more important when firms invest in selecting employees carefully, training people in the system, and other practices. Testing this idea empirically is challenging, however, because measuring productivity is difficult, and human resource practices are adopted endogenously. Several studies (see, e.g., Black and Lynch 2001; Cappelli and Neumark 2001; Bloom and Van Reenen 2007) have shown that the adoption of various workplace practices tends to be done simultaneously, suggesting complementarity between the practices. They are also associated with and likely cause increased productivity in the firms in which they are adopted. However, it is difficult to make any causal statements about these relationships.

Ichniowski et al. (1997) allay this concern to some degree by looking at productivity of individual steel production lines around the time of adoption of modern human resource practices. They show that these practices increase productivity in these factories and that the marginal effect of each practice is increasing in the adoption of other practices.

---

39. Incentives are group-based in these steel mills. However, even when people work in groups, firms may want to use individual incentive pay to keep workers from colluding (either against the firm or against other workers). Bandiera et al. (2009) show that managers on a fruit picking farm allocate workers more efficiently when the managers are given incentive pay. Some of this productivity improvement comes at the expense of the managers' friends, who receive worse assignments under the incentive pay plan.

6.3. Hierarchies

Most people work in a hierarchy with several levels of reporting responsibility. There are many contributing factors to this standard institutional arrangement, and we do not investigate it in any great detail here, because it is the focus of Garicano and Van Zandt (this volume).

As we noted in some detail above, one benefit of hierarchies is that they provide incentives. Hierarchies can also be a substitute for incentives, however, in that they can provide a mechanism for monitoring employees directly. Lucas (1978), formalizing ideas in Manne (1965) and elsewhere, develops a model where some people are simply endowed with superior management skills. These skills can be interpreted as monitoring, decisionmaking, motivating, or any other skill that would be more valuable for a manager than for other employees.

Rosen (1982) distinguishes between the managerial tasks of making choices about what to produce, strategy, and the like ("management") and ensuring that employees carry out these decisions ("supervision"). To best utilize superior management skills, it would be efficient to grow firms ever larger. However, there are diseconomies of scale in supervision, so optimal firm size trades off these two factors. Rosen's (1982) model can explain skewed firm size within an industry and skewed compensation within a firm.

Garicano (2000) models hierarchies as a means of matching problems to those in an organization that can most efficiently solve them. There would be no need to use a hierarchical structure for this issue if everyone knew who was capable of solving which problems. But when there are costs of communicating this knowledge, expertise organized by levels efficiently assigns the right person to the right problem. Hierarchies are arranged with the highest skilled person at the top, the next-highest skilled people at the next level, and so on to the lowest skilled workers at the bottom. Each new problem enters the firm at the lowest level and gets bumped up the hierarchy until it reaches the person who can solve it. Given the increasing importance of services and knowledge workers, this idea of knowledge-based hierarchies has become more important. See Garicano and Van Zandt (this volume) for discussion of recent related work.

7. Conclusion

We have described a great deal of progress in the personnel economics literature. This research has helped explain how firms operate and has helped shape business education curricula in recent years. So it seems sensible to ask, where do we go from here? There is plenty of room for more work, especially empirical work, in all the areas we have discussed. But it seems likely that the highest returns will come from careful analyses of the selection, sorting, and matching processes. How do firms find the right workers? How important is it that firms find the right workers for their particular context? Business school curricula and the business press are filled with many case studies of firms that highlight finding people who match their specific needs (Southwest Airlines, SAS Institute, and Whole Foods Market are prominent examples). How do these and other companies generate economic value by finding the right people?

Another question worth further pursuit is how employees value different fringe benefits. As employees become wealthier and as technology breaks down the work/leisure divide, firms are likely to find noncash compensation more strategically useful. Some types of on-the-job skill development that we discussed can also be thought of as noncash benefits. Why do firms train employees in computer skills and send them to executive education training? Is it to increase their productivity, to reward them, or to signal something to or about them?

In addition to these broad areas, we have also noted some specific questions presented by recent work that are worth pursuing. What explains the lack of evidence to support the risk/incentive trade-off predicted by moral hazard models? Are American executives overpaid? How would we ever know? Other questions will emerge as external and institutional features evolve. For example, if the returns to skill continue to increase, how will firms manage the re-organization process as they pay for greater skill while trying to economize on low-skill jobs? What problems, if any, will result if internal pay differentials grow too large?

Two empirical methods have become useful in answering these and other questions, and we expect them to continue to grow in influence in personnel economics. First, studies of single firms, often involving a field experiment, can provide precise analysis of the effects of various human resource policies. This approach has proven effective in studying incentives, team-based production, and the role of jobs, despite the lack of generalizability of these studies. Well-crafted future studies (and perhaps experiments) can broaden the value of this method to selection, the wage/benefit trade-off, the use of subjective performance evaluation, training, and other areas.

The other method is the exploitation of employer-employee datasets, which have become much more prevalent in recent years.[40] These data can provide rich time series detail about firms' pay structure, growth, employee tenure, and so on. The lack of detail on firms' human resource practices makes it challenging to frame an economic question in a manner that can be addressed across the whole dataset. But careful modeling and/or focusing on certain industries or types of workers often helps make the exercise manageable.

Personnel economics has come a long way in the past few decades. We have learned a great deal about the underlying economics of human resource policies. But through the methods and ideas we have just mentioned, as well as others we have overlooked or that have not yet been discovered, we believe there will be much more learned in the next few decades.

REFERENCES

Abowd, John M., Francis Kramarz, and David N. Margolis. 1999. "High Wage Workers and High Wage Firms." *Econometrica* 67: 251–333.
Abraham, Katharine G., and Henry S. Farber. 1987. "Job Duration, Seniority, and Earnings." *American Economic Review* 77: 278–297.
Acemoglu, Daron, and Joshua D. Angrist. 2001. "Consequences of Employment Protection? The Case of the Americans with Disabilities Act." *Journal of Political Economy* 109: 915–957.
Acemoglu, Daron, and Jorn-Steffen Pischke. 1998. "Why Do Firms Train? Theory and Evidence." *Quarterly Journal of Economics* 113: 79–119.
———. 1999. "The Structure of Wages and Investment in General Training." *Journal of Political Economy* 107: 539–572.

40. See Abowd, Kramarz, and Margolis (1999) for a survey of some of the data and some of the papers that have used them. Also, see Lazear and Shaw (2008) for a series of studies using datasets of this sort from a variety of countries to analyze pay and turnover patterns within and across firms.

Adams, Christopher. 2005. "Agent Discretion, Adverse Selection and the Risk-Incentive Trade-Off." Working paper, Federal Trade Commission, Washington, DC.

Aggarwal, Rajesh K., and Andrew A. Samwick. 1999a. "The Other Side of the Trade-Off: The Impact of Risk on Executive Compensation." *Journal of Political Economy* 107: 65–105.

———. 1999b. "Executive Compensation, Strategic Competition, and Relative Performance Evaluation: Theory and Evidence." *Journal of Finance* 54: 1999–2043.

Akerlof, George A. 1970. "The Market for 'Lemons': Quality Uncertainty and the Market Mechanism." *Quarterly Journal of Economics* 84: 488–500.

Altonji, Joseph G., and Charles R. Pierret. 2001. "Employer Learning and Statistical Discrimination." *Quarterly Journal of Economics* 116: 313–350.

Altonji, Joseph G., and Robert A. Shakotko. 1987. "Do Wages Rise with Job Seniority?" *Review of Economic Studies* 54: 437–459.

Andersson, Fredrik, Matthew Freedman, John C. Haltiwanger, Julia Lane, and Kathryn Shaw. 2009. "Reaching for the Stars: Who Pays for Talent in Innovative Industries?" *Economic Journal* 119: F308–F332.

Antle, Rick, and Abbie Smith. 1986. "An Empirical Investigation of the Relative Performance Evaluation of Corporate Executives." *Journal of Accounting Research* 24(1): 1–39.

Antos, Joseph R., and Sherwin Rosen. 1975. "Discrimination in the Market for Teachers." *Journal of Econometrics* 2(May): 123–150.

Asch, Beth J. 1990. "Do Incentives Matter? The Case of Navy Recruiters." *Industrial and Labor Relations Review* 43: 89S–106S.

Autor, David H. 2001. "Why Do Temporary Help Firms Provide Free General Skills Training?" *Quarterly Journal of Economics* 116: 1409–1448.

Autor, David H., John J. Donohue, and Stewart J. Schwab. 2006. "The Costs of Wrongful-Discharge Laws." *Review of Economics and Statistics* 88: 211–231.

Backes-Gellner, Uschi, Regula Geel, and Johannes Mure. 2011. "Specificity of Occupational Training and Occupational Mobility: An Empirical Study Based on Lazear's Skill-Weights Approach." *Education Economics* 19(5): 519–535.

Baker, George P. 1992. "Incentive Contracts and Performance Measurement." *Journal of Political Economy* 100: 598–614.

Baker, George P., Robert Gibbons, and Kevin J. Murphy. 1994. "Subjective Performance Measures in Optimal Incentive Contracts." *Quarterly Journal of Economics* 109: 1125–1156.

Baker, George P., Michael Gibbs, and Bengt Holmström. 1994. "The Wage Policy of a Firm." *Quarterly Journal of Economics* 109: 921–955.

Bandiera, Oriana, Iwan Barankay, and Imran Rasul. 2007. "Incentives for Managers and Inequality among Workers: Evidence from a Firm-Level Experiment." *Quarterly Journal of Economics* 122: 729–773.

———. 2009. "Social Connections and Incentives in the Workplace: Evidence from Personnel Data." *Econometrica* 77: 1047–1094.

Barro, Jason R., and Robert J. Barro. 1990. "Pay, Performance, and Turnover of Bank CEOs." *Journal of Labor Economics* 8: 448–481.

Becker, Gary S. 1964. *Human Capital.* New York: Columbia University Press.

Bénabou, Roland, and Jean Tirole, 2003. "Intrinsic and Extrinsic Motivation." *Review of Economic Studies* 70: 489–520.

Bergman, Nittai K., and Dirk Jenter. 2007. "Employee Sentiment and Stock Option Compensation." *Journal of Financial Economics* 84: 667–712.

Bergson, Abram. 1978. "Managerial Risks and Rewards in Public Enterprises." *Journal of Comparative Economics* 2: 211–225.

Bernhardt, Dan. 1995. "Strategic Promotion and Compensation." *Review of Economic Studies* 62: 315–339.

Bertrand, Marianne, and Sendhil Mullainathan. 2001. "Are CEOs Rewarded for Luck? The Ones without Principals Are." *Quartery Journal of Economics* 116: 901–932.

Black, Sandra E., and Lisa M. Lynch. 2001. "How to Compete: The Impact of Workplace Practices and Information Technology on Productivity." *Review of Economics and Statistics* 83: 434–445.

Bloom, Nick, and John Van Reenen. 2007. "Measuring and Explaining Management Practices across Firms and Countries." *Quarterly Journal of Economics* 122: 1351–1408.

Bollinger, Christopher R., and Julie Hotchkiss. 2003. "The Upside Potential of Hiring Risky Workers: Evidence from the Baseball Industry." *Journal of Labor Economics* 21: 923–944.

Boning, Brent, Casey Ichniowski, and Kathryn Shaw. 2007. "Opportunity Counts: Teams and the Effectiveness of Production Incentives." *Journal of Labor Economics* 25: 613–650.

Brickley, James A., and Jerold L. Zimmerman. 2001. "Changing Incentives in a Multitask Environment: Evidence from a Top-Tier Business School." *Journal of Corporate Finance* 7: 367–396.

Brown, Charles. 1980. "Equalizing Differences in the Labor Market." *Quarterly Journal of Economics* 94: 113–134.

Brown, Keith C., W. V. Harlow, and Laura T. Starks. 1996. "Of Tournaments and Temptations: An Analysis of Managerial Incentives in the Mutual Fund Industry." *Journal of Finance* 51: 85–110.

Bull, Clive. 1987. "The Existence of Self-Enforcing Implicit Contracts." *Quarterly Journal of Economics* 102: 147–159.

Bull, Clive, Andrew Schotter, and Keith Weigelt. 1987. "Tournaments and Piece Rates: An Experimental Study." *Journal of Political Economy* 95: 1–33.

Bulow, Jeremy I., and Lawrence H. Summers. 1986. "A Theory of Dual Labor Markets with Application to Industrial Policy, Discrimination, and Keynesian Unemployment." *Journal of Labor Economics* 4: 376–414.

Canziani, Patrizia, and Barbara Petrongolo. 2001. "Firing Costs and Stigma: A Theoretical Analysis and Evidence from Microdata." *European Economic Review* 45: 1877–1906.

Cappelli, Peter, and Kevin Chauvin. 1991. "An Interplant Test of the Efficiency Wage Hypothesis." *Quarterly Journal of Economics* 106: 769–787.

Cappelli, Peter, and David Neumark. 2001. "Do 'High-Performance' Work Practices Improve Establishment-Level Outcomes?" *Industrial and Labor Relations Review* 54: 737–775.

Chan, William. 1996. "External Recruitment versus Internal Promotion." *Journal of Labor Economics* 14: 555–570.

Cheung, Steven N. S. 1969. *The Theory of Share Tenancy: With Special Application to Asian Agriculture and the First Phase of Taiwan Land Reform.* Chicago: University of Chicago Press.

Chevalier, Judith, and Glenn Ellison. 1997. "Risk Taking by Mutual Funds as a Response to Incentives." *Journal of Political Economy* 105: 1167–1200.

———. 1999. "Career Concerns of Mutual Fund Managers." *Quarterly Journal of Economics* 114: 389–432.

Courty, Pascal, and Gerald Marschke. 2004. "An Empirical Investigation of Gaming Responses to Explicit Performance Incentives." *Journal of Labor Economics* 22: 23–56.

Crémer, Jacques. 1986. "Cooperation in Ongoing Organizations." *Quarterly Journal of Economics* 101: 33–50.

Deci, Edward L., Richard Koestner, and Richard M. Ryan. 1999. "A Meta-Analytic Review of Experiments Examining the Effects of Extrinsic Rewards on Intrinsic Motivation." *Psychological Bulletin* 125: 627–668.

DeLeire, Thomas. 2000. "The Wage and Employment Effects of the Americans with Disabilities Act." *Journal of Human Resources* 35: 693–715.

Dertouzos, James N., and Lynn A. Karoly. 1992. *Labor Market Responses to Employer Liability*. Santa Monica, CA: RAND.

DeVaro, Jed. 2006. "Internal Promotion Competitions in Firms." *RAND Journal of Economics* 37: 521–542.

DeVaro, Jed, and Fidan A. Kurtulus. 2010. "An Empirical Analysis of Risk, Incentives, and the Delegation of Worker Authority." *Industrial and Labor Relations Review* 63: 641–661.

DeVaro, Jed, and Michael Waldman. 2012. "The Signaling Role of Promotions: Further Theory and Empirical Evidence." *Journal of Labor Economics* 30: 91–147.

Drago, Robert, and Gerald T. Garvey. 1998. "Incentives for Helping on the Job: Theory and Evidence." *Journal of Labor Economics* 16: 1–25.

Dranove, David, Daniel Kessler, Mark McClellan, and Mark Satterthwaite. 2003. "Is More Information Better? The Effects of 'Report Cards' on Health Care Providers." *Journal of Political Economy* 111: 555–588.

Duflo, Esther, Rema Hanna, and Stephen Ryan. 2012. "Incentives Work: Getting Teachers to Come to School." *American Economic Review* 102: 1241–1278.

Dye, Ronald A. 1984. "The Trouble with Tournaments." *Economic Inquiry* 22: 147–150.

Ehrenberg, Ronald G. 1980. "Retirement System Characteristics and Compensating Wage Differentials in the Public Sector." *Industrial and Labor Relations Review* 33: 470–483.

Ehrenberg, Ronald G., and Michael L. Bognanno. 1990. "Do Tournaments Have Incentive Effects?" *Journal of Political Economy* 98: 1307–1324.

Fairburn, James A., and James M. Malcomson. 2001. "Performance, Promotion, and the Peter Principle." *Review of Economic Studies* 68: 45–66.

Falk, Armin, and Andrea Ichino. 2006. "Clean Evidence on Peer Effects." *Journal of Labor Economics* 24: 39–57.

Fama, E. 1980. "Agency Problems and the Theory of the Firm." *Journal of Political Economy* 88: 288–307.

Farber, Henry S. 1994. "The Analysis of Interfirm Worker Mobility." *Journal of Labor Economics* 12: 554–593.

———. 2005. "What Do We Know about Job Loss in the United States? Evidence from the Displaced Workers Survey, 1984–2004." *Economic Perspectives* 29(2): 13–28.

Farber, Henry S., and Robert Gibbons. 1996. "Learning and Wage Dynamics." *Quarterly Journal of Economics* 111: 1007–1047.

Fernie, Sue, and David Metcalf. 1999. "It's Not What You Pay It's the Way That You Pay It and That's What Gets Results: Jockeys' Pay and Performance." *LABOUR: Review of Labour Economics and Industrial Relations* 13: 385–411.

Fershtman, Chaim, and Kenneth L. Judd. 1987. "Equilibrium Incentives in Oligopoly." *American Economic Review* 77: 927–940.

Frank, Robert H. 1984. "Are Workers Paid Their Marginal Products?" *American Economic Review* 74: 549–571.

Freeman, Richard B., and Morris M. Kleiner. 2005. "The Last American Shoe Manufacturers: Changing the Method of Pay to Survive Foreign Competition." *Industrial Relations* 44: 307–330.

Friedman, John N., and Steven Kelman. 2008. "Effort as Investment: Analyzing the Response to Incentives." Working paper, Harvard University, Cambridge, MA.

Gant, Jon, Casey Ichniowski, and Kathryn Shaw. 2002. "Social Capital and Organizational Change in High-Involvement and Traditional Work Organizations." *Journal of Economics and Management Strategy* 11: 289–328.

———. 2003. "Working Smarter by Working Together: Connective Capital in the Workplace." Working paper, Stanford University, Stanford, CA.

Garicano, Luis. 2000. "Hierarchies and the Organization of Knowledge in Production." *Journal of Political Economy* 108: 874–904.

Garicano, Luis, and Esteban Rossi-Hansberg. 2006. "Organization and Inequality in a Knowledge Economy." *Quarterly Journal of Economics* 121: 1383–1435.

Garvey, Gerald, and Todd Milbourn. 2003. "Incentive Compensation When Executives Can Hedge the Market: Evidence of Relative Performance Evaluation in the Cross Section." *Journal of Finance* 58: 1557–1582.

———. 2006. "Asymmetric Benchmarking in Compensation: Executives Are Rewarded for Good Luck But Not Penalized for Bad." *Journal of Financial Economics* 82: 197–226.

Gaynor, Martin, James Rebitzer, and Lowell Taylor. 2004. "Physician Incentives in Health Maintenance Organizations." *Journal of Political Economy* 112: 915–931.

Gibbons, Robert. 1987. "Piece-Rate Incentive Schemes." *Journal of Labor Economics* 5: 413–429.

Gibbons, Robert, and Lawrence Katz. 1991. "Layoffs and Lemons." *Journal of Labor Economics* 9: 351–380.

Gibbons, Robert, and Kevin J. Murphy. 1990. "Relative Performance Evaluation for Chief Executive Officers." *Industrial and Labor Relations Review* 43: 30s–51s.

———. 1992. "Optimal Incentive Contracts in the Presence of Career Concerns: Theory and Evidence." *Journal of Political Economy* 100: 468–505.

Gibbons, Robert, and Michael Waldman. 1999. "Careers in Organizations: Theory and Evidence," in Orley C. Ashenfelter and David Card (eds.), *Handbook of Labor Economics,* volume III. Amsterdam: North-Holland, pp. 2373–2437.

———. 2006. "Enriching a Theory of Wage and Promotion Dynamics inside Firms." *Journal of Labor Economics* 24: 59–107.

Gibbons, Robert, Lawrence Katz, Thomas Lemieux, and Daniel Parent. 2005. "Comparative Advantage, Learning, and Sectoral Wage Determination." *Journal of Labor Economics* 23: 681–724.

Gibbs, Michael, and Wallace Hendricks. 2004. "Do Formal Salary Systems Really Matter?" *Industrial and Labor Relations Review* 58: 71–93.

Green, Jerry R., and Nancy L. Stokey. 1983. "A Comparison of Tournaments and Contracts." *Journal of Political Economy* 91: 349–364.

Greenwald, Bruce C. 1986. "Adverse Selection in the Labor Market." *Review of Economic Studies* 53: 325–347.

Groves, Theodore, Yongmiao Hong, John McMillan, and Barry Naughton. 1994. "Autonomy and Incentives in Chinese State Enterprises." *Quarterly Journal of Economics* 109: 183–209.

Gruber, Jonathan. 2000. "Health Insurance and the Labor Market," in Anthony J. Culyer and Joseph P. Newhouse (eds.), *Handbook of Health Economics.* Amsterdam: North-Holland, pp. 645–706.

Hallock, Kevin F. 2006. "Layoffs in Large U.S. Firms from the Perspective of Senior Managers." *Research in Personnel and Human Resources Management* 25: 137–179.

Hamermesh, Daniel S. 1999. "Changing Inequality in Markets for Workplace Amenities." *Quarterly Journal of Economics* 114: 1085–1123.

Hamilton, Barton H., Jack A. Nickerson, and Hideo Owan. 2003. "Team Incentives and Worker Heterogeneity: An Empirical Analysis of the Impact of Teams on Productivity and Participation." *Journal of Political Economy* 111: 465–497.

Harris, Milton, and Bengt Holmström. 1982. "A Theory of Wage Dynamics." *Review of Economic Studies* 49: 315–333.

Hayes, Rachel M., and Scott Schaefer, 2000. "Implicit Contracts and the Explanatory Power of Top Executive Compensation for Future Performance." *RAND Journal of Economics* 31: 273–293.

Hayes, Rachel M., Paul Oyer, and Scott Schaefer. 2006. "Co-Worker Complementarity and the Stability of Top Management Teams." *Journal of Law, Economics, and Organizations* 22: 184–212.

Healy, Paul M. 1985. "The Effect of Bonus Schemes on Accounting Decisions." *Journal of Accounting and Economics* 7: 85–107.

Holmström, Bengt. 1979. "Moral Hazard and Observability." *Bell Journal of Economics* 10: 74–91.

———. 1982. "Moral Hazard in Teams." *Bell Journal of Economics* 13: 324–340.

———. 1999. "Managerial Incentive Problems: A Dynamic Perspective." *Review of Economic Studies* 66: 169–182.

Holmström, Bengt, and Paul Milgrom. 1991. "Multitask Principal-Agent Analyses: Incentive Contracts, Asset Ownership, and Job Design." *Journal of Law, Economics, and Organization* 7: 24–52.

Ichino, Andrea, and Giovanni Maggi. 2000. "Work Environment and Individual Background: Explaining Regional Differentials in a Large Italian Firm." *Quarterly Journal of Economics* 115: 1057–1090.

Ichniowski, Casey, Kathryn Shaw, and Giovanna Prennushi. 1997. "The Effects of Human Resource Management Practices on Productivity: A Study of Steel Finishing Lines." *American Economic Review* 87: 291–313.

Itoh, Hideshi. 1994. "Job Design, Delegation and Cooperation: A Principal-Agent Analysis." *European Economic Review* 38: 691–700.

Jacob, Brian A., and Steven D. Levitt. 2003. "Rotten Apples: An Investigation of the Prevalence and Predictors of Teacher Cheating." *Quarterly Journal of Economics* 118: 843–877.

Jenter, Dirk, and Fadi Kanaan. 2011. "CEO Turnover and Relative Performance Evaluation." *Journal of Finance*, forthcoming.

Jin, Li. 2002. "CEO Compensation, Diversification, and Incentives." *Journal of Financial Economics* 66: 29–63.

Johnson, D. Gale. 1950. "Resource Allocation under Share Contracts." *Journal of Political Economy* 58: 111–123.

Jovanovic, Boyan. 1979. "Job Matching and the Theory of Turnover." *Journal of Political Economy* 87: 972–990.

Kahn, Charles, and Gur Huberman. 1988. "Two-Sided Uncertainty and Up-or-Out Contracts." *Journal of Labor Economics* 6: 423–444.

Kahn, Lisa B. 2008. "Asymmetric Information between Employers." Working paper, Yale School of Management, Yale University, New Haven, CT.

Kandel, Eugene, and Edward P. Lazear. 1992. "Peer Pressure and Partnerships." *Journal of Political Economy* 100: 801–817.

Kaplan, Steven N., and Bernadette A. Minton. 2008. "How Has CEO Turnover Changed? Increasingly Performance Sensitive Boards and Increasingly Uneasy CEOs." Working paper, University of Chicago.

Katz, Eliakim, and Adrian Ziderman. 1990. "Investment in General Training: The Role of Information and Labour Mobility." *Economic Journal* 100: 1147–1158.

King, Ralph T., Jr. 1998. "Levi's Factory Workers Are Assigned to Teams, and Morale Takes a Hit." *Wall Street Journal,* May 20, p. A1.

Kletzer, Lori G. 1998. "Job Displacement." *Journal of Economic Perspectives* 12: 115–136.

Knoeber, Charles R., and Walter N. Thurman. 1994. "Testing the Theory of Tournaments: An Empirical Analysis of Broiler Production." *Journal of Labor Economics* 12: 155–179.

Kugler, Adriana D., and Gilles Saint-Paul. 2004. "How Do Firing Costs Affect Worker Flows in a World with Adverse Selection?" *Journal of Labor Economics* 22: 553–584.

Larkin, Ian. 2007. "The Cost of High-Powered Incentives: Employee Gaming in Enterprise Software Sales." Working paper, Harvard University, Cambridge, MA.

Lazear, Edward P. 1979. "Why Is There Mandatory Retirement?" *Journal of Political Economy* 87: 1261–1284.

——. 1986a. "Salaries and Piece Rates." *Journal of Business* 59: 405–431.

——. 1986b. "Retirement from the Labor Force," in Orley C. Ashenfelter and Richard Layard (eds.), *Handbook of Labor Economics,* volume 1. Amsterdam: North-Holland, pp. 305–355.

——. 1986c. "Raids and Offer Matching." *Research in Labor Economics* 8: 141–165.

——. 1989. "Pay Equality and Industrial Politics." *Journal of Political Economy* 97: 561–580.

——. 1990. "Job Security Provisions and Employment." *Quarterly Journal of Economics* 105: 699–726.

——. 1992. "The Job as a Concept," in William J. Bruns, Jr. (ed.), *Performance Measurement and Incentive Compensation.* Cambridge, MA: Harvard Business School Press, pp. 183–215.

——. 1998. "Hiring Risky Workers," in Isao Ohashi and Toshiaki Tachibanki (eds.), *Internal Labour Market, Incentives, and Employment.* New York: St. Martin's Press.

——. 1999. "Personnel Economics: Past Lessons and Future Directions." *Journal of Labor Economics* 17: 199–236.

——. 2000a. "Performance Pay and Productivity." *American Economic Review* 90: 1346–1361.

——. 2000b. "The Future of Personnel Economics." *Economic Journal* 110: F611–F639.

——. 2004a. "The Peter Principle: A Theory of Decline." *Journal of Political Economy* 112: S141–S163.

——. 2004b. "Output-Based Pay: Incentives, Retention, or Sorting?" *Research in Labor Economics* 23: 1–25.

——. 2006. "Speeding, Terrorism, and Teaching to the Test." *Quarterly Journal of Economics* 121: 1029–1061.

——. 2009. "Firm-Specific Human Capital: A Skill-Weights Approach." *Journal of Political Economy* 117: 914–940.

Lazear, Edward P., and Sherwin Rosen. 1981. "Rank Order Tournaments as Optimum Contracts." *Journal of Political Economy* 89: 841–864.

Lazear, Edward P., and Kathryn Shaw. 2008. *The Structure of Wages: An International Comparison.* Chicago: University of Chicago Press and National Bureau of Economic Research.

Levin, Jonathan, and Steven Tadelis. 2005. "Profit Sharing and the Role of Professional Partnerships." *Quarterly Journal of Economics* 120: 131–171.

Lluis, Stephanie. 2005. "The Role of Comparative Advantage and Learning in Wage Dynamics and Intrafirm Mobility: Evidence from Germany." *Journal of Labor Economics* 23: 725–768.

Lucas, Robert E., Jr. 1978. "On the Size Distribution of Business Firms." *Bell Journal of Economics* 9: 508–523.

Lumsdaine, Robin, and Olivia Mitchell. 1999. "New Developments in the Economic Analysis of Retirement," in Orley C. Ashenfelter and David Card (eds.), *Handbook of Labor Economics*, volume III. Amsterdam: North-Holland, pp. 3261–3307.

MacLeod, W. Bentley. 2003. "On Optimal Contracting with Subjective Evaluation." *American Economic Review* 93: 216–240.

MacLeod, W. Bentley, and James M. Malcomson. 1989. "Implicit Contracts, Inventive Compatibility, and Involuntary Unemployment." *Econometrica* 57: 447–480.

Malcomson, James M. 1999. "Individual Employment Contracts," in Orley C. Ashenfelter and David Card (eds.), *Handbook of Labor Economics*, volume III. Amsterdam: North-Holland.

Manchester, Colleen Flaherty. 2008. "The Effect of Tuition Reimbursement on Turnover: A Case Study Analysis," in Stefan Bender, Julia Lane, Kathryn L. Shaw, Fredrik Andersson, and Till Von Wachter (eds.), *The Analysis of Firms and Employees*. Chicago: University of Chicago Press and National Bureau of Economic Research, pp. 197–228.

Manne, Henry G. 1965. "Mergers and the Market for Corporate Control." *Journal of Political Economy* 73: 110–120.

Marino, Anthony M., and Jan Zábojník . 2008. "Work-Related Perks, Agency Problems, and Optimal Incentive Contracts." *RAND Journal of Economics* 39: 565–585.

Mas, Alexandre, and Enrico Moretti. 2009. "Peers at Work." *American Economic Review* 99: 112–145.

Meyer, Margaret, Paul R. Milgrom, and D. John Roberts. 1992. "Organizational Prospects, Influence Costs, and Ownership Changes." *Journal of Economics and Management Strategy* 1: 9–35.

Milgrom, Paul, and Sharon Oster. 1987. "Job Discrimination, Market Forces, and the Invisibility Hypothesis." *Quarterly Journal of Economics* 102: 453–476.

Milgrom, Paul, and John Roberts. 1988. "An Economic Approach to Influence Activities in Organizations." *American Journal of Sociology* 94(supplement): S154–S179.

———. 1990. "The Economics of Modern Manufacturing: Technology, Strategy, and Organization." *American Economic Review* 80: 511–528.

Mirrlees, James. 1974. "Notes on Welfare Economics, Information and Uncertainty," in Michael S. Balch, Daniel L. McFadden, and Shih-Yen Wu (eds.), *Essays in Equilibrium Behavior under Uncertainty*. Amsterdam: North-Holland, pp. 243–258.

Murphy, Kevin J. 1999. "Executive Compensation," in Orley C. Ashenfelter and David Card (eds.), *Handbook of Labor Economics*, volume III. Amsterdam: North-Holland, pp. 2485–2563.

———. 2000. "Performance Standards in Incentive Contracts." *Journal of Accounting and Economics* 30: 245–278.

Nagin, Daniel S., James B. Rebitzer, Seth Sanders, and Lowell J. Taylor. 2002. "Monitoring, Motivation, and Management: The Determinants of Opportunistic Behavior in a Field Experiment." *American Economic Review* 92: 850–873.

Nalebuff, Barry J., and Joseph E. Stiglitz. 1983. "Prizes and Incentives: Towards a General Theory of Compensation and Competition." *Bell Journal of Economics* 14: 21–43.

Neal, Derek. 1995. "Industry-Specific Human Capital: Evidence from Displaced Workers." *Journal of Labor Economics* 13: 653–677.

Olsen, Trond E., and Gaute Torsvik. 2000. "Discretion and Incentives in Organizations." *Journal of Labor Economics* 18: 377–404.

Olson, Craig A. 2002. "Do Workers Accept Lower Wages in Exchange for Health Benefits?" *Journal of Labor Economics* 20: S91–S115.

Oyer, Paul. 1998. "Fiscal Year Ends and Non-Linear Incentive Contracts: The Effect on Business Seasonality." *Quarterly Journal of Economics* 113: 149–185.

———. 2004. "Why Do Firms Use Incentives That Have No Incentive Effects?" *Journal of Finance* 59: 1619–1649.

———. 2008. "Salary or Benefits?" *Research in Labor Economics* 28: 429–467.

Oyer, Paul, and Scott Schaefer. 2000. "Layoffs and Litigation." *RAND Journal of Economics* 31: 345–358.

———. 2002. "Litigation Costs and Returns to Experience." *American Economic Review* 92: 683–705.

Oyer, Paul, and Scott Schaefer. 2005. "Why Do Some Firms Give Stock Options to All Employees? An Empirical Examination of Alternative Theories." *Journal of Financial Economics* 76: 99–133.

———. 2010. "Firm/Employee Matching: An Industry Study of American Lawyers." Working paper, Stanford University, Stanford, CA.

Pierce, Brooks. 2001. "Compensation Inequality." *Quarterly Journal of Economics* 116: 1493–1525.

Prendergast, Canice, 1993. "The Role of Promotion in Inducing Specific Human Capital Acquisition." *Quarterly Journal of Economics* 108: 523–534.

———. 1995. "A Theory of Responsibility in Organizations." *Journal of Labor Economics* 13: 387–400.

———. 1999. "The Provision of Incentives in Firms." *Journal of Economic Literature* 37: 7–63.

———. 2000. "What Trade-Off of Risk and Incentives?" *American Economic Review* 90: 421–425.

———. 2002a. "The Tenuous Trade-Off between Risk and Incentives." *Journal of Political Economy* 110: 1071–1102.

———. 2002b. "Uncertainty and Incentives." *Journal of Labor Economics* 20: S115–S137.

———. 2007. "The Motivation and Bias of Bureaucrats." *American Economic Review* 97: 180–196.

Prendergast, Canice, and Robert Topel. 1996. "Favoritism in Organizations." *Journal of Political Economy* 104: 958–978.

Rajan, Raghuram G., and Julie Wulf. 2006. "Are Perks Purely Managerial Excess?" *Journal of Financial Economics* 79: 1–33.

Rosen, Sherwin. 1974. "Hedonic Methods and Implicit Markets: Product Differentiation in Pure Competition." *Journal of Political Economy* 82: 34–55.

———. 1978. "Substitution and Division of Labour." *Economica* 45: 235–250.

———. 1982. "Authority, Control, and the Distribution of Earnings." *Bell Journal of Economics* 13: 311–323.

———. 1986a. "The Theory of Equalizing Differences," in Orley C. Ashenfelter and Richard Layard (eds.), *Handbook of Labor Economics,* volume I. Amsterdam: North-Holland, pp. 641–692.

———. 1986b. "Prizes and Incentives in Elimination Tournaments." *American Economic Review* 76: 701–715.

Ross, Stephen A. 1973. "The Economic Theory of Agency: The Principal's Problem." *American Economic Review* 63: 134–139.

Salop, Joanne, and Steven Salop. 1976. "Self-Selection and Turnover in the Labor Market." *Quarterly Journal of Economics* 90: 619–627.

Sattinger, Michael. 1993. "Assignment Models of the Distribution of Earnings." *Journal of Economic Literature* 31: 831–880.

Schaefer, Scott. 1998. "Influence Costs, Structural Inertia, and Organizational Change." *Journal of Economics and Management Strategy* 7: 237–263.

Schonberg, Uta. 2007. "Testing for Asymmetric Employer Learning." *Journal of Labor Economics* 25: 651–691.

Schöttner, Anja. 2007. "Relational Contracts, Multitasking, and Job Design." *Journal of Law, Economics, and Organization* 24: 138–162.

Shapiro, Carl, and Joseph E. Stiglitz. 1984. "Equilibrium Unemployment as a Worker Discipline Device." *American Economic Review* 74: 433–444.

Shearer, Bruce. 2004. "Piece Rates, Fixed Wages and Incentives: Evidence from a Field Experiment." *Review of Economic Studies* 71: 513–534.

Song, Younghwan. 2007. "Recall Bias in the Displaced Workers Survey: Are Layoffs Really Lemons?" *Labour Economics* 14: 325–345.

Spence, Michael. 1973. "Job Market Signaling." *Quarterly Journal of Economics* 87: 355–374.

Stern, Scott. 2004. "Do Scientists Pay to Be Scientists?" *Management Science* 50: 835–853.

Stiglitz, Joseph E. 1975. "Incentives, Risk, and Information: Notes Toward a Theory of Hierarchy." *Bell Journal of Economics and Management Science* 6: 552–579.

Thaler, Richard, and Sherwin Rosen. 1976. "The Value of Saving a Life: Evidence from the Labor Market," in Nester Terleckyj (ed.), *Household Production and Consumption.* Studies in Income and Wealth 40. New York: Columbia University Press for National Bureau of Economic Research.

Topel, Robert. 1991. "Specific Capital, Mobility, and Wages: Wages Rise with Job Seniority." *Journal of Political Economy* 99: 145–176.

Waldman, Michael. 1984. "Job Assignments, Signaling, and Efficiency." *RAND Journal of Economics* 15: 255–267.

———. 1990. "Up-or-Out Contracts: A Signaling Perspective." *Journal of Labor Economics* 8: 230–250.

Woodbury, Stephen A. 1983. "Substitution between Wage and Nonwage Benefits." *American Economic Review* 73: 166–182.

Woodcock, Simon D. 2008, "Match Effects." Working paper, Simon Fraser University, Burnaby, BC, Canada.

Zábojník, Jan. 1996. "Pay-Performance Sensitivity and Production Uncertainty." *Economic Letters* 53: 291–296.

———. 2002. "Centralized and Decentralized Decision-Making in Organizations." *Journal of Labor Economics* 20: 1–22.

Zhang, Ye. 2007. "Employer Learning under Asymmetric Information: The Role of Job Mobility." Working paper, University of Maryland, College Park.

13

Theory and Evidence in Internal Labor Markets

Michael Waldman

1. Introduction

During the past 30 years economics has made great progress in moving beyond treating the firm as a "black box" and understanding various aspects of its internal operation. One area, in particular, where substantial progress has been made is that of internal labor markets.[1] In this chapter I do not broadly survey the now-extensive literature on this topic (for broad surveys, see Gibbons 1998; Gibbons and Waldman 1999a; Lazear 1999; Lazear and Oyer, this volume) but rather focus on connections between theory and evidence in this literature. In particular, pursuing a theme first explored in Gibbons and Waldman (1999a), I explore the extent to which patterns of empirical evidence can be used to choose among competing theories.

Most of the early literature on internal labor markets was theoretical, and these papers typically fall under one of two main approaches. One approach was to identify and model a fundamental factor concerning the operation of internal labor markets. Important works here include Becker (1962, 1964) on human capital, Holmström (1979, 1982) and Shavell (1979) on agency theory, and Rosen (1982) on the allocation of workers across a job ladder. Clearly these are important contributions. But mostly these papers were not focused on the extent to which the models developed are able to capture important empirical relationships.

I thank Jed DeVaro; Suman Ghosh; Jin Li; Hodaka Morita; Bryan Ricchetti; Jan Zábojník; the volume editors, Bob Gibbons and John Roberts; and participants at the meeting of the NBER Working Group in Organizational Economics devoted to reviewing early drafts of chapters from this handbook at Stanford for helpful comments. I especially thank Bob Gibbons for numerous conversations that have helped develop my thinking on this subject, and Jin Li and Hodaka Morita for help in reviewing the literature.

1. Doeringer and Piore (1971) originally employed the term "internal labor market" to refer to the human resource practices of a firm (or part of a firm) that employs ports of entry, promotion from within, wages attached to jobs, and job ladders. Their analysis focused mostly on blue-collar settings and was mostly descriptive rather than based on statistical analysis. Consistent with more recent literature, I use the term to refer to various issues concerning a firm's labor force when the labor force exhibits long-term attachments to the firm. With this usage the term can be used to describe either blue- or white-collar settings. Alternative terminology would be to refer to "personnel economics" or "careers in organizations" rather than "internal labor markets."

The second approach was more closely tied to the empirical evidence in that the focus was typically on providing an explanation for an important empirical phenomenon. Important papers here include Lazear's (1979) model of mandatory retirement; Lazear and Rosen's (1981) seminal model of labor-market tournaments that provides an explanation for large wage increases associated with promotion; and Waldman (1984a), which explores the signaling role of promotions and provides a competing explanation for large wage increases upon promotion.

But as the literature has matured, two related questions have become central. First, when there are competing theories for a phenomenon, which one best captures the correct real-world explanation? For example, both tournament theory and promotions serving as signals provide explanations for why promotions are typically associated with large wage increases. How should we choose between these theories, or possibly, what would lead us to conclude both are at work? Second, empirical phenomena should not be viewed in isolation. If, for example, tournament theory is the correct explanation for large wage increases at promotion, then this has implications for the correct explanation for other internal labor market phenomena. In other words, many of these phenomena are inherently intertwined, so there should be a single model or a set of related models that explain related phenomena rather than a completely different model for each fact.

More recent literature makes progress on these issues in one of two ways. First, on the empirical side, rather than focusing on a single fact or phenomenon, many papers present a pattern of evidence on related issues. Early papers in this category are the Medoff and Abraham (1980, 1981) papers on performance evaluations and wages. More recent important papers include Baker et al. (1994a,b) on wage and promotion dynamics and the Ichniowski et al. (1997) investigation of human resource practices.

Second, some more recent theoretical studies focus on whether the model is consistent with patterns in the empirical evidence rather than with a single fact or empirical phenomenon. Examples of papers in this category are Milgrom and Roberts (1990), Bernhardt (1995), and Gibbons and Waldman (1999b, 2006). Milgrom and Roberts (1990) show how complementarity across work practices can explain various standard findings concerning innovative work practices, while Bernhardt (1995) and Gibbons and Waldman (1999b, 2006) provide models that explain various findings concerning wage and promotion dynamics inside firms.

This survey focuses on this agenda. That is, it focuses on how patterns of evidence can be used to choose among plausible alternative theoretical approaches, where (not surprisingly) sometimes the evidence points toward a combination of theories being the right answer. I also try to highlight the open questions. Given the focus of the chapter, rather than providing a comprehensive survey of the internal labor market literature, I consider specific topics where the literature is sufficiently mature that focusing on patterns of evidence and theories that can address these patterns is a worthwhile exercise.

The three specific topics I consider are wage and promotion dynamics, human resource practices, and international differences. Sections 2 and 3 consider the literature on wage and promotion dynamics. Section 2 surveys empirical evidence, including basic empirical findings, the role of schooling, and the role of performance evaluations. Section 3 then discusses four candidate models for explaining the evidence and also provides an overview and synthesis. Sections 4 and 5 consider the literature on human resource practices. Section 4 begins with a description of the different types of evidence available and then proceeds to survey the evidence concerning the effects of adoption and patterns of adoption of innovative human resource practices. Section 5 discusses relevant theories. Section 6 considers international differences in internal labor market operation, where most of these differences are closely linked to differences in human resource practices. Here most of the focus is on U.S.-Japanese differences and the various theoretical models that have been put forth to explain these differences. Section 7 concludes.

2. Empirical Evidence on Wage and Promotion Dynamics

This section starts with a discussion of basic empirical findings and then follows with discussions of the role of schooling and performance evaluations. Some evidence concerning wage and promotion dynamics is found in tests of specific theoretical models. Much of this evidence is discussed in Section 3, which focuses on theory.

2.1. Basic Empirical Findings

Although most findings in this section appear in Baker et al. (1994a,b), most of the focus is on findings with support both there and elsewhere. Other important papers in this literature include Lazear (1992), McLaughlin (1994), McCue (1996), and Podolny and Baron (1997). Note that some of these studies are similar to the Baker et al. study in that the data are drawn from a single firm's personnel records, whereas others analyze data drawn from broader cross-sections. Also, like Baker et al., some studies focus on white-collar workers, whereas others consider both blue- and white-collar workers. For each finding I provide a list of papers that find supporting evidence (and where appropriate papers that find contradictory evidence), but because of the rapid growth in this literature I do not attempt to provide an exhaustive list for each finding.[2]

The first finding is that real wage decreases are not rare, but nominal wage decreases and demotions are. That real wage decreases are not rare is found in Baker et al. (1994a,b), McLaughlin (1994), and Card and Hyslop (1997). Baker et al. find that real wage decreases are more frequent in high-inflation environments, which suggests a lag in the wage-adjustment process, but some real wage decreases are seen even with low inflation. The same papers find evidence of a low rate of nominal wage decreases. In terms of demotions, in addition to Baker et al., some studies— including Seltzer and Merrett (2000) and Treble et al. (2001)—find that demotions are rare. A few exceptions, however, find a significant rate of demotions, including the Dohmen et al. (2004) study of Fokker Aircraft's decline and Lin's (2005) study of low-level salespersons in a Taiwanese firm.

A second finding with significant support is serial correlation in promotion rates; that is, a worker promoted quickly from, say, level one to level two will on average earn promotion to level three more quickly. This is sometimes referred to as a fast track. Support for this phenomenon is found in Rosenbaum (1984), Baker et al. (1994a,b), and Podolny and Baron (1997). Belzil and Bognanno (2010) use a structural estimation approach to investigate what drives fast tracks.

---

2. One recent paper specifically worth mentioning is Kauhanen and Napari (2011), which finds empirical results similar to those found in Baker et al. (1994a,b) but which investigates a large linked employer-employee dataset.

They find that fast tracks are mostly driven by individual heterogeneity rather than by early promotions increasing the probability of a subsequent promotion. In other words, their findings suggest that fast tracks are mostly driven by workers with certain characteristics having a high probability of earning multiple promotions, as opposed to an early promotion having a direct causal effect on the likelihood that the worker receives a subsequent promotion.[3]

A third finding is serial correlation in wage changes. Here the evidence is mixed. Evidence in favor of the finding appears in papers focused on relatively homogeneous samples such as the Baker et al. analysis of the managerial workforce of a single firm, the Lillard and Weiss (1979) study of American scientists, and Hause's (1980) study of young Swedish males. Such studies as Abowd and Card (1989), Topel (1991), and Topel and Ward (1992) look at heterogenous samples, such as the Panel Study of Income Dynamics (PSID), and do not find the result. One exception is Baker (1997), which finds serial correlation in wage changes using the PSID. A possible reason that paper finds different results is that it considers a larger panel than the other studies and also uses different econometric tests.

Another finding, this one with strong support, is that promotions are associated with large wage increases. This has been found in numerous studies, including Lazear (1992), Baker et al. (1994a,b), and McCue (1996). There is also strong evidence, however, that wage increases at promotion are small relative to the difference between average wages across adjacent job levels. This result is found in Murphy (1985), Main et al. (1993), and Baker et al. (1994a,b). Evidence in Murphy (1985) nicely illustrates the finding. In a study of large U.S. manufacturing firms Murphy found that (1) the average real increase for vice presidents promoted to president was 21% and (2) the average salary plus bonus for presidents was 60% higher than for vice presidents. Although at first these findings may seem contradictory, as discussed in more detail later, they are actually easy to reconcile, given that on average wage changes are positive in periods where no promotions occur.

The last two findings have less support in the literature, possibly because these issues have been less studied than the previous ones. The first is that large wage increases early at a job level predict subsequent promotions. Baker et al. (1994a,b) demonstrate this result; related evidence is found in McCue (1996). The last finding is that wages exhibit cohort effects; that is, a cohort's average wage as it ages is related to the average starting wage even after controlling for composition differences across cohorts. This is found in Baker et al. (1994a,b) and, more recently, in Oyer (2006), Kahn (2010), and Oreopoulos et al. (2012), which look at economywide or industry-level cohort wages. Also, related findings appear in Beaudry and DiNardo (1991), which is discussed in more detail in Section 3.1.2.

2.2. The Role of Schooling

This section discusses empirical findings that specifically relate to the role of schooling in wage and promotion dynamics. The first result, which I take as noncontroversial so I do not list papers that find it, is that schooling positively affects the starting wage. Certainly, if this were

---

3. In contrast, Ariga et al. (1999) consider fast tracks in a large Japanese firm and find in that case fast tracks are not primarily driven by individual heterogeneity. See also Clemens (2010).

not the case, many of us would likely be unemployed, because the demand for undergraduate and graduate teaching would be significantly reduced.

A second finding is that schooling is positively related to promotion probabilities. Supporting evidence can be found in Baker et al. (1994a,b), McCue (1996), Lluis (2005), and Lin (2006), although McCue's study, which focuses on the PSID, finds a statistically significant relationship only for white men. Lluis (2005) also shows a related finding. As will be discussed in the next section, one explanation for why schooling is positively related to promotion probabilities is schooling is positively related to worker ability, and worker ability is positively related to promotion probabilities. Thus, controlling for worker ability should weaken the positive relationship between schooling and promotion probability. Lluis finds such a result. Specifically, when she includes a lagged value of each worker's wage growth, which should be a noisy measure of ability, the positive relationship between schooling and promotion probabilities becomes weaker.

A third finding with strong support is that schooling is positively related to wage level even after controlling for experience and job assignment (Medoff and Abraham 1980, 1981; Baker et al. 1994a,b). In each case the authors run Mincerian regressions that include job level and find that schooling is positively related to wage level even after controlling for experience and job level.

A final finding, where the evidence is mixed, concerns schooling and the returns to experience. Farber and Gibbons (1996), using data from the National Longitudinal Survey of Youth, regress the wage level on various variables, including schooling, experience, experience squared, a test score unobserved by employers, and various interaction terms. When they include controls for changes in the return to education over time they find that extra schooling does not change the return to experience.[4] In contrast, Rubinstein and Weiss (2007) use three datasets—the Current Population Survey short panel, the PSID, and the National Longitudinal Survey of Youth—directly to consider how earnings growth over various career intervals is related to schooling. They find strong evidence that schooling is positively related to the return to experience. Also, in a study using the Current Population Survey, Habermalz (2006) allows for nonlinearities and finds results consistent with schooling being positively related to the return to experience.[5]

2.3. The Role of Performance Evaluations

The final issue I consider is the role of performance evaluations. Few papers have considered this topic, so many of the results are taken from Medoff and Abraham (1980, 1981). These authors' main focus was on a discrepancy between the way wages depend on labor market experience and firm tenure and the way performance evaluations depend on these two factors. Specifically, they find that within a job wages are strongly positively related to labor market experience and

4. An alternative approach is to use a logarithmic wage specification explored in a large literature starting with Mincer (1974) (for surveys, see Willis 1986; Card 1999). A standard finding in this literature is that log wage is positively related to schooling, which suggests that the absolute return to experience increases with schooling. But in his original study Mincer also adds an experience-schooling interaction and finds a significant negative coefficient. This findings throws some doubt on whether the return to experience is truly increasing with education level.

5. Gibbons and Waldman (2006) argue that the finding of Farber and Gibbons (1996) that the return to experience is not increasing with education may be due to the limited time period studied.

firm tenure, whereas performance evaluations are either unrelated or slightly negatively related to these variables. In interpreting their results they question the idea that much of wage growth is the result of accumulation of human capital, but as I discuss in Section 3.4.1, there are other possibilities.

A related finding is that the magnitude of the negative relationship between performance evaluations and labor market experience depends on the manner in which the test is conducted. Specifically, the negative relationship between performance evaluations and labor market experience is larger in absolute value in cross-sectional analyses than in longitudinal analyses on the same dataset (Medoff and Abraham 1980, 1981; Gibbs 1995). This finding suggests that some of the negative relationship found in cross-sectional analyses is due to the sorting of workers across jobs and firms over time stemming from promotions and exits as workers age.

Another set of findings is that high performance evaluations today predict good future outcomes. For example, Medoff and Abraham (1980, 1981), Dohmen (2004), and DeVaro and Waldman (2012) find that performance evaluations are positively related to future promotions and future wage increases. Also, as is discussed in more detail in Section 3.3.2, DeVaro and Waldman find that, holding performance fixed, the probability of achieving a promotion varies with education level.

A final point here about the Medoff and Abraham interpretation of their results is that it is important to consider what performance evaluations actually measure. If such evaluations are a completely unbiased measure of productivity, then these authors' interpretation of their main findings would almost have to be correct. But that this is the case is not clear cut. It is quite possible that workers are evaluated relative to a specific set of peers, where the comparison group changes over time as workers age and move up the job ladder. As is discussed in more detail in Section 3.4.1, if this is the case, then other possibilities arise concerning what may be driving the main findings of Medoff and Abraham (1980, 1981).

3. Four Candidate Models

This section discusses four theoretical approaches that can be used to address the empirical facts presented in Section 2: (1) symmetric learning and insurance, (2) the tournament approach, (3) promotions as signals, and (4) symmetric learning with human capital accumulation and job assignment.[6] The end of the section provides an overview and synthesis.

3.1. Symmetric Learning and Insurance

This section discusses Harris and Holmström's (1982) model of symmetric learning and insurance (see also Freeman 1977). As is made clear below, this model does well at capturing various

---

6. There are other theoretical approaches one might consider. These include delayed compensation (e.g., Becker and Stigler 1974; Lazear 1979, 1981), the efficiency wage argument (e.g., Calvo 1979, 1985; Shapiro and Stiglitz 1984), influence costs (e.g., Milgrom 1988; Milgrom and Roberts 1988), knowledge hierarchies (e.g., Garicano 2000, Garicano and Hubbard 2005; Garicano and Rossi-Hansberg 2006), social preferences in the workplace (e.g., Frank 1984, 1985; Cabrales et al. 2008), and incentives created by the need for repeated human capital investment (e.g., Kwon 2006). I focus on the four theoretical approaches that I believe are the strongest candidates for explaining the evidence.

facts concerning wage dynamics, but because of a lack of a hierarchical structure, it does poorly in terms of capturing facts that relate to promotions.

3.1.1. Basic Description

In the Harris and Holmström model workers vary in terms of their abilities, but within a schooling group (or some other attribute easily observable at the time of labor market entry) they look observationally equivalent upon entering the labor market. As time passes firms observe workers' outputs and update their beliefs concerning workers' abilities. Because of a stochastic component in the production function, this learning is gradual; because output realizations are public, all firms have the same belief concerning a worker's expected ability in each period.

The other main aspect of the model concerns the contracting environment. Because workers are risk averse and firms are risk neutral, firms would like to insure workers against uncertainty concerning how beliefs about worker ability evolve over time. Harris and Holmström (1982) assume long-term contracting is feasible but also suppose realistically that a worker cannot commit not to leave his or her current employer to accept a higher wage elsewhere.

Equilibrium contracts consist of a downward rigid wage, but the wage may increase over time depending on subsequent output realizations. The downward rigid wage provides partial insurance, where full insurance is not feasible, because workers cannot commit not to leave later for a higher wage elsewhere. Further, at any point in time a worker's wage equals the worker's expected output minus an insurance premium the worker pays for the downward rigidity, where the size of the premium is negatively related to both worker age and the precision of beliefs concerning worker ability. The insurance premium falls with age, because the expected cost of offering a wage floor is lower when there are fewer future periods in which the wage floor might exceed subsequent values of expected worker productivity. Similarly, it falls with the precision of beliefs about worker ability, because the expected cost of a wage floor is lower when future expected productivity is anticipated to vary little.

3.1.2. Theoretical Extensions and Empirical Tests

A related theoretical analysis appears in Weiss (1984). In that analysis realized productivity in any period is stochastic, and expected productivity grows stochastically as workers age, where expected future productivity depends positively on previous productivity. As do Harris and Holmström (1982), Weiss considers the role of insurance contracts. Further, similar to Harris and Holmström's conclusions, Weiss finds that under specific assumptions concerning mobility costs and access to capital markets, the result is a downward rigid wage where wage increases occur if the stochastic process eventually results in sufficiently high expected productivity.

There have been a few empirical tests of the theory. Beaudry and DiNardo (1991) first extend the theory to consider the importance of past labor market conditions on current wages. They find that a worker's current wage should be a positive function of the best labor market conditions experienced since the worker was hired. This prediction contrasts with the spot-contracting prediction that only current labor market conditions should matter. They test the prediction using data from the Current Population Survey and the PSID and find supportive evidence. More recently, Grant (2003) investigates the same prediction using the National Longitudinal Surveys, Clemens et al. (2009) investigate the prediction using data from a single firm that experienced wide swings in demand, and Schmieder and von Wachter (2009) focus on related tests using the Displaced Worker Survey. All three papers find evidence that supports the theory. In contrast, Devereux and Hart (2007) find no support for the prediction using British data.

A different test is investigated in Chiappori et al. (1999). They first extend the model to show that late beginners do better than early starters. That is, holding fixed the wage at date t, the wage at $t + 1$ is negatively correlated with the wage at $t - 1$, so higher recent wage growth on average translates into higher subsequent wage growth. The authors then find supporting evidence using managerial data from a large French state-owned firm. That they find supporting evidence is not surprising, because the prediction is similar to serial correlation in wage increases, which, as discussed earlier, has been found in a number of studies. In addition, one drawback of this test, which is discussed by Chiappori et al., is that there is an alternative explanation. The same prediction follows if wages equal expected productivity and changes in productivity growth are positively correlated over time as in, for example, Gibbons and Waldman (1999b, 2006).

3.1.3. Pros and Cons

There are several positives concerning this theory. First, it explains the Medoff and Abraham (1980, 1981) finding that wages on average rise with experience even though performance evaluations do not. That is, assume performance evaluations not increasing with labor market experience means average productivity does not increase with experience. Then the Harris and Holmström (1982) analysis exactly captures this Medoff and Abraham finding. In their model expected productivity is independent of labor market experience. Yet the average wage increases with experience because of the downward rigidity of wages and because, as discussed, high output realizations push the average wage up over time and the insurance premium falls with experience.

Second, the model is consistent with a number of findings concerning earnings growth not discussed in the previous section but which are found in the literature. For example, the model captures Mincer's (1974) findings that within a schooling group the variance of earnings increases with labor market experience and that within schooling-experience groups the distribution of wages tends to be positively skewed. Third, as discussed above, a few papers have developed tests of the theory, and those tests have in general been supportive.

However, there are also some drawbacks. Probably the most important is that the evidence is not consistent with the model's main prediction. In the Harris and Holmström setting wages are downward rigid, where the prediction is real wage rigidity and not nominal rigidity. But substantial evidence discussed in Section 2 shows that the proportion of real wage decreases is substantial. The other main problem is that, because of its lack of a hierarchical structure or at least alternative job assignments, the model does not address the various empirical findings concerning promotions discussed in Section 2.

3.2. The Tournament Approach

Here I discuss the tournament approach to internal labor market compensation. This literature began with the seminal analysis of Lazear and Rosen (1981), which was the first major theoretical study to focus on the important role of promotions in worker compensation. Most of the discussion focuses on Lazear and Rosen's analysis, although I do discuss a few later papers. As also discussed, there is clear empirical support for the main ideas underlying tournament theory, but in general this literature has not explored the extent to which the theory can explain many of the empirical findings concerning wage and promotion dynamics discussed above.

3.2.1. Basic Description

Lazear and Rosen (1981) consider a setting characterized by two risk-neutral identical workers, where worker output is a function of effort and a stochastic term. In their world effort is not directly observable, so a firm cannot base compensation on the effort choices of its workers. Instead the firm establishes a tournament. It commits to prizes for the winner and the loser, where the winner is the worker who produces more and the two prizes are independent of the difference between the outputs and the absolute levels of the outputs.

Lazear and Rosen show that the difference between the prizes (i.e., the spread) serves as an incentive for effort, where a larger spread means higher equilibrium effort. In turn, the equilibrium spread is the one that generates efficient effort levels. That is, because effort is costly for workers, too much effort is not desirable due to the higher wages a higher effort level requires, so the firm chooses a spread that equates the marginal disutility of effort with the extra productivity associated with effort. Lazear and Rosen interpret their results as providing an explanation for the large compensation increases associated with promotions. In this interpretation promotions and the associated higher compensation serve as prizes, and lower level workers exert effort because doing so increases the probability of receiving these prizes.

Lazear and Rosen (1981) also discuss and analyze the circumstances in which labor market tournaments are preferable to alternative ways of motivating workers when effort is not directly observable. They first show that given risk neutrality, tournaments and piece rates both yield first-best outcomes. They then argue that because the information requirements for conducting tournaments are less than for paying piece rates—the tournament only requires an ordinal ranking of the workers—tournaments may be preferred, as they are less costly to conduct. Lazear and Rosen also consider what happens when workers are risk averse and argue that in some circumstances tournaments will be preferred to piece rates. I come back to this issue below.

3.2.2. Theoretical Extensions and Empirical Tests

A large literature extends Lazear and Rosen's (1981) analysis. Such papers as Green and Stokey (1983) and Nalebuff and Stiglitz (1983) focus on a comparison between the efficiency or profitability of employing tournaments versus contracting directly on output. As was true of Lazear and Rosen's analysis of risk aversion, these two papers do not focus on optimal contracts. In contrast, Mookherjee (1984) shows that under risk aversion the optimal contract typically dominates the optimal tournament. This again raises the question of why tournaments are employed. In addition to Lazear and Rosen's answer, which concerns savings on information costs, Malcomson (1984) argues that tournaments may be employed because individual performance is not verifiable, so individual contracting is difficult to enforce.

Other papers model a tournament that consists of several rounds or contests. Clearly, real-world promotion tournaments do not consist of a single contest, but rather promotion to a higher level job is typically soon followed by competition for a subsequent promotion. Rosen

(1986) models a tournament along this line (see also Meyer 1992). In Rosen's model pairs of workers compete against each other in a round, and then the winners proceed to the next round, where there is again competition between pairs of workers. The tournament ends when a single winner remains. Under the strong assumption that worker effort is constant across rounds, Rosen shows that the wage structure is convex. Specifically, he shows that the wage increase associated with winning the last round of the tournament is larger than the increases associated with winning earlier rounds.[7] The paper thus provides an explanation for why wage increases associated with being promoted to the top levels of firms seem to be especially large, as found, for example, in Murphy (1985) and Baker et al. (1994a,b).[8]

There is also a substantial literature focused on testing the implications of tournament theory. Various papers—including Ehrenberg and Bognanno (1990a,b), who study professional golf tournaments; Becker and Huselid (1992), who study auto racing; and Audas et al. (2004), who study promotions at a large British financial sector employer—find evidence consistent with effort being positively related to the spread. Although of interest, I find this set of findings weak in terms of how strongly they support traditional tournament theory. These tests provide evidence that the individuals in the tournament behave in a fashion consistent with utility maximization (i.e., effort increases when the winning prize is higher). This does not tell us anything about whether, as is true in classic tournament theory, firms commit to optimal prizes in advance of the actual promotion decision.

Another set of papers focus on predictions concerning firm behavior derived from extensions of the basic Lazear and Rosen (1981) model. The first prediction is that the spread or wage increase due to promotion should be positively related to the number of workers at the job level from which the promoted worker is drawn. The logic of this prediction is that, holding the spread fixed, increasing the number of workers competing for a promotion typically reduces equilibrium effort levels, so in response the firm increases the spread.[9] Main et al. (1993), Eriksson (1999), and Bognanno (2001) find supporting evidence, whereas O'Reilly et al. (1988) do not.

A second firm-side prediction is the convexity of the wage structure derived in Rosen's (1986) analysis discussed above. Support for this prediction is found in Lambert et al. (1993) and Eriksson (1999). I find the general support for these two firm-side predictions more persuasive than the support for the worker effort prediction discussed above. The worker effort prediction seems not so closely tied to tournament theory, whereas the firm-side predictions are derived from classic tournament theory's assumption that firms commit to promotion prizes with incentives in mind. However, there are potential alternative explanations. First, as discussed in footnote 17, the idea that the wage increase due to promotion is related to the number of workers at the job from which the promoted worker is drawn can be explained using the promotion-as-signal

---

7. See Prendergast (1999) for an interesting discussion of what drives this result in Rosen's (1986) analysis.

8. Other important theoretical extensions of the basic tournament model include Lazear's (1989) model of sabotage and wage compression (see also Garvey and Swan 1992; Drago and Garvey 1998; Carpenter et al. 2010) and models that show that tournaments can lead firms to favor insiders over outsiders when deciding whom to promote (see Malcomson 1984; Chan 1996, 2006; Waldman 2003).

9. See Prendergast (1999) for a more detailed discussion of the logic of this prediction.

hypothesis. Second, convexity of the wage structure could be due to various factors, such as income effects resulting in higher wage increases on promotion to higher ranks. The logic is that, because of income effects, at these higher ranks higher wages are needed to induce effort.[10]

More recently, DeVaro (2006a,b) uses a structural estimation approach to consider simultaneously worker-effort and firm-side predictions of tournament theory. DeVaro looks at a sample of skilled workers taken from a cross-section of establishments. Using a structural estimation approach that treats promotions, wage spreads, and performance as endogenous, he finds support for both types of predictions. Specifically, he finds results consistent with firms choosing spreads optimally and worker effort being higher when spreads are larger.

3.2.3. Pros and Cons

There are clearly strong positives associated with tournament theory. Probably the most important is the plausibility of the central ideas captured by the argument. Clearly, the possibility of promotion does serve as an incentive for worker effort in real-world firms, and it would be surprising if in thinking about promotion practices firms did not consider the ramifications for worker effort. Further, the approach provides a very plausible explanation for a well-documented internal labor market finding. That is, a quite plausible explanation for large wage increases at promotion is that the large wage increases are used to provide incentives for effort.

The other main positive is that most studies that have tested implications of tournament theory have found supportive evidence. As discussed above, there is substantial evidence that as the model predicts, holding average wages fixed, worker effort is positively related to the spread between winning and losing. Also, studies generally find that compensation varies within and across firms in ways consistent with theoretical predictions. Specifically, evidence supports the prediction that the spread is a positive function of the number of lower level employees and also that there should be a convex relationship between compensation and job level.

The main disadvantage of the tournament approach is that the theory has not been developed in ways that make clear the extent to which the approach can capture various internal labor market findings, such as early wage increases at one job level predicting subsequent promotions, wage increases upon promotion being small relative to wage differences across adjacent levels, and cohort effects being important. But that such findings have not been addressed to date does not mean that some enriched tournament model is not capable of capturing these findings.[11]

Another drawback is that there are certain aspects of standard tournament theory that seem unrealistic. For example, the idea that firms commit to "prizes" that are independent of the attributes and performance of the winner seems inconsistent with empirical evidence in such papers as Baker et al. (1994a,b), where a newly promoted worker's wage seems to depend

10. Recently, Oyer (2007) tests a third firm-side prediction. As mentioned in footnote 8, several extensions of the basic tournament model predict firms favor insiders over outsiders in promotion decisions. Oyer tests this prediction by looking at tenure decisions in economics departments and finds supporting evidence. Specifically, outside the world's top-ten departments, those hired into tenured positions from the outside are more productive on average than those promoted from within. Note, however, this finding could also be explained by asymmetric learning (e.g., Greenwald 1979, 1986) and by influence activities (e.g., Milgrom 1988; Milgrom and Roberts 1988).

11. See Krakel and Schöttner (2008) for a recent paper that moves in this direction by incorporating the possibility of bonus payments into a tournament model.

both on worker attributes and performance. Similarly, the Lazear and Rosen (1981) approach incorporates the market in a very limited way. That is, in initially attracting workers the firm must offer wages that translate into an expected utility at least as high as some reservation value, but there are no similar participation constraints after promotion decisions take place. This also seems inconsistent with Baker et al. (1994a,b) and similar papers, where workers enter and leave at all levels of the job ladder. As discussed further in Section 3.5, possibly the answer to these drawbacks is that there are labor market tournaments, but they take a somewhat different form than initially modeled by Lazear and Rosen.

3.3. Promotions as Signals

Another important approach for investigating the wage and promotion dynamics of internal labor markets is the promotion-as-signal hypothesis, as first modeled in Waldman (1984a) and later extended in Bernhardt (1995). This approach captures a number of empirical findings in the internal labor market literature, although most standard theoretical models in this literature are inconsistent with some important findings in the empirical literature.

3.3.1. Basic Description

Waldman (1984a) puts forth the basic argument. That paper considers a model characterized by asymmetric as opposed to symmetric learning. When workers enter the labor market their ability levels are initially unknown and there is learning. The difference is that only a worker's current employer directly observes ability, while other firms learn about worker ability by observing the actions of the current employer. In Waldman's analysis the key action is the promotion decision.

In Waldman's two-period model workers vary in their innate ability levels but look identical upon labor market entry. Firms are characterized by two jobs—a low-level job where the return to ability is low and a high-level job where it is high. In the first period all workers are assigned to the low-level job, and then at the end of the period a worker's initial employer learns the worker's ability level. In the second period high-ability workers are then promoted to the high-level job, where one of the key results is that fewer workers are promoted than is first-best efficient. The reason is that a promotion serves as a signal that worker ability is high, so after a promotion other firms bid more for the worker's services. Thus, the current employer must pay a promoted worker more to stop the worker from being bid away, but this causes firms to only promote workers who are significantly more productive in the high-level job.[12]

Bernhardt (1995) extends this analysis. The main differences are that in Bernhardt's model workers are in the labor market for more than two periods, there is a richer process of human capital accumulation, and workers vary in terms of their publicly observed schooling levels. What happens is that as a cohort ages workers are promoted in bunches, where the highest ability workers are promoted first and then the next highest, and so forth. Further, as in Waldman's

---

12. One difference between tournament theory and the arguments discussed here and in Section 3.4 is that in tournament theory a promotion does not result in a change in the set of tasks performed, whereas in these other arguments it does. The only relevant empirical work I am familiar with is Pergamit and Veum (1999). In their study of young workers approximately 70% of promoted workers were given additional responsibilities in their current job or position or were moved to a new job or position.

analysis, because of signaling, promotions are associated with large wage increases and fewer workers are promoted than in the first best.

In addition to showing that the main results found in Waldman (1984a) continue to hold in a richer model, Bernhardt also derives a number of new and interesting findings. For example, Bernhardt finds that firms favor more highly educated workers in the promotion process. That is, holding true productivity fixed, workers with more education are promoted first. This arises because even in the absence of a promotion, workers with more education are paid a higher wage, so the signaling role of promotion is smaller for these workers. Bernhardt also shows how his model can explain serial correlation in promotion rates (i.e., promotion fast tracks).

3.3.2. Theoretical Extensions and Related Empirical Tests

There have been many theoretical extensions of this framework and a more limited number of empirical tests. The most important extension appears in Zábojník and Bernhardt (2001).[13] That paper connects the promotion-as-signal idea to the tournament approach (see also Gibbs 1995; Ghosh and Waldman 2010; Zábojník 2010). In the traditional labor market tournament model the firm imposes the promotion tournament to create incentives. In the Zábojník and Bernhardt model the tournament instead arises from asymmetric learning and the resulting signaling aspect of promotions. That is, rather than firms committing to a prize associated with promotion, prizes arise because promotions serve as signals, and large wage increases are needed to stop promoted workers from being bid away. In addition to showing how the labor market tournament approach and the promotion-as-signal approach can be reconciled, Zábojník and Bernhardt show that their model explains various findings in the firm-size-wage-effects literature and the interindustry-wage-differences literature.[14]

On the empirical side there have been a number of tests of asymmetric learning in labor markets but only one that focuses on the promotion-as-signal hypothesis. The classic test of asymmetric learning in labor markets is found in Gibbons and Katz (1991), which builds on Greenwald's (1979, 1986) analysis of adverse selection in labor market turnover. Gibbons and Katz argue that laid-off workers should have lower ability on average than those fired in a plant closing, because adverse selection means laid-off workers are drawn from the low end of the ability distribution, whereas workers fired in a plant closing are drawn from the whole distribution.[15] Based on this logic, they derive three testable implications: (1) predisplacement wages should be uncorrelated with the cause of the displacement, (2) postdisplacement wages should

---

13. Related theory papers include Milgrom and Oster (1987), Ricart i Costa (1988), MacLeod and Malcomson (1988), Waldman (1990), Bernhardt and Scoones (1993), Owan (2004), and Golan (2005, 2009). Also, see Ishida (2004a,b) for interesting analyses that focus on the interaction between education as a signal and promotion as a signal.

14. The Zábojník and Bernhardt (2001) argument also serves as an explanation for the puzzle first identified in Baker et al. (1988): why are promotions used as incentive devices given this creates inefficiencies since the incentive and allocation roles of promotion will sometimes be in conflict? An alternative explanation for this puzzle is found in Fairburn and Malcomson (2001), which is based on the idea that bonus-based incentives are subject to the negative effects of influence activities.

15. To be precise, the Gibbons and Katz (1991) argument allows for both adverse selection as in Greenwald's (1979, 1986) analysis and for the possibility that layoffs serve as a signal like in the promotion-as-signal hypothesis.

be lower for laid-off workers than for those fired in a plant closing, and (3) postdisplacement unemployment duration should be higher for laid-off workers than for those fired in a plant closing. Using data from the Current Population Survey Gibbons and Katz find evidence that supports all three predictions.

There have been numerous follow-up studies, and the evidence is mixed concerning whether the Gibbons and Katz (1991) results are in fact due to asymmetric learning. Acemoglu and Pischke (1998), which is discussed in more detail in Section 6.2, extend the theoretical framework to consider incentives for firms to provide their workers with general human capital and then show supporting evidence using German data. But some studies that have investigated the Gibbons and Katz results argue that their results are explained by something other than asymmetric learning. For example, Krashinsky (2002) argues that the results are due to laid-off workers being displaced from larger establishments that pay higher predisplacement wages, and Song (2007) makes a similar case and also argues that recall bias is important (see also Doiron 1995; Stevens 1997; Grund 1999; and Hu and Taber 2011).

More recently, several papers have developed other predictions of asymmetric learning, and these papers mostly find supporting evidence. Specifically, Schonberg (2007) finds evidence consistent with asymmetric learning for university graduates but not for high school graduates and dropouts,[16] and Kahn (2008), Zhang (2008), and Pinkston (2009) all find general support for asymmetric learning across a variety of tests.

Finally, the only empirical analysis focused directly on the promotion-as-signal hypothesis is found in DeVaro and Waldman (2012) (for related results, see Belzil and Bognanno 2010; DeVaro et al. 2012). Related to a result in Bernhardt (1995), that paper first extends the theory to show that the signaling aspect of promotions should be larger for workers of lower schooling levels, because, even before promotion, workers with higher schooling levels are already thought of as having higher ability. DeVaro and Waldman then use this result to derive three testable implications: (1) holding performance fixed, the probability of a first promotion should be an increasing function of the education level; (2) the wage increase from a first promotion should be a decreasing function of the education level; and (3) the first two relationships should hold more strongly for first promotions than for subsequent ones. Employing the same dataset investigated in Baker et al. (1994a,b), they then find results that support signaling being important for understanding promotion practices concerning bachelors and masters degree holders, whereas the evidence concerning the importance of signaling for high school graduates and doctoral degree holders is mixed. They also consider various alternative explanations for their findings and argue that none of the alternatives explain their empirical results.

---

16. To be precise, Schonberg (2007) develops two testable implications for asymmetric learning. The first, which she finds clear evidence for among university graduates, is the result originally due to Greenwald (1979, 1986) that workers who turn over should be drawn from the low end of the ability distribution. The second is that in a world of asymmetric learning the return to ability should be positively related to tenure at the firm. For this prediction she finds mixed evidence concerning university graduates. However, I do not believe this second prediction is a robust prediction of asymmetric learning models. For example, Pinkston (2009) considers a related theoretical model, but he does not find Schonberg's second prediction. So my interpretation is that Schonberg's findings are consistent with asymmetric learning being important for university graduates.

3.3.3. Pros and Cons

There are clearly some positives associated with the promotion-as-signal hypothesis. The main one is its basic plausibility. Promotions are typically publicly observable events, and workers, especially successful ones, provide their job-assignment histories on their resumes. This practice is consistent with the history of job assignments being important for prospective employers because of its information content, which is exactly the promotion-as-signal argument. It is also plausible that large wage increases at promotion are due at least partly to signaling. That is, if a worker's job-assignment history is an important consideration for prospective employers, then it is plausible that when a worker's current employer improves that history by a promotion, the employer also increases the worker's wage to stop the worker from being bid away.

The approach also has significant empirical support both in terms of various empirical studies and being able to explain some important findings in the empirical wage- and promotion-dynamics literature. First, on net the various empirical studies in the literature support asymmetric learning as an important factor in real-world labor markets. Second, the only empirical investigation focused on the promotion-as-signal hypothesis is found in DeVaro and Waldman (2012), which finds evidence consistent with the hypothesis for bachelors and masters degree holders, although they find mixed evidence for high school educated workers and doctoral degree holders. Third, the hypothesis is consistent with two important empirical findings concerning promotions; that is, there are large wage increases upon promotion, but these wage increases are small relative to wage differences across adjacent job levels.[17]

In addition to the positives discussed above, however, there are also some negatives. Specifically, some of the important empirical findings concerning wage and promotion dynamics are inconsistent with most models of asymmetric learning. Two stand out. First, in most pure asymmetric learning models a worker's salary increase in a period in which there is no promotion is completely determined by observable characteristics, such as schooling, labor market experience, and firm tenure. But numerous studies, such as Baker et al. (1994a,b), make it clear that this is not the case. Second, the approach does not easily explain why the size of wage increases early at a job level forecast speed of promotion. The reason is that in a standard asymmetric-learning model a firm will not reward a worker when no positive information is publicly revealed, so in the absence of promotions the firm should not give higher wage increases to the higher productivity workers.

But for both issues it is possible that richer models of asymmetric learning can match the evidence. For example, Novos (1995) considers a model of asymmetric learning without promotions where, upon starting employment at a firm, a worker privately learns how much disutility the worker will receive from staying at this specific firm, which subsequently affects the worker's probability of accepting a competing wage offer in the future. The result is that the current employer pays a wage increasing in worker ability, even though ability is privately observed by the

---

17. The approach is consistent with wage increases upon promotion being small relative to wage differences across adjacent levels if workers accumulate general human capital as they age. The approach can also explain the finding discussed earlier that wage increases upon promotion are positively related to the number of workers at the level from which the promoted worker is drawn. That is, this prediction is consistent with the promotion-as-signal hypothesis, because the signaling value of a promotion should be positively related to the number of workers who were competing for the promotion.

firm, where it does this to reduce the probability of turnover for the higher ability workers. It is possible that incorporating the Novos approach into an asymmetric-learning model with promotions would result in a model that both captures large wage increases upon promotion due to signaling and is not subject to the two criticisms discussed in the above paragraph.[18]

3.4. Symmetric Learning with Human Capital Accumulation and Job Assignment

The last approach I discuss is the symmetric learning approach to wage and promotion dynamics first explored in Gibbons and Waldman (1999b). That approach combines symmetric learning with human capital accumulation as in Becker (1962, 1964) and job assignment as in Rosen (1982) and Waldman (1984b). This approach is the one most successful at capturing the wide variety of empirical findings concerning wage and promotion dynamics found in the internal labor market literature. But even this approach has some drawbacks.

3.4.1. Basic Description

As indicated, Gibbons and Waldman (1999b) combine symmetric learning, human capital accumulation, and job assignment. In their model workers look identical upon labor market entry but in fact vary in terms of their innate abilities; at the end of each period firms observe worker outputs and update their beliefs concerning each worker's ability. As in Harris and Holmström (1982) discussed in Section 3.1, learning is gradual because of a stochastic term in the production function. Another key assumption is that workers accumulate general human capital as they age with the result that each worker's "effective" ability grows over time, although expected effective ability falls when output is very low. Further, the process of human capital accumulation is multiplicative; that is, workers with higher innate ability accumulate human capital at a faster rate. Also, there are three job levels that vary in terms of the marginal return to effective ability, where the process of human capital accumulation means workers on average move up the job ladder as they age. Finally, wages are determined by spot-market contracting.

Gibbons and Waldman (1999b) show that this framework captures most of the empirical findings concerning wage and promotion dynamics in internal labor markets discussed in Section 2.1. For example, the model explains why real wage decreases are not rare but demotions are. Real wage decreases are not rare, because with learning a worker receives a real wage decrease when realized output is so low that expected effective ability falls. However, this rarely translates into a demotion, because demotion also requires expected effective ability to cross a critical value at which productivity across the two jobs is the same. The model also explains large wage increases upon promotion because promoted workers on average have large increases in expected effective ability. In addition, it shows that large wage increases early at a job level predict quicker than average promotion. This follows because a large wage increase early on means significant

18. Golan (2009), Li (2009), and Pinkston (2009) are other papers with asymmetric-learning analyses not subject to one or both criticisms. Also, the second criticism above implicitly assumes workers with the same observable characteristics. If workers have different observable characteristics, such as heterogenous schooling levels, then it is possible that a large wage increase early on—for example, due to higher schooling—could predict speed of promotion if, as is plausibly the case, workers with higher schooling also on average are promoted more quickly. This argument could explain the Baker et al. (1994a,b) finding that early wage increases predict promotion, because that test does not control for the schooling level. It would be easy to empirically investigate this argument.

growth in expected effective ability; thus, on average, the worker achieves the expected effective ability required for promotion more quickly. The model also explains serial correlation in wage changes, that wage increases at promotion are small relative to the difference between average wages across adjacent job levels, and is consistent with serial correlation in promotion rates.[19]

Gibbons and Waldman (1999b) also show that this framework can explain many of the results concerning performance evaluations discussed in Section 2.3 given the additional assumption that supervisors evaluate individuals relative to other workers with the same labor market experience. This part of their analysis builds on a discussion in Harris and Holmström (1982). For example, Medoff and Abraham (1980, 1981) find that for a given job, wages are positively related to labor market experience, whereas performance evaluations are either unrelated or slightly negatively related to experience. In the Gibbons and Waldman framework, wages for a given job are positively related to labor market experience because general human capital increases with experience. But if workers are evaluated relative to others with the same labor market experience, then performance evaluations for a given job fall with experience, because workers with high expected innate ability are promoted out of the job as they age, while those with low expected ability are promoted into the job. The framework can also explain differences between cross-sectional and longitudinal analyses of the same dataset and explain why performance evaluations predict both future promotions and future wage increases.[20]

3.4.2. Theoretical Extensions and Related Empirical Tests

Important extensions of this framework appear in Gibbons and Waldman (2006). That paper first addresses empirical findings concerning the role of schooling in wage and promotion dynamics. In this model workers vary in terms of their schooling levels, where higher schooling means higher expected innate ability. They show that with this enrichment, the model captures the major empirical findings discussed in Section 2.2. For example, the model provides an explanation for why higher schooling improves promotion probabilities. That is, higher schooling means higher starting levels of expected effective ability, which, in turn, means expected effective ability on average grows faster and passes the critical value required for promotion more quickly. The model also explains why schooling is positively related to the wage even after controlling for experience and job assignment and why the returns to experience may be positively related to schooling, although the evidence on this issue is mixed, as mentioned before.

In the second part of their 2006 paper Gibbons and Waldman address cohort effects (see also Gibbons and Waldman 2004). Remember, cohort effects mean that, even after controlling for differences in the composition of workers in a cohort, a cohort's average wage years after entry into a firm reflects to some degree the cohort's average starting wage. Their 1999b model is not consistent with this finding, but their 2006 paper shows that the framework is consistent with the finding when task-specific human capital is added. Task-specific human capital means

---

19. Gibbons and Waldman (1999b) show serial correlation in promotion rates in their full-information benchmark analysis, but they are unable to show that the framework necessarily exhibits serial correlation in promotion rates given symmetric learning.

20. DeVaro and Waldman (2012) provide evidence using the Baker et al. (1994a,b) dataset consistent with performance evaluations being absolute measures of productivity. This evidence throws some doubt on the explanation given above for the Medoff and Abraham (1980, 1981) findings.

human capital accumulated in one period is more valuable later, when the worker is performing similar tasks. Specifically, Gibbons and Waldman (2006) assume an old worker assigned to the high-level job is more productive when the worker has prior experience on this job. They show that with this enrichment, their framework captures the cohort effects found by Baker et al. (1994a,b) if, during a boom, entering cohorts both earn higher wages and enter the firm on average at higher levels of the job ladder. This approach can also potentially explain the economywide and industry-level cohort effects found in recent papers, such as Oyer (2006), Kahn (2010), and Oreopoulos et al. (2012).[21]

Some recent studies empirically estimate the Gibbons and Waldman (1999b) model using large datasets from other countries (U.S. datasets cannot typically be used for this purpose, because they do not contain job-level information). One such study is Lluis (2005). She uses longitudinal data from the German Socio-Economic Panel and generalized method-of-moments techniques. Her results generally support the framework, although the evidence that learning is important is weak. In particular, the evidence is consistent with learning being important in job assignment for younger workers, but for older workers the evidence is weak.[22] She hypothesizes that the mixed evidence for learning may reflect the apprenticeship system in Germany, because much of the learning about worker ability may occur during the apprentice period. But an alternative explanation, as discussed next, is that her findings are in fact consistent with a more complete analysis of the Gibbons and Waldman framework.[23]

There are also studies related to the Gibbons and Waldman (2004, 2006) arguments concerning task-specific human capital. For example, Dohmen (2004) finds that, consistent with task-specific human capital being important, a worker's performance evaluation falls after a promotion but quickly rises as the worker gains experience at the new job level, while Shaw and Lazear (2008) find a similar result by looking directly at productivity.[24] Also, in an interesting recent paper Gathmann and Schonberg (2010) find support for task-specific human capital in an empirical investigation of the jobs workers leave and those they move to when they switch employers.

21. Other interesting theoretical extensions appear in Clemens (2010) and DeVaro and Morita (2010). Clemens extends the framework by allowing for two lower level jobs rather than one, where one type of lower level job is part of a fast track, because the speed of human capital accumulation is higher, which in turn translates into higher rates of promotion. He also provides empirical evidence using the Baker et al. (1994a,b) dataset that supports the predictions he derives from this approach. DeVaro and Morita focus on internal promotion versus external recruitment (see footnotes 8 and 10 for related discussions) using a symmetric learning model with human capital accumulation and job assignment. They derive various predictions, including increased use of internal promotion at large firms, and then provide empirical support using a large cross-section of British employers.

22. Lima and Pereira (2003) find a similar result using Portuguese data. Their focus is on the wage premiums associated with promotion. They find that toward the bottom of the job ladder learning is an important factor behind these wage premiums, whereas at the top learning is unimportant. Hunnes (2011) uses Norwegian data and an empirical methodology similar to that employed by Lluis (2005). Hunnes finds stronger evidence for learning, but in his analysis the strongest evidence is at the top hierarchical levels. See also Dias da Silva and van der Klaauw (2011).

23. Another related study is Smeets and Warzynski (2008), which provides evidence concerning span of control and dynamics. The authors argue that their findings are consistent with an enriched version of the Gibbons and Waldman (1999b) framework.

24. DeVaro and Waldman (2012) do not find this pattern in their analysis of the Baker et al. (1994a,b) dataset.

In contrast to the general empirical support for task-specific human capital being important, the evidence for the Gibbons and Waldman argument concerning task-specific human capital and cohort effects is more mixed. In a recent paper Kwon et al. (2010) find that cohort effects are due to workers hired during a boom having higher promotion rates rather than the Gibbons and Waldman prediction that during a boom initial job assignments are higher on the job ladder. As conjectured by Kwon et al., possibly these results can be explained by an extension of the Gibbons and Waldman argument where it is job assignments early in the career—rather than just the initial job assignment—that increase productivity later in the career and thus improve assignments and wages later in the career. Also, Schmieder and von Wachter (2010), mentioned in Section 3.1.2, find results using the Displaced Worker Survey that seem to more directly contradict the Gibbons and Waldman argument concerning task-specific human capital and cohort effects.

3.4.3. Pros and Cons

The pros here are straightforward. The theoretical analyses show that the approach can explain a wide set of the empirical findings in the literature on wage and promotion dynamics in internal labor markets. These include what I have referred to as basic empirical findings, findings concerning the role of performance evaluations, and findings concerning schooling. Also, incorporating task-specific human capital, which seems realistic, allows the model to explain cohort effects, although as discussed, the evidence for this part of the argument is mixed.

On the negative side there are two related issues. First, Gibbons and Waldman (1999b, 2006) do not consider the idea that—at least under their assumption that innate ability is a one-dimensional fixed attribute—most learning should occur early in careers. This is potentially problematic if empirical findings for older workers can only be explained by assuming learning is significant. Second, as discussed above, some empirical investigations of the Gibbons and Waldman framework find evidence for symmetric learning only for younger workers.

As a final point, it is unclear to me how significant these issues are. In their 1999b paper Gibbons and Waldman show that many of the empirical findings they focus on can also be explained in their framework under the assumption of full information. It is thus possible the two issues discussed above are not problems for their framework at all. As stated above, in a world where innate ability is a one-dimensional fixed attribute, learning should be mostly confined to the early part of workers' careers. So possibly the correct perspective is that the Gibbons and Waldman framework provides the right explanation for the main empirical findings in Section 2, where at low values of labor market experience it is their symmetric-learning arguments that apply, whereas at high levels their full-information arguments apply. Further theoretical and empirical work exploring this possibility would be helpful.

3.5. Overview and Synthesis

Among the candidate models considered (which were chosen because they were the ones with the most empirical support), clearly the framework that combines symmetric learning, human capital accumulation, and job assignment is the one the literature currently suggests best explains empirical findings concerning wage and promotion dynamics in internal labor markets. Of course, it is possible this model is superior on this dimension only because the other frameworks have not been developed in ways that make clear the extent to which they can explain the empirical evidence. But I believe this is unlikely. The more plausible explanation is that symmetric learning, human capital accumulation, and job assignment are all important elements in the operation of real-world internal labor markets.

But I also believe the evidence does not support the idea that the basic model investigated in Gibbons and Waldman (1999b) is sufficient for explaining all the evidence. Rather, various enrichments seem important.[25] First, both because of its real-world plausibility and because of the growing evidence supporting its presence, incorporating task-specific human capital as in Gibbons and Waldman (2006) seems important. Second, the evidence in favor of asymmetric learning along with recent evidence in favor of the promotion-as-signal hypothesis suggests that asymmetric learning is also important. In other words, most models assume learning is either purely symmetric or purely asymmetric, but in fact there is no reason that real-world learning cannot be a mix of the two. And my sense is that the evidence supports this.[26]

In addition, incentives associated with promotion must also be important. But it is unclear whether it is best to incorporate the type of classic tournament explored by Lazear and Rosen (1981), or whether, along the lines of Zábojník and Bernhardt's (2001) analysis, tournaments based on the promotion-as-signal hypothesis are more realistic. The difference concerns whether the firm commits to optimal values for future high wages associated with promotions or whether these future high wages arise as the result of signaling. Future theoretical and empirical work focused on distinguishing between these possibilities would be of interest.[27]

The evidence also suggests that the Gibbons and Waldman assumption of spot contracting is not fully accurate. Many empirical findings point to the "market" being important in wage determination, so spot contracting will typically give better predictions and explanations than a model in which workers are completely insulated from the aggregate labor market.[28] But there are aspects of the evidence—such as nominal wage rigidity, the type of cohort effects found by Beaudry and DiNardo (1991), and Green Card effects—that suggest that wages do deviate from the market wage in important ways (for a related empirical analysis and discussion, see Gibbs and Hendricks 2004).[29] It is an open question whether these types of deviations can be incorporated convincingly into the theoretical modeling.

There are a few subjects that deserve more attention at both the theoretical and empirical levels. One subject is the connection between wage and promotion dynamics in internal labor markets and the turnover decision. How a worker's career progresses during a stay at a single

25. See Coupe et al. (2006) for an interesting empirical analysis of the academic economist labor market that is consistent with this view.

26. Kahn (2008) is a recent paper that mixes symmetric and asymmetric learning in the manner I have in mind. See also Lazear (1986a), Waldman (1990), and Pinkston (2009).

27. Waldman (2011) discusses the extent to which existing empirical evidence supports the classic approach or that based on the promotion-as-signal hypothesis. That paper also discusses a hybrid approach that combines the two approaches and possibly matches the data better than either of the two earlier approaches viewed in isolation.

28. Lazear and Oyer (2004) show that, even in Sweden's highly regulated labor market, the "market" is important in wage determination.

29. "Green Card effects" refers to rules or guidelines sometimes employed that place bounds on a worker's pay increase in any period. See Milkovich and Newman (1987) and Baker et al. (1994a) for empirical analyses and discussions and Peterson (2010) for a theoretical analysis.

employer should be closely related to voluntary and involuntary turnover decisions and also to how the worker performs at the new job. On the empirical side a few papers develop evidence along these lines. For example, Baker et al. (1994a,b) have results concerning entry and exit rates at different levels and also comparisons of wage growth and promotion outcomes for new entrants versus incumbents, and Treble et al. (2001) provide a similar analysis. But more empirical investigation of this issue would be helpful. Similarly, there is limited theoretical work on this topic, and more theoretical attention to it could prove fruitful, especially if the empirical literature matures to the point that the facts are clear.[30]

A final subject that deserves more attention is bonus payments. Most empirical research in this literature focuses on salaries rather than on bonuses. This is probably because salary data are frequently more readily available, and because some early empirical work in this literature focused on salaries and ignored bonuses. But there are recent findings that suggest bonuses work quite differently than salaries. For example, Lin (2005) finds that bonuses vary more with aggregate economic conditions than do salaries and also that within a level bonuses vary more than do salaries. Also, Belzil and Bognanno (2008) find that promotions cause increases in base pay but not in bonus pay. These results suggest that salary and bonus play somewhat different roles in compensating workers and thus that further empirical and theoretical work on this issue could be fruitful.[31]

4. Empirical Evidence on Human Resource Practices

An important topic in the study of internal labor markets is the type of human resource practices firms employ to increase worker productivity. And in particular, much of the recent literature on this topic has focused on "traditional" versus "innovative" human resource practices. In this section I focus on the empirical literature on the subject. Section 5 discusses the theoretical literature, and Section 6 discusses international differences concerning internal labor markets—most of which can be connected to differences in human resource practices (for an earlier survey on human resource practices, see Ichniowski and Shaw 2003).

4.1. The Basics

The literature on human resource practices makes a distinction between what are referred to as "traditional" and "innovative" practices. Traditional practices are those that were predominant

30. Recent theoretical work that moves in this direction includes Ghosh (2007), Ricchetti (2007), and Peterson (2010).

31. One issue concerning bonuses that has received empirical and theoretical attention is that bonuses are more important at higher levels of job ladders. This is documented empirically in a number of papers, including Baker et al. (1994a,b) and Ricchetti (2007). Possible theoretical explanations include: bonus payments are more important at higher job levels because of diminished career concerns as workers age (see Gibbons and Murphy 1992); bonus payments are more important at higher levels, because bonuses are more important when returns to effort are higher (see Lemieux et al. 2009); and incentives associated with future promotions are smaller at higher levels (see Boschmans 2008). Also, see Ekinci (2011) for an interesting recent theoretical and empirical exercise that integrates these three perspectives.

in the United States prior to the 1980s, whereas innovative practices have become more common recently. Traditional practices are less focused on ensuring that a firm's workers are highly skilled, that incentives for superior performance are high, and that information sharing is high. These practices include hourly pay or salary compensation where there is little connection between pay and performance, narrowly defined jobs and no job rotation, limited screening for other than managerial employees, no work teams or quality circles, little formal on-the-job training, and the use of layoffs when product demand declines.

In contrast, innovative practices are focused more on recruiting and developing workers with high skills, eliciting high performance, and sharing information. These practices include the use of problem-solving teams and quality circles, job rotation, more effort and resources put into worker screening during the recruitment process, more on-the-job training, more use of incentive pay, and higher job security. As discussed in more detail in Section 5, where the theoretical literature is discussed, these practices seem to constitute a set of complementary or interlocking parts whose main goal is the transformation of how decisions are made. That is, one of the goals of the employment of these practices is a shift in decisionmaking away from managers toward production workers.

As discussed in Cole (2000), these practices first emerged among a limited set of large Japanese manufacturers in the 1960s and then became widespread among large Japanese manufacturers in the late 1960s and 1970s. The practices served to improve the quality performance of these large Japanese manufacturers, and to successfully compete, U.S. firms began to adopt these practices starting in the 1980s. Such studies as Osterman (1994, 2000), Lawler et al. (1995), and Cappelli and Neumark (2001) document the adoption of these practices in U.S. firms and, in particular, show the rapid growth in adoption during the 1980s and 1990s (see also Ichniowski et al. 1989; Black and Lynch 1996, 2004; and Gittleman et al. 1998). As an example, Lawler et al. find that the use of problem-solving teams almost doubled among large U.S. firms between 1987 and 1993.

In terms of understanding the time-series evidence, it is also useful to consider in greater detail the nature of the increased employment of these practices over time. First, survey evidence like that found in Osterman (2000) shows that early adopters tended not to revert back over time to the use of more traditional practices. Also, a significant part of the growth in the use of these practices was due to a higher proportion of firms employing them over time. But this is not the sole source of the growth. Rather, there is also clear evidence that firms that employ innovative practices tend to use larger numbers of these practices over time (see again Osterman 2000).

4.2. Different Types of Evidence

Before discussing the effects on firm performance of the adoption of innovative practices, I briefly discuss the different types of evidence that have been brought to bear on the issue. There are a number of different approaches. Early studies that looked at the impact of innovative human resource practices tended to be case studies typically of a single firm or a small set of firms. Well-known studies that take this approach include Krafcik (1988) and Wilms (1995), who look at a single auto assembly plant; Berg et al. (1996), who focus on apparel manufacturing; and Ichniowski (1992), who examines paper manufacturing.

Although these types of studies certainly provide valuable evidence, they can also be limited: inferences are drawn from observations concerning a small number of firms or factories within firms. And in such a study there is the possibility that the effects found are not in fact due to the adoption of innovative work practices but rather to some other difference that is correlated with the employment of these practices. For example, maybe innovative practices tend to be employed on average by higher quality managers, and it is these managers rather than the practices per se that are responsible for the higher productivity frequently associated with innovative practices. This type of scenario provides an alternative explanation for Krafcik's (1988) and Wilms' (1995) findings in their classic studies of the New United Motor Manufacturing, Inc. auto assembly plant.[32]

To avoid some shortcomings of the standard case-study approach, several papers employ what has come to be called "insider econometrics" (for a detailed description of this approach, see Ichniowski and Shaw, this volume). This approach combines the best aspects of the case-study methodology with the positive aspects of systematic statistical analysis. In this approach researchers first do the equivalent of a case study to understand the nature of the production process and the data needed to test well-formulated hypotheses. Then, after collecting the required data, state-of-the-art statistical techniques are employed to investigate which of various hypotheses are supported by the data. This approach provides the highest quality evidence in this area, so much of the discussion that follows focuses on these studies.

In the insider-econometrics approach, there are two distinct sets of papers. One set focuses on single firms, while the other looks at multiple factories and firms in the same industry. Examples of the former include Lazear's (2000) study of piece rates on the productivity of workers installing windshields, the Nagin et al. (2002) study of piece-rate pay and call center productivity, and the Hamilton et al. (2003) study of teams in apparel production (see also Knez and Simester 2001; Bartel 2004; Freeman and Kleiner 2005). Examples of the latter include the Dunlop and Weil (1996) analysis of module versus bundle production in the apparel industry, the Ichniowski et al. (1997) study of various innovative work practices in steel production, and the Boning et al. (2007) follow-up study of steel production (see also MacDuffie 1995; Kelley 1996; MacDuffie and Pil 1996).

A final set of studies are those that conduct nationwide cross-industry surveys of businesses concerning their human resource practices. These studies are useful for documenting the prevalence of innovative human resource practices within a country at a specific time, but they are somewhat limited in terms of understanding the details of what drives the employment of these practices and their impact. Examples of such studies focused on the United States include Huselid and Becker (1996), Black and Lynch (2001, 2004), and Cappelli and Neumark (2001). Studies on other countries include Greenan and Guellec (1997) on France, Michie and Sheehan (1999) on Great Britain, and Eriksson (2003) on Denmark.

---

32. In that case a plant shut down by General Motors was reopened as a joint venture by GM and Toyota employing many of the same workers but using Toyota management. At the reopening innovative work practices were introduced, and productivity improved. But a case-study approach cannot easily determine the extent to which the improved productivity was due to the innovative practices versus other changes associated with the new management.

4.3. Basic Effects of the Adoption of Innovative Work Practices

The extensive empirical investigation of the adoption of innovative human resource practices makes clear that in most cases adoption of such practices increases productivity. Of course, this is not surprising. It is unlikely the employment of these practices would become increasingly common over time unless there was a return associated with their use. In terms of understanding which factors explain the returns and growing use of these practices, however, what is needed is detailed evidence concerning the nature of these returns and patterns of adoption.

One finding is that the increased productivity associated with the use of innovative work practices is not always solely due to the increased productivity of an existing workforce: it can also be partly due to upgrading the workforce. For example, Lazear (2000) investigated worker productivity and firm profitability at the Safelite Glass Corporation after the firm moved from hourly pay to piece-rate pay. Consistent with standard economic theory of incentive pay, worker productivity of the existing workforce rose. But this only accounted for about half of the overall rise in productivity at the firm. The other half was the result of an improved ability to attract highly productive workers and possibly fewer exits of the most productive workers. A second related example is found in the Hamilton et al. (2003) analysis of an apparel factory. In their analysis a move from individual piece rates to team production and team-based incentive pay raised productivity substantially, and in fact the high-productivity workers (i.e., those most likely to be hurt monetarily by moving away from individual piece rates) were the first to voluntarily join the newly forming teams.

The next finding relates to the details concerning the manner in which innovative practices help the productivity of an existing workforce. Specifically, there is clear evidence that adopting a larger number of innovative practices increases productivity more than adopting one or a few practices. This result is not surprising, because if this were not the case, it would be hard to understand why firms that employ innovative practices seem on average to employ larger numbers as time passes. What is of more interest is the substantial evidence indicating that the productivity increase associated with employing a bundle of innovative practices is not simply the sum of increases associated with each practice individually. Rather, the productivity increase associated with employing a bundle of practices frequently significantly exceeds this sum.

A study that nicely captures this idea is the classic Ichniowski et al. (1997) investigation of steel production. That paper employs a panel dataset that covers almost all finishing lines in integrated steel mills in the United States. For these lines they consider 26 different human resource management practices, which they then translate into four systems of practices—a system that employs mostly traditional practices, one that employs mostly innovative practices, and two intermediate systems. One intermediate system uses innovative practices focused mostly on communication and information sharing; the other adds teamwork and formal training. A main finding is that, comparing these four systems, worker productivity increased with the number of innovative practices employed. In fact, the system that employed a full set of innovative practices raised productivity on average more than twice the amount of the system associated with the next highest number of innovative practices. Further, the introduction of any single practice had a statistically insignificant effect on productivity. So the conclusion is that innovative work practices improve productivity, but in addition there seem to be strong complementarities.

Other studies have also found or argued for important complementarities.[33] For example, Knez and Simester (2001) study the introduction by Continental Airlines of an employee bonus based on firmwide performance, where, contrary to the standard free-riding argument, Knez and Simester find evidence consistent with this firmwide performance bonus improving productivity. They argue (and present anecdotal evidence consistent with their argument) that the use of teams or work groups at the firm increased the extent of mutual monitoring, which allowed the firmwide bonus to be successful. Similarly, in their paper on apparel manufacturing, Hamilton et al. (2003) suggest that the simultaneous introduction of module production and group-incentive pay allowed the introduction of teamwork to significantly increase productivity.

In addition to the effects on productivity, there is also a question of how the introduction of innovative practices affects other important outcome variables, in particular, output quality and firm profitability (an increase in productivity does not necessarily translate into increased profits, because innovative practices can also translate into increased costs).[34] As is the case for productivity, there is strong evidence that introducing innovative practices positively affects quality. This has been found in various studies, including MacDuffie (1995), Ichniowski et al. (1997), and Boning et al. (2007).[35] The evidence for a positive impact on profit is weaker, but in some cases one can infer that profits were also positively affected. For example, in their analysis of steel finishing lines, Ichniowski et al. (1997) estimate a significant profit increase for the lines that employed a full set of innovative practices. Of course, that these innovative practices have not been universally adopted suggests that their profitability might vary across different settings. I turn to this issue now.

4.4. Patterns of Adoption and Related Findings

In addition to detailed evidence concerning the effects of adopting innovative work practices, evidence has also been developed concerning patterns of adoption. As discussed earlier, in the United States innovative practices started to be adoped in the early 1980s, and there has been substantial growth since then both in the number of firms employing these practices and the number of practices the average such firm employs. But this diffusion has not been random. One clear pattern concerning adoption is that innovative practices are much more common in new factories and in those that have reopened under new management (e.g., see Kochan et al. 1986; Ichniowski and Shaw 1995; Ichniowski et al. 1997).

There are three possible explanations for this finding. First, there may be transition costs associated with having an operating factory move from using traditional work practices to using innovative practices. Because the first firms to adopt innovative practices should be those where the profitability of adoption is highest, if these transition costs are significant, then at any point in time adoption should be higher at new and reopened factories. Second, there may be an

---

33. See Ennen and Richter (2010) for a recent survey of the empirical literature concerning complementarities in organizations.

34. Wolf and Heinze (2007) find support for the idea that innovative work practices also reduce the gender wage gap.

35. See Frick et al. (2008) for empirical evidence suggesting that at least in some circumstances innovative work practices can lead to decreased rather than increased quality.

agency problem. It is possible that innovative work practices are profitable everywhere, but if a manager has little experience in managing a factory that employs innovative practices, it may not be in the manager's best interests to have the switch occur (e.g., because it makes him or her more easily substituted with a manager who has such experience). Third, it is possible that not all managers are sufficiently familiar with the productivity advantages associated with innovative practices, and it is the managers at new factories and newly reopened factories that, on average, are more likely to know about these advantages.[36]

A second factor that is important in explaining who adopts innovative work practices is the complexity of the production process. In this case the evidence more clearly suggests the reason: the profitability of adoption is higher for more complex production processes. For example, Boning et al. (2007) find that adoption rates for innovative practices are higher and the profitability of adoption is higher for production lines that make more complex shapes. Similarly, Dunlop and Weil (1996) find that innovative work practices—in particular, what they refer to as "module production"—are employed by apparel manufacturers that produce smaller batches and employ quicker turnaround. This is not surprising, because many innovative practices concern increased communication and improved problem solving by production workers, and such practices quite plausibly have higher returns when production is more complex.

A final related finding is that the adoption of innovative practices is more likely and more profitable when the production process employs new computer-aided information technologies. Results along this line appear in numerous studies, including Milgrom and Roberts (1990), Dunlop and Weil (1996), Bresnahan et al. (2002), and Bartel et al. (2007). This finding can be interpreted as an example of the point made earlier that innovative work practices are more valuable and thus more likely to be adopted when production processes are more complex.[37]

5. Theoretical Models Concerning Human Resource Practices

This section discusses various theoretical models that have been put forth to explain the use of innovative human resource practices. Much of the discussion focuses on the issue of complementary work practices, but I also discuss models that do not rely on complementarity.

5.1. Complementary Practices

The main theoretical approach for modeling the role of innovative human resource practices is to assume the practices are complementary. Complementary activities refer to activities such that "if the levels of any of the subset of activities are increased, then the marginal return to

36. One piece of evidence consistent with the first possibility is found in Ichniowski and Shaw (1995). They find that the introduction of new managers who, on average, might be more open to change does not have a statistically significant effect on the likelihood that a production line or factory changes from traditional to innovative practices. However, Lynch (2007) found results consistent with the third possibility. Specifically, she finds that employers who are best situated to learn about new practices are more likely to adopt them.

37. Bloom and Van Reenen (2007, 2010) have found evidence that suggests other factors might also be important for adoption of innovative work practices. For example, their results suggest that innovative practices are more likely to be adopted when product market competition is high, whereas extensive labor market regulation, family ownership, and government ownership tend to result in less use of innovative practices.

increases in any or all of the remaining activities rises" (Milgrom and Roberts 1990: 514). The idea that innovative work practices are complementary immediately explains why innovative practices are frequently employed in bundles and why the marginal return to adopting them can increase (over a range) with the number of practices adopted. For an example of the latter, complementary practices can explain the Ichniowski et al. (1997) finding that the work system containing the highest number of innovative practices was associated with an increase in productivity more than double the increase associated with the system associated with the next largest number of such practices.

An example of this type of argument is the Milgrom and Roberts (1995) analysis of Lincoln Electric. The Lincoln Electric case is a classic example of a firm characterized by what are now called innovative work practices, although it is interesting to note that Lincoln has employed these practices since roughly 1945. Three of the practices employed by Lincoln Electric are as follows. First, Lincoln made heavy use of piece rates. All production and many nonproduction workers at the firm had their compensation at least partly determined by piece rates. Second, a large proportion of the firm's stock was held by the firm's employees (initially accomplished through direct stock purchases and later through an employee stock ownership plan). Third, there was a high degree of job security accomplished through a no-layoff policy.

Milgrom and Roberts (1995) provide an explanation for these three practices using the idea of complementarity. It is well known that piece rates improve worker incentives, but there is the downside known as the "ratchet effect": if outputs are too high, then the firm learns the rate is too high and lowers it for subsequent periods. In turn, if this reduction is anticipated by workers, then the positive incentive effects of the piece rate are reduced.[38] Milgrom and Roberts argue that Lincoln was able to avoid this problem through the high level of employee stock ownership. The idea is that high employee stock ownership reduces the incentive for the firm to lower piece rates and in this way transfer rents from workers to the firm. Finally, because layoffs reduce employee stock ownership, the no-layoff policy was used to commit to a high level of employee stock ownership for future periods.[39]

5.2. Four Additional Arguments Concerning Complementarities

The argument in Milgrom and Roberts (1995) concerning Lincoln Electric is just one example of a theoretical analysis that describes how specific innovative work practices can be complementary. In this section I describe four other important arguments of this type.

The first concerns the use of group-based incentive plans. As discussed in Alchian and Demsetz (1972), the free-rider problem suggests that individual piece rates should be superior to group-based incentive plans. But possibly because of the difficulty of measuring individual output, many firms employ group-based incentive plans rather than individual piece rates for a significant proportion of the workforce. The argument is then that other innovative work practices are employed because they support the use of group-based incentive plans.[40] For

---

38. Theoretical analyses concerning the ratchet effect appear in Lazear (1986b), Gibbons (1987), and Carmichael and MacLeod (2000).

39. Baker et al. (1994c) discuss another complementarity in Lincoln's practices, which is a complementarity between Lincoln's use of piece rates and its use of bonuses.

40. A variant of this argument appears in Che and Yoo (2001). In that paper group-based incentives are optimal in a repeated-game setting, because such incentives lead to high worker effort through peer sanctions or mutual

example, Kandel and Lazear (1992) argue that firms may spend resources on such activities as indoctrination and the formation of quality circles to establish and enforce group norms that ameliorate the free-rider problem through peer pressure (see also the related discussion concerning corporate culture in Kreps 1990).[41] Also, because many highly productive workers might not want to join a firm where incentives are tied to group rather than individual output, another innovative practice potentially complementary to group-based incentive plans is the application of additional effort and resources to worker recruitment.[42]

A second argument focuses on the decentralization of decisionmaking. Many firms that have adopted innovative work practices employ such practices as group-based decisionmaking teams and quality circles that move decisionmaking from managers to lower level employees. In this argument decentralized decisionmaking is employed, possibly because better decisions can be made by those with on-the-spot knowledge; and then other innovative work practices are employed because they support this decentralization (for early discussions of Japanese labor market practices along this line, see Koike 1977, 1988; Aoki 1986, 1988; for more recent analyses, see Morita 2001, 2005).[43] For example, if lower level employees make decisions, then it is important that these employees are cooperative, highly skilled, and provide high effort. Cooperation can be achieved by group-based incentive plans consistent with the argument of Holmström and Milgrom (1991) discussed next, higher skills can be achieved by higher levels of on-the-job training, while group-based incentive plans should induce higher effort than can no-incentive pay. Also, because new ideas can lead to the elimination of jobs, it is also important, as argued by Aoki (1988), that firms offer high levels of employee security. Along the same line, Carmichael and MacLeod (1993) argue that practices like job rotation can add to the range of jobs to which a worker can be assigned, and this can help a firm commit to high levels of job security.

The third argument is that of Holmström and Milgrom (1991, 1994) concerning multitasking. A standard problem in the theory of multitasking is that incentive pay that is based on measurable output inefficiently distorts effort away from important tasks whose value to the firm is not measurable. In particular, Holmström and Milgrom (1994) translate this phenomenon into an argument concerning complementarity. Specifically, if the firm provides high incentive pay associated with measured performance, then it is important that the firm also employ practices that limit the resulting distortions. Holmström and Milgrom argue that one way firms can do this is to couple high incentive pay with worker ownership of assets, because, for

---

monitoring. After showing this result, Che and Yoo then demonstrate that team production and job security are employed because they are complementary to group-based incentives and peer sanctions.

41. Experimental evidence supporting the importance of peer pressure in teams can be found in Falk and Ichino (2006), Mohnen et al. (2008), and Mas and Moretti (2009).

42. The empirical analysis in Hamilton et al. (2003) discussed earlier throws some doubt on certain aspects of this argument (see also related results in Knez and Simester 2001; Burgess et al. 2010). As discussed, in that analysis the firm was able to increase productivity by moving to a group-based incentive plan from individual piece rates. This transition should not happen if, as argued above, group-based incentive plans are only used when individual piece rates are not feasible. Also inconsistent with the above argument, Hamilton et al. find that the high-productivity workers were usually the first to voluntarily join the newly forming teams.

43. See Mookherjee (2006) for a related discussion of decentralized decisionmaking from the standpoint of mechanism design.

example, ownership will cause workers to provide more effort and invest more resources into maintaining the asset. They also argue that, due to complementarity, high incentive pay should be coupled with more discretion on the part of workers concerning what the job entails.

In addition to a theoretical analysis, in their 1994 paper Holmström and Milgrom argue that their framework matches empirical evidence found in a number of studies. Their theoretical approach predicts that high incentive pay, asset ownership by employees, and worker discretion should all covary positively. For example, a change in an exogenous parameter that increases the return to using high incentive pay should increase the degree to which high incentive pay is used, but because of complementarity, it should also increase employee asset ownership and worker discretion. This prediction is supported by empirical findings in Anderson and Schmittlein (1984) and Anderson (1985) concerning the choice between in-house and independent sales agents in industrial selling. They find covariation of exactly the type predicted. That is, independent sales agents had higher incentive pay, more discretion, and (at least in one important dimension) higher asset ownership. Further, the variables predicting the choice between in-house and independent sales agents were also consistent with the theoretical predictions. Holmström and Milgrom (1994) also relate their theoretical predictions to findings in several other studies, including Shepard (1993) and Slade (1996) concerning gas stations and Brickley and Dark (1987) and Krueger (1991) concerning fast food.

The final argument is a variant of the Aghion and Tirole (1997) theory of real versus formal authority. One of their main results is that when choosing whether to use centralized or decentralized decisionmaking, firms face a trade-off between incentives and agency costs. On the one hand, decentralization increases incentives for workers to acquire information. On the other, there is an agency cost, because the interests of the employees and those of the firm are typically not perfectly aligned. As a result of this trade-off, there is a complementarity between an increased use of incentive pay and decentralization accomplished through practices such as problem-solving teams and quality circles. The argument is that higher incentive pay serves to ameliorate the agency problem associated with decentralization by aligning workers' interests with those of the firm.[44]

5.3. Other Theoretical Models

This section discusses theoretical models of innovative work practices that do not focus on complementarities. Rotemberg (1994) focuses on altruism in the workplace. He argues that in the

---

44. One problematic feature of the Aghion and Tirole (1997) framework is that delegation entails the principal giving formal authority to the agent when it is still the principal's organization; that is, the behavior does not seem credible, because in real-world organizations the principal could always undo the delegation decision (for discussions and analyses of this point, see Baker et al. 1999; Gibbons 2003). However, an alternative argument that gives similar predictions is that the principal does not delegate by ceding to the agent irrevocable control but rather commits to delegation by ex ante choosing actions that make it costly for the principal to over-rule the agent. I thank Bob Gibbons for pointing out this argument to me. Also, see Acemoglu et al. (2007) for further theory and interesting empirical evidence on the trade-off between incentives and agency costs in the decentralization decision.

A related argument appears in Van den Steen (2010). In that argument centralized decisionmaking is associated with low incentive pay, because high incentive pay can lead to agents who disobey the orders or instructions of their principals. See also Van den Steen (2009).

presence of altruism, group-based compensation can increase worker productivity. The argument is straightforward. Given group-based compensation and altruism, each worker increases his or her effort level, because the worker internalizes to some extent the effects added effort has on other workers' compensation. Rotemberg also argues that it can be profitable for a firm to induce altruism in this type of setting by allowing time for socialization and other related behaviors. Overall, Rotemberg's argument is a quite plausible additional mechanism to the Kandel and Lazear (1992) peer-pressure argument for how the free-rider problem can be avoided in firms characterized by group-based compensation.[45]

Ortega (2001) provides a new explanation for job rotation (see also Eriksson and Ortega 2006). Rather than focusing on the benefits that job rotation may have on developing an employee's human capital, Ortega argues that the returns to job rotation are mostly in terms of firm learning. In Ortega's model the firm is initially uncertain about the productivity of its various workers at different job assignments, and there is also uncertainty concerning the potential profitability of the various jobs. He shows that in this setting job rotation is superior to job specialization in terms of how much the firm learns along these two dimensions.[46] Hence, job rotation should be employed when the returns in terms of learning are high and costs are low.

In addition to presenting the theory, Ortega argues that it is a good match for empirical evidence on job rotation. He focuses on two pieces of evidence. First, as found by Campion et al. (1994), the use of job rotation is negatively related to a worker's tenure at the firm. Second, as found by Gittleman et al. (1998), job rotation is positively related to whether the firm is using a new technology. Ortega argues that each of these findings is consistent with his theory. First, high tenure means that the firm already has a lot of information about the worker, so the additional information that can be gathered through job rotation is of little value. Second, new technology means job rotation is valuable, because the firm has little information about its current jobs.[47]

Zábojník (2002) focuses on centralization versus decentralization. In particular, this paper considers a setting similar to that considered by Aghion and Tirole (1997) discussed above. The main point is that a firm may decentralize decisionmaking through such practices as problem-solving teams, even when managers are better informed than production workers. The reason is that it can be cheaper to induce workers to provide high effort when the project or method of

---

45. See Bandiera et al. (2005, 2008, 2009) for interesting empirical evidence that supports the idea that social ties among workers can be important.

46. Ortega (2001) builds on Meyer (1994), who also looks at the effect that job assignment can have on the rate at which firms learn about workers' abilities but does not specifically focus on job rotation. For an alternative theoretical approach to job rotation, see Prescott and Townsend (2006).

47. Ortega also argues that the human capital explanation for job rotation is inconsistent with this evidence. But this logic seems less clear. In terms of the human capital theory, it is possible that what is valuable is a little bit of experience in a number of jobs. In turn, this version of the human capital theory is consistent with the evidence, in that high tenure means the worker likely already has at least a little experience in several jobs, so additional job rotation is not needed, whereas new technology means workers do not have the needed experience with the firm's current jobs, so additional job rotation is very valuable. Additionally, to the extent job rotation is a costly investment in human capital acquisition, then standard human capital theory suggests it should be undertaken early in careers, which, in turn, is another reason job rotation should be negatively related to firm tenure. I thank Jan Zábojník for pointing out this last argument to me.

production chosen is that favored by the workers rather than the one favored by the manager. In other words, to the extent workers provide higher effort when they believe the project or method of production has a higher likelihood of success, the firm may be able to increase productivity by letting the workers decide, even when the manager is better informed.[48]

The last paper I consider here is Akerlof and Kranton (2005) (see also Akerlof and Kranton 2008). They take the perspective, common in sociology and psychology, that norms matter. In particular, how an employee behaves in a particular situation (e.g., how much effort a worker expends) depends on the situation and the worker's identity, where identity refers to the worker's social category (e.g., man or woman, black or white) and self-image. The basic idea is that a worker who identifies with the firm or work group will, monetary incentives held fixed, choose higher effort than will a worker who does not identify with the firm or relevant work group.

This perspective can explain the employment of a number of innovative work practices. The idea is that, because a worker provides higher effort when he or she identifies with the firm or work group, the firm has an incentive to adopt practices that serve to foster this type of identification. So, for example, a firm might adopt high levels of screening during the recruitment process, because screening can be used to ensure that new employees are of a type conducive to such identification. Or similarly, the formation of work groups may be beneficial, because workers more easily identify with a work group than with the firm itself. One problem, however, is that Akerlof and Kranton (2008) argue that identification is a substitute for monetary incentives. To the extent this is the case, then we should expect the practices just mentioned not to be used in conjunction with high levels of incentive pay, which is exactly the opposite of what the evidence suggests. But possibly the Akerlof and Kranton discussion of this issue is incomplete in the sense that maybe certain types of incentive pay can be used to help establish identification, which in turn could explain why these practices are used together.

5.4. Overview

The evidence seems quite clear that complementarity is important for understanding the move to innovative work practices. There are several aspects of the evidence that point in this direction. First, innovative work practices are frequently adopted in bundles. Second, there is evidence of an increasing marginal return in terms of productivity to adopting additional practices. Third, the evidence suggests the return to adopting a single practice in isolation is small or possibly even zero. Each of these findings is consistent with the basic idea of complementarity, which is that the return to adopting any specific practice is positively related to the number of other practices adopted.

So the more difficult question is, of the various theories concerning complementarity that have been proposed, which seem most promising as an explanation for the evidence? The literature is far from giving a conclusive answer to this question. But some tentative conclusions can be drawn. First, some theories put forth have some support in the data, so my sense is

---

48. Zábojník (2002) shows this logic is correct when it is costly for firms to induce high worker effort strictly through contracting, which is the case given either liquidity constraints or risk aversion. A related argument appears in Van den Steen (2006). In that argument different priors lead to the same result: delegation can have a positive effect on worker effort, but there is also the cost that delegation reduces coordination both inside and across firms. See also De Paola and Scoppa (2009) for a related analysis.

that the right answer is not that there is a single theory that is correct and the others have no explanatory power. Rather, it is likely that several theories are important for understanding real-world organizations.

For example, as discussed, the Holmström and Milgrom (1991, 1994) theory concerning balancing incentives in a multitasking world seems consistent with various studies on sales agents. However, there is some question concerning whether one of the basic premises of the free-riding argument is correct. That is, given the popularity of group-based incentive plans and the findings in Hamilton et al. (2003) on the returns of moving from individual piece rates to group-based incentive plans, it is questionable whether group-based incentive plans are used primarily when individual piece rates are not feasible (see footnotes 40 and 42 for related discussions). But there are other parts of that argument that seem quite plausible. For example, for whatever reasons group-based incentive plans are adopted, it seems reasonable that activities used to enforce high-effort norms are employed as a way of avoiding the potential free-rider problem.

Second, to the extent that one of the theories is the correct explanation for the bulk of the evidence, my vote is on the argument that decentralized decisionmaking is employed because better decisions can be made by those with on-the-spot knowledge, and, in turn, many innovative practices are employed, because they are complementary with decentralization. On the one hand, this argument ties together the largest number of innovative practices. Specifically, group-based decisionmaking teams and quality circles are explained as practices that directly serve to decentralize decisionmaking, while various other practices (e.g., group-based incentive plans, high levels of on-the-job training, job rotation, and high levels of job security) are employed as ways to support the decentralized decisionmaking. On the other hand, detailed empirical analysis (e.g., Ichniowski et al. 1997) suggests that the extensive use of group-based decisionmaking (i.e., decentralization) is central to the increased productivity associated with innovative work practices.[49]

Finally, a subject that deserves more attention in future research is that of delayering. In a closely related empirical literature it has been shown that over time, hierarchies have become flatter or, equivalently, delayering has occurred—that is, in the typical firm there are fewer layers between the CEO and the bottom of the organization, and the average number of workers reporting to each manager has increased (for an early discussion, see Osterman 1996; for systematic empirical evidence, see Rajan and Wulf 2006; Guadalupe and Wulf 2010). There are several possible explanations for the phenomenon, such as improvements in information technology decrease the need for middle managers, as argued originally by Leavitt and Whisler (1958). My point is that, if a central aspect of innovative work practices is decentralized decisionmaking, it is possible that one reason for delayering is the adoption of these practices and the resulting decentralized decisionmaking, which potentially requires fewer middle managers. Empirical work focused on this possibility would be of significant interest.

---

49. In comparison to production lines that employ traditional work practices, Ichniowski et al. (1997) find that productivity rises 6.7% for lines that employ a full set of innovative work practices and 3.2% for lines that emphasize teamwork and communications. In contrast, productivity on average is only 1.4% higher for lines that emphasize communications with less stress on teamwork. See also Colombo et al. (2007) and Jones and Kato (2011) for evidence that supports the idea that group-based decisionmaking is central for understanding why innovative work practices lead to increased productivity.

6. International Differences

There is a companion literature to the one discussed in Sections 4 and 5 that addresses international differences in how internal labor markets operate. This literature is closely related to the earlier one in that many of the differences can be thought of as differences in human resource practices. In this section I discuss the literature on international differences. In particular, one focus is on trying to understand what can be learned by thinking about the two literatures together. Note that because most of the literature on international differences is focused on U.S.-Japanese differences, that will be the focus here also.[50]

6.1. U.S.-Japanese Differences

Here I describe the major differences that have been identified concerning the operation of U.S. and Japanese internal labor markets. Before proceeding, there are two points worth emphasizing. First, many of these differences are closely related to differences in innovative and traditional human resource practices discussed previously. Second, much of the evidence showing large differences in the operation of U.S. and Japanese internal labor markets is from studies that are now decades old. I come back to these points in Section 6.3.

I start by describing U.S.-Japanese differences in internal labor markets that are closely related to those between traditional and innovative human resource practices.[51] First, such studies as Kagono et al. (1985) and Lincoln et al. (1986) find that decisions are made at lower levels of the hierarchy in Japanese firms than at U.S. firms (see also the earlier work of Clark 1979; Cole 1979). For example, Lincoln et al. conducted a study of 55 U.S. firms and 51 Japanese firms in terms of the hierarchical level at which decisions were made. They found that in the Japanese firms decisions were made at lower hierarchical levels on average than in the U.S. firms. This finding is similar to the earlier discussion of innovative work practices in which some innovative practices serve to move decisionmaking away from managers and to lower level employees.

Second, there is substantial evidence that Japanese firms offer more on-the-job training, and correspondingly Japanese employees have higher levels of firm-specific human capital (e.g., see Koike 1977, 1988; Hashimoto 1994; MacDuffie and Kochan 1995). Further, much of this literature focuses on higher levels of multiskilling in Japanese firms, where "multiskilling" refers to acquiring the human capital needed to do multiple jobs, which occurs, for example, with heavy use of job rotation. Studies that discuss the prevalence of multiskilling in Japanese firms include Koike (1977, 1988), Dertouzos et al. (1989), and Ito (1992). Note that higher levels of on-the-job training and job rotation were also part of the discussion concerning innovative human resource practices.

Third, Japanese firms are characterized by higher levels of continuous process improvement. For example, in Japanese firms, through group decisionmaking teams and quality circles, lower level employees are more frequently solicited for suggestions concerning improvements in the production process (for discussions, see Koike 1977, 1988). Also, Dertouzos et al. (1989) found that in the late 1980s, engineers in Japanese steel production were located in a manner that

---

50. I especially thank Hodaka Morita for suggestions and discussions that were helpful in formulating the discussion in this section.

51. For an overview of the operation of internal labor markets in Japanese firms, see Ariga et al. (2000).

allowed for quicker responses to day-to-day operational problems than was the case in U.S. steel production.

Fourth, long-term employment is higher and turnover rates lower in Japanese firms. This has been found by numerous authors, including Hashimoto and Raisian (1985), Mincer and Higuchi (1988), Blinder and Krueger (1996), and Kato (2001). For example, Hashimoto and Raisian compared U.S. and Japanese labor markets by analyzing data from the Special Labor Force Report for the United States and the Basic Survey of Employment for Japan. They found that long-term job retention rates were higher in Japan and that average job tenure was also higher. These ideas that long-term employment is higher and turnover is lower in Japanese firms are similar to the earlier emphasis on job security in firms that employ innovative work practices.[52]

The last two differences do not have a close relationship with the discussion of traditional and innovative work practices. Fifth, as discussed, for example, in Holzhausen (2000), in Japanese firms promotion to managerial ranks occurs later in careers; correspondingly, there is little differentiation in terms of wage and promotion rates for white-collar workers early in their careers. More specifically in terms of the latter point, in large Japanese firms workers with the same educational background are treated similarly in terms of wages, wage growth, and promotion rates early in their careers, but after approximately 10–15 years of experience, wage growth and promotion decisions depend more heavily on performance evaluations. Of further interest, although outcomes do not vary much early in careers, the evidence suggests that many young white-collar workers in Japan do have a clear sense of their long-term career prospects.

Sixth, within-firm income dispersion is smaller in Japan. For example, Koike (1977, 1988) compares wage differentials between managers and average white-collar workers in Japan and various European countries and finds that Japan has one of the smallest wage differentials. As it is typically believed that within-firm income dispersion is higher in the United States than in Europe, this clearly suggests much higher within-firm income dispersion in the United States than in Japan.[53]

6.2. Candidate Models for Explaining U.S.-Japanese Differences

Some theoretical approaches for explaining U.S.-Japanese differences in internal labor markets rely on models characterized by multiple equilibria.[54] One set of models focuses on the connection between adverse selection and turnover. The best known of these papers is

52. This issue has also been studied more recently in Farber (2007), Kawaguchi and Ueno (2010), Ono (2010), and Kambayashi and Kato (2011). Together the results in these papers suggest that long-term employment in the Japanese economy fell by the end of Japan's Great Recession (which lasted from approximately 1992 to 2007) but that it still remains higher than in the United States.

53. Genda et al. (2010) find another difference that has not previously been emphasized: the disadvantages of entering the labor market during a recession tend to be larger in Japan than in the United States.

54. The first paper I am familiar with that uses a multiple equilibria approach to explain U.S.-Japanese labor market differences is Okuno-Fujiwara (1987). That paper investigates multiple equilibria in a setting of contracting and involuntary unemployment that builds on earlier analyses in Calvo (1979) and Shapiro and Stiglitz (1984).

Acemoglu and Pischke (1998), which builds on Greenwald (1979, 1986) and Gibbons and Katz (1991).[55]

Acemoglu and Pischke consider a labor market setting in which a worker's current employer knows more about a worker's ability than do prospective employers, so turnover is reduced because of the resulting adverse-selection problem. What is new here is the focus on on-the-job training. The adverse-selection problem means that a worker's current employer has monopsony power after the training period. This monopsony power gives the firm an incentive to offer and pay for general training of its workers (while at the same time reducing a worker's incentive to pay for general training). Based on this logic, Acemoglu and Pischke identify the possibility of multiple equilibria. In what might be called the Japanese equilibrium, the adverse-selection problem is severe, causing little turnover and high monopsony power, which, in turn, results in high on-the-job training. In what might be called the U.S. equilibrium, the adverse-selection problem is mild, so turnover is higher, monopsony power is lower, and the result is a lower level of on-the-job training. In addition to developing the theoretical argument, Acemoglu and Pischke present evidence using data on German apprentices that supports the theory.[56]

A second argument appears in Prendergast (1992). Prendergast focuses on delayed promotion and higher firm-specific human capital in the Japanese case. In Prendergast's model each employer has private information about each young worker's long-term career prospects, and the firm must decide whether to reveal this information to workers, which would increase incentives for workers with high potential. In the U.S. equilibrium firms promote young workers with high potential, which signals potential and results in high incentives. In the Japanese equilibrium, instead, the return to training low-ability young workers is high, and firms choose to retain high incentives for low-ability workers by not promoting young workers and in this way not revealing private information. One problem with this argument is that, as mentioned above, even though there are no promotions early in careers in Japan, many young white-collar workers in Japan do seem to have a clear sense of long-term career prospects.[57]

Morita (2001, 2005) also presents a multiple-equilibrium model. His argument serves as an explanation for differences in human capital accumulation, including multiskilling, decentralized decisionmaking, continuous process improvement, and turnover. His model builds on earlier discussions in Koike (1977, 1988) and Aoki (1986, 1988) and is related to one of the arguments concerning decentralization in Section 5.2. Basically, Morita identifies a set of complementarities across these variables that leads to the possibility of multiple equilibria. When workers are multiskilled, they have the knowledge required to make better decisions, so de-

55. Other studies that take an adverse selection and turnover approach to explain U.S.-Japanese differences include Prendergast (1989) and Chang and Wang (1995). Katz and Ziderman (1990) and Chang and Wang (1996) also consider models similar to the ones discussed here but do not relate their analyses to U.S.-Japanese differences.

56. Although the empirical work of Acemoglu and Pischke (1998) concerns Germany, because there are many similarities between German and Japanese labor markets (see Dertouzos et al 1989), their empirical findings can be interpreted as suggesting that adverse selection is also important in the Japanese labor market.

57. A related empirical result is found in Umezaki (2001), who shows a strong correlation in Japan between task assignments when young and subsequent promotion outcomes. In other words, because young workers in Japan with better long-term career prospects seem to be assigned different tasks than others in their age cohort, in contrast to Prendergast's (1992) argument, even in the absence of any initial differentiation of wage and promotion outcomes, young workers should be able to infer their long-term prospects.

centralized decisionmaking becomes more attractive. In turn, the combination of multiskilling and decentralized decisionmaking makes continuous process improvement feasible. Thus, over time the high levels of continuous process improvement mean that each firm is characterized by high levels of firm-specific human capital. Finally, the high levels of firm-specific human capital reduce turnover and increase average job duration.

In Morita's (2001, 2005) argument continuous process improvement is more beneficial when workers have high levels of firm tenure, so the return to adopting continuous process improvement is positively related to the number of other firms that adopt it. That is, when firms adopt continuous process improvement, they are less likely to raid other firms' employees, because skills are not transferable, so job durations are higher. As a result, any given firm has a higher incentive to adopt continuous process improvement. Thus, there can be two equilibria. In the Japanese equilibrium all firms adopt continuous process improvement, which lowers the turnover rate and makes this choice profitable. In contrast, in the U.S. equilibrium firms do not adopt continuous process improvement, which raises the turnover rate and makes choosing continuous process improvement unprofitable. Morita argues that historical events during World War II explain the different equilibrium choices in the two countries.

The last theoretical argument I discuss here is the one put forth in Owan (2004), which employs the promotion-as-signal hypothesis. There are two key assumptions in Owan's model. First, in addition to varying in terms of ability, a firm's workers also vary in the quality of worker-firm matches. Second, a worker's current employer privately learns the worker's ability before learning the quality of the worker-firm match. Given these assumptions, Owan shows that depending on various factors (e.g., the distribution of worker characteristics and the relative value of firm-specific human capital across jobs), one of two possible equilibria will arise. In an early-promotion equilibrium high-ability workers are promoted after the firm learns ability but before learning the quality of worker-firm matches. In a late-promotion equilibrium there are no promotions until the firm learns both ability and the quality of worker-firm matches.

The main point of Owan's (2004) analysis is that the differences between these two potential equilibria match the differences in U.S.-Japanese internal labor market operations discussed above. Think of the late-promotion equilibrium as the Japanese equilibrium and the early-promotion one as the U.S. equilibrium. First, the late-promotion equilibrium clearly matches the late-career promotions and the early-career reduced differentiation in wage and promotion outcomes in Japan. Second, Owan shows that the late-promotion equilibrium has no turnover, because the lack of early promotions serving as a signal causes adverse selection to be severe and the secondary market for workers to shut down, whereas in the early-promotion equilibrium high-ability workers with bad matches leave their initial employers. So the late-promotion equilibrium matches more long-term employment and less turnover in the Japanese case. Third, the lack of promotion signaling in the late-promotion equilibrium means that the asymmetry of information is more severe in this equilibrium, which results in less income dispersion. Thus, the late-promotion equilibrium also matches the smaller dispersion of incomes in the Japanese case.[58] Finally, Owan also provides a discussion for why Japan is characterized by the

---

58. Owan (1999) shows how a related model also explains higher levels of firm-specific human capital in Japan.

late-promotion equilibrium and the United States by the early-promotion equilibrium; as in Morita's (2001, 2005) argument, part of Owan's discussion focuses on historical events.[59]

6.3. Convergence

As is made clear above, much of the literature on U.S.-Japanese differences is based on data or observations that are decades old. This is potentially important. As discussed in Section 4, innovative work practices were introduced in Japan prior to being introduced in the United States, and after the introduction in the latter country, there was and likely still is gradual diffusion of these practices. This suggests that, at least for those differences related to dissimilarities between traditional and innovative human resource practices, the differences are likely much smaller today than they were in the past. Another way to put this is that such studies as Osterman (1994, 2000) and Cappelli and Neumark (2001) show there has been significant growth since the 1980s in the employment of innovative human resource practices in the United States, whereas there is no similar empirical literature suggesting increases during this time in the use of innovative work practices in Japan.[60] Thus, at least for the differences related to innovative human resource practices, there is likely less divergence between the two countries today than there was 20 or 30 years ago.

The idea that some of the differences today are much smaller than they were in the past introduces an interesting possibility concerning what drives these differences. That is, it is likely that the later introduction of innovative work practices in the United States and their gradual diffusion was a major driving force for many of the large differences observed between the United States and Japan in the 1980s and 1990s. As time passed and diffusion continued, differences became smaller—possibly substantially so. Note that I am not claiming here that there is nothing to explain once one takes into account the late introduction and subsequent diffusion of innovative work practices in the United States. Rather, I am arguing that any full picture of what drives differences between the U.S. and Japanese labor markets needs to take the likelihood of convergence into account.

The other issue that this perspective suggests is the relative weight one should put on the various international differences that have been identified concerning the United States and Japan. As innovative work practices have diffused across the former country, some differences that are related to innovative practices have very likely gotten smaller. But for a couple of the differences there is little evidence suggesting convergence. Specifically, in terms of later promotion and less differentiation in wage and promotion outcomes early on, lower income dispersion, and possibly lower turnover seen in Japan, I see little evidence for convergence. So possibly, future empirical work should focus on whether it is correct that convergence has been important for some differences but not for others, whereas future theoretical work might focus more on the differences that seem to be less subject to convergence.

59. See Moriguchi (2003) for a related argument in which the difference in the size of the macroeconomic contractions during the 1930s between the United States and Japan is used to explain subsequent differences between the U.S. and Japanese labor markets.

60. In fact, some recent evidence suggests that some of the distinctive features of Japanese internal labor markets have become less pronounced in recent years. See, for example, Hamaaki et al. (2010), Kawaguchi and Ueno (2010), and Ono (2010).

6.4. Overview

Because many of the differences between U.S. and Japanese internal labor markets are related to differences between traditional and innovative human resource practices in the United States, there should be a close linkage between theories used to explain the movement from traditional to innovative work practices in the United States and theories used to explain differences between the two countries' internal labor markets. In other words, if part of what is driving the differences between U.S. and Japanese internal labor markets is that innovative work practices are more commonly used in the latter country than in the former, then the arguments for what is happening in the United States over time and those concerning U.S.-Japanese differences need to be tightly linked.

The above discussion concerning convergence is consistent with this idea. It attributes at least some of the difference between U.S. and Japanese internal labor markets (and possibly much of it early on) to the later introduction of innovative work practices and subsequent gradual diffusion in the United States. This notion is consistent with the discussion in Section 4, which gave a prominent role to gradual diffusion of innovative work practices in understanding the trends in the use of innovative work practices in the United States. In following up this idea, it might be of interest to compare current U.S. and Japanese internal labor markets but only consider U.S. firms that have adopted innovative work practices. This approach would provide a sense of how much of the U.S.-Japanese differences in internal labor markets is due to gradual diffusion and how much is due to differences that remain even after U.S. firms adopt innovative work practices (for a related analysis, see Ichniowski and Shaw 1999).

In addition, to the extent that there are remaining differences even after taking into account gradual diffusion, the question remains: what drives these differences? Of the theories that I have reviewed, the one that shows the most promise is that presented in Morita (2001, 2005), which is related to the earlier arguments of Koike (1977, 1988) and Aoki (1986, 1988). On the one hand, for various reasons, the other arguments are somewhat lacking in terms of providing a convincing explanation for the gamut of U.S.-Japanese differences. Prendergast's (1992) model relies on young Japanese workers not knowing their career prospects, which seems inconsistent with the evidence, while Owan's (2004) model—although interesting—relies on an ad hoc assumption concerning job-match information being revealed later to firms than information about worker abilities.[61] Also, although there is empirical support for Acemoglu and Pischke's (1998) model, that argument explains a limited number of differences. On the other hand, Morita's argument explains a large number of differences, and it is also heavily focused on information sharing and decentralized decisionmaking, which are central in most descriptions of the differences between the U.S. and Japanese settings.

But even Morita's argument has the drawback that it does not explain one of the key U.S.-Japanese differences: early promotion and early differentiation in the U.S. setting and late promotion and late differentiation in the Japanese case. Possibly, one could extend Morita's argument to capture this important difference by focusing on how different levels of firm-specific

---

61. This assumption is important for Owan's (2004) explanation for why Japan is characterized by late promotions and the United States by early promotion. Since other aspects of Owan's argument are appealing, maybe much of what Owan argues is correct, but there is a different explanation for this particular U.S.-Japanese difference.

human capital affects whether equilibrium is characterized by early or late promotions. But this possibility can only be resolved with further theoretical research.[62] Alternatively, there may be a way to combine Morita's and Owan's arguments.

Finally, although the discussion in this section focuses on differences between U.S. and Japanese internal labor markets (because that is the focus of most of the literature), much of the discussion likely also applies to comparisons of Japanese internal labor markets with those found in many other industrialized countries. That is, it is not just the case that innovative human resource practices spread from Japan to the United States and then gradually diffused in the United States, but rather this later adoption and gradual diffusion is also true of many other industrialized economies. So, to the extent that many of the differences between the operation of U.S. and Japanese internal labor markets discussed above are due to differences in the employment of innovative human resource practices in the two countries, it would be natural to expect that similar differences in internal labor market operations between Japan and other industrialized countries are also due to differences in the employment of innovative human resource practices.[63]

7. Conclusion

The literature on internal labor markets has matured to the point that for some branches of the literature, there is now a very healthy two-way interaction between theory and empirical work. On the one hand, numerous theoretical papers try to provide explanations for empirical phenomena and, more specifically, for patterns found in the data. On the other, numerous empirical papers try to test the most promising theories. In turn, combining theoretical and empirical contributions has the potential to advance our understanding of various issues in internal labor markets in important ways.

In this survey I have focused on this two-way interaction between theory and empirical work. In particular, I examined three topics in the extensive literature on internal labor markets to both show the benefits of a rich interaction between theory and evidence and draw some conclusions in each case about which theoretical approaches look most promising. The first topic I considered is wage and promotion dynamics in internal labor markets. Various distinct theoretical approaches have been put forth concerning this topic. After reviewing the various theories and the relevant empirical literature, my conclusion is that a model that combines symmetric learning, human capital accumulation, and job assignment—as in Gibbons and Waldman 1999b, 2006—holds the most promise for explaining the various empirical findings.

---

62. My idea here is related to the Harris and Holmström (1982) argument discussed in Section 3. Firms would like to partially insure workers against uncertainty concerning true innate ability, and one way to potentially do this is to employ late promotions and little differentiation early in careers. This strategy is feasible in the Japanese case, because the high levels of firm-specific human capital mean that a worker who is revealed to be of high innate ability early on cannot be hired away by another firm. But in the U.S. case, because of the lower levels of firm-specific human capital, this strategy is infeasible—a young worker who is revealed to be of high innate ability who is not promoted or given a high wage would be bid away.

63. One exception may be between Japan and Germany. Dertouzos et al. (1989) argue that even early on, the operation of West Germany's internal labor markets had similarities to those found in Japan that were not seen in most other industrialized countries.

But other theoretical approaches, such as tournament theory and asymmetric learning, also seem important for a full understanding of what drives wage and promotion dynamics inside firms.

The second literature I focused on is that concerning the growing use by firms of innovative human resource practices. After reviewing the empirical and theoretical literatures, my primary conclusion was that—as argued by numerous authors, including Milgrom and Roberts (1990, 1995) and Holmström and Milgrom (1994)—complementarity is a driving force for understanding the growing use of these practices. The evidence is less clear concerning which of the various theories put forth to explain the nature of these complementarities is most important. But the argument that the driving force is a desire to move decisionmaking from managers to lower level employees because better decisions are made by those with on-the-spot knowledge seems to be the argument that best matches the evidence.

The third literature I considered is that on international differences in internal labor markets, where most of this literature focuses on U.S.-Japanese differences. One conclusion here is that at least some of the historical difference between the United States and Japan likely stems from the later initial adoption of these practices and their gradual diffusion in the United States. However, some differences likely remain even after taking this factor into account, and my sense is that the correct explanation for the remaining disparities lies in the differing incentives for decentralized decisionmaking in the two countries, as emphasized initially by Koike (1977, 1988) and Aoki (1986, 1988) and more recently by Morita (2001, 2005).

I have shown how a close partnership between theory and empirical evidence can be used to reach a deeper understanding of the driving forces behind the operation of internal labor markets than can be reached by either empirical evidence or theory taken in isolation. Hopefully, future work concerning wage and promotion dynamics and the use of innovative human resource practices—as well as research on other topics on internal labor markets—will continue to pursue the close two-way interaction between theory and empirical evidence described in this chapter.

REFERENCES

Abowd, J., and D. Card. 1989. "On the Covariance Structure of Earnings and Hours Changes." *Econometrica* 57: 411–445.

Acemoglu, D., and J. Pischke. 1998. "Why Do Firms Train: Theory and Evidence." *Quarterly Journal of Economics* 113: 79–119.

Acemoglu, D., P. Aghion, C. Lelarge, J. Van Reenen, and F. Zilibotti. 2007. "Technology, Information, and the Decentralization of the Firm." *Quarterly Journal of Economics* 122: 1759–1799.

Aghion, P., and J. Tirole. 1997. "Formal and Real Authority in Organizations." *Journal of Political Economy* 105: 1–29.

Akerlof, G. A., and R. Kranton. 2005. "Identity and the Economics of Organizations." *Journal of Economic Perspectives* 19(1): 9–32.

———. 2008. "Identity, Supervision, and Work Groups." *American Economic Review* 98: 212–217.

Alchian, A., and H. Demsetz. 1972. "Production, Information Costs, and Economic Organization." *American Economic Review* 62: 777–795.

Anderson, E. 1985. "The Salesperson as Outside Agent or Employee: A Transaction Cost Analysis." *Marketing Science* 4: 234–254.

Anderson, E., and D. Schmittlein. 1984. "Integration of the Sales Force: An Empirical Examination." *RAND Journal of Economics* 15: 385–395.

Aoki, M. 1986. "Horizontal vs. Vertical Information Structure of the Firm." *American Economic Review* 76: 971–983.

———. 1988. *Information, Incentives, and Bargaining in the Japanese Economy.* Cambridge: Cambridge University Press.

Ariga, K., Y. Ohkusa, and G. Brunello. 1999. "Fast Track: Is It in the Genes? The Promotion Policy of a Large Japanese Firm." *Journal of Economic Behavior and Organization* 38: 385–402.

Ariga, K., G. Brunello, and Y. Ohkusa. 2000. *Internal Labor Markets in Japan.* Cambridge: Cambridge University Press.

Audas, R., T. Barmby, and J. Treble. 2004. "Luck, Effort, and Reward in an Organizational Hierarchy." *Journal of Labor Economics* 22: 379–396.

Baker, G., M. C. Jensen, and K. J. Murphy. 1988. "Compensation and Incentives: Practice vs. Theory." *Journal of Finance* 43: 593–616.

Baker, G., M. Gibbs, and B. Holmström. 1994a. "The Internal Economics of the Firm: Evidence from Personnel Data." *Quarterly Journal of Economics* 109: 881–919.

———. 1994b. "The Wage Policy of a Firm." *Quarterly Journal of Economics* 109: 921–955.

Baker, G., R. Gibbons, and K. Murphy. 1994c. "Subjective Performance Measures in Optimal Incentive Contracts." *Quarterly Journal of Economics* 109: 1125–1156.

———. 1999. "Informal Authority in Organizations." *Journal of Law, Economics, and Organization* 15: 56–73.

Baker, M. 1997. "Growth-Rate Heterogeneity and the Covariance Structure of Life-Cycle Earnings." *Journal of Labor Economics* 15: 338–375.

Bandiera, O., I. Barankay, and I. Rasul. 2005. "Social Preferences and the Response to Incentives: Evidence from Personnel Data." *Quarterly Journal of Economics* 120: 917–962.

———. 2008. "Social Capital in the Workplace: Evidence on Its Formation and Consequences." *Labour Economics* 15: 724–748.

———. 2009. "Social Connections and Incentives in the Workplace: Evidence from Personnel Data." *Econometrica* 77: 1047–1094.

Bartel, A. 2004. "Human Resource Management and Organizational Performance: Evidence from Retail Banking." *Industrial and Labor Relations Review* 57: 181–203.

Bartel, A., C. Ichniowski, and K. Shaw. 2007. "How Does Information Technology Affect Productivity? Plant-Level Comparisons of Product Innovation, Process Improvement, and Worker Skills." *Quarterly Journal of Economics* 122: 1721–1758.

Beaudry, P., and J. DiNardo. 1991. "The Effects of Implicit Contracts on the Movement of Wages over the Business Cycle: Evidence from Microdata." *Journal of Political Economy* 99: 665–688.

Becker, B., and M. Huselid. 1992. "The Incentive Effects of Tournament Compensation Systems." *Administrative Science Quarterly* 37: 336–350.

Becker, G. 1962. "Investment in Human Capital: A Theoretical Analysis." *Journal of Political Economy* 70: 9–49.

———. 1964. *Human Capital.* New York: National Bureau of Economic Research.

Becker, G., and G. Stigler. 1974. "Law Enforcement, Malfeasance and Compensation of Enforcers." *Journal of Legal Studies* 3: 1–18.

Belzil, C., and M. Bognanno. 2008. "Promotions, Demotions, Halo Effects, and the Earnings Dynamics of American Executives." *Journal of Labor Economics* 26: 287–310.

———. 2010. "The Promotion Dynamics of American Executives." *Research in Labor Economics* 30: 189–231.

Berg, P., E. Appelbaum, J. Bailey, and A. Kalleberg. 1996. "The Performance Effects of Modular Production in the Apparel Industry." *Industrial Relations* 35: 356–373.

Bernhardt, D. 1995. "Strategic Promotion and Compensation." *Review of Economic Studies* 62: 315–339.

Bernhardt, D., and D. Scoones. 1993. "Promotion, Turnover, and Preemptive Wage Offers." *American Economic Review* 83: 771–791.

Black, S., and L. Lynch. 1996. "Human Capital Investments and Productivity." *American Economic Review* 86: 263–267.

———. 2001. "How to Compete: The Impact of Workplace Practices and Information Technology on Productivity." *Review of Economics and Statistics* 83: 434–445.

———. 2004. "What's Driving the New Economy? The Benefits of Workplace Innovation." *Economic Journal* 114: 97–116.

Blinder, A., and A. Krueger. 1996. "Labor Turnover in the USA and Japan: A Tale of Two Countries." *Pacific Economic Review* 1: 27–57.

Bloom, N., and J. Van Reenen. 2007. "Measuring and Explaining Management Practices across Firms and Countries." *Quarterly Journal of Economics* 122: 1351–1408.

———. 2010. "Why Do Management Practices Differ across Firms and Countries?" *Journal of Economic Perspectives* 24(1): 203–224.

Bognanno, M. L. 2001. "Corporate Tournaments." *Journal of Labor Economics* 19: 290–315.

Boning, B., C. Ichniowski, and K. Shaw. 2007. "Opportunity Counts: Teams and the Effectiveness of Production Incentives." *Journal of Labor Economics* 25: 613–650.

Boschmans, K. 2008. "Selected Essays on Personnel Economics: Turnover, Promotions, and Incentives." PhD dissertation, University of Antwerp.

Bresnahan, T., E. Brynjolfsson, and L. Hitt. 2002. "Information Technology, Work Organization and the Demand for Skilled Labor: Firm-Level Evidence." *Quarterly Journal of Economics* 166: 339–376.

Brickley, J. A., and F. H. Dark. 1987. "The Choice of Organization Form: The Case of Franchising." *Journal of Financial Economics* 18: 401–420.

Burgess, S., C. Propper, M. Ratto, S. von Hinke, K. Scholder, and E. Tominey. 2010. "Smarter Task Assignment or Greater Effort: The Impact of Incentives on Team Performance." *Economic Journal* 120: 968–989.

Cabrales, A., A. Calvo-Armengol, and N. Pavoni. 2008. "Social Preferences, Skill Segregation, and Wage Dynamics." *Review of Economic Studies* 75: 65–98.

Calvo, G. 1979. "Quasi-Walrasian Theories of Unemployment." *American Economic Review* 69: 102–107.

———. 1985. "The Inefficiency of Unemployment: The Supervision Perspective." *Quarterly Journal of Economics* 100: 373–387.

Campion, M., L. Cheraskin, and M. Stevens. 1994. "Career-Related Antecedents and the Outcomes of Job Rotation." *Academy Management Journal* 37: 1518–1542.

Cappelli, P., and D. Neumark. 2001. "Do 'High Performance' Work Practices Improve Establishment-Level Outcomes?" *Industrial and Labor Relations Review* 54: 737–775.

Card, D. 1999. "The Causal Effect of Education on Earnings," in O. Ashenfelter and D. Card (eds.), *Handbook of Labor Economics,* volume 3. Amsterdam: North-Holland, pp. 1801–1863.

Card, D., and D. Hyslop. 1997. "Does Inflation 'Grease the Wheels of the Labor Market'?" in C. Romer and D. Romer (eds.), *Reducing Inflation: Motivation and Strategy.* Chicago: University of Chicago Press, pp. 71–114.

Carmichael, H. L., and W. B. MacLeod. 1993. "Multiskilling, Technical Change and the Japanese Firm." *Economic Journal* 103: 142–160.

———. 2000. "Worker Cooperation and the Ratchet Effect." *Journal of Labor Economics* 18: 1–19.

Carpenter, J., P. H. Matthews, and J. Schirm. 2010. "Tournaments and Office Politics: Evidence from a Real Effort Experiment." *American Economic Review* 100: 504–517.

Chan, W. 1996. "External Recruitment versus Internal Promotion." *Journal of Labor Economics* 14: 555–570.

———. 2006. "External Recruitment and Intrafirm Mobility." *Economic Inquiry* 44: 169–184.

Chang, C., and Y. Wang. 1995. "A Framework for Understanding Differences in Labor Turnover and Human Capital Investment." *Journal of Economic Behavior and Organization* 28: 91–105.

———. 1996. "Human Capital Investment under Asymmetric Information: The Pigovian Conjecture Revisited." *Journal of Labor Economics* 14: 505–519.

Che, Y., and S. Yoo. 2001. "Optimal Incentives for Teams." *American Economic Review* 91: 525–541.

Chiappori, P. A., B. Salanie, and J. Valentin. 1999. "Insurance, Learning, and Career Profiles: An Empirical Test." *Journal of Political Economy* 107: 731–760.

Clark, R. 1979. *The Japanese Company*. New Haven, CT: Yale University Press.

Clemens, A. 2010. "Position-Specific Promotion Rates and the 'Fast Track' Effect." *Research in Labor Economics*, forthcoming.

Clemens, A., B. Kriechel, and G. Pfann. 2009. "Persistent Effects of Firm Demand on Cohort Wages." Mimeo, University of Chicago.

Cole, R. E. 1979. *Work, Mobility, and Participation*. Berkeley: University of California Press.

———. 2000. "Market Pressures and Institutional Forces," in R. E. Cole and W. R. Scott (eds.), *The Quality Movement and Organization Theory*. Thousand Oaks, CA: Sage, pp. 67–88.

Colombo, M. G., M. Delmastro, and L. Rabbiosi. 2007. "'High Performance' Work Practices, Decentralization, and Profitability: Evidence from Panel Data." *Industrial and Corporate Change* 16: 1037–1067.

Coupe, T., V. Smeets, and F. Warzynski. 2006. "Incentives, Sorting, and Productivity along the Career: Evidence from a Sample of Top Economists." *Journal of Law, Economics, and Organization* 22: 137–167.

De Paola, M., and V. Scoppa. 2009. "Task Assignment, Incentives and Technological Factors." *Managerial and Decision Economics* 30: 43–55.

Dertouzos, M. L., R. K. Lester, and R. M. Solow. 1989. *Made in America*. Cambridge, MA: MIT Press.

DeVaro, J. 2006a. "Strategic Promotion Tournaments and Worker Performance." *Strategic Management Journal* 27: 721–740.

———. 2006b. "Internal Promotion Competition in Firms." *RAND Journal of Economics* 37: 521–542.

DeVaro, J., and H. Morita. 2010. "Internal Promotion and External Recruitment: A Theoretical and Empirical Analysis." *Journal of Labor Economics*, forthcoming.

DeVaro, J., and M. Waldman. 2012. "The Signaling Role of Promotions: Further Theory and Empirical Evidence." *Journal of Labor Economics* 30: 91–147.

DeVaro, J., S. Ghosh, and C. Zoghi. 2012. "Job Characteristics and Labor Market Discrimination in Promotions: New Theory and Empirical Evidence." Mimeo, California State University, East Bay.

Devereux, P. J., and R. A. Hart. 2007. "The Spot Market Matters: Evidence on Implicit Contracts from Britain." *Scottish Journal of Political Economy* 54: 661–683.

Dias da Silva, A., and B. van der Klaauw. 2011. "Wage Dynamics and Promotions Inside and Between Firms." *Journal of Population Economics* 24: 1513–1548.

Doeringer, P., and M. Piore. 1971. *Internal Labor Markets and Manpower Analysis*. Lexington, MA: Heath Lexington Books.

Dohmen, T. J. 2004. "Performance, Seniority, and Wages: Formal Salary Systems and Individual Earnings Profiles." *Labour Economics* 11: 741–763.

Dohmen, T. J., B. Kriechel, and G. A. Pfann. 2004. "Monkey Bars and Ladders: The Importance of Lateral and Vertical Job Mobility in Internal Labor Market Careers." *Journal of Population Economics* 17: 193–228.

Doiron, D. 1995. "Layoffs as Signals: The Canadian Evidence." *Canadian Journal of Economics* 28: 899–913.

Drago, R., and G. Garvey. 1998. "Incentives for Helping on the Job: Theory and Evidence." *Labour Economics* 16: 1–25.

Dunlop, J., and D. Weil. 1996. "Diffusion and Performance of Modular Production in the U.S. Apparel Industry." *Industrial Relations* 35: 334–354.

Ehrenberg, R. G., and M. L. Bognanno. 1990a. "Do Tournaments Have Incentive Effects?" *Journal of Political Economy* 98: 1307–1324.

———. 1990b. "The Incentive Effects of Tournaments Revisited: Evidence from the European PGA Tour." *Industrial and Labor Relations Review* 43: 74S–88S.

Ekinci, E. 2011. "Bonus Payments in a Corporate Hierarchy: Theory and Evidence." Mimeo, Cornell University, Ithaca, NY.

Ennen, E., and A. Richter. 2010. "The Whole Is More Than the Sum of Its Parts—Or Is It? A Review of the Empirical Literature on Complementarities in Organizations." *Journal of Management* 36: 207–233.

Eriksson, T. 1999. "Executive Compensation and Tournament Theory." *Journal of Labor Economics* 17: 262–280.

———. 2003. "The Effects of New Work Practices—Evidence from Employer-Employee Data," in T. Kato and J. Pliskin (eds.), *Determinants of the Incidence and the Effects of Participatory Organizations: Advances in the Economic Analysis of Participatory and Labor-Managed Firms.* Amsterdam: Elsevier, pp. 3–30.

Eriksson, T., and J. Ortega. 2006. "The Adoption of Job Rotation: Testing the Theories." *Industrial and Labor Relations Review* 59: 653–666.

Fairburn, J. A., and J. M. Malcomson. 2001. "Performance, Promotion, and the Peter Principle." *Review of Economic Studies* 68: 45–66.

Falk, A., and A. Ichino. 2006. "Clean Evidence on Peer Effects." *Journal of Labor Economics* 24: 39–57.

Farber, H. S. 2007. "Labor Market Adjustment to Globalization: Long-Term Employment in the United States and Japan." Industrial Relations Section Working Paper 519, Princeton University, Princeton, NJ.

Farber, H. S., and R. Gibbons. 1996. "Learning and Wage Dynamics." *Quarterly Journal of Economics* 111: 1007–1047.

Frank, R. H. 1984. "Are Workers Paid Their Marginal Products?" *American Economic Review* 74: 549–571.

———. 1985. *Choosing the Right Pond: Human Behavior and the Quest for Status.* Oxford: Oxford University Press.

Freeman, R., and M. Kleiner. 2005. "The Last American Shoe Manufacturer: Decreasing Productivity and Increasing Profits in the Shift from Piece Rates to Continuous Flow Production." *Industrial Relations* 44: 307–330.

Freeman, S. 1977. "Wage Trends as Performance Displays Productive Potential: A Model and Application to Academic Early Retirement." *Bell Journal of Economics* 8: 419–443.

Frick, B., U. Gotzen, and R. Simmons. 2008. "The Hidden Costs of High Performance Work Practices: Evidence from a Large German Steel Company." Mimeo, Lancaster University, UK.

Garicano, L. 2000. "Hierarchies and the Organization of Knowledge in Production." *Journal of Political Economy* 108: 874–904.

Garicano, L., and T. N. Hubbard. 2005. "Managerial Leverage Is Limited by the Extent of the Market: Hierarchies, Specialization, and the Utilization of Lawyers' Human Capital." *Journal of Law and Economics* 50: 1–43.

Garicano, L., and E. Rossi-Hansberg. 2006. "Organization and Inequality in a Knowledge Economy." *Quarterly Journal of Economics* 121: 1383–1435.

Garvey, G., and P. Swan. 1992. "Managerial Objectives, Capital Structure, and the Provision of Worker Incentives." *Journal of Labor Economics* 10: 357–379.

Gathmann, C., and U. Schonberg. 2010. "How General Is Human Capital? A Task-Based Approach." *Journal of Labor Economics* 28: 1–49.

Genda, Y., A. Kondo, and S. Ohta. 2010. "Long-Term Effects of a Recession at Labor Market Entry in Japan and the United States." *Journal of Human Resources* 45: 157–196.

Ghosh, S. 2007. "Job Mobility and Careers in Firms." *Labour Economics* 14: 603–621.

Ghosh, S., and M. Waldman. 2010. "Standard Promotion Practices versus Up-or-Out Contracts." *RAND Journal of Economics* 41: 301–325.

Gibbons, R. 1987. "Piece-Rate Incentive Schemes." *Journal of Labor Economics* 5: 413–429.

———. 1998. "Incentives in Organizations." *Journal of Economic Perspectives* 12(4): 115–132.

———. 2003. "Team Theory, Garbage Cans and Real Organizations: Some History and Prospects of Economic Research in Decision-Making in Organizations." *Industrial and Corporate Change* 12: 753–787.

Gibbons, R., and L. Katz. 1991. "Layoffs and Lemons." *Journal of Labor Economics* 9: 351–380.

Gibbons, R., and K. J. Murphy. 1992. "Optimal Incentive Contracts in the Presence of Career Concerns: Theory and Evidence." *Journal of Political Economy* 100: 468–505.

Gibbons, R., and M. Waldman. 1999a. "Careers in Organizations: Theory and Evidence," in O. Ashenfelter and D. Card (eds.), *Handbook of Labor Economics,* volume 3. Amsterdam: North-Holland, pp. 2373–2437.

———. 1999b. "A Theory of Wage and Promotion Dynamics Inside Firms." *Quarterly Journal of Economics* 114: 1321–1358.

———. 2004. "Task-Specific Human Capital." *American Economic Review* 94: 203–207.

———. 2006. "Enriching a Theory of Wage and Promotion Dynamics Inside Firms." *Journal of Labor Economics* 24: 59–107.

Gibbs, M. 1995. "Incentive Compensation in a Corporate Hierarchy." *Journal of Accounting and Economics* 19: 247–277.

Gibbs, M., and W. E. Hendricks. 2004. "Do Formal Salary Systems Really Matter?" *Industrial and Labor Relations Review* 58: 71–93.

Gittleman, M., M. Horrigan, and M. Joyce. 1998. "Flexible Workplace Practices: Evidence from a Nationally Representative Survey." *Industrial and Labor Relations Review* 52: 99–115.

Golan, L. 2005. "Counteroffers and Efficiency in Labor Markets with Asymmetric Information." *Journal of Labor Economics* 23: 373–393.

———. 2009. "Wage Signaling: A Dynamic Model of Intrafirm Bargaining and Asymmetric Learning." *International Economic Review* 50: 831–854.

Grant, D. 2003. "The Effect of Implicit Contracts on the Movement of Wages over the Business Cycle: Evidence from the National Longitudinal Surveys." *Industrial and Labor Relations Review* 56: 393–408.

Green, J. R., and N. Stokey. 1983. "A Comparison of Tournaments and Contracts." *Journal of Political Economy* 91: 349–364.

Greenan, N., and D. Guellec. 1997. "Firm Organization, Technology and Performance: An Empirical Study." *Economics of Innovation and New Technology* 6: 313–347.

Greenwald, B. 1979. *Adverse Selection in the Labor Market.* New York: Garland Press.

———. 1986. "Adverse Selection in the Labour Market." *Review of Economic Studies* 53: 325–347.

Grund, C. 1999. "Stigma Effects of Layoffs? Evidence from German Micro-Data." *Economics Letters* 64: 241–247.

Guadalupe, M., and J. Wulf. 2010. "The Flattening Firm and Product Market Competition: The Effect of Trade Liberalization on Corporate Hierarchies." *American Economic Journal: Applied Economics* 2: 105–127.

Habermalz, S. 2006. "More Detail on the Pattern of Returns to Educational Signals." *Southern Economic Journal* 73: 125–135.

Hamaaki, J., M. Hori, S. Maeda, and K. Murata. 2010. "Is the Japanese Employment System Degenerating? Evidence from the Basic Survey of Wage Structure." ESRI Discussion Paper 232, Economic and Social Research Institute, Dublin.

Hamilton, B. H., J. A. Nickerson, and H. Owan. 2003. "Team Incentives and Worker Heterogeneity: An Empirical Analysis of the Impact of Teams on Productivity and Participation." *Journal of Political Economy* 111: 464–497.

Harris, M., and B. Holmström. 1982. "A Theory of Wage Dynamics." *Review of Economic Studies* 49: 315–333.

Hashimoto, M. 1994. "Employment-Based Training in Japanese Firms in Japan and the United States: Experiences of Automobile Manufacturers," in L. M. Lynch (ed.), *Training and the Private Sector.* Chicago: University of Chicago Press, pp. 109–148.

Hashimoto, M., and J. Raisian. 1985. "Employment Tenure and Earnings Profiles in Japan and the United States." *American Economic Review* 75: 721–735.

Hause, J. 1980. "The Fine Structure of Earnings and the On-the-Job Training Hypothesis." *Econometrica* 48: 1013–1030.

Holmström, B. 1979. "Moral Hazard and Observability." *Bell Journal of Economics* 9: 74–91.

———. 1982. "Moral Hazard in Teams." *Bell Journal of Economics* 13: 324–340.

Holmström, B., and P. Milgrom. 1991. "Multi-Task Principal-Agent Analyses: Incentive Contracts, Asset Ownership and Job Design." *Journal of Law, Economics, and Organization* 7: 24–52.

———. 1994. "The Firm as an Incentive System." *American Economic Review* 84: 972–991.

Holzhausen, A. 2000. "Japanese Employment Practices in Transition: Promotion Policy and Compensation Systems in the 1990s." *Social Science Japan Journal* 3: 221–235.

Hu, L., and C. Taber. 2011. "Displacement, Asymmetric Information and Heterogeneous Human Capital." *Journal of Labor Economics* 29: 113–152.

Hunnes, A. 2011. "Testing the Role of Comparative Advantage and Learning in Wage and Promotion Dynamics." *International Journal of Manpower,* forthcoming.

Huselid, M. A., and B. E. Becker. 1996. "Methodological Issues in Cross-Sectional and Panel Estimates of the Human Resource–Firm Performance Link." *Industrial Relations* 35: 400–422.

Ichniowski, C. 1992. "Human Resource Practices and Productive Labor-Management Relations," in D. Lewin, O. Mitchell, and P. Scherer (eds.), *Research Frontiers in Industrial Relations and Human Resources.* Madison, WI: Industrial Relations Research Association, pp. 239–271.

Ichniowski, C., and K. Shaw. 1995. "Old Dogs and New Tricks: Determinants of the Adoption of Productivity-Enhancing Work Practices." *Brookings Papers on Economic Activity: Microeconomics* 1995: 1–65.

———. 1999. "The Effects of Human Resource Management Systems on Economic Performance: An International Comparison of U.S. and Japanese Plants." *Management Science* 45: 704–721.

———. 2003. "Beyond Incentive Pay: Insiders' Estimates of the Value of Complementary Human Resource Management Practices." *Journal of Economic Perspectives* 17(1): 155–180.

Ichniowski, C., J. J. Delaney, and D. Lewin. 1989. "The New Human Resource Management in US Workplaces: Is It Really New and Is It Only Nonunion?" *Relations Industrielles* 44: 97–119.

Ichniowski, C., K. Shaw, and G. Prennushi. 1997. "The Effects of Human Resource Management Practices on Productivity: A Study of Steel Finishing Lines." *American Economic Review* 87: 291–313.

Ishida, J. 2004a. "Education as Advertisement." *Economics Bulletin* 10: 1–8.

———. 2004b. "Signaling and Strategically Delayed Promotion." *Labour Economics* 11: 687–700.

Ito, T. 1992. *The Japanese Economy.* Cambridge, MA: MIT Press.

Jones, D., and T. Kato. 2011. "The Impact of Teams on Output, Quality and Downtime: An Empirical Analysis Using Individual Panel Data." *Industrial and Labor Relations Review* 64: 215–240.

Kagono, T., I. Nonaka, K. Sakakibara, and A. Okumura. 1985. *Strategic vs. Evolutionary Management: A US-Japan Comparison of Strategy and Organization.* Amsterdam: North-Holland.

Kahn, L. B. 2008. "Asymmetric Information between Employers." Mimeo, Yale University, New Haven, CT.

———. 2010. "The Long-Term Labor Market Consequences of Graduating from College in a Bad Economy." *Labour Economics* 17: 303–316.

Kambayashi, R., and T. Kato. 2011. "The Japanese Employment System after the Bubble Burst: New Evidence," in K. Hamada, A. Kashyap, M. Kuroda, and D. Weinstein (eds.), *Japan's Bubble, Deflation, and Stagnation.* Cambridge, MA: MIT Press, pp. 217–262.

Kandel, E., and E. Lazear. 1992. "Peer Pressure and Partnership." *Journal of Political Economy* 100: 801–817.

Kato, T. 2001. "The End of Lifetime Employment in Japan: Evidence from National Surveys and Field Research." *Journal of the Japanese and International Economies* 15: 489–514.

Katz, E., and A. Ziderman. 1990. "Investment in General Training: The Role of Information and Labour Mobility." *Economic Journal* 100: 1147–1158.

Kauhanen, A., and S. Napari. 2011. "Careers and Wage Dynamics: Evidence from Linked Employer-Employee Data." *Research in Labor Economics*, forthcoming.

Kawaguchi, D., and Y. Ueno. 2010. "Declining Long-Term Employment in Japan." Mimeo, Hitotsubashi University, Tokyo, Japan.

Kelley, M. E. 1996. "Participatory Bureaucracy and Productivity in the Machined Products Sector." *Industrial Relations* 35: 374–399.

Knez, M., and D. Simester. 2001. "Firm-Wide Incentives and Mutual Monitoring at Continental Airlines." *Journal of Labor Economics* 19: 743–772.

Kochan, T. A., H. C. Katz, and R. B. McKersie. 1986. *The Transformation of American Industrial Relations.* New York: Basic Books.

Koike, K. 1977. *Shokuba No Rodokumiai To Sanka* [*Labor Unions and Participation in Workplaces*]. Tokyo: Toyokeizai Shinposha.

———. 1988. *Understanding Industrial Relations in Modern Japan.* New York: St. Martin's Press.

Krafcik, J. 1988. "Triumph of the Lean Production System." *Sloan Management Review* 30(1): 41–52.

Krakel, M., and A. Schöttner. 2008. "Relative Performance Pay, Bonuses, and Job-Promotion Tournaments." Discussion Paper 3702, IZA, Bonn, Germany.

Krashinsky, H. 2002. "Evidence on Adverse Selection and Establishment Size in the Labor Market." *Industrial and Labor Relations Review* 56: 84–96.

Kreps, D. 1990. "Corporate Culture and Economic Theory," in J. Alt and K. Shepsle (eds.), *Perspectives on Positive Political Economy.* New York: Cambridge University Press, pp. 90–143.

Krueger, A. 1991. "Ownership, Agency, and Wages: An Examination of Franchising in the Fast Food Industry." *Quarterly Journal of Economics* 106: 75–101.

Kwon, I. 2006. "Incentives, Wages, and Promotions: Theory and Evidence." *RAND Journal of Economics* 37: 100–120.

Kwon, I., E. Meyersson Milgrom, and S. Hwang. 2010. "Cohort Effects in Promotions and Wages: Evidence from Sweden and the US." *Journal of Human Resources* 45: 772–808.

Lambert, R., D. Larcker, and K. Weigelt. 1993. "The Structure of Organizational Incentives." *Administrative Science Quarterly* 38: 438–461.

Lawler, E. E., S. A. Mohrman, and G. E. Ledford Jr. 1995. *Creating High Performance Organizations: Practices and Results of Employee Involvement and Total Quality Management in Fortune 1000 Companies.* San Francisco: Jossey-Bass.

Lazear, E. 1979. "Why Is There Mandatory Retirement?" *Journal of Political Economy* 87: 1261–1284.

———. 1981. "Agency, Earnings Profiles, Productivity and Hours Restrictions." *American Economic Review* 71: 606–620.

———. 1986a. "Raids and Offer Matching," in R. Ehrenberg (ed.), *Research in Labor Economics,* volume 8. Greenwich, CT: JAI Press, pp. 141–165.

———. 1986b. "Salaries and Piece Rates." *Journal of Business* 59: 405–431.

———. 1989. "Pay Equality and Industrial Politics." *Journal of Political Economy* 97: 561–580.

———. 1992. "The Job as a Concept," in W. Bruns (ed.), *Performance Measurement, Evaluations, and Incentives.* Boston: Harvard University Press, pp. 183–215.

———. 1999. "Personnel Economics: Past Lessons and Future Directions." *Journal of Labor Economics* 17: 199–236.

———. 2000. "Performance Pay and Productivity." *American Economic Review* 90: 1346–1361.

Lazear, E., and P. Oyer. 2004. "Internal and External Labor Markets: A Personnel Economics Approach." *Labour Economics* 11: 527–554.

Lazear, E., and S. Rosen. 1981. "Rank-Order Tournaments as Optimum Labor Contracts." *Journal of Political Economy* 89: 841–864.

Leavitt, H., and T. Whisler. 1958. "Management in the 1980s." *Harvard Business Review* November–December: 41–48.

Lemieux, T., W. B. MacLeod, and D. Parent. 2009. "Performance Pay and Wage Inequality." *Quarterly Journal of Economics* 124: 1–49.

Li, J. 2009. "Job Mobility, Wage Dispersion, and Asymmetric Information." Mimeo, Northwestern University, Evanston, IL.

Lillard, L., and Y. Weiss. 1979. "Components of Variation in Panel Data: American Scientists 1960–1970." *Econometrica* 47: 437–454.

Lima, F., and P. T. Pereira. 2003. "Careers and Wages within Large Firms: Evidence from a Matched Employer-Employee Data Set." *International Journal of Manpower* 24: 812–835.

Lin, M. J. 2005. "Opening the Black Box: The Internal Labor Markets of Company X." *Industrial Relations* 44: 659–706.

———. 2006. "Wages and Learning in Internal Labor Markets: Evidence from a Taiwanese Company." *Contributions to Economic Analysis and Policy* 5(1): Article 2.

Lincoln, R. J., M. Hanada, and K. McBride. 1986. "Organizational Structures in Japanese and US Manufacturing." *Administrative Science Quarterly* 31: 338–364.

Lluis, S. 2005. "The Role of Comparative Advantage and Learning in Wage Dynamics and Intrafirm Mobility: Evidence from Germany." *Journal of Labor Economics* 23: 725–768.

Lynch, L. 2007. "The Adoption and Diffusion of Organizational Innovation: Evidence for the U.S. Economy." Discussion Paper 2819, IZA, Bonn, Germany.

MacDuffie, J. P. 1995. "Human Resource Bundles and Manufacturing Performance: Organizational Logic and Flexible Production Systems in the World Auto Industry." *Industrial and Labor Relations Review* 48: 197–221.

MacDuffie, J. P., and T. Kochan. 1995. "Do US Firms Invest Less in Human Resources? Training in the World Auto Industry." *Industrial Relations* 34: 147–168.

MacDuffie, J. P., and F. Pil. 1996. "The Adoption of High Involvement Work Practices." *Industrial Relations* 35: 423–455.

MacLeod, W. B., and J. M. Malcomson. 1988. "Reputation and Hierarchy in Dynamic Models of Employment." *Journal of Political Economy* 96: 832–854.

Main, B. G. M., C. A. O'Reilly III, and J. Wade. 1993. "Top Executive Pay: Tournaments or Teamwork?" *Journal of Labor Economics* 11: 606–628.

Malcomson, J. M. 1984. "Work Incentives, Hierarchy, and Internal Labor Markets." *Journal of Political Economy* 92: 486–507.

Mas, A., and E. Moretti. 2009. "Peers at Work." *American Economic Review* 99: 112–145.

McCue, K. 1996. "Promotions and Wage Growth." *Journal of Labor Economics* 14: 175–209.

McLaughlin, K. J. 1994. "Rigid Wages." *Journal of Monetary Economics* 34: 383–414.

Medoff, J., and K. Abraham. 1980. "Experience, Performance, and Earnings." *Quarterly Journal of Economics* 95: 703–736.

———. 1981. "Are Those Paid More Really More Productive?" *Journal of Human Resources* 16: 186–216.

Meyer, M. A. 1992. "Biased Contests and Moral Hazard: Implications for Career Profiles." *Annales d'Economic et de Statistique* 25/26: 165–187.

———. 1994. "The Dynamics of Learning with Team Production: Implications for Task Assignment." *Quarterly Journal of Economics* 109: 1157–1184.

Michie, J., and M. Sheehan. 1999. "HR Practices, R&D Expenditures and Innovative Investment: Evidence from the U.K.'s Workplace Industrial Relations Survey." *Industrial and Corporate Change* 8: 211–233.

Milgrom, P. 1988. "Employment Contracts, Influence Activities and Efficient Organization Design." *Journal of Political Economy* 96: 42–60.

Milgrom, P., and S. Oster. 1987. "Job Discrimination, Market Forces, and the Invisibility Hypothesis." *Quarterly Journal of Economics* 102: 453–476.

Milgrom, P., and J. Roberts. 1988. "An Economic Approach to Influence Activities in Organizations." *American Journal of Sociology* 94: S154–S179.

———. 1990. "The Economics of Modern Manufacturing: Technology, Strategy, and Organization." *American Economic Review* 80: 511–528.

———. 1995. "Complementarities and Fit: Strategy, Structure, and Organizational Change in Manufacturing." *Journal of Accounting and Economics* 19: 179–208.

Milkovich, G. T., and J. M. Newman. 1987. *Compensation.* Plano, TX: Business Publications.

Mincer, J. 1974. *Schooling, Experience, and Earnings.* New York: National Bureau of Economic Research.

Mincer, J., and Y. Higuchi. 1988. "Wage Structures and Labor Turnover in the United States and Japan." *Journal of the Japanese and International Economies* 2: 97–133.

Mohnen, A., K. Pokorny, and D. Sliwka. 2008. "Transparency, Inequity Aversion, and the Dynamics of Peer Pressure in Teams: Theory and Evidence." *Journal of Labor Economics* 26: 693–720.

Mookherjee, D. 1984. "Optimal Incentive Schemes with Many Agents." *Review of Economic Studies* 51: 433–446.

———. 2006. "Decentralization, Hierarchies and Incentives: A Mechanism Design Perspective." *Journal of Economic Literature* 44: 367–390.

Moriguchi, C. 2003. "Implicit Contracts, the Great Depression, and Institutional Change: A Comparative Analysis of U.S. and Japanese Employment Relations, 1920–1940." *Journal of Economic History* 63: 625–665.

Morita, H. 2001. "Choice of Technology and Labor Market Consequences: An Explanation of US-Japanese Differences." *Economic Journal* 111: 29–50.

———. 2005. "Multi-Skilling, Delegation and Continuous Process Improvement: A Comparative Analysis of US-Japanese Work Organizations." *Economica* 72: 69–93.

Murphy, K. J. 1985. "Corporate Performance and Managerial Remuneration: An Empirical Analysis." *Journal of Accounting and Economics* 7: 11–42.

Nagin, D., J. Rebitzer, S. Sanders, and L. Taylor. 2002. "Monitoring, Motivation and Management: The Determinants of Opportunistic Behavior in a Field Experiment." *American Economic Review* 92: 850–873.

Nalebuff, B. J., and J. E. Stiglitz. 1983. "Prizes and Incentives: Towards a General Theory of Compensation and Competition." *Bell Journal of Economics* 14: 21–43.

Novos, I. 1995. "Imperfections in Labor Markets and the Scope of the Firm." *International Journal of Industrial Organization* 13: 387–410.

Okuno-Fujiwara, M. 1987. "Monitoring Costs, Agency Relationships, and Equilibrium Modes of Labor Contracts." *Journal of the Japanese and International Economies* 1: 147–167.

Ono, H. 2010. "Lifetime Employment in Japan: Concepts and Measurements." *Journal of the Japanese and International Economies* 24: 1–27.

O'Reilly III, C., B. Main, and G. Crystal. 1988. "CEO Compensation as Tournament and Social Comparison: A Tale of Two Theories." *Administrative Science Quarterly* 33: 257–274.

Oreopoulos, P., T. von Wachter, and A. Heisz. 2012. "The Short- and Long-Term Career Effects of Graduating in a Recession." *American Economic Journal: Applied Economics* 4: 1–29.

Ortega, J. 2001. "Job Rotation as a Learning Mechanism." *Management Science* 47: 1361–1370.

Osterman, P. 1994. "How Common Is Workplace Transformation and Who Adopts It?" *Industrial and Labor Relations Review* 47: 173–188.

———. 1996. *Broken Ladders: Managerial Careers in the New Economy.* New York: Oxford University Press.

———. 2000. "Work Reorganization in an Era of Restructuring: Trends in Diffusion and Effects of Employee Welfare." *Industrial and Labor Relations Review* 53: 179–196.

Owan, H. 1999. "Internal Organization, Bargaining, and Human Capital." PhD dissertation, Stanford University, Stanford, CA.

———. 2004. "Promotion, Turnover, Earnings, and Firm-Sponsored Training." *Journal of Labor Economics* 22: 955–978.

Oyer, P. 2006. "Initial Labor Market Conditions and Long-Term Outcomes for Economists." *Journal of Economic Perspectives* 20(3): 143–160.

———. 2007. "Is There an Insider Advantage in Getting Tenure?" *American Economic Review* 97: 501–505.

Pergamit, M., and J. Veum. 1999. "What Is a Promotion?" *Industrial and Labor Relations Review* 52: 581–601.

Peterson, J. 2010. "Essays on Employee Turnover." PhD dissertation, Cornell University, Ithaca, NY.

Pinkston, J. 2009. "A Model of Asymmetric Employer Learning with Testable Implications." *Review of Economic Studies* 76: 367–394.

Podolny, J. M., and J. N. Baron. 1997. "Resources and Relationships: Social Networks and Mobility in the Workplace." *American Sociological Review* 62: 673–693.

Prendergast, C. 1989. "Theories of Internal Labor Markets." PhD dissertation, Yale University, New Haven, CT.

———. 1992. "Career Development and Specific Human Capital Collection." *Journal of the Japanese and International Economies* 6: 207–227.

———. 1999. "The Provision of Incentives in Firms." *Journal of Economic Literature* 37: 7–63.

Prescott, E. S., and R. M. Townsend. 2006. "Private Information and Intertemporal Job Assignments." *Review of Economic Studies* 73: 531–548.

Rajan, R., and J. Wulf. 2006. "The Flattening Firm: Evidence from Panel Data on the Changing Nature of Corporate Hierarchies." *Review of Economics and Statistics* 88: 759–773.

Ricart i Costa, J. 1988. "Managerial Task Assignments and Promotions." *Econometrica* 56: 449–466.

Ricchetti, B. M. 2007. "Essays in Labor and Organization Economics." PhD dissertation, Cornell University, Ithaca, NY.

Rosen, S. 1982. "Authority, Control, and the Distribution of Earnings." *Bell Journal of Economics* 13: 311–323.

———. 1986. "Prizes and Incentives in Elimination Tournaments." *American Economic Review* 76: 701–715.

Rosenbaum, J. 1984. *Career Mobility in a Corporate Hierarchy.* New York: Academic Press.

Rotemberg, J. J. 1994. "Human Relations in the Workplace." *Journal of Political Economy* 102: 684–717.

Rubinstein, Y., and Y. Weiss. 2007. "Post Schooling Wage Growth: Investment, Search and Learning," in E. A. Hanushek and F. Welch (eds.), *Handbook of the Economics of Education,* volume 1. Amsterdam: North-Holland, pp. 1–67.

Schmieder, J., and T. von Wachter. 2009. "Does Wage Persistence Matter for Employment Fluctuations? Evidence from Displaced Workers." *American Economic Journal: Applied Economics* 2: 1–21.

Schonberg, U. 2007. "Testing for Asymmetric Employer Learning." *Journal of Labor Economics* 25: 651–691.

Seltzer, A., and D. Merrett. 2000. "Personnel Policies at the Union Bank of Australia: Evidence from the 1888–1900 Entry Cohorts." *Journal of Labor Economics* 18: 573–613.

Shapiro, C., and J. E. Stiglitz. 1984. "Equilibrium Unemployment as a Worker Discipline Device." *American Economic Review* 74: 433–444.

Shavell, S. 1979. "Risk Sharing and Incentives in the Principal and Agent Relationship." *Bell Journal of Economics* 10: 55–73.

Shaw, K., and E. Lazear. 2008. "Tenure and Output." *Labour Economics* 15: 705–724.

Shepard, A. 1993. "Contractual Form, Retail Price, and Asset Characteristics in Gasoline Retailing." *RAND Journal of Economics* 24: 58–77.

Slade, M. 1996. "Multitask Agency and Organizational Form: An Empirical Exploration." *International Economic Review* 37: 465–486.

Smeets, V., and F. Warzynski. 2008. "Too Many Theories, Too Few Facts? What the Data Tell Us about the Link between Span of Control, Compensation and Career Dynamics." *Labour Economics* 15: 687–703.

Song, Y. 2007. "Recall Bias in the Displaced Workers Survey: Are Layoffs Really Lemons?" *Labour Economics* 14: 335–345.

Stevens, A. H. 1997. "Persistent Effects of Job Displacement: The Importance of Multiple Job Losses." *Journal of Labor Economics* 15: 165–188.

Topel, R. H. 1991. "Specific Capital, Mobility, and Wages: Wages Rise with Job Seniority." *Journal of Political Economy* 99: 145–176.

Topel, R. H., and M. P. Ward. 1992. "Job Mobility and the Careers of Young Men." *Quarterly Journal of Economics* 107: 439–479.

Treble, J., E. V. Cameren, S. Bridges, and T. Barmby. 2001. "The Internal Economics of the Firm: Further Evidence from Personnel Data." *Journal of Labor Economics* 8: 531–552.

Umezaki, O. 2001. "Nihon Kigyo Ni Okeru Howaito Karah No Shokuba Soshiki To Jinteki Shigen Kanri" ["Work Organization and Human Resource Management of White-Collar Workers in the Japanese Firm"]. PhD dissertation, University of Osaka.

Van den Steen, E. 2006. "The Limits of Authority: Motivation versus Coordination." Research Paper 4626-06, Sloan School of Business, Massachusetts Institute of Technology, Cambridge, MA.

———. 2009. "Authority versus Persuasion." *American Economic Review* 99: 448–453.

———. 2010. "Interpersonal Authority in a Theory of the Firm." *American Economic Review* 100: 466–490.

Waldman, M. 1984a. "Job Assignments, Signalling, and Efficiency." *RAND Journal of Economics* 15: 255–267.

———. 1984b. "Worker Allocation, Hierarchies, and the Wage Distribution." *Review of Economic Studies* 51: 95–109.

———. 1990. "Up-or-Out Contracts: A Signaling Perspective." *Journal of Labor Economics* 8: 230–250.

———. 2003. "Ex Ante versus ex Post Optimal Promotion Rules: The Case of Internal Promotion." *Economic Inquiry* 41: 27–41.

———. 2011. "Classic Promotion Tournaments versus Market-Based Tournaments." *International Journal of Industrial Organization*, forthcoming.

Weiss, Y. 1984. "Wage Contracts When Output Grows Stochastically: The Roles of Mobility Costs and Capital Market Imperfections." *Journal of Labor Economics* 2: 155–173.

Willis, R. J. 1986. "Wage Determinants: A Survey and Reinterpretation of Human Capital Earnings Functions," in O. Ashenfelter and R. Layard (eds.), *Handbook of Labor Economics,* volume 1. Amsterdam: North-Holland, pp. 525–602.

Wilms, W. 1995. *NUMMI: An Ethnographic Study.* New York: Free Press.

Wolf, E., and A. Heinze. 2007. "How to Limit Discrimination? Analyzing the Effects of Innovative Workplace Practices on Intra-Firm Gender Wage Gaps Using Linked Employer-Employee Data." Discussion Paper 07-077, ZEW–Centre for European Economic Research, Mannheim, Germany.

Zábojník, J. 2002. "Centralized and Decentralized Decision Making in Organizations." *Journal of Labor Economics* 20: 1–22.

———. 2010. "Promotion Tournaments in Market Equilibrium." *Economic Theory*, forthcoming.

Zábojník, J., and D. Bernhardt. 2001. "Corporate Tournaments, Human Capital Acquisition, and the Firm Size-Wage Relation." *Review of Economic Studies* 68: 693–716.

Zhang, Y. 2008. "Employer Learning under Asymmetric Information: The Role of Job Mobility." Mimeo, Indiana University–Purdue University Indianapolis, Indianapolis, IN.

PART IV

Within Firms: Structures and Processes

14

Technological Innovation and Organizations

Pierre Azoulay and Josh Lerner

1. Introduction

In a handbook that takes a broad view of organizational structure, it might be wondered whether a chapter devoted to the relationship between technological innovation and organization is appropriate. After all, is not innovation just one relatively modest facet of economic activity?

There are two responses to this question. First, since the 1950s, economists have understood that technological innovation is critical to economic growth. Our lives are more comfortable and longer than those of our great-grandparents on many dimensions. At the heart of these changes has been the progress of technology. Innumerable studies have documented the strong connection between technological progress and economic prosperity both across nations and over time. Since the work of Abramowitz (1956) and Solow (1957), the importance of technological change has been generally understood, an understanding that has been deepened by studies in recent years documenting numerous positive effects of technological progress in specific areas, such as information technology (Bresnahan et al. 2002).

Second, innovation represents a particularly extreme ground for understanding organizational economics. This setting is one where information and incentive problems, which exist in the backdrop of many models of organizational structure and effectiveness, are front and center. These problems are at the heart of the innovation process. As Holmström (1989: 307) observes in his classic essay:

> One would expect modern finance theory to give good general advice on how to manage investments into research and development. But a quick look at finance textbooks reveals answers that are based on a very stylized conception of the problem and rather less illuminating than one would hope.

We thank Harvard Business School's Division of Research for financial support. Bob Gibbons, John Roberts, and participants in a meeting of the NBER Working Group in Organizational Economics devoted to reviewing early drafts of chapters from this handbook provided helpful comments. All errors and omissions are our own.

Thus, if we can understand organizational issues in the innovation setting—where performance often cannot be accurately measured, where knowledge often flows between entities, and where contracts may not be enforceable—we are likely to have a better understanding of these questions more generally. In this sense, the study by an economist of the relationship between innovation and organizational structure is akin to that of a physicist studying reactions in extremely young stars to gain insights that will be useful here on earth.

In this chapter, we begin by examining the relationship among internal organization, innovation inputs, and research productivity. We then turn to the relationship between contracting and innovation, and finally to the consequences of innovation for organizations.

Technological innovation is a large topic with many empirical and theoretical challenges. Nonetheless, we can highlight several conclusions that emerge from our discussion:

- Our understanding of contracting and innovation is probably the most developed of any of the major topics delineated here. At least in part, this reflects the close connections between theoretical and empirical research on this topic.

- In far too many other topics, however, there has been a disconnect between the insights of theoreticians and the work by empirical researchers.

- Most of what economists know about technological innovation and organizations does not stem from the mining of traditional datasets. On the contrary, some of the more lasting insights come from the collection of original fine-grained data at the project level. Case studies also inform the state of economists' knowledge on these topics (see Baker and Gil, this volume).

- An essential difficulty facing large-sample empirical research has been an inability to distinguish between association and causation, and, in some cases, a failure even to think carefully about this distinction. Empirical research is likely to advance considerably if some of the experimental methodologies employed in labor economics and related fields can be adopted here.

- Many valuable insights into these questions can be gleaned from fields outside economics, including sociology and more traditional managerial studies.

- The greatest gains in future years will be achieved by looking inside the "black box" of the firm and understanding the internal workings of the innovation process.

Reflecting the substantial size of this topic, we have limited our discussion in several important ways. First, we have focused on technological, not organizational, innovations. Readers interested in the adoption of new management techniques and their consequences for firm performance could turn to the work of Nick Bloom, John Van Reenen, and their collaborators (Bloom and Van Reenen [2010] provide a concise introduction to this fascinating topic). We have also focused only on research concerning the development of new ideas and approaches, and not on the diffusion of those ideas. Finally, we have ignored industry-level perspectives, such as the study of shake-outs and the industry life cycle, which have been the subject of other reviews (Klepper 2008).

2. Research and Development Productivity and Internal Organization

What makes an organization more or less innovative? For a long time, the literature on this topic focused solely on the relationship between innovation and firm size, following Schumpeter's (1942) conjecture that large firms had an inherent advantage at innovative functions relative to smaller enterprises. From the vantage point of twenty-first–century economists, the Schumpeterian hypothesis has not stood the test of time. It turns out to have been the intellectual by-product of an era that saw large firms and their industrial laboratories (e.g., IBM, AT&T, and DuPont) replace the independent inventors who accounted for a large part of innovative activity in the late nineteenth century and early twentieth (Lamoreaux and Sokoloff 2009).

At an anecdotal level, the Schumpeterian hypothesis does not accord with casual empiricism, as in several new industries (medical devices, communication technologies, semiconductors, software), industry leadership is firmly in the hands of relatively young firms whose growth was largely financed by public equity markets (e.g., Boston Scientific, Cisco, Intel, and Microsoft). But more systematic tests of Schumpeter's argument have been inconclusive too. A vast empirical literature, reviewed by Cohen and Levin (1989), has failed to uncover a robust relationship between firm size and innovation inputs.

What explains the relative failure of the empirical program started by Schumpeter's mid-century prophecy? An important reason is institutional change in the form of the emergence of vibrant markets for ideas that heralded a new division of innovative labor between large and small firms (Teece 1986; Gans and Stern 2000; Arora et al. 2002; Gans et al. 2002). If would-be innovators have the ability to cooperate with incumbent firms to appropriate the returns from technological innovation, regressing research and development (R&D) expenditures on firm sales will not be very illuminating.

Long before the emergence of modern ideas markets, some of Schumpeter's contemporaries, however, had some misgivings about the ability of large firms to generate technological innovations. For instance, Jewkes (1958: 55) argued:

> It is erroneous to suppose that those techniques of large-scale operation and administration which have produced such remarkable results in some branches of industrial manufacture can be applied with equal success to efforts to foster new ideas. The two kinds of organization are subject to quite different laws. In the one case the aim is to achieve smooth, routine, and faultless repetition, in the other to break through the bonds of routine and of accepted ideas. So that large research organizations can perhaps more easily become self-stultifying than any other type of large organization, since in a measure they are trying to organize what is least organizable. The director of a large research institution is confronted with what is perhaps the most subtle task to be found in the whole field of administration.

This section is devoted to fleshing out Jewkes's intuition by reviewing work by economists and other social scientists studying how other organizational characteristics impinge on the process of technological innovation. For organizing the discussion, we distinguish between studies of that focus on the *intensive margin* (the degree of effectiveness achieved by firms as they attempt to organize their innovative activities) from those that focus on the *extensive margin* (whether firms are able to innovate at all in the face of technological transitions).

2.1. Beyond Firm Size: Opening the Innovation Black Box

Perhaps the earliest indication that the internal organization of firms deserved more attention than it had traditionally received from economists came from empirical studies of the
innovation production function in the often-cited National Bureau of Economics Research
conference volume edited by Zvi Griliches (1984), *R&D, Patents, and Productivity*. Pakes and
Griliches (1984) found that when estimating patent production functions, the magnitude of
the coefficient on R&D investment fell drastically in the within-firm dimension of the data.
Similarly, Scott (1984) found that fixed firm effects explained about 50% of the variance in
R&D intensity. Of course, firm effects constitute a measure of economists' ignorance, and since
1984 a sizable body of research has emerged to explain the magnitude and relative stability over
time of these firm effects. The literature has focused on three broad features of organizations:
(1) the design of incentive systems; (2) firms' abilities to manage spillovers of knowledge, with a
particular emphasis on the causes and consequences of job mobility among engineers and scientists; and (3) firms' choice of organizational structure, including (but not limited to) acquisition
behavior.

2.2. Motivating Innovation: The Role of Incentive Systems

Firms provide incentives to their employees in all realms of economic life. Why would the
design of incentive systems for innovative tasks differ from that appropriate for "humdrum"
tasks? Holmström (1989) provides a number of reasons that make the provision of incentives
for innovation a difficult task. First, innovation projects are risky and unpredictable; second,
they are long-term and multistage; third, it might not be clear ex ante what is the correct action
for the agent to take; and finally, they tend to be idiosyncratic and difficult to compare to other
projects.

To this list, we would add two additional characteristics: innovators tend to bring to their
labor a certain degree of intrinsic motivation, and innovation is very often a team activity.

Manso (2011) is the first economist to formalize the trade-off between the exploration
of untested actions and the exploitation of well-known actions, which has long been a focus
of organization theorists (March 1991). He uses a class of decision problems called "bandit
problems," in which the agent does not know the true distribution of payoffs of the available
actions. Exploration of new untested actions reveals information about potentially superior
actions but is also likely to waste time with inferior actions. Exploitation of well-known actions
ensures reasonable payoffs but may prevent the discovery of superior actions. Embedding the
bandit problem into a traditional principal-agent model, Manso focuses on the features of
incentive schemes that encourage exploration. He finds striking departures from the standard
pay-for-performance contracts that are optimal when the principal is focused on eliciting effort
for known actions. The principal should tolerate early failure and reward long-term success; she
should provide some job security to the agent and should provide feedback on performance to
the agent.

Ederer and Manso (2011) devise a laboratory experiment in which subjects are randomly
assigned to incentive plans, including (1) a flat wage, (2) a standard pay for performance contract, and (3) a pay for future performance contract. They find that forward-looking incentives

result in more exploration and higher profits. These results suggest that appropriately designed incentives do not lead to a crowding-out effect, contrary to earlier arguments that incentives are likely to undermine creativity (e.g., Amabile 1996).

To test the potency of exploration incentives to stimulate innovative activities in a real-world setting, one of the main difficulties is to find agents who are at risk of receiving either exploration- or exploitation-type incentives. Azoulay et al. (2011) focus on alternative funding mechanisms for elite biomedical scientists that appear to provide just this kind of variation. The lifeblood of academic life sciences in the United States is provided by so-called R01 grants awarded by the National Institutes of Health. These grants are relatively short term (the modal length is 3 years), and renewal is both competitive and not forgiving of failure. In addition, brilliant scientists can be appointed as investigators of the Howard Hughes Medical Institute. HHMI investigators continue to be housed in the same institutions but labor under a very different set of incentives. They are explicitly told to "change their fields" and are given the resources, time (5-year renewable appointments, with a lax first review and a 2-year phase down in case of termination), and autonomy (they do not need prior authorization to change the direction of their research) to accomplish this.

Compared with a set of equally eminent scientists at baseline, the authors find that the program appears effective in boosting the rate of production of particularly creative scientific papers—those in the top percentile of the citation distribution. The impacts are even larger for other outcomes, such as the production of trainees who go on to win early-career prizes or election to the National Academy of Sciences.

In the absence of random assignment, the conclusions must remain tempered, despite the care taken to match control scientists with treated scientists, based on observable characteristics. But taken as a whole, these two papers certainly suggest that tolerance for early failure and rewards for good performance over the long term are effective ways to motivate agents engaged in idiosyncratic, nonrepetitive tasks. Of course, many questions remain to be addressed. For example, how does one design incentives to attract the most creative agents? Also, in a setting with multiple agents, what is the optimal balance between individual and team incentives to motivate exploration? In particular, can exploration-type incentives be effective when the principal must rank the agents she oversees to determine a prize, such as in a promotion tournament? These are important questions for future research.

Another generic theme is that of incentive balance, when several tasks compete for the agent's attention, but the principal's ability to infer effort from output is much higher for one set of tasks relative to another set. The main result from this literature is that it may be optimal to provide low-powered incentives in such situations, to avoid distorting the agent's allocation of effort toward the task that is easier to meter. Cockburn et al. (1999) illustrate the implications of this principle in the setting of drug discovery R&D. Pharmaceutical firms would like their researchers to generate many useful patents, but if the scientists are not connected to sources of knowledge located outside the firm, their creativity will eventually run dry. Conversely, if the scientists solely focus on staying on the frontier of science, the firm will find itself running a (possibly very good) biology department but will have little tangible output (actual new drugs) to show for its R&D investment. Cockburn et al. show that pharmaceutical firms resolve this tension by keeping incentives for basic and applied output in balance. On the one hand, scientists will be rewarded and promoted based on their individual standing in their scientific subfield, using traditional academic criteria, such as publications and citations. On the other hand, research teams will be rewarded on the basis of their applied output. In practical terms, a group that generates more useful patents than expected in a given year will see its budget increase the following year. Cockburn et al. (1999) find that firms tend to adopt both or neither of these practices, rather than adopting one without the other.

Innovation settings differ from more traditional ones because employee-technologists often work on something because they find it personally rewarding. Intrinsic motivation is important, because it has implications for job design and wage setting. In a fascinating survey of life scientists on the job market, Stern (2004) finds that pharmaceutical firms who give their scientists freedom to choose their own projects and otherwise remain connected to open science pay 15% less on average, holding scientist ability constant. This finding provides a rationale for firms to harness their employees' preferences in the way they organize research activities, in addition to the crowding-out effect of extrinsic incentives often stressed by psychologists (Amabile 1993).

Of course, firms need to balance the wage savings associated with employee autonomy against the probability that some of the knowledge generated internally will leak out to their competitors. As it turns out, the management of knowledge spillovers from innovative activities is a topic that has also received considerable attention.

2.3. Spillovers of Knowledge and Internal Organization

In his famous 1962 essay, Kenneth Arrow focused economists' attention on the nonrival nature of knowledge and the attendant disclosure problem. Ever since, economists have been focused on firms' ability to actively manage knowledge spillovers. The starting point for the discussion is that knowledge is not as public a good as initially thought, and therefore, distance between the transmitter and the receiver of knowledge matters in determining the extent of spillovers. Jaffe et al. (1993) observed that despite their ethereal nature, knowledge spillovers might leave a paper trail in the form of citations to prior art recorded in patents. By constructing a large dataset of patents and matching the location of inventors for both cited and citing patents, they documented that these citation patterns exhibit a pronounced degree of localization.[1]

However, physical proximity is not necessarily the only, or even the most relevant, concept of distance that economists should consider when attempting to estimate the magnitude of knowledge spillovers. To the three dimensions of physical space, it seems worthwhile to add technological space: advances in the state of knowledge in one particular technological area are likely to spur relatively more developments in technological areas that are thematically related. Jaffe (1986) was the first to construct a measure of technological distance between firms by using the distribution of firms' innovative efforts across patent classes, and he found that the R&D productivity of a focal firm was indeed positively correlated with the R&D of technological neighbors.

Social distance might also impinge on the extent of spillovers. Here the network metaphor is particularly apt, whether one thinks about degrees of separation between scientists in a

---

1. As documented by Thompson and Fox-Kean (2005), this exercise is fraught with difficulties because of the difficulty of finding nonciting patents that can serve as a control group and capture the agglomeration patterns that are due to other factors than knowledge spillovers.

coauthorship network, of the relationship between a corporate parent and its subsidiaries, or about the vertical linkages between buyers and suppliers. Adams and Jaffe (1996), focusing on the chemical industry, showed that the effects of parent firm R&D on plant-level productivity decrease with both geographic and technological distance between the research lab and the plants. Moreover, spillovers from technologically related firms are significant in magnitude but are diluted by the firms' own R&D intensity. This article stands out in the vast empirical literature, because it simultaneously attends to the three concepts of distance mentioned above.

In a similar vein, Azoulay et al. (2010) estimate the magnitude of spillovers generated by the untimely death of 112 academic superstars in the life sciences on their coauthors' research productivity. They find a lasting and significant decline in publication output, which is surprisingly homogeneous across a wide range of coauthor characteristics. But they do not observe a differential effect of a prominent collaborator's death for co-located coauthors. They interpret their findings as providing evidence that part of the scientific field embodied in the "invisible college" of coauthors working in a particular area dies along with the star.

A second fundamental idea in the study of knowledge spillovers is that of *absorptive capacity:* absorbing spillovers from other firms requires doing research yourself (Cohen and Levinthal 1989, 1990). Using a dataset that combines the Federal Trade Commission's line of business information with Levin et al. (1987) survey data, these authors find that spillovers from input suppliers can be absorbed with less R&D investment than spillovers from government and university labs. In the setting of pharmaceutical drug discovery, Cockburn and Henderson (1998) document strong correlations between the extent of ties between firms and academic science (mostly through coauthorship of scientific articles) and these same firms' research productivity. Moreover, building absorptive capacity has implications for the organization of R&D activity. Henderson and Cockburn (1994) use detailed data at the research program level from ten pharmaceutical firms and show that firms that adopted the practices of open science to motivate and reward scientists increased their research productivity (as measured by important patents per dollars invested) significantly during the 1980s.

A more recent literature stresses that there are other ways—beyond performing basic R&D—for firms to absorb outside knowledge. In a fascinating case study of the semiconductor industry, Lim (2011) shows that IBM's competitors were able to quickly imitate its design of copper interconnects by working closely with equipment suppliers, collaborating with some key academic labs, and hiring newly minted PhDs and postdoctoral fellows in the relevant scientific subfields.

2.4. The Mobility of Engineers and Human Capital Externalities

In her seminal study of the computer and semiconductor cluster in Silicon Valley, Annalee Saxenian (1994) drew the attention of economists to the high rates of job hopping among engineers. She ascribed the sustained success of Silicon Valley firms to the rapid movement of technical professionals among firms in the region and pointed out that an accident of Californian legal history precluded the enforcement of noncompete agreements in the state. Since then, an ever-expanding empirical literature has documented more systematically that job hopping is indeed a source of knowledge spillovers, and that these spillovers tend to be geographically localized (Almeida and Kogut 1999; Fallick et al. 2006).

What is less clear from this evidence, however, is whether these spillovers correspond to true externalities or whether there exist mechanisms through which the labor market can internalize the effects. Pakes and Nitzan (1983) present a model in which engineers bond themselves to their firms by accepting lower entry wages. Moen (2005), using matched employee/employer data from Norway, compares the wage-experience profiles of engineers and nontechnical white collar workers and finds that they are steeper for the former group of employees than for the latter. This suggests that the potential externalities associated with labor mobility are partially internalized in the labor market.

Our knowledge of the practices used by firms to manage outgoing and incoming knowledge spillovers is still fragmentary. The best-known evidence probably pertains to the role of scientific superstars documented by Zucker et al. (1998). These authors document a robust correlation between the rates of founding of new biotechnology firms and proximity to scientists who are leaders in the relevant subfields of biology. In the same spirit, Lacetera et al. (2004) show that pharmaceutical firms are more likely to change the organization of their drug discovery operations toward the open science model after hiring academic superstars. In this line of research, the direction of causality has not been clearly established, for a number of reasons. First, high-quality data on employee mobility is hard to come by. A popular approach has been to rely on patent or publication data to ascertain the movement of employees across firms, but it is obviously problematic to base mobility on potentially endogenous output measures (Almeida and Kogut 1999; Rosenkopf and Almeida 2003). Second, even if mobility could be measured with less error, there is always the possibility that scientists' or engineers' movements in and out of firms are driven by expectations regarding future firm productivity. A productive avenue for mobility research is to gather much more detailed data on individuals to extract exogenous variation in exposure to talent. Life cycle events, such as marriage, birth of children, and becoming "empty nesters" might provide such variation. An alternative is to focus instead on policy changes that affect rates of mobility among technical personnel. Marx et al. (2009) exploit Michigan's inadvertent reversal of its noncompete enforcement legislation to demonstrate that noncompetes decrease inventor mobility by 34%. Although this effect is not by itself surprising, the study's design can be thought of as providing a plausible first stage to study the effect of engineers' mobility on productivity.

2.5. Organizational Structure

In their efforts to broaden the range of organizational characteristics that impinge on the innovation process, economists and other social scientists have focused on various aspects of organizational structure. We focus here on three of the most salient: the choice between centralized and decentralized R&D activities, the effect of takeover and acquisitions on innovation, and the design and composition of R&D project teams.

2.5.1. Corporate R&D Laboratories versus Decentralized Innovation
Managerial scholars have long debated the relative merits of centralized R&D labs and decentralized R&D activities (Rosenbloom and Spencer 1996). Centralized R&D labs can potentially engage in nonlocal search activities and focus on long-term projects, but they run the risk of slowly evolving into ivory towers. Decentralizing R&D investment into divisions prevents

employee-technologists from losing sight of market imperatives, but it might result in a slow degradation of technological and scientific competencies. Some recent studies appear to support the view that centralized R&D more effectively supports wide-ranging innovative activities.

Using a sample of 71 large research-intensive corporations, Argyres and Silverman (2004) show that firms with centralized R&D labs generate more highly cited patents than do firms with decentralized or hybrid R&D structures. Lerner and Wulf (2007) combine information about structure with data on incentives provided to corporate R&D managers among Fortune 500 firms. They find that long-term incentives (stock options and restricted stock) result in patents than are more heavily cited, but this relationship is driven solely by firms with centralized R&D.

Together, these studies suggest that aligning the incentives of corporate R&D staff with those of the firm as a whole can mitigate the risk that research output loses relevance, with important caveats. First, patent citations are far from an ideal measure of the relevance of the research to the firm's product markets; sales from innovative products would be a more appropriate metric. Second, the choice of structure is potentially endogenous, and the studies provide suggestive conditional correlations, not estimates of causal effects. The relative virtues of centralized and decentralized R&D structures remain a relatively open question.

2.5.2. Takeovers, Mergers, and Acquisitions: Much Ado about Nothing?

In the 1970s and 1980s, the rise of Japan as an industrial giant stirred a debate in the United States and Europe about the effects of takeovers and merger activity on the rate and direction of R&D undertaken by firms. This prompted several studies probing the link between corporate restructurings and the intensity of R&D among U.S. manufacturing firms. Although the zeitgeist that provided the impetus for these studies has changed radically in the past 20 years, two papers by Bronwyn Hall stand out as particularly informative (Hall 1990, 1991).

As usual, the devil lies in the details of the econometric exercise, but in both cases, the effects she uncovers are of a relatively small magnitude—certainly smaller than what the hyperbolic statements of policymakers at the time would have implied. Hall finds that public firms involved in acquisitions where both partners are in the manufacturing sector have roughly the same pattern of R&D spending as the sector as a whole, and that the acquisition itself does not cause a reduction in R&D activity. Moreover, the target's R&D capital seems to be valued more highly by the acquirer than by the stock market itself (Hall 1991). In a second paper, Hall also studies the effects of leveraged buyouts. Here, she finds a more pronounced negative effect of increased leverage on R&D intensity, but because the firms taken over as a prelude to leveraged buyouts tend to be in less R&D-intensive segments, it seems unlikely that the leveraged buyout wave of the 1980s and early 1990s had a significant negative effect on R&D expenditures (Hall 1990).

2.5.3. Performance of R&D Project Teams: The Role of Social Structure

Employee-technologists are very often organized in project teams. Economists have long studied the provision of incentives in teams, including peer pressure (Kandel and Lazear 1992) and collective rewards (Che and Yoo 2001). Here we draw attention to a distinct attribute of R&D teams that has been shown to play a role in explaining their performance: the structure of the social networks to which team members belong.

Economists have contributed very little to this vibrant area of social science research. In light of the relevance of the results to the rate of technological innovation inside organizations, we chose to include a bare-bones exposition of the key idea, partly in the hope of stimulating economists' interest in the topic. Sociologists characterize social networks as cohesive or closed when many redundant contacts exist among network members. In a closed network, information flows quickly from one individual to another. In contrast, social networks can be rich in structural holes, that is, when some individuals can broker ties between subgroups that would have otherwise no opportunity for communication (Burt 1992). A central trade-off arises because network closure among team members makes coordination easier—which is beneficial in the execution phase of a project. At the same time, assembling in a team individuals whose social worlds do not overlap provides learning benefits, because it ensures that team members will be exposed to diverse sources of information (Burt 2004). In a fascinating paper, Reagans et al. (2004) provide evidence from a contract research organization that sheds light on how organizations can resolve this tension. Using the fact that employees participate in several distinct teams over the period during which they collected the data, these authors show that the most effective project teams have both high internal density (i.e., strong ties exist among team members) and high external range (i.e., team members have ongoing relationships with employees belonging to a diverse set of other project teams).

Of course, an economist might be skeptical of the empirical results for a variety of standard reasons. We might rightly wonder about simultaneity or omitted variables, though the authors have designed the study while attending to these concerns. More importantly, the outcome variable—time to project completion—is not ideal, especially as other research has found that employees in brokerage positions extract higher wages from their employers. Nonetheless, the effects the authors uncover are important in magnitude and statistically significant. Given the explanatory power of social network theories, it would seem that economists ignore these findings to their own detriment.

2.6. The Extensive Margin: When Established Firms Fail to Innovate at All

Rather than ask whether large firms invest more in R&D relative to small ones, another line of research focuses on evaluating theoretically and empirically the costs and benefits of market incumbency.

One branch of the literature provides an explanation for the dominance of entrepreneurial firms in new industries. Aron and Lazear (1990) present a model in which new firms pursue high-variance strategies and hence are more likely to introduce new products. Prusa and Schmitz (1994) test their argument by examining the introduction of new software programs. The authors suggest that new firms appear to be more effective at creating new software categories, whereas established firms have a comparative advantage in extending existing product lines. It should be noted that models like that of Aron and Lazear pertain to innovation generally, not necessarily to technological innovation.

A distinct stream of research explores the conditions under which market incumbents can adapt in the face of technological change. Here there has been a closer connection between theoretical work and empirical studies. The theoretical debate is well known and has been reviewed elsewhere (e.g., Reinganum 1989). In brief, models of technology races make sharply different predictions about the innovation incentives of incumbents and entrants depending on (1) the nature of uncertainty (i.e., can investment shift the timing of the new product's introduction?) and (2) whether the innovation is radical or incremental (i.e., is the new product so obviously superior that demand for the old product disappears?) (Gilbert and Newberry 1982; Reinganum 1983).

Because these features are hard for researchers to measure, empirical work has attempted to test the implications of racing models rather than compare the models directly. Lerner (1997), in his empirical examination of the disk drive industry, is a good example of this approach. For each product generation, he finds that firms who followed the leader in the previous generation display the greatest propensity to innovate. Interestingly, the same pattern does not exist in situations where strategic incentives are muted, as is the case when the firm is a division within a vertically integrated firm. Lerner interprets these findings as providing support for Reinganum's model of technological racing, but it is not clear that innovation in the disk drive industry should be construed as radical. In particular, the old and new generations of products tend to coexist for a period of time, because they typically appeal to distinct customer segments.

Christensen (1997) provides a different interpretation of the same phenomenon. According to his analysis, the new product generation initially poorly serves the needs of the incumbent's customers, but its quality eventually catches up. This presents an ideal situation for entrants to exploit incumbents' blind spots, which stem from their single-minded focus on existing customers. Christensen goes on to recommend that established firms systematically create "skunkworks" to incubate their next generation of products, far from the paralyzing influence of the old business.

Economists will naturally be skeptical of such a blanket recommendation. The disk drive industry is characterized by a weak appropriability regime (patents can be invented around), and it would be hazardous for an entrant to try to license an innovation to an established firm. The conclusions may be therefore highly contingent on particular industry characteristics. Nonetheless, the reasons behind the apparent bias of incumbents in favor of home-grown technology is a recurrent theme of the managerial literature, and its persistence and effects are worthy of attention by economists.

Other strands of the managerial literature put forth a conception of radical and incremental innovations based on supply-side considerations: A radical innovation is one that destroys, or at least does not build on, the technological capabilities of incumbent firms (Tushman and Anderson 1986). In her study of the photolithographic industry, Henderson (1993) notes that it is entirely possible for innovations to be incremental in an economic sense but radical in an organizational sense, and she provides evidence that incumbents have particular difficulty adapting to such architectural changes. Using qualitative evidence, she explores the mechanisms that might explain the incumbents' lack of success in commercializing architectural innovations. She advances two types of explanations. The first focuses on dysfunctional incentives and stilted communication channels; the second emphasizes behavioral biases that affect the managers of incumbent firms. One lesson from recent advances in behavioral corporate finance is that cognitive biases can magnify the salience of agency problems in firms (Baker et al. 2007). The study of internal capital markets—especially in the presence of informed but biased R&D managers—seems a very promising area for future research. So far, the growing literature on internal capital markets (reviewed by Gertner and Scharfstein, this volume) has been largely focused on resource allocation in diversified publicly listed conglomerates. Although attention has increasingly been paid to the role of divisional boundaries on R&D investment and productivity (e.g., Seru 2010), further progress in this area will probably require access to finer-grained, project-level data.

Before moving on to other issues, we can venture a few conclusions. First, most of what economists know about technological innovation and organizations does not stem from the mining of traditional datasets. On the contrary, some of the more lasting insights come from the collection of original data at a level that is usually finer grained than the whole organization. Case studies also inform the state of economists' knowledge on these topics. Second, the empirical literature has been rather casual in its treatment of endogeneity issues, though there are of course exceptions (e.g., Stern 2004). What is missing are more systematic attempts to estimate the causal effect of various features of firms' internal organization on innovative outcomes.

3. Contracting and Innovation

One of the most fertile areas of research in recent years has been the relationship between innovation and contracting. Thanks to a variety of theoretical work, we now better understand the critical importance of contracting in the innovation process and the ways in which contract structure can affect the innovations being undertaken.

3.1. Why Is Contracting Important for Innovation?

One of the dominant features of many high-technology industries has been a reliance on contracting. In many cases, start-up firms, rather than going head-to-head with established incumbents, will choose to license technologies to their peers. Such industries as telecommunications and biotechnology have been profoundly shaped by this business model.

It is natural to wonder what the rationale for this approach in technology-intensive industries is. Gans and Stern (2000) suggest that there are several reasons firms will choose a cooperative strategy, including avoidance of thinner profit margins and duplicative investments associated with head-to-head competition. They argue that a cooperative strategy is more likely for start-ups in three cases: when intellectual property rights are stronger (which puts the start-up firm in a better bargaining position with potential licensors), when intermediaries who can facilitate and reduce the costs of such transactions are present, and when established firms have made expensive investments (e.g., in a sales force) that the start-up would need to duplicate. The authors show that these patterns not only hold theoretically but also in a survey of the commercialization strategies of more than 100 start-up firms.

This rationale for cooperative commercialization is compelling, but efforts to contract on technology often encounter many challenges. In many instances, academic technology managers or corporate executives seeking to commercialize early-stage technologies have encountered real difficulties. They may find investors unwilling to invest the time and resources to examine early-stage technologies, or offering only modest payments in exchange for large stakes in innovations that the scientists, technology transfer officers, and company executives believe to be quite valuable.

Much of this reluctance stems from the information problems that surround innovations, particularly in technologically advanced industries, which often scare off potential investors. The work of Guedj and Scharfstein (2004) highlights the importance of these information problems. The paper documents the extent of agency problems among young biotechnology firms, which emerges from a comparison with established pharmaceutical companies. The authors show that the young firms—particularly those with large cash reserves—are more likely than their more established peers to push drug candidates forward in clinical trials, but the success rate in these trials is much lower. The evidence points to an agency problem, in which managers of single-product early-stage firms are unwilling to drop the development of their only viable drug candidates, and the difficulty that outside shareholders have in monitoring innovative activities.

The consequences of these difficulties have been illustrated by Shane (1995) and Majewski (1998), who examine the decisions of biotechnology firms to raise capital through public markets and alliances. Through their different methodologies, these authors show that firms turn to alliance financing when asymmetric information about the biotechnology industry is particularly high. During these periods—which are measured through such proxies as the variance of the returns of biotechnology securities—firms are likely to delay the time until their next equity issuance and to rely on alliances rather public offerings as a source of external financing. The authors argue that the greater insight on the part of the pharmaceutical company into the nature of the biotechnology firm's activities allows it to make successful investments at times when uninformed public investors are deterred by information problems.

3.2. Contract Structure and Innovation

Much academic interest in recent years has surrounded the question of how firms contract for innovations and the implications of these contracts. The seminal work of Aghion and Tirole (1994) has inspired a variety of investigations.

This work builds on the tradition, beginning with Grossman and Hart (1986) and Hart and Moore (1988), that depicts incomplete contracting between a principal and an agent. A typical assumption is that it is impossible for the two parties to write a verifiable contract, enforceable in a court of law, that specifies the effort and final output of the two parties. This is because there are many possible contingencies, not all of which can be anticipated at the time the contract is drafted. Due to this nonverifiability problem, these models suggest that it is optimal for ownership of the project to be assigned to the party with the greatest marginal ability to affect the outcome. This party, who will retain the right to make the decisions that cannot be specified in the contract ex ante, should also receive any surplus that results from the project. Because of this incentive, the party will make the decisions that maximize—or come close to maximizing—the returns from the project.

Aghion and Tirole (1994) adapt this general model to an R&D alliance between two firms. In their basic model, the authors assume that the research unit is without financial resources of its own, cannot borrow any funds, and has no ability to commercialize the innovation itself. As a result, it turns for financing to a customer, a firm that may intend to use the product itself or to resell it to others but cannot make the discovery independently. The success of the research project is an increasing function, though at a decelerating rate, of both the effort provided by the research unit and the resources provided by the customer.

Developing a contract between the two parties is challenging. Even though the ownership of the product can be specified in an enforceable contract, and the resources provided by the customer can also be so specified, uncertainty precludes writing a contract for the delivery of a specific innovation. Similarly, an enforceable contract cannot be written that specifies the level of effort that the research unit will provide.

Aghion and Tirole (1994) consider two polar cases: when the research unit has the ex ante bargaining power and when the customer does. When the research unit has the bargaining power, the ownership of the research output will be efficiently allocated. If the marginal impact of the research unit's effort on the innovative output is greater than the marginal impact of the customer's investment, then the research unit will receive the property rights. If not, the research unit will transfer ownership to the customer in exchange for a cash payment. This result is similar to that of Grossman and Hart (1986).

When the customer has the bargaining power, a different pattern emerges. If it is optimal for the customer to own the project, it will retain the project. If, however, the total amount of value created would be greater were property rights to be allocated to the research unit, the ideal outcome will not be achieved, because the cash-constrained research unit will not have enough resources to compensate the customer. As a result, an inefficient allocation of the property rights occurs, with the customer retaining the rights to the invention.

This work has inspired a variety of empirical investigations. Lerner and Merges (1998) examine the determinants of control rights in a sample of 200 alliances between biotechnology firms and established pharmaceutical firms. This setting is particularly auspicious, because it exhibits wide variation in contractibility (e.g., early-stage versus late-stage projects) and bargaining power (e.g., does the start-up have other products in development or is it essentially a single-product firm?). They analyze the share of 25 key control rights allocated to the financing firm by regressing the assigned number of rights on independent variables denoting the project stage and financial conditions, as well as on controls for a variety of alternative explanations. The results are generally consistent with the framework developed by Aghion and Tirole (1994): the greater the financial resources of the R&D firm, the fewer control rights are allocated to the financing firm; in contrast, there is no evidence that early-stage projects are associated with more control rights being assigned to the research-based firm.

Lerner and Malmendier (2010) expand on this line of research. They point out that the key variable in Lerner and Merges (1998) is a bit of a grab bag. Among these 25 decision rights, which ones really matter? They also point out that Aghion and Tirole's (1994) canonical model should not be taken too literally. Rather, they ask what central incentive problem the proper assignment of these rights should alleviate. Based on insights gained from conversations with practitioners, they conjecture that pharmaceutical firms are especially worried that their biotechnology partners will inappropriately cross-subsidize other projects using the payments received as part of a specific drug development project. They go on to develop a simple model in the spirit of Aghion and Tirole but tailored to the specifics of the context at hand. This leads them, in turn, to focus on the allocation of a specific contractual clause: a termination right coupled with broad transfer of intellectual property and associated payments. The model makes some specific predictions: (1) such clauses should be more frequently observed when the direction of research is less contractible (e.g., when the alliance does not center on a "lead compound" with a specific chemical formula); and (2) this correlation should be much weaker, or even go away, when the biotechnology firm is not financially constrained (e.g., when the biotechnology firm has low net income). These sharp predictions are borne out in the empirical analysis and appear robust to a number of carefully examined alternative explanations.

Whereas Aghion and Tirole (1994) do not explicitly depict a role for the public market, Lerner et al. (2003) argue that variations in the availability of public financing will affect the bargaining power of R&D firms. During periods when public financial markets are readily accessible, these firms may be able to finance projects through either public equity issues or alliances. But during periods when equity issues are more difficult, R&D firms may have few alternatives to undertaking alliances. In the latter periods, it is also reasonable to assume that the R&D firm's bargaining power will be considerably reduced.[2]

The authors examine these patterns in biotechnology, noting that equity financing in the industry has undergone dramatic variations over the years. These shifts have been largely in the nature of industrywide shocks. The authors show that in periods when public equity financing is readily available, the agreements are more likely to grant key control rights to the R&D firm. This pattern—consistent with the theory of Aghion and Tirole (though, of course, with other theories as well)—holds even after controlling for variations in the quality of the technology in the agreement. Lerner et al. (2003) then examine whether the agreements are successful in terms of the progress of the product under development. Alliances that grant the bulk of the control to the R&D firm are more successful, an effect that is more pronounced in weak financing markets, as Aghion and Tirole (1994) predict.[3]

Finally, the authors examine the likelihood of renegotiation. If it would have maximized innovative output to assign control to the small biotechnology company, but this allocation of control was precluded by financial market conditions, there should then be a distinct pattern in renegotiations. In particular, when financing conditions for biotechnology firms improve, the agreements that assign the bulk of the control to the financing firm should be disproportionately renegotiated. The empirical results are consistent with this pattern.[4]

Robinson and Stuart (2007) take a different approach, examining 125 alliances involving genomics research at young biotechnology firms. The authors consider a variety of characteristics of these contracts, including the use of equity, extent of up-front payments, contractual provisions employed, provisions regarding termination, and length of the agreement. Although it is difficult to do justice to so many disparate analyses in a brief summary, the key findings are the resemblance between strategic alliances and venture capital contracts[5] and the importance of contractual provisions that are difficult to verify. The authors interpret the latter conclusion as

2. As noted above, the posited relationship between the strength of the public equity market and the bargaining power of the R&D firm is not explicitly modeled in the Aghion-Tirole model. Under the plausible assumption that in the subset of parameters where the R&D firm chooses an alliance instead of public equity issue, the strength of the market still affects the R&D firm's bargaining power in choosing the terms of the alliance, an extension to their model could deliver this result. The claim that control rights are more likely to be transferred to the financing firm during periods of diminished public equity market activity is also supported by theoretical work by Aghion and Bolton (1992) and Holmström and Tirole (1997).

3. Of course, if we assume that having the R&D firm control the alliance is inevitably efficient, then it is hard to distinguish the Aghion-Tirole hypothesis from one where the lack of financial resources leads the R&D firm to make important concessions. The results regarding the renegotiations of alliances, however, seem less consistent with this alternative hypothesis.

4. See Elfenbein and Lerner (2003) for another example of an analysis of these issues.

5. This point has also been raised in the work of legal scholars, such as Bernard Black, Ronald Gilson, and Robert Merges. For one example, see Merges (1995).

raising doubts about the substantial literature on incomplete contracts most closely associated with Grossman, Hart, and Moore.

3.3. Spin-offs and Firm Boundaries

A consequence of the ability of start-up firms to enter into contracts with established firms is that industry structure may change. The prospect of garnering profits through licensing—or alternatively, through successful head-to-head competition—may lead individuals to leave established firms and begin new concerns. A variety of work has examined these changes to industry structure and the consequences for innovation.

Much of this literature highlights the difficulties that firms face when managing multiple projects in a single organization. This literature has been largely motivated by the diversification discount puzzle: the empirical observation that diversified firms appear to trade at prices that are significantly below those of comparable portfolios of specialist firms.

Much of the literature has highlighted the presence of agency problems in firms. Jensen (1986), for instance, suggests that CEOs have a tendency to use the cash flows from the business to overinvest in unprofitable projects. Scharfstein and Stein (2000) argue that the presence of agency problems at both the CEO and divisional manager level may lead to firms overinvesting in weaker projects and neglecting stronger ones, particularly when there is a substantial divergence in the projects and when the CEO has low-powered incentives.[6]

Several works have explicitly examined the trade-off between undertaking an innovative project in a major corporation and in a start-up firm. Typically, they assume that an employee makes a valuable discovery while working for an established firm. These models usually assume that substantial informational asymmetries preclude the established firm from learning (at least initially) about the project's prospects. In some cases, the difficulties of contracting and bargaining lead to an independent firm being established. Wiggins (1995) predicts that projects that are high risk, take longer to develop, and are less capital intensive will be more likely to be pursued in independent firms. Although employing a somewhat different theoretical setup, Anton and Yao (1994) similarly conclude that more radical innovations will be more likely to be pursued in start-ups.[7]

These issues are captured nicely in a model by Hellmann and Perotti (2011), who explore the challenges that an inventor who has developed an incomplete idea faces. They argue that if the would-be entrepreneur can find a third party (e.g., a venture capitalist) to evaluate his idea, he will be able to validate his concept and decide whether to invest more resources into it. But the third party may be tempted to report to the inventor that the idea is worthless, and then steal the idea and commercialize it herself. They argue that the likelihood a third party will respond truthfully depends on the extent to which her skills are complementary with, or simply identical to, those of the inventor.

---

6. Although the work is not cast in this manner, the findings of Steven Klepper highlighting the importance of disagreements among individuals as a driver of new firm formation (e.g., Klepper and Thompson 2005) may be seen as consistent with these arguments.

7. Dix and Gandelman (2007) and Hellmann (2007) are two more recent examinations of these questions.

Alternatively, the entrepreneur may take the idea to his employer. Although this approach may not be as efficient in some respects (the firm may not have as much expertise as a third party), Hellmann and Perotti argue that firms can more readily develop a reputation for trustworthiness and honesty. They argue that these commitments are least likely to be honored when the invention is very valuable: in these instances, individual investors are more likely to try their luck in the treacherous open market.

Acemoglu et al. (2003) take a somewhat broader view of these questions. They depict a world where firms can engage in two activities: adopting existing technologies from the world's best innovators and developing innovations themselves. They argue that managerial skill is relatively unimportant in the adoption process but is critically important to successful innovation. As a result, in countries where technology is more advanced—and hence, the returns from imitation are lower—it becomes critically important to select the right managers. Thus, they suggest, as countries approach the technological frontier, technology-intensive industries should become increasingly Darwinian, with younger firms, shorter relationships among firms, and more weeding out of managers.

On the empirical side, Gompers et al. (2005) contrast two views of the spin-off process. In one view, individuals already working for entrepreneurial firms—particularly those already backed by venture capitalists and located in hotbeds of venture capital activity—may find launching their own venture less daunting than others might for a number of reasons. These reasons include: they have already been exposed to a network of suppliers of labor, goods, and capital, as well as a network of customers (Saxenian 1994); they have already learned by doing how to establish an entrepreneurial firm; or individuals with a higher taste for risky activities may have already found their way to entrepreneurial firms, consistent with models of the sorting processes (Jovanovic 1979; Holmes and Schmidt 1990; Gromb and Scharfstein 2002).

Alternatively, individuals become entrepreneurs because the large bureaucratic companies for which they work are reluctant to fund their entrepreneurial ideas. As discussed above, established firms may be incapable of responding to radical technological changes that upset the established ways of organizing their businesses, or these hierarchical organizations may have a hard time assessing such investment opportunities (Stein 2002; Berger et al. 2005). After systematically examining which publicly traded firms had employees depart to start new venture-backed firms, Berger et al. and Stein conclude the findings appear to be more consistent with the view that entrepreneurial learning and networks are critical factors in the creation of venture-backed firms.

Azoulay (2004) examines instead the question of how the innovative process affects firms' vertical integration decisions. Pharmaceutical companies have long outsourced at least part of the process by which new drugs are evaluated (known as clinical trials) to specialists in these procedures. He argues that these trials typically are dominated by one of two tasks, routine compilation of data on the drugs' effectiveness and more fundamental analyses of the pharmaceuticals' workings.

The analysis suggests that firms respond to this variation. They will choose to undertake the project in-house, or alternatively outsource it, depending on the nature of activities that will dominate the trial process. In the more cutting-edge projects involving the production of new knowledge, they are more likely to use their own employees. A key driver of this choice, Azoulay

(2004) argues, is the difficulty of measuring contractor performance when undertaking truly innovative activities: the difficulty of designing appropriate incentives for innovation leads to the choice of firm boundaries.

3.4. New Organizational Structure and Innovation

Another area of considerable research interest has been the growth of new organizational structures to promote innovation. These have many intriguing features, which will well reward ongoing research.

Perhaps the most intriguing of these topics is the open source process of production and innovation, which seems very unlike what most economists expect. Private firms usually pay their workers, direct and manage their efforts, and control the output and intellectual property thus created. In an open source project, however, a body of original material is made publicly available for others to use, under certain conditions. In many cases, anyone who makes use of the material must agree to make all enhancements to the original material available under these same conditions. This rule distinguishes open source production from, say, material in the public domain and "shareware." Many contributors to open source projects are unpaid. Indeed, contributions are made under licenses that often restrict the ability of contributors to make money on their own contributions. Open source projects are often loosely structured, with contributors free to pursue whatever area they feel most interesting. Despite these unusual features, recent years have seen a rise of major corporate and venture capital investments into open source projects.

Economics research into open source has focused on two issues. The first has been the motivation of contributors. Lerner and Tirole (2002) argue that the standard framework of labor economics can be adapted to capture activity in the open source environment. Even if there are no short-run monetary returns from working on open source projects, they argue that participation can have important signaling benefits in the long run. The paper highlights the importance of programmers' desire to signal their quality—that is, the desire to impress prospective employers and financiers, as well as obtain peer recognition—as a spur to contributing to open source projects. The presence of these signaling incentives will lead to more success for open source projects where contributions are more visible to the relevant audience (e.g., peers or employers) and where the talent of the contributor is better discerned from his or her contributions. These observations lead to a series of predictions about the likely success and structure of open source projects.

The empirical evidence, particularly the survey work of Hann et al. (2004), is largely consistent with the belief that individual contributors to open source projects do ultimately benefit financially from their participation in these projects. The results suggest that the sheer volume of contributions to the Apache project have little impact on salary. But individuals who attain high rank in the Apache organization enjoy wages that are 14–29% higher, regardless of whether their work directly involves the Apache program.

The second issue on which economists have focused concerns the legal rules under which open source projects operate. The licenses differ tremendously in the extent to which they enable licensors and contributors to profit from the code that is contributed.

Lerner and Tirole (2005) argue that permissive licenses, where the user retains the ability to use the code as she sees fit, will be more common in cases where projects have strong appeal to the community of open source contributors—for instance, when contributors stand to benefit considerably from signaling incentives or when the licensors are well trusted. Conversely, restrictive licenses, such as the General Public License, will be commonplace when such appeals are more fragile. Lerner and Tirole also examine the licenses chosen in 40,000 open source projects. The authors find that, consistent with theory, restrictive licenses are more common for applications geared toward end users and system administrators. Similarly, projects whose natural language is not English—whose community appeal may be presumed to be much smaller—are more likely to employ restrictive licenses.

But many issues posed by open source are not unique to this setting. Open source can be seen as at the end of a spectrum of technology-sharing institutions. Many of these other institutions have encountered similar conflicts. Leaders of patent pools, for instance, have had to deal with the conflicting goals of the potential members, sometimes reconciling their disparate goals successfully and in other cases failing to overcome these gaps. To cite another example, the challenges of enlisting cooperation from commercial firms while guarding against opportunistic behavior are familiar to leaders of standard-setting organizations. These institutions have lengthy and well-documented track records; for example, the first patent pool dates back to the 1850s.

The modern study of patent pools has its origins in the work of Shapiro (2001), who uses Cournot's (1838) analysis to point out that patent pools raise welfare when patents are perfect complements and harm it when they are perfect substitutes. Although this observation is a useful first step in the antitrust analysis of patent pools, patents are rarely perfect complements or perfect substitutes. Indeed, antitrust authorities sometimes are unsure about the relationships among the patents. Moreover, frequently observed features of pools, such as provisions demanding independent licensing, cannot be analyzed in a setting where only the polar cases exist.

Lerner and Tirole (2004) build on this work, analyzing the strategic incentives to form a pool in the presence of current and future innovations that either compete with or are complementary to the patents in the pool. The authors begin with a very stylized model (though one that allows the full range between the two polar cases of perfectly substitutable and perfectly complementary patents) and then consider progressively more realistic scenarios. A major focus of the analysis is the process through which competition authorities examine patent pools. Recent antitrust doctrines are that only "essential patents" should be included in pools and that patent owners retain a right to license their invention separately from the pool (known as "independent licensing"). Among other conclusions, the paper highlights the effectiveness of the demands for independent licensing: a pool is never affected by the possibility of independent licensing if and only if the pool is welfare enhancing.

Lerner et al. (2008) empirically focus on patent pools. They construct a sample of 63 pools established between 1895 and 2001 and determine the structure of these agreements. They then analyze the determinants of the features of these agreements and highlight the extent to which the structure does appear to be consistent with theoretical predictions.

These areas are certainly not the only ones of interest to researchers in terms of new organizational forms and innovation. Open source and academia have many parallels. The most obvious parallel relates to motivation. As in open source, the direct financial returns from writing academic articles are typically nonexistent, but career concerns and the desire for peer recognition provide powerful inducements. In recent years, academic institutions have begun more aggressively experimenting with new organizational forms, whether in the hopes of more thoroughly diffusing their discoveries (e.g., the Biological Resource Centers; Furman and Stern 2011) or to more effectively profit from their intellectual property.

Another fascinating and important area is the study of standard-setting bodies. This topic is important because how open a standard is can critically affect its evolution. The rapidity with which the standard is adopted and the incentives to innovate may be shaped by this decision. For instance, the Internet today runs on a nonproprietary architecture largely because the Internet Engineering Task Force in its early years had a strict policy of only incorporating technology where the developer agreed to license it on reasonable and nondiscriminatory terms. Had the Standard-Setting Organization had a more permissive policy (as indeed they adopted in the mid-1990s), the development of the Internet may have been very different (Bradner 1999). Although there have been some initial looks at standard-setting bodies and how they affect innovation (Lerner and Tirole 2006; Chiao et al. 2007; Greenstein and Stango 2007; Simcoe 2012), much more needs to be done.

4. The Financing of Innovation

Another cluster of relevant research has been in finance literature. Although the relationship between finance and innovation has been studied in many contexts not particularly relevant to organizational economics—for instance, work on the market reaction to the announcement of R&D projects and the value relevance of R&D expenditures in accounting statements—other work is very germane.

In this section, we highlight two relevant bodies of work. The first of these stresses the importance of capital constraints and the financing of innovation. The second focuses on financial intermediaries—particularly venture capitalists—and their role in fomenting innovation.[8]

Another source of uncertainty surrounds the ability of capital constraints—or limits on the ability to raise external financing—to affect the innovation process. Even if a firm has a great idea, it may be unable to raise the capital to market it.

4.1. Capital Constraints and Innovation

The examination of financial constraints has been an important topic in corporate finance. In practitioner accounts and theoretical models, the state of financial markets may limit a firm's ability to raise outside capital. This inability to raise capital may stem from information gaps or an inability to reach a satisfactory contract on the outcomes of a venture. In this environment, good projects may find it impossible to get financing on reasonable terms if the firm does not have enough internal funds.

---

8. Even here, there is other work we do not discuss. One example is work on R&D financing organizations, such as those typically seen in the biotechnology industry (Beatty et al. 1995).

A variety of empirical studies of financial constraints explore the investment behavior of firms and its sensitivity to changes in internally generated funds. Fazzari et al. (1988) find that firms with low or no dividend payout ratios are more likely to have investment that was sensitive to changes in free cash flow. The authors interpret their results as demonstrating that capital constraints likely affect companies that do not pay dividends, as they forego investment when internal cash is not available. In a similar vein, Lamont (1997) looks at companies that have oil-related production and nonoil-related businesses. He finds that investments in the nonoil-related businesses are dramatically affected by swings in the world price of oil. This is true even though the firm's nonoil businesses were largely uncorrelated with the prospects for their oil businesses. He interprets this result as suggesting the capital constraints limit the ability of firms to raise outside financing.

Since Arrow (1962), it has been understood that not only investments in physical goods but also innovation should be affected by an inability to raise capital. The substantial information problems surrounding R&D projects make it difficult to raise external capital to finance them. As a result, firms with promising projects may be unable to pursue them.

The sensitivity of innovation to capital constraints has been corroborated in a number of studies. For instance, Himmelberg and Petersen (1994) look at a panel of small firms and show that the sensitivity of R&D investment to cash flow seems to be considerably greater than that of physical investment. This suggests that the problems discussed above are if anything more severe for innovation as opposed to more traditional capital investments.

Economists have also studied the impact of debt on R&D spending. The classic study in this mold, Hall (1990), shows that firms that take on more debt and increase their leverage tend to reduce R&D spending. Similar conclusions are offered by Greenwald et al. (1992).

Thus, even if a firm develops an invention, it may not have the resources to commercialize it. The difficulty of raising capital stemming from the information problems surrounding the proposed innovation may preclude the development of innovations that would be otherwise successful.

4.2. Financial Intermediaries and Innovation

A second relevant stream of the finance literature on innovation has examined the relationship between intermediaries and innovation. Much of the attention here has focused on venture capital organizations, that is, independently managed, dedicated capital focusing on equity or equity-linked investments in privately held high-growth companies.

Venture capital has attracted extensive theoretical scrutiny. These works suggest that venture capitalists promote innovation by mitigating agency conflicts between entrepreneurs and investors. The improvement in efficiency might be due to the active monitoring and advice that is provided (Hellmann 1998; Marx 2000; Cornelli and Yosha 2003), the screening mechanisms employed (Chan 1983), the incentives to exit (Berglöf 1994), the proper syndication of the investment (Admati and Pfleiderer 1994), or investment staging (Sahlman 1990; Bergemann and Hege 1998).

Theorists have suggested a variety of mechanisms by which venture capital may affect innovation, but the empirical record is more mixed. It might be thought that establishing a relationship between venture capital and innovation would be straightforward. For instance, one could look at regressions across industries and time to determine whether, controlling for R&D spending, venture capital funding has an impact on various measures of innovation. But even a simple model of the relationships among venture capital, R&D, and innovation suggests that this approach is likely to give misleading estimates.

Both venture funding and innovation could be positively related to a third unobserved factor, the arrival of technological opportunities. Thus, there could be more innovation at times when there was more venture capital, not because the venture capital caused the innovation, but rather because the venture capitalists reacted to some fundamental technological shock that was sure to lead to more innovation. To date, only two papers have attempted to address these challenging issues.

The first of these papers, Hellmann and Puri (2000), examines a sample of 170 recently formed firms in Silicon Valley, including both venture-backed and nonventure firms. Using questionnaire responses, the authors find empirical evidence that venture capital financing is related to product market strategies and outcomes of start-ups. They find that firms that are pursuing what they term an "innovator strategy" (a classification based on the content analysis of survey responses) are significantly more likely to obtain venture capital and to obtain it more quickly. The presence of a venture capitalist is also associated with a significant reduction in the time taken to bring a product to market, especially for innovators. Furthermore, firms are more likely to list obtaining venture capital as a significant milestone in the lifecycle of the company compared to other financing events.

The results suggest significant interrelations between investor type and product market dimensions, and a role for venture capital in encouraging innovative companies. Given the small size of the sample and the limited data, Hellmann and Puri (2000) can only modestly address concerns about causality. Unfortunately, the possibility remains that more innovative firms select venture capital for financing, rather than venture capital causing firms to be more innovative.

In contrast, the second paper, Kortum and Lerner (2000), examines whether these patterns can be discerned on an aggregate industry level rather than on the firm level. These authors address concerns about causality in two ways. First, they exploit the major discontinuity in the recent history of the venture capital industry: in the late 1970s, the U.S. Department of Labor clarified the Employee Retirement Income Security Act, a policy shift that freed pensions to invest in venture capital. This shift led to a sharp increase in the funds committed to venture capital. This type of exogenous change should identify the role of venture capital, because it is unlikely to be related to the arrival of entrepreneurial opportunities. They exploit this shift in instrumental variable regressions. Second, they use R&D expenditures to control for the arrival of technological opportunities that are anticipated by economic actors at the time but are unobserved by econometricians. In the framework of a simple model, they show that the causality problem disappears if they estimate the impact of venture capital on the patent-R&D ratio, rather than on patenting itself.

Even after addressing these causality concerns, the results suggest that venture funding does have a strong positive impact on innovation. The estimated coefficients vary according to the techniques employed, but on average a dollar of venture capital appears to be three to four times more potent in stimulating patenting than a dollar of traditional corporate R&D. The estimates therefore suggest that venture capital, even though it averaged less than 3% of corporate R&D from 1983 to 1992, is responsible for a much greater share—perhaps 10%—of U.S. industrial innovations in this decade.

Some of the most interesting theoretical work in recent years has focused not on the question of whether venture capitalists spur innovation but rather on the societal consequences of the relationship between venture-backed entrepreneurship and innovation. Landier (2006) presents a model in which entrepreneurial ventures succeed or fail on the basis of ability and luck.[9] He argues that as the venture progresses, the entrepreneur is likely to learn about the probable eventual success of the venture, but that the decision to continue or abandon it will not be the same in all environments. In particular, the decision depends critically on how expensive it would be to raise capital for a new venture from investors after a failure. In this setting, Landier shows, multiple equilibria can arise. If the cost of capital for a new venture after a failure is not very high, entrepreneurs will be willing to readily abandon ventures, and failure is commonplace but not very costly. Alternatively, if the cost of capital for failed entrepreneurs is high, only extremely poor projects will be abandoned. Thus, societies may differ dramatically in the prevalence of experimentation in high-risk, innovative ventures.

5. Conclusion

In this chapter, we review the key features of the literature on innovation and organizational structure. We highlight the key areas where work as been undertaken, as well as the limitations of the literature to date.

Stepping back, two metathemes emerge across the strands of literature reviewed above. The first is that there is now a much more fruitful back-and-forth between theoretical and empirical work than was the case at the inception of the field. The patent race literature, for example, was only loosely motivated by empirical observations and did not (at least initially) necessarily provide much grist for the empiricist's mill (e.g., Cockburn and Henderson 1994). Similarly, much of the early empirical work on the relationship between firm size and innovation was atheoretical.

In recent years, these two approaches have been moving more closely together. Consider, for example, the response to the rise of an active market for early development projects in the biopharmaceutical sector. These changes have made salient—in theorists' minds—the possibility of appropriating at least part of the returns from innovation on the ideas market, rather than on the product market. In addition, they have stimulated both theoretical work and empirical investigations that test these theories' specific predictions, either in different papers (Gans and Stern 2000; Gans et al. 2002) or sometimes in a single paper combining theory and evidence (Lerner and Malmendier 2010). These developments bode well for future research in this area.

The second theme pertains to the style of empirical work practiced by applied economists studying innovation and organizations. Although aware of the perils involved in sweeping generalizations, it seems clear to us that we are lagging behind other subfields of microeconomics in our treatment of endogeneity and unobserved heterogeneity. It is possible that our subject matter provides inherently fewer opportunities to exploit natural experiments, relative to the type of questions studied by health, development, or labor economists. An alternative explanation is that we have collectively been too reluctant to place identification at the center of our preoccupations. This reluctance is not always for the worse. Researchers often face trade-offs between

---

9. See also Gromb and Scharfstein (2002) for a thoughtful theoretical analysis that touches on many of these issues.

the importance of the problem they tackle and the degree of confidence they can achieve in providing answers to this problem.

At the same time, we suggest that putting relatively more emphasis on the establishment of causal relationships—as opposed to the careful documentation of conditional correlations—would be a welcome development. One hallmark of the fields of technical change and organizational economics is that researchers often laboriously produce the data that they analyze rather than simply consuming existing sources of administrative data, such as the Current Population Survey or the Panel Survey of Income Dynamics. Thus, in the quest for exogenous sources of variation, we face potentially fewer constraints than do researchers in other subfields of economics, provided that we channel more effort into addressing identification problems at the time of a project's inception. Stern's (2004) study of compensating differentials in the entry-level science labor market is an exemplar of this particularly creative genre. More studies in that vein on the traditional concerns of the field (e.g., the estimation of knowledge spillovers) would enable us to step back and sort out what we can confidently claim to know from what is at most informed speculation.

REFERENCES

Abramowitz, Moses. 1956. "Resources and Output Trends in the U.S. since 1870." Occasional Paper 52, National Bureau of Economic Research, New York.

Acemoglu, Daron, Philippe Aghion, and Fabrizio Zilibotti. 2003. "Vertical Integration and Distance to Frontier." *Journal of the European Economic Association* 1: 630–638.

Adams, James D., and Adam B. Jaffe. 1996. "Bounding the Effects of R&D: An Investigation Using Matched Establishment-Firm Data." *RAND Journal of Economics* 27: 700–721.

Admati, Anat R., and Paul Pfleiderer. 1994. "Robust Financial Contracting and the Role for Venture Capitalists." *Journal of Finance* 49: 371–402.

Aghion, Phillipe, and Patrick Bolton. 1992. "An Incomplete Contract Approach to Financial Contracting." *Review of Economic Studies* 59: 473–494.

Aghion, Phillipe, and Jean Tirole. 1994. "On the Management of Innovation." *Quarterly Journal of Economics* 109: 1185–1207.

Almeida, Paul, and Bruce Kogut. 1999. "The Localization of Knowledge and the Mobility of Engineers in Regional Networks. *Management Science* 45: 905–917.

Amabile, Teresa M. 1993. "Motivational Synergy: Toward New Conceptualizations of Intrinsic and Extrinsic Motivation in the Workplace." *Human Resource Management Review* 3: 185–201.

———. 1996. *Creativity in Context.* Boulder: Westview Press.

Anton, James J., and Dennis A. Yao. 1994. "Expropriation and Inventions: Appropriable Rents in the Absence of Property Rights." *American Economic Review* 84: 190–209.

Argyres, Nicholas S., and Brian S. Silverman. 2004. "R&D, Organization Structure and the Development of Corporate Technological Knowledge." *Strategic Management Journal* 25: 925–958.

Aron, Debra J., and Edward P. Lazear. 1990. "The Introduction of New Products." *American Economic Review* 80(papers and proceedings): 421–426.

Arora, Ashish, Andrea Fosfuri, and Alfonso Gambardella. 2002. *Markets for Technology: The Economics of Innovation and Corporate Strategy.* Cambridge, MA: MIT Press.

Arrow, Kenneth. J. 1962. "Economic Welfare and the Allocation of Resources for Innovation," in Richard R. Nelson (ed.), *The Rate and Direction of Inventive Activity: Economic and Social Factors.* Princeton, NJ: Princeton University Press, pp. 609–625.

Azoulay, Pierre. 2004. "Capturing Knowledge within and across Firm Boundaries: Evidence from Clinical Development." *American Economic Review* 94: 1591–1612.

Azoulay, Pierre, Joshua Graff Zivin, and Jialan Wang. 2010. "Superstar Extinction." *Quarterly Journal of Economics* 125: 549–589.

Azoulay, Pierre, Joshua Graff Zivin, and Gustavo Manso. 2011. "Incentives and Creativity: Evidence from the Academic Life Sciences." *RAND Journal of Economics* 42: 527–554.

Baker, Malcolm, Richard Ruback, and Jeffrey Wurgler. 2007. "Behavioral Corporate Finance: A Survey," in Espen Eckbo (ed.), *Handbook of Corporate Finance: Empirical Corporate Finance*. Amsterdam: Elsevier/North-Holland, pp. 145–187. [Formerly Working Paper 10863, National Bureau of Economic Research, Cambridge, MA.]

Beatty, Anne, Philip G. Berger, and Joseph Magliolo. 1995. "Motives for Forming Research & Development Financing Organizations." *Journal of Accounting and Economics* 19: 411–142.

Bergemann, Dirk, and Ulrich Hege. 1998. "Venture Capital Financing, Moral Hazard, and Learning." *Journal of Banking and Finance* 22: 703–735.

Berger, Allen N., Nathan H. Miller, Mitchell A. Petersen, Raghuram G. Rajan, and Jeremy C. Stein. 2005. "Does Function Follow Organizational Form? Evidence from the Lending Practices of Large and Small Banks." *Journal of Financial Economics* 76: 237–269.

Berglöf, Erik. 1994. "A Control Theory of Venture Capital Finance." *Journal of Law, Economics, and Organization* 10: 247–267.

Bloom, Nick, and John Van Reenen. 2010. "Why Do Management Practices Differ across Firms and Countries?" *Journal of Economic Perspectives* 24(1): 203–224.

Bradner, Scott. 1999. "The Internet Engineering Task Force," in Chris DiBona, Sam Ockman, and Mark Stone (eds.), *Open Sources: Voices from the Open Source Revolution*. Sebastopol, CA: O'Reilly Media, pp. 47–52.

Bresnahan, Timothy F., Erik Brynjolfsson, and Lorin M. Hitt. 2002. "Information Technology, Workplace Organization, and the Demand for Skilled Labor: Firm-Level Evidence." *Quarterly Journal of Economics* 117: 339–376.

Burt, Ronald S. 1992. *Structural Holes: The Social Structure of Competition*. Cambridge, MA: Harvard University Press.

———. 2004. "Structural Holes and Good Ideas." *American Journal of Sociology* 110: 349–399.

Chan, Yuk-Shee. 1983. "On the Positive Role of Financial Intermediation in Allocation of Venture Capital in a Market with Imperfect Information." *Journal of Finance* 38: 1543–1568.

Che, Yeon-Koo, and Seung-Weon Yoo. 2001. "Optimal Incentives for Teams." *American Economic Review* 91: 525–541.

Chiao, Benjamin, Josh Lerner, and Jean Tirole. 2007. "The Rules of Standard Setting Organizations: An Empirical Analysis." *RAND Journal of Economics* 38: 905–930.

Christensen, Clayton. 1997. *The Innovator's Dilemma*. Cambridge, MA: Harvard Business School Press.

Cockburn, Iain, and Rebecca Henderson. 1994. "Racing to Invest? The Dynamics of Competition in Ethical Drug Discovery." *Journal of Economics and Business Strategy* 3: 481–519.

———. 1998. "Absorptive Capacity, Coauthoring Behavior, and the Organization of Research in Drug Discovery." *Journal of Industrial Economics* 46: 157–182.

Cockburn, Iain, Rebecca Henderson, and Scott Stern. 1999. "Balancing Incentives: The Tension between Basic and Applied Research." Working Paper 6882, National Bureau of Economic Research, Cambridge, MA.

Cohen, Wesley M., and Richard Levin. 1989. "Empirical Studies of Innovation and Market Structure," in Richard Schmalensee and Robert Willig (eds.), *Handbook of Industrial Organization,* volume II. Amsterdam: North-Holland, pp. 1059–1107.

Cohen, Wesley M., and Daniel A. Levinthal. 1989. "Innovation and Learning: The Two Faces of R&D." *Economic Journal* 99: 569–596.

Cohen, Wesley M., and Daniel A. Levinthal. 1990. "Absorptive Capacity: A New Perspective on Learning and Innovation." *Administrative Science Quarterly* 35: 128–152.

Cornelli, Francesca, and Oved Yosha. 2003. "Stage Financing and the Role of Convertible Debt." *Review of Economic Studies* 70: 1–32.

Cournot, Augustin. 1838. *Recherches sur les Principes Mathématiques de la Théorie des Richesses.* Paris: Hachette.

Dix, Manfred, and Néstor Gandelman. 2007. "R&D Institutional Arrangements: Start-up Ventures versus Internal Lab." *Manchester School* 75: 218–236.

Ederer, Florian P., and Gustavo Manso. 2011. "Is Pay-for-Performance Detrimental to Innovation?" SSRN working paper. Available at Social Science Research Network: http://ssrn.com/abstract= 1270384 or http://dx.doi.org/10.2139/ssrn.1270384.

Elfenbein, Dan, and Josh Lerner. 2003. "Ownership and Control Rights in Internet Portal Alliances." *RAND Journal of Economics* 34: 356–369.

Fallick, Bruce, Charles A. Fleischmann, and James B. Rebitzer. 2006. "Job Hopping in Silicon Valley: Some Evidence Concerning the Micro-Foundations of a High Technology Cluster." *Review of Economics and Statistics* 88: 472–481.

Fazzari, Steven M., R. Glenn Hubbard, and Bruce C. Petersen. 1988. "Financing Constraints and Corporate Investment." *Brookings Papers on Economic Activity: Microeconomics* 1: 141–205.

Furman, Jeffrey L., and Scott Stern. 2011. "Climbing Atop the Shoulders of Giants: The Impact of Institutions on Cumulative Research." *American Economic Review* 101: 1933–1963.

Gans, Joshua S., and Scott Stern. 2000. "Incumbency and R&D Incentives: Licensing the Gale of Creative Destruction." *Journal of Economics and Management Strategy* 9: 485–511.

Gans, Joshua S., David H. Hsu, and Scott Stern. 2002. "When Does Start-up Innovation Spur the Gale of Creative Destruction?" *RAND Journal of Economics* 33: 571–586.

Gilbert, Richard J., and David M. G. Newberry. 1982. "Preemptive Patenting and the Persistence of Monopoly." *American Economic Review* 72: 514–526.

Gompers, Paul, Josh Lerner, and David Scharfstein. 2005. "Entrepreneurial Spawning: Public Corporations and the Formation of New Ventures, 1986–1999." *Journal of Finance* 60: 577–614.

Greenstein, Shane, and Victor Stango (eds.). 2007. *Standards and Public Policy.* Cambridge: Cambridge University Press.

Greenwald, Bruce, Michael Salinger, and Joseph E. Stiglitz. 1992. "Imperfect Capital Markets and Productivity Growth." Working paper, Bellcore, Morristown, NJ; Boston University; and Stanford University, Stanford, CA.

Griliches, Zvi (ed.). 1984. *Patents, R&D, and Productivity.* Chicago: University of Chicago Press.

Gromb, Denis, and David Scharfstein. 2002. "Entrepreneurship in Equilibrium." Working Paper 9001, National Bureau of Economic Research, Cambridge, MA.

Grossman, Sanford J., and Oliver D. Hart. 1986. "The Costs and Benefits of Ownership: A Theory of Lateral and Vertical Integration." *Journal of Political Economy* 94: 691–719.

Guedj, Ilan, and David Scharfstein. 2004. "Organizational Scope and Investment: Evidence from the Drug Development Strategies and Performance of Biopharmaceutical Firms." Working Paper 10933, National Bureau of Economic Research, Cambridge, MA.

Hall, Bronwyn H. 1990. "The Impact of Corporate Restructuring on Industrial Research and Development." *Brookings Papers on Economic Activity: Microeconomics* 1990: 85–124.

———. 1991. "The Effect of Takeover Activity on Corporate Research and Development," in Alan J. Auerbach (ed.), *Takeovers: Causes and Consequences.* Chicago: University of Chicago Press, pp. 69–87.

Hann, Il-Horn, Jeff Roberts, Sandra Slaughter, and Roy Fielding. 2004. "An Empirical Analysis of Economic Returns to Open Source Participation." Working paper, Carnegie-Mellon University, Pittsburgh, PA.

Hart, Oliver D., and John Moore. 1988. "Incomplete Contracts and Renegotiation." *Econometrica* 56: 755–785.

Hellmann, Thomas. 1998. "The Allocation of Control Rights in Venture Capital Contracts." *RAND Journal of Economics* 29: 57–76.

———. 2007. "When Do Employees Become Entrepreneurs?" *Management Science* 53: 919–933.

Hellmann, Thomas, and Enrico Perotti. 2011. "The Circulation of Ideas in Firms and Markets." *Management Science* 57: 1813–1826.

Hellmann, Thomas, and Manju Puri. 2000. "The Interaction between Product Market and Financing Strategy: The Role of Venture Capital." *Review of Financial Studies* 13: 959–984.

Henderson, Rebecca. 1993. "Underinvestment and Incompetence as Responses to Radical Innovation: Evidence from the Photolithographic Industry." *RAND Journal of Economics* 24: 248–270.

Henderson, Rebecca, and Iain Cockburn. 1994. "Measuring Competence—Exploring Firm Effects in Pharmaceutical Research." *Strategic Management Journal* 15: 63–84.

Himmelberg, Charles P., and Bruce C. Petersen. 1994. "R&D and Internal Finance: A Panel Study of Small Firms in High-Tech Industries." *Review of Economics and Statistics* 76: 38–51.

Holmes, Thomas J., and James A. Schmidt, Jr. 1990. "A Theory of Entrepreneurship and Its Application to the Study of Business Transfers." *Journal of Political Economy* 98: 265–294.

Holmström, Bengt. 1989. "Agency Costs and Innovation." *Journal of Economic Behavior and Organization* 12: 305–327.

Holmström, Bengt, and Jean Tirole. 1997. "Financial Intermediation, Loanable Funds, and the Real Sector." *Quarterly Journal of Economics* 112: 663–691.

Jaffe, Adam B. 1986. "Technological Opportunity and Spillovers of R&D: Evidence from Firms' Patents, Profits, and Market Value." *American Economic Review* 76: 984–1001.

Jaffe, Adam B., Manuel Trajtenberg, and Rebecca Henderson. 1993. "Geographic Localization of Knowledge Spillovers as Evidenced by Patent Citations." *Quarterly Journal of Economics* 108: 578–598.

Jensen, Michael C. 1986. "Agency Costs of Free Cash Flow, Corporate Finance, and Takeovers." *American Economic Review* 76(papers and proceedings): 323–329.

Jewkes, John. 1958. "The Sources of Invention." *The Freeman: Ideas on Liberty* 58(4): 45–57.

Jovanovic, Boyan. 1979. "Firm-Specific Capital and Turnover." *Journal of Political Economy* 87: 1246–1260.

Kandel, Eugene, and Edward P. Lazear. 1992. "Peer Pressure and Partnerships." *Journal of Political Economy* 100: 801–817.

Klepper, Steven. 2008. "Product Life Cycle," in Steven N. Durlauf and Lawrence E. Blume (eds.), *The New Palgrave Dictionary of Economics,* second edition. London: Palgrave Macmillan. Available at: http://www.dictionaryofeconomics.com/article?id=pde2008_P000331.

Klepper, Steven, and Peter Thompson. 2005. "Spinoff Entry in High-Tech Industries: Motives and Consequences." Working Paper 0503, Florida International University, Miami.

Kortum, Samuel, and Josh Lerner. 2000. "Assessing the Contribution of Venture Capital to Innovation." *RAND Journal of Economics* 31: 674–92.

Lacetera, Nicola, Iain Cockburn, and Rebecca Henderson. 2004. "Do Firms Change Their Capabilities by Hiring New People? A Study of the Adoption of Science-Driven Drug Research," in Joel Baum and Anita McGahan (eds.), *Business Strategy over the Industry Lifecycle: Advances in Strategic Management,* volume 21. New York: JAI/Elsevier Science, pp. 133–159.

Lamont, Owen. 1997. "Cash Flow and Investment: Evidence from Internal Capital Markets." *Journal of Finance* 52: 83–109.

Lamoreaux, Naomi R., and Kenneth L. Sokoloff. 2009. "The Decline of the Independent Inventor: A Schumpeterian Story?" in Sally H. Clarke, Naomi R. Lamoreaux, and Steven Usselman (eds.), *The Challenge of Remaining Innovative: Lessons from Twentieth Century American Business.* Stanford: Stanford University Press, pp. 43–78.

Landier, Augustin. 2006. "Start-up Financing: Banks vs. Venture Capital." Working paper, Massachusetts Institute of Technology, Cambridge, MA.

Lerner, Josh. 1997. "An Empirical Exploration of a Technology Race." *RAND Journal of Economics* 28: 228–247.

Lerner, Josh, and Ulrike M. Malmendier. 2010. "Contractibility and the Design of Research Agreements." *American Economic Review* 100: 214–246.

Lerner, Josh, and Robert Merges. 1998. "The Control of Technology Alliances: An Empirical Analysis of the Biotechnology Industry." *Journal of Industrial Economics* 46: 125–156.

Lerner, Josh, and Jean Tirole. 2002. "Some Simple Economics of Open Source." *Journal of Industrial Economics* 52: 197–234.

———. 2004. "Efficient Patent Pools." *American Economic Review* 94: 691–711.

———. 2005. "The Scope of Open Source Licensing." *Journal of Law, Economics, and Organization* 21: 20–56.

———. 2006. "A Model of Forum Shopping." *American Economic Review* 96: 1091–1113.

Lerner, Josh, and Julie Wulf. 2007. "Innovation and Incentives: Evidence from Corporate R&D." *Review of Economics and Statistics* 89: 634–644.

Lerner, Josh, Hillary Shane, and Alexander Tsai. 2003. "Do Equity Financing Cycles Matter? Evidence from Biotechnology Alliances." *Journal of Financial Economics* 67: 41g–446.

Lerner, Josh, Marcin Strojwas, and Jean Tirole. 2008. "The Design of Patent Pools: The Determinants of Licensing Rules." *RAND Journal of Economics* 38: 610–625.

Levin, Richard C., Alvin K. Klevorick, Richard R. Nelson, and Sidney G. Winter. 1987. "Appropriating the Returns from Industrial Research and Development." *Brookings Papers on Economic Activity* 3 (special issue on microeconomics): 783–831.

Lim, Kwanghui. 2011. "The Many Faces of Absorptive Capacity: Spillovers of Copper Interconnect Technology for Semiconductor Chips." *Industrial and Corporate Change* 18: 1249–1284.

Majewski, Suzanne E. 1998. "Causes and Consequences of Strategic Alliance Formation: The Case of Biotechnology." PhD dissertation, Department of Economics, University of California, Berkeley.

Manso, Gustavo. 2011. "Motivating Innovation." *Journal of Finance* 66: 1823–1860.

March, James G. 1991. "Exploration and Exploitation in Organizational Learning." *Organization Science* 2: 71–87.

Marx, Leslie M. 2000. "Contract Renegotiation in Venture Capital Projects." Working paper, University of Rochester, Rochester, NY.

Marx, Matt, Debbie Strumsky, and Lee Fleming. 2009. "Mobility, Skills, and the Michigan Non-Compete Experiment." *Management Science* 55: 875–889.

Merges, Robert P. 1995. "Intellectual Property and the Costs of Commercial Exchange: A Review Essay." *Michigan Law Review* 93: 1570–1615.

Moen, Jarle. 2005. "Is Mobility of Technical Personnel a Source of R&D Spillovers?" *Journal of Labor Economics* 23: 81–114.

Pakes, Ariel, and Zvi Griliches. 1984. "Patents and R&D at the Firm Level: A First Report," in Zvi Griliches (ed.), *Patents, R&D, and Productivity.* Chicago: University of Chicago Press, pp. 55–72.

Pakes, Ariel, and Shmuel Nitzan. 1983. "Optimal Contracts for Research Personnel, Research Employment and the Establishment of 'Rival' Enterprises." *Journal of Labor Economics* 1: 345–365.

Prusa, Thomas J., and James A. Schmitz, Jr. 1994. "Can Companies Maintain Their Initial Innovation Thrust? A Study of the PC Software Industry." *Review of Economics and Statistics* 76: 523–540.

Reagans, Ray E., Ezra W. Zuckerman, and Bill McEvily. 2004. "How to Make the Team: Social Networks vs. Demography as Criteria for Designing Effective Projects in a Contract R&D Firm." *Administrative Science Quarterly* 49: 101–133.

Reinganum, Jennifer F. 1983. "Uncertain Innovation and the Persistence of Monopoly." *American Economic Review* 73: 741–748.

———. 1989. "The Timing of Innovation: Research, Development, and Diffusion," in Richard Schmalensee and Robert Willig (eds.), *Handbook of Industrial Organization,* volume I. Amsterdam: North-Holland, pp. 849–908.

Robinson, David, and Toby E. Stuart. 2007. "Financial Contracting in Biotech Strategic Alliances." *Journal of Law and Economics* 50: 559–596.

Rosenbloom, Richard S., and William J. Spencer (eds.). 1996. *Engines of Innovation: U.S. Industrial Research at the End of an Era.* Boston: Harvard Business School Press.

Rosenkopf, Lori, and Paul Almeida. 2003. "Overcoming Local Search through Alliances and Mobility." *Management Science* 49: 751–766.

Sahlman, William A. 1990. "The Structure and Governance of Venture Capital Organizations." *Journal of Financial Economics* 27: 473–524.

Saxenian, Annalee. 1994. *Regional Advantage: Culture and Competition in Silicon Valley and Route 128.* Cambridge, MA: Harvard University Press.

Scharfstein, David S., and Jeremy C. Stein. 2000. "The Dark Side of Internal Capital Markets: Divisional Rent-Seeking and Inefficient Investment." *Journal of Finance* 55: 2537–2564.

Schumpeter, Joseph A. 1942. *Capitalism, Socialism and Democracy.* New York: Harper and Row.

Scott, John T. 1984. "Patents and R&D at the Firm Level: A First Report," in Zvi Griliches (ed.), *Patents, R&D, and Productivity.* Chicago: University of Chicago Press, pp. 233–245.

Seru, Amit. 2010. "Firm Boundaries Matter: Evidence from Conglomerates and R&D Activity." *Journal of Financial Economics,* forthcoming.

Shane, Hillary. 1995. "Asymmetric Information and Alliance Financing in the Biotechnology Industry," in *Three Essays in Empirical Finance in High-Technology Firms.* PhD dissertation, Wharton School, University of Pennsylvania, Philadelphia.

Shapiro, Carl. 2001. "Navigating the Patent Thicket: Cross Licenses, Patent Pools, and Standard Setting." *Innovation Policy and the Economy* 1: 119–150.

Simcoe, Timothy. 2012. "Standard Setting Committees: Consensus Governance for Shared Technology Platforms." *American Economic Review* 102: 305–336.

Solow, Robert M. 1957. "Technological Change and the Aggregate Production Function." *Review of Economics and Statistics* 39: 312–320.

Stein, Jeremy C. 2002. "Information Production and Capital Allocation: Decentralized versus Hierarchical Firms." *Journal of Finance* 57: 1891–1921.

Stern, Scott. 2004. "Do Scientists Pay to Be Scientists?" *Management Science* 50: 835–853.

Teece, David J. 1986. "Profiting from Technological Innovation: Implications for Integration, Collaboration, Licensing and Public Policy." *Research Policy* 15: 285–305.

Thompson, Peter, and Melanie Fox-Kean. 2005. "Patent Citations and the Geography of Knowledge Spillovers: A Reassessment." *American Economic Review* 95: 450–460.

Tushman, Michael. L., and Philip Anderson. 1986. "Technological Discontinuities and Organizational Environments." *Administrative Science Quarterly* 31: 439–465.

Wiggins, Steven N. 1995. "Entrepreneurial Enterprises, Endogenous Ownership, and the Limits to Firm Size." *Economic Inquiry* 33: 54–69.

Zucker, Lynne G., Michael R. Darby, and Marilynn B. Brewer. 1998. "Intellectual Human Capital and the Birth of U.S. Biotechnology Enterprises." *American Economic Review* 88: 290–306.

15

Hierarchies and the Division of Labor

Luis Garicano and Timothy Van Zandt

1. Introduction

Knight (1921) saw the function of entrepreneurs (and others "of higher skill") as making informed decisions in a world of uncertainty. Indeed, this would describe also the role of middle- and low-level managers, their assistants, and the technicians who collectively manage a large organization through decentralized decision processes.

This chapter reviews some research in economics on such managerial decision processes. Such research is not a mere technological exercise, akin to studying production on an assembly line. Rather, organizational processes are integral to the external interaction between an organization and other actors and to the internal functioning of the organization. Externally, these organizational processes constitute the decisionmaking by organizations, which is of inherent interest to economists, for whom organizations are among the actors in broader economic models. Internally, such coordination processes are what define organizations—what make organizations organized—and the division of decisionmaking tasks and the flows of information among members of an organization are what define organizational structure.

1.1. Complexity and Bounded Rationality

This topic is inherently tied to "bounded rationality," where this term is defined broadly to include human limits on decisionmaking in complex situations. If the mythical unboundedly rational, all-capable owner-entrepreneur-manager existed, there would be no organizational processes to talk about, no need to delegate the coordination in organizations to several or many agents, and therefore no organization structure other than a center and everyone else. There would be few of the incentive problems that delegation creates and that are the focus of much of the theory of organizations. An organization could be modeled as a single rational agent, as in the classic "black box" theory of the firm.

That said, the research we review in this chapter is not about sophisticated models of the bounded rationality or behavioral biases of a single person but rather about the decentralization of organizational processes that such bounded rationality entails. The "microbiology" of the individual manager is sacrificed to understand the organism-level "macrobiology" of the organization.

The basic elements of a model of organization processes are (1) a specification of the task or decision problem that the organization faces and (2) the capabilities of the potential managers and other organizational resources available for handling the task. A common feature of the models that we review is that the *complexity*—the difficulty of the task or decision problem compared to the capabilities of the individuals—is modeled explicitly. This contrasts with some behavioral approaches to bounded rationality.

Most of the literature we review has then closed such a model using a *constrained-optimal* approach. That is, the modeler characterizes the feasible decision procedures that are optimal—or that at least are good by some criterion, if it is too difficult to characterize optimal procedures—according to a performance criterion that may reflect computational or communication costs. It is logically consistent to have a model of bounded rationality in which agents cannot fully optimize and then to characterize optimal solutions to the design problem—because it is the theorist, not the agents in the model, who is performing the optimization. Yet what do we learn from such a characterization of constrained-optimal organizations?

Our approach is little different from the rationality assumption in most models of individual behavior in economics. We know that agents cannot be perfectly rational, but they are goal oriented, and this economic motivation is an important driver of human behavior. The rationality assumption is a powerful way to make these observations salient. Likewise, we understand that organizations are not constrained optimal, but organizations evolve and are designed in ways that are driven by performance goals and constraints. Hence, it can be elucidating to conclude that, for example, a particular hierarchical form or type of decentralization is prevalent because it is a good way for an organization to do well in a complex environment when the decisionmaking is done by managers, each of whom has limited capacity for absorbing information and making decisions. A powerful way to analyze this is for the theorist to outline explicitly the firms' decisionmaking task and performance goals and the constraints on the individual managers, and then to characterize the constrained-optimal organizational forms and processes.

1.2. A Division of the Literature

We have divided the literature into three groups, which focus on different questions about organizations and feature different kinds of models.

1. *Knowledge hierarchies.* This group focuses on the benefits of and limits to specialization of the knowledge and skills that managers in an organization have, and the process of dividing tasks among specialized managers. In a typical model, the firm faces a flow of independent problems. Decentralization takes the form of different problems being handled by different people. In its simplest form, with homogenous problems and managers, this is a queuing problem. We devote our attention, however, to models with heterogeneous problems and managers, in which organizational performance depends on how well problems are handled by the right managers, that is, by how well the problems are matched to the knowledge available in the organization.

The other two groups have in common that they focus on aspects of joint and interrelated decisionmaking. As a consequence, a typical model has a task or decision problem that is decomposable but that cannot be divided into unrelated problems. Decentralization takes the form of different decisions being made by or different calculations being performed by different managers.

2. *Team theory.* Limits to communication and to the cognitive capability of an individual manager imply that interrelated decisions are made by different people with different information. This group of papers focuses on the design of optimal decision rules, given such decentralized information, and also compares different information structures and different assignments of decision variables. A typical model has the flavor of a Bayesian game (which captures the decentralization of information) with common payoffs.

3. *Information processing.* The task of making a decision involves not merely communication but also time-intensive thinking and information processing. The sharing of such information-processing tasks is a motive for decentralizing decisionmaking to managers who a priori do not even have private information. This final group of papers studies the structure of such decentralized information processing. A typical model has the flavor of a simple model of distributed computation. It starts with an information-processing task or decision problem and with a decomposition of such a problem into steps, which are then assigned to different managers.

2. Historical Debates

2.1. Markets versus Planning Bureaus

The term "organization" is often interpreted as a tightly coordinated bureaucracy in which individuals have specific functions and common purpose. However, more broadly, an organization is any collection of individuals or groups whose actions are coordinated and for which there is some criterion for evaluating the collective outcome, even if it is a weak criterion, such as Pareto efficiency. Hence, markets and bureaucratic structures, such as firms, are alternate forms of organizations.

Having thus included market mechanisms in the theory of organization, we can say that the first prominent discussions in economics about alternate forms of organizations and their relative efficiency for decisionmaking were debates about socialism from about 1910 to 1940.

Some early visions of planning under socialism held that economic activity would be directed entirely by a central authority, without any role for prices. However, it was later suggested that prices were necessarily part of efficient resource allocation mechanisms, because they arise naturally in such a constrained optimization problem. This argument is essentially that of both Barone (1935, originally published in 1908) and Mises (1951, originally published in 1922), although the former proposed a price-based planning mechanism, and the latter claimed that price-based planning was not possible because of the lack of private ownership and exchange of the means of production. (For details on the origin of these ideas, see Hayek 1935.)

The role of prices was soon accepted by many economists, along with the additional point that the computation of solutions to the planning problem, even using prices, was too large a task to be done centrally by a planning bureau and would require the communication of too much information to the planning bureau. Hayek (1940: 125–126) summarizes this consensus. Therefore, later stages of the debate argued about whether socialist economies could use decentralized price mechanisms to allocate resources. Taylor (1929), Lange (1936, 1937), Dickinson (1939), and others proposed iterative mechanisms in which the adjustment of prices was controlled by the planning bureau. Hayek (1940) and others contended that such mechanisms would be too slow and cumbersome, but these authors never presented a model of how private-property markets reach equilibrium. Hence, the computational efficiency of the proposed planning mechanisms and of markets in capitalist economies could not be compared. This important gap has yet to be filled.

2.2. Markets versus Firms

In the 1930s, while some economists were comparing the efficiency of socialism and private-property market economies, other economists, such as Kaldor (1934), Robinson (1934), and Coase (1937), were drawing attention to the fact that even in private-property market economies, many transactions take place inside firms and are not regulated by price mechanisms. They suggested that the boundaries of firms are determined, in part, by the relative efficiency of markets and bureaucracies for processing information. However, this issue was also unresolved, because the authors discussed the process of managing a firm but did not make a direct comparison with how markets perform similar tasks.

One of the themes of that brief literature, which has consistently reappeared in the theory of organizations, is that information-processing constraints may be a limit to firm size. It was first observed that with centralized information processing (meaning that a single entrepreneur processed all information and made all decisions), there would be diseconomies of scale because of the fixed information processing capacity of firms. However, it was also noted that as firms grow, more managers are hired, and information processing is decentralized. Kaldor (1934: 68) responded that full decentralization of the coordination task is still not possible:

> You cannot increase the supply of co-ordinating ability available to an enterprise alongside an increase in the supply of other factors, as it is the essence of co-ordination that every single decision should be made on a comparison with all the other decisions made or likely to be made; it must therefore pass through a single brain.

This idea suggests that information-processing constraints will lead not only to decentralized information processing but also to decentralized decisionmaking, in which multiple agents make decisions based on differing information.

These themes have been further developed by Williamson (1975, 1985) and others in the field of transaction economics and in the models of organizational processes described in this chapter.

3. The Cognitive Role of Hierarchies

A theme of information-processing models in Section 6 is that, even if the managers in an organization have identical skills and knowledge, there are advantages to dividing up complex tasks among such managers. However, another important value of team decisionmaking is that it allows for specialization among the knowledge workers while providing mechanisms for the utilization of dispersed knowledge. We take up this theme first.

The main source of the increasing returns to knowledge specialization, as Rosen (1983) argued, is that an individual's investment in knowledge is a fixed cost that is independent of its subsequent utilization. Indeed, Sherwin Rosen (2002: 10) in his presidential address to the American Economic Association argued "for the economy as a whole, the most important reason by far for specialization and division of labor are scale economies in utilizing acquired skills."

Such a force would seem to push the economy to complete specialization: each individual would acquire one piece of knowledge and use it as intensively as possible. However, such complete horizontal specialization makes it impossible to match problems to solutions. Suppose a pediatrician only knows how to treat one type of tumor. How do we match the right child with this specialist? As specialization increases, it becomes harder to know who knows what. Organizations must find ways to determine who has the relevant knowledge.

This section considers a literature that focuses on the benefits of knowledge specialization and the problem of then allocating dispersed knowledge to determine the implications of these two forces on organizations. For these questions, it is sufficient to consider organizations that are a means of dealing with a flow of unrelated problems, each of which requires specific knowledge to be solved. The important modeling consideration is that knowing which knowledge a problem requires is itself a task that requires knowledge.

The organizational problem under these circumstances is then as follows. In the course of production, the organization must deal with a stream of problems. To solve them, specialized knowledge is required. Problems may differ by how difficult they are (some may be harder than others), in how often they come up (some are routine, the other are exceptional), and so forth. Agents can acquire specialized knowledge about problems, and the organization may determine the order in which different agents confront these problems and how they communicate with one another. The organization may also invest scarce resources in labeling problems.

Garicano (2000) combines these elements in a model of knowledge-based hierarchies. The hierarchical form, in which workers deal with the routine problems and managers deal with the exceptions, arises as an optimal way to structure the organization of knowledge. Crémer et al. (2007) extend this idea by allowing problems to be labeled through codes to facilitate the allocation of knowledge, as discussed by Arrow (1974). Each piece of the organization may develop variants of a given code or language, and then managers serve in these organizations as translators. We discuss these two ideas in turn.

These theories generate sharp predictions concerning the impact of information technology on organizations. Consider first knowledge hierarchies. The key trade-off is between the costs of communication and the costs of training and knowledge acquisition. By creating a hierarchy, training costs per worker are reduced, but communication costs rise. Thus, the cost of acquiring knowledge and of communicating affect the structure of the hierarchy. Lower training or acquisition costs lead to less reliance on the manager's knowledge, as more problems can be solved by frontline employees and thus less communication is necessary; conversely, lower communication costs are "deskilling": frontline employees need to acquire less knowledge, because relying on the knowledge of those above is now cheaper.

Similarly, drops in information and communication costs affect the scope of firms through the cost of common codes. With low information cost, specialized codes become less necessary, and expanding the scope of the code can result in synergies without substantive information losses.

We discuss both theories next, along with some relevant empirical evidence.

3.1. Knowledge-Based Hierarchies: Management by Exception

Garicano (2000) shows that when matching problems and solutions is hard, hierarchies conserve the time of more-able agents by allowing them to use the time of less-able agents to deal with the routine problems. Alfred Sloan (1924), a former head of General Motors, wrote: "We do not do much routine work with details. They never get up to us. I work fairly hard, but on exceptions." We study here under what conditions this is the case and the implications of such a view for organizational design.

The model of production and problem solving is as follows. A firm handles a flow of production tasks, which can be scaled, so that any worker can be fully occupied with her own flow. Each task requires specialized knowledge and production time to complete; if completed, it results in output (gross profit not including the cost of knowledge and production). We measure the quantity of knowledge by the effort, cost, and/or time required to acquire it. The production time, which could as well be thought of as managerial processing time, incorporates the time it takes to determine whether one has the knowledge required for the task and then (if so) to perform the task. In fact, the assumption in the model is that this production time is the same whatever the outcome of such processing, as if the sole or main part of such production were to understand what the task entails and how it matches one's knowledge.

We take a continuous approximation, as if the tasks were perfectly divisible, and index the tasks by $z \in [0, \infty)$. We assume that different tasks involve the same proportions of knowledge, production time, and output. We normalize the units, so that these three quantities are equal to one another for each task, and we can set them to 1 per unit interval of tasks. What varies across tasks is their frequency, which is measured by a density $f(z)$, with cumulative distribution function F and induced measure ν. We index the tasks in decreasing order of frequency, so that f is a decreasing function.

Consider first the case in which there is no team production, in the sense that each worker in the firm either solves a task by herself or not at all. Suppose that such a worker acquires the knowledge necessary to solve the tasks in a set $A \subset [0, \infty)$. (We refer to A as the "worker's knowledge.") A particular problem arrives, and the worker can solve it with probability $\nu(A)$. At the level of flows, she completes fraction $\nu(A)$ of the one unit of tasks that reach her per unit time.

Her training or knowledge acquisition cost is c per unit of knowledge. That is, her cost of learning all tasks in set A is c times its Lebesgue measure $\mu(A)$. She should acquire knowledge about the most frequent tasks; given that the tasks are ordered from most to least frequent, this means the tasks in an interval $[0, \bar{z}]$ for some cutoff $\bar{z}$. The cost of such knowledge is $c\bar{z}$, and because each completed task generates one unit of knowledge, the value of such knowledge is $F(\bar{z})$. Her optimal cutoff is the solution to $\max_{\bar{z}} F(\bar{z}) - c\bar{z}$. It is the same for all workers.

Suppose now that workers may work in teams, so that a worker can ask other workers for help with the problems that he cannot solve. The worker who is asked can provide help at a time cost $h < 1$. This cost does not affect the time that the original worker devotes to the problem. We assume $h < 1$ to capture the idea that the original worker's acquired understanding of the task facilitates the analysis of the task by other workers.

Crucially, again, a worker cannot know in advance whether he will be able to deal with a particular task until he has tried it—that is, he spends h when he is asked, regardless of whether the help is actually useful (e.g., a car mechanic often spends as much or more time on a car he cannot fix as on one he can). Consider, for example, a team where worker 1 knows problems in the set A_1 and worker 2 knows those in the set A_2. Suppose they help each other. Worker 1 then spends fraction $t_1^h = h(1 - v(A_2))$ of his time helping worker 2. Each worker has one unit of time, so the fraction t_i^p of time that worker i spends in production on the tasks that reach him directly is $t_i^p = 1 - t_i^h$.

The total flow of problems that reach the workers is then $t_1^p + t_2^p$, and they are successful with any task in the set $A_1 \cup A_2$. Therefore, the joint output is[1]

$$(t_1^p + t_2^p)v(A_1 \cup A_2) - c(\mu(A_1) + \mu(A_2)).$$

In general, to find the optimal organization among a large pool of workers, we can divide the workers into classes, indexed by i, such that workers within the same class i have the same knowledge A_i, spend the same time t_i^p in production and the same time t_i^h helping, and have the same rules ℓ_i for communication. These rules prescribe whom (which other class) they are supposed to ask first, whom next, and so forth. Then the team design problem is to choose A_i, t_i^p, t_i^h, and ℓ_i for each class, along with the measure β_i of workers in each class, to maximize per capita output—subject to the time constraint $1 \geq t_i^h + t_i^p$ and to the organization size constraint $\sum \beta_i = 1$.

Garicano (2000) shows that the solution is a simple hierarchy, where only the first layer of workers are involved in production and in asking questions, and the rest are problem solvers— that is, they spend all their time solving problems that are passed on to them from below. Moreover, production workers know the most common problems $[0, z_0]$; moving up the hierarchy, each successive layer i knows increasingly exceptional problems $[z_{i-1}, z_i]$, as shown in Figure 1. The key characteristic of this structure is management by exception.

To understand this last result, consider instead a hierarchical arrangement where agents in some layer know problems $[z, z + \varepsilon]$ (among others), which come up more often than a same-size interval $[z', z' + \varepsilon]$ of problems known by those who ask them questions. That is, $z < z'$ and hence $f(z) > f(z')$. This arrangement can be improved by swapping these intervals. Learning costs are unchanged, as all agents learn the same number of problems as before. Production is unchanged, because the total amount of knowledge is unchanged. But communication costs are lower, as those asking questions are now less likely to confront a problem they do not know. The crucial insight is that, by relying on management by exception, some specialization in knowledge can be attained while minimizing communication costs.

This principle of management by exception is very common in organizations. For example, in a hospital environment, residents (junior doctors) deal with the patient as she arrives, and the

---

1. Note that the analysis ignores for simplicity the stochastic aspect of problem arrival (i.e., there is no queuing in front of a manager when multiple workers requesting help arrive) and assumes that a certain measure of problems arrive with certainty at each level. See Beggs (2001) for a treatment of this aspect of the queuing problem.

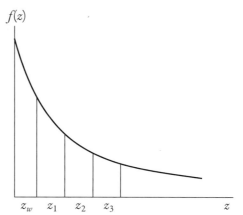

Figure 1. Management by exception: Workers specialize in production and deal with the routine problems (those in z_w). Managers help these workers to deal with increasingly exceptional problems. Managers in layer 1 acquire knowledge z_1; those in layer 2, z_2; and those in layer 3, z_3.

residents ask an attending physician for help only when the patient presents a difficult problem. In the production floor of a factory, production workers operate the machines, mechanical coordinators help them when the machine breaks down or stops, and production engineers are only called in when workers and coordinators both fail to deal with the production problem.[2] We discuss some more specific examples when we review the empirical literature below.

Note that the organization that emerges is pyramidal: each successively higher layer contains fewer workers. This is because an increasing share of the problems have been solved as one moves up the pyramid. Quantitatively, if there are n_0 workers in the first layer, then the flow of problems the organization can handle is n_0. For each layer $i > 0$, fraction $1 - F(z_{i-1})$ of these make it to layer i, so $n_i = (1 - F(z_{i-1}))n_0$.[3]

To explore the comparative statics of this type of hierarchy, Garicano (2000) proposes a version of the model with an exponential distribution $F(z) = 1 - e^{-\lambda z}$ and solves for the optimal hierarchy. With the results established so far, we have only to determine the knowledge thresholds $\{z_0, z_1, \ldots\}$, such that level i has knowledge $[z_{i-1}, z_i]$, that maximize the overall payoff. However, this optimization problem can be solved using a decentralized "referral market" solution with shadow prices, developed in the dynamic model of Garicano and Rossi-Hansberg (2012). We follow this approach, because it is simpler and provides more intuition.

In this referral market, the salary of a problem solver is the result of the knowledge he adds to problems that could not be solved before him. Production agents who have a problem they cannot solve pass it on, in exchange for a referral fee r_0 that equals the expected value generated per problem passed up the hierarchy. In the context of the firm, where we think those exchanges would be likely to take place, r_0 is a transfer price or a shadow price. The earnings of a production agent are given by the problems that his knowledge allows him to solve on his own, plus the value

2. The example is taken from the observation of a Procter and Gamble plant in Spain.

3. A variant of this model can be obtained when knowledge is overlapping; that is, where the agent's knowledge must be a superset of the knowledge of those below, for example, because the knowledge of the easier problems is required for the more difficult ones, knowledge is acquired through learning by doing, or the superiors supply instruction. Such a variant is described in Garicano (2000) and used as a building block in Garicano and Rossi-Hansberg (2006).

of the problems he confronts but cannot solve, minus his training costs:

$$w_0 = \max_{z_0} F(z_0) + (1 - F(z_0))r_0 - cz_0. \tag{1}$$

Likewise, a problem solver in layer i receives a referral fee r_i for problems he cannot solve and thus pushes futher up the hierarchy. Given the knowledge z_{i-1} of the layers lower in the hierarchy and this referral fee, the optimal knowledge threshold z_i for layer i solves

$$\max_{z_i} \frac{1}{h} \left(\frac{F(z_i) - F(z_{i-1}) + \left(1 - F(z_i)\right) r_i}{1 - F(z_{i-1})} - r_{i-1} \right) - c(z_i - z_{i-1}). \tag{2}$$

That is, he has the capacity to take on $1/h$ problem passed from below. He pays r_{i-1} for each of these. He solves each problem with probability

$$\frac{F(z_i) - F(z_{i-1})}{1 - F(z_{i-1})};$$

this hazard function is the conditional probability the solution is in his interval, given that it was not below. If he does not solve it, which happens with the complementary probability $(1 - F(z_i))/(1 - F(z_{i-1}))$, he can refer the problem to the next layer, receiving the fee r_i. His training cost is $c(z_i - z_{i-1})$.

Replacing $F(z) = 1 - e^{-\lambda z}$ and denoting the amount of knowledge of a level-i problem solver by $\hat{z}_i = z_i - z_{i-1}$, (2) is equivalent to

$$\max_{\hat{z}_i} \frac{1}{h} \left(1 - e^{-\lambda \hat{z}_i}(1 - r_i) - r_{i-1}\right) - c\hat{z}_i. \tag{3}$$

The first-order condition of the production worker problem is

$$\lambda e^{-\lambda z_0}(1 - r_0) = c, \tag{4}$$

and the first-order condition for a problem solver in layer i is

$$\frac{1}{h}\lambda e^{-\lambda \hat{z}_i}(1 - r_i) = c. \tag{5}$$

Note that the marginal cost of learning is the same for all agents, and that the marginal benefit has the same form for all agents—that is, except for the price of problems, nothing depends on how much those in previous layers learned. This lack of memory is a consequence of the constant hazard rate of the exponential distribution: conditional on a problem not having been observed in a given interval, the probability that it is in the next one is constant and is equal to λ in the limit where those intervals are very small. The stationarity of the first-order conditions suggests that the referral fee does not change with the layer, that is, $r_i = r$. The guess can be indeed verified, and it follows immediately that $\hat{z}_i$ is also the same for all $i > 0$, and we denote the common value by $\hat{z}_s$. A worker who asks once indeed finds it optimal to ask again and again, until she finds the solution in this exponential case (the value of asking is analogous to the hazard rate—the probability that the problem will be known by the next layer, given that it was not known by the layer below). We can then simply solve the model and obtain closed-form solutions for all variables. The equilibrium referral fee is $r = 1 - h - (ch/\lambda) \log h$, and the amount of knowledge of each production agent and that of each problem solver are, respectively,

$$z_0^* = \frac{1}{\lambda} \log \left(\frac{h\lambda}{c} - h \log h \right), \tag{6}$$

$$\hat{z}_s^* = \frac{1}{\lambda} \log \left(\frac{\lambda}{c} - \log h \right), \tag{7}$$

with earnings at all layers given by

$$w = 1 - \frac{c}{\lambda} \left(1 + \log \left(\frac{h\lambda}{c} - h \log h \right) \right). \tag{8}$$

From (6)–(8) we obtain comparative statics for the tasks dealt with at each level and the spans of control (the ratio of workers in one level to workers in the next) in the optimal organization. First, a reduction in communication costs h increases the range of expertise of problem solvers (z_s) and reduces the range of expertise of production workers (z_0). Essentially, asking for help becomes cheaper relative to acquiring knowledge. As a consequence, the frequency $F(z_0)$ of decisionmaking of production workers decreases, and that of problem solvers increases. It also increases the span of control of problem solvers at each level, that is, the ratio n_i/n_{i-1}. Essentially, when communication costs are reduced, workers are less empowered.

Second, consider a reduction in the cost c of acquiring knowledge. This reduction could be the consequence of the introduction of expert systems and electronic diagnostics: each worker can solve, for a given investment in acquiring knowledge, a larger proportion of problems. For example, a machine operator can solve more problems for a given investment in learning if the machine is fitted with a diagnostic system. A reduction c increases the range of expertise of both problem solvers and production workers. As a consequence, the frequency of decisionmaking by production workers increases, and the frequency of decisionmaking by problem solvers ($1 - F(z_w)$) decreases, but more of the problems that reach any level are solved by that level. The reduction in c also increases the span of control of problem solvers. Again, the organization has become flatter, but workers are now more, rather than less, empowered. Production workers now can acquire knowledge more cheaply, so they ask relatively fewer questions. This increases the span of control of each problem solver, reduces the number of layers of problem solvers required, reduces the delay needed to obtain solutions to problems, and decreases the frequency with which problem solvers intervene in the production process.

Finally, changes in the density function as indexed by λ are (the inverse of) changes in the complexity of the production process. A more complex production process is one in which problems further out in the tails are more likely to be confronted. One can show that an increase in the complexity of the production process (a fall in λ) may increase or decrease the range of expertise of problem solvers (z_s) and production workers (z_w). However, it unambiguously increases the frequency of decisionmaking by problem solvers $(1 - F(z_w))$ and decreases the frequency of decisionmaking by production workers $(F(z_w))$. It also reduces the span of control of problem solvers as they have to deal with more problems.

Garicano and Hubbard (2007b) extend the analysis to a world where there is both horizontal and vertical (or hierarchical) specialization. With multiple fields and uncertainty about which field will be necessary for production, generalists and specialists coexist—generalists arbitrage unpredictable differences in demand among fields and receive more stable earnings, whereas specialists use knowledge more intensively and earn more when the demand for their field is high. In such a world, an increase in the returns to horizontal specialization (e.g., because the size of the economy increases, and aggregate uncertainty about the allocation of demand across fields declines) reduces the value of the arbitrage among fields performed by generalists and increases equilibrium field specialization. As individuals become "narrower but deeper," the benefit of leveraging their expertise increases. That is, increasing the returns to specialization also increases the value of leveraging individuals' talent, and thus also increases both knowledge depth and the span of control of specialized problem solvers.

We now turn our attention to the second way that organizations (and hierarchy) structure the acquisition of knowledge by specialists: through specialized languages.

3.2. Organizational Languages: Managers as Translators

An alternative way to match problems with knowledge is by investing in labeling problems. As Arrow (1974) pointed out, agents often use technical languages to communicate with others about contingencies that are specific to their common environment. These specialized languages, or codes, economize in knowledge and communication costs within a group but at the cost of limiting communication with agents from outside the group. Communication across groups requires the use of specialized translators who span multiple languages and facilitate communication (e.g., for the reallocation of resources).[4] Crémer et al. (2007) present an analysis of this problem. As they point out, the essential trade-off determining the scope of the language chosen is one between specialization and coordination. An organization that wants to capture more synergies by expanding its scope must acquire a more vague and imprecise common language to facilitate coordination among its units. The use of managerial hierarchies as integration devices weakens this trade-off somewhat.

We consider a simple version of the model by Crémer et al. (2007), which allows us to illustrate some of the main results of the analysis by making some functional form assumptions. In our story, a firm serves clients, whose types x are distributed on $[0, 1]$. On the front line are the salespersons, but they must communicate with a specialist—engineers in our story—to serve any client. The problem is to efficiently communicate the type of the client to the engineer.

---

4. Crémer (1993) generalizes this idea in his discussion of culture. Essentially, in his view, culture is a stock of shared firm-specific human capital, a knowledge stock shared by a substantial portion of the employees of the firm but not by the general population. This stock has three elements: a common code, a shared knowledge of facts, and a shared knowledge of rules of behavior. As in Arrow's narrower discussion of codes, such a stock reduces communication costs. For example, a decision by an individual that commits her firm can be facilitated if there is a stock of facts (rules) that can help the agent predict the behaviors of others.

Communication is by a simple language in which each word denotes a set of client types, and each agent can only use a limited number of words, which thus define a partition of the set of types. For concreteness and simplicity, here let there be only 2 words.

Thus, the salesperson communicates that the type is above $\hat{x}$ (this is one word) or below $\hat{x}$ (this is the other word). The more types of clients included in a word, the less useful it is; to capture this, we assume the diagnosis cost that the engineer must incur to serve the client is equal to the breadth of the word (the measure of the set of types the word represents). This is the additional information that the engineer must acquire about the client after learning only that the type lies in the set corresponding to the word.

It is easy to see that the optimal code will be such that one word contains the more frequent events and the other word contains the less frequent ones. Furthermore, in an optimal code, broader words describe less frequent events. If not, the more frequent event in the broad word can be swapped with a less frequent one from a less broad word with a reduction in diagnosis costs.

Suppose that the distribution is given by a density f that is increasing (with cumulative distribution function F). Then the two words determine a simple partition into two intervals, $[0, \hat{x}]$ and $[\hat{x}, 1]$. The upper interval contains the more frequent words and hence is smaller: $\hat{x} > 1/2$. The optimal code problem reduces to

$$\min_{\hat{x}} F(\hat{x})\hat{x} + (1 - F(\hat{x}))(1 - \hat{x}).$$

Suppose now that there are two services, A and B. Each of them is composed of one salesperson and one engineer. They can organize in three possible ways:

1. separation (the two services use different codes);

2. integration (the two services share the same code); or

3. hierarchy (there exists a hierarchical structure supplying an interface between the services).

We establish next the circumstances under which each form is optimal. For expositional reasons, it is best to focus first on the comparison between the two pure forms, separation and integration, and then introduce the third form. But first we explicitly model the source of synergies.

To generate a need for coordination, there must be a potential synergy among the two services, which we model as follows. Customers arrive randomly, and there may be excessive load in one service and excessive capacity in the other. If that happens, the two services benefit from diverting some business from the overburdened service to the other. Formally, suppose that salespersons from services A and B deal with clients from two different distributions F_A and F_B, where $F_i(x) = (1 - b_i)\, x + b_i x^2$, where $b_A = b$ and $b_B = -b$, and $b \in [0, 1]$ measures the difference between the two distributions. When $b = 0$, both distributions are uniform; when $b > 0$, the distribution in A is skewed toward the lower end, and in B it is skewed toward the upper end. Let $\hat{x}_i$ be the cutoff between words of each service, with (by symmetry) $\hat{x}_B = 1 - \hat{x}_A$, and let $D_i(x)$ be the expected diagnosis cost in service i.

In a given period, salesperson i receives a random number y_i of clients, with the following distribution:

$$y_i = \begin{cases} 0 & \text{with probability } p, \\ 1 & \text{with probability } (1-2p), \\ 2 & \text{with probability } p, \end{cases}$$

where p belongs to the interval $[0, 1/2]$. This arrival process captures the effect of the variability in the expected number of clients of each type. Suppose that each engineer has the ability to attend to the needs of at most one client. If p is low, then each salesperson is likely to find one client per period. When p is high, although on average one client is arriving, it is quite likely that either none or two will arrive. Thus, p measures the importance of the synergy between the two services: a high p means that the services are likely to need to share clients, whereas a low p means that each service is likely to have its capacity fully utilized.

Finally, we assume that the profit that can be obtained when a client's problem is solved is 1. The per-client diagnosis costs is $\lambda \in (1, 2)$, so that if the engineer knows that the client's characteristics fall in an interval of size s, her diagnosis cost is $s\lambda$. This ensures positive profits. It also ensures that information must transit through a salesperson before being sent to an engineer; indeed, an engineer without information on the client's problem would have diagnosis costs greater than the profits obtained from solving it.

The organizational choice here is between segregating the services, so that salespersons from service A only communicate sales leads to engineers in A; and integrating them so that a salesperson from A may communicate sales leads to either engineer. Should services communicate with each other, even at the expense of a common code?

In a *separated organization*, where the two services use different codes and there is no communication, each service uses a code adapted to its own distribution of types. Then $\hat{x}_A < 1/2$ and $\hat{x}_B > 1/2$. The expected profit given separate codes $\mathcal{C}_s$ is

$$\Pi_S(p, b, \lambda | \mathcal{C}_s) = 2(1-p)(1-\lambda D(b)).$$

Consider next an *integrated organization*. This requires that a salesperson from service A explain to an engineer in B the needs of his client, and vice versa. Indeed, because $\lambda > 1$, sending the problem to the engineer without explanation is not profitable. However, in this case the codes must be common in both services. What are the diagnosis costs in this case? The common language is the one that would be chosen when the density of tasks is the average of the two densities of the two services. In this case, because both services have opposing distributions, the average problem density is uniform. The optimal code has two equally imprecise words, with each word identifying the sales lead as coming from one-half of the distribution. The total profits given joint code $\mathcal{C}_j$ are then

$$\Pi_I(p, b, \lambda | \mathcal{C}_j) = 2(1 - p(1-p))\left(1 - \frac{\lambda}{2}\right).$$

Finally, in a *hierachical organization*, the two services may exploit the synergy by employing a fifth agent who provides translation between the two services. Each service adopts a separate code. When interservice communication is needed, the translator steps in. For instance, if salesperson A has two clients, he communicates to the translator the type of the "extra" client in the code used in service A. The translator will search for x, and then she will transmit the information to engineer B in the code used in service B. Hiring a translator requires incurring a fixed cost μ, but because the translator is specialized in language, we assume that her diagnosis cost is lower than that of the engineers. For simplicity we make the extreme assumption that the translator's λ is zero. (The qualitative results of the analysis go through even if her λ is strictly positive, as long as it is lower than the engineers' λ.) Then

$$\Pi_H(p, b, \lambda | \mathcal{C}_t) = 2(1 - p)(1 - \lambda D^t(b)) + 2p^2 \left(1 - \lambda D^t(b)\right) - \mu,$$

where $\mathcal{C}_t$ is the code with translation, and μ is the fixed cost of the translator.

It can then be shown that if the cost of diagnosis is low, then the optimal organization is an integrated one with a common code. The synergies are captured, and the cost of having a language that is not well adapted are low. If diagnosis costs are high, separation is preferred, as it is important to ensure that a well-adapted language is used for each service. Finally, for in-between diagnosis costs, hierarchical structures are preferred. Organizations can attain some synergies, and languages are reasonably adapted to each separate environment.

An implication of the analysis is that hierarchies and codes are substitute modes of coordination: developments (e.g., improvements in information technology) that facilitate communication across units reduce the need for vertical communication and are likely to result in reductions in layers in firms. Moreover, the analysis allows for a comparison between horizontal and vertical coordination mechanisms. Horizontal mechanisms require common codes and thus result in less precise communication, given bounded rationality; vertical ones allow for more specialization of languages and knowledge sets but clearly increase delay, because communication takes one more step.

This work leaves an important unresolved aspect of codes to be analyzed. As Arrow (1974) argued, codes create an irreversible commitment by an organization, because they involve specific investments. As a result, a code (and a culture in the sense of Crémer 1993) results in an identity and a capability for the organization—to the extent that it adapts well to a current reality by developing a particular cognitive culture and structure for information processing, history does matter. Moreover, the presence of corporate culture imposes fixed costs of selective intervention—a merger cannot do as well if one exists—and thus it also has implications for the theory of the firm. This idea, which is close to what the management literature has called the "capabilities" of the firm, has been rarely explored in economics and should be the object of future work.

3.3. Empirical Evidence on Knowledge Hierarchies

The premise of the theories we discussed in Section 3.1 is that productive knowledge is embodied in individuals who have limited time. The efficient allocation of tasks must then be such that the time of more-knowledgeable individuals is only used when it cannot be substituted for the time of less-knowledgeable agents. This is accomplished through knowledge hierarchies in which less-knowledgeable agents deal with routine problems, and the experts deal with the exceptions. We review the empirical evidence on two issues: (1) Do hierarchies indeed take this shape and allocate tasks in the manner suggested by the theory? (2) Do changes in the return to expertise, and thus to the depth of knowledge acquisition, affect the hierarchical structure of firms? Some related evidence, involving the wages at different positions of the hierarchy, is discussed later in the chapter.

3.3.1. Case Evidence

Knowledge hierarchies are prevalent in manufacturing. In a Kawasaki manufacturing plant in Japan operators do routine tasks; when a problem comes up that they cannot solve, it is recorded for later analysis by managers and engineers (Schonberger 1986). Similarly, at a Procter and Gamble plant in Barcelona, operators confronted with a problem first ask mechanical supervisors for help and then, if unsuccessful, the managers (most of whom are mechanical engineers). Variants of this organizational structure seem to be the norm at most manufacturing plants.

Customer service at software companies, hospitals, and banks is similarly structured. For example, in software development firms, the technical department is structured so that junior workers handle all calls initially, and they transfer upward the calls they cannot handle (Orlikowski 1996). In an experimental study using customer complaints randomly distributed to hospital employees, managers were randomly assigned 37% of initial complaints, but dealt, in a second instance, with 70% of the unsolved ones (Stevenson and Gilly 1991). The loan approval process in banks, as studied by Liberti and Mian (2009), has similar characteristics. Credit dossiers flow from the less to the more senior managers. The more risky, complex, and valuable the credit is, the more likely it is that it will be approved by a higher level of management. A similar phenomenon can be observed in medical services, where patients are first seen by a nurse, then by a resident, and only if necessary by an attending physician.

Using efficiently the existing knowledge of agents in the hierarchy is also a crucial factor in the structure of professional service firms (e.g., consulting, law, or investment banks). For example, at McKinsey the most routine parts of the assignment are dealt with by business analysts or associates; the more unusual and exceptional the assignment is, the more engaged managers and partners become. In fact, the whole business model of professional services is explicitly based on leveraging the highly valuable time of senior personnel through the use of relatively inexpensive associates (Maister 1993). Similarly, in research and development, the time of senior research scientists is leveraged through the use of large teams of junior scientists and postdocs who engage in the more routine tasks. In universities and other research institutions, knowledge hierarchies are highly prevalent, particularly in the physical sciences. This type of organization is also found in software development firms and open source software development, where bugs are dealt with by junior programmers and, if they prove complicated, go up the ladder to senior programmers.

Another interesting example of knowledge hierarchies can be found in military and intelligence services. Some information from the field is, if routine, dealt with by the frontline or field officer. If the information is unusual, it goes up the organizational ladder to a more knowledgeable officer, who decides what action to take. Information that is truly exceptional continues up to the top of the hierarchy (Wilensky 1967). Again, this conserves the time of the senior officers for the exceptional problems.

Knowledge hierarchies are also prevalent in upper-level management. The practice of having middle managers deal with the more routine management problems so that the very top managers only intervene in unusual circumstances is a well-established management practice: management by exception (Sloan 1924). In an empirical study of senior management Simons (1991) finds that management control systems are mostly used to allow senior managers to leverage their time by ensuring their attention is focused on those problems only they can deal with.

3.3.2. Systematic Evidence

A key implication of Garicano (2000) is the distinct impact of the two aspects of information and communications technology on the organization of firms. Improved knowledge access empowers frontline workers and flattens firms; cheaper communication does the opposite. Bloom et al. (2009) test this implication in a multinational sample of production firms and find strong empirical support for it. Specifically, they find that CAD/CAM, a key information technology in manufacturing, empowers production workers; that enterprise resource planning, the key new IT technology, empowers middle managers; and that communication technology shifts decisions away from both middle managers and workers and toward the top of the organization. This finding that information technology empowers lower-level managers, reducing layers and increasing spans, may also provide an explanation for the trend toward fewer hierarchical levels between division managers and CEOs and toward larger CEO span (Rajan and Wulf 2006).

Garicano and Hubbard (2007a) provide further evidence on the link between knowledge utilization and the structure of firms. Specifically, they first show that an increase in the returns to horizontal specialization will increase the returns to hierarchy, by increasing knowledge depth and the value of protecting the (now more valuable) individual's knowledge. They show that it follows that both the share of individuals who work in hierarchies and the ratio of lower-level to upper-level individuals should increase with market size, and test this (and other related propositions) using a unique dataset: confidential data on thousands of law offices from the 1992 Census of Services. These data are a large sample taken from all law offices located in the United States at the time, and contain office-level information on both the hierarchical organization of lawyers (i.e., how many lawyers are partners versus associates) and the field specialization of lawyers. These data are unique because they contain both information on individual hierarchical organizations and the breadth of their human capital for an entire industry.

They find that the empirical evidence is consistent with these propositions. The share of lawyers who work in hierarchies (i.e., in an office with at least one associate) is greater in larger local markets. This increase is correlated with increases in lawyers' field specialization in a way that is consistent with our model; specifically, the share of lawyers who work as partners in hierarchies remains constant, but the average number of associates who work under these partners increases. These findings seem robust, in that they hold also when looking only across small, isolated markets and persist when holding firm size constant. They appear mostly when analyzing lawyers who primarily serve business rather than individual clients. Finally, Garicano and Hubbard (2007a) find that these patterns are far weaker when examining the hierarchical margin between lawyers and nonlawyers, a margin where the division of labor among individuals is constrained by regulation. This additional analysis provides evidence that is consistent with the view that the role of hierarchy in law offices is, in part, to support vertical specialization, because these results are stronger at hierarchical margins where the division of labor is not constrained and are strongest in segments where vertical specialization is most valuable.

4. Decomposing Decision Problems

4.1. Introduction

The debates in the 1930s on socialism and on the management of firms, reviewed in Section 2, both observed that decentralizing information processing and decisionmaking economizes on communication costs and distributes the decision tasks. Such decentralization requires that decision problems be decomposable into tasks that can be assigned to different agents.

In the knowledge hierarchies literature reviewed in Section 3, such decomposition is straightforward, because the organizational task consists of a flow of unrelated problems. In the other research streams we study in this survey, a single problem is decomposed into interrelated steps, and hence, the composition itself is a more fundamental feature of the model. In fact, the formal study of such decompositions—as an end in itself—was prevalent in the theory of organizations from the mid-1950s to the early 1970s, aided by advances in mathematical optimization methods.

In this section, we present in some detail a decomposition of a resource allocation problem. We focus on resource allocation, because it links several literatures and approaches (team theory, communication mechanisms, and information processing), because it is a fundamental economic problem both within and across organizations, and because the decomposition itself results in recognizable hierarchical procedures.

4.2. A Canonical Resource Allocation Problem

Consider a one-good resource allocation problem without externalities, framed as a payoff maximization problem of an organization, such as a firm. The firm has n production shops or operatives, indexed $i = 1, \ldots, n$. The link among the shops is that each shop i receives an amount x_i of a resource that is in fixed supply x_R. Each shop also takes independent local decisions y_i. Fix a domain $X = \mathbb{R}$ or $X = \mathbb{R}_{++}$ for allocations and a domain Y for the local decisions. Then the firm's decision problem is

$$\max_{\langle x_1, y_1, \ldots, x_n, y_n \rangle \in X^n \times Y^n} \sum_{i=1}^{n} \pi_i(x_i, y_i), \tag{9}$$

$$\text{subject to} \sum_{i=1}^{n} x_i = x_R.$$

The data in the problem are the shops' payoff functions $\{\pi_1, \ldots, \pi_n\}$ and the amount x_R of the resource.

This canonical resource allocation problem has numerous interpretations. For example, each shop is a division in a firm; $\langle x_1, \ldots, x_n \rangle$ is an allocation of a quantity x_R of a common resource, such as capital; y_i is a local decision variable for division i; and π_i is the profit function of division i. Alternatively, each shop is a production shop; $\langle x_1, \ldots, x_n \rangle$ is an assignment of production targets to the shops; x_R is the total required output; y_i is a local decision variable, such as inputs; and $\pi_i(x_i, y_i)$ measures inversely the cost of production; and the problem is to minimize the total cost of producing x_R. The resource could also be a consumption good, and each shop i could be a consumer whose weighted utility in an aggregate welfare function is π_i.

4.3. Decomposition between Local Decisions and the Resource Allocation

For each shop i, define $u_i \colon X \to \mathbb{R}$ by

$$u_i(x_i) = \max_{y_i \in Y} \pi_i(x_i, y_i). \tag{10}$$

We can think of the problem in (10) as a local decision made by shop i. The central office or headquarters focuses on the necessary coordination among the shops by solving

$$\max_{\langle x_1, \ldots, x_n \rangle \in X^n} \sum_{i=1}^{n} u_i(x_i), \quad \text{subject to} \quad \sum_{i=1}^{n} x_i = x_R. \tag{11}$$

This decomposition and its implied communication is illustrated in Figure 2. Shop i must determine the entire function u_i and then communicate it to the central resource manager, who then solves (11) and communicates the resource allocation to the shops. We can think of the functions u_i as demands for resources communicated by the shops, and the resource manager responds with a resource allocation that balances the demands.

The benefits of such decomposition—compared to having a single person or office solve (9)—may be twofold. First, if the functions π_i are private information of the shops, then

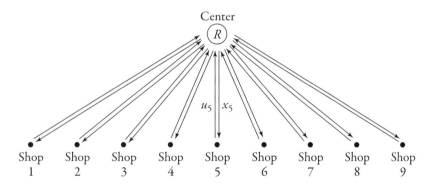

Figure 2. Decomposition between local and global decisions. Shop i makes local decision y_i, given resource allocation x_i received from the center; u_i measures shop i's maximized payoff (contribution to the firm), given any resource allocation.

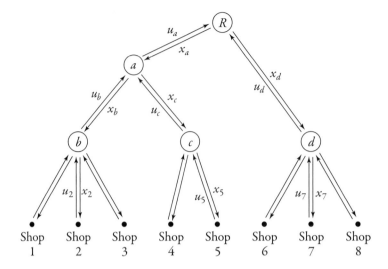

Figure 3. Hierarchical decomposition of the resource allocation problems. Payoff functions are aggregated through an upward flow of information. Allocations are disaggregated through a downward flow of information.

communicating the single-variable function u_i is less complex than communicating the two-variable function π_i. Second, each of the single-variable optimization problems in (10) and the n-variable problem in (11) are less complex than the $2n$-variable optimization problem in (9). Thus, the information-processing task is shared among more agents.

4.4. A Hierarchical Decomposition

The allocation of resources in the mechanism in Section 4.3 is centralized in the sense that the resource allocations emanate directly from the resource manager and are based on the pooled information of the shop managers. However, resource allocation procedures in organizations often have the hierarchical upward and downward flows of information seen in Figure 3. Examples include the capital budgeting processes of large firms and procedures for allocating resources in large nonmarket organizations such as governments, firms, and universities.

At the bottom of the hierarchy are the shops (or operatives, or whatever are the ultimate recipients of resources). In the upper tiers of the hierarchy are managers or administrators, grouped into offices; these are the nodes, such as a, c, and R, in Figure 3. We refer to the entire set of shops below one of these offices as a "division." Information about the shops is aggregated by a flow of information up the hierarchy, and resources are recursively disaggregated by a flow of information down the same hierarchy.

Consider, for example, the capital budgeting cycle of a chain of local newspapers. Each reporter, writer, and salesperson (etc.) puts in requests for computer acquisitions with justifications. The head of the news department of each newspaper aggregates these requests and puts together an overall budget request, summarizing the department's needs. The director of each newspaper aggregates the requests from the newspaper's news, editorial, sales, and advertising departments, putting together a summary of the newspaper's needs, which is sent to central headquarters. There, the office of the director of capital budgeting aggregates these reports to compare the needs. At that point, the director does not decide on the computer acquisitions of each employee. Instead, she divides her capital budget among the newspapers. Each of these newspaper directors divides her budget among the departments, and then each department manager allocates the budget to the members of her department.

Such a decentralized procedure can replicate the decisions of a centralized procedure, as we now explain. In Figure 3, node b represents, for example, a news department in one of the newspapers. The subordinates of b, which we denote by Θ_b, are the reporters. Reporter 2's message to b is a summary of the payoff $u_2(x_2)$ that any allocation for computers would generate for the company (given optimal local decisions that the reporter would make). The aggregate payoff function for the news department, which we denote by $u_b = \bigoplus_{k \in \Theta_b} u_k$, is the following value function:

$$u_b(x_b) \equiv \sup_{\{x_k | k \in \Theta_b\}} \sum_{k \in \Theta_b} u_k(x_k), \quad \text{subject to} \sum_{k \in \Theta_b} x_k = x_b.$$

That is, it is the highest payoff to the firm that the reporters under b can generate when resources x_b are subdivided optimally among those reporters.

The aggregation of payoff functions is an associative and commutative binary operation, which we denote by $\oplus$. Thus, when office a, which in our story could represent the management of a newspaper, aggregates the reports u_b and u_c from the newspaper's two departments and thereby computes $u_a = u_b \oplus u_c$, it ends up with the same result as if it had directly aggregated the reports from the lowest level. That is,

$$u_a = u_b \oplus u_c$$
$$= (u_1 \oplus u_2 \oplus u_3) \oplus (u_4 \oplus u_5)$$
$$= u_1 \oplus u_2 \oplus u_3 \oplus u_4 \oplus u_5,$$

and so no information is lost by the hierarchical aggregation of information.

Consider now the disaggregation of resource allocations. Consider the example in Figure 3 and suppose that office a (the management of a newspaper) has to allocate an amount x_a of the resource to the shops below it (its reporters) to maximize the total payoff. It can either do so directly or instead (i) allocate amounts x_b and x_c of the resource to offices b and c to maximize the sum $u_b(x_b) + u_c(x_c)$ of their aggregate payoffs, and then (ii) instruct each department b and c to divide its allocation among its reporters to maximize the sum of those reporters' payoffs to the firm. Once again, there is no loss from this decomposition of the resource allocation decisions.

This property can be stated formally as follows. Let J be the set of offices (nonleaf nodes) in the hierarchy and, for $j \in J$, let θ_j be the shops below j in the hierarchy ("division j"). Let $\{x_i^*\}_{i=1}^n$ be a balanced resource allocation. For each office $j \in J$, let $x_j^* = \sum_{i \in \theta_j} x_i^*$ be the total resource allocation to the shops below j in the hierarchy. Then $\{x_i^*\}_{i=1}^n$ solves the overall resource allocation problem in (11) if and only if, for each $j \in J$, $\{x_k^*\}_{k \in \Theta_j}$ solves j's local resource allocation problem:

$$\max_{\{x_k \in \mathbb{R}\}_{k \in \Theta_j}} \sum_{k \in \Theta_j} u_k(x_k), \quad \text{subject to} \sum_{k \in \Theta_j} x_k = x_j^*.$$

Thus, the hierarchically decentralized upward flow of payoff functions and downward flow of resource allocations, as shown in Figure 3, yields the same allocations as a centralized procedure, as shown in Figure 2. The benefits of such decentralization are not made explicit in this model, but the informal idea once again is that it is useful to be able to share complex tasks among multiple managers.

4.5. An Example with Quadratic Payoffs

To make the preceding section more concrete and to provide an example to be extended in other models in this chapter, we describe the aggregation of payoffs and disaggregation of resource allocations for the particularly simple example of quadratic payoffs. Specifically, we assume that each shop i's payoff has the form

$$u_i(x_i, \gamma_i) = \bar{u}_i - b_i^{-1}(x_i - \gamma_i)^2, \tag{12}$$

where $b_i > 0$ and $\bar{u}_i, \gamma_i \in \mathbb{R}$. Then the aggregate payoff function of division $j \in J$ is

$$u_j(x_j, \gamma_j) \equiv \bar{u}_j - b_j^{-1}(x_j - \gamma_j)^2,$$

where

$$\bar{u}_j = \sum_{k \in \theta_j} \bar{u}_k, \qquad b_j = \sum_{k \in \theta_j} b_k, \quad \text{and} \quad \gamma_j = \sum_{k \in \theta_j} \gamma_k.$$

We can see from these formulas that such aggregation of payoff functions involves merely addition—a simple example of an associative binary operation. The optimal allocation by office $j \in J$ to subordinate in $k \in \Theta_j$ is

$$x_k^* = \gamma_k + \frac{b_k}{b_j}(x_j - \gamma_j). \tag{13}$$

Intuitively, γ_k is the ideal allocation that maximizes k's payoff, and γ_j would be the total allocation if all subordinates received their ideal allocations. Then $x_j - \gamma_j$ is the total amount by which allocations would have to be adjusted to achieve resource balance. This adjustment is apportioned to the subordinates according to the weights b_k/b_j.

4.6. But What Does the Administrative Staff Do?

We have thus seen the possibility of decomposing a resource allocation problem, as depicted in Figure 3. However, it does not explain why this would be advantageous. To identify the advantages of such decentralization, we should model the bounded capacities of the individual administrators. We consider two approaches in Section 5:

1. The first, discussed in Section 5, uses team theory to tell a story analogous to the returns to knowledge specialization studied in Section 3: managers are bounded in the amount of information they may have; decentralization allows the organization to bring to bear more information on the problem. The difference between this model and that of the previous sections is that the different managers have heterogenous information about different parts of a single coordination problem, and hence are working together to solve the problem.

2. The second approach, discussed in Sections 6 and 7, models the actual information-processing activities by which managers turn raw data into decisions. Managers are bounded in what they can do in any amount of time; decentralization allows the firm to use more, or more recent, data.

5. Team Theory: Decisionmaking with Dispersed Information

By "team theory," we mean the statistical theory of teams, as in Marschak and Radner (1972). (This term has also been used more loosely to describe any model without conflict of interest, or even any model with some kind of collective decisionmaking.) We begin with an overview of team theory as a Bayesian game of common interest, followed by an explanation of why this can be a model of organizations. We discuss Geanakoplos and Milgrom (1991), which is a model of hierarchical disaggregation of resource allocations, in more detail.

5.1. Overview

Team theory considers group decisionmaking when the members have private information but share the same goals. Ideally, the group would pool its information and make decisions that are optimal conditional on the pooled information. However, how should the members of the group make decisions when such pooling of information is impractical due to communication constraints?

The simplest interesting class of problems is when there are n players who observe private signals about the state of nature and then simultaneously choose actions. This is a Bayesian game in which players have the same payoffs for every realization of the state and every action profile.

A richer example is the resource allocation model studied in Groves and Radner (1972), Radner (1972), Arrow and Radner (1979), and Groves (1983). The basic decision problem is the resource allocation problem (9) outlined in Section 4.3, and the organizational structures typically resemble the decomposition given there, with a central production manager allocating resources and each unit manager controlling the unit's local decision variable. These models consider fixed, finite exchanges of information that do not resolve all uncertainty before decisions are made. A small sample of other models is Beckmann (1958), Groves and Radner (1972), Marschak (1972), Crémer (1980), Aoki (1986), and Green and Laffont (1986).

Team theory can incorporate both implicit and explicit constraints on the information-processing capacity of individual agents. As an example of implicit constraints, Crémer (1980) studies a quadratic version of the resource allocation problem and characterizes the optimal grouping of shops when resources can only be allocated within groups of a fixed size. The story is that any manager who allocates resources only has the capacity to do so for a fixed number of shops. As an example of explicit constraints, suppose that, in an extension of Crémer (1980), information about shops is available as noisy signals of the shops' payoff parameters. A manager has the capacity to process a fixed number of signals but can compute any statistically optimal decision rule conditional on this information. One could characterize how many shops should be assigned to each manager and which signals a manager should observe.

5.2. Hierarchical Resource Allocation with Dispersed Information

The hierarchically decomposed resource allocation procedures in Section 4.4 are an interesting setting in which to incorporate dispersed information and to understand the optimal team decision rules. In such hierarchies, the decisionmaking is the recursive downward disaggregation of resource allocations. The upward aggregation of payoff information determines the information that each office has when choosing how to allocate resources. In the procedures studied in Section 4.4, such aggregation yields all information each office needs to optimally allocate resources. However, it would be natural that offices lack such full information—perhaps because information is lost during the aggregation.

In Section 7, we examine a model of aggregation of information that leads to such a loss. We begin, however, with a paper by Geanakoplos and Milgrom (1991) (henceforth, GM91), which imposes exogenous constraints on the information available to each node of the hierarchy and thereby focuses on the optimal decision rules for the disaggregation of resource allocations. By incorporating some flexibility about the information available to each manager, the model also yields results about the benefits of decentralization and about optimal hierarchical structures.

Consider, then, a hierarchy such as shown in Figure 3. Write the payoff of shop i as $u_i(x_i, \phi_i)$, where ϕ_i is a random parameter that captures the uncertainty about i's payoff function. Replace the upward aggregation of information by an exogenous information set ϕ_j for each office $j \in J$. A decision rule or strategy for office j gives j's allocation to each subordinate k as a function $x_k(x_j, \phi_j)$ of j's own allocation and of the realization of j's information. We look for decision rules that maximize the total expected profit of the firm.

Because the disaggregation of resources is recursive, this game is sequential rather than static. Therefore, a manager's resource allocation to a subordinate conveys some of the manager's information. This could throw a wrench into the model, because (i) the inference and resulting decision rules could be complicated and (ii) without a model of communication complexity, the resource allocation could encode an arbitrary amount of information, thereby circumventing the implicit information processing constraints in the model. Therefore, GM91 restrict attention to information structures in which a subordinate's information about shops below that subordinate in the hierarchy are a sufficient statistic for her superior's information about those shops. This restriction is reasonable and would hold, for example, if the shops' payoffs are independently distributed and if each manager's information is obtained by a lossy aggregation of information received from his subordinates.

The optimal decision rules can then be derived recursively from the bottom of the hierarchy moving up. For any office j, let $u_j(x_j, \phi_j)$ be the maximum expected profit conditional on the realization ϕ_j of j's information and on the resources j receives, given that j and the offices subordinate to j follow optimal decision rules. Then office j solves

$$\max_{\{x_k\}_{k \in \Theta_j}} \sum_{k \in \Theta_j} E[u_k(x_k, \phi_k) \mid \phi_j], \tag{14}$$

and $u_j(x_j, \phi_j)$ is the value function for this maximization problem.

This model is nice enough in the abstract, but to say more about optimal hierarchies and the distribution of information in a hierarchy, a more quantifiable model is needed. Many functional forms for the payoffs would be intractible, because, in (14), $u_k(x_k, \phi_k)$ can depend in a complicated way on k's information ϕ_k, leading to a complicated interrelationship among the information from different offices—in the derivation of both the optimal decision rules and the maximized expected profit.

To avoid this problem, we would like a functional form whereby $u_k(x_k, \phi_k)$ equals the full-information maximized payoff on the subhierarchy rooted at k plus a loss that depends on ϕ_k but not on x_k—and hence that does not matter for the solution to (14). That is, each office should then allocate resources as if the offices below had complete information, and we can attribute a loss to each office that equals the difference between the maximized payoff the office would achieve if it had full information and the actual payoff it achieves. The overall profit of the hierarchy equals the full-information maximized payoff plus the sum of the offices' losses.

Both quadratic payoffs and logarithmic payoffs have exactly this property. GM91 assume quadratic payoffs, as in Section 4.5:

$$u_i(x_i, \gamma_i) = \bar{u}_i - b_i^{-1}(x_i - \gamma_i)^2, \tag{15}$$

where γ_i is a random variable, but $\bar{u}_i$ and b_i are known constants. The kind of certainty equivalence that one expects from such quadratic payoffs holds in this recursive model. That is, the optimal decision rules have manager j set[5]

$$x_k^* = \hat{\gamma}_k^j + \frac{b_k}{b_j}(x_j - \hat{\gamma}_j^j), \tag{16}$$

where $\hat{\gamma}_k^j = E[\gamma_k \mid \phi_j]$, and $\hat{\gamma}_j^j = E[\gamma_j \mid \phi_j] = \sum_{k \in \Theta_j} \hat{\gamma}_k^j$. (That is, whereas γ_k is a random variable, $\hat{\gamma}_k^j$ is the expectation of this variable conditional on j's information.) The loss of office j can be shown to be[6]

$$L_j\big(\langle \gamma_k, \hat{\gamma}_k^j \rangle_{k \in \Theta_j}\big) = -b_j^{-1}(\gamma_j - \hat{\gamma}_j^j)^2 + \sum_{k \in \Theta_j} b_k^{-1}(\gamma_k - \hat{\gamma}_k^j)^2. \tag{17}$$

---

5. This allocation rule is part of Proposition 1 in GM91 and is analogous to equation (A8) in Crémer (1980).

6. See Van Zandt (1996) for details on this particular form, which is similar to equation (9) in GM91 and equation (A12) in Crémer (1980).

GM91 write the expected payoff as the no-information expected payoff plus the sum of the values of the managers' information. This is done as follows. Suppose that no manager has any information. Then for all $j \in J$, $\hat{\gamma}_j^j = E[\gamma_j] \equiv \bar{\gamma}_j$, and for all $k \in \Theta_j$, $\hat{\gamma}_k^j = E[\gamma_k] \equiv \bar{\gamma}_k$. Hence, manager j's loss is $L_j\big(\langle \gamma_k, \bar{\gamma}_k \rangle_{k \in \Theta_j}\big)$. Define the ex post value of manager j's information to be the difference

$$\tilde{v}_j \equiv L_j\big(\langle \gamma_k, \bar{\gamma}_k \rangle_{k \in \Theta_j}\big) - L_j\big(\langle \gamma_k, \hat{\gamma}_k^j \rangle_{k \in \Theta_j}\big)$$

between j's loss if j had no information and j's actual loss. Then the total payoff equals the no-information total payoff plus $\sum_{j \in J} \tilde{v}_j$. Let U_R^{ni} be the expected value of the no-information payoff and let $v_j = E[\tilde{v}_j]$, which we call the "value of j's information." Then the expected value of the total payoff is equal to $U_R^{\mathrm{ni}} + \sum_{j \in J} v_j$. A little algebra shows that

$$U_R^{\mathrm{ni}} = \bar{u}_R - b_R^{-1}(x_R - \bar{\gamma}_R)^2 - \sum_{i=1}^{n} b_i \operatorname{Var}(\gamma_i) \tag{18}$$

and

$$v_j = -b_j \operatorname{Var}(\hat{\gamma}_j^j) + \sum_{k \in \Theta_j} b_k \operatorname{Var}(\hat{\gamma}_k^j) . \tag{19}$$

The organization design problem in GM91 is to specify a hierarchy and information acquisition for each manager, given constraints on the possible information structures that a manager can acquire, to maximize the expected payoff minus the managerial wages. Observe that the value of a manager's information does not depend on his resource allocation; therefore, it is irrelevant whether a manager's information acquisition is decided after he learns his allocation or before.

A necessary condition for optimality is that the *value of each manager,* which we define to be the decrease in expected payoffs when the manager is fired, be no less than the manager's wage. In this hypothetical firing of a manager, we assume that the information structure for the remaining managers is not modified, and that the fired manager's immediate subordinates receive allocations from the manager's immediate superior, if he has one. If the manager is instead the root, then the manager's subordinates become the root managers of independent organizations. Because the role of managers is to acquire information in order to allocate resources, we assume that independent firms obtain their zero-information optimal allocation.[7] The value of a manager other than the root depends on the information her immediate superior has about her immediate subordinates' payoff functions. An easily calculated upper bound on the value of a manager is the value v_j of the manager's information.

5.3. Benefit of Decentralization

The benefit of decentralization in this model is that it allows more information to be brought to bear on decisionmaking. As a particularly simple example, suppose that each manager can

---

7. Under symmetry assumptions, then, the allocation to each firm is proportional to the firm's size.

observe the aggregate payoff parameters of 3 immediate subordinates. Then a single manager can solve the allocation problem without error only if she allocates resources to 3 shops. However, q managers, organized in *any* hierarchy—including a uniform hierarchy—such that each has a span of 3, can solve without error the resource allocation problem for $2q + 1$ shops.[8]

5.4. Economies of Scale

The informationally integrated unit in GM91 is the hierarchy, and the size of this unit, for the purpose of characterizing economies of scale, is the number n of shops. In this section, an optimal hierarchy or firm size is one that maximizes per-unit profit (expected shop payoffs minus managerial costs).

The information-processing constraints in GM91 do not limit firm size without additional assumptions and regularity restrictions on hierarchies. This is because one can always merge two firms by making one a subsidiary of the other in a way that increases total expected payoffs but does not change the managerial costs. Specifically, the root manager of one firm is made a subordinate of any manager in the other firm. Even without acquiring information about the subsidiary, the immediate superior of the subsidiary can make advantageous transfers to the subsidiary based only on information about her own shops. For example, with quadratic payoffs, the manager equates the expected marginal payoffs of her immediate subordinates, conditional on her information. In the absence of information about the subsidiary, the expected marginal payoff of any transfer to the subsidiary is deterministic; however, the expected marginal payoff of transfers to the manager's other immediate subordinates depends on the realization of her information.

The hierarchy that results from the merger just described is typically not balanced. This model may have a bounded firm size under the restriction that the hierarchy be balanced; under the assumption that managers have access to only disaggregate information with a bound on the total amount of information, given a positive managerial wage; and under the following symmetry assumptions:

1. $b_i = 1$ for all i.
2. $\{\gamma_i\}_{i \in I}$ are iid, with mean 0 and variance σ^2.
3. For any collection of shops, total resources are 0. (Coordination involves only transfers between shops.)
4. $\bar{u}_i = \sigma^2$. (This is merely a normalization that sets the no-information expected payoff to 0.)

Rather than providing a formal proof of the bounded firm size under these assumptions, we outline the intuition. If a manager has access to only disaggregate information, then the value of information is low, unless she is sufficiently close to some shops, in the following sense: she must have at least one subordinate whose division does not have too many shops. If the hierarchy is balanced, so that all subordinate divisions are the same size, then there is a bound on the size of any of the root's subordinates. Then the total size of the hierarchy can be large only if the root

---

8. In any tree with q interior nodes that all have s children, there are a total of qs children, $q - 1$ of which are interior nodes. Hence, there are $q(s - 1) + 1$ terminal nodes.

has many subordinates. However, the root manager's per-subordinate value of information goes to zero as the number of her subordinates increases, given the bound on the total amount of the root's disaggregate information. Hence, it is better to take a very large hierarchy, in which the root manager is essentially irrelevant, and divide it among two root managers.

6. Decentralized Computation in Hierarchies

In the model of GM91, the limitations on the information that any manager can have are exogenous. Furthermore, the likely source of some of the managers' information, through an upward aggregation of information in the hierarchy, is not modeled.

The next approach instead starts with raw data and managerial processing capacities as the primitives. Any information that a manager may end up with comes through explicitly modeled information processing.

6.1. A Model of Decentralized Batch Processing

The nature of information-processing constraints is that people are bounded in the amount they can process in a given amount of time. It is possible to suppress the temporal aspect of these constraints and simply bound the total amount of processing an agent can do, as in Geanakoplos and Milgrom (1991) and Marschak and Reichelstein (1995, 1998). However, we focus on models that emphasize this temporal aspect.

One approach that emphasizes computational delay is decentralized batch processing, known in computer science as parallel or distributed batch processing (see Zomaya 1996). Kenneth Mount and Stanley Reiter, starting in 1982, have advocated this as a model of human organizations. Models of organizations based on decentralized batch processing include Malone and Smith (1988), Mount and Reiter (1990, 1996), Radner (1993), Bolton and Dewatripont (1994), Friedman and Oren (1995), Reiter (1996), Meagher and Van Zandt (1998), Van Zandt (1998), Beggs (2001), and Orbay (2002). The value of decentralizing information processing in these papers is typically that it reduces delay; in the periodic models of Radner (1993), Bolton and Dewatripont (1994), and Van Zandt (1998), it also increases the rate (throughput) at which problems can be computed.

The first part of a decentralized batch-processing model is a function $f: Y \to Z$ to be computed. The input domain Y is typically multidimensional, in which case all data in the vector $y \in Y$ are available when the computation starts. The other part of a decentralized batch-processing model is a decentralized computational model, which consists of the following components:

1. a set of elementary operations—functions that, when composed, can yield f;

2. a description of how the processing activities of agents are coordinated and how information is communicated between agents—this may include a communication protocol;

3. a set of potential information-processing agents, each of whom is characterized primarily by the time it takes the agent to perform each elementary operation and each operation in the communication protocol.

Given a decentralized batch-processing model, a *procedure* (algorithm) specifies how one or more agents calculate $f: Y \to Z$ by performing elementary operations and sharing information.

For the resource allocation problem in Section 4, the function to be computed is $f: \mathcal{U}^n \times X \to X^n$, where $f(u_1, \ldots, u_n, x_R)$ is the solution to (11), and $\mathcal{U}$ is the set of potential payoff functions. Assume that $\mathcal{U}$ is a set of strictly convex and differentiable payoff functions such that $\mathcal{U}$ is closed under the operation $\oplus$ and such that the resource allocation problem (11) has a solution for all $\{u_i \in \mathcal{U}\}_{i=1}^n$ and $x_R \in X$.

As explained in Section 6.2, we have some discretion in choosing the set of elementary operations. The following suit the objectives of this section:

1. (aggregation of two payoff functions) $f_1: \mathcal{U}^2 \to \mathcal{U}$, where $f_1(u_a, u_b) = u_a \oplus u_b$;

2. (derivative of a payoff function) $f_2: \mathcal{U} \times X \to \mathbb{R}$, where $f_2(u, x) = u'(x)$; and

3. (inverse derivative of a payoff function) $f_3: \mathcal{U} \times \mathbb{R} \to \mathbb{R}$, where $f_3(u, p) = u'^{-1}(p)$.

These elementary operations are sufficient to compute $f(u_1, \ldots, u_n, x_R)$ as follows.

1. The aggregate payoff function $u_R := u_1 \oplus \cdots \oplus u_n$ can be calculated with $n - 1$ operations f_1.

2. The shadow price $p_R := f_2(u_R, x_R)$ of the resource can be calculated with one operation f_2.

3. The allocation of each shop i can then be computed by setting the shop's marginal payoff equal to the shadow price: $x_i := f_3(u_i, p_R)$. A total of n operations f_3 are needed.

Table 1 summarizes the elementary operations and the number that are performed to calculate $f(u_1, \ldots, u_n, x_R)$.

Next we specify the means by which agents communicate and are coordinated. We choose the simplest specification:

1. Agents are coordinated by synchronously executing instructions (the organization's managerial procedures).

2. There are neither individual nor network communication costs or delays.

Table 1. Elementary operations and serial and parallel delay for the resource allocation problem

Calculation	Elementary operation	Number of operations	Parallel delay
$u_R := u_1 \oplus \cdots \oplus u_n$	$f_1(u_A, u_B) = u_A \oplus u_B$	$n - 1$	$\lceil \log_2 n \rceil$
$p_R := u'_R(x_R)$	$f_2(u, x) = u'(x)$	1	1
$\{x_i := u_i'^{-1}(p_R)\}_{i=1}^n$	$f_3(u, p) = u'^{-1}(p)$	n	1
	Total:	$2n$	$2 + \lceil \log_2 n \rceil$

Note: $\lceil \cdot \rceil$ denotes the round-up operation.

Finally, we specify the capacities of the potential information-processing agents. We have already assumed that they are unconstrained in their communication abilities. We also assume the following:

1. Agents have identical computational abilities and wages.
2. Each elementary operation takes the same amount of time (a *cycle*).
3. Each agent is paid only when performing an operation, at a fixed wage per operation.
4. Each agent has unbounded memory.

Overall, we have the simplest possible specification of the communication among and coordination of agents. The lack of communication costs and delays means that agents have equal access to all raw data and partial results. Therefore, it does not matter which agents perform which operations each cycle—as long as no agent performs more than one operation at a time. Such a model is called a "parallel random access machine" in computer science.[9]

6.2. Discussion of the Computational Model

We have chosen a very simple model in terms of both the decomposition of the problem into elementary operations and the interaction among information-processing agents. In this section, we explain some of the options and considerations.

Consider first the selection of elementary operations. One of the reasons for decomposing the computation problem into elementary operations, whether processing is serial or parallel, is to compare the delay and processing costs of different types and sizes of problems. To do so, we must decompose the different problems into a common set of operations. Van Zandt (2003b), for example, compares the information processing for different numbers n of shops. Therefore, the aggregation $u_1 \oplus \cdots \oplus u_n$ of all the payoff functions should not be a single elementary operation, because this operation is different for different values of n. This is why the elementary operations we defined are all independent of n.

However, there are many sets of elementary operations that satisfy this invariance condition and that are sufficient to calculate $f: \mathcal{U}^n \times X \to X^n$. We must balance other goals when choosing among the possible specifications. On the one hand, a coarse decomposition is simpler. On the other hand, a fine decomposition permits more decentralized processing (the assignment of different elementary operations to different agents) and a more complete and realistic description of the actual activities of the agents.

The other simple features of this computational model suppress some potentially interesting issues, such as the problem of economizing memory and communication costs, the coordination of agents who are not synchronized, the scheduling of tasks when agents must be paid even when idle, and the assignment of tasks to agents with heterogeneous computational abilities and wages.

Note, however, that the computational delay could be due either (i) to human delays in reading, understanding, and interpreting information or (ii) to human delays in calculating with

---

9. See Zomaya (1996) for an overview of the parallel random access machine and other models of parallel computation. Our model is also a special case of the one in Mount and Reiter (1990). Their formalization deals with certain technical issues related to real-number computation and to the measurement of communication costs, which our model suppresses.

information they have already "loaded" into their brains. (In a model with "reading delays," there would be an implicit communication cost: the managerial wages for the time it takes agents to read messages.)

Communication costs are important for two themes in much of the economics literature on decentralized batch processing:

1. Decentralizing information processing entails a trade-off between delay and communication costs. As more administrators share the operations and hence more operations are performed concurrently, delay is decreased but communication costs increase.

2. The pattern of communication among individual administrators, which has been interpreted as an organization's structure, also affects costs. Without communication costs, this microcommunication is indeterminate; when all agents have equal access to all information at all times, the identities of the agents who perform the operations each cycle are not relevant to the performance of the procedure. However, Van Zandt (2003a) contends that organizational structure should be derived from the macrostructure of decisionmaking more than from the microstructure of message exchange among individual agents.

6.3. Decentralization and Delay

This section describes two batch-processing procedures and illustrates how decentralization reduces delay. In the first procedure, a single agent (the "entrepreneur") calculates the resource allocation. The $2n$ operations listed in Table 1 must be performed sequentially by this agent, so the delay is $2n$.

Compare this procedure with decentralized information processing, in which potentially many agents compute the resource allocation jointly. In the first stage, $u_R := u_1 \oplus \cdots \oplus u_n$ is calculated. The efficient algorithms for associative computation with a parallel random access machine are illustrated in Figure 4. In the first cycle, the payoff functions are divided into pairs, and each pair is assigned to a different agent, who calculates the aggregate of the two payoff functions. In each subsequent cycle, the aggregate payoff functions computed in the previous cycle are grouped into pairs, and again each pair is assigned to an agent who calculates the aggregate. The number of partial results is reduced by half in each cycle, so there is a single pair in cycle $\lceil \log_2 n \rceil$, whose aggregate is u_R. (The brackets $\lceil \cdot \rceil$ denote the ceiling or round-up operation.) Hence, the delay is $\lceil \log_2 n \rceil$ rather than the $n - 1$ cycles it takes a single agent to compute u_R. However, the computation of u_R still requires $n - 1$ operations.

The next step is to compute $p_R := f_2(u_R, x_R)$, which one agent does in one cycle. Finally, the n operations $\{x_i := f_3(u_i, p_R)\}_{i=1}^n$ can be assigned to n different agents and executed concurrently in one cycle. As summarized in Table 1, the total delay when the computation is decentralized is $2 + \lceil \log_2 n \rceil$, compared to $2n$ when a single agent calculates the allocations. This reduction in the delay is the benefit of decentralization.

The only administrative (computational) costs in this model are the wages of the agents. These are proportional to the total number of operations, which is $2n$ whether the computation is performed by one agent or many. Hence, there is no administrative overhead incurred by decentralization. This is because we assume that there are no communication costs and that agents are paid only for the operations they perform. Under different assumptions, such as in Radner (1993), increasing the number of agents who jointly calculate f reduces the delay but increases the administrative costs.

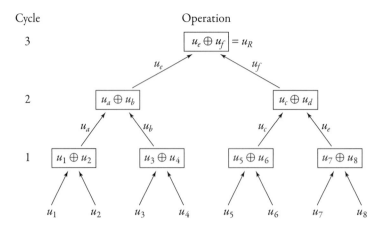

Figure 4. Associative computation by a parallel random access machine.

How does this batch-processing model relate to Figure 3? The aggregation of payoff functions in Figure 3 is similar to the decentralized aggregation of payoff functions in our batch-processing model. However, the disaggregation of resource allocations in Figure 3 has no analogue.

Consider first the aggregation of payoff functions. If we treat each interior node in Figure 3 as an information-processing agent in our computational model, then it takes an agent $j \in J$ who has s_j immediate subordinates a total of $s_j - 1$ cycles to compute her aggregate payoff function. Agents b, c, and d can start this calculation at the same time; they finish after two, one, and two cycles, respectively. Then agent a computes $u_a := u_b \oplus u_c$ in the third cycle, and agent R computes $u_R := u_a \oplus u_d$ in the fourth cycle. The total delay of 4 is less than the delay of 7 for a single agent. This result is similar to the parallel computation of u_R that is shown in Figure 4. (Although the nodes in Figure 4 are operations, it is possible to assign each operation to a different agent, in which case the nodes in Figure 4 correspond to agents.)

In contrast, there is no analogue in this batch-processing model to the hierarchical disaggregation of resource allocations. In the computational procedure described in this section and shown in Table 1, resources are allocated to all shops in a single step, once the shadow price p_R is calculated. Suppose instead that, as in Figure 3, there is a recursive disaggregation of resource allocations. Starting with the root, each agent j receives the allocation x_j for its division, calculates its shadow price $p_j := u'_j(x_j)$, and then allocates resources to each subordinate $k \in \Theta_j$ by setting x_k so that $u'_k(x_k) = p_j$. With such a procedure, the shadow price is the same at every node, and the only useful operations are the calculation of the overall shadow price $p_R := u'_R(x_R)$ and of the individual shops' allocations $x_i := u'^{-1}_i(p_R)$. The calculations of intermediate shadow prices and allocations increases not only the number of operations (by twice the number of intermediate nodes) but also the delay (by twice the number of intermediate tiers).

7. Real-Time Decentralized Information Processing

7.1. Measuring the Cost of Delay

For the moment, ignore the question of why resource allocations might be disaggregated hierarchically. Instead, motivate the next step by supposing that we have a batch-processing model with communication costs and that we have derived the set of efficient procedures, in which there is a trade-off between delay and administrative cost (as is done, e.g., in Radner 1993; Van Zandt 1998). To determine which procedures are optimal or to study how information-processing constraints affect economies of scale, we need to measure the administrative cost and the cost of delay. Administrative cost is easy to measure—for example, by managerial wages. Delay, however, is not an input that we can buy at a constant unit price. Instead, it has a decision-theoretic cost—higher delay means that decisions are based on older information.

To quantify the cost of delay, we need a temporal decision problem in which current decisions are computed from lagged information. A decision procedure is then a decision rule together with a computational procedure for computing the decision rule. The computation of the decision rule must adapt to the timing of the arrival of information and that of the decision epochs. This problem is one of real-time or on-line control.

We obtain a simple temporal version of the resource allocation problem in (11) by assuming there are discrete time periods $t \in \{\ldots, -1, 0, 1, \ldots\}$ and that, at the beginning of each period t, new payoff functions $\{u_{1t}, \ldots, u_{nt}\}$ are realized and observed and a deterministic quantity x_{Rt} of the resource must be allocated. That is, the payoff in period t when the allocation of x_{Rt} is $\{x_{1t}, \ldots, x_{nt}\}$ equals $\sum_{i=1}^{n} u_{it}(x_{it})$. We are assuming that the resource constraint must be satisfied each period; hence, there is no intertemporal allocation of resources. However, the informational structure is dynamic, because allocations are computed from past observations of the payoff functions.

We can use the same computational model as in Section 6 for the computation of the decision rules, but we need to specify the relationship between a cycle (the unit of time in the computation model) and a period (the unit of time in the decision problem). We assume that a cycle and a period are the same; this assumption simplifies notation but is not important for the qualitative results.

We measure the net performance in each period by the expected payoff of the decision rule minus the administrative cost of the computational procedure, and we call it the "profit." To determine the expected payoff of a decision rule, we need assumptions about the stochastic process $\{u_{1t}, \ldots, u_{nt}\}_{t=-\infty}^{\infty}$. However, for the purpose of this section—which is to derive a qualitative rather than quantitative value of decentralized decisionmaking—the reader should simply imagine that we have imposed statistical assumptions such that decision rules that use old information tend to have a lower expected payoff than those that use recent information.

In this real-time setting, the following stationary procedures resemble batch processing and compute the allocation for each period from data of homogeneous lags. The resource allocation for each period t is calculated, in the manner described in Section 6, from the payoff functions $\{u_{1,t-d}, \ldots, u_{n,t-d}\}$ collected in period $t - d$.[10] The lag d is the delay in performing these computations, which is given in Table 1. With serial processing (one agent), the allocation in each period is calculated from the payoff functions from $2n$ periods ago, whereas with decentralized computation, each allocation is calculated from the payoff functions from $2 + \lceil \log_2 n \rceil$

---

10. With specific statistical assumptions, as in Van Zandt (2003a), we could allow the decision rule to take into account the expected change in the payoff functions between periods $t - d$ and period t.

Because the shadow price is calculated from $\{u_{i,t-d_1}\}_{i=1}^{n}$, the final step in which the marginal payoff is set equal to the shadow price must use these same payoff functions (rather than more recent ones) to balance the allocation.

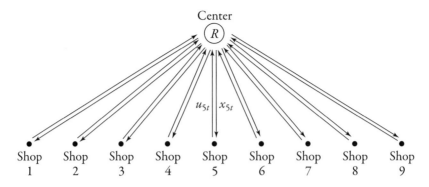

Figure 5. A two-tier centralized hierarchy.

periods ago. Such decentralization leads to lower delay and hence more recent information and a higher payoff.

We consider this decision procedure to be a two-tier hierarchy, as shown for $n = 9$ in Figure 5. The single administrative node, which is the root node R or center, is an office in which reside the agents who compute the decision rule. Each period, this office collects the current payoff functions from the shops and sends the current allocation to the shops. In period t, the organization is busy computing the allocations for periods $t + 1, \ldots, t + d$. Although these computations overlap temporally, they are independent and do not use common data. As in Section 6.3, there is decentralized information processing in the central office, because the procedure is computed in parallel, but decisionmaking is not decentralized, because, in each period, all the shops' allocations are computed from the same data. In particular, there is no hierarchical disaggregation of resource allocations.

7.2. A Procedure with Decentralized Decisionmaking

In this real-time model, we are not restricted to procedures, such as those of Section 7.1, in which each period's decisions are calculated from data of the same lag. We now specify a procedure without this property.

We first present the hierarchical structure that we ascribe to the procedure. Assume there are integers $s_1, s_2 \geq 2$ such that $n = s_1 s_2$. Consider a balanced three-tier hierarchy in which the span of an office in tier $h \in \{1, 2\}$ is s_h. Thus, the root (in tier 2) has s_2 immediate subordinates, which are offices in tier 1, and each of these offices has s_1 immediate subordinates, which are shops in tier 0. There are thus $s_1 s_2 = n$ shops. Such a hierarchy is shown in Figure 6 for $n = 9$ and $s_1 = s_2 = 3$.

In this decision procedure, each office calculates resource allocations in much the same way as the center does in the procedure defined in Section 7.1. However, an office in tier 1 uses as its quantity of resources an amount that is sent by the center. The center uses as its payoff information the aggregate payoff functions calculated by the tier-1 offices. These aggregate payoff functions are also used by the tier-1 offices to determine the suballocations of resources to their subordinate shops.

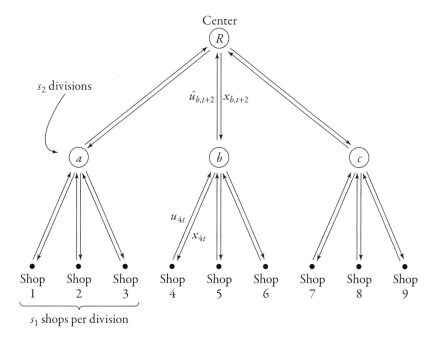

Figure 6. Information flow at the beginning of period t in a three-tier hierarchy.

Disregard the root of this hierarchy and imagine that we have simply divided the organization into s_2 independent units, which we call "divisions," even though they are independent. Each division contains s_1 shops. Because these divisions operate independently and resource allocations to the divisions are not coordinated, each division allocates a fixed fraction of the total resources. For example, if the allocations represent net trades, then the total amount of the resources available to the whole organization and to each division is 0. Denote division j's available resources in period t by x_{jt}.

Each of these divisions allocates resources using a two-tier hierarchy as described in Section 7.1, but with s_1 shops rather than n shops. These calculations are shown in the left column of Table 2. The delay is denoted by d_1 and is equal to $2 + \lceil \log_2 s_1 \rceil$. The aggregate payoff function and shadow price calculated by division j for the purpose of allocating resources in period t are denoted by $\hat{u}_{jt}$ and p_{jt} and are equal to $\bigoplus_{i \in \theta_j} u_{i,t-d_1}$ and $\hat{u}'_{jt}(x_{jt})$, respectively.

These divisions and their decision procedures correspond to the three subtrees under the center in Figure 6. The advantage of splitting the organization this way is that the delay $2 + \lceil \log_2 s_1 \rceil$ of each division is smaller than the delay $2 + \lceil \log_2 n \rceil$ of the unified two-tier organization in Section 7.1. However, gains from trade (coordination) among the divisions are lost.

To exploit some of these gains from trade, we add the central office, shown as the root node R in Figure 6. The center also uses a decision procedure like the two-tier procedure described in Section 7.1, but the center's immediate subordinates are the division offices instead of the shops. The data that the center uses are the aggregate payoff functions $\{\hat{u}_{jt}\}_{j \in \Theta_R}$ of the divisions, which are partial results of the divisions' decision procedures. The center's delay is $d_2 \equiv 2 + \lceil \log_2 s_2 \rceil$. Its calculations are shown in the right column of Table 2.

Table 2. Calculations by the divisions and the center in the three-tier hierarchy

	Division j	Center
Begin, ..., end	$t - d_1, \ldots, t - 1$	$t - 2 - d_2, \ldots, t - 3$
Delay	$d_1 = 2 + \lceil \log_2 s_1 \rceil$	$d_2 = 2 + \lceil \log_2 s_2 \rceil$
Data	$\{u_{i,t-d_1}\}_{i \in \theta_j}, \; x_{jt}$	$\{\hat{u}_{j,t-d_2}\}_{j \in \Theta_R}, \; x_{Rt}$
Aggregation	$\hat{u}_{jt} := \bigoplus_{i \in \theta_j} u_{i,t-d_1}$	$\hat{u}_{Rt} := \bigoplus_{j \in \Theta_R} \hat{u}_{j,t-d_2}$
Shadow price	$p_{jt} := \hat{u}'_{jt}(x_{jt})$	$p_{Rt} := \hat{u}'_{Rt}(x_{Rt})$
Allocation	$x_{it} := u'^{-1}_{i,t-d_1}(p_{jt})$	$x_{jt} := \hat{u}'^{-1}_{j,t-d_2}(p_{Rt})$

Note: $\lceil \cdot \rceil$ denotes the round-up operation.

As information is recursively aggregated and passed up the hierarchy, it becomes older. As one might guess, the cumulative lag of the raw data that goes into the center's decisions equals $d_1 + d_2$.

For example, toward the end of August a division office finishes aggregating information about its immediate subordinates' resource needs and sends this information to its immediate superior. At the same time, it receives a budget for September, which in the next few days it disaggregates in order to assign a September budget to each of its subordinates. The center calculated the division's September budget using information sent by that division and the other divisions at the end of July, but the division office disaggregates the budget using more recent information, which it aggregated during August.

7.3. The Benefits and Costs of Decentralized Decisionmaking

In Section 7.2, we presented the three-tier hierarchy as a comparison of (i) independent two-tier hierarchies, between which there is no coordination, and (ii) a three-tier hierarchy, in which these two-tier hierarchies are coordinated by a central office. Now we compare (iii) a two-tier hierarchy that has no hierarchical disaggregation and (iv) a three-tier hierarchy with the same number of shops. That is, we compare Figures 5 and 6. To simplify this comparison, assume that s_1, s_2, and n are powers of two, so that the round-up operations in the formulas or the delay in the previous sections can be ignored.

It may appear that one difference between the two- and three-tier hierarchies is that, in the latter, the aggregation of payoff functions is hierarchically decomposed and hence more decentralized. However, remember that each node in these hierarchies is an office containing multiple information-processing agents, and the aggregation of payoff functions is always maximally decentralized in each node. Thus, the hierarchical decomposition of the aggregation of payoff functions, which is explicit in Figure 6, also exists in the center in Figure 5. In particular, observe that in a three-tier hierarchy, the center finishes calculating in period $t - 4$ the aggregate payoff function $\hat{u}_{Rt}$ that it uses to allocate resources for period t. Furthermore, $\hat{u}_{Rt} = \bigoplus_{i=1}^{n} u_{i,t-d_1-d_2}$. Hence, the aggregate payoff function is calculated in

$$d_1 + d_2 - 4 = (2 + \log_2 s_1) + (2 + \log_2 s_2) - 4 = \log_2 n$$

periods in the three-tier hierarchy. This delay is exactly the same as that in the two-tier hierarchy.

The actual difference between the two- and three-tier hierarchies is the disaggregation of resource allocations. The center in a three-tier hierarchy, after calculating its aggregate payoff function $\hat{u}_{Rt}$ and then its shadow price p_{Rt}, does not allocate resources directly to the shops in one step. Instead, it calculates allocations for the divisions, whose offices then calculate suballocations for the shops. We interpret this procedure as decentralized decisionmaking. Its advantage may be summarized as follows.

When a division receives x_{jt} from the center in period $t-2$, it does not have to allocate x_{jt} using the information $\hat{u}_{j,t-d_2}$ that the center used to compute x_{jt}. Instead, it uses its most recently calculated aggregate payoff function $\hat{u}_{jt}$. That is, the data used to allocate resources in each division in a three-tier hierarchy are $2+\log_2 s_1$ periods old, and hence $\log_2 n - \log_2 s_1 = \log_2 s_2$ periods more recent than the data used to compute allocations in the two-tier hierarchy.

The intermediate disaggregation of resource allocations adds two extra steps: the calculations of the divisions' allocations and the divisions' shadow prices. This leads to two disadvantages of the three-tier hierarchy compared to the two-tier hierarchy:

1. In the three-tier hierarchy, gains from trade among shops in different divisions are exploited by the center. The cumulative lag of the center's data that it uses to allocate resources is

$$d_1 + d_2 = (2+\log_2 s_1) + (2+\log_2 s_2) = 4 + \log_2 n.$$

   This delay is two periods greater than the center's lag in the two-tier hierarchy. The extra lag is a *decision-theoretic cost* of decentralized decisionmaking.
2. The three-tier hierarchy also has higher managerial costs. The center's calculations in the three-tier hierarchy involve $2s_2$ operations per period. Each division's calculations involve $2s_1$ operations per period. Hence, the total number of operations is $2s_2 + s_2(2s_1) = 2s_2 + 2n$. In contrast, the number of operations in the two-tier hierarchy is only $2n$. The wages paid for the $2s_2$ additional operations in the three-tier hierarchy are a *managerial cost* of decentralized decisionmaking.

The benefits and costs are summarized in Table 3.

We have now described real-time decision procedures that correspond to two- and three-tier hierarchies that are balanced (each node in the same tier has the same number of subordinates). Van Zandt (2003a) generalizes the real-time procedures to arbitrary hierarchies. Increased decentralization of decisionmaking corresponds to additional intermediate tiers. The benefits and costs of three- versus two-tier hierarchies arise again as additional tiers are added.

7.4. Optimal Hierarchies and Economies of Scale

To go beyond this qualitative treatment of the benefits and costs of decentralization, we need to make concrete assumptions about the functional forms and shocks affecting payoffs. Van Zandt (2003a,b) develops a model with quadratic costs. Although the possibility of decentralizing

Table 3. The benefits and costs of decentralized decisionmaking (three-tier versus two-tier hierarchies)

Two-tier	delay	$2 + \log_2 n$
Three-tier	delay of each division	$2 + \log_2 s_1$
Difference	**decrease** in division's delay	$\log_2 s_2$
Two-tier	delay	$2 + \log_2 n$
Three-tier	center's cumulative delay	$(2 + \log_2 s_1) + (2 + \log_2 s_2)$
Difference	**increase** in center's delay	2
Two-tier	operations of center	$2n$
Three-tier	operations center and divisions	$2s_2 + s_2(2s_1)$
Difference	**increase** in operations	$2s_2$

decisionmaking in these hierarchical organizations allows for larger hierarchies, organization size is still bounded. This is because the combined effect of cumulative delay and administrative costs means that in large enough hierarchies, the value of the root office's information processing is less than the office's administrative costs.

Furthermore, as the environment changes more rapidly, optimal hierarchies become smaller and more internally decentralized. A speed-up of managerial processing, such as through improved information technology, has the opposite effect.

8. Equilibrium Assignment of Talent to Teams and Hierarchies

8.1. Introduction

We have studied hierarchies that exist in isolation—organizations devised optimally to process information, acquire knowledge, and monitor individuals. But hierarchies exist in the market. The assignment of individuals to positions and jobs in a hierarchy is the other side of the occupational distribution in the labor market. For example, changing skill quantities in the job market due to offshoring or immigration will affect equilibrium wages, the assignment of individuals to teams, and the hierarchical organization of firms. Thus, an understanding of hierarchy can help us arrive at a better understanding of the impact of technology on the labor markets, as it will allow us to introduce in the analysis the changes in the organization of firms that result from a new technology or from the impacts of offshoring, brain drains, or different skill training and selection mechanisms in different countries. In sum, although decisionmaking and how it is affected by hierarchy are the focus in most of this chapter, we now move to exploring how hierarchy helps us understand more macro- or market-level facts—notably, the distribution of earnings, the distribution of firm sizes, trade patterns, the relation between growth and talent allocation, and so forth.

Neoclassical models of production, which use a variant of the generic form $Y = f(K, H)$, where K is physical capital and H is human capital, do not take a stand on the organization of production. That is, what matters is the total amount of physical and human capital employed;

no attention is paid to decisionmaking, information flows, and the allocation of responsibility. The internal organization of the firm is meant to be a separate object of study. But in fact, labor market and firm organization are the two sides of the same coin. The link between the two is the scale of operations effect: the marginal value of a worker's ability is given by the amount of resources he manages, as we discuss below. More broadly, the productivity of each individual is determined by other individuals with whom he works in a team. Thus, a worker's position in a hierarchy determines his marginal value of ability, and as a result determines labor and goods market outcomes, such as wages and productivity. Knowing the aggregate value of the human capital employed does not tell us its productivity; we need to know how and with whom these units of human capital are used. The firm size distribution and the earnings and productivity patterns in industries are jointly determined by the same underlying mechanism—the equilibrium assignment of individuals to firms and hierarchical positions.

The first two accounts of the scale of operations are by Mayer (1960) and Simon (1976). Their aim is explaining the skewness in the distribution of income. Specifically, as Mayer put it, how does a normal distribution of ability generate such a skewed distribution of income? The answer he provided (verbally) is that it must be the result of a scale of operations effect, through which those with higher ability are assigned more resources. This scale effect affects, in turn, the marginal value of ability. For example, a better concert pianist has higher earnings not only because consumers are willing to pay more for better performances but also because she plays in larger halls (scale).[11] Similarly, a more able lawyer wins more cases, and is assigned the largest ones; finally, earnings of entrepreneurs are skewed, because only the more talented agents have a positive span, and the differences in ability are multiplied by that span.

Simon (1976) first develops a model of hierarchy with the purpose of explaining the salaries of CEOs. The stylized fact that motivated his quest was the finding that the elasticity of CEO pay to firm size was around 0.37. (The survey by Rosen (1992) on CEO pay finds it to be 0.25.) There is no assignment or equilibrium aspect in his mechanical model. However, it does suggest some of what may be underlying these regularities. Specifically, Simon assumes that the span of control s is exogenous and fixed at all levels and that the exogenous salary multiple between levels is $b > 1$. Then the size of an L-level firm, as measured by the number of employees, is given by $N = 1 + s + s^2 + \cdots + s^{L-1} = (s^L - 1)/(s - 1) \simeq s^L/(s - 1)$. Similarly, the salary of the CEO is $w_{CEO} = w_0 b^{L-1} = w b^L$, where $w = w_0/b$. Letting the elasticity of compensation to size be $\varepsilon_{wN} = d \log w_{CEO}/d \log N$, simple computations imply that $\varepsilon_{wN} = \log b/ \log s$. Empirically, ε_{wN} is about 0.35. For example, with $b = 2$ and $s = 7$, we have $\varepsilon_{wN} = 0.3572$; with $s = 5$, and $b = 1.75$, $\varepsilon_{wN} = 0.35$. Of course, these simple calculations produce more questions than they answer—most notably, where do b and s come from?[12]

---

11. The "superstar" model of Rosen (1981) provided a formal model and a complete analysis of this scale of resources effect in the market.

12. Some more recent work in the spirit of Simon (1976) on CEO pay, notably Gabaix and Landier (2008), estimates a matching model with exogenously given firm sizes to empirically characterize the size-pay elasticity and to study whether the change in firm sizes may have caused the explosion in CEO pay. To do this, they use extreme value theory to estimate the earnings function that is derived from CEO-firm matching process. This work falls outside of the scope of this survey, as the size and the internal organization of firms are exogenously given.

8.2. Distribution of Income and the Allocation of Talent

Papers by Lucas (1978), Rosen (1982), Waldman (1984), and Garicano and Rossi-Hansberg (2006) aim to provide microeconomically founded models of the assignment of agents to positions in a neoclassical world. Essentially, the starting point of all this literature is the observation that the economy wide problem of assigning resources to talent generates skewness through the scale of operations effects. We briefly discuss these papers in what follows; the discussion is necessarily somewhat superficial, and, as in our previous sections, the reader is directed to the primary sources for a full account.

Some of the questions that these papers aim to deal with are: What determines the matching of individuals with positions and teams? What determines the salaries associated with those positions? How do changes in labor markets interact with changes in the organization of teams and/or firms? Four observations motivate this literature: (i) the distribution of firms' size is skewed to the right and is remarkably stable; (ii) the distribution of earnings is also quite stable and skewed to the right; (iii) earnings of top executive officers are enormous in magnitude and positively correlated with firm size; (iv) earnings within firms are positively correlated with rank.

8.2.1. Heterogeneous Managers of Homogeneous Workers

The first formal treatment of firms in equilibrium is Lucas (1978). Lucas argues that the observed size distribution is a solution to the problem: allocate productive factors over managers of different ability so as to maximize output. He departs minimally from the neoclassical production model in that, essentially, a manager is required to run a firm formed by a set of undifferentiated workers and capital. A manager with skill α shifts up the production that can be obtained by combining that labor and capital. Lucas' aim is not so much to have a theory of organization as a theory of why organization matters.

We present here the simplest possible version of Lucas's model, one that is considerably simpler than his but captures its essence. The resource allocation problem is essentially to divide the workforce, formed by N agents, into managers and workers, and to allocate the factors of production (labor N and capital K) across managers. To simplify the exposition, we ignore capital K. Managerial ability q is distributed according to a distribution ϕ of talent, $\phi : R^+ \rightarrow [0, 1]$, with cumulative distribution function Φ. Ability is defined and measured by how much an agent can raise the output of a team: a manager who has ability q and is allocated n workers produces $y = qf(n)$. Larger teams produce more, $f' > 0$, but there are decreasing returns to managerial talent, $f'' < 0$, and this results in limits to firm scale.[13] The firm's profits are then given by

$$\pi = qf(n) - wn, \tag{20}$$

where w is the wage of a worker. The first-order condition for the choice of firm size n is given by:

$$qf'(n) = w. \tag{21}$$

---

13. We apologize for changing the notation in the Lucas (1978) paper. We change it to ensure consistency with the notation of other papers we survey later. Also, Lucas's analysis focuses on the planners' problem, whereas our presentation focuses on the competitive equilibrium. There are no externalities or other factors, and the two formulations are equivalent, although the competitive one is simpler.

The solution of this first-order condition is a function $n(q)$, with $n'(q) > 0$ and possibly $n(q) = 0$, which describes the number of workers managed by agent q. The most skilled agents will choose to be entrepreneurs, because they benefit from their higher ability in two ways. First, for a given firm size n, they earn more. Second, the most skilled individuals hire a larger team $n(q)$ to leverage their ability or spread it over more agents. Note that the assumption $f'' < 0$ is key; if there are no decreasing returns to scale, the most able entrepreneur can manage all workers. Of course, the model is silent as to what leads to such congestion; the literature on hierarchies surveyed to this point addresses the source of these diseconomies.

Optimal occupational choice requires that an agent become an entrepreneur if

$$\pi = qf(n(q)) - wn(q) > w.$$

Thus, there exists a cutoff skill level q^* such that those with $q > q^*$ are entrepreneurs and the rest are workers. Finally, equilibrium requires that markets clear—that is, the supply and demand of workers must be equalized. The supply of workers is $\Phi(q^*)$, and the demand of workers by all available managers, $\int_{q^*}^{\infty} n(q)d\Phi(q)$. Thus we have

$$\Phi(q^*) = \int_{q^*}^{\infty} n(q)d\Phi(q). \tag{22}$$

Solving the model involves finding two constants, the cutoff level q^* and the equilibrium wage w. If, for example, the returns to scale shift up, then each entrepreneur wants to have a larger team, and $n(q)$ shifts up; equilibrium requires that both w and q^* move up. From the model we can obtain three interesting empirical distributions: of wages in the economy, of firm sizes, and of occupations.

Beyond the pathbreaking theoretical contribution that this simple model represents,[14] Lucas (1978) derives some interesting results. There is obviously a scale of operations effect ($n' > 0$ in equilibrium, as smarter managers manage larger firms). Moreover, there is a close connection between talent distribution and firm size distribution; for example, if one is Pareto, the other one is also Pareto. Also, under some restrictions on the productivity of talent, the model is consistent with Gibrat's law. Finally, there is a tight relation between managerial rents (or earnings) and firm size. However, the model has some problems. First, the relation between size and earnings obtained from the model is linear in n, that is, $R(x) = Cn(x)$. However, empirically, managerial compensation varies with the log of the number of employees, leading to the conclusion that multiple layers are needed to fit the data. Moreover, workers are undifferentiated, when in fact we know that talent is heterogeneous and thus the matching of workers to managers matters. Finally, contrary to the spirit of the rest of this chapter, the managerial technology is a black box—What are managers actually doing in these firms? Why do they raise workers' productivity?

---

14. Because of its tractability, the model has been widely used in macroeconomics. For example, the literature relies on Lucas (1978) to back up productivity heterogeneity from firm size heterogeneity. See Hopenhayn and Rogerson (1993: 928) and Atkeson and Kehoe (2007: 73).

8.2.2. Homogeneous Managers of Heterogeneous but Perfectly Substitutable Workers

Rosen (1982) expands on the Lucas technology by introducing heterogeneous workers. He adds an extra stylized fact to be understood—the within-firm correlation between pay and rank. Rosen argues that the way to explain the skewness of the earnings distribution is to combine a recursive productive technology with an assignment model like that of Lucas. From Rosen's perspective, the critical factor in the production technology must be that management makes discrete, indivisible decisions ("a great soldier is useless if in the wrong war") and thus, managerial talent filters down—a better decision benefits all workers. However, the technology must recognize that supervision involves scale diseconomies and congestion, which limit the scope of managerial ability and, eventually, firm size. The scale economies of management require that the most able people go to top positions in large firms. The diseconomies of supervision limit management effectiveness and allow the coexistence of many firms. Thus, the technology must capture three components: decisionmaking, supervision, and production. As we shall see, the model is essentially like the Lucas model, except that now workers are heterogeneous—it is not just the size of the team but the total efficiency units that matters. The model also has multiple numbers of layers. To capture this aspect, Rosen lets the output of one layer be intermediate output that is then aggregated by an upper level, so recursively, all layers actually have the same production function. Although this assumption is convenient, it again blackboxes what is going on at different levels.

To simplify the analysis, Rosen (1982) treats skill as one factor—all supervisory and worker skills are a linear transformation of the same underlying skill—and assumes the production function has constant returns to scale. As a result, output is simply a function of the efficiency units of labor (quality-adjusted quantity) controlled by managers; there is no matching, and who works with whom is not identified. Instead, the analysis determines the quality-adjusted span of control. Under these assumptions, the technology of Rosen in a two-layer world is a generalization of the Lucas technology:

$$\pi = q_m f(Q) - wQ, \tag{23}$$

where q_m is the ability of the manager, and Q is the efficiency units of labor managed by a manager with skill q_m. Everything proceeds as in Section 8.2.1, except that now workers with skills q_i earn wq_i. As a result, the wage schedule now increases in skill (it was flat in Lucas). The output of level-2 agents is an input to the level-3 agents, and thus, multiple layers can be built.

The occupational choice conditions are analogous to those of Lucas: $q_m f(Q(q_m)) - wQ(q_m) > wq_m$. The supply and demand are somewhat different: now we count efficiency units of labor, as one worker has q units. The market clearing condition becomes

$$\int_0^{q^*} q \, d\Phi(q) = \int_{q^*}^{\infty} Q(q) d\Phi(q) \tag{24}$$

(note the difference in the left-hand side, adding up over units of skill, rather than over agents). Some of the results in Lucas are again delivered here: more talented people command more resources as production and labor controlled rise more than proportionally with skills, and so does the reward for skill; earnings are skewed to the right, relative to the underlying skill distribution;

and the presence of multilevel firms tends to skew the distribution of rewards even more. In addition, whereas Lucas failed at matching the elasticity of pay to firm size, Rosen's model can match any constant empirical elasticity. Moreover, the microfoundation of the analysis is more extensive. What is missing from the analysis, however, is a full characterization of the equilibrium, as the multilayer firm problem is sketched but not solved. Further, the introduction of "intermediate-layer output" as the output of middle-layer managers is somewhat unsatisfactory. This is a black-box modeling device that obscures more than it clarifies.

Thus, as in Lucas (1978), only the quantity of resources, and not the quality of which they are composed, matters. But absent an element of imperfect substitutability between workers of different skill, these models do not allow for a full analysis of either the equilibrium assignment of individuals to one another or of earnings distributions. If skilled and unskilled workers are perfect substitutes, in equilibrium, then managers should be indifferent between working with a few relatively skilled workers or many unskilled workers. Assignment patterns between individual managers and workers would then be indeterminate. A more complete analysis of assignment patterns requires introducing production with imperfect substitutability. Kremer (1993) provides a building block for this improvement.[15]

8.2.3. Matching: Teams of Heterogeneous Workers

The starting point of Kremer's (1993) analysis is the observation that strong complementarities are common in production, as many production functions have a "weak link" aspect to them, so that output is given by the output of the least productive worker. For example, a space shuttle is as strong as the weakest of its O-rings. This type of production function can easily rationalize the common observation that (contrary to what happens in Rosen's (1982) hierarchy) even a large number of low-skill workers cannot substitute for one high-skill worker—100 bad lawyers are not better in dealing with a divorce filing than 1 excellent lawyer. There is no consideration of managerial skill, however, in this model, as all the matching takes place (as in Becker's 1973 marriage model) between similarly placed agents.

Production in Kremer's (1993) model requires n tasks, all of which must be correctly performed. Each worker's talent q_i determines the probability of success on her task; workers are further combined with k units of capital; productivity is B units of output per worker. The firm's problem is then

$$\max_{k,q_i} k^a n B \prod_{i=1}^{n} q_i - \sum_{i=1}^{n} w(q_i) - rk,$$

where $a \in (0, 1)$.

Clearly, positive sorting holds in equilibrium, as $\frac{d^2 y}{dq_i dq_j} > 0$, where y is output as given by the profit function. Firms with high-ability workers at the first $n - 1$ positions choose able

---

15. In the more general model of Waldman (1984), no restrictions on the interaction between managers' and workers' skills are imposed, but that only allows him to characterize the correlation between ability levels and hierarchical position and the skew of the wage distribution to the right with respect to the ability distribution. The specific model he analyzes rules out complementarities between worker and manager skills and as a result has equilibria where workers are more skilled than managers.

workers for the last one. When workers of the same skill are matched together, the first-order conditions are

$$\frac{dw}{dq} = q^{n-1}nBk^a,$$

$$ak^{a-1}q^nnB - r = 0.$$

Substituting the second equation into the first gives a differential equation in w', which can be solved to obtain the wage schedule, $w(a) = (1-a)q^nBk^a + c$. It is clear that $nw(q) = (1-a)Y + nc$; because capital reward is aY, zero profits implies $c = 0$. This is an equilibrium: firms are indifferent to hiring workers of different skills as long as the labor force in each firm is homogeneous.

Thus, when tasks are symmetric and complementary, an extreme form of segregation emerges in equilibrium, where individuals work only with others like themselves. This mechanism rationalizes large productivity differentials between rich and poor, as complementarities expand on the initial ability differentials across countries, regions, or firms. Moreover, different firms occupy different rungs in the quality of talent distribution; there is thus a positive correlation between wages of workers within firms (which is indeed observed empirically). Also, better quality workers must be used at later stages of production, where the impact of mistakes is larger. Finally, teams with more skill must be engaged in more complicated production processes, because a mistake is more likely in them.

8.2.4. Hierarchical Teams of Heterogeneous Workers

A further step in integrating the theory of hierarchy into an analysis of labor markets involves having workers who are not perfect substitutes for one another, so that matching is necessary, as in Kremer (1993). This refinement involves pinning down the specific talent of the specific worker who occupies a particular job and matches with one specific manager.

Kremer and Maskin (1996) first present a framework with matching and allocation of agents to different positions. However, there is no mechanism through which managers can exploit scale effects associated with their human capital: by definition, one agent is in the more productive position and one in the less productive one, so production is not hierarchical.

Imperfect substitutability is natural in a context like the problem-solving knowledge-based hierarchy in Garicano (2000). A hard problem can only be solved (or a hard decision taken) by a highly knowledgeable agent. Having multiple less-knowledgeable agents does not help, in the same way that several good high school students cannot deal with a hard topology problem if none of them has learned topology. Garicano and Rossi-Hansberg (2004, 2006) embed the model of knowledge-based hierarchies in Garicano (2000) in a context where workers are heterogeneous. In this model, workers are involved in production and managers in problem solving. From the result in Section 3, we can easily obtain the following elements of this production function. First, individuals of different skills are not perfect substitutes for one another; unlike in Rosen (1982), this extends to individuals acting as workers as well as managers. Second, managers' and workers' skills are complementary. Third, output is asymmetrically sensitive to managerial and worker skill; the asymmetric sensitivity follows naturally from the fact that teams are formed by workers and a manager, whose skill increases the productivity of all workers to which this skill is applied.

The model in Garicano and Rossi-Hansberg (2006) has multiple levels and endogenous knowledge. We present here a simpler version with only two layers and exogenous knowledge or skill, following Garicano and Rossi-Hansberg (2004), and discuss later the broader model's implications. This simpler version amounts to specializing the production technology in Section 3 to a case with heterogenous, but given, z, but limiting the analysis to a two-layer set-up. We label this exogenous skill or knowledge q to make it consistent with the rest of the section.

Suppose for now that organizations can only have one or two layers, so that agents can choose either to work on their own or with other agents. Teams are formed by managers, who specialize in problem solving, and production workers, who know only the routine tasks and specialize in production. Hence, a team of $n + 1$ agents, where n of them are production workers with knowledge q_p, has n units of production time. We normalize q so that skill is indexed by the percentile in the distribution of agents; that is, the population q is distributed according to a uniform distribution in $[0, 1]$.[16] The task distribution is $F[q]$, so that an agent with skill q can solve a fraction $F(q)$ of the problems that come up in the course of production.

The output produced by a team is then simply $F(q_m)n$, where q_m is the knowledge or skill of its manager. This is subject to the time constraint of the manager: the manager spends a fraction of time h communicating with each worker in his team when she cannot perform a task, which happens with probability $1 - F(q_p)$. The time constraint of managers is then given by $hn(1 - F(q_p)) = 1$. Thus, the span of the manager is limited by the knowledge of production workers; if production workers are more knowledgeable, they will need help less often, and managers will be able to supervise larger teams.[17]

A manager with skill q_m maximizes his earnings $\pi = F(q_m)n - w(q_p)n$ subject to his time $hn(1 - F(q_p)) = 1$. Substituting in the constraint yields

$$\pi = \frac{F(q_m) - w(q_p)}{(1 - F(q_p))h}. \tag{25}$$

Solving for an equilibrium in this economy is a continuous assignment problem (Sattinger 1993) with two twists relative to standard assignment problems. First, who is assigned to whom is not a given but is an equilibrium outcome. In standard assignment models, this identity of the agents is assumed. In contrast, here we are matching a mass of workers with a mass of managers— where those roles and masses are not given by assumption. Second, agents can decide not to be matched and produce on their own; their output is $F(q)$ in this case.

---

16. This normalization is not in the original Garicano and Rossi-Hansberg (2004), as they were not aware that the model could be simplified in this manner.

17. Note that there are no decreasing returns to scale directly in this production function, but only through the congestion in the time constraint of the manager. We thus have a trade-off between congestion and skill: a manager can increase team size if he so desires, but he needs to hire more skilled workers to do so. Thus, matching matters: having more agents does not, in fact, help to increase production, because they need extensive supervision. The only way to increase output is to hire more skilled agents who need less help.

Optimality requires positive sorting; that is, workers with more knowledge must be assigned to managers with more knowledge. Formally, $y = F(q_m)n = F(q_m)/((1 - F(q_p))h)$, and $\partial^2 y/\partial q_m \partial q_p > 0$. A more knowledgeable manager must spread his higher knowledge over a larger number of workers, and that requires workers to be more knowledgeable, so that they can deal with more problems on their own.

To characterize the equilibrium in this economy, we need to describe three objects: the allocation of agents to occupations (i.e., production workers, specialized problem solvers, and self-employed), the team composition (i.e., the matching between workers and managers, and the optimal spans of control of managers), and the earnings function.[18]

The slope of wage equation must be such that the first-order condition holds:

$$w'(q_p) = \frac{f(q_p)(F(q_m) - w(q_p))}{(1 - F(q_p))h}, \quad \text{for all } q_p \leq q^*. \tag{26}$$

This equation, as in Kremer's (1993) O-ring production function, results in a wage function $w(q)$ that uniquely determines the wage of each individual q for a given match q_p, q_m.

The wage slope for those agents who do not join in a hierarchy (independents) is given by $w'_I(q) = f(q)$, and it is clear that $w'(q_p) < w_I(q_p)$ for all workers (because for agents who are workers, $w(q_p) < F(q_p)$, and $(F(q_m) - F(q_p))/(1 - F(q_p)) < 1$). Using the Envelope Theorem, we have that the earnings function of managers is

$$\pi'(q_m) = \frac{f(q_m)}{(1 - F(q_p))h} > f(q_m) = w'_I(q_m).$$

For optimal occupational choice, it is necessary that for a marginal worker $w(q^*) = F(q^*)$ and for a marginal manager $\pi(q) = F(q)$. An equilibrium will be characterized by a pair of thresholds (q^*, q^{**}), such that all agents with skill $q < q^*$ become production workers, all agents with skill above q^{**} become managers, and those in between are self-employed.

Consider now the market clearing condition. Again, it is significant that worker-manager matching takes place in equilibrium. Instead of summing over all workers and managers, we need pointwise equalization of supply and demand:

$$\int_0^{q_p} d\Phi(q) = \int_{q^{**}}^{m(q_p)} n(m(q))d\Phi(q), \quad q_p \leq q^*, \tag{27}$$

where $m(q_p)$ denotes the skill of the manager assigned to workers with skill q_p. Because (27) holds for all $q_p \leq q^*$, $n = 1/((1 - F(q_p))h)$ and $\Phi(q) = q$ by normalization, we can differentiate with respect to q_p to obtain $m'(q_p) = h(1 - F(q_p))$. This result, together with $m(0) = q^{**}$ and $m(q^*) = 1$, determines the equilibrium assignment function $m(q)$.

18. Two of these objects, occupational choice and optimization, are as in Lucas (1978) and Rosen (1982), but the matching and wage functions are now pinned down in the equilibrium.

The model provides all the implications in Lucas (1978) and Rosen (1982), and some more. Among the common ones are the correspondence between firm size distribution and wage distribution and the fact that managerial wages grow faster than ability thanks to the scale effects (although workers' wages grow more slowly). Among the new results are that, the model pins down, for the first time, the occupational distribution in the economy: the less-skilled agents are workers, the medium-skilled agents are independent or self-employed, and the most-skilled agents are managers or problem solvers. Moreover, the team composition is specific. It is not merely that more skilled managers have more subordinates; those subordinates are also of better quality. Finally, the model's microfoundation in a hierarchical production function allows for comparative statics with respect to information costs. Specifically, as shown in Garicano and Rossi-Hansberg (2004), better communication costs increase firm size, wage inequality, and the share of workers and managers in an economy where the three types of agents coexist.

8.3. Economywide Applications

We discuss the implications of these models for broader economic issues, such as the impact of outsourcing, information technology, or rent seeking for the structure of wages, firms, and occupations in the economy. The discussion is necessarily brief, but with it we hope to illustrate a key point of this chapter and of the entire handbook: a better understanding of the "inside the firm" economics improves our understanding of broader economic questions.

8.3.1. *Information Technology and Wage Inequality*

Garicano and Rossi-Hansberg (2006) analyze the implications of information and communication technology for occupational distribution, firm size distribution, and wage distribution. Their framework is similar to the one discussed in Section 8.2 except that it allows for both acquisition and communication of information and also for multiple layers. They find that better information access and better communication technology have different implications for wage inequality and occupational distributions. Improvements in communication technology lead teams to rely more on problem solvers. As a result, wage inequality among workers decreases, but wage inequality among top managers and between managers and workers increases. Organizations also change as spans of control and the number of layers increase. Conversely, reductions in the cost of accessing information increase the number of problems solved by agents in all layers. This increases the marginal productivity of talent at all levels, and thus wage inequality in any particular occupation; it also reduces the number of layers in firms but also increases spans. They find empirical support for this hypothesis in the covariation of the patterns of information and communication technology over the past 30 years (first information technology and then communication technology advanced) and the patterns of wage inequality (first growing within worker classes and then between).

8.3.2. *Trade and Offshoring*

Grossman and Maggi (2000) study how different talent distributions in different countries affect patterns of international specialization and trade. They show that countries with more homogeneous talent distributions specialize in O-ring style production functions (i.e., activities with strong complementarities and for which all talents matter), and countries with more heterogeneous talent distributions specialize in the Lucas (1978) type of production functions ("superstar" functions, where only the talent of those most talented matters). They use this insight to rationalize the U.S. and Japanese specialization and trade patterns.

Antràs et al. (2006) apply a production function similar to the one in Garicano and Rossi-Hansberg (2004) discussed above to study the impact of the appearance of international production teams (offshoring) on wages and occupations. They show that the matches of all workers in the South improve when teams can be formed by production workers and problem solvers from different countries, while only the matches of the best workers in the North improve. As a result, wage inequality among workers increases in the South. In the North, overall wage inequality also increases when communication technology is sufficiently cheap and managerial skill is, as a result, particularly scarce (so that economizing on managerial skill through the use of talent is particularly important).

8.3.3. Growth

Murphy et al. (1991) present a dynamic version of the Lucas model (1978) to analyze the allocation of talent and its consequences for growth. There is a sector that works just like the Lucas sector, where entrepreneurs can leverage their abilities. The key departure from Lucas is that the technology in the next period increases with increasing ability of the entrepreneur allocated to the sector in the previous period—that is, growth depends on the talent allocated to each sector. There is an alternative sector that is pure rent seeking—its members earn a share of what rent seekers earn. Rent seeking leads to three distortions: it absorbs labor; it causes less-able entrepreneurs to become workers; and it causes the most-able entrepreneurs to become rent seekers. They show that a reduction in the share of profit extracted by rent seekers leads not only to higher levels of output (as fewer agents rent seek) but also to higher growth rates, as the talent of the most talented entrepreneurs increases.[19]

9. Conclusion

In this chapter, we have surveyed a literature that makes substantive progress toward explaining some empirical regularities of first-order importance: hierarchies are a crucial way to organize the division of labor in all organizations and present quite similar features across functions, sectors, and countries. We have argued that these striking regularities have to do with the large advantages that, given boundedly rational agents, hierarchies provide due to parallel information processing and aggregation and management by exception. Hierarchies allow managers to process and integrate very large amounts of information and knowledge in undertaking production tasks, and to coordinate large numbers of agents. As we have shown in this chapter, this is true *even if agents are angels* and have the best interests of the organization in mind, simply because hierarchies can bring to bear more knowledge and information on the production problems than any single manager can.

To focus on these bounded rationality issues, this chapter has abstracted from the monitoring and incentive functions of hierarchy. Mookherjee (this volume) takes the complementary view and studies managers as supervisors when agents' incentives are misaligned.

19. Garicano and Rossi-Hansberg (2012) also present a growth model, but it is more in the spirit of the models discussed in Section 3, as it has no a priori talent heterogeneity.

Clearly, both literatures are incomplete and focus only on half of the problem. Agents are boundedly rational, yes, but they also have different preferences and interests than the principal. As a result, hierarchies do facilitate the division of knowledge, process information, and ensure the smooth disaggregation of decisions, but they also serve to ensure the enforcement of rules of behavior by large groups of individuals. The literature to this point has failed to study how these two roles of hierarchy interact and what the implications of solving coordination and motivation problems together are for organizations. This is probably one of the most promising and exciting areas for future research in the economics of organizations.

REFERENCES

Antràs, Pol, Luis Garicano, and Esteban Rossi-Hansberg. 2006. "Offshoring in a Knowledge Economy." *Quarterly Journal of Economics* 121: 31–77.

Aoki, Masahiko. 1986. "Horizontal vs. Vertical Information Structure of the Firm." *American Economic Review* 76: 971–983.

Arrow, Kenneth J. 1974. *The Limits of Organization*. New York: W. W. Norton.

Arrow, Kenneth J., and Roy Radner. 1979. "Allocation of Resources in Large Teams." *Econometrica* 47: 361–385.

Atkeson, Andrew, and Patrick J. Kehoe. 2007. "Modeling the Transition to a New Economy: Lessons from Two Technological Revolutions." *American Economic Review* 97: 64–87.

Barone, Enrico. 1935. "The Ministry of Production in the Collectivist State," in Friedrich A. von Hayek (ed.), *Collectivist Economic Planning*. London: George Routledge and Sons. pp. 245–290. Originally published in 1908.

Becker, Gary S. 1973. "A Theory of Marriage: Part I." *Journal of Political Economy* 81: 813–846.

Beckmann, Martin. 1958. "Decision and Team Problems in Airline Reservations." *Econometrica* 26: 134–145.

Beggs, Alan W. 2001. "Queues and Hierarchies." *Review of Economic Studies* 68: 297–322.

Bloom, Nick, Luis Garicano, Raffaella Sadun, and John Van Reenen. 2009. "The Distinct Effects of Information Technology and Communication Technology on Firm Organization." CEP Discussion Paper 927. Centre for Economic Performance, London School of Economics and Political Science, London.

Bolton, Patrick, and Mathias Dewatripont. 1994. "The Firm as a Communication Network." *Quarterly Journal of Economics* 109: 809–839.

Coase, Ronald H. 1937. "The Nature of the Firm." *Economica* 4: 386–405.

Colombo, Massimo G., and Marco Delmastro. 2004. "Delegation of Authority in Business Organization." *Journal of Industrial Organization* 52: 53–80.

Crémer, Jacques. 1980. "A Partial Theory of the Optimal Organization." *Bell Journal of Economics* 11: 683–693.

———. 1993. "Corporate Culture and Shared Knowledge." *Industrial and Corporate Change* 2: 351–386.

Crémer, Jacques, Luis Garicano, and Andrea Prat. 2007. "Language and the Theory of the Firm." *Quarterly Journal of Economics* 122: 373–407.

Dickinson, Henry D. 1939. *Economics of Socialism*. Oxford: Oxford University Press.

Friedman, Eric J., and Shmuel S. Oren. 1995. "The Complexity of Resource Allocation and Price Mechanisms under Bounded Rationality." *Economic Theory* 6: 225–250.

Gabaix, Xavier, and Augustin Landier. 2008. "Why Has CEO Pay Increased So Much?" *Quarterly Journal of Economics* 123: 49–100.

Garicano, Luis. 2000. "Hierarchies and the Organization of Knowledge in Production." *Journal of Political Economy* 108: 874–904.

Garicano, Luis, and Thomas N. Hubbard. 2007a. "Managerial Leverage Is Limited by the Extent of the Market: Hierarchies, Specialization, and the Utilization of Lawyers' Human Capital." *Journal of Law and Economics* 50: 1–44.

———. 2007b. "The Returns to Knowledge Hierarchies." NBER Working Paper 12815, National Bureau of Economic Research, Cambridge, MA.

Garicano, Luis, and Esteban Rossi-Hansberg. 2004. "Inequality and the Organization of Knowledge." *American Economic Review* 94: 197–202.

———. 2006. "Organization and Inequality in a Knowledge Economy." *Quarterly Journal of Economics* 121: 1383–1435.

———. 2012. "Organizing Growth." *Journal of Economic Theory* 147: 623–656.

Geanakoplos, John, and Paul Milgrom. 1991. "A Theory of Hierarchies Based on Limited Managerial Attention." *Journal of the Japanese and International Economies* 5: 205–225.

Green, Jerry, and Jean-Jacques Laffont. 1986. "Alternative Limited Communication Systems," in Walter P. Heller, Ross M. Starr, and David A. Starett (eds.), *Uncertainty, Information and Communication (Essays in Honor of K. J. Arrow)*, volume 3. Cambridge: Cambridge University Press, pp. 255–271.

Grossman, Gene M., and Giovanni Maggi. 2000. "Diversity and Trade." *American Economic Review* 90: 1255–1275.

Groves, Theodore. 1983. "The Usefulness of Demand Forecasts for Team Resource Allocation in a Dynamic Environment." *Review of Economic Studies* 50: 555–571.

Groves, Theodore, and Roy Radner. 1972. "Allocation of Resources in Teams." *Journal of Economic Theory* 4: 415–441.

Hayek, Friedrich A. von. 1935. "The Nature and History of the Problem," in Friedrich A. von Hayek (Ed.), *Collectivist Economic Planning*. London: George Routledge and Sons, pp. 239–255.

———. 1940. "Socialist Calculation: The Competitive 'Solution.'" *Economica* 7: 125–149.

Hopenhayn, Hugo, and Richard Rogerson. 1993. "Job Turnover and Policy Evaluation: A General Equilibrium Analysis." *Journal of Political Economy* 101: 915–938.

Kaldor, Nicholas. 1934. "The Equilibrium of the Firm." *Economic Journal* 44: 70–71.

Knight, Frank H. 1921. *Risk, Uncertainty and Profit*. Boston: Houghton Mifflin.

Kremer, Michael. 1993. "The O-Ring Theory of Economic Development." *Quarterly Journal of Economics* 107: 35–78.

Kremer, Michael, and Eric Maskin. 1996. "Wage Inequality and Segregation by Skill." NBER Working Paper 5718, National Bureau of Economic Research, Cambridge, MA.

Lange, Oskar. 1936. "On the Economic Theory of Socialism: Part I." *Review of Economic Studies* 4: 53–71.

———. 1937. "On the Economic Theory of Socialism: Part II." *Review of Economic Studies* 4: 123–142.

Liberti, Jose M., and Atif R. Mian. 2009. "Estimating the Effect of Hierarchies on Information Use." *Review of Financial Studies* 22: 4057–4090.

Lucas, Robert E. 1978. "Asset Prices in an Exchange Economy." *Econometrica* 46: 1429–1445.

Maister, David H. 1993. *Managing the Professional Service Firm*. New York: Free Press.

Malone, Thomas W., and Stephen A. Smith. 1988. "Modeling the Performance of Organizational Structures." *Operations Research* 36: 421–436.

Manne, Henry G. 1965. "Mergers and the Market for Corporate Control." *Journal of Political Economy* 73: 110–120.

Marschak, Thomas. 1972. "Computation in Organizations: The Comparison of Price Mechanisms and Other Adjustment Processes," in C. B. McGuire and Roy Radner (eds.), *Decision and Organi-*

zation. Amsterdam: North-Holland, pp. 237–281. Second edition published in 1986 by University of Minnesota Press.

Marschak, Thomas, and Stefan Reichelstein. 1995. "Communication Requirements for Individual Agents in Networks and Hierarchies," in J. Ledyard (ed.), *The Economics of Informational Decentralization: Complexity, Efficiency and Stability.* Boston: Kluwer Academic.

———. 1998. "Network Mechanisms, Informational Efficiency, and Hierarchies." *Journal of Economic Theory* 79: 106–141.

Marschak, John, and Roy Radner. 1972. *The Economic Theory of Teams.* Amsterdam: North-Holland.

Mayer, Thomas. 1960. "The Distribution of Ability and Earnings." *Review of Economics and Statistics* 42: 189–195.

Meagher, Kieron, and Timothy Van Zandt. 1998. "Managerial Costs for One-Shot Decentralized Information Processing." *Review of Economic Design* 3: 329–345.

Mises, Ludwig von. 1951. *Socialism: An Economic and Sociological Analysis.* New Haven: Yale University Press. Originally published as *Die Gemeinwirtschaft* in 1922.

Mount, Kenneth, and Stanley Reiter. 1990. "A Model of Computing with Human Agents." Discussion Paper 890, Center for Mathematical Studies in Economics and Management Science, Northwestern University, Evanston, IL.

———. 1996. "A Lower Bound on Computational Complexity Given by Revelation Mechanisms." *Economic Theory* 7: 237–266.

Murphy, Kevin M., Andrei Shleifer, and Robert W. Vishny. 1991. "The Allocation of Talent: Implications for Growth." *Quarterly Journal of Economics* 106: 503–530.

Orbay, Hakan. 2002. "Information Processing Hierarchies." *Journal of Economic Theory* 105: 370–407.

Orlikowski, Wanda J. 1996. "Improvising Organizational Transormation over Time: A Situated Change Perspective." *Information Systems Research* 7: 73–92.

Radner, Roy. 1972. "Allocation of a Scarce Resource under Uncertainty: An Example of a Team," in C. B. McGuire and Roy Radner (eds.), *Decision and Organization.* Amsterdam: North-Holland. pp. 217–236. Second edition published in 1986 by University of Minnesota Press.

———. 1993. "The Organization of Decentralized Information Processing." *Econometrica* 62: 1109–1146.

Rajan, Raghuram G., and Julie Wulf. 2006. "The Flattening Firm: Evidence from Panel Data on the Changing Nature of Corporate Hierarchies." *Review of Economics and Statistics* 88: 759–773.

Reiter, Stanley. 1996. "Coordination and the Structure of Firms." Working paper. Northwestern University, Evanston, IL.

Robinson, Austin. 1934. "The Problem of Management and the Size of Firms." *Economic Journal* 44: 240–254.

Rosen, Sherwin. 1981. "The Economics of Superstars." *American Economic Review* 71: 845–858.

———. 1982. "Authority, Control and the Distribution of Earnings." *Bell Journal of Economics* 13: 311–323.

———. 1983. "Specialization and Human Capital." *Journal of Labor Economics* 1: 43–49.

———. 1992. "Contracts and the Market for Executives," in Les Werin and Hans Wijkander (eds.), *Contract Economics.* Cambridge, MA: Oxford and Blackwell, pp. 181–211.

———. 2002. "Markets and Diversity." *American Economic Review* 92(1): 1–15.

Sattinger, Michael. 1993. "Assignment Models of the Distribution of Earnings." *Journal of Economic Literature* 31: 831–880.

Schonberger, Richard. 1986. *World Class Manufacturing: The Lessons of Simplicity Applied.* New York: Free Press.

Simon, Herbert A. 1976. *Administrative Behavior: A Study of Decision-Making Processes in Administrative Organizations,* second edition. New York: Free Press.

Simons, Robert. 1991. "Strategic Orientation and Top Management Attention to Control Systems." *Strategic Management Journal* 12: 49–62.

Sloan, Alfred. 1924. "The Most Important Thing I Ever Learned about Management." *System: The Magazine of Business* 46(August).

Stevenson, William B., and Mary C. Gilly. 1991. "Information Processing and Problem Solving: The Migration of Problems through Formal Positions and Networks of Ties." *Academy of Management Journal* 34: 918–928.

Taylor, Fred M. 1929. "The Guidance of Production in the Socialist State." *American Economic Review* 19: 1–8.

Van Zandt, Timothy. 1996. "Organizations with an Endogenous Number of Information Processing Agents: Supplementary Notes." Working paper, Princeton University, Princeton, NJ.

———. 1998. "The Scheduling and Organization of Periodic Associative Computation: Efficient Networks." *Economic Design* 3: 93–127.

———. 2003a. "Real-Time Hierarchical Resource Allocation with Quadratic Payoffs." Mimeo. INSEAD, Paris.

———. 2003b. "Structure and Returns to Scale of Real-Time Hierarchical Resource Allocation." Mimeo. INSEAD, Paris.

Waldman, Michael. 1984. "Worker Allocation, Hierarchies, and the Wage Distribution." *Review of Economics and Statistics* 51: 95–109.

Wilensky, Harold L. 1967. *Organizational Intelligence: Knowledge and Policy in Government and Industry.* New York: Basic Books.

Williamson, Oliver E. 1975. *Markets and Hierarchies, Analysis and Antitrust Implicatons.* New York: Free Press.

———. 1985. *The Economic Institutions of Capitalism.* New York: Free Press.

Zomaya, Albert Y. (ed.). 1996. *Parallel and Distributed Computing Handbook.* New York: McGraw-Hill.

16

Internal Capital Markets

Robert Gertner and David Scharfstein

1. Introduction

Resource allocation is at the core of economics. Economists mostly concern themselves with resource allocation across organizational boundaries mediated through contracts or markets. Yet a great deal of resource allocation occurs within organizations. Businesses allocate capital and other scarce resources across and within business units, including production capacity, R&D capabilities, physical inputs, and human capital.

The most extensive research on internal resource allocation is by financial economists. These studies largely focus on the differences between internal and external capital allocation. Indeed, the insight that the key feature of conglomerates is the replacement of external capital markets with internal capital allocation has led to a large literature, including theoretical work that predicts differences in investment behavior between conglomerate and single-business firms and empirical work that tests these theories. The empirical work on internal capital markets is arguably the most fully developed body of empirical work in organizational economics, and it is the focus of our chapter.

In Section 2 we present an example to motivate the importance of studying internal capital markets. We then proceed to a richer discussion of the institutional literature on internal capital allocation in Section 3. We follow with a detailed survey of the theoretical and empirical literature on internal capital markets (Sections 4–6). This review includes the early empirical work in the area, as well as more granular studies of particular industries, relationships among managers, and the functioning of business groups. We conclude the chapter by discussing models of the capital allocation process, including capital budgeting rules, the shape of hierarchies, and communication (Section 7).

Despite our focus on internal capital allocation, it is important to keep in mind that firms allocate more than just capital. Firms allocate workers who have specialized firm-specific know-how and cannot be easily replaced with outside hires. Price does not appear to be the principal means by which firms allocate workers to jobs. Goods and services are also allocated in firms.

Vertically integrated firms differ greatly in the mechanisms used. For example, upstream divisions may sell exclusively to internal downstream divisions, or they may also sell outside the firm. Downstream divisions may be required to purchase exclusively from the upstream division or may be able to purchase externally.[1] In the most complete study of transfer pricing practices, Eccles (1985) demonstrates the links among transfer pricing practices, performance measurement, organizational structure, and strategic planning processes. This area is ripe for future research.

2. An Example

We begin with an example of a start-up biotechnology firm whose sole asset is a drug compound, SF-920, discovered by its founder-scientist. The firm is ready to begin early stage clinical trials but has little financial or physical capital, few employees other than the founder-scientist, and no contracts for the provision of goods or services. The firm needs to raise financial capital to fund the clinical trials, hire additional employees, and enter into contracts for goods or services. The difficulty of raising capital to fund investment is the subject of much theoretical work in finance. This literature has focused on the problems arising from asymmetric information and agency, and the contractual and governance responses to these problems.[2]

The founder may know more than outside investors about the likelihood that SF-920 will succeed in clinical trials. There are a number of market responses to this asymmetric information problem. First, the firm will likely raise capital from a relatively more informed capital supplier, most likely a venture capitalist or "angel" investor with special knowledge of the biotech industry. Second, the firm will not raise all the capital it needs to bring a drug from early stage clinical trials to FDA approval. Doing so would send a signal to investors that the founder was not confident that the drug would pass early stage clinical trials.

The founder's objectives may also differ from those of outside investors, giving rise to agency problems. For example, the founder may derive nonpecuniary benefits from having a drug approved, or the founder may be overly optimistic about the likelihood the drug will succeed. As a result, the founder may be reluctant to abandon development, even when value maximization dictates that she should. There are both contractual and governance responses to this agency problem. The venture capitalist will fund only part of the cost of bringing the drug to market and will likely seek some control through board membership and contractual provisions of the financing. These market responses go some way toward resolving asymmetric information and agency problems.

Because these mechanisms help mitigate asymmetric information and agency problems, the founder may be able to raise financial capital to start her firm and hire employees, enter into contracts for goods and services, and purchase or lease equipment for scientific research.

Now suppose instead that the same scientist develops the compound in her role as an employee of an existing biotechnology firm that already has two other compounds in clinical trials,

---

1. Recent empirical evidence suggests that nonexclusivity is the norm. Hortaçsu and Syverson (2009) document that among vertically integrated firms, a large percentage of upstream production is sold to third parties, and a large percentage of downstream plants' requirements of inputs they produce upstream are purchased from third parties. See also Mullainathan and Scharfstein (2001) for evidence from the chemicals industry.

2. For excellent surveys, see Harris and Raviv (1991) and Shleifer and Vishny (1997).

numerous employees (including a CEO), capital equipment, and various contracts for goods and services. The scientist would like to get the firm to fund the clinical trial. First, note that the scientist cannot just decide to raise capital from outside investors. She would need approval from her superiors to do this, as firms have the authority to prevent their employees or divisions from raising capital externally.[3] Senior management can also prevent the scientist from running the clinical trial. But if they choose to go ahead and run the trial, they might choose to finance it with funds the firm already has, possibly by reallocating funds originally intended for other clinical trials, or they could seek external capital. The scientist would also need the approval of her superiors to hire people to run the clinical trials and to enter into contracts for necessary goods and services. Management might choose to reallocate employees working on other clinical trials to help in the management of the SF-920 trial and to use supply relationships they already have for the necessary goods and services.

As the example should make clear, there are stark differences in how standalone firms and divisions within larger firms obtain resources. First, authority relationships within firms provide senior management with exclusive control over people and capital. Although delegation of this authority is feasible, it only rarely occurs with respect to capital; senior management typically exercises its decisionmaking authority over large capital commitments. Furthermore, price mechanisms are not used to allocate capital resources, at least not directly. Although it is quite common to measure divisional performance net the cost of capital it employs and compensate division managers based on accounting measures that net out capital costs, the price of the capital is set formulaically, and the division managers do not choose how much capital they want as a function of its price. At most, division managers state their demands at the given price, and then senior management decides how much of the request to honor. Another common characteristic of internal capital markets is that business units do not have direct access to the excess cash flow they generate. Instead, they must upstream the cash and seek funds for capital investment through the capital allocation process. Additionally, internal capital markets often include quantity rationing through a fixed corporate capital budget. And there can be significant differences in the way information flows from divisions to headquarters compared to that in a firm with a single division.

The external capital market differs significantly from the internal capital market. In general, external capital providers have less direct control over the allocation of resources once they have been provided. Managers often have discretion over the use of cash beyond contractual obligations, enabling them to use retained earnings to invest in new projects. However, in some environments, particularly for early stage firms raising capital from one or several investors, these capital providers can exercise somewhat greater control over the allocation of resources internally through board control and possibly their power to replace management. For larger firms, where ownership is diffuse, the ability to control the use of internal resources once they have been provided is fairly limited.

---

3. The distinction we focus on is that the division can only go to headquarters for capital, whereas the independent firm can seek any outside source of capital. In both cases, one can think that the firm rather than the scientist owns the rights to SF-920, so the scientist could not take the compound with her if she were to quit either firm.

This distinction has been central to formal models of internal versus external capital markets, as well as to empirical analysis. But before we proceed to the recent research that attempts to explain choices between internal and external capital markets and measure their impact, we discuss the institutional literature on resource allocation that preceded it.

3. Institutional Literature on Capital Allocation

There is a rich descriptive literature on the resource allocation process and its relation to strategy. An early antecedent to the academic literature is Alfred P. Sloan's (1964) classic book, *My Years with General Motors,* in which he describes his transformation of General Motors into a multidivisional firm and the resource allocation processes the company used. The academic literature starts with Bower's (1970) classic ethnographic study, *Managing the Resource Allocation Process.* Bower's book and the work that builds on it, such as Burgelman (1983), develop and refine a descriptive model of how a company's key strategic decisions are made through the process by which capital and other scarce assets are allocated to divisions and projects. Bower characterizes internal resource allocation as a bottom-up process in which front-line managers identify investment opportunities and seek the support of middle managers, who choose which project to champion and put before senior managers for ultimate approval. Bower argues that although front-line managers may have deep knowledge of their particular areas of responsibility, the process does not readily incorporate information from other parts of the company and thereby fails to take advantage of potential synergies across business units. Given that projects are generated from the bottom up, the resource allocation process often misses new opportunities outside the limited window from which front-line managers view the world. Senior management, however, can influence the set of projects that percolate up to them for approval through communication of strategic direction, choice of organizational structure, and implementation of measurement systems and incentives.

One of Bower's (1970) most important contributions is to identify the central role that resource allocation plays in strategy. Strategy may be formulated as grand plans by senior management, but the process of resource allocation—the decisions of which initiatives to undertake and which to reject—is where strategic choices are often made. In Bower's view, a strategy formulation process that does not integrate effectively into the resource allocation process cannot be successful.

Bower's model is largely descriptive and does not try to relate differences in market outcomes with differences in resource allocation processes or between internal and external resource allocation. Nor does he try to identify and empirically document biases in the process. Furthermore, Bower's model largely abstracts from incentive problems, in effect assuming that the problem is one of aggregating diffuse knowledge within the organization. Communication is implicitly assumed to be imperfect, but the reasons for this are not explored.

Sull (1999) and Christensen (1997) go on to document some problems that can arise when firms adhere to the bottom-up process identified by Bower. Sull shows how Firestone failed to adjust to the reduced demand for nonradial tires in the 1970s. He shows that incentives can become misaligned in a bottom-up process when the capital allocation decisions involve taking away a division's resources. Lower level management did not recommend disinvestment, and senior management relied on lower management for recommendations.

Christensen (1997) documents how leading firms often fail to respond to potentially disruptive technological change because they listen to existing customers who are largely satisfied rather than learning about the market opportunities for major innovations. Christensen identifies the bottom-up resource allocation process as one of the sources for these strategic errors.

Despite the ostensible importance of resource allocation process for strategy and performance, this literature appears not to have gone much beyond case studies. And to our knowledge, the field of organizational behavior has given relatively little attention to the question of how resources are allocated in organizations. We now turn to a description of economic theories of capital allocation and the empirical work that follows from these theories. Many papers we discuss are described in Stein's (2003) excellent survey of corporate investment, as well as in a more recent survey by Maksimovic and Phillips (2007).

4. Theoretical Perspectives on Capital Allocation

The idea that firms replace price-based relationships with authority-based relationships dates back to Coase (1937). Although Coase is not specific about how these authority-based relationships work, they should have implications for how capital is allocated in firms. Williamson (1975) begins the economic literature that examines the implications for internal capital allocation. He describes the multidivisional firm as a "miniature capital market," with two main advantages over external capital markets. First, headquarters can more easily monitor its business units than external investors can monitor the companies in which they invest, "thereby securing a higher level of adherence to profit maximization than the unassisted capital market could realize." Second, headquarters is better at "assigning cash flows to high yield uses. Thus cash flows . . . are not automatically returned to their sources but instead are exposed to internal competition" (Williamson 1975: 147). Elements of these ideas also appear in Weston (1970) and Donaldson (1984).

In the context of the drug-development example in the previous section, Williamson's view amounts to saying that the headquarters of a large biopharmaceutical firm ("pharma") will do a better job allocating its drug development budget across internal projects than the capital market would do in allocating funds across smaller single-project drug-development companies ("biotech"). There are two reasons, according to Williamson. First, pharma headquarters can better assess the value of any given project and can better ensure that funds are used appropriately than can investors in a biotech firm. Second, pharma headquarters does a better job than the capital markets in choosing among competing drug-development projects; headquarters can reallocate cash flows generated by previously successful projects to fund projects with better prospects, whereas investors in biotech firms cannot redeploy cash flows from previously successful firms to other firms with better prospects.

The formal theoretical work on internal capital markets is by and large a fleshing-out of both these claims. There are two key elements of most of these models, though often both are not present: (1) agency and information problems between headquarters and external sources of capital and (2) agency and information problems between headquarters and internal users of capital (business units or project managers).

Why, as Williamson (1975) suggests, would headquarters be better than external capital markets at evaluating and monitoring projects in the firm? One possibility, suggested by Gertner et al. (1994) is that headquarters—in contrast to a bank or noncontrolling shareholder—has unconditional control rights over the management of projects in the firm. Thus, if a CEO has an idea that would improve a project in the firm, he has the authority to have the improvement implemented by the project manager. More precisely, he has the authority to fire the manager if she does not comply, thereby giving the CEO bargaining power to have the idea implemented without having to pay the manager much in exchange for implementation. This provides the CEO with strong incentives to become informed about where to allocate resources lower down in the organization. In contrast, a bank loan officer only has control conditional on very poor performance (default), and therefore has no authority to fire a manager for not implementing his idea. Without this authority he has to pay the manager in some way to implement the idea, which in turn discourages the loan officer from coming up with ideas for project improvement. However, the greater authority of the CEO gives the him the capacity to extract rents from the manager, which discourages his effort and may lead him to identify fewer valuable investment opportunities.

Stein (1997) builds on this model of a more informed headquarters to explore its implications for capital allocation across business units. In his model, business unit managers (and the managers of standalone companies) always want to invest as much as possible, because they derive private benefits from investment. Thus, the capital market, which is poorly informed about business-level investment opportunities, rations credit to protect against overinvestment. For example, each standalone firm might only be able to raise one unit of capital, even though one of the firms has much better investment prospects. However, if these standalone firms become part of a two-division firm in which headquarters makes the capital allocation decisions, the firm can raise two units of capital overall, and the well-informed headquarters can deploy more capital in the division with the better investment prospects. In Stein's terminology, the benefit of an internal capital market is that it can engage in both "winner picking" and "loser sticking," preventing divisions with poor investment opportunities from overinvesting. This idea is a formalization of Williamson's notion of the benefits of internal capital markets.

This argument would appear to hinge on the assumption that the CEO has strong incentives to maximize value. However, Stein (1997) shows that one can have an efficient internal capital market even if the managers at headquarters are empire builders, provided they prefer better projects to worse ones, controlling for the level of investment. Thus, it will be in the interest of headquarters to have a large capital budget but make sure that it is deployed in the most efficient way possible. In Stein's (1997: 131) words, "a partial solution to the agency problem of empire building managers is to take control from them and give it to an empire building supervisor, who is no more noble but has less parochial interests." Stein then uses this model to consider the optimal scale and scope of the firm.

This positive view of internal capital allocation also appears in the work of Maksimovic and Phillips (2002) but for entirely different reasons. Unlike most models in this literature, there are no agency and information problems. Instead, their model is driven by the assumptions that there are decreasing returns to scale at the business unit level, and importantly, that managers have general skills that they can apply across business units, even if they are in different industries. Under these assumptions, it is optimal for headquarters to deploy its skills across multiple, possibly unrelated, businesses rather than on one business unit with diminishing returns. In this model, it is efficient to have multiple businesses under one roof; the capital allocation process just amounts to allocating capital to its highest value use. These authors then derive empirical implications that they argue are consistent with the data.

There are other models of the financial benefits of corporate diversification, but they are not about capital allocation, so we do not focus on them. As an example, Lewellen (1971) argues that a benefit of diversification is that asset values are less variable, which lowers the probability of financial distress and enables firms to finance themselves with more leverage, thereby allowing firms to take greater advantage of the interest tax deduction.[4] In contrast, Hadlock et al. (2001) argue that because asset values are less variable, equity issues are associated with less adverse selection, which facilitates more equity issuance, with a less negative price impact (which they verify empirically).

The idea that internal capital markets function smoothly seems at odds with the common view espoused in the finance and strategy literature that the conglomerate form of organization—the primary purpose of which is to allocate resources—was a failure. One of the main theories behind the assembly of a conglomerate of unrelated businesses was precisely that they would allocate capital more efficiently than the external capital market (Hubbard and Palia 1999). ITT, which in its prime had acquired more than 350 businesses in industries as diverse as insurance and baking, was a leading example of such a conglomerate. However, beginning in the 1980s, with concerns rising about whether conglomerates had become too large to be effectively managed, conglomerates began paring themselves down. Many conglomerates were subjected to hostile takeovers and leveraged buyouts, with acquirers appearing to reap large gains by disassembling them and selling the parts off to industry and financial buyers (Bhagat et al. 1990). Many of the acquisitions that were done to assemble the conglomerates were, in the end, unsuccessful (Porter 1987; Kaplan and Weisbach 1992). Conglomerates appeared to be valued at less than the sum of their parts (e.g., Berger and Ofek 1995). Scholars attributed these difficulties to incentive problems in conglomerate divisions, as compensation was only loosely tied to divisional performance, and to failures of the internal capital allocation process (Baker and Wruck 1989; Baker 1992; Kaplan et al. 1997). It is against this backdrop that theories of the dark side of internal capital markets were developed. Rajan et al. (2000), Scharfstein and Stein (2000), and Wulf (2009) are early attempts to model inefficiencies in capital allocation. All the models are based on some sort of rent-seeking behavior on the part of divisional managers, which headquarters responds to by distorting the allocation of capital away from the first best. Meyer et al. (1992) also model rent-seeking behavior by division managers who try to get headquarters to allocate more capital to their divisions. But in equilibrium they are unsuccessful, and even though the rent-seeking activities are in themselves inefficient, they do not result in a distorted capital budget.

In both Rajan et al. (2000) and Scharfstein and Stein (2000) capital allocation is distorted toward poorly performing divisions at the expense of the better divisions. In Rajan et al. (2000) this distortion is an attempt by value-maximizing managers at headquarters to encourage cooperation among divisions. This result follows from a set of assumptions in their model that imply that when capital budgets and investment opportunities are very diverse, divisional managers have increased incentives to engage in the types of investments that benefit only their own divisions. These incentives are reduced with more equalized capital budgets.

---

4. Inderst and Mueller (2003) present an optimal contracting model in which diversification reduces cash flow variability and enables firms to pledge more cash flows to debt investors.

In contrast, Scharfstein and Stein (2000) rely on two tiers of agency problems—between headquarters and division managers (as in Rajan et al. 2000) but also between headquarters and shareholders. Division managers, particularly those in poorly performing divisions, have incentives to engage in activities that enhance their bargaining power with headquarters. Headquarters, in turn, can try to prevent this sort of behavior through cash compensation. However, if divisional managers obtain private benefits from a larger capital budget, headquarters may choose to compensate divisional managers with more capital instead of cash. As an agent of shareholders, managers at headquarters may perceive this approach as a less costly form of compensation, because they do not bear the full cost of the distortion. To the extent that the managers of the divisions with poor investment opportunities need more compensation to discourage rent-seeking activities, the capital budget will be distorted in their favor.[5]

Rajan et al. (2000) and Scharfstein and Stein (2000) both hinge on some very particular assumptions that are hard to verify empirically. In the main, these papers have been cited to motivate a set of empirical tests that examine whether the better divisions of conglomerates receive too small a share of the capital budget relative to the efficient level. An important distinction between the models, which we discuss further in our review of the empirical literature in Section 5, is that Scharfstein and Stein (2000) predict that capital allocation will be more distorted in firms in which there are greater agency problems between top management and shareholders.

Rotemberg and Saloner (1994), De Motta (2003), Brusco and Panunzi (2005), and Ozbas (2005) also present models in which an internal capital market with winner picking creates problems. Rotemberg and Saloner (1994) and Brusco and Panunzi (2005) show that if a divisional manager is concerned that the fruits of her innovative efforts will not be rewarded because capital will be allocated to other divisions, then she may not exert much effort in the first place. De Motta (2003) highlights an alternative mechanism through which an internal capital market could reduce managerial incentives while doing an effective job of winner picking among projects. In his model, managers try to signal quality to the external capital market through greater effort. If there are multiple divisions, there is a free-rider problem among divisions; it is less important for any one division manager to boost the market's impression of firm quality through its effort. Moreover, if headquarters is relatively informed about manager quality, there is less incentive to signal to headquarters through greater effort.[6] Ozbas (2005) presents a model in which winner picking encourages divisional managers to overstate the value of their projects, and he considers various ways that headquarters can reduce this incentive through, for example, more rigid (less information-sensitive) capital allocations and job rotation across divisions.

Matsusaka and Nanda (2002) and Inderst and Mueller (2003) analyze models in which internal capital markets have both costs and benefits. In Matsusaka and Nanda (2002) the benefit of an internal capital market is that firms can use the excess cash flows of one division to fund those of another without having to bear the deadweight costs of going to the capital market to raise funding. The cost of an internal capital market is that empire-building managers may

---

5. Bernardo et al. (2006) also present a model of "socialistic" capital allocation that fully endogenizes incentive compensation, effort, and the allocation of capital.

6. This idea is related to the model of Gromb and Scharfstein (2002), which analyzes the costs of internal entrepreneurship ("intrapreneurship") versus new firm formation (entrepreneurship).

overinvest excess cash flow. This cost is the same as in Inderst and Mueller (2003), whereas the benefit they model is that the reduced variability of cash flows in a multidivisional firm enables it to commit to pay out more cash to debtholders and thereby increases its ability to raise debt financing. Neither of these models has strong predictions about how capital will be allocated across divisions.

Finally, there is a line of theoretical work developed in the mainstream organizational economics literature that considers the resource allocation process of multidivisional firms. Athey and Roberts (2001) study a model in which division managers choose effort (which impacts the performance of the manager's own division) and projects (which affect other divisions' performance). They study the implications for incentive schemes and the allocation of decision rights over project selection. Dessein et al. (2010) develop a model of organizations with both business-unit managers, who choose effort, and functional managers, who identify opportunities for synergies that create externalities among business units. They study the joint choices of incentive schemes and the allocation of authority among managers. The model demonstrates the trade-offs between generating strong local incentives and taking advantage of projects that have externalities among business units.

5. Early Empirical Perspectives on Internal Capital Markets

Early empirical work on conglomerates suggests that at the time of diversifying acquisitions, the stock market perceived them as increasing value (Schipper and Thompson 1983; Matsusaka 1993). Indeed, Hubbard and Palia (1999) show that, during the 1960s, when there was an announcement that a financially unconstrained firm was undertaking a diversifying acquisition of a financially constrained firm, the acquirer's stock price rose more than the average diversifying acquisition. This phenomenon suggests that the market perceived internal capital markets as being more efficient than external capital markets, at least for the firms involved in the transactions during the 1960s. However, the poor performance of conglomerates and their disassembly during the 1980s and 1990s spawned a literature trying to understand why they appear to have failed.

The first round of empirical research tried to establish that conglomerates are indeed inefficient by documenting that firm value decreases with increasing degrees of diversification (Montgomery and Wernerfelt 1988; Lang and Stulz 1994) and that the market value of conglomerates is less than the value of a matched portfolio of standalone firms (Berger and Ofek 1995). This latter fact has come to be known as the "conglomerate discount" or "diversification discount." Berger and Ofek estimate a discount of about 13–15%, using data from the United States, and discounts of varying degrees have been documented in numerous other countries (Servaes 1996; Fauver et al. 1998; Claessens et al. 1999; Lins and Servaes 1999, 2002).

Although it is well established that conglomerates trade for less than the sum of their parts, some papers have argued that this fact is not evidence of the inefficiency of the conglomerate form of organization. In particular, Campa and Kedia (2002), Graham et al. (2002), Hyland and Diltz (2002), and Villalonga (2004a) argue that the conglomerate discount is really driven by the fact that firms that choose to be conglomerates are weaker in the first place. Indeed, Chevalier (2004) shows that single-segment firms that were acquired by conglomerates traded at a discount relative to other single-segment firms even before they were acquired. And Lamont and Polk (2001) show that about half of the conglomerate discount does not stem from lower cash flows but rather from the market requirement for higher returns on diversified firms. Thus, some of the discount may be the result of inefficient valuation rather than inefficient management. Finally, Villalonga (2004b), using much more disaggregated, establishment-level data, shows that the conglomerate discount may not even exist on average.

Houston et al. (1997), Lamont (1997), Shin and Stulz (1998), Scharfstein (1998), and Rajan et al. (2000) are the earliest papers to look directly at the functioning of internal capital markets. Lamont (1997), though early on the scene, arrived there somewhat inadvertently. His main focus is on whether the well-documented relationship between cash flow and investment exists because of capital market imperfections or because cash flow proxies for the value of investment opportunities. This question arose in the first studies of the effect of cash flow on investment, such as Fazzari et al. (1988) and Hoshi et al. (1991). Lamont's empirical approach is to look at the investment behavior of the divisions of diversified oil firms that operate outside the oil industry. He shows that in response to a drop in the price of oil, which adversely affected the cash flow of oil divisions, firms cut the capital budgets of their non-oil divisions, even though the divisions were either unrelated to the oil industry or benefited from a drop in the oil price (e.g., the petrochemical industry). Although this finding demonstrates that corporate cash flow affects investment because of capital market imperfections, it also demonstrates that there is an internal capital market in which the cash flows of one division have implications for the investments of other divisions. In fact, Lamont showed that prior to the drop in oil prices, when oil firms were earning large profits from their oil divisions, the non-oil divisions of these firms invested more than their industry counterparts. The steep reduction in oil prices led firms to cut the capital budgets of their non-oil divisions down to the industry average, thus possibly implying that firms had been overinvesting in their non-oil divisions because of the excess cash generated by the high price of oil. This possibility is suggestive of inefficiencies in internal capital markets.

Shin and Stulz (1998) build on Lamont's (1997) study by examining the divisional investment behavior of a large sample of diversified firms. Using segment-level data reported in annual financial statements, Shin and Stulz find that a segment's investment does not just depend on its own investment opportunities (as measured by Tobin's Q) and cash flow but also depends on the cash flow of other segments, even though the segments are in different two-digit Standard Industrial Classification (SIC) codes. It is possible that this finding is part of an efficient reallocation of corporate resources as suggested by Stein (1997) and other models. However, cash flow does not appear to be more prone to be reallocated to divisions in high-Q industries. The authors suggest that this negative finding could be evidence of an inefficient internal capital market.

Rajan et al. (2000) take a different approach to examining the efficiency of internal capital allocation. Consistent with their theory, they find that diversified firms invest more in their industry segments that are below the firm average industry Q than would a standalone firm operating in that industry. Similarly, they invest less in industry segments that are above the firm's average industry Q. These differences are more pronounced in firms that operate in industries with very diverse Q values, which is also an implication of the Rajan et al. (2000) model as well as an implication of Scharfstein and Stein (2000). Moreover, the greater is the misallocation of resources according to this measure, the greater the conglomerate discount will be. Thus, for example, we would expect that a firm that operates in a high-growth technology business would invest less than its industry peers if at the same time it owns a slow-growth consumer foods business. However, if the firm operates in two different high-growth technology businesses, the empirical results would suggest less divergence in the investment behavior of these segments from standalone industry participants. Moreover, the conglomerate discount should be smaller for the latter firm than for the former.

Scharfstein (1998) and Ozbas and Scharfstein (2010) start with a similar observation. These papers show that diversified firms tend to invest more than their standalone peers in low-Q industries and less than standalone firms in high-Q industries.[7] Importantly, they show that these differences are more pronounced for firms in which top management has low ownership stakes. This finding is consistent with the implications of Scharfstein and Stein (2000), who argue that inefficiencies in capital allocation stem from two-tiered agency problems—those between headquarters and shareholders and those between headquarters and division managers. This paper provides direct evidence for the effect of top-tier agency problems on capital allocation. Sautner and Villalonga (2010) confirm the importance of good corporate governance for efficient capital allocation in a study of the effects of a change in German tax law that reduced ownership concentration. They find a reduction in their measure of internal capital market efficiency after the change in the tax law. Other recent work, which we discuss later in this section, examines in greater detail the effect on the capital allocation process of agency problems between division managers and headquarters, a key element of most models of internal capital market inefficiency.

A series of papers analyzes the functioning of internal capital markets by looking at what happens after a corporate restructuring. Gertner et al. (2002) document similar behavior by comparing the investment of businesses before and after they are spun off from a conglomerate. This approach has the advantage of using actual business-unit data rather than segment-level data, which may not correspond to an actual business unit. The paper documents an increased sensitivity of investment to industry Q after the spinoff. Moreover, low-Q divisions cut their investment after the spinoff, and high-Q divisions increase their investments. The effects are larger for businesses that are unrelated to the former parent, and for those whose stock price announcement effect of the spinoff is larger. Ahn and Denis (2004) also find increases in investment efficiency after spinoffs. Of course, the sample is biased toward conglomerates whose internal capital markets have likely been most problematic. These papers should be viewed as providing evidence that spinoffs may be driven by a failure of capital allocation, rather than as evidence about the average performance of internal capital markets.

---

7. The basic results in Scharfstein (1998) and Ozbas and Scharfstein (2010) are substantively similar; however, there are two main advantages of the latter paper, which is why we discuss it in more detail. First, it more systematically measures the relatedness of segments by measuring vertical relationships, which is done by using the input-output matrix of trade flows between industries published by the Bureau of Economic Analysis. Two industries are vertically unrelated if they do not sell (buy) more than 10% of the outputs (inputs) to (from) each other. This is an improvement over Scharfstein's (1998) subjective measure of relatedness, and the standard two-digit SIC measure of relatedness. This latter approach classifies many related industries as unrelated, and unrelated industries as related. For example, oil and gas extraction (two-digit SIC code 13) is considered unrelated to petroleum refining (two-digit SIC code 29), because they are in different two-digit SIC codes. And it considers drugs to be related to industrial inorganic chemicals, because they are both in two-digit SIC code 28. A second advantage of Ozbas and Scharfstein (2010) is that it examines a much larger sample over a longer time horizon.

Dittmar and Shivdasani (2003) examine the flip side of divestitures—the impact of the divestiture on the investment behavior of the remaining business segments. The segments that appeared to be underinvesting increased investment, whereas those that appeared to be overinvesting reduced investment. Moreover, the conglomerate discount of the remaining parent decreased following the divestiture. Peyer and Shivdasani (2001) show that when firms undertake leveraged recapitalizations (whereby they borrow to buy back a significant fraction of outstanding equity), internal capital markets appear to become less efficient. Segment-level investment becomes less sensitive to industry Q and more sensitive to segment-level cash flows.

These studies, and others like it, have been criticized by Chevalier (2004) and Whited (2001). Chevalier's main criticism is that some of the observed investment patterns of the segments of diversified conglomerates exist even before they were acquired by a conglomerate. For example, prior to a merger the investment of the target firm is sensitive to the cash flow of the acquirer, even though they are in different two-digit SIC codes. And targets tend to invest less than their industry peers if the target industry's Q is greater than the acquirer's industry Q. Shin and Stulz (1998) and Rajan et al. (2000) find the same result once the segments are part of the same conglomerate. That these patterns exist in the data prior to the businesses being part of the same conglomerate casts some doubt on the factors that drive the results in Shin and Stulz (1998), Rajan et al. (2000), and related papers. Moreover, Whited (2001), using a method she developed to correct for measurement error (relying on third- and higher-order moments of the joint distribution of the regressors), claims that the main results in the literature are not robust to correcting for measurement error.

However, as Stein (2003) points out, although these criticisms may cast some doubt on whether the average conglomerate exhibits inefficient investment behavior, they do not explain the cross-sectional findings. For example, Rajan et al. (2000) show that the cross-subsidization of investment is greater in firms with a larger conglomerate discount. And Scharfstein (1998) and Ozbas and Scharfstein (2010) relate investment inefficiencies to low managerial ownership stakes.

The early literature has been followed by three main research streams. One stream of work attempts to provide a more granular perspective on capital allocation, with more detailed investment data, a focus on a single industry, or a focus on a single firm. In particular, extensive work has been done on capital allocation in banks both domestically and across borders. The second stream of work more directly measures the effect of incentives and rent-seeking behavior at lower levels in the organization. And the third stream analyzes the functioning of internal capital markets in business groups, such as Korean chaebol and family-controlled pyramidal enterprises.

6. Granular Perspectives on Internal Capital Markets

6.1. Industry Studies

Although the main body of work on internal capital markets uses segment-level data from Standard & Poor's Compustat to examine capital expenditures of diversified conglomerates, a stream of the literature has developed that analyzes investment behavior in a particular industry. This approach has the advantage of providing a specific industry context for analysis and in some cases more detailed information on the nature of the investment.

6.1.1. Banking

Although much of the literature on internal capital allocation in banks follows the initial contributions to the literature on nonfinancial firms, Houston et al. (1997) deserves credit for being one of the founding papers in the empirical literature on internal capital markets. This paper was the first to show the existence of an internal capital market in banks by documenting that the lending behavior of banks in multibank holding companies is more sensitive to the cash flow of the holding company than it is to its own cash flow, and that a subsidiaries' lending is negatively related to the lending of other subsidiary banks of the holding company. A more recent paper by Ashcraft (2008) analyzes the "source-of-strength doctrine," whereby bank holding companies are required by their regulator (the Federal Reserve) to support troubled depository subsidiaries. He finds that bank subsidiaries of multibank holding companies are safer than either stand-alone banks or those that are subsidiaries of single-bank holding companies. This paper also points to an active internal capital market in banks, albeit one that may have been driven by regulation.

Other papers speak to the importance of internal capital markets in banking, but the authors do not position their papers as being about internal capital markets. Peek and Rosengren (1997) is a good example. Following a strategy similar to that of Lamont (1997), the paper shows that the collapse of the Japanese real estate market and the resulting large losses Japanese banks incurred in Japan induced these banks to cut their commercial real estate lending in the United States in the 1990s, while U.S. banks continued to lend. Thus, shocks in Japan were transmitted to the United States through the internal capital market of Japanese banks. Schnabl (2012) documents similar effects in Peru, where global banks reduced their lending to their Peruvian subsidiaries in response to the global banking crisis that emerged following the Russian debt default in 1998.

Transmission mechanisms of this sort were also explored by Morgan et al. (2004). In contrast to Peek and Rosengren (1997), the authors show that the internal capital market can have a stabilizing effect on lending. Their paper examines the effect of the introduction of interstate banking in the United States—state laws that allowed out-of-state banks to add branches in the state—on the variability of economic growth in the state. Morgan et al. find that it reduces the variability of economic growth: out-of-state banks stabilize lending because their own profitability is presumably less variable than that of in-state banks. Profits from banking activity outside a state provides banks with the capital they need to lend in a state subject to adverse shocks. Of course, if the shock is on a broader scale, the shock could have adverse effects on a state that was not initially impacted by the shock. This transmission mechanism is similar to the one documented by Schnabl (2012) in Peru.

Campello (2002) analyzes the effect of internal capital markets on the performance of monetary policy. He compares the response of small standalone banks to Fed monetary tightening to that of small banks that are part of larger multibank holding companies. The lending by the small banks appears to be much more sensitive to their cash flow during these periods, as they have limited access to nondeposit forms of financing to offset the decline in reserves. In contrast, larger bank holding companies can more easily raise other forms of financing and downstream the capital to their small banks. As a result, lending by these small banks is less sensitive to their own cash flows during periods of monetary tightening. Campello comes to an ambiguous conclusion about whether this allocation of capital across banks in the holding company is efficient.

Cetorelli and Goldberg (in press) undertake a related exercise by comparing the monetary policy response of U.S.-based global banks to that of U.S. domestic banks. They find that U.S. global banks are able to undo some of the contractionary effects of monetary policy tightening by borrowing from their foreign branches. Thus, lending in the United States does not decline for these banks, while it does for similarly sized domestic banks, which cannot tap foreign affiliates for funding.

6.1.2. Supermarkets

Chevalier and Scharfstein (1996) study the effect of financial constraints on the pricing behavior of supermarket chains. They argue that financial constraints will induce supermarkets to raise prices even though doing so compromises long-run market share, because raising prices increases short-run profits, given the existence of customer switching costs. Among other results consistent with this prediction, they find that when oil-producing states in the United States (e.g., Texas) experienced a recession following the large drop in oil prices in 1986, local supermarket chains increased their prices relative to national chains. Both local and national chains experienced a reduction in profits in oil states, but the national chains were able to use the profits they were earning elsewhere to avoid the pressure of raising prices to increase short-run profits. This finding is similar to that of Morgan et al. (2004) on the stabilizing effect of large multistate banks on state-level lending behavior.

6.1.3. Discount Department Stores

Khanna and Tice (2001) present evidence suggesting that in the discount department store industry, diversified firms—those with significant operations outside the discount department store industry—made more efficient investment decisions than focused firms in response to entry by Walmart. Walmart's entry reduced the value of being an incumbent. The authors argue that the efficient response to Walmart's entry was either to exit immediately or to stay and fight. They argue that this strategy was better than the in-between strategy of staying in the business for a few years and then giving up as Walmart came to dominate the local market. Diversified firms were more likely to exit early on, redeploying their capital to other, more profitable, divisions. If they did choose to stay in the market, they invested more in the markets that remained profitable despite Walmart's entry. Khanna and Tice (2001) argue that these findings are largely consistent with Stein's (1997) model in which diversified firms in related industries make more efficient capital allocation decisions because headquarters has the incentive to redeploy capital to its most efficient use.

6.1.4. Chemicals

Mullainathan and Scharfstein (2001) focus on capital investment in vertically integrated chemical manufacturers. In particular, they compare the capacity decisions of standalone manufacturers of vinyl chloride monomer (VCM), the key input in the production of polyvinyl chloride (PVC), to VCM producers that are vertically integrated into PVC production. They find that while the capacity of standalone producers of VCM is very sensitive to downstream industry demand, the integrated manufacturers' VCM capacity depends mainly on the internal demand of their upstream PVC producers. This structure could be inefficient in that integrated producers of VCM miss out on market opportunities because they are focused only on internal demand.

Or it is possible that it is efficient for these integrated producers to cater to the idiosyncratic demands of their upstream units. That integrated VCM producers are more prone to hold capacity during periods when there is excess VCM capacity suggests that there may be some inefficiency. In any case, it is clear that integration can have profound effects on the investment behavior of the units.

6.1.5. Research and Development

Seru (in press) analyzes whether diversified conglomerates inhibit innovative activity. He first establishes that conglomerate divisions produce fewer and less-innovative patents than standalone firms, but he recognizes that standalone firms might be more innovative simply because they are at an earlier stage in their development. Thus, he compares the change in patenting of the targets of successful diversifying acquisitions to the patenting of targets where the acquisition is initiated but fails to be completed. Consistent with the cross-sectional results, Seru finds that the number and novelty of the patents by the targets of completed acquisitions falls relative to the targets of the failed acquisitions. This difference is larger for conglomerates that have a more active internal capital market using the measure developed by Billett and Mauer (2003). These empirical results are consistent with theories of the firm in which the possibility that headquarters reallocates output of the division to other uses discourages effort (Gertner et al. 1994; Rotemberg and Saloner 1994; Brusco and Panunzi 2005). It is also consistent with a theory of the firm in which headquarters is not well informed about the value of innovative activity at the divisional level and therefore only funds the safest research projects because they are easiest to verify (Stein 2002; Mathews and Robinson 2008).

6.2. Direct Evidence of Divisional Rent Seeking

The early empirical work on internal capital markets documents inefficiencies in capital allocation and interprets these inefficiencies as stemming from rent-seeking behavior by divisional managers. However, it provides little direct evidence that more influential divisional managers are able to attract more capital. A series of recent papers tries to provide more direct evidence along these lines.

The findings generally support the view that the influence of divisional managers is important. The most direct evidence comes from surveys in which CFOs report that "corporate politics" plays an important role in capital allocation (Graham et al. 2011). These surveys do not explore the ways in which corporate politics matter. How they matter is the focus of much of the recent research.

Xuan (2009) finds evidence that politics matter by looking at the behavior of new CEOs. He shows that when a CEO who gets promoted from her prior position as a divisional manager (a "specialist" CEO), she tends to favor other divisions in the capital allocation process at the expense of her prior division. The investment allocations of these CEOs tend to be less efficient than those of more generalist CEOs. Xuan interprets these findings as evidence that specialist CEOs need to curry favor with politically powerful division managers.

Glaser et al. (2010) provide more direct evidence of the importance of politically connected divisional managers. Studying a single large diversified conglomerate, they show that divisional managers have more capital allocated to their divisions in response to large cash windfalls at the corporate level if the division manager has a longer tenure in the firm or his division is geographically closer to headquarters.

Duchin and Sosyura (in press) study corporate politics using a large set of firms. They document that various measures of divisional manager connections to the CEO (e.g., membership in the same nonprofit organizations, degrees from the same universities, and previous employment at the same firm) are related to higher investment at the divisional level. These connections also reduce the sensitivity of investment to measures of divisional Q when there are greater agency problems between headquarters and management. This finding is consistent with Scharfstein and Stein (2000) who argued that capital allocation is less efficient if there are two tiers of agency problems—one between divisional managers and CEOs and the other between the CEO and shareholders.

While these papers focus on informal connections between divisional managers and CEOs as a measure of influence, Cremers et al. (2011) analyze the effect of more formal connections to headquarters. In particular, they study a German banking group, composed of 181 member banks, which each have voting rights in the management of headquarters. These voting rights can be disproportionate to the size of the member bank and could well exceed the member bank's claims on the cash flows of headquarters. They find that when a member bank has disproportionately high voting rights relative to its cash flow rights, headquarters reallocates more capital to the member bank, away from less influential banks.

6.3. Business Groups

Another stream of research focuses on the functioning of "internal" capital markets in business groups. This is not exactly an internal capital market in the sense that capital is being allocated across divisions of a single business entity; instead it is allocated across independent firms that are tied together because they are owned by a common large (possibly controlling) shareholder. This structure could take the form of a shareholder directly controlling each business through a large ownership stake and high voting rights. Or it could take the form of a pyramidal structure whereby one of the firms, which has a controlling shareholder, also owns a large (but not necessarily a 100% stake) in another firm. These structures are common around the world, as documented by La Porta et al. (1999). Much of the empirical work has been about Indian business groups and Korean chaebol.

To our knowledge, Almeida and Wolfenzon (2006) is the sole theoretical paper on the internal capital markets of business groups. They develop a model in which business groups efficiently allocate capital for the same sorts of reasons developed by Stein (1997). However, they point to a potential unintended consequence of an efficient internal capital market on the functioning of the external capital market: it could reduce the supply of funding to standalone firms with high-value projects. With weak investor protection, a business group may prefer to reallocate funds from a poor project to a mediocre internal project rather than invest in a high-return external project where its rights as an investor are poorly protected. In contrast, a standalone firm with a poor project has no alternative but to invest in the standalone firm with the high-return project. In this model, business groups appear to be efficient, given the existing structures, but could be inefficient from a broader, general equilibrium, perspective.

There are papers that point to the value of business groups in the allocation of capital and others that raise doubts about their effectiveness. Gopalan et al. (2007) analyze capital reallocation across firms in business groups in India. These firms report interfirm loans within the business group, which tend to be quite large, thus suggesting an active market for capital within business groups. They find that most intragroup loans are made to weaker firms in the group on more favorable terms than arm's-length lending would suggest. The motive for lending seems to be more support for weak firms to avoid bankruptcy than to fund investment projects to stimulate growth. These loans are more likely to be provided to firms with higher insider holdings. The efficiency implications of this activity are ambiguous, but the authors show that when a firm in a business group fails, other firms in the group have greater difficulty raising external capital and investing.[8]

Bertrand et al. (2002) take a less sanguine view about the value of transfers among firms in Indian business groups. They examine whether controlling shareholders of these business groups engage in "tunneling," a term introduced by Johnson et al. (2000) in modeling behavior whereby profits are moved from firms where the controlling shareholder has low cash flow rights to others where he has high cash flow rights. Tunneling could happen through transfer prices or the sort of low-interest loans documented by Gopalan et al. (2007), as described above. They show that industry shocks that should increase the profits of firms where the controlling shareholder has low cash flow rights also increase the cash flow of firms where the controlling shareholder has high cash flow rights. But the opposite is not true; when positive shocks hit the industry of the firms where the controlling shareholder has high cash flow rights, there is no corresponding increase in the cash flows of the other firms.

Likewise, there appear to be somewhat competing views about the function of Korean chaebol. Shin and Park (1999) show that the investment of member firms of a chaebol is insensitive to their own cash flow, whereas independent firms' investment is sensitive to their own cash flow. This result is reminiscent of the finding of Hoshi et al. (1991) on Japanese keirestu. Yet Shin and Park also find that chaebol firms tend to invest more than independent firms in low-Q industries, much like the finding of Scharfstein (1998) and Ozbas and Scharfstein (2010) for U.S. conglomerates. On the bright side, however, Almeida and Kim (2011) find that chaebol firms invested more during the 1997 Asian financial crisis than a matched sample of independent firms. This difference did not exist during noncrisis periods.

Perhaps one way to reconcile the competing views of business groups is that they may destroy value during normal times (through tunneling or inefficient investment), but during a crisis—either firm-specific or economy wide—business groups can help alleviate distress. Nevertheless, there remain many open questions about how well the business group, which is the predominant form of corporate organization around the world, functions generally and with respect to the allocation of capital.

7. The Process of Internal Capital Allocation

The functioning of internal capital markets should, in theory, depend on how the allocation of capital is organized—the layers of approval required to undertake an investment, the type of information that must be provided for an investment to be authorized, and the extent to which control over investment is centralized or decentralized. The internal capital market

---

8. Hoshi et al. (1990) document superior performance of distressed Japanese firms that are members of a *keiretsu* business group and those that are not.

models discussed above do not address these important questions; they essentially assume that decisionmaking is centralized and is based on information provided to headquarters.

Some work on internal capital markets has attempted to address the question of optimal design of an internal resource allocation process. Other work, although not directly addressing the design of a capital allocation process, analyzes the optimal design of organizational communication and the allocation of control rights. This work could prove useful in understanding the process of internal capital allocation.

An early paper that models the capital allocation process is that of Harris and Raviv (1996). The model is of a single division manager, who receives private benefits from investment, and of headquarters, which seeks to maximize firm value. The manager has private information about the economic value of the project. The problem is to give the manager enough latitude to incorporate her information into the investment decision, but not so much latitude that she will significantly overinvest, given the private benefits she receives from such investment. Harris and Raviv show that the optimal process involves an initial allocation to the manager, along with an option for the manager to ask for an increase in her capital allocation. If the requested increase is modest, the manager is given her request. But if it is above a certain threshold, the division is audited with positive probability to ensure that the request is warranted. If it is warranted, then the request is granted, but otherwise it is not. One implication of this analysis is that there is overinvestment in low-value projects, because managers know they can deploy the initial allocation even if the project valuation is low. There can also be underinvestment in high-value projects, because if there is a request above the initial allocation, it is not optimal to grant the manager her full request.

Dessein (2002) analyzes a similar question. A better-informed agent has interests that are systematically misaligned with those of the principal. Dessein compares delegating a decision to the agent or receiving a cheap talk report from the agent and then having the principal decide. The incentive conflict limits the amount of information that can credibly be conveyed to the principal, so the principal's trade-off is between delegation that uses all the local information but results in decisions that are misaligned or communication that incorporates limited information but avoids the misalignment. The main result in the paper is that if the incentive conflict is not too large, delegation dominates.

Marino and Matsusaka (2005) study a similar problem to Dessein (2002) in an internal capital market setting, but they allow for signaling by the agent through the size of a request for funds. Senior managers must accept or reject proposals. Larger requests signal better projects, so signaling creates a cost through excessive investment. Again delegation is typically preferred.

Malenko (2012) extends the Harris and Raviv (1996) analysis to continuous time and an infinite horizon. Like the Harris and Raviv model, the optimal mechanism derived by Malenko captures some key features of the way that capital is allocated in corporations. Malenko shows that it is optimal to give a manager a capital budget and allow him to spend freely from that budget when the projects are below a certain threshold. But if the project size exceeds the threshold, the manager is required to seek approval from headquarters to go ahead with the project, and the project is financed out of headquarters' budget.

Another issue in the design of a capital allocation process is the extent to which it should be centralized in a hierarchy or decentralized throughout the organization. Stein (2002) presents a model that is useful in addressing this important question. The model hinges on the distinction between "hard" information, which can be documented and used to convince bosses about the value of a project, and "soft" information, which cannot be easily verified. A salient example of hard information in banking is a borrower's credit score; an example of soft information is a borrower's trustworthiness.

When information is soft, the disadvantage of a hierarchy with multiple layers of management is that managers may decide, based on their own information, to choose other projects proposed by other managers. This possibility reduces the incentive for lower level managers to put in effort identifying good projects based on soft information. This problem can be mitigated by designing a relatively flat hierarchy, whereby decisions over individual projects are relatively decentralized, and managers have more control over whether the project is approved.

Hierarchies may generate too little soft information, but they can result in excessive hard information production. A project is much more likely to be approved if it can be supported by hard information. Thus, even if soft information is intrinsically more valuable, managers will spend excessive time documenting their proposals with hard information. The model therefore has implications for how organizational structure affects the type of information that is gathered as well as the optimal choice between hierarchical and decentralized decisionmaking.

The Stein (2002) paper was motivated by the observation that small banks (which can be thought of as a decentralized model of decisionmaking) tend to do more relationship lending than do large banks, as indicated by Berger et al. (1999). Berger et al. (2005) present a collection of evidence indicating that large banks rely more heavily on hard information. In particular, large banks lend to firms that maintain better accounting records, operate at a greater distance from the bank, and meet with their loan officers less frequently.[9] Liberti and Mian (2009) examine information flows within a bank rather than across banks as in Berger et al. (2005). Using detailed information from the credit dossiers of individual borrowers, they are able to show that when loans require more levels of approval, the loan approval decision is more sensitive to hard than to soft information.

A large complementary literature in organizational economics studies information flows and the allocation of control rights in organizations. Some ideas in this literature could prove useful in understanding the capital allocation process, although the empirical implications of this literature are far from clear. For example, Dewatripont and Tirole (2005) develop a model where there are misaligned incentives and communication is costly for both the sender and recipient. The more effort each one exerts, the greater the likelihood that soft information becomes hard. In other words, business-unit managers can try to explain to senior managers why they think a particular project is attractive. They can provide costly evidence, senior management can ask questions that impact the reliability of the evidence, and the like. The authors show that in these situations communication and effort can be strategic complements. It is worthwhile for the recipient to invest a great deal in listening only if the sender spends a great deal to provide useful information and vice versa. Dewatripont and Tirole also introduce the notion of cue communication—the sender conveys cues, such as his expertise, which then makes soft information credible.

---

9. One might be concerned that the results are driven by endogenous assignment of firms to banks, but Berger et al. (2005) do a good job of instrumenting for the size of the bank by looking at regulatory changes that affect bank size.

Several recent papers study the allocation of control rights in organizations with dispersed information. Rantakari (2008) and Alonso et al. (2008) build models with a trade-off between local adaptation and interdivision coordination. They study horizontal communication among division managers with decentralized decisionmaking and compare it to vertical communication with headquarters and centralized decisionmaking. Rantakari focuses on asymmetries among divisions in the importance of coordination and shows that asymmetric organizational structures with some divisions decentralized and others centralized can be optimal. In Alonso et al. (2008), vertical cheap talk communication is more effective than horizontal communication, because incentives are more aligned, but there is a loss in adaptation from centralized decisionmaking. As coordination becomes more important, horizontal communication actually improves, because division managers' interests become more aligned and more information is incorporated in decentralized decisionmaking. Thus, even if coordination is important, centralized control is not necessarily the optimal outcome.

Van den Steen (2010) provides one justification for centralization based on disagreements among managers of complementary projects. In his model, the combination of externalities and disagreement leads to optimal concentration of authority over projects. Common ownership (through its residual control rights) and low-powered incentives make it easier to enforce authority, thereby generating a complementarity among centralization, internal control, and low-powered incentives. The idea that lack of coordination in a decentralized firm is not simply an information problem but results from differences of opinion may be important. Communication may be insufficient to resolve such differences, and therefore, centralized authority may be required. This would be especially true if differences of opinion are coupled with differences in judgment, which could be modeled as more accurate prior beliefs. The assumption that agents have different priors may therefore also be an avenue to incorporate judgment into formal models of organizational structure.

8. Conclusion

The research on internal capital markets centers squarely on the question of how firms allocate resources. Although this issue would seem to be the central question in organizational economics, it has not received much attention from mainstream organizational economists. Instead, much of the work on resource allocation has been undertaken by financial economists, writing about the conduct and performance of diversified conglomerates. The field would be richer if there were more integration between the work of financial economists and organizational economists, as has been argued by Bolton and Scharfstein (1998). This work need not focus exclusively on the allocation of resources for investment in capital and R&D. It could also address issues related to the transfer of goods and services within firms, as well as the assignment of workers to various jobs within firms. Of course, this is no easy task, but it is one worth taking on.

REFERENCES

Ahn, S., and D. Denis. 2004. "Internal Capital Markets and Investment Policy: Evidence from Corporate Spinoffs." *Journal of Financial Economics* 71: 489–516.

Almeida, H., and C. S. Kim. 2011. "The Effect of Internal Capital Markets on Corporate Investment: Evidence from the Asian Financial Crisis." Working paper, University of Illinois, Urbana-Champaign.

Almeida, H., and D. Wolfenzon. 2006. "Should Business Groups Be Dismantled? The Equilibrium Costs of Efficient Internal Capital Markets." *Journal of Financial Economics* 79: 99–144.

Alonso, R., W. Dessein, and N. Matouschek. 2008. "When Does Coordination Require Centralization?" *American Economic Review* 98: 145–179.

Ashcraft, A. B. 2008. "Are Bank Holding Companies a Source of Strength to Their Banking Subsidiaries?" *Journal of Money, Credit and Banking* 40: 273–294.

Athey, S., and J. Roberts. 2001. "Organizational Design: Decision Rights and Incentive Contracts." *American Economic Review* 91(papers and proceedings): 200–205.

Baker, G. P. 1992. "Beatrice: A Study in the Creation and Destruction of Value." *Journal of Finance* 47: 1081–1119.

Baker, G. P., and K. Wruck. 1989. "Organizational Changes and Value Creation in Leveraged Buyouts: The Case of O.M. Scott & Sons Company." *Journal of Financial Economics* 25: 163–190.

Berger, A. N., R. S. Demsetz, and P. E. Strahan. 1999. "The Consolidation of the Financial Services Industry: Causes, Consequences, and Implications for the Future." *Journal of Banking and Finance* 23: 135–194.

Berger, A. N. Miller, M. Petersen, R. G. Rajan, and J. C. Stein. 2005. "Does Function Follow Organizational Form? Evidence from the Lending Practices of Large and Small Banks." *Journal of Financial Economics* 76: 237–269.

Berger, P., and E. Ofek. 1995. "Diversification's Effect on Firm Value." *Journal of Financial Economics* 37: 9–65.

Bernardo, A., J. Luo, and J. Wang. 2006. "A Theory of Socialistic Internal Capital Markets." *Journal of Financial Economics* 80: 485–509.

Bertrand, M., P. Mehta, and S. Mullainathan. 2002. "Ferreting out Tunneling: An Application to Indian Business Groups." *Quarterly Journal of Economics* 117: 121–148.

Bhagat, S., A. Shleifer, and R. W. Vishny. 1990. "Hostile Takeovers in the 1980s: The Return to Corporate Specialization." *Brookings Papers on Economic Activity: Microeconomics* 1990: 1–84.

Billett, M., and D. Mauer. 2003. "Cross Subsidies, External Financing Constraints, and the Contribution of the Internal Capital Market to Firm Value." *Review of Financial Studies* 16: 1167–1201.

Bolton, P., and D. S. Scharfstein. 1998. "Corporate Finance, the Theory of the Firm, and Organizations." *Journal of Economic Perspectives* 12(4): 95–114.

Bower, J. 1970. *Managing the Resource Allocation Process: A Study of Corporate Planning and Investment,* revised edition. Cambridge, MA: Harvard Business School Press.

Brusco, S., and F. Panunzi. 2005. "Reallocation of Corporate Resources and Managerial Incentives in Internal Capital Markets." *European Economic Review* 49: 659–681.

Burgelman, R. 1983. "A Process Model of Internal Corporate Venturing in the Diversified Major Firm." *Administrative Science Quarterly* 28: 223–244.

Campa, J., and S. Kedia. 2002. "Explaining the Diversification Discount." *Journal of Finance* 57: 1731–1762.

Campello, M. 2002. "Internal Capital Markets in Financial Conglomerates: Evidence from Small Bank Responses to Monetary Policy." *Journal of Finance* 57: 2773–2805.

Cetorelli, N., and L. Goldberg. In press. "Banking Globalization and Monetary Transmission." *Journal of Finance.*

Chevalier, J. A. 2004. "What Do We Know about Cross-Subsidization? Evidence from Merging Firms." *B.E. Journal of Economic Analysis and Policy* 4: 1, 3.

Chevalier, J. A., and D. S. Scharfstein. 1996. "Capital Market Imperfections and Countercyclical Markups: Theory and Evidence." *American Economic Review* 86: 703–725.

Christensen, C. 1997. *The Innovator's Dilemma.* Cambridge, MA: Harvard Business School Press.

Claessens, S., S. Kjankov, J. P. H. Fan, and L. H. P. Lang. 1999. "The Benefits and Costs of Internal Markets: Evidence from Asia's Financial Crisis." Working paper, World Bank, Washington, DC.

Coase, Ronald H. 1937. "The Nature of the Firm." *Economica* 4: 386–405.

Cremers, M., R. Huang, and Z. Sautner. 2011. "Internal Capital Markets and Corporate Politics in a Banking Group." *Review of Financial Studies* 24: 358–401.

De Motta, A. 2003. "Managerial Incentives and Internal Capital Markets." *Journal of Finance* 58: 1193–1220.

Dessein, W. 2002. "Authority and Communication in Organizations." *Review of Economic Studies* 69: 811–838.

Dessein, W., L. Garicano, and R. Gertner. 2010. "Organizing for Synergies," *American Economic Journal: Microeconomics* 2: 77–114.

Dewatripont, M. 2006. "Costly Communication and Incentives." *Journal of the European Economic Association* 4: 253–268.

Dewatripont, M., and J. Tirole. 2005. "Modes of Communication." *Journal of Political Economy* 113: 1217–1238.

Dittmar, A., and A. Shivdasani. 2003. "Divestitures and Divisional Investment Policies." *Journal of Finance* 58: 2711–2743.

Donaldson, G. 1984. *Managing Corporate Wealth.* New York: Praeger.

Duchin, R., and D. Sosyura. In press. "Divisional Managers and Internal Capital Markets." *Journal of Finance.*

Eccles, R. 1985. *The Transfer Pricing Problem: A Theory for Practice.* New York: Lexingon Books.

Fauver, L., J. Houston, and A. Naranjo. 1998. "Capital Market Development, Legal Systems and the Value of Corporate Diversification: A Cross-Country Analysis." Working paper, University of Florida, Gainsville.

Fazzari, S. M., R. G. Hubbard, and B. C. Petersen. 1998. "Financing Constraints and Corporate Investment." *Brookings Papers on Economic Activity* 1988: 141–195.

Gertner, R. H., D. Scharfstein, and J. C. Stein. 1994. "Internal versus External Capital Markets." *Quarterly Journal of Economics* 109: 1211–1230.

Gertner, R. H., E. Powers, and D. Scharfstein. 2002. "Learning about Internal Capital Markets from Corporate Spinoffs." *Journal of Finance* 57: 2479–2506.

Glaser, M., F. Lopez-de-Silanes, and Z. Sautner. 2010. "Opening the Black Box: Internal Capital Markets and Managerial Power." Available at Social Science Research Network: http://papers.ssrn .com/sol3/papers.cfm?abstract_id=966325.

Gopalan, R., V. Nanda, and A. Seru. 2007. "Affiliated Firms and Financial Support: Evidence from Indian Business Groups." *Journal of Financial Economics* 86: 759–795.

Graham, J. R., M. L. Lemmon, and J. Wolf. 2002. "Does Corporate Diversification Destroy Value?" *Journal of Finance* 57: 695–720.

Graham, J. R., C. R. Harvey, and M. Puri. 2011. "Capital Allocation and Delegation of Decision-Making Authority within Firms." Working Paper 17370, National Bureau of Economic Research, Cambridge, MA.

Gromb, D., and D. Scharfstein. 2002. "Entrepreneurship in Equilibrium." Working Paper 9001, National Bureau of Economic Research, Cambridge, MA.

Hadlock, C., M. Ryngaert, and S. Thomas. 2001. "Corporate Structure and Equity Offerings: Are There Benefits to Diversification?" *Journal of Business* 74: 613–635.

Harris, M., and A. Raviv. 1991. "The Theory of Capital Structure." *Journal of Finance* 46: 297–355.

———. 1996. "The Capital Budgeting Process: Incentives and Information." *Journal of Finance* 51: 1139–1174.

Hortaçsu, A., and C. Syverson. 2009. "Why Do Firms Own Production Chains?" Working paper, University of Chicago.

Hoshi, T., A. Kashyap, and D. Scharfstein. 1990. "The Role of Banks in Reducing the Costs of Financial Distress in Japan." *Journal of Financial Economics* 27: 67–88.

———. 1991. "Corporate Structure, Liquidity, and Investment: Evidence from Japanese Industrial Groups." *Quarterly Journal of Economics* 106: 33–60.

Houston, J., C. James, and D. Marcus. 1997. "Capital Market Frictions and the Role of Internal Capital Markets in Banking." *Journal of Financial Economics* 46: 135–164.

Hubbard, R. G., and D. Palia. 1999. "A Reexamination of the Conglomerate Merger Wave in the 1960s: An Internal Capital Markets View." *Journal of Finance* 54: 1131–1152.

Hyland, D. C., and J. D. Diltz. 2002. "Why Firms Diversify: An Empirical Examination." *Financial Management* 31: 1–81.

Inderst, R., and H. M. Mueller. 2003. "Internal versus External Financing: An Optimal Contracting Approach." *Journal of Finance* 58: 1033–1062.

Johnson, S., R. LaPorta, F. Lopez-de-Silanes, and A. Shleifer. 2000. "Tunneling." *American Economic Review* 90(papers and proceedings): 22–27.

Kaplan, S., and M. Weisbach. 1992. "The Success of Acquisitions: Evidence from Divestitures." *Journal of Finance* 47: 107–138.

Kaplan, S., M. Mitchell, and K. Wruck. 1997. "A Clinical Exploration of Value Creation and Destruction in Acquisitions: Organization Design, Incentives, and Internal Capital Markets." Working paper, University of Chicago.

Khanna, N., and S. Tice. 2001. "The Bright Side of Internal Capital Markets." *Journal of Finance* 56: 1489–1528.

Lamont, O. 1997. "Cash Flow and Investment: Evidence from Internal Capital Markets." *Journal of Finance* 52: 83–109.

Lamont, O., and C. Polk. 2001. "The Diversification Discount: Cash Flows vs. Returns." *Journal of Finance* 56: 1693–1721.

Lang, L.H.P., and R. Stulz. 1994. "Tobin's *q,* Corporate Diversification, and Firm Performance." *Journal of Political Economy* 102: 1248–1280.

LaPorta, R., F. Lopez-de-Silanes, and A. Shleifer. 1999. "Corporate Ownership around the World." *Journal of Finance* 54: 471–517.

Lewellen, W. G. 1971. "A Pure Financial Rationale for the Conglomerate Merger." *Journal of Finance* 26: 521–537.

Liberti, J., and A. Mian. 2009. "Estimating the Impact of Hierarchies on Information Use." *Review of Financial Studies* 22: 4057–4090.

Lins, K., and H. Servaes. 1999. "International Evidence on the Value of Corporate Diversification." *Journal of Finance* 54: 2215–2239.

———. 2002. "Is Corporate Diversification Beneficial in Emerging Markets?" *Financial Management* 31: 5–31.

Maksimovic, V., and G. M. Phillips. 2002. "Do Conglomerate Firms Allocate Resources Inefficiently across Industries? Theory and Evidence." *Journal of Finance* 57: 721–767.

———. 2007. "Conglomerate Firms and Internal Capital Markets," in B. Espen Eckbo (ed.), *Handbook of Corporate Finance: Empirical Corporate Finance.* Handbooks in Finance Series. Amsterdam: Elsevier/North-Holland.

Malenko, A. 2012. "Optimal Design of Internal Capital Markets." Working paper, Massachusetts Institute of Technology, Cambridge, MA.

Marino, A., and J. Matsusaka. 2005. "Decision Processes, Agency Problems, and Information: An Economic Analysis of Capital Budgeting Procedures." *Review of Financial Studies* 18: 301–325.

Mathews, R. D., and D. T. Robinson. 2008. "Market Structure, Internal Capital Markets, and the Boundaries of the Firm." *Journal of Finance* 63: 2703–2736.

Matsusaka, J. 1993. "Takeover Motives during the Conglomerate Merger Wave." *RAND Journal of Economics* 24: 357–379.

Matsusaka, J., and V. Nanda. 2002. "Internal Capital Markets and Corporate Refocusing." *Journal of Financial Intermediation* 11: 176–216.

Meyer, M., P. Milgrom, and J. Roberts. 1992. "Organizational Prospects, Influence Costs, and Ownership Changes." *Journal of Economics and Management Strategy* 1: 9–35.

Montgomery, C. A., and B. Wernerfelt. 1988. "Tobin's q and the Importance of Focus in Firm Performance." *American Economic Review* 78: 246–250.

Morgan, D. P., B. Rime, and P. E. Strahan. 2004. "Bank Integration and State Business Cycles." *Quarterly Journal of Economics* 119: 1555–1585.

Mullainathan, S., and D. Scharfstein. 2001. "Do Firm Boundaries Matter?" *American Economic Review* 91(papers and proceedings): 195–199.

Ozbas, O. 2005. "Integration, Organizational Processes, and Allocation of Resources." *Journal of Financial Economics* 75: 201–242.

Ozbas, O., and D. Scharfstein. 2010. "Evidence on the Dark Side of Internal Capital Markets." *Review of Financial Studies* 23: 581–599.

Peek, J., and E. Rosengren. 1997. "The International Transmission of Financial Shocks: The Case of Japan." *American Economic Review* 87: 495–505.

Peyer, U., and A. Shivdasani. 2001. "Leverage and Internal Capital Markets: Evidence from Leveraged Recapitalizations." *Journal of Financial Economics* 59: 477–515.

Porter, M. E. 1987. "From Competitive Advantage to Corporate Strategy." *Harvard Business Review* 65: 43–59.

Rajan, R., H. Servaes, and L. Zingales. 2000. "The Cost of Diversity: The Diversification Discount and Inefficient Investment." *Journal of Finance* 55: 35–80.

Rantakari, H. 2008. "Governing Adaptation." *Review of Economic Studies* 75: 1257–1285.

Rotemberg, J., and G. Saloner. 1994. "Benefits of Narrow Business Strategies." *American Economic Review* 84: 1330–1349.

Sautner, Z., and B. Villalonga. 2010. "Corporate Governance and Internal Capital Markets." Working Paper 10-100, Harvard Business School, Cambridge, MA.

Scharfstein, D. S. 1998. "The Dark Side of Internal Capital Markets II: Evidence from Diversified Conglomerates." NBER Working Paper 6352, National Bureau of Economic Research, Cambridge, MA.

Scharfstein, D. S., and J. C. Stein. 2000. "The Dark Side of Internal Capital Markets: Divisional Rent-Seeking and Inefficient Investment." *Journal of Finance* 55: 2537–2564.

Schipper, K., and R. Thompson. 1983. "Evidence on the Capitalized Value of Merger Activity for Acquiring Firms." *Journal of Financial Economics* 11: 85–119.

Schnabl, P. 2012. "The International Transmission of Bank Liquidity Shocks: Evidence from an Emerging Market." *Journal of Finance,* forthcoming.

Seru, A. In press. "Firm Boundaries Matter: Evidence from Conglomerates and R&D Activity." *Journal of Financial Economics.*

Servaes, H. 1996. "The Value of Diversification during the Conglomerate Merger Wave." *Journal of Finance* 51: 1201–1225.

Shin, H., and Y. S. Park. 1999. "Financing Constraints and Internal Capital Markets: Evidence from Korean Chaebols." *Journal of Corporate Finance* 5: 169–191.

Shin, H., and R. Stulz. 1998. "Are Internal Capital Markets Efficient?" *Quarterly Journal of Economics* 113: 531–552.

Shleifer, A., and R. W. Vishny. 1997. "A Survey of Corporate Governance." *Journal of Finance* 52: 737–783.

Sloan, A. 1964. *My Years with General Motors.* New York: Doubleday.

Stein, J. C. 1997. "Internal Capital Markets and the Competition for Corporate Resources." *Journal of Finance* 52: 111–133.

———. 2002. "Information Production and Capital Allocation: Decentralized vs. Hierarchical Firms." *Journal of Finance* 57: 1891–1921.

———. 2003. "Agency, Information and Corporate Investment," in G.M. Constantinides, M. Harris, and R. Stulz (eds.), *Handbook of the Economics of Finance.* Amsterdam: Elsevier, pp. 111–162.

Sull, D. 1999. "The Dynamics of Standing Still: Firestone Tire & Rubber and the Radial Revolution." *Business History Review* 73: 430–464.

Van den Steen, E. 2010. "Interpersonal Authority in a Theory of the Firm." *American Economic Review* 100: 466–490.

Villalonga, B. 2004a. "Does Diversification Cause the Diversification Discount?" *Financial Management* 33: 5–27.

———. 2004b. "Diversification Discount or Premium? New Evidence from the Business Information Tracking Series." *Journal of Finance* 59: 475–502.

Weston, J. F. 1970. "Diversification and Merger Trends." *Business Economics* 5: 50–57.

Whited, T. 2001. "Is It Inefficient Investment That Causes the Diversification Discount?" *Journal of Finance* 56: 1667–1692.

Williamson, O. 1975. *Markets and Hierarchies: Analysis and Antitrust Implications.* New York: Macmillan.

Wulf, J. 2009. "Influence and Inefficiency in the Internal Capital Market." *Journal of Economic Behavior and Organization* 72: 305–321.

Xuan, Y. 2009. "Empire-Building or Bridge-Building? Evidence from New CEOs' Internal Capital Allocation Decisions." *Review of Financial Studies* 22: 4919–4948.

17

What Do Managers Do?
Exploring Persistent Performance Differences among Seemingly Similar Enterprises
Robert Gibbons and Rebecca Henderson

1. Introduction

Decades of research using a wide variety of detailed plant- and firm-level data has provided strong evidence of persistent performance differences among seemingly similar enterprises (hereafter, PPDs among SSEs). Bartelsman and Doms (2000) reviewed the sizeable initial literature on this issue, and a recent review by Syverson (2011) highlighting much new research has only strengthened the result.

As one striking example, Syverson (2004a) finds that "within 4-digit SIC [Standard Industrial Classification] industries in the U.S. manufacturing sector, the average difference in logged total factor productivity (TFP) between an industry's 90th and 10th percentile plants is 0.651 . . . [meaning that] the plant at the 90th percentile of the productivity distribution makes almost *twice* as much output *with the same measured inputs* as the 10th percentile plant." And the United States is not exceptional: Hsieh and Klenow (2009) "find even larger productivity differences in China and India, with average 90-10 TFP ratios over 5:1" (Syverson 2011: 326–327, emphasis in the original).

Indeed, the existence of PPDs among SSEs is so well established that recent work in trade, industry dynamics, and productivity growth has increasingly taken this fact as a fundamental starting point. For example Melitz's (2003: 1695) celebrated paper begins: "Recent empirical research using longitudinal plant- or firm-level data from several countries has overwhelmingly

We are very grateful for help from Dan Barron, Nick Bloom, Sylvain Chassang, Eliza Forsythe, Marina Halac, Casey Ichniowski, Nico Lacetera, Ruitian Lang, Hongyi Li, Jin Li, Maria Polyakova, Mike Powell, Jan Rivkin, John Roberts, Annalisa Scognamiglio, Kathryn Shaw, Chad Syverson, John Van Reenen, Sarah Venables, and seminar audiences at Brown, Columbia, Dartmouth, Emory, Harvard, London Business School, London School of Economics, University of Michigan, University of Minnesota, Stanford, Sydney, Tilburg University, University of Toronto, Vanderbilt, Washington University, and Yale. This project would not have been possible without years of crucial support from the Massachusetts Institute of Technology Sloan School's Program on Innovation in Markets and Organizations, especially Nancy Beaulieu, Nelson Repenning, John Sterman, and Tommy Wang.

substantiated the existence of large and persistent productivity differences among establishments in the same narrowly defined industries."

The question of what *causes* these performance differences, however, is still wide open. Syverson (2011) offered a long list of possibilities, including differences in management practice, higher quality labor and capital, differential investment in information technology and research and development (R&D), learning by doing, firm structure, productivity spillovers, regulatory behavior, and differences in competitive regime. Here we focus on the first of these: the role of management practices as a source of PPDs among SSEs.

We choose this focus for four reasons, which we state briefly here and unpack below. First, in large-sample studies, differences in management practices are correlated with differences in productivity. Second, focused-sample studies at the plant and even the line level suggest that these large-sample results are robust to controls for many other factors that Syverson identifies as potential determinants of productivity. Third, choosing management practices as a key driver of PPDs surfaces an important question rarely asked in economics but central to strategic management: why do best practices not diffuse more readily? Finally, we hope that our specific discussion of management practices and PPDs will help shape a broader research agenda in organizational economics about what, exactly, managers do.

We begin from the observation that many competitively significant management practices cannot be reduced to well-defined action rules that can be specified ex ante and verified ex post. Instead, the implementation of these management practices is critically dependent on context. For example, for many years the singularly successful retailer Nordstrom asked its sales associates to "use their good judgment in all situations." Similarly, Toyota's chief request of its production workers was that they seek to "continuously improve the production process." The state-dependent actions necessary to meet these expectations cannot be the subject of a formal contract. We therefore focus on relational contracts—roughly, understandings that the parties share about their roles in and rewards from cooperating together, but understandings so rooted in the details of the parties' relationship that they cannot be shared with a court.

Viewed broadly, we see our perspective on management practices as consistent with decades of work on management and authority, such as Barnard (1938), Simon (1947), Penrose (1959), Cyert and March (1963), and Arrow (1974). As one crisp summary, Mintzberg (2004) separates a manager's activities into analysis (deciding what to do) and administration (getting the organization to do it). Although both are surely important, the strong theme we see in the literature from Barnard to Arrow focuses on the latter, as do we here. In short, we see relational contracts as a key way that managers get organizations to get things done. Furthermore, we see many competitively significant management practices as relying on relational contracts that themselves are hard to build and change, leading to the slow diffusion of management practices that could improve organizational performance.

The core of this chapter is therefore (1) evidence that some important management practices rely on relational contracts, (2) evidence that relational contracts can be hard to build and change, and (3) examples of recent theories that begin to address some of these issues. To prepare for these core aspects of the chapter, in Sections 2 and 3 we briefly review the two literatures mentioned above that motivate our argument. In Section 2 we summarize evidence that PPDs among SSEs exist and are economically significant across a wide range of industries and geographies. These results have been shown to be robust to concerns that they reflect problems of selection, or simultaneity, or the distinction between productivity in revenue versus physical terms. These productivity differences have also been shown to be persistent over time and surprisingly resistant to increased competition. That is, as we describe in Section 2, an increase in competition does tend to increase an industry's average productivity and decrease its productivity dispersion, but such dispersion is by no means eliminated, even in very competitive environments.

In Section 3 we then summarize evidence that performance differences are importantly correlated with variation in management practices. We complement the recent large-sample work in economics by drawing particularly on focused-sample research in industrial relations and human resource management that has explored the role of high-commitment work systems in driving productivity, as well as on focused-sample research in strategy and organizational studies that has studied the role of white-collar work practices in explaining competitive advantage. As we describe, such focused-sample work can offer especially sharp measures of control variables, dependent variables, and the independent variables of interest (i.e., management practices); see Ichniowski and Shaw (this volume) for more on such "insider econometrics."

In the remainder of the chapter we consider relational contracts. We begin Section 4 by sketching the basic theory of relational contracts, which is closely related to more established work on repeated games. We then describe qualitative examples of competitively significant management practices that rely on relational contracts—at Lincoln Electric and Toyota for blue-collar work and at Merck for white-collar work.

Section 5 turns to the question of why management practices associated with persistent performance differences do not diffuse more readily. We begin by reviewing the extensive literature on this topic, which has developed along four lines. First, managers may have problems of *perception*—they do not know they are behind. Second, managers may have problems of *inspiration*—they know they are behind, but they do not know what to do about it. Third, managers may have problems of *motivation*—they know they are behind and they know what to do, but they lack incentive to adopt new practices. Fourth, managers may have problems of *implementation*—they know they are behind, they know what to do, and they are trying hard to do it, but they nonetheless cannot get the organization to get it done.[1]

Given the evidence from Section 4 that important management practices may depend on relational contracts, we continue Section 5 by sketching recent models in which superior performance indeed rests on relational contracts, but these contracts are either too expensive or not even feasible for some enterprises to implement. In short, in these models, bad performance is due to bad parameters among enterprises that are only seemingly similar (i.e., there is unmeasured heterogeneity in the costs of using the key relational contracts).

Our central interest, however, is in the important class of cases where practices do not diffuse even though they are widely acknowledged to be competitively significant, knowledge of how to implement them is reasonably widespread, and firms are striving mightily to adopt them. (Think of the mature phases of the Toyota Production System or total quality management, for example.) Such cases are not well explained either by the perception, inspiration, or motivation arguments for why practices do not diffuse or by relational-contract models in which the rela-

---

1. We thank Jan Rivkin for explaining his "four 'tion" labels to us and allowing us to adapt them here for our purposes.

tional contracts that underlie high performance are either too expensive or not feasible for some firms. Instead, for the class of cases that is our central interest, we require an implementation argument.

The remainder of the chapter therefore focuses on implementation difficulties that arise through relational contracts. In particular, we suggest two approaches to modeling such issues. We present the first approach in the remainder of Section 5. In very recent relational-contracting models, such as those where path dependence in relational contracting can produce measured performance differences among ex ante identical enterprises, several interesting possibilities arise: cooperation can be hard to build well, in the sense that achieving perfunctory cooperation can make it harder to achieve consummate cooperation; cooperation, once built, can be fragile; and cooperation may be difficult to build in the first place. In all these models, however, the parties play the optimal equilibrium of the game as a whole, and they understand this equilibrium from the beginning of the game. That is, although we have moved beyond explanations of bad performance based on bad parameters, now we have explanations based on bad luck.

Our second approach to modeling implementation difficulties that arise through relational contracts is much more speculative; in fact, we know of no existing models. In Section 6 we therefore draw from both case studies and lab experiments to suggest that the implementation of some relational contracts requires solving problems of not only *credibility* but also *clarity*. The credibility problem is familiar: should one party believe another's promise? The clarity problem is new: can one party understand another's promise? Furthermore, these problems seem likely to interact: for example, if one party does something unexpected, does the other attribute it to miscommunication or gaming?

We emphasize that the clarity problem is likely to be particularly acute in exactly those settings where relational contracts are needed because formal contracts are imperfect or infeasible: where parties recognize that their roles in and rewards from cooperation are not easy to articulate ex ante or verify ex post. More precisely, the existing relational-contracts literature—including the models described in Section 5 (both those focused on bad parameters and those focused on bad luck)—focuses on the credibility problem that arises when the parties' roles in and rewards from cooperation cannot be verified ex post. The additional issue we raise in Section 6 is the clarity problem that arises when these roles and rewards cannot be articulated ex ante. We conclude Section 6 with some highly speculative thoughts about how this clarity problem might be modeled. As our discussion makes clear, we view this section as a very early report on a research agenda that is promising but just beginning.

Of course, much of our argument echoes earlier work, especially outside economics. For example, there are enormous literatures on organizational culture and its potential connection to organizational performance; see Schein (1985) and Barney (1986), respectively. Even closer to our themes, Ostrom (1990) analyzed self-organized and self-governed institutions for managing common-pool resources, Rousseau (1995) studied "psychological contracts" within organizations, and Adler and Heckscher (2006) saw the firm as a collaborative community. Finally, inside economics, Leibenstein (1969, 1987) suggested that underperforming enterprises (those inside the production possibility frontier, or "X-inefficient") might be stuck in Defect-Defect equilibria, whereas superior performers might have learned to play Cooperate-Cooperate. Not surprisingly, these contributions from outside economics made little use of formal models. Furthermore, although Leibenstein's argument appealed to multiple equilibria familiar from repeated-game models, neither his work nor subsequent models spoke directly to "stuck in" or "learned to." Kreps (1990, 1996) pointed toward formal models of the latter issues, but the literature then went quiet.

To conclude this introduction, we return to our rationales for writing this chapter, which are encapsulated by the two parts of our title. Working backward, we begin with the existence of persistent performance differences among seemingly similar enterprises. As Syverson (2011: 326) notes, "the magnitudes involved are striking," from which it is a short step to Lucas's (1988: 5) remarks about analogous differences in income and growth across countries: "I do not see how one can look at figures like these without seeing them as representing *possibilities*. . . . This is what we need a theory . . . *for:* to provide some kind of framework for organizing facts like these, for judging which represent opportunities and which necessities" (emphasis in the original). In short, one needn't aspire to move a 10th percentile firm to the 90th; moving up a quartile would be a big deal, so we need to know whether (and, if so, how) it can be done.

Continuing backward, we reach managers. In particular, we believe that a better understanding of the role of management practices in PPDs among SSEs could have significant policy implications. Since at least Cyert and March (1963), students of organizations have struggled to understand how organizations make decisions; see Gibbons et al. (this volume) for more. To put it mildly, firms do not always appear to costlessly and constantly optimize their choices from a fixed and known production possibility set, and yet the economic analyses underlying regulation and other policies often assume this to be so. We expect there to be useful analogies between how a firm struggles to improve its productivity, as considered in this chapter, and how a firm responds to regulations and incentives created by policies: in both cases, not only analysis but also implementation will be involved, and this could change the way we think about policy regarding research funding, patent law, trade liberalization, antitrust rules, and beyond. Both for these policy reasons and more generally, we hope this chapter facilitates future empirical and theoretical work on what managers actually do.

2. PPDs among SSEs Exist and Are Economically Significant

The evidence that PPDs among SSEs exist and are economically significant has been ably reviewed by Bartelsman and Doms (2000) and Syverson (2011). They describe the extensive empirical literature in the area, discussing in some depth the econometric and data quality issues inherent in accurately measuring heterogeneity in productivity across firms and plants.

This body of research establishes that there exist very significant productivity differences across plants in a wide range of industries and geographies. Furthermore, these findings on productivity differences have been shown to be robust to concerns about selection and simultaneity, as well as the distinction between physical- and revenue-based productivity. They have also been shown to be persistent over time and to be surprisingly resistant to the pressure of increasing competition.

In this section we highlight some of the central papers in the literature. Given these existing surveys, our intention is to be illustrative, not exhaustive. We complement the economics literature with some discussion of research drawn from the strategy and management literatures, including some valuable focused studies. In short, because different samples offer different advantages, we take a collage approach to summarizing the evidence on PPDs.

2.1. Firm-Level Analyses

Early work focused on the relative contribution of "firm" versus "industry" effects in explaining firm-level profitability. Building on the pioneering work of Schmalensee (1985), Rumelt (1991) and McGahan and Porter (1997, 1999) found that business unit effects were significantly more important than industry effects in explaining the dispersion of returns. More recently Hawanini et al. (2003) confirm the role of stable firm effects in explaining the variance in business performance over time and show that this result is robust to multiple measures of value creation. Intriguingly, they show that these results are driven by the performance of firms at the two tails of the distribution: when they drop the top two and the bottom two performers in each industry and re-estimate the models, firm effects fall by 35–54%, depending on the dependent variable, whereas industry effects increase by nearly 100–300%.

Some of the most compelling evidence of persistent firm effects in the data surfaced in the pioneering work of Griliches and Mairesse, who set out to study the effects of R&D on productivity at the firm level. Though not the primary focus of their research, they discovered surprisingly large between-firm heterogeneity in the data (e.g., in deflated sales, number of employees, physical plant, and R&D capital stock) even after accounting for the firm's industrial sector and adjusting for labor inputs. This heterogeneity endured econometric analysis: estimated parameters from a simple model of the production function revealed a large amount of between-firm variability in the firm-specific intercepts and in the slope coefficient for R&D capital (Griliches and Mairesse 1981, 1982, 1985; Griliches 1986).

2.2. Plant-Level Analyses

Differences in productivity measured at the firm level immediately raise the question of the degree to which firms are similar. Research at the plant level has addressed this issue by including increasingly sophisticated controls for potential sources of heterogeneity, including product mix, capital vintage, labor quality, and market power. We begin by recounting some key accomplishments of the early literature; see Bartelsman and Doms (2000) for more. We follow this with a description of recent contributions considering the distinction between physical and revenue productivity and the econometric challenges inherent in this research.

The exploration of productivity measured at the plant level has a long history, since at least Salter (1960), who studied the pig-iron industry during 1911–1926. Salter found that labor productivity was widely dispersed and that the most productive plant was two times more productive than the average plant. Similarly, Chew et al. (1990) examined productivity dispersion across 41 operating units of a single commercial food division in a large multidivisional corporation. These 41 operating units all used essentially the same production technology, were all located in the United States, and all produced nearly identical products for very similar customers. However, even after controlling for such factors as local labor market characteristics, size of the local market, unionization, capital vintage, product quality, and local monopoly power, the top-ranked unit was still twice as productive as the bottom-ranked unit. (Figure 1 shows the raw productivities across units, where the top-to-bottom ratio is 3:1.)

Continuing with focused studies, Dunlop and Weil (1996) analyzed 42 business units in the United States that produced a narrow range of apparel products. The raw performance data on

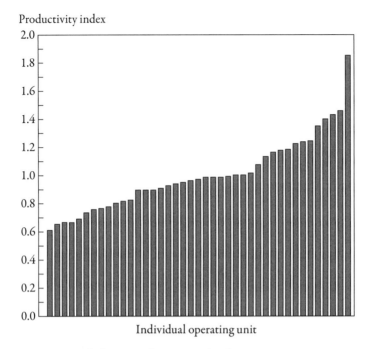

Figure 1. Multifactor productivity index for operating units in a single commercial food division. Redrawn from Chew et al. (1990).

lead time (the total time from ordering inputs to finished products) and operating profits (as a percentage of shipments) exhibited substantial inter-unit variability (coefficients of variation of 0.80 for lead time and 0.69 for operating profits). In a similar spirit, Arthur (1994) reduced product diversity even further in a study of 29 steel mills but still found substantial coefficients of variation in labor efficiency (0.43) and scrap rates (1.0).

Turning to broader samples, more recent work, using census data from different industries and countries, suggests that the productivity dispersion found in focused-sample studies is widespread. For example, Dwyer (1998), using panel data from the U.S. census of textile plants in 21 distinct industries, documented 85-15 percentile TFP ratios ranging from 2 to 4 and showed that this dispersion did not decrease over the 1972–1987 time period. Using plant-level data from an even broader set of industries, Syverson (2004a) showed that the average 90-10 percentile labor productivity ratio for 443 (four-digit) manufacturing industries in 1977 was 7:1; whereas the average 90-10 percentile TFP ratio ranged from 2.7:1 to 1.9:1.

Moving outside the United States, Klette (1999) found significant within-industry differences in permanent plant productivity (as measured by fixed effects) in 13 of 14 Norwegian manufacturing industries studied during 1980–1990. Using similar data, Biorn et al. (2002) estimated a four-factor production function by industry on 4 years of panel data and found that 72–84% of the gross variance in productivity could be attributed to heterogeneity at the plant level. In their analyses of manufacturing establishments in the United Kingdom, Disney et al. (2003) found that establishments in the top decile are 156% more productive than establishments in the bottom decile when productivity is measured according to real gross output per hour of manual labor; this 90-10 productivity advantage was reduced to 91% when log TFP is the productivity measure.

One might be concerned that these productivity results are measured in revenue rather than in physical product. Using a revenue-based measure of TFP, a local monopolist facing limited competition could appear to be more productive than its rival merely because it is able to obtain higher margins for its products. Idiosyncratic demand shifts could also cause high-profitability firms to appear more technically efficient than they really are. However, research controlling for these effects suggests that substantial heterogeneity in productivity remains even when output is measured in physical units. For example, Foster et al. (2008) use a Census of Manufacturers dataset for 1977, 1982, 1987, 1992, and 1997 containing measures of physical output for 11 industries with physically homogeneous goods (e.g., cardboard boxes and white pan bread). The authors document large and persistent within-industry dispersion in physical quantity-based productivity measures. In fact, dispersion in physical quantities is greater than dispersion in revenue-based TFP: after removing product-year fixed effects, the standard deviation for revenue TFP is 22 log points, and for physical productivity TFP the standard deviation is 26 log points.

These focused- and broad-sample results also appear to be robust to problems of selection and simultaneity (Olley and Pakes 1996). For example, Van Biesebroeck (2008) compared five different econometric techniques for estimating productivity. All five techniques produced remarkably similar results regarding productivity heterogeneity in Columbian clothing and apparel industries, with on average one quarter of all firms having TFP less than 45% of median productivity and one quarter of all firms having TFP greater than 42% of median productivity.

2.3. Persistence over Time and under Competitive Pressure

The research we have reviewed thus far has established the existence of cross-sectional productivity differences in many industries and countries. In this section, we review evidence that these productivity differences persist over time. We first review studies based on census data that demonstrate persistence in both the top and the bottom of productivity distributions. We then move on to describe studies that consider the effects of competition in the evolution of productivity distributions; this research suggests that heterogeneous productivity far from disappears as a result of competitive pressure.

In longitudinal data the evidence for the persistence of productivity differentials over time is very strong. In early work, Bailey et al. (1992) computed plant-level TFP for plants in 23 industries at four points in time (1972, 1977, 1982, and 1987), assigning each plant to a quintile of the productivity distribution in each of the survey years. They found substantial persistence in these distributions: 76% of plants in the top quintile in 1972 remained in the top two quintiles in 1977, and 58% of plants in the top quintile in 1972 remained in the top two quintiles in 1982.[2] Persistence was less strong in the bottom of the productivity distribution: 48% of plants in the bottom quintile in 1972 appeared in the bottom two quintiles in 1977, and 54% of plants in the bottom quintile in 1972 remained in the bottom two quintiles in 1982.

---

2. In the transition matrix, plant productivities are weighted by their employment. With unweighted data, the percentage of 1972 top-quintile plants remaining in the top two quintiles in 1977 is 62%.

Foster et al. (2006) found similar results for firms in retail trade. The authors employed quinquennial census data (1987, 1992, and 1997) to compute establishment-level productivity adjusted for four-digit industry effects. They found that "for continuing businesses these differences are highly persistent" (Foster et al. 2006: 757), although exit was also high with the entry of national chains. Similarly, Disney et al. (2003) computed the productivity dispersion of manufacturing establishments for a fixed cohort of surviving firms over time. In 1982, the 90-10 spread for the 1982 cohort ranged from 1.48 (ln TFP) to 1.62 (ln labor productivity). Five years later, the spreads for the firms remaining from the 1982 cohort had fallen to 0.81 and 1.43 (ln TFP and ln LP, respectively) but were not close to zero. Even 4 years later, in 1991, the heterogeneity among surviving firms from the 1982 cohort had fallen only a bit further, with 90-10 spreads now 0.66 and 1.28, respectively. Thus, after almost a decade, substantial heterogeneity persisted among those firms that had not exited from an initial cohort of firms.

Turning to the effect of competition, in cross-sectional data, increased competition is associated with increased productivity levels levels and reduced productivity dispersion. For example, Syverson (2004b) analyzes cross-sectional data on plants in the ready-mix concrete industry. Very high transportation costs in cement effectively create many distinct geographical markets, and Syverson uses the density of the local construction industry—which varies significantly across markets—as an instrument for local market competition. He finds that, in more competitive markets, average productivity is higher and productivity dispersion is lower (in particular, the productivity distribution is truncated from below). However, even in quite competitive markets, there is substantial dispersion in productivity.

There is also longitudinal evidence that productivity dispersion is highly persistent, even in the face of competitive pressure. Although increasing competition raises average productivity, as weak firms exit and strong firms expand, productivity differences are highly persistent, with some studies even suggesting that greater competitive intensity is associated with a higher degree of plant-level heterogeneity. For example, Eslava et al. (2004) use plant-level data from Columbia for 1982–1998 to study the effects of market reforms (trade, labor, and financial) on productivity, profitability, and the reallocation of market share. The authors find TFP dispersion increasing for exiting, entering, and continuing firms in each of the 17 years of their panel, and the persistence in TFP was greater in the years following market reforms. See Holmes et al. (2012) for citations to recent papers with similar findings.

2.4. Focused Studies

Further evidence that productivity differences are real and persistent comes from studies that focus on fewer firms but use much more detailed data, attempting to control at the finest level for differences in capital and labor productivity. For example, the Chew et al. (1990) study of commercial food units was discussed above. As another example, Ichniowski et al. (1997) studied 36 finishing lines in steel minimills. They included more than 25 technological controls in their analysis of the determinants of productivity, including capital vintage, computerization, learning curve effects, line speed and width, the quality of the steel input, equipment design, and scheduled downtime for maintenance. They still found very significant productivity differences across lines (which they attribute to differences in human resource management policies, so we return to this paper in Section 3).

Similarly, in a series of highly detailed field studies of semiconductor manufacturing (Appleyard et al. 2000; Macher and Mowery 2003, 2009; Macher 2006) Mowery, Macher, and colleagues collected data on defect rates, yield, and cycle time. Consistent with their argument that embedded routines and processes underlie dynamic capabilities, the authors find evidence that interfirm differences in performance are greater than intrafirm differences:

> The average within-firm yield coefficient of variation is 1.44, while the between-firm coefficient of variation is 4.42. Similarly, the average within-firm cycle time coefficient of variation is 0.66, while the between-firm coefficient of variation is 2.14. Our performance metrics thus appear to capture firm-specific differences that are both substantial and enduring. [Macher and Mowery 2009: S51]

In summary, the literature suggests that (1) even after the imposition of tight controls, establishment-level TFP exhibits large dispersion in many industries, countries, and time periods; (2) within-industry productivity rankings are persistent, particularly in the right tail of the productivity distribution; and (3) increased competition leads to aggregate productivity growth but not in a manner that substantially reduces productivity dispersion.

We now turn to the possible role of variation in management practices as one important cause of persistent differences in productivity.

3. PPDs and Variation in Management Practices

Syverson's (2011) review not only documents the existence of PPDs but also categorizes their potential sources into two groups: internal factors (management "levers" in organizations) and external factors (market and environmental factors beyond managerial control). An important next step is to assess the importance of these factors. However, even now a large literature argues that variation in management practices may be an important source of PPDs among SSEs, and it is to this literature that we now turn.

Perhaps the simplest way that managers could be partially responsible for measured performance differences is that some managers are just better than others. Such managerial fixed effects have been discussed at least since Walker (1887) and Mundlak (1961). See Bertrand and Schoar (2003) for recent work blending the two—that is, a study of how particular managers adopt particular practices. Our focus, however, is on management practices—that is, things that any manager (or, at least, most managers) might do, rather than on managerial ability per se.

Regarding management practices, Bloom and Van Reenen (2007) began an important research program. Their initial paper reports results from an establishment-level survey of management practices in 732 manufacturing firms located in four countries. They present data on 18 management practices (including the degree to which the firm uses high-powered incentive systems, teamwork, selective recruiting, and skills training) and show that measures of management practice are highly correlated with TFP, profitability, Tobin's Q, sales growth, and survival rate. They show that although 44% of the overall variation in management practices can be ascribed to country and/or three-digit industry effects, the remaining 56% is within country and industry. Furthermore, they demonstrate that management practices can explain a substantial portion of the variation in the permanent component of firm productivity (estimated from longitudinal data on the production function). Finally, they find that management scores are significantly higher for firms in competitive markets; see Section 5.1.2.

Since their initial paper, Bloom, Van Reenen, and co-authors have substantially deepened this program, including expanding the dataset to include more firms, more countries, and more kinds of organizations (Bloom et al. 2012b); expanding the conception of management to include organizational structure (Bloom et al. 2012d); and exploring the connection between management and information technology productivity (Bloom et al. 2012c). In addition, they have made progress on identification issues, both through an instrumental variables approach (Bloom et al. 2010) and a field experiment (Bloom et al. 2012a). Finally, they have summarized their work in various outlets (Bloom and Van Reenen 2010, 2011).

Given all this work, one might wonder whether anything else has been or could be done. Our answer is strongly in the affirmative to both questions, for reasons like those described in the Ichniowski and Shaw (this volume) discussion of insider econometrics. Specifically, although large samples can offer important strengths, focused samples can offer complementary strengths, such as (1) more detailed controls, (2) sharper performance measures, and (3) more nuanced understandings of what managers actually do. In the econometric framework $Y = X\beta + Z\gamma + \epsilon$, these strengths correspond to Z, Y, and X, respectively. For our purposes, the first two are important, and the third is crucial: we perhaps could not have conceived of this chapter without the detailed accounts of management practices given by the kinds of focused-sample research we describe below. This is one of the chief returns that focused-sample researchers sometimes get from their days in the field talking with dozens of sources.

As a complement to large-sample research, this section describes focused-sample work. (Indeed, the field experiment by Bloom et al. [2012a] has many attributes of a focused study and so could be included here, but see Ichniowski and Shaw [this volume] for a description.) In Section 3.1 we focus on blue-collar work in general and on "high-performance work systems" in particular; in Section 3.2 we turn to studies that have explored the role of management practices in driving productivity differentials in white-collar work. Throughout this discussion, we are illustrative rather than exhaustive, and we pay special attention to studies that illustrate the benefits of focused samples in providing detailed control variables (Z), sharper performance measures (Y), and nuanced measures of management practices (X). As in Section 2, however, no sample is perfect, so we again take a collage approach to summarizing the evidence.

Any interpretation of these results in both the blue-collar and white-collar processes literature must be tempered by the recognition that the adoption of any particular configuration of organizational practices is almost certainly not a random event. On the contrary, the endogeneity of (and documented complementarity among) these organizational practices naturally limits any claims of causality. Nevertheless, we take two important findings from these carefully conducted studies: (1) there is substantial variation in internal practices and (2) there is significant correlation between internal practices and performance.

3.1. Blue-Collar Work: High-Performance Work Systems and Productivity

A long tradition among labor economists and others studying blue-collar work has suggested that high-performance work systems are closely correlated with superior organizational performance (e.g., Kochan et al. 1986, Huselid 1995, MacDuffie 1995, Huselid and Becker 1996,

Ichniowski et al. 1997, Pfeffer 1998, Appelbaum et al. 2000, Black and Lynch 2001).[3] For example, a large literature has developed around the study of Toyota, a firm that was perceived for many years to be an order of magnitude more effective than its competitors.[4] Similarly, Southwest Airlines has been widely studied as an example of best practice (e.g., see Gittell 2003). Both firms have significantly outperformed their competitors, and in both cases the difference has been widely ascribed to the ways in which they manage their blue-collar labor force.

There is no single definition of "high-performance work system," but three overarching elements can be identified in the literature. In general, firms with high-performance work systems (1) implement effective incentive systems, (2) pay a great deal of attention to skills development, and (3) use teams and create widespread opportunities for distributed communication and problem solving. Table 1 lists some of the particular practices identified by some key studies in the field.[5]

The first of these categories, *high-powered incentives,* includes both financial incentives (e.g., employee stock-ownership plans, performance-based pay, piece rates, and group-incentive plans) and longer term psychological or cultural incentives (e.g., long-term job security; plausible promotion opportunities; reduced wage and status differentials between workers and management; and proactive conflict-resolution methods in place of autocratic, centralized control). The second, *skills development,* includes such actions as selective hiring processes, the extensive training of employees, job rotation, and more flexible job assignments. Finally, *dense communication, local problem solving* includes such practices as the widespread use of teams; the decentralization of information gathering and processing; the allocation of decision rights to frontline manufacturing employees (through self-directed teams, offline problem solving, or quality control groups); and improved communication and coordination among different employee work groups, so that they have access to resources that may assist problem solving. Several studies have found widespread variance in the adoption of such practices (e.g., see Huselid 1995).

Studies that focus on specific industries allow researchers to develop industry-appropriate productivity measures and to collect more detailed and precise data, often at the plant or even line level. Focusing on a single industry also allows researchers to control for heterogeneity, while the smaller scale of these studies mitigates selection and response-bias problems. For example,

---

3. Regarding this distinction between large- and focused-sample studies, it is worth noting that Huselid (1995), Huselid and Becker (1996), and Black and Lynch (2001) are in fact large-sample studies of work practices, similar in some ways to the Bloom–Van Reenen research on management practices. Huselid and Becker (1996) find that a one standard deviation increase in the use of high-performance work systems is associated with a $15,000 increase in market value/employee. Black and Lynch (2001) find that unionized establishments that adopted human resource practices promoting joint decisionmaking coupled with incentive-based compensation had significantly higher productivity than did other similar nonunionized plants, whereas unionized establishments that maintained more traditional labor-management relations had lower productivity.

4. More than 300 books and more than 3,000 articles have been published about Toyota and managerial systems. See, for example, the international bestseller by Jeffrey Liker (2004), *The Toyota Way: 14 Management Principles from the World's Greatest Manufacturer,* and the companion book *The Toyota Way Fieldbook* (Liker and Meier 2006), which targets managers trying to implement the 14 principles in their own companies.

5. Becker and Gerhart (1996) provide a similar meta-summary of the practices included in additional studies of high-performance work systems.

Table 1. Management practices underlying high-performance work systems

Practice[a]	Huselid (1995)	MacDuffie (1995)	Ichniowski et al. (1997)	Pfeffer (1998)	Appelbaum et al. (2000)	Black and Lynch (2001)	Bloom and Van Reenen (2007)
High-powered incentives							
Incentive pay	X	X	X	X	X	X	X
Employment security			X	X	X	X	X
Merit-based promotions	X				X		X
Reduced status distinctions		X		X	X		
Performance review	X						X
Skills development							
Skills training	X	X	X	X	X	X	X
Selective recruiting	X	X	X	X	X	X	X
Flexible job assignments		X	X		X		
Dense communication and local problem solving							
Teamwork	X	X	X	X	X	X	X
Communication			X		X	X	
Information sharing	X			X	X		
Total quality management/ process control		X				X	X

Note: X indicates the inclusion of a particular practice in a study's definition of management practices comprising a high-performance work system.

a. These practices are not necessarily mutually exclusive. For instance, some authors specifically focus on the importance of communication and information sharing in developing well-functioning teams, others directly measure the use of such teams, and still others measure a specific type of team that might be used in lean manufacturing, total quality management programs, or statistical process control. These measures may all be capturing similar successful work practices.

Lazear (2000) studied workers installing auto windshields, finding that those who were under a piece-rate system were significantly more productive than those who were not. The change to a piece-rate system led to a 44% increase in worker productivity. About half of the increase in productivity appeared to be purely an effect of the greater incentives provided by the piece-rate mechanism; the remaining increase in productivity was due to a selection effect. See Ichniowski and Shaw (this volume) and Lazear and Oyer (this volume) for details.

In a global study of automotive assembly plants between 1987 and 1990, MacDuffie (1995) contacted 90 assembly plants in 16 countries, representing 60% of the industry's production capacity. He found statistically significant correlations among three sets of high-performance practices and productivity and quality: work system design, corporate-level human resource management policies, and the (minimal) use of inventory buffers. Their "work systems" variables capture measures of communication and local problem solving, with additional focus on specific managerial innovations, such as total quality management and statistical process control; their "human resource management policies" variable overlaps heavily with work practices

Table 2. Sample questions used to identify the presence of teamwork and communication

Variable name	Dummy variable question
Teamwork	
High participation	Are a majority of operators involved in formal or informal work teams or other related problem-solving activities?
Multiple teams	Do operators participate in more than one problem-solving team?
Formal team practice	Are operators organized into formal work teams either on the line or for the purposes of problem-solving activities according to an established policy with at least some operators involved in team activities?
Communication	
Information sharing	Are operators and union representatives, if any, provided with financial information on a regular basis?
Meet workers	Do line managers meet off-line with operators to discuss issues of concern, including issues related to performance and quality?
Meet union	Do union representatives and managers meet often to discuss concerns and cooperate in finding solutions to issues?

Source: Table 1 in Ichniowski et al. (1997).

associated with improving workers' skills and incentives; and their "inventory buffers" variable is specific to the lean manufacturing methods associated with the Toyota Production System. The nature of the capital stock, scale, model mix, parts complexity, and product design age together explained 48.3% of the variation in labor productivity, but adding their three "management practice" variables increased the adjusted R^2 to 54.3%, and adding in two- and three-way interaction effects further increased this measure to 64.9%. Subsequent work (MacDuffie et al. 1996) showed that these practices diffused only slowly: in the 43 plants common to both the 1989 and 1993 surveys, the overall 100-point work practices index increased from only 34.6 to 46.9.

Another example of an intra-industry study of the value of high-performance work systems comes from the work of Ichniowski, Shaw, and their co-authors in the steel industry (Ichniowski et al. 1997, Ichniowski and Shaw 1999, Gant et al. 2002, Boning et al. 2007). Ichniowski et al. (1997) examined the effect of human resource management practices on the productivity of integrated steel-finishing lines. The authors collected data from 36 homogenous steel-finishing lines to form a panel dataset of 2,190 monthly observations. Discussion with engineering experts and careful controls for the technology and product mix of any particular line led the authors to focus on uptime as a particularly clean measure of productivity. The study focuses on innovative practices in seven areas of personnel management: incentive pay, recruiting and selection, teamwork, employment security, flexible job assignment, skills training, and communication, each measured using a range of qualitative variables. For example, the presence of teamwork and communication were identified by asking the questions listed in Table 2.

The authors define four distinct systems of work practices. System 4 is the traditional system and lacks most of the innovative work practices. System 3 includes some low-to-moderate levels of teamwork and improved labor-management communication. System 2 includes the innovations of system 3 with higher levels of teamwork and also introduces extensive skills training. Finally, system 1 incorporates all eight innovative work practices described by the authors. The authors find strong evidence that human resource management practices exist in bundles, and they use cross-section and fixed-effects specifications to suggest that it is bundles— *and not individual practices*—that have an economically and statistically significant effect on productivity.

Their data suggest that relative to system 4, systems 3, 2, and 1 improve line productivity by 1.4%, 3.2%, and 6.7%, respectively.[6] Using detailed cost data from one line, the authors estimate that the 6.7% productivity difference between systems 1 and 4 implies increased profits of $2.24 million annually. In an attempt to identify causality, the authors also use a fixed-effects specification to explore productivity changes in a particular line following the adoption of new work practices. Their data show that lines upgrading from system 4 to systems 3 and 2 improved their productivity by 2.5% and 3.5%, respectively.[7] Controlling for selection effects (because lower performing lines are more likely to switch regimes) raises these numbers to 4.3% and 6.8%. Here again the data suggest that "better" practices are surprisingly slow to diffuse: 36% of the monthly observations in the sample used the traditional system for all 5 years, and 58% still had no teams by the end of the sample.

Hamilton et al. (2003) used weekly productivity and personnel data for employees at a garment factory between 1995 and 1997 to investigate the effects of the introduction of a team-based production system on productivity. Between 1995 and 1996, both team and individual production methods were employed side by side under the same management and union, sewing essentially identical garments. They found that the adoption of teams over a 3-year period at a single plant was associated with an average increase in productivity of 14% (4% stemming from higher ability workers more likely to join teams and 10% attributable to team-production effect).

The focused-sample studies of blue-collar work practices discussed in this section demonstrate detailed and customized controls (e.g., model mix, parts complexity, and design age in MacDuffie's study of automotive assembly), sharp and meaningful measures of productivity (e.g., windshields installed per day in Lazear's study of piece rates in the autoglass industry), and sophisticated measurement of organizational practices (e.g., teamwork and communication among workers in the Ichniowski et al. study of steel-finishing lines). Even in these studies, with detailed and careful measurement of the Zs, Ys, and Xs, there is evidence of a strong relationship between management practices and productivity.

3.2. Management Practices in White-Collar Work

An extensive stream of empirical work has explored the implications of variation in white-collar work processes on productivity. However, in contrast to research on the blue-collar workforce, much of the work in this tradition abstracts from questions of incentives and skills to focus primarily on questions of decisionmaking and integrated communication.

---

6. These estimates come from a regression using detailed technology controls, including customer type, maximum line speed, maximum width of line, nine dummies corresponding to specific equipment used in the line, equipment age, computer control of operations, and a measure of the value of major new equipment.

7. All lines classified as system 1 are new lines and hence could not be included in analyses of line changes over time.

For example, Clark and Fujimoto (1991) and Iansiti and Clark (1994) draw on detailed data collected at the level of individual product development projects to show that product development productivity in the world automobile industry between 1981 and 1988 was strongly correlated with the use of "heavyweight project teams"—an organizational structure in which the senior team leader has finite-duration matrixed authority over the members of his or her team and is responsible for supporting rich communication and rich problem solving processes across functional groups. The authors show that the use of heavyweight project teams is correlated with higher development productivity, faster lead times, and higher quality projects. Successful firms also do simultaneous product and process engineering, and they rely on bilateral and face-to-face communication, and the constant and early release of information. For example, these authors show that Japanese firms (which were in general more likely to employ these techniques) took an average of 24 months to develop a new vehicle, whereas American firms (which were the least likely to use them) took 34.

In a study of R&D productivity in the pharmaceutical industry, Henderson and Cockburn (1994) used qualitative research methods to develop measures of management practice and study their effects on research productivity. Using data from structured interviews and internal company documents, the authors created the variable PROPUB to measure the use of incentives designed to persuade researchers to "act almost as if they were academic scientists" and to publish in the research literature. They created a second managerial variable, DICTATOR, to measure the degree to which decisionmaking about resource allocation was concentrated in a single individual. The authors show that adding PROPUB and DICTATOR to their regression predicting research productivity increased the R^2 statistic by 34% (from 0.49 to 0.66).[8] Despite the apparent power of these practices, they diffused only slowly across their sample (Cockburn et al. 2000).

Researchers in healthcare delivery have also increasingly examined organizational factors as a potential explanation for the wide variability in the adoption of clinical best practices and organizational performance. For example, in 2000, a highly motivated anesthesiologist from the Johns Hopkins University School of Medicine named Peter Pronovost set out to reduce medical errors in intensive care units (see Pronovost and Vohr 2010). He chose to focus initially on central line catheter-related bloodstream infections. Existing research had shown that consistent compliance with a few basic safety procedures could significantly reduce the rates of this type of infection. Another contributing factor in the study choice of catheter-related bloodstream infections was the large personal cost to the patient (morbidity and risk of mortality) and medical costs associated with these events (estimated annually in the United States to be 80,000 infections, 28,000 deaths, and $2.3 billion in additional costs). Finally, informal observation of clinicians in surgical intensive care units at Johns Hopkins suggested that these basic safety procedures were not in use.

Over time, based on his experience at Johns Hopkins, Pronovost developed a set of complementary management practices designed to reduce errors (specifically, catheter-related bloodstream infections) in hospital intensive care units. This set of management practices included (1) a checklist of five steps to be taken when inserting central line catheters, (2) organizational tools to support continuous quality improvement (e.g., performance data collection and

---

8. This analysis included a wide variety of program-level controls for productivity, including resources spent by program, therapeutic area, and the scale and scope of the research effort as a whole.

feedback), and (3) a culture change program that was delivered in house and was designed to foster collaborative teamwork between clinicians and nonclinicians in reducing errors. In 2003, Pronovost and colleagues entered into a research collaboration involving nearly all acute care hospitals in Michigan (108 intensive care units). They designed and executed a pre- and post-experiment involving the three-pronged intervention. Over 18 months, median (mean) catheter-related bloodstream infections were reduced from 2.7 (7.7) to 0 (1.4) infections per 1,000 catheter-days (Pronovost et al. 2006). These reductions were sustained at 36 months postintervention (Pronovost et al., 2010) and were associated with significant decreases in hospital mortality (Lipitz-Snyderman et al. 2011).

Researchers in education have similarly begun to document more systematically the role of management practices in school effectiveness. For example, a recent stream of work from Roland Fryer and co-authors has attempted to identify the key ingredients in charter school success in New York City. Several studies have previously found a significant and sizeable effect of charter school attendance on student achievement, especially in poor urban settings (e.g., see Hoxby and Murarka 2009; Angrist et al. 2012). However, it is much less common for researchers to conduct a detailed look inside the "black box" of charter schools. Dobbie and Fryer (2012) collected extensive school-level data on student outcomes and school inputs (physical and human capital), school curriculum, and several management practices from 35 New York City charter schools and found that an index of five policies explains roughly 50% of the variation in student achievement. These policies include increased instructional time, data-driven instruction, quality teacher feedback, high-dosage tutoring, and a culture of high expectations.

4. Many Important Management Practices Are Relational

The evidence that heterogeneity in management practices may be one important source of PPDs among SSEs raises an important question: why, then, do best practices not diffuse? After all, changing management practices would seem much less costly than, say, upgrading capital equipment or buying the latest information technology.

As outlined in Section 1, we believe that one possible answer to this question may be that, first, the implementation of many competitively significant management practices requires a relational contract (again, roughly, a shared understanding of each party's role in and rewards from achieving cooperation) and, second, that such contracts are hard to build and change. Here in Section 4 we use field research and case studies to buttress the first part of this suggestion: we describe particularly successful blue- and white-collar work practices that rely on relational contracts. In Section 5 we then argue that these relational contracts can be hard to build and change, again drawing on qualitative evidence, this time partly from firms that had significant difficulty implementing competitively significant management practices.

In some sense, we have made our tasks in Sections 4 and 5 harder, because we allowed our descriptions of management practices in Section 3 to be deceptively precise, such as "commit to employment security," "develop teamwide communication," and so on. Such blithe descriptions can give the impression that management practices are like light switches—choices that can be easily switched on or off—so that a manager's greatest challenge lies in designing practices, rather than in implementing them. Here we argue that this view is mistaken and that many (most?) competitively significant management practices require both managers and employees to act in ways that cannot be fully specified ex ante or verified ex post, so organizations must rely on relational contracts to implement these practices.

One concrete example of this idea is provided by the case of Nordstrom (Spector and McCarthy 2012). For many years Nordstrom's employee handbook was a single sheet of paper on which was written:

> Welcome to Nordstrom
>
> We're glad to have you with our Company. Our number one goal is to provide outstanding customer service. Set both your personal and professional goals high. We have great confidence in your ability to achieve them.
>
> **Nordstrom Rules: Rule #1: Use good judgment in all situations.**
>
> **There will be no additional rules.**
>
> Please feel free to ask your department manager, store manager, or division general manager any question at any time.

Throughout this period Nordstrom was an extraordinarily successful firm, plausibly because their employees were extremely good at "exercising good judgment in all situations." Nordstrom's sales associates have reputedly accepted the return of snow tires (Nordstrom does not sell snow tires), driven for hours to deliver merchandise so that customers can be ready to attend family occasions, and changed the tires of customers stranded in the company parking lot. These actions, and others like them, have given Nordstrom a reputation for excellent customer service that is the envy of its competitors and that has created deep customer loyalty. Notice, however, that "exercising good judgment" is not something that can be easily defined. By its very nature it is not an action rule that can be readily described ex ante or verified ex post. Instead it is a process of noticing what this particular customer needs at this particular time and then deciding to take a particular action in response. No formal contract could fully specify what it means to "exercise good judgment," and it therefore seems plausible that the firm relies on relational contracts instead.

In this section we attempt to extend this insight and build the case that many—perhaps most—competitively significant management practices rely on relational contracts. In Section 4.1, we lay some formal groundwork by describing the repeated trust game from Kreps (1990) and briefly discussing relational-contract models that have built on this intuition. We then present three qualitative examples of management practices supported by relational contracts. In Section 4.2, we discuss two blue-collar examples—the bonus system at Lincoln Electric and the use of the andon cord in the Toyota Production System. And in Section 4.3, we discuss a white-collar practice—the nature of "pro-publication" management in the pharmaceutical industry.[9]

4.1. Modeling Relational Contracts

Repeated game models of collusion among firms have been explored since at least Friedman (1971). The repeated trust game from Kreps (1990) has the same underlying intuition but is

---

9. These descriptions draw on Gibbons and Henderson (2012), "Relational Contracts and Organizational Capabilites," *Organization Science,* by permission from the Institute for Operations Research and the Management Sciences, 7240 Parkway Drive, Suite 300, Hanover, MD 21076, USA.

cast in a setting closer to our own and so allows us to develop some basic terminology. In Kreps's analysis, each period begins with player 1 choosing either to Trust or Not Trust player 2. If player 1 chooses Trust, then player 2 can choose either Honor or Betray; if player 1 chooses Not Trust, then the period ends. The payoffs to players 1 and 2 are (C, C) following (Trust, Honor), (S, D) following (Trust, Betray), and (P, P) following Not Trust, where $D > C > P$. That is, in the language of the prisoner's dilemma, D is player 2's payoff from defection (betraying 1's trust), C is her payoff from cooperation (honoring 1's trust), and P is her payoff from punishment (when 1 chooses not to trust). For simplicity, we assume that player 1's payoffs are the same values C from cooperation and P from punishment, but all that really matters is that 1's payoffs satisfy $C > P > S$ (where, again drawing on the prisoner's dilemma, S is 1's sucker payoff from having his trust betrayed). Finally, to focus on the case where cooperation maximizes the players' total payoffs, we assume that $2C > S + D$.

In a one-shot trust game, player 2 will choose Betray, because $D > C$, so player 1 will choose Not Trust, because $P > S$. In the repeated game, however, the parties may be able to sustain cooperation, provided player 2 is not too impatient. For example, if player 1 begins by playing Trust but switches forever to Not Trust if player 2 ever plays Betray, then it is optimal for player 2 to play Honor if the present value of the payoff sequence $(C, C, C, \ldots)$ exceeds the present value of the payoff sequence $(D, P, P, \ldots)$. If player 2's discount rate is r, then it is optimal for her to cooperate if $r < (C - P)/(D - C)$; in this case, one could say that the players have a shared understanding that is "self-enforcing." See Gibbons and Henderson (2012) for details, modest enrichments, and evidence from both experiments and contracts between firms that such relational considerations matter in practice.

The repeated trust game allows us to understand the basic intuition behind relational contracts, but it does not allow the parties to make payments to each other. Because employment relationships are perhaps our chief setting of interest (and because, as we will see, allowing for such payments has an important impact on the analysis), henceforth we focus mainly on models where payments are feasible. (Strictly speaking, the possibility of such payments is what distinguishes relational-contract models from repeated-game models.) The first such models were by Bull (1987) and MacLeod and Malcomson (1989), who analyzed intuitive equilibria but conducted these analyses before the literature learned from Abreu (1988) to analyze *optimal* equilibria. That is, it is one thing to determine that a particular set of strategies (say, reverting to the static Nash equilibrium after defection) can sustain cooperation if the parties are sufficiently patient, but it is quite another to determine what is the best equilibrium outcome the parties can achieve if they are not especially patient. The latter equilibrium need not have the simple form assumed in the former equilibrium. Indeed, for repeated-game models, the optimal equilibrium can involve quite sophisticated punishment strategies; see Abreu (1988) and Abreu et al. (1990).

Levin (2003) rebooted the relational-contracts literature by proving the striking result that the possibility of payments between the parties makes optimal equilibria quite simple in many relational-contract models, as opposed to optimal equilibria in repeated game models. For example, in the canonical repeated agency model, where both parties are risk neutral and have deep pockets, suppose the principal promises to pay the agent a bonus b as a function of the agent's output y. Levin showed that the optimal equilibrium is stationary, in the sense that the bonus in period t is a stationary function of only the output in period t, $b(y_t)$. Furthermore, this bonus function $b(y_t)$ might itself be simple (as well as stationary across periods), such as paying no bonus if output is below a critical value y^* and a bonus of b^* if output is above y^*. See Malcomson (this volume) for much more on this subject.

The simplicity of optimal equilibria in the canonical relational agency model has facilitated the application of such models in many settings, including some of those described in Section 5.2. Furthermore, the rebooting of this literature has led to richer models in which the optimal equilibrium is not stationary, including some of those described in Section 5.3. Before turning to such models, however, we first illustrate the relational contracts underlying some famously successful management practices.

4.2. Relational Contracts in Blue-Collar Settings: Lincoln Electric and Toyota

Lincoln Electric is an Ohio-headquartered manufacturer of arc welders and has relied successfully on incentive pay for more than 75 years.[10] Most workers earn a piecework wage and receive an annual bonus that generally averages half the worker's annual pay. The board decides on the companywide bonus pool, and individuals then receive shares according to a merit rating based on four factors—dependability, quality, output, and ideas and/or cooperation. Because of its incentive plan, and perhaps also for other reasons, Lincoln has succeeded fabulously in its industry, including driving established firms, such as General Electric, out of the market.

At first glance it might appear that Lincoln's piece rate and bonus could easily be duplicated, but our simple description again masks the presence of several nuanced relational contracts between the company and its employees that are central to the effectiveness of Lincoln's incentive plan. For instance, the company encourages workers to continuously improve piecework processes, but it reserves the right to change piece rates when there is "a change in methods." A worker who develops a faster method for a particular piecework process thus has a clear incentive to keep this knowledge concealed. If the worker's output suddenly skyrockets, managers might notice and readjust piece rates, but the worker could also produce the same amount of output in less time and with less effort while maintaining the outward appearance of constant hours and output. Both workers and managers might be better off in the long run if workers were to share possible process improvements, but workers are likely to share their knowledge only if they believe that they will receive some "fair return" from doing so. Thus arises Lincoln's relational contract about when and how to change the piece rate.

The annual bonus also has important discretionary components. Although it may be possible to develop relatively concrete measures of some aspects of any particular worker's performance, the value of each individual worker's ideas and cooperation may be quite difficult to quantify. To the degree that Lincoln wishes to encourage exactly this kind of less quantifiable behavior, any effective incentive contract will include a significant discretionary component. Furthermore, even if the merit rating on which the annual bonus is based were to be constructed from purely objective measures, the board ultimately sets the firmwide bonus pool. Although the board makes use of a bonus reserve to minimize variance in actual bonuses paid, the average bonus has still ranged from 78% to 129% of wages since 1945. In short, the board ultimately has complete discretion in setting the bonus pool, so workers must rely on a relational contract

---

10. This account draws on Fast and Berg (1975).

Table 3. Relational contracts at Lincoln Electric

Actor	Action		
	Cooperate	Defect	Punish
Worker	1. Work on improving piecework process 2. Share ideas and improvements	1. Shirk on process improvement effort 2. Keep improvements hidden from co-workers and managers	1. Stop or reduce process innovation effort 2. Keep ideas and innovations secret, inhibiting further innovation 3. Quit
Manager	1. Adjust piece rate only when there is a genuine change in methods 2. Credit workers for ideas in assessing merit ratings 3. Set total bonus pool for all workers large enough to reward workers' contributions	1. Claim there is a change in methods to adjust for workers who have innovated new methods 2. Deny workers good merit ratings 3. Limit the cumulative total bonus pool despite obvious contributions	1. Lower workers' merit ratings (and thus lower bonuses) 2. Fire workers

that the board will, indeed, pay the expected bonus. Table 3 summarizes some elements of the relational contracts that we believe to be in place at Lincoln.

A similar reliance on relational contracts is evident in our next case study, from the Toyota Production System, an exemplar from the automotive industry of the high-performance work systems described in Section 3.1.[11] As we outlined in Section 3, much of this performance differential appears to have been driven by the firm's management practices rather than by any structural advantage. Indeed, Toyota's success came in the face of competition that possessed many significant assets—including well-established brands and distribution channels, extensive technical knowledge, and in some cases local government support.

Extensive research has demonstrated that one important source of the extraordinary levels of productivity and quality obtained by Toyota in the late 1980s and the 1990s was the firm's ability to make continuous improvements to its production processes. Shop-floor workers were grouped into problem-solving teams that were encouraged to identify bottlenecks and inefficiencies in the production process and to explore potential solutions to them. Workers were asked to be alert for potential opportunities for improvement and to be creative and innovative in their search for solutions. Successful participation in these teams relied on a set of behaviors that could not be articulated ex ante or verified ex post, and hence could not be rewarded through a formal contract. The use of the andon cord as a tool to improve the production process is a particularly compelling example. Every worker on the Toyota production line has access to an andon cord, a rope that can be pulled to alert a supervisor to the fact that the worker believes there is a problem on the line. Once the andon cord is pulled, if the supervisor cannot resolve

---

11. This account draws on Liker and Franz (2011).

Table 4. Cooperation, defection, and punishment in the use of the andon cord at Toyota

Actor	Action		
	Cooperate	Defect	Punish[a]
Worker	1. Pull the andon cord when worker sees a problem 2. Offer suggestions on improvements to the production process (that might make worker's job redundant)	1a. Never pull the andon cord (out of fear of being punished) 1b. Pull the andon cord to stop the line and avoid work when there is no true problem 2. Keep improvements hidden from co-workers and managers	1. Sabotage the manufacturing line 2. Pull andon cord frequently 3. Engage in absenteeism
Supervisor	1. Recognize potential problem when andon cord pulled and aid in problem-solving 2. Implement improvements without necessarily cutting jobs 3. Accept authority of work teams to make some shop-floor decisions	1. Punish workers for pulling andon cord (even appropriately) 2. Cut workforce once they discover potential innovations 3. Interfere in work teams and override their decisions	1. Penalize workers (financially or socially) for pulling andon cord 2. Remove the andon cord

a. The punishment is undertaken in response to the perceived defection by the other actor (i.e., worker or supervisor).

the problem that the worker has identified in a reasonably short time, the entire production line may be brought to a halt. This event is enormously costly. Giving individual workers the power to stop the line on the basis of something as nebulous as "whenever you see a problem" implies, we believe, the existence of a relational contract between workers and the firm. Any worker pulling the andon cord must exercise considerable judgment in identifying potential problems and must believe that he or she will not be penalized for potentially stopping the line. No formal contract can specify the conditions under which stopping the line is an appropriate thing to do. Table 4 sketches some key elements that may underlie the relational contract that supports the use of the andon cord at Toyota.

4.3. Relational Contracts in White-Collar Work: Pro-Publication Management at Merck

A similarly complex relational contract has been operational for many years, we believe, in some leading pharmaceutical firms, such as Merck, that have implemented the "pro-publication" management practice described in Section 3.2.[12] For many decades, research-based pharmaceutical firms attempted to discover new drugs through a large-scale process of trial and error, so-called

12. This account draws heavily on Henderson (1994).

random drug discovery. For example, researchers might inject hundreds of compounds into rats or dogs in the hope of finding one that lowered cholesterol or reduced hypertension. If a compound showed promising activity, then medicinal chemists would synthesize large numbers of related compounds for further testing, in an attempt to find potential drug candidates that were both more efficacious and less toxic. Highly skilled medicinal chemists were the backbone of most companies' research efforts.

Beginning in the 1980s, university-based researchers working in biology and biochemistry began to uncover the biochemical mechanisms underlying many diseases. Early work exploring the causes of hypertension, for example, uncovered the fact that blocking the renin angiotensive cascade lowered blood pressure. This discovery, and others like it, enabled firms to move from animals to using chemical reactions as screens to discover new drugs. In place of "find me something that will lower blood pressure in rats," firms could now request "find me something that inhibits the action of the angiotensin II–converting enzyme."

This science-based approach promised to be—and, ex post, proved to be—much more productive than the approach it replaced, but it required those firms who embraced it to significantly change the ways in which they managed research. First, the firms had to hire scientists with quite different sets of skills, including molecular biologists, physiologists, and biochemists. Second, whereas random drug discovery required the firm's scientists to maintain only a cursory understanding of the current scientific literature, the science-based approach required them not only to stay current with the promising mechanisms being discovered in the academic literature but also to conduct such leading-edge science themselves, in house.

This shift required research scientists to behave almost as if they were academic scientists. On the one hand, staying current with the academic literature or, more importantly, understanding the current literature, could not be accomplished by simply reading journal articles. In a classic instance of what Cohen and Levinthal (1990) have called "absorptive capacity," researchers wishing to stay at the leading edge found that they not only needed to attend academic conferences but also to conduct leading-edge science themselves (e.g., to be invited to such conferences, or to participate in informal discussions at them). Some pharmaceutical firms even began to encourage their scientists to publish in the peer-reviewed literature—even though protecting the firm's intellectual property through patents was a substantial part of the ultimate goal.

At the same time, scientists in science-based pharmaceutical firms could not act completely like academics. They also had to actively support their colleagues in the attempted discovery of new drugs. Making a major scientific breakthrough—even winning a Nobel prize—without simultaneously generating knowledge that could be quickly applied to the search for new drugs would not constitute consummate success. Instead, those firms that chose to adopt the science-based approach—and the scientists who worked for them—had to learn how to balance the behaviors characteristic of a successful research scientist with those characteristic of a successful drug hunter.

This was not a balance that could be easily specified in a formal contract. It was widely understood that staying connected to the academic world required publishing in journals and attending conferences, but no one could specify ex ante exactly how many papers a scientist should publish and which conferences he or she should attend, particularly when every scientist's research trajectory was likely to be different. How could anyone tell ex ante exactly what the balance between fundamental research and drug hunting should be at any given moment,

Table 5. Cooperation, defection, and punishment in science-driven drug discovery

Actor	Action		
	Cooperate	Defect	Punish[a]
Scientist	Behave almost like an academic scientist, but be sure to develop useful knowledge for discovering new drugs	Either shirk (represent lack of results as unlucky research) or behave like an academic scientist (pursue problems for their own sake, build external reputation)	Behave like an academic scientist, or ignore research and become a drug hunter
Manager	Reward the scientist who displays high-science behavior even if no new drugs result	Fail to increase resources for scientists who publish; reward only those who produce drugs	Fire the scientist or cut funding

a. The punishment is undertaken in response to the perceived defection by the other actor (i.e., scientist or manager) and perhaps depends on the nature of that defection.

or develop a verifiable measure of whether a researcher was being "sufficiently helpful" to his or her drug-hunting colleagues? This uncertainty was symmetric: scientific researchers might be motivated as much by the chance to work on interesting problems and to control their own time as by money or promotion, but specifying in advance exactly what kinds of rewards would be given in response to exactly what kinds of behaviors proved to be very difficult.

In practice, those pharmaceutical firms that successfully developed "pro-publication" management (as Cockburn et al. [2000] have termed it) not only fared better in the production of major patents (Henderson and Cockburn 1994) but also appear to have developed a sophisticated relational contract with their researchers. Table 5 sketches our sense of its key elements.

Taken together, we hope that these three examples make plausible the idea that many—perhaps most—competitively significant management practices rely heavily on relational contracts for their execution. Such shared understandings ask both managers and employees to perform actions that cannot be easily specified ex ante or verified ex post, and as such cannot be enforced by formal contracts.

5. Could Relational Contracts Be Part of the Implementation Problem?

It is one thing to assert that competitively significant management practices may rely on relational contracts but quite another to suggest that this dependence is one of the reasons that such practices are slow to diffuse and hence that performance differences persist. To believe the latter, we would need to know why the relational contracts underlying key management practices might themselves be slow to diffuse. In this section and the next we discuss three approaches to exploring this possibility.

To put these three approaches in context, we begin in Section 5.1 by briefly summarizing existing explanations for the slow diffusion of management practices—without reference to relational contracts. As noted in Section 1, this existing literature has proposed four broad answers to the question of why competitively significant management practices do not diffuse more rapidly. First, incumbent managers may have problems of *perception*—they do not know they are behind. Second, managers may have problems of *inspiration*—they know they are behind, but they do not know what to do about it. Third, managers may have problems of *motivation*—they know they are behind and they know what to do, but they lack incentive to adopt new practices. Fourth, managers may have problems of *implementation*—they know they are behind, they know what to do, and they are trying hard to do it, but they nonetheless cannot get the organization to get it done.

The first of our three approaches to understanding why some relational contracts might be slow to diffuse is related to the motivation problem: if the relational contracts that facilitate high performance in some enterprises are simply too costly or not feasible for others to adopt, then low-performing enterprises will know they are behind and know what could be done, but they will find it unprofitable or infeasible to do it. In this scenario, high- and low-performing enterprises may seem similar but actually differ in some important parameter. In short, this approach is consistent with the idea from Section 4 that high-performance management is often importantly relational, but this approach then attributes PPDs to unmeasured heterogeneity in the costs of adopting the key relational contracts.

We discuss models of this kind in Section 5.2. In particular, we describe models with four sources of heterogeneity—differences in discounting, in the competitive environment, in network structure, and in player types—that might lead to heterogeneity in the kinds of relational contracts that firms can adopt. These models offer interesting applications of the basic logic from Levin's (2003) canonical model, and they suggest further topics that could be explored with related techniques.

In contrast, the models in Section 5.2 cannot account for the important class of cases in which managers believe that the adoption of a particular management practice would improve productivity, they have a deep understanding of the nature of the practice, they are striving mightily to adopt it, and yet they still fail to implement the practice successfully. In Section 1 we mentioned the mature phases of the Toyota Production System and total quality management as examples from this class; now, after Section 4.2, we can add science-driven drug discovery, such as at Merck, to the list.[13]

Our second and third approaches to understanding why some relational contracts might be slow to diffuse both explore implementation difficulties that arise through relational contracts. In particular, our second approach includes a variety of recent models that enrich Levin's canonical model and deliver nonstationary optimal equilibria. In contrast, our third approach is more speculative and has not yet been modeled, as far as we know.

We discuss the second approach in Section 5.3 by describing models such as those where path dependence in relational contracting can produce persistent performance differences among ex ante identical enterprises. As noted in Section 1, several interesting possibilities arise: cooperation can be hard to build well, in the sense that achieving perfunctory cooperation can make it

13. For example, there have been more than 300 books and thousands of articles written about Toyota, yet until quite recently many automobile companies appeared to have great difficulty imitating its practices (Pil and MacDuffie 1996). Similarly, the practice of science-driven drug discovery diffused only slowly across the pharmaceutical industry despite widespread agreement about its effectiveness (Cockburn et al. 2000).

harder to achieve consummate cooperation; cooperation, once built, can be fragile; and cooperation may be difficult to build in the first place. In all these models, however, the parties play the optimal equilibrium of the game as a whole, and they understand this equilibrium from the beginning of the game. Thus, although we have moved beyond the bad parameters that cause bad performance in Section 5.2, now we have explanations of bad performance based on bad luck—that is, from path dependence or other events over the course of the relationship, among enterprises that were identical ex ante.

Finally, because our third approach is more speculative, with no relational-contract models we know of, we discuss it separately, in Section 6. Indeed, we begin not with theory but instead with brief descriptions of cases in which firms had difficulty building or changing relational contracts. Based in part on these cases, we suggest that the implementation of some relational contracts requires solving problems of not only *credibility* but also *clarity*. The credibility problem is familiar: should one party believe another's promise? The clarity problem is new: can one party understand another's promise? In fact, the clarity problem is tougher than this statement, for the usual reasons associated with common knowledge: I need to understand that you understand my promise, and so on.

We emphasize that the clarity problem is likely to be particularly acute in exactly those settings where relational contracts are needed because formal contracts are imperfect or infeasible: where parties recognize that their roles in and rewards from cooperation are not easy to articulate ex ante or verify ex post. More precisely, the existing relational-contract models described in Section 5 (both those focused on bad parameters in 5.2 and those focused on bad luck in 5.3) share the focus of the entire relational-contracts literature on what happens when the parties' roles in and rewards from cooperation cannot be verified ex post. This literature's focus on what happens without verifiability ex post has been very productive; we think it is now time to start studying what happens when these roles and rewards cannot be fully articulated ex ante. We say more about how one might do this in Section 6.

5.1. Existing Explanations for the Slow Diffusion of Management Practices

An extensive literature has attempted to account for the fact that many competitively significant management practices do not diffuse rapidly. As noted above, four major lines of argument involve the perception, inspiration, motivation, and implementation problems. For ease of exposition, we proceed from perception to motivation and then to inspiration and implementation.

5.1.1. The Perception Problem

A first stream of work hypothesizes that significant heterogeneity in management practices persists because managers are subject to problems of perception. It argues that managers may literally not be aware that heterogeneity in management practices exists or that these differences shape productivity. For example, Henderson and Clark (1990) suggest that in the photolithographic alignment equipment industry, incumbent firms failed to recognize the threat posed by the next generation of products, because their employees focused their attention on the components of each technology, failing to understand that their competitors had developed the ability to understand the performance of the system as a whole. Christensen (1997) suggested that incumbent firms in the disk-drive industry invested their attention and resources in satisfying the needs of their existing customers, and in doing so failed to appreciate the ways in which their competitors had developed skills that allowed them to meet new customer needs using new technology. Tripsas and Gavetti (2000) drew on a detailed history of the competition between Polaroid and Kodak to show that the two firms conceived of photography in very different terms, which led them to make very different investments. More recent work has amplified and extended these results, suggesting that both the cognitive frames of individual managers and the ways in which information processing is structured in the firm may lead firms to have quite different perceptions of their environments and the capabilities of their competitors (Kaplan et al. 2003; Kaplan 2011).

5.1.2. The Motivation Problem
A second stream of explanation has focused on the degree to which heterogeneity in the adoption of management practices persists because managers have motivation issues, either because of differences in competitive intensity across industries or because of differences in agency costs in firms. This perspective has most recently found support in the work of Bloom and Van Reenen (2007); see also Reinganum (1989) and Bresnahan et al. (2011) for alternative formulations. Bloom and Van Reenen report statistically significant correlation between the adoption of their measures of management practices and competition, measured by three separate proxies: import penetration, the Lerner index, and self-reported survey results on the level of competition. After controlling for firm and market characteristics, firms with five or more competitors have management z-scores 0.140 higher than firms with fewer competitors. Bloom et al. (2012e) find even stronger results for estimates with industry-country fixed effects in panel data.

5.1.3. The Inspiration Problem
The third stream of explanation for persistent heterogeneity in management practice flows from the seminal work of Sidney Winter and his collaborators. It suggests that many competitively significant management practices fail to diffuse because, even though managers may be aware that their competitors have developed practices that it would be valuable to adopt, they are hampered in adopting new practices by an inspiration problem: much of the knowledge fundamental to building management practices is tacit, or deeply embedded in individuals or organizational routines, so it is simply unclear how to mimic a high performer (e.g., see Nelson and Winter 1982; Winter 1987, 1988, 2006; Zollo and Winter 2002).

Winter (2006: 131) likens the problem of transferring organizational knowledge to the difficulty of baking a cake from a recipe: "'Knowing how to bake a cake' is clearly not the same thing as 'knowing how to bring together in one place all of the ingredients for a cake'." As to the sequence of actions required to turn the ingredients into cake, he notes that even though it is technically feasible to write out these tasks in great detail, hands-on experience under an experienced chef is a much easier and more effective way to learn to cook than any amount of book learning. This idea has been explored empirically by several researchers. For example, Anand and Khanna (2000) suggested that one of the reasons some banks are much better at making acquisitions than others is because there is a great deal of "causal ambiguity" in the knowledge required to make good acquisitions, and because some banks have greater absorptive capacity (i.e., more knowledge of the area in question) and so are better equipped to understand new ideas. Similarly, various studies have shown that both access to knowledge and performance are correlated with the movement of key individuals (e.g., see Almeida and Kogut 1999; Lacetera et al. 2004; Breschi and Lissoni 2009), suggesting that management practices are much easier to "learn" if one has access to individuals who have experienced them first hand.

Detailed studies of particular management practices confirm the idea that many practices have important "sticky" or causally ambiguous elements. For example, Gant et al. (2002) conducted a study of the drivers of innovation across four steel-finishing plants. They find that more innovative plants are characterized by an emphasis on worker-level decisionmaking, team-based work, and greater communication in general, with particular emphasis on horizontal communication among workers on the shop floor. Their detailed diagrams of communication patterns show that innovative plants have more horizontal communication and denser interaction networks than do other plants and suggest that once we examine communication at a sufficiently fine-grained level, it turns out to be a highly complex set of behaviors that might indeed be hard to reproduce.

5.1.4. The Implementation Problem

Finally, introducing the implementation problem (and to some extent blending it with an inspiration problem), a fourth reason it might be difficult to imitate a high performer is based on the idea that effective management practices are subject to strong complementarities; for example, see Milgrom and Roberts (1990, 1995) and Brynjolfsson and Milgrom (this volume). When the elements of a management practice are highly interactive, there can be little return from getting most elements right but large return from getting them all right. As a result, a firm could know that it is behind, know what it needs to do, be trying hard to do it, and yet not be able to coordinate the many pieces of the organization sufficiently to get the job done.

As evidence in this spirit, recall from Section 3.1 that the work of Ichniowski et al. (1997) suggests that high-performance work practices are most tightly correlated with productivity when they are bundled together. Similarly, Pil and MacDuffie (1996) find that firms are more likely to adopt what they deem high-involvement work practices (use of teams, problem-solving groups, and job rotation) when they previously had in place certain complementary human resource practices (selective hiring, contingent compensation, training, and reduced status barriers between management and production workers). Finally, Bresnahan et al. (2002) find evidence of complementarities among workplace organization (a measure of teamwork and decentralized work practices), information technology, and more skilled workers.

Levinthal, Rivkin, and Siggelkow, among others, build on these observations to develop models of bounded search over rugged landscapes consistent with the idea that firms that search locally may find it very difficult to adopt new bundles of practices even under quite weak assumptions as to bounded rationality and costly search (Levinthal 1997; Rivkin and Siggelkow 2003; Siggelkow and Rivkin 2005). Rivkin (2000), for example, suggests that it can be exceedingly difficult to search through a space of strategies with numerous elements that are highly interactive, and that imitators may suffer large penalties from even small errors in attempting to match a particular combination of practices. Similarly Brynjolfsson and Milgrom (this volume) suggest that the existence of complementarities plausibly makes changing management practices—when change must occur simultaneously across the entire bundle of practices if it is to improve performance—costly or infeasible.

5.1.5. Summary

Taken together, these four streams of research—on the perception, motivation, inspiration, and implementation problems—offer compelling explanations for why management practices may not readily diffuse. But none of these research streams has paid much (if any) attention to relational contracts. Given the suggestion from Section 4 that competitively significant management practices are often relational, in the rest of this chapter we begin to explore how relational-contract models might complement existing work in these research streams. In particular, in Section 5.2 we explore models related to the motivation problem: if the relational contracts that facilitate high performance in some enterprises are simply too costly or not feasible for others to adopt, then low-performing enterprises will know they are behind and know what could be done, but they will find it unprofitable or infeasible to do it.

In Sections 5.3 and 6, we then shift to our main focus—implementation difficulties that arise through relational contracts. We see our approach to the implementation problem as importantly complementary to the rugged-landscape models of Levinthal, Rivkin, and Siggelkow. More specifically, a firm that can engage in only local search may have difficulty on a rugged landscape, perhaps getting stuck at a local peak, whereas any firm that can hill-climb locally can find the global peak of a landscape, where all monotonically increasing paths lead to the top. But our canonical setting—say, something like Levin's relational agency model—is just such a smooth landscape, so local search would suffice. Instead, in our approaches, relational contracts pose implementation difficulties because the enterprise may have trouble moving at all (not to mention searching locally): getting the organization to move requires the right relational contracts, and these may be hard to build.

5.2. Unobserved Heterogeneity in the Costs of Using Relational Contracts

One relational explanation for persistent performance differences is that some enterprises find it too costly or infeasible to use the relevant relational contracts.[14] Here we draw from recent literature to explore four potential sources of such heterogeneity: differences in discounting, in the intensity of competition, in network structure, and in the types of managers or employees. This literature is making nice progress; our summary is designed not to be a comprehensive listing but rather to be suggestive of the potential fruitfulness of this approach.

Perhaps the most intuitive source of variation in the effectiveness of relational contracting is variation in discounting: impatient players are more tempted to defect. (Of course, a player's discount rate need not reflect her personal rate of time preference; it could instead reflect, say, the frequency of repeated interactions.) As one of many recent papers that produces this comparative-static result but is otherwise focused on different issues, consider Board (2011), where a firm builds a group of suppliers over time and then, once the group is established, sources each period from the low-cost provider from the group. A more patient firm optimally

---

14. By focusing here and hereafter on models of PPDs sustained by relational contracts, we are certainly not rejecting alternative theories, including those related to the perception or inspiration problems. Indeed, we cannot resist noting some of the fascinating learning theories that could be seeds for the latter models, such as Smith and Sørensen (2000), Jeitschko and Taylor (2001), Bar-Isaac (2003), Bonatti and Hörner (2011), Callander (2011), and Ali and Kartik (2012).

builds a larger group of suppliers and thus has lower expected procurement cost per period. An econometrician who could not control for the size of the supplier group or the firm's discount rate would therefore measure persistent differences in the firm's input costs that are created by the quality of its relational contracts with its suppliers.

As an illustration of how variation in competitive intensity could affect relational contracting, consider Powell (2012), who explores the interaction between relational contracts inside an organization and competition in the market outside. In particular, Powell builds on the MacLeod and Malcomson (1989) result that the key to sustaining a relational contract is the net surplus that the relationship creates over and above the parties' outside opportunities (for details, see Malcomson, this volume). Powell embeds many firms in one market, where each firm consists of a principal-agent relationship in which the principal creates incentives for the agent through a relational incentive contract. For a given firm, the net surplus from its principal-agent relationship depends on the market price of output, which in turn depends on the aggregate output produced by the other firms in the market. Loosely speaking, competition in the market may thus be bad for productivity in a firm, if a lower market price of output reduces the net surplus in the firm's agency relationship. More specifically, if market 1 consists of firms 1a and 1b and market 2 of firms 2a and 2b, then firms 1a and 2a might be internally identical and yet able to sustain different relational contracts—because of differences in the productivities of firms 1b and 2b.[15]

As illustrations of how variation in network structure could affect relational contracting, consider the emerging literature on repeated games in networks. This literature suggests that the network structure of interactions, the network structure of information, optimal network structures, and endogenous network structures may shape the kinds of relational contracts that can be constructed (e.g., see Lippert and Spagnolo 2011; Fainmesser 2012; Jackson et al. 2012; Wolitzky 2012). This emerging literature may also allow important connections to empirical work, such as the Gant et al. (2002) paper described in Section 5.1, which relates work-group networks to productivity. Our point here is simply that differences in network structure in firms might be hard to measure and hence may be a source of PPDs among enterprises that are only seemingly similar. A further step would be to see network structure as not only endogenous but perhaps also responsive to management practices.

Finally, as an initial illustration of how private information about a player's type can affect relational contracting, consider Halac (2012), who adds persistent private information to Levin's (2003) analysis of relational contracting by endowing the principal with private information about her outside option (and hence about the value of the relationship, from which follows the maximum feasible strength of incentives for the agent). Unlike Levin's case of complete information, where it is immaterial whether the principal or the agent has the bargaining power, Halac derives different reneging temptations and hence different (and possibly testable) time

---

15. See also Board and Meyer-ter-Vehn (2012) for more on how industry equilibrium might affect relational contracting in individual firms. In particular, identical firms hiring identical workers in a given labor market may offer different relational contracts in equilibrium. Workers accept inferior contracts only until high performance gets them an offer from a firm offering a superior contract. Firms offering inferior contracts eventually lose their workers, but they profit in the short run from the high effort the workers supply in the attempt to generate an outside offer.

paths for incentive strength and termination probability, depending on which party has the bargaining power. In particular, when the principal has the bargaining power, in the efficient equilibrium, incentives strengthen gradually, as the agent becomes convinced of the principal's type. Consistent with persistent performance differences, both of the principal's types in Halac's model value the relationship enough to stick with it, so after the bad type reveals herself, the relationship may not terminate but rather settle into perfunctory rather than consummate cooperation. See Watson (1999, 2002) for other models where relationships start small to screen types.

Another set of models endows the agent, rather than the principal, with persistent private information. For example, in MacLeod and Malcomson (1988), workers know their own abilities, but initially firms do not. The technology of production is such that, under full information, it would be efficient for higher ability workers to exert more effort. The result is akin to heats in a track meet. In the first round, only the least-able workers fail to qualify for the second round (i.e., fail to get promoted); all other workers work just hard enough to qualify. Of those in the second round, the least able fail to qualify for the third, and the others work just hard enough to qualify. Eventually, the continuous distribution of ability is broken into intervals, corresponding to the groups of workers who failed to qualify for each successive round. Having reached its steady-state level, each such group is playing an efficiency-wage continuation equilibrium—where the firm pays a high wage each period but will fire the worker if output is below a critical value. Of course, different groups of workers are playing (appropriately) different efficiency-wage continuation equilibria: a group with high average ability receives a higher wage and produces greater output than does a group with low ability, so an econometrician will measure persistent productivity differences if ability is not a control variable. See Malcomson (2012) and Yang (2012) for further models in this spirit. As with variation in network structure, a further step in this literature would be to see the distribution of workers' types as responsive to management practices—whether via screening during hiring or skill development during employment.

5.3. Consummate Cooperation Can Be Hard to Build and Sustain

We turn next to our second approach to understanding why some relational contracts might be slow to diffuse. Whereas the relational-contract models in Section 5.2 bear some resemblance to the motivation problem—in that the relational contracts that facilitate high performance for some enterprises are simply too costly or are not feasible for others to adopt, so underperformers know they are behind and know what needs to be done but are not trying to do it—the models we describe here are our first stab at our main interest: implementation difficulties arising from relational contracting.

In this section we focus on path dependence and other events during a relationship that can cause ex ante identical enterprises to perform differently. As will become clear, this literature is very recent but also very exciting. We hope it continues to grow.

In Section 5.3.1 we describe how learning about persistent private information potentially causes a principal-agent relationship to settle for perfunctory cooperation, when the principal knows that consummate cooperation is feasible but too expensive to discover. This model thus produces persistent performance differences among ex ante identical enterprises. In Section 5.3.2 we describe how learning about independent identically distributed (iid) private shocks can cause nonstationary dynamics if the shock persists. In particular, in this model short-run shocks can produce long-run or even permanent distortions. Finally, in Section 5.3.3 we describe several models in which cooperation, once built, is nonetheless fragile. Of course, a publicly observed change in the payoffs can cause initial cooperation to collapse, but interesting recent models explore much more subtle threats to cooperation involving learning in various ways.

In all these models, the parties play the optimal equilibrium and have a shared understanding of this equilibrium from the beginning of the game. In Section 6 we discuss our third approach to why some relational contracts might be slow to diffuse, this time exploring how clarity problems might hamper the parties' attempt to develop a shared understanding.

5.3.1. *Persistent Performance Differences among ex ante Identical Enterprises*

We now consider Chassang's (2010a) model of building a relationship. As in the type models in Section 5.2, such as Halac (2012) and MacLeod and Malcomson (1988), persistent private information inspires an initial learning phase. The key difference between the Chassang and type models, however, is that here the agent's private information is about production possibilities, not about an aspect of the agent himself, such as his ability. Our interest in this seemingly slight difference in modeling is that now the principal's attempt to learn and utilize the agent's information can produce persistent performance differences among ex ante identical enterprises (i.e., among enterprises with the same production possibilities) as follows.

Chassang shows that in the optimal equilibrium of the game as a whole, play converges to one of several heterogeneous steady states, based on the stochastic results of the initial learning phase. Furthermore, these steady-state continuation equilibria correspond to equilibria of the underlying game without private information. In this sense, Chassang's model can be interpreted as an equilibrium theory of equilibrium selection, potentially rationalizing Leibenstein's (1969, 1987) conjecture that underperforming enterprises might be stuck in Defect-Defect, whereas superior performers might have learned to play Cooperate-Cooperate.[16]

Formally, in each period, the principal first chooses whether to invest or not, where investing imposes a cost k on the principal but delivers a benefit b to the agent. Not investing delivers zero to both parties and means that no further actions are feasible that period. If the principal does invest, then the actions $a \in A$ might be feasible for the agent: each period, each action is feasible with (independent) probability p. Both parties observe which actions are feasible, and the principal observes the action the agent chooses.

There are two kinds of actions, unproductive and productive: $A = A_U \cup A_p$. An unproductive action costs nothing for the agent to take but produces no output for the principal, whereas a productive action costs c to take and produces output $\tilde{y}(a)$, where $\tilde{y}(a) = y(a) > 0$ with probability q and $\tilde{y}(a) = 0$ with probability $1 - q$. It is common knowledge that the number of productive actions is $\#A_p$ and that a given productive action produces $y(a_p)$ when it produces positive output, but initially only the agent knows which actions are productive.

---

16. The remainder of this description of Chassang (2010a) draws on Gibbons (2010) with permission from the *Annual Review of Economics,* Volume 2, © 2010 by Annual Reviews, http://www.annualreviews.org.

As a simple case, suppose it is common knowledge that there are two productive actions, a_0 and a_1, with $y(a_0) < y(a_1)$. In the first period, a_0 might be feasible but a_1 not, or the reverse, or both might be feasible, or neither. To induce the agent to take a productive action that has not been revealed as such, instead of an unproductive action, the principal threatens not to invest in several future periods if this period's output is zero. Note that this punishment will occur on the equilibrium path, because a productive action could produce zero output. In this sense, learning (i.e., identifying a new action as productive) is expensive. In contrast, if an action has produced a positive output then the principal knows that the action is productive, so if the agent takes this action in a later period and it produces zero output, then the principal does not need to punish the agent.

Because learning is expensive (and all the more so after at least one productive action has been identified), it can be optimal to stop learning before all productive actions are identified. Because opportunities to learn arrive randomly, otherwise identical dyads may stop learning after identifying different sets of productive actions. Thus, this model can produce persistent performance differences among ex ante identical dyads because of path-dependence in building a relationship.

5.3.2. Long-Run Distortions from Short-Run Shocks

In this section we consider Li and Matouschek's (2011) relational-agency model. The key feature of their model is that the principal's opportunity costs of paying the agent are stochastic and privately observed by the principal. Even though the principal's opportunity costs are iid, the optimal relational contract generates periodic conflicts during which effort and expected profits decline gradually. To manage a conflict, the principal uses a combination of informal promises and formal commitments that evolves with the duration of the conflict.

More specifically, suppose that the principal promises the agent a bonus if he provides the agreed-upon effort level, but she makes this promise contingent on her privately observed opportunity costs being low. If the principal does not pay the bonus, then the agent has to punish her. The challenge is to structure the punishment in the most efficient way.

Consider a period in which effort and expected profits are at their highest level and suppose that the principal then faces high opportunity costs in a number of consecutive periods. In the first phase of the conflict, the agent punishes the principal by gradually reducing effort. Since the production function is concave, these effort reductions become increasingly costly. At some point, it becomes more efficient for the agent to punish the principal by insisting on a contractible wage that is not contingent on the principal's opportunity costs. In the second phase of the conflict, effort is therefore constant but contractible wages are increasing over time. Finally, contractible wages reach their highest sustainable level and the conflict enters its third and final phase during which effort and wages are constant. This final phase lasts until there is a period with low opportunity costs. In that period, the principal pays her debts to the agent with a single large bonus payment and the agent returns immediately to the efficient-effort level.

Li and Matouschek also consider an extension of their model in which the principal is liquidity constrained: the payments she can make in any period are constrained by the amount of effort provided in that period. They show that such liquidity constraints slow down recoveries, since the principal can no longer pay her debts to the agent with a single bonus payment and instead spreads this payment over multiple periods.

Li and Matouschek find support for their predictions from two cases we discuss in Section 6.1: Credit Suisse First Boston (CSFB) and (further history from) Lincoln Electric. For example, at CSFB, in line with this model, management's response in the first year of a shock was to promise superior bonuses when times got better, but their response in the second year was to offer guaranteed pay raises immediately. During this evolution of management's responses, the bankers did not switch abruptly from cooperation to defection, but they might well have decreased their effort, again in line with the model.

5.3.3. Might Cooperation Be Hard to Sustain, Even Once Initiated?

As a stark example where cooperation collapses, imagine enriching the repeated trust game from Section 4.1 so that player 2's payoffs begin as (C, D, P), but in each period there is a probability that 2's payoffs are publicly observed to have shifted permanently to (C, D', P), where $D' > D$ and $r > (C - P)/(D' - C)$. In this case, cooperation will end after player 2's payoffs shift, but cooperation can nonetheless start at the beginning of the game, provided that r is sufficiently below $(C - P)/(D - C)$, relative to the probability that player 2's payoffs shift.

Richer versions of this idea explore how cooperation can collapse from transitory shifts in player 2's payoffs, slower learning about permanent shifts in 2's payoffs, or other subtler causes. For example, McAdams (2011) models a stochastic partnership under symmetric information. There can be learning about the partnership's productivity, which can evolve, and the partners' actions can affect future productivity. A vicious cycle can arise where a negative shock bodes ill for the future, reducing the value of the ongoing relationship and possibly causing the partners to work less hard now, thereby further imperiling the relationship.

Whereas the state variable in the McAdams model is public information, Chassang (2010b) studies the effect of the global-games perturbation, where each party receives a low-noise, conditionally independent private signal of the state. In particular, Chassang analyzes a dynamic exit game, where staying is akin to cooperation and exiting is akin to defection. The extreme equilibria—those with most staying and most exiting—involve threshold strategies, where a player stays for the next period only if her noisy signal is sufficiently high. In such equilibria, each player is uncertain about the other's behavior, and this makes it difficult to coordinate their expectations about play. Even as the noise goes to zero, the conditions needed for cooperation are stricter than they would be under complete information. Moreover, these conditions now depend on new considerations: now not only the predatory incentive (to defect when one's partner is cooperating) but also the preemptive incentive (to avoid cooperating when one's partner defects) matter for whether cooperation can be sustained.

As the first of two more applied examples, in the related model of deterrence of Chassang and Padro i Miquel (2010), weapons stocks are unambiguously helpful in deterring war under complete information, but they may be harmful with vanishingly little private information if they greatly reduce the payoff from being the second party to engage in war, even if they also somewhat reduce the payoff from being the first. And in the second example, Chassang and Takahashi (2011) analyze a related model of the repeated prisoner's dilemma. Here the sucker payoff from being the victim of defection—not just the temptation payoff from being the defector—matters for whether cooperation can be sustained. Furthermore, in the Chassang and Takahashi model, grim-trigger strategies need not be the best way to sustain cooperation: selective punishment strategies that punish defectors while attempting to reward cooperators sustain higher levels of cooperation by reducing the overall cost of being the victim of defection.

Finally, cooperation can also collapse when there is private monitoring, such as in the subjective-evaluation agency models by Levin (2003), MacLeod (2003), Fuchs (2007), and Maestri (2012). A key insight of this literature is that there must be inefficiency on the equilibrium path: to provide incentives, the agent must do worse when outcomes are poor; but to induce truthful revelation of outcomes, the principal must be indifferent across alternative output reports. See Malcomson (this volume) for more on private monitoring in relational incentive contracts.

6. The Clarity Problem

In Sections 5.2 and 5.3 we explored the credibility problem in relational contracting: should one party believe another's promise? In this section we finally reach the clarity problem in relational contracting: can one party understand another's promise? Both of these problems arise naturally if formal contracts are infeasible or imperfect because the parties are unable to articulate ex ante or to verify ex post their roles in and rewards from cooperating together. So far, the relational-contracts literature has focused on the credibility problem that arises when roles or rewards cannot be verified ex post. Here we begin to explore the possibility that roles or rewards cannot be fully articulated ex ante.

As an example familiar to many, consider the tenure criteria in an academic department. In principle, a department could use solely formal criteria (here meaning objective weights on objective measures); for example, department policy could be "you get tenure if and only if you have at least three papers in *Econometrica* by the fall of your sixth year." More typically, however, a department's tenure process allows some role for judgment and discretion—perhaps for reasons similar to those that led Lincoln Electric to complement its objective piece rate with a discretionary bonus, as described in Section 4.2. At Lincoln, decades of shared experience seem to have given managers and workers a shared sense for how the bonus program is supposed to be run (although see Section 6.1.2 for an interesting twist in this story). Likewise, in many departments, senior faculty seem to have a shared sense for what their department's tenure criteria are. The issue we explore in this section, however, is the possibility that these senior faculty cannot easily communicate their shared sense to a new assistant professor, or even to an outside senior hire. Clearly, such phrases as "have an impact on your field," "publish good papers in good journals," or "contribute appropriately to the work of the department" are only a beginning.

As a second example, recall from Section 4.3 the relational contract that supports pro-publication behavior by scientists and managers at science-driven pharmaceutical firms like Merck. Notice how much shared information is required. First, there is extensive task knowledge about the state-dependent actions that constitute pro-publication behavior. Each scientist has to learn not only what kinds of knowledge are potentially useful in the search for new drugs, but also how to behave almost like an academic scientist—including subtle expertise about which conferences to go to, what kinds of papers to publish, and, most importantly, how to make trade-offs between behaving like an academic and actively engaging in drug discovery. Likewise, each manager has to learn what kinds of rewards and recognition matter to research scientists—employees who famously care more about the design and reception of their work than they do about monetary rewards. All this learning, by scientists and managers, is significantly complicated by the fact that appropriate behaviors will likely vary across fields (e.g., cardiology versus neurology), across disciplines (e.g., chemists versus biologists), and with the particular circumstances of the firm (e.g., How strong are the firm's market and patent positions? How close is it to finding other new drugs?).

In short, as Winter and others studying the inspiration problem described in Section 5.1.3 have emphasized, task knowledge is often both extensive and difficult to communicate. We further emphasize that management practices relying on relational contracts have additional information requirements, which we call relational knowledge. Roughly, if task knowledge concerns what is supposed to happen, relational knowledge is its complement: what will happen if parties do not do what they are supposed to (i.e., in game-theoretic terminology, what is supposed to happen off the equilibrium path)? We note that, hard as it might be to communicate task knowledge, there is a sense in which relational knowledge is more difficult to communicate, because events off the equilibrium path are not supposed to happen, so there may be less opportunity for the parties to learn from experience about relational knowledge than about task knowledge.

Given the shared task and relational knowledge underlying pro-publication behaviors by scientists and managers, we find it impressive that Merck and some other pharmaceutical firms managed to succeed at this management practice. We also find it unsurprising that other firms were slower or less successful at implementing this practice; see Cockburn et al. (2000). What we ask readers to imagine here, however, is how Merck got this practice going in its early days. We find it easy, for example, to imagine a recruiter trying to explain the novel approach to a newly minted postdoc (who, let's say, would otherwise be considering academic jobs) by appealing to a rough metaphor, such as "it's almost like being an assistant professor." We return to both of these ideas—difficulties in communication and the related reliance on metaphors—in Section 6.2.

Motivated by these examples of tenure and pro-publication behaviors, we proceed in two steps. First, in Section 6.1, we provide brief descriptions of case studies that can be interpreted as examples where the parties may not have had a shared understanding of their intended relational contract. Then, in Section 6.2, we discuss recent evidence and theory about how parties might build a shared understanding. If the parties have identical interests, this work explores the resolution of the clarity problem in its pure form, without any complications from the simultaneous presence of the credibility problem that arises from imperfectly aligned interests. Exploring the interaction between these two problems is a leading issue for further research, both theoretical and empirical: if one party does something unexpected, does the other attribute it to miscommunication or gaming?

6.1. Case Studies of Imperfectly Shared Understandings

In this section we discuss the possibility that parties may not have a shared understanding of their roles in and rewards from cooperating together. In Section 6.1.1 we consider examples where the possibility of misunderstanding surfaced relatively early in the relationship. In Section 6.1.2 we turn to examples that arose after decades of a successful relationship.[17]

---

17. This section draws on Gibbons (2010) with permission from the *Annual Review of Economics,* Volume 2, © 2010 by Annual Reviews, http://www.annualreviews.org.

6.1.1. Imperfectly Shared Understandings Early in Relationships

Empirically, it seems unsurprising that parties may not have a shared understanding early in their relationship. Theoretically, however, we know of no models exploring how this possibility affects relational contracting. That is, even in relational-contract models with learning, such as those discussed in Section 5, one party may be disappointed at what the other turns out to have known all along, but the parties are never surprised to find that they have misunderstood each other. We return to this issue in Section 6.2.3.

We use two case studies to illustrate the possibility of imperfectly shared understandings relatively early in relationships. Naturally, these case studies also admit other interpretations. In particular, both case studies we describe here can be interpreted as cousins of the types models in Section 5.2, such as Halac's (2012) model, where the principal has private information about her value from continuing the relationship.

First, consider Stewart's (1993) account of how Credit Suisse, a large European bank, bought the U.S. investment bank First Boston, taking the company private under the name CS First Boston (CSFB). At the time of the deal, there was much speculation about how the new firm would handle the inevitable differences in culture and firm policies, especially with regard to bankers' compensation. Although we cannot know the details of managers' attempts to identify and resolve these differences, the events that unfolded in the years immediately following the change in ownership reveal a lack of shared understanding about the determination of the bankers' annual bonus payments.

In the first 2 years that Credit Suisse controlled CSFB, all firms in the investment-banking industry performed poorly, and CSFB bankers received bonuses that were lower than the historical average but comparable to bonuses paid at other investment banks. In the third year, however, CSFB performed better than previously and yet worse than its competitors, and Credit Suisse paid bonuses that were above bonuses at CSFB in the first two years but lower than those at other firms in the third year. A crisis ensued. In brief, CSFB bankers asserted that the bonus policy in their industry was to match the market, meaning that bonuses should be competitive with bonuses at other top-bracket firms. In contrast, the Swiss asserted that in *their* industry the bonus policy was pay for performance, meaning that a banker's bonus depended on how he and his bank performed. Note that these two policies make identical pay prescriptions when all firms in the industry have the same performance, as was broadly true in the first 2 years.

We make no attempt to adjudicate the parties' competing claims in this case. Nonetheless, we do draw two lessons from this case. First, it seems unlikely that the parties had common knowledge ex ante about the determinants of the bonus (since they could not then offer each other conflicting claims about what they had understood). Second, in expressing their claimed understandings, both parties use metaphors: match the market and pay for performance. That is, although one could imagine solely formal bonus plans receiving such labels (e.g., "pay the same total bonus pool as at Goldman Sachs" or "pay 30% of profits as bonuses"), such formal contracts were clearly not what the parties were saying they had understood to be in place.

As a second example, consider the Danish hearing-aid firm Oticon. In 1990 the firm launched radical empowerment of its product-development projects with a memo from CEO Lars Kolind titled "Think the Unthinkable" that envisioned project groups as akin to mini-businesses, each with its own resources, timeline, goals, and incentives. The initial results were strong and were attributed to the new organization; subsequent commentators used language like "bringing the market inside the firm" (for a discussion, see Foss 2003).

We don't know whether Oticon's executives explicitly used the market metaphor to introduce the new organization, but suppose they did (or, suppose the metaphor was used by contemporaneous commentators). Oticon's project managers could then interpret the market metaphor as an initial approximation (akin to "almost like being an assistant professor") or as something closer to a literal promise to run the firm as an open market. If the former, then they would have expected the metaphor to be refined as events unfolded, clarifying just how much autonomy project managers actually would have in the new organization; if the latter, then they may have been surprised and upset (perhaps akin to the Wall Street bankers at CSFB) when the firm's Projects and Products Committee (staffed by the CEO and three senior managers) tightened control after the firm's portfolio of projects spiraled into disarray. The reaction of the firm's employees to the change suggests that the latter was the closer to the case.

Again, the possibility we take from this case is that the parties did not have a shared understanding ex ante. Perhaps no one thought that the market had literally been brought inside the firm, in the sense that project managers were now identical to entrepreneurs in their control over project decisions, and perhaps everyone understood that the old way of running the firm (before "Think the Unthinkable") no longer applied. But the gap between these extremes is very large, and we find it easy to imagine that project managers might have thought or hoped that the new way the firm was to be run would be closer to the former than the latter.

6.1.2. Imperfectly Shared Understandings in Decades-Old Relationships
In 1981, the cover of Johnson & Johnson's annual report read "Decentralization = Creativity = Productivity" (Aguilar and Bhambri 1986: 1). For decades before and after, J&J was comprised of many disparate and nearly autonomous healthcare businesses, ranging in size from a handful to thousands of employees. Although the substantial freedom given to each business was widely believed to increase innovation and initiative, it also made coordination more difficult.

This tension is by no means unique to J&J. For example, Alfred P. Sloan's (1963: 429–435) account of his years at General Motors is similar:

> It has been a thesis of this book that good management rests on a reconciliation of centralization and decentralization, or "decentralization with co-ordinated control." . . . It must be apparent that co-ordinated decentralization is not an easy concept to apply. . . . The balance which is struck between corporate and divisional responsibility varies according to what is being decided, the circumstances of the time, past experience, and the temperaments and skills of the executives involved. . . . [T]he responsibility for determining administrative organization is a continuing one.

One example of this tension between initiative and coordination at J&J arose as hospitals found it increasingly burdensome to work directly with so many separate businesses, requesting that J&J instead create a single organization that could handle sales and distribution for all its relevant divisions. Although J&J's competitors moved rapidly to this structure, the firm delayed making the change for several years, plausibly because it believed that having corporate headquarters create this new sales and distribution business would raise serious questions as to the nature of the relational contract between headquarters and the existing businesses: if headquarters was prepared to limit these businesses' historical autonomy in this way now, what would happen in the future?

Our reading of this episode in J&J's history is that there was, of course, never any doubt about whether corporate headquarters *could* make this change in the organization structure, but there was concern about whether and how it *should*—in the sense that doing so might be interpreted by some as reneging on an understanding of how the tension between initiative and coordination was to be managed at J&J. Presumably, this episode concerning sales and distribution to hospitals was not the first time this tension surfaced at J&J, nor was it the last (e.g., see Barrett 2003). As Sloan put it, the "responsibility for determining administrative organization is a continuing one." Or, in our terms, even decades of shared experience may not fully clarify a crucial relational contract.

As a second example where decades of a successful relationship nonetheless left key decisions in doubt, we update the history of Lincoln Electric begun in Section 4.2. As Hastings (1999) describes, in the early 1990s rapid international expansion led to serious financial difficulties at Lincoln. For example, in 1992 the firm as a whole lost $46 million, even though operations in Cleveland had an excellent year. These losses forced Lincoln to consider how large a bonus pool to pay the Cleveland workers. (Recall that Lincoln's bonus is completely discretionary and not governed by contract or formula.) Broadly similar to CSFB, there were two possible views on the bonus Lincoln should pay in Cleveland: a large bonus based on Cleveland's excellent results, or a small or zero bonus based on results for the firm as a whole. Because Lincoln's overseas expansion was recent, this distinction between Cleveland profits and aggregate profits had never arisen.

In the event, Lincoln's managers decided to conform to the Cleveland workers' interpretation of the contract and paid $52 million in bonuses at the end of 1992, even though the firm had to take on debt of $250 million (63% of equity). Lincoln's financial difficulties continued into the following year, while the Cleveland operation continued to excel. Lincoln's management team launched an intensive communication effort to implore the Cleveland workers to expand their efforts and hours even further to make up for the firm's aggregate losses and failed production efforts abroad and to rescue the company from violating covenant agreements. Workers responded by redoubling their efforts and raising the capacity utilization of the Cleveland plant from roughly 75% to nearly full capacity. This required current workers to work weekends and holidays and to give up vacation time. These efforts played a major role in the firm's being able to honor its loan agreements, and the firm paid out $55 million in bonuses at the year's end despite again having aggregate losses.

We interpret these events as suggesting that in some important respects the relational contract that had developed at Lincoln was incomplete. When the company operated only in Cleveland, the question of whether the bonus should reflect plantwide or firmwide profits was immaterial; it was only after the company was operating around the world that it became clear that management and employees might have different understandings of their relational contract. Under these conditions Lincoln's decision to honor their employees' understanding of the relational contract represented a substantial investment in strengthening their relationship—an investment whose power was illustrated in the following year by the employees' continued commitment to the firm.

6.2. Toward Modeling the Clarity Problem

As noted above, this second approach to understanding implementation difficulties that might arise through relational contracts—based on the clarity problem rather than, say, path dependence—is much more speculative; in fact, we know of no existing models. However, we are mindful of Krugman's (1995: 27) dictum that "like it or not, . . . [in economics] the influence of ideas that have not been embalmed in models soon decays." We therefore hazard the following avenues for future research.

6.2.1. Team-Theoretic Experiments and Models

There are some fascinating laboratory studies and models of parties trying to develop a shared understanding. To date, however, most of these analyses assume that the parties have identical interests. We discuss this work here, because it gives exciting hints about what might be done with imperfectly aligned interests, as in our settings of interest.[18]

In a pair of beautiful laboratory investigations, Weber and Camerer (2003) and Selten and Warglien (2007) study how parties learn to communicate. Weber and Camerer show one subject 16 pictures of people in office settings, and a light goes on next to one of the pictures. The other subject sees the same 16 pictures but in a different order and without the light. After the light goes on, the first subject picks up a phone and speaks to the second; each subject gets a payoff if the second subject can touch the correct picture in a specified amount of time. After the specified time has elapsed, the second subject learns which picture had the light next to it.

Selten and Warglien conduct a parallel exercise but with a much simpler state space: instead of 16 pictures that are somewhat hard to describe, they use 6 simple figures in a cross-product structure—a circle or a triangle on the outside of each figure, and nothing or a dot or a plus on the inside. If the subjects could use a phone, the exercise would be too easy, because the first subject would simply say "circle with a dot in it." But, having simplified the state space, Selten and Warglien also simplify the message space, allowing the first subject to send characters from a small, abstract message space, such as {7, J, &, *, $}. The advantage of simplifying the message space in this way is that Selten and Warglien can easily capture the language used by the subjects over time. For example, the second subject might learn that 7J means a circle with a dot in it.

Formally, both these papers report on observations of players attempting to build a shared language during repetitions of a game like the following: (1) player 1 observes the state of the world, $s \in S$; (2) player 1 sends a costless message to player 2, $m \in M$; (3) player 2 chooses an action $a \in S$; (4) payoffs to each player are $U(s, a) = 1$ if $a = s$ and $U(s, a) = 0$ otherwise; (5) player 2 observes s. Thus, player 1 would like to send a message $m(s)$ that tells player 2 that the state is s (so that player 2 will then choose the action $a = s$). The problem is that, at least in the early going, player 2 has little basis for understanding player 1's messages, especially in the setting used by Selten and Warglien.

Both papers find that different pairs of players develop different languages, even though these pairs are playing in the same environment (except for the random realizations of the states of the world over time). Because these are common-interest games, we interpret the knowledge being communicated as task knowledge, not relational knowledge. In particular, there is no concern with defection or punishment in a common-interest setting. Nonetheless, consistent with the large literature on the difficulties of communicating tacit knowledge, different

18. This section draws on Gibbons and Henderson (2012), "Relational Contracts and Organizational Capabilities," *Organization Science,* by permission from the Institute for Operations Research and the Management Sciences, 7240 Parkway Drive, Suite 300, Hanover, MD 21076, USA, as well as on Gibbons (2010) with permission from the *Annual Review of Economics,* Volume 2, © 2010 by Annual Reviews, http://www.annualreviews.org.

pairs of players take different lengths of time to develop a shared understanding, and different pairs hold different shared understandings once they reach them. From this lab evidence, we find it only a small stretch to imagine that similar forces could cause reasonable people to hold different understandings in situations like those at Lincoln Electric or CSFB. Of course, the issue at these two companies involved bonuses, so these were not common-interest settings; rather, the problem of credibility also arose because there was imperfect alignment of interests.

Turning to theory, in a game with Pareto-ranked Nash equilibria and zero payoff to all players out of equilibrium, a focal point may command everyone's attention. But what if multiple Nash equilibria offer the best payoff, or some of the payoffs out of equilibrium are very negative (making coordination failure very costly)? Furthermore, what if the parties cannot easily discuss the opportunities they perceive (as when an organization has congealed into functional silos, and, say, the production and marketing groups have only a rudimentary language in common)?

Crawford and Haller (1990) provide a pioneering analysis of such issues in a repeated coordination game. One of their important insights is that, absent a common language about actions (e.g., about the detailed production and marketing activities that might be useful in concert), the parties' shared experience may facilitate coordination by allowing decentralized partners to label their action spaces in terms of past play.

Blume and Franco (2007) continue in this spirit, analyzing an n-player, m-action coordination game with k "successes" (Nash equilibria paying 1 to all players) and $m^n - k$ "failures" (action-tuples where all players receive 0). The parties know the number of successes but not the action-tuples that will achieve them. Each player observes his own actions and payoffs but not the actions of other players. The optimal strategy entails mixing (until a success is reached), so that the players do not all change their actions in lock-step (which would cause the players to revisit unsuccessful action-tuples). As a result of this mixing, different groups of n players could take different durations to find a success.

Whereas Blume and Franco call their work "Decentralized Learning from Failure," Ellison and Holden (2012) take a more hierarchical approach, in which a principal instructs an agent. Each period, (1) the agent observes the state of the world, $s \in S$; (2) the agent chooses an action $a \in A$; (3) the principal sends a message $m \in M$ to the agent; and (4) both parties receive the payoff $\pi(a, s)$. A novel aspect of the model is that the principal cannot communicate about a state until that state has been realized. More specifically, the principal's message dictates that if a future state is within a specified neighborhood of this period's state, then the agent should take a specified action. When messages are of this form, there are more and less useful realizations of s that may occur in early periods; in particular, a useful realization is one that allows the principal to specify a broad neighborhood. As a result, dyads whose early realizations of s are useful will perform better.

Finally, as a first step away from common interests, there are a few papers that consider the costs that parties bear in trying to communicate with each other, focusing more on whether the parties will choose to incur these costs and what quality of communication will then occur, rather than on what language is then used to communicate. The initial paper in this spirit is Dewatripont and Tirole (2005), who treat the problem as one of moral hazard in teams: will a sender and a receiver both invest sufficiently to allow an intelligible message to be sent by the one and understood by the other?

Closer to our concerns, Li (2012) studies a setting where the clarity problem is difficult to resolve in organizations, because (1) propagation of tacit knowledge requires shared experience between individuals, and thus can diffuse only gradually across the group and (2) propagation of shared knowledge is privately costly, so self-interest may stymie the propagation of knowledge. Initial conditions in an organization may then have a persistent effect on the extent to which knowledge is propagated across the organization and thus the extent to which the clarity problem is resolved for the organization as a whole. For example, if an organization expands too quickly for the diffusion of knowledge to keep up with the expansion, the resultant incomplete propagation may persist even after the period of rapid growth has ended.

6.2.2. Categories, Metaphors, and Beliefs

We conclude this section with a speculative discussion about the sources and consequences of differing beliefs about relational contracts.

To illustrate what people might do when struggling to articulate a proposed relational contract ex ante, we return to the two settings discussed at the beginning of Section 6. First, in attempting to communicate tenure standards, senior faculty might cite specific examples, such as "Jane got tenure, but Joe did not." Second, in the early days of pro-publication management at Merck, we imagined a recruiter saying "It's almost like being an assistant professor." We see these as complementary approaches to communicating a state-dependent action rule $a^*(s)$: the former conveys specific examples such as $a^*(s_1) = a_1$ and $a^*(s_2) = a_2$, whereas the latter offers an alternative rule $a(s)$ that is somehow close to $a^*(s)$.

Research in cognitive psychology and linguistics has explored related issues concerning categories and metaphors. Rosch (1973, 1975) departed from the view that categories are defined by a set of properties shared by all their members, showing that there can be more- and less-representative members. Later work such as Osherson et al. (1990) explored category-based induction. For example, if you are told that lions and tigers use norepinephrine as a neurotransmitter, what is your belief that rabbits do, too?

Turning to metaphors like the Merck example, Lakoff and Johnson (1980: 3) argue that "Metaphor is pervasive in everyday life, not just in language but in thought and action." Lakoff (1987: xi) then builds on Rosch's theory of prototypes to connect categories and metaphors to human reasoning: "categorization [is] the main way that we make sense of experience." With both category-based induction and metaphors, two things seem plausible: first, there can be better or worse examples $a^*(s_1) = a_1$ and $a^*(s_2) = a_2$ and metaphors $a(s)$; second, reasonable people might draw different conclusions from specific examples and metaphors. See Mullainathan et al. (2008) for an initial economic model of some of these ideas.

We so far see four interesting opportunities for further work on communicating relational contracts via categories and metaphors. First, differences in beliefs about what will happen off the equilibrium path can lead to different equilibria. For example, Greif (1994) interprets the cultural origins of institutional structures governing commercial transactions as a difference in beliefs about what would happen if a trader claimed malfeasance by an agent. In Genoa, individualist cultural beliefs encouraged the use of family firms to mitigate the costs of defection, whereas among the Maghribi an expectation of community enforcement made family firms unnecessary. Fudenberg and Levine (2006) explore related issues.

Second, if multiple rules $a^*(s)$ can fit a finite history $\{a^*(s_1) = a_1, \ldots, a^*(s_n) = a_n\}$, there may be a role for reinterpretation of the history to clarify the proposed equilibrium going forward. Sabel (1993) describes something like this in industrial districts in Pennsylvania, and Bates et al. (1998) do likewise for conflicts in Zambia and the Balkans. See also Gibbons (2010: 358) for a discussion of how, in the early 1990s, Hewlett-Packard attempted to reinterpret decades without a layoff as a guiding value rather than an ironclad commitment.

Third, recall from the CSFB and Oticon cases in Section 6.1.1 that the parties began a relationship but later claimed to have different beliefs about what equilibrium they were playing. Such scenarios may be loosely related to Fudenberg and Levine's (1993) definition of self-confirming equilibrium, in which players' understandings of each other's strategies need agree only on the equilibrium path. However, in a self-confirming equilibrium, events off the equilibrium path never occur. See Ryall (2003) and de Figueirdeo et al. (2006) for applications to strategy and the American Revolution, respectively.

Finally, one can ask what happens after people misunderstand one another. In Ettinger and Jehiel's (2010) theory of deception, parties have only coarse knowledge of one another's strategies. Their approach connects nicely with the fundamental attribution error (Ross 1977), in which parties over-attribute another person's behavior to that person's permanent type, rather than to transitory shocks to that person's environment. Heath and Staudenmayer (2000) and Repenning and Sterman (2002) discuss related attribution errors in attempts to coordinate and cooperate, respectively. Further work on attribution errors seems likely to be one important way to explore how the problems of clarity and credibility may interact.

7. Conclusion

In this chapter we have explored the role of relational contracts in sustaining persistent performance differences among seemingly similar enterprises. We began by reviewing the evidence that PPDs among SSEs exist and are economically significant across a wide range of industries and geographies, and we summarized the evidence that these performance differences are correlated with variation in management practices. Critically, we suggested that the successful performance of many of these practices cannot be easily articulated ex ante or verified ex post, and we used three qualitative accounts to suggest that many (most?) competitively significant management practices rely on the presence of relational contracts.

We then turned to the question of why managerial practices, if they do indeed play a significant role in enabling PPDs, do not diffuse more readily. We reviewed the rich literature exploring this question and suggested that it can be complemented by a focus on the difficulties firms may encounter in building relational contracts. Here we described three barriers firms may face: bad parameters, bad luck, and bad communication. First, the relational contracts operated by leading firms may be infeasible or prohibitively costly for underperformers to implement. In this case, measured PPDs are due to bad parameters (i.e., unmeasured heterogeneity in the costs or benefits of the relevant relational contract). Second, the sequence of events during a relationship can produce measured performance differences among ex ante identical enterprises: achieving perfunctory cooperation can make it harder to achieve consummate cooperation; cooperation, once built, can be fragile; and cooperation may be difficult to build in the first place. Third and less conventionally, we suggested that the problem of clarity—difficulty in communicating the extensive task and relational information that underlies many relational contracts—may also play a role in making it difficult to build unfamiliar relational contracts.

At our most ambitious, we hope that our specific discussion of relational contracts, managerial practices, and PPDs will help define and encourage research in organizational economics about what, exactly, managers do. At a broad level, we find the distinction between analysis (deciding what to do) and administration (getting the organization to do it) extremely useful. Returning to our specific focus, if the impediments to building the relevant relational contracts include bad parameters, bad luck, and bad communication, we could imagine managers working to reduce each of these impediments. For example, regarding bad parameters, in Section 5.2 we mentioned models in which network structure and worker types play key roles in limiting the feasible set of relational contracts, and managers might work to change such parameters. Similarly, regarding the models of bad luck in Section 5.3, managers might work to change the likelihood of bad luck—such as building a rainy-day fund so that being liquidity constrained is less likely. Finally, regarding bad communication (i.e., the clarity problem discussed in Section 6), managers might take seriously that they and others not only talk but also think in categories, metaphors, and codes, all of which can lead first to miscommunication and then to attribution errors.

Of course, all these approaches—to changing parameters, luck, and communication—are not only possible managerial activities but also possible avenues for research. And while theoretical work on these issues would be exciting, this chapter as a whole cries out for empirical work focused sharply on relational contracting. Gibbons and Henderson (2012) give some illustrations of relational contracts in laboratory experiments and field data on contracts between firms, but there is perilously little analogous work inside organizations. One promising start, however, is Bloom et al. (2012d), who use the large-sample methodology of Bloom and Van Reenen described in Section 3, but complement it with auxiliary data on trust scores between regions. Bloom et al. find that multinational subsidiaries located in a country that the parent firm's country tends to trust will be more decentralized (measured, say, by expenditure constraints) than subsidiaries located in a country that the parent firm's country does not trust. We see this as an enormously promising start toward empirical work on the issues we have raised here, but clearly much more remains to be done.

Finally, moving from our main focus on productivity to the neighboring notion of profitability, much of what we have described can be cast in reduced form as saying that relational contracts are an investment that might improve an enterprise's productivity. But investments are costly, and there are typically many such investments a firm could make. One intriguing question is therefore whether and how investments in relational contracts might act as substitutes or complements to other more conventional assets. Both Toyota and Southwest Airlines, for example, appear to have used investment in relational contracts as routes to enter industries that had for many years been dominated by firms with harder assets—superior brands and prime geographic locations. We suspect that exploring the interaction between relational contracts and other forms of investment will be a productive target for future research.

REFERENCES

Abreu, Dilip. 1988. "On the Theory of Infinitely Repeated Games with Discounting." *Econometrica* 56: 383–396.

Abreu, Dilip, David Pearce, and Ennio Stacchetti. 1990. "Toward a Theory of Discounted Repeated Games with Imperfect Monitoring." *Econometrica* 58: 1041–1063.

Adler, Paul, and Charles Heckscher. 2006. "Towards Collaborative Community," in Charles Heckscher and Paul Adler (eds.), *The Firm as a Collaborative Community.* New York: Oxford University Press, pp. 11–105.

Aguilar, Francis, and Arvind Bhambri. 1986. "Johnson & Johnson (B): Hospital Services." Harvard Business School Case 384-054. Boston: Harvard Business School Press.

Ali, Nageeb, and Navin Kartik. 2012. "Herding with Collective Preferences." *Economic Theory,* forthcoming.

Almeida, Paul, and Bruce Kogut. 1999. "Localization of Knowledge and the Mobility of Engineers in Regional Networks." *Management Science* 45: 905–917.

Anand, Bharat, and Tarun Khanna. 2000. "Do Firms Learn to Create Value? The Case of Alliances." *Strategic Management Journal* 21(special issue: Strategic Networks): 295–315.

Angrist, Josh, Parag Pathak, and Christopher Walters. 2012. "Explaining Charter School Effectiveness." NBER Working Paper 17332, National Bureau of Economic Research, Cambridge, MA.

Appelbaum, Eileen, Thomas Bailey, Peter Berg, and Arne Kalleberg. 2000. *Manufacturing Advantage: Why High-Performance Work Systems Pay Off.* Ithaca, NY: Cornell University Press.

Appleyard, Melissa, Nile Hatch, David Mowery. 2000. "Managing the Development and Transfer of Process Technologies in the Semiconductor Manufacturing Industry," in Giovanni Dosi, Richard Nelson, and Sidney Winter (eds.), *The Nature and Dynamics of Organizational Capabilities.* London: Oxford University Press, pp. 183–207.

Arrow, Kenneth. 1974. *The Limits of Organization.* New York: W. W. Norton.

Arthur, Jeffrey. 1994. "Effects of Human Resource Systems on Manufacturing Performance and Turnover." *Academy of Management Journal* 37: 670–687.

Bailey, Martin, Charles Hulten, David Campbell, Timothy Bresnahan, and Richard Caves. 1992. "Productivity Dynamics in Manufacturing Plants." *Brookings Papers on Economic Activity: Microeconomics* (1992): 187–267.

Bar-Isaac, Heski. 2003. "Reputation and Survival: Learning in a Dynamic Signaling Model." *Review of Economic Studies* 70: 231–251.

Barnard, Chester. 1938. *The Functions of the Executive.* Cambridge, MA: Harvard University Press.

Barney, Jay. 1986. "Organizational Culture: Can It Be a Source of Sustained Competitive Advantage?" *Academy of Management Review* 11: 656–665.

Barrett, Amy. 2003. "Staying On Top." *Business Week,* May 5, pp. 60–68.

Bartelsman, Eric, and Mark Doms. 2000. "Understanding Productivity: Lessons from Longitudinal Microdata." *Journal of Economic Literature* 38: 569–594.

Bates, Robert, Rui de Figueiredo, and Barry Weingast. 1998. "The Politics of Interpretation: Rationality, Culture, and Transition." *Politics and Society* 26(2): 221–256.

Becker, Brian, and Barry Gerhart. 1996. "The Impact of Human Resource Management on Organizational Performance: Progress and Prospects." *Academy of Management Journal* 39: 779–801.

Bertrand, Marianne, and Antoinette Schoar. 2003. "Managing with Style: The Effect of Managers on Firm Policies." *Quarterly Journal of Economics* 118: 1169–1208.

Biorn, Eric, Kjersti-Gro Lindquist, and Terje Skjerpen. 2002. "Heterogeneity in the Returns to Scale: A Random Coefficient Analysis with Unbalanced Panel Data." *Journal of Productivity Analysis* 18: 39–57.

Black, Sandra, and Lisa Lynch. 2001. "How to Compete: The Impact of Workplace Practices and Information Technology on Productivity." *Review of Economics and Statistics* 83: 434–445.

Bloom, Nicholas, and John Van Reenen. 2007. "Measuring and Explaining Management Practices across Firms and Countries." *Quarterly Journal of Economics* 122: 1351–1408.

———. 2010. "Why Do Management Practices Differ across Firms and Countries?" *Journal of Economic Perspectives* 24(1): 203–224.

———. 2011. "Human Resource Management and Productivity," in Orley Ashenfelter and David Card (eds.), *Handbook of Labor Economics,* volume 4. Amsterdam: Elsevier and North-Holland, pp. 1697–1767.

Bloom, Nicholas, Carol Propper, Stephen Seiler, and John Van Reenen. 2010. "The Impact of Competition on Management Quality: Evidence from Public Hospitals." NBER Working Paper 16032, National Bureau of Economic Research, Cambridge, MA.

Bloom, Nicholas, Benn Eifert, David McKenzie, Aprajit Mahajan, and John Roberts. 2012a. "Does Management Matter? Evidence from India." Working paper, Stanford University, Stanford, CA.

Bloom, Nicholas, Christos Genakos, Raffaella Sadun, and John Van Reenen. 2012b. "Management Practices across Firms and Countries." *Academy of Management Perspectives* 26: 12–33.

Bloom, Nicholas, Raffaella Sadun, and John Van Reenen. 2012c. "Americans Do I.T. Better. US Multinationals and the Productivity Miracle." *American Economic Review* 102: 167–201.

———. "The Organization of Firms across Countries." 2012d. *Quarterly Journal of Economics,* forthcoming.

———. 2012e. "Management as Technology." Working paper, Stanford University, Stanford, CA.

Blume, Andreas, and April Franco. 2007. "Decentralized Learning from Failure." *Journal of Economic Theory* 133: 504–523.

Board, Simon. 2011. "Relational Contracts and the Value of Loyalty." *American Economic Review* 101(7): 3349–3367.

Board, Simon, and Moritz Meyer-ter-Vehn. 2012. "Relational Contracts in Competitive Labor Markets." Working paper, University of California at Los Angeles.

Bonatti, Alessandro, and Johannes Hörner. 2011. "Collaborating." *American Economic Review* 101: 632–663.

Boning, Brent, Casey Ichniowski, and Kathryn Shaw. 2007. "Opportunity Counts: Teams and the Effectiveness of Production Incentives." *Journal of Labor Economics* 25: 613–650.

Breschi, Stefano, and Francesco Lissoni. 2009. "Mobility of Inventors and Networks of Collaboration: An Anatomy of Localised Knowledge Flows." *Journal of Economic Geography* 9: 439–468.

Bresnahan, Timothy, Erik Brynjolfsson, and Loren Hitt. 2002. "Information Technology, Workplace Organization and the Demand for Skilled Labor: Firm-level Evidence." *Quarterly Journal of Economics* 117: 339–376.

Bresnahan, Timothy, Shane Greenstein, and Rebecca Henderson. 2011. "Schumpeterian Competition and Diseconomies of Scope: Illustrations from the Histories of Microsoft and IBM," in Josh Lerner and Scott Stern (eds.), *The Rate and Direction of Inventive Activity, 50th Anniversary Volume.* Cambridge, MA: National Bureau of Economic Research, pp. 203–271.

Bull, Clive. 1987. "The Existence of Self-Enforcing Implicit Contracts." *Quarterly Journal of Economics* 102: 147–159.

Callander, Steven. 2011. "Searching and Learning by Trial and Error." *American Economic Review* 101: 2277–2308.

Chassang, Sylvain. 2010a. "Fear of Miscoordination and the Robustness of Cooperation in Dynamic Global Games with Exit." *Econometrica* 78: 973–1006.

———. 2010b. "Building Routines: Learning, Cooperation, and the Dynamics of Incomplete Relational Contracts." *American Economic Review* 100: 448–465.

Chassang, Sylvain, and Gerard Padró i Miquel. 2010. "Conflict and Deterrence under Strategic Risk." *Quarterly Journal of Economics* 125: 1821–1858.

Chassang, Sylvain, and Satoru Takahashi. 2011. "Robustness to Incomplete Information in Repeated Games." *Theoretical Economics* 6: 49–93.

Chew, Bruce, Kim Clark, and Timothy Bresnahan. 1990. "Measurement, Coordination and Learning in a Multiplant Network," in Robert Kaplan (ed.) *Measures for Manufacturing Excellence.* Boston: Harvard Business School Press, pp. 129–162.

Christensen, Clayton. 1997. *The Innovator's Dilemma*. Boston: Harvard Business School Press.

Clark, Kim, and Takahiro Fujimoto. 1991. *Product Development Performance: Strategy, Organization, and Management in the World Auto Industry*. Boston: Harvard Business School Press.

Cockburn, Iain, Rebecca Henderson, and Scott Stern. 2000. "Untangling the Origins of Competitive Advantage." *Strategic Management Journal* 21(special issue): 1123–1145.

Cohen, Wesley, and Daniel Levinthal. 1990. "Absorptive Capacity: A New Perspective on Learning and Innovation." *Administrative Science Quarterly* 35: 128–152.

Crawford, Vincent, and Hans Haller. 1990. "Learning How to Cooperate: Optimal Play in Repeated Coordination Games." *Econometrica* 58: 571–595.

Cyert, Richard, and James March. 1963. *A Behavioral Theory of the Firm*. Oxford: Blackwell.

De Figueiredo, Rui, Jack Rakove, and Barry Weingast. 2006. "Rationality, Inaccurate Mental Models, and Self-Confirming Equilibrium: A New Understanding of the American Revolution." *Journal of Theoretical Politics* 18(4): 384–415.

Dewatripont, Mathias, and Jean Tirole. 2005. "Modes of Communication." *Journal of Political Economy* 113(6): 1217–1238.

Disney, Richard, Jonathan Haskel, and Ylva Heden. 2003. "Restructuring and Productivity Growth in UK Manufacturing." *Economic Journal* 113(July): 666–694.

Dobbie, Will, and Roland G. Fryer. 2012. "Getting beneath the Veil of Effective Schools: Evidence from New York City." Working paper, Harvard University, Cambridge, MA.

Dunlop, John, and David Weil. 1996. "Diffusion and Performance of Modular Production in the U.S. Apparel Industry." *Industrial Relations* 35: 334–355.

Dwyer, Douglas. 1998. "Technology Locks, Creative Destruction, and Nonconvergence in Productivity Levels." *Review of Economic Dynamics* 1: 430–437.

Ellison, Glenn, and Richard Holden. 2012. "A Theory of Rule Development." *Journal of Law, Economics, and Organization,* forthcoming.

Eslava, Marcela, John Haltiwanger, Adriana Kugler, and Maurice Kugler. 2004. "The Effects of Structural Reforms on Productivity and Profitability Enhancing Reallocation: Evidence from Columbia." *Journal of Development Economics* 75: 333–371.

Ettinger, David, and Philippe Jehiel. 2010. "A Theory of Deception." *American Economic Journal: Microeconomics* 2: 1–20.

Fainmesser, Itay. 2012. "Community Structure and Market Outcomes: A Repeated Games-in-Networks Approach." *American Economic Journal: Microeconomics* 4: 32–69.

Fast, Norman, and Norman Berg. 1975. *The Lincoln Electric Company*. Harvard Business School Case 9-376-028. Boston: Harvard Business School Press.

Foss, Nicolai. 2003. "Selective Intervention and Internal Hybrids: Interpreting and Learning from the Rise and Decline of the Oticon Spaghetti Organization." *Organization Science* 14: 331–349.

Foster, Lucia, John Haltiwanger, and C. J. Krizan. 2006. "Market Selection, Reallocation, and Restructuring in the U.S. Retail Trade Sector in the 1990s." *Review of Economics and Statistics* 88: 748–758.

Foster, Lucia, John Haltiwanger, and Chad Syverson. 2008. "Reallocation, Firm Turnover, and Efficiency: Selection on Productivity or Profitability?" *American Economic Review* 98: 394–425.

Friedman, James. 1971. "A Non-Cooperative Equilibrium for Supergames." *Review of Economic Studies* 38: 1–12.

Fuchs, William. 2007. "Contracting with Repeated Moral Hazard and Private Evaluations." *American Economic Review* 97: 1432–1448.

Fudenberg, Drew, and David Levine. 1993. "Self-Confirming Equilibrium." *Econometrica* 61: 523–545.

———. 2006. "Superstition and Rational Learning." *American Economic Review* 96: 630–651.

Gant, Jon, Casey Ichniowski, and Kathryn Shaw. 2002. "Social Capital and Organizational Change in High-Involvement and Traditional Work Organizations." *Journal of Economics and Management Strategy* 11: 289–328.

Gibbons, Robert. 2010. "Inside Organizations: Pricing, Politics, and Path Dependence." *Annual Review of Economics* 2: 337–365.

Gibbons, Robert, and Rebecca Henderson. 2012. "Relational Contracts and Organizational Capabilities." *Organization Science,* forthcoming.

Gittell, Jody Hoffer. 2003. *The Southwest Airlines Way: Using the Power of Relationships to Achieve High Performance.* New York: McGraw-Hill.

Greif, Avner. 1994. "Cultural Beliefs and the Organization of Society: A Historial and Theoretical Reflection on Collectivist and Individualist Societies." *Journal of Political Economy* 102: 912–950.

Griliches, Zvi. 1986. "Productivity, R&D, and Basic Research at the Firm Level in the 1970s." *American Economic Review* 76: 141–154.

Griliches, Zvi, and Jacques Mairesse. 1981. "Productivity and R&D at the Firm Level." NBER Working Paper 826, National Bureau of Economic Research, Cambridge, MA.

———. 1982. "Comparing Productivity Growth: An Exploration of French and US Industrial and Firm Data." NBER Working Paper 961, National Bureau of Economic Research, Cambridge, MA.

———. 1985. "R&D and Productivity Growth: Comparing Japanese and U.S. Manufacturing Firms." NBER Working Paper 1778, National Bureau of Economic Research, Cambridge, MA.

Halac, Marina. 2012. "Relational Contracts and the Value of Relationships." *American Economic Review* 102: 750–779.

Hamilton, Barton, Jack Nickerson, and Hideo Owan. 2003. "Team Incentives and Worker Heterogeneity: An Empirical Analysis of the Impact of Teams on Productivity and Participation." *Journal of Political Economy* 111: 465–497.

Hastings, Donald. 1999. "Lincoln Electric's Harsh Lessons from International Expansion." *Harvard Business Review* 77: 162–178.

Hawanini, Gabriel, Venkat Subramanian, and Paul Verdin. 2003. "Is Performance Driven by Industry or Firm-Specific Factors? A New Look at the Evidence." *Strategic Management Journal* 24: 1–16.

Heath, Chip, and Nancy Staudenmayer. 2000. "Coordination Neglect: How Lay Theories of Organizing Complicate Coordination in Organizations." *Research in Organizational Behavior* 22: 155–193.

Henderson, Rebecca. 1994. "The Evolution of Integrative Capability: Innovation in Cardiovascular Drug Discovery." *Industrial and Corporate Change* 3: 607–630.

Henderson, Rebecca, and Kim Clark. 1990. "Architectural Innovation: The Reconfiguration of Existing Product Technologies and the Failure of Established Firms." *Administrative Science Quarterly* 35: 9–30.

Henderson, Rebecca, and Iain Cockburn. 1994. "Measuring Competence? Exploring Firm Effects in Pharmaceutical Research." *Strategic Management Journal* 15(S1): 63–84.

Holmes, Thomas, David Levine, and James Schmitz. 2012. "Monopoly and the Incentive to Innovate When Adoption Involves Switchover Disruption." *American Economic Journal: Microeconomics* 4: 1–33.

Hoxby, Caroline, and Sonali Murarka. 2009. "Charter Schools in New York City: Who Enrolls and How They Affect Their Students' Achievement." NBER Working Paper 14852, National Bureau of Economic Research, Cambridge MA.

Hsieh, Chang-Tai, and Peter Klenow. 2009. "Misallocation and Manufacturing TFP in China and India." *Quarterly Journal of Economics* 124: 1403–1448.

Huselid, Mark. 1995. "The Impact of Human Resource Management Practices on Turnover, Productivity, and Corporate Financial Performance." *Academy of Management Journal* 38: 635–672.

Huselid, Mark, and Brian Becker. 1996. "Methodological Issues in Cross-Sectional and Panel Estimates of the Human Resource-Firm Performance Link." *Industrial Relations* 35: 400–422.

Iansiti, Marco, and Kim Clark. 1994. "Integration and Dynamic Capability: Evidence from Product Development in Automobiles and Mainframe Computers." *Industrial and Corporate Change* 3: 557–605.

Ichniowski, Casey, and Kathryn Shaw. 1999. "The Effects of Human Resource Systems on Productivity: An International Comparison of U.S. and Japanese Plants." *Management Science* 45: 704–722.

Ichniowski, Casey, Kathryn Shaw, and Giovanni Prennushi. 1997. "The Effects of Human Resource Management Practices on Productivity: A Study of Steel Finishing Lines." *American Economic Review* 87: 291–313.

Jackson, Matthew, Tomas Rodriguez-Barraquer, and Xu Tan. 2012. "Social Capital and Social Quilts: Network Patterns of Favor Exchange." *American Economic Review,* forthcoming.

Jeitschko, Thomas, and Curtis Taylor. 2001. "Local Discouragement and Global Collapse: A Theory of Coordination Avalanches." *American Economic Review* 91: 208–224.

Kaplan, Sarah. 2011. "Strategy and PowerPoint: The Epistemic Culture and Machinery of Strategy Making." *Organization Science* 22: 320–346.

Kaplan, Sarah, Fiona Murray, and Rebecca Henderson. 2003. "Discontinuities and Senior Management: Assessing the Role of Recognition in Pharmaceutical Firm Response to Biotechnology." *Industrial and Corporate Change* 12: 203–233.

Klette, Tor. 1999. "Market Power, Scale Economies and Productivity: Estimates from a Panel of Establishment Data." *Journal of Industrial Economics* 47: 451–476.

Kochan, Thomas, Harry Katz, and Robert McKersie. 1986. *The Transformation of American Industrial Relations.* New York: Basic Books.

Kreps, David. 1990. "Corporate Culture and Economic Theory," in James Alt and Kenneth Shepsle (eds.), *Perspectives on Positive Political Economy.* New York: Cambridge University Press, pp. 90–143.

———. 1996. "Markets and Hierarchies and (Mathematical) Economic Theory." *Industrial and Corporate Change* 5: 561–595.

Krugman, Paul. 1995. *Development, Geography, and Economic Theory.* Cambridge, MA: MIT Press.

Lacetera, Nicola, Iain M. Cockburn, and Rebecca Henderson. 2004. "Do Firms Change Capabilities by Hiring New People? A Study of the Adoption of Science-Based Drug Discovery." *Advances in Strategic Management* 21: 133–159.

Lakoff, George. 1987. *Women, Fire, and Dangerous Things: What Categories Reveal about the Mind.* Chicago: University of Chicago Press.

Lakoff, George, and Mark Johnson. 1980. *Metaphors We Live By.* Chicago: University of Chicago Press.

Lazear, Edward. 2000. "Performance Pay and Productivity." *American Economic Review* 90: 1346–1361.

Leibenstein, Harvey. 1969. "Organizational or Frictional Equilibria, X-Efficiency, and the Rate of Innovation." *Quarterly Journal of Economics* 83: 600–623.

———. 1987. *Inside the Firm: The Inefficiencies of Hierarchy.* Cambridge, MA: Harvard University Press.

Levin, Jonathan. 2003. "Relational Incentive Contracts." *American Economic Review* 93: 835–857.

Levinthal, David. 1997. "Adaptation on Rugged Landscapes." *Management Science* 43: 934–950.

Li, Hongyi. 2012. "Developing Shared Knowledge." Working paper, University of New South Wales, Sydney.

Li, Jin, and Niko Matouschek. 2011. "Managing Conflicts in Relational Contracts." Mimeo, Northwestern University, Evanston, IL.

Liker, Jeffrey K. 2004. *The Toyota Way: 14 Management Principles from the World's Greatest Manufacturer.* New York: McGraw-Hill.

Liker, Jeffrey K., and James Franz, 2011. *The Toyota Way to Continuous Improvement.* New York: McGraw-Hill.

Liker, Jeffrey K., and David Meier. 2006. *The Toyota Way Fieldbook.* New York: McGraw-Hill.

Lipitz-Snyderman, Allison, Donald Steinwachs, Dale Needham, Elisabeth Colantuoni, Laura Morlock, and Peter Pronovost. 2011. "Impact of a Statewide Intensive Care Unit Quality Improvement Initiative on Hospital Mortality and Length of Stay: Retrospective Comparative Analysis." *BMJ* 342: d219.

Lippert, Steffen, and Giancarlo Spagnolo. 2011. "Networks of Relations and Word-of-Mouth Communication." *Games and Economic Behavior* 72(1): 202–217.

Lucas, Robert. 1988. "On the Mechanics of Economic Development." *Journal of Monetary Economics* 22: 3–42.

MacDuffie, John Paul. 1995. "Human Resource Bundles and Manufacturing Performance: Organizational Logic and Flexible Production Systems in the World Auto Industry." *Industrial and Labor Relations Review* 48: 197–221.

MacDuffie, John Paul, Kannan Sethuranman, and Marshall Fisher. 1996. "Product Variety and Manufacturing Performance: Evidence from the International Automotive Assembly Plant Study." *Management Science* 42: 350–369.

Macher, Jeffrey. 2006. "Technological Development and the Boundaries of the Firm: A Knowledge-Based Examination in Semiconductor Manufacturing." *Management Science* 52: 826–843.

Macher, Jeffrey, and David Mowery. 2003. "Managing Learning by Doing: An Empirical Study in Semiconductor Manufacturing." *Journal of Product Innovation Management* 20: 391–410.

———. 2009. "Measuring Dynamic Capabilities: Practices and Performance in Semiconductor Manufacturing." *British Journal of Management* 20: S41–S62.

MacLeod, Bentley. 2003. "Optimal Contracting with Subjective Evaluation." *American Economic Review* 93: 216–240.

MacLeod, Bentley, and James Malcomson. 1988. "Reputation and Hierarchy in Dynamic Models of Employment." *Journal of Political Economy* 96: 832–854.

———. 1989. "Implicit Contracts, Incentive Compatibility, and Involuntary Unemployment." *Econometrica* 57: 447–480.

Maestri, Lucas. 2012. "Bonus Payments versus Efficiency Wages in the Repeated Principal-Agent Model with Subjective Evaluations." *American Economic Journal: Microeconomics* 4: 34–56.

Malcomson, James. 2012. "Relational Incentive Contracts with Persistent Private Information." Working paper, University of Oxford.

McAdams, David. 2011. "Performance and Turnover in a Stochastic Partnership." *American Economic Journal: Microeconomics* 3: 107–142.

McGahan, Anita, and Michael Porter. 1997. "How Much Does Industry Matter, Really?" *Strategic Management Journal* 18 (summer special issue: Organizational and Competitive Interactions): 15–30.

———. 1999. "The Persistence of Shocks to Profitability." *Review of Economics and Statistics* 81: 143–153.

Melitz, Marc. 2003. "The Impact of Trade on Intra-Industry Reallocations and Aggregate Industry Productivity." *Econometrica* 17: 1695–1725.

Milgrom, Paul, and John Roberts. 1990. "The Economics of Modern Manufacturing: Technology, Strategy, and Organizations." *American Economic Review* 80: 511–528.

———. 1995. "Complementarities and Fit: Strategy, Structure, and Organizational Change in Manufacturing." *Journal of Accounting and Economics* 19: 179–208.

Mintzberg, Henry. 2004. *Managers not MBAs: A Hard Look at the Soft Practice of Managing and Management Development.* San Francisco: Berrett-Koehler.

Mullainathan, Sendhil, Joshua Schwartzstein, and Andrei Shleifer. 2008. "Coarse Thinking and Persuasion." *Quarterly Journal of Economics* 123: 577–619.

Mundlak, Yair. 1961. "Empirical Production Function Free of Management Bias." *Journal of Farm Economics* 43: 44–56.

Nelson, Richard, and Sidney Winter. 1982. *An Evolutionary Theory of Economic Change.* Cambridge, MA: Harvard University Press.

Olley, G. Steven, and Ariel Pakes. 1996. "The Dynamics of Productivity in the Telecommunications Equipment Industry." *Econometrica* 64: 1263–1297.

Osherson, Daniel, Edward Smith, Ormond Wilkie, Alejandro López, and Eldar Shafir. 1990. "Category-Based Induction." *Psychological Review* 97(2): 185–200.

Ostrom, Elinor. 1990. *Governing the Commons: The Evolution of Institutions for Collective Action.* New York: Cambridge University Press.

Penrose, Edith. 1959. *The Theory and Growth of the Firm.* New York: John Wiley and Sons.

Pfeffer, Jeffrey. 1998. *The Human Equation: Building Profits by Putting People First.* Boston: Harvard Business School Press.

Pil, Frits, and John MacDuffie. 1996. "The Adoption of High-Involvement Work Practices." *Industrial Relations* 35: 423–455.

Powell, Michael. 2012. "Productivity and Credibility in Industry Equilibrium." Working paper, Northwestern University, Evanston, IL.

Pronovost, Peter, and Eric Vohr. 2010. *Safe Patients, Smart Hospitals.* New York: Hudson Street Press.

Pronovost, Peter, Dale Needham, Sean Berenholtz, David Sinopoli, Haitao Chu, Sara Cosgrove, Bran Sexton, Robert Hyzy, Robert Welsh, Gary Roth, Joseph Bander, John Kepros, and Christine Goeschel. 2006. "An Intervention to Decrease Catheter-Related Bloodstream Infections in the ICU." *New England Journal of Medicine* 355: 2725–2732.

Pronovost Peter, Christine Goeschel, Elizabeth Colantuoni, Sam Watson, Lisa Lubomski, Sean Berenholtz, David Thompson, David Sinopoli, Sara Cosgrove, Bryan Sexton, Jill Marstellar, Robert Hyzy, Robert Welsh, Patricia Posa, Kathy Schumacher, and Dale Needham. 2010. "Sustaining Reductions in Catheter Related Bloodstream Infections in Michigan Intensive Care Units: Observational Study." *BMJ* 340: c309.

Reinganum, Jennifer. 1989. "The Timing of Innovation: Research, Development and Diffusion," in Richard Schmalensee and Robert Willig (eds.), *Handbook of Industrial Organization,* volume 1. Amsterdam: North-Holland, pp. 849–908.

Repenning, Nelson, and John Sterman. 2002. "Capability Traps and Self-Confirming Attribution Errors in the Dynamics of Process Improvement." *Administrative Science Quarterly* 47: 265–295.

Rivkin, Jan. 2000. "Imitation of Complex Strategies." *Management Science* 46: 824–844.

Rivkin, Jan, and Nicolaj Siggelkow. 2003. "Balancing Search and Stability: Interdependencies among Elements of Organizational Design." *Management Science* 49: 290–311.

Rosch, Eleanor. 1973. "Natural Categories." *Cognitive Psychology* 4: 328–350.

———. 1975. "Cognitive Representations of Semantic Categories." *Journal of Experimental Psychology: General* 104(3): 192–233.

Ross, Lee. 1977. "The Intuitive Psychologist and His Shortcomings: Distortions in the Attribution Process," in Leonard Berkowitz (ed.), *Advances in Experimental Social Psychology,* volume 10. New York: Academic Press, pp. 173–220.

Rousseau, Denise. 1995. *Psychological Contracts in Organizations: Understanding Written and Unwritten Agreements.* Thousand Oaks, CA: SAGE.

Rumelt, Richard. 1991. "How Much Does Industry Matter?" *Strategic Management Journal* 12: 167–185.

Ryall, Michael. 2003. "Subjective Rationality, Self-Confirming Equilibrium, and Corporate Strategy." *Management Science* 49: 936–949.

Sabel, Charles. 1993. "Studied Trust: Building New Forms of Cooperation in a Volatile Economy," in

Richard Swedberg (ed.), *Exploration in Economic Sociology*. New York: Russell Sage Foundation, pp. 104–144.

Salter, Wilfred E. G. 1960. *Productivity and Technical Change*. Cambridge: Cambridge University Press.

Schein, Edgar. 1985. *Organizational Culture and Leadership*. San Francisco: Jossey-Bass.

Schmalensee, Richard. 1985. "Do Markets Differ Much?" *American Economic Review* 75: 341–351.

Selten, Reinhard, and Massimo Warglien. 2007. "The Emergence of Simple Languages in an Experimental Coordination Game." *Proceedings of the National Academy of Sciences (USA)* 104: 7361–7366.

Siggelkow, Nicolaj, and Jan Rivkin. 2005. "Speed and Search: Designing Organizations for Turbulence and Complexity." *Organization Science* 16: 101–122.

Simon, Herbert. 1947. *Administrative Behavior: A Study of Decision-Making Processes in Administrative Organization*. New York: Free Press.

Sloan, Alfred P. 1963. *My Years with General Motors*. New York: Doubleday. Reprinted in 1990 by Crown Publishing Group, New York.

Smith, Lones, and Peter Sørensen. 2000. "Pathological Outcomes of Observational Learning." *Econometrica* 68: 371–398.

Spector, Robert, and Patrick McCarthy. 2012. *The Nordstrom Way to Customer Service*, second edition. Hoboken, NJ: Wiley.

Stewart, James. 1993. "Taking the Dare." *New Yorker*, July 26, pp. 34–39.

Syverson, Chad. 2004a. "Product Substitutability and Productivity Dispersion." *Review of Economics and Statistics* 86: 534–550.

———. 2004b. "Market Structure and Productivity: A Concrete Example." *Journal of Political Economy* 112: 1181–1222.

———. 2011. "What Determines Productivity?" *Journal of Economic Literature* 49: 326–365.

Tirole, Jean. 1996. "A Theory of Collective Reputations (with Applications to the Persistence of Corruption and to Firm Quality)." *Review of Economic Studies* 63: 1–22.

Tripsas, Mary, and Giovanni Gavetti. 2000. "Capabilities, Cognition, and Inertia: Evidence from Digital Imaging." *Strategic Management Journal* 21: 1147–1161.

Van Biesebroeck, Johannes. 2008. "The Sensitivity of Productivity Estimates: Revisiting Three Important Debates." *Journal of Business and Economic Statistics* 26: 311–328.

Walker, Francis. 1887. "The Source of Business Profits." *Quarterly Journal of Economics* 1: 265–288.

Watson, Joel. 1999. "Starting Small and Renegotiation." *Journal of Economic Theory* 85: 52–90.

———. 2002. "Starting Small and Commitment." *Games and Economic Behavior* 38(1): 176–199.

Weber, Roberto, and Colin Camerer. 2003. "Culture Conflict and Merger Failure: An Experimental Approach." *Management Science* 49: 400–415.

Winter, Sidney. 1987. "Knowledge and Competence as Strategic Assets," in David Teece (ed.), *The Competitive Challenge: Strategies for Industrial Innovation and Renewal*. Cambridge, MA: Ballinger, pp. 159–184.

———. 1988. "On Coase, Competence, and the Corporation." *Journal of Law, Economics, and Organization* 4: 163–180.

———. 2006. "Toward a Neo-Schumpeterian Theory of the Firm." *Industrial and Corporate Change* 15: 125–141.

Wolitzky, Alex. 2012. "Cooperation with Network Monitoring." *Review of Economic Studies,* forthcoming.

Yang, Huanxing. 2012. "Nonstationary Relational Contracts with Adverse Selection." *International Economic Review,* forthcoming.

Zollo, Maurizio, and Sidney Winter. 2002. "Deliberate Learning and the Evolution of Dynamic Capabilities." *Organization Science* 13: 339–351.

18

Corporate Governance
A Critical Assessment
Benjamin E. Hermalin

1. Introduction

People invest in organizations. They invest their human capital, and they invest their physical capital. In exchange, they expect some return, and all else equal, they would like the organizations in which they invest to maximize that return. A problem arises, however, when the people who invest in an organization are not the same people who control the organization. Lack of control makes the investors vulnerable to mismanagement of the organization, misallocation of its resources, or even misappropriation of their returns. In short, investors fear that their returns will not be maximized, because their desires are not necessarily aligned with those of the controlling parties. In response to these fears, investors will wish to put in place various institutions to constrain the controlling parties to better act in their interests. In short, they will put in place some sort of governance structure for the organization.

Although this problem is endemic to all organizations (consider, e.g., the concerns of a philanthropist worried that a charitable organization will not make the best use of her money), it has proved to be of critical importance with respect to corporations (especially, for-profit corporations).[1] In the corporate setting, the parties typically deemed to have control are management and, if they exist, dominant shareholders. In some cases, the controlling parties are both (e.g., companies dominated by a single family, as the Ford Motor Company was historically by the Ford family or as many companies around the world are today).

The potential misalignments of incentives in corporations are many. For instance, managers are more inclined to tolerate their own incompetence than are shareholders. They are also unlikely to see eye-to-eye with shareholders about managerial amenities, such as lavish offices, corporate jets, and the like. The terms of an asset transfer from one firm to another could be disadvantageous to the first firm (and hence the majority of its investors), but advantageous to its dominant shareholder if the other company is one in which she owns an even greater proportion.[2]

---

1. There is a limited literature on the governance of nonprofit corporations. See, for example, Bowen (1994) and Ehrenberg (2004).

2. Johnson et al. (2000) refer to such transfers as "tunneling."

Concerns about corporate governance,[3] in particular, the issues that arise when investors and controlling parties are not one and the same, are longstanding. Smith (1776) is an early, if not the earliest, example in economics:

> The directors of such companies, however, being the managers rather of other people's money than of their own, it cannot well be expected that they should watch over it with . . . anxious vigilance . . . . Negligence and profusion, therefore, must always prevail, more or less, in the management of the affairs of such compan[ies]. [Book V, Part III, Article I, "Of the Publick Works and Institutions which are necessary for facilitating particular Branches of Commerce," paragraph 18]

The modern era of economic interest in corporate governance appears to have started in the 1920s, when initially the focus was on financial reporting.[4] Berle and Means (1932) was perhaps the most important early modern work, and it directly influenced a number of reforms undertaken by the New York Stock Exchange (NYSE).[5] Berle and Means were among the first to note that the stark separation of ownership and control, common to the modern corporation, created a number of potentially serious problems. The 1950s and 1960s saw economists looking at issues of executive compensation and starting to model the divergence of interests between owners and managers (see Lewellen 1968 as an example and survey of the former; Williamson 1963 is a noteworthy example of the latter). An article of great importance in the evolution of the field was Jensen and Meckling (1976), which, in addition to surveying some of the literature to that point, identified many of the issues that have continued to occupy economists working on corporate governance to this day. As with much of life, good timing is essential, and the renewed interest in corporate governance generated by Jensen and Meckling occurred just as the tools of information economics, game theory, and contract theory were coming to the fore in economics. These tools led to an explosive growth in the literature on organizations generally (as this handbook attests) and on corporate governance specifically. For instance, Becht et al. (2003) cite more than 550 works in their survey of corporate governance, almost all of which are dated 1980 or later; surveying just the literature on boards of directors, Adams et al. (2010) cite approximately 170 works, with the overwhelming majority having been written after 2000.[6]

This vast literature has generated many survey pieces. In addition to the two just mentioned, a sample of such surveys includes Shleifer and Vishny (1997), Tirole (2001), Farinha (2003), and Zingales (2008) on the literature overall; John and Senbet (1998) and Hermalin and Weisbach (2003) on boards of directors; Bertrand (2009) on CEOs; Devers et al. (2007) and Edmans and Gabaix (2009) on executive compensation; Bhagat and Jefferis (2002) on econometric issues; Denis and McConnell (2003) on international governance; and Durisin and Puzone (2009) on the intellectual structure of governance research. One can rightly ask whether another survey

---

3. Becht et al. (2003: 5) suggest that the term "corporate governance" was first used in 1960. The field is obviously considerably older.

4. An important work in this regard was Ripley (1927), which was initially a series of articles in the *Atlantic Monthly*. Baskin and Miranti (1997: 197) describe Ripley's work as a "widely read polemic." Scholz (1928: 178) discusses "the commotion which was aroused in financial and official circles" by its publication.

5. See Baskin and Miranti (1997: 200) for a discussion of the influence of Berle and Means on policy.

6. Adams et al. (2010: 64) report that more than 200 papers on boards—not all of which they cite—were written in 2003–2008 alone.

is needed; in particular, given the existence of the aforementioned surveys, the social benefit—even accounting for my egotistical exaggeration of my writing's value—is modest, and given the huge literature, the cost—to me at least—immense. Consequently, I propose a different course of action: this chapter presents an overarching framework from which to assess the issues of corporate governance and a means of framing the existing literature, both empirical and theoretical. Such an approach will, I believe, also be more conducive to suggesting future lines of research than a more traditional survey chapter.

Briefly, the chapter is organized as follows. The next section considers the scope of corporate governance, arguing that it is primarily the study of what happens when investors seek to protect themselves against mismanagement, misallocation, and misappropriation of their investments by those who control the corporations in which they wish to invest. The section thereafter seeks to tie these three Ms to the various economic literatures that have explored these contract and agency problems. Section 4 deals with the fact that governance institutions are arrived at *endogenously*. This has important implications for how empirical work needs to be conducted. Perhaps more importantly, it also has important implications for how that work is interpreted. This second point is explored further in Section 5, where the consequences of the fact that different governance structures govern different firms are discussed. Section 6 focuses on the dispersion of ownership and its consequences. The last two sections are essentially conclusions. The first of these suggests that both the literature and policy have placed too great an emphasis on improving shareholder control. The second sketches directions for future research.

2. What Is Corporate Governance?

I suggested in the previous section that corporate governance is concerned with protecting the interests of investors when they are not the ones wholly in control of the organization. Such a view echoes Shleifer and Vishny (1997: 737):

> Corporate governance deals with the ways in which suppliers of finance to corporations assure themselves of getting a return on their investment. How do the suppliers of finance get managers to return some of the profits to them? How do they make sure that managers do not steal the capital they supply or invest it in bad projects? How do suppliers of finance control managers?

For companies in which a few dominant shareholders have control, one could replace "managers" in this quote with "dominant shareholders." One could, and perhaps should, also extend it to cover all suppliers of capital, including human capital. That said, the economic literature has been almost exclusively focused on the suppliers of finance (Roberts and Van den Steen 2003 and Tirole 2001 are notable exceptions).

One could, following Tirole, take an even more encompassing view: Corporate governance is the means by which the externalities that controlling parties generate are regulated.[7] With respect to the very largest corporations, we are all affected to some degree by the actions of those in control. Typically, however, the set of individuals affected is more compact: its employees,

---

7. Tirole (2001: 4) writes "I will . . . define corporate governance as the design of institutions that induce or force management to internalize the welfare of stakeholders."

customers, suppliers, local community, and, of course, investors—a set typically referred to as the firm's "stakeholders."

Although one might properly be concerned with stakeholders' welfare, such a broad view is not, in my opinion, the best way to look at corporate governance. First, the potential externalities of the controlling parties' actions are many and include such matters as environmental degradation, the health and safety features of the products and services provided, and even the contribution to rush-hour congestion through transportation decisions. Further, these externalities may generate subsequent effects, so like the proverbial butterfly that triggers a hurricane, everyone is potentially affected by each corporate decision. This is simply too broad a perspective to be workable in terms of analysis or policy setting.

Second, even if one limits the set of externalities at issue, the set of those affected is not necessarily clear. If a firm closes a plant, who would we say has been affected? The workers, certainly, and, perhaps, their local community as well. But what about the workers of companies that supplied the plant and who now face reduced hours or layoffs? What about their communities? Or what about a distant community whose economy is, in part, reliant on remittances from those who work at the plant? In this regard, a plus for focusing on investors is that they are readily identifiable.

Third, if the focus is on externalities, broadly defined, then what distinguishes corporate governance from other forms of environmental or health and safety regulation? Even a cursory examination suggests that there is some value in studying corporate governance apart from the general study of state regulation of economic activity.

One way in which corporate governance stands apart from state regulation generally is that corporate governance involves, to a great extent, the way private parties choose to regulate their own dealings. In contrast, the only way in which all stakeholders, broadly defined, can have a say is if the state intervenes on their behalf. Hence, the focus in the chapter is on the institutions that the private parties—investors and managers—wish to put in place to govern their relations. Although corporate governance is highly regulated by the state, at least in most of the world and in all OECD countries, it is possible to consider corporate governance independently of any state action. Indeed, there is much to be gained by studying corporate governance assuming away state regulation. Only by knowing what private parties would otherwise put in place can we properly assess the wisdom—or lack thereof—in state regulation of firms' governance structures. To be sure, one cannot wholly ignore the state—or at least the law—with respect to corporate governance; in particular, some institutions could not be created privately absent certain features of corporation law or political institutions.[8] Nevertheless, the relevant parties still possess considerable freedom in designing the institutions that govern their relation.

8. See, for instance, Hansmann and Kraakman (2000a,b) and Kornhauser and MacLeod (this volume) on this topic. Hansmann and Kraakman argue that private contracting could not replicate the corporation's legal personhood. The ability of the corporation to own property in its own name—as opposed to having said property owned collectively by the shareholders—is essential for a corporation to function. Beyond simplifying the sale of shares, it also simplifies the corporation's ability to sell and acquire assets. Perhaps most importantly, legal personhood prevents a shareholder from selling his or her portion of the assets or pledging them as collateral, and similarly, it prevents any creditor of a shareholder from seizing the firm's assets as a form of recovery should the shareholder default on his or her debts. This is what Hansmann (this volume) refers to as "entity shielding."

Fligstein (2008) discusses some of the political and societal structures necessary for a corporate governance regime aimed at maximizing firm value to be acceptable.

3. Threats and Responses

Investors fear losing returns due to mismanagement of the organization, misallocation of its resources, or even outright misappropriation. Of these, the last is arguably the biggest threat, at least as measured in terms of the response. A moment's reflection plus some quick back-of-the-envelope calculations will show that expenditures on procedures and methods to detect and discourage misappropriation are the lion's share of resources devoted to the control of the corporation. Every large organization has numerous procedures and methods to detect theft. Examples include auditing of transactions, requiring multiple levels of approval for transactions, and direct monitoring of employee activity. A nontrivial portion of various governance regulations, such as Sarbanes-Oxley, are concerned with these processes.[9]

Misappropriation can occur at any level of the organization. In economics, the study of misappropriation mitigation at the lower levels has been essentially indirect, with the focus on such matters as management of hierarchies, budgeting, and collusion.[10] With respect to misappropriation at the top, the literature has focused on how securities should be designed to mitigate the threat of misappropriation—of nondisgorgement of funds, more specifically. For example, one topic has been how debt can induce those in control to disgorge the returns due investors. Townsend (1979), Jensen (1986), and Hart and Moore (1998) are some examples of this literature.[11]

A related concern is that a dominant shareholder may engage in self-dealing in one form or another. As Johnson et al. (2000), among others, observe, there is a danger that a controlling shareholder could engage in transfer pricing between companies she controls in a manner that is self-enriching (e.g., she has a firm of which she owns 50% buy inputs from a firm of which she owns 75% at an inflated price). If she is an executive, she could also approve excessive compensation for herself. There are other abuses of minority shareholders that could arise, such as freeze-outs (i.e., effectively compelling them to sell at less than true market value).[12] Here, the principal response to this threat has been legal: it is laws on the protection of minority-shareholder rights that mainly serve to limit such behavior.

Although the distinction between misappropriation and misallocation is fuzzy—has the CEO stolen from shareholders when he has the company purchase a corporate jet?—we can view misallocation as a catch-all for various agency problems that arise because management and investors have differing preferences concerning the use of corporate resources, including managerial time. If we treat management's allocation choices as a hidden action,[13] then basic agency theory (e.g., Holmström 1979; Shavell 1979; Grossman and Hart 1983) provides a sense of the responses. In particular, we would postulate that companies would provide executives

---

9. The accounting literature on auditing is vast. A few notable contributions are Baiman and Demski (1980), Fellingham and Newman (1985), Antle and Demski (1988), and Demski and Sappington (1989).

10. See, for instance, Williamson (1975), Tirole (1986), and Mookherjee and Reichelstein (1997).

11. See also Tirole (2006: 132–144) for a survey and discussion of the relevant literature.

12. For more on freeze-outs, see Hermalin and Schwartz (1996) and the citations therein. There is also considerable cross-country variation in the law governing minority-shareholder protections; see La Porta et al. (1997).

13. If allocation decisions are observable to investors, then presumably management and investors will bargain to an efficient agreement concerning these decisions; that is, misallocation will not occur.

with various forms of incentive compensation. (Although it is important to note that incentive compensation is not the only way to respond to the threat of moral hazard; a point to which I return later.)

Executive compensation has been much studied (for two recent surveys, see Bertrand 2009; Edmans and Gabaix 2009). Although I will return to the topic later for a more critical discussion, it is worth mentioning some of the more important work in this area. The popular press and others (e.g., Bebchuk and Fried 2004) have bemoaned the seemingly endless rise in executive compensation. For historical perspectives on this phenomenon, see Hadlock and Lumer (1997) and Frydman and Saks (2010). The literature has also sought to empirically test whether compensation practices are consistent with basic agency theory, with mixed results. For example, agency theory predicts that the optimal compensation scheme should seek to eliminate noise from the performance measure. Bertrand and Mullainathan (2001) find that CEO compensation schemes fail to do so. In contrast, Gibbons and Murphy (1990) do find evidence of relative-performance compensation, a means of reducing noise. As Bertrand (2009) observes, one reaction to the rapid run-up in CEO compensation and the poor record of basic agency theory has been the development of new models of compensation based on changes in the executive labor market or other trends. A partial list of these include Murphy and Zabojnik (2003); Murphy and Zabojnik (2004), Hermalin (2005), Gabaix and Landier (2008), and Terviö (2008).[14]

The third investor concern, mismanagement, deals with the competence of the managers. Managers or would-be managers vary in ability. If talent were known ex ante, then some market mechanism would allocate managers to firms (for such models, see, e.g., Gabaix and Landier 2008; Terviö 2008). In equilibrium, investors are happy with their manager's ability in the sense that they are unwilling to effect an alternative outcome.

Alternatively, managerial ability could be unknown, including, possibly, by the manager. This is the approach taken in Holmström's (1999) seminal article on career concerns.[15] How well a newly appointed CEO will do is uncertain, but if his previous record is publicly known, then everyone should hold the same beliefs about his ability at the start of his tenure as CEO.[16] In addition to Holmström (1999), other articles adopting a career-concern approach include Holmström and Ricart i Costa (1986), Stein (1989), Hermalin and Weisbach (1998), and Hermalin (2005).[17] In these models, players learn information that improves their estimate of

---

14. Bertrand (2009: 136–138) offers a critical assessment of the Gabaix and Landier (2008) model with respect to its fit with the empirical evidence.

15. The article first appeared in 1982 in a now out-of-print *festschrift* for Lars Wahlbeck.

16. The underlying logic of career concerns models does not rely on the CEO's being equally ignorant of his ability as other players. Provided there is no scope for him to clearly signal his type, the CEO will still have incentives to engage in the signal-jamming activities discussed here. The technical difficulties that would, however, arise are daunting, which is why the equal-ignorance assumption prevails in these models.

Another variation—unexplored to the best of my knowledge—would be for the CEO to hold a biased estimate of his ability, consistent with some of the excessive optimism and overconfidence models in the behavioral economics literature. See, for example, Malmendier and Tate (2005). Bertrand (2009: 142–144) contains a nice survey of the literature on "cognitively challenged CEOs."

17. The paper by Gibbons and Murphy (1992) is an empirical study of career concerns. It finds evidence to support the idea that firms increase explicit compensation to compensate for the reduced career concerns CEOs have toward the ends of their careers.

the CEO's ability. Because the CEO is rewarded if his estimated ability increases (e.g., he receives higher salary offers) or punished if his estimated ability falls (e.g., he gets fired), the CEO has an incentive to manipulate what information is learned by the other players. This manipulation can be beneficial to the firm (the CEO works harder, as hypothesized by Fama 1980), but it can also create agency problems (see, in particular, Stein 1989). For instance, the CEO may boost signals of his ability in the short term in ways that have long-term adverse effects that outweigh the net present value of any benefit the boost might create. An example of this is a CEO who behaves in a myopic fashion to boost performance in the short term at the expense of long-term value (see Stein 1989). Alternatively, the CEO may choose actions based on how much or little they reveal of his ability rather than based on the investors' best interests (see Holmström and Ricart i Costa 1986). In other words, investors' desires to limit mismanagement can create costly agency problems.

Another feature of these models is that improving the estimation of CEO ability exposes the CEO to risk.[18] Under certain circumstances, he will require compensation for bearing that risk, which in turn could motivate investors to limit that risk even at the cost of reducing the probability that a bad CEO will be fired. Hermalin and Weisbach (1998) and Hermalin (2005) consider, in different contexts, what the consequences of this tension are for the design of governance structures. In particular, these last two articles examine, among other issues, how the choice of corporate directors—the people who actually dismiss the CEO—balances the desire to be able to get rid of low-ability CEOs against the potential agency problems and compensation demands that monitoring induces.

Monitoring is another response to agency problems. Generally, the job of monitoring top management has been seen as a responsibility of a company's board of directors (although the takeover market and proxy contests can also take on this role). Directors are also supposed to guard against misappropriation and misallocation. As noted earlier, the literature on directors is voluminous (for surveys, see Hermalin and Weisbach 2003; Adams et al. 2010).

This section has briefly considered the various threats investors face and the range of responses they may take (more precisely, the economics literature that considers how to respond). What it has ignored is what determines the choice and degree of response. In particular, because those in control naturally do not wish to be constrained, they can be expected to push back against the various responses, seeking to modify or limit them. This is the topic of the next section.

4. The Determination of Responses: Corporate Governance in an Equilibrium Framework

As noted, investors wish to limit the ability of controlling parties to behave contrary to the investors' interests. Such limits are not in the controlling parties' private interests, and the

---

18. This can be seen intuitively by imagining that the estimate of ability was based on a signal that is complete noise. Consequently, the posterior estimate would equal the prior estimate. Given there is no change in the estimate, there is no uncertainty and, hence, no risk. In contrast, if the signal is informative (not noisy), then the posterior estimate will put considerable weight on it, meaning, from an ex ante perspective, that the posterior estimate is quite variable, which translates into risk for the CEO.

controlling parties can, thus, be expected to resist their imposition. Or, if they cannot block their imposition, then controlling parties will seek compensation for them. This suggests that the corporate governance institutions we observe are the consequence of some—perhaps implicit—bargaining game between investors and controlling parties.

In economics, the standard presumption is that if the private parties are symmetrically informed *at the time* they bargain, they will typically reach an efficient outcome.[19] Because the optimal solutions to agency problems are almost always second best, the efficiency standard is second-best efficiency; a standard often referred to as "constrained Pareto optimality." Specifically, given the constraints inherent in dealing with agency issues, the outcome is optimal only in the sense that money has not been left on the table. That is, there is no alternative contract or institution the parties could adopt that at least one party favors more than the original and the other no less than the original. Moreover, if we assume—as seems reasonable in this context—an ability to make transfers between the parties, then there is no alternative contract or institution that would generate greater total welfare in equilibrium than the one the parties put in place.

Admittedly, the view that governance institutions could be constrained Pareto optimal is not without controversy. It is a perspective that is certainly at odds with how many commentators on corporate governance see corporate governance.[20] How can one use the adjective "optimal" with regard to practices—such as apparently impotent boards and apparently undeservedly huge executive compensation—that seem so suboptimal? Where is the optimality in spectacular governance failures such as Enron, WorldCom, and Parmalat? These commentators are overlooking one or more the following:

1. Even if there were no constraints, this does not imply that investors would get everything they want. As noted, there is bargaining between investors and management, which presumably reflects relative market position. If capital is plentiful but managerial talent scarce, then the returns generated by combining capital and talent will tend to flow disproportionately to the talent.[21]

2. Even if there were no constraints, there are costs to governance, and some amount of failure should occur even in the first-best solution. By way of analogy, auto-related fatalities can be reduced by requiring automobiles to travel more slowly. But there is an opportunity cost to the extra time spent traveling. Hence, society accepts some failures (auto-related fatalities), because eliminating or reducing them would be too costly.

3. There are constraints and they are not trivial. As an analogy, we would not say that Henry Aaron, Babe Ruth, and other Hall-of-Fame hitters were failures because more than 65% of their at-bats ended in failure.[22] Major-league pitchers, backed up by major-league fielders, represent a serious constraint with respect to hitting safely.

19. See Hermalin et al. (2007: especially 21–46) for a survey of the relevant literature.
20. As examples of work suggesting current governance is highly suboptimal, see Lorsch and MacIver (1989), Bebchuk and Fried (2003, 2004), and MacAvoy and Millstein (2003).
21. In this regard, it is worth speculating about the extent to which the run-up in executive salaries at the beginning of this century was due to the availability of cheap capital. Did the relative bargaining positions of talent and capital tip toward talent?
22. Henry Aaron's career average was .305. Babe Ruth's was .342.

4. Finally, the corporation is not the only way to organize an enterprise. Alternatives include sole proprietorships, partnerships, cooperatives, and state-owned enterprises.[23] For more than 400 years, at least, the corporate form has successfully competed with these other forms and has, economically, come to dominate all alternatives.[24] Hence, there is a limit on just how bad corporate governance can be.[25]

I am not, however, suggesting one adopt a panglossian approach to governance. It is doubtful that we live in the best of all possible worlds; that is, there could be scope for improvement via regulatory action (more on this point later). My point is rather that the efficacy of regulatory action is more limited than many commentators would suggest.

Investors and management choose the institutions by which their relation is governed. Hence, governance institutions are *endogenous*. As such, any regression analysis that attempts to determine the effect of one or more of these institutions on firm performance—for instance, a regression of return on assets (ROA) on the proportion of the board of directors who are outside directors—needs to control for the joint endogeneity of the dependent and independent variables.[26] Although researchers have not always been careful in this regard, the better work does attempt to deal with this endogeneity (for a more complete treatment of this issue, see Bhagat and Jefferis 2002).

A more fundamental issue, though, is the following: how should one interpret a regression of financial performance on governance attributes? A common presumption in the literature, for example, is that outside directors are better monitors of management than are inside directors. Naïvely, one might seek to test this hypothesis by regressing a measure of financial performance on a measure of the relative number of outside directors. The "rationale" is that, if the hypothesis is correct, firms that score higher on the measure of outside directors will tend to score better

---

23. See Hansmann (this volume) for a survey of the literature on why different organizational forms are chosen.

24. The East India Company is often taken to be the first corporation, chartered on December 31, 1600, by Queen Elizabeth I (Baskin and Miranti 1997). Another early corporation was the Vereenigde Oost-Indische Compagnie (usually referred to in English as the Dutch East India Company), which was established in 1602. Neither is as old as Stora Kopparberg, a Swedish mining company that sold its first share in 1288 and was chartered by King Magnus IV of Sweden in 1347. Malmendier (2009: 1077) argues "the earliest predecessor of the modern business corporation was . . . the Roman *societas publicanorum*." *Societates publicanorum* rose to prominence in the last two centuries BCE.

25. This is not to claim that corporate governance is better than the governance of other forms of enterprise. Rather, it is the observation that it cannot be so bad as to outweigh whatever benefits the corporate form offers over these other forms. In this regard, it is worth noting that one of the benefits of the modern corporate form, limited liability, cannot be what has made the corporate form survive. Limited liability did not come into being until the British enacted the Limited Liability Act of 1855, roughly 255 years after the first corporation was chartered there (for further discussion and detail, see Diamond 1982).

26. The outside directors of a corporation are those directors who are not current or former officers of the corporation (i.e., part of its management team). Inside directors are directors who are current or former officers. In the literature the two groups are often referred to as "outsiders" and "insiders," respectively. It is generally assumed that outsiders' interests are more aligned with investors than are insiders'; in particular, the presumption is that outsiders exercise some control over management. See, for example, Hermalin and Weisbach (2003) and Adams et al. (2010) for a discussion of the relevant literature.

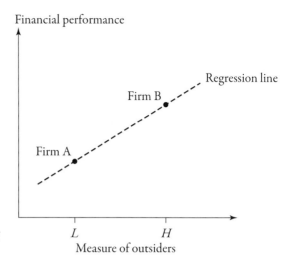

Figure 1. A hypothetical regression of financial performance against a measure of outside director presence on the board.

in terms of financial performance.[27] That is, if the data resemble those in Figure 1, then there is support for the hypothesis.[28]

A problem with such an interpretation is that if more outside directors really mean better financial performance, why does firm A in Figure 1 choose to have a low measure of outside directors? That is, if the hypothesis is true, then it would appear firm A is leaving money on the table. Surely the investors and management of firm A would have had a larger "pie" to divide had they emulated firm B in terms of outside directors. In short, one cannot accept both the hypothesis that governance structures are constrained Pareto optima and the hypothesis that the regression in Figure 1 is a valid test of whether more outside directors improves financial performance.

Furthermore, as Demsetz and Lehn (1985) and others have noted, if one accepts that the observed governance structures are constrained Pareto optima, then it is no longer clear that any

27. Baysinger and Butler (1985), Rosenstein and Wyatt (1990), Brickley et al. (1994), and Durchin et al. (2009), among others, find evidence that measures of outside directors are positively correlated with firm performance. Hermalin and Weisbach (1991) and Yermack (1996) also study the issue but find little evidence that firm performance is related to board composition. Other studies have investigated the relation between other attributes of the governance structure and firm performance: Yermack (1996) and Eisenberg et al. (1998) find a negative relation between board size and firm performance (Coles et al. [2008], however, find that firm performance is increasing in board size for certain types of firms); Stulz (1988) and Morck et al. (1988) find a positive relation between managerial stock ownership and firm performance (up to a certain threshold of ownership, at which point the relation reverses; see Becht et al. 2003: 63 and Section 6 for a more detailed appraisal of the managerial stock ownership literature); Jarrell and Poulsen (1987), Mahoney and Mahoney (1993), and Bebchuk and Cohen (2005) find having directors serve staggered terms of multiple years (as opposed to all serving annual terms) has a negative effect on firm performance. See some of the aforementioned survey articles for additional studies of the relation between governance attributes and firm performance.

28. To be more precise, imagine in Figure 1 that the dependent variable is the residual of financial performance regressed on the relevant controls other than the measure of outsiders.

Financial performance

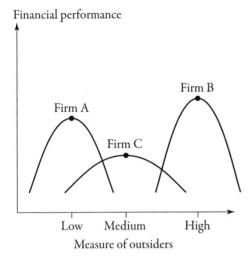

Figure 2. Given firms choose governance optimally, should governance and performance be correlated? Parabolas illustrate the indicated firms' optimization problems.

relation should exist in the data between governance structures and performance. If the relevant parties are solving an optimization program unique to their firm, then, as Demsetz and Lehn observe, we could readily expect to see data like that shown in Figure 2. In this second figure, in addition to the scatter plot of the "data," I have also drawn parabolas to indicate, heuristically, the different optimization programs faced by the investors and controlling interests of these three firms.[29]

Consistent with the idea that the parties achieve constrained Pareto optima, each firm in Figure 2 is shown resting on the top of its respective hill; that is, no set of parties could do better. Clearly, a regression should reveal no relationship between the variables in question. Yet many carefully executed empirical studies find evidence of correlation; moreover, this correlation tends to be positive: measures that arguably indicate stronger governance (e.g., smaller boards, or higher governance indices) go hand-in-hand with better firm performance and vice versa.[30] Why, in a world of constrained Pareto optimal governance structures, do we observe these positive correlations?

29. See Adams et al. (2010) for a survey of models that seek to explain the optimal mix of outside and inside directors. In this literature, there are three basic explanations: (1) bargaining between management and investors (directors) results in a compromise (see, e.g., Hermalin and Weisbach 1998; Cyert et al. 2002); (2) getting management (the CEO) to reveal information or otherwise take actions risky to their careers (see, e.g., Almazan and Suarez 2003; Dominguez-Martinez et al. 2008); or (3) as a means of inducing efficient information sharing among directors (see, e.g., Adams and Ferreira 2007; Harris and Raviv 2008). In all these models, restricting the proportion of outside directors is essentially a means of committing the board to future actions that cannot be contracted on formally.

30. See, for example, Bhagat and Jefferis (2002), Becht et al. (2003), and Adams et al. (2010), among others, for surveys covering this empirical literature. Examples of articles finding a negative correlation between board size and performance (i.e., that small boards are associated with better performance) include Yermack (1996) and Eisenberg et al. (1998) (but for partially contradictory evidence see Coles et al. 2008). Examples of articles finding a positive correlation between indices of good governance and performance include Gompers et al. (2003) and Bebchuk et al. (2009).

Could the view that Figure 1 is showing something causal be resuscitated by assuming that firms sometimes get out of equilibrium or that there are large adjustment costs? The problem with an out-of-equilibrium explanation is the following. If firms are truly seeking to be at the peaks of their respective parabolas but get knocked off the peak for various reasons, why aren't they equally likely to land to the right of the peak as to the left? That is, an out-of-equilibrium explanation of the data in Figures 1 must posit that firms are more likely to slip to the left—have less than the optimal measure of outside directors—than to the right—have more than the optimal measure. To be sure, such a bias is possible. Indeed, the Hermalin and Weisbach (1998) model predicts that corporations will "drift to the left" over the tenure of a CEO.[31] The Hermalin and Weisbach model does not, however, also predict that financial performance will fall as the corporation drifts to the left.

Adjustment costs would seem to offer another explanation for why firm A does not emulate firm B in Figure 1. But then one is left with the puzzle of how firm A came to be so far from the optimum board structure in the first place. Perhaps L was, at some point in the past, the optimal measure of outside directors. But if so, then H was suboptimal, and we are left wondering how firm B came to be so far from the optimum. An evolutionary twist might help: a greater percentage of outsiders on the board is a "mutation" largely enjoyed by new firms, such as B. Older firms, such as A, see that this is a positive mutation, but find it hard to adjust. Evolution and organizational adjustment are important phenomena (see, e.g., Hermalin, "Leadership and Corporate Culture," this volume), but it seems unlikely this could be the explanation, given the long time such heterogeneity has existed. (For example, Hermalin and Weisbach [1988] find considerable variation as far back as the 1970s, and such variation continues to exist to this day.)

Where, then, does this leave us? The fact that many studies do find a significant and positive relation between governance and performance suggests there could be something in the data that cannot be dismissed. But what is in the data, and how do we reconcile it with the previous discussion? One answer is that we are thinking about the data backwards: Rather than good governance causing good performance, perhaps it is good performance—more specifically, the potential for or likelihood of good performance—that is causing good governance.

To have a tangible framework in which to explore the idea that good governance is the consequence of the potential for good performance, consider the following model. Investors deal with a single manager. The manager's utility is

$$u = D + v(R - D, g),$$

where R denotes the firm's resources, D denotes the amount the manager diverts to uses he desires but that are unproductive from the firm's perspective, $v : \mathbb{R}^2 \to \mathbb{R}$, and g is a measure of the strength or effectiveness of governance. The variable g could represent the percentage of independent directors on the board or on key board committees, a measure of the directors' diligence, a measure of the effectiveness of the monitoring and auditing systems in place, some

31. There is also empirical evidence for a leftward drift; that is, for the proportion of outside directors to tend to decrease with the length of the CEO's tenure. See Hermalin and Weisbach (1988), Baker and Gompers (2003), Ryan and Wiggins (2004), and Boone et al. (2007).

measure of the strength of the incentives given the manager, or perhaps some index of governance strength (e.g., that proposed by Gompers et al. 2003). One interpretation, in particular, is worth considering: given the many dimensions of governance, think of g as the firm's total expenditure on governance. Provided the owners set the dimensions of governance optimally, spending more on governance must correspond to stronger governance.

As with all exogenous functions in this chapter, $v(\cdot, \cdot)$ is assumed to be twice continuously differentiable. The function represents the benefit the manager derives from behaving in a manner desired by the investors (i.e., not diverting funds or assets for private use). This benefit is, in part, a function of the level of governance.[32] All this simply reflects the idea that governance structures operate to reward the manager for good behavior. Consistent with the view that better performance is better rewarded, assume $v_1(\cdot, g) > 0$ for all $g > 0$.[33]

To keep the analysis straightforward, assume that, for any g, there is a unique value of D that maximizes the manager's utility. That is, it solves

$$\max_D D + v(R - D, g).$$

This maximization has a unique solution if the manager's utility exhibits diminishing marginal return to diversion (i.e., if $v_{11}(\cdot, g) < 0$ for all g). Let $D(g)$ denote that solution. Again to keep the analysis straightforward, corner solutions are ruled out.[34]

Stronger governance means an increase in the governance parameter that results in a reduction in agency behavior; that is, it leads the manager to choose a smaller D. Formally, assume the following.

Assumption 1 *Let g and g' be two different levels of governance, $g > g'$, and let D and D', respectively, be the levels of private use chosen by the manager in response to those governance levels. Then $D < D'$.*

A sufficient condition for Assumption 1 to hold is that the marginal utility of not diverting resources is increasing in the level of governance; that is, $v_{12}(\cdot, \cdot) > 0$. That more governance then leads to better behavior follows from well-known concepts in comparative statics (see, e.g., Topkis 1978; Milgrom and Roberts 1990), which in this context can be summarized by the following lemma.

Lemma 1 *Let $f : \mathbb{R}^2 \to \mathbb{R}$ be at least twice differentiable in its arguments. Suppose that $f_{12}(\cdot, \cdot) > 0$. Let $\hat{x}$ maximize $f(x, z)$, and let $\hat{x}'$ maximize $f(x, z')$, where $z > z'$. Then $\hat{x} \geq \hat{x}'$. Moreover, if $\hat{x}'$ is an interior maximum, then $\hat{x} > \hat{x}'$.*

---

32. Of course, because a cost is just a negative benefit, this formulation also incorporates specifications in which the governance structure punishes the manager for behaving at odds with the shareholders' preferences.

33. I am employing the convention that subscripts on functions denote partial derivatives; that is, f_n denotes the derivative with respect to the nth argument of function f, and f_{nm} denotes the second derivative with respect to the nth and mth arguments.

34. Specifically, if $g > 0$, we want $D(g) < R$. Hence, assume $v_1(0, g) > 1$ for all positive g. However, to avoid dealing with corner solutions in the level of governance, assume $v_1(0, 0) = 1$; hence, the absence of governance implies $D(0) = R$. To assure $D(g) > 0$ for R great enough, assume $\lim_{R \to \infty} v_1(R, g) < 1$ for all g. An example of a v function satisfying all assumptions given so far is $v(R - D, g) = 2g\sqrt{R - D}$.

Suppose that the corporation's returns r are distributed on the interval $[\underline{r}, \infty)$, $\underline{r} > -\infty$, according to the conditional distribution function $F(\cdot | R - D, \tau)$, where $\tau \in \mathbb{R}$ is the corporation's type (more on τ below). Assume $\mathbb{E}\{r | R - D, \tau\}$ exists for all possible values of $R - D$ and τ. Using integration by parts, observe that

$$\mathbb{E}\{r | R - D, \tau\} = \underline{r} + \int_{\underline{r}}^{\infty} \big(1 - F(r | R - D, \tau)\big) dr = \underline{r} + \int_{\underline{r}}^{\infty} S(r | R - D, \tau) dr,$$

where $S(r | X, \tau) \equiv 1 - F(r | X, \tau)$ is the survival function. It is natural to assume that the more net resources utilized, the greater the expected return. In fact, let us make the somewhat stronger assumption that an increase in net resources improves the distribution of returns in the sense of strict first-order stochastic dominance; that is, $\partial S(r | X, \tau) / \partial X > 0$ for all $X, r \in (\underline{r}, \infty)$, and τ. Finally, as our definition of corporate type, assume that this improvement is stronger the greater is τ. In other words, the marginal expected return from an increase in net resources utilized is greater for higher type corporations than lower type corporations. In terms of calculus, this definition of type can be written as

$$\frac{\partial^2 S(r | X, \tau)}{\partial \tau \partial X} > 0 \tag{1}$$

for all $X, r \in (\underline{r}, \infty)$, and τ.

The realized profit of the corporation is return less the cost of governance, $C(g)$. Writing $X(g)$ for $R - D(g)$, the investors' choice of governance will be the solution to the program

$$\max_{g} \underline{r} + \int_{\underline{r}}^{\infty} S(r | X(g), \tau) dr - C(g). \tag{2}$$

The cross-partial derivative of (2) with respect to g and τ is

$$\int_{\underline{r}}^{\infty} \frac{\partial^2 S(r | X(g), \tau)}{\partial X \partial \tau} X'(g) dr > 0, \tag{3}$$

where the inequality follows from (1) and from the fact that $D(\cdot)$ is a decreasing function, and thus, $X(\cdot)$ an increasing function. Expression (3) and Lemma 1 imply the following proposition.

Proposition 1 *The level of governance a corporation has is nondecreasing in its type (i.e., in its marginal expected return from net resources).*

By imposing more structure on the model, it is possible to ensure that the solution to (2) is always an interior solution. This would allow us to conclude as follows.

Corollary 1 *If the level of governance that maximizes the investors' expected net returns is an interior solution within the space of feasible governance levels, then the level of governance a corporation has is increasing in its type.*

Proposition 1 and its corollary explain the difference between firms A and B in Figures 1 and 2. An additional dollar of net resources is more valuable to firm B than firm A; that is, B is a higher-type firm than A. What has not yet been explained is why the data resemble Figure 1 and not Figure 2. Explaining that requires an additional assumption: a corporation that employs no net resources will enjoy a zero return (one typically does not get something for nothing). Hence, the distribution of returns when no net resources are employed is independent of type. In terms of calculus, this means $\partial S(r|0, \tau)/\partial \tau \equiv 0$ for all r and τ. This insight and expression (1) imply

$$\frac{\partial S(r|X, \tau)}{\partial \tau} = \frac{\partial S(r|X, \tau)}{\partial \tau} - \frac{\partial S(r|0, \tau)}{\partial \tau} = \int_0^X \frac{\partial^2 S(r|x, \tau)}{\partial \tau \partial X} dx > 0 \qquad (4)$$

for all r and $X > 0$. Observe that (4) demonstrates that an increase in type, holding net resources constant, improves the distribution of returns in the sense of first-order stochastic dominance.

Let $g(\tau)$ be the solution to program (2). Utilizing the Envelope Theorem, it follows that

$$\frac{d}{d\tau}\left(\underline{r} + \int_{\underline{r}}^{\infty} S\left(r|X(g(\tau)), \tau\right) dr - C(g(\tau))\right) = \int_{\underline{r}}^{\infty} \frac{\partial S\left(r|X(g(\tau)), \tau\right)}{\partial \tau} dr > 0,$$

where the inequality follows from (4). In words, higher-type firms have greater expected profits in equilibrium than do lower-type firms. This explains why the performance of firm B, a higher-type firm, is better than that of firm A, a lower-type firm. To summarize, I have shown that higher-type firms will have both greater levels of governance and greater profit (in expectation) than lower-type firms. Thus, governance level and profits should be positively correlated; the data should, in fact, resemble those shown in Figure 1.

Proposition 2   *In this model, in which all corporations are making optimal decisions, there will be a positive correlation between level of governance and corporate profits.*

Note the path of causation: A corporation with a high marginal return to net resources—which will therefore be, ceteris paribus, a corporation with greater profits on average—is a corporation with a higher marginal cost of agency. It therefore puts in place a higher level of governance than would a corporation with a low marginal return to net resources (low marginal cost of agency).

5. The Many Dimensions of Governance

Governance is the product of decisions in many dimensions: board structure, security design, incentive schemes, and the like. This observation raises another issue: if the different dimensions are substitutes and different firms face different factor-price vectors, then there could be considerable heterogeneity in the governance practices in any sample of firms. To see this readily illustrated, consider the following extreme "model." Let $g = \max\{\gamma_1, \gamma_2\}$, where γ_i is the amount of governance on dimension i. A corporation will, therefore, set the more expensive dimension to zero. If the more expensive dimension is the first for some firms, but the second for others, then the sample will contain a subset of firms that use only the first method of governance and another subset that use only the second. This situation can create complications

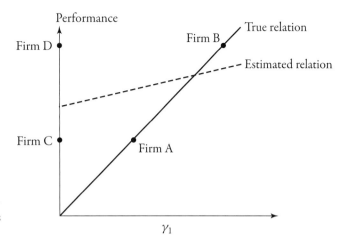

Figure 3. The empirical consequence of governance structures having many dimensions.

for empirical work, because empirical work often focuses on the effect of governance on a single dimension only. Because the firms that elect to have zero of the dimension under study are not necessarily poorly governed firms (they could have invested heavily in the other, unstudied dimension), the coefficient on the dimension being studied will be biased downward. Figure 3 illustrates the potential problem. In that figure, there are four data points. Firms A and B achieve their governance objectives by investing along the first dimension (e.g., proportion of outside directors); Firms C and D achieve their governance objectives by investing along the second dimension (e.g., incentive compensation). Firms B and D are high-type firms, and so perform well, whereas firms A and C are low-type firms, and so perform less well. But because firms C and D achieve their governance objectives differently than do A and B, a regression of performance on γ_1 will suggest that the relation between these variables is less strong than it truly is for those firms that invest in governance along the first dimension.

Observe that controlling for governance on both dimensions—that is, running the regression

$$\text{Performance} = \beta_0 + \beta_1\gamma_1 + \beta_2\gamma_2 + \varepsilon$$

does not correct the problem identified in Figure 3. Relative to the true relation for those firms utilizing a given dimension, the coefficients β_1 and β_2 will be biased downward.

Heterogeneity is a particularly important issue in the study of pay-for-performance incentive contracting. Agency theory (e.g., Holmström 1979; Shavell 1979; Grossman and Hart 1983) teaches us that one way to better align the incentives of investors (the principal) and managers (the agent) is to make the agent's compensation contingent on signals that are informative about the agent's action in a way that induces the agent to take actions the principal desires. Because investors desire that management takes actions that boost their returns, a natural set of signals on which to base compensation are various performance metrics (e.g., profit or ROA). The extent to which different metrics are utilized depends on their informativeness (see, e.g., Holmström 1982; Kim 1995), which could differ across different firms or industries. Consequently, one should expect variation in the incentive contracts employed across firms and industries. One should also expect variation because high-type firms will wish to provide their managers stronger incentives than will low-type firms, as discussed above. Even with otherwise identical firms, variation in incentives can arise in equilibrium as a consequence of product-market competition (Hermalin 1994). More generally, the discipline of product-market competition can be a substitute for incentive compensation, thus serving as another source of heterogeneity.[35] These theoretical predictions of heterogeneity in incentive compensation are given empirically validity by Kole (1997), who examined executive compensation contracts and documents considerable variation across them.

What is the implication of this variety for empirical work? Consider a possible regression specification:

$$\text{Comp}_n = \beta_0 + \beta_1 \times \text{Perf}_{1n} + \cdots + \beta_J \times \text{Perf}_{Jn} + \varepsilon_n, \qquad (5)$$

where Comp_n is the compensation of the nth executive (typically firm n's CEO) and Perf_{jn} is the jth performance metric (e.g., ROA) for the nth executive's firm.[36] What is the interpretation of (5)? Presumably, the coefficients (the βs) are the terms of the compensation contract.[37] But which firm's? If, as theory and evidence indicate, different firms will utilize different contracts, then there is a fundamental misspecification in (5), because (5) rests on the erroneous assumption that all firms are using the same compensation contract.

The consequences of this misspecification are similar to the problem identified in Figure 3. If firms A and B tend to base compensation on Perf_1, while C and D tend to base it on Perf_2, then the situation will resemble that shown in Figure 4. The true sensitivity of pay to performance for those firms that base compensation on Perf_1 is the slope of the "true" line.[38] The econometrician will, however, measure it as the slope of the estimated line. Consequently, the estimates of all coefficients are biased downward insofar as they understate the true sensitivity of pay to performance measures for those firms that base compensation on those performance measures.

---

35. The idea that market competition serves to discipline managers is sometimes attributed to Hicks (1935) as the "quiet-life" hypothesis. Formalizing it has not proved easy (see Allen and Gale 2000 for a discussion of the intellectual history of the quiet-life hypothesis). Part of the problem, as noted by Hermalin (1992), is that product-market competition introduces a number of contradictory effects. Important articles in this area include Hart (1983), Scharfstein (1988), Schmidt (1997), and Allen and Gale (2000). Empirical studies include Bertrand and Mullainathan (2003) and Giroud and Mueller (2008). The latter, in particular, finds evidence that product-market competition mitigates managerial slack. A related literature (see, e.g., Aghion et al. 2005 and cites therein) considers the complementary question of how competition affects incentives to innovate and become more productive.

36. An actual regression of this sort could also have numerous nonperformance controls (e.g., for industry or firm size). They have been omitted from (5) to avoid unnecessary clutter. In addition, the dependent variable is often the log of compensation; taking logs would not change the point being made here. Finally, what compensation is and how it is best measured is a tricky empirical issue (see, e.g., Jensen and Murphy 1990; Hall and Liebman 1998; Hermalin and Wallace 2001). These details are, however, not relevant for the point being made here.

37. Except under strong conditions (see Holmström and Milgrom 1987), a linear compensation scheme is not guaranteed to be the optimal scheme. Indeed, it is straightforward to construct examples in which linear compensation would be suboptimal. Given that real-life compensation is not linear (bonuses, e.g., are rarely—if ever—negative and stock options pay off nonlinearly), the use of a linear specification is, in itself, questionable.

38. True is in quotes because there are multiple true relations—in this case one for firms A and B and another for firms C and D.

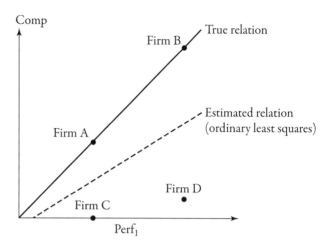

Figure 4. Downward bias in measures of sensitivity of pay to performance.

Hermalin and Wallace (2001) attempt to deal with this issue by allowing the coefficients in (5) to vary across firms (such an analysis requires, obviously, panel data). Consistent with the concerns raised above and in Figure 4, they show, using a two-step estimator of a hierarchical linear model based on Wong and Mason (1991), that the estimated coefficients are greater under such a specification than using ordinary least squares (OLS).[39] In other words, as predicted, failure to treat the coefficients—that is, the parameters of the compensation contract—as varying across firms leads to a downward bias in their estimation. In addition, consistent with the idea that the different dimensions of governance could be substitutes and that firms vary with respect to the performance measures to which they make compensation sensitive, Hermalin and Wallace find a negative correlation between the coefficients on the two performance measures they investigate. Thus, firms that make CEO pay highly sensitive to one measure tend, all else being equal, not to make it particularly sensitive to the other and vice versa.

Even if the different dimensions of governance are complements—so a high-type firm will tend to have more governance in all dimensions than a low-type firm—(5) is still misspecified. To see this, suppose there is only one performance measure r, which is distributed normally with mean $a\tau$ and variance σ^2, where $a \in \mathbb{R}_+$ is the CEO's action and τ again denotes the firm's type. Suppose the CEO's utility is $-\exp(\frac{1}{2}a^2 - y)$, where y is her income. Limit attention to affine incentive contracts: $y = \beta_0 + \beta_1 r$. Hence, the CEO's equilibrium expected utility is a monotonic transformation of[40]

$$\beta_0 + \frac{1}{2}\beta_1^2(\tau^2 - \sigma^2). \tag{6}$$

39. Because they estimate a distribution of coefficients, a more precise summary of their results is that the distribution estimated using their specification lies to the right (has a greater mean) than under OLS.

40. The CEO's expected utility is readily seen to be a monotonic transformation of

$$\beta_0 + \beta_1 a\tau - \frac{1}{2}\beta_1^2\sigma^2 - \frac{1}{2}a^2.$$

Hence, the CEO maximizes her expected utility by choosing $a = \beta_1\tau$.

Suppose, perhaps unrealistically, that investors have all the bargaining power and are thus able to hold the CEO to her reservation utility. If $\underline{u}$ is her (suitably transformed) reservation utility, then, from (6), it must be that $\beta_0 = \underline{u} - \beta_1^2(\tau^2 - \sigma^2)/2$. Equilibrium expected compensation and firm expected profit are thus, respectively,

$$\underline{u} + \frac{1}{2}\beta_1^2(\tau^2 + \sigma^2) \quad \text{and} \quad \beta_1\tau^2 - \frac{1}{2}\beta_1^2(\tau^2 + \sigma^2) - \underline{u}.$$

Investors will set β_1 to maximize the latter expression; hence, $\beta_1 = \tau^2(\tau^2 + \sigma^2)^{-1}$. Observe β_1 is increasing in τ; that is, consistent with the discussion above, higher type firms employ stronger governance than do lower type firms. Moreover, as claimed, different firms are using different contracts—the implicit assumption in (5) of a common compensation contract is invalid.

The adverse consequences of this misspecification in (5) can be illustrated by the following simulation. Set $\underline{u} = 0$ and $\sigma^2 = 1$. Construct a "sample" of 10,001 firms, where $\tau_1 = 1$ and $\tau_n = \tau_{n-1} + 1/10,000, 1 < n \leq 10,001$. For each firm randomly generate r as a normal random variable with mean $a_n\tau_n$, or substituting, mean $\tau_n^4(\tau_n^2 + \sigma^2)^{-1}$. Calculate the corresponding compensation for each firm, and then estimate (5) using OLS from these data.[41] Multiple runs of this simulation all came back with estimates of β_1 between .575 and .580. The true β_1s range from .5 to .8, with 82% of them being greater than .58; that is, the estimated sensitivity of pay to performance from (5) dramatically understates the actual sensitivity in the sample.[42]

This insight is more than just nit-picking. The question one is investigating when estimating the sensitivity of pay to performance is not whether there is a positive relation—it is virtually inconceivable that they are negatively correlated in reality—but rather, how sensitive? Do executives operate under high-powered incentives or not? Jensen and Murphy (1990), who estimate an equation similar to (5), argue that CEOs operate under fairly low-powered incentives; they estimate that CEO wealth changes by $3.25 per $1,000 increase in shareholder wealth. They cite earlier studies that found a pay-to-performance elasticity of approximately 0.1, a number consistent with their own estimates. They argue that such estimates of sensitivity are "inconsistent with the implications of formal agency models of optimal contracting" (Jensen and Murphy 1990: 227). They go on to suggest that outside political forces "implicitly regulate executive compensation by constraining the type of contracts that can be written between management and shareholders."[43] Haubrich (1994) disputes this conclusion. He conducts numerical simulations using parameterized versions of the Grossman and Hart (1983) model, calibrated using real-life data, to show that the Jensen and Murphy estimates need not be at odds with optimal contracting.[44] Hall and Liebman (1998) also estimate an equation similar to (5) and find a greater sensitivity of pay to performance than did Jensen and Murphy. They ascribe the difference in findings between the two studies to their focus on a later period of time, during which CEOs held more stock and stock options than before. Bebchuk and Fried (2003, 2004) also

41. The Mathematica program used for this is available from the author upon request.

42. The true average of the β_1s is .678.

43. Bebchuk and Fried (2004) refer to these as "outrage" costs; although, in contrast to Jensen and Murphy, they believe these are not sufficiently deterring high levels of compensation.

44. See also Haubrich and Popova (1998) for another calibration exercise that reaches a similar conclusion.

argue that the pay-to-performance sensitivity is too low, but do so from the perspective that managers have too much power and are being unduly rewarded, almost independently of their performance. Hall and Murphy (2003) take issue with that view, but they, too, suggest that firms may fail to be setting the sensitivity of pay to performance optimally (they suggest that the costs of stock options are misperceived as being "free"—see, in particular, Hall and Murphy 2003: 66–69).[45] What the discussion here suggests, however, is that the debate over executive compensation is being conducted under a possibly misleading understanding of what the data actually say. If there are systematic biases of the sort identified above, then the sensitivity of pay to performance could be higher than heretofore estimated (at least for those corporations that rely on that means of governance).[46]

This section has sought to make the following points. The inherent heterogeneity in governance solutions—both in structure and intensity—is a first-order problem for the empirical study of governance (as well as a source of puzzles for theoreticians). Cross-sectional regressions, in particular, must be viewed with great caution, as they are subject to misinterpretation.

6. Dispersed Shareholders, Managerial Power, and Governance

Many of the complaints about governance are that managers have too much power vis-à-vis the shareholders (see, e.g., Lorsch and MacIver 1989; Bebchuk and Fried 2004). Since at least Berle and Means (1932), this disparity in power has been attributed to the dispersion of ownership. In particular, any one shareholder holds too few shares to have any power him or herself; that is, alone, he or she does not possess the votes to control the board of directors and, through it, management. A lone shareholder could, in theory, seek to build a coalition of shareholders with sufficient power to control the board of directors, but—traditionally at least—such action is costly. Because our lone shareholder bears the cost, but shares in the benefit, the usual theory of positive externalities applies: any one shareholder will undersupply efforts to rein in management. Not surprisingly, attempts to gain control of the board of directors by existing shareholders are relatively rare events.[47]

As Grossman and Hart (1980) observed, a similar problem confronts an outside actor who attempts to take over a corporation. If the motivation for such a takeover is the outside actor's belief that it can generate greater returns from the assets of the corporation, then it will behoove the outside actor to launch a takeover bid provided it will get a sufficient share of the increase in returns it generates. The problem is that an existing shareholder will reason as follows. "Because I

45. For more complete surveys of the debate on executive pay, especially whether it is appropriately sensitive to performance, see Devers et al. (2007) and Edmans and Gabaix (2009).

46. For large corporations (e.g., Fortune 500 companies), reliance on incentive compensation (e.g., use of bonuses or stock options) has tended to be the norm. For smaller corporations, however, this has been—historically at least—less universally true. See, for example, Hermalin and Wallace (2001) for data on the savings and loan industry. See also Hall and Murphy (2003) for a discussion on the growing use of stock-option compensation during the 1980s and 1990s.

47. Over a 16-year period, Mulherin and Poulsen (1998) find there were only 270 proxy contests (attempts to change the board of directors) at NYSE and Nasdaq-listed firms (an average of 16.875 contests per year). Of these, roughly half led to changes in management. This rate of "success" clearly overstates the ex ante probability of success, because presumably such contents are not undertaken unless there is a reasonable chance of success.

own such a small proportion of shares, the odds that my tendering my shares will be pivotal to the success of the takeover bid are so small as to be negligible. Hence, if I retain my shares, I will enjoy the benefits of the improved management. I, therefore, should not sell unless the bid price equals the expected present value of the returns I will enjoy under this improved management." Given this reasoning, existing shareholders will sell only if given all the gains created by the outside actor. This, however, eliminates the gains from launching a takeover bid in the first place. Of course, takeovers do occur, so there must be ways around this free-riding problem. Grossman and Hart (1980) suggest some means of reducing the free-riding problem by limiting the returns to those shareholders who hold out (the ex post minority).[48]

Such free-riding problems are less pronounced if there is a shareholder whose holdings are relatively large. The governance literature has thus devoted considerable attention to large shareholders (blockholders).[49] The classic article in this regard is Shleifer and Vishny (1986), which considers how the presence of a large blockholder can serve to overcome the free-riding problems identified above. The presence of a large blockholder is not, however, unambiguously good for governance. A large blockholder can use its power for evil as well as good. In a reverse of the free-riding problem, if the blockholder can use its power to engage in self-dealing with the corporation (e.g., induce the corporation to buy inputs at inflated prices from a supplier it fully owns), then the blockholder gets all the benefit but incurs only a portion of the cost. This problem is potentially more severe when there is a pyramid structure of ownership, which permits a shareholder to control the votes but have a more limited financial exposure.[50] Such ownership structures are more common in Europe and Asia than in the United States. See Becht et al. (2003: 24–29) for more on blockholders.

A remark is in order at this juncture. Although dispersed ownership would seem to limit shareholders' ability to control management effectively, it is nevertheless an equilibrium phenomenon. In other words, as Demsetz and Lehn (1985) note, ownership structure is endogenous. Consequently, if we observe dispersed ownership, then we must at least entertain the idea that the costs of dispersion are not necessarily that great (or that the net benefits of concentration are not that great). Otherwise, it is hard to see how the system could have persisted—$100 bills do not linger long on the sidewalk. This is not—I hasten to add—to claim that dispersed ownership is not a binding constraint with respect to achieving the ideal in governance, but rather that its cost cannot be excessive.

This last point can be readily illustrated. Let return r be distributed normally with mean $\mu + g$ and variance σ^2. Suppose, initially, the firm has a large shareholder. She oversees management. Suppose she is undiversified and, so, concerned about risk. In particular, assume her utility is $-\exp(C(g) - \alpha r)$, where $C(g)$ is the cost she incurs to monitor—provide level of governance

48. See Hermalin and Schwartz (1996) for a discussion of the relevant law concerning freeze-outs of minority shareholders and some of the economic implications of the law in this regard.

49. A related literature looks at the roles of main banks in German and Japanese governance. See, for example, Hoshi et al. (1990), Hellwig (1991), and Kaplan (1994a,b). Hellwig (2000) contains a partial survey of this literature.

50. As an example, suppose an individual owns 51% of company A, which in turn owns 51% of company B, which in turn owns 51% of company C. Given that the individual controls A, which controls B, which controls C, the individual controls C. But he or she has a claim on just $.51^3 \approx 13\%$ of company C's returns.

g—and $\alpha \in (0, 1]$ is her share of the company. A monotone transformation of her expected utility is

$$\alpha(\mu + g) - \frac{1}{2}\alpha^2\sigma^2 - C(g). \tag{7}$$

Suppose that $C : \mathbb{R} \to \mathbb{R}$ is strictly convex. Application of Lemma 1 reveals that the g that maximizes her expected utility cannot increase as α decreases (and is falling in α when it is positive).

Imagine, initially, that this shareholder owns 100% of the company (she is its founder, perhaps). Assume she can sell shares to diversified and atomistic shareholders, who can therefore be considered to be risk neutral. They will pay the expected return $\mu + g$ times the portion of the firm they purchase; hence, the large shareholder gets $(1 - \alpha)(\mu + g)$ with certainty. Her expected utility is, then

$$\mu + g - \frac{1}{2}\alpha^2\sigma^2 - C(g). \tag{8}$$

If the large shareholder could commit to a level of governance, then clearly she does best to choose the g that maximizes (8). That could be time inconsistent, however: when she actually chooses g, her relevant utility is given by (7) and her incentive would be to maximize it. Let us suppose that is what will happen. Let $g(\alpha)$ maximize (7). New investors anticipate this and take it into account when bidding for shares; hence, they pay $(1 - \alpha)(\mu + g(\alpha))$ for the portion of the firm they buy. The proportion of the corporation that the large shareholder retains maximizes

$$\mu + g(\alpha) - \frac{1}{2}\alpha^2\sigma^2 - C(g(\alpha)).$$

Utilizing the Envelope Theorem, the first-order condition for maximizing that expression with respect to α is equivalent to

$$(1 - \alpha)g'(\alpha) - \alpha\sigma^2 \leq 0, \tag{9}$$

with equality holding only if the optimal α is positive. Observe that $\alpha = 1$ cannot be a solution to (9). The large shareholder will sell some portion of the company even though that guarantees a worsening of governance. The intuition is clear. Starting from $\alpha = 1$, a small reduction in α has a second-order effect on the level of governance (and, thus, share value), but a first-order effect on the risk she must bear. Not surprisingly, therefore, she will sell some of her shares.

Observe that the large shareholder would be strictly better off if she could commit to a governance level before selling her shares (i.e., commit to the g that maximizes (8)). Let g^* be the level of governance that maximizes (8). If such commitment were possible, then the large shareholder would sell 100% of her stake. If we assume that the large shareholder's commitment to g^* is part of a contract with the purchasers, then it is readily shown to be renegotiation proof. If the large shareholder sought to reduce governance by Δ, then she could induce the purchasers to agree only if they receive Δ in compensation. Given that g^* maximizes (8), $\Delta = 0$ must maximize $-\Delta - C(g^* - \Delta)$.

Here, as shown, the large shareholder's commitment to a governance level is renegotiation proof. This result is unlikely to be general or robust to the introduction of more real-world issues. First, as has been shown in a variety of important settings, many ideal contracts are not renegotiation proof (a particularly pertinent example with respect to governance would be Fudenberg and Tirole 1990). Second, new information could arise that renders a previously optimal contract suboptimal. Admittedly, in theory, the original contract could be designed so as to allow the incorporation of any new information. In reality, however, bounded rationality, legal constraints, and difficulties in verifying all relevant new information mean that no contract could incorporate all new information, which means renegotiation could be Pareto improving. If parties can benefit from renegotiating, then it seems reasonable to suppose that they will.[51]

One reason commitment is difficult is that people cannot be bound to a firm. For example, the large shareholder above could quit her job as the supplier of governance. Given this, the parties would again be limited to time-consistent governance levels. Even if the large shareholder could not quit without penalty under her employment contract, as a matter of law such penalties are limited (both by the ability of the large shareholder to seek bankruptcy protection and by the law's abhorrence of penalty clauses—see, e.g., Hermalin et al. 2007: 99–126). The ability of key executives to quit gives them a lever with which to force the firm to renegotiate with them. In theory, a firm might seek to develop a reputation for never renegotiating, but as a practical matter achieving such a reputation is daunting and, thus, unlikely.[52]

Inability to commit or to avoid renegotiation can potentially explain many oddities of governance. For instance, suppose that investors put in place what they believe to be the optimal governance system. Over time, the firm's CEO proves himself to be of high ability. As such, the CEO gains bargaining power—he has proved himself a rare commodity, which, because he cannot be bound to the firm, provides him market power. One thing he will want is more money. Another potential goal is laxer governance (perhaps, e.g., for career concern issues as discussed earlier). Paying the CEO more is a first-order loss for the investors. Relaxing the governance system, given that it was at an optimum, is a second-order loss. Hence, investors will initially be more yielding to the CEO's demand for laxer governance than his demand for more pay. Hermalin and Weisbach (1998) use this insight to explain why a long-serving CEO can gain influence over the board of directors: At any point in time, the incumbent board believes it is engaging in the optimal level of monitoring. As such, giving in to the CEO's demand to add a director friendly to him to the board, which will lower monitoring somewhat, is a second-order loss for

51. This principle is actually not universally accepted in the literature; some authors have argued that, in some circumstances, there can be off-the-equilibrium-path outcomes that the parties would like to renegotiate but cannot (i.e., on some off-the-equilibrium paths the parties leave money on the table). See Hermalin et al. (2007: 84–86) for a discussion and survey of the relevant literature.

52. One factor that makes developing such a reputation daunting is that, although the firm is infinitely lived, the directors—the people actually doing the negotiating—are not. Again, theory permits short-lived individuals to carry an infinitely lived firm's reputation—see, for example, the relevant sections of Hermalin ("Leadership and Corporate Culture," this volume)—but it by no means guarantees they can do so. Furthermore, it is possible that directors would not wish to promote a norm of no renegotiation: many of them are themselves CEOs of other firms; others of them make a nontrivial income serving as directors and could therefore wish to avoid developing a reputation of being too hard-nosed (given that some set of CEOs play a role in their obtaining their board seats). See Adams et al. (2010) for a discussion of the incentives directors have to avoid being seen as "boat rockers."

the incumbent board and, thus, preferable to giving in to the CEO's demand for more pay. In other words, the CEO's utility can be increased either through more money or less governance, and on the initial margin, the latter costs the investors less than the former.

7. More Thoughts on Shareholder Control

The famous German banker Carl Fürstenberg (1850–1933) once remarked: "Shareholders are stupid and impertinent—stupid because they give their money to somebody else without any effective control over what this person is doing with it and impertinent because they ask for a dividend as a reward for their stupidity" (quoted in Hellwig 2000: 109). Although exaggerated, as witticisms often are, the remark nonetheless illuminates a basic truth: The legitimacy of shareholder complaints about their lack of control is limited—no one compelled them to purchase equity, and they are, in expectation at least, compensated for the risks they bear. Consequently, one should be cautious about extolling the virtues of increasing shareholder control, especially if imposed via regulatory fiat.

In particular, most of the governance relations we observe emerged as the consequence of (at least implicit) bargaining between investors and controlling parties. The general presumption in economics is that private parties will arrive at a better contract than one that can be imposed by the state. There are, to be sure, exceptions to this presumption (for a discussion, see, e.g., Hermalin et al. 2007: 18–56). But even if these exceptions apply, their existence does not necessarily entail intervention on behalf of the shareholders.

Another reason to be cautious about interventions that strengthen the shareholders' control is that shareholders are not the only investors in the firm. There are other providers of financial capital, such as the debtholders. Another class of investors are the workers who invest human capital (as noted above and in Tirole 2001; Roberts and Van den Steen 2003).

With respect to debtholders, there is the well-known asset substitution problem (Harris and Raviv 1991): given limited liability, shareholders have an incentive to want the firm to take on risk, even at the expense of expected return, as the firm nears bankruptcy. Hermalin and Wallace (1994) provide illustrative empirical evidence on this matter. In the 1980s, stock savings and loans (thrifts) held far riskier portfolios than did mutual savings and loans. Consequently, the probability of a stock savings and loan going bankrupt was 4.5 times that of a mutual, even though evidence shows that stock savings and loans were more efficiently operated than mutuals ceteris paribus.

Similarly, at any point in time, the interests of investors of financial capital and those of investors of human capital need not coincide. For instance, changed circumstances can make physical capital more valuable in alternative uses than in its current uses, but such a reallocation of physical capital could severely reduce the return on investment to human capital. If the financial investors have sufficient control of the enterprise, they could decide to reallocate the physical capital at the expense of the human capital investors (the workers). Indeed, in some circumstances, they could use this power to expropriate some of the return to human capital (e.g., threaten reallocation to reduce wages). Shleifer and Summers (1988) raise this issue in terms of assessing the social desirability of takeovers. Roberts and Van den Steen (2003) present some formal models that explore these issues. In short, when the concerns of other investors are taken into account, it is not obvious that less-than-full shareholder control is a bad thing.

With respect to the concern that shareholders have too little control, I would argue the following:

1. The degree of shareholder control could reflect a rational trade-off between the benefits of control and the wish to hold a diversified portfolio. (See previous section.)

2. The degree of shareholder control also reflects initial and ongoing negotiations between shareholders and management. (See Section 4.) In particular, shareholders may trade off less control in exchange for less managerial remuneration. (Again, see previous section.)

3. The degree to which shareholders lack control may be overstated because of issues with the empirical tests used to gauge the strength of governance. (See Section 5.)

4. Because there are other investors, giving shareholders (or a subset of shareholders) too much control can adversely affect these other investors (including minority shareholders) and thus their willingness to invest.

8. Where Does the Field Go Next?

To conclude this chapter, let me briefly outline what I see as promising directions for future research in the area of corporate governance.

8.1. New Empirical Approaches

Although of value, much of the existing empirical literature in corporate governance is plagued with problems. Identification is an especially difficult problem, given that almost all variables of interest are endogenous. New identification strategies would be of great value. For example, the logic of regression discontinuity design (for a survey, see Lee and Lemieux 2010) could be used: firms that just satisfy certain regulatory restrictions are likely the firms for which these restrictions are binding and, hence, arguably value reducing. Their behavior and performance should, ceteris paribus, vary from those that satisfy the restrictions "with room to spare."[53] In the same vein, imposition of restrictions can serve as a "natural" experiment. This approach will be especially valuable when some firms are "assigned" to the treatment group (i.e., they must adjust their governance structures to come into compliance) and others are assigned to the control group (i.e., they do not need to adjust their structures to be in compliance).

In addition, interpreting regression results is complicated by the heterogeneity in governance structures. As Demsetz and Lehn (1985), among others, have noted, causal interpretations of

---

53. Cuñat et al. (in press) is noteworthy in this regard as a paper that utilizes the regression discontinuity approach. They use close votes on proxy ballots concerning corporate governance provisions as a means of identifying the market's valuation of unanticipated good news about governance. Although provocative, their results are somewhat difficult to interpret, because the ballot measures in question are not binding. Hence, it is difficult to know what information a close vote reveals to the market. One possible interpretation, given by the authors, is that such a firm will have better governance policies than previously expected. Another is that the market learns the shareholders are "tougher" (paying attention to management and more willing to challenge it) than previously thought. Because management realizes it faces tougher shareholders, it is less inclined to act at odds with shareholder wishes for fear of retribution (e.g., shareholders are judged more likely to vote against management in a proxy contest or in a hostile takeover).

regressions between governance structures and firm performance are especially problematic in this regard (even assuming that the joint endogeneity issue has been resolved). As I have sketched out in this chapter, economic theory offers ways to think about such regressions, but more work is needed both with regard to developing the theory and to its use in the design of empirical tests. Heterogeneity is also an issue insofar as it makes the results of cross-sectional regressions suspect; there is strong reason to believe many such regressions will have coefficients that are biased downward. Various hierarchical models and other variations on random-coefficients models should be employed. Such models dictate the use of panel datasets.

8.2. Theory

Many aspects of governance represent applications of agency and other contracting theory. There are dimensions to governance, however, that fall outside the general frameworks or that otherwise exhibit novel features. One direction is to expand the canon beyond the typical single principal–single agent perspective (e.g., shareholders and CEO). Governance involves multiple principals (e.g., large and small shareholders, and equity and debtholders), hierarchical structures (e.g., shareholders–board of directors–management), and teams of agents, among other features. Better modeling of governance with multiple classes of investors, especially taking human capital investment seriously, is another priority. Theory should also explore the dynamic aspects of governance: How do governance institutions evolve over time, optimally and in practice? To what extent is governance a nexus of contracts aimed at controlling the management of the firm in an ever-changing environment? To what extent is governance a substitute for formal contracting, reflecting the inherent impossibility of complete contracting over long horizons with unforeseen contingencies? Finally, what do less neo-classical concepts, such as leadership, corporate culture, and various cognitive biases, have to say about the structure of corporate governance?

8.3. Perspective

A common view in governance research is that the aim of governance is to improve shareholder control. For a number of reasons, it is not clear that should necessarily be the aim of governance. A more appropriate view could be that governance is about balancing the (possibly disparate) needs of investors to have some measure of protection against mismanagement, misallocation, and misappropriation against the various costs of providing these protections.

Given the importance of the topic, governance research continues to be valued. With a large number of open questions, there are plenty of *terrae incognitae* left to be explored.

REFERENCES

Adams, Renée B., and Daniel Ferreira. 2007. "A Theory of Friendly Boards." *Journal of Finance* 62: 217–250.
Adams, Renée B., Benjamin E. Hermalin, and Michael S. Weisbach. 2010. "The Role of Boards of Directors in Corporate Governance: A Conceptual Framework and Survey." *Journal of Economic Literature* 48: 59–108.

Aghion, Philippe, Nick Bloom, Richard Blundell, Rachel Griffith, and Peter Howitt. 2005. "Competition and Innovation: An Inverted-U Relationship." *Quarterly Journal of Economics* 120: 701–728.

Allen, Franklin, and Douglas Gale. 2000. "Corporate Governance and Competition," in Xavier Vives (ed.), *Corporate Governance: Theoretical and Empirical Perspectives.* Cambridge: Cambridge University Press, pp. 23–84.

Almazan, Andres, and Javier Suarez. 2003. "Entrenchment and Severance Pay in Optimal Governance Structures." *Journal of Finance* 58: 519–547.

Antle, Rick, and Joel S. Demski. 1988. "The Controllability Principle in Responsibility Accounting." *Accounting Review* 63: 700–718.

Baiman, Stanley, and Joel S. Demski. 1980. "Economically Optimal Performance Evaluation and Control Systems." *Journal of Accounting Research* 18 (supplement): 184–220.

Baker, Malcolm, and Paul A. Gompers. 2003. "The Determinants of Board Structure at the Initial Public Offering." *Journal of Law and Economics* 46: 569–597.

Baskin, Jonathan Barron, and Paul J. Miranti, Jr. 1997. *A History of Corporate Finance.* Cambridge: Cambridge University Press.

Baysinger, Barry D., and Henry N. Butler. 1985. "Corporate Governance and the Board of Directors: Performance Effects of Changes in Board Composition." *Journal of Law, Economics, and Organization* 1: 101–124.

Bebchuk, Lucian Arye, and Alma Cohen. 2005. "The Costs of Staggered Boards." *Journal of Financial Economics* 78: 409–433.

Bebchuk, Lucian Arye, and Jesse M. Fried. 2003. "Executive Compensation as an Agency Problem." *Journal of Economic Perspectives* 17(3): 71–92.

———. 2004. *Pay without Performance.* Cambridge, MA: Harvard University Press.

Bebchuk, Lucian Arye, Alma Cohen, and Allen Ferrell. 2009. "What Matters in Corporate Governance?" *Review of Financial Studies* 22: 783–827.

Becht, Marco, Patrick Bolton, and Ailsa Röell. 2003. "Corporate Governance and Control," in George Constantinides, Milton Harris, and René Stulz (eds.), *The Handbook of the Economics of Finance.* Amsterdam: North-Holland, pp. 1–109.

Berle, Adolph A., and Gardiner C. Means. 1932. *The Modern Corporation and Private Property.* New York: Macmillan.

Bertrand, Marianne. 2009. "CEOs." *Annual Review of Economics* 1: 121–149.

Bertrand, Marianne, and Sendhil Mullainathan. 2001. "Are CEOs Rewarded for Luck? The Ones without Principals Are." *Quarterly Journal of Economics* 116: 901–932.

———. 2003. "Enjoying the Quiet Life? Corporate Governance and Managerial Preferences." *Journal of Political Economy* 111: 1043–1075.

Bhagat, Sanjai, and Richard H. Jefferis. 2002. *The Econometrics of Corporate Governance Studies.* Cambridge, MA: MIT Press.

Boone, Audra L., Laura Casares Field, Jonathan L. Karpoff, and Charu G. Raheja. 2007. "The Determinants of Corporate Board Size and Composition: An Empirical Analysis." *Journal of Financial Economics* 85: 66–101.

Bowen, William G. 1994. *Inside the Boardroom: Governance by Directors and Trustees.* New York: John Wiley and Sons.

Brickley, James A., Jeffrey L. Coles, and Rory L. Terry. 1994. "Outside Directors and the Adoption of Poison Pills." *Journal of Financial Economics* 35: 371–390.

Coles, Jeffrey L., Naveen D. Daniel, and Lalitha Naveen. 2008. "Boards: Does One Size Fit All?" *Journal of Financial Economics* 87: 329–356.

Cuñat, Vincente, Mireia Gine, and Maria Guadalupe. In press. "The Vote is Cast: The Effect of Corporate Governance on Shareholder Value." *Journal of Finance.*

Cyert, Richard M., Sok-Hyun Kang, and Praveen Kumar. 2002. "Corporate Governance, Takeovers, and Top-Management Compensation: Theory and Evidence." *Management Science* 48: 453–469.

Demsetz, Harold, and Kenneth Lehn. 1985. "The Structure of Corporate Ownership: Causes and Consequences." *Journal of Political Economy* 93: 1155–1177.

Demski, Joel S., and David E. M. Sappington. 1989. "Hierarchical Structure and Responsibility Accounting." *Journal of Accounting Research* 27: 40–58.

Denis, Diane K., and John J. McConnell. 2003. "International Corporate Governance." *Journal of Financial and Quantitative Analysis* 38: 1–36.

Devers, Cynthia E., Albert A. Cannella, Jr., Gregory P. Reilly, and Michele E. Yoder. 2007. "Executive Compensation: A Multidisciplinary Review of Recent Developments." *Journal of Management* 33: 1016–1072.

Diamond, Aubrey L. 1982. "Corporate Personality and Limited Liability," in Tony Orhnial (ed.), *Limited Liability and the Corporation*. London: Croom Helm, pp. 22–43.

Dominguez-Martinez, Silvia, Otto H. Swank, and Bauke Visser. 2008. "In Defense of Boards." *Journal of Economics and Management Strategy* 17: 667–682.

Durchin, Ran, John G. Matsusaka, and Oguzhan Ozbas. "When Are Outside Directors Effective?" 2009. Working Paper, Marshall School of Business, University of Southern California, Los Angeles.

Durisin, Boris, and Fulvio Puzone. 2009. "Maturation of Corporate Governance Research, 1993–2007: An Assessment." *Corporate Goverance: An International Review* 17: 266–291.

Edmans, Alex, and Xavier Gabaix. 2009. "Is CEO Pay Really Inefficient? A Survey of New Optimal Contracting Theories." *European Financial Management* 15: 486–496.

Ehrenberg, Ronald G. 2004. *Governing Academia.* Ithaca, NY: Cornell University Press.

Eisenberg, Theodore, Stefan Sundgren, and Martin T. Wells. 1998. "Larger Board Size and Decreasing Firm Value in Small Firms." *Journal of Financial Economics* 48: 35–54.

Fama, Eugene F. 1980. "Agency Problems and the Theory of the Firm." *Journal of Political Economy* 88: 288–307.

Farinha, Jorge. 2003. "Corporate Governance: A Survey of the Literature." Centro de Estudos de Economia Industrial Working Paper DP 2003-06, Faculdade de Economia, Universidade do Porto, Porto, Portugal.

Fellingham, John C., and D. Paul Newman. 1985. "Strategic Considerations in Auditing." *Accounting Review* 60: 634–650.

Fligstein, Neil. 2008. "Myths of the Market." in Alexander Ebner and Nikolaus Beck (eds.), *The Institutions of the Market: Organizations, Social Systems, and Governance.* Oxford: Oxford University Press, pp. 131–156.

Frydman, Carola, and Raven E. Saks. 2010. "Executive Compensation: A New View from a Long-Term Perspective, 1936–2005." *Review of Financial Studies* 23: 2099–2138.

Fudenberg, Drew, and Jean Tirole. 1990. "Moral Hazard and Renegotiation in Agency Contracts." *Econometrica* 58: 1279–1320.

Gabaix, Xavier, and Augustin Landier. 2008. "Why Has CEO Pay Increased So Much?" *Quarterly Journal of Economics* 123: 49–100.

Gibbons, Robert, and Kevin J. Murphy. 1990. "Relative Performance Evaluation for Chief Executive Officers." *Industrial and Labor Relations Review* 43: 30S–51S.

———. 1992. "Optimal Incentive Contracts in the Presence of Career Concerns: Theory and Evidence." *Journal of Political Economy* 100: 468–505.

Giroud, Xavier, and Holger M. Mueller. 2008. "Does Corporate Governance Matter in Competitive Industries?" Working paper, New York University, New York.

Gompers, Paul A., Andrew Metrick, and Joy Ishii. 2003. "Corporate Governance and Equity Prices." *Quarterly Journal of Economics* 118: 107–155.

Grossman, Sanford J., and Oliver D. Hart. 1980. "Takeover Bids, the Free-Rider Problem, and the Theory of the Corporation." *Bell Journal of Economics* 11: 42–64.

———. 1983. "An Analysis of the Principal-Agent Problem." *Econometrica* 51: 7–46.

Hadlock, Charles J., and Gerald B. Lumer. 1997. "Compensation, Turnover, and Top Management Incentives." *Journal of Business* 70: 153–187.

Hall, Brian J., and Jeffrey B. Liebman. 1998. "Are CEOs Really Paid Like Bureaucrats?" *Quarterly Journal of Economics* 113: 653–691.

Hall, Brian J., and Kevin J. Murphy. 2003. "The Trouble with Stock Options." *Journal of Economic Perspectives* 17(3): 49–70.

Hansmann, Henry, and Reinier Kraakman. 2000a. "The Essential Role of Organizational Law." *Yale Law Journal* 110: 387–440.

———. 2000b. "Organizational Law as Asset Partitioning." *European Economic Review* 44: 807–817.

Harris, Milton, and Artur Raviv. 1991. "The Theory of Capital Structure." *Journal of Finance* 46: 297–355.

———. 2008. "A Theory of Board Control and Size." *Review of Financial Studies* 21: 1797–1832.

Hart, Oliver D. 1983. "The Market Mechanism as an Incentive Scheme." *Bell Journal of Economics* 14: 366–382.

Hart, Oliver D., and John H. Moore. 1998. "Default and Renegotiation: A Dynamic Model of Debt." *Quarterly Journal of Economics* 113: 1–41.

Haubrich, Joseph G. 1994. "Risk Aversion, Performance Pay, and the Principal-Agent Problem." *Journal of Political Economy* 102: 258–276.

Haubrich, Joseph G., and Ivilina Popova. 1998. "Executive Compensation: A Calibration Approach." *Economic Theory* 12: 561–581.

Hellwig, Martin. 1991. "Banking, Financial Intermediation, and Corporate Finance," in Alberto Giovannini and Colin Mayer (eds.), *European Financial Integration.* Cambridge: Cambridge University Press, pp. 35–63.

———. 2000. "On the Economics and Politics of Corporate Finance and Corporate Control," in Xavier Vives (ed.), *Corporate Governance: Theoretical and Empirical Perspectives.* Cambridge: Cambridge University Press, pp. 95–134.

Hermalin, Benjamin E. 1992. "The Effects of Competition on Executive Behavior." *RAND Journal of Economics* 23: 350–365.

———. 1994. "Heterogeneity in Organizational Form: Why Otherwise Identical Firms Choose Different Incentives for Their Managers." *RAND Journal of Economics* 25: 518–537.

———. 2005. "Trends in Corporate Governance." *Journal of Finance* 60: 2351–2384.

Hermalin, Benjamin E., and Alan Schwartz. 1996. "Buyouts in Large Companies." *Journal of Legal Studies* 25: 351–370.

Hermalin, Benjamin E., and Nancy E. Wallace. 1994. "The Determinants of Efficiency and Solvency in Savings and Loans." *RAND Journal of Economics* 25: 361–381.

———. 2001. "Firm Performance and Executive Compensation in the Savings and Loan Industry." *Journal of Financial Economics* 61: 139–170.

Hermalin, Benjamin E., and Michael S. Weisbach. 1988. "The Determinants of Board Composition." *RAND Journal of Economics* 19: 589–606.

———. 1991. "The Effects of Board Composition and Direct Incentives on Firm Performance." *Financial Management* 20(4): 101–112.

———. 1998. "Endogenously Chosen Boards of Directors and Their Monitoring of the CEO." *American Economic Review* 88: 96–118.

———. 2003. "Boards of Directors as an Endogenously Determined Institution: A Survey of the Economic Literature." *Economic Policy Review* 9: 7–26.

Hermalin, Benjamin E., Avery W. Katz, and Richard Craswell. 2007. "Contract Law," in A. Mitchell Polinsky and Steven Shavell (eds.), *Handbook of Law and Economics,* volume 1. Amsterdam: North-Holland, pp. 3–138.

Hicks, John R. 1935. "Annual Survey of Economic Theory: The Theory of Monopoly." *Econometrica* 3: 1–20.

Holmström, Bengt. 1979. "Moral Hazard and Observability." *Bell Journal of Economics* 10: 74–91.

———. 1982. "Moral Hazard in Teams." *Bell Journal of Economics* 13: 324–340.

———. 1999. "Managerial Incentive Problems—A Dynamic Perspective." *Review of Economic Studies* 66(226): 169–182.

Holmström, Bengt, and Paul Milgrom. 1987. "Aggregation and Linearity in the Provision of Intertemporal Incentives." *Econometrica* 55: 303–328.

Holmström, Bengt, and Joan Ricart i Costa. 1986. "Managerial Incentives and Capital Management." *Quarterly Journal of Economics* 101: 835–860.

Hoshi, Takeo, Anil Kashyap, and David Scharfstein. 1990. "Bank Monitoring and Investment: Evidence from the Changing Structure of Japanese Corporate Banking Relationships," in R. Glenn Hubbard (ed.), *Asymmetric Information, Corporate Finance, and Investment.* Chicago: University of Chicago Press, pp. 105–126.

Jarrell, Gregg, and Annette Poulsen. 1987. "Shark Repellents and Stock Prices: The Effects of Antitakeover Amendments since 1980." *Journal of Financial Economics* 19: 127–168.

Jensen, Michael C. 1986. "Agency Costs of Free Cash Flow, Corporate Finance, and Takeovers." *American Economic Review* 76 (Papers and Proceedings): 323–329.

Jensen, Michael C., and William H. Meckling. 1976. "Theory of the Firm: Managerial Behavior, Agency Costs, and Capital Structure." *Journal of Financial Economics* 3: 305–360.

Jensen, Michael C., and Kevin J. Murphy. 1990. "Performance Pay and Top-Management Incentives." *Journal of Political Economy* 98: 225–264.

John, Kose, and Lemma W. Senbet. 1998. "Corporate Governance and Board Effectiveness." *Journal of Banking and Finance* 22: 371–403.

Johnson, Simon, Rafael La Porta, Florencio Lopez-de-Silanes, and Andrei Shleifer. 2000. "Tunneling." *American Economic Review* 90: 22–27.

Kaplan, Steven N. 1994a. "Top Executive Rewards and Firm Performance: A Comparison of Japan and the United States." *Journal of Political Economy* 102: 510–546.

———. "Top Executives, Turnover, and Firm Performance in Germany." *Journal of Law, Economics, and Organization* 10: 142–159.

Kim, Son Ku. 1995. "Efficiency of an Information System in an Agency Model." *Econometrica* 63: 89–102.

Kole, Stacey R. 1997. "The Complexity of Compensation Contracts." *Journal of Financial Economics* 43: 79–104.

La Porta, Rafael, Florencio Lopez-de-Silanes, Andrei Shleifer, and Robert W. Vishny. 1997. "Legal Determinants of External Finance." *Journal of Finance* 52: 1131–1150.

Lee, David S., and Thomas Lemieux. 2010. "Regression Discontinuity Designs in Economics." *Journal of Economic Literature* 48: 281–355.

Lewellen, Wilbur G. 1968. *Executive Compensation in Large Industrial Corporations.* New York: National Bureau of Economic Research.

Lorsch, Jay W., and Elizabeth MacIver. 1989. *Pawns or Potentates: The Reality of America's Corporate Boards.* Boston: Harvard Business School Press.

MacAvoy, Paul W., and Ira M. Millstein. 2003. *The Recurrent Crisis in Corporate Governance.* New York: Palgrave Macmillan.

Mahoney, James M., and Joseph T. Mahoney. 1993. "An Empirical Investigation of the Effect of Corporate Charter Amendments on Stockholder Wealth." *Strategic Management Journal* 14: 17–32.

Malmendier, Ulrike. 2009. "Law and Finance 'at the Origin.'" *Journal of Economic Literature* 47: 1076–1108.

Malmendier, Ulrike, and Geoffrey Tate. 2005. "CEO Overconfidence and Corporate Investment." *Journal of Finance* 60: 2661–2700.

Milgrom, Paul, and John Roberts. 1990. "Rationalizability, Learning, and Equilibrium in Games with Strategic Complementarities." *Econometrica* 58: 1255–1277.

Mookherjee, Dilip, and Stefan Reichelstein. 1997. "Budgeting and Hierarchical Control." *Journal of Accounting Research* 35: 129–155.

Morck, Randall, Andrei Shleifer, and Robert W. Vishny. 1988. "Management Ownership and Market Valuation: An Empirical Analysis." *Journal of Financial Economics* 20: 293–315.

Mulherin, J. Harold, and Annette B. Poulsen. 1998. "Proxy Contests and Corporate Change: Implications for Shareholder Wealth." *Journal of Financial Economics* 47: 279–313.

Murphy, Kevin J., and Jan Zabojnik. 2003. "Managerial Capital and the Market for CEOs." Marshall School of Business Working Paper, University of Southern California, Los Angeles.

———. 2004. "CEO Pay and Appointments: A Market-Based Explanation for Recent Trends." *American Economic Review* 94: 192–196.

Ripley, William Z. 1927. *Main Street and Wall Street.* Boston: Little, Brown and Co.

Roberts, John, and Eric Van den Steen. 2003. "Human Capital and Corporate Governance," in Joachim Schwalbach (ed.), *Corporate Governance: Essays in Honor of Horst Albach,* second edition. Berlin: Berliner Wissenschafts-Verlag, pp. 126–142.

Rosenstein, Stuart, and Jeffrey G. Wyatt. 1990. "Outside Directors, Shareholder Independence, and Shareholder Wealth." *Journal of Financial Economics* 26: 175–192.

Ryan, Harley, and Roy Wiggins. 2004. "Who Is in Whose Pocket? Director Compensation, Bargaining Power, and Board Independence." *Journal of Financial Economics* 73: 497–524.

Scharfstein, David. 1988. "Product-Market Competition and Managerial Slack." *RAND Journal of Economics* 19: 147–155.

Schmidt, Klaus M. 1997. "Managerial Incentives and Product Market Competition." *Review of Economic Studies* 64: 191–213.

Scholz, Karl. 1928. "Book Review." *Annals of the American Academy of Political and Social Science* 135: 178.

Shavell, Steven. 1979. "Risk Sharing and Incentives in the Principal and Agent Relationship." *Bell Journal of Economics* 10: 55–73.

Shleifer, Andrei, and Lawrence H. Summers. 1988. "Breach of Trust in Hostile Takeovers," in Alan J. Auerbach (ed.), *Corporate Takeovers: Causes and Consequences.* Chicago: University of Chicago Press, pp. 33–67.

Shleifer, Andrei, and Robert W. Vishny. 1986. "Large Shareholders and Corporate Control." *Journal of Political Economy* 94: 461–488.

———. 1997. "A Survey of Corporate Governance." *Journal of Finance* 52: 737–783.

Smith, Adam. 1776. *An Inquiry into the Nature and Causes of the Wealth of Nations.* London: W. Strahan and T. Cadeli, in the Strand.

Stein, Jeremy C. 1989. "Efficient Capital Markets, Inefficient Firms: A Model of Myopic Corporate Behavior." *Quarterly Journal of Economics* 104: 655–669.

Stulz, René M. 1988. "Managerial Control of Voting Rights: Financing Policies and the Market for Corporate Control." *Journal of Financial Economics* 20: 25–54.

Terviö, Marko. 2008. "The Difference That CEOs Make: An Assignment Model Approach." *American Economic Review* 98: 642–668.

Tirole, Jean. 1986. "Hierarchies and Bureaucracies: On the Role of Collusion in Organizations." *Journal of Law, Economics, and Organization* 2: 181–214.

———. 2001. "Corporate Governance." *Econometrica* 69: 1–35.

———. 2006. *The Theory of Corporate Finance.* Princeton, NJ: Princeton University Press.

Topkis, Donald M. 1978. "Minimizing a Submodular Function on a Lattice." *Operations Research* 26: 305–321.

Townsend, Robert M. 1979. "Optimal Contracts and Competitive Markets with Costly State Verification." *Journal of Economic Theory* 20: 265–293.

Williamson, Oliver E. 1963. "Managerial Discretion and Business Behavior." *American Economic Review* 53: 1032–1057.

———. 1975. *Markets and Hierarchies: Analysis and Antitrust Implications.* New York: Free Press.

Wong, George Y., and William M. Mason. 1991. "Contextually Specific Effects and Other Generalizations of the Hierarchical Linear Model for Comparative Analysis." *Journal of the American Statistical Association* 86: 487–503.

Yermack, David. 1996. "Higher Valuation of Companies with a Small Board of Directors." *Journal of Financial Economics* 40: 185–212.

Zingales, Luigi. 2008. "Corporate Governance." in Steven N. Durlauf and Lawrence E. Blume (eds.), *The New Palgrave Dictionary of Economics,* second edition. Basingstoke: Palgrave Macmillan. Also available online. DOI:10.1057/9780230226203.0323.

19

Incentives in Hierarchies

Dilip Mookherjee

1. Introduction

The twentieth century witnessed the emergence of large organizations in the private, public, and nonprofit sectors. Alfred Chandler's (1962, 1977) classic studies *Strategy and Structure* and *The Visible Hand* document the historical transformation of American industrial enterprises from small or medium-sized owner-managed firms in the early nineteenth century into large business conglomerates controlled by a hierarchy of professional managers by the middle of the twentieth century. Likewise, government agencies managed by professional bureaucracies have grown in size and scope throughout the course of the twentieth century, accompanying the growth of the role of governments in taxation, regulation, and delivery of public services.

The internal organization of private firms and government agencies is therefore a topic of considerable interest for both academics and policy practitioners interested in such issues as determinants of productivity, income distribution, human resource development, and efficiency of government. It is now commonly accepted that the size and internal structure of firms is an important determinant of their productivity and profitability. As various management best sellers indicate, firms seem to vary considerably in how well managed they are. Organizations that are too large are widely believed to be overly bureaucratic, unresponsive, and their top management "out of touch" with ground reality—and this is believed to be the key problem with socialist economies with large state-owned firms or large government bureaucracies, compared with more decentralized market economies. Yet conventional economic theory has difficulty explaining why this is so; or why some organizations are not as well managed as others; or the exact manner in which size, structure, and operating rules of organizations determine their effectiveness and productivity. Relevant attributes of organizational structure include the shape (e.g., the number of vertical layers, spans of control); allocation of authority and responsibility across managers; grouping of functions and managers into different departments; processes by which information is distributed, processed,

I thank Alberto Motta; Masatoshi Tsumagari; and the volume editors, Robert Gibbons and John Roberts, for useful comments.

and communicated across managers; the way that managers are evaluated and compensated; and how all this eventually affects the way decisions are made and coordinated across the organization.

The internal organization of large firms is also a topic of considerable interest for those interested in inequality and social mobility, given the large fraction of the workforce in modern economies employed as white-collar occupations involving managerial, secretarial, or supervisory jobs. Theories of income distribution need to grapple with the question of what roles managers play in organizations, how they are evaluated and compensated, and how these roles vary across different layers of management as well as between white-collar and blue-collar workers.

Managerial hierarchies pose a significant challenge for conventional economic theory, raising such issues as the separation of ownership from management and the functional role of managers in productive enterprises. What prevents owners from managing the firms they own? Alfred Marshall (1920: Book IV, Ch. XII) listed organization as a fourth critical factor of production besides land, labor, and capital, and subsequently included management as a key ingredient of organization. Yet more than a century later, models of management are still not part of the central corpus of the neoclassical theory of the firm. In the context of industrial or service enterprises that account for the bulk of all economic activity in developed countries, fixed factors such as land do not play an important role, creating challenges for explaining limits to the size of firms. Although many believe that time and attention of top managers is one of the most important fixed factors that account for limits to the size of firms, modeling this trait has posed a significant challenge for economic theory. Part of the reason is the difficulty of modeling cognitive capacities of managers to process information, make decisions, and get things done—that belong to the realm of bounded rationality that Herbert Simon (1955) and Oliver Williamson (1981) have emphasized are key to understanding organizations and the role that managers play in them.

Nevertheless, the nineteenth century view of a firm as an entity whose sole objective is to maximize profits has now evolved to a nexus of contracts among a large number of important stakeholders and functionaries (see, e.g., Milgrom and Roberts 1992). The firm is viewed as an organization or collective of different agents with dispersed information, responsibilities, and noncongruent interests. Accordingly, problems of asymmetric information and incentives play an important role in the modern theory of the firm. Yet contemporary mainstream theory of information economics as represented by the principal-agent paradigm is still struggling to explain why authority and responsibility are distributed across different managers in an organization, instead of being centralized. The Revelation Principle, which plays a central role in standard principal-agent theory (e.g., Myerson 1982), states that any allocation of authority in an organization can be replicated by a degenerate centralized organization in which all agents communicate their private information to the owner or a central headquarter office ("principal"). The principal then processes this information and makes all relevant decisions, subsequently sending instructions to all agents concerning what they should do. In this kind of organization the only role of agents is to communicate information and receive instructions; the mechanism needs to be designed to encourage honest and obedient behavior from all of them. In this setting there is no role for a managerial hierarchy: all authority is vested in the principal.

To create a theory of managerial organizations, it is necessary to go back to the foundational question: What do managers do? How or why do they do these tasks better than the principal can? To quote Chandler:

> Just what, then, are the functions of the excutives responsible for the functions of the enterprise? They coordinate, appraise and plan. They may, at the same time, do the actual buying, selling, advertising, accounting, manufacturing, engineering or research, but in the modern enterprise the execution or carrying out of these functions is usually left to such employees as salesmen, buyers, production supervisors and foremen, technicians and designers. In many cases, the executive does not even personally supervise the working force but rather administers the duties of other executives. In planning and coordinating the work of subordinate managers or supervisors, he allocates tasks and makes available the necessary equipment, materials, and other physical resources necessary to carry out the various jobs. In appraising their activities, he must decide whether the employees or subordinate managers are handling their tasks satisfactorily. If not, he can take action by changing or bringing in new physical equipment and supplies, by transferring or shifting the personnel, or by expanding or cutting down available funds. Thus, the term, *administration*, as used here, includes executive action and orders as well as the decisions taken in coordinating, appraising, and planning the work of the enterprise and in allocating its resources. [Chandler 1962: 8]

Therefore, managers perform at least three important functions: they (1) process information helpful in decisionmaking by the firm regarding production, marketing, technology, employment, and suppliers; (2) supervise (i.e., generate and supply information used to evaluate and compensate employees and suppliers); and (3) make decisions concerning production, marketing, and contracting with employees and suppliers on behalf of the owners.

The first two functions pertain to the role of managers as processors or generators of information useful in decisionmaking by others. Only the last function includes the role of managers as decisionmakers. This pertains to the notion of hierarchy as a inverted-tree-like asymmetric pattern of distribution of authority within an organization. As emphasized in the writings of Coase (1937) and Simon (1951), a firm conceptualized as a hierarchical relation between an owner and employee is distinct from a more symmetric market relationship between the owner and an outside contractor. In this vein, Van den Steen (2010) defines hierarchical or interpersonal authority as a situation where the owner or boss tells the employee what actions to take, which the latter is expected (or incentivized) to obey. The employee may be inclined to select other actions on the basis of her own information or her personal motivation; the terms of employment include monitoring of actions or their consequences, combined with suitable rewards and penalties, to induce the employee to obey the owner's instructions. In contrast, an external contractor retains more control over her own actions.

It is evident that this notion of hierarchical authority is closely related to that of centralization of decisionmaking: the owner decides what the employee should do and incentivizes the latter to obey. And a market relationship with an external contractor involves greater delegation of decisionmaking to the latter. However, one cannot identify firms as distinct from market relationships solely in terms of the distribution of decisionmaking authority. Intrafirm relationships can allow delegation of some decisionmaking authority to employees, just as market relationships may involve some instructions sent by clients to suppliers. For this reason, most modern theories of the boundaries between firms and markets emphasize ownership of assets as the defining characteristic. If the employee works with some complementary assets, Van den Steen (2010), for instance, defines a firm or hierarchy as a situation where assets are owned by the employer, and the employer exercises hierarchical authority over the employee. In contrast, in a market relationship between the firm owner and an external contractor, the productive assets are owned by the latter, and the former does not exercise authority over the contractor in the same way as she does over her employees. Van den Steen's theory provides reasons for synergistic connections between asset ownership and decisionmaking authority patterns, so that they tend to be distributed in a similar way (e.g., explaining why asset owners tend to retain more decisionmaking authority).

It is important to clarify at the outset that the literature surveyed in this chapter does not address the question of boundaries between firms and markets or any of the issues relating to asset ownership. Instead it is concerned solely with the question of distribution of decisionmaking authority among sets of agents who work together for productive reasons and enter into contracts with one another that define and shape their interactions. It applies equally to intrafirm organization and to contractual relationships among different firms or suppliers. Most of our interest is in models of organizations with at least three players: in the context of a firm, an employer, owner, or principal (P); a manager-cum-employee (M); and an employee or productive agent (A), who works alone or in collaboration with M to generate a productive benefit for P. In the context of supplier contracting networks, P could be the customer, M could be a prime contractor, and A a subcontractor. In models focusing on the supervisory role of managers, M supervises the actions of A and sends reports to P, which the latter uses in evaluating and compensating A. These models are considered in Section 2. Subsequent sections address the allocation of decisionmaking authority between P and M. A completely centralized organization is one where P retains all authority. The role of M and A is to send reports to P and await instructions from the latter. Alternatively, P could delegate authority to M over decisions concerning production and contracting with A, and evaluate and compensate M on the basis of some measure of performance of the firm or division in question. Later sections address hierarchical allocations of authority in more complex organizations involving more productive agents, multiple products, horizontal layers (i.e., divisions or branches), and vertical layers. The aim is to (1) describe the performance of any given hierarchical pattern of allocating authority under suitable assumptions concerning monitoring and incentive mechanisms available, (2) compare the performance across different patterns of delegation and organizational patterns for a given scale of the organization, and (3) ultimately address the question of organizational diseconomies of scale.

To set this in perspective, it is useful to delineate many issues not addressed in it, many of which are addressed by other chapters in this volume. Because theories of costly information processing are still in a state of relative infancy and have yet to be combined with incentive problems, the theories described here will abstract from them. Garicano and van Zandt (this volume) provides an overview of models which focus on the role of managers as processors of information *per se*. This issue is also partially addressed by Bolton and Dewatripont (this volume).

My main focus is on models of hierarchies in which incentive considerations play an important role. Accordingly, many interesting models of hierarchies based on team theory (Radner and Marschak 1972), which abstracts from incentive considerations, are not included. In addition, models based on (exogenously) incomplete contracts will not be covered in detail, as they are included in Bolton and Dewatripont (this volume); they also overlap with the discussion by Segal and Whinston (this volume) of property rights. Also ignored are models of interaction between formal and informal contracts, as in the work of Baker et al. (1999).

Nevertheless, some form of contractual incompleteness is essential for delegation to have some benefits. Hence, Section 4 describes contracting models where strategic renegotiation, complexity, or communication costs are explicitly incorporated to explain why contracts may be incomplete and then discuss their implications for the performance of different kinds of hierarchies. Many of these branches of the literature have posed challenges for conventional economic theory and are nowhere near being settled. Despite these problems, I have sought to include them for the sake of completeness, for those interested in pursuing these avenues in future research and the possibility that they may generate useful applications in the future.

Section 2 describes the literature on supervision hierarchies, following the work of Calvo and Wellisz (1978), in which managers are modeled as supervisors. The rationale for supervision is that it helps limit the asymmetry of information between employees and owners, thus limiting the scope for opportunistic behavior by the former. Owing to limitations of time or expertise, owners may seek to supplement their own supervisory activities with information supplied by third-party supervisors. Yet these hired supervisors also need to be motivated to apply effort in supervision and thus need to be supervised themselves. This creates the rationale for a hierarchy of supervisors. Much of this literature has sought to explore implications for limits to the size of firms, as firms with a larger scale of operations employ more workers and thus need a larger hierarchy of supervisors, causing organizational diseconomies of scale, owing to resultant losses of control across successive vertical layers of managers. This intuitive idea, expressed originally by Williamson (1967), however, has turned out to be quite difficult to model. We also describe some recent literature on supervision hierarchies following Tirole (1986), which focuses on problems of collusion between supervisors and supervisees, ways of combating these problems, and their implications for performance.

Section 3 turns to models of delegation of decisionmaking authority to managers. The focus in this section is on the attendant cost or "control loss" incurred by the principal, owing to incentive problems (i.e., noncongruence of goals and information between owners and managers). The benefits of delegation are not studied in this approach, as these are presumed to arise from unmodeled costs of centralizing all information processing and decisionmaking responsibilities with the principal. The advantage of this approach is that it utilizes tools of mechanism design theory, which rely on the assumption of complete contracts, in an environment where the Revelation Principle applies: the principal is assumed to be able to commit to a comprehensive contract; there are no costs of communication or contractual complexity; and agents behave noncooperatively. These models help show the precise circumstances under which delegation arrangements can be structured in a way to avoid any loss of control, so that they can implement optimal allocations. Briefly, this requires three sets of conditions: risk neutrality of managers, ability of the principal to monitor measures of performance pertaining to the allocation of effort or payments between managers and their subordinates, and ability to prevent collusion (in the form of unobserved side payments or communication). Violation of any of these conditions—financial constraints faced by managers, lack of suitable accounting systems, or collusion—constitute potential sources of control loss. The implications of collusion are subsequently considered in this section. This branch of the literature is less settled, owing to the inherent complexity of the issue and different ways it has been formulated by numerous authors.

Section 4 subsequently addresses the question of the benefits of delegation in conjunction with its costs. This necessitates a framework in which the Revelation Principle no longer applies and contracts are incomplete. I describe models based, respectively, on limited commitment ability of the principal and on costs of communication or contractual complexity. Either of these frameworks is shown to generate a theory of delegation, trading off its costs and benefits. When the underlying problem is the possibility of strategic renegotiation, delegating control is beneficial from an incentive standpoint, but it raises problems of coordinating the agent's actions with information that subsequently becomes available to the principal. In contexts involving complexity or communication costs, delegation permits actions to be responsive to information available to agents that they cannot communicate to the principal or to third-party contract enforcers. This has to be traded off against the costs of control loss considered in Section 3. The value of delegation thus depends on the determinants of control loss, such as managerial financial constraints, problems of monitoring, or collusion. The theory also suggests the value of intermediate organizational structures, where some decisions, such as contracting and evaluation, are centralized, while authority over production decisions is delegated to employees.

The abovementioned sections deal with the simplest possible model of a hierarchy involving three vertical layers, consisting of a single principal at the top, a single manager in the middle, and one or two productive agents at the bottom. Models of larger and more complex hierarchies are considered in Section 5; these models build on the simpler ones in earlier sections. They focus on problems of horizontal coordination across departments, scale diseconomies, and grouping of activities into departments (e.g., U-form versus M-form hierarchies).

Finally, Section 6 concludes with an assessment of the achievements and shortcomings of the literature and possible research directions for the future.

2. Organizational Scale Diseconomies and Supervision Hierarchies

Williamson (1967) initiated the modern literature on the limits to size of hierarchical firms arising from the control losses associated with internal management problems. His theory is based on a behavioral theory of how losses of information and control arise across vertical layers of management. The other ingredient in the theory is the limit to the span of control of any given manager; that is, the number of subordinates that any manager can oversee owing to problems of limited time and attention. Given the limits of span of control, it is not possible for the firm to grow without adding vertical layers of management. But then the vertical control losses cascade across the various layers, implying rising inefficiency as the firm grows.

The source of these control losses are not explained by Williamson's model. He provides as motivation errors in serial reproduction demonstrated in social psychology experiments, wherein losses in information can occur when it passes through a succession of individuals, despite each individual in the chain being satisfied they have passed on all important features of their own information with little or no change. Hence, top managers in organizations tend to be progressively out of touch with events at the ground level, as the number of vertical layers increase. Other sources of control loss are asymmetric information and opportunistic behavior by subordinates, which were not, however, part of the formal model. We start by describing Williamson's formulation, followed by the effort of Calvo and Wellisz (1978) to provide a microfoundation for vertical control losses owing to incentive problems.

2.1. The Williamson-Calvo-Wellisz Model

The simplest version of Williamson's model has an exogenously given span of control s at each layer. At the top level $(i = 1)$ of the firm there is one owner or principal, supervising s managers at level $i = 2$, each of whom are supervising s level-3 managers in turn, and so on. At the very bottom layer n, there are thus s^{n-1} employees, the production workers of the firm. All layers $i = 1, \ldots, n - 1$ consist of managers or supervisors, layer i consisting of s^{i-1} managers. The production function yields the firm's output as a Cobb-Douglas function of the number of production workers s^{n-1} and a level of total factor productivity that reflects a proportional loss of output owing to control loss at each management layer: $y = (\bar{a}s)^{n-1}$, where $\bar{a} \in (0, 1)$ is the vertical control loss parameter reflecting communication and incentive problems.

Williamson also assumes an exogenous rate of wage progression across layers of the hierarchy; $\beta > 1$ is the ratio of wages at one level to the level below. Hence, if w_0 denotes the wage of production workers, level $n - 1$ managers earn βw_0, and level i managers earn $w_0 \beta^{n-i}$.

If the firm faces product price P on the output market (net of raw material costs per unit of output) and wage rate w_0 for production workers on the labor market, it selects a size (or number of layers n) to maximize $P(\bar{a}s)^{n-1} - w_0 \sum_{i=1}^{n} s^{i-1}\beta^{n-i}$. This expression yields an equation for the number of layers as a function of span of control, the vertical control loss parameter $\bar{a}$, the wage rate for production workers, and the rate of wage growth across layers:

$$n^* = 1 + \frac{1}{\log \bar{a}} \left[\log \frac{w_0}{P} + \log \frac{s}{s - \beta} + \log \left(\frac{\log s}{\log \bar{a}s} \right) \right]. \tag{1}$$

Firm size is finite if $\bar{a} < 1$ and tends to ∞ as control losses disappear $(\bar{a} \to 1)$. It is also increasing in s, the span of control.

An extended version of this model makes the span of control s endogenous by postulating that the vertical control loss at any layer is increasing in s. This captures the intuitive idea that limits on time and attention of any supervisor cause loss of control per subordinate when the supervisor has to supervise more people. Hence, $\bar{a}$ is decreasing in s. With the specific functional form $\bar{a}(s) = \exp[-ks^2]$, Williamson (1967) shows that larger firms have higher n and lower s, but this result seems to depend on the specific functional form chosen.

Williamson's model has the virtue of delivering predictions concerning size and structure of firms based on technology and product and labor market characteristics that can be empirically tested. However, the key ingredients of the theory—vertical control loss $\bar{a}$ and the rate of wage progression β in the hierarchy—are taken as given. Much of the literature described in this chapter can be viewed as an attempt to endogenize these factors on the basis of incentive considerations and thereby provide a microfoundation for the Williamson model. As we shall see, this goal has yet to be fully achieved.

Calvo and Wellisz (1978) were among the first to attempt endogenization, using a model of supervision and wage incentives. In this model, all workers and supervisors are identical: they have a utility function $u(c) - v(a)$, where u is a smooth, strictly increasing, concave function of consumption or earnings c; v is a smooth, strictly increasing, convex function representing disutility of effort $a \in [0, 1]$, which is the fraction of the week worked; and $u(0) = v(0) = 0$. A production worker applying effort a generates revenue Pa for the employer, where P is a given parameter depending on output price, raw material costs, and technology.

The supervision process is as follows. Supervisors allocate their time equally between monitoring all their subordinates. If the number of supervisors at level i is denoted by M_i, and if they work a_i fraction of the week, the amount of time devoted to supervision per level-$(i + 1)$ employee is $\frac{a_i M_i}{M_{i+1}}$. With probability $p_{i+1} \equiv g(\frac{a_i M_i}{M_{i+1}})$, the true value of a_{i+1}, the time worked by any level-$(i + 1)$ employee will become known, where g is a strictly increasing function satisfying $g(0) = 0$ and $g(\infty) \in (0, 1]$. Here it is assumed that supervisors report their findings honestly to the employer.

Let w_{i+1} denote the wage paid for full-time work to a level-$(i + 1)$ employee. This will be determined endogenously, as explained below. If the employer learns from supervisor reports that an employee at level $i + 1$ worked a_{i+1}, this employee is paid $a_{i+1} w_{i+1}$. If no information is available, the employee is presumed to have worked full time and is paid a wage of w_{i+1}. Hence, workers detected shirking are punished by having wages withheld for the fraction of time they are reliably known to have shirked.

Consider a worker who is monitored with probability p and paid a full-time wage of w. This worker will choose to work a^* fraction of the time, which maximizes $pu(wa) + (1 - p)u(w) - v(a)$. Clearly, this expression is increasing in p and is also a function of w: let it be denoted by $a^*(p; w)$. The worker will agree to work for the firm if $V(p, w) \equiv pu(wa^*(p, w)) + (1 - p)u(w) - v(a^*(p, w)) \geq \underline{u}$, a given positive level of utility that forms the worker's outside option. Clearly $V(p, w)$ is increasing in w and decreasing in p.

Consider first a firm where the owner herself supervises all production workers, in what we may call a "one-layer hierarchy." Assume that the owner has a fixed amount of time, normalized to unity, available to supervise the workers. The optimal size of such a firm is defined by the solution to the following problem: choose n, the number of production workers, and a wage w, to maximize $nPa^*(p, w) - [pwa^*(p, w) + (1 - p)w]n$, subject to $p = g(\frac{1}{n})$ and the participation constraint for workers. It is easy to verify that there is an interior optimum for both n and w for this problem. In particular, as n rises, the monitoring probability p falls, inducing workers to shirk. As n tends to ∞, p tends to 0, and workers then tend to apply zero effort, in which case firm profits tend to $-\infty$ (because the firm needs to pay a positive wage to attract workers). Hence, firm size is bounded if it is owner managed (i.e., a one-layer hierarchy). Denote by π_1^* the maximized level of profit achieved by the owner in this case.

One way for the firm to expand is to hire third-party supervisors. In a two-layer hierarchy, the owner employs a number of supervisors and asks them to monitor production workers. The owner herself monitors the supervisors, which ensures that the supervisors exert effort in monitoring production workers, which in turns motivates the latter to apply effort in production. The incentive problem for choice of effort by supervisors (as well as the participation constraint) is exactly analogous to that of production workers. In a two-layer hierarchy the owner selects the number of supervisors and the number of production workers supervised by each supervisor, as well as the wages at each layer. Hiring level-1 supervisors relieves the owner with regard to supervisory responsibility, thus enabling the firm to employ more production workers and ensure that their efforts do not get diluted owing to the shrinking probability of being monitored when the owner alone has to conduct all supervision. This model formalizes the notion of vertical control loss and how it increases in the span of control. The Calvo-Wellisz model thus allows a simple and elegant model of these critical variables that were assumed exogenous in the Williamson model. Moreover, the wage structure in the hierarchy is also endogenously determined.

The salient question is whether these control losses arising for incentive reasons limit the size of the firm. Let π_n^* denote the level of maximum profit earned by the owner in an n-layer hierarchy. The interesting result in the Calvo-Wellisz (1978) paper is that this model does not provide a limit to the size of the firm. The key proposition is the following. *Suppose $\pi_1^* > P$, that is, it is more profitable for the owner to hire production workers and form a one-layer hierarchy rather than do all the production work herself. Then $\pi_n^* \to \infty$ as $n \to \infty$.*

Here is an outline of the argument. It suffices to show there is a way of expanding the number of production workers indefinitely by raising n, which leads to unbounded profits. This method involves replicating the optimal incentive arrangement for production workers for every layer of supervisor in an n-layer hierarchy. Specifically, letting a^*, w^*, n^* denote the optimal values of a, n, w, respectively, in a one-layer hierarchy, select a constant span of control $s^* = n^*$ at each level of the hierarchy, and pay the same wages at all levels. Hence, the number of supervisors at a pair of successive levels $i-1$ and i is selected so that $\frac{a^* M_{i-1}}{M_i} = \frac{1}{n^*}$. Provided supervisors at level $i-1$ are working a^* each, each level-i supervisor is monitored with the same probability $p^* \equiv \frac{1}{n^*}$ as are production workers in a one-layer hierarchy. Hence, it is optimal for each such supervisor to agree to work for this firm, and work a^* fraction of the time. Letting W^* denote the expected wage cost per employee $p^* w^* a^* + (1 - p^*) w^*$, expanding the firm from $n-1$ to n layers results in an increase in profit by

$$Pa^*(M_n - M_{n-1}) - M_n W^* = M_n[Pa^*(1 - \frac{M_{n-1}}{M_n}) - W^*] = M_n[Pa^* - P\frac{1}{n^*} - W^*]$$

$$= \frac{M_n}{n^*}[(Pa^* - W^*)n^* - P] = \frac{M_n}{n^*}[\pi_1^* - P],$$

which grows without limit as $M_n \to \infty$. Essentially, the mechanism in place in a one-layer hierarchy can be replicated independently for each supervisor at each layer. Hence, the model shows that incentive problems do not necessarily constitute a source of control loss that limits the size of firms. Formalizing the simple Williamsonian intuition will require some additional ingredients.

Of course the preceding model is somewhat special in a number of respects, such as the symmetry between workers and supervisors and their respective incentive problems. It turns out, however, that the basic result is robust to many variations that make the model more realistic (Datta 1996; Tsumagari 1999). Both these papers consider contexts in which supervisory effort cannot be directly monitored. Datta studies a context in which supervisors are evaluated indirectly by monitoring the output of production workers directly or indirectly under their supervision. Here the Calvo and Wellisz (1978) replication arguments continue to apply under plausible assumptions: supervisors are evaluated on the basis of the performance of their respective divisions and internalize the effect of their own shirking on their subordinates' efforts. Tsumagari considers a context in which supervisors have overlapping jurisdictions, with cross-checking of reports of different supervisors. In this context the firm can expand horizontally rather than vertically, with each supervisor being cross-checked against reports of adjacent supervisors; again, firm size is unbounded under reasonable conditions.

Another variation was suggested by Calvo and Wellisz (1978) themselves, in which supervisees know in advance exactly when they are being monitored, so the fraction of time they work equals the fraction of time they are monitored. This implies that to get n production workers to work any fixed positive a fraction of the week, it is necessary to have them supervised by the same number of supervisors working a fraction of the week, and the same is true in turn for the supervisors themselves, so ultimately the owner will have to personally spend at least na fraction of the week. Given the limit on the total time available to the owner, it is impossible to let n grow indefinitely while a is bounded away from zero. In that case firm size is limited. However, this constraint no longer holds once there is some scope for random audits, wherein workers do not know in advance when or whether they will be monitored. In that case one supervisor working a fraction of the week can supervise and ensure that $n > 1$ subordinates will also work a fraction of the week. The logic of the model described above then kicks in to ensure that the firm can grow indefinitely.

Qian (1994) returns to this question with a formulation that combines aspects of the Calvo-Wellisz model with Williamson's (1967) model. The critical departure from the Calvo-Wellisz model is the production function. Because the number of production workers in the n-layer Calvo-Wellisz hierarchy equals M_n, the gross revenue of the firm in the Calvo-Wellisz model equals $PM_n a_n$ if the layer-i employees apply effort a_i. Qian assumes instead a gross revenue that equals $PM_n a_n a_{n-1} \ldots a_1$. In other words, there is an additional source of revenue loss $a_{n-1} \ldots a_1$ arising from the existence of supervisors at intermediate levels of the hierarchy. Qian uses a variant of the incentive model of Calvo and Wellisz, whereby any shirking of the employee below the mandated effort level a^* is punished with a zero wage. Consequently, an employee monitored with probability p needs to be paid an efficiency wage of $\underline{w} \equiv \frac{v(a^*)}{p} = s v(a^*)$ to induce an effort of a^*, where $s \equiv \frac{1}{p}$ denotes the span of control of the employees' supervisor. The costs of increasing the span of control are thus represented by a corresponding linear increase in the efficiency wage for a given level of effort.

Using this formulation, Qian (1994) studies the problem of determining the optimal hierarchy (i.e., number of layers, span of control at every layer, and efforts and corresponding wages at each layer). If feasible effort a for any employee is zero or one, then clearly every employee must be induced to work ($a = 1$), and the formulation coincides with Calvo and Wellisz (1978). In this case, there is no limit to firm size. The other case that Qian investigates is where a can be any number in the unit interval, and $v(a) \to \infty$ as $a \to 1$. In that case it is impossible to get anyone to work full time, and every agent must put in an interior $a \in (0, 1)$ in any optimal arrangement, with a bounded away from 1. Given the specification of the production function, however, this case implies that the supplementary control losses $a_{n-1} \ldots a_1$ arising from the existence of intermediate supervisors must cascade, implying that the firm's revenue eventually converges to zero as the number of layers grows without bound. A limit to the size of the firm obtains. But it is due entirely to vertical control losses, which remain unexplained. It is not clear why the effort of the supervisors has any effect over and above the way they influence the effort of those they supervise. Perhaps managers do other things apart from supervise workers, but these are not included or explained. Hence the Calvo and Wellisz puzzle of limits to firm size is not really resolved in this model. This shortcoming motivates the consideration of the possibility of collusion between supervisors and workers, a factor ignored by the preceding models.

2.2. Collusion and Supervision

The literature on collusion and supervision was pioneered by Tirole (1986). His model has a principal P and an agent A who produces revenue $\theta + a$ for P, where $\theta \in \{\theta_L, \theta_H\}$ is a productivity realization that is observed by A before choosing a level of effort a. Productivity can be either low (θ_L) or high (θ_H), where $\theta_H > \theta_L > 0$. P's net payoff is the expected value of $\theta + a - w$, where w is the wage paid to A. A's payoff is $u(w - v(a))$, where v is an increasing convex function of $a \geq 0$, and u is a strictly increasing concave function. A has a reservation utility normalized to 0.

P can hire a supervisor S, who may observe the realization of θ, though he cannot observe the agent's effort a. The information that S can observe in the process of supervision is represented by a signal σ with three possible realizations: θ_L, θ_H, and ϕ. If $\sigma = \theta_i$, $i = L, H$, the true state is exactly θ_i: in this case S learns the true state with certainty. However, the signal may also equal ϕ in either state: in this case S does not learn the true state. Tirole assumes that the signal represents hard information: S can submit definite evidence to P concerning the realization of the signal when it reveals the true state. S cannot fabricate evidence when there is none (i.e., he cannot produce any evidence when $\sigma = \phi$). The only option for behaving strategically is to suppress evidence: S can claim $\sigma = \phi$ when he did receive evidence of the true state. Unlike the Calvo-Wellisz model, supervisory effort per se generates no disutility for S. The latter's utility is $V(c)$, where c denotes the financial return of S, and V is a strictly increasing concave function. S also has a given outside option level of utility.

P lacks the capacity or time to supervise the agent herself. In this situation, she would design an incentive contract for A, which, as per the standard model of incentives with adverse selection, motivates the first-best effort a^* satisfying $v'(a^*) = 1$ when A observes $\theta = \theta_H$, and a lower level of effort $\underline{a}$ when A observes $\theta = \theta_L$. In the former state A earns an incentive rent (i.e., obtains a wage high enough to end up with a payoff above his outside option). In the latter state A earns zero rent (i.e., a net payoff equal to the outside option). In this equilibrium, A is indifferent in the high-productivity state between producing the revenue of $(\theta_H + a^*)$ and $(\theta_H + \underline{a})$. The rent earned by A in the high-productivity state is the price or bonus paid by P to induce A to apply high effort in this state, rather than slacking off on effort (reducing a from a^* to $\underline{a} - (\theta_H - \theta_L)$ and pretending that the state is θ_L instead of θ_H).

When S is hired and does not collude with A, he reports the realization of the signal truthfully to P. This reduces the informational asymmetry between P and A, enabling P to avoid paying the incentive rent to A when there is firm evidence that the true state is θ_H. This is the benefit P obtains from hiring S, which has to be traded off against the cost of hiring S. If S's outside option is low enough (e.g., if it is zero), the cost of hiring S is low enough that it is profitable for P to hire S. Here S earns a fixed salary of c, just equal to the level necessary to induce him to accept the job.

But now A has an incentive to bribe S to suppress evidence of the high-productivity state, and so qualify for the incentive rent. S does not mind accepting the bribe, as the salary c is fixed, while

A gains the incentive rent as a result of the suppression of evidence. Tirole (1986) assumes that there are no frictions in collusion—it can be modeled as an enforceable side-contract between S and A, which cannot be observed by P. Moreover, A knows exactly what evidence is available to S, so in the case where S receives evidence, there is no asymmetric information between S and A. Effectively, then, S and A will then jointly behave as if they were a single player, earning a pecuniary equivalent payoff of $c + w - v(a)$ equal to the sum of their respective payoffs. The second-best payoff achieved by P is thus no longer achievable in the presence of collusion.

Tirole goes on to solve for the third-best contract, which maximizes P's expected payoff, subject to both individual and joint collusive incentives of S and A. An argument analogous to the Revelation Principle shows that P can confine attention to contracts that are collusion proof (i.e., in which S and A have no incentive to enter into a collusive agreement), and S reports his evidence truthfully to P. This is achieved partly by P offering S a selective reward for disclosing evidence of high productivity, as well as reducing the power of A's incentives and rents, both of which reduce the stakes for collusion. A has less to gain by bribing S to suppress evidence of high productivity, and S is less willing to suppress this evidence. The net consequence is that S will be forced to bear the risk associated with the availability of evidence, for which P will have to pay S a risk premium if S is risk averse. And A will be provided with less effort incentive. On both counts P's profitability will decline, compared with the second-best outcome. The extent to which this decline occurs depends on how risk averse S is. If S is risk neutral, P does not lose at all: P can effectively sell the firm to S and thereby overcome the problem of collusion entirely—there is no loss of either profitability or productivity. At the other extreme, if S is infinitely risk averse, no risk can be imposed on S at all, which implies no incentive rents can be paid to A; the firm ends up with low productivity and profitability. Nevertheless, even in this case it pays P to hire S if the latter has a zero outside option, owing to the advocacy role he plays on behalf of A (by providing evidence of state θ_L when it occurs, which is in the joint interest of S and A). In general, when S is somewhat but not infinitely risk averse, the three-layer hierarchy is more profitable than the two-layer one in which S is not hired, though the agent may become less productive owing to the reduction in the power of incentives.

Tirole's model provides an useful illustration of the problem of collusion and its consequences. Worker incentives are lower in the three-layer hierarchy compared with the two-layer one. The costs of collusion are the rents P has to pay the supervisor to deter collusion and the lower effort of the worker. The severity of these costs depends on the risk aversion of the supervisor. Despite these collusion costs, they are outweighed by the benefits of hiring a supervisor. We shall see in subsequent sections that similar results arise in the literature on delegation. Interesting applications of this theory to auditing and regulation have been developed. For instance, Kofman and Lawaree (1993) extend Tirole's model to include external and internal auditors and explain the role of the former in cross-checking reports made by internal auditors who may be colluding with workers. Laffont and Tirole (1993) develop a comprehensive theory of regulation of natural monopolies based on the role of regulators who monitor firms' technology and cost-cutting efforts and can be potentially bribed to not disclose their findings publicly.

Comparatively less attention has been devoted to the question of whether collusion can serve as a source of control loss that limits the size of firms. Datta (1996) sketches an example where collusion limits firm size. Supervisors are evaluated by audits of production workers in their divisions. Firms must grow by adding vertical layers owing to endogenous limits on the span of control, and collusion is deterred by inconsistency of audit reports at successive vertical layers.

The larger the firm gets, the lower the likelihood of such inconsistencies becomes. In contrast, collusion does not limit the size of the firm in the Tsumagari (1999) model based on overlapping jurisdictions of different supervisors. In his model, the firm grows horizontally; hence, there is no problem of cascading control losses.

In summary, models of supervision hierarchies have illustrated some of the difficulties in explaining limits to firm size. Collusion is probably important in understanding why larger organizations tend to be less productive and why middle managers earn large rents. But we still do not have tractable models of determinate firm size and structure based on collusion and supervision.

3. Delegation and Loss of Control with Complete Contracts

The previous section focused on the supervisory role of managers, pertaining to the generation of information concerning the activities of subordinates that helps evaluate and motivate the latter. Supervision per se does not include any responsibility for actual decisions. Conceptually there is little difference between supervisors and external consultants, whom the principal may rely on to generate information relevant to the decisions she makes. The models do not explain why authority over decisions may be delegated. In the supervision models, the principal still contracts with all workers and suppliers personally and makes all relevant production, technology, marketing, and sourcing decisions.

In this and succeeding sections I focus on the question of delegation of key operating decisions to managers. As the quote from Chandler (1962) in Section 1 indicates, although managers may play some role in the production process themselves, they rarely do so at higher levels of the hierarchy. Their functions include contracting and supervision of subordinates, allocating resources, and coordinating the activities of departments under their control, apart from long-term planning. The principal or owners rarely become personally involved in the internal administration of the enterprise.

From an analytical perspective, we therefore need to understand the implications of delegation of contracting with subordinates to managers, where the term "contracting" includes production and sourcing decisions, coordination of production and allocation of resources, recruitment, and supervision and evaluation of employees and suppliers. In this section I do not pose the question of why the principal does not carry out these tasks herself (i.e., what the value of delegation of contracting is). Instead, I simply assume that decisions will be delegated and study how the principal ought to evaluate and compensate a self-interested manager. This is precisely the problem of potential loss of control. The questions posed by these models are: What are the determinants of this loss of control? What are the strategies for ameliorating it?

In Section 3.1, I assume the conditions underlying the Revelation Principle are valid: there are no costs of communication, complexity, or information processing; the principal can commit to a comprehensive contract; and agents do not collude. Under these circumstances the Revelation Principle (e.g., Myerson 1982) tells us that centralized decisionmaking—where the principal contracts and communicates with all agents personally and makes all relevant decisions based on reports of private information of the agents—can always perform at least as well as any method of decentralizing these responsibilities. Hence, delegation can never outperform centralization. The question addressed instead is: can delegation of key responsibilities to self-interested managers achieve the same level of profit for the principal as any centralized mechanism? If so, delegation is costless and is a way of implementing the optimal mechanism.

We shall subsequently explore the consequences of dropping different assumptions underlying the Revelation Principle. The latter part of this section explores the effects of collusion among agents, preserving all the other assumptions. Section 4 examines the consequences of inability of the principal to commit to a mechanism or of costs of communication and complexity. Because subsequent sections build on this one, it makes sense to explain the results in some detail.

3.1. The Basic Model

The standard model in this section is a simple adverse selection contracting problem. Analogous questions in a moral hazard setting have been studied by Baliga and Sjöström (1998) and Macho-Stadler and Perez-Castrillo (1998). There is one Principal P, one or two agents A (or A_i, $i =$ 1, 2), and a third-party manager M. Extension of these models to incorporate more agents, managers, or layers will be covered in Section 5. The agents carry out productive tasks that generate a revenue or gross benefit B for P. In the single-agent case, A delivers a good or service $a \geq 0$ that generates a benefit $B(a)$. In the two-agent case A_i delivers $a_i \geq 0$, and the benefit is $B(a_1, a_2)$. The two goods delivered could be perfect substitutes, in which case B depends only on $a_1 + a_2$: in this case the mechanism design problem reduces to a procurement auction with variable quantities. Or the two goods could be perfect complements: $B = \min\{a_1, a_2\}$. More generally, a_1 and a_2 could be neither perfect substitutes nor perfect complements, as represented by a production function with a constant elasticity of substitution.

Agents are privately informed regarding their cost of production before they need to commit to deciding whether to participate in the mechanisms concerned. In other words, contracting occurs at the interim stage, where each agent knows his own cost but not the cost realizations of others. Most authors assume that each agent's unit cost does not vary with the level of production, and this unit cost is uncertain. Some authors assume that these costs can take one of two possible values. Others assume they are distributed on an interval of the real line, with a standard monotone hazard rate assumption on the distribution, which ensures that global incentive constraints can be ignored. Specifically, if θ_i is the unit cost incurred by A_i, it is distributed according to a cumulative distribution function F_i and density f_i on an interval $[\underline{\theta}_i, \bar{\theta}_i]$, where $\theta_i + \frac{F_i(\theta_i)}{f_i(\theta_i)}$ is nondecreasing in θ_i, an assumption satisfied by the uniform, exponential, and many other well-known distributions. Throughout it is assumed that θ_1, θ_2 are independently distributed. Moreover, most formulations assume risk neutrality and zero outside option utilities for agents. Hence, P's payoff is $B(a_1, a_2) - t_1 - t_2 - t_M$, where t_1, t_2, and t_M denote transfers made by P to A_1, A_2, and M, respectively. The payoff of A_i is $T_i - \theta_i a_i$ and of M is T_M, where T_i and T_M denote net transfers received by A_i and M, respectively. In the centralized mechanism without any collusion, $T_i = t_i$ and $T_M = t_M$, but this is not the case in decentralized mechanisms or in the presence of collusion, owing to side-transfers between the agents.

Many authors have studied what we shall call the "restricted version" of the standard problem, in which each agent's cost takes one of two possible values, and the inputs produced by the two agents are perfect complements. Other authors have studied the continuous version of this problem, in which costs are distributed according to a density on an interval on the real line, and no restriction is imposed on the benefit function.

Decisionmaking responsibility can be delegated either to one of the productive agents or to the third-party manager M. The latter may also act as a supervisor of the productive agents, receiving a private signal of their cost realizations. Agents and the manager all act in a self-interested fashion.

In this section I assume that it is possible for anyone with contracting authority to commit to a comprehensive contract, which includes details of communication protocols (i.e., the message sets, who communicates with whom and when, etc.), production assignments, and transfers. Owing to the Revelation Principle, it will suffice to focus on revelation mechanisms in the centralized regime, where agents report their private information and receive instructions concerning production assignments. The outputs a_i they deliver are assumed to be costlessly monitored; transfers can be conditioned on these outputs, and/or reports communicated. In the decentralized regime, assumptions concerning sequencing, communication, and observability will be made explicit in due course.

3.2. Single Agent, No Collusion

Here A produces a at cost θa, P's net payoff is $B(a) - t$, and A's is $t - \theta a$. In this setting the following mechanisms can be compared: (1) centralization, denoted by $(P^* - A)$, where "*" depicts the decisionmaker and a "−" indicates a line of hierarchical control; (2) agent-based decentralization, denoted by $(P - A^*)$; and (3) manager-based decentralization, denoted by $(P - M^* - A)$. In $(P^* - A)$, P retains all decision rights. In $(P - A^*)$, P contracts with A but delegates production decisions to A. In $(P - M^* - A)$, P delegates contracting and production decisions to M and contracts with M alone. M contracts in turn with A. M is evaluated and compensated by P based on the revenue generated. Other mechanisms are also possible, such as $(P^* - (M, A))$, where M's role is purely supervisory or consultative and thus is on the same hierarchical level as A, depicted by the parentheses around the set of agents M and A at that level. Here P contracts with both M and A, and M's responsibility is limited to submitting a report to P concerning the signal concerning A's cost. P uses this information to evaluate and compensate A.

It is obvious that centralization $(P^* - A)$ and agent-based decentralization $(P - A^*)$ achieve equivalent outcomes, in what is often referred to as the "Taxation Principle." Under the former, P designs an incentive-compatible revelation mechanism $a(\theta)$, $t(\theta)$, in which A is always motivated to report truthfully. Equivalent outcomes are achieved in agent-based decentralization by P instead offering A a nonlinear incentive mechanism $t(a)$ equal to $t(\theta)$ if $a = a(\theta)$ for some θ and 0 otherwise. The incentive compatibility of the original revelation mechanism implies that this nonlinear function is well defined and motivates A to select the same production in every state as did P in the centralized regime. The converse is equally straightforward, amounting to the proof of the Revelation Principle. Generalizations of this result to contexts with production or monitoring uncertainty (i.e., where P's revenue or measured performance is not a but is some function $R(a, \epsilon)$, where ϵ is a random variable unobserved by A at the time of selecting a) have been provided by Melumad and Reichelstein (1989).

Matters are somewhat more interesting when P has the opportunity of using the services of M to supervise the agent. If M and A do not collude, P can obtain M's information costlessly in the centralized mechanism $P^* - (M, A)$, because M does not have any incentive to hide his information. Here the outcome is the same as if P contracted with A with the same information as M. This is no longer the case in the decentralized variant $(P - M^* - A)$, because M can act strategically with respect to his information. This result is easy to see if M is perfectly informed about the cost realization θ: in that case M can procure any quantity a from A at cost θa, and the problem is equivalent to P contracting with A in the absence of M. The same result is also evident when M's information about θ is identical to P's. Hence, delegation to M is typically costly in this setting.

3.3. Two Agents, No Collusion

We now come to a model involving two productive agents and a single principal, considered by various authors in diverse settings of regulation and internal organization (Baron and Besanko 1992; Gilbert and Riordan 1995; Melumad et al. 1992, 1995; Laffont and Martimort 1998; Severinov 2008). This model is extended in subsequent sections on collusion and incomplete contracts, so it makes sense to present the results in some detail.

The chief question concerns implications of delegating contracting and production decisions to one of the two agents. In the regulation context, the regulated entity may be a downstream service provider who procures a essential input from an upstream firm. The question is whether the regulator should regulate both firms directly as well as all aspects of production and transfers between them or whether only the downstream firm ought to be regulated and is free to procure its inputs from the upstream provider. In a team-production setting within a firm, the employer could retain all authority and treat the different team members symmetrically. Alternatively, she could appoint one of them as the manager and delegate decisions concerning contracting with other agents to the manager. An additional alternative is to hire a manager M^* who plays no productive role but supervises the producing agents.

In this setting, the alternatives are (1) centralization $(P^* - (A_1, A_2))$; (2) agent-based delegation $(P - A_1^* - A_2)$, where P delegates to A_1 the responsibility of communicating and contracting with A_2; and (3) manager-based delegation $(P - M^* - (A_1, A_2))$, where P delegates to M the responsibility of contracting with A_1, A_2. Variants of these include $(P - (A_1^*, A_2^*))$, where P contracts with the two agents but delegates to them the right to make their own production decisions. Another is $(P^* - (M, A_1, A_2))$, where P retains all decision rights, and the sole responsibility of M is to communicate reports to P.

Consider the comparison between the centralized $(P^* - (A_1, A_2))$ and decentralized $(P - A_1^* - A_2)$ variants. There are many variants of the decentralized version, differing with respect to the precise sequencing of contracting, and the information available to P concerning the performance of the manager-cum-worker A_1.

A key result here is that *delegation to A_1 is optimal (i.e., can achieve the same expected profit as centralized contracting), if (1) the sequence of contracting is "top-down" in the sense that P contracts with A_1[1] before A_1 communicates or contracts with A_2; (2) P monitors both the gross revenue B*

---

1. This contract includes both a commitment from A_1 to participate in the mechanism, and submission of a report concerning his own state.

and either the payment t_2 made by A_1 to A_2 or the input a_1 delivered by A_1 alone; and (3) A_1 is risk neutral and is not subject to any limited liability constraint.[2]

The argument is constructive: P can offer A_1 a contract that makes the latter a residual claimant on profits earned by the former, adjusted by a subsidy for payments made to A_2 or on the extent of input supplied by the latter. The subsidy corrects for the tendency of A_1 to procure too little from the other agent, owing to her tendency to maximize her own information rents. This problem is key with delegation, closely related to the phenomenon of "double marginalization of rents" (DMR) in the industrial organization literature on vertical contracting relationships (see, e.g., Tirole 1988). Contracting with adverse selection gives rise to monopsony distortions: owing to the trade-off between productive efficiency and incentive rents, too little tends to be procured by those in middle tiers.

Nevertheless, these papers show that the problem can be overcome under the specified assumptions of risk neutrality, appropriate sequencing of contracts to prevent collusion, and monitoring of contributions of the manager vis-à-vis the rest of the team. When the latter takes the form of monitoring of payments, the incentive system for the manager resembles that of decentralized profit or cost centers within firms (Melumad et al. 1992). Observability of aggregate cost of the division suffices to overcome the DMR problem. It is not necessary for P to observe further details of the side-contracts designed by A_1 or the communication of the latter with his subordinates.

Nevertheless, some monitoring of side-contracts (or A_1's output a_1) is essential, as long as there is some substitutability between a_1 and a_2. Only in the case of perfect complementarity (a Leontief production function) can the DMR problem be avoided if P does not monitor any aspect of the transactions between A_1 and his subordinates. And even in that case, there would be a tendency for A_1 to generate too much aggregate revenue. This tendency provides a possible explanation for the empire-building tendencies of managers, which shareholders seek to limit in various ways (e.g., using a compensation formula where fractional bonus coefficients are used to reduce the manager's inclination to overexpand operations). The conflict of interest between owner and manager arises owing to the informational rents earned by the manager, which the manager sees as a benefit, but the shareholders see as a cost. Baron and Besanko (1992), who study the case of perfect complementarity, avoid this problem by centralizing the production decision while delegating A_1 only the responsibility for contracting and communicating with A_2. The DMR problem is then avoided by reducing the extent of responsibility delegated.

The other assumptions (1) and (3) also play an essential role in ensuring the optimality of delegation. Delegation enlarges the extent of asymmetric information between P and A_1, as the latter is now privately informed both about his own cost θ_1 and those of his subordinates θ_2. This knowledge would expand the informational rents that A_1 would earn vis-à-vis P, on top of the rents that A_2 earns. This scenario is another version of the DMR problem. It is avoided with assumption (1) of top-down contracting, because A_1 contracts with P before he learns the realization of θ_2. These additional rents can then be "taxed" away at the time of contracting. For this it is necessary that A_1 end up with a negative payoff in some states of the world (e.g., when both θ_1 and θ_2 end up too high). This situation would not be possible

---

2. Severinov (2008) shows that additional conditions on the degree of complementarity between the inputs supplied by the two agents are needed if cost types have a discrete rather than a continuous distribution.

if there were a limited liability constraint requiring A_1's payoff be nonnegative in all states of the world. This observation is the central point made by McAfee and McMillan (1995), which underlies their model of organizational diseconomies of scale. Such a context is similar to one where A_1 communicates with A_2 before contracting with P, so the former knows the state of the world before committing to participate in the contract offered by P. In that world, A_1 will earn additional informational rents owing to the privacy of his information concerning the realization of θ_2. There is then a cascading of information rents across successive vertical layers of the hierarchy.

Similarly, if A_1 were risk averse, she would incur risk associated with the realization of her subordinates' costs in the delegation arrangement, for which P would have to compensate A_1 with an additional risk premium. This is the main idea underlying the Faure-Grimaud and Martimort (2001) and Faure-Grimaud et al. (2000) model of the cost of delegation. The point is qualitatively similar to that made by Tirole (1986) in a different setting, as well as by McAfee and McMillan (1995). It is particularly relevant to the case of managers in firms who are likely to be risk averse and subject to limited liability concerns. The optimality result seems applicable, if at all, to the case of supply chains in defense procurement or healthcare contracting, in which P is the government and the agents correspond to large corporations with deep pockets and ample access to capital markets.

3.4. Delegation to Information Intermediaries

Consider next the costs of delegating management of a firm with two (or more) productive workers to a third-party supervisor or intermediary M who does not carry out any productive tasks. As Chandler (1962) noted, most top executives in large organizations are not involved in any productive activity themselves. The value of hiring such professional managers presumably lies in their ability to supervise and coordinate the activities of productive agents. So suppose that M receives signals about the realization of costs of different agents. Presumably, M is better informed than P; otherwise, it would not pay for P to hire the former.

An interesting problem here is comparing the costs and benefits of P managing the firm herself (the $(P^* - (A_1, A_2))$ organization) with those of delegating management to M (the $(P - M^* - (A_1, A_2))$ organization).[3] The advantage of delegation is that it takes advantage of M's expertise and supervision. The disadvantage is that M will behave strategically with respect to this information vis-à-vis P and extract corresponding informational rents.

It is simplest to consider the case where M is perfectly informed about the costs of the two agents. Then the delegated organization reduces to the problem of P contracting with a single consolidated agent, who produces both inputs (a_1, a_2) at a cost of $\theta_1 a_1 + \theta_2 a_2$ (because this will be the cost that M incurs in procuring these inputs from the agents). Hence, the comparison

---

3. There is a third alternative $(P^* - (M, A_1, A_2))$, in which P retains control and treats M as a supervisor rather than a manager. In the absence of collusion, P can costlessly acquire M's information and then use it to contract with the agents. However, for the reasons provided by Tirole (1986), this arrangement would be vulnerable to collusion between M and the agents. In the presence of collusion, which we consider in Section 3.5, it turns out that this alternative is closely related to the one we are considering now, where authority is delegated to M.

is between P contracting with two separate agents, each of whom produces one of the inputs, with a consolidated agent, who produces both at the same aggregate cost.

This problem has been considered by Baron and Besanko (1992), Gilbert and Riordan (1995), Mookherjee and Tsumagari (2004), and Severinov (2008). The main result is the following. *If M is perfectly informed about agents' costs, delegation to M is better than P managing the firm herself without involving M, if the two inputs a_1 and a_2 are complements in the sense that $\frac{\partial^2 B}{\partial a_1 \partial a_2} \geq 0$ and the costs have iid exponential distributions with a lower bound of 0. The converse is true if a_1 and a_2 are perfect or near-perfect substitutes (i.e., infinite or near-infinite elasticity of substitution).*[4]

The intuitive explanation is the following. When P contracts with separate suppliers, each supplier exerts an externality on the other supplier through their cost reports. This information is internalized when the suppliers are consolidated into a single entity. If the inputs are near-perfect substitutes, then the two agents are competing suppliers, and a lower cost report by one agent tends to decrease the production target awarded to (and hence the payoff earned by) the other agent. Internalizing this externality implies that cost reports will tend to become higher—which lowers P's profits. Consolidation here suppresses competition. However, when the two inputs are complements, a lower cost report by one agent expands the production target and the payoff of the other agent. Internalization of this externality results in lower cost reports—which works to P's advantage. Here consolidation fosters cooperation.

There is another effect of consolidation: two one-dimensional adverse selection problems are replaced by a single multidimensional problem. The consolidated agent can consider coordinated deviations of cost reports along the two dimensions that was not possible when the agents were separate. This adds to the problems of control of *M*. These problems are not severe when the two agents are ex ante symmetric and have exponentially distributed costs (this scenario contains uniformly distributed cost as a special case).[5]

3.5. Delegation and Collusion

How are the preceding results modified in the presence of collusion among agents? One heuristic view is that centralized contracting is generally vulnerable to collusion (e.g., it undermines P's efforts to induce competition among agents when they supply substitutes), whereas delegation is not vulnerable, as the latter already incorporates a form of side-contracting between agents. Hence, collusion increases the relative value of delegation and renders it optimal in a wider class of circumstances. Extending the models considered above allows us to appraise the extent to which this view is correct. In fact, once we allow for collusion among agents, the Revelation Principle no longer applies. Is it possible that delegation can then be superior to centralization?

4. Again, this result holds for the case of continuously distributed costs. The result as stated is an implication of Proposition 5 in Mookherjee and Tsumagari (2004). Severinov (2008) considers the case of a discrete set of cost types and provides detailed results concerning how the comparison depends on the degree of substitutability and asymmetry across agents. However, the results are broadly similar to the continuous distribution case.

5. Da Rocha and de Frutos (1999) and Severinov (2008) provide examples where delegation performs worse than centralization, owing to asymmetries between the agents, even when they perform complementary tasks.

The first note of caution is that the results concerning the incentive-constrained optimality of delegation ($P - A_1^* - A_2$) described above relied on particular assumptions regarding the nature of side-contracting that are inconsistent with collusive behavior. For instance, P must be able to observe side-payments between the two agents or their relative contribution to the firm's revenues. The profit center arrangement implies A_1's compensation increases by less than a dollar for every dollar's increment in payments to A_2. This will tempt A_1 to pad costs or payments to A_2, in exchange for under-the-table kickbacks. The manager must be prevented from communicating with the subordinate before contracting with the owner. Preventing either of these actions will typically be difficult for P. In the absence of the ability to monitor side-payments between the agents, I have already noted that the firm will be prone to the empire-building tendency of the manager, and delegation is then no longer a second-best option.

However, centralization is also vulnerable to collusion. For instance, consider the case of a procurement auction designed by P between two competing and ex ante symmetric agents. The second-best mechanism is a second-price auction, which creates strong incentives for the suppliers to enter into a hidden agreement to raise their cost reports. Whether centralization or delegation is more vulnerable to collusion is therefore a nontrivial question.

The answer depends partly on the precise way that collusion is modeled. Most of the literature follows Tirole (1986) and ignores possible problems with the enforceability of side-contracts. The usual handwaving justification offered for this assumption is that the agents are engaged in a long-term relationship with one another and can thus enter into self-enforcing agreements. Additional problems arise with the allocation of bargaining power within the coalition of colluding agents. Owing to asymmetric information among the agents regarding their respective costs, the Coase Theorem does not apply to the analysis of ex ante optimal side contracts: the allocation of bargaining power affects decisions they make concerning the cost reports they decide to send P in a coordinated fashion. This is one complicating feature of this class of models compared with the context studied by Tirole (where there was effectively complete information within the coalition of the agent and the supervisor, so that their joint behavior could be represented simply by that of a consolidated entity earning the sum of their respective payoffs). There is a nontrivial contracting-within-contracting aspect to the problem.

A related question concerns how the allocation of bargaining power between colluding agents varies between the centralized and decentralized contracting regimes. Laffont and Martimort (1998) postulate that it is symmetric in the centralized regime and asymmetric in the decentralized one. This idea seems intuitive, insofar as the two agents are at the same layer of the hierarchy in the centralized world and at different layers in the decentralized one. However, the idea seems to be based on the notion that the structure of unobserved side-contracting (which is hidden, illegal, or informal) reflects the structure of the regular or permitted contracts in the respective hierarchies. Their theory provides no account of why this may be so.

The Laffont and Martimort (1998) model focuses on the restrictive case of the standard model with two agents (i.e., where costs take two possible values for each agent, and tasks are perfectly complementary). In centralization with collusion, the two agents enter into an ex ante side-contract, which agrees on a coordinated set of cost reports submitted to P and associated hidden side-transfers between themselves. This side-contract is chosen to maximize the sum of their ex ante payoffs, subject to incentive and participation constraints within the coalition. The incentive constraint states that each agent has an incentive to report his cost truthfully within the coalition; the participation constraint states that each agent must attain at least the expected utility he would attain by not entering the collusive agreement and playing the mechanism designed by P noncooperatively.

In contrast in the delegation setting, Laffont and Martimort assume that A_1 makes a take-it-or-leave-it offer of an unobserved side-contract, in which the agents again coordinate the cost report that A_1 makes to P on their joint behalf and enter into side-transfers unobserved by P. There are two main differences in the nature of this side-contracting problem. First, the objective function is different: it is the expected utility of A_1 alone. Second, the participation constraint is different. Because P does not offer a formal contract to A_2 and delegates this authority to A_1, A_2 does not have the option of participating in another mechanism, should he refuse the side-contract offered by A_1.

Using the restrictive version of the standard model with ex ante symmetric agents, Laffont and Martimort (1998) find that delegation and centralization both achieve equivalent (second-best) profits for P, irrespective of whether there is collusion. This is no longer the case when there is an additional constraint of symmetric treatment of the agents—which they interpret either as a "fairness" requirement or the result of communication or information processing costs (wherein P can only keep track of the aggregate cost $\hat{\theta}_1 + \hat{\theta}_2$ reported by the two agents, rather than their separate cost reports). They find then that delegation still achieves second-best profit, but centralization does not. The control of collusion requires asymmetric treatment of the two agents, which is not permitted in the centralized regime but is possible in the delegation setting owing to the asymmetry in bargaining power that it allows through a side-contract.

Bargaining power shifts to A_1 in the delegation setting for two reasons in the Laffont and Martimort (1998) theory. The first results from the assumption that the implied welfare weight on A_2's expected payoff is zero under delegation but is equal to that on A_1's payoff under centralization. This consideration is based on an implicit assumption of a change in the bargaining protocol itself as a result of a shift in the formal contracting regime. The second reason for a diminution of A_2's relative bargaining power is that he no longer has a backup option of participating noncooperatively.

This second reason for the reduction in bargaining power of A_2 is intrinsic to the nature of the contracting: delegation gives no back-up noncooperative option to A_2 should he refuse to collude, unlike centralization. The first reason is less intrinsic: it seems conceivable that the bargaining protocol itself does not change as a result of the formal contracting regime. For instance, if the two agents belong to a union, cartel, or industry association with fairness norms, which require equal treatment, and this association mediates the collusion, the allocation of welfare weights would not change across the two regimes. Therefore, it seems more natural to keep the bargaining protocol itself unchanged by the contracting regime and focus only on the second reason for alteration in bargaining power, which is entirely intrinsic to the regimes concerned.

For this reason, most of the subsequent literature assumes that welfare weights do not change between centralization and delegation; only the participation constraint for the side-contract differs. It is assumed that in both regimes, the same agent A_1 makes a take-it-or-leave-it offer of side contract to A_2.

If collusion is modeled in this way, it is evident that delegation cannot outperform centralization. A version of the Revelation Principle reappears: any outcome achieved by delegation can be replicated under centralization with P designing a contract that is null for A_2 (i.e., offers no transfers or production assignments to this agent). Then the nature of the constraints in P's contracting problem are exactly the same, because the induced side-contracting games are identical.

The question to be resolved, then, is whether delegation is costly relative to centralization. In other words, is it valuable for P to contract with both agents rather than just one of them? Doing so allows her to manipulate the bargaining power within the coalition.

One additional ingredient of the models need to be mentioned: the treatment of participation constraints in the contract offered by P. Some authors (e.g., Mookherjee and Tsumagari 2004) assume these are ex post (i.e., the agents decide whether to agree to participate after exchanging cost reports within the coalition). Others, such as Faure-Grimaud et al. (2003) and Celik (2009), assume these constraints are interim: participation decisions must be made at the outset, before the agents have had an opportunity to communicate with each other.

Mookherjee and Tsumagari consider the standard model with continuous types with two agents; they compare centralized contracting ($P^* - (A_1, A_2)$) with delegation to one of the productive agents ($P - A_1^* - A_2$) and to delegation to an intermediary ($P - M^* - (A_1, A_2)$), who is perfectly informed about the agents' costs.[6] Using ex post participation constraints (in the sense described above, where agents can collude on their participation decisions as well as on reports), they find the same rankings between these regimes hold as in the case of no collusion. Specifically, centralized contracting is always superior to delegation to one of the agents, while the ranking of the former vis-à-vis delegation to M depends on whether the two agents supply substitute or complementary inputs. Similar results also obtain in the discrete types case, where M is not perfectly informed about the agents' costs, provided M is sufficiently well informed. These results provide an explanation of Chandler's (1962) observation that authority tends to be predominantly delegated by owners to managers who are pure intermediaries and not personally involved in productive tasks; their principal responsibility is to supervise and coordinate complementary tasks carried out by different workers.

Faure-Grimaud et al. (2003) and Celik (2009) consider analogous questions in a setting with one agent A and one supervisor M, a discrete set of cost types, and where M is better informed than P but not perfectly informed about A's cost. Although both sets of authors assume participation decisions in the mechanism offered by P must be made at the interim stage, their models differ with respect to details of the information structure. Faure-Grimaud et al. study the two cost type case, where M receives a signal that also takes two possible values. They find that delegation to M (i.e., ($P - M^* - A$)) and centralization ($P^* - (M, A)$) achieve equivalent payoffs for P. In contrast, Celik considers a case with three cost types, where M's information consists of a partition of the state space. He finds that delegation to M does strictly worse. Hence, the cost of delegation in these papers seems very sensitive to the fine details of the information structure.

The results of Mookherjee and Tsumagari (2004) and Celik (2009) are similar and have a similar intuition. Collusion renders inoperable the second-best optimality of delegation, owing

---

6. Baliga and Sjöström (1998) compare centralized contracting with delegation to one of the agents in a setting with moral hazard with limited liability, rather than adverse selection. They find that the two are equivalent in a wide variety of circumstances, though not in all.

to the DMR problem (i.e., the adverse selection problem between the manager and his subordinate). The incidence of this problem can be reduced by raising the bargaining power of the subordinate vis-à-vis the manager. This can be achieved by P contracting with both agents, so as to allow A_2 (or A in the case of the Celik model) a positive outside option if he refuses the side-contract offered by A_1 (or M in the case of the Celik model). However, it is not easy to provide a simple intuition for why the same does not happen in the case considered by Faure-Grimaud et al. (2003).

Motta (2009) argues that the analyses of Faure-Grimaud et al. (2003) and Celik (2009) impose the overly restrictive assumption that contracts offered by P in the centralized regime are always accepted by both M and A on the equilibrium path. He shows that if we continue to assume that both parties must decide on whether to participate in P's mechanism at the interim stage (i.e., before they can collude), then a centralized mechanism exists in which the second-best outcome can be achieved. This result is true for either of the type or information structures considered by Faure-Grimaud et al. (2003) and Celik (2009). The mechanism constructed by Motta (2009) involves offering a menu of contracts to A in which some options selected by A are associated with M not being employed to supervise A. These are tantamount to allowing an amnesty scheme or self-reporting by A, which obviates the necessity of supervision. Motta shows that such schemes are useful in combating collusion, irrespective of how bargaining power is distributed within the coalition. Hence, using such mechanisms, which further augment the bargaining power of A, allows the problem of collusion to be completely overcome in the centralized regime, irrespective of the structure of information available to M. At the same time, delegation continues to be unable to achieve the second-best outcome, owing to the weak bargaining power of A in that regime. This observation suggests that centralization is superior to delegation in the presence of collusion, when agents cannot collude in their participation. Whether this continues to be so for the more relevant case, where agents and supervisors can collude in their participation decisions as well, has not yet been studied.

In summary, the dust has yet to settle on how to model collusion and what it implies for the optimality of delegation. If delegation and centralization do not change bargaining weights of colluding participants, delegation cannot be superior to centralization. Whether it is inferior to centralization depends on the context and fine details of the nature of collusion.

4. Contractual Incompleteness, Renegotiation, and Complexity

The preceding section considered contexts of complete contracts, in which the principal can commit to a comprehensive mechanism in which there are no restrictions on (1) the ability of agents to communicate their private information or (2) the principal to process this information, make decisions, and communicate corresponding instructions back to agents. These assumptions, combined with noncooperative behavior of agents, allow the Revelation Principle to hold, implying that delegation cannot outperform centralization. To understand the benefits of delegation, it is therefore necessary to explore settings where the assumptions underlying the Revelation Principle fail to apply. Because the last section showed that collusion among agents does not provide a convincing theory of the benefits of delegation, it is necessary to explore some of the other assumptions. This requirement confirms the well-known proposition (going back to Williamson [1975] and reiterated by Hart [1995]) that one needs an incomplete contract framework to have a cogent theory of allocation of control rights in an organization.

Contractual incompleteness is, however, a very broad notion, and there are different approaches to modeling it. The simplest approach is to exogenously rule out complete contracts and impose "realistic" restrictions on contracts (e.g., limiting their duration or the kinds of contingencies they can incorporate). Aghion and Tirole (1997), Dessein (2002), Alonso et al. (2008), Bester and Krähmer (2008), and Rantakari (2008) use this approach to model the costs and benefits of delegation. Most of these models model communication between A and P under centralization as a cheap-talk game, where the latter is unable to commit ex ante to decisions following any particular set of reports received. This restriction is the principal drawback of centralization, which limits the amount of information that the agent communicates, owing to the desire of the latter to manipulate the principal's subsequent decision. In contrast, decentralization results in decisions that depend more sensitively on the agent's information but tend to serve A's personal interests rather than P's. We pass over this interesting literature, because it is described in some detail in Bolton and Dewatripont (this volume). Hereafter I focus instead on theories where incompleteness arises endogenously from either of two additional frictions: inability of the principal to commit, and costs of communication or contractual complexity.

4.1. Commitment Problems

In many contexts it can be difficult for P to commit to deviate from ex ante promises and behave in a certain way in particular ex post contingencies, even though the latter can be anticipated and specified in advance. The reason is that ex ante decisions promised by P may not be optimal ex post, as the former may have been prompted by the need to provide certain kinds of incentives to A. Once the required actions have been chosen by A, then P may wish to revert to a different decision, which is in the subsequent ex post mutual interest of P and A. Delegation of authority to an independent third party may be a way to overcome this commitment problem.

Examples of this time-inconsistency problem in the context of monetary policy have been familiar to macroeconomists since the work of Kydland and Prescott (1977). Governments with a short-term interest in expansionary monetary policy tend to create excessive inflation when they possess discretionary control. This problem forms the primary motivation for delegation of monetary policy to an independent central bank (Rogoff 1985). The solution to the problem of commitment to an anti-inflationary monetary policy is for the government to delegate day-to-day policymaking to bureaucrats or technocrats with a known commitment to anti-inflationary policy and insulate them from short-term political pressure. Similar problems also arise in fiscal policy, such as the problem of bailouts of public sector firms or soft budget constraints (see, e.g., Dewatripoint and Maskin 1995; Qian and Weingast 1997), and in income tax audits (Melumad and Mookherjee 1989). Crémer (1995) provides an interesting model of commitment problems in organizations along similar lines, in the context of design of employment contracts: owners will find it difficult to follow through on threats to fire high-quality agents detected shirking, if these agents are expected to be superior relative to others who might replace them. Delegation of employment decisions to a manager who is provided strong incentives to fire unproductive workers via an incentive scheme may be a way of committing to implement termination threats that induce workers not to shirk.

One problem with this explanation of delegation is that it is based on an implicit assumption that it is easier for principals to commit to delegating the allocation of control rights than it is to commit to detailed decisions if they retain the rights themselves. There may be problems arising even with these delegation arrangements, wherein P may seek to reallocate control rights ex post or attempt to influence the decisions made by agents to whom authority has been delegated (for a detailed analysis, see Katz 1991). In Cremer's model, for instance, if employment decisions were delegated to a manager who is supposed to be penalized for retaining unproductive workers, the owner would have an ex post incentive for not applying this penalty when the worker in question was discovered to be of high quality. Neither the worker nor manager would have an interest in opposing P's opportunistic intervention. Hence, there could be problems with the enforcement of commitments to delegate. It is not clear whether and why it is easier to commit to delegate authority than to actual decisions.

A tighter argument for the value of delegation on the basis of renegotiation problems is provided by Beaudry and Poitevin (1995) and Poitevin (1995, 2000) in the context of a standard principal-agent production problem. Opportunities for (ex post Pareto-improving) renegotiation are provided in both centralized and decentralized environments. They show that the decentralized regime is less vulnerable to renegotiation and can accordingly generate a higher level of payoff for P.

The argument is simplest in a single-agent setting. Suppose the agent A produces a at a cost of θa, which generates revenue $B(a)$ to P, and A is privately informed about the realization of θ. Under centralization the contracting game is as follows. In stage 1 P offers a contract $a(\theta)$, $t(\theta)$. In stage 2 A observes the realization of θ, decides whether to participate, and submits a cost report to P. In stage 3 P can offer a new contract to A. If A accepts, the game continues with the new contract in force. Otherwise, the previous contract continues to apply. The output and transfer are then determined by the prevailing contract and the report already submitted by A.

Attention can be restricted to contracts that are not renegotiated on the equilibrium path. It can then be shown that the equilibrium renegotiation-proof allocation must be separating (i.e., P will learn the true cost of A at the end of stage 2).[7] Hence, P will subsequently offer an ex post efficient allocation in stage 3. Thus, the second-best solution (i.e., the allocation associated with a commitment contract) cannot be supported in the presence of opportunities for renegotiation as long as it involves ex post distortions.

Now consider delegation, wherein P offers A an incentive contract $t(a)$ in stage 1. In stage 2 A observes θ, decides whether to participate, and selects a. In stage 3 P observes a and can offer a new contract. But given that a has already been chosen, the only scope for renegotiation is over the transfer payment. But there cannot be any scope for an ex post Pareto-improving renegotiation over the transfer payment alone. Hence, the second-best allocation can be implemented under delegation. It follows that delegation typically dominates centralization, as it is less vulnerable to renegotiation. The key difference is that under centralization, decisions over production and transfers are made by P following communication from the agent. Under delegation, renegotiation can happen after the production decision has already been made by A.

Does this difference suggest that delegation generally outperforms centralization? Poitevin (1995) points out that this is not the case when P also receives relevant information after signing

---

7. See Beaudry and Poitevin (1995: 315, proposition 5) for details.

the initial contract. Suppose P learns the value of a market parameter η that enters the revenue function $B(a; \eta)$ at the same time that A learns the realization of cost θ. Delegating production decisions to A without any communication from P regarding the realization of η would then imply independence of production decisions with regard to the realization of market information. Conversely, the benefit of centralization based on communication of cost information from A would be that production decisions would be responsive to market information, at the cost of being vulnerable to renegotiation with A. There are now four possible organizational alternatives: pure centralization (decisions are made by P without communication from A), pure decentralization without communication (production decisions are made by A without communication from P about the realization of η), and corresponding versions with communication (which Poitevin calls a "hierarchy"). A hierarchy is more responsive to information about both cost and market parameters, at the cost of being more vulnerable to renegotiation.

4.2. Communication and Complexity Costs

Melumad et al. (1992, 1997) explore the implications of costly communication or contractual complexity for the costs and benefits of delegation vis-à-vis centralization, in the context of the standard production model with one principal and two agents. Their 1992 paper focuses on communication costs, which are argued to arise from expertise of agents not shared by P, which makes it impossible for the agents to communicate all they know to the latter. Languages used by P and agents may not be exactly the same, and they could lack a rich enough shared vocabulary. There could also be limits on P's ability to process the reports sent by the agents in a given time limit within which decisions need to be made.

Such restrictions are incorporated as an (exogenous) finite limit on the message set available to any agent for communicating with P (under either centralization or decentralization), while the agent's private information is real valued. Thus, full revelation is impossible: agents must compress what they know into messages in a way that entails loss of information. The finite limit could represent a common finite alphabet used for communication. Alternatively, if sending each bit of information takes one unit of time, then a given time limit for making decisions imposes an upper bound to the number of bits that can be communicated. This approach is similar to the one used in computer science to measure communicational complexity, that is, the tree complexity of communication protocols (Karchmer 1989; Segal 1995). Nevertheless, Melumad et al. (1992) do not model the underlying sources of the communication restrictions. Instead they impose a common restriction on the size of message sets that applies uniformly to both centralization and decentralization, and then they compare their performance under any given size restriction. This approach follows in the tradition of earlier models of Green and Laffont (1986, 1987). A similar approach was adopted by Laffont and Martimort (1998), in which P was assumed to only be able to receive aggregates of cost reports sent by different agents.

The Melumad et al. (1992) model imposes a number of additional restrictions on communication and contracting. Only one round of communication takes place, either sequentially or simultaneously. Other conditions ensure zero control loss from delegation in a full communication setting: risk neutrality, suitable monitoring, and sequencing of contracts to eliminate collusion and the DMR problem. Then for any finite message-set restrictions, delegation is shown to outperform centralization. A similar result is obtained in their follow-up 1997 paper, in which restrictions on communication are derived from restrictions on complexity of contracts, where the latter is measured by the total number of contingencies (which correspond to message combinations under centralization, and message-action combinations under decentralization). The underlying idea is that finite communication restrictions prevent agents from fully revealing their real-valued cost realizations to P under centralization. Delegating decisionmaking authority to agents enables decisions to be based on more localized information, resulting in a flexibility gain. Offsetting this gain is the incentive (DMR) problem, which cannot be fully overcome, owing to limits on communication. The trade-off is then based on a comparison of the flexibility gain and the control loss, and the former prevails under the conditions stated.

At the same time, if P lacks the ability to monitor detailed production assignments or transfers between the agents, examples can be constructed where the control losses inherent in delegation may outweigh the gains in flexibility, ensuring that centralization is superior. Hence, the theory provides contexts in which either one of the two modes is superior, depending on the ability of P to monitor the side contract.

These results provide a rationale for studying conditions for delegation to be optimal with complete contracts: the very conditions that ensure this turn out to ensure that delegation is superior to centralization when communication or contractual complexity is costly. When delegation with complete contracts is inferior, it may also be so when contracts are incomplete, owing to communication or complexity costs. In general, there is a trade-off between the flexibility advantage of delegation (which arises only when contracts are incomplete) and its control loss (which also arises when contracts are complete).

Nevertheless, several problems remain with this theory, as discussed in a recent paper by Mookherjee and Tsumagari (2008). For one, the restriction to a single round of communication is ad hoc: most real-world organizations are characterized by interactive multistage communication between agents. The mechanism design problem includes the design of communication protocols. Mookherjee and Tsumagari consider a context in which agents take time to read and write messages, and production decisions need to be made within a finite time horizon, combined with time taken to read and write messages. This consideration allows a wide range of finite communication protocols, varying with regard to the number of rounds and message-set size at each round.

Mookherjee and Tsumagari (2008) develop a theory of mechanism design that allows a broad class of finite communication protocols with multiple stages, as well as a wide range of mechanisms where different components of contracting, communication, and production can be centralized or decentralized. Based on an assumption that messages exchanged between agents are costlessly verifiable by P, they show that centralized contracting can generally perform as well as decentralized contracting. At the same time, decentralized production and communication systems generally outperform centralized ones, owing to the greater flexibility they allow in the choice of production and coordination of information across agents. In other words, it indicates the optimality of an intermediate form of organization, where contracting and monitoring are centralized while production decisions are decentralized, as in the prototypical Japanese firm (e.g., Aoki 1990).[8]

---

8. However, when communication between agents is difficult to verify by employers, they provide an example where decentralized contracting outperforms centralized contracts.

5. More Complex Hierarchies

The preceding two sections have been concerned with foundational issues in the modeling of costs and benefits of delegating control to managers or intermediaries. Accordingly, they focused on simple contexts involving one principal or owner; one manager; and one or two agents, who play a productive role. In this section I describe models of more complex hierarchies, involving more agents or departments, which help address a number of additional questions concerning the organization of hierarchies. An example of such a question concerns the grouping of activities into different departments. In *Strategy and Structure*, Chandler (1962) described the evolution of many large, vertically integrated firms producing a multitude of products in various regions or markets from unitary (U-form) to multidivisional (M-form) organizations. In the former, departments are organized along functional lines: departments concentrate plants and activities producing the same input or intermediate good. In the latter, they are organized by product, market, or region, with each division being internally vertically integrated and relatively independent of other divisions (except for overhead, capital, or top management, which are allocated by top management across divisions). Socialist economies likewise can be organized by ministries producing specific intermediate inputs (as in the erstwhile Soviet economy) or by regions, each of which is relatively self-contained (as in the Chinese economy). Chandler argued that the shift away from the U-form freed up the time and effort of central management from day-to-day management of operations in each division, required by the need to coordinate the activities of different divisions. By using the M-form, they could delegate internal management of divisions to divisional managers and focus on long-range issues. However, this form meant giving up the advantages of scale economies and specialization made possible by the concentration of similar activities within the same division in the U-form.

Understanding this dimension of organizational design requires extension of the models described in previous sections to incorporate multiple divisions and problems of horizontal coordination across these divisions. The previous models can be thought of as organizations consisting of a single division, with a focus on problems of vertical control and coordination.

Rotemberg (1999) provides an interesting model in which the key trade-off between a U-form and a M-form hierarchy involves coordination versus control. A firm produces two products A and B and two associated intermediate inputs 1 and 2, each of which is required in the production of either good. There are four agents or plant managers, represented by a combination of a product and an input used for that product. Rotemberg assumes that a pair of agents will have a common supervisor and will thereby form a division. Implicit here is an exogenous upper bound on the span of control: a supervisor cannot oversee more than two agents. This restriction rules out a fully centralized firm with a single division that contains all four agents. Rotemberg assumes, therefore, that the firm has two divisions and two corresponding supervisors, who jointly own it. Another important assumption is that the supervisors operate independently and cannot share any information with each other.

In the U-form, divisions are organized by the inputs produced: division i produces input i and includes the two plants iA and iB producing this input, where $i = 1, 2$. In the M-form, they are organized by products: division j produces product j and includes the plants $1j$ and $2j$ producing the two inputs needed for this product, where $j = A, B$. Each plant ij has to choose a level of activity x^i_j and a method m^i_j. The inputs used in the production of each product need to be coordinated: there is a loss function for each product j that depends on the difference in activity levels x_j^1, x_j^2. The M-form allows better coordination, because it groups different plants involved in the same product group into the same department.

The optimal method of producing the same input across different products is the same. Incentive problems arise with respect to the choice of method, about whose costs the respective plant managers are privately informed. The main advantage of the U-form is that the supervisor controls two agents producing the same input, thus allowing the report of each agent to discipline the other. Hence, the U-form allows for better control of incentive problems.

The model has a number of interesting predictions. The U-form involves less high-powered incentives for plant managers, owing to the better information available to the corresponding supervisor. As the firm expands in scale, it adds more plants in each division. In the M-form there are now multiple plants producing the same input, which helps reduce the incentive problem. But the U-form continues to be subject to coordination losses. Hence, for sufficiently large scale, the M-form must dominate. This result helps explain how American firms shifted from one form to the other as described by Chandler (1962): the coordination problems with the U-form became worse relative to the control problems as firms grew in scale.

Mookherjee and Reichelstein (1997, 2001) provide a model of hierarchies that generalizes the standard production model of preceding sections to the context of many agents, departments, and products. They provide general sufficient conditions on the structure of the organizational production function or technology for a hierarchy with an arbitrary number of branches and layers to be able to achieve second-best profits for P. The mechanism they use extends the profit or cost center mechanism described in Section 3 for the case of two agents who form a single division. With multiple divisions that constitute different branches of the hierarchy at any given layer, the mechanism has to ensure horizontal coordination across these branches as well as vertical coordination and control across layers in any given branch. In addition to the assumptions concerning the sequencing of contracts and absence of collusion and of risk aversion or limited liability constraints, the key assumption required is that the organization of the hierarchy is consistent with the technology being used. This stipulation means that the technology is recursively decomposable into the production of intermediate inputs at different stages of production, and each plant has constant returns to scale.

Absent incentive problems, this consistency condition implies that an optimal production plan can be formed for the firm as a whole, with (one-dimensional) cost reports (or budgets or forecasts) sent by agents that flow up the hierarchy, which are aggregated at each layer and passed up by each manager to his manager in turn. Subsequently, production targets are formed at the top of the hierarchy, and these then flow down the hierarchy. Each divisional manager forms a contingent production plan, allocating production responsibility across subordinate divisions on the basis of their respective cost reports and the aggregate production target assigned to the division. Mookherjee and Reichelstein (1997, 2001) show that the same kind of mechanism can be used even in the presence of incentive problems, where each agent is self-interested. It requires an initial phase to be added wherein contracts flow down the hierarchy; the manager at any layer offers a contract to each subordinate, which the latter must respond to prior to offering contracts to their subordinates in turn. The assumptions required are the same as those that ensure optimality of delegation in a three-layer hierarchy: top-down contracting, monitoring of costs, and risk neutrality of all agents. The construction resembles the Calvo and Wellisz (1978) method of replicating the three-layer hierarchy to accommodate more layers and branches. Under these conditions, then, there is no limit to the size of the hierarchy.

Applied to the question of U-form versus M-form, this model provides conditions when either can be optimal. The U-form is optimal if it is consistent with the technology being used—as would be the case if the firm produces a single product by combining different inputs, each of which is produced by multiple plants. Each division then corresponds to the production of a particular input. The M-form is consistent with the technology if the firm produces multiple products, each of which combines a number of inputs (some of which are used in different products). The divisions are then organized along product lines. Each division is independent of the others, except for allocation of some overhead facilities or capital resources by headquarters. When the technology takes this form, it is evident that the U-form is not consistent with it. This approach thus suggests the role of changing technology and product variety in explaining evolution from U-form to M-form organizations. With the emergence of multiple products produced by the same firm, the U-form would experience problems relative to the M-form in coordinating production of different inputs used in any given good. Specifically, it would no longer be possible to use a budgeting system based on one-dimensional cost and quantity aggregates for each division.

An alternative perspective on U-form versus M-form organizations is provided by Maskin et al. (2000). Their theory abstracts from coordination issues altogether and focuses on the informational and incentive implications of these alternatives. Similar to the basic Rotemberg (1999) model, the Maskin et al. model has a three-layer hierarchy producing two products $i = 1, 2$ in two different regions $r = A, B$. There are four plants, corresponding to a combination of a product and a region. Productivity shocks arise at the economy, regional, and industrial levels. The organizational structure assigns responsibility to managers to devote costly effort to improving productivity. Observed performance levels are the confluence of effort and shocks, giving rise to moral hazard problems. In both the U-form and M-form a top manager deals with the economywide shock. The essential difference arises at the middle layer of the hierarchy. In the U-form the departments are organized by industry, so there is a manager at the middle layer in each department whose effort affects the productivity of the two plants in the corresponding industry. In the M-form the departments are organized by region, so the middle manager's effort affects the performance of the two plants in two different industries, which happen to be located in the same region. Bottom-level managers' efforts affect the plants they are assigned to. In the U-form (resp. M-form), these correspond to different regions (resp. industries) within the same industry (resp. region). The two organizational forms thus differ in the assignment of tasks across managers. In the M-form, for instance, only one manager (located in the middle tier) in the organization is dealing with the regional shocks, whereas there are two managers in the U-form (located at the bottom layer in two different industry divisions) who deal with regional shocks.

Managers are risk averse, giving rise to a trade-off between risk-sharing and effort incentives in the design of their compensation schemes. "Yardstick" competition is an important way of dealing with these incentive problems, wherein an agent's performance is measured relative to that of peers whose performance is subject to similar (i.e., correlated) shocks. Maskin et al. (2000) show that the U-form and M-form offer identical opportunities for evaluating performance of managers in the top and bottom tiers, but they differ with regard to managers in the middle tier. If performance at the regional level (aggregating across industries) is more comparable (i.e., correlated) across regions, rather than performance at the industrial level (aggregating across regions), then the M-form allows more effective use of yardstick competition for middle managers. For top managers, there is no opportunity for yardstick competition (as in the model, this is the only firm in the economy). And for bottom-level managers, there exists one other manager in the firm whose performance provides a comparable yardstick in both organizations. The model thus predicts that performance differences will arise owing to differential managerial effort incentives at intermediate levels of the hierarchy. Maskin et al. (2000) go on to provide empirical evidence from Chinese firms that the structure of productivity shocks is such that performance is more comparable across regions than across industries. This result suggests the superiority of the M-form, thus providing a potential explanation for superior performance of the Chinese over the Soviet version of socialism.

6. Conclusion

The literature overviewed in this chapter pertains mainly to the microfoundations of an incentive-based theory of hierarchies. The holy grail of this field has been a formalization of Williamson's (1967) ideas of control loss in hierarchies based on incentive problems, and how it affects the size and structure of organizations. This effort has proved difficult, mainly because addressing this question requires understanding what managers do and the costs and benefits of delegating authority to them. Only when a basic model of management exists can the theory be used to address detailed questions concerning the nature of control loss and how it varies with the size and structure of the organization.

The models described in this chapter focus on a particular source of control loss in hierarchies: that arising from incentive problems associated with supervision and delegation of authority. They address questions about the design of compensation for supervisors, how these designs relate to the compensation of production workers, and attendant problems of collusion. The models help pose the question of choice among different organizational designs, highlighting the different dimensions involved in these designs even in the simplest contexts involving one or two productive agents and one manager: breadth (span of control) and depth (number of vertical layers); the extent of responsibility delegated at each level and related compensation rules and monitoring systems; and how contracts, communication, and production planning are sequenced. So far most of the models have been rudimentary, with only one or two production workers, one manager, and one owner. At the next step one expects these models will be used as building blocks for more complex organizations and design issues in the presence of more agents, managers, products, and intermediate goods.

Despite their simplicity, the models enable the age-old question of centralization versus decentralization to be posed in different concrete ways. They have also generated a wide range of applications in fields as diverse as management accounting (profit centers and budgeting [Mookherjee and Reichelstein 1997], transfer pricing [Edlin and Reichelstein 1995; Vaysman 1996, 1998; Baldenius and Reichelstein 2004], and auditing [Melumad and Mookherjee 1989; Kofman and Lawaree 1993]), fiscal decentralization (hard versus soft budget constraints [Dewatripont and Maskin 1995; Qian and Roland 1998], treatment of externalities [Klibanoff and Poitevin 2009], or accountability in local governments [Seabright 1996; Bardhan and

Mookherjee 2000, 2006]), procurement and regulation (Baron and Besanko 1992; Gilbert and Riordan 1995; Severinov 2008), and comparisons between Soviet-style and Chinese-style socialism (Qian and Weingast 1997; Maskin et al. 2000; Jin et al. 2005).

Nevertheless, much remains to be done. There is considerable scope and need to use these models to address more applied questions in industrial organization and enable closer integration with empirical work on the internal organization of firms. What are the effects of changes in information technology, competition in the product market, or openness to trade on the internal structure of firms? These issues have been discussed extensively in fields of management (e.g., Hammer and Champy 1993) and have been the subject of recent empirical studies (e.g., Brynjolfsson and Hitt 2000; Caroli and Van Reenen 2001; Bresnahan et al. 2002; Acemoglu et al. 2006; Rajan and Wulf 2006). With the exception of Acemoglu et al. (2006), most of this literature lacks a theoretical framework. A closer integration of theory and empirics would enrich these analyses and permit better understanding of normative implications.

Even in the context of purely theoretical analysis, significant challenges and open questions remain. An integration of incentive issues with costly information processing would represent a major step forward at the conceptual level. It would help formalize hierarchy design as a trade-off between information processing advantages with the incentive and control disadvantages of delegating authority. Issues concerning the design of more complex hierarchies still remain to be addressed, for example, models of delegation that address questions of size and structure of hierarchies and related implications for compensation, rents, and performance at different levels. The simple models described in this chapter suggest roles for collusion, limited liability, or managerial risk aversion as sources of control loss in hierarchies. They need to be embedded in more complex settings to develop detailed predictions concerning how the size and structure of firms are affected by technology and market parameters. This effort would then help realize the goal of constructing a Williamsonian model of hierarchies with secure microfoundations that can be empirically tested.

REFERENCES

Acemoglu, D., P. Aghion, L. Lelarge, J. Van Reenen, and F. Zilibotti. 2006. "Technology, Information and the Decentralization of the Firm." NBER Working Paper 12206, National Bureau of Economic Research, Cambridge, MA.

Aghion, P., and J. Tirole. 1997. "Formal and Real Authority in Organizations." *Journal of Political Economy* 105: 1–29.

Alonso, R., W. Dessen, and N. Matouschek. 2008. "When Does Coordination Require Centralization?" *American Economic Review* 98: 145–179.

Aoki, M. 1990. "Toward an Economic Model of the Japanese Firm." *Journal of Economic Literature* 28(1): 1–27.

Baker, G., R. Gibbons, and K. Murphy. 1999. "Informal Authority in Organizations." *Journal of Law, Economics, and Organization* 15: 56–73.

Baldenius, T., and S. Reichelstein. 2004. "External and Internal Pricing in Multidivisional Firms." Working Paper 1825(R), Graduate School of Business, Stanford University, Stanford, CA.

Baliga, S., and T. Sjöström. 1998. "Decentralization and Collusion." *Journal of Economic Theory* 83: 196–232.

Bardhan, P., and D. Mookherjee. 2000. "Capture and Governance at National and Local Levels." *American Economic Review* 90(Papers and Proceedings): 135–139.

———. 2006. "Corruption and Decentralization of Infrastructure Delivery in Developing Countries." *Economic Journal* 116: 107–133.

Baron, D. P., and D. Besanko. 1992. "Information, Control, and Organizational Structure." *Journal of Economics and Management Strategy* 1: 237–275.

Beaudry, P., and M. Poitevin. 1995. "Contract Renegotiation: A Simple Framework and Implications for Organization Theory." *Canadian Journal of Economics* 28: 302–335.

Bester, H., and D. Krähmer. 2008. "Delegation and Incentives." *RAND Journal of Economics* 39: 664–682.

Bresnahan, T., E. Brynjolfsson, and L. Hitt. 2002. "Information Technology, Workplace Organization, and the Demand for Skilled Labor: Firm-Level Evidence." *Quarterly Journal of Economics* 117: 339–376.

Brynjolfsson, E., and L. Hitt. 2000. "Beyond Computation: Information Technology, Organizational Transformation and Business Performance." *Journal of Economic Perspectives* 14(4): 23–48.

Calvo, G., and S. Wellisz. 1978. "Supervision, Loss of Control and the Optimal Size of the Firm." *Journal of Political Economy* 86: 943–952.

Caroli, E., and J. Van Reenen. 2001. "Skill-Biased Organizational Change." *Quarterly Journal of Economics* 116: 1148–1192.

Celik, G. 2009. "Mechanism Design with Collusive Supervision." *Journal of Economic Theory* 144(1): 69–95.

Chandler, A. 1962. *Strategy and Structure.* Cambridge, MA: MIT Press.

———. 1977. *The Visible Hand.* Cambridge, MA: Harvard University Press.

Coase, R. 1937. "The Nature of the Firm." *Economica* 4: 386–405.

Crémer, J. 1995. "Arm's Length Relationships." *Quarterly Journal of Economics* 110: 275–295.

Datta, S. 1996. "On Control Losses in Hierarchies." *Rationality and Society* 8(4): 387–412.

Da Rocha, J. M., and M. A. de Frutos. 1999. "A Note on the Optimal Structure of Production." *Journal of Economic Theory* 89: 234–246.

Dessein, W. 2002. "Authority and Communication in Organizations." *Review of Economic Studies* 69: 811–838.

Dewatripont, M., and E. Maskin. 1995. "Credit and Efficiency in Centralized and Decentralized Economies." *Review of Economic Studies* 62: 541–555.

Edlin, A., and S. Reichelstein. 1995. "Specific Investment under Negotiated Transfer Pricing: An Efficiency Result." *Accounting Review,* April 1995.

Faure-Grimaud, A., and D. Martimort. 2001. "Some Agency Costs of Intermediated Contracting." *Economics Letters* 71: 75–82.

Faure-Grimaud, A., J. J. Laffont, and D. Martimort. 2000. "A Theory of Supervision with Endogenous Transaction Costs." *Annals of Economics and Finance* 1: 231–263.

———. 2003. "Collusion, Delegation and Supervision with Soft Information." *Review of Economic Studies* 70: 253–280.

Gilbert, R., and M. Riordan. 1995. "Regulating Complementary Products: A Comparative Institutional Analysis." *RAND Journal of Economics* 26: 243–256.

Green, J., and J. Laffont. 1986. "Incentive Theory with Data Compression," in W. Heller, R. Starr, and D. Starrett (eds.), *Essays in Honor of Kenneth Arrow,* volume 3. Cambridge: Cambridge University Press, pp. 239–254.

———. 1987. "Limited Communication and Incentive Compatibility." in T. Groves, R. Radner, and S. Reiter (eds.), *Information, Incentives and Economic Mechanisms.* Minneapolis: University of Minnesota Press, pp. 308–329.

Hammer, M., and J. Champy. 1993. *Reengineering the Corporation.* New York: Harper-Collins.

Hart, O. 1995. *Firms, Contracts, and Financial Structure.* Oxford and New York: Oxford University Press and Clarendon Press.

Jin, H., Y. Qian, and B. Weingast. 2005. "Regional Decentralization and Fiscal Incentives: Federalism, Chinese Style." *Journal of Public Economics* 89: 1719–1742.

Karchmer, M. 1989. *Communication Complexity and Circuit Depth.* Cambridge, MA: MIT Press.

Katz, M. 1991. "Game-Playing Agents: Unobservable Contracts as Precommitment." *RAND Journal of Economics* 22: 307–328.

Klibanoff, P., and M. Poitevin. 2009. "A Theory of (De)Centralization." Working paper, Kellogg School of Management, Northwestern University, Chicago.

Kofman, F., and J. Lawaree. 1993. "Collusion in Hierarchical Agency." *Econometrica* 61: 629–656.

Kydland, F., and E. Prescott. 1977. "Rules Rather than Indiscretion: Time Consistency of Optimal Plans." *Journal of Political Economy* 85: 473–492.

Laffont, J. J., and D. Martimort. 1998. "Collusion and Delegation." *Rand Journal of Economics* 29: 280–305.

Macho-Stadler, I., and J. D. Perez-Castrillo. 1998. "Centralized and Decentralized Contracts in a Moral Hazard Environment." *Journal of Industrial Economics* 46: 489–510.

Marshall, A. 1920. *Principles of Economics,* eighth edition. London: Macmillan.

Maskin, E., Y. Qian, and C. Xu. 2000. "Incentives, Information and Organizational Form." *Review of Economic Studies* 67: 359–378.

McAfee, P., and J. McMillan. 1995. "Organizational Diseconomies of Scale." *Journal of Economics and Management Strategy* 4: 399–426.

Melumad, N., and D. Mookherjee. 1989. "Delegation as Commitment: The Case of Income Tax Audits." *RAND Journal of Economics* 20: 139–163.

Melumad, N., and S. Reichelstein. 1989. "Value of Communication in Agencies." *Journal of Economic Theory* 47: 334–368.

Melumad, N., D. Mookherjee, and S. Reichelstein. 1992. "A Theory of Responsibility Centers." *Journal of Accounting and Economics* 15: 445–484.

———. 1995. "Hierarchical Decentralization of Incentive Contracts." *RAND Journal of Economics* 26: 654–672.

———. 1997. "Contract Complexity, Incentives and the Value of Delegation." *Journal of Economics and Management Strategy* 6: 257–289.

Milgrom, P., and J. Roberts. 1992. *Economics, Organization and Management.* Upper Saddle River, NJ: Prentice Hall.

Mookherjee, D., and S. Reichelstein. 1997. "Budgeting and Hierarchical Control." *Journal of Accounting Research* 35: 129–155.

———. 2001. "Incentives and Coordination in Hierarchies." *B. E. Journal of Theoretical Economics* 1(1). Available at: http://works.bepress.com/dilip_mookherjee/1.

Mookherjee, D., and M. Tsumagari. 2004. "The Organization of Supply Networks: Effects of Delegation and Intermediation." *Econometrica* 72: 1179–1220.

———. 2008. "Mechanism Design with Limited Communication: Implications for Decentralization." Mimeo, Department of Economics, Boston University, Boston.

Motta, A. 2009. "Collusion and Selective Supervision." Working paper 93, Universita Degli Studi Di Padova, Padua.

Myerson, R. 1982. "Optimal Coordination Mechanisms in Generalized Principal Agent Problems." *Journal of Mathematical Economics* 10: 67–81.

Poitevin, M. 1995. "Contract Renegotiation and Organizational Design." Working paper 95-3, Center for Inter-University Research and Analysis of Organizations, Montreal.

Poitevin, M. 2000. "Can the Theory of Incentives Explain Decentralization?" *Canadian Journal of Economics* 33: 878–906.

Qian, Y. 1994. "Incentives and Loss of Control in Optimal Hierarchy." *Review of Economic Studies* 61: 527–544.

Qian, Y., and G. Roland. 1998. "Federalism and the Soft Budget Constraint." *American Economic Review* 88(5): 1143–1162.

Qian, Y., and B. Weingast. 1997. "Federalism as a Commitment to Preserving Market Incentives." *Journal of Economic Perspectives* 11: 83–92.

Radner, R., and J. Marschak. 1972. *Economic Theory of Teams.* New Haven, CT: Yale University Press.

Rajan, R., and J. Wulf. 2006. "The Flattening Firm: Evidence from Panel Data on the Changing Nature of Corporate Hierarchies." *Review of Economics and Statistics* 88: 759–773.

Rantakari, H. 2008. "Governing Adaptation." *Review of Economic Studies* 75: 1257–1285.

Rogoff, K. 1985. "The Optimal Degree of Commitment to an Intermediate Monetary Target." *Quarterly Journal of Economics* 100: 1169–1189.

Rotemberg, J. 1999. "Process versus Function Based Hierarchies." *Journal of Economics and Management Strategy* 8: 453–487.

Seabright, P. 1996. "Accountability and Decentralization in Government: An Incomplete Contracts Model." *European Economic Review* 40(1): 61–89.

Segal, I. 1995. "Communication Complexity and Coordination by Authority." Mimeo, Department of Economics, University of California, Berkeley.

Severinov, S. 2008. "The Value of Information and Optimal Organization." *RAND Journal of Economics* 39: 238–265.

Simon, H. 1951. "A Formal Model of the Employment Relation." *Econometrica* 19: 293–305.

———. 1955. "A Behavioral Model of Rational Choice." *Quarterly Journal of Economics* 69(1): 99–118.

Tirole, J. 1986. "Hierarchies and Bureaucracies: On the Role of Collusion in Organizations." *Journal of Law, Economics, and Organization* 2: 181–214.

———. 1988. *The Theory of Industrial Organization.* Cambridge, MA: MIT Press.

Tsumagari, M. 1999. "Supervision and Firm Structure." Working paper, Department of Economics, Keio University, Tokyo, Japan.

Van den Steen, E. 2010. "Interpersonal Authority in a Theory of the Firm." *American Economic Review* 100: 466–490.

Vaysman, I. 1996. "A Model of Cost-Based Transfer Pricing." *Journal of Accounting Studies* 1: 73–108.

———. 1998. "A Model of Negotiated Transfer Pricing." *Journal of Accounting and Economics* 25: 349–384.

Williamson, O. 1967. "Hierarchical Control and Optimal Firm Size." *Journal of Political Economy* 75: 123–138.

———. 1975. *Markets and Hierarchies: Analysis and Antitrust Implications.* New York: Free Press.

———. 1981. "The Economics of Organization: The Transaction Cost Approach." *American Journal of Sociology* 87: 548–577.

20

Strategy and Organization

John Roberts and Garth Saloner

1. Introduction

A firm's business strategy is a set of choices about what business it will be in, which products and services it will offer, which customers it will seek to serve, where it will operate, and which of the activities that are needed to realize these plans it will undertake itself rather than leave to others. A strategy sets direction and provides a standard against which later options can be evaluated. It is not a complete specification of all the decisions a firm must make, but it does fix enough of these choices to facilitate coordination of later decisions. It also can have a role in motivation.

Strategy has a central role in business management and, correspondingly, in business schools. It has not featured very much in economics, however, although industrial economics and game theory have had major influences on the study—and even the practice of—strategic management.[1]

In particular, organizational economics has largely developed without paying much explicit attention to strategy. Most chapters in this volume can be thought of as studying how to organize to maximize profits in a very general context. However, realizing a firm's strategy implies that it needs to carry out certain activities (product development, production, sales, etc.), and different strategy choices lead to different required activities. It seems likely that what the firm is trying to do might have a significant impact on how it is organized. The purpose of this chapter is to examine the (mostly very recent) research that has paid attention to the connection between strategy and organization and to point to what seem to be interesting issues for organizational economists in this area.

The fundamental assumption on which this chapter is based is that firm performance is determined by three broad factors: the economic, legal, regulatory, social, and technological *environment* in which it operates; the *strategy* it adopts to deal with that environment; and the

The authors are indebted to Robert Gibbons and Heikki Rantakari for numerous helpful comments and suggestions and to the participants in a meeting of the NBER Working Group in Organizational Economics devoted to reviewing early drafts of chapters from this handbook.

1. Popular treatments and textbook expositions include Dixit and Nalebuff (1991), McMillan (1992), Brandenberger and Nalebuff (1996), Saloner et al. (2001), McAfee (2002), and Besanko et al. (2009).

organization it puts in place, through which it seeks to implement its strategy. High performance involves finding "fit" among these three, where one cannot assume that there is a single best choice of strategy and organization for all environments. Success also requires maintaining alignment over time by altering the strategy and organization as the environment changes (Lawrence and Lorsch 1967).

This chapter is organized as follows. Section 2 is devoted to establishing what strategy is, the roles it serves, its connection to some related managerial concepts, and how it comes about and changes. Section 3 examines what we mean by organization, some central issues and trade-offs in organizational design, the problem of establishing fit, and the basic connection between organization and competitive advantage at the level of a single-business firm or business unit. Section 4 looks at the multiproduct firm, its reasons for existence, and the connection between organization and corporate strategy.

2. Strategy

We begin by establishing what we mean by strategy. The management literature has offered a variety of definitions. We start by looking at the concept historically.

2.1. What Is Strategy?

While we do not propose to provide a history of the field of strategic management here, some background is useful in setting the context for this chapter. As a field of academic study the genesis of modern strategic management can be found in the Harvard Business School's general management approach to the subject of business policy. In 1912 Harvard Business School introduced its first course in the subject, designed to recognize the interrelationship among problems faced in specialized functions and the need for coordination among departments to achieve broad company objectives (for a more detailed discussion, see Ghemawat 2006). In the 1950s C. Roland Christensen and others stressed the notion that the firm's strategy should fit with the competitive environment, and by the late 1950s Kenneth R. Andrews was proposing an approach to strategy that called for a broad view of the firm and its objectives.

In his 1971 classic, *The Concept of Corporate Strategy,* Andrews wrote:

> Corporate strategy is the pattern of decisions in a company that determines and reveals its objectives, purposes, or goals, produces the principal policies and plans for achieving those goals, and defines the range of business the company is to pursue, the kind of economic and human organization it is or intends to be, and the nature of the economic and noneconomic contribution it intends to make to its shareholders, employees, customers, and communities. [Andrews 1971: 13]

The role of the general manager in this perspective is to set direction; to establish organizational structure, commitment, and policies to pursue the company's goals; and to ensure that the entire process is managed with an eye to corporate social responsibility and good corporate governance.

The next major innovation in the field occurred with Michael Porter's development of systematic frameworks for the analysis of industry structure and the firm's competitive positioning, culminating in his *Competitive Strategy* (Porter 1980). Although a great deal of economics bears on issues of relevance to Andrews's concept of strategy, it was the direct overlap of the domains of Porter's competitive strategy and the economics of industrial organization that caused the first major infusion of economic thinking (and economists) into the field of strategic management.

Although many still equate strategy and competitive strategy, here we take a broader view, perhaps closer in spirit to Andrews than to Porter. In particular, we consider not only the product market competitive forces that are the focus of Porter but also the firms' choices of the resources to acquire and the productive capabilities to develop.[2] We take this perspective, because it is a more natural vantage point for a discussion of strategy and organization, but also because we believe, though relatively neglected, it is arguably more important for a comprehensive general management perspective of the firm. At the same time, we adhere to Porter's fundamental position that strategy is about winning. While Andrews begins with strategy at the level of a corporation as a whole, we begin with strategy at the level of an individual business unit and build up to corporate strategy.

Recent research has begun to offer formal definitions and models of strategy, and we examine these below. However, for now, we proceed on a less formal, more practice-oriented, level to develop a clear understanding of the phenomena under discussion.

For practical purposes, a well-considered statement of a business unit's strategy has four main elements (Saloner et al. 2001).[3] First is a specification of the *goal* that that firm is trying to achieve—what it means to win. This is important, because it suggests the appropriate measures to collect. In economics we usually assume that profit maximization is the goal, but it need not be. For example, through the 1980s, large Japanese firms acted as if their principal objectives were to maintain and expand their employment. Moreover, firms often find it useful to adopt more proximate, less formulaic, objectives. For Komatsu, the Japanese heavy equipment company, the stated goal was to "Encircle [Beat] Caterpillar!"(Bartlett and Rangan 1988).

The next element of a strategy statement is a specification of *scope:* what products or services the firm will offer; which customers it will try to attract; how it will select and deal with suppliers; where it will do business geographically; what technology it will use; and which of the activities that must be carried out to realize these plans the firm will do in-house, and which it will leave to others. Economics has investigated aspects of many of these choices, but typically not the first one, of what business to be in.[4] Yet that is one of the most crucial decisions that the people leading a company must make.

The third element is an indication of why customers will deal with the firm on terms that let it achieve its goals—a statement of its *competitive advantage.* In a commercial setting, competitive advantage often comes down to how the firm will create value. Most often, it does so by offering a combination of low costs and perceived quality that allows it to serve its target market uniquely well (Porter 1980; Saloner et al. 2001). Sources of competitive advantage are typically thought to include the firm's position in the markets in which it deals, the capabilities it has to undertake various activities well, and, in some contexts, the resources it controls. For example, being a

2. The input-focused approach to strategy is often called the "resource-based" view of the firm. See Section 3.6.

3. See Collis and Rukstad (2008) for a more recent, but similar, experienced-based specification.

4. Granted, the literature on entry treats the decision to enter a business, but it rarely considers alternative businesses among which a choice must be made.

monopolist in a business with significant barriers to entry is a strong positional advantage. Enjoying large cost advantages because of learning effects or economies of scale allows charging attractively low prices that are still profitable. Having particular expertise in key aspects of business (e.g., in developing great new products, as at Apple) is a capability that gives competitive advantage. A crucial patent or a particularly productive mine are resources that can convey competitive advantage.

Finally, the strategy should have an explicable *logic:* why the firm will be able to realize its claimed competitive advantage within the scope of its strategy and thereby achieve its goals. This logic requires that there should be coherence among the firm's goals, competitive advantage, and strategic scope; that the organization through which it seeks to implement its strategy should be fit for its purpose; and that these factors should all fit with the environment (e.g., customers, competitors, suppliers, legal and regulatory policies, and social concerns) in which the business operates.

If a strategy is to succeed more than briefly, it must involve a sustainable competitive advantage; one that will endure despite the efforts of competitors. We return to this subject in Section 3.6.

At the level of the corporation, a strategy is a specification of the array of businesses in which the firm will be active, supported by a theory of how, by having the constituent businesses under common ownership and management, the firm will add value over what they would generate on their own. We return to corporate-wide issues in Section 4.

2.2. Relationship to Other Common Strategy Notions

CEOs often talk about future directions for a business in terms of their "vision." By this term they mean a description of a desired future state. As Bennis and Nanus (1985: 89) stated: "a vision articulates a view of a realistic, credible, attractive future for the company." A vision typically paints a picture of the future competitive landscape and a position the business in question might attain in it. Because strategy is fundamentally about winning, the putative future position is a favorable one, achieved by choosing the products and services the business offers in a way that creates advantage for the firm over the products and services offered by its rivals.

Nokia's leaders in the first years of the 1990s had the vision that "voice will go wireless," and they focused their firm, which had been a remarkably diverse conglomerate, completely on mobile telephony (Doornik and Roberts 2001: 4). Bill Gates's somewhat tardy recognition in the middle of that decade of the potential significance of the Internet led Microsoft as well to reshape its business fundamentally.

As the term suggests, a vision is often suggestive rather than specific. By describing a desired future state, it incorporates some sense of what part of the product space the business will occupy and how it will achieve competitive advantage relative to its rival when it does so. So vision contains at least some elements of objectives, scope, and competitive advantage. Moreover, to be at all compelling, it must contain at least some defensible rudimentary logic. But because it is nonspecific, a vision typically falls short of fully describing a business strategy.

A compelling vision is neither necessary nor sufficient for a successful business strategy. A firm that is well positioned with clear competitive advantage can succeed by tweaking its current strategy at the margin. And a CEO with a dazzling vision but without a coherent plan for pursuing it is unlikely to be successful.

Instead, a vision is typically the starting point for coming up with a novel strategy. By articulating what the business might become, it provides the basis both for an analysis of the product and service definitions and requirements that will be needed and for an examination of whether the business has the capabilities, resources, and organization—or can develop them—to pull it off. More importantly, coming up with the vision provides the creative spark that drives a new business strategy.

Coming up with an innovative vision can account for a significant fraction of the value a firm creates by propelling it down an entirely new path it might not otherwise have taken. It is harder to be enthusiastic about the much more ubiquitous mission statement. In contrast to the business strategy, the mission statement is a public declaration of whom the firm aspires to serve and how. In principle, therefore, the mission statement might be expected to share many elements with the business strategy. In particular, the mission statement might contain useful elements of objectives, scope, and competitive advantage.

In practice, however, mission statements tend to be bland and largely uninformative. Because they are public documents, their crafters often lack the courage to place any class of stakeholders above any others, so that the business appears to serve customers, employees, shareholders, and the public equally. And because they are typically designed to be enduring statements of purpose, they are far more general than are descriptions of strategic scope, for example, "to develop people to work together to create value for the Company's shareholders by doing it right with fun and integrity"[5] could be the mission statement of any number of companies.

Still, mission statements are interesting, because they belie a kind of collective corporate need for definition around why the business exists and who it serves. These issues would seem to be salient in a not-for-profit organization, where there is often a natural ambiguity about its raison d'être and the identity of its primary stakeholders. Their ubiquity in for-profit firms, where shareholders' value maximization is often the unambiguous overarching goal, suggests executives share a common struggle to put even basic parameters around their businesses. Often the creation of the mission statement is a response to uncertainty and even conflict within the organization about whom it will and will not serve and, more generally, about what the company is trying to do; elements that ought to be clear from the objectives and scope of the strategy.

In the short term, at least, one might expect that this kind of uncertainty and conflict would be adjudicated in an agreed-on plan of action. Indeed, most businesses are guided by a *strategic plan* (or business plan) that sets goals with horizons of perhaps 1 year and 5 years for sales, by product and region, for existing and still-to-be-developed products and services. As well, the plan usually describes specific actions to be taken to meet those goals. The strategic plan also typically translates the hoped-for business performance into a set of pro forma financial statements and financial requirements for the business. Finally, the functional areas of the business typically develop functional strategic plans (a marketing plan, financial strategy, etc.) to support the business strategy.

We discuss in Sections 2.4 and 2.5 the process by which plans are developed and how strategy evolves. For now, suffice it to say that, although one might expect a strategic plan

5. The quotation is from the Canadian Natural Resources Limited website, www.cnlr.com/about (accessed November 5, 2006).

naturally to include a goal, scope, competitive advantage, and logic, it is not uncommon for these plans to neglect at least some of these elements. In what follows we use the term "strategy" as incorporating those elements, as distinct from vision, mission, or the strategic plan.

2.3. The Role of Strategy

As the above discussion of ambiguity, uncertainty, and conflict suggests, there is a role for strategy in ensuring that the members of an organization take actions that advance the goals of the business. There are fundamentally two ways in which strategy can serve this role that have been discussed in the literature: by facilitating the coordination of decisions and by providing motivation in the absence of complete contracting.

2.3.1. Coordination

In the presence of interdependencies among the functions of the organization, even in the absence of disagreement or of conflict of interest, strategy can serve to coordinate. For example, a firm with a choice between providing top-quality products aimed at the high end of the market and low-cost mass-produced products aimed at the low end will need to coordinate product design, pricing, marketing, sourcing, manufacturing, and channel strategy to support the choice it makes. Even if everyone in the business has the same information about all options facing the firm, the same beliefs about the outcomes that will result from any set of actions, and the same ability to calculate costlessly the profitability of every course of action, there still will typically be multiple equilibria: one in which everyone coordinates on the high-end approach and another in which coordination occurs on the low-end approach. In this case the strategy that picks which coordinated approach to pursue helps avoid Pareto-dominated outcomes (Milgrom and Roberts 1992).

In most practical settings the coordination problem in the firm concerns much more than simply which of a set of well-defined coordinated outcomes to choose. In most businesses of any size, for example, manufacturing does not possess the knowledge of customer wants and willingness to pay that the sales organization has, and sales has little information about the costs of production of different products at varying volumes. So managers in neither area even understand what coordinated outcomes are possible. In the presence of significant costs of communicating and processing all such information, the role for central coordination increases in significance.

However, it is not clear that this enhanced role for coordination should take the form of a statement of strategy in the way that we have defined it above. For example, one could imagine a structure in which decentralized information is communicated to a center, with a complete set of optimal actions being communicated back, but strategy is definitely not such a comprehensive plan. The sort of thing we have been calling a "strategy" would make more sense if additional decentralized decisionmaking is desired even after some aspects of a coordinated outcome have already been specified. In the military analogy, once it has been decided which hill is to be taken (and whether from the ground or from the air), it can be left to the commanders in the field to decide precisely how to do it.

Van den Steen (2011) has recently offered a formal model of strategy as a coordination device that captures much of this discussion and yields additional implications. For him, a Strategy[6] is a specification of a minimal set of choices that are sufficient to guide all other choices that the members of an organization must make to reach an objective. The above discussion treated these choices as involving the (proximate) goal, aspects of the scope of the firm's activities, and how it plans to compete successfully (the competitive advantage, supported by the logic).

To model this idea, Van den Steen considered an organization with K individuals, each of whom can make a binary decision $D_k \in \{A, B\}$. Each decision may be right or wrong, depending on the state $T_k \in \{A, B\}$. In addition, pairs of decisions i and j can be complements or substitutes, depending on a state variable $V_{ij} \in \{S, C\}$, where $V_{ij} = V_{ji}$, so there are $K(K-1)/2$ such pairs. If the two actions are substitutes, then the decisions AB and BA are aligned; in the case of complements, then the decisions AA and BB are the right ones. Each state has probability 1/2 and the states are independent. All agents share these beliefs. Payoffs are separable. A correct decision $D_k = T_k$ yields payoff $\alpha_k > 0$ to all individuals. Incorrect decisions yield zero. If a pair i, j of decisions are aligned, then they generate $\gamma_{ij} > 0$ for everyone; if they are not aligned, they yield $-\gamma_{ij} < 0$. All this is common knowledge. Let θ denote a realization of the $K + K(K-1)/2$ states. Given a particular subset of the states S, we write (θ_S, θ_{-S}) to represent the whole vector.

The correctness of individual decisions is meant to model the need for fit with an external environment; the patterns of alignment model internal coherence. The common payoff focuses the model on coordination rather than on incentives.

There is also an additional agent, called the "strategist," who shares the common payoffs of the K decisionmakers. Before any actions are taken, the strategist may obtain signals on any number of the states. Having done so, she can fix any subset of the decisions and communicate her choices to the other agents. These actions by the strategist are assumed to have infinitesimal costs: everyone lexicographically prefers that the strategist make fewer investigations and also fewer decisions and announcements, but the actual payoffs from the decisions are overwhelmingly more important. Once the strategist has acted, then each individual k receives a signal about the state pertaining to his decision D_k and about the $K-1$ interaction states involving decisions D_k and D_j, j different from k. For simplicity, assume these signals are the same as the ones the strategist would see if she investigated. So, in particular, both members of any pair of agents see the same signal about the interaction between their actions. Then those agents whose decisions have not been fixed by the strategist all simultaneously make their decisions, and the payoffs are realized.

Note that, without the first stage (no strategist), this is a game of incomplete information.[7] Players' strategies in the game map their private information (their signals) into their decisions. From the point of view of each agent k, every other agent j is equally likely to have seen A as B as the signal on j's choice D_j and to have seen C as S on each of the interactions that j's choice has with other actors' choices (except that k knows that j saw the same signal as he did on the jk interaction). In this context, a very salient equilibrium involves each party k conjecturing

---

6. In this discussion only, we capitalize "Strategy" in the sense it is being used in this chapter to distinguish it from players' strategies in the game Van den Steen (2011) analyzes.

7. As is the game after the strategist has made her choices.

that every other party j follows the signal j received for his individual decision, so everyone effectively is expected to play A with probability 1/2 and B with probability 1/2. Then playing in this way is actually optimal for each player. In this case, the choices end up being coordinated only a fraction of the time (half the time when $K = 2$). This result indicates the nature of the coordination problem that the strategist is meant to help solve.

Van den Steen (2011) then formally defined a Strategy as a nonempty set X of choices by the strategist of states to examine and decisions to specify such that, given the objective $D(\theta)$ being pursued, the signals that she receives, and the beliefs of the other agents once they have observed her choices:[8]

1. the choices the strategist makes in X are those that realize the target $D(\theta_X, \theta_{-X})$ for any possible realization θ_{-X} of the states she has not examined;

2. for each individual decision k not in X and any θ_{-X}, it is an equilibrium of the game specified above for individual k to choose the decision that realizes his part of $D(\theta_X, \theta_{-X})$; and

3. there does not exist a strict subset X^* of X such that conditions (1) and (2) hold with X^* in place of X.

So the Strategy achieves coordination on the desired outcome and is a minimal set of choices that can do so.

The first result is that, in any equilibrium of the full game, the choices of the strategist define a Strategy in the above sense that induces the (common) payoff-maximizing outcome. The proof is simple. With only infinitesimal costs to inspection and announcements, the strategist can achieve essentially the joint maximizing outcome by her own actions alone. Further, whatever choice she makes must implement the optimal outcome in any subgames starting after her choices are announced: otherwise, it cannot be equilibrium behavior, because she shares the payoffs. Finally, given her lexicographic preferences, she will pick a minimal set of decisions achieving these goals.

Van den Steen (2011) then examined the comparative statics of his model, focusing on the case $K = 2$ but allowing for a third stage in the game in which any decision can be reversed at a cost c, where c measures the irreversibility of choices. The parameters are the payoffs from the individual decisions and from alignment, the precision of the signals, and the cost of reversing. The first result is that the value of developing a Strategy (i.e., the expected payoff to the game when it includes the first stage less the payoff to the game without the first stage) is increasing in the payoff to alignment, the precision of the signals about the nature of the interaction, and the cost of reversing. In addition, these three features are complementary: raising any of them enhances the effect of increasing the others on the value of developing a Strategy. If there is little gain to aligning choices or the form of the interaction is very uncertain, then there is little to be gained by trying to coordinate: decisions might just as well be made on their own. And if it is cheap to achieve coordination ex post, in the third stage, then coordination ex ante through a Strategy is relatively less valuable. As Van den Steen suggested, these results should

---

8. These beliefs about the actual state of the world may depend on the individuals' beliefs about what the strategist has seen, given her observed choices.

probably be thought of as a check that his formulation is reasonable. Yet they yield an interesting point: having a Strategy is really important only if there are both important interactions and significant irreversibility. Also, because we think of strong interactions as creating multiple coherent patterns of organization features (see Sections 3.2 and 3.3), Strategy really matters only when internal alignment—finding a good pattern—is important. To the extent we think of external fit in terms of decisions being well adapted to markets and internal alignment as a matter of organizational coherence, Strategy in this sense matters only when the organizational design problem is relatively complex. If interactions are unimportant, individual decisions can be made reasonably well on the basis of individual signals about the external environment: they need no Strategy to guide them.

Van den Steen (2011) also investigated a rich set of issues about when particular decisions will be part of the Strategy, what form the Strategy takes, and the role of process and leadership in Strategy, but these issues are not so relevant here. The key results here are those relating to the value of Strategy in coordination and its link to organization.

In a more dynamic coordination context, Strategy can play an ongoing role in helping those inside the firm know which new opportunities to ignore without undertaking extensive investigation—because they clearly do not fit with the Strategy—and which to explore more thoroughly. To our knowledge, this idea has not been modeled, although some of the models we discuss next about strategy as a motivational device have something of this flavor.[9]

2.3.2. Motivation and Commitment

The above discussion of coordination assumes no disagreement or incentive issues within the firm. The presence of either issue introduces an additional role for strategy. One reason is that if it is difficult for the firm to provide incentives for employees to take actions that are dependent on the firm's adhering to particular products and markets approached in a specific way, it might be advantageous to commit to a specific strategy. As Aguilar (1988: 71) put it:

> Consistency of word and deed on the leader's part is absolutely necessary if others are to commit themselves to the personal and business risks associated with new and unproven courses of action. The general manager who runs hot and cold will fail to encourage confidence in others . . . Nobody wants to go out on a limb and risk being abandoned at the first sound of cracking wood.

Rotemberg and Saloner (1994) offered a model of when it may be valuable for senior management to commit to a narrow business strategy—one that excludes some things the firm may already have been doing. They contemplated a setting in which employees must exert costly effort to generate innovative ideas for the business. They further supposed that, because of the difficulty of contracting on either effort or the ideas themselves, employees reap the rewards of their innovative efforts only when their ideas are actually implemented. Rotemberg and Saloner considered two settings in which the strategy the firm pursues can affect whether the ideas are implemented. In one the firm is not able to pursue all the directions in the future that it has in the past (because, e.g., it faces financial constraints). Knowing that, employees working in each

---

9. We are indebted to Heikki Rantakari for this point.

of the directions currently being pursued may doubt that their efforts will be rewarded, because their innovations will not be implemented if the firm changes direction, and they then will be reluctant to exert costly effort to innovate in the first place. In the second case employees in one line of business may generate innovations that render innovations made by those in the other less valuable. Knowing that, the latter have less incentive to innovate. In either case it may be in the interests of the firm to commit to a narrower range of future paths to credibly convince employees that their innovative ideas are likely to be implemented. The authors argued that if strategy commits the firm to a specific scope for at least some time, it can achieve this goal (see also Rotemberg and Saloner 1995).

In a related paper, Rotemberg and Saloner (2000) argued that an alternative way to achieve commitment, and hence motivation, is to hire a CEO whose "vision" for the company favors certain directions over others. They modeled this predilection on the part of the CEO as a bias in favor of certain kinds of projects over others. A biased CEO can be relied on to consistently implement projects he favors, leaving employees with little doubt that their innovations in those directions will be implemented. Rotemberg and Saloner argued that a company with a visionary CEO of this kind can actually outperform one that simply follows a narrow strategy, because the latter completely eschews certain potentially profitable directions in the interests of commitment, whereas a biased CEO will ultimately implement highly profitable projects if they are sufficiently good to overcome his bias.

The essence of these arguments is that if employees earn rents when the projects they have worked on are implemented, and if their innovative efforts are not contractible, they will be more likely to put forth effort if they believe the top executive's strategy or vision favors the direction into which their projects fit. Van den Steen (2005) showed that one need not rely on some unexplained bias on the part of the CEO to make the managers' and employees' expectations about future direction matter. In his model, because he did not impose common prior beliefs about the likelihood of various states of the world, people simply disagree about the likelihood of success of possible projects. Van den Steen showed that in such a setting employees will work harder for managers who hold beliefs that agree with their own about what sort of projects are more likely to succeed, because they know their ideas will be more likely to be implemented. Further, if they agree with the manager on which state is more likely, they will work even harder the more certain the manager is in his beliefs, because his expected payoff from adoption is higher, and so he adopts more projects. Interestingly, employees will work hard even for managers with whom they disagree, as long as the managers' convictions are very strongly held. At least they know where they stand and that implementation of projects the manager likes is assured, even though they personally have little confidence in the likelihood of these succeeding. Even so, if we back up a stage and consider the employment decision, employees will choose to work for firms whose managers hold beliefs similar to their own, so that sorting then creates organizational alignment around the direction that is favored by the manager. As a result, employees working for a strongly visionary manager will work harder and be more satisfied than others. Then it is worthwhile to hire such a manager, even if one believes the manager is too much of a "true believer." The resulting shared beliefs are an aspect of corporate culture that emerges quite naturally in this model (see Van den Steen 2010a,b).

Just as alignment of beliefs about strategy between those who take actions and those who must implement them can increase motivation, so, too, can alignment of preferences. CEOs who put weight on what their employees want (even at the expense of profit) give employees the confidence that the firm will continue to pursue strategies that allow the employees to bring their nascent efforts to fruition. Whether the reason that senior managers act this way is because the CEO is "fair minded" and follows through on her implicit promises (Shleifer and Summers 1988), is empathic and cares about the utility of the employees (Rotemberg and Saloner 1993), or is "enthusiastic" and cares about the direction of the firm and about the benefits of like-minded workers (Hart and Holmström 2002), motivation is enhanced through alignment of preferences.

In Rotemberg and Saloner (1994) firms limit themselves to narrow strategies because it is a commitment that induces employees to worker harder. It is also possible that firms might benefit from narrow strategies for precisely the opposite reason: fear that the firm might later broaden its strategy if the current strategy is unsuccessful might cause employees to work harder to ensure continuation of the current strategy. For that fear to be founded, senior management must have the flexibility to change strategy in the future rather than being committed to the current one.

This alternative motivation for hard work can happen if the value of employees' human capital itself is strategy-specific, or at least there are complementarities between the human capital employees develop (or come with) and the strategy the firm is pursuing. For example, salespeople nurture networks that are complementary to the products and services that the firm is providing, and access to those networks is more valuable if the firm continues to provide those products and services. If the value of employees' human capital is strategy-specific and the rents they receive are greater if the firm continues with its current strategy, the employees then have an incentive to work hard to ensure the continuation of the strategy. Fear that the firm will change strategy will induce effort.

This point is demonstrated by Mailath et al. (2004) in a model where the firm considers a merger between two related businesses. In their model if firms A and B are in related businesses producing competing differentiated products, if A does not perform well in its current strategy, senior management might be tempted to shift in the direction of B's products. If management does so, A's current employees would suffer a reduction in the value of their strategy-specific human capital. Consequently they will work hard to ensure the success of the current strategy. If, however, the firms were to merge, an ex post shift in A's strategy would be less profitable, as it would come at the expense of B, a cost that the merged firm would internalize. Thus, in a merged firm a change in A's strategy is less credible, with the result that the fear of changing the strategy is less of a disciplining device.

The difference between the motivations for pursuing narrow strategies in these two lines of research is that in the Rotemberg-Saloner and Van den Steen models the firm wants to induce employees to make new strategy-specific investments, whereas in Mailath et al. (2004), the employees, as a result of existing human capital, have a vested interest in the status quo.

Finally, Ferreira and Rezende (2007) offered a model in which publically announcing a strategy to outsiders can induce commitment to it, because changing an announced strategy causes the managerial labor market to reduce its estimate of the manager's ability. In their setup, the strategy is a plan about how business will be conducted in the future, and the problem is to induce noncontractible investments that are specific to that plan. Commitment to the plan makes inducing the investment easier.

2.4. The Process of Strategy Formulation

There is a great deal of variety in way that strategy is formulated in practice. This variety reflects the differing needs of firms of different sizes and in different industries, but it also reflects the lack of a single accepted best practice in this area.

2.4.1. Large, Established Single-Business Firms

These firms are the most interesting place to start, because size introduces significant issues of communication and delegation, and usually of ownership and control as well. It is common in these settings to ascribe the responsibility for coming up with a vision for the business and translating it into a business strategy to the CEO. Quigley (1993) gave credence to this top-down view, citing a Korn/Ferry International study of 1,500 senior managers in 20 countries, in which 98% say the most important CEO trait is the ability to convey a strong sense of vision, and the most important skill (by a margin of 25% over any other) is strategy formulation to achieve the vision.

Some strategic management scholars ascribe a much smaller role to senior management. Mintzberg has repeatedly argued that the role of senior management is much closer to that of formalizing and documenting strategic changes that have already been brought about by others in the organization. He uses the term "emergent" strategy to capture the idea that strategy grows from small initiatives spread throughout the organization undertaken at the discretion of employees, rather than as the result of a master plan (e.g., Mintzberg and Waters 1985). Of course, "small initiatives" might be consistent with the existing strategy and could advance that strategy in the spirit of the formal models described above. However, in contrasting "emergent strategies" with "deliberate" ones, Mintzberg suggests that strategy is better described as a "bottom-up" than a "top-down" phenomenon.[10]

Burgelman (1983, 1991) attempted to reconcile the top-down and bottom-up views of strategy formulation, based on his observations of different companies, most notably Intel. In his formulation senior management does indeed specify a strategy, but managers lower down in the organization sometimes use their delegation of authority to explore initiatives that are outside the stated strategy. If these initiatives are successful, they sometimes later become incorporated in the formal strategy. Burgelman's framework incorporates a curious mix of behaviors: senior management that directs strategy and junior managers who flaunt those directives and take actions outside the scope of the current strategy that ultimately change the strategy.

However, this combination of behaviors arises naturally in models in which the firm employs visionary leaders who are biased, enthusiastic, or have strong beliefs of the kind described above. The strength of the visionary leader in those models in motivating employees to exert effort that is consistent with the vision is tempered by the fact that objectively good initiatives might not be undertaken for fear that they would not be implemented, and indeed, employees wishing to

---

10. The organizational ecology literature in sociology (Hannan and Freeman 1984) proposes an even smaller role for senior management in determining the strategic course of the firm. In that literature firms of different organizational forms are inherently suited to pursuing particular courses of action (the way that they compete is a function of inherent firm attributes). In that sense the strategy *is* the organizational form. Some firms win and others lose, not because senior management has chosen and implemented a winning strategy, but because the competitive environment selects the organizational forms that are better suited to the industry context.

pursue such initiatives might be starved of the resources to do so. It might then be better to have an intermediate layer of middle managers who have an objective view of the world ("professional managers" in the terminology of Hart and Holmström 2002). Such managers understand that senior management will not favor initiatives that are inconsistent with their idiosyncratic or biased view of the world, but they might provide the resources for promising initiatives outside the scope of the current strategy. The point is that these initiatives, if sufficiently successful, might overcome the predilections of the bosses and be adopted, changing the course of the strategy in the process.

A formal model of such a hierarchy was developed in Rotemberg and Saloner (2000). In addition, although he did not formally develop the role of the middle managers in such a setting, in Van den Steen's model (2005) employees with strong opinions that differ from their boss's will pursue their own inclinations, and if sufficiently successful, will have their projects implemented despite being outside the preferred strategy of the CEO. For middle managers to be objective, their appointment must be supervised by a group that does not share the CEO's bias—a board of directors, perhaps.

2.4.2. Start-Ups

Strategy in small companies is more straightforward, because top management is both well informed about strategy-relevant characteristics and in a position to monitor employees' actions. In these settings strategy does tend to spring from the mind of the CEO—a top-down view is clearly the relevant one here—and tends to be formulated without a formal or inclusive process.

Start-ups, by which we mean nascent organizations assembled to pursue a novel idea or business approach, are small companies that introduce different issues, because the strategies that most start-ups end up pursuing are either completely different from what was originally conceived or are significant modifications thereof. Yet the provision of critical resources—capital, labor, channels of distribution, etc.—will in part depend on an assessment of the likely success of the strategy. Consequently, although start-ups are compelled by resource-providers to be able to articulate strategy even at an early stage, they often exhibit two features not always seen in more established companies (at least not to the same degree). First, the strategy is a work in progress, often evolving rapidly as the founders learn about their markets, their competitors, and the tastes of resource providers. Second, whereas disciplined, more mature businesses often drive toward focus by ejecting elements of scope that will be distracting, even start-ups that are resource-poor often explicitly experiment among several strategic alternatives because of the high value of the real options they have, resulting from the uncertainty inherent in matching a start-up's potential to its market. This lack of initial focus also means that young firms are sometimes unable to align their human capital to their strategies as closely as more established entities can, and they may require more generalist skills. (This view is consistent with Lazear [2005], who argued that entrepreneurs are jacks-of-all-trades, although in that paper the reason given—that entrepreneurs must tackle diverse tasks—is different.)

2.4.3. Corporate Strategy

Strategy in multibusiness firms must encompass both the complexity of strategy formulation for each individual business, discussed above, and the alignment and coordination of strategy across businesses. We defer discussion of this topic to the section on multibusiness firms in Section 4.1.

2.5. Strategic Change

Organizations must manage a natural tension between immutable strategy and change. The benefits to coordination and motivation described above can be realized only if the firm sticks to its strategy. Employees lower down in the organization know what to do, and they know that their initiatives will be implemented, only if the strategy they are following in taking those actions is not a moving target. At the same time, in the presence of changes in the firm's environment and its own internal capabilities, a given strategy will not remain optimal forever. One might imagine that the firm might adapt the strategy to optimize continuously against such changes, but in practice it takes time to communicate strategy effectively. This, plus limitations on the kinds of subtleties that can be effectively communicated, tend to lead to infrequent but significant changes to strategy.

This line of thought suggests a kind of "punctuated equilibrium" view of strategy, in which periodic changes to strategy are significant events, between which strategy is stable. In this view of the world the general manager is expected to manage, on the one hand, as though the strategy is fixed (at least for now) while, on the other, continually assessing whether environmental or internal developments are such that a significant shift in strategy is needed.

The frequency with which strategy should be changed must be industry and firm dependent. In more rapidly changing industries, firms will find the balance between the benefits of responding to changes in their external environment and the costs of strategic change tilting in favor of more frequent changes. The same will be true of firms that are smaller (because they are less complex and can execute change more quickly) or have more centralized structures (so change is more easily coordinated).

Some strategic change will consist of small, local adjustments in response to changes in internal and external factors. Although the changes may be sporadic because of the adjustment costs described above, they may well approximate a continuous process. However, the most interesting episodes of strategic change involve discontinuous realignments of strategy and organization. Because a strategy involves a coherent goal, scope, competitive advantage, and logic, and an execution of that strategy that is aligned with organization structure (as discussed in more detail in Section 3), strategic change may require a set of people, policies, products, positioning, etc. that is at once different from the status quo yet internally consistent. Strikingly, however, the issue is not continuous versus discrete change, because the abilities to do each are complementary: being able to make large changes is more valuable the better one is able to fine-tune after the major shift, and vice versa (Milgrom and Roberts 1995b).

A final potential motivation for strategic change that one hears, at least among practitioners, is to "shake things up." As described above, a firm that steadfastly pursues a given strategy for a long time will tend to align its organization, processes, and people around that strategy. Sorting is likely to result in people with like beliefs, and the only innovations that are undertaken are ones that are consistent with the direction the company has been pursuing. It is sometimes suggested that opening the firm up to a process of strategic change can result in increased innovation, creativity, and motivation, both through the process of thinking through change and its implementation.

This whole area of the meaning of strategic change, its frequency, and nature has not been the subject of much formal economic analysis.

3. Organization

Choice of a strategy determines a set of activities that must be carried out to implement it. Executing these activities requires putting in place an organization through which decisions and actions of the people involved can be coordinated and motivated: managed organizations exist to coordinate and motivate.

3.1. The Elements of Organization

A useful typology of the features of any formal, managed organization involves four elements, each of which affects coordination and motivation (Roberts 2004). The first is the people who belong to the organization, with their knowledge, skills, preferences, and individual beliefs, and with their networks of relationships with others, both inside and outside the organization. Next comes the organizational architecture, including such matters as the specification of the organizational chart with its information about who reports to whom, how tasks are collected to define jobs and how people are assigned to them, how jobs are collected together into units and units into larger entities, how broad the spans of control are, and how deep the hierarchy is. Architecture also involves such matters as the allocation of authority over various decisions; the financial, ownership, and governance structures of the organization; and its formal boundaries and relationships with other, cooperating entities. The third set of features involves the routines, processes and procedures, both formal and informal, official and actual, through which information is gathered and disseminated, decisions are made, assets are acquired, resources are allocated, work is done, performance is tracked, and people are rewarded. Finally, there is the culture of the organization, involving shared beliefs and values, mental models, special vocabulary, and behavioral norms. Each of the many features of the organization is at least partially controllable and so may be used to influence behavior and affect the realization of the strategy.

Various chapters in this volume deal with specific aspects of organizations in detail. For example, Baron and Kreps (this volume), Lazear and Oyer (this volume), and Waldman (this volume) deal with human capital and personnel issues; Gertner and Scharfstein (this volume) study resource allocation; Bresnahan and Levin (this volume) examine the vertical boundaries of the firm; Garicano and Van Zandt (this volume) and Mookherjee (this volume) study hierarchy and delegation; Hermalin ("Culture and Leadership," this volume) reflects on culture in organizations; Gibbons and Henderson (this volume) look at routines and capabilities; Bolton and Dewatripont (this volume) study authority; Gibbons et al. (this volume) examine organizational decisionmaking; and Gibbons and Roberts ("Economic Theories of Incentives in Organizations," this volume) study motivation and incentives. Thus, rather than dig into these issues here, we instead focus on higher level issues, except in the specific context of multiproduct firms in Section 4.

There are two extreme views on the connection between strategy and organization. One is encapsulated in Alfred Chandler's dictum: "Structure follows strategy" (Chandler 1962: 14). Chandler's theory arose from his studies of the emergence of the multidivisional form in the early twentieth century. More ambitious strategies—operating over an unprecedentedly broad geographic expanse or in multiple product or factor markets—implied much more complex problems of coordination and motivation than had previously been encountered. Confronting these problems led to the development of new organizational models that would permit execution of the new strategies.

In the other view, in ongoing companies the organization that is in place constrains strategic choice and may even determine it, so that strategy follows structure. First, it is obvious that the people in the firm limit its options: a steel manufacturer cannot easily convert to being an investment bank, no matter how profitable banking might be, because the steelmakers lack the skills and relationships to be bankers and the capital stock of the company is ill-suited to the new role. Culture has similar inertial effects. In addition, the capabilities on which competitive advantage may rest are embedded in the routines of the organization (Nelson and Winter 1982), so what the firm can do depends on who its members are and what it has done before. Moreover, because organizational change is hard and dangerous (Barnett and Carroll 1995), the existing organizational design affects the attractiveness of any new strategy through the costs of adjustment. Finally, and most fundamentally, the existing organizational architecture, routines, and culture will shape the decisions that affect strategy: the information that those empowered to make decisions have and the explicit and implicit incentives they face will lead them to make choices that will, in effect, determine the emergent strategy (Bower 1970; Burgelman 1983). In this context, John Browne, former Group Chief Executive of energy giant BP, has said, "our organization is our strategy."[11]

In fact, both positions have an element of truth. In established firms, the extant organization does influence what is possible. In contrast, Chandler's dictum is often right in the context of new ventures: the entrepreneur decides what to do, then how to do it. But even here matters are not crystal clear. As discussed above, actual start-ups often go through an extended process of exploratory learning as they attempt to figure out what the market actually wants, and the nascent organization influences the path and scope of this learning.

Ideally, the strategy and the organization are developed together in a holistic fashion and are jointly determined, so they fit each other and also fit the economic, technological, legal, regulatory, and social environment in which the company operates.

3.2. Fundamental Trade-Offs in Organizational Design

Organizational design involves fundamental trade-offs, two of which we highlight here as illustrative of some of the basic issues.

3.2.1. Initiative and Cooperation

In thinking of the organization as a mechanism to coordinate and motivate in pursuit of the strategy, Holmström's conception of the necessity of inducing two sorts of behavior—initiative and cooperation—is useful. Initiative is the clever, diligent, honest pursuit of one's own responsibilities. Cooperation is behavior that advances others' interests or overall organizational success, as opposed to contributing to one's own assigned responsibilities. High levels of initiative are almost definitionally valuable in any organization. At the same time, because managed organizations tend to arise in contexts where interdependencies abound and that are problematic for formal contracting, cooperative behavior can be extremely valuable as well. The difficulty is that

---

11. Private discussion with John Roberts, circa 1999.

often the two compete for peoples' time, so that inducing one makes it more costly to induce the other. Thus, for a given level of resources being dedicated to motivating behavior and a given state of managerial technology, there will be some maximum amount of initiative that can be induced for any level of cooperation, and one expects that this frontier is downward sloping. This framework can be a useful tool for analysis (Roberts 2004).

In some organizations, initiative is paramount. The trading desk of an investment bank might be an example, although some of the risk taking that went on in the run-up to the financial crisis of 2008 does seem to have shown a lack of concern with the success of the overall organization—a shortage of cooperation. In other contexts, motivating cooperation may be of greater value. For example, a company facing similar operating issues in many different locations might get great value out of managers' sharing their experiences with different possible solutions to common problems.

One approach to modeling motivating the provision of both cooperation and initiative would naturally be done in the context of a multitasking agency framework (Holmström and Milgrom 1991; Baker 1992; see also Gibbons and Roberts, "Economic Theories of Incentives in Organizations," this volume). The key would be that providing formal, explicit incentives for initiative should typically be much easier than for cooperation, because the former may be easily measured, whereas the latter may be subject only to very noisy or easily manipulable measures. For example, in many situations, cooperation consists simply of avoiding opportunism aimed at others inside the firm, and determining when someone has passed on such an opportunity will be hard. Or if cooperation is providing help in solving a problem in another part of the company, it will be hard to determine whether someone did not contribute because of lack of cooperation or lack of anything useful to offer.

In this case, the logic of multitasking indicates that any formal incentives for both activities must be quite muted if the marginal cost of providing the one is increasing in the amount of the other (Holmström and Milgrom 1991). Two other alternatives seem possible, however. One would be to rely on a boss's subjective evaluations on the provision of cooperation while providing explicit formal incentives for initiative. The other would be to develop norms of cooperation in situations where, even if the boss cannot observe enough to form useful subjective evaluations, peers are aware of one another's behavior. This was done at BP to encourage the sharing of resources and knowledge across business units (Roberts 2004). Both approaches presumably would involve relational contracts in a repeated setting.[12]

Van den Steen (2006) looked at a closely related trade-off—between motivating individual effort and coordinating decisions—that arises in situations where the parties fundamentally disagree about what the right decisions are.[13] He considers a setup very much like that in Van den Steen (2011) discussed above, where a principal and an agent must each make a binary decision, and the agent can exert costly, unobservable effort. The payoff from the project depends on the individual decisions (whether they match the state or not), on whether the two decisions are the same (coordination), and on the agent's effort. The principal can either make both decisions just on her own or make one and leave the other to the agent, who then observes

12. Baker et al. (1994) in fact carry out a related analysis when the supply of each activity is unaffected by the amount of the other being provided. This assumption generally simplifies the analysis considerably.

13. Formally, they have differing prior beliefs about the likelihood of various states of nature.

the principal's choice. Letting the agent make his own decision motivates him to provide effort if the quality of the decision and effort are complements, because he believes the decisions he makes are better than those the principal makes (by revealed preference plus differing beliefs). As for coordination, one obvious potential way to achieve it is to use monetary incentives (which would work in a setting where there was simply a common prior, but the agent received private benefits from making decisions). Here it does not, because although giving the agent more residual income increases his interest in coordination, it also intensifies his interest in making the right decision (from his point of view), even at the expense of coordination. In the present setup these two effects cancel out, and monetary incentives are useless. So if coordination is to be assured, the principal must make both decisions, although this reduces the agent's effort incentives. The result is a trade-off and, for a given share of the project returns paid to the agent, a downward-sloping frontier relating motivation and coordination.

3.2.2. Exploration and Exploitation

March (1991) identified two fundamental learning processes in organizations. One involves exploitation: realizing the opportunities inherent in the current strategic, organizational, and environmental contexts. The second is exploring for new opportunities outside the current agenda. Effective exploitation is needed to succeed in the ongoing business, but exploration is also vital in a world of change, where competitive advantage can erode and demand may disappear. Perhaps this search need not always be pursued intensely, instead being concentrated in times of crisis, when there is a great need for redefinition and renewal; see Tushman and O'Reilly (1996, 2011) for examples. Still, at least sometimes the firm must both explore and exploit.

The difficulty is that the two compete for resources and, further, organizational designs that support exploration are typically inimical to exploration (Roberts 2004). The competition for resources is often an uneven one, because the resources are being generated by the current business—the exploiters—who are likely to resist resources being shifted away from the uses they have for them to pay for the explorers. Also, all the normal measurement, control, and reward systems will show the exploiters in a better light compared to the explorers. The former can demonstrate immediate, measurable results that are easily understood. The explorers offer little but hope and dreams while burning up cash. To support exploration, the measures should be in terms of milestones and growth—not cost, revenues, and efficiency. The reward schemes and the culture should favor risk taking, imagination, and innovation—not the rigor, discipline, and focus that mark exploitation—and they must avoid punishing well-intentioned failure. Taking a multitasking point of view, it is clear that it is much harder to induce exploration than exploitation (Roberts 2004).

At the same time, the exploratory efforts must be linked back to the business. Otherwise the glorious, sad history of Xerox's Palo Alto Research Center (PARC) may be repeated. PARC invented a remarkable list of technologies, including the computer mouse and graphical user interfaces that Apple Corporation copied for the Macintosh, yet Xerox was never able to figure out how to use any of them profitably.

Management scholars have identified a set of actions that appear to be conducive and perhaps even necessary to support exploration. These include setting up separate new business units outside the existing business, having the new units report to top-level executives directly, and allowing them to develop their own organizational designs (see the references in Tushman and O'Reilly 2011).

A variety of economics papers have investigated the problem of motivating innovation, but only one apparently has looked at the problem of exploration and exploitation. Manso (2011) considered a repeated agency problem where, in each period, the agent has three choices: shirk; try the established way of carrying out his responsibilities, which has a known probability of success; or try a new way, whose probability of success is unknown. Each option carries a positive probability of success and of failure, but the new way is, in expectation, inferior to the old. So exploitation is favored in a one-shot game. However, suppose that if the new way is tried and it succeeds, then the updated posterior on its probability of success exceeds the known probability of success of the established way. In this case, the principal may want the agent to explore the new way, with the intention of adopting it in the second period if it is a success and otherwise reverting to exploiting the old way.

To motivate exploitation of the old way optimally involves a contract design that is absolutely standard from the literature on unobservable, costly effort. However, motivating exploration necessitates muted first-period incentives, because success is more likely if the agent exploits, and so success is bad news about his choice. In fact, it may even be necessary to reward first-period failure if the agent finds it easier to exploit than to explore.

3.3. Finding Fit

For success, the strategy and organization need to fit each other. What is involved?

3.3.1. The Problem

Sometimes fit questions are simple, even if firms do not always come up with the right answers. For example, suppose a firm adopts a strategy that calls for very high service being provided to a group of customers with whom it wants to build long-term relationships and from whom it will seek to learn about their evolving preferences to develop new offerings. Then it would be unwise to pay salespeople significant commissions based on short-term sales revenues, although such incentives would be ideal in a context where current sales were all that really mattered (Anderson and Schmittlein 1984; Holmström and Milgrom 1991). Financing the firm predominantly with debt may be desirable in a stable, mature industry, where the firm has few good options for investing its cash flow but where managers might prefer not to pay out the cash to shareholders (Jensen 1986). Yet equity may be preferred in a more volatile environment with better growth opportunities.

Despite such examples, the task of finding the best fit among all the elements of organization and of the organization as a whole with the strategy and environment is, in principal, arbitrarily complicated, because the elements of strategy and organization interact in potentially complex ways that affect performance.

For example, consider Southwest Airlines and Singapore Airlines. Both are in the passenger airline business, and both are very successful, but they have radically different strategies and organizations. Singapore Airlines focuses on long-haul, international flights through its hub in Singapore and provides extremely high levels of service, especially to business and first class customers, with little discounting of prices. To support this approach, it requires that its female flight attendants be slim and physically attractive, trains them extensively not just in service but also in grooming, and requires them to retire at a young age. (Male flight attendants receive training in service but are not subject to the other conditions.) It also makes a point of having the most modern fleet of airplanes (it was the first to buy the Airbus 380), equipping the airplanes with every luxury, having luxurious lounges in airports, and offering excellent food and drinks on board. Meanwhile, Southwest is purely domestic, operating point-to-point flights with only economy seating and very sharp prices. Service is friendly but not in any sense outstanding (there are no assigned seats, and no food is offered on the planes). Flight attendants appear to be selected for good humor and a willingness to work hard. Costs are kept low by a variety of measures, including especially high utilization of the aircraft, achieved in large part by fast turnarounds at the gate. To facilitate quick turnarounds, the aircrew and flight attendants will clean the plane rather than waiting for cleaners, and they even handle baggage. To further economize by eliminating variation, Southwest operates only one type of aircraft, the Boeing 737, a small single-aisle model whose design dates back almost 50 years. In each case, the strategy and organization fit together, and the success of each enterprise can be attributed to this fit. But crucially, until very recently no airline has managed to match either Singapore's strategy and organization or Southwest's, despite the presumptive gains from doing so in an industry where most participants fail to earn their cost of capital. Finding fit is apparently hard, even when models are available.

In fact, recent empirical work on organizations and management indicates tremendous heterogeneity across various elements of design. For example, Bloom and Van Reenen and various coauthors (e.g., see Bloom and Van Reenen 2007; Bloom et al. 2010, 2011b) have found extensive differences in the extent of delegation and decentralization (e.g., authority to hire various sorts of employees and spending limits for buying spare parts) in particular populations of establishments around the world. They have also examined various management practices (e.g., promotion on merit or future promise versus other criteria, setting goals and providing feedback, and recording quality problems and acting on the knowledge) and have found wide divergences in practice. Whether to decentralize or not involves important trade-offs, so that either answer on this dimension might be correct, if not obvious. However, for most management practices they study, there is clearly a right way to do things in most circumstances, but relatively few firms do it. Again, finding fit is apparently hard.

3.3.2. Rugged Landscapes and the Difficulty of Finding Fit

This logic has been captured in the "rugged landscapes" literature that begins with the work of Levinthal (1997). Levinthal's model, which is based on work by Kauffman (1993) on complexity, treats the choice of organization as selection of the values for N different binary (0 or 1) attributes, so there are 2^N different possible organizational designs. The payoff to a particular choice of the nth variable is a random number drawn from a uniform distribution on $[0, 1]$ that depends on the value of the choice of that variable as well as the specification of the values of K other variables. So in the $N = 3$, $K = 2$ case, the payoff to, say, $x_1 = 1$ is a different random number for each possible specification of x_2 and x_3, whereas with $K = 0$, the payoff to x_1 depends only on the value of x_1. Then the overall performance for a given organization is the average of the payoffs across the N variables.

If $K = 0$, then changing the value of one attribute does not change the payoff of any others, so the maximum change in the overall performance is $1/N$. In this case there is typically a unique optimal organizational design. As K increases, changing a single attribute's level changes more and more of the payoffs to other attributes, and thus the overall performance can change much more. If $K = N - 1$, then any change in a single variable changes the contribution of all the others. Thus, with $K > 0$, adjacent points can have very different performance levels, and the graph of the performance function can be uneven and irregular: a "rugged landscape." Moreover, the number of local maxima increases probabilistically with K.

In such a setup, local search is of limited value, because improving performance by changing the value of one variable gives no information on the effects of any other changes, and as N and K become large, global search becomes very complex.[14] These factors suggest that firms that happen upon "good" configurations may have a lasting competitive advantage, because imitation will be hard: even getting one element of the design wrong may give radically different performance. Less positively, firms may also find replication of their success in another location or line of business very difficult, because altering one element of the strategy and organization (location, product) may change the effectiveness of all other elements. And finding fit again after the environment has changed may be very difficult.

The rugged landscapes modeling of the problem of selecting strategy and organization is about as far as possible from the standard models of economics that yield nice, smooth, concave optimization problems. This newer model has pluses and minuses. On the one hand, dropping unwarranted but conventional assumptions of divisibility and decreasing returns is clearly desirable. On the other hand, the approach assumes that there is no logic or theory that can be used to guide the selection. This conclusion seems to be too nihilistic.

3.3.3. Complementarity and Fit

In a series of papers, Milgrom and Roberts (e.g., 1988b, 1990, 1995b) have argued that finding fit will often involve recognizing and exploiting complementarities that exist among elements of strategy and organization. Two elements of choice are complementary when increasing one weakly increases the return to increasing the other. Complementarity ideas accord with the rugged landscape in accentuating the possibly multitudinous interactions among organizational design variables. They also are consistent with the design problem involving indivisibilities and nonconcavities. So the complementarity approach shares key features of the rugged landscapes framework, namely, that multiple local optima are normal and that improving performance may require changing many aspects of design simultaneously. But crucially, this approach assumes that there are important regularities in the interactions among the attributes of the organization and a resulting recognizable logic to organizational performance and design.

In particular, with complementary choice variables, any change in the environment that favors increasing a particular variable will also favor increasing all other variables that are complementary to it. Further, increasing them all will yield a greater change in payoffs than would be estimated by looking at the individual changes in isolation. Thus, there is a tendency for all or none of a set of complementary practices to be adopted together. In addition, the search for performance improvement is simplified, because at least half the gains from moving from any particular specification of the choices to the optimum can be found just by searching over those quadrants where all variables are higher than at the base point and where all are lower (Milgrom

---

14. The problem is NP complete (Rivkin 2000).

and Roberts 1995a). Yet, as in the rugged landscapes literature, failure to adjust even one variable optimally may lead to large losses relative to the overall optimum, and local improvements may not find the overall optimum. Thus, some of the difficulties of imitation survive.

There is now a wealth of papers using complementarity in studying strategy and organization. Milgrom and Roberts (1988b) argued that the strategic issue of the breadth of the firm's product line is complementary with such organizational choices as producing to order (rather than for inventory) and communicating more closely with customers. Milgrom and Roberts (1990) argued for complementarities among the frequency of new product introduction, the flexibility of the manufacturing system, reduced inventories, and the extent of outsourcing, with greater reliance on these being driven by improvements in information and communications technologies. Milgrom and Roberts (1995a) added a group of human resource management practices to the "modern manufacturing" nexus. These practices include long-term employment, high investment in training, finer pre-employment screening, worker empowerment, and increased horizontal communication. The same paper also points to complementarities among Lincoln Electric's low-cost strategy and many of its distinctive organizational features: piece rates, bonus payments for quality and cooperation, no layoffs, internal ownership, open communication, no executive perks, and large inventories of work in process.

Testing empirically whether choices are actually complementary is tricky, because of unobserved heterogeneity problems (Athey and Stern 1998; see also Brynjolfsson and Milgrom, this volume). However, numerous empirical studies have observed patterns of payoffs to differing or changing strategic and organizational designs that are consistent with complementarity. For example, MacDuffie (1995) found that a distinctive set of human resource management practices was associated with the move to Toyota-style lean production in U.S. auto assembly plants, as Milgrom and Roberts's models had suggested. Ichniowski et al. (1997) found that a bundle of human resource management practices positively affected performance in steel finishing only when they were all adopted. Whittington et al. (1999) found the payoffs to changing elements of strategy and organization in a broad survey of European firms had a similar pattern: only by making all the changes was performance improved, but then the improvements were significant. Bresnahan et al. (2002) found that investments in IT were much more productive when matched with changes in organization that are arguably complementary. See Brynjolfsson and Milgrom (this volume), Lazear and Oyer (this volume), Ichniowski and Shaw (this volume), and Waldman (this volume) for other examples of complementarity among features of strategy and organization.

3.4. Some Dynamics

Of course, establishing alignment among strategy, organization, and the environment is not a once-and-for-all proposition. As the environment changes, the strategy and organization may need to be adjusted to maintain performance. This raises the issue of how finely the strategy and organization ought to be crafted to perform in a single environment. If some organizational designs will deliver reasonably good performance across a range of environmental conditions, while others perform exceptionally well over a limited range but badly if the environment changes more substantially, then there can be a trade-off between maximizing performance in a given environment and achieving good performance over time in the face of environmental change (so long as organizational change is costly). This trade-off is similar to that noted by Stigler (1939) for the choice of cost curves in the face of variable demand. We are not aware of formal efforts to model the trade-off.

Although changing environmental conditions may call for organizational change, numerous observers have noted an apparent tendency for organizations to alternate between centralized and decentralized modes. Typically, these oscillations are taken by business commentators as reflecting managerial failure. A more positive approach has been suggested by Nickerson and Zenger (2003). A version is the following: Suppose the behavior that drives performance is not observable, and further suppose that the relationship between action and outcomes is so subtle and complex that agents cannot easily figure out how to behave to improve performance. Thus, inducing the right behavior is not possible using normal means. However, suppose that the formal organizational architecture and the associated routines and processes shape behavior over time. For example, when the organization is decentralized, initiative might tend to increase but cooperation tend to decrease. Now suppose there are only two coherent patterns of organizing: decentralized or centralized. Either a decision is made at the center or at the operating level; there is no half-way option. Thus, if we let the behavior be indicated by $a \in [0, 1]$, we specify that da/dt is positive if the organizational choice x is centralized ($x = 1$) and is negative if it is decentralized ($x = 0$). Further, suppose that $\lim_{t \to \infty} a(t, x) = x$, so behavior drifts to extremes. Finally, suppose that the performance is concave in a, that the optimal behavior is somewhere between that induced by centralization and decentralization, and that changing x is costly. Then just like a thermostat or an (s, S) solution to an inventory problem, the solution is to set $x = 1$ for a period of time, so that a drifts up, eventually reaching a critical level at which it is too far above the desired level, then to switch to $x = 0$ for a time, during which a drifts down until it has fallen to another critical level, whereupon x is reset to 1. So the organizational design optimally bounces back and forth.

3.5. Recent Trends in Organizational Design

For at least two decades, scholarly, journalistic, and practitioner observers of business organizations have been describing a broad pattern of changes. Here we present the perceived trends, as noted largely in case studies, and then look at the econometric evidence for them.

3.5.1. Perceived Trends

Architectural elements of the changes include reducing the overall size of the organization (downsizing, downscoping, outsourcing, and reliance on alliances); breaking up units into smaller sizes with more focused responsibilities; decreasing the number of hierarchic layers (delayering); increasing spans of control (the number of direct reports to an individual manager), especially at the top of the hierarchy; increasing operational and strategic delegation and, sometimes simultaneously, increasing authority at the center (via assumption of some powers previously held by the delayered middle managers); developing cross-functional and cross-business teams; and adopting more flexible, project-oriented structures. Routines and process changes include increased communication (horizontally among units and within teams; vertically across the hierarchy; and externally with suppliers, customers, and allies); heavy investment in information and communications technologies; and altered human resource practices, including tighter pre-employment screening, more training, greater reliance on (often group) performance pay, more flexible job designs, greater encouragement of linkages among people, and greater reliance on frontline employees' using their own knowledge, judgment, and intelligence.[15] Generally, the drivers of these changes are seen to be increased competition through globalization of markets and industries and changes in information and communication technologies. Increased competition requires firms to be able to change more quickly and respond faster to market developments. Technology enables operating and managing in new ways to meet the new challenges.

3.5.2. Econometric Evidence

Most patterns described above are drawn from individual case studies and/or small-numbers studies. The first systematic empirical examination of these changes on a broad scale appears to be Whittington et al. (1999). They surveyed a group of medium to large British and European manufacturing firms, receiving responses from about 450 CEOs. Their questions asked about current (1996) organizational practices on ten of the dimensions noted above[16] and about changes since 1992. They found broad support for the asserted patterns of change but significant variation in the range and extent of actual changes. Strikingly, after bundling the changes into three groups—changing structures, changing processes, and changing boundaries—they found evidence that making changes in only one or two of these tended to be associated with weaker financial performance, whereas changing all three was associated with stronger performance.

Bresnahan et al. (2002) examined U.S. data from a similar period and found that information technology investment was associated with increasing decentralization; increased employee empowerment; an increased value to employee skill, leading to more screening and training; and on the strategic side, increased new product introduction. Also like Whittington et al. (1999), they found feedbacks consistent with complementarity among these features.

More recently, several empirical studies have examined more specific aspects of organizational and strategic change, sometimes linking these to increased competition. Rajan and Wulf (2006), Gaudalupe and Wulf (2010), and Guadalupe et al. (2012) all examined changes in the hierarchical structure of firms, using U.S. data. Rajan and Wulf studied a sample of 300 very large U.S. firms from 1986 to 1998. Their first finding was that the number of people reporting directly to the average CEO rose significantly, from an average (median) of 4.4 (4) in 1986 to 8.2 (7) in 1998. They also found that the number of layers in the hierarchy between the CEO and the lowest level manager with profit and loss responsibility (division heads) fell by more than a quarter over the period, while the number of division heads reporting directly to the CEO increased three times, and many of these frontline managers were newly appointed as corporate officers. These changes took place despite little change in the size of the divisions they headed. Instead, the delayering involved removing middle managers, such as chief operating officers, whose number fell by 20% during this period. Finally, the compensation of the division heads rose as they moved closer to the CEO, suggesting that their responsibili-

---

15. See Whittington et al. (1999) for references to the management literature describing these changes and Roberts (2004) for more detailed descriptions of the changes.

16. The dimensions queried were delayering, project structure, operational decentralization, strategic decentralization, human resource innovations, information technology, horizontal linkages, outsourcing, strategic alliances, and downscoping.

ties were increased. Rajan and Wulf (2006) discussed several possible drivers of these changes, but did not test any of them. Potential drivers included increased product market competition requiring quicker responses, improved corporate governance driving out slack and dismantling empires, and improved information technology allowing a broader span of control at the top.

Guadalupe and Wulf (2010) explicitly identified increased competition as leading to these changes, utilizing a quasi-natural experiment. They studied the effect of increased Canadian competition for U.S. firms occasioned by the passage of the North American Free Trade Agreement, which removed U.S. tariffs on imports from Canada. Using a multi-industry panel of more than 300 firms during 1986–1999, they employed a differences in differences strategy made possible because different industries had enjoyed different levels of tariff protection before the tariffs were removed. They were able to show that increased competition led to decreased numbers of hierarchical layers and larger CEO spans of control.

Most recently, Guadalupe et al. (2012) looked at the composition of the set of executives reporting directly to the CEO in a panel of 300 large U.S. firms from 1986 to 2006. They found that the number of such executives doubled on average, but that three-quarters of this growth was among senior functional managers (e.g., chief marketing officer, chief information officer), rather than among general managers responsible for pieces of business. We return to this paper in our discussion of the organization of multiproduct firms in Section 4.2.1.2.

At a lower hierarchic level, Colombo et al. (2007) examined the effects on profitability of adopting high-performance work practices, including plant-level profit sharing, pay for skills, total quality management, team work, job rotation, and employee involvement in decisions, in a panel of single-plant Italian metalworking firms in the 1990s. (Many studies have documented the spread of such practices over the past decades, but few have measured their impact on performance.) They also looked at the effects of reducing the number of supervisory layers between the plant manager and the workers and of delegation of operational and strategic authority to the plant manager. In doing this, they controlled for the adoption of various advanced manufacturing technologies. The sample was relatively small (109 firms), and there seem to have been significant selection issues associated with it. Still, they obtained some interesting results.

In particular, they found that, among the high-performance work practices, only profit sharing and total quality management were individually significant in affecting profitability, with both having positive effects. However, there was significant colinearity in their data, because the practices tended to be adopted in bundles, making estimating individual effects tricky. In any case, the null hypothesis that the collection of high-performance work practices together had no effect was easily rejected. The effect of involving the plant manager in decisions rather than holding them all with the manager's superior was also positive and significant, whereas the number of layers had an inverse-U shaped effect: bureaucratic firms with many layers gained by delayering, but those with few layers gained by adding intermediate levels.

In two recent papers Cuñat and Guadalupe have investigated the effect of increased competition on incentive compensation inside firms. The first of these (Cuñat and Guadalupe 2005) examined data from the 1990s on the compensation of the highest-paid executive (director), other executive directors, and the average employee from a panel of more than 22,000 U.K. manufacturing firms, ranging in size from the largest firms in the country to ones with only five employees. They utilized a quasi-natural experiment, namely, the sharp and sudden appreciation of the British pound in 1996, which increased foreign competition for these firms (but differentially so for firms in more open sectors). Their differences in differences estimations found a strong effect: increased competition led to greater sensitivity of pay to firm profit at all levels, but especially at the top of the firm.

Cuñat and Guadalupe (2009) used a matched employer-employee panel of 831 large U.S. manufacturing firms and 7,571 executives from 1992 to 2000. The data involve detailed information on firm characteristics and on the base and performance-related pay of the five highest-paid executives in each firm. Foreign competition is measured by import penetration in different lines of business. The results are that increased foreign competition lowered base pay and increased the sensitivity of pay to performance. In addition, the in-firm dispersion of total pay among executives increased, largely through greater increases in performance sensitivity for higher ranks, and executive total compensation increased. Further, increased competition led firms to hire more able executives. Together these studies point to a strong role for competition in driving compensation and staffing decisions, a key aspect of organizational design.

Although competition's impact on organization is beginning to be documented, there is much less work examining its effects on strategy. Exceptions are case studies, such as Skil's withdrawing from the mass market channels for power tools in the face of competition from Black & Decker (Porter and Ong 1988), Intel's decision to abandon the dynamic random-access memory business it had created and focus only on microprocessors in the face of Japanese competition (Burgelman 1994), and IBM's move to accentuate services over hardware sales (Applegate et al. 2009). There are also a few studies at the industry level. Notable are Freeman and Kleiner (2005), Bartel et al. (2007), and Bugamelli et al. (2008), each of which showed manufacturing firms in particular industries increasing innovation in response to competition from low-wage countries.

The first cross-industry study in this area appears to be Bloom et al. (2011a). They examined the impact of Chinese imports from 2000 to 2007 on strategy and aspects of organization in a set of many hundreds of European firms.[17] During this period, following China's entry to the World Trade Organization, the share of imports from China to the United States and Europe more than doubled. These products were typically technologically unsophisticated, mass produced, and of basic quality.

The authors found that imports from China to a given country and product market reduced employment in the importing country, as many domestic firms contracted or went out of business. However, those firms that stayed in business shifted to a strategy emphasizing innovation (higher quality) by increasing their patenting and research and development expenditures. They also increased their total factor productivity growth and their investments in information technology. Meanwhile, on the organizational side, they improved their management practices on the 18 dimensions first identified in Bloom and Van Reenen (2007): monitoring (do firms continuously collect, analyze, and use information); targets (do firms have balanced, well-understood, and binding targets); and incentives (do firms reward high-performers and retrain and/or sanction poor performers). The attention to both strategic and organizational features makes Bloom et al. (2011a) especially notable.

---

17. The number varied across different datasets related to different dimensions of the estimated effects.

3.6. Organization and Competitive Advantage

As discussed in Section 2.1, competitive advantage is the set of reasons that other parties will deal with the firm on terms that let it realize its goals. As also noted, at any point in time, competitive advantage is likely to lie in the firm's mix of quality and price that attracts its target customers, because they prefer this offer to the alternatives in the market. However, for such an advantage to be sustainable in the face of competition, the firm must have some advantages that are not replicable. Lasting competitive advantage is inconsistent with everyone having access to the same production and market opportunities.

A favorable market position can be a significant source of sustainable advantage. Examples are a monopoly position protected by barriers to entry or uniquely low costs arising from learning economies that resulted from being a first-mover. Porter's (1980) application of industrial organization economics to strategy accentuated positional advantage and market power as the source of rents.

The resource-based view of the firm, originating with Rumelt (1984) and Wernerfeldt (1984), accentuates looking at input markets over the output markets that are the focus of Porter-style work. It sees the sources of rents in the unique resources and capabilities that the firm has at its disposal.

Unique resources, such as patents or access to particularly productive ore deposits, can be a source of lasting advantage. There is, however, always an issue of whether the firm is getting the most out of these resources by using them itself rather than selling or licensing them. Moreover, human resources are a particularly difficult source of lasting competitive advantage, because employees' ability to seek alternative employment means they are apt to claim a large share of the rents they generate. Interdependencies among employees, which imply they need to move together to carry their rent-generating potential elsewhere, combined with problems coordinating their bargaining with alternative employers, may restrict their ability to seize the rents they generate (Mailath and Postlewaite 1990). But Wall Street's experience with teams of hot traders moving to other banks, Hollywood's history of star performers and directors collecting the bulk of the returns that the studios cannot hide, and Silicon Valley's norm of engineers moving en masse to create new companies are all suggestive of the problems with making money on the basis of unique human resources. Clearly, to the extent that unique human resources are the source of profits, the recruitment, retention, and motivation of these people are crucial activities to which the organization must be shaped.

The other widely recognized source of competitive advantage are the unique capabilities of the firm that let it produce better or cheaper products or services and develop superior new ones. In standard economic models, these capabilities are black-boxed in the production function. Once we start to unpack the box, the connection between capabilities and organization emerges. Capabilities rely on the knowledge and skills of different people in the firm (not any single individual, or that person alone would be the source of rents). Thus, to cite a standard example, Sony's capabilities in miniaturization in the 1970s and 1980s that let it develop breakthrough products did not reside in any one person but in a collection of people inside the firm and in the standardized routines it had for developing compact products. Activating the capabilities relies on these people working together, so the capabilities depend on the networks among individuals as well as the formal architecture of teams, departments, and divisions. Motivating people may draw on numerous other aspects of the organizational design. Finally, as emphasized by Nelson and Winter (1982), the capabilities become encoded in the routines of the firm.

From this point of view, the strategic question is not so much which markets to enter and how to position the firm's offerings in those markets, but rather what resources to acquire and which capabilities to build. Of course, neither formulation stands on its own: deciding on developing a capability requires evaluating the uses to which it could be put, and choosing a product strategy depends on being able to generate the product in question. Yet the focus on capabilities seems better suited for considering a variety of issues, such as the persistence of performance differentials among apparently similar firms (see Gibbons and Henderson, this volume). It also leads to conceptions of the fundamental problems facing firms that are quite different from the industrial organization approach, because skill development and acquisition, knowledge management, and the management of innovation and learning are key activities. It further puts the focus much more on the organization—people, architecture, routines, and culture—than is natural under Porter's industrial organization approach.

The economics literature contains streams of work that connect to these issues. For example, Prendergast (1993) examines how promotion policies can affect the development of firm-specific human capital. Meanwhile, a variety of organizational approaches have been studied in the context of encouraging innovation. These include incomplete ownership contracts in Aghion and Tirole (1994), agency contracts in Manso (2011), and the allocation of authority in Rantakari (2012a). See Lazear and Oyer (this volume) and Waldman (this volume) for more on human resource management and see Azoulay and Lerner (this volume) on innovation.

4. The Multiproduct Firm, Corporate Strategy, and Organization

The previous sections focused on strategy and organization for firms operating in a single market. Now we turn to multiproduct firms. Of course, almost all firms are "multiproduct" if products are defined as in Arrow-Debreu by the date, location, and state of the world in which they are available, as well as by their physical characteristics. However, we focus on situations where more common notions of market definition mean that the firm is operating in several distinct (possibly unrelated) markets. These might be defined by the set of physical products or services being offered or, in the case of a multinational firm, by geography.

Corporate strategy is about multiproduct firms. It involves answering two questions. First, which businesses should be created or brought inside a single firm? To answer this, in turn, we need to explain how having these businesses under common ownership and management will allow them to do better than they could do on their own (or bundled with some other group of businesses). The organizational issues at the corporate level are then to figure out how to structure the connections among these businesses to realize the opportunities for better performance and how to allocate decisionmaking and rewards within the firm. These issues involve the role of corporate headquarters and its relations with the units. At least until recently, formal economic theory has had little to say on these questions.

4.1. Why Are There Multiproduct Firms?

Chandler (1969) documented that corporate diversification occurred on a major scale in the United States during the 1930s. He seems to have believed that this broadening of scope arose from the desire to maintain growth when the markets in which the firms were already active showed no growth prospects (Chandler 1969: 275). After World War II the United States experienced the development of conglomerate mergers—ones involving unrelated products, such as bringing baking and telephone service provision inside one firm. Early attempts to explain these combinations (Marris 1964; Mueller 1969) rested on "managerialist" theories. Today these would be modeled as moral hazard on the part of managers who prefer (for whatever reason) that their firms grow faster than shareholders' interests would warrant and faster than can be achieved in the market(s) in which they are already active.

4.1.1. Teece's Theory of the Multiproduct Firm

The first attempt to build a systematic theory of firm scope based on profit-maximizing behavior is due to Teece (1982). Strikingly, although Google Scholar lists more than 1,300 references to this paper, only a handful of the referencing papers are in economics journals and only a couple, all appearing recently, are in the most-cited journals: economists have largely ignored the issue of the horizontal scope of the firm. This is quite remarkable, given the huge amounts of attention devoted to explaining vertical integration.

Teece wrote in the spirit of Williamson (1975) and of Nelson and Winter (1982). There is no formal model, but much serious theorizing and good sense. He began by arguing that, under standard assumptions, many arguments that might be adduced to explain the existence of multiproduct firms are not valid. Economies of scope plus efficiency lead to joint production, but if contracts are complete, there is no need for this to occur inside a single firm. Instead, the producers of the various goods can contract over the shared inputs giving rise to the scope economies. Bringing two random income streams together by merging the corresponding companies may reduce variance, but shareholders can achieve that gain for themselves if the capital markets are working properly. Similarly, the merging of income streams does not increase the value of the firm by reducing default risk: all that happens is that bondholders gain and stockholders lose, with the total value being unaffected. The fall in the stockholder wealth comes from the reduced value of the option that stock represents, where this reduced value is occasioned by the reduced variance.

Teece's (1982) arguments to explain the existence of multiproduct firms focus on the existence of excess resources in firms—resources that would not be efficiently used in the current line(s) of business. These may be indivisible physical assets; financial assets; human resources; or, importantly, knowledge. Machine capacity may exceed the demands of the current business, so the machine is often idle. The firm may be generating cash in excess of what can profitably be reinvested in its current business. Experience may have increased the productivity of workers or managers, meaning that they are not fully occupied in the current business. Knowledge and knowhow often have the character of a public good that allows them to be used repeatedly without being "used up."

These excess resources should be put to other uses. If they cannot be efficiently transferred to other users contractually, they may be better used within the firm by its diversifying into new lines of business.

Teece (1982) then presented transaction cost arguments concerning the likelihood that particular resources can or cannot be effectively transferred contractually. Although nonspecialized indivisible assets can be shared contractually, specialized physical assets are subject to hold-up.

Protecting them may then be the basis for diversification, if they can be used in multiple products. Knowhow with multiple uses that is embodied in human assets is hard to transfer for a variety of reasons: not only is it subject to all the usual problems with selling information, but also much of it is likely to be tacit, so its transfer may necessitate moving people (at least temporarily). Finally, following Williamson (1975), Teece argued that internal capital allocation may be better than what the market can achieve, because the managers may have deeper knowledge and may have better incentives than do bankers (see Gertner and Scharfstein, this volume). In any case, multiproduct firms may be efficient.

We might note that industrial organization economics provides some other potential advantages to a multiproduct firm, but again Teece's arguments about the role of contracting apply. For example, static Nash behavior between providers of substitutes (or complements) will lead to prices that do not maximize total joint profits. Bringing the two firms under common control would then be profitable. But if the firms can contract over the prices they will charge, this alternative might be at least as effective as merger. Similarly for situations of multimarket contact: two multiproduct firms might coordinate better than two pairs of standalone enterprises, but again, contract may be an alternative.

What is missing from Teece's (1982) theory is an analysis of the limits of the multiproduct firm. He starts from an existing firm with excess assets, which enters new businesses presumably until it runs out of spare resources. But many multiproduct firms grow by acquisition. Perhaps this behavior is a matter of buying assets to use with other assets already inside the firm that are in excess supply and are not easily transferrable. This story was one given for conglomerate mergers: the managers of the conglomerates were supposedly better than those outside the firm and had the capacity to manage more assets better than outsiders could. Ultimately, however, there must be some cost to adding new businesses inside a single firm. Otherwise, we face a version of Williamson's selective intervention problem (Williamson 1985). If the managers of a multiproduct firm can mimic the market when that is appropriate, but manage internally assets that cannot be transferred efficiently through contract, then there is no limit to the scope of the firm.

4.1.2. Limits on the Scope of the Firm

Williamson (1985) presented a variety of arguments against the possibility of a comprehensive policy of selective intervention that would limit the size of firms. In the case where an owner-managed firm is being absorbed, the primary one is the difficulty or inadvisability (for multitasking reasons) of committing to marketlike incentives. If two organizations where ownership and management are already separated are being brought together, he focuses on the costs of bureaucracy, including an excessive propensity to manage, excessive forgiveness, and log-rolling, all of which might be more extensive in a merged organization.

Milgrom and Roberts (1988a) identified another potential cost of having decisions made inside an organization: the affected parties would have strong incentives to try to influence the decisionmaker in ways that would not be possible if the decision were made in another organization to which both parties did not belong. These influence activities could be expected to be greater as the range of decisions being taken and the number of interested parties increase, so they would increase with the size and possibly with the complexity of the organization. These activities can be costly in a variety of ways: resources are expended on them, decisions may be affected by them in ways that do not promote efficiency, and organizational processes may be twisted to reduce the extent of influence activities (see Gibbons et al., this volume). These influence costs could then put a limit on the (horizontal) scope of the firm.

Meyer et al. (1992) then developed an explicit influence cost–based argument concerning horizontal scope as an explanation of the trend in the 1980s for multiproduct firms to shed businesses that had become poor performers, even if their weakness was public knowledge, so they could not fetch a high price. They argued that divisions that had fallen on hard times would be especially likely to exert influence in attempts to grab corporate resources to keep themselves going, to the detriment of overall efficiency. If separation into distinct companies limited or prevented this influence activity, this would give a reason for spinoffs or sale of such weak units. (For further discussion of these issues, see Gertler and Scharfstein, this volume.)

Although such arguments as those adduced by Williamson (1985) and by Milgrom and Roberts (1988a) for the cost of integration may eminently plausible, it would be more theoretically appealing if the costs and benefits of integration were to emerge in a single model. In a recent contribution, Friebel and Raith (2010) offer such a theory of the multiproduct firm. Like that of Teece (1982), their approach rests on difficulties of contracting, but it has a much more organizational flavor.

4.1.3. Friebel and Raith on the Multiproduct Firm

Friebel and Raith (2010) modeled the choice between having two separately owned firms (each run by a manager, who contracts with the unit's owner) and a consolidated firm (where the two managers are still in charge of their divisions and there is also a central owner and/or CEO who contracts with the two managers). The advantage of the multiproduct firm is that it can potentially allocate resources better than the separate firms can.

Specifically, contracting problems are assumed to prevent transferring assets between separate companies, but the bringing the assets under common ownership eliminates the need for contracting over them. The CEO can then allocate the resources as seems fit, leaving them in the divisions where they were initially lodged or moving one unit's resources into the other.

The costs of consolidation are informational and incentive ones. First, the manager of each unit can exert costly, unobservable effort to increase the value of resources used in that unit. To motivate this effort, managerial compensation, even in the standalone context, should be tied to the performance of the manager's unit. In fact, bringing the two firms under common management partially alleviates this moral hazard problem, because the possibility of resources being transferred increases the returns to effort more than the threat of losing resources decreases effort incentives. However, some own-performance pay is still needed.

Second, the consolidated firm faces another problem. Specifically, the value of using resources in each division is private information to the unit's manager. Thus, the managers need to be induced to provide accurate information to headquarters to allow efficient reallocation between the divisions of the merged firm. But now the own-unit performance pay creates problems. In particular, the managers must get some nonnegative return when admitting that the value of resources in their units are low rather than claiming the value is high and that they should be receiving resources, not giving them up. If the managers' pay were independent of their units' performance, they would presumably be willing to report truthfully. With the performance pay, however, the incentives are to hang on to resources. The performance pay generates an endogenous incentive for empire building, because having more resources helps generate better returns and rewards. To offset this and generate incentives for correct revelation, rewards must also be linked to overall firm performance (or, equivalently, the performance of the other unit). Doing so raises the cost of providing incentives. These problems are avoided if the firms are distinct and each unit's resources are certain to be used there. Thus, the gain in the efficiency of capital allocation comes at organizational costs of misaligned incentives for effort and truthful communication.

Depending on the magnitudes of these incentive costs and of the benefits of reallocation, either single or multiproduct firms may be better. In particular, if the difference in the productivity of resources between high- and low-value uses is increased, then the gains to reallocation are greater. This situation favors bringing the units under common direction. Also, if the economies of scale in the use of resources increase, common management is favored for similar reasons. This might be the case if the two units are more similar in their production processes, so that their resources are more likely to be complementary. Further, stepping outside the formal model, if the managers can be held accountable for their reports, then the multiproduct solution is favored, because the cost of inducing correct revelation falls. Such accountability might be possible in a repeated framework corresponding to an ongoing venture.

4.1.4. Other Approaches

The possibility of transferring resources more effectively presents one clear motive for multiproduct firms, but surely not the only one. For example, if there are economies of scope in marketing, then product line extensions would seem attractive. If the salespersons are employees of the firm for multitasking incentive reasons (Anderson and Schmittlein 1984; Holmström and Milgrom 1991), then the line extension must be done inside a single firm. The countervailing costs might be the diminishing returns to more finely segmenting markets. More generally, formal models building on the difficulty of contracting to share assets (versus reallocating them) would be potentially interesting, with knowledge sharing being a particularly obvious candidate.

There is a huge literature, largely in finance, that studies mergers and acquisitions, a major mechanism through which multiproduct firms are created and expanded. It seeks to understand whether mergers create or destroy value (as they would if driven by executives' enjoying private benefits from having larger empires), when they occur, and what the characteristics of the targets and acquirers are. This literature is too large to address here. For a recent paper with extensive references, see Basu (2010).

4.1.5. Multinationals

The particular case of the multinationals as multiproduct firms has received separate attention from the scholarly communities in international trade, economic geography, and international business. The first issue here is why firms become multinationals, that is, make foreign direct investments by acquiring or establishing facilities and subsidiaries in other countries. The existence of foreign markets for the firms' products is not enough, as there are options of exporting (perhaps using a local distributor for sales and service) and of licensing a foreign affiliate. The literature here, growing out of the work of Dunning (1977) and ably surveyed by Markusen (1995), focuses on shared excess resources, mostly knowledge, originally held in the home country, and on the difficulties of contracting on the transfer and use of knowledge. These factors lead firms to establish their own production facilities in foreign markets. Formal models of such "horizontal internationalization," wherein firms produce goods in different locations to be sold either locally or exported, begin with Helpman (1984) and Markusen (1984). The issue of vertical internationalization, with firms establishing plants in foreign countries to supply inputs, is a different matter that takes us too far from the chapter's subject of strategy and organization.

The second issue with multinationals is their internal organization. Again, the literature on this subject is largely separate from organizational economics but is relevant to its concerns. We now turn to this topic.

4.2. Structuring the Multiproduct Firm

The literature considers two broad questions about how to organize a multiproduct firm. First, how should activities be grouped for purposes of coordination and motivation? This issue was first addressed by Chandler (1962), who described the replacement of functional organizational designs by multidivisional architectures. More recent work has examined when each of these may be optimal and when even more complex designs may be best. We examine this topic in this section. The second issue is, where should the authority to make various decisions be lodged? In the context of centralization versus decentralization, this question goes back for decades, but there has been recent work of substantial note explicitly in the context of a multibusiness firm. This is the subject matter of Section 4.3.

When modern corporations first emerged in the nineteenth century, they were organized functionally (Chandler 1962). All manufacturing activities were grouped together and reported to a head of manufacturing, who in turn reported to the CEO; similarly for sales, marketing, procurement, engineering, and so on. Williamson (1975) dubbed this the unitary or U-form organization.

Beginning in the early years of the twentieth century companies developed and adopted the multidivisional or M-form of organization (Chandler 1962). In this model, "business units" are established that, in the first instance, offer a particular product. The business units take fundamental responsibility for all activities directly necessary to bring their products to market (later versions of the model have had business units defined by customer segments, technologies, geographies, and probably other criteria). Thus, each business unit handled its own product development, engineering, procurement, manufacturing, marketing, sales, and service. Meanwhile, finance, accounting, legal, and possibly other support services stayed under the control of headquarters, as well as the definition of the scope of the individual businesses, the establishment of strategic direction, and monitoring of division performance.[18] The prototypical example is General Motors under Alfred P. Sloan. Each of the divisions—Chevrolet, Pontiac, Oldsmobile, Buick, and Cadillac—had its assigned target market, was to avoid competing with its brethren, and was measured on its performance, much as if it were a standalone company. The divisions developed, manufactured, and sold their own models within these mandates, while headquarters allocated capital, monitored performance, and set strategy, avoiding involvement

---

18. Earlier there were also holding companies that owned several distinct businesses (each arranged functionally), but the headquarters of a holding company played a very limited role relative to the role it played in the M-form.

in operating details. This organizational design ultimately spread across American industry and then to Europe and Asia, eventually becoming the dominant form for large, complex firms around the world.

4.2.1. U-Form versus M-Form

Chandler (1962) and Williamson (1975, 1985) both discussed the U-form and M-form as alternatives. Chandler argued on the basis of historical observation, to which Williamson added transaction cost insights, that it was increasing size and complexity in multiproduct, multilocational firms that rendered the U-form incapable of coordinating effectively at reasonable cost. With only the CEO having authority and responsibilities across functions, the top became overloaded. At the same time, the need for coordination across what were to be the divisions meant that a holding company, with a headquarters that took only the most minimal role, was also inadequate. Structure then followed strategy: the more ambitious strategies required a new organizational design.

The relative attractions of the U-form versus the M-form were first modeled by operations researchers in the 1980s. A notable example is Malone and Smith (1988), who considered a model of the production of m products, each of which requires that a common set of tasks be undertaken. Product orders arrive randomly and must be assigned to workers who are capable of handling the necessary tasks. Among the several organizational alternatives considered by Malone and Smith are (1) a product-based hierarchy in which the m product managers (who decide on the tasks to be undertaken) directly assign workers who are under their individual commands to the tasks and (2) a functional hierarchy in which all workers capable of carrying out a task report to a functional manager, with the functional managers being told what tasks need doing by a top-level product manager (the CEO). The analysis, based on queuing theory, evaluated the design options on the length of the average queue, the amount of communication necessary for coordination, and the costs of disruption when a worker is unavailable. The model suggested that if production became more efficient and coordination more costly, then the product hierarchy would be favored, because it involved lower communication costs. The authors suggested this as an explanation for the shift from U-form to M-form.

Aghion and Tirole (1995) developed the first formal model in economics of U-form versus M-form and the first to adduce incentive reasons as a key element in the choice. The authors built a model of how overload at the center leads to the choice of the M-form that is based on their well-known model of real versus formal authority (Aghion and Tirole 1997).[19] There are two products, production of each of which requires the carrying out of two different activities (say, manufacturing and sales). Each agent can perform two tasks. Thus, the principal hires two agents and assigns each to two specific tasks. The U-form has each agent performing one activity (sales or manufacturing) twice, once for each product, and the M-form has each agent perform both of the two activities associated with one of the products.

Performing each activity involves a search over a number of alternatives to determine the unique best way to undertake the specific activity. Search involves effort, and both the principal and the agents can exert effort to increase the probability of learning the values of all alternatives and thus determine which is best. The agents' efforts are not observable, and incentive pay

---

19. This model is discussed in detail in several chapters, including Bolton and Dewatripont (this volume).

is ruled out. Instead, the agents are motivated to provide effort by career concerns related to potential outside employers' inferring their search abilities. The cost to the principal of exerting effort E is $g(E, k)$, where k is a parameter affecting the marginal cost of effort, with $\partial g/\partial E > 0$ and $\partial^2 g/\partial E \partial k > 0$. There is also a cost for training the agents that is assumed to be strictly lower for the U-form, because each agent must learn how to undertake only one activity.

If the principal is successful in determining the best alternative for all four activities (which occurs with probability E), she will produce both products (she has formal authority in terms of Aghion and Tirole 1997). In this case the market learns nothing of the agents' abilities. If the principal is completely uninformed (which occurs with probability $1 - E$), then she may rely on the agents' possibly being informed and suggesting the way to do things. The payoffs to different alternatives are such that it is worthwhile to produce a product only if the best way to do each of the two associated activities has been found. In the M-form, if either agent learns the best ways to carry out both his responsibilities, then the corresponding product will be produced and the market will raise its beliefs about the agent's abilities. Failure to produce a particular product is thus bad news about the corresponding agent's ability. However, failure to produce a product in the U-form can occur because either agent failed to find the best way to carry out his activity associated with that product. Thus, failure to produce is not as bad news about either agent as it is under the M-form, and so the implied incentives are weaker. From this logic, it follows that the agents in equilibrium will work harder in the M-form for any given E.

Aghion and Tirole (1995) placed assumptions on the curvature of the agents' effort-cost functions and on the payoff increase for the agents in the U-form from two goods being produced rather than one. They then showed that as the parameter of the principal's cost function k rises, increasing the marginal cost of E (which is meant to model the principal becoming overloaded), it becomes more valuable to induce more effort from the agents. This situation favors the M-form. Then, for any specific advantage in training costs (scale economies) that the U-form enjoys, there is a cut-off k^* beyond which the M-form is preferred.

This Aghion-Tirole model is a sensible rendering of the overloaded hypothesis, but (as the authors note) the main conclusion is not very robust to variations in the modeling. Further, the reputation mechanism and wage setting mechanism are not modeled, so the assumption on the relative returns to having two products produced rather than one is ad hoc. In addition, one would want to allow for incentive contracts. Still, this model is a valuable first step that deserves to be better known.

Rotemberg (1999) offered a different take on the issue. In his model, the U-form has an advantage in control: the functional manager, observing more people doing a given job, can more effectively determine the best way to do that job (of which the workers have private knowledge) and require that it be adopted. The M-form has better coordination across functions within a division (in fact, by assumption, within-division coordination is perfect). Rotemberg showed that making compensation more dependent on division performance in the M-form can overcome some of the incentive problems, making workers more willing to reveal their private information. Still, despite the superiority of the M-form at coordination, the U-form can be superior if the importance of getting things done the right way is great enough. However, as the number of employees increases, the M-form ultimately becomes superior, as solving the coordination problem becomes more important.

Maskin et al. (2000) built a model of M-form versus U-form in which different organizational designs generate different information that affects the incentives that can be provided to middle managers. Thus, this approach does not link very directly to the size-complexity-coordination arguments on which earlier modelings were based. The M-form is modeled as a two-function, two-product, three-level hierarchy with a top executive and two mid-level executives, each of whom is responsible for one product and has two frontline functional people reporting to her, one from each function. In the U-form, the managers in the middle have functional responsibilities, and each has two frontline reports, one involved with each product. Each of the various agents can exert nonobservable effort and has a separable utility function over income and the cost of effort. The output of any frontline worker is simply the sum of the unobservable efforts across the three levels plus random noise attached to each effort:

$$y_{ij} = e + \eta + e_i + \delta_i + e_j + \theta_j,$$

where $i = 1, 2$ denotes the function, and $j = A, B$ denotes the product.

Maskin et al. (2000) showed that the provision of incentives at the top and bottom of the hierarchy is unaffected by the choice of U-form or M-form. However, the problem of motivating the middle manager does depend on the architecture. Specifically, the M-form involves relative performance evaluation between the two business unit managers, whereas the U-form has relative performance evaluation between the two functional managers. Which is better depends on how effective this relative performance evaluation is in each case, which is a matter of the amount of residual noise in the performance measures left after the comparison. If it is more effective to compare two division managers than to compare across functions, the M-form is favored. The authors suggested that this might reasonably seem be the case: comparing two product managers is likely more informative than comparing the head of manufacturing's performance to that of the head of marketing (because the corresponding noise terms are more correlated in the former case). This observation does not, however, offer much insight into why the M-form has historically become more important and the U-form less so.

Other approaches to the issue of M-form versus U-form include that of Besanko et al. (2000), who assumed that the M-form permits more effective performance pay but argue that the U-form may be superior if it is sufficiently important to manage cross-product spillovers within functions and there is enough asymmetry in the system. Another approach is that of Qian et al. (2006), who examined how the organizational structure affects the information available for coordination and thus the effectiveness of different sorts of experimentation and innovation.

4.2.2. Matrix Structures

In recent years firms have developed more complex organizational models. A major innovation is the matrix form. In it, at least two dimensions into which the business can be divided are identified. The most frequent are geography and product. Then a particular business in a particular region reports both to a manager with responsibility for that product across geographies and also to a manager responsible for that geography across products. A prime instance is one of the most-studied examples of matrix organization, ABB (Asea Brown Boveri) in the late 1980s and early 1990s (Bartlett 1999). ABB was in a broad range of businesses, from railroad engines to electrical transformers and factory automation equipment, and it operated in most European countries and later also in the Americas and Asia. Its organization design had a global product manager for each of its dozens of product areas (e.g., high-voltage transformers or steam turbines) as well as a country head for each of the countries or regions in which it operated. Then each product area in each geographic area was set up as a separate company, with its own balance sheet and income statement, and the president of that company reported to both the country head and the product manager. The latter was charged with coordinating across countries, determining where investments would be made, and which countries would handle exports to countries without their own manufacturing capabilities. The country head had responsibility for coordinating across businesses in the country, particularly with regard to human resources, labor relations, and governmental affairs, as well as for profit and loss in the country. Both managers were involved in setting performance standards and carrying out performance evaluations for the company presidents. Other multinationals, including Citibank, have had even more complex matrices, involving three or more dimensions.

The importance of these more complex forms is suggested by the recent work of Guadalupe et al. (2012). They examined the changes in the titles (and pay) of the executives who reported directly to the CEO in a sample of U.S. firms. They found a doubling of the number of direct reports from 1986 to 2006, but crucially, much of the growth was from central functional managers being brought into the top executive team, rather than general managers of business units. Presumably, the functional managers were charged with coordination across the companies' businesses on a functional basis. Yet business managers remained an important class of direct reports. This trend certainly suggests strongly that large U.S. firms are moving away from the pure U-form and M-form.

The first attempts to explore formally the relative merits of the matrix form of organization versus a simple product structure or a geographic structure are due to Baron and Besanko (1996, 2001). They considered a firm selling P different products in G geographic areas. Demand for good i in geography j is a linear function of the quantity of the good and of the total amounts of other goods sold by the company in the region and of this good sold in other regions. Similarly, the marginal cost of each good in each region depends on its quantity and the sum of the quantities of other goods sold in the region and the total amount of this good sold in other regions.

Each product in each region has an associated frontline manager. There is also potentially a manager for each region, overseeing all products in the region, and a manager for each product overseeing all regions. Finally, there is a top manager. The top manager designs the organization—which comes down to determining how much influence each middle manager will have over the pay of the frontline managers—and instructs the two middle managers to design bonus contracts for the front line to coordinate the spillovers in the dimension for which that manager is responsible. The payoff to the frontline manager is then a weighted average of the bonuses offered by the two middle managers. The design solution depends on how the spillovers interact.

If all markets are symmetric, a matrix is optimal if coordinating the geographic spillovers requires changing outputs in the opposite direction to that required to coordinate the product spillovers. In this case, both the product and geography managers have a positive influence on the frontline managers' pay. An example would be where there are economies of scale for a particular product, calling for increased production in each individual geography beyond what would otherwise be produced, and competition within a product across geographies (perhaps from customers going to other regions to buy), which calls for reducing output in each geography. In contrast, if the spillovers work in the same direction, then either a pure product or a pure geographic organization is optimal (one or the other middle manager's weight in determining the local manager's pay is zero). Which one should prevail depends on the strength of the two types of spillovers. In particular, the simultaneous existence of both scale and scope economies, which is often suggested as a basis for multinational, multiproduct strategies, is inconsistent with a matrix organization being optimal. Baron and Besanko (1996, 2001) also examined the effect of asymmetries across markets and of local or global competition.

Harris and Raviv (2002) offered another approach to the issue of matrix organization based on coordination along different dimensions rather than the incentive issues that drive the Baron-Besanko model. Coordination of spillovers across activities requires managerial expertise, which is costly. The trade-off is then between the costs of coordination and its benefits. Different organizational designs permit more or less coordination but involve different demands on management.

Reinterpreting the Harris-Raviv setup in terms of the Baron-Besanko formulation, consider a firm that offers two physical products $i = 1, 2$ in two geographic markets $j = A, B$. Product i in market j, denoted P_{ij}, is produced by a local manager. There are four potential bilateral interactions across pairs of markets and products: between P_{iA} and P_{iB}, $i = 1, 2$, each of which occurs with probability p, and between P_{1j} and P_{2j}, $j = A, B$, each of which occurs with probability r. All the random variables are independent. Finding and coordinating a pairwise interaction brings a benefit of 1. Additionally, if all four pairwise interactions are present, there is also an additional benefit of s to coordinating across all four pairs.

The organization consists of a CEO, who is capable of coordinating any interactions and is uniquely able to coordinate across all four pairs, plus zero, two, or four middle managers, each of whom can coordinate a single pairwise interaction. The middle managers each cost F, and the CEO's expenditure of time on coordination has an opportunity cost $Q < s$ to the firm. If there are no middle managers, the local managers report directly to the CEO, who may or may not attempt coordination. This flat organization is called "centralized" if coordination is attempted and "decentralized" if it is not. With two middle managers there can be either a product organization, with one manager coordinating P_{1A} and P_{1B} and the other handling interactions of product 2 across the two markets, or a geographic organization, with one manager coordinating across products in region A and the other handling region B. In either of these cases the CEO may or may not coordinate the interactions not covered by the middle managers and the companywide interaction. These hierarchies are accordingly labeled "centralized" or "decentralized." Finally, with four middle managers we have a matrix structure, with each pairwise interaction handled by a middle manager and, because $s > Q$, the CEO coordinating the companywide interactions if the four managers have each discovered a pairwise interaction.

The authors determined the optimal structure as a function of the costs F of middle managers and the opportunity cost Q of involving the CEO. For high values of F, the flat structure without middle managers is used, and whether the CEO attempts to coordinate depends on how large Q is. For low values of F, a matrix is favored, with the upper boundary of the set of parameters leading to a matrix form being a convex piecewise linear set. It is also possible to have the two hierarchical forms with the CEO involved in coordination, and also the decentralized hierarchy involving middle managers coordinating the more likely interaction (i.e., a product organization if $p > r$).

The Baron-Besanko model is all about incentives and Harris-Raviv ignores them entirely to focus on coordination via managerial expertise and costs. It seems likely that both effects are in fact at work, and a model of matrix organization that encompassed both would seem a natural next step. Drawing on the literature on common agency (Bernheim and Whinston 1986) would seem an obvious step.

4.2.3. Other Forms

Beyond the basic U-form, M-form, and matrix structures, firms are adopting other designs that would seem worthy of formal modeling. For example, Bartlett and Ghoshal (1998) describe an organizational design for multinational corporations that they call the "transnational model." It involves a significant amount of delegation to national business units (to facilitate adaptation to local conditions), differentiated assignments to different local business units and coordination across them (to achieve economies of scale), extensive horizontal communication among business units, and a managerial center that sets broad strategy and coordinates and allocates resources across units. They contrast this model with two earlier ones. In one, decision authority and most activity was highly centralized and standardized with the aim to maximize global efficiency through economies of scale. This model was exemplified by Japanese multinational corporations, such as Matsushita and Toyota in the 1970s. The other involved extreme decentralization to national business units in search of effective adaptation to local conditions. This model was common among European multinational corporations, such as Philips and Unilever, after World War II. The first example of the transnational identified by Bartlett and Ghoshal was ABB in the 1980s (see Section 4.2.2), although other examples are now available.

One such is Tenaris, the leading manufacturer of high-quality seamless steel pipes and tubing globally. As described in Catalano and Roberts (2004), Tenaris has an elaborate "front-and-back" model involving production units—factories as organizational units—in various countries; geographically defined sales units for the countries in which it has production facilities; global, customer-defined sales units; several administrative functions that are managed globally; a global procurement operation; and a "supply chain" unit that manages the allocation of production among factories and the fulfillment of orders. This remarkably complex design was the result of explicit planning, not accretion or uncoordinated variation, although the geographic dispersal of production resulted from acquisitions. It was meant to provide responsiveness to local market conditions, efficiency across markets, and a high level of coordination.

4.3. The Optimal Locus of Decisionmaking in Complex Organizations

There is a large literature on the allocation of authority over decisions between hierarchical superiors and lower levels, much of which is discussed in other chapters in this volume (see Bolton and Dewatripont; Garicano and Van Zandt; Gibbons et al.; Mookherjee, all in this volume). Here we limit consideration to analyses that focus on the particular context of multibusiness firms.

4.3.1. A First Pass at the Problem

Athey and Roberts (2001) offered one of the first formal investigations of the interactions among businesses within a multiproduct firm and how these might affect organizational design. Their analysis is incomplete but quite suggestive.

They considered a firm with two divisions.[20] Each is headed by a manager, who must exert unobservable effort to create value in his individual division plus make a decision, about which he is privately informed, that may have noisy effects on the performance of both units. Crucially, contracting is constrained by there being only a single (noisy) performance measure for each manager ("unit profit"), and this measure confounds the effects of that manager's effort and the two managers' decisions. Athey and Roberts noted that if the decisions had no performance effects, then the optimal pay scheme would have each manager's pay depend heavily on own-performance and, if the noise in the performance measures is positively correlated, would also have each manager's pay depend negatively on the other's performance (relative performance evaluation). In contrast, if effort is not productive (or can be observed), then the pay system should simply focus on making the managers internalize the externalities in their decisions. This approach would tend to make pay depend positively on both performance measures if there are spillovers. There is thus a conflict: good incentives for effort create very bad incentives for decisions, and good incentives for decisions are bad ones for effort.

For the more general case, where both effort and decisions matter, Athey and Roberts (2001) argued that a number of organizational adaptations may be desirable in different contexts. In particular, they suggested that it may be desirable to centralize decisions, either with one of the managers or with a third agent who does not need to exert effort and so can be straightforwardly motivated to make good decisions. Athey and Roberts assumed in this context that the managers' information about the decisions can be made verifiable at a cost. In particular, they did not model the process of communication that would need to occur if the managers' decision-relevant information cannot be communicated verifiably. These issues are picked up in later work.

4.3.2. The Alonso-Dessein-Matouschek and Rantakari Model

Among the first papers to model strategic communication in the context of allocating decision authority are Alonso et al. (2008) and Rantakari (2008). These both considered models of whether decisions in two businesses should be centralized with a single decisionmaker in light of two factors: (1) a need to coordinate decisions between the two units because of externalities and (2) a need to adapt the individual decisions to local conditions that are specific to that business. Informational constraints that limit communication possibilities and differing interests between the two units together create incentive problems. The optimal organization solves the problem of maximizing total profits across the two units.

4.3.2.1. The Symmetric Case. For simplicity, we initially focus on the Alonso et al. (2008) version, which examines only a symmetric case, as opposed to Rantakari's (2008) richer model that explicitly allows for some asymmetries across units and considers a richer set of organi-

---

20. Athey and Roberts (2001) did not explain why the divisions are within a single firm, although the externalities they assume between divisions might provide a basis for an explanation.

zational designs. We return to the Rantakari version later to examine some further alternative organizational structures that can arise there.

Even for the simpler case, the analysis is complicated. Alonso et al. (2008) considered a model with two businesses, each led by a manager, whose payoffs v_i, $i = 1, 2$, depend on both the fit of their individual decisions d_1 and d_2 to local conditions (independent random variables θ_1 and θ_2) and the fit of the two decisions with each other:

$$v_i(d_i, d_j) = -(d_i - \theta_i)^2 - \delta(d_i - d_j)^2.$$

Here δ measures the relative importance of coordinating the two decisions as opposed to responding to local conditions. The payoffs of manager i are exogenously fixed at $\lambda v_i + (1 - \lambda)v_j$, where $0.5 \leq \lambda \leq 1$. Here $(1 - \lambda)$ measures the extent to which the manager cares about the other unit.

The issue Alonso et al. (2008) addressed is when it is best to decentralize and let the two managers make the decisions on their own and when the decisions should be centralized with a third agent (headquarters), whose payoff is simply the sum of the two managers' payoffs, $v_1 + v_2$. In either case, they allow for communication: between the managers when the decisions are decentralized to them, so they can coordinate their choices, or between the individual managers and headquarters, to inform the central decision. In both cases, the communication is cheap talk (Crawford and Sobel 1982): manager i can claim any value m_i for θ_i in $[-s_i, s_i]$, the interval over which θ_i is uniformly distributed, because neither the other manager nor headquarters can observe θ_i, although the distributions are common knowledge. There are no contracts allowed over the decisions or communication protocols. All that can be chosen is who will have decision rights, and once this is set (which is before the managers learn their private local information), these rights cannot be changed.

Although the interactions are relatively complex, the final performance under either structure is determined by the quality of the final decisions, which in turn depend on (1) the amount of information made available to the decisionmaker regarding the local conditions and (2) biases, if any, in the actual use of that information. These factors differ across the two structures.

The analysis proceeds in several steps. First, the decisions that result from any given set of beliefs about the θ_i values are derived. In the centralized case, these values are the ones that maximize the expected value of the headquarters' payoffs. The decision d_i turns out to be a weighted average of the expected values of θ_i and θ_j conditional on the messages received. The weighting on θ_j in determining d_i is 0 if δ is 0, when no coordination is required, so d_i is just the expected value of θ_i conditional on the message m_i. As δ goes to infinity, the weighting converges to 1/2, so each d_i is just the expected value of $\theta_1 + \theta_2$, conditional on m_1 and m_2.

In the decentralized case, the decisions are the Bayesian Nash equilibrium choices by the two managers, given the beliefs they hold after communicating with each other and knowing their own θ_i values. Manager 1's decision is a convex combination of his local conditions θ_1, his posterior belief about θ_2, and Manager 2's posterior belief about θ_1. The weighting depends both on λ and δ. As δ increases, each manager puts less weight on his private information and more weight on a weighted average of the posterior beliefs. As δ goes to infinity, the division managers rely only on the communicated information and set $d_1 = d_2 = E(\theta_1 + \theta_2 \mid m_1, m_2)$. Note that, for given posteriors, these are exactly the same decisions that headquarters implements as δ goes to infinity.

The next step is to determine the communication strategies. Each player has an incentive to exaggerate his private information, with $m_i/\theta_i > 1$ as long as $\theta_i \neq 0$. This is because both the headquarters (in the centralized case) and the other manager (in the decentralized case) have incentives to take decisions that are smaller in magnitude than the given manager would like. From the point of view of manager i, the headquarters puts more weight on coordinating d_i and d_j (instead of adapting d_i to θ_i) than i wants. Because $E(\theta_j) = 0$, if i were to report correctly, then the headquarters' tendency would be to make decisions that are smaller in magnitude than i wants. So manager i exaggerates. When decisionmaking is decentralized, manager j puts more weight on adapting d_j to θ_j rather than coordinating the decisions than manager i wants, and again i is led to exaggerate. Thus, the incentives for misrepresentation are qualitatively similar in both cases. However, under centralization, manager i's incentive to exaggerate is increasing in the own-division bias and in the need for coordination, whereas under decentralization, manager i's incentive to exaggerate is increasing in his own-division bias but decreasing in the need for coordination.

In equilibrium, the private information is not completely revealed. Instead, equilibrium communication is characterized by a collection of intervals in (θ_1, θ_2) space in which the information lies, with a given value of the private information θ_i leading to an announcement that it lies in a certain interval. These intervals become smaller with decreases in the magnitude of the value of the sender's private information, with $m_i = \theta_i$ if $\theta_i = 0$. There are multiple equilibria, indexed by the number of intervals. The most efficient one obtains as the number of intervals grows without bound.

In this most efficient equilibrium, the difference in the quality of information transmission under the two decisionmaking regimes (as measured by the difference of the inverse of the residual variance of θ after communication has occurred under decentralization versus centralization) is decreasing in the own-bias λ and increasing in the need for coordination δ. If $\lambda = 1/2$, then the two regimes are equally effective, as they are as δ goes to infinity. For $\lambda > 1/2$, the centralized regime has better decisionmaking, because an increase in the own-division bias λ has a more detrimental effect on horizontal than on vertical communication. This difference arises because, under centralization, an increase in λ increases the bias of the senders but does not affect the decisionmaking of the receiver. In contrast, under decentralization, an increase in λ also leads to more biased decisionmaking by the receiver. Meanwhile, for any value of the bias, centralized decisionmaking performs better than decentralized, but the two coincide in the limit.

The difference in the precision of communication in the two regimes is essentially driven by the qualitatively different purpose of communication in each. Under centralization the managers communicate to headquarters to induce it to adapt the decisions to their local needs, whereas under decentralization the managers naturally know their local needs but need to communicate with each other to achieve better coordination between the decisions.

The expected profits are now determined through the interplay of the incentives governing the decisions and the quality of the communication. Alonso et al. (2008) showed that the performance of the centralized regime compared to the decentralized one can be written as the difference in performance due to worse adaptation to the local conditions under the centralized regime plus 2δ times the performance advantage due to better coordination that the centralized regime enjoys.

The simple intuition is that decentralization always achieves better adaptation, because the information needed for adaptation is directly available to the division managers, whereas some of it is lost when transmitted to headquarters. Meanwhile, coordination will be better under centralization. By being in control of the decisions, headquarters always achieves the right level of coordination. In contrast, imprecise communication between the division managers under decentralization leads to some coordination failures. Further, these effects are amplified by the own-division biases of the division managers, making their decisions inherently excessively adaptive at the expense of coordination, even given perfect information.

The expression for the relative efficiency turns out to be highly nonlinear in the parameters λ and δ. If $\lambda = 1/2$, so the managers are not biased toward their own profitability, then the two regimes perform equally well. The same is true if coordination does not matter ($\delta = 0$) or, in the limit, if all that matters is coordination: $\delta \to \infty$. However, because of the complex interplay of the effects on communication and on decisionmaking, the effects of increasing the importance of either adaptation or coordination are not monotonic. For positive values of λ that are close enough to $1/2$ (very small bias), decentralization is superior for any δ. This is because the quality of information utilization is good (and similar) under either regime, and so the collocation of information and decisionmaking under decentralization is definitive. Thus, great need for coordination does not necessarily lead to centralization if the individual manager's incentives are good. Similarly, decentralization is superior for any positive λ if the value of coordination is small enough. Essentially, even when the need for coordination is very small, communication is noisy under both structures. Under centralization this noise affects the ability of headquarters to adapt the decisions to the local conditions, whereas under decentralization it affects the ability of the division managers to coordinate their actions. Because for small δ coordination is much less important than adaptation, the centralized structure suffers more from imperfect communication than the decentralized one does. Thus, strong bias is not a problem if the need for coordination is small.

However, for higher values of each variable, centralization can be best. If the division managers are very biased, vertical communication is much more efficient than horizontal. In addition, because increases in own-division biases distort decisionmaking by the division managers but not by headquarters, decisionmaking under centralization is significantly more efficient than decisionmaking under decentralization when the bias is large. Because of these two factors, centralization outperforms decentralization when the division managers are very biased and coordination is important.

This model indicates that the organizational design problem in the multiproduct firm involves extremely complicated trade-offs. Still, Alonso et al. (2008) suggested that their results are consistent with two classic cases of organizational change in multiproduct firms instigated in response to strategic change, namely, General Motors in the 1920s under Alfred Sloan and British Petroleum's Exploration and Production stream in the 1990s under John Browne. In both cases, an increase in the need for coordination led to the creation of mechanisms to facilitate horizontal communication and a rebalancing of incentives toward group versus individual incentives.

4.3.2.2. Allowing for Asymmetries. Rantakari's (2008) model is very similar to that of Alonso et al. (2008), except the unit i's payoffs are

$$\Pi_i = -k_i((1 - r_i)(\theta_i - d_i)^2 + r_i(d_j - d_i)^2),$$

so the two units may differ. Here, r_i measures the relative importance of coordination to division i. It is called the "dependency" of i. The parameter k_i measures the overall importance of decisionmaking to unit i and is related to its size. In parallel with Alonso et al. (2008), the θ_i are independently distributed over $[-s_i, s_i]$, where s_i measures the environmental volatility faced by unit i. In contrast with Alonso et al., each manager is interested only in the profits of his own division (in terms of Alonso et al. [2008], $\lambda = 1$).

Rantakari (2008) investigated the two alternatives of centralization and decentralization studied by Alonso et al. (2008) but was also able to examine the effects of situations where the sizes of the units differ and, more centrally, where the importance of coordination differs between them. Generally, except for low values of both r_1 and r_2, where coordination does not matter much, the decentralized regime does worse than the centralized one, because the latter coordinates better. He also studied two further organizational options that are of interest in the asymmetric case. One, partial decentralization, involves the center choosing d_i, while d_j is left to division j. The other, directional authority, involves subjugating one division to the other, with manager i making both decisions. Shifting the decision authority changes both the decision rules and the equilibrium communication, and each of these forms may be optimal. In particular, Rantakari provided two examples. One involves IBM's managing the PC business in the 1980s, where the partial decentralization model was initially employed, with the PC group allowed to have its head and the mainframe business controlled by the center. Later the PC business was centralized, too. The second involves Microsoft's belated refocusing on the Internet and the development of Internet Explorer. This new business was centralized initially, then brought into one of the main business units in an example of directional authority. In each case, the behavior is in line with the model's predictions.

4.3.2.3. Dynamics. A more recent paper by Rantakari (2012b) uses a version of this same basic model to look at the impact of environmental volatility on several aspects of organizational design: the allocation of decision rights to the managers or headquarters, managerial compensation contracts, managerial investments in learning their local conditions, and the extent of operational integration. The divisional payoff function now is

$$\Pi_i(\theta_i, d_i, d_j) = K(\beta) - \beta(d_i - d_j)^2 - \alpha(d_i - \theta_i),$$

where β is the measure of operational integration. The payoff increases in β through K, reflecting gains from standardization, but the need for coordination also increases with β. The importance of local adaptation is measured by α. Managers now are initially uninformed about their local conditions, but each can get a signal about his θ_i in $[-s, s]$, at a cost that is increasing in the accuracy of the signal. Also, the total profit can be distributed linearly between the two managers in any way. In particular, each might be paid on only his own division's performance, they could share total returns equally, or anything in between. The problem is to select the degree of operational integration, whether the decisions are centralized or decentralized, and the compensation of the managers to maximize expected total returns.

The analysis proceeds in a similar fashion to Alonso et al. (2008) and Rantakari (2008), allowing for the extra choice variables. The key results are in how the solution responds to changes in the uncertainty or volatility in the environment, as measured by the length of the interval $[-s, s]$. In particular, Rantakari showed that an increase in volatility decreases the level of operational integration, decreases the use of firmwide incentives for a given governance structure, and increases the preference for decentralization. If the increase in volatility leads to decentralization, the use of firmwide incentives can increase. In addition, centralization arises as the preferred governance structure only when information is sufficiently costly relative to volatility and is always coupled with a significant level of operational integration and significant use of firmwide incentives.

This model is especially interesting in the context of multinationals. It shows that if the world is well understood and stable, the optimal organization will tend to be centralized in its decisionmaking, with a great deal of operational integration and many firmwide incentives. This specification corresponds to the model Bartlett and Ghoshal (1998) described that aimed at global efficiency through standardization and coordination. In contrast, if conditions in the two markets can differ significantly, then a model with decentralized decisionmaking by the local business units, less operational integration, and pay based more on individual unit performance is favored. This is the model Bartlett and Ghoshal described for trying to achieve high levels of local adaptation.

4.3.3. Horizontal Boundaries of the Firm

The analyses by Alonso et al. (2008) and by Rantakari (2008, 2012b) potentially provide the basis for alternatives to Teece's (1982) theory of the emergence of the multiproduct firm. Such theories would be driven by the effectiveness of communication and of decisionmaking within versus across firm boundaries. If there were only one firm, it could select the incentives for both division managers. If it makes pay depend only on total profits ($\lambda = 1/2$), then the firm would avoid any costs of misaligned incentives. Thus, a useful theory that would allow separate firms to be optimal (and one that would generate both decentralization and centralization in a multiproduct firm) would have to involve some mechanism that makes it valuable for pay to be biased toward own-division results. Inducing effort is an obvious possibility.

Almost by definition, having two separate firms involves the decentralization regime. However, one could imagine allowing the firms to communicate about their local circumstances and also to coordinate their pay systems if there is still value to coordinating decisions (but see Holmström 1999). To make the two-firm alternative interesting, there would again need to be some reason to keep them from agreeing on setting each λ to eliminate own-unit bias. An obvious option is whatever element in the theory prevents a single firm from simply setting $\lambda = 1/2$. In addition, it would be natural to assume that the firms' contracting over each other's actual pay might be problematic, and so only Nash equilibrium choices of pay systems might be possible.

A recent paper by Dessein et al. (2010) offers a related model that does provide an organizationally based theory of the multiproduct firm. They described their model as being concerned with the allocation of decision authority when there are benefits both to responsiveness to local variation in individual product markets in some dimensions or activities (e.g., marketing) and also gains to standardization of other activities across markets (e.g., product designs). The choice is between having the two local managers handle both the marketing and design for their individual markets, in which case the opportunity for achieving gains to standardization is lost (these managers cannot coordinate with one another), or appointing a third manager to oversee the dimension on which standardization may be valuable. The former choice is called "nonintegration" and the latter "integration."

Each manager must be motivated to supply unobservable effort, and they are risk averse, with exponential utility and quadratic costs for the effort applied to each activity. The gains to standardization (in terms of cost reduction) and its costs (in terms of lessened desirability of the product in the individual markets, resulting in lower revenues) are random. Initially these costs and benefits become public information once the organization design is fixed, but the authors also study the case in which they are private information to the manager concerned and so give rise to strategic communication.

Dessein et al. (2010) first computed the (second-best) effort contracts that prevail when the two divisions are not integrated. Each manager receives a fraction of any cost savings and revenue gains in that manager's unit. If integration is attempted, then the manager charged with standardization determines the amount of effort to be put into cost reduction for each good, as well as whether to standardize. Paying this manager just for cost reductions, however, leads to excessive standardization, because the manager making the standardization decision does not bear the cost of the lost revenues. To offset this, the integration manager must also be paid on revenues. However, because the manager is risk averse, paying on revenues has a risk cost that leads to reducing the strength of cost incentives for this manager relative to the nonintegrated case.

Thus, there is an incentive cost to integration that may outweigh the potential gains of standardization. Having strategic communication about the costs and benefits of standardization increases the relative attractiveness of nonintegration.

Note that this model provides an alternative theory of the multiproduct firm if the gains from integration can be realized only by using a manager who needs to be motivated through pay.

5. Conclusion

We have examined the notions of business and corporate strategies and their connection to organization. Although an increasing amount of economic research, both theoretical and empirical, has addressed this subject in recent years, there is still much to do, and it is a fertile area for further work.

REFERENCES

Aghion, Philippe, and Jean Tirole. 1994. "The Management of Innovation." *Quarterly Journal of Economics* 109: 1185–1209.
———. 1995. "Some Implications of Growth for Organizational Form and Ownership Structure." *European Economic Review* 39: 440–456.
———. 1997. "Formal and Real Authority in Organizations." *Journal of Political Economy* 105: 1–29.
Aguilar, Francis Joseph. 1988. *General Managers in Action.* New York: Oxford University Press.

Alonso, Ricardo, Wouter Dessein, and Niko Matouschek. 2008. "When Does Coordination Require Centralization?" *American Economic Review* 98: 145–179.

Anderson, Erin, and David Schmittlein. 1984. "Integration of the Sales Force: An Empirical Examination." *RAND Journal of Economics* 15: 385–395.

Andrews, Kenneth R. 1971. *The Concept of Corporate Strategy.* Homewood, IL: Richard D. Irwin.

Applegate, Lynda, Robert Austin, and Elizabeth Collins. 2009. "IBM's Decade of Transformation: Turnaround to Growth." Case 805130, Harvard Business School, Cambridge, MA.

Athey, Susan, and John Roberts. 2001. "Organizational Design: Decision Rights and Incentive Contracts." *American Economic Review* 91(2): 200–205.

Athey, Susan, and Scott Stern. 1998. "An Empirical Framework for Testing Theories about Complimentarity [sic] in Organizational Design." Working Paper 6600, National Bureau of Economic Research, Cambridge, MA.

Baker, George. 1992. "Incentive Contracts and Performance Measurement." *Journal of Political Economy* 100: 598–614.

Baker, George, Robert Gibbons, and Kevin J. Murphy. 1994. "Subjective Performance Measures in Optimal Incentive Contracts." *Quarterly Journal of Economics* 109: 1125–1156.

Barnett, William, and Glenn Carroll. 1995. "Modeling Internal Organizational Change." *Annual Review of Sociology* 29: 217–236.

Baron, David, and David Besanko. 1996. "Global Strategy and Organization." Research Paper 1394, Stanford Graduate School of Business, Stanford, CA.

———. 2001. "Strategy, Organization, and Incentives: Global Corporate Banking at Citibank." *Industrial and Corporate Change* 10: 1–36.

Bartel, Ann, Casey Ichniowski, and Kathryn Shaw. 2007. "How Does Information Technology Really Affect Productivity? Plant-Level Comparisons of Product Innovation, Process Improvement and Worker Skills." *Quarterly Journal of Economics* 122: 1721–1758.

Bartlett, Christopher. 1999. "ABB's Relays Business: Building and Managing a Global Matrix." Case 394016, Harvard Business School, Boston.

Bartlett, Christopher, and Sumatra Ghoshal. 1998. *Managing across Borders: The Transnational Solution,* second edition. Boston: Harvard Business School Press.

Bartlett, Christopher, and U. Srinivasa Rangan. 1988. "Komatsu Limited." Case 385277, Harvard Business School, Boston.

Basu, Nilanjan. 2010. "Trends in Corporate Diversification." *Financial Markets and Portfolio Management* 14: 87–102.

Bennis, Warren, and Bert Nanus. 1985. *Leaders: Strategies for Taking Charge.* New York: Harper and Row.

Bernheim, Douglas, and Michael Whinston. 1986. "Common Agency." *Econometrica* 54: 923–942.

Besanko, David, Pierre Regibeau, and Katharine Rockett. 2000. "A Multi-Task Principal-Agent Approach to Organizational Form." CEPR Discussion Paper 2443, Centre for Economic Policy Research, London.

Besanko, David, David Dranove, Mark Shanley, and Scott Schaefer. 2009. *The Economics of Strategy,* ninth edition. New York: John Wiley and Sons.

Bloom, Nicholas, and John Van Reenen. 2007. "Measuring and Explaining Management Practices across Firms and Countries." *Quarterly Journal of Economics* 122: 1341–1408.

Bloom, Nicholas, Raffaella Sadun, and John Van Reenen. 2010. "Recent Advances in the Empirics of Organizational Design." *Annual Review of Economics* 2: 105–137.

Bloom, Nicholas, Mirko Draca, and John Van Reenen. 2011a. "Trade Induced Technical Change? The Impact of Chinese Imports on Innovation, IT and Productivity." Working Paper 16717, National Bureau of Economic Research, Cambridge, MA.

Bloom, Nicholas, Benn Eifert, Aprajit Mahajan, David McKenzie, and John Roberts. 2011b. "Does Management Matter: Evidence from India." Working Paper 16658, National Bureau of Economic Research, Cambridge, MA.

Bower, Joseph. 1970. *Managing the Resource Allocation Process.* Boston: Harvard Business School Press.

Brandenberger, Adam, and Barry Nalebuff. 1996. *Co-opetition: A Revolution Mindset That Combines Competition and Cooperation: The Game Theory Strategy That's Changing the Game of Business.* New York: Currency Doubleday.

Bresnahan, Timothy, Erik Brynjolfsson, and Lorin Hitt. 2002. "Information Technology, Workplace Organization, and the Demand for Skilled Labor: Firm-Level Evidence." *Quarterly Journal of Economics* 117: 339–376.

Bugamelli, Matteo, Fabiano Schivardi, and Robert Zizza. 2008. "The Euro and Firm Restructuring." Working Paper 14454, National Bureau of Economic Research, Cambridge, MA.

Burgelman, Robert. 1983. "Corporate Entrepreneurship and Strategic Management: Insights from a Process Study." *Management Science* 29: 1349–1364.

———. 1991. "Intraorganizational Ecology of Strategy Making and Organizational Adaptation: Theory and Field Research." *Organization Science* 2: 239–262.

———. 1994. "Fading Memories: A Process Theory of Strategic Business Exit in Dynamic Environments." *Administrative Science Quarterly* 39: 24–56.

Catalano, Charles, and John Roberts. 2004. "Tenaris: Creating a Global Leader from an Emerging Market." Case IB60, Stanford Graduate School of Business, Stanford, CA.

Chandler, Alfred. 1962. *Strategy and Structure: Chapters in the History of the American Industrial Enterprise.* Cambridge, MA: MIT Press.

———. 1969. "The Structure of American Industry in the Twentieth Century: A Historical Review." *Business History Review* 43: 225–298.

Collis, David J., and Michael G. Rukstad. 2008. "Can You Say What Your Strategy Is?" *Harvard Business Review* 86: 82–90.

Colombo, Massimo, Marco Delmastro, and Larissa Rabbiosi. 2007. "'High Performance' Work Practices, Decentralization, and Profitability: Evidence from Panel Data." *Industrial and Corporate Change* 16: 1037–1067.

Crawford, Vincent, and Joel Sobel. 1982. "Strategic Information Transmission." *Econometrica* 50: 1431–1451.

Cuñat, Vincente, and Maria Guadalupe. 2005. "How Does Product Market Competition Shape Incentive Contracts?" *Journal of the European Economic Association* 3: 1058–1082.

———. 2009. "Globalization and the Provision of Incentives inside the Firm: The Effect of Foreign Competition." *Journal of Labor Economics* 27: 179–212.

Dessein, Wouter, Luis Garicano, and Robert Gertner. 2010. "Organizing for Synergies." *American Economic Journal: Microeconomics* 2(4): 77–114.

Dixit, Avinash, and Barry Nalebuff. 1991. *Thinking Strategically: The Competitive Edge in Business, Politics and Everyday Life.* New York: W. W. Norton.

Doornik, Katherine, and John Roberts. 2001. "Nokia Corporation: Innovation and Efficiency in a High-Growth Global Firm." Case IB32, Stanford Graduate School of Business, Stanford, CA.

Dunning, John. 1977. "Trade, Location of Economic Activity and the MNE: A Search for an Eclectic Approach," in Bertil Ohlin, Per-Ove Hesselborn, and Per Magnus Wijkman (eds.), *The International Allocation of Economic Activity.* London: Macmillan, pp. 395–418.

Ferreira, Daniel, and Marcelo Rezende. 2007. "Corporate Strategy and Information Disclosure." *RAND Journal of Economics* 38: 164–184.

Freeman, Richard, and Morris Kleiner. 2005. "The Last American Shoe Manufacturers: Decreasing Productivity and Increasing Profits in the Shift from Piece Rates to Continuous Flow Production." *Industrial Relations* 44: 307–342.

Friebel, Guido, and Michael Raith. 2010. "Resource Allocation and Organizational Form." *American Economic Journal: Microeconomics* 2(2): 1–33.

Ghemawat, Pankaj. 2006. *Strategy and the Business Landscape: Core Concepts,* second edition. Englewood Cliffs, NJ: Prentice-Hall.

Guadalupe, Maria, and Julie Wulf. 2010. "The Flattening Firm and Product Market Competition: The Effect of Trade Liberalization on Corporate Hierarchies." *American Economic Journal: Applied Economics* 2(4): 105–127.

Guadalupe, Maria, Hongyi Li, and Julie Wulf. 2012. "Who Lives in the C-Suite? Organizational Structure and the Division of Labor in Top Management." Working Paper 12-059, Harvard Business School, Boston.

Hannan, Michael, and John Freeman. 1984. "Structural Inertia and Organizational Change." *American Sociological Review* 49: 149–164.

Harris, Milton, and Artur Raviv. 2002. "Organization Design." *Management Science* 48: 852–865.

Hart, Oliver, and Bengt Holmström. 2002. "A Theory of Firm Scope." Harvard Department of Economics, Cambridge, MA.

Helpman, Elhanan. 1984. "A Simple Theory of International Trade with Multinational Corporations." *Journal of Political Economy* 92: 451–471.

Holmström, Bengt. 1999. "The Firm as a Subeconomy." *Journal of Law, Economics, and Organization* 15: 74–102.

Holmström, Bengt, and Paul Milgrom. 1991. "Multitask Principal-Agent Analyses: Incentive Contracts, Asset Ownership, and Job Design." *Journal of Law, Economics, and Organization* 7: 24–52.

Ichniowski, Casey, Kathryn Shaw, and Giovanna Prennushi. 1997. "The Effects of Human Resource Management Practices on Productivity: A Study of Steel Finishing Lines." *American Economic Review* 87: 291–313.

Jensen, Michael. 1986. "The Agency Cost of Free Cash Flow, Corporate Finance and Takeovers." *American Economic Review* 76(2): 323–329.

Kauffman, Stuart. 1993. *The Origins of Order.* New York: Oxford University Press.

Lawrence, Paul, and Jay Lorsch. 1967. *Organization and Environment.* Boston: Harvard Business School.

Lazear, Edward. 2005. "Entrepreneurship." *Journal of Labor Economics* 23: 649–680.

Levinthal, Daniel. 1997. "Adaptation on Rugged Landscapes." *Management Science* 43: 934–950.

MacDuffie, John Paul. 1995. "Human Resource Bundles and Manufacturing Performance: Organizational Logic and Flexible Production Systems in the World Auto Industry." *Industrial and Labor Relations Review* 48: 197–221.

Mailath, George, and Andrew Postlewaite. 1990. "Workers versus Firms: Bargaining over a Firm's Value." *Review of Economic Studies* 57: 369–380.

Mailath, George, Volker Nocke, and Andrew Postlewaite. 2004. "Business Strategy, Human Capital, and Managerial Incentives." *Journal of Economics and Management Strategy* 13: 617–633.

Malone, Thomas W., and Stephen A. Smith. 1988. "Modeling the Performance of Organizational Structures." *Operations Research* 36: 421–436.

Manso, Gustavo. 2011. "Motivating Innovation." *Journal of Finance* 66: 1823–1860.

March, James. 1991. "Exploration and Exploitation in Organizational Learning." *Organization Science* 2: 71–87.

Markusen, James. 1984. "Multinationals, Multi-Plant Economies, and the Gains from Trade." *Journal of International Economics* 16: 205–226.

Markusen, James. 1995. "Incorporating the Multinational Enterprise into the Theory of International Trade." *Journal of Economic Perspectives* 9(1): 169–189.

Marris, Robin. 1964. *The Economic Theory of Managerial Capitalism.* New York: Free Press of Glencoe.

Maskin, Eric, Yingyi Qian, and Chenggang Xu. 2000. "Incentives, Information, and Organizational Form." *Review of Economic Studies* 67: 359–378.

McAfee, R. Preston. 2002. *Competitive Solutions: The Strategist's Toolkit.* Princeton, NJ: Princeton University Press.

McMillan, John. 1992. *Games, Strategies and Managers: How Managers Can Use Game Theory to Make Better Business Decisions.* Oxford: Oxford University Press.

Meyer, Margaret, Paul Milgrom, and John Roberts. 1992. "Organizational Prospects, Influence Costs and Ownership Changes." *Journal of Economics and Management Strategy* 1: 9–36.

Milgrom, Paul, and John Roberts. 1988a. "Bargaining Costs, Influence Costs and the Organization of Economic Activity," in James Alt and Kenneth Shepsle (eds.), *Perspectives on Positive Political Economy.* Cambridge: Cambridge University Press, pp. 57–89.

———. 1988b. "Communication and Inventories as Substitutes in Organizing Production." *Scandinavian Journal of Economics* 90: 275–289.

———. 1990. "The Economics of Modern Manufacturing: Technology, Strategy and Organization." *American Economic Review* 80: 511–528.

———. 1992. *Economics, Organization and Management.* Englewood Cliffs, NJ: Prentice-Hall.

———. 1995a. "Complementarities and Fit: Strategy, Structure and Organizational Change in Manufacturing." *Journal of Accounting and Economics* 19: 179–208.

———. 1995b. "Continuous Adjustment and Fundamental Change in Business Strategy and Organization," in Horst Siebert (ed.), *Trends in Business Organization: Do Participation and Cooperation Increase Competitiveness?* Tübingen, Germany: J.C.B. Mohr (Paul Siebeck), pp. 231–258.

Mintzberg, Henry, and James Waters. 1985. "Of Strategies, Deliberate and Emergent." *Strategic Management Journal* 6: 257–272.

Mueller, Dennis. 1969. "A Theory of Conglomerate Mergers." *Quarterly Journal of Economics* 83: 643–659.

Nelson, Richard R., and Sidney G. Winter. 1982. *An Evolutionary Theory of Economic Change.* Cambridge, MA: Belknap Press of Harvard University Press.

Nickerson, Jackson, and Todd Zenger. 2003. "Being Efficiently Fickle: A Dynamic Theory of Organizational Choice." *Organization Science* 13: 547–566.

Porter, Michael. 1980. *Competitive Strategy: Techniques for Analyzing Industries and Competitors.* New York: Free Press.

Porter, Michael, and Cheng Ong. 1988. "Skil Corp." Case 389005, Harvard Business School, Boston.

Prendergast, Canice. 1993. "The Role of Promotion in Inducing Specific Human Capital Acquisition." *Quarterly Journal of Economics* 108: 523–553.

Qian, Yingyi, Gérard Roland, and Chenggang Xu. 2006. "Coordination and Experimentation in M-Form and U-Form Organizations." *Journal of Political Economy* 114: 366–402.

Quigley, Joseph. 1993. *Vision: How Leaders Develop It, Share It, and Sustain It.* New York: McGraw-Hill.

Rajan, Raghuram, and Julie Wulf. 2006. "The Flattening Firm: Evidence from Panel Data on the Changing Nature of Corporate Hierarchies." *Review of Economics and Statistics* 88: 759–773.

Rantakari, Heikki. 2008. "Governing Adaptation." *Review of Economic Studies* 75: 1257–1285.

———. 2012a. "Employee Initiative and Managerial Control." *American Economic Journal: Microeconomics,* forthcoming.

———. 2012b. "Organizational Design and Environmental Volatility." *Journal of Law, Economics, and Organization,* forthcoming.

Rivkin, Jan. 2000. "Imitation of Complex Strategies." *Management Science* 46: 824–844.

Roberts, John. 2004. *The Modern Firm: Organizational Design for Performance and Growth*. Oxford: Oxford University Press.

Rotemberg, Julio. 1999. "Process- versus Function-Based Hierarchies." *Journal of Economics and Management Strategy* 8: 453–487.

Rotemberg, Julio, and Garth Saloner. 1993. "Leadership Style and Incentives." *Management Science* 39: 1299–1318.

———. 1994. "Benefits of Narrow Business Strategies." *American Economic Review* 84: 1330–1349.

———. 1995. "Overt Interfunctional Conflict (and Its Reduction though Business Strategy)." *RAND Journal of Economics* 26: 630–653.

———. 2000. "Visionaries, Managers, and Strategic Direction." *RAND Journal of Economics* 31: 693–716.

Rumelt, Richard. 1984. "Towards a Strategic Theory of the Firm," in Richard B. Lamb (ed.), *Competitive Strategic Management*. Englewood Cliffs, NJ: Prentice-Hall, pp. 566–570.

Saloner, Garth, Andrea Shepard, and Joel Podolny. 2001. *Strategic Management*. New York: John Wiley and Sons.

Shleifer, Andrei, and Larry Summers. 1988. "Breach of Trust in Corporate Takeovers," in Alan Auerbach (ed.), *Corporate Takeovers: Causes and Consequences*. Chicago: University of Chicago Press, pp. 33–68.

Stigler, George. 1939. "Production and Distribution in the Short Run." *Journal of Political Economy* 43: 305–327.

Teece, David. 1982. "Towards an Economic Theory of the Multiproduct Firm." *Journal of Economic Behavior and Organization* 3: 39–63.

Tushman, Michael, and Charles O'Reilly. 1996. "The Ambidextrous Organization: Managing Evolutionary and Revolutionary Change." *California Management Review* 38(4): 8–30.

———. 2011. "Organizational Ambidexterity in Action: How Managers Explore and Exploit." *California Management Review* 53(4): 5–22.

Van den Steen, Eric. 2005. "Organizational Beliefs and Managerial Vision." *Journal of Law, Economics, and Organization* 21: 256–283.

———. 2006. "The Limits of Authority: Motivation versus Coordination." Working Paper 4626-06, Sloan School of Management, Massachusetts Institute of Technology, Cambridge, MA.

———. 2010a. "Culture Clash: The Costs and Benefits of Homogeneity." *Management Science* 56: 1718–1738.

———. 2010b. "On the Origin of Shared Beliefs (and Corporate Culture)." *RAND Journal of Economics* 41: 617–648.

———. 2011. "A Theory of Strategy and the Role of Leaders in It." Harvard Business School, Boston.

Wernerfeldt, Birger. 1984. "The Resource-Based View of the Firm." *Strategic Management Journal* 5: 171–180.

Whittington, Richard, Andrew Pettigrew, Simon Peck, Evelyn Fenton, and Martin Conyon. 1999. "Change and Complementarities in the New Competitive Landscape: A European Panel Study, 1992–1996." *Organization Science* 10: 583–600.

Williamson, Oliver. 1975. *Markets and Hierarchies: Analysis and Antitrust Implications*. New York: Free Press.

———. 1985. *The Economic Institutions of Capitalism*. New York: Free Press.

PART V

Between Firms

21

Vertical Integration and Market Structure

Timothy Bresnahan and Jonathan Levin

1. Introduction

Vertical integration occupies a central role in organizational economics. Williamson (2005) calls it the "paradigm" problem for explaining the distribution of firms and markets in modern economies. In this chapter, we review research on vertical integration decisions and their consequences, and offer some perspective on the current state of knowledge.[1]

Our discussion bridges two very different literatures. Research in organizational economics generally treats vertical integration as an efficient response to contracting frictions. This approach is often associated with Coase (1937) and Williamson (1971). Research in industrial organization has taken a complementary approach, emphasizing patterns of integration at the market or industry level. Some of this work, following Stigler (1951), draws attention to scale and scope economies as rationales for integration, while other strands emphasize strategic motives and the idea that integration can be a tool for consolidating or extending market power.

Theoretical work in the first tradition argues that certain features of transactions create particular problems for arm's-length contracting. These can include difficulty anticipating future contingencies, ambiguity in the nature of tasks and decisions to be carried out, the need to use specific assets, or an inability to measure and verify transaction outcomes. In Section 2, we describe some of the "building-block" models that link these types of transactional frictions to problems of hold-up, decisionmaking externalities, and incentive distortions, and offer explanations for when and why internal organization might lead to more efficient outcomes.

We thank the volume editors, Robert Gibbons and John Roberts, for helpful discussions and unusual patience, and the Ewing Marian Kauffman Foundation (Bresnahan) and the National Science Foundation (Levin) for their support.

1. Readers may also be interested in the surveys by Gibbons (2005), Joskow (2005), Klein (2005), Shelanski and Klein (1995), and Lafontaine and Slade (2007). Perry (1989) is an earlier survey of industrial organization research on vertical integration. Helpman (2006) and Antràs and Rossi-Hansberg (2009) review recent work on multinationals and cross-country integration decisions.

The ideas in these models have been the starting point for a long sequence of empirical studies dating back at least to Monteverde and Teece (1982), Masten (1984), Joskow (1985, 1987), and others. The typical strategy in the empirical literature has been to relate observed integration decisions to measures of contractual frictions, or more often, proxies for these frictions. In a very few cases, an attempt is made to link the integration decision to economic outcomes (e.g., productivity, investment, and innovation), or observed transaction costs (e.g., the incidence of disputes).

Many studies along these lines report statistically significant correlations between integration decisions and proxies for contracting difficulties. In Section 3, we discuss the extent to which these findings can be viewed as strong supportive evidence for the theory. We highlight a number of difficulties in relating the evidence to the theory. One is that the relevant theoretical variables (e.g., the importance of noncontractible decisions or the marginal returns to specific investments) can be inherently hard to measure (Whinston 2003). In other cases, the sources of variation that identify the parameters of interest appear to reflect important omitted variables. Finally, even if one accepts the directional results, the lack of evidence linking integration decisions to realized transaction costs makes it hard to assess the quantitative importance of the effects.

Empirical research also has faced a tension between testing specific predictions derived from the theory and trying to explain broad industry patterns of integration. Most contractual theories of integration aim to isolate particular mechanisms. The models tend to focus on simple environments, for example, two parties structuring a supply relationship with the surrounding market held fixed. Thus, the clearest empirical analogues are marginal decisions at the firm boundary, such as whether a firm should make or buy a particular input. Moving from this level of analysis to explain the organization of an entire industry requires additional steps, because the availability of suppliers or the existence of functioning markets or contracts needs to be treated as an outcome of the analysis rather than a fixed parameter.

This higher level industry perspective on vertical integration has been adopted in much of the industrial organization literature. Here, decisions about integration are often considered in the context of broader models of industry structure, competition, or technological change, but typically with much less attention to contractual issues and the ways in which vertical integration might differ from sophisticated contractual arrangements. In Section 4, we discuss this research, which has an empirical component as well, consisting most often of industry case studies or historical analyses of industry evolution. Using the case studies to communicate the key analytical themes, we distill three reasons industry structure and firm structure are interdependent.

The first relates to the presence of scale or scope economies. Many theories of industry structure are framed in terms of trading off the successful exploitation of scale economies versus the benefits of competition. If that trade-off calls for a large number of distinct firms in one or both of the industries where firms might be vertically integrated, the contracting problems emphasized in some organizational economics theories decline in importance. This leads to models in which market size or thickness is an important determinant of vertical integration.

Second, competitive strategy can be a key factor in vertical integration decisions. A rich set of models in industrial organization emphasize the use of vertical integration as a way to raise entry barriers in one or both of the associated markets. Another class of models focuses on mixed structures, where a firm in industry A might be vertically integrated with a firm in industry B while also serving other firms in B as a disintegrated market supplier. Such structures create complex strategic problems of supplying, or being supplied by, one's competitor. These models lack foundational theories regarding why integration, rather than a complex contract, is needed to implement a particular strategy, but they nevertheless capture trade-offs that commonly arise in industry case studies and are discussed frequently in competition policy.

Third, the industrial organization literature has taken up the special case of vertical integration with complementary innovators. This literature deals with the trade-off between the benefits of coordination associated with integrated production and the benefits of getting multiple diverse draws, which favors separation into multiple independent inventors. The distinction has organizational implications, because contracting to coordinate ex ante calls for identifying and selecting a partner ex ante. Market organization of innovation can use ex post market selection. We use the production of scientific research as an example to illustrate this trade-off and how it brings together organizational and industry-level ideas.

We conclude our review by noting that the two literatures on vertical integration have remained largely separate despite the potential benefits of cross-pollination. We provide some suggestions for how insights from organizational economics might inform traditional analyses of market structure, and how a broader industry-level perspective at times might enrich organizational economics.

2. Contractual Theories of Vertical Integration

In his famous essay on the nature of the firm, Coase (1937) proposed to study why and how economic activity divides between firms and markets. He argued that firms exist to reduce the costs of transacting through markets. Their size and scope depends on the extent to which they offer a transaction cost advantage. Therefore, a decision to vertically integrate rather than sourcing inputs or selling outputs should reflect the respective transaction costs of internal and market organization.

To go further, one needs an explanation for why market transactions are inefficient and why the inefficiencies cannot be remedied with better contracts or pricing mechanisms. One also needs to explain why integration might yield an improvement in some cases but not all. Finally, a satisfactory theory should match observed patterns of integration and offer some hope for empirical testing and measurement. Essentially all contractual theories, from transaction cost economics to formal models of hold-up, decision rights, and incentives, reflect these goals.

2.1. Transaction Cost Theories

The transaction cost theory of integration was developed by Williamson (1971, 1975, 1985), Goldberg (1976), Klein et al. (1978), Joskow (1985), and others beginning in the 1970s. The theory expands on Coase's original idea by describing a wide set of transaction inefficiencies and potential organizational responses.[2]

---

2. Tadelis and Williamson (this volume) provide a more detailed account of transaction cost economics. See also Joskow (2005) and Williamson (2010) for recent overviews.

A starting observation is that market contracts are inherently incomplete. Parties can plan for some contingencies but not every one of them. Thus, in a great many transactions there will be room for opportunistic and inefficient behavior as the transaction proceeds. The concern may be especially severe when complexity or uncertainty make it difficult to specify contractual safeguards or when parties cannot walk away without incurring substantial costs.

Transaction cost theory argues that integration can be an effective response when these features are present. One reason given by Williamson (1971) relates to decisionmaking. When a dispute arises in an organization, it can be settled by a senior manager. In contrast, a dispute between separate entities must be resolved by negotiation or litigation. To the extent that managerial authority makes it easier to resolve disputes or make adaptations, integration can be the efficient response to uncertainty or contractual incompleteness (Williamson 1971, 1979).

A related rationale for integration is that it might mitigate potential hold-ups. If parties anticipate the possibility of future haggling or disputes, they may have little incentive to make specific investments for fear the investment could be wasted or expropriated (Klein et al. 1978; Williamson 1985). To the extent that integration allows a firm to protect specific investments, it again can be an efficient response to contractual incompleteness.

These stories provide a motive for vertical integration but not a corresponding cost. Williamson (1975, 1985) suggests a related but distinct set of inefficiencies inside organizations. These include low-powered incentives, and rent-seeking and informational bottlenecks that arise in managerial hierarchies. An implicit assumption in transaction cost theory is that these problems are relatively insensitive to the complexity, uncertainty, or specificity of particular transactions. So integration becomes optimal when hazards are more severe, but nonintegrated production may be preferred for relatively straightforward transactions.[3]

An important point in many transaction cost analyses is that the set of potential organizational responses to transaction frictions is very large. In addition to full vertical integration and spot contracting, responses can include contracts of varying duration and specificity, joint ventures, partial ownership through financial investment, partial control through seats on a board or voting arrangements, or shared ownership of assets or intellectual property. In fact, part of the appeal of transaction cost economics is that it offers such a broad and inclusive framework for matching organizational responses to transaction frictions. From an empirical perspective, however, this richness poses some challenges.

The sharpest predictions of the theory are that such transaction characteristics as specificity, uncertainty, and complexity should favor vertically integrated production. Perhaps the canonical example of specificity is a coal-fired electricity plant located next to a coal mine (Joskow 1985), which is also a good example to illustrate the subtleties of empirically testing transaction cost theories of integration. Coal-fired electricity plants are expensive to build, have a long lifetime, and are designed to burn particular types of coal. Before investing, the owners want to ensure a steady and reliable input supply. There are, however, a variety of ways to do this. Some plants vertically integrate, while others sign long-term contracts with the neighboring mine. There is relatively little evidence that the integrated plants outperform their counterparts

---

3. Williamson (1985) also emphasizes that the frequency of a transaction can be important, in the sense that one-time transactions are less likely to be integrated than repeated transactions.

(Kerkvliet 1991). So even in cases where specificity is apparent, vertical integration may be only one of several possible responses and not necessarily the most effective.

This same point can be seen in another classic example from the transaction cost literature: the acquisition of the Fisher Body Corporation by General Motors (Klein et al. 1978; Coase 1988, 2000; Klein 1988, 2000, 2007; Langlois and Robertson 1989; Casadesus-Masanell and Spulber 2000; Freeland 2000). Fisher Body supplied metal car bodies to GM in the early days of the auto industry. In 1919, GM acquired a stake in Fisher and the companies signed a contract committing Fisher to supply its output exclusively to GM. The contract was for 10 years, on cost-plus terms. After it was signed, production expanded as the demand for cars grew, and in 1926, GM purchased the remainder of Fisher Body, dissolving the contract and integrating the firms.

The question of why GM decided to integrate Fisher Body has been the subject of extensive debate. Klein et al. (1978) interpret the episode as a canonical example of a hold-up leading to integration. They observe that the relationship involved substantial specific investments in manufacturing and human capital. They also argue that rising demand raised Fisher's opportunity costs, so that they began to hold up GM by, among other things, using a relatively costly manufacturing process. This left GM with no option but integration. Coase (2000) and Freeland (2000) provide a very different interpretation. They point out that Fisher and GM had a tight relationship. A Fisher brother sat on GM's board, and GM paid for the construction of at least one Fisher plant. Rather than a hold-up arising from the cost-plus contract, Freeland and Coase argue that the cause of integration may have been a dispute about whether to expand an existing plant or build a new one that fit GM's expansion plans.

The episode demonstrates the subtleties in trying to formulate sharp empirical tests based on transaction cost theory. The historical research makes it clear that even before integration, Fisher and GM were closely intertwined. It is not obvious that things would have proceeded much differently if the companies had integrated in 1919 or not at all. Moreover, although different accounts are at odds over many issues, they are all consistent with the broad claims of transaction cost economics. In this sense, the same inclusiveness of the theory that makes it useful for organizing historical accounts also makes it difficult to reject.

A somewhat different issue, but one that turns out to be important for applied work, is that transaction cost theory tends to treat individual transactions in isolation, holding fixed the characteristics of the transaction and the surrounding market conditions. The difficulty in applied work is that transaction characteristics and market structure are often best viewed as endogenous variables. For instance, firms may have a choice about whether to use standard or customized inputs or to cooperate with other firms in their industry to create standardized contracts or technologies. We return to this point in more detail in Sections 2.5 and 4.3.

2.2. The Property Rights Model

The property rights model (Grossman and Hart 1986; Hart and Moore 1990; Hart 1995) is one of the first formal theories of integration that makes precise assumptions about the limits of contracting.[4] The model focuses on how integration changes the incentives to make specific

---

4. Segal and Whinston (this volume) provide an overview of the property rights model as well as many extensions and related models.

investments. In the property rights theory, a firm is defined as a collection of physical assets. Decisions to integrate upstream or downstream are associated with shifts in asset ownership. An example would be a manufacturer that purchases a supplier and takes control of its physical plant or one that integrates downstream and takes ownership of distribution outlets. Contracts are assumed to be incomplete. When open issues arise, ownership strengthens a party's bargaining position. As a result, it has a stronger incentive to undertake ex ante specific investments.

The standard version of the property rights model has three stages. The relevant parties first decide who should own which assets. Other decisions, or some of them, are left to be decided later. Then the parties make investment decisions. The investments are specific—some of their value is lost if the relationship breaks down. After investments are sunk, the parties bargain over the outstanding terms and trade. Bargaining is assumed to be efficient, so the surplus-maximizing trade is made regardless of asset ownership.

Although bargaining leads to an efficient trading outcome irrespective of the distribution of assets, ownership does affect the terms of trade. Because it conveys the right to use an asset in the event of breakdown, ownership of an asset means that a party gets a larger share of the bargaining surplus. Under the typical assumptions about payoffs, this leads to sharp predictions about investment incentives. A move toward integration increases the investment incentives of the acquiring party but lowers the incentives of the acquired party. Determining whether integration is optimal, and which party should be the owner, requires a comparison of the costs and benefits, which can be complex.

Although the hold-up mechanism seems similar to transaction cost theory, the property rights model leads to distinct empirical predictions (Whinston 2003). For instance, transaction cost theory predicts that integration will be a response to specificity, where specificity refers (somewhat loosely) to a gap between the value of the ongoing relationship and the value of the parties' outside alternatives. In the property rights model, the gap per se is not consequential for predictions about ownership (Holmström and Roberts 1998). Instead, the relevant quantity is the degree to which ownership affects the marginal returns to noncontractible specific investments.

Perhaps because of these subtleties, the specific predictions of the theory have not received a great deal of empirical attention. Whinston (2003) emphasizes the difficulty in measuring or proxying for the marginal returns to investment. Moreover, ownership in the model conveys *residual* rights of control—that is, the right to make decisions that are not otherwise specified in a contract. In many settings, it is not obvious how to characterize or measure the importance of these rights. Similarly, the model focuses on investments that are both noncontractible and inalienable. Identifying important investments that are inherently nontransferable (e.g., investments in human capital) and yet important enough to drive vertical integration decisions can be tricky.

Holmström (1999) also has emphasized another issue with the property rights model, which may help explain why it has been more influential as a theoretical building block than as a framework for empirical work. Taken literally, the model suggests that individuals (e.g., the ones investing in human capital) should own the productive assets. Clearly, this is not the right frame of reference for thinking about large organizations that own many assets and coordinate many activities, where shares of ownership are often widely dispersed and separation of ownership and control is common.[5] One could associate the actors in the property rights theory with larger entities and still think about hold-up of specific investments as being a rationale for vertical integration, but in the context of the model, one then needs an explanation for why investments cannot be shared or contractually specified.

2.3. Decision Rights Models

One major contribution of the property rights model is that it offers a precisely formulated argument for why and when ownership conveys the right to make decisions. Many earlier accounts (e.g., Simon 1951) simply assume that managers enjoy a degree of authority to make decisions.[6] In the property rights model, a firm's owner has to bargain with employees, who are free to walk away. If they do, however, they leave the firm's assets behind. This can give a firm's owner some degree of bargaining power over the firm's employees. In contrast, a supplier that walks away takes productive assets with it. Of course, in the property rights model, the key decision rights are never exercised because of the efficient bargaining assumption, so ownership matters only through ex ante investment incentives.

An alternative, and in some ways simpler, modeling approach assumes that bargaining is not efficient, or that there is no bargaining at all. Examples of this approach include Hart and Holmström (2010) and Baker et al. (2011). In these models, ownership is associated with the right to make certain residual decisions (the presence of physical assets is no longer very important). Roughly, these models predict that ownership should be allocated in a way that ensures more efficient ex post decisions (see Segal and Whinston, this volume).

In Hart and Holmström (2010), for instance, there are two business units that can benefit from coordinating their actions. Integration means that the units are placed under a single manager. The manager can force the units to coordinate, but (by assumption) may fail to respect the private preferences of the divisional employees. If instead the units operate under separate ownership, the respective managers will cater to their employees, but the units may fail to coordinate. There is a trade-off between the coordination benefits of internal organization and the incentive or appropriation benefits of nonintegration.[7]

This type of decision rights approach hearkens back to a much older, although less contractually grounded, set of models in industrial organization. For instance, in the classic double

---

5. The separation of ownership and control in large organizations relates closely to many of the issues raised in this chapter, though we will not pursue it here. (Berle and Means (1932) is an early and classic reference.)

6. This view has been controversial. For instance, Alchian and Demsetz (1972: 777) write:

It is common to see the firm characterized by the power to settle issues by fiat, by authority, or by disciplinary action superior to that available in the conventional market. This is delusion. The firm does not own all its inputs . . . [An employer] can fire or sue, just as I can fire my grocer by stopping purchases from him or sue him for delivering faulty products.

7. Similar trade-offs also appear in the literature on internal capital markets (e.g., Stein 1997). A related model in Hart (2009) explores how integration might provide a way to avoid costly hold-ups, as in the transaction cost account of Klein (1996). In Hart's model, vertically related parties write a contract to trade at a future date. But they are unable to get the price right for every contingency. A situation can therefore arise where one party might threaten to walk away, triggering a (costly) renegotiation. The optimal ownership structure therefore is one that minimizes the likelihood of a hold-up.

marginalization model of Spengler (1950), a nonintegrated upstream supplier will choose its markup without regard to the profits of a downstream producer. The resulting trade is inefficient. Integration helps resolve the inefficiency, because pricing decisions are coordinated in a way that leads to a jointly profit-maximizing transfer price.[8]

The double marginalization model and related models of incentive conflicts in vertical supply chains share the feature that integration shifts authority from separate managers to a single coordinating entity. What it leaves unexplained is why integration does a better job of restoring efficiency than a sophisticated nonintegrated contract (Tirole 1988). Nevertheless, it is a workhorse for applied economists, because of its clear predictions (e.g., the potential inefficiency will be larger and the incentive to integrate greater when there is substantial market power both upstream and downstream). In this sense, the approach taken in recent decision rights models may be a promising framework for empirical research, particularly for studies where it is possible to observe decision processes and outcomes in integrated and nonintegrated situations.

2.4. Incentive Theory Models

A complementary set of vertical integration models focus on how integration decisions shift the financial incentives of workers and managers. As a simple example, we can consider a firm contracting with a sales agent. Suppose for the moment that nonintegration is associated with the agent having high-powered incentives—for instance, a contract under which the agent buys the product at a fixed price and keeps the proceeds from its sales. Conversely, integration means that the agent becomes a salaried employee with low-powered incentives. Whether integration is optimal will depend on how important it is to provide incentives for the sales agent and whether monitoring can substitute for high-powered financial incentives.

This type of agency model has been the dominant paradigm in research on franchising arrangements and related distribution integration decisions. It has several attractive features. First, internal organization often does seem to feature low-powered incentives relative to market-based exchange. Second, the basic logic of incentive theory models is familiar, and the relevant quantities—the sensitivity to incentives, the difficulty of measuring or monitoring behavior, the degree of risk aversion, and so forth—are in principle objects that can be proxied or quantified.

One element that is missing, however, is why integration should be equated with low-powered incentives in the first place. Holmström and Milgrom (1994) provide an answer. Their argument is that financial incentives generally are part of a broader incentive environment. Other elements might include decisions about asset ownership, or the set of tasks that are permitted or excluded. Holmström and Milgrom show that under certain conditions, asset ownership by the agent (e.g., nonintegration) can be complementary to providing high-powered financial incentives. Conversely, taking assets away (integration) makes it desirable to use low-powered incentives. From this perspective, integration is likely to be associated with broader shifts in incentives and other organizational variables, even if asset ownership per se is not the primary driver of incentives (see also Holmström 1999).

---

8. Related models focus, for instance, on the inability of nonintegrated firms to coordinate investment or marketing decisions, or to price complementary products efficiently. Tirole (1988) and Perry (1989) provide extensive coverage of these types of models.

The incentive system model is particularly useful for thinking through shifts in incentives and organizational design that might accompany integration decisions. For example, privately funded start-up firms in Silicon Valley often compensate their workers and managers with equity or options. The work atmosphere can be intense. These firms attract workers and managers who are drawn to the high-pressure, high-powered incentives of starting a new business. If a large firm acquires the start-up, it may seek to align the start-up's activities and efforts with its own. Measuring alignment can be difficult, so the logic of the model suggests that an acquisition will be followed by a shift to lower-powered incentives and perhaps the subsequent departure of some of the original managers and employees.

The challenge that arises in making the theory operational for empirical work is that its predictions are again very rich. Many outcome variables should move together as a response to underlying shifts in the environment. As a result, most of the research linking agency considerations to integration decisions has tended to focus on simpler, although perhaps less interesting, predictions.

2.5. Capabilities Theories

The theories we have described focus mainly on decisions at the boundary of the firm and often deal with cases where firms integrate to internalize the transfer of some tangible good or service. In contrast, research on business strategy and organization theory frequently emphasizes the idea that firms may seek to expand or acquire other firms to leverage their internal capabilities or exploit superior management capabilities (e.g., Penrose 1959; Cyert and March 1963; Wernerfelt 1984). These theories rest on two premises. The first is that organizations develop certain capabilities or know-how that is embodied by managers and employees or in organizational routines. The second is that capabilities or knowledge cannot easily be traded or shared across firm boundaries.

These ideas have received less attention in economic theory, although there is a range of work that speaks to related issues. In the Lucas (1978) model of firm size, managerial talent is a scarce resource that can be leveraged by creating hierarchical organizations. Lucas uses the model to derive predictions about the size distribution of firms in the economy. Subsequent work has adapted his model to study the optimal organization of hierarchies (e.g., Garicano 2000). Clark (1985) and Bloom and van Reenen (2007) provide evidence that managerial practices can be an important factor in explaining productivity differences across firms.[9]

These theories address the first piece of the capabilities view—that firms differ in managerial know-how, and this difference is important for production—but not the second. That is, they do not address why integration, as opposed to contractual arrangements, is required to leverage managerial talent. One natural hypothesis is that managerial authority tends to coincide with firm boundaries, an idea that is captured in the model of Hart and Holmström (2010) discussed in Section 2.3, and is a common presumption in less formal analyses.

---

9. These papers look at comparable firms and have an observable definition of "better" managerial capabilities. As Clark (1985) points out, to understand complementarities between different organizations, one needs a definition of managerial capabilities that includes the task to be carried out as well as effectiveness at pursuing that task.

A complementary line of research argues that vertical integration allows information flows that cannot occur across firm boundaries (Malmgren 1961). For instance, Arrow (1975) considers a model in which information can be transmitted within an integrated firm but not between disintegrated firms. Again, the model sidesteps the question of why transmitting information or knowledge across firm boundaries might be difficult. One potential justification is that employees who interact regularly in a firm develop a body of shared knowledge that facilitates further communication.

Another difficulty with sharing knowledge or information across firm boundaries is that once information is shared, it cannot be rescinded, creating an appropriability problem. Indeed, Cohen and Levinthal (1990) argue that the ability to absorb information can itself be an important organizational capability. In Section 4.4 we argue that identifying situations in which firms have an advantage in coordinating the production and dissemination of knowledge is particularly useful for thinking about the organization of innovative industries.

3. Empirical Evidence on Vertical Integration Decisions

Since the 1980s, many empirical studies have attempted to test or apply contractual theories of integration. The studies vary in the details but share common features. The general approach is to predict observed integration decisions using transaction characteristics identified in the theory. The integration decisions lie at the firm boundary—whether to buy certain inputs, to use a contracted sales force, to franchise retail outlets, or instead to bring these services in house. These decisions typically are at the firm level, holding fixed the nature of the goods and services being contracted over, the contracting environment, and the surrounding market structure.

These papers also share common measurement challenges. Testing contractual theories of integration requires empirical measures of concepts, such as the degree of specificity, the importance of noncontractible investment, and the potential for opportunism and hold-up. Testing also requires variation in their incidence. The variation might be across firms or across the transactions of a single firm. But its source needs to be plausibly exogenous to the integration decision itself. It is also necessary to identify the set of possible contracting outcomes. This undertaking is complicated by the possibility, noted above, of a wide range of contractual solutions to a given problem. Most studies try to capture moves closer to or further from integration with some sort of binary classification and avoid fine distinctions among contractual arrangements.

Virtually all studies we discuss report statistically significant correlations between integration decisions and proxies for theoretically relevant transaction characteristics. This correlation has been viewed as quite favorable for contractual theories. A more skeptical perspective, however, is that these analyses often do not provide a very sharp test of the theory. In some cases, the empirical proxies used to capture complexity, specificity, or the potential for opportunism do not have an obvious relationship to the theoretical concepts. In other cases, the source of identifying variation seems to be earlier or concurrent decisions made at the firm or industry level.

Perhaps the main limitation of this work, however, is that very few studies provide any quantitative (and sometimes not even qualitative) sense of the transaction costs or incentive distortions associated with different contractual forms. As a result, it is frequently unclear whether the difference between integration and nonintegration is really that important in any economic sense. In Section 3.6, we argue that this last concern requires combining evidence on integration decisions with specific ex post measures of transaction costs or performance, and that this approach is a key direction for future research.

3.1. Sourcing Complex and Specific Inputs

Some of the earliest empirical studies look at industrial make-or-buy decisions in search of evidence that firms might seek to integrate the production of complex or specific inputs. Two classic examples are Monteverde and Teece (1982) and Masten (1984).[10] Both studies relate make-or-buy decisions to empirical proxies for hold-up and opportunism and thus are usefully representative of a much larger empirical literature.

Monteverde and Teece (1982) studied how Ford and General Motors source auto components. They used a probit regression to relate sourcing to measures of transaction specificity and complexity. A component is "specific" if the procuring firm is the exclusive purchaser of that component. An engineering cost estimate is used to proxy for complexity, or technical know-how. Because many components consist of parts procured in different ways, Monteverde and Teece defined a component as "made" rather than "bought" if the cost fraction of the component produced internally exceeds a given threshold. Their main finding was that both specificity and complexity are positively correlated with internal sourcing.

Masten (1984) examined a single large aerospace project that required nearly 2,000 inputs. Masten also constructed measures of specificity and complexity, in his case on an input-by-input basis. Here too, an input is specific if the general contractor is the exclusive user. Inputs are classified as complex or not complex, based on a survey of the procurement team. Masten found that both measures are highly correlated with sourcing. In fact, more than 90% of the specific and complex inputs were sourced internally versus less than 1% of the nonspecific and noncomplex inputs.

These pioneering studies highlight some of the challenges in testing contractual theories of integration. One challenge is to find empirical measures of transaction frictions that correspond closely to the conceptual ideas in the theory. For instance, both studies use measures of technical or engineering complexity as proxies to indicate that purchasing a component is complicated. The relationship is clearly imperfect. Computers are very technically complex, and yet most firms readily source computers from external vendors. From a theoretical perspective, it would be better to define complexity in terms of communication or information about a transaction. Are there many possible contingencies? Does performance involve a great many details that are difficult to communicate or incorporate in a contract? Is it difficult to identify the responsible party if problems arise? Is there substantial room for asymmetric information? These notions each require a different approach to make them operational. For example, the idea that complex transactions may involve asymmetric information calls for an empirical treatment recognizing that one party may have superior information at the time of contracting. This idea, so important

---

10. Related work on industrial or government procurement decisions includes Walker and Weber (1984), Masten et al. (1989, 1991), Crocker and Reynolds (1993), and Levin and Tadelis (2010).

in the rest of the economics literature on asymmetric information, appears essentially nowhere in the empirical literature on vertical integration.[11]

Defining "specificity" is also problematic. Monteverde and Teece (1982) and Masten (1984) use what is most naturally viewed as an outcome, the demand for an input by only one customer, to proxy for a primitive, namely the specificity of the investments associated with the exchange relationship. The fact that the input has a sole user may reflect some fundamental and fixed attribute of the input (and in a study that focuses narrowly on a single firm, that may be the obvious source of variation on which to focus), but it may also reflect broader market forces. For example, variation in the efficient scale of production relative to demand needs may play a large role in determining whether an input is classified as specific. If the input is efficiently produced at large scale relative to the demand of individual users, we might expect to see several firms using the same input, even if it is produced by only a single supplier, creating the type of bilateral market power emphasized in the theory. If production of the input is flexible, users may adopt customized versions, irrespective of whether the market to supply the input is highly competitive or very concentrated.

Note that the important part of this argument for analytical purposes is not the specific point about scale. It is the movement of the argument from firm to market. In the firm-level theory, an input is made rather than bought because producing it requires specialized equipment, knowledge, or a specialized location, or because the input itself has no alternative use, and moreover because this specialization leaves parties open to opportunism if the input is bought instead of made. In the market-level alternative theory, some inputs are sold to multiple buyers because that is the efficient market organization, and this causes their use to be less specific. This arrangement might be optimal because of scale economies in production, because the market is organized in a way that facilitates the pricing and distribution of standardized products, or because regulatory or legal uncertainty favors standardized transactions.[12]

These problems illustrate the difficulty of distinguishing aspects of a transaction that are primitive from those that follow from design decisions or market equilibrium. Baldwin and Clark (2005) have tried to tackle this problem from an engineering perspective. They argue that within a production process it is possible to identify the engineering interfaces that are more or less amenable to a market transaction. One suspects this approach could prove powerful in certain instances, particularly if it is possible to measure performance along a chain of production (e.g., failure rates or delays).

---

11. Many of the most successful approaches to asymmetric information are based on datasets in which the econometrician, by gathering data later, can observe an outcome that only one party could observe at the time of contract (e.g., Einav et al. 2010). This approach is beginning to be deployed in the few studies of vertical integration that examine outcomes of this sort. Below, we look at a paper by Arora et al. (2009) that studies pharmaceutical development for licensed (i.e., contracted) versus in-house chemical entities. They interpret the observed lack of difference in success rates between licensed and in-house developed drugs as evidence against any "lemons" theory of asymmetric information in the licensing market.

12. One can also raise issues of causality with reference to a single firm. If the market supplies a small set of input varieties, a producer may be able to tailor its design to use these varieties rather than a specific input. Similarly, Novak and Stern (2009) point out that if there are complementarities in production, manufacturers may internally source clusters of inputs if they anticipate difficulties in coordinating design changes that require large-scale modifications.

We have emphasized the difficulties in measuring transaction frictions, but difficulties in measurement also arise on the left-hand side of transaction cost regressions. In the case of auto manufacturing, U.S. manufacturers traditionally relied on a partial outsourcing model in which suppliers compete for contracts each year. Japanese firms adopted a very different approach involving close relationships with a set of closely coordinated suppliers (Asanuma 1989). The economic and engineering problems faced by firms in this industry in different countries are not all that different, but history and broader institutional issues led these firms to adopt different organizational modes. Depending on the study country, one might arrive at very different views of what it means to buy rather than make a component.

3.2. Specificity, Market Thickness, and Hold-Up

Empirical researchers arguably have had more success in linking integration decisions, or at least the use of more complete vertical contracts, to measures of market structure (e.g., the availability of multiple suppliers in the upstream market). Two emblematic studies are Stuckey (1983) and Joskow (1987). These studies get around many of the problems discussed above by identifying settings where parties make large investments in specific assets—in each case, specialized production facilities—and there appears to be substantial potential for hold-up in subsequent price negotiations stemming from the limited availability of trading partners.[13]

Stuckey (1983) focuses on aluminum manufacturing. The primary input in this process, bauxite, is very costly to transport. Thus, it is efficient to locate aluminum refineries close to bauxite mines, and indeed the largest refineries are mine-mouth plants. Because refineries and mines require substantial sunk investments and have long lifetimes, Stuckey argues that integration is a natural response to the threat of costly breakdowns. He documents that integration of co-located mines and refineries is indeed common. Hennart (1988) provides an interesting comparison: the production of tin. Relative to aluminum, tin production has much lower capital and transport costs, less specialization of refineries, and also much less vertical integration.

Joskow (1987) studies coal-fired electric utilities. He points out that utilities located in the eastern United States have relatively easy access to multiple coal suppliers, while utilities located in the West have fewer options. As a result, western utilities are more exposed to costly hold-ups and are more likely to take contractual precautions. Geographic variation in market structure therefore provides a source of identifying variation. The dependent variable in the study is the duration of supply contracts, as vertical integration is relatively uncommon. Joskow shows that utilities in the East have relatively short contracts, whereas those in the West can last 15 years or more. Over such a long duration, the value of energy can be expected to vary widely. Thus, the costs of long-term contracting might be considerable, especially if the contractual price only poorly tracks the spot prices that would have prevailed (Joskow 1988). Presumably this cost is weighed against the benefit of protecting investments in choosing contract duration.[14]

---

13. Acemoglu et al. (2010) take a less direct approach to assessing the relationship between investments and integration, but one that is motivated by property rights theory, studying the relationship between technological intensity and integration in British manufacturing.

14. A related line of work uses variation across firms within an industry, or across local markets, to test whether integration decisions are related to the number of available suppliers or to upstream concentration. See, for instance, Lieberman (1991), Ohanian (1994), or the additional studies discussed in Section 4.

In the aluminum and coal examples, asset specificity is closely related to market structure. In Stuckey (1983), co-location and high transport costs ensure that refineries have few alternative suppliers. In Joskow, firms in the West cannot rely on a thick spot market and competition to avoid hold-up. In each case, a concentrated market structure (i.e., few ex post options) provides an empirical proxy for potential opportunism.

The availability of alternative suppliers can depend a great deal on the relevant time horizon. A firm may have many options if it plans well in advance, but few on short notice, creating what Masten et al. (1991) refer to as "temporal specificity." Pirrong (1993) argues that differences in the incidence of temporal specificity can explain organizational arrangements in ocean shipping for different commodities. Grain and fertilizer are at one extreme. They can be carried using general-purpose vessels and have liquid spot markets. The thickness of the market leaves little room for haggling over prices, and both commodities are commonly shipped under spot contracts. In contrast, iron ore requires specialized vessels to ship, and the number of mines and steelmakers is limited. Integration and long-term contracts are the norm. Either steelmakers own their own shipping subsidiaries, or they secure a shipper for a long period of time, with the agreement typically negotiated prior to the construction of the specialized ship.

3.3. Decision Rights and Coordination

One of the central ideas in transaction cost theory and in models of the optimal allocation of decision rights is that integration might help firms adapt to contingencies that are anticipated in a broad sense but not in specific detail. Testing this proposition calls for a setting in which such contingencies arise frequently and with enough similarity to facilitate statistical analysis, but with sufficient variation to prevent easy contracting in advance. Several studies have made progress by looking at integration decisions in transportation industries, where scheduling poses a coordination problem that often has to be solved in real time in a fashion that allows adaptation to changing circumstances and events.[15]

Forbes and Lederman (2009) study the relationships between major U.S. airlines and their regional affiliates. Some carriers own their regional affiliates, while others use long-term contracts. The organizational structure is revised infrequently, but numerous issues (e.g., scheduling) must be resolved on an ongoing basis. Forbes and Lederman focus on the possibility that weather disruptions might be a particular source of conflict. They argue that when there is a disruption, a carrier may want to adapt local flights to keep their network running as smoothly as possible. Regional carriers may not internalize broader problems on the network. Forbes and Lederman use cross-route variation in weather patterns to proxy for the incidence of conflict. They find that major carriers are more likely to use wholly owned regional operators on routes with worse weather. Integration is also more common on routes that are more intricately linked to the network, where the need for coordination is arguably larger.[16]

15. Gil (2007) provides a related analysis of adaption in the movie industry, where the market for any given movie is initially uncertain but realized over time, leading to a question of how long theatres should continue to exhibit the movie when the box office receipts are being shared with (disintegrated) movie distributors.

16. Forbes and Lederman (2009) do not provide much direct evidence on the costs of integration that encourage carriers to sometimes rely on contracts with nonintegrated affiliates. They hypothesize that arm's-length

In a subsequent paper, Forbes and Lederman (2012a) tighten this story by relating integration decisions to ex post measures of performance, in this case flight delays. They find that integrated regionals experience fewer delays than nonintegrated ones, particularly on airport days with adverse weather conditions. The finding is consistent with the idea that the national airline, not the regional carrier, disproportionately bears the costs of delay and that opportunistic behavior by the regional carrier hinders adaptation in certain contingencies. Although delays do not translate immediately into dollar costs of disintegrated supply, the paper is unusual, and admirable, in completing the link from plausibly exogenous market conditions to integration decisions to ex post performance.[17]

Problems of adaptation also feature prominently in studies by Lafontaine and Masten (2002), Nickerson and Silverman (2002), and Baker and Hubbard (2003, 2004) on organizational arrangements in the trucking industry. In trucking, costs are reduced by minimizing driving distance and maximizing the likelihood of full loads. These features mean that efficient matching of trucks and loads can create substantial value, and often the matching needs to be done in real-time, based on the location of trucks and loads. One conjecture is that when load matching is more important, we might expect a greater prevalence of trucking employees driving company-owned trucks rather than independent operators contracting for loads.

Consistent with this broad hypothesis, Nickerson and Silverman (2002) find that employee drivers are more common in "less-than-truckload" (LTL) carriage, where they argue there is more need for coordinated scheduling. Baker and Hubbard (2003, 2004) find a similar relationship between the use of employee drivers and difficulty in finding backhauls, where again the potential for miscoordination and haggling may be greater. In an interesting extension, Baker and Hubbard (2003) look at the adoption of information technology in the form of on-board computers. They point out that on-board computers had ambiguous implications for organization form. On the one hand, by allowing companies to track driver locations, they facilitated load matching and more efficient capacity utilization, favoring an integrated structure. On the other hand, they allowed for improved monitoring of driver activities, facilitating arm's-length contracting.

The Baker and Hubbard (2003, 2004) papers and Pirrong's (1993) work on shipping raise the interesting question of whether vertically integrated control structures have a natural advantage in solving complex coordination or matching problems. In transportation, scheduling and load-matching problems are frequently tackled using optimization models that incorporate various constraints on allocation and dispatch. Economists immediately understand that solutions to these types of problems have a market analogue, for instance with multipliers on different constraints corresponding to implied prices for different routes. What is the incentive to shift from market control to operations research control? Pirrong points to the problem of having sufficiently thick markets to generate reliable prices. Another rationale might be the

---

contracting keeps the employees of the regional firm at a distance from the generally quite powerful unions of the parent carrier.

17. In a further related study, Forbes and Lederman (2012b) analyze an industry shift from revenue sharing contracts with regional carriers to capacity utilization (or "per flight") payments. They show that this shift was associated with the adoption of flexible regional jets and argue that the change in contract was needed to reduce haggling with the regional carriers over what flights to fly.

difficulty of solving complex scheduling and matching problems in a decentralized fashion, although arguably this type of problem might be addressed with more sophisticated market mechanisms.

3.4. Agency, Incentives, and Monitoring

Empirical researchers have also explored the extent to which incentive contracting theories of integration have predictive power. The large literatures on retail franchising decisions and sales force integration are typical in this regard.[18] Here, researchers have attempted to link organizational decisions by the parent firm—such as whether franchise outlets are to be company owned—to the importance of franchisor and franchisee effort and to difficulties in monitoring this effort. Because direct measures of the marginal returns to effort and the ability to monitor typically are hard to come by, most researchers rely on proxies. For example, studies have found that more remote outlets (e.g., those in rural areas, without neighboring outlets, or farther from headquarters) are more likely to be franchised as opposed to company owned (e.g., Brickley and Dark 1987; Minkler 1990; Kehoe 1996). Other studies report correlations between franchise ownership and such variables as employee-to-sales ratio or the experience required of new franchisees.

A common issue in interpreting these findings is that (once again!) the empirical proxies may not relate very tightly to a particular theory. For example, the cost of monitoring remote outlets may be higher, making it desirable to provide higher powered revenue incentives. Alternatively, remote outlets also may be less integral to the chain's reputation, making it less important for the parent to exercise control. The set of individuals interested in obtaining a remote franchise and the potential customers at remote outlets also may be different from nearby franchises.[19] This ambiguity can lead to multiple explanations for a reported correlation.

Some studies have been able to mitigate the proxy problem by identifying cases where there is compelling cross-franchise or cross-location variation in the nature of tasks. Shepard's (1993) study of gasoline stations in Massachusetts is a good example. Shepard views the choice of organizational form for gasoline stations as resolving a trade-off between resolving double-marginalization problems in pricing and providing incentives for the station operators. She argues that incentives are likely to be more important at stations that offer ancillary services, such as auto repair or full-service gasoline. Consistent with this logic, Shepard finds that the stations offering ancillary services are less likely to be company owned.[20]

---

18. On franchising decisions, see, for example, Caves and Murphy (1976), Brickley and Dark (1987), Norton (1988), Minkler (1990), Lafontaine (1992), Lafontaine and Shaw (2005), and Yeap (2006). Studies of sales force integration include Anderson and Schmittlein (1984), John and Weitz (1988), and Regan (1999).

19. Other studies proxy for franchisee effort using such measures as the employee-sales ratio (Norton 1988) or the amount of franchisee experience required (Lafontaine 1992). Related work adopts proxies for the importance of franchisor effort, such as advertising expenditures (Lafontaine and Shaw 2005) or the number of years a chain went before franchising any outlets (e.g., Lafontaine 1992). It is not entirely obvious why the variation in these variables should be unrelated to other factors influencing franchisee ownership.

20. Yeap (2006) takes a similar approach to studying franchising decisions by fast-food chains. Her central finding is that restaurants where food preparation is done on site and table service is supplied are more likely to be franchised. See also Slade (1996).

Studies of retail organization also face difficult problems of selection. For instance, a common hypothesis in research on franchising is that parent companies should tend to own outlets where revenue is highly variable, as a way to shelter franchisees from risk. The evidence, however, is highly inconclusive (Lafontaine and Slade 2007). Of course, finding a convincing proxy for risk is not easy, but even apart from this measurement problem, one may be concerned about selection. For instance, franchise operators may vary substantially in their risk attitudes, and those with greater risk tolerance (or perhaps greater wealth) may be drawn to the more risky outlets and also prefer to have ownership.[21]

A broader issue with the contractual literature on franchising is that it does not provide much evidence on whether outlet ownership has first-order operational effects. After all, a statistical relationship between incentives and ownership structure does not necessarily establish that the incentive problems under one organizational form are large. From an incentive perspective, a company-owned McDonald's might be radically different from a franchisee-owned McDonald's, or it might be pretty much the same. To assess the difference, one needs to know whether there really is substantial variation in effort or behavior across franchises and whether it co-varies with organizational form. Absent such information, it is difficult to infer whether agency considerations are really the central issue driving franchising decisions or whether such issues as capital structure and financing are more important. The best way to address these questions would be to incorporate direct measures of outlet performance into the analysis.

3.5. Knowledge and Information Transfers

In contrast to empirical work on transaction specificity and incentives, the literature that tries to link vertical integration decisions to knowledge and information flows is less well developed. One likely reason is that the relevant variables—organizational capabilities or know-how, managerial ability, and internal processes—can be difficult to measure, a prerequisite for empirical work. (Bloom and van Reenen's (2007) survey measures of management practices are an interesting and promising exception.) As discussed earlier, the theory is also less sharply organized in terms of generating specific testable hypotheses.

One area where there has been some progress is the study of organizational structures in the pharmaceutical industry. Knowledge creation in pharmaceuticals happens in the early stages of drug discovery and in subsequent stages of development and clinical trials, and there are further stages of production and distribution. Several studies have found evidence for economies of scope at various stages of the chain, which they attribute to firms developing specialized capabilities.

Henderson and Cockburn (1996) focus on the first stage of drug discovery, using data on development projects gathered from large pharmaceutical firms. Their dataset is unusual in that it contains information on projects that do not succeed as well as those that do. The number of patents provides a measure of success. By this measure, projects taking place in firms with larger overall research programs appear to be more successful, and Henderson and

---

21. The same concern can be voiced about Shepard's (1993) study to the extent that the operators of auto repair stations are relatively entrepreneurial and may prefer to be owners—although Shepard does try to provide auxiliary evidence that weighs against selection bias.

Cockburn argue that this can be attributed in part to scope economies. Their work suggests that complementarities across research projects may help explain the boundaries of pharmaceutical firms.

Subsequent to their study, the industry underwent a major shift toward early-stage drug discovery taking place outside the large pharmaceutical firms, in academic laboratories or smaller entrepreneurial firms. This shift creates a potential market or contracting friction. Relatively few firms appear able or willing to push drugs through to commercial use, whether because of scale economies or differences in capabilities at the later stages of drug development. As a result, a licensing market has emerged, where drugs invented in one firm are transferred for development or commercialization in another. A natural concern is that the licensing market might suffer from problems of expropriation or asymmetric information.

Arora et al. (2001) investigate whether licensing transactions might be subject to a "lemons" problem of asymmetric information. They gather a dataset that includes ex post outcomes that might not have been forecastable by (all) parties at the time of contract. They look at the later stages of drug trials and commercialization for licensing agreements signed before phase I clinical trials. It appears that, contrary to the lemons hypothesis, success rates do not differ between products that are out-licensed and those retained in-house for further development. Arora et al. also conclude, perhaps less surprisingly, that there are economies of scale and scope at the firm level in the later stages of drug development.

Concerns about organizational capabilities are also the key to Azoulay's (2004) case study of outsourcing in the pharmaceutical industry, where firms increasingly rely on contract research organizations to perform clinical trials for new drugs. Azoulay looks at how the decision to outsource varies with the nature of the trial. He argues that the incentive systems and capabilities of large pharmaceutical firms and contract research organizations are fundamentally different. Contract research organizations are organized to efficiently gather and analyze large quantities of routine data, whereas pharmaceutical firms are better equipped to manage trials that require the production of new knowledge rather than just new data. The data appears to be consistent with this story. For instance, Azoulay finds that studies that involve more academics, and hence may be more skewed toward knowledge production rather than data production, are much less likely to be outsourced.

These interesting results suggest connections between knowledge transfer and organizational capabilities and integration in one specific industry. Even so, one might argue that these papers are not yet fully testing what is arguably the most interesting hypothesis related to integration in innovative industries. Specifically, smaller, newer firms might have the advantage of flexibility and diversity (particularly with respect to new drug ideas), whereas larger established firms might have superior commercialization and regulatory skills. These differences might be behind the pattern of licenses, alliances, and entry and growth of firms of different types.

3.6. When and How Do Vertical Integration Decisions Matter?

We have already highlighted one of the main limitations of the empirical literature. By and large, it focuses on the decision of whether to vertically integrate, but not on the implications of this decision for economic outcomes or realized transaction costs. This focus leads to questions about when integration has first-order incentive effects (e.g., in the case of franchising), effects on decisionmaking or adaptation (e.g., in the case of sourcing different types of inputs), or important effects on innovation and productive efficiency.

Quantifying the effects of integration decisions poses some challenges. One difficulty, of course, is the econometric problem of selection. If firms choose to integrate when they think it will lead to productivity benefits, finding the right variation to identify the effect of integration on productive efficiency is going to be difficult. In the case of coal contracts, for example, one might like to measure the costs and benefits of longer contracts holding fixed the market environment. Most of the utilities with short-duration contracts, however, are in the eastern United States, whereas those with longer duration contracts are co-located or are in the western United States.

A second difficulty with measuring the effects of integration is that most empirical studies focus on borderline cases, where integration is a close call. Of course, integration may have both a large efficiency benefit and a large efficiency cost, but this is not guaranteed. Thus, a more promising strategy may be to look at decisions that are complementary to integration. For instance, as emphasized by Holmström and Milgrom (1994), small variations in the environment might lead firms to make large changes to a cluster of policies if there are important complementarities.

These difficulties notwithstanding, there is a variety of evidence that sheds some light on differences across integrated and nonintegrated firms. One example comes from research on manufacturing productivity.[22] For instance, Hortaçsu and Syverson (2007) compare integrated and nonintegrated concrete and cement plants. They find that integrated plants are larger and more productive in the cross-section, that plants that become integrated are more productive, and that the event of becoming integrated is associated with an increase in productivity. They argue that the source of these productivity advantages may be tied to better logistics coordination, a benefit that is associated more with size than with vertical integration per se.[23]

Further evidence along these lines is provided by Atalay et al. (2012), who use establishment-level data from a broad range of industries. They again show that integration, plant size, capital intensity, and labor productivity are positively correlated. The paper also includes a striking finding about commonly owned plants in vertically related industries. There is relatively little transfer of physical goods from one plant to another. Instead, plants within the same firm in vertically related industries are overwhelmingly involved in merchant operations, in which they transact across the firm's boundary.

---

22. Less work has been done on behavioral or operating differences between integrated and nonintegrated manufacturers. For instance, Mullainathan and Scharfstein (2001) study the capacity decisions of vinyl chloride monomer manufacturers, some of whom are integrated downstream into the production of waterproof plastic, of which this monomer is an input. They present evidence that nonintegrated vinyl chloride monomer producers react more strongly to market demand for the monomer, whereas integrated producers focus on internal demand needs, and they argue that this might be explained by differences in managerial focus and attention.

23. Related work by Van Biesebroeck (2006) on automobile manufacturing finds that component integration is associated with higher productivity, especially in plants that have adopted flexible manufacturing techniques. His results also are consistent with the view that integration facilitates greater coordination in the production process.

This observation strongly suggests that much common ownership of vertically related plants is driven by the sharing of intangible assets (e.g., managerial skills, know-how, or other information) or is related to the financing of the firm.[24] This general story is also consistent with work on large diversified firms, such as that of Schoar (2002), who provides evidence that plants in diversified firms are more productive than those in single-segment firms.[25] This sort of evidence pushes us away from a primarily operational or commodity-flow understanding of vertical integration.

Relating these papers to the theory calls for telling where exactly the trade-offs arise in making integration decisions. To what extent can managerial know-how be leveraged, and where do the benefits drop off? Does an increase in scale or scope feed back into productivity? These analyses also do not make much contact with the types of contractual concerns on which theorists have focused. They also differ from those discussed above in that there is little explicit measure of what happens at the firm boundary or at the divisional boundary within a vertically integrated firm. Instead, an inference is drawn from firm scale and scope. Thus, the interpretation in terms of the underlying theory is necessarily indirect, although a natural trend is toward theories that involve spreading a fixed managerial input over a range of production activities (e.g., Lucas 1978).

The productivity and incentive consequences of vertical integration have also received attention in research on healthcare organizations. In the United States, healthcare systems have become significantly more integrated over the past 25 years, through partnerships between general and specialist physicians, physicians and hospitals, and hospitals and specialty care units, among others. Although one explanation for this integration is that physicians and hospitals are attempting to improve their bargaining power vis-à-vis insurers and exercise market power, another line of thought holds that integrated systems are able to successfully resolve contractual inefficiencies and can provide more efficient, coordinated care.

The current literature seems to be broadly inconclusive (Gaynor 2006), but some studies offer interesting specific findings, some of which are consistent with contractual theories. Afendulis and Kessler (2007), for instance, look at the problem of integrating diagnostic services and treatment. They find that in the case of coronary artery disease, patients seen by cardiologists whose practices also provide surgical treatments were more likely to receive angioplasties; these patients received generally more expensive care but did not have better health outcomes. Afendulis and Kessler interpret this result as consistent with moral hazard or incentive contracting theories of integration.

In more recent work, Afendulis and Kessler (2011) look at how changes in Medicare reimbursement policy affected skilled nursery facilities that were and were not integrated with

---

24. In an effort to make this finding more direct, Hortaçsu and Syverson (2007) also examine the white collar (nonproduction) workers in the plants they study. Their inclusion might tie the inference closer to a theory about management. However, many of the white collar workers in manufacturing plants are not, typically, managers of the manufacturing production process, but rather managers of the market or nonmarket processes by which intermediate inputs flow into the plant and outputs flow out of it.

25. More surprisingly, however, she finds that existing plants become less productive following an increase in firm diversification. She hypothesizes that this result also can be explained by management, to the extent that a new acquisition leads to a shift in managerial focus away from existing lines of business. This interpretation is consistent with another systematic merger fact, which is that many mergers are followed by spin-offs of the acquired business (Ravenscraft and Scherer 1987).

hospitals. They find that a shift to prospective payment (essentially fixed-price reimbursement rather than cost-based reimbursement) led to significantly greater declines in healthcare costs for the integrated facilities. The mechanism that enables integrated hospitals to better respond to changes in external financial incentives is not entirely clear, and indeed, studies have reached mixed conclusions on whether hospitals that are more broadly integrated generally have lower costs (Ciliberto and Dranove 2006; Cuellar and Gertler 2006).

Ciliberto (2006) uses integrated and nonintegrated hospitals to offer a more specific test of hold-up theories, by looking at the decision to invest by offering outpatient and diagnostic services. These services rely on referrals from primary care physicians, so the hypothesis is that hospitals that are integrated with their physicians might be better positioned to internalize referrals, which might support investments in service provision. Ciliberto indeed finds that vertically integrated hospitals added more of these services following integration. The effect is strongest in areas where HMO penetration is higher, which is roughly consistent with the idea that the returns to integration might increase with the prospect of hold-up.

What are the efficiency consequences of this finding? The perspective Ciliberto (2006) takes is that the potential for hold-up leaves nonintegrated hospitals investing too little in outpatient and diagnostic services, and integration resolves the inefficiency. An alternative interpretation, closer to the view in Afendulis and Kessler (2007), is that offering these services provides a mechanism for physicians to capture rents. These rents could arise from failures of the physicians to act as the perfect agents of patients in making referrals or from problems in the setting of prices paid for these services by third-party payers.

The example illustrates the difficulty of moving from even cleanly measured behavioral effects to efficiency or welfare interpretation in a complex market and organizational environment, such as health care. Nevertheless, we expect that this topic will, and should, receive a great deal of attention in coming years.

4. Vertical Integration and Market Structure

A recurring theme in our discussion of the empirical literature on vertical integration is the connection between integration decisions and market structure. This link has not been the focus of contractual theories of vertical integration, but it is a major focus of research in industrial organization. In this section, we distill some of the key ideas and relate them to work in organizational economics.

The theories we examine bring several different sets of ideas to the foreground. One set of ideas relates to the determination of horizontal market structure, typically based in firm-level costs or in strategic interaction among firms. In some circumstances, cost efficiencies or strategy decisions that impact horizontal structure also affect vertical organization. Another set of ideas concerns the creation of institutions supporting market exchange and the importance of these institutions for supporting disintegrated forms of production. The final set of ideas pertains specifically to innovative industries and the efficient organizational and market structure for coordinating and spurring innovative activity.

Apart from their focus on industry-level outcomes, the industrial organization theories we describe differ from the organizational theories in paying far less attention to the foundations of contract theory. They tend to assume, without spelling out exact reasons, that integration offers more control or a greater ability to coordinate decisionmaking than a market contract does. For this reason, one can think of the two sets of theories as complementary inputs in a full explanation of vertical integration, even if this complementarity has not always been fully recognized.

4.1. Scale Economies and the Extent of the Market

An important line of research in industrial organization relates vertical integration to fixed costs and market size. This approach has its roots in Adam Smith's dictum that the division of labor is limited by the extent of the market (Young 1928; Stigler 1951; Bresnahan and Gambardella 1998). The central idea is that vertical integration decisions are closely connected to the horizontal structure of the constituent industries.

This point can be understood in a simple model that involves the production of two complementary inputs subject to scale economies. Suppose the market for the final product is so small (relative to the scale economies) that it can support only a single firm in each of the two input markets. Because of the horizontal structure in each of the two markets, the vertical relationship between the two producers is bilateral monopoly. If this relationship leads to inefficiencies because of haggling, hold-up, incentive distortions, or any of the other reasons explored above, the efficient vertical relationship calls for integration. The same problem, however, may not arise if the product market expands. Suppose that final demand becomes sufficiently large (relative to scale economies) to support a competitive market structure in both layers. With this horizontal market structure, the bilateral monopoly problem need not arise, and the efficient vertical structure may involve disintegrated specialists.

Note that this argument blends two very different bodies of theory. It requires a theory of horizontal industry structure, drawn from industrial organization, and a theory of bilateral contracting, drawn from organizational economics. Like most theories we discuss in this section, the elements are simple. But they focus attention on the joint determination of firm and industry structure and the interaction between ideas from the two fields.

Stigler (1951) developed this basic idea into a theory of industry evolution. He argued that in the early and innovative phases of an industry, firms have to be vertically integrated, because there are no markets for the relevant inputs—the costs of organizing those markets, he assumes, are higher than the costs of coordinating the production of the inputs within the firm. As the industry becomes larger, what had formerly been internal inputs are supplied by new, vertically disintegrated industries. In addition to the trade-off between efficient horizontal scale and vertical market power, Stigler's theory adds the idea that market institutions to support disintegrated trade are themselves endogenous and have to be developed over time.

Many historical accounts of particular industries resonate with Stigler's theory. One example is Rosenberg's (1994, 1998) account of how design procedures for chemical processing plants evolved over time. Initially, manufacturing firms that operated chemical processing plants undertook plant design themselves. Plant design is complex and represents a plant-level fixed cost, but much of the knowledge needed to design a single plant can be used to design other plants. Thus, the potential existed for a separate disintegrated design industry that could allow the acquisition of this knowledge to be shared across multiple plants.

As Rosenberg (1994, 1998) points out, this potential was not immediately realized, because it required the creation of a new market boundary—identifying exactly what services specialized engineering firms would provide in plant design. Ultimately, however, specialized engineering firms did emerge. Their emergence subsequently changed the degree of scale economies in chemical manufacturing, because firms no longer needed to have many plants to spread the fixed costs of maintaining a plant design capability. The change in scale economies helped facilitate a less concentrated industry structure in a number of distinct chemical processing industries (Arora et al. 2001).

Another example in which one can see evidence for Stigler's (1951) ideas comes from the integrated circuit industry. Integrated circuits must be designed and then manufactured. A few decades ago, the creation of an interface between computer-aided design and computer-aided manufacturing permitted the design and manufacture to be done either by the same firm or by different firms. As the manufacturing facilities are very large, and some products have very short production runs, the creation of the interface led to a great deal of vertical disintegration. Firms that specialize in design but do not manufacture are now able to contract with firms that specialize in manufacturing but not in design.

Scale economies play a role here, because many products with small markets may be produced in the same large manufacturing facility. There are also individual products with very large markets, such as Intel microprocessors. Firms selling the products with the largest markets, such as Intel, are vertically integrated. This permits them to strategically align manufacturing process improvements with product design improvements, presumably with less contractual frictions than might arise in a situation of bilateral monopoly between layers of production. So the variation in the extent of the market across products (rather than over time) generates patterns of integration consistent with the Stigler theory.

In addition to historical case studies of individual industries, some attempts have been made to statistically test relationships between vertical integration and varying measures of scale economies or horizontal concentration. Holmes (1999) takes an interesting approach by asking whether vertical disintegration is more prevalent in geographic areas where manufacturing industries are localized. For each plant, he measures localization as the amount of employment at neighboring plants in the same industry. Roughly, the idea is that in areas where an industry is localized, there is the potential for specialized suppliers to thrive and support a disintegrated vertical production structure. Holmes finds that vertical disintegration (measured by the share of purchased inputs in production) is indeed higher in areas where there is extensive local employment in a given industry, broadly consistent with Stigler's hypothesis.

An alternative cross-sectional approach has been to test whether industries that are more highly concentrated or have larger firms are also more vertically integrated. The Levy (1984) paper is an older but carefully executed study along these lines. Levy looks at the relationship, across three-digit industries between vertical integration (as measured by value added divided by sales) and covariates, such as average firm size, demand growth, and concentration. He reports that industries with larger firms, more demand growth, and more concentration are all more likely to feature vertical integration (see also Elberfeld 2002). Even with careful execution, however, these types of correlations are very difficult to interpret as sharp evidence for or against any particular theory, because there are so many factors that can influence cross-industry relationships between vertical integration and other industry characteristics.[26]

One of the elaborations of Stigler's (1951) general approach to thinking about vertical integration occurs when complementary goods are produced with very different levels of scale economies. This can lead to the common industry structure in which one or a few firms supply a general specialty or platform input that is complementary to a potentially large number of products or inputs produced by other firms (Stigler 1951; Bresnahan and Gambardella 1998). A typical trade-off here is that any efficiency benefits that might come from the platform provider integrating into complementary markets must be weighed against the potential for reduced competition.

For instance, consider a setting in which differentiated products rely on the same complementary platform. Standard models of market structure in differentiated products industries give rise to an equilibrium in which firms enjoy some market power to cover the fixed costs of product differentiation, and a trade-off occurs between achieving scale economies in a particular product versus having product variety and competition across products. If the horizontal industry equilibrium has many more firms than scale economies in the complementary layer permit, vertical integration that forecloses the platform to competing products may have the effect of eliminating the benefits of competition and differentiation in the market where they are feasible.

An example considered by Stigler (1951) is the production and transportation of manufactured goods. Efficient industry structure in production is likely to involve many distinct firms, whereas parts of the transportation system are subject to increasing returns and thus are supplied by only a few firms. Both competition and product diversity drive the production layer toward multiple firms. Although some manufactured goods (e.g., iPads) may be produced by only a few firms and others (e.g., lag bolts) by many, in the aggregate we expect a large number of firms producing a wide variety of goods. In contrast, scale economies play a much larger role in determining the equilibrium industry structure for transportation by limiting the number of railroads, canals, or roads that can link any two places as well as the number of ports or airports that can be built at any given city.

Note that there is some tension between the industrial organization theories of market structure in the types of industries we are considering (i.e., those with differentiated products) and the organizational economics theories. The industrial organization theories take certain firm boundaries as given. For instance, they offer no explanation for why a single firm could not control and produce a wide range of differentiated products. Instead, they begin with the assumption that no firm could integrate all manufacturing processes, even if it remains an open question whether each manufacturing firm owns ships or railroad cars. Although this argument can be seen as merely one of common sense, it implicitly relies on some notion of organizational diseconomies of scale or scope.

---

26. Acemoglu et al. (2009) take a somewhat different approach by asking whether firms in countries that are more financially developed are more or less likely to be vertically integrated. They find no direct relationship between financial development and the prevalence of integrated firms, but they do find a higher prevalence of integration in countries that have both greater financial development and higher contracting costs.

This gap has been met partially by organizational economics theories that explain organizational diseconomies of scale. Williamson's (1985) suggestion that bureaucratic decisionmaking is one disadvantage of large firms, Simon's (1947) idea that larger firms must undertake more communication, and Radner's (1992) idea that more complex and larger teams will make worse decisions have all received some exploration in this regard.[27] These questions, which have received only modest attention in organizational economics, become particularly important when we consider the joint determination of firm and industry structure.[28]

4.2. Role of Strategy in Determining Industry Structure

The simple framework discussed above suggests a relationship between horizontal concentration and vertical integration that is driven by efficiency considerations—the size of scale economies relative to the size of the market. What it neglects is the possibility that firms might make strategic efforts to limit competition. An industry can be very concentrated and feature considerable market power because of scale economies or because business strategy limits the number of active firms (e.g., by affecting the potential for entry).[29] Indeed, that organizational economics theories have focused so much on efficiency rationales for vertical integration suggests that we might want to reformulate Coase's crack about monopoly theories: nowadays if an economist finds something—a business practice of one sort or another—that she does not understand, she looks for an efficient contracts explanation![30]

Once we allow for the possibility of strategic investments, the relationship described above between market size and concentration can become less clear. Consider the class of industries that feature what Sutton (2007) has called "endogenous sunk costs." These are industries in which firms can undertake strategic investments (e.g., in technological innovations or brand building) to make their products more attractive. If the investment opportunities in endogenous sunk costs are sufficient (in a sense made precise in the literature), then industry structure remains concentrated, even as demand grows without limit. The link from increased market size to reduced horizontal concentration to vertical disintegration is broken.

A very large literature on industrial organization also has pointed to the potentially important role of vertical integration or vertical contracts themselves in helping to limit competition or more generally influence horizontal market structure. A classic example might be a monopoly supplier of an input that integrates or signs an exclusive contract with the supplier of a complementary input to maintain monopoly power in the first market or create it in the second. The literature has debated two questions about this type of situation. First, is it even possible for

27. See, among others, Simon (1951), Calvo and Wellisz (1978), Williamson (1985), Radner (1992), Anton and Yao (1995), and McAfee and McMillan (1995). Some evidence on the source of scope diseconomies in technology industries can be found in Bresnahan et al. (2012).

28. Another partial solution comes from the industrial organization theories themselves. Models of horizontal disintegration through competitive entry call for separate firms in order to have competitive outcomes. Vertically integrating all firms in a competitive industry with the same complementor would defeat the competitive purpose.

29. See, for example, Berry and Reiss (2007) and Sutton (2007).

30. Coase's (1972: 67) original line was: "If an economist finds something—a business practice of one sort or another—that he does not understand, he looks for a monopoly explanation."

the monopoly supplier to raise prices by integrating? Second, is it anticompetitive, and as such, should antitrust policy seek to prevent this type of strategic foreclosure?[31]

Whinston (2007) provides a lucid and thorough treatment of these issues, which go well beyond the scope of this chapter. We note, however, that this literature—although potentially highly germane if one wants to understand the joint determination of firm and industry structure—has by and large not connected with organizational economics rationales for integration. Indeed, it often treats vertical integration and restrictive vertical contracts in roughly a parallel fashion. It is true that in formulating antitrust policy, the potential organizational efficiency benefits of allowing a contract or merger to go through are sometimes weighed against the competitive costs, but generally these are treated as distinct phenomena.

We also note that in addition to strategic theories in which firms integrate as a way to gain market power in anticompetitive fashion, there are arguments for why strategic integration might be welfare enhancing. For instance, Teece (1986) has suggested that firms can sometimes integrate to consolidate "good" market power. If a firm has an invention in an area with poor patent protection, for example, it might vertically integrate into a downstream business with entry barriers and avoid losing the return on its innovation through competition.[32] Another class of theories, discussed for instance in Perry (1989), consider how vertical integration can facilitate certain forms of price discrimination that might be efficient (e.g., by allowing a supplier to integrate downstream and sell its input at different prices to the integrated downstream producer than it does to the general market).

4.3. Market Institutions and Vertical Integration

The point made by Stigler (1951) that market institutions need to be invented before a wide variety of firms can participate in them remains only partially explored in organizational economics. Distinct literatures have taken up this question, many of which raise interesting issues about vertical integration and market structure.

A textbook benefit of a well-functioning market is that the price mechanism coordinates the needs of many parties and determines an efficient use of resources. If matching is less efficient, a buyer and seller might agree to go around the market. This idea is captured in Carlton's (1979) model of supply assurance as a rationale for vertical integration. He considers a setting in which market frictions upset the functioning of the spot market for inputs, so that buyers cannot be assured of reliable supply. If the problem is severe, buyers want to integrate upstream, or

---

31. The Hart and Tirole (1990) paper is a classic reference on the first question, which turns on the question of commitment: after integrating forward, can the supplier really commit to shutting off supply to rival downstream firms? On the second question, the classic argument against government intervention is the "one monopoly rent" story associated with the Chicago School. The basic argument is that, in some circumstances, a monopolist supplier can achieve the same profit regardless of whether it integrates forward and raises the downstream price or simply raises the input price. Whinston (2007) discusses a range of conditions under which this argument does not hold, and vertical integration or exclusive contracts indeed can be anticompetitive.

32. Of course, the same argument applies to any tactic that might generate market power, and the Teece (1986) proposal has become a general management doctrine for creating rents at the firm level. See, for example, the widely cited article by Amit and Schoemaker (1993).

alternatively formulate a nonmarket forward contract to assure supply.[33] So Carlton's theory provides a potential explanation in which vertical integration might be linked to the existence of a well-functioning market interface between layers of production (see also Green 1986).

A related observation can be made in the context of transaction cost analyses of integration. If we consider, for instance, the studies of transportation industries, such as trucking or shipping discussed above, a central problem being solved is logistical—the efficient short-run allocation of heterogeneous suppliers to heterogeneous tasks. The existence of market institutions—standard contractual forms, preexisting agreements on exactly what service will be exchanged, or the availability of comparable reference prices on which to base negotiation—can be crucial to support a disintegrated structure, because they are necessary to support efficient, predictable, and potentially competitive agreements at low cost.

The existence of market institutions to support disintegrated exchange is not a given. In many cases, market institutions tend to co-evolve with industry structure. Financial markets provide an exceptionally rich set of examples. Consider, for instance, a loan from a bank to an individual to allow the individual to purchase a house. Historically in the mortgage market, the same bank extended the loan and then undertook collections and received interest and principal payments from the borrower. In this setting, selling a loan portfolio would have been an idiosyncratic and unusual transaction. Yet over time, the development of relatively standard securitization contracts allowed the initial originators of loans (banks and later also less well-capitalized companies) to sell their loans to investors, creating a vertically disintegrated market structure, albeit one with some potential incentive problems on the part of loan originators.

The securitization example is useful: one can in fact point to a range of institutions required to support a disintegrated market structure. These include not only standardized contracts to facilitate sales of loans but also effective institutions for transferring foreclosure rights in the event of a default, rating agencies to limit the potential for adverse selection in the sale of loans, and functioning markets to allow investors who have bought securities to later sell them. From this perspective, standard transaction cost variables, such as complexity and specificity, look somewhat different. A particular transaction—say, the sale of a loan portfolio—might seem highly complex and specific at one point in time, but much less so once market institutions are developed to support it.[34]

The more general point here is that transaction costs depend on existing market institutions—institutions that facilitate search and matching, and institutions that facilitate contractual and pricing arrangements. As a result, a disintegrated market structure—particularly the creation of a disintegrated industry with frequent arm's-length exchanges—often requires the creation of market institutions: standards for products and contracts, and mechanisms for matching buyers and sellers, determining prices, disseminating information, and so forth. Although these issues fall outside the traditional theory of the firm, they become hard to avoid

33. Bolton and Whinston (1993) provide an alternative model, based on the property rights theory, that also shows how supply assurance motives can lead firms to vertically integrate.

34. At the same time, the creation of market institutions is facilitated by having a degree of standardization in the underlying products. It may be relatively easy to develop an effective market for loan resale if the loans themselves are relatively standardized in most dimensions.

when one takes the theory to empirical settings, and perhaps they deserve more attention from organizational economists interested in firm boundaries.

4.4. Coordination and Innovation

A wide range of economically important innovations depend on complementary but distinct inventions. Computers would not be particularly valuable without applications software, to take one famous example. New products are more valuable if process innovations allow them to be produced cheaply. The invention of mass production itself would have been much less valuable without transportation technologies that permitted large plants to serve geographically dispersed customers. Research on platform industries, on product and process innovations, and on general-purpose technologies all emphasize the importance of coordinating complementary invention and raise the question of whether this should take place within large organizations or across disparate innovative firms.[35] The resulting trade-offs provide an interesting example of how organizational theories of integration intersect with considerations of market structure.

A potential benefit of integrating the invention of complementary technologies is that investments may be better coordinated. A basic price theory intuition is that creators of complementary inventions may end up in a position of bilateral or multilateral monopoly, and they may fail to coordinate their pricing and other ex post decisions. This can lead to a form of hold-up where the full returns on ex ante investment are not appropriated. Kenneth Arrow (1974) famously pointed out one particular problem with contracting over innovation, which is that firms seeking to reach an agreement may find it difficult to exchange information in a way that protects their ideas. For these reasons, vertical integration, or a similar contract to internalize externalities in complementary invention, can increase the private return from innovative activity.

A second and distinct argument for integration comes from game theory. The multiple invention problem is a coordination game, and it might have failures to coordinate if the different inventors cannot be sure ex ante of one another's plans for invention. In addition, separate firms may have an incentive to delay investments in order to assess which technologies or standards will emerge as grounds for coordination. These forces work against decentralized innovation and favor ex ante partner selection and contracting.

A countervailing force comes from the economics of invention with uncertain goals or methods. Suppose that, in one or more of the complementary inventions, the highest value direction of technical progress is ex ante uncertain. Different potential inventors can have different views about the appropriate direction, based on their private information. In such circumstances, ex ante selection among alternative invention projects can be inefficient, even when there is a fixed cost of inventive effort.[36] The alternative is to have invention competition and then let the market choose the best alternative. The advantage of ex post invention market

---

35. In the case of truly infrastructural inventions, such as those in transportation, communications, or basic scientific research, government has also played a considerable role in coordinating innovation. In this chapter, however, we focus on the trade-off between markets and integrated firms.

36. See Nelson (1961), Evenson and Kislev (1976), Metcalfe (1986), and Klepper (1996) for models of competition with uncertainty about the direction of technical progress with ex post market selection.

selection is that it can choose the best innovative efforts out of a number of initiatives based on their technical success or their success in meeting market needs. As a result, a market form of organization may have considerable value when there is substantial uncertainty about the optimal direction of technical progress or about the source of that progress,

The computer industry, which over time has witnessed both a high degree of vertical integration and considerable disintegration, provides a useful case study of these considerations.[37] The first highly valuable segment of the industry, mainframe computers for corporate data processing, was pioneered in the 1950s. IBM, which dominated the market for four decades, was highly vertically integrated in invention and production. Its inventions included not only the computer but also a large number of complementary hardware and software components useful in business data processing.[38] As a result, the boundary of the firm coincided with the boundary between general and specific technologies. IBM sought to supply all general-purpose components for its corporate customers, including the tools that would let them invent specific applications.

What factors might have led to all of the general components, each of which needed ongoing invention, being supplied by one firm? The key was the ex ante identification of a desired direction of technical progress for the system as a whole. At the time of IBM's entry into computing, the basic technical knowledge associated with the computer itself was largely public.[39] IBM was already the leading seller of business data-processing products and subsequently built a research and invention capability in computers.[40] As a result, IBM had knowledge not only of the technical opportunity but also of demand needs. This information gave a single firm considerable ex ante knowledge about the set of feasible directions for improvements in the overall system and the set of products that would be valuable to its customers. IBM picked reasonable innovative goals from the intersection of these two sets, allowing it to coordinate multiple inventions in the general mainframe components—computer, tape drive, programming languages, and operating system—going forward.[41]

---

37. See Bresnahan and Greenstein (1999) and Bresnahan and Malerba (2002). See also Langlois and Robertson (1992) on the value of vertical disintegration at the PC industry segment's founding.

38. These components included data-processing complements (e.g., tape or disk storage devices), input and output devices (e.g., printers), and especially software (e.g., operating systems and database management systems). Throughout IBM's tenure as the leading firm in this segment, customers had a high opinion of the way the complements making up an IBM system worked together but not of the technical level of its computers themselves.

39. It is important to point out that this discussion refers to the creation of computer systems for business use, not to the original invention of the computer itself. Many essential elements of the computer itself were invented before IBM's entry. The view, taken by IBM and others, that these essential elements were in the public domain, was extremely controversial. The controversy was heightened by IBM's late entry into the computer business and appropriation of existing knowledge. See Bresnahan and Malerba (2002) for a discussion. The point here depends on the fact that IBM, already knowledgeable about demand needs, could easily appropriate knowledge associated with the invention of the computer itself, not on the propriety of that appropriation.

40. The earlier business products were mechanical and electromechanical products, such as card sorters.

41. Industry historians will point out that this story misses important nuances. For example, the later emergence of applications software companies, especially semi-custom software developers such as EDS, meant that the distinction between the general and the specific is not such a bright line. Our point that the IBM system was largely one of vertical integration of the general components is robust, however.

The same trade-off worked the other way at the founding of another important computer industry segment, the personal computer. In that instance, ex ante knowledge about the overlap of technically feasible inventions and demand needs was much weaker, making coordination difficult. None of the founders of the personal computer industry—the designers of computers, disk drives, programming tools, or operating systems—had a clear view of the appropriate direction of technical change ex ante. As a result, the original industry structure was not vertically disintegrated, with considerable independent innovation in each component. Coordination was achieved ex post invention through market institutions, such as voluntary compliance with interconnection standards.[42]

Eventually, the invention of certain key applications, such as the word processor and the spreadsheet, helped clarify the direction of technical change—namely, toward business applications. That increased clarity led to efforts to coordinate supply by contract, notably in the IBM PC.[43] Those contracts, however, did not specify the direction of technical change, nor were they exclusive on either side. Innovation in the different components continued to be organized more along market lines than by contract.[44] Indeed, some of the leading firms involved in IBM PC contracts, including IBM itself, were later replaced by others through market selection. The advantage of vertical disintegration of invention, even of the general-purpose components, was the possibility of component-by-component invention races and the extensive use of ex post market selection, also on a component-by-component basis.

This vertical industry structure and component-by-component market selection process continued through a number of rounds of fundamental innovation. Indeed, some dominant firms supplying important PC markets were replaced through competition for the market on a component-by-component basis.[45] As long as the overlap between technical opportunity and demand needs was hard to see ex ante the next round of innovation, the less-coordinated model had considerable advantage.

Another example of the trade-offs in coordinating innovative activity comes from the organization of scientific research. Here the relevant boundary is between firms that undertake research with the express purpose of commercialization, and universities and other organizations that undertake research with potentially broader objectives. The resulting industry structure often locates basic research in noncommercial organizations, with applied research taking place in firms in a vertically disintegrated structure (though the distinction is frequently blurred). In a pioneering article, Dasgupta and David (1997) emphasize two points about this structure: first, that the reward structure for academic scientists is very different than it is for commercial inventors; second, that noncommercial research institutions are organized very differently than are firms.

---

42. Once again, we skip important nuances. Some firms, most successfully Apple, had a more vertically integrated model. See Langlois and Robertson (1992) for more details, and for the observation that the more vertically integrated efforts failed precisely because of their integration.

43. IBM entered with a computer and sought to contract with the leading firm in each important complementary technology, successfully so in disk drives, spreadsheets, programmer tools, and microprocessors. In operating systems or word processors, the leading firm would not sign and IBM found other partners.

44. Even hardware specifications of the computer itself were set in the market by firms other than IBM. See Bresnahan and Greenstein (1999) for details.

45. See Langlois and Robertson (1992) and Bresnahan and Greenstein (1999) for details.

The structure of incentives facing scientists rewards them less with money and more with freedom, prestige, and status (Stern 2004). These peculiar goals are reflected in a large number of distinctive scientific institutions, including peer review, status based on priority rather than ultimate commercial success, and openness in publication and the permission of replication. Because these institutions were designed by scientists rather than by managers (i.e., individuals interested primarily in the commercialization of science), they lead to a situation in which even commercial scientists' rewards can depend more on other scientists than on the managers in their own organizations. The incentives created by scientific institutions can enhance productivity—openness, for example, lowers the costs of access to existing knowledge by a large group of potential inventors, while competition to be first pushes each discipline toward more rapid technical progress. But it also can have disadvantages, for example, if peer review leads to rewards for work that is highly regarded by one's peers but not particularly useful or interesting to others outside one's narrow field. In contrast, the system of incentives for commercial innovation is more straightforward, as the market provides a primary metric for success.

These differences lead to tensions when basic and applied research take place in a disintegrated fashion. Commercially oriented managers experience difficulty incentivizing scientists to engage in work that is not rewarded by their discipline (e.g., work on specific rather than general problems) or to interact with others outside their field. For scientists who are considering commercializing their inventions or discoveries, there can be a commercial incentive to keep innovations secret rather than to publish, weakening the reward system of academic science (Murray and Stern 2007). And successful structures at the boundary of science and commercialization, such as university licensing programs kicked off by the Bayh-Dole Act permitting university scientists to patent inventions that result from government-funded research, sometimes have been criticized for distorting basic scientific research incentives.

Nevertheless, there are considerable reasons to think that a system whereby basic scientific research was left to commercial firms would be problematic. Perhaps the most obvious are the lack of immediate commercial reward to foundational research and the spillovers that result from many scientific breakthroughs. Even when scientific research produces inventions that are in principle appropriable, they may not be appropriable in their initially planned use. A large and diverse firm might be able to capture some spillovers from scientific research but not all of them. A famous example comes from Bell Laboratories. Bell Labs worked not only on basic engineering projects but also on basic science, discovering (among other things) the transistor effect. Although the Bell System certainly had uses for a wide range of inventions, the breadth of use for the transistor was too wide even for highly diverse Bell, so the firm put that fundamental innovation into the public domain as part of a strategy to avoid government interference.

5. Conclusion

We have discussed a wide range of economic theory and empirical work related to the vertical integration or disintegration of production. Theories from organizational economics have tended to focus on the contractual issues that affect the integration decisions of individual firms, posing an interesting contrast to resource- or capabilities-based theories of integration, and to industrial organization theories that emphasize the relationship between integration decisions and the determination of horizontal market structure. We have argued that the intersection of these areas—in particular, how transaction cost issues interact with other forces to determine the overall structure of industries and markets—deserves more attention. We also see considerable room for progress in formulating empirical tests of the various theories and in measuring the incidence and importance of transaction costs under alternative contractual or organizational arrangements. As better data on contracts and organizations become available, most notably in emerging areas (e.g., the online world and rapidly industrializing economies), we expect there will be many opportunities along these lines.

REFERENCES

Acemoglu, Daron, Simon Johnson, and Todd Mitton. 2009. "Determinants of Vertical Integration: Financial Development and Contracting Costs." *Journal of Finance* 63: 1251–1290.

Acemoglu, Daron, Philippe Aghion, Rachel Griffith, and Fabrizio Zilibotti. 2010. "Vertical Integration and Technology: Theory and Evidence." *Journal of the European Economic Association* 8: 989–1033.

Afendulis, Christopher, and Daniel Kessler. 2007. "Tradeoffs from Integrating Diagnosis and Treatment in Markets for Health Care." *American Economic Review* 97: 1013–1020.

———. 2011. "Vertical Integration and Optimal Reimbursement Policy." Working Paper 17316, National Bureau of Economic Research, Cambridge, MA.

Alchian, Armen A., and Harold Demsetz. 1972. "Production, Information Costs, and Economic Organization." *American Economic Review* 62: 777–795.

Amit, Raphael, and Paul Schoemaker. 1993. "Strategic Assets and Organizational Rent." *Strategic Management Journal* 14: 33–46.

Anderson, Erin, and David C. Schmittlein. 1984. "Integration of the Sales Force: An Empirical Examination." *RAND Journal of Economics* 15: 385–395.

Anton, James J., and Dennis A. Yao. 1995. "Start-Ups, Spin-Offs and Internal Projects." *Journal of Law, Economics, and Organization* 11: 362–378.

Antràs, Pol, and Esteban Rossi-Hansberg. 2009. "Organizations and Trade." *Annual Review of Economics* 1: 43–64.

Arora, Ashish, Andrea Fosfuri, and Alfonso Gambardella. 2001. *Markets for Technology: The Economics of Innovation and Corporate Strategy.* Cambridge, MA: MIT Press.

Arora, Ashish, Alfonso Gambardella, L. Magazzini, and Fabio Pammolli. 2009. "A Breath of Fresh Air? Firm Types, Scale, Scope and Selection Effects in Drug Development." *Management Science* 55: 1638–1653.

Arrow, Kenneth J. 1974. *The Limits of Organization.* New York: W. W. Norton.

———. 1975. "Vertical Integration and Communication." *Bell Journal of Economics* 6: 173–183.

Asanuma, Banri. 1989. "Manufacturer-Supplier Relationships in Japan and the Concept of Relation-Specific Skill." *Journal of the Japanese and International Economies* 3: 1–30.

Atalay, Enghin, Ali Hortaçsu, and Chad Syverson. 2012. "Why Do Firms Own Production Chains?" Working paper, University of Chicago.

Azoulay, Pierre. 2004. "Capturing Knowledge within and across Firm Boundaries: Evidence from Clinical Development." *American Economic Review* 94: 1591–1612.

Baker, George P., and Thomas N. Hubbard. 2003. "Make versus Buy in Trucking: Asset Ownership, Job Design and Information." *American Economic Review* 93: 551–572.

———. 2004. "Contractibility and Asset Ownership: On-Board Computers and Governance in U.S. Trucking." *Quarterly Journal of Economics* 119: 1443–1479.

Baker, George P., Robert Gibbons, and Kevin Murphy. 2011. "Relational Adaptation." Working paper, Massachusetts Institute of Technology, Cambridge, MA.

Baldwin, Carliss, and Kim Clark. 2005. *Design Rules,* volume 1: *The Power of Modularity.* Cambridge, MA: MIT Press.

Berle, Adolf, and Gardiner Means. 1932. *The Modern Corporation and Private Property.* New York: Macmillan.

Berry, Steven, and Peter Reiss. 2007. "Empirical Models of Entry and Market Structure," in Mark Armstrong and Robert Porter (eds.), *Handbook of Industrial Organization,* volume 3. Amsterdam: North-Holland, pp. 1845–1886.

Bloom, Nicholas, and John van Reenen. 2007. "Measuring and Explaining Management Practices across Firms and Countries." *Quarterly Journal of Economics* 122: 1351–1408.

Bolton, Patrick, and Michael Whinston. 1993. "Incomplete Contracts, Vertical Integration, and Supply Assurance." *Review of Economic Studies* 60: 121–148.

Bresnahan, Timothy, and Alfonso Gambardella. 1998. "The Division of Inventive Labor and the Extent of the Market," in Elhanan Helpman (ed.), *General Purpose Technologies and Economic Growth.* Cambridge, MA: MIT Press, pp. 253–281.

Bresnahan, Timothy, and Shane Greenstein. 1999. "Technological Competition and the Structure of the Computer Industry." *Journal of Industrial Economics* 47: 1–40.

Bresnahan, Timothy, and Franco Malerba. 2002. "The Value of Competitive Innovation," in Chong-En Bai and Chi-Wa Yuen (eds.), *Technology and the New Economy.* Cambridge, MA: MIT Press, pp. 49–94.

Bresnahan, Timothy, Rebecca Henderson, and Shane Greenstein. 2012. "Schumpeterian Competition and Diseconomies of Scope: Illustrations from the Histories of Microsoft and IBM," in Josh Lerner and Scott Stern (eds.), *The Rate and Direction of Technical Change Revisited.* Chicago: University of Chicago Press, pp. 203–276.

Brickley, James A., and Frederick H. Dark. 1987. "The Choice of Organizational Form: The Case of Franchising." *Journal of Financial Economics* 18: 401–420.

Calvo, Guillermo, and Stanislaw Wellisz. 1978. "Supervision, Loss of Control and the Optimal Size of the Firm." *Journal of Political Economy* 86: 943–952.

Carlton, Dennis. 1979. "Vertical Integration in Competitive Markets under Uncertainty." *Journal of Industrial Economics* 27: 189–209.

Casadesus-Masanell, Ramon, and Daniel F. Spulber. 2000. "The Fable of Fisher Body." *Journal of Law and Economics* 43: 67–104.

Caves, Richard E., and William F. Murphy, II. 1976. "Franchising: Firms, Markets, and Intangible Assets." *Southern Economic Journal* 42: 572–586.

Ciliberto, Federico. 2006. "Does Organizational Form Affect Investment Decisions?" *Journal of Industrial Economics* 54: 63–93.

Ciliberto, Federico, and David Dranove. 2006. "The Effect of Physician-Hospital Affiliations on Hospital Prices in California." *Journal of Health Economics* 25: 29–38.

Clark, Kim. 1985. "The Interaction of Design Hierarchies and Market Concepts in Technological Evolution." *Research Policy* 14: 235–251.

Coase, Ronald H. 1937. "The Nature of the Firm." *Economica* 4: 386–405.

———. 1972. "Industrial Organization: A Proposal for Research," in Victor R. Fuchs (ed.), *Policy Issues and Research Opportunities in Industrial Organization.* New York: National Bureau of Economics Research, pp. 59–73.

———. 1988. "The Nature of the Firm: Influence." *Journal of Law, Economics, and Organization* 4: 33–47.

———. 2000. "The Acquisition of Fisher Body by General Motors." *Journal of Law and Economics* 43: 15–31.

Cohen, Wesley, and Daniel Levinthal. 1990. "Absorptive Capacity: A New Perspective on Learning and Innovation." *Administrative Science Quarterly* 35: 128–152.

Crocker, Keith, and Kenneth J. Reynolds. 1993. "The Efficiency of Incomplete Contracts: An Empirical Analysis of Air Force Engine Procurement." *RAND Journal of Economics* 24: 126–146.

Cuellar, Alison Evans, and Paul J. Gertler. 2006. "Strategic Integration of Hospitals and Physicians." *Journal of Health Economics* 25: 1–28.

Cyert, Richard, and James March. 1963. *A Behavioral Theory of the Firm.* Englewood Cliffs, NJ: Prentice-Hall.

Dasgupta, Partha, and Paul David. 1997. "Information Disclosure and the Economics of Science and Technology," in George Feiwel (ed.), *Arrow and the Ascent of Modern Economic Theory.* New York: New York University Press, pp. 539–591.

Einav, Liran, Amy Finkelstein, and Jonathan Levin. 2010. "Beyond Testing: Empirical Models of Insurance Markets." *Annual Review of Economics* 2: 311–336.

Elberfeld, Wallter. 2002. "Market Size and Vertical Integration: Stigler's Hypothesis Reconsidered." *Journal of Industrial Economics* 50: 23–43.

Evenson, Robert E., and Yoav Kislev. 1976. "A Stochastic Model of Applied Research." *Journal of Political Economy* 84: 265–281.

Forbes, Silke, and Mara Lederman. 2009. "Adaptation and Vertical Integration in the Airline Industry." *American Economic Review* 99: 1831–1849.

———. 2012a. "Does Vertical Integration Affect Firm Performance? Evidence from the Airline Industry." *RAND Journal of Economics* 41: 765–790.

———. 2012b. "Contract Form and Technology Adoption in a Network Industry." *Journal of Law, Economics, and Organization,* forthcoming.

Freeland, Robert F. 2000. "Creating Holdup through Vertical Integration: Fisher Body Revisited." *Journal of Law and Economics* 43: 33–66.

Garicano, Luis. 2000. "Hierarchies and the Organization of Knowledge in Production." *Journal of Political Economy* 108: 874–904.

Gaynor, Martin. 2006. "Is Vertical Integration Anticompetitive? Definitely Maybe (But That's Not Final)." *Journal of Health Economics* 25: 175–180.

Gibbons, Robert. 2005. "Four Formal(izable) Theories of the Firm?" *Journal of Economic Behavior and Organization* 58: 200–245.

Gil, Ricard. 2007. "'Make-or-Buy' in Movies: Integration and ex-post Renegotiation." *International Journal of Industrial Organization* 25: 643–655.

Goldberg, Victor. 1976. "Regulation and Administered Contracts." *Bell Journal of Economics* 7: 426–448.

Green, Jerry. 1986. "Vertical Integration and Assurance of Markets," in G. Frank Mathewson and Joseph E. Stiglitz (eds.), *New Developments in the Analysis of Market Structure.* Cambridge, MA: MIT Press, pp. 177–207.

Grossman, Sanford, and Oliver Hart. 1986. "The Costs and Benefits of Ownership: A Theory of Vertical and Lateral Integration." *Journal of Political Economy* 94: 691–719.

Hart, Oliver. 1995. *Firms, Contracts, and Financial Structure.* Clarendon Lectures in Economics. Oxford and New York: Oxford University Press and Clarendon Press.

———. 2009. "Hold-Up, Asset Ownership, and Reference Points." *Quarterly Journal of Economics* 124: 267–300.

Hart, Oliver, and Bengt Holmström. 2010. "A Theory of Firm Scope." *Quarterly Journal of Economics* 125: 483–513.

Hart, Oliver, and John Moore. 1990. "Property Rights and the Nature of the Firm." *Journal of Political Economy* 98: 1119–1158.

Hart, Oliver, and Jean Tirole. 1990. "Vertical Integration and Market Foreclosure." *Brookings Papers on Economic Activity: Microeconomics* 1990: 205–276.

Helpman, Elhanan. 2006. "Trade, FDI, and the Organization of Firms." *Journal of Economic Literature* 44: 589–630.

Henderson, Rebecca, and Iain Cockburn. 1996. "Scale, Scope, and Spillovers: The Determinants of Research Productivity in Drug Discovery." *RAND Journal of Economics* 27: 32–59.

Hennart, Jean-Francois. 1988. "A Transaction Costs Theory of Equity Joint Ventures." *Strategic Management Journal* 9: 361–374.

Holmes, Thomas. 1999. "Localization of Industry and Vertical Disintegration." *Review of Economics and Statistics* 81: 314–325.

Holmström, Bengt. 1999. "The Firm as a Subeconomy." *Journal of Law, Economics, and Organization* 15: 74–102.

Holmström, Bengt, and Paul Milgrom. 1994. "The Firm as an Incentive System." *American Economic Review* 84: 972–991.

Holmström, Bengt, and John Roberts. 1998. "The Boundaries of the Firm Revisited." *Journal of Economic Perspectives* 12: 73–94.

Hortaçsu, Ali, and Chad Syverson. 2007. "Cementing Relationships: Vertical Integration, Foreclosure, Productivity, and Prices." *Journal of Political Economy* 115: 250–301.

John, George, and Barton A. Weitz. 1988. "Forward Integration into Distribution: An Empirical Test of Transaction Cost Analysis." *Journal of Law, Economics, and Organization* 4: 337–355.

Joskow, Paul L. 1985. "Vertical Integration and Long-Term Contracts: The Case of Coal-Burning Electric Generating Plants." *Journal of Law, Economics, and Organization* 1: 33–80.

———. 1987. "Contract Duration and Relationship Specific Investments." *American Economic Review* 77: 168–175.

———. 1988. "Price Adjustment in Long Term Contracts: The Case of Coal." *Journal of Law and Economics* 31: 47–83.

———. 2005. "Vertical Integration," in Claude Ménard and Mary Shirley (eds.), *Handbook of New Institutional Economics.* Dordrecht and New York: Springer, pp. 319–348.

Kehoe, Michael R. 1996. "Franchising, Agency Problems, and the Cost of Capital." *Applied Economics* 28: 1485–1493.

Kerkvliet, Joe. 1991. "Efficiency and Vertical Integration: The Case of Mine-Mouth Electric Generating Plants." *Journal of Industrial Economics* 39: 467–482.

Klein, Benjamin. 1988. "Vertical Integration as Organized Ownership: The Fisher Body–General Motors Relationship Revisited." *Journal of Law, Economics, and Organization* 4: 199–213.

———. 1996. "Why Hold-Ups Occur: The Self-Enforcing Range of Contractual Relationships." *Economic Inquiry* 34: 444–463.

———. 2000. "Fisher–General Motors and the Nature of the Firm." *Journal of Law and Economics* 43: 105–141.

———. 2007. "The Economic Lessons of Fisher Body–General Motors." *International Journal of the Economics of Business* 14: 1–36.

Klein, Benjamin, Robert Crawford, and Armen Alchian. 1978. "Vertical Integration, Appropriable Rents, and the Competitive Contracting Process." *Journal of Law and Economics* 21: 297–326.

Klein, Peter G. 2005. "The Make-or-Buy Decision: Lessons from Empirical Studies," in Claude Ménard and Mary Shirley (eds.), *Handbook of New Institutional Economics.* Dordrecht and New York: Springer, pp. 435–464.

Klepper, Steven. 1996. "Entry, Exit, Growth, and Innovation over the Product Life Cycle." *American Economic Review* 86: 562–583.

Lafontaine, Francine. 1992. "Agency Theory and Franchising: Some Empirical Results." *RAND Journal of Economics* 23: 263–283.

Lafontaine, Francine, and Scott Masten. 2002. "Contracting in the Absence of Specific Investments of Moral Hazard: Understanding Carrier-Driver Relations in the US." Working Paper 8859, National Bureau of Economic Research, Cambridge, MA.

Lafontaine, Francine, and Kathryn L. Shaw. 2005. "Targeting Managerial Control: Evidence from Franchising." *RAND Journal of Economics* 36: 131–150.

Lafontaine, Francine, and Margaret E. Slade. 2007. "Vertical Integration and Firm Boundaries: The Evidence." *Journal of Economic Literature* 45: 629–685.

Langlois, Richard, and Paul L. Robertson. 1989. "Explaining Vertical Integration: Lessons from the American Automobile Industry." *Journal of Economic History* 69: 361–375.

———. 1992. "Networks and Innovation in a Modular System: Lessons from the Microcomputer and Stereo Component Industries." *Research Policy* 21: 297–313.

Levin, Jonathan, and Steve Tadelis. 2010. "Contracting for Government Services: Theory and Evidence from U.S. Cities." *Journal of Industrial Economics* 58: 507–541.

Levy, D. T. 1984. "Testing Stigler's Interpretation of 'Division of Labor Is Limited by the Extent of the Market.'" *Journal of Industrial Economics* 32: 377–389.

Lieberman, Marvin B. 1991. "Determinants of Vertical Integration: An Empirical Test." *Journal of Industrial Economics* 39: 451–466.

Lucas, Robert. 1978. "On the Size Distribution of Business Firms." *Bell Journal of Economics* 9: 508–523.

Malmgren, Harald B. 1961. "Information, Expectations and the Theory of the Firm." *Quarterly Journal of Economics* 75: 399–421.

Masten, Scott E. 1984. "The Organization of Production: Evidence from the Aerospace Industry." *Journal of Law and Economics* 27: 403–417.

Masten, Scott E., James W. Meehan, Jr., and Edward A. Snyder. 1989. "Vertical Integration in the U.S. Auto Industry: A Note on the Influence of Transaction Specific Assets." *Journal of Economic Behavior and Organization* 12: 265–273.

———. 1991. "The Costs of Organization." *Journal of Law, Economics, and Organization* 7: 1–25.

McAfee, Preston, and John McMillan. 1995. "Organizational Diseconomies of Scale." *Journal of Economics and Management Strategy* 4: 399–426.

Metcalfe, J. S. 1986. "Technological Variety and the Process of Competition." *Economie appliquée* 39: 493.

Minkler, Alanson P. 1990. "An Empirical Analysis of a Firm's Decision to Franchise." *Economics Letters* 34: 77–82.

Monteverde, Kirk, and David J. Teece. 1982. "Supplier Switching Costs and Vertical Integration in the Automobile Industry." *Bell Journal of Economics* 13: 206–213.

Mullainathan, Sendhil, and David Scharfstein. 2001. "Do Firm Boundaries Matter?" *American Economic Review* 91: 195–199.

Murray, Fiona, and Scott Stern. 2007. "When Ideas Are Not Free: The Impact of Patenting on Academic Science," in Adam Jaffe, Josh Lerner, and Scott Stern (eds.), *Innovation Policy and the Economy,* volume 7. Cambridge, MA: National Bureau of Economic Research, pp. 33–69.

Nelson, Richard R. 1961. "Development Efforts." *Review of Economics and Statistics* 43: 351–364.

Nickerson, Jack A., and Brian S. Silverman. 2003. "Why Aren't All Truck Drivers Owner-Operators? Asset Ownership and the Employment Relation in Interstate For-Hire Trucking." *Journal of Economics and Management Strategy* 12: 91–118.

Norton, Seth W. 1988. "An Empirical Look at Franchising as an Organizational Form." *Journal of Business* 61: 197–218.

Novak, Sharon, and Scott Stern. 2009. "Complementarity among Vertical Integration Decisions: Evidence from Automobile Product Development." *Management Science* 54: 1963–1979.

Ohanian, Nancy. 1994. "Vertical Integration in the US Pulp and Paper Industry, 1900–1940." *Review of Economics and Statistics* 76: 202–207.

Penrose, Edith. 1959. *The Theory of the Growth of the Firm.* New York: John Wiley and Sons.

Perry, Martin K. 1989. "Vertical Integration," in Richard Schmalensee and Robert Willig (eds.), *Handbook of Industrial Organization.* Amsterdam: North-Holland, pp. 183–258.

Pirrong, Stephen Craig. 1993. "Contracting Practices in Bulk Shipping Markets: A Transactions Cost Explanation." *Journal of Law and Economics* 36: 937–976.

Radner, Roy. 1992. "Hierarchy: The Economics of Managing." *Journal of Economic Literature* 30: 1382–1415.

Ravenscraft, David, and Frederic Scherer. 1987. *Mergers, Sell-Offs and Economic Efficiency.* Washington, DC: Brookings Institution.

Regan, Laureen. 1999. "Vertical Integration in the Property-Liability Insurance Industry: A Transaction Cost Approach." *Journal of Risk and Insurance* 64: 41–62.

Rosenberg, Nathan. 1994. *Exploring the Black Box: Technology, Economics and History.* Cambridge: Cambridge University Press.

———. 1998. "Chemical Engineering as a General Purpose Technology," in Elhanan Helpman (ed.), *General Purpose Technologies and Economic Growth.* Cambridge, MA: MIT Press, pp. 167–192.

Schoar, Antoinette. 2002. "Effects of Corporate Diversification on Productivity." *Journal of Finance* 57: 2379–2403.

Shelanski, Howard A., and Peter G. Klein. 1995. "Empirical Research in Transaction Cost Economics: A Review and Assessment." *Journal of Law, Economics, and Organization* 11: 335–361.

Shepard, Andrea. 1993. "Contractual Form, Retail Price, and Asset Characteristics in Gasoline Retailing." *RAND Journal of Economics* 24: 58–77.

Simon, Herbert A. 1947. *Administrative Behavior.* New York: Macmillan.

———. 1951. "A Formal Theory of the Employment Relationship." *Econometrica* 19: 293–305.

Slade, Margaret E. 1996. "Multitask Agency and Contract Choice: An Empirical Exploration." *International Economic Review* 37: 465–486.

Spengler, Joseph J. 1950. "Vertical Integration and Antitrust Policy." *Journal of Political Economy* 58: 347–352.

Stein, Jeremy. 1997. "Internal Capital Markets and the Competition for Corporate Resources." *Journal of Finance* 52: 111–133.

Stern, Scott. 2004. "Do Scientists Pay to Be Scientists?" *Management Science* 50: 835–853.

Stigler, George. 1951. "The Division of Labor is Limited by the Extent of the Market." *Journal of Political Economy* 59: 185–193.

Stuckey, John. 1983. *Vertical Integration and Joint Ventures in the Aluminum Industry.* Cambridge, MA: Harvard University Press.

Sutton, John. 2007. "Market Structure: Theory and Evidence," in Mark Armstrong and Robert Porter (eds.), *Handbook of Industrial Organization,* volume 3. Amsterdam: North-Holland, pp. 2301–2368.

Teece, David. 1986. "Profiting from Technological Innovation: Implications for Integration, Collaboration, Licensing and Public Policy." *Research Policy* 15: 285–305.

Tirole, Jean. 1988. *The Theory of Industrial Organization.* Cambridge, MA: MIT Press.

Van Biesebroeck, Johannes. 2006. "Complementarities in Automobile Production." Working Paper 12131, National Bureau of Economic Research, Cambridge, MA.

Walker, Gordon, and David Weber. 1984. "A Transaction Cost Approach to Make-or-Buy Decisions." *Administrative Science Quarterly* 29: 373–391.

Wernerfelt, Berger. 1984. "A Resource-Based View of the Firm." *Strategic Management Journal* 5: 171–180.

Whinston, Michael. 2003. "On the Transaction Cost Determinants of Vertical Integration." *Journal of Law, Economics, and Organization* 19: 1–23.

———. 2007. *Lectures on Antitrust Economics.* Cambridge, MA: MIT Press.

Williamson, Oliver E. 1971. "The Vertical Integration of Production: Market Failure Considerations." *American Economic Review* 61: 112–123.

———. 1975. *Markets and Hierarchies: Analysis and Antitrust Implications.* New York: Free Press.

———. 1979. "Transaction-Cost Economics: The Governance of Contractual Relations." *Journal of Law and Economics* 22: 233–261.

———. 1985. *The Economic Institutions of Capitalism.* New York: Free Press.

———. 2005. "The Economics of Governance." *American Economic Review* 95: 1–18.

———. 2010. "Transaction Cost Economics: The Natural Progression." *American Economic Review* 100: 673–690.

Yeap, Clarissa A. 2006. "Residual Claims and Incentives in Restaurant Chains." Center for Economic Studies Working Paper CES 06–18, U.S. Census Bureau, Washington, DC.

Young, Allyn. 1928. "Increasing Returns and Economic Progress." *Economic Journal* 38: 527–542.

22

Ownership and Organizational Form

Henry Hansmann

1. Introduction

In contemporary market economies, productive enterprise is undertaken predominantly by large numbers of independent firms. Although in theory these firms could be organized in myriad ways, in practice they typically adopt one or another of a small number of standard forms. In this chapter we examine the basic elements of those forms and analyze the economic forces that induce their adoption.

Section 2 begins by exploring the basic legal nature and economic role of the firm. We focus on the firm as a contracting entity, and on the relationship between two different boundaries of the firm: the control boundary and the asset boundary. Sections 3–9—the heart of the chapter—then turn to the ownership of the firm. We examine why it is that a firm is typically owned by one or another class of its patrons—that is, its suppliers and customers—and seek to explain the choice of the ownership class as a trade-off between costs of market contracting and costs of ownership. We focus, in this connection, not just on investor-owned firms but as well on the surprisingly numerous forms of supplier-owned firms, customer-owned firms (including mutual companies), and employee-owned firms (including professional partnerships) that are found in modern economies. We also consider, in the same framework, nonprofit firms and governmental enterprise.

Section 10 briefly explores the patterns of owners' and creditors' rights that constitute the basic standard forms for legal entities and the reasons for evolution in those forms. Section 11 asks why law is important to firm structure and governance. Section 12 concludes.

2. What Is a Firm?

The economics literature has long described a firm as a "nexus of contracts" (Jensen and Meckling 1976). As it has come to be used, this expression is ambiguous. Often it is invoked simply to emphasize that most of the important relationships in a firm (including, in particular, those among the firm's owners, managers, and employees) are essentially contractual in character. This insight is important, but it does not distinguish firms from other networks of contractual relationships.

2.1. Control: The Firm as a Nexus for Contracts

The more fundamental fact is that a firm is a nexus *for* contracts. More precisely, a firm is a common party to a group of contracts—what might be termed a "contracting entity." Although authority in a single firm is often exercised through a cascade of relationships, as in the conventional pyramidal organization chart, that is not the way that a firm's contractual relations are organized. General Motors, for example, is the common party to millions of contracts with the firm's investors, employees, suppliers, and customers. Employees of the Chevrolet division each have a contract of employment with General Motors, and not with the Chevrolet division, much less with departments or supervisors in the division. The same is true of suppliers of steel to GM or any of its divisions, and of dealers that purchase cars produced by GM.

Figure 1 offers a simple illustration. The nodes numbered 1 through 12 are distinct persons—either natural persons (individuals) or firms. The dark connecting lines indicate contractual relationships. For concreteness, we might assume that persons 1 through 4 are employees, persons 5 and 6 are lenders of capital, persons 7 and 8 are suppliers of other productive inputs, and that persons 9 through 12 are customers. Together, these persons constitute the patrons of the firm—that is, persons who have a contractual relationship with the firm as either a supplier or a customer. Figure 1a shows a single firm, designated A, with each of the 12 persons as patrons. In Figure 1b, in contrast, the same persons are patrons of two distinct firms, designated B and C (which might or might not themselves be connected by contract, as indicated by the dashed line).

A much-studied question, famously raised by Coase (1937), concerns the efficient scope (or boundary) of an individual firm. One interpretation of this boundary question is to ask which persons should be made patrons of a given firm. Under what circumstances, for example, is the one-firm structure in Figure 1a more efficient than the two-firm structure in Figure 1b? The answer to this question concerns, importantly, the appropriate scope of control for the managers of a firm. The owners of a firm, or their designated managers, have authority to exercise the discretion—that is, the residual control rights—afforded by the various contracts to which the firm is a common party. In choosing between the alternative firm structures in Figure 1, for example, it is important to know whether it is more efficient to have discretionary authority over all contractual rights in the hands of a common management, as in Figure 1a, or divided, as in Figure 1b. Moreover, just as a firm can enter into contracts in its own name, it can also own assets in its own name; consequently, the firm's discretionary powers extend beyond its contractual rights to include the residual control rights that are a concomitant of ownership (Grossman and Hart 1986).

The determinants of the firm's boundaries in terms of control, and related issues of incentives, are surveyed in Bresnahan and Levin (this volume), Gibbons and Roberts ("Incentives in Organizations," this volume), Lafontaine and Slade (this volume), and Segal and Whinston (this volume). Considerations beyond the scope of control are involved in choosing a firm's boundaries, however. In particular, there is the question of how the firm's contractual commitments are to be bonded.

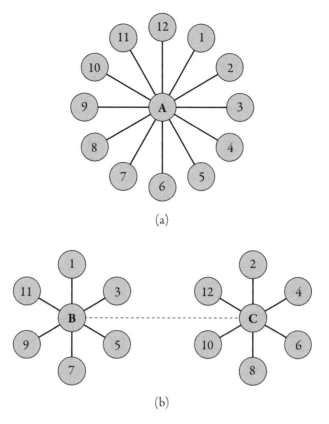

(a)

(b)

Figure 1. The firm as a nexus for contracts.

2.2. Bonding: The Firm as Asset Partitioning

As a general default rule of law, the contracts entered into by a firm—or by any legal entity,[1] including a natural person—are bonded by the assets owned by that firm, in the sense that a patron with an unsatisfied claim against the firm can seize the firm's assets to satisfy that claim. An important distinction between the organizational structures shown in Figure 1, then, is that in Figure 1a the contractual claims of both patron 1 and patron 2 are bonded by all the assets (including contractual rights, e.g., accounts receivable) of Firm A, whereas in Figure 1b the same bonding assets are partitioned into two separate pools, with the claims of patron 1 bonded by the assets of Firm B, while the claims of patron 2 are bonded by the assets of Firm C.

This distinction becomes particularly salient when one firm owns another. Suppose, for example, that the two firms in Figure 1b are organized as separate business corporations but

1. The term "legal entity" is used broadly here to comprise all the law's standard forms for enterprise organization, from marriages, trusts, and partnerships to business corporations, nonprofit corporations, and municipal corporations. Thus, the terms "legal entity" and "contracting entity" are used synonymously. Because the term "legal entity" has various and often vague definitions in the law, however, some legal authorities would not consider all these forms to be legal entities.

that firm C is a wholly owned subsidiary of firm B (a relationship which we can now take to be indicated by the dashed line connecting them). In that situation, there is effectively no difference between the organizational structures in Figures 1a and 1b in terms of control: the managers of B can exercise as much control over the decisions of C as they could if C and B were merged into a single firm, as in Figure 1a. (The most direct means of establishing control is simply to install employees of B as the directors of C.) Yet the structures in Figures 1a and 1b would nonetheless remain very different in terms of creditors' rights. If C becomes insolvent, then a creditor of C—that is, any patron of C with an unsatisfied claim against the firm—can proceed only against the assets of firm C. The patron has no claim on the assets of firm B, even if B is quite solvent, and even though B entirely owns and controls C. This is a consequence, of course, of the limited liability that is granted the owners of business corporations. In this sense, limited liability partitions the assets of Firms B and C between their respective creditors, giving Firm B's creditors exclusive claim on that firm's assets.

But there is another aspect of asset partitioning that, though less often commented on, is more fundamental than limited liability. To see this, suppose that firm B goes bankrupt while firm C remains solvent (i.e., C's assets are more than adequate to pay what is owed to C's own creditors). Then C's creditors will be paid in full out of C's assets before any of those assets become available to satisfy B's creditors. Put differently, firm C's assets—and hence its creditors—are shielded from the creditors of firm B by virtue of the fact that B is a separate corporation. This is an example of the general characteristic of *entity shielding* that is a feature of all legal entities: creditors of the firm have priority of claim, over the creditors of the firm's owners, on all the firm's assets. Entity shielding is, in a sense, the converse of limited liability, which is a form of *owner shielding* that gives the creditors of a firm's owners first (or exclusive) claim—over the creditors of the firm—on assets owned directly by the firm's owners.

It is asset partitioning—entity shielding and limited liability—that make the situations in the two diagrams in Figure 1 fundamentally different, even when Firm B owns Firm C. What is the advantage of the two-firm structure of Figure 1b? Most importantly, it can reduce the organization's overall cost of capital. Suppose, for example, that a firm in the airline business decides that, to realize some valuable synergies, it will also enter the hotel business. Then it is likely to be advantageous to set up the hotel business as a separately incorporated subsidiary, like C in Figure 1b, while the airline is operated by the parent, like B in that figure, or by a separate subsidiary of the parent. The reason is that creditors of the hotel business (lessors of land and buildings, vendors of furnishings, suppliers of linens, etc.) may be quite familiar with the prospects of the hotel industry in general, and with the management (and competitors) of C's hotels in particular, and hence in a good position to estimate the risks of doing business with C. At the same time, they may be quite unfamiliar with the airline industry, and hence poorly positioned to appraise the risks of being a creditor of B. With C separately incorporated, C's creditors can adjust their terms of business according to the risks posed just by C and can largely ignore the likely fortunes of B. Likewise, creditors of B (e.g., lessors of aircraft and vendors of jet fuel) can focus principally on the risks of the airline industry, which they are well positioned to understand, and can largely ignore the likely fortunes of the hotel operations undertaken through the subsidiary C. Thus, the aggregate cost of credit—or, more generally, the aggregate cost of contracting—for the airline and hotel operations may well be reduced by organizing those operations as separate entities, even though they are under common overall management.

In short, by partitioning an organization's assets so that some are pledged to the patrons of one line of business while others are pledged to the patrons of another line of business, the two-corporation structure can reduce monitoring costs for creditors by allowing them to focus just on the assets and operations with which they have greatest familiarity.[2] But the same two-corporation structure may also bring added costs, relative to the single corporation structure, by creating the potential for opportunistic behavior on the part of the parent firm B and its owners. Most obviously, B's owners might be tempted to drain assets out of C and into B, to the detriment of C's creditors, if it begins to look as if C will fail.[3] Various legal rules and contractual devices are designed to inhibit such opportunism, but they are imperfect. As a consequence, organizing the two commonly controlled businesses as separate corporations, rather than as mere divisions in a single corporation, is efficient—holding other considerations constant—when the reduction in the costs of creditor monitoring exceeds the increased costs of opportunism on the part of the firms' owners.[4]

Although we have focused on a corporate subsidiary to illustrate the role of the legal entity as a device for asset partitioning, the same considerations are involved in partitioning the assets of a firm from the assets of the firm's owners in general. In the conventional business corporation with multiple shareholders, for example, limited liability shields the personal (and other business) assets of the firm's owners from the claims of the firm's creditors, while entity shielding protects the firm's assets from the claims of the shareholders' personal creditors and other business creditors. In firms with multiple owners, both these forms of asset partitioning not only offer the monitoring economies described above but also facilitate the transferability of shares by making the creditworthiness of the firm largely independent of the personal creditworthiness of the firm's owners.

Limited liability has, until recently, been the principal focus of the literature on the economic relationship between organizational forms and creditors' rights (Halpern et al. 1980; Woodward 1985; Easterbrook and Fischel 1991). Yet entity shielding—although until recently largely ignored (and even lacking a name) in the Anglo-American literature in both law and economics—is the more elemental rule (Hansmann and Kraakman 2000a,b; Hansmann et al. 2006). All standard legal forms for enterprise organization today offer entity shielding; that is, they give the creditors of the organization first claim on the organization's assets, ahead of the individual creditors of the firm's owners. Limited liability, in contrast, is not universal. For

2. Thus, legal entities can serve a function long recognized for security interests in specific assets (Jackson and Kronman 1979).

3. Opportunistic behavior of the reverse character, exploiting entity shielding rather than limited liability, is the problem if it is the parent corporation B that might fail. In that situation, B's owners have an incentive to pass more of B's assets down to C, hence shielding them from B's creditors and permitting them to be used as security for further borrowing on the part of C. This tactic was central to the financial debacle at Enron, which created more than a thousand subentities for the purpose of extensive nontransparent leveraging. The bankruptcy doctrine of substantive consolidation is a crude means of dealing with this form of opportunism.

4. Other factors, such as the likelihood of incurring the administrative costs of bankruptcy for one or another entity, must also be entered into the efficiency calculus (Hansmann et al. 2006).

example, the partnership offers entity shielding but not limited liability. And the partnership, not the corporation, was the dominant form for organizing commercial activity in Western society from the Middle Ages until the late nineteenth century.[5]

All this is logical. Limited liability demarcates the assets on which the creditors of the firm do not have a claim. Entity shielding demarcates the assets on which the creditors of the firm do have a (prior) claim—that is, the pool of assets that affirmatively bond the firm's contractual commitments.

2.3. The Boundaries of the Firm: Control versus Assets

In all the standard legal forms for enterprise organization—such as partnerships, business corporations, nonprofit corporations, and trusts—the organization's scope of control and its pool of bonding assets are, as a default rule, coterminous, in the sense that the organization's bonding assets comprise all the contractual and property rights over which the organization has control and, conversely, all the firm's contracts are (unless otherwise specified) backed by all the organization's bonding assets. The reason is that legal entities serve, critically, as devices for signaling the assets that back contractual commitments. As illustrated in the discussion of the hypothetical organization that is engaged in both the airline and the hotel businesses, however, the efficient scope of control may be different from the efficient size of a pool of bonding assets. We might say that, in such cases, the efficient boundary of the firm for control purposes (the "control boundary" of the firm) is different from the efficient boundary for bonding purposes (the "asset boundary" of the firm).[6]

In particular, as the airline-hotel example shows, the efficient asset boundary may be smaller than the efficient control boundary. In that case, the different business activities may be organized into two (or more) distinct entities, with one owned entirely by the other or with both owned by a third entity (e.g., a holding company). Subsequent sections focus principally on entities with multiple owners. But, for the reasons discussed above, entities with a single owner—such as a business corporation with a single shareholder—can also be efficient and are extremely common. General Electric, for example, has about 1,500 separately incorporated subsidiaries, most of which it wholly owns.

3. Ownership of the Firm

In principle, the choice of a firm's owners is largely distinct from the determination of the boundaries of the firm: ownership can be structured in any of a host of different ways for a firm with any given control and asset boundaries. In practice, however, the two questions are related, because the owners of the firm are nearly always a subgroup of the firm's patrons, that is, of the persons with whom the firm has a contractual relationship as suppliers or customers.

---

5. The historical evolution is actually somewhat more complex. The partnership, though lacking limited liability, had a weak form of owner shielding throughout most of the past millennium. See Section 10.

6. Iacobucci and Triantis (2007) draw a similar distinction between what they term the "economic" and the "legal" boundaries of firms; they survey some further considerations in dividing activities across two or more separate corporate entities.

3.1. Owned versus Unowned Firms

The "owners" of a firm—as that term is conventionally used and as it is used here—are persons who possess two rights: the right to control the firm and the right to appropriate the firm's residual earnings. There are obvious incentive reasons for putting these two rights into the same hands: if those who control the firm are not entitled to its residual earnings, they have little incentive to maximize those earnings, and hence may manage the firm inefficiently. Consequently, most firms have owners. There are, however, some firms, such as nonprofit firms, in which the right to control is separated from the right to receive residual earnings, making the firms ownerless (or, viewed differently, self-owned). The discussion that follows focuses first on the assignment of ownership in firms with owners and then examines the reasons some firms do not have owners. The approach overall will echo that followed by Hansmann (1988, 1996).

In speaking of the persons who have the right to control the firm, we mean here the persons who have what might be termed "ultimate," or "formal," control rights. In a business corporation, for example, the owners—the firm's shareholders—may lack the right to manage the firm directly and simply have the right to elect the firm's board of directors and to approve major transactions, such as mergers or dissolution of the firm. In a publicly traded corporation with dispersed shareholdings, even those rights may in practice be exercised feebly, making the firm's management effectively self-appointing. For this reason, it is often said that such corporations exhibit a "separation of ownership from control." In the discussion that follows, however, such a statement is an oxymoron: ownership by definition comprises control. However attenuated the ultimate or formal control rights may be, in their structure or in their exercise, the persons who hold them are, for purposes of the discussion here, the firm's owners, so long as they also have the right to appropriate the firm's residual earnings. Consequently, the shareholders of a business corporation are clearly its owners, however modest their effective control over the firm's managers may be. An important reason for this usage is that, as discussed below, the economic considerations that lie behind the choice of a firm's owners seem to apply to both strong and weak owners.

3.2. Ownership by Patrons

In theory, anyone could own a firm. In practice, however, the assignment of ownership follows very distinct patterns. In particular, the owners of a firm are nearly always one or another subset of the firm's patrons—that is, persons who have some transactional relationship with the firm, either as suppliers or customers, apart from their possession of the rights of ownership. Often that transactional relationship is the supply of capital to the firm, in which case we have the conventional investor-owned firm. Not infrequently, however, ownership of the firm is instead placed in the hands of another class of patrons. This is the case, for example, with producer cooperatives, consumer cooperatives, mutual companies, employee-owned firms, and governments (which, when democratic, are essentially a form of consumer cooperative). Indeed, such noninvestor-owned firms play an astonishingly large role in modern economies, from consumer goods wholesaling and agricultural marketing to retail franchising, financial services, and the service professions; we consider a number of representative examples below.

Consequently, in exploring the assignment of ownership, the focus here is on (1) why firms are owned by their patrons, (2) what determines which class of patrons is given ownership, (3) why that class often—but by no means always—is a subset of the suppliers of capital, and (4) why some firms, such as nonprofit firms, have no owners at all.

3.3. The Efficient Assignment of Ownership

The evident reason ownership of firms is typically assigned to one or another class of the firm's patrons is to reduce the costs of contracting between the firm and those patrons. The circumstances surrounding the contractual relationship between a firm and its patrons—such circumstances as market power, asymmetric information, or the need for the patrons to make transaction-specific investments—often place the firm in a position to behave opportunistically toward its patrons if it deals with them on an arm's-length (or "market") basis. Making the patrons the owners of the firm reduces or eliminates the incentive for the firm to exploit that position.

If this were the only consideration in the assignment of ownership, then efficiency would call for assigning ownership to the class of patrons for whom the costs of market contracting would be highest, or perhaps for simply sharing ownership of the firm among all its various types of patrons. But ownership, too, has its costs, including most obviously (though not necessarily most importantly) the agency costs associated with delegation of authority to the firm's managers. Some patrons are better positioned than others to keep those costs low. Consequently, when choosing which class of a firm's patrons are to be its owners, there can be a trade-off between reducing the costs of contracting and reducing the costs of ownership. Moreover, the costs of market contracting for any given class of patrons may be affected by which group, among the firm's other patrons, is given ownership. Efficiency therefore calls for assigning ownership in a fashion that minimizes the total costs of contracting and of ownership for all the firm's patrons combined. That is, in a firm with n groups of patrons, the efficient assignment of ownership is to the group that satisfies

$$\min_j C_j^o + \sum_{i=1}^n C_{ij}^c,$$

where C_j^o is the cost of ownership when patrons in group j own the firm, and C_{ij}^c is the aggregate cost of contracting for patrons in group i when group j owns the firm.

Of course, the costs of market contracting can commonly be reduced or eliminated not just by having the firm owned collectively by its patrons but conversely by having the firm own its patrons, as when a firm integrates upstream to own its suppliers or downstream to own its customers. Often, however, there are strong incentives (well captured by Grossman and Hart 1986) for keeping each patron under separate ownership, whether the patrons are individuals (where ownership by the firm implies slavery) or small businesses. It is the latter situations, where the firm is owned by a numerous subset of its patrons, that are our focus here.

3.4. Market Selection

If ownership is relatively easy to reassign from one group of patrons to another, and if organizational law, taxation, and regulation do not strongly influence the choice of ownership form, then—by virtue of market selection and self-conscious choice—the patterns of ownership we observe should generally be efficient. As it is, these conditions are reasonably well satisfied in the United States[7] and apparently hold to a rough approximation in most other developed market economies as well. Consequently, existing patterns of ownership should offer evidence as to the relative importance of the various costs of contracting and ownership. With this in mind, let us proceed to look first at the costs of contracting and then at costs of ownership, considering examples of industries where these costs seem conspicuous in determining which patrons own the firm.

4. The Costs of Contracting

There are a variety of costs associated with arm's-length contractual transactions that can be reduced by bringing the contracting parties under common ownership. We focus here on four that seem particularly important in explaining the patterns of ownership observed in market economies.

4.1. Simple Market Power

Situations in which a firm occupies a position of monopoly or monopsony vis-à-vis one or another class of its patrons offer conspicuous examples of the assignment of ownership to reduce the costs of contracting. Many types of firms organized as producer or consumer cooperatives fall into this category. Prominent among these are agricultural marketing cooperatives, which handle a large fraction of basic crops—from corn and wheat to oranges and nuts—grown in the United States and other developed economies. These cooperatives clearly arose in response to the economies of scale that gave purchasers of crops substantial market power in comparison to the otherwise highly fragmented farmers who grew them. For example, one or two elevators commonly suffice to collect, store, and transfer to a railroad all the grain grown by farmers in a given locality—a situation that stimulated U.S. farmers to establish cooperative ownership of local grain elevators from the late nineteenth century on (Refsell 1914). The consumer cooperatives that have long distributed electricity to many communities in the American West constitute another clear example, with the cooperatives avoiding both the costs of monopoly and those of public rate regulation.

Stock exchanges have historically provided yet another example. The liquidity offered by the exchanges depends on a high volume of trading, resulting in large economies of scale and consequent market power. In response, exchanges have commonly been organized as cooperatives, collectively owned by their major customers, who are the brokers and dealers with rights to trade on the exchange. The recent trend toward converting major exchanges from broker cooperatives to investor ownership evidently reflects changes in the technology of trading that increase the competition offered by alternative trading forums to the established exchanges, reducing the exchanges' market power (Lee 1998; Pirrong 2000). Whether this reduction in market power is permanent or only temporary remains to be seen.

---

7. That is not to say they hold perfectly. Most conspicuously, some service professionals have been constrained by law, or by the profession's internal discipline, to practice only in employee-owned firms. This was largely the case for doctors in the United States until 1973, for example, and remains the case for lawyers today.

4.2. Ex Post Market Power ("Lock-in")

Another source of the costs of contracting that create an incentive for assigning ownership to a particular class of patrons is the ex post small numbers situation (Williamson 1985) that results when patrons must make transaction-specific investments after choosing the firm with which they will transact. Franchising offers an illustration. Franchisees commonly must make substantial investments that are specific to the franchisor with which they have a licensing agreement. The familiar result is to provide scope for the franchisor to behave opportunistically toward its franchisees. The problem is aggravated by the need to give the franchisor substantial discretion to alter its mode of operation (e.g., the particular products it offers) and to discipline errant franchisees. The problem can be solved by having the franchisor own the franchisees. But this arrangement eliminates the strong incentives for local efficiency that derive from having each store owned by its local manager (Grossman and Hart 1986). Consequently, the opportunism problem is commonly addressed in the reverse fashion, by making the franchisees, collectively, owners of the franchisor.

Franchisee-owned franchisors are in fact common. At one time most consumer hardware in the United States was marketed through seven national franchise systems (e.g., True Value Hardware or Ace Hardware), each of which was collectively owned by its several thousand franchisees, which were local independently owned hardware stores. Similar franchisee-owned franchisors have been prominent in other industries, including grocery wholesaling, baking supplies, van lines, and news reporting. And the two dominant credit card systems, VISA and MasterCard, have for most of their lives been collectively owned by the thousands of local franchisee banks that issue, and provide the credit behind, their cards.[8] In each of these cases, simple monopoly power—from the economies of advertising and wholesaling—evidently provided part of the stimulus for franchisee ownership. But that incentive has been strengthened by the investments in brand-specific facilities and goodwill that local franchisees must make and that render it costly to switch to another franshisor or to operate as an independent firm.

Because franchisee ownership mitigates the problem of franchisor opportunism without altering the other advantageous structural features of a franchise relationship, it might seem the natural form of organization for all mature franchise systems. Nonetheless, most franchise systems—most notably, those in the fast-food business—remain investor-owned rather than franchisee-owned. We return to the reasons for this when we examine the costs of ownership.

The lock-in problem also provides an incentive for collective tenant ownership of apartment buildings (as in cooperative and condominium housing) and for collective employee ownership of the firms that employ them (as in partnerships of professionals, which are discussed in Section 6; Roberts and Van den Steen 2001).

4.3. Asymmetric Information

A firm's customers or suppliers may also be vulnerable to costly opportunism because they are unable to observe or verify important aspects of the firm's performance of its contractual com-

---

8. In 2006, faced with threatened antitrust enforcement based on the overlapping ownership of the VISA and MasterCard systems that had evolved, MasterCard converted to investor ownership via a public offering of stock, though the franchisee banks retained voting control over the firm.

mitments. Again, patron ownership reduces the firm's incentive to exploit this informational advantage and hence may reduce the costs of contracting. Simple but clear examples are provided by fertilizer and hybrid seed grain when these products were first commercially marketed to farmers early in the twentieth century. It was difficult for farmers to evaluate the content of the fertilizers or seed grain offered for sale, and investor-owned producers exploited this vulnerability. In response, manufacture and sale of these products was undertaken by farmer-owned supply cooperatives. Investor-owned firms regained dominance in these industries only when, partly as a result of federal disclosure regulation, quality became observable and verifiable.

Life insurance offers another example. A whole-life insurance contract requires the insured to make payments to the insurer throughout her lifetime, in return for the insurer's promise to pay a large sum to a third-party beneficiary on the insured's death. This arrangement creates a natural incentive for the insurer to invest the premiums in highly risky ventures, or simply pay them out as dividends to the owners, because if the firm's reserves ultimately prove inadequate to cover its liabilities and it goes bankrupt, the losses will be borne largely by the policyholders. As a consequence, only mutual firms (policyholder cooperatives) were able to sell whole-life insurance policies in the United States before states began regulating insurance company financial reserves in the middle of the nineteenth century.

The most conspicuous example of ownership as a response to the costs of asymmetric information, however, is the conventional investor-owned business corporation. If a firm borrows most or all of its capital from nonowners via conventional debt contracts, the contracts must generally be long term; otherwise, the firm may face repeated liquidity crises or hold-up by the lenders. But if the loans are long term, the borrowing firm, like the early life insurance companies just discussed, has an incentive to behave opportunistically, investing the borrowed funds in excessively risky ventures or simply distributing them as dividends and leaving the resulting risk of bankruptcy to be borne largely by the lenders. In contrast to the situation with life insurance, moreover, this problem cannot easily be solved by public regulation of firms' investments. That approach works in life insurance, because the firm's capital is held almost entirely in the form of financial investments whose risk profile is relatively easy to observe, and because the amount of capital that an insurance company must maintain to pay its future obligations to its policyholders is relatively easy to calculate. For other types of firms, however, regulation of investments for the sake of protecting creditors has proven largely impossible, as indicated by the progressive historical abandonment of both legal and contractual obligations for firms to maintain stated levels of legal capital.

The more workable solution, instead, has generally been to make the lenders of capital, or a major subset of them, owners of the firm, hence removing the incentive for the firm to behave opportunistically toward them (Klein et al. 1978; Williamson 1985: 298–325; Tirole 2001).

4.4. The Risks of Long-Term Contracting

Contracts between a firm and its patrons do not just allocate risk but sometimes create risk as well, particularly when the contracts have very long terms. Life insurance again offers a clear example. A whole-life insurance contract may have an expected term of several decades. Consequently, if both premiums and death benefits are fixed in nominal dollars, the ultimate value of the contract to both the insured and the insurer will depend heavily on inflation rates, productivity growth rates, and mortality rates over the intervening period, all of which are difficult to predict and were particularly unpredictable when the life insurance industry first began to develop in the early nineteenth century. The result is that life insurance contracts are essentially a gamble between insurer and insured on these macroeconomic factors, creating private risk that far exceeds social risk and raising the cost of the contract to both parties. This risk can be substantially eliminated by giving collective ownership of the life insurance company to its policyholders, in the form of mutual companies, so that what policyholders lose on the gamble as insureds they gain as owners of the insurer, and vice versa. This incentive for mutual life insurance companies arguably helps explain their continued dominance of the industry long after public regulation of reserves largely removed the risk of default by the insurers.

5. The Costs of Ownership

The efficient assignment of ownership, as noted, must consider not just the costs of contracting but also the costs of ownership. Ownership, in turn, has two elements: receipt of residual earnings and exercise of control. Some costs of ownership, such as risk bearing, are associated with the former, whereas others, such as agency costs and those of collective decisionmaking, are associated with the latter.

5.1. Risk Bearing

For any given firm, some types of patrons are better situated than others to bear the risks of ownership. For large firms with publicly tradable shares, investor ownership has this strong and familiar advantage. However, most firms are insufficiently large to have freely tradable shares. Rather, if they are investor owned, they must be closely held. As a consequence, customer ownership may offer comparable risk-spreading benefits.

More importantly, the risks of ownership are sometimes inversely correlated with other risks facing the firm's customers. Apartment buildings offer an example. It is common for retirees to sell their single-family homes and move into an apartment building, perhaps located in a climatically mild region, such as Florida or Arizona. But if the retiree has an income that is fixed in nominal terms, as with a defined benefit pension plan, renting an apartment exposes the retiree to the risk of inflation or other factors that might raise nominal rents. Ownership of an apartment building by its tenants, as in a cooperative or condominium, financed by a mortgage with payments fixed in nominal terms involves a large undiversified investment with risks that offset those imposed by the pension contract. In consequence, the apartment tenants may have low costs of risk bearing relative to other potential owners.

But in general, allocation of risk may not be a first-order consideration in the ownership of enterprise. Here as elsewhere, incentives seem to dominate risk bearing. A conspicuous illustration is offered by the millions of family-owned farms that dominate the production of staple grain crops in the United States. These farms are extremely capital intensive, sell their products in highly volatile markets, and are quite undiversified (often depending heavily on a single crop). In addition, competition is rigorous, and the rate of technological progress is rapid, with the result that individual producers are constantly being squeezed out of business. Yet large-scale corporate farming under investor ownership has never made noticeable inroads on the sector despite the enormous advantages such a change would offer in risk bearing. The reason, evidently, is that seasonality of crops frustrates specialization of labor and hence economies of scale,[9] and family ownership—in effect, employee ownership—provides strong incentives for high productivity. And, importantly, families are willing to bear the extraordinary risks involved.

5.2. Agency Costs of Controlling Managers

Some classes of patrons are also in a better position than others to minimize the agency costs of controlling a firm's managers. In particular, some agents make better monitors than do others. Franchisees, for example, are good monitors of their common franchisor: franchisees necessarily know their franchisor's business well. They are in constant contact with the franchisor and are aware of its performance. Moreover, good management of the franchisor has a large impact on the franchisee's own success. For similar reasons, farmers are good monitors of the marketing and supply cooperatives of which they are members.

By the same logic, employees should be good monitors of the management of the firm where they work. (One should have in mind here not just blue-collar assembly line workers, but key personnel, such as plant supervisors, division chiefs, and managers in engineering, finance, and marketing.) Yet employees rarely have ownership of large firms, which instead (at least in the United States and the United Kingdom) are often owned by dispersed small shareholders who are relatively poor monitors.[10] Consequently, monitoring capacity is evidently not decisive in the allocation of ownership.

5.3. Collective Decisionmaking

In firms with multiple owners, some means—typically involving voting—must be used to aggregate the preferences of the owners for purposes of exercising control. Whatever the means chosen, it will bring costs of two types. First, there are the costs of the decisionmaking process itself. These include the time and effort needed to inform the various owners of the issues, to discuss the matters among the owners, and to make and break coalitions among subsets of the owners. Second, there are the costs of the substantive decisions taken, which may be inefficient as a consequence of problems in the process. For example, if majority voting is the method of decisionmaking employed, the result may be to take the decision representing the median rather than the mean of the owners (modeled in Hart and Moore 1996). Or the decision may be skewed toward the interests of those owners who are better informed about their own interests or who are strategically positioned to control the agenda. The more heterogeneous the interests of a firm's co-owners, the higher the costs of both types are likely to be.

---

9. The tasks done on a farm (e.g., plowing, planting, weeding, fertilizing, and reaping) change with the seasons, with most efforts concentrated on one task at any given time. Consequently, farm workers cannot specialize in one of these tasks but must be generalists, capable of handling some aspect of each task. Increasing the size of a farm consequently provides only modest opportunity for increasing the specialization of labor (Smith 1776: Book I, Chapter 1).

10. Of course, shareholders of publicly traded corporations have the great advantage of information provided by market institutions, though this information does not necessarily tell them where problems lie in the firm's management.

The patterns of ownership that we observe suggest that these costs of collective decisionmaking weigh heavily. In firms with only two or three owners, heterogeneity of interests is common. The prototypical example is the classic partnership, in which ownership is shared between one partner who provides the firm's financing and another who manages the business. Evidently, with these small numbers, differences of interest can be resolved through negotiation. With larger numbers of owners, however, homogeneity of stakes is the overwhelming rule.[11] Ownership is virtually always confined to a single class of patrons, such as investors of capital, employees, suppliers of other inputs, or customers. In the class of patrons who serve as owners, moreover, ownership interests are, or are structured to be, highly homogeneous. Thus, in business corporations with more than a handful of owners, the interests of the owners are typically homogenized by giving them all shares of a single class of common stock with uniform rights. Agricultural marketing cooperatives generally handle only a single type of crop, such as wheat or corn or cranberries, passing up economies of scope and risk diversification for the sake of having owner-members with essentially identical interests in all the firm's decisions. Employee-owned firms are generally owned by a single homogeneous class of workers—whether the drivers in a bus company or the senior lawyers in a law firm—who perform similar jobs and exhibit little vertical hierarchy among themselves.

There are, to be sure, many otherwise investor-owned firms in which employees have substantial shareholdings. In general, however, the employee-held shares in these firms are either too few to provide any voice in management or are held via a vehicle (e.g., an employee stock ownership plan) that effectively strips them of control (e.g., by denying the employee-held shares a vote for the firm's directors).[12] This suggests strongly that, even though there may be net efficiency gains from sharing profits between employees and investors in a firm, shared control brings costs of collective decisionmaking that generally exceed any additional reduction in the costs of employee contracting that might result.

Additional evidence of the costs of collective decisionmaking can be found in other devices frequently employed to avoid conflicts of interest among the owners of a firm. A conspicuous example is the use of crude focal points, such as a simple norm of equality, to simplify decisionmaking. Thus, equality of compensation, or compensation according to a simple objective formula, is typical among the members of employee-owned firms. A striking instance is the once-common practice of allocating shares of earnings to partners in leading law firms strictly according to age, hence eliminating any financial incentive for productivity—all for the sake, apparently, of avoiding the internal conflicts that would accompany any effort to establish a more individuated compensation scheme.[13]

---

11. Although casual observation suggests that the number of firms with ownership shared among heterogeneous patrons falls off very rapidly when more than two owners are involved, we seem to lack systematic empirical evidence on the point. There may be a huge drop between the number of firms with two owners and those with three, or the number of firms may instead fall more continuously as the number of owners increases to as many as five or six. At stake is how much traction the Coase Theorem has in multi-actor settings.

12. The most conspicuous experiment in true shared control between capital and labor—United Air Lines as it was reorganized in 1994—ended a decade later in conspicuous failure. The apparent reason was irreconcilable conflict among the three ownership groups: public investors, pilots, and members of the mechanics' union. Conflict between the two groups of employee-owners (pilots and mechanics) was a major part of the problem.

13. Another explanation offered for lock-step compensation in law firms—that it is a form of risk sharing (Gilson and Mnookin 1985)—not only seems inconsistent with observed behavior toward risk in other industries,

Franchise operations arguably also offer evidence of the difficulty of creating institutions that discriminate among owners of a firm. As noted above, collective ownership of franchisors by their franchisees, though common in the sale of such goods as hardware and groceries, is rare among franchises for services, such as fast food. One plausible reason is that service franchises require that the quality of performance by franchisees be rigorously policed to avoid negative reputational externalities. This policing requires in turn that the franchisor be prepared to impose severe sanctions on errant franchisees, including, in particular, termination. The difficulty in deviating from a strong norm of simple equality of treatment among co-owners evidently renders franchisee-owned firms incapable of deploying such sanctions rigorously.[14]

Although it seems apparent from casual empiricism that the costs of collective decisionmaking play a decisive role in determining which allocations of ownership are efficient, the precise source of these costs is less clear. In particular, it is not obvious whether the principal source of these costs lies in the processes of decisionmaking or in the nature of the substantive decisions reached. One might expect important insight into the nature and magnitude of these costs to come from the literature on political processes, but that is not the case. In fact, it may be easier to study the costs of political-type collective decisionmaking mechanisms in firms than in governments. This is in part because firms are so numerous and operate under strong market conditions, and in part because, via the allocation of ownership, firms offer a clear choice between markets and politics as a means of aggregating the interests of the members of different classes of patrons.

6. Employee-Owned Firms

Employee ownership has attracted particular attention in the industrial organization literature and is a helpful focus for testing the relative importance of the various costs and benefits of alternative ownership structures. Employee-owned firms have long been particularly conspicuous in the service professions, including law, accounting, engineering, investment banking, advertising, and medicine, though in recent decades there has been a decided switch toward investor ownership in many of these industries, including the last three among those just mentioned. Various theories have been offered to explain these unusual and shifting patterns of ownership. Despite the prominence of professional service firms in modern economies, however, there is no consensus on these theories.

One theory is that employee ownership serves to increase work incentives for hard-to-monitor employees (Alchian and Demsetz 1972). A sophisticated variant on this theory is offered by Morrison and Wilhelm (2004, 2005, 2007), who seek to explain employee ownership in investment banking, and its recent decline, in terms of incentives for senior employees to commit credibly to train their juniors under circumstances in which customers cannot directly evaluate the quality of the services that the employees are capable of providing. But this theory faces several obstacles. The most obvious and familiar of these obstacles—and one that faces

---

such as farming, but is also inconsistent with the patterns of specialization observed in law firms (Garicano and Hubbard 2009).

14. Other factors also help explain the absence of franchisee-owned franchisors in particular industries. For example, the high capital requirements of oil production and refining are presumably an obstacle to putting major oil companies under the collective ownership of their gas station franchisees.

any such effort to explain patron ownership as a means of dealing with moral hazard on the part of the patrons themselves rather than the firm—is the $1/N$ problem. In a firm with N worker-owners, a worker on average gets only $1/N$ of the returns to her increased effort. Although incentives for mutual monitoring might overcome this problem (Kandel and Lazear 1992), the evidence is that it does not in professional partnerships (Gaynor and Gertler 1995; Prendergast 1999; Von Nordenflycht 2007).[15] Another difficulty with the worker incentive theory is that service professionals, relative to other employees, appear relatively easy to monitor. Corporate lawyers, for example, commonly work alone or in small teams and document the use of their time (and the client to be billed for it) at 6-minute intervals. This contrasts markedly with, say, an assistant manager in the finance department of a large industrial firm, whose marginal contribution to the firm's annual revenues would be extremely difficult to measure. This is not to say, of course, that employee ownership has no positive effect on incentives, but only that it does not seem to explain why employee ownership arises in the service professions and not elsewhere.

A rather different theory is offered by Levin and Tadelis (2005), who explain employee ownership of professional service firms not as a means of reducing the costs of contracting between the firm and its employees, but rather as a means of reducing the costs of contracting between the firm and its customers. They focus on employee-owned professional service firms that have equal profit sharing or some other form of cross-subsidy from more productive to less productive worker-owners. They argue that the clients of professional service firms have particular difficulty observing the quality of the services rendered them, creating a risk that law firms will increase their quantity of service provision by employing low-quality lawyers. That incentive, they suggest, can be offset by the otherwise inefficient incentive (Ward 1958) for profit-sharing employee-owned firms to hire workers whose marginal productivity is (otherwise) inefficiently high, making those firms more trustworthy for their customers than are investor-owned firms. A concern with this theory, however, is that it seemingly requires strong assumptions about customers' understanding of the firms' internal incentive structure.

A simpler theory than the two just mentioned—and one that is more consistent with the role of noninvestor-owned firms in other sectors—is that employee ownership in professional service firms serves not to prevent the employees from behaving opportunistically toward the firm or its customers, but to prevent the firm from behaving opportunistically toward its employees. One potential source of opportunism is the employees' investment in firm-specific skills, such as knowledge of the firm's particular personnel, procedures, and clients. Another is the inability of employees, after the passage of years, to signal to other prospective employers their abilities. (Because their current employer, to whom the employees' abilities are presumably well known, has little incentive to communicate those abilities truthfully to competitors in the labor market, the firm has the ability to pay the employees less than their marginal product.)[16] Both these

15. Indeed, it is hard to find evidence in general that employee profit sharing or ownership significantly improves productivity (Weitzman and Kruse 1990).

16. Another incentive for employee ownership may come from the market power that established professional service firms arguably often have over their customers—market power that derives from the customers' inability to judge the value or cost of services, and from the customers' perceived costs of switching suppliers (i.e., customers' supplier-specific investments; Morrison and Wilhelm 2007). If it is relatively easy for the employees to establish

problems, to be sure, may be much less serious among service professionals than among the employees of, for example, large manufacturing firms. But for professional service firms, the costs of employee ownership appear especially low because of the unusual homogeneity of interests among the employees who share ownership—a homogeneity that derives from their similarity in jobs and talent and from the absence of internal hierarchy. Moreover, the relatively low requirements for firm-specific capital in professional service firms permit the employees themselves to provide the necessary capital and avoid the costs of raising it on the market from nonowners. In short, under this theory, costs of ownership (in particular, the costs of collective decisionmaking) are far more important than costs of contracting in determining the presence or absence of employee ownership in any given industry.

If this is the correct explanation for employee ownership in professional service industries, then why has there been a recent trend toward investor ownership in some, but not all, of those industries? One possibility is that the quality of professional services, and of individual professionals, is becoming easier for customers to value, hence reducing firms' ability to avoid paying employees a competitive wage (and reducing their market power as well).[17] Another is that the capital requirements for some of these industries are growing. There is evidence of both phenomena, for example, in the investment banking industry (Morrison and Wilhelm 2005, 2007).

7. Nonprofit Firms

For some goods and services, the costs of contracting between firms and one or another class of their patrons is potentially extremely high, but at the same time the class of patrons in question cannot be organized to serve as effective owners at any feasible cost. In these cases, the efficient solution may be to create a nonprofit firm, that is, a firm without owners. In these firms, control is separated from the claim to residual earnings by imposing a bar (the "nondistribution constraint") on distributions of the firm's net earnings or assets to persons who control the firm. The consequence is that all the firm's revenues must be devoted to providing services. By removing strong incentives for the firm's managers to earn profits, the incentive to exploit the firm's patrons is reduced.

Asymmetric information between a firm and its customers is typically the source of the contracting costs involved. More particularly, the problem is often that the firm's customers cannot observe the quantity of product or service that the firm provides in return for the price they pay. Such a situation arises commonly when an individual, out of philanthropic motives, seeks to purchase services to be delivered to needy third parties in distant places. Payments to an organization like Oxfam to deliver food to famine victims in Africa are an example. The contributors are in no position to determine how their individual contributions are used. If such a firm were owned by someone other than its customers, the firm would have an incentive to provide few or no services in return for the payments it receives. Prospective customers, expecting this behavior, would refuse to patronize the firm. At the same time, however, the

---

ownership of the firm (i.e., the costs of ownership are low), then the employees can capture these monopoly rents for themselves.

17. See the previous note.

firm's customers (referred to as "donors") are too transient and dispersed to be organized, at any acceptable cost, as owners capable of monitoring effectively the firm's managers. Consequently, customer ownership is not a viable solution. A similar problem faces firms producing public goods, such as cancer research or commercial-free broadcasting: a contributor may be able to observe both the quantity and quality of services that the firm is producing but cannot determine whether, at the margin, her own contribution induced an increase in quantity or quality.

Of course, once those who control the firm are deprived of the profit motive, one must ask what incentive they have to put any effort whatsoever into managing the firm, much less into producing a level of quantity and quality acceptable to customers. The best explanation is that, in the absence of competing "high-powered" profit incentives, the managers' actions are guided by "low-powered" nonpecuniary incentives, including pride, professionalism, and identification with the goals of the organization (Glaeser and Shleifer 2001).

The nonprofit form seems most commonly to be a response to the problems of contracting when quantity is (at the margin) unobservable. In particular, this problem generally occurs in organizations supported by donations, from the Salvation Army to the performing arts to universities. But there are also situations in which the nonprofit form is evidently a response to unobservable or unverifiable quality.[18] In such situations, one can find nonprofit firms that derive all their revenue from prices charged to their customers. Nursing homes for the elderly—where, for example, sedating patients into inexpensive tractability is a tempting strategy for the producers—are evidently an example.

However, the observed distribution of nonprofit firms across industries cannot be assumed to be a strong reflection of their comparative efficiency vis-à-vis other ownership types. In comparison with firms with owners, transactions in control (and particularly conversions out of the nonprofit form) may not occur when they would be efficient. In principle, a nonprofit corporation can sell its business as a going concern to a proprietary firm and either donate the proceeds to another nonprofit organization and liquidate, or invest the proceeds in another activity that the nonprofit can manage more efficiently. By virtue of the nondistribution constraint, however, the managers who control a nonprofit cannot gain financially from such a transaction; they may in fact suffer from it both in financial (salary) and in nonpecuniary (interest and status of employment) terms. In this regard, it is particularly significant that the managers of a nonprofit firm do not bear the opportunity cost of the capital that the firm has accumulated. Moreover, a nonprofit firm can survive indefinitely, even if it earns only a zero net rate of return on its (self-owned) capital, and can in fact grow if it earns any positive rate of return, no matter how small. Consequently, survivorship cannot be taken as an indication of the efficiency of the nonprofit form as confidently as it can with proprietary forms of ownership.

This problem is compounded by the evolution of industries over time. The nonprofit form is sometimes the best or only way to organize production in the early stages of developing a new service, before effective mechanisms to monitor and pay for the service have been developed. When those mechanisms subsequently come into place, proprietary firms can take over production, and the nonprofit form becomes anachronistic. Yet, because market mechanisms are weak in inducing exit by nonprofit firms, they may long continue to account for a large share of the in-

---

18. Glaeser and Shleifer (2001) interpret their model, which is the best we have, in terms of unverifiable quality, though it can as easily be interpreted in terms of unobservable quantity.

dustry's production. A conspicuous example is offered by nonprofit savings banks, which arose in the United States (and elsewhere) in the early nineteenth century, because (as with life insurance), in the absence of public regulation, depositors could not trust that their savings would still be intact for withdrawal after many years in a proprietary bank's possession. Although regulation and deposit insurance long ago removed this reason for the nonprofit form, it continued to have a large presence in the industry until recent times (Rasmusen 1988; Hansmann 1996: 246–264). Similarly, there is evidence that nonprofit hospitals—originally institutions supported by donations that provided services to the poor—retain a large market share today, not because they are more efficient than proprietary hospitals but because of weak mechanisms to induce exit (Hansmann et al. 2003).

The distinction between formally nonprofit firms and firms that simply have extremely weak owners is vanishingly small at the margins. Mutual life insurance companies, for example, are in formal terms collectively owned by their policyholders (i.e., they are consumer cooperatives) and hence are in principle proprietary firms. Yet the firms' highly fragmented policyholders have little incentive or ability to exercise effective control over the firms' managers. As a consequence, most U.S. life insurance companies, from the time of their initial formation, have effectively been nonprofit firms, controlled by self-perpetuating boards of directors and holding a growing pool of assets whose value the policyholders do not entirely appropriate. Similarly, there is today little meaningful difference in the United States between mutual savings and loan associations, which are formally depositors' cooperatives, and mutual savings banks, which (despite the term "mutual") are formally nonprofit entities.

Large business corporations with highly dispersed shareholdings that are largely free from the market for corporate control, as some U.S. firms arguably have been over substantial periods, may likewise be little different from nonprofit entities with respect to the costs of ownership—which, for nonprofit firms, consist principally of managerial agency costs. There are, in fact, some industrial firms that are formally organized as nonprofit corporations or very close to it. The most conspicuous examples are the "industrial foundations" that are common in northern Europe (though effectively proscribed by tax law in the United States). These are business firms that are either organized as a nonprofit firm or are entirely controlled by one. The available empirical evidence fails to show that these industrial foundations are less efficient than their investor-owned counterparts (Thomsen and Rose 2004), lending some support to the judgment that, even at the extreme, the agency costs of delegated management are relatively modest in comparison with other costs of ownership and with the costs of market contracting.[19] Even with no owners at all—or, as we might say, even with a true "separation of ownership from control"—firms can be managed with fair efficiency.

---

19. Even if these results prove robust and are not idiosyncratic to the Danish environment, it is possible that the particular dual-level structure of these firms is an important factor. The industrial firms in the sample are themselves organized as business corporations, with a controlling majority of their shares held by a separate nonprofit foundation. Thus, in a sense, the industrial firms are proprietary firms with an owner—namely, the foundation. And though the foundation is nonprofit, its management may think of the operating company principally as a source of revenue for the foundation and hence seek to assure that the company is managed with substantial efficiency. In a sense, this structure is an extreme form of a company with a dual board system—an outside supervisory board that chooses an inside managerial board—which is itself a formal extension of the idea of having a single board with a majority of outside directors. For analogous results involving nonprofit hospitals in the United States, see Hansmann et al. (2003).

8. Governments

Governments fit comfortably into the analytic framework described here. In effect, governments are territorial consumer cooperatives. This is most obvious at the local level, where (in the United States) geographically contiguous residents are relatively free to form themselves into a municipal corporation. Municipalities commonly provide a package of collective-consumption services to their residents for a price collected as taxation. As Tiebout (1956) long ago suggested, these packages of services might instead be offered by proprietary firms for an annual fee. But if the consumers purchase real estate within the territory served by the firm, they become locked in to the service provider and hence subject to exploitation. And if the service provider itself owns all the real estate and rents it to residents, there will be poor incentives for the residential and commercial occupants of the property. The simple solution is to have the residents own their own homes and businesses and then collectively own the local service provider. (Municipalities are, of course, not fully owned by their residents, but rather are on the previously discussed borderline between cooperative and nonprofit entities.)

9. Resulting Patterns of Organization and Ownership

We have relatively little rigorous empiricism on the trade-offs among the costs of ownership and the costs of contracting just surveyed. The general patterns of ownership that we observe do, however, permit some broad inferences about the relative magnitudes of these costs.

9.1. The Firm as a Political Institution

Perhaps most strikingly, the costs of collective decisionmaking through nonmarket mechanisms are evidently high and play a strong and even decisive role in determining which forms of ownership are viable. It is rare to see ownership in the hands of a heterogeneous class of patrons regardless of the costs of contracting that those owners face. Conversely, noncapitalist firms, such as employee-owned firms, are evidently quite viable when the class of patron-owners is highly homogeneous, even if the costs of contracting that those patrons would face if they were not the firm's owners appear relatively small. This observation supports the conclusion that investor-owned firms are dominant in the economy largely because, relative to other classes of patrons, the interests of capital suppliers can easily be made highly homogeneous (Jensen and Meckling 1979).

9.2. Weak versus Strong Owners

The patterns of ownership that we observe also support the inference that, among the factors that determine those patterns, the agency costs of delegated management are distinctly secondary.

   To be more precise, let us imagine a firm with two classes of patrons. For class A, the costs of contracting are high, and so are the agency costs of delegated management; for class B, in contrast, both types of costs are low. For example, class A might be purchasers of whole-life insurance, or savings bank depositors, in the early nineteenth century, while class B might be a small group of investors who can provide financing for the insurance company or the bank. Or class A might be a group of widely dispersed small investors, and class B might be a reasonably homogeneous group of senior employees at the firm. In such a situation, the observed distribution of ownership suggests that it is generally more efficient to give ownership to class A: the costs of contracting avoided are greater than the agency costs of delegated management that are incurred. The reason, apparently, is that the difference in costs between tightly controlling owners and owners who are no more than nominal is modest compared to the potential costs of market contracting. Put differently, it is clearly important, in terms of overall efficiency, that vulnerable patrons not face a firm that is owned by persons who will exploit their vulnerability. It appears much less important that the patrons themselves, when made the firm's owners, be able to exercise much control over the firm. This is not to say, of course, that managerial agency costs are entirely unimportant; too much of modern scholarship on corporate governance says otherwise. Rather, it is just to say that managerial agency costs do not seem to be of first-order importance in determining the class of patrons to which ownership is most efficiently assigned.

9.3. Regulation and Capitalism

The literature on corporate governance appropriately emphasizes the importance of capital market regulation for facilitating efficient investor ownership of enterprise. But regulation of other markets in which firms operate is also important in this regard. By reducing the costs of contracting for patrons other than investors, regulation of product and supply markets makes investor ownership feasible for industries that might otherwise be heavily populated with cooperative, nonprofit, or governmental firms. Conspicuous examples are life insurance and savings banking, discussed above, and consumer goods in Sweden, where the absence of antitrust law long fostered a large cooperative sector.

10. Further Structural Attributes of the Firm

Earlier it was observed that, as a consequence of the protean character of the standard legal forms for enterprise organization (the business corporation, the partnership, the limited liability company, the cooperative corporation, the nonprofit corporation, etc.), there is only a modest correspondence between those forms and the choice of the class of patrons to whom ownership is assigned.[20] There are, however, some strong regularities across legal entity forms in the patterns of relationships that owners and other patrons have to the firm. This is most conspicuous with respect to claims on firm assets.

Asset partitioning in organizations exhibits a greater variety of forms than just those described in Section 2. Owner shielding, for example, has exhibited a variety of different forms over time, of which three have been (and remain) particularly common:[21]

> *Complete owner shielding* ("limited liability"). The personal assets of a firm's owner are completely shielded from the claims of the firm's creditors, as in a modern business corporation.

20. As a further indication of this vagueness, the nonprofit form is sometimes even stretched to be used for fully owned organizations, such as cooperative housing and stock exchanges.

21. We deal here only with liability toward voluntary (contractual) creditors, not involuntary (tort) creditors. The two types need not be treated the same, and it is arguable that limited liability for tort claimants is in general an inefficient rule that survives because of severe collective action problems affecting potential tort victims (Hansmann and Kraakman 1990).

Weak owner shielding. Firm creditors have a claim on the personal assets of the firm's owners, but only a claim that is subordinated to the claims of the owners' personal creditors. This rule is traditional for partnerships.

No owner shielding. Firm creditors can proceed against the personal assets of the firm's owners on equal terms with the owners' personal creditors. This has been the rule for U.S. partnerships since 1978.

Likewise, for commercial firms there are two principal forms of entity shielding:[22]

Weak entity shielding. The personal creditors of a firm's owners have a claim on the assets of the firm, but that claim is subordinated to the claims of the firm's own creditors. This rule is characteristic for partnerships.

Strong entity shielding. This form is like weak entity shielding, except that personal creditors cannot force liquidation of the firm but rather must wait until it voluntarily dissolves to assert their (subordinated) claim to its assets. This rule is characteristic for corporations.

Closely tied to asset partitioning is the question of whether the owners of the firm have individual withdrawal rights. Passing over complexities, there are two principal possibilities:

Free withdrawal. An individual owner of the firm can, at will, terminate his membership in the firm and withdraw his share of firm assets. This rule is the default in a general partnership.

No withdrawal. An individual owner cannot withdraw his share of firm assets until the firm itself is dissolved by its owners acting as a group (though the owner may be able to transfer his ownership share to another person). This rule is typical in a business corporation.

Though there are variations, these rights tend to come in particular combinations, of which two have historically been the most common. The first, the general partnership, combines weak (or no) owner shielding, weak entity shielding, and free withdrawal. The second, the corporation, combines complete owner shielding (limited liability), strong entity shielding, and no withdrawal. The elements of each of these two packages are complementary, largely based on avoidance of owner opportunism toward personal or business creditors. In the partnership, personal liability compensates firm creditors for the instability in the firm created by the right of the owners and their personal creditors to force liquidation of firm assets. In the corporation, strong entity shielding and the absence of withdrawal rights provide creditors with a reliable base of assets to compensate for the lack of a claim on owners' personal assets.

Although the corporate form was employed in ancient Rome (Malmendier 2005) and medieval Genoa (Ferrarini 2005), it did not supplant the partnership for most commercial activities until the twentieth century. This was not just a demand-side evolution, driven by the need to accumulate larger amounts of firm-specific capital, because even small service firms—of the type once commonly formed as partnerships—are now organized as corporations. Rather, it is arguably in part a consequence (though the issue remains a bit clouded) of (1) better creditor

22. Nonprofit corporations exhibit yet a third form, complete entity shielding, in which creditors of the firm's (beneficial) owners have no claim at all on firm assets.

protection, both through bankruptcy law and through financial contracting and monitoring, and (2) better owner protection, through greater judicial sophistication in guarding minority shareholders. Better owner protection renders it less costly for those shareholders to give up their withdrawal rights, which offer valuable protection against expropriation by controlling owners (Blair 2003; Hansmann et al. 2006; Lamoreaux and Rosenthal 2006).

11. The Role of Law

The mushrooming "law and finance" literature, seeded by the eponymous article of La Porta et al. (1998), explores the empirical relationship between legal systems and the development of corporate capitalism. That literature has focused heavily on the importance of particular substantive provisions of the law, such as rules that govern shareholders' ability to control corporate managers (antidirector rights). By and large, however, that literature does not ask closely what makes rules of law important. To be sure, the law and finance literature examines the degree to which the law is effectively enforced. But that is a characteristic of the legal system in general, not of organizational law in particular. The harder question—one that arises at the intersection of Coase's two most famous articles (Coase 1937, 1960)—is why specific rules of organizational law should be important, given the possibility of contracting around those rules.[23]

As noted above, rules of law are necessary to define the control and asset boundaries of the firm, because these boundaries provide the background social conventions necessary for contracting to take place. Nearly all other aspects of entity structure, however, can in theory be determined by contract among the organizers of the entity and placed in the firm's charter (articles of association) or in shareholder agreements. In particular, this includes the designation of the firm's owners and the allocation of earnings and control among them, as well as all details of the firm's internal governance structure. Thus, in principle, the modern statutory business trust offers all that is really necessary in a legal form for enterprise organization: it provides for contracting authority and strong entity shielding but lacks even default rules for most other aspects of entity structure, which are left to be specified in the firm's governing instrument. Yet the business trust is used almost exclusively for just two specialized purposes: asset securitization and mutual funds. Other types of organizations instead choose to form under much more heavily articulated statutes—such as a general business corporation statute, a limited liability company statute, or a cooperative corporation statute—that offers specific rules governing nearly all aspects of organizational structure. Moreover, although closely held firms often adopt specially crafted charter terms, publicly traded business corporations rarely take advantage of the broad freedom given them to deviate from the default terms of the corporation statutes, no matter how controversial those terms are, adopting instead all the standard statutory provisions.

Just why firms do not more commonly use individually tailored governance structures is not entirely clear. Nor is it clear why, if firms adopt standard-form structures, the standard forms they adopt are publicly provided via statute rather than (like many other standard form

---

23. Acemoglu and Johnson (2005) offer evidence that, in the long run, such rules of law are not in fact important.

contracts) privately drafted. Network externalities in marketing shares or in obtaining legal advice is one potential explanation (Kahan and Klausner 1997). Another is that state-provided organizational law may be a solution to a severe problem of incomplete contracting. Firms with long expected lifetimes, such as publicly traded business corporations, need to revise their governance structure as surrounding circumstances (e.g., the character of financial markets, or the nature of applicable tax and bankruptcy and labor law) change over time. But recontracting among the firm's participants—majority shareholders, minority shareholders, managers, and creditors—to amend the firm's own charter is a highly imperfect means to such adaptations. The available mechanisms for charter amendment are unlikely to lead to efficient results; one group or another will have either too much veto power over changes or too much leeway to force changes on the other participants. By deferring to the legally provided default terms, firms delegate this process of continual charter revision to the state, which—at least if it is a small and economically marginal state, such as Delaware—is a reasonably neutral party that is likely to avoid strong capture by any of the interests involved in corporations, including controlling shareholders, public shareholders, managers, creditors, and employees (Hansmann 2006; Listokin 2009).

12. Conclusion

Viewed as contracting entities, firms are assemblages of owners' rights and creditors' (more generally, patrons') rights. A classical firm has a simple structure in this regard. Ownership of the firm is in the hands of a single and highly homogeneous subset of the firm's patrons. All the firm's other patrons have contractual claims on the firm that are backed by a single undivided pool of bonding assets, which consists of all productive assets and contractual claims of the firm. Historically, there have been two principal variants of this classical form: the general partnership and the business corporation.

The historical tendency, for at least the past century, has been to complicate this simple structure with respect to creditors' rights by providing for subdivision of the firm's assets into smaller pools that can be separately pledged to particular subsets of the firm's patrons. One route to this end has been increasing flexibility in the formation of subsidiary entities. Another has been increasing flexibility in the mechanisms for giving security interests in particular assets to selected creditors. The trade-off here is between the costs of monitoring the assets that back a given contractual claim and the costs of giving notice of the various claims on firm assets—the first of which generally decrease, and the second of which generally increase, as asset partitioning becomes more refined. That trade-off has gradually shifted in favor of greater subpartitioning as information costs of giving notice have decreased. The result has been increasing dissociation between the control boundaries and the asset boundaries of firms.

Even though better access to information has thus led to more articulated contracting between firms and their nonowner patrons, it has not permitted similar refinements in the political-type collective choice mechanisms employed to aggregate the preferences of a firm's owners, which seem difficult to improve on. Although there has been experimentation with more articulated approaches to sharing or apportioning ownership rights among patrons with heterogeneous interests in a firm, they have fared poorly. Efforts that have been made in this direction include, conspicuously, German-style codetermination, employee stock ownership plans, and tracking stock.[24] None has taken hold in the absence of legal compulsion or substantial subsidies. Perhaps more complex ownership structures will someday become feasible. For the present, however, ownership of the firm must evidently remain in the hands of patrons with highly homogeneous interests. Therefore, because it is particularly easy to homogenize the interests of contributors of financial capital, free enterprise economies are likely to remain largely (though not exclusively) capitalist economies for the foreseeable future.

REFERENCES

Acemoglu, Daron, and Simon Johnson. 2005. "Unbundling Institutions." *Journal of Political Economy* 113: 949–995.

Alchian, Armen A., and Harold Demsetz. 1972. "Production, Information Costs, and Economic Organization." *American Economic Review* 62: 777–795.

Blair, Margaret M. 2003. "Locking in Capital: What Corporate Law Achieved for Business Organizers in the Nineteenth Century." *UCLA Law Review* 51: 387–455.

Coase, Ronald H. 1937. "The Nature of the Firm." *Economica* 4: 386–405.

———. 1960. "The Problem of Social Cost." *Journal of Law and Economics* 3: 1–44.

Easterbrook, Frank, and Daniel Fischel. 1991. *The Economic Structure of Corporate Law*. Cambridge, MA: Harvard University Press.

Ferrarini, Guido. 2005. "Origins of Limited Liability Companies and Company Law Modernisation in Italy: A Historical Outline." *Law of Business and Finance* 6: 187–216.

Garicano, Luis, and Thomas N. Hubbard. 2009. "Specialization, Firms, and Markets: The Division of Labor within and between Law Firms." *Journal of Law, Economics, and Organization* 25: 339–371.

Gaynor, Martin, and Paul J. Gertler. 1995. "Moral Hazard and Risk Spreading in Partnerships." *RAND Journal of Economics* 26: 591–613.

Gilson, Ronald J., and Robert Mnookin. 1985. "Sharing among the Human Capitalists: An Economic Inquiry into the Corporate Law Firm and How Partners Split Profits." *Stanford Law Review* 37: 313–392.

Glaeser, Edward, and Andrei Shleifer. 2001. "Not-for-Profit Entrepreneurs." *Journal of Public Economics* 81: 99–115.

Grossman, Sanford, and Oliver Hart. 1986. "The Costs and Benefits of Ownership: A Theory of Vertical and Lateral Integration." *Journal of Political Economy* 94: 691–719.

Halpern, Paul, Michael Trebilcock, and Stewart Turnbull. 1980. "An Economic Analysis of Limited Liability in Corporation Law." *University of Toronto Law Journal* 30: 117–150.

Hansmann, Henry. 1988. "Ownership of the Firm." *Journal of Law, Economics, and Organization* 4: 267–304.

———. 1996. *The Ownership of Enterprise*. Cambridge, MA: Harvard University Press.

———. 2006. "Corporation and Contract." *American Law and Economics Review* 8: 1–19.

---

24. An important consequence of the mandatory inclusion of labor representatives on the supervisory boards of German firms under codetermination has evidently been the weakening of those boards and a de facto devolution of substantially greater—and arguably inefficient—autonomy to managerial boards (Roe 1994).

The dividends paid on tracking stock are based on only the portion of a corporation's earnings attributable to designated activities.

Hansmann, Henry, and Reinier Kraakman. 2000a. "Organizational Law as Asset Partitioning." *European Economic Review* 44: 807–817.

———. 2000b. "The Essential Role of Organizational Law." *Yale Law Journal* 110: 387–440.

Hansmann, Henry, Daniel Kessler, and Mark McClellan. 2003. "Ownership Form and Trapped Capital in the Hospital Industry," in Edward Glaeser (ed.), *The Governance of Not-For-Profit Organizations.* Chicago: University of Chicago Press, pp. 45–70.

Hansmann, Henry, Reinier Kraakman, and Richard Squire. 2006. "Law and the Rise of the Firm." *Harvard Law Review* 119: 1333–1403.

Hart, Oliver, and John Moore. 1996. "The Governance of Exchanges: Members' Cooperatives vs. Outside Ownership." *Oxford Review of Economic Policy* 12(4): 53–69.

Iacobucci, Edward, and George Triantis. 2007. "Economic and Legal Boundaries of Firms." *University of Virginia Law Review* 93: 515–570.

Jackson, Thomas, and Anthony Kronman. 1979. "Secured Financing and Priorities among Creditors." *Yale Law Journal* 88: 1143–1182.

Jensen, Michael, and William Meckling. 1976. "Theory of the Firm: Managerial Behavior, Agency Costs, and Ownership Structure." *Journal of Financial Economics* 3: 305–360.

———. 1979. "Rights and Production Functions: An Application to Labor-Managed Firms and Codetermination." *Journal of Business* 52: 469–506.

Kahan, Marcel, and Michael Klausner. 1997. "Standardization and Innovation in Corporate Contracting (or 'The Economics of Boilerplate')." *Virginia Law Review* 83: 713–770.

Kandel, Eugene, and Edward Lazear. 1992. "Peer Pressure and Partnerships." *Journal of Political Economy* 100: 801–817.

Klein, Benjamin, Robert Crawford, and Armen A. Alchian. 1978. "Vertical Integration, Appropriable Rents, and the Competitive Contracting Process." *Journal of Law and Economics* 21: 297–326.

Lamoreaux, Naomi R., and Jean-Laurent Rosenthal. 2006. "Corporate Governance and the Plight of Minority Shareholders in the United States before the Great Depression," in Edward Glaeser and Claudia Goldin (eds.), *Corruption and Reform.* Chicago: University of Chicago Press, pp. 125–152.

La Porta, Rafael, Florencio Lopez-de-Silanes, Andrei Shleifer, and Robert W. Vishny. 1998. "Law and Finance." *Journal of Political Economy* 106: 1113–1155.

Lee, Ruben. 1998. *What Is an Exchange?* Oxford: Oxford University Press.

Levin, Jonathan, and Steven Tadelis. 2005. "Profit Sharing and the Role of Professional Partnerships." *Quarterly Journal of Economics* 120: 131–172.

Listokin, Yair. 2009. "What Do Corporate Default Rules and Menus Do? An Empirical Examination." *Journal of Empirical Legal Studies* 6: 279–308.

Malmendier, Ulrike. 2005. "Roman Shares," in William Goetzmann and K. Geert Rouwenhorst (eds.), *The Origins of Value: The Financial Innovations That Created Modern Capital Markets.* New York: Oxford University Press, pp. 31–43.

Morrison, Alan, and William Wilhelm, Jr. 2004. "Partnership Firms, Reputation, and Human Capital." *American Economic Review* 94: 1682–1692.

———. 2005. "The Demise of Investment Banking Partnerships: Theory and Evidence." Working paper, Said Business School, University of Oxford, Oxford.

———. 2007. *Investment Banking: Institutions, Politics, and Law.* Oxford: Oxford University Press.

Pirrong, Craig. 2000. "A Theory of Financial Exchange Organization." *Journal of Law and Economics* 43: 437–471.

Prendergast, Canice. 1999. "The Provision of Incentives in Firms." *Journal of Economic Literature* 37: 7–63.

Rasmusen, Eric. 1988. "Stock Banks and Mutual Banks." *Journal of Law and Economics* 31: 395–422.

Refsell, Oscar. 1914. "The Farmers' Elevator Movement." *Journal of Political Economy* 22: 872–895, 969–991.

Roberts, John, and Eric Van den Steen. 2001. "Human Capital and Corporate Governance," in Joachim Schwalbach (ed.), *Corporate Governance: A Volume in Honor of Horst Albach*. Berlin: Springer-Verlag, pp. 128–144.

Roe, Mark. 1994. *Political Foundations of Corporate Governance*. Cambridge: Cambridge University Press.

Smith, Adam. 1776. *An Inquiry into the Nature and Causes of the Wealth of Nations*. London: W. Strahan and T. Cadell.

Thomsen, Steen, and C. Rose. 2004. "Foundation Ownership and Financial Performance: Do Companies Need Owners?" *European Journal of Law and Economics* 18: 343–364.

Tiebout, Charles. 1956. "A Pure Theory of Local Public Expenditures." *Journal of Political Economy* 64: 416–424.

Tirole, Jean. 2001. "Corporate Governance." *Econometrica* 69: 1–35.

Von Nordenflycht, Andrew. 2007. "Is Public Ownership Bad for Professional Service Firms? Ad Agency Ownership, Performance, and Creativity." *Academy of Management Journal* 50: 429–445.

Ward, Benjamin. 1958. "The Firm in Illyria: Market Syndicalism." *American Economic Review* 48: 566–589.

Weitzman, Martin, and Douglas Kruse. 1990. "Profit Sharing and Productivity," in Alan Binder (ed.), *Paying for Productivity: A Look at the Evidence*. Washington, DC: Brookings Institution, pp. 95–142.

Williamson, Oliver. 1985. *The Economic Institutions of Capitalism: Firms, Markets, Relational Contracting*. New York: Free Press.

Woodward, Susan E. 1985. "Limited Liability in the Theory of the Firm." *Journal of Institutional and Theoretical Economics* 141: 601–611.

23

Contracts between Legal Persons

Lewis A. Kornhauser and W. Bentley MacLeod

The duty to keep a contract at common law means a prediction that
you must pay damages if you do not keep it—and nothing else.

Oliver Wendell Holmes,
"The Path of the Law," *Harvard Law Review*, 1897

1. Introduction

Contract law and the economics of contract have, for the most part, developed independently of
each other. While contract law has existed for centuries, if not millennia, the economic analysis
of contract is both very recent and largely divorced from the content and structure of contract
law.[1] Current reviews of contract theory, such as Laffont and Martimort (2002) and Bolton and
Dewatripont (2005), do not discuss either the substantive law of contract or the role that courts
play in enforcement. In this chapter, we begin to bridge this gap.

We briefly review the notion of a contract from the perspective of a lawyer and then use
this framework to organize the economic literature on contract. The review thus provides
an overview of the literature for economists who are interested in exploring the economic
implications of contract law. The title, "Contracts between Legal Persons," limits the review
to that part of contract law that is generic to any legal person. A legal person is any individual,
firm, or government agency with the right to enter into a binding agreement. Our goal is to
discuss the role of the law in enforcing these agreements under the hypothesis that legal persons
have well defined goals and objectives.[2]

The possession of well-defined preferences does not imply that legal persons never make
mistakes. In fact, a key ingredient to understanding the observed form of contract law requires
the introduction of some imperfections in decisionmaking. Since the seminal work of Herbert
Simon (1982), there has been little disagreement that a complete understanding of human

We thank Elliott Ash, Kevin Davis, Robert Gibbons, Avery Katz, John Roberts, and participants at the fourth
annual Research Triangle Conference on Law and Economics for comments on earlier drafts of this chapter. We
also thank Elliott Ash, Wilfredo Lim, and Teck Yong Tan for research assistance.

1. The introduction of Laffont and Martimort (2002) provides a nice historical overview of the development
of incentives contracts.

2. For example, the field of corporate governance (see Hermalin ("Corporate Governance"), this volume) is
concerned with the design of legal institutions that ensure that firms have preferences corresponding to maximizing
firm value.

institutions requires the incorporation of errors in decisionmaking. However, there is little agreement regarding the best way to achieve this goal. In this review, we follow the widely accepted hypothesis that imperfect and asymmetric information are key ingredients of any theory of contract form. We show that these elements are sufficient to tie together the various strands of the literature. We then outline a plan for future research.

The review is divided into three substantive parts. Section 2 focuses on the primary legal concepts on which contract law rests—including the notion of a legal person and what is meant by an enforceable agreement. We focus on the substantive remedial regime that determines how contracts are enforced and on two features of the process of adjudication—fact-finding and interpretation—that determine what obligations the parties have and when they have been breached.

Section 3 examines how the implicit assumptions underlying the economic literature on contract compares to the substantive law of remedy. Economic models of contract make stylized assumptions regarding how the law enforces contracts. In many cases, these assumptions are consistent with existing law. In some cases, particularly when the contract requires a person to act in a particular way, the implicit assumptions are inconsistent with existing law in such jurisdictions as the United States. This inconsistency is manifested in some recent work that builds on results in mechanism design. The same inconsistency may help explain, as Tirole (1999) observes, the gap between the predictions of these models and observed contract forms. In addition, Section 3 discusses the literature on economic analysis of law that begins to bridge the gap between the spare assumptions on remedial regime in the economic literature and the complexity of the law.

Section 4 discusses the sparse literature on fact finding and interpretation. This literature asks two questions:

1. When parties write an incomplete contract, how should a court determine the obligations that the parties have?

2. How do courts find facts? In terms of the economic literature, what is the technology of verification?

Section 5 concludes the chapter.

We deploy the conceptual scheme of contract law summarized in Section 2.2 to organize a summary of the literature on the economics of contract. Our characterizations of some of the underlying economics literature may thus seem a bit askew, but we hope that the legal perspective will open additional avenues of research.

2. Contract Law

In this section, we set out the legal view of contract. We begin with the legal view of agency for two reasons. First, it provides a sharp contrast with the economic view. Second, as most contracts are between firms, we require a conception of a firm and of when a transaction is between firms rather than within a firm. Our conception of a firm relies on some basic legal concepts that have consequences for the legal treatment of different types of transactions. We proceed in Section 2.2 to a characterization of contract law.

2.1. Legal Personality

The economic agent is characterized by her preferences; the legal agent is characterized by her legal capacities to hold and convey property, to make contracts, and to sue and be sued. These capacities are central to each of the different legal forms that a firm might take: sole proprietorship, partnership, business corporation, trust, or not-for-profit corporation.[3] Natural persons (who have reached the age of majority and are mentally competent) also have these properties. Hansmann (this volume) discusses the importance of asset ownership (and, implicitly, some aspects of exposure to suit). As Hansmann notes, legal personality segregates a set of assets owned by the entity. Consider, for example, a corporation C. C owns some set of assets A that are subject to claims from other persons. Liability of C is limited (to the asset pool A), because the corporate form protects the assets of other legal persons, in particular, the owners of C, from valid legal claims against C.[4]

We focus on the legal person's right to make contracts and to sue and be sued. Legal persons act through natural persons. When the legal person is simply a natural person, both action and identification of which acts are attributable to her is relatively straightforward. Many legal persons, however, are complex; they are constituted by and encompass large numbers of other legal persons, both natural and artificial. For example, law firms 30 years ago were typically organized as partnerships. Each partner was a natural person as were all employees of the partnership (but not all its clients, many of whom were corporations). Some actions of the partners and their employees were attributable to the partnerships, and others were not. Similarly, a business corporation has shareholders, managers, directors, employees, and customers; some members of each of these classes may be natural persons, but others may be corporations. It may also own, wholly or in part, other corporations. Corporations, of course, act only through individuals, some but not all of whose acts are attributable to the corporation.

Two bodies of law solve these problems of attribution: organizational law and agency law. Organizational law addresses problems of the internal organization of the firm or legal person. Often, in conjunction with constitutional documents of the firm—in business corporations the articles of incorporation and the by-laws—organizational law identifies a decision procedure for the firm. In business corporations, this decision procedure is complex, with final authority for most decisions given to the board of directors, though some decisions require shareholder approval and many decisions are delegated to management.[5] The law of agency determines which actions may bind the legal persons. Under what circumstances is the fictitious person responsible for the acts of its agents (e.g., employees)? Even a natural

---

3. The attributes of legal personality of the different forms of business organization vary somewhat. So, for example, partnerships are not treated as "persons" for tax purposes, whereas corporations are. More importantly, a partnership can be terminated at will by any partner at any time, whereas corporate death (or dissolution) is more complex. For a brief introduction to the concept of legal personality, see Clark (1986: 15–21).

4. The protection of assets of other legal persons is not complete. In some circumstances, a claimant T on C's assets may either "pierce the corporate veil" and make claims against the assets of the owner of C when A is insufficient to satisfy T's claim or claim assets that have been transferred to third parties.

5. On corporate law generally, see Clark (1986).

person might benefit from having an agent, someone who can enter contracts for her and make other decisions. The law of agency governs which actions of the agent belong to the agent and which to the principal.[6] We ignore here actions that lead to harm to third parties and focus on exchange.[7] If the agent has actual or apparent authority[8] to act on behalf of the principal (here the legal person), then the principal is bound by the agent's actions, while generally, the agent has no liability to the contracting party. The principal grants authority either expressly or implicitly; in some instances, it may appear that the agent has authority even when she does not. Agency law places the risk of error on the principal. In what follows, we shall generally assume that the legal person acts through agents with actual authority.

Legal persons may also sue or be sued. We might differentiate contracts between firms from contracts between the firm and its employees and from contracts between parts of the firm in terms of the remedies available to resolve disputes. In essence, the law treats this last class of transactions—transactions internal to the firm (but not employment contracts)—differently from market transactions.[9] Several distinct questions arise here. Consider some actor X. We may ask first: what rights does X have? Second, what forum is available to adjudicate these rights? More specifically, are state courts available to adjudicate these rights? Third, and finally, if state courts are available, is X able to assert these rights in this forum? In any given dispute, the law provides complex answers to these questions. We provide a brief sketch of the legal terrain (in the United States) with respect to disputes arising from exchange.

In economics, a legal person C is usually a business corporation, though in some contexts, C might be a natural person or a governmental entity. Suppose C is a business corporation. Hence, C has relations with its employees and its subsidiaries, both sets of which are sets of legal persons, with outside firms and outside consumers. Disputes may thus arise from interactions among

---

6. Clark (1986: 113–117) offers a brief introduction to agency principles. See also American Law Institute (2006).

7. When an individual acts as an agent on behalf of someone else, two questions arise. We emphasize the question raised in the text: under what circumstances is the principal responsible for the acts of its agents? This question might arise in at least two contexts: contract and tort. In the first case, agency law generally determines when the acts of the agent bind the principal to contracts that the agent makes on her behalf. When an agent harms a third party, tort liability arises, and the doctrine of vicarious liability determines when the tort victim also has a claim against the principal. For economic analysis of vicarious liability see Sykes (1981), Kornhauser (1982), and Arlen and MacLeod (2005).

The second question asks under what circumstances is the agent relieved of responsibility for her actions. Again, the analysis of contract and tort differs. Usually, agents are not responsible to the promisee for the contracts that they enter on behalf of their principals. They might, however, be liable to the principal if they acted outside the scope of their authority. See American Law Institute (2006: §§ 6.01, 6.04, 6.10, 6.11). In tort, agents generally are responsible for actions that harm third parties, though public officials in the United States benefit from a qualified immunity from tort liability for actions taken in furtherance of their official duties. See generally American Law Institute (2006: § 7.01).

8. On apparent authority see American Law Institute (2006: § 3.03).

9. Contracts between the firm and its employees are generally governed by contract law, employment law, or labor law.

employees, subsidiaries, or groups of employees, or between agents of the firm and outside suppliers or consumers.

The first question concerns the substantive rights the disputants have. The legal person to a large extent makes its own law to govern its internal disputes; Williamson (1991) makes this point. Thus, our corporation C has the power to determine, within limits,[10] the substantive rights that employees and subsidiaries have against it and the substantive rights that employees and subsidiaries have against one another. C's power to makes its own law, however, may be limited by state law, or state law may create a set of default rules to govern without explicit internal law. Employment law provides a good example. Internal rules may not violate employment discrimination rules, and the doctrine of at-will employment serves as a default rule in most jurisdictions in the United States. Of course, C and the outside firms with which it contracts also have the power, subject to the same caveats, to make their own law to govern their exchange; this power is granted by contract law.

Turn now to the second question of forum. Suppose two persons A and B, employees or subsidiaries of C, have a dispute arising under C's internal rules. As the employment contract usually delegates authority to the firm, the state courts will not resolve this dispute (unless the dispute implicates some statutory right of the employee). Nor would the parent corporation usually allow its subsidiaries to resort to the courts to resolve an internal dispute.

Now consider two unincorporated divisions D and D' of C. Neither D nor D' is a legal person for purposes of state law. However, even if they have engaged in an exchange with an "outsider" that constitutes a contract, neither D nor D' has the power to sue or be sued with respect to such a claim. To be concrete, suppose Chevrolet and Pontiac, both unincorporated subdivisions of General Motors, jointly hire an advertising firm; the agreement between Chevrolet and Pontiac provides a formula for allocating the costs incurred by the advertising firm. Any dispute between Chevrolet and Pontiac must be resolved within General Motors. (If these subdivisions were corporate subsidiaries of General Motors, each with a distinct legal identity, then each would have the right to sue or be sued. General Motors, however, might prohibit its subsidiaries from exercising this right.) One may view many of the contributions to this handbook (e.g., Hansmann, this volume) as reviews of the internal procedures and policies that firms use to govern internal disputes.

2.2. The Law of Contract

2.2.1. Defining the Basic Concepts

A contract, in the legal literature, is "an agreement between two or more parties creating obligations that are enforceable or otherwise recognizable at law" (*Black's Law Dictionary;* Garner and Black 2005).[11] The economics literature, in contrast, provides no definition of a

---

10. Contract law provides the parties with great latitude in structuring their relationship, but other parts of state law do constrain the substantive rights. The Thirteenth Amendment to the Constitution of the United States bans slavery, for instance. More relevantly, U.S. law includes statutes that require equal treatment by race, gender, age, and disability as well as restrictions on minimum wages and various terms and conditions of employment.

11. The *Restatement Second of Contracts* (American Law Institute 1981: § 1) offers a similar definition: "a promise or set of promises for the breach of which the law gives a remedy or the performance of which the

contract.[12] To the economist, "contract" refers to an incentive structure, often an optimal or constrained optimal incentive structure.[13]

Fruitful interchange between the two literatures thus requires that we specify at the outset a common vocabulary that permits the introduction of a legal framework into the economic analysis of contract. We introduce four concepts: *an exchange environment, a contractual instrument, contract law,* and *contractual behavior.* We then offer a definition of a contract.

An exchange environment is specified by the preferences of the agents, the information structure among the agents and any third-party enforcer, and the production technology that determines the effects of various investments by the parties on the costs and benefits of exchange. The exchange environment identifies the constraints under which the agents act.

A contractual instrument contains the terms the parties bargained for, while contract law may imply terms that the parties have neglected to make explicit; interpret terms that, in the light of performance, are ambiguous; or, more rarely, impose a term contrary to the one negotiated by the parties. Further, the remedial rules of contract law largely determines the structure of any renegotiation. Contractual behavior refers to the actions of parties to the contract in light of the contractual instrument and the prevailing law of contract. We reserve the term "contract" for the set of obligations that result from the application of contract law to the contractual instrument.

We may think of a contractual instrument as a (partial) list of events and associated obligations for each party. Though the law usually enforces oral agreements, we assume that the agreement has a written form. Thus, a contractual instrument is embodied in a fixed text that is publicly available, so that the parties and any third-party enforcer know the contents of this text. The contractual instrument in conjunction with contract law determines the contractual obligations the parties have. We might say, that is, that the contractual instrument, as understood against the background law of contract, determines the contract between the parties. This contract is, in the sense of Arrow and Debreu (1954), a complete contingent claims contract; it specifies what each party must do in every possible state of the world, though, of course, the specified actions may not be optimal ones.

---

law in some way recognizes as a duty." On this issue specifically, and on contract law generally, see Farnsworth (2004).

Different legal systems have different criteria for determining the set of agreements that the law will enforce. In common law jurisdictions, such as the United States and Britain, these constraints are few. The agreement must be sufficiently detailed for the court to determine the content of the bargain; in most cases an agreement that required the transfer of goods at some future date without specifying the quality or quantity of the goods or the price at transfer would be unenforceable. In addition, for a promise to perform a future action to constitute an agreement, the promisee must give "consideration," but almost any return promise or action is now understood as consideration. See generally Farnsworth (2004: 47–53). Note also that some agreements must be in writing to be enforceable.

12. The index to Bolton and Dewatripont (2005) has no entry for contract law, and the text provides no formal definition. The index to Salanie (1997) does have an entry "contract, definition of," but the designated page does not provide a clear definition.

13. Salanie's (1997) discussion in his introduction is consistent with this interpretation. Ayres and Gertner (1992) characterize the economic literature in a similar fashion.

This chapter begins to disentangle the role of the contractual instrument from the role of contract law in the structure of mechanisms. We also specify the constraints that contract law imposes on mechanism design by articulating some of the real features of contract law.

2.2.2. What Does Contract Law Do?

One ambiguity remains in our vocabulary. Contract law refers both to the substantive rules governing contracting behavior and to the institutions that interpret and enforce them. Substantive contract law identifies what private parties must do to create a legally binding agreement and guides the courts in the interpretation and enforcement of contractual instruments. In this chapter, we focus on two institutional aspects of contract law that characterize the tasks of courts and on a subset of the substantive law of contract. In effect, the court performs three distinct tasks when it adjudicates a contract dispute. First, it finds the facts. It determines what actions the parties took and what state of the world or nature was realized. Second, it interprets the contractual instrument. Interpretation requires the court to determine what obligations the contractual instrument imposed in the realized state of the world.[14] If the contractual instrument was complete, coherent, and uncontradictory, some term specified these obligations. If the contractual instrument was incomplete, then it will not have specified any obligations in the realized state of the world. In this case, the court must nonetheless determine the obligations of the parties. In other instances, the contractual instrument may be poorly drafted and impose conflicting or ambiguous obligations in some state of the world.[15] Again, the court must determine what obligations the parties actually have. Third, if the court determines that one party (or more) has failed to meet its obligations under the contractual instrument, as interpreted by the court, it must enforce the contract; the court imposes the remedy dictated by the substantive law.[16] Remedies may take many forms. The substantive rules of contract law determine the form of the remedy.

This discussion of the functions of courts suggests that we assess regimes of contract law along three different axes—the process of fact determination, the interpretative practice, and the substantive remedial regime.

2.2.3. Fact Finding

A contractual instrument specifies, against the legal backdrop, the obligations of each party. Often the obligations of the parties are state-contingent; what each party must do varies with the state of the world. Resolution of every contract dispute thus requires determination of the actions that each party took and of the realized event.

---

14. Of course, the content of the contractual instrument and the substance of contract law determine in part what facts the court must find.

15. A poorly drafted contractual instrument might, in one or more contingencies, also specify an inefficient or otherwise inappropriate obligation. Some poorly drafted contracts impose in some events inconsistent obligations on a party (i.e., it requires the party both to do and not to do some act).

16. "Impose a remedy" here means to announce a judgment for the plaintiff (promisee) that specifies an amount of damages to be paid or an action to be taken by the defendant (promisor). If the defendant does not satisfy the judgment, the plaintiff must return to court for an order to direct the sheriff to seize assets sufficient to satisfy the damage award or to seize the defendant as in contempt of court. Thus, strictly speaking, the sheriff, not the court, enforces remedies.

Fact-finding procedures apply across a wide of range of types of disputes, and they are governed by distinct bodies of law (that generally go under the names of civil or criminal procedure and evidence). We may assess these procedures along two dimensions: their accuracy and their cost. In an ideal world, fact finding would be perfectly accurate and costless. In the real world, the invocation of courts is costly, and courts themselves sometimes err in their fact finding.[17]

As we discuss below, the economic theory of contract generally distinguishes observable actions from verifiable actions. Courts costlessly observe verifiable actions with perfect accuracy; courts cannot observe unverifiable actions at any cost.[18] Most actions and events, in contrast, are only verifiable at some cost and to some degree of accuracy.

2.2.4. Interpretive Practices

Contract disputes often entail more than a dispute over facts. They often include disputes over the content of the contractual obligations the parties faced. A party's obligations may be unclear for several reasons: the contractual instrument may have been ambiguous, so that it is unclear whether an action *a* satisfies the contractually specified obligation; the contractual instrument may have been inconsistent and required that the party undertake an action that was not feasible in the realized state of the world or that the party undertake inconsistent actions; or the contractual instrument may not have contemplated the realized state of the world and so specified no obligation at all. Finally, contract law itself may have been unclear or ambiguous.

Contract interpretation is the legal practice that determines the obligations of the parties. These practices are complex and difficult to specify. To begin, we consider a procedural aspect of interpretive practices: the information on which the court relies in deciding what obligations the parties have under the contractual instrument.[19] The practice may be more or less inclusive in its informational base. It might refer only to the fixed text of the contractual instrument, or it might rely on additional information. It might, for instance, rely on statements during the precontractual negotiations of the parties. It might rely on the precontractual practice (if any) of the parties (i.e., it might look to prior behavior of the parties under contractual instruments dealing with the same or similar subject matter). The court might look to the course of dealing of the parties under the contractual instrument in dispute. Alternatively, the court might look to general trade practice; that is, it might consider how individuals who regularly engage in exchanges of the type governed by the disputed contractual instrument behaved under similar circumstances. We distinguish textualist practices of interpretation (in which the court refers only to the written text of the contractual instrument) from contextualist practices of interpretation (in which the court refers to some information external to the contractual instrument as well as to the text). This simple distinction is sufficient to classify the existing literature, discussed in Section 4.2; this literature has been inattentive to the problem of interpretation.

Of course, even courts that adopt identical informational bases might have different interpretive practices. After all, an interpretive practice is a map from the space defined by the

---

17. We note in passing that the parties may, in the contractual instrument, alter the usual default fact-finding procedures.

18. The economic literature treats unverifiable actions as a constraint on the contractual instrument.

19. Katz (2004) discusses this issue.

informational base into the set of obligations. Court C might impute one obligation to a given set of facts, while court C′ imputes a different obligation to the same set of facts.

We may better understand these imputation practices by considering the different objectives a court might pursue in interpreting the relevant informational base. The court might pursue at least three different objectives. First, it might seek to determine what the parties agreed to (or, if they did not contemplate the realized event, would have agreed to). To accomplish this aim, a court must recover both the interests of the parties and their relative bargaining power.[20] Second, the court might seek to determine what "normal" or "average" parties to exchanges of this type would agree to. To accomplish this aim, the court must determine the preferences of the normal contracting parties. Third, the court might seek to determine an efficient contract. Efficiency here might refer to ex ante incentives to invest, or it might refer to efficient risk sharing. Again, the court needs to recover or to impute the preferences of the parties.

In the stylized world of the economics of contract literature, the parties are rational; they would themselves thus write an efficient contract. It might thus appear that the third interpretive aim simply recapitulates either of the prior two aims. This appearance, however, is deceptive for two reasons. First, though rational parties would seek to maximize their surplus, they might divide that surplus in many different ways. Hence, the first two aims require the court to infer the nature of a specific bargain.

Second, the contractual instruments of rational parties are clear and well specified. In the commercial world, however, parties are not fully rational; they may make mistakes. Consequently, contract terms may be vague, unclear, or contradictory (in the sense of requiring a party to take inconsistent actions in some state of the world). The court, in interpreting the contractual instrument, must confront these imperfections and determine what obligations the parties in fact had under the contract.

2.2.5. Remedial Regimes

After the court determines what happened and what obligations the parties had under the contractual instrument, it determines whether each party met its obligations under the instrument (as interpreted under the prevailing contract law). If the court finds that some party did not perform as required, it offers a remedy. Again, contract law has a rich set of remedial rules. We might understand a remedial regime as giving the promisor an option: to perform or not to perform but to make a damage payment. Remedial regimes differ in the option price, or the level of damages that the promisor must pay in the event of nonperformance. We contrast two remedial regimes: (expectation) damages and no damages (against a backdrop of secure property rights).[21]

The standard remedy[22] for breach of contract in common law jurisdictions is expectation damages.[23] The principle of expectation damages awards the promisee her (subjective) value

---

20. In fact, the court needs a complete theory of how the parties would bargain.

21. Hermalin, Katz, and Craswell (2006) surveys the economic literature on contractual remedies.

22. Two types of deviations may occur. In some cases, lesser damages may be imposed, and in some cases, specific performance (see the next note) may be imposed. In addition, the remedial rules of contract law are, to a certain extent, default rules. The parties may specify a level of damages in the contractual instrument that would substitute for the court measurement.

23. In civil law countries, there is a large group of contracts for which the default remedy is specific performance, a requirement that the nonperforming party meet her obligation. This requirement might be enforced by

of performance. Of course, the court generally cannot observe this subjective valuation; the common law has developed some clever rules to implement the principle that, in many cases, contrive to deliver to the promisee her subjective value of performance without actually measuring it.[24] In many cases, however, the actual measure of the promisee's expectation leads to undercompensation. This undercompensation results in part from the procedural rule in the United States that each party bears her own costs of litigation. This practice contrasts with the practice in Britain, where the losing party bears the winner's costs of litigation as well as paying substantive damages.

Expectation damages nevertheless applies to most agreements. It differs dramatically from the common assumption in the economics of contract literature that the obligation specified in the contractual instrument will be enforced. The rule of expectation damages will lead to radically different consequences than does the rule of perfect enforcement assumed in the economics of contract literature.[25]

Finally, the law may simply protect the property rights of the parties and not enforce any agreements at all. In this regime, the parties have no access to the fact-finding or interpretive capacities of courts. Courts do, however, protect persons against bodily harm and property from appropriation by other individuals (and the government). When a promisor fails to perform, the promisee can enforce the contract only through reputational devices or refusals to deal. This regime corresponds to a regime of pure "relational" contracts.

2.3. Discussion

These brief comments suggest a rich panoply of regimes of contract law against which exchange might occur. We consider a few ideal types, all against a backdrop of security of property rights. At the extremes are anarchy and utopia, the two regimes commonly assumed in the economics of contract. Under anarchy, there is no third-party fact finding, interpretation, or enforcement, though each party remains secure in her property holdings. Under utopia, fact-finding is perfectly accurate and costless, interpretation is clear and costless, and enforcement is costless and perfect (in the sense that each party performs her stated obligation). In the world of anarchy, contracts must be self-enforcing; in utopia, the parties can costlessly bind themselves to any obligation they choose.

---

charging the breaching party with civil contempt, which in common law countries might lead to jail time or to large fines.

24. Consider, for example, the rule of "cover," which permits an aggrieved buyer to purchase the contracted-for goods on the spot market and to receive as damages the difference between the market price at which she covered and the contract price. This rule delivers the promisee her expectation by delivering her the goods at the contract price (on the assumption that the contracted-for goods were standardized goods available in a sufficiently thick spot market).

Notice that, generally, the law may offer a number of different remedial options from which the aggrieved party may choose. Section 7 of Article 2 of the Uniform Commercial Code illustrates well both the panoply of options and the elective nature. In addition, an aggrieved party might rely on either restitution or promissory estoppel rather than pure contract remedies.

25. As noted above, courts applied the remedy of specific performance to contracts for "unique" goods. One might, however, understand the rule of specific performance as an instance (or implementation) of the expectation principle: by delivering the contracted-for performance, the promisor delivers the promisee her expectation. At-will employment, in contrast, does not deliver the value of the performance to the agent.

Courts, however, decide cases in neither an anarchic nor an utopian world but in a world in which fact finding, interpretation, and enforcement are both costly and error-ridden. Contracts here need not be self-enforcing, but they will not be perfectly enforced. Observed contracts reflect this middle ground (as well as the oddities that result from the efforts of boundedly rational or irrational agents).[26]

3. Enforcement and Remedy in Economic Models of Contract

In this section, we examine the enforcement assumptions implicit in the economic literature on contract. Economic analyses of contract usually make one of three assumptions. The literature on relational contracts assumes that the parties have no remedies available to them other than the enforcement of unconditional monetary transfers. The agency literature assumes, consistent with the substantive legal regime, that an aggrieved party will receive compensation equal to her expectation from the contract. The incomplete contracts literature, in contrast, assumes that an aggrieved party will receive specific performance (i.e., that the courts will enforce all terms in the contract as written). As we discuss in more detail below, specific performance is not the general remedial rule in Anglo-American common law systems, and hence several of the contract forms that have been suggested as efficient solutions to the hold-up problems could not be implemented in the United States.

It is worth pointing out that in economics, the only role that damages play is to ensure that individuals choose to perform their obligations. Kornhauser (1983) observes that contract damages can play a second role, namely, to encourage careful planning by parties. However, this point requires a theory of endogenously incomplete contracts, a relatively new literature. This issue is discussed further in Section 4.

---

26. We have ignored some complications that arise when parties are insolvent. Our discussion thus far has assumed that the promisor is fully solvent; it can meet all claims on it. Under this assumption, the promisee understands that the promisor will either perform or pay damages as measured by the contract rule. In many actual transactions, however, and in some models, the promisor is potentially insolvent. Insolvency triggers a shift in the set of legal rules that govern disputes over contracts. Fried (1996) sets out the rules governing contracts in bankruptcy. He argues that the rules provide the trustee in bankruptcy with incentives to reject some contracts with expected gains from trade.

Consider a contract at time t_0 between a Seller S and a Buyer B for the delivery of one widget at a price p at time t_2. Suppose S files for bankruptcy at time t_1; S is insolvent. If the contract was performed by both parties prior to t_1, there is no problem. Suppose therefore that S has not performed by t_1. There are two possibilities: (1) B has fully performed prior to t_1, or (2) B has not fully performed by t_1 (in which case the contract is executory). In situation (1), B is an unsecured creditor with no priority over any other unsecured creditors. Of course, B may have taken a security interest in some asset of S's; then B would have a prior claim on that asset. In principle, an economic analysis of contracting must now ask: under what circumstances would we expect to see either party take a security interest in some asset? Turn now to situation (2). S faces a choice. She may either assume the contract or reject it. If she rejects the contract, then B is once again treated as an unsecured creditor of S. If S, however, assumes the contract, there are again two possibilities. S might perform the assumed contract, in which case there is no problem; or S might later breach the contract. (At the time t_1 of the bankruptcy, the market price for widgets might be $p - 2$; S therefore makes a profit by assuming the contract. At t_2, though, the market price may have risen to $p + 2$, and S might do better if she breaches.) If S breaches subsequent to assumption of the contract, then B is an unsecured creditor of S, but she now has priority over unsecured creditors whose debts were incurred prior to bankruptcy.

In Section 3.1 we consider relational contracts. Section 3.2 discusses the general question of remedy. Section 3.3 considers expectation damages. These are damages that require the harmed party to pay the plaintiff an amount equal in value to the loss suffered by the breach. Section 3.4 examines liquidated damages. In these clauses, the contracting parties specify their own remedial regimes. Section 3.5 discusses the remedy of specific performance. Section 3.6 compares expectation damages and specific performance. Section 3.7 provides a brief summary.

3.1. Relational Contracts and the Absence of a Remedial Regime

Relational contracts use the threat to terminate a relationship as a contract enforcement device.[27] The literature here has antecedents in both the legal and the economic literature. In a classic study on the sociology of law, Macaulay (1963) observed that many business relationships appear to work well, even though they have no formal contract, or the contractual instrument they have is extremely unclear or inconsistent.[28] The evidence in Macaulay (1963) suggests that parties performed because of the expectation of future business rather than because of the threat of legal remedies.[29]

Simon's (1951) classic paper on employment contracts initiated the economic literature on relational contracts. Simon was not concerned with the enforceability of the contract but with how complexity can lead to one or the other contract form. Malcomson (1981: 852) begins his analysis of the employment contract with the observation that the complexity of performance requirements makes it impossible to enforce performance standards. This impossibility creates a problem of ex post hold-up (MacLeod 2002). Malcomson (1981) points out that legal enforcement of employment contracts is limited; the firm must pay an employee who arrives at work, but the court will not generally assess the quality of the employee's labor. Hence, dismissal is the sole sanction available to the employer. This characterization is consistent with the common law rule of employment at will.[30]

These ideas have resulted in a large literature on relational contracts that builds on the hypothesis that courts cannot be relied on to enforce sanctions conditional on the performance of complex tasks. Employment at will is the common-law default rule in the United States but not generally in other jurisdictions. Moreover, even in the United States the law has evolved a number of exceptions to at-will employment that allow employees to seek damages from employers (Miles 2000). Though some recent literature explores the role of employment protection in labor market performance (MacLeod 2011), for the most part, the economics literature equates employment law with a turnover tax.[31] As we observed above, one of the important roles of

27. See MacLeod (2007) and Malcomson (this volume) for detailed reviews of the literature on relational contracts.

28. This confusion can occur when buyer uses her own purchase order and the seller uses his own invoice, each of which includes boilerplate terms. This practice leads to the famous "battle of the forms" problem in contract law. See Farnsworth (2004: 161–170).

29. See also Posner (1997) for a discussion of the role of norms and how they may shape behavior in contractual relationships.

30. See Feinman (1978) for a history of evolution of the doctrine of employment at will.

31. Blanchard and Tirole (2008) provide a nice analysis of employment policy for the purposes of informing French public policy. They explicitly explore the role of employment insurance and view employment protection as mainly a turnover cost. The fact-finding role of the courts is not discussed at all.

the courts is its fact-finding function; hence, equating employment law with a turnover tax is a rather crude representation of the legal system.

The formal analysis of relational contracts begins with Telser (1980), who introduced the idea that a relational contract can be modeled as a repeated game. He shows that if both parties have sufficient gains from trade, then they will both perform when the consequence of nonperformance is a cessation of trade. His model assumes that both parties might breach the contract, and that this event is observable by both parties. Though Telser does not use all the formalism of repeated game theory, his analysis is consistent with the characterizations of the equilibria of repeated games in Abreu (1988).

Abreu (1988) shows that one can characterize all equilibria in a repeated game with a two-step procedure. First, parties agree on the equilibrium action in each period. In the context of a contract, this stage can be viewed as specifying the performance obligations. Next, Abreu shows that this agreement can be the outcome of playing a subgame perfect equilibrium if, in every period, parties cannot gain by not performing, and then playing the worst subgame perfect equilibrium for the cheater. In other words, when breach occurs, the nonperforming party faces the worst equilibrium possible under the rules of the game.

In this framework, the efficiency of an agreement is constrained by the size of the possible punishment. The Folk Theorem formalizes the idea that, as the frequency of interaction increases, eventually the gain from cheating is less than the cost, and hence an efficient agreement can be reached. In this theory, the discount rate between periods represents the frequency of interaction. In this class of models, increasing the discount rate is equivalent to holding the volume of trade constant per period and having more transactions of smaller value within a single period. In that case, the cost of cheating does not change, but because the value of each individual transaction is smaller, the gain from breach falls.

A crucial assumption is that breach can be perfectly observed. One might wonder whether the set of feasible allocations depends on the allocation of the cost of cheating between the two parties. MacLeod and Malcomson (1989) showed that only the total gains from future trade affect the set of feasible allocations. By carefully designing the breach obligation, combined with a bonus payment by the buyer to the seller at the end of each period, parties can choose any allocation of the surplus.

When performance is not perfectly observable, the problem is much more complex. It may no longer be optimal for one party always to perform. Consequently, it is no longer optimal for the breaching party to face the maximal penalty. The modern theory of relational contracts explores the interplay between uncertainty regarding the breach obligation and the possible punishments available in a relationship. In summary, the main technical difference between the theory of damages under relational contracts and damages under contractual instruments in the shadow of the law is that the maximal punishment under a relational contract is limited by the potential gains from future trade. The insights of the contract design and damages literature also apply to relational contracts when the gains from trade are sufficiently large.

Before proceeding to our discussion of damages, it is worthwhile discussing two papers that are often cited as examples of relational contracting, namely, Klein and Leffler (1981) and Shapiro and Stiglitz (1984). These papers do not explicitly address the question of what is an optimal contract. Rather, they begin with an observed contract form and then ask what the market implications are if parties restrict themselves to this contractual instrument. In the case of Klein and Leffer (1981), they consider the simple sales contract: the seller sells a good at a fixed price. They then suppose that product quality is potentially imperfect and that the market can observe product quality in the past. They explore the consequences for a competitive market when buyers shun sellers who have produced low-quality goods in the past. They show that this shunning strategy implies that high-quality sellers will have brand names with positive rents associated with them. Sellers will choose not to supply low-quality goods for fear of losing the return on their brand name.

Shapiro and Stiglitz (1984) assume that firms offer fixed-wage contracts but have the ability to dismiss workers at will. When there is uncertainty regarding worker performance or a delay in observing performance, then under such a contract, employed workers must earn higher utility than do newly unemployed workers (and hence there is involuntary unemployment). As MacLeod and Malcomson (1989) show, involuntary unemployment follows from the assumption about contract form and not from the assumption of costly monitoring (for an excellent discussion of the issues see Carmichael 1989). These papers illustrate an important branch of the literature that explores the properties of observed contractual instruments and how features of the contractual instrument (mainly the price) vary with characteristics of the environment (see also Lafontaine and Slade, this volume). For the most part, it is still an open empirical question why some contract forms are chosen rather than others.

3.2. Remedy Generally

Courts do not automatically enforce contracts; rather, the party harmed by nonperformance invokes the court. As such, legal enforcement is more properly viewed as providing parties with a set of decision rights. This idea has its origin in Aghion and Bolton (1992). They observe that bankruptcy can be viewed as a situation in which the control rights to a firm moves from the owners to the debt holders. Similarly, MacLeod (2007) observes that contract breach can be viewed as providing the harmed party the right to seek damages in a court of law.

Contract law determines the remedy available to an aggrieved party; the parties, through the contract design, assign the right to invoke the court for nonperformance. We can illustrate the problem with a version of the simple buyer-seller example. We also use this example to discuss remedies for contract breach.

Consider a buyer-seller relationship where the seller chooses a level of effort or quality $q > 0$ that determines the probability $\lambda(q, E)$ that there has been performance as a function of q and possibly of other events E that occur after q is chosen. Let B_P be the ex ante benefit from performance, B_B the ex ante benefit if there is breach, and $c(q)$ the cost to the seller of performing ($c(0) = 0$, $c'(q)$, $c''(q) > 0$, $\forall q$). Given a price p, the payoffs to the buyer and seller are

$$U_B(q) = B_P\lambda(q, E) + B_B(1 - \lambda(q, E)) - r_B - p,$$

$$U_S(q) = p - c(q) - r_S.$$

The terms r_S, $r_B \geq 0$ are the reliance expenditures made by the buyer and seller, respectively, after the contractual instrument has been signed, but before trade and production. These investments provide a motivation for writing a contract, as formally modeled by Grout (1984) and Hart and Moore (1988).

In addition to protecting investments, the contract must also provide appropriate incentives for the seller to choose the efficient level of effort or output, q^*, given by

$$(B_P - B_B)\lambda'(q^*, E) = c'(q^*). \tag{1}$$

Suppose that the buyer cannot directly observe effort q, in which case we have a model that is technically identical to a principal-agent model with risk-neutral agents, and hence, from a contract theory perspective, is trivial. We suppose that it is efficient to trade, and hence any state-contingent price is of the form

$$p_s = B_s - R, \quad s \in \{P, B\},$$

which effectively shifts all risk to the seller, and thus it induces the seller to choose the efficient level of effort. The term R is the rent that the buyer obtains from the relationship. It would be set as a function of the relative ex ante bargaining power of the two parties.[32]

This contractual instrument is not a legal document—it merely specifies the transfers as a function of the seller's decision to perform. It supposes either a costless legal system or a world where individuals do not breach their obligations. In practice, this agreement could be implemented in a number of ways. Consider, for example, two contractual instruments that could govern a simple exchange. The first instrument is denoted by p^A. It defines the price that a buyer pays in advance in exchange for a promise by the seller to deliver a good that conforms to the contract specifications. The second contractual instrument, p^P, is the price that the buyer promises to pay the seller on delivery of a conforming good. Notice that neither contractual instrument is complete, in the sense that neither specifies what will happen in the event of breach. Nevertheless, these contractual instruments are very common in practice, and courts are expected to be able to adjudicate the disputes that arise in these cases.

Notice that, though these are very simple contractual instruments, they have quite different properties when viewed as contractual instruments. In the case of instrument p^A, the buyer has paid, and hence the performance obligation rests in the hands of the seller. If she does not perform, then the buyer must sue and must take care to collect evidence regarding the seller's performance. Thus, it is the buyer who must make the investment to sue. If the seller can be shown not to perform, then the courts must determine the appropriate damages.

In the case of instrument p^P the situation is reversed. In this case, once the seller has performed, the buyer must perform her promise to pay. If not, then the seller would have to sue the buyer to collect the amount due. Note that, in the second case, once performance has been verified, then the question of damages is straightforward—the buyer is obliged to pay the amount agreed on, plus possibly any expenses arising from the delay in payment. We use these two generic contractual instruments to discuss the various remedies for breach of contract that have been proposed by the literature.

---

32. Under this contract, we have: $U_B = R - r_B$ and $U_S = B_P\lambda(q, E) + B_B(1 - \lambda(q, E)) - R - r_S - c(q)$.

3.3. Expectation Damages

The rule of expectation damages attempts to measure the loss arising from breach of contract. In the case of contractual instrument p^P, if the buyer does not pay, the loss to the seller is p^P, and hence, expectation damages provides the same remedy as specific performance. In the case of contract p^A, if the seller performs, the buyer obtains a return B_P and a return of B_B if there is breach. The loss due to breach would be $D = B_P - B_B$. As we can see from (1), this rule ensures that the seller has an incentive to choose effort efficiently. Crocker and Masten (1988) provide some evidence that in the case of long-term gas contracts, parties prefer expectation damages as a way of ensuring efficient ex post adaptation to changing conditions.

The rule also provides an incentive for efficient matching. For example, suppose that the seller has another buyer of a good for whom the value is $B' > B_P$. If the seller breaches, she would have to pay the buyer B_P, but she could sell the good for B' for a gain of $B' - B_P$. Thus, she would breach when it is efficient to do so.[33] However, as Schwartz (1979) observes, this well-known argument does not necessarily imply that specific performance is inefficient. In the absence of transaction costs, the seller could always renegotiate the contract to share some of the gains from breach with the buyer.[34] In practice, this argument is problematic, because parties are unlikely to be truthful regarding their valuations; hence, such renegotiation is not likely to be efficient. Myerson and Satterthwaite (1983) have shown that even in the context of a simple exchange for a single good, if parties have private information regarding their valuations and are fully rational, then it is impossible to obtain efficient trade in all cases. Ayres and Talley (1995) build on this result to show how liability rules should be chosen to enhance the efficiency of contract renegotiation.

The early literature on legal-damage rules (Shavell 1980; Rogerson 1984) observes that even though expectation damages result in efficient breach, it may not provide appropriate incentives for relationship-specific investments. These papers are the beginning of a significant economics literature that compares the impact of remedies on the efficiency of a contractual instrument. This literature used the categorization of remedies by Fuller and Perdue (1936). That classic work reviews existing law and suggests that observed remedies can be categorized into three types:

1. Value that the harmed party expected to obtain from the contract or expectation damages in both the legal and economic literatures.

2. The harmed party's reliance on the contract, generally measured by the specific investment r. The economics literature terms these losses "reliance damages."

3. Specific performance, according to which the promisor is ordered to perform the obligation.

The economics literature has accepted these three categories as the prototype representation of U.S. contract law. There are a series of papers, including Chung (1991), Spier and Whinston

---

33. See Hermalin, Katz, and Craswell (2006: 102–114) for a discussion of this well-known result as well as a more comprehensive review of the literature on expectation damages and related measures of damages.

34. Alternatively, the second buyer could purchase from the original buyer.

(1995), Edlin (1996), Edlin and Reichelstein (1996), Che and Chung (1999), and Schweizer (2006), that explore the relative efficiency of these three rules. This approach is convenient, because it allows one to carefully compare these rules under a variety of conditions. Depending on the environment, each of the damage rules may be efficient, but in general the rule of specific performance is typically found to be the most efficient, consistent with prescriptions of legal scholars, such as Schwartz (1979) and Ulen (1984). This observation raises the obvious question of why the courts do not use specific performance.

To begin with, Craswell (2000) observes that the damage rules used in economic models are rather crude representations of the law. In the case of expectation damages, the parties could have avoided court costs by specifying in advance the monetary damages for breach, a practice called "liquidation damages." Moreover, a court cannot force the exchange of a good; we need to ask exactly how to implement the doctrine of specific performance. Given that the best the court can do is impose monetary penalties, why don't the parties avoid court costs by specifying such payments for all possible contingencies—in other words, why do they leave gaps in a contract? Finally, advance specification of the performance obligation is not the only choice available to parties. The parties might instead delegate ex post authority for certain decisions to one of the parties. How are such contracts enforced? In the next three subsections we address each of these concerns in turn.

3.4. Liquidated Damages

Under contractual instrument p^A the seller promises to perform, otherwise there is a breach of contract. If there is nonperformance, the buyer would sue the seller, and under the rule of expectation damages parties should expect a judgment equal to $B_P - B_B$. Equation (1) shows that this remedy provides first-best effort incentives. Going to court to recover $B_P - B_B$ is an expensive exercise. If parties knew the outcome of a court case with certainty, then the costs of litigation could be avoided with an out-of-court settlement, the typical outcome in practice (see Spier 2006).

If the value of performance is private information, then from the Myerson and Satterthwaite (1983) theorem, it may not be possible to avoid conflict and a court case. The parties might adopt a number of solutions to this problem. First, the parties might specify liquidated damages—the amount that the seller should pay in the event of nonperformance. These damages, specified in advance, provide a way for the buyer to signal to the seller her private valuation. In principle, liquidated damages reduces the uncertainty associated with a court case, and hence they increase the prospects for settlement.

In economics, liquidated damages is equivalent to a form of performance pay—the explicit linking of performance to compensation. However, these are two different contractual instruments. A liquidated damages clause substitutes the parties' measure of damages for the default judicial remedy of expectation damages. The clause directs the courts on the measure of damages if breach occurs—if the seller supplies either no goods or nonconforming goods—and the buyer decides to litigate. In principle, the liquidated damages clause should govern but a clause must satisfy several conditions to be enforceable; consequently, the court has substantial discretion in the application of the clause. Indeed, the court will not enforce a penalty clause (a liquidated damages clause that sets the amount of compensation too high).[35]

In contrast, performance pay is a contractual obligation that leaves the court little discretion. If the seller supplies nonperforming goods, that would not be a breach of contract as long as the seller also makes the agreed-upon compensation to the buyer. In this case, breach of contract only occurs over promised transfers, a task for which the courts are generally competent. In economics, the principal-agent models rely exclusively on contracts of this type. This class of models covers a large part of the economics of contract, and so it is worthwhile to discuss their enforceability.

Historically, principal-agent models build on the theory of optimal risk bearing. Risk-averse individuals who face diversifiable risks are expected to purchase insurance. An insurance contract specifies payments to be made when certain events occur.[36]

Agency contracts are particularly applicable to the procurement of services. A physical good is one that can be delivered and inspected before the buyer accepts the good. However, for services, production and delivery are simultaneous, and hence, third parties can never directly observe performance. Rather, one has signals of performance, which might include the amount of apples harvested, monthly sales, number of customer complaints, the amount by which students improve their test scores, and so on. In each of these cases, the principal can link compensation to a measure of performance. Such contracts are also very common in employment. (MacLeod and Parent (1999) find that more than 25% of U.S. workers are on some form of performance pay.)

Holmström (1979) has shown that the optimal contract in a prototypical principal-agent model entails making compensation vary with any useful measure of performance. The question then is whether such a contract is enforceable. In the case of commissions paid to a sales person there has been some litigation regarding the question of whether firms can dismiss employees and then not be required to pay commissions on sales that were completed while the individuals were employees.[37] Many states in the United States have applied the doctrine of good faith and fair dealing to such cases to rule that the firm did indeed have an obligation to make good on such promised payments. More generally, because agency contracts typically require the principal to make monetary payments as a function of well-defined events that are observable by the courts,

35. To be enforceable, a liquidated damages clause must be set at a level that approximates actual damage suffered, and the amount of damages must be, at the time of formation of the contract, uncertain and hence difficult to anticipate. On liquidated damages generally, see American Law Institute (1981: § 375). Goetz and Scott (1977) also provide an introduction to the law.

36. The genesis of the principal-agent model is Arrow's (1963) observation that, in the case of health care, the government is in the best position to insure individuals against the costs of medical care in the event of an accident. However, Pauly (1968) observed that this policy recommendation overlooks an important market incompleteness—namely, these contracts do not control the level of care that individuals use to avoid risks. He argued that insurance contracts create moral hazard: insured individuals have less incentive to take precautions than uninsured persons have. This observation spawned a large literature that today is called either "agency theory" or the "principal-agent problem." See Bolton and Dewatripont (2005: 129–169).

37. See Miles (2000) for a discussion of these doctrines and the extent to which performance contracts are enforceable.

then we would conclude that these contracts are consistent with existing legal regime. We are sure that this conclusion is a great relief for our dear reader (as it was for us), given the importance of agency theory in modern economics.

3.5. Specific Performance

The economics literature generally assumes that contracts are enforceable in the sense that, if a party has an obligation *a,* then the party will in fact do *a.* In legal terms, the economics literature assumes that the default legal remedy is "specific performance." The discussion in the last section has indicated that this assumption is generally false. The standard common law remedy for breach of contract is expectation damages.

Consider first specific performance in the context of the sales contract given by p^P in which the buyer promises to pay p^P on delivery of the good. If Seller delivers and Buyer fails to pay, specific performance merely requires the payment of a sum of money, a task that the courts are competent to do. Notice that the first-best outcome can be achieved with a price $p^P = B_P$ when $\lambda(q^*, E)B_P \geq c(q^*)$. Also notice that the remedy of expectation damages would provide the same outcome.

Now consider the contractual instrument p^A, where the seller promises to deliver a good after payment has been made. Suppose Seller fails to deliver or delivers a good that is not of the appropriate quality. What does specific performance mean in this case? If the contract merely called for the transfer of physical or real property, then the courts could competently enforce the transfer. In the case of real property they would simply order that a transfer has occurred and have this put into public record. At that point the new owner would simply rely on the sheriff's office to enforce her ownership rights. In such cases the courts often use specific performance as a remedy.[38]

What does specific performance mean when the courts cannot directly control the actions of the seller? In these cases, the mechanism design literature, such as Aghion, Dewatripont, and Rey (1994) and Edlin and Reichelstein (1996), observes that the enforcement of specific performance entails the (judicial) threat of penalties that are sufficiently large that the parties choose to perform as promised.[39] If it is the case that, at the effort q^*, one has $\lambda(q^*, E) = 1$, then any penalty greater than $U_S(q^*) - U_S(0) = c(q^*)$ would ensure performance. Notice that this is equivalent to a performance pay contract of the form:

$$P(q) = \begin{cases} p^* & \text{if } q \geq q^* \\ -C & \text{if } q < q^*. \end{cases} \qquad (2)$$

Under this contract, the seller pays a penalty $-C$ if performance is inadequate. Given that rewards are deterministic, the seller can always elect to avoid the penalty by choosing q^*. Such

---

38. See Farnsworth (1999). If the prior owner does not vacate the premises, the sheriff will, on an appropriate order of the court, evict. Similarly, if a losing defendant in a contract action fails to pay the ordered expectation damages, the sheriff, on an appropriate court order, will levy and execute on the defendant's assets to satisfy the judgment.

39. See Edlin and Reichelstein (1996: 482).

a contract might make sense if the buyer wished to ensure performance for a wide variety of costs to the seller. In the absence of a penalty, the seller might choose to default. Such contracts are implicitly used in economic models where the goal is to implement a price-quantity pairing where there is possibly some asymmetric information (e.g., Maskin and Riley 1984; Laffont and Tirole 1986).

As Edlin and Reichelstein (1996) observe, this rule is easy to implement in practice—the courts need only verify whether performance occurred and then impose a sufficiently large penalty if not. They then provide conditions under which specific performance can ensure efficient investment and trade, significantly extending the earlier results of Rogerson (1984) and Shavell (1984). The benefit of the rule is that it provides a method for enforcing effort revelation when the courts cannot observe relevant information or when one party is credit constrained.

However, the *penalty doctrine* (see Farnsworth 1999) directs courts not to enforce liquidated damage clauses that require payments (e.g., C in the contractual instrument given in (2)) that are out of proportion to actual damages. This doctrine allows courts to reduce or waive liquidated damages.[40] This rule can be used to explain some features of observed contractual instruments. As an example, consider long-term contracts for inputs to a manufacturing process. Joskow (1988) describes in some detail the market for the supply of coal to electric utilities. If parties are risk neutral, then in principle they could agree to terms that might allow the contract price for coal to vary significantly from the spot price. An interesting feature of observed contract prices is that they closely follow the spot price for coal. This raises the question of why parties engage in costly contract design, rather than use the spot price. MacLeod and Malcomson (1993) provide a solution to this problem: if each party needs to make a relationship-specific investment that affects their own payoffs, but not the other's (the so-called "self-investment" case), then it is efficient to have a fixed-price contract. However, over time the price of coal can fluctuate a great deal. Parties could put into place large penalties to enforce trade at the contract price, but these may not be enforceable under the penalty doctrine. MacLeod and Malcomson (1993) show that if parties can index the contractual instruments so that it follows the market price, then it is unnecessary to put in place penalties for breach of contract. Moreover, parties would still have the incentive to make efficient investments into relationship-specific capital, because their investments do not affect the price paid or received in the future. Edlin (1996) has another solution that may work in some circumstances. He shows that Cadillac contracts that call for very high performance can ensure efficient investment under the rule of expectation damages.

These results do not resolve the issue of why courts are reluctant to enforce penalty clauses. Thus, there is an unresolved tension between the results of Aghion, Dewatripont, and Rey (1994) and Edlin and Reichelstein (1996) showing that the doctrine of specific performance allows for the implementation of efficient arrangements, while in practice courts are reluctant to enforce such contracts. One possible reason for this reluctance is that courts must adjudicate all disputes, including disputes involving poorly drafted and incomplete contracts. We now turn to this issue.

---

40. See Posner and Rosenfield (1977) for an early analysis of these issues.

3.6. Specific Performance and Expectation Damages Compared

Both Schwartz (1979) and Ulen (1984), distinguished legal scholars, have argued that the courts should use specific performance rather than expectation damages as the default remedial rule. In an important paper on mechanism design, Aghion, Dewatripont, and Rey (1994) show in a model with hold-up that the rule of specific performance can ensure efficient investment and exchange. Schwartz and Scott (2003) reiterate this point in a law review. Indeed, the economics literature suggests that specific performance has superior efficiency properties compared to expectation damages.

This conclusion, however, may underestimate judicial and party ingenuity. Consider the case of construction contracts. The complexity of construction presents a particularly challenging environment to achieve first-best outcomes even with specific performance. Bajari and Tadelis (2001) introduce a simple and elegant way to formally introduce unforeseen events into a model of construction contracts. The idea is that the time and money spent drafting a contract can be viewed as relationship-specific investment in the quality of the contractual instrument. Let I be the investment in planning, and let $\rho(I)$ be the probability that only foreseen events occur. It is assumed that $\rho' > 0$, and hence the quality of planning increases with I. With probability $1 - \rho(I)$ an unforeseen event occurs. They then compare two contract forms—fixed price and cost plus. Under a fixed-price contract the seller is responsible for delivering an acceptable product at the agreed-on price. Thus, the seller receives all the returns from any cost-saving actions.

In contrast, under a cost-plus contract, the buyer pays all costs of production, thereby reducing the incentives to the seller of making unobserved cost-reducing investments. If all events are foreseeable, then the fixed-price contract implements the first-best, whereas if events are unforeseeable, then the cost-plus contract is more efficient. Thus, if the costs of planning are sufficiently low that unforeseen events occur with low probability, then a fixed-price contract is optimal; the opposite holds with respect to cost-plus contracts. The model delivers a theory of contract form as a function of the complexity of the environment, as measured by the cost of planning.

Bajari and Tadelis (2001) assume, following the literature, that courts enforce agreement with specific performance as given. Chakravarty and MacLeod (2009) build on their model and explore how such contracts are enforced. They begin with the structure of the American Institute of Architects (AIA) form of construction contracts.

This class of contractual instruments is interesting, because they are widely used in the U.S. construction industry and have evolved over 100 years in response to both experience in the field and the outcome of litigation involving construction disputes. Hence, these contractual instruments are likely to satisfy the economists' assumption that the form of observed contractual instruments can be explained as an efficient solution to the problem of implementing trade, given transaction costs and the characteristics of the contracting parties. Chakravarty and MacLeod (2009) show that these contracts can indeed be viewed as efficient under the following conditions:

1. The buyer's design is costly in the sense of Bajari and Tadelis (2001).

2. The seller's investment in cost reduction is not observable, though realized costs are observable.

3. Buyer's preferences are private information, and they can change between the time of contract and project implementation.

4. Courts use expectation damages but may excuse performance.

In practice construction must occur in the shadow of the law, and it is natural to ask whether efficient trade is possible within existing law. The literature on mechanism design reviewed above suggests that specific performance may be a necessary ingredient for efficient trade. Chakravarty and MacLeod (2009) find that this is not the case—these contractual instruments are able to implement the efficient allocation with a generalized version of expectation damages:

$$\text{Damages} = \text{Foreseeability} \times \text{Expectation},$$

where Foreseeability is a number between 0 (unforeseen) and 1 (perfectly foreseen) representing the extent to which a loss is anticipated. If an event is unforeseeable, and/or impractical to remedy, then the law excuses the breaching party from performance. In contrast, if the event is foreseen, then the rule of expectation damages applies. Both these extremes are consistent with current law. The rule is more general because, when an event is only partially foreseeable, then damages should be reduced. This rule is implemented in the AIA forms by leaving the damages in some cases to be determined by mutual consent.

Thus, even within the economics of contract literature, the superiority of specific performance as a remedy remains an open question. The resolution of the debate over the appropriate default remedy will likely entail a better understanding of the interplay between the fact-finding function of the courts and the contractual environment. Notice, for example, that the rule of specific performance can lead to opportunistic behavior on the part of the seller. If the seller learns that the buyer has had an unfortunate event (say, her plant burns down), then she can take advantage of the buyer's low valuation b to threaten delivery under the contract in order to extract a larger damage payment. If one can anticipate such behavior, then the contract can be design to mitigate its costs. If benefits and costs are private information, then as Myerson and Satterthwaite (1983) have shown, it is not possible to implement the ex post efficient allocation.

One of the messages of the literature on asymmetric information is that there are inevitably costs to revealing information. There is a growing literature that uses models of asymmetric information to understand the process of litigation.[41] This literature is not yet integrated into the literature on contract design. Hence, we conclude that contracts that vary with well-defined performance measures are in general enforceable. However, contracts that entail large penalty payments or rely on specific performance are in general not enforceable.

3.7. Summary

The basic message of this section is that the economic theory of contract does not rely on the complex institution that is contract law. For the standard principal-agent problem this does not entail great loss of generality. Performance pay contracts are in general enforced. However, more recent models that rely on strong forms of specific investment are not in general consistent with existing law.

---

41. See Cooter and Rubinfeld (1989) and Spier (2006) for excellent reviews of the literature.

This observation may help explain the tension that exists between the property rights approach to the theory of the firm (Grossman and Hart 1986; Rajan and Zingales 1998; and Hart and Moore 1999) and the mechanism design approach to contract (Moore 1992; Maskin and Tirole 1999; Tirole 1999). The former implicitly recognizes that contracts may be limited in their ability to allocate bargaining power, something that can be better achieved with ownership rights.

Parties to a contract are concerned with ensuring that they are able to rely on the contract and thus make appropriate relationship-specific investments. In addition, there is always an element of asymmetric information between parties and the courts that may also lead to transaction costs that may be reduced with the appropriate allocation of bargaining power. Rogerson (1992) has made some progress on integrating asymmetric information and hold-up, but much work remains. In particular, the contract literature has not incorporated the fact-finding activity of a court case into contract design. In the next section we discuss the literature that explores these activities in more detail.

4. Adjudication

Section 3 examined the shadow cast by the substantive remedial rules of contract law.[42] This section examines the judicial role in dispute resolution. Resolution of a contract dispute requires a court to determine what obligations the parties have and whether any obligation has been breached. The first task requires the court to interpret the contractual instrument. The second task requires the court to determine what in fact happened. Phrased differently, contract disputes may arise for two distinct reasons. The parties may disagree about what happened; in economic terms, they disagree about the realized state of the world (including the actions undertaken by each party). Or the parties may disagree about the content of their obligations.

Disagreement about the state of the world may arise even when contractual instruments are complete. Disagreement about the obligations of the parties, in contrast, assumes either that the contractual instrument is incomplete or otherwise defective (perhaps ambiguous or inconsistent).

We organize our discussion into two parts. Section 4.1 examines the literature on fact finding. As virtually nothing has been written about the role of the court as a finder of facts in

---

42. We ignore here a substantial literature on the shadow cast by rules of bankruptcy. The law of bankruptcy looms when one party cannot afford to make a transfer required by a contract. In the case of agency theory, given that the state provides a complete description of the environment, this constraint is anticipated and incorporated into the design of the contractual instrument. See Sappington (1983) and Innes (1990) for two early important contributions and Lewis and Sappington (1999) for a more recent contribution and discussion of this literature. The contract design ensures that, even in this case, there is no real role for the courts, because the transfers are always feasible. The contract design must reflect this constraint. There is a vast literature in corporate finance that explores the consequence for contract design when parties face limited liability. See Gale and Hellwig (1985), Bolton and Dewatripont (2005) and Doornik (2010) for a comprehensive review of this vast literature. These papers can be viewed as contributing to our understanding of contracting in the shadow of the law, where the shadow is cast by the rule that limits penalties to the financial wealth of defendants. This limitation was not always the case. In the past debtors might be sent to prison or face other physical penalties. It is an open question why there has been a historical evolution toward limiting liability to one's assets. See Hansmann (this volume) for further discussion on the historical evolution of limits to financial liability.

contract disputes, we review a related literature on fact finding generally. Section 4.2 addresses interpretation.

4.1. Fact Finding

4.1.1. *Fact Finding in the Economics of Incomplete Contracts*
The economic literature on contract classifies facts into four classes: verifiable, jointly observable, observable by one party but not the other, and neither verifiable nor observable.[43] A verifiable fact is one that is known (or knowable) publicly, that is, to both parties and to any third-party adjudicator. A jointly observable fact is known to both parties to the contract but is not publicly available. Obviously, a fact that is observable by one party but not the other occurs in contractual environments with asymmetric information. Some facts (e.g., the precise state of the world) may be not observable. The existence of observable but nonverifiable facts constrains parties in the drafting of contractual instruments (and courts in the imposition of contractual obligations). An obligation cannot be conditioned on a fact that is not verifiable.

This classification is very extreme. Either a fact is verifiable (generally at 0 cost), or it is not verifiable (at any cost). The situation in actual exchange environments is more nuanced. A fact may be more or less verifiable at greater or lesser cost. One might say that a "more verifiable" fact is one for which the court or other third party receives a more accurate signal. Moreover, courts can use burdens of proof and burdens of persuasion to influence the quality of signals that parties provide as well as distributing the consequences of erroneous signals.

Before considering the structure of judicial fact finding, we note that much of the economic literature investigates the consequences of nonverifiability for the form of a contractual instrument. One might, for example, understand the entire principal-agent literature this way. Agent effort is not verifiable (nor observable to the principal); consequently, the parties require a contract that conditions the agent's wage on other verifiable facts.

4.1.2. *Judicial Fact Finding*
A contractual instrument specifies, against the legal backdrop, the obligations of each party. Often the obligations of the parties are state contingent: what each party must do varies with the state of the world. Resolution of every contract dispute thus requires determination of the actions that each party took and of the realized event.

Fact-finding procedures apply across a wide of range of types of disputes, and they are governed by distinct bodies of law (that generally go under the names of "civil" or "criminal" procedure and evidence).[44] We may assess these procedures along two dimensions: their accuracy and their cost. In an ideal world, fact finding would be perfectly accurate and costless. In the real world, the invocation of courts is costly, and courts themselves sometimes err in their fact finding.[45]

As we discuss below, the economic theory of contract generally distinguishes observable actions from verifiable ones. Courts costlessly observe verifiable actions with perfect accuracy;

43. A more complete account would include dates: when a fact is known by whom.
44. We ignore some evidentiary rules that are specific to contract law, such as the statute of frauds, which requires writing to enforce certain classes of contracts. On the statute of frauds, see Farnsworth (2004: 353–410).
45. We note in passing that the parties may, in the contractual instrument, alter the usual default fact-finding procedures.

courts cannot observe unverifiable actions at any cost.[46] Most actions and events, in contrast, are only verifiable at some cost and to some degree of accuracy.

A few models—Milgrom and Roberts (1986), Shin (1998), and Dewatripont and Tirole (1999)—examine how accuracy varies with the fact-finding procedure. These models contrast adversarial procedures (in which each party presents evidence favorable to itself) with inquisitorial procedures (in which a nonpartisan agent gathers evidence). These models identify conditions under which adversarial procedures dominate inquisitorial ones.

These models require further elaboration to yield insights for an economic theory of contract. In Milgrom and Roberts (1986), the parties are fully informed about the state of the world. In the legal context, in contrast, each party generally has only partial and asymmetric information about the state.

All three papers address questions of imperfect and asymmetric information. Moreover, Shin's (1998) model addresses adjudication directly. From a legal perspective, however, these models are in a reduced form. Each assumes that the agents and the principal acquire information about the correct final decision that in Shin is dichotomous, whereas in Dewatripont and Tirole (1999) it is trichotomous. The decision in Shin thus corresponds to the disposition of an adjudication (i.e., the judgment that the plaintiff prevails or fails). The disposition in a contract dispute depends both on the state of the world and on the obligations imposed by the contract. These obligations, however, result from the process of interpretation, discussed in Section 4.2.

Common law adjudicatory institutions reflect this structure. Facts in contract disputes in the United States are typically found by juries. Judges determine the law; that is, judges interpret the contractual instrument and determine the contractual obligations of the parties.

4.2. Contract Interpretation

Virtually all models in both the economics of contract and the economic analysis of contract law make two critical assumptions about contractual behavior. First, the models assume that contractual instruments are perfectly drafted: contractual instruments are clear and consistent on their face. Second, the models assume that parties to the contract have foresight and correctly anticipate the consequences of their actions, including those of the court. Neither assumption is warranted: contractual instruments are inevitably incomplete, unclear, and often inconsistent. They require interpretation. Moreover, the practice of interpretation is not completely transparent. As Goetz and Scott (1980) observe, courts have a complex set of rules that often entail changing clearly specified performance obligations.

The economic theory of incomplete contracts does admit one important role for interpretation. When an uncontracted-for event occurs, a court must fill the gap in the incomplete contractual instrument. The court must specify the obligations of the parties to determine whether breach has occurred. The gap-filling ruling is often called a "default rule."

The literature on incomplete contracts and that on the economic analysis of contract law have studied default rules from two complementary perspectives. In the incomplete contracts literature, this study has been implicit rather than explicit; it occurs in the analysis of the causes of the incompleteness of contractual instruments. The economic analysis of contract law, in

---

46. The economics literature treats unverifiable actions as a constraint on the contractual instrument.

contrast, has generally asked which default rules provide the optimal background against which parties should draft their incomplete contractual instruments. We discuss the choice of optimal default rules in Section 4.2.2 and the role of interpretation in contractual incompleteness in Section 4.2.4.

Gap filling, however, is not the sole purpose of interpretation. In Section 4.2.4, we discuss the sparse literature that adopts a more general approach to interpretation. As noted in Section 2.2, we can understand interpretation as a mapping from some set of interpretative materials that include the contractual instrument (but may include other texts and actions) into a set of contractual obligations for each possible event.

In economics, the dividing line between contract theory and other areas of the theory of organization (e.g., corporate governance or human resource management) typically turns on the notion that courts merely enforce the terms of a written agreement. In contrast, corporate governance focuses on the design of decision rights for officers of the corporation. In fact, a legally binding contractual instrument must explicitly deal with the allocation of decision rights over the relationship. That is, parties to a legally binding agreement provide each other the right to take the other party to a court of law for the adjudication of the contractual instrument in the event of a breach. In the absence of courts, parties would have to rely on other instruments to enforce an agreement, such as reputation effects; threats to reduce trade in the future; or even possibly threats of violence, as discussed in MacLeod (2007).

4.2.1. What Is Interpretation?

In the most basic sense, a contract is a complete list of terms k_θ that specify, for each state θ of the world, the obligation a_θ of each party: in state θ, the seller must undertake action s_θ and the buyer must undertake action b_θ. A contractual instrument, in contrast, is a partial list of terms. The list of terms in a contractual instrument is partial in at least two senses. Most obviously, the instrument may not specify an obligation for every state of the world. In addition, a contractual instrument may not fully specify the obligations of each party even when it covers a state of the world. Interpretation is the process through which the court completes the contractual instrument to yield a contract.

The contractual instrument and its partial list of terms may present several different interpretive problems:

1. Missing terms. The realized state θ may not be on the partial list of states included in the contractual instrument.

2. Ambiguous terms. A contractual instrument may specify an agent's obligation ambiguously, or it may specify the event ambiguously.

3. Inconsistent terms. There is an event E for which are two clauses k_i, k_j that specify conflicting obligations. If event E occurs, it is not clear which action, b_i or b_j, should be carried out.

4. Impossible terms. A term imposes an obligation that is impossible to perform in the realized event, even though that event is contemplated in the terms.

5. Unwanted terms. The contractual instrument may, for state θ, specify obligations that, when θ is realized, the parties do not prefer to some other obligations.

Each of these defects present an interpretive problem for the court. As economic models typically assume, suppose that the model parties use an accurate representation of their relationship. Then these defects cannot occur. As a consequence, though there is a substantial amount of law arising from these five contractual defects, there is little economic analysis of these problems. We discuss each of these interpretive tasks in turn.

When the contractual instrument is missing a term, it is, in the most basic sense, incomplete. The statement that "the *contract* is incomplete" is, in contrast, a rather crude and not particularly helpful statement. After all, a simple rule of interpretation ensures that every contractual instrument is complete. Given any contractual instrument K, let E^c be the set of states for which there is no specified obligation. If an event $E \subset E^c$ occurs, then we can complete the contractual instrument by supposing that neither party has an obligation in this event. As one can always do this, one can always suppose, following Ayres and Gertner (1992), that contracts are obligationally complete. Hence, for each contractual instrument, either parties perform as specified in the agreement, or one party believes there is breach of contract, in which case she has the right to an adjudication.

Notice that, when $E \subset E^c$, a court could adopt a different rule to complete the contractual instrument. The court might, for instance, require each party to perform the obligations that are specified in some other term k. Whatever specification the court implies is called a "default rule." We discuss default rules in Section 4.2.2.

A term may be ambiguous in two different ways. Typically, a term k in a contractual instrument does not address a single state θ. Rather, it groups states into events E. Given ordinary language, however, it may be unclear whether some state θ is in E. Alternatively, the contractual instrument may have described the obligation of one of the parties ambiguously. The parties may describe a party's obligation in at least two different ways. Ideally, each term would specify a single obligation of the party, but often, a contractual instrument gives the party discretion. The term might provide a list of tasks that the agent may perform. Or the parties may describe a performance that the agent must accomplish. Suppose a contractual instrument simply states "deliver the fresh fish by 3 p.m. today to 230 Mercer Street, New York City." This instrument uses a performance to describe the action set; it does not list the multitude of ways that the agent might actually deliver the fish by 3 p.m.—by cart at 2:59, by bicycle at 2:58, etc.[47] The manner of specification may affect the interpretive task for the court. It may be unclear whether the action undertaken by the party falls within the description of the obligation.

A contractual instrument may also include inconsistent terms. For example, the contractual instrument may specify that the seller supply 100 units when the price of wheat is less than $5 per bushel and 50 units when the price of corn is greater than $4 per bushel. If the price of each is $4.50 per bushel, is the seller in compliance when she supplies 50 units? A court must resolve these inconsistencies.

Impossible terms are a particularly egregious example of an inconsistent term. This is a very common case for simple contractual instruments, such as an agreement to supply q at a price p. Events may make it impossible to supply q. In the well-known English case *Caldwell v. Taylor*, for example, the plaintiff had rented the defendant's opera house for a performance on a given

---

47. Notice that these descriptions are incomplete. A complete description of the tasks would identify the route the deliveryman took and the type of cart or bicycle he might use.

date; shortly before that date, the opera house burned down, rendering performance of the defendant's contractual obligation impossible.

When economists speak of incomplete contracts, they often mean contracts with unwanted terms: the parties have, for some state θ, specified obligations that are inefficient. There are some actions available to each party that would yield a higher total surplus to be divided among them.[48] The court must now decide whether to reform the contractual instrument and require the parties to undertake the efficient actions rather than those specified in the contractual instrument.

4.2.2. Default Rules

A default rule determines the obligations of the parties when an event occurs about which the contractual instrument is silent. To reach this conclusion, of course, the court must first interpret the contractual instrument as not having addressed the realized event. Two questions arise: Why is the contractual instrument silent? How should the court specify the missing term?

At first thought, the silence of a contractual instrument is perplexing. Consider, for example, a paradigm supply example. Suppose a caterer contracts for the delivery of fresh fish to a location for an event in the afternoon, at an agreed-on price p. The contractual instrument is very simple: it requires the supplier to deliver by 3 p.m. and emphasizes the importance of timely delivery, because the fish is for an important event. Now suppose the normally reliable supplier is involved in a traffic accident and fails to deliver the fish, which results in irreparable harm to the caterer's reputation for reliability.

The court must determine what damages, if any, should be assessed against the supplier for breaching the promise to deliver the fish. Our example presents a classic problem of an incomplete contractual instrument. To an economist, the prevalence of these disputes is puzzling, because the parties surely understand that accidents sometimes happen. The dispute does not arise from asymmetric information. As the accident was foreseen, why haven't the parties included terms in the agreement that cover such cases? A complete contractual instrument would have clauses that specify payments that would be made when there is nonperformance. In this section we review the various models that have been introduced to explain why contractual instruments are incomplete. In Section 4.2.4 we discuss the role of the law in completing such incomplete contractual instruments.

Four reasons have been offered for the silence of contractual instruments. First, Goetz and Scott (1980) suggest that if breach is a very low probability event, then parties may find that the ex ante cost of negotiating breach terms is greater than the benefit. In this case, they choose to delegate the damage decision to the court (for a formalization of this argument see Shavell 1984). In these cases, they would like the court to set damages equal to the amount they would have agreed on ex ante. As we shall see in Section 4.2.4, costs of drafting provide a general answer to the first question of silence and unwanted terms.

Second, contractual instruments may be strategically incomplete. Ayres and Gertner (1989), Aghion and Hermalin (1990), and Spier (1992) show that a buyer with asymmetric information

---

48. This inefficiency might arise in two ways. The parties may simply have made a mistake and specified the wrong acts. Or the contract term may be overbroad; it specifies a uniform action for all states in some event E when efficiency requires that the actions differ.

about her own valuation may not include a term that specifies liquidated damages, fearing that it will reveal how much she values the good. The seller could use this information to increase the price. Hermalin and Katz (1993) suggest that courts should allow parties to use fill-in-the-blank contractual instruments to enhance performance.

Third, and related, Bernheim and Whinston (1998) show that parties may choose to leave contractual instruments incomplete because doing so will increase future gains from trade and thus increase the set of outcomes that can be supported by a subgame perfect equilibria. The parties can then place more reliance on the value of a future relationship for enforcement and thereby avoid costly enforcement via a court. Scott (2003) provides some evidence from case law that is consistent with the results of Bernheim and Whinston (1998); namely, parties do seem to use contract incompleteness to enhance the set of feasible allocations. Baker, Gibbons, and Murphy (1994) have what can be viewed as a countervailing result. Namely, they show that if one adds a legally binding agency instrument, then it can increase the set of self-enforcing agreements. Using this idea, Schmidt and Schnitzer (1995) show that when one party breaches a relational contract, then, rather than separate, the parties might choose to use a contractual instrument that is enforceable in court. This option would reduce the cost of breaching and thereby reduce the set of agreements enforceable with a relational contract.

Finally, Bolton and Faure-Grimaud (2005) introduce an explicit planning model and work out how these costs give rise to the incompleteness of contractual instruments. Tirole (2009) interprets the cost of planning as a form of limited cognition and then explores the consequence of planning costs or limited cognition on contract design. He shows that, if one can hide one's information, then the introduction of limited cognition can lead to adverse selection, as in the model of Spier (1992).

The answer to the second question of the judical response to the silence of the contractual instrument is equally complex but less developed. The complexity arises because contractual parties will bargain in the shadow of the law. The content of the default rules will determine whether parties contract over specified events or leave the instrument silent. Change the default rule, and one changes the content of a contractual instrument. Shavell (1984) shows that, in principle, courts can choose default rules that allow short contractual instruments to induce optimal contractual behavior.

In practice, the actual design of specific default rules is controversial. A prominent view is that courts should fill in gaps using so-called "majoritarian defaults." Under a majoritarian default rule, the court supplies the term that the majority of individuals would prefer. Economic analysts of contract law justify this choice on the grounds that it minimizes drafting costs (Goetz and Scott 1983). Given that the majority of contracts are not litigated, it is not at all obvious that such a notion is well defined or knowable to contracting parties.

Even if knowable, the determination of the optimal default rule ex post is challenging. Mechanism design theory reveals the inherent tension between ex post and ex ante efficiency. The implementation of ex ante efficient contracts often entails the use of actions that are sometimes ex post inefficient. If an event occurs that is not addressed in the contractual instrument, how does one tell if it is a foreseen event that parties have delegated to the courts to fill or one that is unforeseen? If the event is unforeseen, then as Hart (1990) observes, the consequences of reaching that state can have no effect on ex ante decisions. In that case, the efficient rule is always to choose an ex post efficient allocation. As we have discussed above, a defining feature of expectation damages is that it is an attempt to achieve ex post efficiency. Hence, though the rule of expectation damages does not necessarily achieve ex ante efficiency, the fact that it approximates an ex post efficient allocation makes it an appropriate rule for unforeseen gaps in a contractual instrument.

Ayres and Gertner (1989, 1992) and Bebchuk and Shavell (1991) argued that, in contractual environments with asymmetric information, courts should adopt a penalty default that induces the informed party to reveal her private information. These papers consider models with two types of buyers and assume that the optimal level of seller's investment is a function of the buyer's type. The buyer's type is assumed to be private information. The authors show that a default rule that penalized buyers with a high type would, under the appropriate circumstances, induce low-type buyers to reveal their type. This model, however, failed to clearly distinguish penalty from majoritarian defaults. If low-type buyers constituted a majority of the buyer population, then they would be indifferent between the two rules considered by the court.

4.2.3. Unwanted Terms

The economic literature on incomplete contracts has offered an explanation of the presence of unwanted terms. They may arise simply because of the complexity of the contractual environment. This complexity requires that the parties invest time and resources into the creation of a contractual instrument.

Defining exactly what one means by "complex" remains an open question, or more precisely, there are many definitions of complexity that depend on context. The formal model of contract we describe above supposes that a contractual instrument is a collection of event-obligation pairs. Events are subsets of the state space, which even for very simple problems becomes astronomically large (see Williamson (1975: 21); MacLeod 2002). Thus, even with small costs of adding clauses, contractual instruments are likely to be very incomplete. This idea is formalized in the work of Townsend (1979) and Dye (1985) in the context of a simple risk-sharing contract. They show that the fixed costs of adding terms implies that there can be only a finite number of events specified in any contractual instrument. This finite number of terms partitions an infinite state space into a finite number of events. Consequently, it lumps together a number of states. An ideal contract would require distinct acts for some of these states; the contractual instrument has produced an overbroad term that may require the inappropriate actions in some realization, and thus the first-best outcome cannot be achieved.

Rather then exogenously fixing the cost of adding an event, Anderlini and Felli (1994, 1999) endogenize these costs with a model of computational complexity. They also show that the optimal contractual instrument trades off the cost of planning against contractual completeness. Battigalli and Maggi (2002) extend this work and discuss how contract complexity affects the choice between rigid and flexible contract terms. In their model, the parties may be unable to specify the optimal action.

This literature derives results on contractual form by assuming an interpretive practice of the courts. Specifically, the literature assumes that a court will enforce the contractual instrument as written: it will not reform the instrument and substitute ex post the term that the parties would in fact want. Of course, courts may not adopt this interpretive practice. Section 4.2.4 suggests that this interpretive practice is in fact not optimal.

4.2.4. Interpretation Generally

The focus on default rules arises naturally in a world in which contracting parties are fully rational and have perfect foresight. Interpretation will play a larger role in worlds where agents err and draft defective contractual instruments.

Even within the limits of perfectly foresighted parties, optimal interpretation requires more than simply filling gaps. Shavell (2007) formalizes interpretation as a function from the set of contractual instruments into itself. An interpretive method takes the contractual instrument—a list of pairs of events and obligations—into another list of event-obligation pairs.[49]

To understand the role of interpretation, we must consider the drafting options available to the parties. Consider some state θ. The parties may draft a specific term that specifies obligations for θ only; they may draft a general term that specifies obligations for some event E with $\theta \in E$, or the parties may ignore θ and leave a gap in the contractual instrument. Both gaps and general terms arise because it is costly to draft a term.

It follows immediately that the optimal method of interpretation has several properties: (1) specific terms are enforced literally; (2) gaps are filled with majoritarian defaults; and (3) general terms are, in some cases, overridden—the majoritarian default rule may be applied to some $\theta \in E$. These results hold for a wide class of exchange environments. There are, however, several caveats. First, there is no renegotiation. Second, there is perfect contract enforcement. Finally, it is not obvious how to link the formal language in this model to observed phenomena. What is a majoritarian default, and how can it be measured? In fact, if these concepts were well defined, a contract could simply be prefaced by directions to the court that they should fill gaps with majoritarian defaults. The difficulty is that the real work of the courts is to figure out what is a majoritarian default, something about which the theory is currently silent.

4.2.5. Delegation, Renegotiation, and Interpretation

Interpretation determines the obligations of the parties to a contract ex post. There are two other mechanisms for the ex post specification of obligations that serve as partial substitutes for judicial interpretation of contractual instruments. Unlike judicial interpretation, these two ex post methods—delegation and renegotiation—have received extensive treatment in the economic literature.

Each of these three methods permits the parties to impose or to alter an obligation ex post. They differ in the identification of the agent that determines the content of the ex post obligation. Delegation gives one of the parties the exclusive right to determine the obligation, perhaps within limits specified in the contractual instrument. Renegotiation permits the parties jointly to determine the content of the obligation ex post. Under interpretation, a third party, the court, has the sole power to specify ex post the content of the obligation.[50]

Despite this common attribute, interpretation differs in one important respect: interpretation is always available. Delegation (and the decisions of the delegate) and renegotiation occur

---

49. As Shavell observes and we noted in Section 2.2, an interpretive method might take more than the text of the contractual instrument as its domain: the court might refer to additional texts and actions to determine the obligations of the parties.

50. A contractual instrument might identify a third party other than the court. Many contractual instruments provide for arbitration, a third-party mechanism.

in the shadow of the law. It is important to understand how legal institutions shape the operation of delegation and renegotiation. The extent and operation of delegation in a contractual instrument only has the range and force permitted by a court after interpretation. Similarly, the outcome of a renegotiation depends on the point of disagreement, and that point is determined by the interpretive practice of the court and the remedial rules of contract law.

We focus on delegation of authority. As Lafontaine and Slade (this volume) observe, contractual instruments commonly include an allocation of control rights or authority. We shall see that the reasons for such delegation mirror the reasons that provoke interpretation. This literature may thus shed light on how best to model interpretive questions.

There are essentially three reasons for the allocation of authority to one party or another: unforeseen or costly-to-foresee contingencies, asymmetric information, and the allocation of ex post bargaining power.

The first formal model of authority, indeed the first modern contract model, is due to Simon (1951).[51] He considered a model in which parties sign a contractual instrument, the buyer learns the state of nature, and then the level of output that the seller is to provide the buyer is determined. Formally, the optimal allocation $\{q(x),\, p\}$ solves

$$\max_{\{q(x),\, p\}} E\{B(x, q(x))\} - p,$$

subject to

$$p - E\{C(q(x))\} \geq u^0,$$

where x is a random variable, $C(q)$ is the cost of producing q, $B(x, q)$ the benefit of q in state x, p is the price, and u^0 is the seller's outside option. Simon (1951) supposes that x is not contractible and is known only to the buyer. Hence, the buyer is constrained to choose between two contractual instruments. The first is a sales contract, where price p and quantity q are set in advance. The second is an employment contract, a contractual instrument in which the seller (employee) agrees to supply any amount in a set Q at a price p. The benefit of this contractual instrument is that the buyer can adjust q as a function of information received after the contractual instrument is signed.[52]

In terms of enforcement, notice that the employment contract has two elements. First, the buyer, after observing x, creates a performance obligation $q(x)$ for the seller. If the seller does not perform, then the seller has breached. In employment relationships, such breach does not typically lead to damages but to the dismissal of the employee. Thus, the employment contract is enforceable only to the extent that dismissal is a sufficiently large penalty. A second element to the contractual instrument (i.e., the requirement that $q(x) \in Q$) might be enforced by requiring that the seller can only be dismissed with just cause. If the employer asks for an action outside of the set Q, then the seller has a right to refuse to carry out such actions.

---

51. Notions of authority and control are also central to the theory of the firm (see Gibbons 2005).

52. Simon has in mind an elemental theory of bounded rationality that is captured by the hypothesis that x cannot be explicitly contracted on—a theme that the profession would not explore again until the 1980s. The main result is that when uncertainty is sufficiently important (variance of x is sufficiently large), then the employment contract is most efficient; otherwise, parties will use a sales contract.

An obvious application of the model is to the theory of the firm—a theory that predicts when contracts are within the firm and when they are between firms. Alchian and Demsetz (1972) argued that Simon's employment contract could not be construed as an explanation for why we have firms. They observe that the buyer and seller are free to reach any agreement they wish, and should circumstances change, the contract terms can be renegotiated. Thus, as MacLeod (2002) shows formally, the introduction of renegotiation ensures that Simon's sales contract can always achieve the first-best outcome. This result suggests that, for a complete model of authority, one needs to add additional ingredients. One such ingredient is asymmetric information.

There are two ways in which asymmetric information may lead to an allocation of authority rights. The first of these has its roots in Williamson's (1975) idea that contractual relations are plagued by ex post opportunistic behavior that leads to costly contract renegotiation. These costs are formally captured in the Myerson and Satterthwaite (1983) model. If there is two-sided asymmetric information, and one is not sure if it is efficient to trade, then it is not possible to implement the efficient allocation. Ayres and Talley (1995) and McKelvey and Page (2002) show that one way to enhance the efficiency of bargaining with two-sided asymmetric information is to modify the status quo point in the event of a disagreement.

Asymmetric information is often invoked to explain why there may be costly contract negotiation. A less emphasized implication is that investing in more information can reduce negotiation costs. In particular, if there is one-sided asymmetric information, then it is possible to achieve an efficient allocation by allocating all bargaining power to the informed party. Chakravarty and MacLeod (2009) note that this observation is consistent with the standard clauses in AIA form contracts that allocate authority for design changes to the buyer, while requiring the buyer to compensate the seller for any measured out-of-pocket costs arising from the change. This rule makes sense, because although in principle one can measure construction costs with careful bookkeeping, the subjective valuation a buyer assigns to design is difficult, if not impossible, to measure.

This difficulty is reflected in the common law enforcement of sales contracts that place an obligation on sellers to respond to changes in delivery terms requested by the buyers, and it provides an explanation of why specific performance is not used in these cases. It is efficient to grant authority to the buyer to modify her requirements, while protecting the seller with expectation damages that ensure her profits are not reduced by the buyer's actions.

The United States Uniform Commercial Code is quite explicit regarding damages when the buyer refuses to accept delivery of goods:

§ 2-708. Seller's Damages for Nonacceptance or Repudiation.
    (1) Subject to subsection (2) and to Section 2-723:
    (a) the measure of damages for nonacceptance by the buyer is the difference between the contract price and the market price at the time and place for tender together with any incidental or consequential damages provided in Section 2-710, but less expenses saved in consequence of the buyer's breach; and
    (b) the measure of damages for repudiation by the buyer is the difference between the contract price and the market price at the place for tender at the expiration of a commercially reasonable time after the seller learned of the repudiation, but no later than the time stated in paragraph (a), together with any incidental or consequential damages provided in Section 2-710, less expenses saved in consequence of the buyer's breach.

(2) If the measure of damages provided in subsection (1) is inadequate to put the seller in as good a position as performance would have done then the measure of damages is the profit (including reasonable overhead) which the seller would have made from full performance by the buyer, together with any incidental damages provided in this Article (Section 2-710), due allowance for costs reasonably incurred and due credit for payments or proceeds of resale.

Notice that section 1(b) states that damages should be reduced by the amount saved by the buyer's breach. More generally, under the common law, the seller has an obligation to mitigate the loss. This would include stopping production at the time the buyer sends a letter repudiating the contract. Under the rule of specific performance, the seller would have the right to continue production and then demand the seller to pay for the goods (which might be optimal if the market price were less than the agreed-on price for the goods).

Aghion and Tirole (1997) introduce an innovative model of the authority relationship that extends this theme. Their idea is that authority arises from the access to information necessary to act. In their model, the principal with formal authority will delegate authority to an agent who has better information. However, the principal will reserve the right to overrule an agent when he is better informed. This model can be viewed as another way of explaining employment contracts. The law gives the employer broad discretion when allocating tasks to the employee, and the employer always has the formal right to change an employee's task as long as it is within the scope of work.

Finally, the allocation of authority also affects the allocation of bargaining during contract renegotiation that can occur when contractual instruments are incomplete and there is the potential for hold-up. The property rights literature of Grossman and Hart (1986) and Hart and Moore (1990) implicitly builds on the idea that courts do not generally enforce contract breach through specific performance. Rather than regulate the relationship by contract, they observe that the bargaining power of parties can be allocated by ownership rights over assets. Rajan and Zingales (1998) extend this idea to relationships within the firm, where an organization can choose how much power agents have to grant access to firm resources.

5. Conclusion

A theory of contracts studies the relation among four theoretical objects: exchange environments, contractual instruments, contract law, and contractual behavior. The relation among these concepts is complex. In the short term, the exchange environment and contract law are exogenous; we thus seek to explain both contractual instruments and the resulting contractual behavior in terms of the exogenously given contractual environment and contract law. From a wider perspective, however, both contract law and, to a lesser extent, the exchange environment are endogenous. To a large extent, we choose the legal rules that govern contractual instruments. Similarly, agents choose the environment in which they contract; moreover, they might act to alter the exchange environment in which they find themselves.

Each aspect of the literature on contract focuses on a different explanatory question. The mechanism design literature asks: for a given contractual environment, does a mechanism exist that induces efficient contractual behavior? In this literature, a mechanism conflates contractual instruments and contract law; it examines contracts, the set of obligations that result from the operation of contract law on contractual instruments. Nevertheless, the literature assumes a legal system that is basically utopian.

The incomplete contracts literature, in contrast, seeks to explain the structure of observed contractual instruments. It often begins with some observed contractual instrument and then asks: in what exchange environment is a specified contractual instrument optimal for the parties? Once again, the structure and competence of the legal system is largely idealized. The incomplete contracts literature explains the oddities of contractual instruments largely without reference to any features of contract law.

The literature on the economic analysis of contract law, finally, abandons the assumption of an ideal legal system. Rather, it often asks: given a contractual instrument in a specific exchange environment, how does the legal rule influence contractual behavior? Here the legal system is not ideal, though the literature has primarily relaxed only the assumption of perfect enforcement.

Each of these literatures has provided significant insight into contractual behavior and the structure of contractual instruments. The mechanism design literature, for instance, has provided clear, formal accounts of specific transaction costs, such as asymmetric information, and analyzed the extent to which these features of the contractual environment impede efficient exchange. The assumption of an ideal legal system, however, limits the practical insights available from these models. An assumption of perfect enforcement, for example, implies that contractual behavior always conforms to the obligations embodied in the contractual instrument. Indeed, rational parties need never invoke an ideal legal system; the shadow of the law is sufficient to regulate behavior. Similarly, the assumption that interpretation is unambiguous, clear, and foreseeable implies that parties can always implement perfectly their intentions.

The economic analysis of contract law adopts complementary simplifying assumptions. It generally studies very simple exchange environments; we have little idea how the ideal legal rule would vary across exchange environments. Similarly, it generally focuses on the effects of legal rules on contractual behavior but ignores the effects of legal rules on contractual instruments. It has provided few explanations for variation in available remedies across exchange environments and contractual instruments. Why, for instance, are common law employment contracts at-will rather than protected by expectation damages? Moreover, the formal study of interpretation is in its infancy. Models have very crude representations of the rules of interpretation, in part because the literature has not exploited the language formulated in Battigalli and Maggi (2002).

This sketch of these literatures points clearly to promising paths of future research. We need to meld the sophisticated analyses of exchange environments and contractual instruments to the simple models of nonideal legal institutions. The mechanism design literature might investigate the set of achievable allocations under nonideal legal systems. Imperfect enforcement will impede the realization of first-best allocations. How good must contract enforcement be to yield the first-best outcome? How costly is imperfect enforcement?

Relaxing the assumption of unambiguous interpretation is apt to be both more difficult and more fruitful. Contracting agents rarely use new or innovative language in their contractual instruments. Contractual terms that have been subject to extensive interpretation provide a more certain environment against which to contract. This observation suggests that many contractual terms might be suboptimal relative to the world in which interpretation is unambiguous and costless. Thus, at least some features of observed contracts likely respond to the failings of the courts and contract law.

In terms of a way forward, the first step is to work more on models that help us build empirical representations of the legal system. Theories create conceptual categories that should have analogues in practice. Second, what are the testable implications of these theories? There is surprisingly little discussion of how one could formulate an empirical hypothesis that can be brought to the data.

One of the real difficulties with attempting to study contract law is that it is impossible to build data on the universe of contracts. Litigated cases are the exception, rather than the norm. Moreover, when drafting a contract, parties draw on both litigated cases and industry practice. Hence, as Manski (1993) showed in the context of social networks, it will be very difficult to identify the causal impact of contract law on contract performance.

REFERENCES

Abreu, D. 1988. "On the Theory of Infinitely Repeated Games with Discounting." *Econometrica* 56: 383–396.

Aghion, P., and P. Bolton. 1992. "An Incomplete Contracts Approach to Financial Contracting." *Review of Economic Studies* 59: 473–494.

Aghion, P., and B. Hermalin. 1990. "Legal Restrictions on Private Contracts Can Enhance Efficiency." *Journal of Law, Economics, and Organization* 6: 381–409.

Aghion, P., and J. Tirole. 1997. "Formal and Real Authority in Organizations." *Journal of Political Economy* 105: 1–29.

Aghion, P., M. Dewatripont, and P. Rey. 1994. "Renegotiation Design with Unverifiable Information." *Econometrica* 62: 257–282.

Alchian, A., and H. Demsetz. 1972. "Production, Information Costs, and Economic Organization." *American Economic Review* 62: 777–795.

American Law Institute. 1981. *Restatement of the Law, Second, Contracts*. St. Paul, MN: American Law Institute.

———. 2006. *Restatement of the Law, Third, Agency*. St. Paul, MN: American Law Institute.

Anderlini, L., and L. Felli. 1994. "Incomplete Written Contracts: Undescribable States of Nature." *Quarterly Journal of Economics* 109: 1085–1124.

———. 1999. "Incomplete Contracts and Complexity Costs." *Theory and Decision* 46: 23–50.

Arlen, J., and W. B. MacLeod. 2005. "Torts, Expertise, and Authority: Liability of Physicians and Managed Care Organizations. *RAND Journal of Economics* 36: 494–519.

Arrow, K. J. 1963. "Uncertainty and the Welfare Economics of Medical Care." *American Economic Review* 53: 941–973.

Arrow, K. J., and G. Debreu. 1954. "Existence of an Equilibrium for a Competitive Economy." *Econometrica* 22: 265–290.

Ayres, I., and R. Gertner. 1989. "Filling Gaps in Incomplete Contracts: An Economic Theory of Default Rules." *Yale Law Journal* 99: 87–130.

———. 1992. "Strategic Contractual Inefficiency and the Optimal Choice of Legal Rules." *Yale Law Journal* 101: 729–773.

Ayres, I., and E. Talley. 1995. "Solomonic Bargaining: Dividing a Legal Entitlement to Facilitate Coasean Trade." *Yale Law Journal* 104: 1027–1117.

Bajari, P., and S. Tadelis. 2001. "Incentives versus Transaction Costs: A Theory of Procurement Contracts." *RAND Journal of Economics* 32: 387–407.

Baker, G., R. Gibbons, and K. J. Murphy. 1994. "Subjective Performance Measures in Optimal Incentive Contracts." *Quarterly Journal of Economics* 109: 1125–1156.

Battigalli, P., and G. Maggi. 2002. "Rigidity, Discretion, and the Costs of Writing Contracts." *American Economic Review* 92: 798–817.

Bebchuk, L. A., and S. Shavell. 1991. "Information and the Scope of Liability for Breach of Contract: The Rule of Hadley v. Baxendale." *Journal of Law, Economics, and Organization* 7: 284–312.

Bernheim, B. D., and M. D. Whinston. 1998. "Incomplete Contracts and Strategic Ambiguity." *American Economics Review* 68: 902–932.

Blanchard, O. J., and J. Tirole. 2008. "The Joint Design of Unemployment Insurance and Employment Protection: A First Pass." *Journal of the European Economic Association* 6: 45–77.

Bolton, P., and M. Dewatripont. 2005. *Contract Theory*. Cambridge, MA: MIT Press.

Bolton, P., and A. Faure-Grimaud. 2005. *Thinking Ahead: The Decision Problem*. Technical Report 11867. Washington, DC: National Bureau of Economic Research.

Carmichael, H. L. 1989. "Self-enforcing contracts, shirking and life cycle incentives." *Journal of Economic Perspectives* 3(4): 65–83.

Chakravarty, S., and W. B. MacLeod. 2009. "Contracting in the Shadow of the Law." *RAND Journal of Economics* 40: 533–557.

Che, Y.-K., and T.-Y. Chung. 1999. "Contract Damages and Cooperative Investments." *RAND Journal of Economics* 30: 84–105.

Chung, T.-Y. 1991. "Incomplete Contracts, Specific Investments, and Risk Sharing." *Review of Economic Studies* 58: 1031–1042.

Clark, R. C. 1986. *Corporate Law*. Boston: Little, Brown.

Cooter, R. D., and D. L. Rubinfeld. 1989. "Economic Analysis of Legal Disputes and Their Resolution." *Journal of Economic Literature* 27: 1067–1097.

Craswell, R. 2000. "Against Fuller and Perdue." *University of Chicago Law Review* 67: 99–161.

Crocker, K. J., and S. E. Masten. 1988. "Mitigating Contractual Hazards—Unilateral Options and Contract-Length." *RAND Journal of Economics* 19: 327–343.

Dewatripont, M., and J. Tirole. 1999. "Advocates." *Journal of Political Economy* 107: 1–39.

Doornik, K. 2010. "Incentive Contracts with Enforcement Costs." *Journal of Law, Economics, and Organization* 26: 115–143.

Dye, R. A. 1985. "Costly Contract Contingencies." *International Economic Review* 26: 233–250.

Edlin, A. S. 1996. "Cadillac Contracts and Up-Front Payments: Efficient Investment under Expectation Damages." *Journal of Law, Economics, and Organization* 12: 98–118.

Edlin, A. S., and S. Reichelstein. 1996. "Holdups, Standard Breach Remedies, and Optimal Investment." *American Economic Review* 86: 478–501.

Farnsworth, E. A. 1999. *Contracts,* third edition. Boston: Little, Brown and Company.

———. 2004. *Contracts,* fourth edition. New York: Aspen Publishers.

Feinman, J. M. 1978. " The Development of the Employment at Will Rule." *American Journal of Legal History* 20: 118–135.

Fried, J. M. 1996. "Executory Contracts and Performance Decisions in Bankruptcy." *Duke Law Journal* 46: 517–574.

Fuller, L. L., and W. Perdue. 1936. "The Reliance Interest in Contract Damages: 1." *Yale Law Journal* 46: 52–96.

Gale, D., and M. Hellwig. 1985. "Incentive-Compatible Debt Contracts: The One-Period Problem." *The Review of Economic Studies* 52: 647–663.

Garner, B. A., and H. C. Black. 2005. *Black's Law Dictionary,* abridged eighth edition. St. Paul, MN: Thomson/West.

Gibbons, R. 2005. "Four Formal(izable) Theories of the Firm?" *Journal of Economics, Behavior, and Organization* 58: 200–245.

Goetz, C. J., and R. E. Scott. 1977. "Liquidated Damages, Penalties and Just Compensation Principle— Some Notes on an Enforcement Model and a Theory of Efficient Breach." *Columbia Law Review* 77: 554–594.

———. 1980. "Enforcing Promises: An Examination of the Basis of Contract." *Yale Law Journal* 89: 1261–1322.

———. 1983. "The Mitigation Principle: Toward a General Theory of Contractual Obligations." *Virginia Law Review* 69: 967–1024.

Grossman, S. J., and O. D. Hart. 1986. "The Costs and Benefits of Ownership: A Theory of Vertical and Lateral Integration." *Journal of Political Economy* 94: 691–719.

Grout, P. 1984. "Investment and Wages in the Absence of Binding Contracts: A Nash Bargaining Approach. *Econometrica* 52: 449–460.

Hart, O. D. 1990. "Is 'Bounded Rationality' an Important Element of a Theory of Institutions?" *Journal of Institutional and Theoretical Economics* 14: 696–702.

Hart, O. D., and J. Moore. 1988. "Incomplete Contracts and Renegotiation." *Econometrica* 56: 755–785.

———. 1990. "Property Rights and the Nature of the Firm." *Journal of Political Economy* 98: 1119–1158.

———. 1999. "Foundations of Incomplete Contracts." *Review of Economic Studies* 66: 115–138.

Hermalin, B. E., and M. L. Katz. 1993. "Judicial Modification of Contracts between Sophisticated Parties: A More Complete View of Incomplete Contracts and Their Breach." *Journal of Law, Economics, and Organization* 9: 230–255.

Hermalin, B. E., A. W. Katz, and R. Craswell. 2006. "Law and Economics of Contracts," in A. M. Polinsky and S. Shavell (eds.), *Handbook of Law and Economics.* Amsterdam: North-Holland.

Holmström, B. 1979. "Moral Hazard and Observability." *Bell Journal of Economics* 10: 74–91.

Innes, R. D. 1990. "Limited Liability and Incentive Contracting with ex-ante Action Choices. *Journal of Economic Theory* 52: 45–67.

Joskow, P. L. 1988. "Price Adjustment in Long-Term-Contracts—The Case of Coal." *Journal of Law and Economics* 31: 47–83.

Katz, A. W. 2004. "The Economics of Form and Substance in Contract Interpretation." *Columbia Law Review* 104: 496–538.

Klein, B., and K. Leffler. 1981. "The Role of Market Forces in Assuring Contractual Performance." *Journal of Political Economy* 89: 615–641.

Kornhauser, L. A. 1982. "An Economic Analysis of the Choice between Enterprise and Personal Liability for Accidents." *California Law Review* 70: 1345–1392.

———. 1983. "Reliance, Reputation, and Breach of Contract." *Journal of Law and Economics* 26: 691–706.

Laffont, J. J., and D. Martimort. 2002. *The Theory of Incentives.* Princeton, NJ: Princeton University Press.

Laffont, J. J., and J. Tirole. 1986. "Using Cost Observation to Regulate Firms." *Journal of Political Economy* 94: 614–641.

Lewis, T. R., and D.E.M. Sappington. 1999. "Using Decoupling and Deep Pockets to Mitigate Judgment-Proof Problems." *International Review of Law and Economics* 19: 275–293.

Macaulay, S. 1963. "Non-Contractual Relations in Business: A Preliminary Study." *American Sociological Review* 28: 55–67.

MacLeod, W. B. 2002. "Complexity and Contract," in E. Brousseau and J.-M. Glachant (eds.), *Economics of Contract in Prospect and Retrospect.* Cambridge: Cambridge University Press, pp. 213–240.

———. 2007. "Reputations, Relationships and Contract Enforcement." *Journal of Economics Literature* 45: 597–630.

MacLeod, W. B. 2011. "Great Expectations: Law, Employment Contracts, and Labor Market Performance," in O. Ashenfelter and D. Card (eds.), *Handbook of Labor Economics,* volume 4. Amsterdam: Elsevier.

MacLeod, W. B., and J. M. Malcomson. 1989. "Implicit Contracts, Incentive Compatibility, and Involuntary Unemployment." *Econometrica* 57: 447–480.

———. 1993. "Investments, Hold-up, and the Form of Market Contracts." *American Economic Review* 83: 811–837.

MacLeod, W. B., and D. Parent. 1999. "Job Characteristics and the Form of Compensation." *Research in Labor Economics* 18: 177–242.

Malcomson, J. M. 1981. "Unemployment and the Efficiency Wage Hypothesis." *Economic Journal* 91: 848–866.

Manski, C. F. 1993. "Identification of Endogenous Social Effects: The Reflection Problem." *Review of Economic Studies* 60: 531–542.

Maskin, E., and J. Riley. 1984. "Monopoly with Incomplete Information." *RAND Journal of Economics* 15: 171–196.

Maskin, E., and J. Tirole. 1999. "Unforeseen Contingencies and Incomplete Contracts." *Review of Economic Studies* 66: 83–114.

McKelvey, R. D., and T. Page. 2002. "Status Quo Bias in Bargaining: An Extension of the Myerson-Satterthwaite Theorem with an Application to the Coase Theorem." *Journal of Economic Theory* 107: 336–355.

Miles, T. J. 2000. "Common Law Exceptions to Employment at Will and U.S. Labor Markets." *Journal of Law, Economics, and Organization* 16: 74–101.

Milgrom, P., and J. Roberts. 1986. "Relying on the Information of Interested Parties." *RAND Journal of Economics* 17: 18–32.

Moore, J. 1992. "Implementation, Contracts, and Renegotiation in Environments with Complete Information," in J. J. Laffont (ed.), *Advances in Economic Theory: Sixth World Congress*, volume I. Cambridge: Cambridge University Press, pp. 182–282.

Myerson, R. B., and M. A. Satterthwaite. 1983. "Efficient Mechanisms for Bilateral Trading." *Journal of Economic Theory* 29: 265–281.

Pauly, M. V. 1968. "The Economics of Moral Hazard." *American Economics Review* 58: 531–537.

Posner, R. A. 1997. "Social Norms and the Law: An Economic Approach." *American Economic Review* 87: 365–369.

Posner, R. A., and A. M. Rosenfield. 1977. "Impossibility and Related Doctrines in Contract Law—Economic Analysis." *Journal of Legal Studies* 6: 83–118.

Rajan, R. G., and L. Zingales. 1998. "Power in a Theory of the Firm." *Quarterly Journal of Economics* 113: 387–432.

Rogerson, W. P. 1984. "Efficient Reliance and Damage Measures for Breach of Contract." *RAND Journal of Economics* 15: 39–53.

———. 1992. "Contractual Solutions to the Hold-up Problem." *Review of Economic Studies* 59: 777–793.

Salanie, B. 1997. *The Economics of Contracts: A Primer.* Cambridge, MA: MIT Press.

Sappington, D. 1983. "Limited Liability Contracts between Principal and Agent." *Journal of Economic Theory* 29: 1–21.

Schmidt, K. M., and M. Schnitzer. 1995. "The Interaction of Explicit and Implicit Contracts." *Economic Letters* 48: 193–199.

Schwartz, A. 1979. "The Case for Specific Performance." *Yale Law Journal* 89: 271–306.

Schwartz, A., and R. E. Scott. 2003. "Contract Theory and the Limits of Contract Law." *Yale Law Journal* 113: 541–619.

Schweizer, U. 2006. "Cooperative Investments Induced by Contract Law." *RAND Journal of Economics* 37: 134–145.

Scott, R. E. 2003. "A Theory of Self-Enforcing Indefinite Agreements." *Columbia Law Review* 103: 1641–1699.

Shapiro, C., and J. E. Stiglitz. 1984. "Equilibrium Unemployment as a Worker Discipline Device." *American Economic Review* 74: 433–444.

Shavell, S. 1980. "Damage Measures for Breach of Contract." *Bell Journal of Economics* 11: 466–490.

———. 1984. "The Design of Contracts and Remedies for Breach." *Quarterly Journal of Economics* 99: 121–148.

———. 2007. "Liability for Accidents," in P. Polinsky and S. Shavell (eds.), *Handbook of Law and Economics,* volume 1A. Amsterdam: Elsevier, pp. 139–182.

Shin, H. S. 1998. "Adversarial and Inquisitorial Procedures in Arbitration." *RAND Journal of Economics* 29: 378–405.

Simon, H. A. 1951. "A Formal Theory of the Employment Relationship." *Econometrica* 19: 293–305.

———. 1982. *Models of Bounded Rationality.* Cambridge, MA: MIT Press.

Spier, K. E. 1992. "Incomplete Contracts and Signalling." *RAND Journal of Economics* 23: 432–443.

———. 2006. "Litigation," in A. M. Polinsky and S. Shavell (eds.), *Handbook of Law and Economics.* Amsterdam: North-Holland.

Spier, K. E., and M. D. Whinston. 1995. "On the Efficiency of Privately Stipulated Damages for Breach of Contract: Entry Barriers, Reliance, and Renegotiation." *RAND Journal of Economics* 26: 180–202.

Sykes, A. O. 1981. "An Efficiency Analysis of Vicarious Liability under the Law of Agency." *Yale Law Journal* 91: 168–206.

Telser, L. G. 1980. "A Theory of Self-Enforcing Agreements." *Journal of Business* 53: 27–44.

Tirole, J. 1999. "Incomplete Contracts: Where Do We Stand?" *Econometrica* 67: 741–782.

———. 2009. "Cognition and Incomplete Contracts." *American Economic Review* 99: 265–294.

Townsend, R. 1979. "Optimal Contracts and Competitive Markets with Costly State Verification." *Journal of Economic Theory* 22: 265–293.

Ulen, T. S. 1984. "The Efficiency of Specific Performance: Towards a Unified Theory of Contract Remedies." *Michigan Law Review* 83: 341–403.

Williamson, O. E. 1975. *Markets and Hierarchies: Analysis and Antitrust Implications.* New York: Free Press.

Williamson, O. E. 1991. "Comparative Economic Organization: The Analysis of Discrete Structural Alternatives." *Administrative Science Quarterly* 36: 269–296.

24

Inter-Firm Contracts
Evidence
Francine Lafontaine and Margaret E. Slade

1. Introduction

1.1. Background

Economics is sometimes described as the study of markets. Many market transactions, however, do not take place in arm's-length spot markets but instead are governed by long- or short-term contracts. Because those contracts restrict the actions of one or both parties, there must be offsetting benefits. Otherwise, parties would not voluntarily enter into agreements that limit their flexibility. In this chapter, we review empirical analyses of interfirm contracts, paying particular attention to the reasons for entering into contractual relationships and the associated costs and benefits. We consider not only studies of the incidence of such contracts—when different types of contracts and contract terms are chosen—but also studies of the effects of those choices on outcomes, such as profits, prices, sales, and firm survival. Because our goal is to review the empirical literature, we rely throughout on authors' institutional knowledge and their definitions and classification schemes for contracts and contract terms.

Given that interfirm contracts are found most extensively in the context of procurement and distribution, most contracts analyzed herein occur between firms that are vertically related. In particular, one party supplies either an input or a service to the other. Nevertheless, some contracts, such as licensing agreements, arise between firms in the same product market. Yet in the context of a licensing relationship, one firm, the licensor, in fact provides an input (a production technology and associated services) to the other, and in that sense the relationship is also vertical. With few exceptions, we do not discuss alliances and joint ventures, which are more common forms of relationships among firms in the same horizontal market. The interested reader is referred to Azoulay and Lerner (this volume) and Ménard (this volume) for a discussion of these types of relationships. Similarly, to keep the scope of the chapter manageable, we focus

We thank the volume editors, Robert Gibbons and John Roberts, as well as several colleagues, including Kenneth Corts, Ricard Gil, Desmond Ho-Fu Lo, Julie Mortimer, Emmanuel Raynaud, and participants in workshops at the National Bureau for Economic Research for helpful comments. We thank our respective institutions for their support. Margaret Slade also acknowledges financial support from the Leverhulme Foundation.

on procurement and distribution contracts rather than on contracts that occur between firms and their capital providers, be they banks or individuals. The latter tend to involve a different set of issues and are discussed further in Gertner and Scharfstein (this volume).

In our review of the empirical literature on interfirm contracting, we emphasize analyses of agreements that are framed in the context of transaction costs and contract theory. However, we also consider contributions that predate those developments. Many studies that fall into the latter category are analyses of contract terms known as vertical restraints, where one link in a vertical chain constrains the activities of another. Historically, such constraints have been viewed either as mechanisms by which firms can achieve (or at least move toward) the vertically integrated outcome without resorting to integration or as devices that enable them to enhance their market power.[1] By emphasizing the incentive aspects of vertical restraints, our coverage attempts to bring the findings from the vertical-restraints literature into the fold of organizational economics and the empirical analysis of interfirm contracts.

Interfirm contracts are often similar in structure to the contracts used within firms, including executive and certain types of labor compensation schemes. Empirical studies of within-firm contracts, however, are also beyond the scope of this chapter. Interested readers should consult Azoulay and Lerner (this volume) and Waldman (this volume). A related literature that is beyond the scope of the present survey is that which focuses on the contractual relationships of firms with growers in various agricultural sectors, including the hog and broiler industries. Because growers are usually individual farmers, this literature tends to emphasize agent risk aversion and heterogeneity, much in the same way as the within-firm contracting literature does.[2] Similarly, and for similar reasons, we do not consider contracts with talent, whether in the context of sports or movie production. Finally, we generally exclude studies of contracts where one party is the government. Both motivations and constraints can be quite different in such contexts.[3] We focus instead on those transactions that parties have chosen to organize across firms.

The fact that we are considering agreements between firms already has implications for the parties' incentives (see, e.g., Gibbons 2005: 12). In particular, in such contexts, the parties are usually residual claimants, although their profits are likely to depend on each other's actions. Moreover, risk plays a less salient role in many of the models and empirical applications than it might if the transactions involved individuals.[4] Similarly, many firms are, at least in theory, longer lived than individuals.[5] Thus, the shadow of the future probably looms larger in their relationships with other parties, including, of course, other firms.

---

1. For analyses of vertical integration, see Bresnahan and Levin (this volume) and Lafontaine and Slade (2007). For a discussion of market-power motives for vertical restraints, see Lafontaine and Slade (2008).

2. Interested readers should consult, for example, Knoeber (1989), Allen and Lueck, (2002), Dubois and Vukina (2004), and Vukina and Leegomonchai (2006) for more on contracts used in these settings.

3. For more on government procurement contracts, however, see Banerjee et al. (this volume) and Moe (this volume).

4. Of course, risk is an important factor in analyses where one of the parties is a small firm, for example, an owner-operator or a partnership.

5. In reality the failure rate of firms is quite high, such that their life expectancy is probably lower than that of individuals. However, what matters is that managers and owners make decisions as if the firm were long lived, either because they do not know when the firm might fail or because they internalize the effects of their decisions on the value of the firm's assets upon failure.

1.2. Types and Terms of Common Contracts

Here, we introduce some standard forms of contracts and then go on to discuss some related contracting issues. Contracts can take many forms. Nevertheless, certain standard formats or contract types appear in many industries, time periods, and regions of the world. We devote most of our chapter to those standard forms and practices, of which the following are typical.

Perhaps the simplest contract is a *pricing contract* that just specifies a price at which a good or service can be bought or sold. Such contracts can be very short lived, in which case they are not very different from spot market interactions, or they can last for many decades. In the latter case, researchers have studied not only the contracts themselves but also their duration and the ways in which they can adapt to changed circumstances. Pricing contracts are common when the product is homogeneous, such as many fuel and nonfuel minerals, and in traditional franchising, such as gasoline and automobile sales.[6] Finally, a special case of pricing contract involves only one item, such as a project, in which case it is referred to as a "fixed-price contract."

Cost-plus contracts are very different from pricing contracts in that they do not specify a price. Instead the seller is paid her costs plus a fraction of those costs to compensate for the effort involved. This type of contract is often used to procure one item, such as a project or service, that is often unique to a buyer. Moreover, a cost-plus contract is frequently contrasted with a fixed-price contract, which is the other standard method of financing a single project. The choice between the two involves a trade-off between the flexibility of a cost-plus contract and the incentives for cost control that a fixed-price contract gives the supplier.

A *share contract* is a third standard type. This sort of contract is most often affine in revenues. Specifically, it tends to involve a fixed fee (which can be positive or negative) that is paid by the downstream firm, in addition to each party receiving a share of revenues. Share contracts are commonly found in business-format franchising,[7] such as fast food and real estate sales, but also in many other contexts, such as technology licensing and retail leasing. Because each party receives a share of revenues rather than profits, such contracts are distortionary. As a result, it was once thought that they were inefficient and would disappear in modern economies. It is now well understood, however, that share contracts, which are also associated with countervailing benefits, are here to stay.

Vertical restraints are not types of contracts. Rather, they are restrictions, such as exclusive dealing, tying, and resale price maintenance, that are included in contracts and that limit the activities of one or more parties to the contract. Vertical restraints are most commonly found in retail settings, where they limit the downstream firm's activities. Most studies of vertical restraints have emphasized their potential for increasing horizontal market power. We do not consider that part of the literature. Instead we survey the studies of vertical restraints that emphasize their incentive properties in a vertical context and how they can be used to reallocate decision rights. Vertical restraints are thus special cases of the ways in which control rights are specified.

---

6. Traditional franchising refers to vertical relationships where a product is produced upstream and sold downstream by a separate firm under a franchise contract (e.g., gasoline and autos). It can be distinguished from business-format franchising, which is discussed below under share contracts.

7. One can contrast business-format franchising, where no production takes place upstream, with traditional franchising. With the former, the upstream firm sells a way of doing business and the right to use a trademark, whereas the latter involves upstream production and an associated dealer network.

Most of the studies that we survey involve explicit contracts. This is to be expected, because researchers typically analyze data on the terms and clauses that are written into contracts. Nevertheless, many "contracts" are unwritten but well understood by the parties. *Implicit contracts* are especially important in areas where the legal system is weak or corrupt, but they are also a common feature of modern economic systems.

Once a contract is agreed upon, enforcement becomes an issue. Moreover, many of the same mechanisms can be used to enforce explicit and implicit contracts, and those mechanisms tend to be implicit. In particular, most derogations are dealt with informally, and legal breach-of-contract proceedings are relatively rare. At least two mechanisms are commonly used to sustain agreements implicitly. The first is relational, which means that both parties expect to benefit from a continuing one-on-one relationship. This might be accomplished by ensuring that both expect to receive a stream of future rents. The second is reputational and involves group enforcement. In this case, failure to conform to accepted behavior will damage a party's reputational capital more generally.

The chapter is organized as follows. In Section 2, we very briefly review some theoretical arguments that have been used to explain the structure of interfirm contracts. Our coverage of the theories is nontechnical. The interested reader can find a much more complete and rigorous treatment of that literature in Kornhauser and MacLeod (this volume) and Malcomsom (this volume). In Section 3, we review some econometric issues that arise in the empirical assessment of inter-firm contracts. We emphasize some of the pitfalls that researchers face and solutions that have been adopted. To keep the chapter tractable, we do not revisit these issues when discussing the evidence. Our hope is that the reader will keep in mind that such issues affect the quality of the evidence in individual papers. We reserve the heart of the chapter for Section 4, which contains a detailed review of the empirical literature on the incidence and effects of contract forms and terms, such as fixed fees, revenue shares, contract duration, and price-adjustment clauses. Concluding remarks are found in Section 5.

2. The Theories

Given our description of the many forms that contracts between firms can assume, it is not surprising that no single model can capture all the complexities. Nevertheless, much of the empirical literature aims to assess whether the predictions of just a few theories hold in the specific contexts from which their data are obtained. Because our objective in this section is to provide a framework that can be used to organize the empirical work, our discussion of the theories is short and nontechnical. As mentioned previously, readers interested in more complete and advanced treatments are referred to Kornhauser and MacLeod (this volume) and Malcomsom (this volume).

Throughout our discussion of the theories, we consider a vertical chain with at most three links: an upstream supplier, a manufacturer or franchisor, and a downstream retailer. We assume that the manufacturer is the principal who must decide how to interact with her agent, either her supplier or retailer. (Throughout the chapter, we refer to the middle link in our vertical chain, the manufacturer, as "she," and use "he" for both suppliers and retailers.) Explicit interfirm contracts govern these relationships in all but the extreme cases of vertical integration (in which case there no longer are separate firms in the vertical chain), and pure arm's-length transactions in markets (which only require agreement on spot prices and quantities purchased).

Contracts are normally designed so that, ex ante, it is in the parties' best interest to accept them. Nevertheless, contingencies can arise ex post that can cause one of the parties to want to break the contract. We begin with a discussion of explicit contracts that are legally enforceable, either by the courts or through some agreed-on arbitration scheme. Not all contracts are legally enforceable, however, either because the appropriate institutions do not exist or because reliance on third-party enforcement is prohibitively expensive. We therefore conclude this section with a discussion of contracts that are self-enforcing ex post as well as ex ante.

2.1. Agency Models

Agency theory is the theoretical lens that has been most relied on in the empirical literature to study the existence and the terms of one of the categories of contracts described above, namely, share contracts. The reliance on this theoretical framework in the empirical literature on share contracts is due in part to the fact that very early models were developed to explain sharecropping. As such, they focused their attention on contracts that had the property of being linear in (or rather an affine function of) output, as is the case for sharecropping. Stiglitz (1974), for example, derived implications about factors that would affect the choice of share parameter α in such a contract, implications that could be taken to data directly in a number of contexts where contracts take this form. In that sense, the theory "met the empiricists half-way."

In the pure risk-sharing version of his model, Stiglitz showed that increases in risk would lower the share of output α that the more risk-averse party, assumed to be the agent, should be awarded under the optimal second-best contract. More typically, however, the agency or moral hazard model of contracting involves a risk- and work-averse agent who must exert an unobservable effort. In this case, Stiglitz (1974: 244) showed that "if workers are risk averse, then $0 < \alpha < 1$, and α is larger the greater is the responsiveness of effort to an increase in the share α. . . . If workers are risk neutral, $\alpha = 1$." Thus, early agency-theoretic models yielded testable implications concerning the effect of risk, risk aversion, and the importance of agent effort on the optimal second-best contract terms (i.e., the share parameter).

One drawback of this theoretical framework, however, is that the focus on single principal-agent pairs leads to the conclusion that contracts should be tailored to the characteristics of individual agents and local circumstances. In other words, the theory suggests that differences in agent risk aversion, local exposure to risk, and other characteristics of the agent or transaction should lead the principal to offer different contract terms. Yet in many contexts, observed contracts are not tailored in these ways. Building on the work of Reid (1977), Rubin (1978), and Eswaran and Kotwal (1985), Bhattacharyya and Lafontaine (1995) argued that in many instances, it is not sufficient to give incentives to the agent. In the case of franchising, for example, the principal must also be given incentives to exert effort on, say, maintaining brand value. When this is true, there is moral hazard on both sides. Nevertheless, assuming that the principal is risk neutral, the second-best contract can still be implemented as an affine function of output. The share parameter, however, is now meant to give incentives to both parties. Bhattacharyya and Lafontaine (1995) show that, although traditional agency models give rise to different contracts for each principal-agent pair, under double-sided moral hazard and risk neutrality, the share parameter is much more likely to be the same or very similar across agents and/or sets of circumstances. Moreover, the prediction still holds from the traditional agency model that the share going to the agent should increase with the importance of the agent's effort. This share, however, is now also decreasing in the importance of the principal's effort.

In reality, of course, contract design is much more than just an issue of choosing a share parameter. In particular, effort is not the only factor that is costly; contract administration, for example, is associated with documentation and enforcement costs. An ideal contract would therefore provide appropriate effort incentives to each party, share the risk in an optimal fashion, and elicit an appropriate quality and quantity of the goods or services that are traded while at the same time keeping administration costs at a minimum. In addition, unless the contract is very simple and short term, it should also provide efficient methods of adapting to unexpected changes in the economic environment. It is difficult to imagine that any single model could deal with this level of complexity. However, as noted by several authors, there are important complementarities among the various goals that the principal is trying to achieve. This suggests that we are likely to observe fixed packages of contract attributes. In other words, if there are n attributes, each of which can be high or low, we do not observe 2^n contract types. Instead, we usually observe only a few contracts, which often can be positioned along a linear scale between two extremes. The choice of the share parameter α in the theoretical model can then be viewed as a choice of location along such a scale. Table 1 illustrates this point. Assume that the agent receives compensation $s(x) = \alpha x + f$. In a procurement situation, where x is cost, $\alpha < 0$ is the share of costs that the agent pays, and $f > 0$ is a fixed price or payment that he receives. In a retailing or sales situation, x is output or sales revenue, $\alpha > 0$ is the agent's or retailer's share, and $f > 0$ is his fixed wage. Equivalently, in a franchise or licensing contract, $(1 - \alpha)$ and $-f$ are the royalty rate and fixed fee, respectively, that the agent pays to the principal. With both procurement and retailing then, $|\alpha|$ represents the power of the agent's incentives. In the procurement case, a higher share of cost borne by the agent gives him incentives to keep costs low. In the retailing or sales context, a higher share of sales revenues going to the agent, or a lower royalty rate paid to the principal, induces the agent to exert more effort toward increasing revenues. However, increasing the power of the agent's incentives necessarily implies reducing the power of the principal's incentives.[8]

Table 1 also can be used to illustrate how changes in exogenous factors lead to changes in contract terms (e.g., to changes in α). For example, it is usually assumed that the agent is the more risk-averse party, which means that when market or project risk increases, the need to insure the agent also rises, and $|\alpha|$ should fall as a consequence. In addition, as the marginal product of one party's effort rises, that party should be given a higher fraction of residual claims, which will cause $|\alpha|$ to rise or fall, depending on whether that party is the agent or principal. Finally,

---

8. See, for example, Shepard (1993), who places the three contract types in gasoline retailing in the United States along a scale with one standard contract, company-owned stations, representing vertical integration and at the other extreme, open dealers, a form of trade between independent firms. She puts lessee dealers—which she equates with franchising—somewhere between these two extremes. Similarly, Slade (1998a,b) describes the four standard contracts used in beer retailing in the United Kingdom and in gasoline retailing in the United States, respectively, along a similar continuum. Finally, in the labor context, Ichniowski et al. (1997) group human resource practices into four human resource management systems that they describe as different points along a scale from "most traditional" to "most innovative."

Table 1. A moral-hazard classification of contracts

	$\alpha = 0$	$0 < |\alpha| < 1$	$|\alpha| = 1$
Contract type			
	Cost plus vertical integration	Sharing	Fixed price market transaction
Characteristic			
Risk bearer	Principal	Agent and principal	Agent
Effort incentives	Low for agent; high for principal	Intermediate for agent and principal	High for agent; low for principal
Flexibility	High	Intermediate	Low
Documentation effort	High	Intermediate	Low
Quality incentives	High	Intermediate	Low

Source: Adapted from Bajari and Tadelis (2001).
Note: When positive, α is the share of output or revenue that the agent receives, and when negative, it is the share of costs that the agent pays.

when the principal is responsible for the costs, it is easier to implement changes in product design, because a fully compensated agent is less likely to object. However, cost-plus contracts are more costly to administer, because the agent must document all expenses.[9]

This simple classification scheme, moreover, can encompass a situation in which the agent must perform multiple tasks (as in Holmström and Milgrom 1991) in a straightforward way. To illustrate, the agent might have to exert effort on quality as well as on quantity production, and the former might be more difficult to measure than the latter. With a share contract of the form that we have been discussing, compensation tends to be based on (measurable) quantity. Thus, as quality measurement difficulties increase, $|\alpha|$ should fall. A move toward lower powered incentives occurs because high-powered incentives cause the agent to neglect the important quality dimension that is not emphasized by the compensation scheme.

The two extremes of our simple classification scheme, $\alpha = 0$ and $|\alpha| = 1$, also are worth noting, as they represent limiting contracting forms. First, if $\alpha = 0$, the agent bears none of the costs of production in the procurement case as, for example, in a cost-plus contract. In a retailing context, the agent is paid a fixed salary only. This case can be equated with vertical integration to the extent that fixed salaries are found mostly within firms. The opposite extreme, with $|\alpha| = 1$, is equivalent to spot market transactions, because the agent is the residual claimant with respect to his product or service. Furthermore, $\alpha = -1$ is also a linear or fixed-price contract, where the buyer pays either the prevailing market price or the one that is specified in the contract, namely f.[10] All these situations are encompassed in Table 1.

Finally, even though our classification scheme focuses on the case of a single principal and agent, in empirical settings the principal may use a single contract with all or most of its agents.

9. Most of these comparative-static results are derived formally in Lafontaine and Slade (2007) for retailing and in Bajari and Tadelis (2001) for procurement.
10. Note that this is a linear contract for a single item.

If the optimal share parameter for each agent does not differ much, one can move from a theory where $\alpha \in [0, 1]$ is for a single agent to a group-level empirical analysis, where the many agents of a principal all operate under the same contract terms. As mentioned above, Bhattacharyya and Lafontaine (1995) show that share parameters are likely to vary less under double- than single-sided moral hazard. Moreover, the principal is more likely to use the same contract for all agents if the costs of administering different contract terms for different agents are high, either from an administrative perspective or because agents might be particularly concerned about opportunism when contracts differ (see McAfee and Schwartz 1994). Finally, in many of the settings where contracts are uniform across agents, they are offered on a take-it-or-leave-it basis. Though this is again outside the simple model above, the types of agent that will accept the offered contract are likely to be somewhat similar, in terms of risk aversion and taste for effort, for example, such that contract uniformity across agents again need not be costly for the principal (see Lo et al. 2011).

2.2. Transaction Costs

Transaction costs are the costs of establishing and administering business relationships within and between firms or individuals. Transaction cost theories can be traced back to Coase (1937), who focused on the costs of transacting under different organizational forms, particularly, the costs of writing and enforcing contracts. The theories have been developed further by Williamson (1971, 1979, 1983), Klein et al. (1978), and others.

The insight from transaction cost economics that is most often addressed in the empirical literature is as follows. Parties to a transaction often make investments that have greater value inside than outside the relationship. In other words, the value of the assets in their intended use is higher than their value in alternative uses. Examples include specialized tools that can only be used to produce the products of one manufacturer, training that increases worker productivity exclusively in using those tools, and supplier facilities that have been located in close geographic proximity to purchasers. Specific investments give each party to a relationship a degree of monopoly or monopsony power. Indeed, even when there are many potential trading parties ex ante, when investments are specific, parties are locked in ex post.

When specific assets are involved, interaction in spot markets is unlikely. Instead, parties are expected to turn to long-term contacts or vertical integration to protect themselves and their assets. If those contracts were complete, specificity would not create problems. The complete contract would specify exactly what will occur and who will control the assets under all possible contingencies. However, writing complete contracts is costly, and not all contingencies can be foreseen. Thus, real-world contracts are normally incomplete. Unfortunately, the combination of incompleteness and specificity gives the parties incentives to endeavor to capture the rents associated with the specific assets. Thus, they are likely to haggle with one another, thereby increasing the costs of writing and administering the contract. They are also more likely to attempt to renegotiate the contract or, more generally, engage in opportunistic behavior. These possibilities, which are the essence of the hold-up problem, clearly pose problems for long-term contracting. Moreover, those problems are exacerbated in volatile environments, making it more likely that the firms will turn to vertical integration to protect their specific assets.

Here again, forms of contracts that lie between full vertical integration (or hierarchy) and spot market transactions—hybrid organizational forms, as they are often called in this literature (see Williamson 1985, 1996)—are viewed as intermediate solutions to the problem of minimizing haggling, opportunistic behavior, and exploitation. These organizational forms thus are apt to be relied on when these problems are present yet not too severe. The theory moreover predicts that the contracts will be of longer duration when transaction costs are larger. However, as contract duration increases, the probability that the economic environment will change grows. When transaction costs are important and firms still choose to organize their activity via contract, the theory predicts that these longer duration contracts are more apt to incorporate flexibility. This can be done, for example, by including price and quantity adjustment clauses that specify how those variables can be altered, as well as provisions for efficient breach if the relationship becomes disadvantageous.

Finally, the theory provides a number of testable predictions concerning the circumstances under which transaction costs are likely to be important. Specifically, transaction costs are apt to be more problematic when transactions are complex, when they involve specific investments, when those specific assets are more durable, when the quality of those assets is difficult to verify, when the environment is uncertain, and when the quasi-rents generated by the relationship are large.[11]

2.3. Property Rights

Property rights theories, which are more recent and more formal than transaction cost arguments, were developed by Grossman and Hart (1986), Hart and Moore (1990), Hart (1995), and others.[12] Those theories emphasize how asset ownership affects investment incentives. More specifically, they demonstrate how the allocation of property rights, which confer the authority to make decisions concerning the use of assets when unforeseen contingencies arise, changes *ex ante* investment incentives.

Because property rights theories deal with relationship-specific assets, incomplete contracts, and ex post bargaining,[13] they are often thought to be closely related to transaction cost models. However, there are important differences. In particular, unlike the transaction cost literature, the property rights literature has not focused on ex post haggling, renegotiation, and opportunistic behavior. Instead, authors have developed formal models that have shown how costless ex post bargaining affects ex ante investment in noncontractible assets. Whinston (2003) moreover shows that the predictions from the two sets of theories can be quite distinct. However, if one equates the probability of vertical integration with $(1 - \alpha)$ in a contract, some of the comparative statics listed in Table 1 in relation to our discussion of agency theory emerge under property rights models as well. In particular, Grossman and Hart (1986) show that as the importance of the manufacturer's investment (or alternatively, decisions or effort) grows, manufacturer ownership (vertical integration or low-powered incentives for the supplier) becomes more desirable, whereas as the importance of the supplier's investment grows, supplier

11. For more on transaction costs, see Tadelis and Williamson (this volume).
12. For an in-depth discussion of property-rights theories, see Segal and Whinston (this volume).
13. Property rights theories can therefore also be traced back to Coase's (1937) seminal contribution.

ownership (vertical separation or high-powered incentives for the supplier) is more apt to dominate. These predictions are consistent with those of double-sided moral hazard models in particular.[14]

While the theoretical property rights literature historically has focused on asset ownership as the mechanism that confers control or decision rights as well as payoff rights, contract clauses can reallocate control rights away from asset owners. And indeed, Baker et al. (2011) depart from the assumption of costless bargaining ex post found in the Grossman-Hart-Moore framework to analyze maladaptation during the contract execution phase (see also Baker et al. 2008; Hart and Moore 2008). Their approach yields predictions concerning contract design and the allocation of decision rights separately from asset ownership. This theme—that contract clauses can allocate decision rights across fixed firm boundaries—is familiar also from an earlier empirical literature on vertical restraints, to which we now turn.

2.4. Vertical Restraints

We have thus far considered how contract design, which determines, for example, the power of the incentives that are given to each party as well as contract duration and flexibility, varies with the economic environment. Clauses that determine who can make important decisions, such as choose product prices and product lines, are also written into contracts. Any restriction imposed by one member of a vertical relationship on the other member is a vertical restraint. Here we focus on the possible efficiency aspects of traditional price and nonprice vertical restraints. The former refers to resale price maintenance, where, for example, a manufacturer either sets the price or sets a maximum or minimum price that retailers can charge, whereas the latter includes exclusive dealing, exclusive territories, quantity forcing, and tying. In all cases, the presence of these clauses in a contract constrains the behavior of some party to the contract while keeping fixed the boundaries of the firms.

There is an important body of literature in economics that considers the effects of such restraints. This is because they have been viewed with some suspicion by the antitrust authorities, raising concerns that they might be used to create or increase market power. The market power considerations for such restraints are beyond the scope of this chapter.[15] From an organizational economics perspective, however, our interest is in considering when firms want to adopt such restraints for efficiency reasons. We thus take the view that such restraints are clauses that principals write into their contracts with agents to align up- and downstream incentives.

Empirically, vertical restraints most often arise in retail settings, with the upstream firm or manufacturer restricting its downstream retailers' choices. For example, a manufacturer might limit its retailer's product line or geographic market, or it might set the retail price. In describing the reasons these restraints might be used, we therefore focus on retail rather than procurement contracts. The restraints that appear in retail contracts can alleviate many different types of incentive problems. We discuss a representative few that are by no means exhaustive.

---

14. For more on the similarities between property-rights and moral-hazard models, see Lafontaine and Slade (2007).

15. Interested readers are referred to Lafontaine and Slade (2008).

First, the typical succession-of-monopoly problem arises when an upstream monopolist sells an input to a downstream firm at a price above marginal cost. If the downstream firm has market power, it is well known that it will choose a price that is higher, and a quantity that is lower, than the price and quantity that would maximize joint profits. The manufacturer can alleviate this problem in a number of ways, including setting the price or requiring certain minimum quantities.

Second, manufacturers who invest in improving retail outlets, promoting retail products, or training outlet managers might worry that dealers will free ride on those investments. For example, dealers might encourage customers who visit their store to switch to a competing brand that has a lower price—thereby making the sale easier—or that has a higher retail margin—thereby making the sale privately more profitable. Exclusive dealing resolves this problem by making it impossible for the dealer to propose an alternative brand to customers. In such a context, exclusive dealing is a mechanism that enables manufacturers to protect their investments against potential dealer opportunism. Furthermore, in its absence, potentially profitable investments might not be undertaken.[16]

Third, a dealer-incentive issue arises in situations where the manufacturer wants the dealer to invest ex ante in specific facilities or human capital that would allow him to provide better service to consumers. As per the property rights models mentioned above, unless the dealer can be assured that his investments are fully protected, he will choose to underinvest or not invest at all. Combined with a long contract duration, a vertical restraint, such as an exclusive territory, can provide the type of reassurance that the dealer needs.[17]

Finally, dealer services offered at the point of sale during the contract period can enhance the demand for a manufacturer's or franchisor's product. Retailers of course also benefit from providing such services. However, when there are multiple outlets in a retail chain, retailers do not fully internalize the benefit associated with their own decisions, as some of their satisfied customers will patronize other units of the same chain rather than returning to their unit in the future. In contrast, retailers bear the full cost of supplying the services. As a result, retailers are expected to provide a service level that is too low from the perspective of the upstream firm. In other words, in the context of retail chains, not only do dealers have incentives to free ride on the value of the brand, a vertical externality, they also have incentives to free ride on services offered by other dealers, a horizontal externality. Furthermore, the problem worsens as the fraction of repeat business that retailers face falls.

When this problem takes the form of a franchisee wanting to use lower quality inputs in the production process, it can be resolved with input-purchase requirements (tying) or approved-supplier programs as long as defection from such programs is not too difficult to detect.

When dealer service issues take other forms, Telser (1960) argued that minimum price restraints could solve the dealer service incentive problem by preventing retailers from competing on price and leading them to compete instead on quality or customer service. Klein and Murphy

16. This, of course, is a form of the standard underinvestment problem analyzed in the property rights literature.

17. For this solution to work, the upstream firm must be able to verify downstream investment and to terminate the contract if it is unsatisfactory. At the same time, the upstream firm must be able to commit to not terminating opportunistically.

(1988) instead proposed that manufacturers could use vertical restraints, such as minimum re-sale prices or exclusive territories, to ensure that their dealers earn above-normal returns, thereby creating rents that the dealers would lose if their contracts were terminated. Such rent, in combination with ongoing quality or service monitoring and the threat of termination, could entice dealers to provide desired levels of quality or service. In either case, because the quality and service levels in question are valued by customers—if it were otherwise, manufacturers would not value them—quantities sold and hence consumer satisfaction should be enhanced.

This last argument, which states that upstream firms can use vertical restraints in their retail contracts as part of a mechanism that creates rent for retailers (rent that retailers can lose if they do not abide by the terms of their contract and are thus terminated) was one of the early applications of the notion of self-enforcing contracts in the context of interfirm contracts, a topic to which we now turn.

2.5. Self-Enforcement

In many situations, parties to a contract cannot rely on formal enforcement of contractual terms. This can occur because formal institutions do not exist (or when they do, they are not effective), or because reliance on third-party enforcement is prohibitively costly. In such cases, parties must rely on informal enforcement. The notion of self-enforcing contracts, which was developed by Klein and Leffler (1981), Bull (1987), Klein and Murphy (1988), MacLeod and Malcomsom (1989), and others, builds on the legal concept of relational contracting (see Macneil 1978; Baker et al. 2002; Levin 2003).[18] Very generally, the idea is that the breaching party must face some future loss when breach occurs. This could occur, for example, when a contract that is advantageous to the breaching party is terminated or when that party's reputational capital is damaged. Furthermore, the punishment can be inflicted by the party who is harmed in a bilateral relationship (in which case the contract is said to be "relational"), or enforcement can rely on group punishment (in which case other parties participate in sanctioning unacceptable behavior).

A relational contract is one that is sustained on the value of future interaction between the parties. In this literature, interaction is usually modeled as a repeated game with imperfect monitoring of the agent's effort.[19] Because the agent's actions are unobservable, contracts cannot be written on effort. Moreover, because outcomes, while observed by the parties, are not verifiable, contracts on outcomes cannot be enforced by third parties. However, it is assumed that effort shifts the distribution of outcomes. In particular, high effort causes good outcomes to become more likely. In that setting, if the reward to good behavior is sufficiently high, the agent will eschew cheating in favor of high effort. In the context of interfirm contracting, this implies that the agent must earn higher than competitive rewards. In other words, he is not taken down to his reservation value. Relational contracting models are therefore similar to efficiency wage models.[20]

---

18. For a recent survey of formal and informal enforcement, see MacLeod (2007).
19. See Telser (1980) for an early model of self enforcement in a repeated game context.
20. Akerlof and Yellen (1986) provide a collection of important contributions on efficiency wages.

Although an important mechanism, relational considerations are not the only means of sustaining contracts informally. Indeed, the notion of reputation as an asset that can be damaged by failure to live up to others' expectations is very general. Furthermore, many reputational models rely on group punishments rather than one-on-one interactions as a mechanism to sustain cooperation (see, e.g., Klein and Leffler 1981). If group punishment is to be effective, however, others must be able to attribute blame when a relationship dissolves. This can be accomplished by invoking social norms, as in Okuno-Fujiwara and Postlewaite (1995), or by word-of-mouth communication, as in Greif (1989). Furthermore, published scores based on past performance, such as credit ratings, can play a useful communication role.

As we noted earlier, the notion of self-enforcement has been used to explain a number of empirical regularities in interfirm contracting. In particular, Klein (1980, 1995) notes that explicit constraints on franchisee behavior are sustained by the value of the bilateral relationship, whereas implicit constraints on franchisor opportunism are sustained by group punishment. Similarly, Klein and Murphy (1988) argue that vertical restraints can play an important self-enforcement role. Specifically, a manufacturer who offers minimum resale prices or exclusive territories to dealers might do so to ensure that the latter earn rent. The presence of such rent in a manufacturer-dealer relationship creates something that the dealer will lose if he is caught misbehaving and is terminated as a consequence. The restraint thus ensures that the dealer will not go against the manufacturer's stated service requirements.

3. Methods of Assessment

Our focus in this chapter is on empirical assessment of models of interfirm contracts. Unfortunately, there are numerous pitfalls that researchers must face when attempting to tease out causal relationships rather than merely uncovering simple correlations, and some of the studies we discuss rely on simple econometric methods that are not adequate for the task. We highlight some of the pitfalls before turning to a discussion of the empirical studies, organizing our discussion of potential problems around incidence and effects.

3.1. Incidence

Most of the literature on incidence—that is, the literature that tries to identify circumstances under which parties to a contract will choose to rely on one contract form or another, or on one contract term or another—uses what amounts to a comparative institutions approach (see notably Williamson 1991). In other words, the papers consider how firms choose among a specific set of contractual alternatives. Examples include studies of franchising, where the alternative for a franchisor is to integrate vertically (e.g, Brickley and Dark 1987; Lafontaine 1992), while the alternatives for a franchisee might be to operate as an independent business person (e.g., Williams 1999; Mazzeo 2004) or work as an employee. In other cases, the authors examine whether a particular contracting practice is relied on—for example, one might consider whether contracts include take-or-pay provisions, as in Masten and Crocker (1985), or whether upstream firms grant exclusive territories, as in Brickley (1999). In these cases, the alternative is the absence of the contract clause of interest. Finally, in a few cases, contracting practices can be captured better by a continuous variable. Such is the case for, for example, contract duration

(Joskow 1987; Brickley et al. 2003), the share parameter in franchise contracts (Lafontaine 1992; Lafontaine and Shaw 1999), and the proportion of franchised outlets in franchised chains (Brickley and Dark 1987; Lafontaine 1992; Lafontaine and Shaw 2005).

When the dependent variable is continuous, authors have used ordinary least squares or in some cases a limited dependent-variable estimator, such as a Tobit, to examine how the characteristics of the contracting parties and the transaction affect the continuous choice. In this literature, most authors ignore the potential endogeneity issue. Nevertheless, it can be a problem. To illustrate, certain types of investments, which can become characteristics in the regression model, might be undertaken only if the contract is of long enough duration, which could be the dependent variable. Thus, a franchisee might not invest as much in specific assets (e.g., retrofitting a building to accommodate a particular style of restaurant) if her franchise contract is of short duration. This reverse causality would bias estimates in regressions of contract duration on investment levels (see, e.g., Brickley et al. 2003). The standard solution to the endogeneity problem is to use an instrumental variables technique. Of course, this method is only viable if valid instruments can be found. Unfortunately, the problem of finding good instruments is particularly acute in these studies, as in most empirical studies in organizational economics, because the factors that lead firms to choose particular characteristics are also likely to affect desired contracting practices or terms.

When the set of contractual alternatives is limited to just two (or a few), the standard empirical study uses a discrete choice model to relate the decision to use a contract term to the characteristics of the transaction and of the contracting parties. Methods for dealing with discrete dependent variables are well known. There are, however, several problems that are apt to surface in discrete choice studies of contractual practices, problems whose solutions are more complex than when the dependent variable is continuous.

First, the ubiquitous endogeneity problem surfaces again. To illustrate, outlet characteristics are usually included among the explanatory variables that determine the method of transacting between manufacturer and retailer (for gasoline retailing see, e.g., Shepard 1993; Slade 1996; Pinkse and Slade 1998). When an upstream firm decides to change the nature of the contract with the retailer, however, it might well decide to also change some of the outlet's characteristics and vice versa. This could be the case with gasoline retailing, for example, where stations that are changed from full to self-service also often increase their number of pumps and may be changed from independent to lessee dealer at the same time. In such circumstances, the direction of causality is particularly unclear. A standard method for overcoming the endogeneity problem in this context is to use two-stage least squares, where the probability that a transaction is organized in a given way is assessed under a linear probability model.[21] However, the linear probability model has other undesirable features, including the fact that it is usually not possible to constrain the predicted probabilities to lie between 0 and 1. Other solutions to the problem of endogenous explanatory variables in the presence of limited dependent variables normally require strong assumptions (see, e.g., Wooldridge, 2002: 472–477).

A related empirical problem arises from the fact that contract terms play a role in attracting particular contracting parties—that is, we see endogenous matching as well as selection. For example, if agents are heterogeneous with respect to risk aversion, some might simultaneously

21. Of course, the problem of finding valid instruments is just as acute here as with continuous choice.

choose risky (safe) projects and contractual packages that are high (low) powered. If this selection problem is ignored, it can lead to the conclusion that when risk increases, agents are offered less insurance. In other words, the estimated coefficients will not only be biased but can also have the wrong sign. The bias can be eliminated if we include all relevant characteristics of contracting parties in the regression equation. Unfortunately, it is rarely possible to measure all relevant variables. In particular, risk aversion presents an often insurmountable problem. The solution suggested by Ackerberg and Botticini (2002) requires instruments that affect the matching process but not the contract choice.

Second, the errors in a discrete choice model are likely to be spatially correlated, in the sense that the off-diagonal entries in the variance/covariance matrix at a point in time are nonzero. For example, retail outlets located in a city center might experience common shocks that are not experienced by the retail outlets in the suburbs; or outlets that sell brands of a common manufacturer might have common private information. One possible remedy is to use the correction for spatial and time-series correlation of an unknown form developed in Pinkse et al. (2006) in a discrete choice context.

Finally, a much broader problem with empirical studies of contract terms is that authors typically focus on just one component of the contract at a time. Unfortunately, contracts may be better described as sets of contract terms, where each choice interacts with the others. The issue of complementarity among contract terms has been mentioned in both the theoretical and empirical literatures, but the data requirements and empirical difficulties associated with correctly addressing those concerns have meant that only limited progress has been achieved on this front. We come back to this issue in Section 4.9.

3.2. Effects

The empirical literature on contracting has focused more on incidence than on the consequences of contracting decisions. This may seem surprising, given the interest in establishing the value of various contractual alternatives. Indeed, what matters at the end of the day is performance: is it beneficial for firms to rely on a given contract type, or do those that include a particular term in their contracts with their suppliers or retailers do better than those that do not? If so, should we suggest that the transaction be organized in this way? If not, why not? In other words, are there normative conclusions that can be drawn from analyses of interfirm contracts?

Unfortunately, studies of the effects of contract terms on firm performance or other outcome variables (e.g., prices, sales, profits, growth, and survival) are relatively rare for a reason. First, studies of profitability or cost differences require detailed data that are typically proprietary. For that reason, much of the literature focuses on firm growth or survival, which may not be as related to performance as one would want. Second, and more importantly, the endogeneity issue is particularly problematic in these studies. Simply put, the effects of various contractual decisions are difficult to identify empirically, given that firms do not make contractual choices randomly. Instead, parties to a contract choose certain options based on what they expect will give the best outcome in a given situation. This choice, of course, is exactly what the literature on incidence relies on and tries to capture. Unfortunately, it also raises important issues when assessing the effects of contractual practices.

There are well-established techniques, such as Heckman's (1978, 1979) selection and endogenous dummy variable models and treatment-effects models, that can be used to deal with endogenous decisions on organizational form.[22] But those techniques require valid instruments, and such instruments are particularly difficult to come by in the settings we are concerned with. After all, firm and transaction characteristics are to some extent the result of decisions made by managers, and in that sense all are endogenous. Authors thus often rely on various arguments to justify treating certain firm characteristics as exogenous, or at least predetermined, even in the incidence literature. When it comes to consequences, it is particularly difficult to argue that a variable postulated to affect the likelihood that a contract term is used will not also directly affect performance. To make matters worse, in the absence of nonsuspect instruments, it is impossible to perform a formal assessment of the validity of any instrument. Still, we see promise in the increasing availability of various forms of spatial information about competitor and own-outlet characteristics in the same or other markets as potential sources of instruments.[23]

At the same time, due to the concern with endogenous selection, many studies of effects rely on external sources of variation in organizational form for identification. Specifically, they look for mandated changes in contracting practices (i.e., legislation) to assess effects. Some studies of this type use techniques developed in the natural experiments literature, whereas others use an event-study approach.

In the former category, for example, researchers have used data on firms that operate in regions where legislators ban a particular practice or restraint (the treatment group), as well as data on firms that operate in regions where the practice is not banned (the control group). Because the ban comes from outside the relationship, it is often assumed to be exogenous. But even though the endogeneity problem is lessened in this situation compared to cases where the firms choose the contract terms, it is not eliminated. To illustrate, suppose that franchised chains do better when they do not face state termination restrictions; that is, when they can terminate their franchise relationships at will. One might be tempted to conclude that the imposition of termination restrictions causes lower franchisor performance. However, it is also possible that termination restrictions are imposed exactly in those states where franchisors do poorly and thus have particularly strained relationships with their franchisees, leading franchisees to lobby for protection. Under those circumstances, the causality runs from poor performance to legislation.

If the underlying omitted factors that affect both the use of a particular form of contract and the performance variable of interest are time invariant—as might be the case, for example, for a manager's innate ability or the difficulty of monitoring a particular task—the endogeneity problem can be overcome through the use of panel data. In particular, with panel data, one can use a fixed-effects estimator to remove the influence of time-invariant unobserved regional, brand, or outlet characteristics that cause the endogeneity problem. With this procedure, however, the effect of a contracting practice is identified solely through time-series variation. In other words, one is essentially assessing how changes in the use of a contracting practice lead to changes in performance. Unfortunately, there is often little time-series variation in organizational form. Furthermore, with panel data it is tempting to use lagged endogenous variables as instruments

---

22. See Wooldridge (2002: 551–642) for a comprehensive discussion of econometric methods used for policy evaluation.

23. For a general discussion of how spatial data can be used to generate instruments in parametric and nonparametric contexts, see Pinkse et al. (2001) and Pinkse and Slade (2010). For contracting applications in a parametric context, see Schneider (2010) and Kosová et al. (2012).

in the hopes that they are predetermined. This hope will be thwarted, however, if the errors are serially correlated, as is highly likely.

An alternative approach is to use a before-and-after estimation strategy—a time-series model. This approach requires access to data on firm performance that include periods before and after a legally mandated change, such as the banning of a practice. The problem with this approach is that many things change over time, and although it is tempting to attribute any significant performance change to the new legal requirement, this attribution might not be valid.

Some studies use a before-and-after approach on a cross-section of firms when the data are not a panel. Those studies typically rely on data on stock prices to measure firm performance (i.e., event studies). Unfortunately, this approach reduces the set of firms whose actions can be examined empirically to publicly traded firms. This is problematic to the extent that the contracting practices of interest are used by relatively small firms, as in the case of franchise contracts.

Finally, recent work on within-firm incentives addresses the issues of selection and endogeneity by relying on data from field experiments (e.g., Lazear 2000; Shearer 2004; Bandiera et al. 2007). Unfortunately, it is very unlikely that researchers can obtain experimental data that would be suited to the study of many questions involving how firms interact with one another. As best we can ascertain, no study of interfirm contracts relies on such data.

Perhaps in part because experimental data are hard to come by, in the empirical literature in industrial economics authors increasingly use assumptions about utility functions, cost functions, and market equilibrium to generate estimating equations that allow them to identify underlying taste and technology parameters. These parameters are then used to perform counterfactual (what if) analyses. In recent years, this methodology has been applied to the study of effects of contracting practices, in particular by Asker (2005) on exclusive dealing, Brenkers and Verboven (2006) on exclusive dealing and exclusive territories, Villas-Boas (2007) and Bonnet and Dubois (2010) on nonlinear wholesale pricing, Mortimer (2008) on share contracts, Crawford and Yurukoglu (2012) on bundling, and Ho et al. (2012) on full-line forcing. As with all structural analyses, the requirements of the models in terms of data and industry knowledge are very stringent, even more so in these vertical settings, as the researcher needs to model horizontal games among upstream and among downstream firms as well as bargaining games among links in the vertical chain. Other problems with this approach include the fact that cost savings arising from better incentive alignment are difficult to capture in such models, and that evaluation of effects obtained from such models are valid only to the extent that the assumptions embedded in the model are valid. Despite these problems, we view this type of modeling as a fruitful area for future research on the effects of vertical contracting. Still, given the strong assumptions required to make these models tractable, we expect that reduced-form analyses with strong identification strategies will continue to be an important source of insights.

4. The Evidence

In this section, we discuss the empirical evidence on interfirm contracting, organizing this discussion around a series of themes related to contract types and contract terms or practices. We begin each section with a discussion of evidence concerning the incidence of a choice or practice, followed by a discussion of evidence on the consequences of the same choice or practice. In the latter case, we focus on consequences from the firm's perspective, rather than from a public policy or total welfare perspective, as efficiency for the firm is the typical concern in the organizational economics literature. This is not to say that public policy concerns are absent from the empirical literature on interfirm contracts, but simply that the goal of organizational economics is to uncover the benefits that the firm derives from using different contracting options.

4.1. Pricing Contracts

Many simple contracts specify a price at which a variable quantity of an input can be purchased. Perhaps because they are so common, or because they do not differ much from spot market transactions, linear pricing contracts tend to be studied less often than, for example, share contracts, at least relative to their occurrence. In this section, we discuss some work on incidence, much of which comes from traditional franchising. Note that in this context, the alternative to contracting considered by the franchisor tends to be vertical integration (rather than spot transactions). In that sense, much of the vast literature on the make-or-buy decision in procurement includes tests of simple pricing contracts when the input under the buy option is supplied under contract.[24] The manufacturer's decision, however, is treated simply as a buy in that literature, and thus the form and terms of the contract that ties the supplier to the manufacturer are typically not emphasized or even described in any detail. Exceptions include work on shipping and contracting in mineral markets, both of which we discuss below.

4.1.1. Incidence

Several authors have examined the choice of contractual form in gasoline retailing. Often this involves the choice between transacting at a wholesale price (a pricing contract), which gives the station operator high-powered incentives, and vertical integration, which normally involves salaried employment. Most studies estimate discrete choice equations for organizational form (pricing contract versus vertical integration). The object and focus of each study, however, are different. To illustrate, Shepard (1993) finds that higher powered incentives (pricing contracts) are more apt to be relied on when monitoring is difficult, as is the case, for example, for stations with repair facilities. Slade (1996), in contrast, casts her analysis in a multitask setting and finds that higher powered contracts are less likely to be offered when tasks are complementary, where complementarities can occur in demand (as measured by cross-price elasticities) or through covariation in sources of risk. Both studies lend support to moral hazard models that emphasize incentive issues in choosing efficient contracts.

There is also evidence, however, that contract choice in gasoline retailing is influenced by competitive concerns. For example, Pinkse and Slade (1998) find that contract types (pricing contract versus vertical integration) tend to cluster in geographic space, which is consistent with a model in which market share motives (which are associated with similarity of offerings)[25] outweigh market power motives (which are associated with differentiation). Furthermore, Slade

---

24. See Bresnahan and Levin (this volume) and Lafontaine and Slade (2007) for recent reviews of the empirical literature on vertical integration.

25. Because there is a strong relationship between contract type and station offerings, contract clustering implies attribute clustering. See also Kalnins and Lafontaine (2004) on contract clustering in fast-food chains.

(1998b) finds evidence that supports strategic delegation of the pricing decision.[26] In particular, she finds that delegation (i.e., a pricing contract) is chosen more often in contexts where competition among operators is less aggressive, a situation in which delegation is predicted to yield a greater increase in profits. It is important to recognize, however, that these findings, which imply that contracting practices are affected by the intensity of local competition, are more likely to surface in such industries as gasoline retailing, which tend to be less competitive than those in which business-format franchising is the norm.

Shipping is another industry in which linear pricing contracts are common. Unlike gasoline retailing, however, with shipping the choice is often contracting versus market transaction. In addition to specifying rates (or formulas for rates), shipping contracts can contain incentive provisions, such as penalties for delays and take-or-pay clauses. Researchers who have studied such contracts have paid particular attention to the role of market thickness in determining contract choice, under the hypothesis that, when markets are thin, the advantages of contracting increase relative to spot market transactions. Pirrong (1993), who assesses ocean bulk-shipping contracts, and Hubbard (2001), who examines long- and short-haul trucking contracts, find support for this hypothesis. Furthermore, Hubbard finds that the thickness effect is strong for long but weak for short hauls and explains this regularity by the fact that, when hauls are short, the costs of writing contracts exceed the benefits.

4.1.2. Effects

Several studies of consequences consider how retail prices vary with contract choice (e.g., company ownership versus franchising with linear or affine prices versus spot market transactions). For example, Shepard (1993) compares consumer prices for gasoline in leasee-dealer (contract) and company units and finds evidence that, for some products, prices charged at leasee dealerships are higher. In contrast, Hastings (2004) makes a similar comparison and finds no difference in price levels.

The above studies consider the effect of contract choice on retail prices, which are relatively easy to observe. Normally, it is more difficult to assess prices in long-term procurement contracts, because data on those prices are not usually available to the public. A comparison of contract and spot prices is possible, however, for nonferrous metals (e.g., copper, lead, and zinc), because those commodities were traded in North America under two price systems. Indeed, spot and long-term contract prices, which coexisted between the end of World War II and the late 1970s, are available from public data sources. The price on which long-term contracts were based was known as the U.S. producer price, whereas the spot price was the cash settlement price from the London Metal Exchange. Both prices are transactions prices, because there was very little discounting off published prices. Nevertheless, although both prices were highly visible, differences between the two were often sizable and persistent. Not surprisingly, economists have compared the behavior of these two prices. Slade (1991), for example, has shown that on average there was little difference in the levels of these two prices but substantially greater variability in the spot price. Hubbard and Weiner (1989) find that the increased reliance on the spot price that occurred prior to the demise of the producer price led to faster adjustment of prices to supply and

---

26. With company operation, prices are chosen by the principal or company, whereas with franchising, they are chosen by the agent or station operator.

demand shocks. Note that prices in these industries are notoriously volatile. It therefore seems that firms entered into long-term supply contracts partially to reduce the amplitude of price fluctuations and to facilitate planning. However, as geographic markets became more integrated and competition increased as a consequence, it became more difficult, and less desirable, to maintain a two-price system for such homogeneous commodities.

Wolak (1996) explores similar issues in electric utility steam-coal markets and finds that, even though contract prices were systematically higher in that market, buyers entered into long-term contracts to insure against unforeseen supply interruptions and unwanted input price variability.

4.1.3. Government Intervention and Effects

In the above studies, the choice of contract type (vertical integration versus linear or affine pricing contract versus arm's-length transaction) was made by the firms involved in the transaction. There have been many instances, however, where local governments have intervened and prohibited certain types of contracts. Perhaps the most famous is the case of gasoline divorcement in the United States, where divorcement means prohibition of company operation (vertical integration) but not prohibition of ownership. In other words, firms were forced to transact using wholesale prices (to use a pricing contract) even with the branded stations that they owned. Divorcement laws, which have been passed by a number of U.S. state legislatures, usually result from lobbying on the part of franchised dealers, who claim that, when a company acts as both supplier and horizontal competitor, its behavior is influenced by considerations of foreclosure. The empirical literature (e.g., Barron and Umbeck 1984; Vita 2000; Blass and Carlton 2001), in contrast, shows that prices and costs rose and hours became shorter after oil companies were prevented from operating stations directly.

A different sort of divorcement is examined in Slade (1998a)—the forced move that occurred in the British beer industry from franchising with two-part tariffs (contracting) to market interaction under linear prices. In the British beer industry, similar to the U.S. gasoline industry, tenanted pubs are owned by the brewer but operated by the publican, and the publican sets the price. Slade finds that draft beer prices rose after divestiture and attributes the rise to double marginalization—successive oligopoly markups—that is apt to occur after the removal of fixed fees.

The evidence thus indicates that government intervention that prohibits contractual arrangements involving certain modes of operation or ownership structures (including some that replace vertical integration with pricing contracts and contracts involving two-part tariffs by arm's-length transactions) is inefficient. This is so not only for the firms involved, who would have voluntarily chosen the new arrangements had they considered them profitable, but also for consumers (see also Lafontaine and Slade 2008).

4.2. Contract Duration

The period over which a contract is binding can be very short, or it can span many decades. It is therefore natural for researchers to be interested in uncovering the determinants and effects of the choice of duration. Transaction cost theory is the main framework relied on to generate predictions concerning contract length. Specifically, the theory implies that contracts will be longer when firms have more specific investments at stake, because the need to protect those investments is greater. They will be shorter, in contrast, when environments are more uncertain, because flexibility assumes greater importance in that case. To our knowledge, however, although this framework has generated studies of incidence (or, put differently, duration decisions), there are no empirical analyses of the consequences of such decisions for prices, quantities, or other performance measures.

In his seminal papers, Joskow (1985, 1987) relates the duration of contracts between U.S. electric utilities and coal companies, which can last as briefly as 1 year or as long as 50 years, to various proxies that capture the amount of relationship-specific investment (and thus quasi-rent) involved. He finds that mine-mouth plants (i.e., plants that choose to locate next to specific coal mines with the expectation that they will obtain their coal from those mines)—a classical case of site specificity—operate under much longer contracts than do other plants. Specifically, his baseline specification shows that mine-mouth contracts are on average 12–16 years longer. In addition, he finds that plants that use more coal, and those that operate in the East in contrast to the West or Midwest, use longer term contracts. He argues that the former reflects the increased difficulty of finding alternative buyers or sellers for large quantities, whereas the latter reflects differences in the types of coal produced and in the production and transportation options available in the three regions. In sum, Joskow finds strong support for the hypothesis that differences in relationship-specific investments determine the duration of electric utility–coal contracts.

Like Joskow, in their study of natural gas sales contracts, Crocker and Masten (1988) find that firms use longer term contracts when they face a greater likelihood of hold-up; for example, when they have fewer buyer, seller, or transportation options. However, the authors consider not only the benefit of long-term contracts in protecting specific assets but also the cost of using longer term contracts, which relates to the loss of flexibility in dealing with unforeseen events. Consistent with their hypothesis, they find that contract duration was reduced substantially by the 1973 oil embargo, which increased the amount of uncertainty in the market for natural gas. Saussier (2000) documents similar effects in his sample of coal procurement contracts for Électricité de France, even after endogenizing the degree of asset specificity in the transaction. Finally, Pirrong (1993) finds that contracts used in bulk shipping are of longer duration when markets are thin and carriers are specialized, and Hubbard's (2001) finding that shippers rely more on contract carriage compared to spot transactions for long hauls when local markets are thin has a similar interpretation. All these findings support transaction cost determinants of procurement-contract duration.

With business-format franchising contracts, which last about 15 years on average, duration varies substantially across firms both within and between sectors (see, e.g., Lafontaine 1992; Blair and Lafontaine 2005). Brickley et al. (2003) analyze the factors that affect the duration of franchise contracts and find that better-established franchisors rely on longer term contracts, as do those franchisors who require greater investment levels from their franchisees and those who face higher recontracting costs. They explain the result on franchisee investment using asset-specificity arguments and interpret the franchisor-experience effect in terms of reduced uncertainty. In other words, their analyses yield results that are consistent with those obtained in the procurement literature.

4.3. Flexibility and Adjustment Clauses

With long-term contracts, it is crucial to incorporate flexibility. The sort of flexibility that can be built into contracts includes, among other things, adjustment clauses for price or quantity and clauses that make breach easier. Moreover, flexibility is related to duration in the sense that shorter contracts are in essence more flexible. Not surprisingly then, like empirical analyses of duration, studies of flexibility are mainly cast in a transaction cost framework.

4.3.1. Incidence

Provisions for price adjustment in contracts can take many forms.[27] Most schemes, however, can be classified as either redetermination or renegotiation mechanisms, where the former specifies a formula and the latter specifies a process.[28] The choice between the two must take into account the trade-off between flexibility, which favors renegotiation, and freedom from opportunism, which favors redetermination. As conditions are apt to change more during the life of a longer term contract, transaction cost theory predicts that such contracts will include terms that yield more flexibility. Crocker and Masten (1991) assess that choice in natural gas contracts and find that flexible adjustment (renegotiation) is indeed more apt to be chosen in longer duration contracts. However, conditional on contract length, they find no evidence that increases in quasi-rents or market volatility affect the choice of adjustment mechanism.

In their study of contracts between producers and consumers of petroleum coke, Goldberg and Erickson (1987) found that more than 90% of the contracts contained some form of adjustment mechanism. Moreover, those mechanisms ranged from price indexing based on crude oil prices, to renegotiation when that price was above or below some limits, to negotiation at fixed periods. After 1973, however, when the volatility of the market increased markedly, indexing clauses that were meant to be in force for the duration of the contract became less common, as they were replaced by renegotiation clauses. These authors also found that, after 1973, the period between price changes fell substantially, and termination became easier. This evidence also can be rationalized in terms of transaction costs.

Adjustment clauses are but one form of flexibility that can be built into contracts. Contracts also differ in the degree of detail, penalties, legal sanctions, and other specifics that they include, making some documents long and complex, while others are short and simple. Murrell and Paun (2008) study contract complexity in agreements among Romanian firms and find that complexity increases (decreases) with seller (buyer) relationship-specific investment and with the quality of the legal system. Similarly, Lyons (1994) assesses the probability that British engineering subcontractors will formalize their relationships with customers rather than relying on more informal agreements. He finds evidence that pricing contracts tend to be more formal in cases where subcontractors are more vulnerable to customer opportunism; namely, when customers account for larger shares of the engineering firm's output and when output tends to be more specifically designed to the customer's requirements or requires significant specific investment on the part of the engineering firm. These findings and those of Murrell and Paun (2008) are interpreted as supportive of modified versions of transaction cost economics.

---

27. For an early discussion, see Goldberg (1976).
28. This distinction is due to Crocker and Masten (1991).

4.3.2. Effects

A large segment of the literature on adjustment clauses attempts to distinguish between efficiency and market-power-enhancing effects of contract flexibility. The most favored nation (MFN) clause, which guarantees buyers (sellers) the lowest (highest) price that is offered to others in a region, is perhaps the most studied. Given the antitrust authorities' stance on the anticompetitive nature of such contracts (see, e.g., Salop (1986) on the Ethyl case), it is not surprising that most authors have modeled the use of MFN clauses as practices that facilitate oligopolistic coordination. In particular, MFN clauses are expected to eliminate the possibility of selective price discounts and thus enhance cartel stability. However, Crocker and Lyon (1994) argue that MFN provisions facilitate efficient price adjustment in long-term contracts. In contrast to most research in this area, which is theoretical, they use data from natural gas contracts to distinguish empirically among competing explanations.[29] After noting that market power and thus collusion opportunities reside with buyers in this market, Crocker and Lyon claim that the evidence in favor of efficiency rather than collusion is twofold. First, they find that the use of MFN becomes much more likely as the number of buyers increases, which they argue is inconsistent with the notion that MFN clauses facilitate buyer collusion. Second, they show that the nondiscrimination regions over which MFN clauses are defined are small and correspond more closely to sellers' alternative market opportunities than to buyers'. Yet to be effective as practices that facilitate buyer collusion, MFN clauses would need to be applied to the set of competitors that buyers face rather than the set of competitors that sellers face. In addition, they note that MFN adoption patterns parallel those of clauses indexing gas prices to those of other fuels—evidence, they argue, that further supports their efficiency argument.

The effect of take-or-pay provisions, which obligate buyers to pay for a contractually specified minimum quantity, called a "take percentage," even when delivery is not taken, has also been studied. With these provisions, flexibility increases as take percentages fall, but protection of specific investments also declines, creating a tension between these two goals. Various explanations for the existence of take-or-pay provisions (e.g., risk sharing) have been proposed. However, Masten and Crocker (1985) argue that they provide an efficient means for contract breach. They test this hypothesis in natural gas markets. Specifically, they explain take percentages as functions of buyer and seller numbers and find that take percentages fall (flexibility increases) when sellers are few and buyers are many. These results are consistent with their efficiency rationale for the provision, as both of those factors raise the alternative value of gas reserves and make breach more desirable. Mulherin (1986) also argues that take-or-pay and MFN clauses are efficiency rather than market-power enhancing in natural gas markets and provides some empirical evidence consistent with the idea that the use of these clauses is related to bilateral contracting hazards.

A different, but related, question concerns just how flexible stipulated contract prices really are. To answer this question, Joskow (1988, 1990) compared realized coal contract prices to market prices. He found that, because most coal contracts were indexed to cost factors, in periods of stable or predictable growth in demand, contract prices were relatively flexible to changing cost conditions, and thus contractual relationships did not break down. When demand turned

---

29. See also Arbatskaya et al. (2004), who, in a noncontractual context, use informal techniques and data obtained from newspaper advertisements to argue that low-price guarantees do not facilitate collusion.

down, however, the market price for coal was reduced, and substantial deviations between market and contract prices arose. In other words, the contract prices and associated pricing rules did not track changes in market conditions well. Nevertheless, in spite of unfavorable conditions for buyers, most long-term contracts remained in effect. In some cases, parties were able to renegotiate their contracts, relying either on scheduled reopener provisions or on changed quantity commitments. But this occurred because the contract or specific conditions permitted it. In general, the formal contract terms remained binding: with clear contractual promises, litigation and breach were the exception, not the rule.

4.4. Fixed Price versus Cost Plus

Recall that, with a cost-plus contract, the seller is paid a percentage of costs, where the percentage exceeds 100. The fixed-price contract, in contrast, pays the seller a fixed amount that is determined ex ante. Most empirical studies of cost-plus contracts involve neither a choice between contracting and vertical integration nor between contracting and spot market transactions. Instead, the choice is between two forms of contracts. Specifically, taking the existence of a contract for granted, it is the decision to rely on a particular type of contract—cost plus versus fixed price—that is assessed. As little is known about the effects of this decision, we limit our discussion to incidence.

4.4.1. Incidence

Since cost-plus contracts adjust automatically to changed circumstances affecting costs, they are more flexible, and one would expect them to prevail when (1) projects are highly uncertain, (2) the technology is complex or untested, (3) quality is important but difficult to verify, and (4) trading parties trust each other. In contrast, since fixed-price contracts are associated with better incentives for cost control, they are more apt to be chosen when (1) the project is fairly standard, (2) the measurement of costs is problematic, and (3) important changes in specification are not anticipated.

Some researchers have examined whether these theoretical predictions hold up in practice. Leffler and Rucker (1991) assess private timber harvesting contracts, Banerjee and Duflo (2000) look at contracts for Indian customized software, Kalnins and Mayer (2004) and Shi and Susarla (2011) assess contracts for the provision of information technology services and computer-related hardware, Corts and Singh (2004) and Kellogg (2011) look at contracts between oil exploration and production companies on the one hand, and independent drilling contractors on the other, and Bajari et al. (2009) consider private sector construction contracts. To summarize, they find evidence that cost-plus contracts are preferred when presale measurement costs are high and monitoring is relatively cheap (Leffler and Rucker 1991); when firms are older, where age is equated with reputation (Banerjee and Duflo 2000); when costs are uncertain ex ante, the cost of measuring quality ex post is high, and the project does not involve the buyer's hardware or proprietary technology (Kalnins and Mayer 2004); and when development rather than exploratory wells are involved, because drilling activities for the former are more complex (Corts and Singh 2004). Bajari et al. (2009), moreover, find that more complex projects are more likely to be awarded via negotiation than through an auction mechanism, which, they note, amounts to saying that complex projects will be cost-plus rather than fixed price. Finally, Shi and Susarla

(2011) find that vendors that can be trusted to negotiate fairly or to keep costs low are more likely to be awarded fixed-price and cost-plus contracts, respectively. All these findings are supportive of the theoretical predictions.

Theoretical predictions concerning other effects, however, are more ambiguous. In particular, the issue of how previous experience with the same trading partner affects the choice of contract cannot be signed a priori. Indeed, as Corts and Singh (2004) argue, whether repeated interaction makes fixed-price or cost-plus contracts more attractive depends on how such interaction affects incentive provision relative to contracting costs. On the one hand, experience with a partner can lower the need for high-powered incentives and thus favor reliance on cost-plus contracts. On the other hand, it can lower contracting/recontracting costs and thus favor fixed-price contracting.[30] Like the predictions, the empirical findings concerning previous interaction are also somewhat mixed. Specifically, Banerjee and Duflo (2000) find that the choice of contract for software procurement is unaffected by whether the software firm has previously worked for a client, whereas Corts and Singh (2004), Kalnins and Mayer (2004), Kellogg (2011), and Shi and Susarla (2011) find that frequent interaction leads firms to rely more on cost-plus contracting in drilling and information technology service procurement. The results of these studies thus suggest that, at least in these industries, repetition reduces the need for high-powered incentives more than it reduces contracting costs. We return to these issues in Section 4.8.

4.5. Share Contracts

With a share contract, which may involve fixed fees, each party receives a portion of some output variable, usually revenues. Relative to their occurrence, share contracts have received a large amount of attention in the empirical literature. Much of this literature, however, has been about contracts that arise within firms (e.g., executive compensation) or in contexts where at least one of the two parties is an individual (e.g., sharecropping or compensation of talent in the legal, real estate, or movie production industries). Still, other analyses have focused on interfirm share contracts, such as those used in business-format franchising and technology licensing. The main question addressed in the empirical work is the rationale for these contracts or the question of incidence. However, interest in assessing consequences has grown recently.

4.5.1. Incidence

Table 2 summarizes several studies that examine how firms choose to interact with other firms using a share contract versus some other option(s). The table shows the sector of the economy in which the firms operate, the authors of the study, the date of its publication, what the parties share under the share contract, the type of data or empirical technique used, the dependent variable for the study, and the principal conclusions that the authors draw.

The research in Table 2 illustrates the different settings in which sharing among firms arises in the economy. In addition, the results from the studies support three main conclusions. First, share contracting is often used in contexts in which incentive issues are important. Specifically, parties choose to share the outcome of their efforts when both of them need to cooperate in a form of team production and neither contribution is easily assessed by the other. This is one of

---

30. See also Crocker and Reynolds (1993), who examine government procurement contracts, on this issue.

Table 2. Empirical evidence on the incidence of share contracts

Reference	Industry setting	Share of	Data/analysis	Main focus	Main conclusions of study
Licensing					
Contractor (1981)	International technology by U.S. manufacturers	Licensee revenues	Cross-section	Returns and costs of contract, contract terms	Royalties based on licensee sales occur in 80% of agreements, average 4%, and are the most important source of licensor returns.
Caves et al. (1983)	Technology by U.S. chemical, electrical, and equipment manufacturers	Licensee revenues	Cross-section/ survey data	Contract terms	Incomplete rent extraction occurs due to uncertain value of technology to licensee and incomplete contracts. Firms licensing core technologies impose more restrictions on licensees.
Macho-Stadler et al. (1996)	Spanish licensees, all industries	Licensee revenues	Cross-section/ administrative data	Contract terms	Royalty payments are more important in contracts involving know-how.
Bessy and Brousseau (1998)	Technology in French manufacturing	Licensee revenues	Cross-section/ survey data	Propensity to license, contract terms	Contracting practices vary due to different goals of licensing firms and industry settings where licensing occurs.
Anand and Khanna (2000)	Technology in U.S. manufacturing	Licensee revenues	Cross-section	Contract features	Technology licensing is highly concentrated in a few manufacturing sectors. Robust cross-industry differences exist in incidence of licensing, use of exclusives, cross-licensing, ex ante deals, and repeat transactions. Authors suggest differences in strength of intellectual property rights drive these differences.

Continued

Table 2. *Continued*

Reference	Industry setting	Share of	Data/analysis	Main focus	Main conclusions of study
Franchising					
Caves and Murphy (1976)	Various retailing and service sectors	Franchisee revenues	Descriptive	Propensity to franchise	Reliance on franchising versus company ownership reflects divergent efficient scales of activities and need for incentives locally.
Brickley and Dark (1987)	Various retailing and service sectors	Franchisee revenues	Cross-section	Propensity to franchise	Reliance on franchising versus company ownership reflects a trade-off among agency problems, including downstream effort and free-riding incentives.
Lafontaine (1992)	Various retailing and service sectors	Franchisee revenues	Cross-section	Propensity to franchise, contract terms	Double-sided moral hazard is best supported. Risk effect is absent or has wrong sign. Empirical model explains reliance on franchising better than it does contract terms.
Lafontaine (1993)	Various retailing and service sectors	Franchisee revenues	Cross-section	Propensity to franchise, contract terms	Information asymmetries between franchisor and franchisee and the resulting need for signaling franchisor type do not explain contract terms or stake of franchisor.
Scott (1995)	Various retailing and service sectors	Franchisee revenues	Cross-section	Propensity to franchise	Company ownership is a substitute instrument to royalty payments for franchisor incentives to maintain quality.
Lafontaine and Shaw (1999)	Various retailing and service sectors	Franchisee revenues	Panel data	Contract terms	Considerable heterogeneity exists in financial contract terms (royalty rates and franchise fees) across franchised chains, but there is persistence over time within. When changed, they may go up or down with no systematic pattern.
Lafontaine and Shaw (2005)	Various retailing and service sectors	Franchisee revenues	Panel data	Propensity to franchise	Reliance on franchising goes up during the first 7 or so years in franchising—a period of adjustment—then remains quite stable over time. Large differences in reliance on franchising across franchisors are explained by differences in brand name value.
Lafontaine and Oxley (2004)	International, various sectors	Franchisee revenues	Cross-section	Contract terms	U.S. franchisors use the same terms with franchisees in Mexico as in the United States.

Movie distribution					
Cachon and Larivière (2005)	Movie video	Video store revenues from movie	Cross-section	Reliance on revenue sharing, contract terms	Revenue sharing is a better channel coordination mechanism.
Filson et al. (2005)	Movie	Theater revenues	Cross-section	Reliance on revenue sharing	Revenue sharing in this industry is best explained by risk sharing.
Gil and Lafontaine (2012)	Movie	Theater revenues	Panel data	Contract terms	Sharing allows better week-to-week pricing of the movie by upstream firm, and thus it yields better downstream incentives to keep movies on the screen.
Mortimer (2008)	Movie video	Video store revenues from movie	Cross-section	Reliance on revenue sharing	Revenue sharing enhances upstream and downstream profits and contributes to increased consumer welfare.
Commercial leasing					
Wheaton (2000)	Retail real estate	Retailer revenues	Cross-section	Reliance on revenue sharing	Revenue sharing is the solution to a double-sided moral hazard problem.
Gould et al. (2005)	Retail real estate	Retailer revenues	Cross-section	Reliance on revenue sharing, contract terms	Revenue sharing induces efficient actions from anchor and nonanchor stores and developers in the presence of externalities.
Joint ventures					
Bai et al. (2004)	All industries	Joint venture revenues	Cross-section	Contract terms	Revenue sharing terms are consistent with double-sided moral hazard.

the conclusions that authors who have examined franchising, licensing, real estate leasing, and joint venture contracts in particular have reached.

Second, we find another type of explanation arising in settings where the value of the good being exchanged is unknown to both parties at the time of contracting and depends on factors outside their control.[31] This is the case, for example, for movie distributors selling copies of movies to video rental stores (Cachon and Larivière 2005; Mortimer 2008). The level of revenues that the video rental store can earn from stocking copies of the video is unknown at the time of contracting. If the video rental store must purchase all copies of the video at a fixed price ex ante, it will be wary of buying too many copies. Just as auction participants underbid if they are concerned about the value of the good that they are buying (i.e., underbidding is the best response to the "winner's curse"), the downstream firm, worried about overevaluating revenue streams for a video, will "underbid." In this context, underbidding will take the form of choosing a lower quantity (i.e., purchasing fewer videos). From the distributor's perspective, this practice increases the chances of stock-outs downstream and thus hurts the revenue stream of the movie distributor as well as that of the video rental store. Specifying the price of the video as a function of the revenues it brings in ex post, which is what revenue sharing achieves, can thus serve as a flexible pricing device that prevents underbuying. Moreover, it reduces the need for ex ante search and for renegotiation ex post (Leffler and Rucker 1991; Lafontaine and Masten 2002; Gil and Lafontaine 2012).[32]

Third, and finally, the findings of these studies are important in what they do not support: the notion that risk sharing is an important factor explaining the use of share contracting. In fact, authors have tended to find a positive relationship between sharing and risk in contexts where alternative contracts would much better insure the risk-averse party. This relationship is inconsistent with risk sharing but consistent with the notion that uncertainty exacerbates monitoring problems and induces different levels of delegation, which in turn leads to more sharing (Lafontaine 1992; Lafontaine and Bhattacharyya 1995; Prendergast 2002).

A smaller group of studies considers how share parameters vary across contracts. These include Lafontaine (1992, 1993), Lafontaine and Shaw (1999), and Brickley (2002) on franchising and Wheaton (2000) and Gould et al. (2005) on retail-lease contract terms. In general, these authors find results consistent with the findings from the empirical literature on the choice of organizational form (i.e., the decision to use sharing). Lafontaine (1992), for example, finds that the explanatory variables used to capture double-sided moral hazard issues have the same sign in royalty rate (share parameter) regressions as they do in regressions for the extent of franchising in a chain. However, the variables in question explain much less of the variance in royalty rates and franchise fees than they do in the proportion of outlets that are franchised.[33] Similarly, for licensing contracts, Taylor and Silbertson (1973), Contractor (1981),

---

31. See Goldberg (1976) for an early statement of this argument.

32. The argument also relates to the measurement-cost argument of Barzel (1982) and to the self-enforcement argument of Kenney and Klein (1983, 2000) on the use of block booking.

33. One factor that explains some of the variance in royalty rates is the franchisor's reliance, in some sectors, on input sales as an alternative form of profit extraction. Lafontaine (1992) finds that royalty rates are lower, for example, in chains that sell more to their franchisees. Rao and Srinivasan (1995) provide related evidence that royalty rates are lower for franchisors in retail compared to those that sell services.

and Caves et al. (1983) find that the variation in fixed fees and royalty rates across industries is difficult to explain. However, Gil and Lafontaine (2012) show that, in the context of movie distribution, the shares to distributors vary in predictable ways when viewed as a mechanism to extract downstream value. Specifically, distributor shares are higher (and decline more slowly) for movies that are expected to do better at the box office. They are lower, however, for movies shown in older and larger theaters and for those shown in theaters whose owners have more local market power.

Finally, and not surprisingly, state laws that protect franchisees in business-format franchising have been found to affect the use of franchising as well as the terms of these contracts. Specifically, Brickley et al. (1991) find that franchising is used less relative to company ownership in states that have enacted franchise termination laws. They also find that the value of franchised companies operating in a state is negatively affected by the passage of such a law. Moreover, Brickley (2002) shows that franchisors headquartered in states with termination laws—laws that make franchisee termination more costly—charge higher royalty rates and lower franchise fees, such that the prices paid for franchises by franchisees are higher in those states. These results are all consistent with the notion that franchisors value termination rights, a result that suggests that franchisee behavior in business-format franchising is controlled at least in part by the threat of losing future benefits from the relationship. We come back to these issues briefly below.

In sum, the literature on incidence has shown that share contracting between firms tends to occur most often when incentive problems arise for both parties to a contract. In addition, the empirical literature suggests that in some contexts, sharing is a response to the difficulties of setting the right price and minimizing renegotiation costs in markets where transactions are heterogeneous and values are uncertain a priori.

4.5.2. Effects

A typical study of consequences considers the effects of sharing on firm outcomes relative to what would have happened under another organizational form (e.g., a comparison of firm profitability, service quality, or survival between company and franchised units of a chain, or for chains that franchise versus those that do not). Shelton's (1967) analysis is a classic in this respect. He uses data on costs, revenues, and profits for outlets in a single chain to examine the effect of switching from franchising to company ownership and from company ownership back to franchising. He finds no difference in revenues across the two governance regimes. However, under company ownership, costs are higher, and thus profits are lower, than under franchising.

The main advantage of Shelton's study is that its within-outlet design holds most things constant as the mode of organization changes. Its main drawback is that units in this chain are operated under company ownership only during periods of transition. In other words, franchising is the preferred mode, and company ownership is only a transitory phase. Consequently, company ownership is likely to be inefficient, and inefficiently implemented, in this particular chain. This circumstance, then, might explain Shelton's findings.

Other authors have looked for price or cost differences between franchised and company units of chains when the firm chooses which outlets are franchised and which are operated by the company. In particular, Krueger (1991) found that company employees were paid slightly more and faced somewhat steeper earnings profiles than did employees in franchised units. He argued that the lower powered incentive contracts of the managers of company restaurants make it necessary to offer greater incentives to employees in the form of efficiency wages and steeper earnings profiles. Freedman and Kosová (2012) revisit this question using data on housekeeper compensation in the hotel industry, a context where they argue agency issues are apt to be especially pronounced. They find even stronger evidence of differences in pay schemes between franchised and corporately run hotels, with greater emphasis on performance pay and steeper earnings profiles in franchised hotels. Finally, Kosová et al. (2012) compare revenues, occupancy rates, and prices among the hotels of a large multichain company. They find significant differences between these outcomes for franchised and nonfranchised hotels in aggregate data patterns and in analyses that treat organizational form as exogenous. However, the differences are small even in aggregate data, and when they use information about the company's other local operations to instrument for organizational form at a given hotel, the differences between franchised and company operations become statistically and economically insignificant.[34]

Some studies have also looked for quality differences between franchised and company units of the same chain. Bradach (1998: 109), in particular, interviewed managers in five fast-food chains and concluded that the two arrangements exhibited similar levels of (standard adherence) uniformity. For the two firms in his sample that used third-party evaluators to assess quality, the average score was 94.6 (out of 100 points) for the franchised units and 93.9 for the company units in the first chain, and 89.7 and 90.6, respectively, for the second. He concluded that there was no quality difference between franchised and company-owned restaurants within these chains. Using data on quality ratings published by *Consumer Reports,* Michael (2000) found that quality was negatively associated with franchising in both the restaurant and hotel industries, and concluded that free riding was a problem for franchised chains. Jin and Leslie (2009) also found evidence that hygiene scores (a measure of quality) were higher among company-owned restaurants than among the franchised units of the same chains. A new policy requiring that restaurants post their hygiene scores, however, eliminated this difference.

Whether franchising affects firm survival is a question that has received some attention in the literature as well. Most studies have been concerned with whether affiliation with a franchised chain augments the likelihood of survival for an entrepreneur. For example, Bates (1995a,b) used the Characteristics of Business Owners (CBO) database produced in 1992 by the U.S. Census Bureau to assess the rate of failure among a representative sample of small businesses, both franchised and nonfranchised. He found that failure rates of franchised small businesses were greater than those of independent businesses, though not significantly so. Specifically, he observed that over a 5-year period, 34.7 percent of franchised businesses failed as opposed to 28.0 percent for independents. Bates (1998) then further distinguished units sold to new franchisees and those sold to existing franchisees. He found that the vast majority (84 percent) of new franchised units are opened by existing multi-unit operators, and that these units were very likely to survive, much more so than independent businesses. New units opened by new franchisees, however, were less likely to survive than were independents.

---

34. In contrast, Arruñada et al. (2009) find that company-owned car dealerships in Spain are much less productive than franchised car dealerships. However, they explain these performance differences not based on organizational form per se but rather on the pro-labor legal environment, which affected the terms of labor contracts more in vertically integrated dealerships, making them particularly inefficient.

Early empirical evidence had suggested that franchising attracts people who would not have chosen to open a business by themselves (Hunt 1972; Stanworth 1977). Consistent with these findings, Williams (1999) used the same CBO database to document differences in human capital, such as formal training and business experience, between individuals who choose to purchase a franchise and those who go in business for themselves. He found that those who opt for franchising tend to have higher education and more work experience but lower levels of business experience than those who opt for independent businesses. He then showed that those who choose franchising are substantially better off as franchisees than they would have been if they had tried to start businesses on their own.

As for franchisor, as opposed to franchisee, survival, several studies have documented a high rate of failure for them (e.g., Shane 1996; Stanworth 1996; Lafontaine and Shaw 1998). To our knowledge, no study compares the exit rates of franchised and nonfranchised companies explicitly. Instead, authors examine factors that affect the likelihood of survival of franchised chains. Lafontaine and Shaw (1998), for example, show that the chain's characteristics at the time it begins franchising, including contract terms (e.g., royalty rates and franchise fees), have little predictive power regarding success or failure. The number of years in business prior to the start of franchising was one of the very few factors that increased the likelihood of success in franchising. Silvester et al. (1996) found that a franchisor's initial financial investment in the business and his or her strategy of choosing franchisees with prior experience also affect the survival and growth of the chain. Azoulay and Shane (2001) suggest that offering exclusive territories to franchisees increases the likelihood of survival for young franchised chains. Finally, using a unique unbalanced panel dataset covering about 1,000 franchise chains annually from 1980 to 2001, Kosová and Lafontaine (2010) show that the usual variables from the industry dynamics literature, namely age and size, affect franchised chain growth and survival most, even after controlling for chain fixed effects and other characteristics, such as contract terms. They also confirm the result in Lafontaine and Shaw (1998) for the effect of the number of years that the franchisor spends developing the franchise concept before starting to franchise. As for the chain's contracting practices, they find that a larger proportion of company units in the chain is positively related to growth and survival in franchising. Moreover, though these effects were not always statistically significant, they find that higher ongoing revenue streams for franchisors (in the form of royalties or other such fees) and lower up-front requirements for franchisees are positively associated with both franchise chain growth and continued involvement or survival in franchising.

Few studies have considered the consequences of share contracting outside of franchising. One such study, by Mortimer (2008), analyzes the move from linear pricing to revenue sharing in video rental stores, a change that was brought about by a fall in the cost of monitoring transactions on a per movie basis. Not surprisingly, since the change was voluntarily undertaken by the up- and downstream firms—studios and retailers—she finds that it enhanced profits for both. More interestingly, using a structural econometric model of firms' contracting choices, she is able to quantify the benefits for both upstream and downstream firms. She finds that both up- and downstream firm profits increased by 10% for popular, and even more so for less popular, titles. She also shows that small retailers benefit more from revenue sharing than larger retailers do, and that consumer welfare increased as a result of the adoption of revenue sharing in this industry. Both of these effects would have been hard to predict a priori. A second study, by Gil (2009), shows that for movies whose revenues are most difficult to predict, namely, nonblockbuster movies, reliance on revenue sharing in movie distribution contracts does not fully align distributor and exhibitor incentives. Consequently, movies of vertically integrated distributors are shown longer in distributors' own theaters than in vertically separated theaters despite the systematic reliance on revenue sharing in this industry.[35]

4.6. Vertical Restraints

Vertical restraints are restrictive contract clauses that one link in a vertical chain imposes on another. Usually, the manufacturer or upstream firm restricts the retailer or downstream firm in some way. Vertical restraints are therefore instruments of control. There are many other ways in which one level in the vertical chain can exercise control over another or transfer certain rights across firm boundaries. Those methods are discussed in Section 4.7. Here we limit discussion to the traditional vertical restraints that the antitrust literature has focused on.

In contrast to the share-contracting literature, the bulk of the vertical restraints literature evaluates the consequences of employing various forms of restraints, not the incidence. This emphasis is likely due to its focus on competition policy. Still, although the literature has often just mentioned where these restraints occur and then examined their effects, a few studies have tried to arrive at some conclusions as to why these are used by analyzing where they occur most. We begin with a few examples of the use of specific vertical restraints and then discuss some reasons for employing them.

4.6.1. Incidence

Exclusive dealing—where a manufacturer requires that a retailer sell only her products—is perhaps the most common form of vertical restraint. Indeed, all franchising involves some form of exclusive dealing arrangement. However, one also finds exclusive dealing outside of franchise relationships. For example, the GM–Fisher Body contract involved exclusive dealing (Klein et al. 1978), as did the contracts between boat captains and tuna processors studied by Gallick (1984). Exclusive dealing also is used by manufacturers with their distributors: Heide et al. (1998) found that 46 of the 147 manufacturers they surveyed—all of them from the industrial machinery and equipment or the electronic and electric equipment sectors—used exclusive dealing clauses in their contracts with distributors.

An exclusive territory is granted when a manufacturer assures a downstream firm that he will be the exclusive reseller of a brand in a geographic market. As noted by Marvel (1982), exclusive territories often accompany exclusive dealing clauses. Not surprisingly then, they are commonly granted to industrial sales forces and wholesale distributors. It is also customary, for example, for cleaning-service franchises to grant exclusive territories. In fact, about 3 out of every 4 franchised chains grant some form of exclusive territory to their franchisees (Blair and Lafontaine 2005: 223). In their studies of manufacturing firms in the industrial machinery and equipment and the electronic and electric equipment sectors, Dutta et al. (1999) found that 69 of the 147 firms in their final sample used territorial restrictions.

---

35. See Lach and Shankerman (2008) for estimates of the effects of royalty rates on effort and outcomes in a different context, namely public and private universities licensing activities.

"Tying" refers to situations in which a manufacturer requires its customers to purchase product B as a condition for obtaining what they really want, namely, product A. Well-known examples include IBM, which required that purchasers of computers also buy punch cards, and movie distributors who practiced block booking in the early days of the industry. Block booking is a form of bundling that requires that exhibition houses rent packages of, rather than individual, films. Perhaps the most famous recent tying case involved Microsoft's attempt to tie the use of Internet Explorer to its Windows operation system (see Whinston 2001).

With resale price maintenance (RPM), the upstream firm exerts control over the price that the downstream firm can charge. RPM takes many forms including setting a specific price or a price floor or ceiling. Because RPM is or has been illegal in most countries, examples often come from antitrust challenges, which have included cases involving firms in such sectors as gasoline distribution, recreational equipment, and brewing and distilling. Franchisors in particular have been known to exert downward pressure on the prices charged by their franchisees (i.e., maximum RPM; see Blair and Lafontaine 2005), while in other contexts, manufacturers, including high-end electronics and fashion firms, have successfully implemented minimum pricing requirements.

Going beyond mere examples, Ippolito (1991) examined the population of all 203 reported cases of RPM in the United States between 1975 and 1982, a period during which a fairly broad interpretation of what constitutes RPM was adopted by the courts, and during which she argues the courts adhered quite strictly to the per se standard. She shows first that vertical restraints are often used together. Firms simultaneously relied on other vertical restraints in 122 of the RPM cases, most frequently using territorial, tying, or customer restrictions (49, 31, and 32 of the cases, respectively). Cases of RPM also often involved other charges, in particular, horizontal price fixing in 30 and refusal to deal in 40 of the cases. In addition, Ippolito finds evidence that a nontrivial portion of RPM cases (65% of all private and 68% of all public cases in her data) arise in contexts where products can be classified as complex, new, or infrequently purchased, which are the types of products where the special services theory for RPM is most likely to hold. She also finds another largely overlapping segment of both private and public cases arising in contexts where dealers can influence the quality of the final good or the customer's experience in important ways. Here again, manufacturer-controlled pricing can alleviate the fundamental principal-agent problem that efficiency motives and organizational economics emphasize. Yet another set of (mostly franchising) cases seems well explained by concerns over vertical sales-effort externality problems. She concludes that collusion is not the primary explanation for the RPM practices that were prosecuted during this period.

Heide et al. (1998) focus on exclusive dealing, which historically has not been treated as harshly as RPM by the U.S. antitrust authorities. As a result, they were able to obtain survey data that they used to examine what leads manufacturers to use exclusive dealing in their contracts with distributors. They found that manufacturers who were more concerned that their promotional efforts, training, or general support of distributors might benefit their competitors were much more likely to adopt exclusive dealing arrangements. In contrast, when it was difficult for manufacturers to assess whether their dealers sold other manufacturers' products (i.e., when monitoring the behavior of dealers was difficult ex post), or when manufacturers perceived that their customers had a preference for multiproduct distribution, they were less likely to rely on exclusive dealing. Again, these results are consistent with the type of efficiency or principal-agent arguments one finds in the organizational economics literature.

Finally, Zanarone (2009) compares contracts used by 19 car manufacturers with their dealers in Italy before and after the European Commission prohibited the use of location clauses in car distribution in 2002. These clauses prevented dealers from selling cars outside their territories. Zanarone shows that once exclusive territories became illegal, the number of car manufacturers who imposed price ceilings, required dealers to abide by a variety of explicit standards, and required dealers to contribute to an advertising fund that the manufacturer controlled went up significantly. He explains the latter two changes as direct responses to the reduced dealer incentives to advertise and provide pre-sales services. As for price ceilings, he suggests that they may have become necessary to prevent dealers from circumventing their quantity floors, something they could do, he argues, by selling aggressively outside their territories while maintaining above-normal prices in their own, perhaps isolated, markets.

4.6.2. Effects

The results of studies that have examined the effects of vertical restraints on firm performance and on downstream prices and quantities have been summarized in Cooper et al. (2005) and Lafontaine and Slade (2008). In both cases, the authors find that, on the whole, vertical restraints imposed by manufacturers on their resellers tend to be associated with lower costs, greater consumption, higher stock returns, and better chances of upstream firm survival. In other words, they are efficient devices for aligning incentives, eliminating free riding, and controlling opportunistic behavior, as the studies on the incidence of these practices summarized above also suggest. Moreover, there is little evidence of foreclosure.

The evidence also suggests strongly that mandated restraints, such as the exclusive territories that car manufacturers are required to provide to their dealers in most states, lead to higher prices, higher costs, shorter hours of operation, lower consumption, and fewer dealerships. For example, in his study of the effect of state laws protecting the territories of car retailers, all of whom operate under exclusive dealing contracts, Smith II (1982) found that car prices and dealership values rose, while hours of operation fell, after the state laws were enacted. In line with the results in Zanarone (2009) mentioned above, Brickley (2002) finds that franchisors adjust the terms of their contracts after the passage of laws protecting franchisees against termination such that, when all is said and done, franchisees are no better off.[36] So although the focus of the latter is not traditional vertical restraints, the conclusions reached are the same as in that literature.

The authors of both survey papers conclude that manufacturer and consumer welfare tend to be aligned when it comes to vertical restraints, as manufacturers have every incentive to develop lean distribution systems that get their products to their customers at the lowest possible cost. In contrast, retailers and distributors do better (or at least anticipate doing better) in the more protected, or less competitive, environments that government-mandated restraints sometimes afford them.

---

36. Similarly, the benefits of increased state regulation governing car manufacturer-dealer relations accrue to incumbent dealers at the time they are enacted, in that these dealers either derive greater profits or other benefits directly, or can resell their dealerships at higher prices. Thus, the state regulation encourages potentially excessive investment levels by dealers. See Lafontaine and Scott Morton (2010).

Although the results from the reviews of the literature on effects of vertical restraints are striking, they cannot be definitive if for no other reason than the small number of studies from which these conclusions are drawn, especially when one considers the number of different restraints and industries covered. Tests of the effects of vertical restraints are rare despite the intense interest of antitrust authorities in these issues, because of the challenges associated with endogeneity and the difficulty in obtaining the right type of data. In particular, efficiency motives for these restraints imply changes in costs, yet cost data are often unavailable. The recent work by Asker (2005) on exclusive dealing, Crawford and Yurukoglu (2012) on bundling, Ho et al. (2012) on full-line forcing, and finally Ferrari and Verboven (2012) on restricted licensing and franchise fees, much of which post dates the surveys mentioned above, relies on structural approaches (along with detailed data and institutional knowledge) to estimate demand and costs and evaluate the effects of the restraints. Consistent with the literature reviewed in the surveys mentioned above, Asker (2005), Brenkers and Verboven (2006), and Ho et al. (2012) find that the restraints cannot be explained by anticompetitive motives—respectively, foreclosure, strategic delegation, and leveraging of monopoly power. Also consistent with prior literature on the cable industry, Crawford and Yurukoglu (2012) find that bundling of services is costly to consumers in that industry.

Clearly, much more work is needed in this area. Hopefully, this discussion of the literature on vertical restraints will encourage empirical researchers to consider those restraints as well as other types of contract clauses in their analyses of governance and to bring vertical restraints more squarely into the realm of organizational economics and contract theory.

4.7. Control Rights Allocation

All studies of contracting practices in some sense are about the allocation of control rights. Indeed, except for the very simplest fixed-price contracts, virtually all contracts specify who can make certain decisions and/or who owns and controls the use of certain assets. For example, the choice between company operation and franchising, whether traditional or business-format, also largely determines who has the right to hire employees and set wages and prices. Similarly, the vertical restraints discussed in Section 4.6 allocate decision rights to one party or the other. Some empirical analyses of contracts, however, focus more directly on the issue of how different control rights are allocated. Moreover, the more recent studies of this type often test aspects of the theory of incomplete contracts, which emphasizes the importance of allocating decision or control rights to those parties whose decisions, investments, and/or efforts will have the greatest impact on final outcomes. These studies then explain the presence of various clauses based on the potential impact of allocating decision rights to the parties involved. To our knowledge, there has been no attempt to empirically assess the effect of this allocation.[37] As a result, this section focuses on incidence only.

---

37. Ciliberto's (2006) analysis of joint ventures, which he treats similarly and for which he finds similar results as for vertical integration, could be viewed as an exception. He notes that in the relationship between hospital and physicians, the asset is the physician's patients. Under a joint venture, he argues that the hospital gains some control over this asset. He then shows that joint ventures between hospitals and doctors positively affect hospital investment in new technologies, just like vertical integration does.

Some of the empirical work on contractual agreements that predates the development of incomplete contract theory includes detailed descriptions of the various components of contracts, often in the form of frequency tables for various clauses from a cross-section of contractual agreements. For example, Udell (1972) analyzes a total of 172 contracts for 167 distinct contract provisions in business-format franchise contracts, many of which entail the allocation of control rights. He finds, among other things, that 59% of the contracts include exclusive-territory clauses, 58% specify the days (hours) of operation for the franchised unit, thereby allocating to the franchisor the right to make such decisions, and 60% include clauses stipulating that the franchisor controls the products, services, or menus offered by the franchisee. Similarly, Contractor (1981) provides information on the frequency of various restrictions imposed on licensees in international license contracts.

Table 3 summarizes information about the main contract clauses described in these and in more recent studies, such as Lerner and Merges (1998) and Ryall and Sampson (2009), who analyze control rights allocation in technology alliances in the biotech industry and the telecommunications and microelectronic industries, respectively. The table also includes a study by Arruñada et al. (2001), who focus on the contracting practices of car manufacturers with their dealers in Spain.[38] In these studies, authors often comment that contracting practices are not easily labeled or classified. Not surprisingly then, categorization schemes vary across studies, making them particularly difficult to summarize. In addition, often due to data constraints, different studies focus on certain aspects of agreements while ignoring others. Finally, some studies are concerned with franchising, while others are about licensing and yet others about procurement. In spite of this heterogeneity, a few themes emerge from Table 3.

First, and not surprisingly, we find that there is much variety in contracting practices, even within contract types (i.e., when one examines only franchising arrangements, only licensing agreements, and so on). This variety reflects the use of these contracts by numerous firms engaged in a variety of business activities.

Second, despite the variety, we find that the same issues are addressed repeatedly: typically, the contracts specify the terms of the exchange, including prices and sometimes quantities, and then limit the rights of the agent (licensee, franchisee, or supplier) explicitly to a time and place. They also give the principal the capacity to monitor the behavior of the agent and to terminate the contract at will or under certain conditions. Finally, they spell out what happens after termination. In other words, these contracts resemble leasing arrangements, with the principal providing an asset—whether it be a brand and business format, a technology, or simply some desirable business (as in the case of information technology procurement)—and then spelling out the limits within which the agent can use and profit from this asset. These limits, in turn, protect the principal's ongoing interest in the value of the asset.

Third, the data in the table reflect the fact that the number or extent of restrictions imposed on the agent typically increases with the value of the asset involved in the transaction (see also Table 2). Thus, when a firm licenses its core technology, Caves et al. (1983) find that it imposes more restrictions on its licensees than when the technology is more peripheral to the licensor's business. Brickley (1999) analyzes the tendency of a large sample of franchisors to rely

38. See also Elfenbein and Lerner (2003) on contracts for portal alliances. This paper is not included in the table, because the paper does not provide simple frequencies for the contract clauses they focus on.

Table 3. The allocation of control rights

Reference	Data/setting	Asset ownership[a]	Control over (sample clauses)
Udell (1972)	172 fast-food franchise contracts in the United States, 167 clauses	Franchisor owns/leases property, 62%; intangible trademarks, brand, 52%; building design and décor, 21%	*Input purchases:* Equipment, may or must, 66%; supplies, may or must, 52%; vendor approval, 50% *Monitoring:* Franchisor right (obligation) to inspect, 71% (13%); to audit books, 44%; periodic reports by franchisee, 76%; must use franchisor's bookkeeping system, 58%; penalties for violations, 20% *Vertical restraints:* Franchisor controls price, 28%; franchisee cannot own competing business, 27.5% *Operations:* Standards, 64%; cleanliness, 72%; operating manual part of contract, 43%; franchisors sets: days, 58%, hours, 57%, product line, 60%; franchisee must be full time, 13% *Sale/transfer rights:* Franchisor approval required, 74%; franchisor right of first refusal, 32%; right of inheritance, 33% *Duration/termination:* Duration, 10–20 years; option to renew, 54%; conditions for termination, 98%; conditions for immediate cancellation, 42%; grace period, 69%; noncompete years, 56%; noncompete distance, 49%
Contractor (1981), first sample	International technology licensing, 37 U.S. licensors, all industries	Technology flow-back clauses, 71%	*Input purchases:* Materials to be purchased from licensor or designated agents, 12% *Monitoring:* Quality control on: materials, 29.4%, finished product, 55.9%; royalties on sales revenue lead to creative accounting *Vertical restraints:* Territorial limitations on manufacture, 82%; limitation on: export quantity, 15%, export price, 6%; export through designated agent, 23%; exclusive dealing, 23%
Contractor (1981), second sample	102 international technology licensing agreements, all industries	Patent mentioned, 64%; technology flow-back clause, 40%	*Vertical restraints:* Territorial limitations on: sales, 43%, output, 16%, both, 7% *Duration/termination:* Mean duration, 12.6 years
Caves et al. (1983)[b]	257 contracts of 28 licensors in chemical, electrical, and equipment manufacturing	Transfer of technology, 75%; purchase right to infringe on licensor patent, 25%; technology flow-back clauses, 43%	*Vertical restraints:* Licensee may not sell outside specified markets, 34%; production location restriction, 34%; exclusive territory for licensee, 33% *Duration/termination:* If performance clause (growth) is not met, exclusivity clause is terminated

Continued

Table 3. *Continued*

Reference	Data/setting	Asset ownership[a]	Control over (sample clauses)
Dnes (1992)[c]	19 franchised systems in the United Kingdom, traditional and business format	Lease control, 63%	*Input purchases:* Franchisor controls: displays, (14/15), store design, (14/15) *Monitoring:* Inspection, 15/18; periodic reports by franchisee, 15/15 *Vertical restraints:* Maximum prices, 14/15 *Operations:* Best endeavors by franchisee and franchisor, 15/15; franchisor can hire management or all personnel, 7/15 *Sale/transfer rights:* Franchisor approval required, 15/15; franchisor right of first refusal, 8/15 *Duration/termination:* Duration: 5–26 years; noncompete, 12/15; franchisor may repurchase franchisee assets on termination, 10/15
Bessy and Brousseau (1998)	46 license agreements	Technology flow-back, 65%	*Vertical restraints:* Exclusive territory, 72%; territorial restriction, 59% *Sale/transfer rights:* No resale of technology, 37% *Duration/termination:* Duration: patent life, 20%, <7 years, 35%, 7–12 years, 28%, >12 years, 17%
Lerner and Merges (1998)	Random sample of 200 technology alliances in biotech	Pharma takes equity stake, 51%; know-how transfer, 45%; partial or full ownership of patent by pharma, 82%	*Monitoring:* Seat on R&D firm's board, 21% *Vertical restraints:* Pharma has exclusive right to market, 80% *Operations:* Pharma has right to manufacture, 63%; pharma controls top project management, 6% *Sale/transfer rights:* Pharma has right to sublicense, 26% *Duration/termination:* Mean minimum length, 3.9 years; right to extend, 22%; right to terminate alliance without cause, 32%; right to shelve projects, 93%
Anand and Khanna (2000)	1,365 license agreements, U.S. manufacturing	Cross-licensing agreements, 13%	*Vertical restraints:* Exclusive territory for licensee: world, 11%, other, 26% *Duration/termination:* Duration always less than 10 years
Arruñada et al. (2001)	23 Spanish car distribution networks accounting for 99% of market in 1993–1995	Dealer owns dealership, car, and parts inventory, 100%	*Input purchases:* Manufacturer has right to set size and design of showroom, 100%; machinery and tools, including workshop design, 100% *Monitoring:* Fulfillment of sales targets, 100%; premises inspection, 100%; dealer must provide data, 87%; right to audit, 52%, right to poll dealer clients, 74% *Vertical restraints:* Manufacturer has right to set maximum prices, 100%; dealer exclusive territory, 52%; nonlinear pricing (sales discounts), 87% *Operations:* Manufacturer sets: sales targets, 100%, number of trial vehicles, 52%, inventory levels, 100%; advertising requirements, 100%; has right to set personnel, number and qualifications, 100%; training, for salesforce, 65%, training for after sales personnel, 100%; manufacturer can specify stock of spare parts, 100% *Sale/transfer rights:* Changes in ownership of dealership can lead to termination if not authorized, 100% *Duration/termination:* Contract specifies conditions for termination, 100%

Study	Sample		
Bai et al. (2004)	200 joint venture contracts, 1986–1996, in China; all industries but agriculture and mining	Intellectual property exchanged, 100%	*Input purchases:* Domestic procurement decisions by Chinese partner, 98%; overseas procurement by foreign partner, 97% *Operations:* Foreign partner recruits local (Chinese) staff; 10%
Ryall and Sampson (2009)	52 joint technology development contracts in the telecom and microelectronic industries	Intellectual property rights defined, 33%; equity between partners, 30%; joint venture creation, 11%	*Monitoring:* Seven types of clauses, with frequencies between 15% and 46% *Operations:* Output specifications, 42%; timeframe for completion, 52%; number of employees (specific employees) to be contributed, 15% (27%) *Duration/termination:* Termination date fixed, 81%; right to terminate for underperformance (separate from breach), 33%
Zanarone (2009)	19 Italian car distribution networks pre– and post–EU competition policy change (1995, 2002)	Dealer owns dealership, car, and parts inventory	*Vertical restraints (1995, 2002):* Dealer exclusive territory (100%, 0%); price ceiling (5%, 57%); quantity floor (15%, 52%) *Operations (1995, 2002):* Manufacturer sets advertising contributions (15%, 52%), advertising budget (26%, 15%), number of personnel (52%, 47%), qualification of personnel (15%, 36%), customer satisfaction targets (27%, 52%), mandatory training (68%, 73%), standards (10%, 63%)

Notes: Percentages indicate the proportion of contracts with specific clause. Missing categories in the last column mean that the paper was silent on these potential dimensions of the contract.

a. A flowback clause means that the licensee is required to share with the licensor any advances or improvements in the technology, usually free of charge.

b. The authors conducted a second survey, of licensees, but do not quantify the allocation of control rights in this survey. Elfenbein and Lerner (2003) examine control rights in portal alliances, but they do not provide descriptive statistics on the frequency of various control rights.

c. Ratios are used to describe Dnes (1992) because of changing sample sizes.

on area-development agreements (which he equates with the provision of an exclusive territory, though in reality they also entail some expansion rights) or their decision to allow passive ownership (which dictates whether the franchisee can pursue other work or business activities while a franchisee). Brickley also analyzes their decision to mandate advertising levels. He argues and finds that franchisors are more likely to impose restrictions when there are significant externalities across outlets in a chain—that is, when the brand is high value. Similarly, Arruñada et al. (2001) find that contracts allocate more rights to manufacturers when the potential cost of dealer moral hazard is higher and when manufacturers' opportunism is better controlled by reputation. The evidence in Lafontaine and Shaw (2005) goes even further, as it establishes that the likelihood that there will be a contract (i.e., the probability that a principal will be willing to "lease the asset" to an agent) decreases with the value of the asset, which in their study is the value of a business format and franchise brand.

4.8. Rent, Reputation, and Repetition

As with any repeat-business situation, the rent that parties earn in their relationship, or the difference between the profits that they can expect if they remain in their relationship compared to what they could earn outside of it, can play a crucial role in the maintenance and day-to-day functioning of the relationship. Firms can rely on this difference, along with some monitoring, to ensure that their contractual partners behave as requested or expected. Alternatively, firms can rely on the reputation of their contracting partner, and the cost the partner would bear if this reputation were damaged, to ensure performance.

4.8.1. Incidence
In a series of interviews, and subsequent analyses, Contractor (1981) found that licensor executives did not attempt to maximize their own profits by extracting all rent from licensees. Caves et al. (1983) similarly note that contracts generally fail to capture for licensors the full rent that licensees can be expected to obtain. These authors conclude that leaving rent with licensees can mitigate moral hazard and attending control issues. Specifically, they note that licensees are expected to provide inputs that raise the value of the technology, inputs whose provision cannot be specified or priced easily in the contract. "With the licensee gaining no specific recompense for these inputs, letting him share the general profits benefits the licensor by mitigating their underprovision" (Caves et al. 1983: 264). Similarly, in his series of interviews of railroad carriers and shippers, Palay (1984) found that those involved in the transport of such goods as cars, where the transport itself requires specific investments, were much more willing to make necessary adjustments to their agreement than parties involved in the transport of goods requiring no such equipment. He notes that shippers, in particular, wanted to keep carriers viable.

The franchising literature also provides empirical support for the idea that franchisees earn rent. In particular, Brickley et al. (1991), Dnes (1992), Kaufmann and Lafontaine (1994), and Michael and Moore (1995) find evidence suggesting that rent, combined with the threat of termination, plays an important role in franchising.

To illustrate, Brickley et al. (1991) exploit variation in the existence and timing of state laws requiring good cause for termination of franchise contracts to show that franchisors use franchising less in states where they face laws that restrict their ability to terminate franchisees.

This tendency holds especially for franchisors operating in industries with mostly transient customers, as the consumption decisions of such customers do not directly discipline franchisees that free ride. Those authors also find evidence that the passage of a law requiring good cause for termination in California in 1980 was associated with relatively large losses for the shareholders of publicly traded franchisors with operations in that state. Based on these results, the authors conclude that those laws, by making it more difficult to use termination, increase the cost of controlling quality in chains.

Kaufmann and Lafontaine (1994) examine the profit and loss statements from typical McDonald's outlets and the resale prices of a small set of such outlets. They conclude that McDonald's indeed leaves rent with its franchisees, rent that the franchisees lose if they are found in violation of firm policy and are terminated.[39] Moreover, McDonald's does not require franchisees to pay up front for the full amount of ex post rent. In other words, it allows franchisees to earn rent from an ex ante perspective. The authors explain this tactic in part based on the type of franchisees that McDonald's desires, namely, individuals who will devote themselves to their role as owner-operators of their restaurants. The authors also note that the company reserves the right to decide which franchisees are granted expansion rights, that is, which franchisees are allowed to own additional McDonald's restaurants, based on a franchisee's degree of compliance with firm policies. The prospect of additional ex ante rents thus also creates incentives for current franchisees at McDonald's, encouraging those who aspire to grow their businesses to continue to function within the bounds set by their franchise contracts. Moreover, the option of adding restaurants is made especially valuable, because the contract requires franchisees to work full time at their business and "keep free from conflicting enterprises or any other activities which would be detrimental to or interfere with the business of the Restaurant" (McDonald's Franchise Agreement 2003: 105).

Finally, Dnes (1992) dedicates a whole chapter in his book to what he calls the "wider" franchise contract, where he discusses the relational aspects of the contract, namely, a number of business understandings that have evolved over time in franchise relationships. These include a tendency in some franchise networks to let franchisees sell unauthorized goods, to grant implicit territorial protection, to support a distressed franchisee directly (e.g., by reducing royalty or lease payments or providing discounts), and to repurchase franchised outlets if needed. These aspects of the franchise relationship are implicit and are sustained only to the extent that the value of the relationship to both parties is sufficient to prevent them from altering their "understandings."

4.8.2. Effects

A different perspective on the issues of repetition and reputation is obtained from studies of industries where relationships are shorter term than in the franchising context, but where firms choose to repeatedly do business with the same partner. Anand and Khanna (2000), for example, find that 30% of licensing deals in their data involve firms with prior relationships or otherwise related firms, whereas 34% of international deals are concluded by firms with prior relationships. In their study of contracts for customized software, Banerjee and Duflo (2000) find that 41% of external projects involve firms that have worked with the same clients before. Repetition is not

---

39. Michael and Moore (1995) show that other franchise systems also leave rents with their franchisees.

ubiquitous in interfirm contracting, however. For example, only 6% of the technology alliances in Lerner and Merges (1998) involve firms that have been alliance partners before.

Most relational and reputational contracting models rely on repeated interaction to sustain cooperation, a factor that lends itself to empirical assessment. As discussed earlier, Banerjee and Duflo (2000), Corts and Singh (2004), Kalnins and Mayer (2004), Kellogg (2011), and Shi and Susarla (2011) examine the effect of repeated interaction on the choice of fixed-price or cost-plus contracts. The last four find that repetition reduces the need for high-powered incentives, but Banerjee and Duflo find no significant effect of repetition on contract choice. However, they find a strong effect for reputation, measured by the age of the software firm producing the customized product for the client. Specifically, young firms (which, they argue, have less reputational capital) are much more likely to be hired under a fixed-price contract than are older firms. This result suggests that firms use high-powered incentives for agents who have no reputation at stake but are more willing to rely on more flexible lower powered cost-plus contracts when the supplier comes to the relationship with more reputational capital. Shi and Susarla (2011) find that larger suppliers, who also presumably have more reputational capital, are more often hired under cost-plus contracts. Robinson and Stuart (2007) find that pharmaceutical companies take a smaller equity position in their biotech partners when partners are central or well embedded in the network of prior alliances in the sector. They interpret this result in terms of reputational capital as well, which, they argue, allows firms to rely less on explicit control mechanisms, such as equity.

The issues that underlie relational and reputational contracting assume particular importance in environments where the legal system is not well developed, such as developing economies. McMillan and Woodruff (1999a, b) examine relational contracting in Vietnam and find that prior experience with a trading partner and prior information gathering on that partner (presumably when the information gathered is good) are associated with increased provision of credit, which they equate with enhanced trust. Furthermore, because they find that customers who are located through business networks also receive more credit, they conclude that networks are used in group sanctions or punishments. However, they also find that retaliation is not as forceful as one would expect in a standard repeated game framework, as renegotiation often follows breach.[40]

Whereas the studies mentioned above examine the effects of repetition or reputation on the mode of contracting, Gil and Marion (2012) consider effects on costs directly. Specifically, they examine how the stock of prior interactions between contractors and subcontractors in highway construction affect the bidding behavior of contractors. They find that prior interactions with the subcontractors included in a bid allow contractors to bid more aggressively and participate in more auctions. They interpret these results as evidence that prior interactions improve relationship-specific productivity. They note, however, that past interactions may improve learning or lower coordination costs, rather than provide the type of incentives through repeated business effects that authors are trying to capture in this literature. And indeed, Kellogg (2011) documents important productivity benefits associated with repeat interactions in on-shore drilling. Gil and Marion (2012), however, then show that the effect of prior relationships

---

40. See also Gil (2012) and Gil and Lafontaine (2012) on contracting and renegotiation, and, for example, Lafontaine et al. (2011) for an analysis of the effect of regulatory uncertainty on contracting in the hotel industry.

on bids and auction participation depends crucially on the number and dollar value of contracts expected to be up for bid in the relevant region in the coming year. They conclude that past interactions affect costs only when firms also have expectations of future business opportunities. Along similar lines, Lyons (2001) finds evidence that firms can support specific investments by reputation and rent through the establishment of partnership agreements, whereby firms agree to work together in the future, or preferred supplier agreements, which also imply longer term relationships.

Viewed as a whole, this empirical literature suggests that explicit incentives become less important when either reputation or repeated interaction, and associated rents, are present and thus can be used to support transactions. Conversely, explicit incentives become especially important in the absence of reputation or expectations of future interactions, as long as the legal system is capable of enforcing those explicit provisions. But Ryall and Sampson (2009) find that repeat interactions are associated with an increase in contract detail in their sample of technology development agreements, suggesting a type of complementarity between formal and informal contracting. Similarly, Lafontaine and Raynaud (2002) argue that self-enforcement mechanisms complement residual claims allocations in providing incentives to franchisees. This issue of complementarity among contract terms or contracting practices has taken many forms in the literature. We turn to it in the next section.

4.9. Complementarities

Most of the literature on contract terms focuses only on some aspects of contractual relationships (e.g., financial terms, quantity clauses, contract duration, or control rights). Though authors emphasize individual contract characteristics, individual terms are often but one component of complex sets of contracting practices that interact and work together as a group. This interaction is similar to that characterizing human resource practices as described by Ichniowski et al. (1997). Indeed, in his study of the practices of five fast-food restaurant chains, Bradach (1997) argues that the mechanisms and systems that franchisors rely on to govern their relationships with their franchisees interact with one another, as do the mechanisms employed in the managerial employment contract on the company-owned side of these firms. He further suggests that the two separate forms of governance complement one another, so that franchisors who use both company and franchised units can better address what he describes as the main managerial challenges that retail chains face.

Formally, complementarities occur when the marginal profitability of one action (e.g., practice or contract clause) increases with the level of another. In other words, there are synergies among the choices. Although the idea that one needs to consider complementarities in analyses of the choice of mode of governance has gained momentum since the mid-1990s, in reality, this notion did not go unnoticed by early authors in this literature. For example, Goldberg and Erickson (1987) note that because many decisions about contractual provisions and about organizational form are made simultaneously, they can interact, and thus empirical studies should strive to jointly estimate decisions concerning the set of contractual provisions and organizational decisions.

Overall, the empirical evidence supports these claims. In particular, Lafontaine and Raynaud (2002), who approach the problem descriptively, review the agency and self-enforcement arguments for franchise contracts and describe in some detail the set of clauses that support each. Echoing Klein (1995), they conclude that explicit and implicit incentive-provision mechanisms are themselves complements rather than substitutes. They note that while the ownership stake of a franchisee and his residual claims give him reasons to work hard on the day-to-day operations of the business, these same residual claims can also lead him to free ride. Free riding can take the form, for example, of cutting costs in a way that can harm the brand and thus the chain, or of catering to local customers to a degree that is excessive from the chain's point of view. The self-enforcing aspects of the contract give the franchisor an opportunity to control exactly those behaviors that can arise as side effects from the allocation of residual claims and ownership rights to franchisees. Hueth et al. (2008) show a similar tendency for explicit and implicit contracting to be positively correlated in their study of California fruit and vegetable intermediaries' contracts. Finally, as mentioned above, Ryall and Sampson (2009) find that contracts are more detailed when a firm engages in many deals with the same or different partners. They interpret this finding to mean that formal contracting complements relational aspects of contractual relationship in high-tech industries.[41]

If one can characterize the relationship among the contracting parties using just a few important characteristics, it becomes possible to examine all possibilities. Brickley (1999), for example, examines three specific nonfinancial contract terms, namely, restrictions on passive ownership, area development plans, and mandatory advertising requirements. He finds that the occurrence of these provisions is positively correlated and thus concludes that they are apt to be complementary instruments of control.

In most real-world contexts, however, there are numerous contract terms to consider. This complication, in turn, leads to the problem of dimensionality: if there are n factors to assess, then there are $n(n-1)/2$ possible two-way interactions, which in many cases is intractable. One must therefore put some structure on the problem. Unfortunately, this is not always done in a satisfactory manner. To illustrate, a standard practice in estimating a linear equation for the choice of organizational form, for example, is to include the set of other contractual provisions in the choice equation. Although this practice allows each provision to affect the firm's choice of organizational form, it does not allow for interactions among factors leading to that decision. Moreover, although most discrete choice models that include other contracting practices among the regressors imply that the marginal effect of one clause depends on the others (because the model is nonlinear), that dependency is not flexible. Instead, it is mostly determined by the assumed distribution of the error term.[42]

An alternative and promising way to address the problem is to group contracts among a smaller set of types, focusing on major groups rather than on small variants within groups. This, of course, is the comparative institutions approach emphasized by Williamson (1991, 1996) applied to contracts and contract terms, where the latter often lend themselves quite well to grouping.[43]

41. See also Lin et al. (2011) on the interaction between performance-based and ownership-based incentives in the hotel industry.

42. To illustrate, with a logit, if there are n practices or clauses, once the pattern of complementarity or substitutability between an arbitrary clause x_i and the remaining $n-1$ clauses is determined, all other relationships are known.

43. This approach has been useful in other contexts as well. For example, clustering or grouping is the approach used by Ichniowski et al. (1997) in their study of the productivity effects of human resource management practices.

To illustrate, Bessy and Brousseau (1998) use cluster analysis to classify their sample of technology licensing contracts into five categories from simple transactional contracts to complex multidimensional and very incomplete contracts. They argue that the characteristics of industries and intellectual property regimes largely explain the choice that firms make among these different types of contracts. Arruñada et al. (2001) also group sets of rights found in the car dealership contracts that they study. They find positive correlations among their categories of rights (completion, monitoring, and termination), and between these and the financial terms of the contract, namely, the level of discounts offered to dealers. They also find that these correlations are much lower after controlling for characteristics of the transaction, however, suggesting that these characteristics, and thus the same underlying factors, affect the use of different contract terms. Still, they find a significant positive relationship between completion and termination rights, and between monitoring rights and discount levels (incentives), even after controlling for common sources of variation. Similarly, Kaplan and Strömberg (2003) show that their 213 venture capital contracts can easily be classified into five separate groups, and that the clusters thus generated are easily ordered in terms of either cash flow rights that are relinquished by the founder or board and voting rights allocated to the venture capitalist. Thus, the first (fifth) cluster is one where the venture capitalist (founder) obtains most of the cash flow and control rights. In other words, the rights "move" together to create the desired set of incentives and venture capitalist control.

In essence, researchers also group contract clauses when they contrast, say, franchising versus company ownership, cost-plus versus fixed-price contracts, or independents versus affiliated businesses. Of course, looking at these categories as discrete alternatives is not a perfect solution. In particular, there may remain much variation among the members of each group. For example, franchise contracts can differ importantly across chains, and this variety is interesting in its own right. Still, franchising is also fundamentally different from company operation, so that contrasting these governance modes facilitates assessment of incidence and effects. Empirical studies of franchising find that factors suggested by theory explain the choice of how much to franchise better than they do financial contract terms. This finding further supports the idea that contractual relationships may best be understood as combinations of contractual practices rather than as phenomena requiring that every component be analyzed separately.[44] Consistent with this approach, Bajari and Tadelis (2001) suggest that, even though they are limit cases, fixed-price and cost-plus contracts are fundamentally different from linear contracts, where the supplier is reimbursed for a portion of his costs (i.e., the case where $0 < |\alpha| < 1$ in the notation in Table 1). The Lafontaine and Slade (2007) approach of relating the decision to vertically integrate or contract with an independent agent to the agency-theoretic model predicting the optimal share parameter also relies on the introduction of some nonconvexity (in this case a cost of contracting) when the share parameter α is not zero.

Finally, the theoretical (e.g., Holmström and Milgrom 1991) and empirical (e.g., Slade 1996) literature on multitasking is also an examination of complementarity and substitutability, because it shows how the characteristics of one task affect compensation for another. Thus, models that assess compensation for one activity in isolation are incapable of capturing the full

---

44. That franchise contract terms do not vary much with time, or at all across franchisees that join at a given time suggests that firms adjust to different circumstances more by the choice among the two types of contracts than by designing new forms of the same contract type.

picture in this case. Moreover, the theory makes it clear that the problem worsens when the outputs of some tasks are difficult to measure and are thus not compensated directly. Under these circumstances, low-powered incentives for all tasks may be preferred, because such incentives are not associated with a diversion of effort from hard- to easy-to-measure tasks.

One should perhaps not be surprised that contract types can often be classified as described above. After all, in most industries, contracting parties and their lawyers have devised a set of templates or standard forms that many industry members rely on. As Bajari and Tadelis (2001) note, the central clauses found in such standard forms have the advantages that they are well understood in the industry, and their interpretation has been clarified through a substantial body of case law. Moreover, these templates can still provide much flexibility when it comes to specifics (see MacLeod 2007; Kornhauser and MacLeod, this volume). Perhaps what is more surprising is that the use of such templates seems to offer at least a partial solution to the dimensionality problem inherent to the study of contracts in the presence of complementarities.

5. Conclusion

In this chapter, we have reviewed a large body of empirical literature that deals with interfirm contracts. We have made a conscious effort to include within the purview of the chapter some literature that predates the development of many of the theoretical models that now guide much of this work. By doing so, we hope to have brought some focus back onto these earlier, often more descriptive, contributions to our understanding of interfirm contracts. We also hope to have convinced researchers interested in questions of organizational theory that the literature on vertical restraints is an important component of the larger literature on how firms organize their relationships.[45]

Even though our chapter and references cover a lot of ground, we have also chosen to exclude certain areas of research. In particular, we have focused on firms' relationships with other firms in their supply chain rather than on their relationships with the providers of capital, be they banks or venture capitalists. Readers interested in organizational issues related to firm finance should consult Gertner and Scharfstein (this volume). Due to constraints on length, we have chosen to emphasize mostly early and recent work on particular issues rather than review the entirety of the literature on a topic. This approach gives readers an appreciation for where the literature started and where it now stands, providing the most relevant information for those interested in contributing further to this literature. Finally, to keep the discussion manageable, we have focused on the literature in economics, although we have tried to include some of the more recent or relevant contributions from the growing literature on contracts that appears in management journals.[46]

In addition to taking stock of the literature, our goal is to generate interest in the area of interfirm contracts. This chapter has highlighted the need for much more empirical research on a variety of topics. Indeed, our understanding of numerous issues is still quite primitive. Those

45. Although many theoretical analyses of vertical restraints rely on considerations of incentive provision, this body of literature is not well integrated into the more orthodox study of organizational economics.

46. See also Argyres et al. (2007) and the references therein for more on the management literature on contracts.

issues include how firms choose the many terms of their contracts; when and why contract terms tend to vary significantly across firms but little over time within firms; how contracting practices interact with one another; and how explicit and implicit contracting are affected by learning, reputation, and the value of future trade. In particular, we stress that in contrast to the theory, the entire area of dynamics (e.g., relational and reputational contracting) is underexplored from an empirical point of view. In addition, there is a need to develop empirical models that can capture flexible patterns of complementary interactions while remaining empirically tractable.[47] Given the importance of interfirm contracts in the economy, we hope that our summary of the evidence will encourage researchers to develop further theory and empirical work in the area, and a stronger link between the two.

REFERENCES

Ackerberg, Daniel A., and Maristella Botticini. 2002. "Endogenous Matching and the Empirical Determinants of Contract Form." *Journal of Political Economy* 110: 564–591.

Akerlof, George A., and Janet L. Yellen. 1986. *Efficiency Wage Models of the Labor Market.* Cambridge: Cambridge University Press.

Allen, Douglas W., and Dean Lueck. 2002. *The Nature of the Farm: Contracts, Risk, and Organization in Agriculture.* Cambridge, MA: MIT Press.

Anand, Bharat, and Tarun Khanna. 2000. "The Structure of Licensing Contracts." *Journal of Industrial Economics* 48: 103–135.

Arbatskaya, Maria, Morten Hviid, and Greg Shaffer. 2004. "On the Incidence and Variety of Low-Price Guarantees." *Journal of Law and Economics* 47: 307–332.

Argyres, Nicholas, Janet Bercovitz, and Kyle Mayer. 2007. "Complementarity and Evolution of Contractual Provisions: An Empirical Study of IT Services Contracts." *Organization Science* 18: 3–19.

Arruñada, Benito, Luis Garicano, and Luis Vázquez. 2001. "Contractual Allocation of Decision Rights and Incentives: The Case of Automobile Distribution." *Journal of Law, Economics, and Organization* 17: 257–284.

Arruñada, Benito, Luis Vázquez, and Giorgio Zanarone. 2009. "Institutional Constraints on Organizations: The Case of Spanish Car Dealerships." *Managerial and Decision Economics* 30: 15–26.

Asker, John. 2005. "Diagnosing Foreclosure Due to Exclusive Dealing." Mimeo, Stern School of Business, New York University.

Azoulay, Pierre, and Scott Shane. 2001. "Entrepreneurs, Contracts, and the Failure of Young Firms." *Management Science* 47: 337–358.

Bai, Chong-En, Zhigang Tao, and Changqi Wu. 2004. "Revenue Sharing and Control Rights in Team Production: Theories and Evidence from Joint Ventures." *RAND Journal of Economics* 35: 277–305.

Bajari, Patrick, and Steven Tadelis. 2001. "Incentives versus Transaction Costs: A Theory of Procurement Contracts." *RAND Journal of Economics* 32: 387–407.

Bajari, Patrick, Robert McMillan, and Steven Tadelis. 2009. "Auctions versus Negotiations in Procurement: An Empirical Analysis." *Journal of Law, Economics, and Organization* 25: 372–399.

---

47. One could perhaps borrow from the empirical literature on differentiated products to structure such models. For example, the distance-metric approach of Pinkse et al. (2001) could be used to organize the numerous possible interactions. To illustrate, if it were possible to assign characteristics (or clauses or attributes) to groups (e.g., factors that measure the importance of the agent's effort or the riskiness of the market, or clauses related to control), one could model a common (presumably) substitution pattern within each group but allow a flexible pattern of complementarity or substitutability across groups.

Baker, George, Robert Gibbons, and Kevin J. Murphy. 2002. "Relational Contracts and the Theory of the Firm." *Quarterly Journal of Economics* 117: 39–84.

———. 2008. "Strategic Alliances: Bridges between Islands of Conscious Power." *Journal of the Japanese and International Economies* 22: 146–163.

———. 2011. "Relational Adaptation." Mimeo, Massachusetts Institute of Technology, Cambridge, MA.

Bandiera, Oriana, Iwan Barankay, and Imran Rasul. 2007. "Incentives for Managers and Inequality among Workers: Evidence from a Firm-Level Experiment." *Quarterly Journal of Economics* 122: 729–773.

Banerjee, Abhijit, and Esther Duflo. 2000. "Reputation Effects and the Limits of Contracting: A Study of the Indian Software Industry." *Quarterly Journal of Economics* 115: 989–1017.

Barron, John M., and John R. Umbeck. 1984. "The Effects of Different Contractual Arrangements: The Case of Retail Gasoline." *Journal of Law and Economics* 27: 313–328.

Barzel, Yoram. 1982. "Measurement Cost and the Organization of Markets." *Journal of Law and Economics* 25: 27–48.

Bates, Timothy. 1995a. "A Comparison of Franchise and Independent Small Business Survival Rates." *Small Business Economics* 7: 377–388.

———. 1995b. "Analysis of Survival Rates among Franchise and Independent Small Business Startups." *Journal of Small Business Management* 33: 25–36.

———. 1998. "Survival Patterns among Newcomers to Franchising." *Journal of Business Venturing* 13: 113–130.

Bessy, Christian, and Eric Brousseau. 1998. "Technology Licensing Contracts Features and Diversity." *International Review of Law and Economics* 18: 451–489.

Bhattacharyya, Sugato, and Francine Lafontaine. 1995. "Double-Sided Moral Hazard and the Nature of Share Contracts." *RAND Journal of Economics* 26: 761–781.

Blair, Roger D., and Francine Lafontaine. 2005. *The Economics of Franchising.* New York: Cambridge University Press.

Blass, Asher A., and Dennis W. Carlton. 2001. "The Choice of Organizational Form in Gasoline Retailing and the Cost of Laws That Limit That Choice." *Journal of Law and Economics* 44: 511–524.

Bonnet, Céline, and Pierre Dubois. 2010. "Inference on Vertical Contracts between Manufacturers and Retailers Allowing for Nonlinear Pricing and Resale Price Maintenance." *RAND Journal of Economics* 41: 139–164.

Bradach, Jeffrey L. 1997. "Using the Plural Form in the Management of Restaurant Chains." *Administrative Science Quarterly* 42: 276–303.

———. 1998. *Franchise Organizations.* Boston: Harvard Business School Press.

Brenkers, Randy, and Frank Verboven. 2006. "Liberalizing a Distribution System: The European Car Market." *Journal of the European Economic Association* 4: 216–251.

Brickley, James. 1999. "Incentive Conflicts and Contractual Restraints: Evidence from Franchising." *Journal of Law and Economics* 42: 745–774.

———. 2002. "Royalty Rates and Upfront Fees in Share Contracts: Evidence from Franchising." *Journal of Law, Economics, and Organization* 18: 511–535.

Brickley, James A., and Frederick H. Dark. 1987. "The Choice of Organizational Form: The Case of Franchising." *Journal of Financial Economics* 18: 401–420.

Brickley, James A., Frederick H. Dark, and Michael S. Weisbach. 1991. "The Economic Effects of Franchise Termination Laws." *Journal of Law and Economics* 34: 101–132.

Brickley, James A., Sanjog Misra, and R. Lawrence Van Horn. 2003. "Contract Duration: Evidence from Franchising." *Journal of Law and Economics* 49: 173–196.

Bull, Clive. 1987. "The Existence of Self-Enforcing Implicit Contracts." *Quarterly Journal of Economics* 102: 147–159.

Cachon, Gérard P., and Martin A. Larivière. 2005. "Supply Chain Coordination with Revenue-Sharing Contracts: Strengths and Limitations." *Management Science* 51: 30–44.

Caves, Richard E., and William F. Murphy. 1976. "Franchising: Firms, Markets, and Intangible Assets." *Southern Economic Journal* 42: 572–586.

Caves, Richard E., Harold Crookell, and J. Peter Killing. 1983. "The Imperfect Market for Technology Licenses." *Oxford Bulletin of Economics and Statistics* 45: 249–268.

Ciliberto, Federico. 2006. "Does Organizational Form Affect Investment Decisions?" *Journal of Industrial Economics* 54: 63–93.

Coase, Ronald H. 1937. "The Nature of the Firm." *Economica* 4: 386–405.

Contractor, Farok. 1981. *International Technology Licensing: Compensation, Costs and Negotiation.* Lexington, MA: Lexington Books.

Cooper, James, Luke M. Froeb, Dan O'Brien, and Michael G. Vita. 2005. "Vertical Antitrust Policy as a Problem of Inference." *International Journal of Industrial Organization* 23: 639–664.

Corts, Kenneth, and Jasjit Singh. 2004. "The Effect of Repeated Interaction on Contract Choice: Evidence from Offshore Drilling." *Journal of Law, Economics, and Organization* 20: 230–260.

Crawford, Gregory S., and Ali Yurukoglu. 2012. "The Welfare Effects of Bundling in Multi-Channel Television Markets." *American Economic Review* 102: 643–685.

Crocker, Keith J., and Thomas P. Lyon. 1994. "What Do 'Facilitating Practices' Facilitate? An Empirical Investigation of Most-Favored-Nation Clauses in Natural Gas Contracts." *Journal of Law and Economics* 37: 297–322.

Crocker, Keith J., and Scott E. Masten. 1988. "Mitigating Contractual Hazards: Unilateral Options and Contract Length." *RAND Journal of Economics* 19: 327–343.

———. 1991. "*Pretia ex Machina?* Prices and Process in Long Term Contracts." *Journal of Law and Economics* 34: 69–99.

Crocker, Keith J., and Kenneth J. Reynolds. 1993. "The Efficiency of Incomplete Contracts: An Empirical Analysis of Air Force Engine Procurement." *RAND Journal of Economics* 24: 126–146.

Dnes, Antony W. 1992. *Franchising: A Case-Study Approach.* Aldershot, U.K.: Ashgate Publishing.

Dubois, Pierre, and Tomislav Vukina. 2004. "Grower Risk Aversion and the Cost of Moral Hazard in Livestock Production Contracts." *American Journal of Agricultural Economics* 86: 835–841.

Dutta, Shantanu, Jan B. Heide, and Mark E. Bergen. 1999. "Vertical Territorial Restrictions and Public Policy: Theories and Industry Evidence." *Journal of Marketing* 63: 121–137.

Elfenbein, Daniel, and Josh Lerner. 2003. "Ownership and Control Rights in Internet Portal Alliances, 1995–1999." *RAND Journal of Economics* 34: 356–369.

Eswaran, Mukesh, and Ashok Kotwal. 1985. "A Theory of Contractual Structure in Agriculture." *American Economic Review* 75: 352–367.

Ferrari, Stijn, and Frank Verboven. 2012. "Vertical Control of a Distribution Network: Evidence from Magazines." *RAND Journal of Economics* 43: 26–50.

Filson, Darren, David Switzer, and Portia Besocke. 2005. "At the Movies: The Economics of Exhibition Contracts." *Economic Inquiry* 43: 354–369.

Freedman, Matthew, and Renáta Kosová. 2012. "Agency and Compensation: Evidence from the Hotel Industry." *Journal of Law, Economics and Organization,* forthcoming.

Gallick, Edward C. 1984. "Exclusive Dealing and Vertical Integration: The Efficiency of Contracts in the Tuna Industry." Federal Trade Commission Bureau of Economics Staff Report. Washington, DC: Federal Trade Commission.

Gibbons, Robert. 2005. "Incentives between Firms (and within)." *Management Science* 51: 2–17.

Gil, Ricard. 2009. "Revenue Sharing Distortions and Vertical Integration in the Movie Industry." *Journal of Law, Economics, and Organization* 25: 579–610.

———. 2012. "The Interplay between Formal and Relational Contracts: Evidence from Movies." *Journal of Law, Economics, and Organization,* forthcoming.

Gil, Ricard, and Francine Lafontaine. 2012. "Using Revenue Sharing to Implement Flexible Pricing: Evidence from Movie Exhibition Contracts." *Journal of Industrial Economics* 60: 187–219.

Gil, Ricard, and Justin Marion. 2012. "Self-Enforcing Agreements and Relational Contracting: Evidence from California Highway Procurement." *Journal of Law, Economics, and Organization,* forthcoming.

Goldberg, Victor P. 1976. "Regulation and Administered Contracts." *Bell Journal of Economics* 7: 426–448.

Goldberg, Victor, and John Erickson. 1987. "Quantity and Price Adjustment in Long-Term Contracts: A Case Study of Petroleum Coke." *Journal of Law and Economics* 30: 369–398.

Gould, Eric D., B. Peter Pashigian, and Canice J. Prendergast. 2005. "Contracts, Externalities, and Incentives in Shopping Malls." *Review of Economics and Statistics* 87: 411–422.

Greif, Avner 1989. "Reputation and Coalitions in Medieval Trade: Evidence on the Maghribi Traders." *Journal of Economic History* 69: 857–882.

Grossman, Sanford J., and Oliver D. Hart. 1986. "The Costs and Benefits of Ownership: A Theory of Vertical and Lateral Integration." *Journal of Political Economy* 94: 691–719.

Hart, Oliver. 1995. *Firms, Contracts, and Financial Structure.* New York: Oxford University Press.

Hart, Oliver, and John Moore. 1990. "Property Rights and the Nature of the Firm." *Journal of Political Economy* 98: 1119–1158.

———. 2008. "Contracts as Reference Points." *Quarterly Journal of Economics* 123: 1–48.

Hastings, Justine. 2004. "Vertical Relationships and Competition in Retail Gasoline Markets: Empirical Evidence from Contract Changes in Southern California." *American Economic Review* 94: 317–328.

Heckman, James J. 1978. "Dummy Endogenous Variables in a Simultaneous Equation System." *Econometrica* 46: 931–960.

———. 1979. "Sample Selection Bias as a Specification Error." *Econometrica* 47: 153–161.

Heide, Jan B., Shantanu Dutta, and Mark Bergen. 1998. "Exclusive Dealing and Business Efficiency: Evidence from Industry Practice." *Journal of Law and Economics* 41: 387–407.

Ho, Justin, Katherine Ho, and Julie Mortimer. 2012. "The Use of Full-Line Forcing Contracts in the Video Rental Industry." *American Economic Review* 102: 686–719.

Holmström, Bengt, and Paul Milgrom. 1991 "Multi-Task Principal-Agent Analyses: Incentive Contracts, Asset Ownership, and Job Design." *Journal of Law, Economics, and Organization* 7: 24–51.

Hubbard, R. Glenn, and Robert J. Weiner. 1989. "Contracting and Price Adjustment in Commodity Markets: Evidence from Copper and Oil." *Review of Economics and Statistics* 71: 80–89.

Hubbard, Thomas N. 2001. "Contractual Form and Market Thickness in Trucking." *RAND Journal of Economics* 32: 369–385.

Hueth, Brent, Ethan Ligon, and Tigran Melkonyan. 2008. "Interactions between Explicit and Implicit Contracts: Evidence from California Agriculture." Mimeo, University of Wisconsin, Madison.

Hunt, Shelby D. 1972. "The Socioeconomic Consequences of the Franchise System of Distribution." *Journal of Marketing* 36: 32–38.

Ichniowski, Casey, Kathryn L. Shaw, and Giovanna Prennushi. 1997. "The Effects of Human Resource Management Practices on Productivity: A Study of Steel Finishing Lines." *American Economic Review* 87: 291–313.

Ippolito, Pauline M. 1991. "Resale Price Maintenance: Empirical Evidence from Litigation." *Journal of Law and Economics* 34: 263–294.

Jin, Ginger Z., and Phillip Leslie. 2009. "Reputation Incentives for Restaurant Hygiene." *American Economic Journal—Microeconomics* 1: 237–267.

Joskow, Paul. 1985. "Vertical Integration and Long-Term Contracts: The Case of Coal-Burning Electric Generation Plants." *Journal of Law, Economics, and Organization* 1: 33–80.

———. 1987. "Contract Duration and Relationship-Specific Investment: Empirical Evidence from Coal Markets." *American Economic Review* 77: 168–185.

———. "Price Adjustment in Long-Term Contracts: The Case of Coal." *Journal of Law and Economics* 31: 47–83.

———. 1990. "The Performance of Long-Term Contracts: Further Evidence from Coal Markets." *RAND Journal of Economics* 21: 251–274.

Kalnins, Arturs, and Francine Lafontaine. 2004. "Multi-Unit Ownership in Franchising: Evidence from the Fast-Food Industry in Texas." *RAND Journal of Economics* 35: 747–761.

Kalnins, Arturs, and Kyle Mayer. 2004. "Relationships and Hybrid Contracts: An Analysis of Contract Choice in Information Technology." *Journal of Law, Economics, and Organization* 20: 207–229.

Kaplan, Steven, and Per Strömberg. 2003. "Financial Contracting Theory Meets the Real World: An Empirical Analysis of Venture Capital Contracts." *Review of Economic Studies* 70: 281–315.

Kaufmann, Patrick J., and Francine Lafontaine. 1994. "Costs of Control: The Source of Economic Rents for McDonald's Franchisees." *Journal of Law and Economics* 37: 417–454.

Kellogg, Ryan. 2011. "Learning by Drilling: Inter-Firm Learning and Relationship Persistence in the Texas Oilpatch." *Quarterly Journal of Economics* 126: 1961–2004.

Kenney, Roy, and Benjamin Klein. 1983. "The Economics of Block Booking." *Journal of Law and Economics* 26: 497–540.

———. 2000. "How Block Booking Facilitated Self-Enforcing Film Contracts." *Journal of Law and Economics* 43: 427–436.

Klein, Benjamin. 1980. "Transaction Cost Determinants of 'Unfair' Contractual Arrangements." *American Economic Review* 70: 356–362.

Klein, Benjamin. 1995. "The Economics of Franchise Contracts." *Journal of Corporate Finance* 2: 9–37.

Klein, Benjamin, and Keith Leffler. 1981. "The Role of Market Forces in Assuring Contractual Performance." *Journal of Political Economy* 89: 615–641.

Klein, Benjamin, and Kevin M. Murphy. 1988. "Vertical Restraints as Contract Enforcement Mechanisms." *Journal of Law and Economics* 31: 265–297.

Klein, Benjamin, Robert G. Crawford, and Armen A. Alchian. 1978. "Vertical Integration, Appropriable Rents and the Competitive Contracting Process." *Journal of Law and Economics* 21: 297–326.

Knoeber, Charles R. 1989. "A Real Game of Chicken: Contracts, Tournaments, and the Production of Broilers." *Journal of Law, Economics, and Organization* 5: 271–292.

Kosová, Renáta, and Francine Lafontaine. 2010. "Firm Survival and Growth in Retail and Service Industries: Evidence from Franchised Chains." *Journal of Industrial Economics* 58: 542–578.

Kosová, Renáta, Francine Lafontaine, and Rozenn Perrigot. 2012. "Organizational Form and Performance: Evidence from the Hotel Industry." *Review of Economics and Statistics,* forthcoming.

Krueger, Alan B. 1991. "Ownership, Agency and Wages: An Examination of the Fast Food Industry." *Quarterly Journal of Economics* 106: 75–101.

Lach, Saul, and Mark Schankerman. 2008. "Incentives and Invention in Universities." *RAND Journal of Economics* 39: 403–433.

Lafontaine, Francine. 1992. "Agency Theory and Franchising: Some Empirical Results." *RAND Journal of Economics* 23: 263–283.

———. 1993. "Contractual Arrangements as Signaling Devices: Evidence from Franchising." *Journal of Law, Economics, and Organization* 9: 256–289.

Lafontaine, Francine, and Sugato Bhattacharyya. 1995. "The Role of Risk in Franchising." *Journal of Corporate Finance* 2: 39–74.

Lafontaine, Francine, and Scott Masten. 2002. "Contracting in the Absence of Specific Investments and Moral Hazard: Understanding Carrier-Driver Relations in US Trucking." NBER Working Paper w8859, National Bureau of Economic Research, Cambridge, MA.

Lafontaine, Francine, and Joanne Oxley. 2004. "International Franchising Practices in Mexico: Do Franchisors Customize Their Contracts?" *Journal of Economics and Management Strategy* 13: 95–123.

Lafontaine, Francine, and Emmanuel Raynaud. 2002. "Residual Claims and Self Enforcement as Incentive Mechanisms in Franchise Contracts: Substitute or Complements?" in Erie Brousseau and Jean-Michel Glachant (eds.), *The Economics of Contract in Prospect and Retrospect.* Cambridge: Cambridge University Press, pp. 315–336.

Lafontaine, Francine, and Fiona Scott Morton. 2010. "State Franchise Laws, Dealer Terminations, and the Auto Crisis." *Journal of Economic Perspectives* 24(3): 233–250.

Lafontaine, Francine, and Kathryn L. Shaw. 1998. "Franchising Growth and Franchisor Entry and Exit in the U.S. Market: Myth and Reality." *Journal of Business Venturing* 13: 95–112.

———. 1999. "The Dynamics of Franchise Contracting: Evidence from Panel Data." *Journal of Political Economy* 107: 1041–1080.

———. 2005. "Targeting Managerial Control: Evidence from Franchising." *RAND Journal of Economics* 36: 131–150.

Lafontaine, Francine, and Margaret E. Slade. 2007. "Vertical Integration and Firm Boundaries: The Evidence." *Journal of Economic Literature* 45: 629–685.

———. 2008. "Empirical Assessment of Exclusive Contracts," in Paolo Buccirossi (ed.), *Handbook of Antitrust Economics.* Cambridge, MA: MIT Press, pp. 391–414.

Lafontaine, Francine, Rozenn Perrigot, and Nathan Wilson. 2011. "Institutional Quality and Organizational Form Decisions: Evidence from within the Firm." Mimeo, University of Michigan, Ann Arbor.

Lazear, Edward P. 2000. "Performance Pay and Productivity." *American Economic Review* 90: 1346–1361.

Leffler, Keith B., and Randal R. Rucker. 1991. "Transaction Costs and the Efficient Organization of Production: A Study of Timber-Harvesting Contracts." *Journal of Political Economy* 99: 1060–1087.

Lerner, Josh, and Robert Merges. 1998. "The Control of Technology Alliances: An Empirical Analysis of the Biotechnology Industry." *Journal of Industrial Economics* 46: 125–156.

Levin, Jonathan. 2003. "Relational Incentive Contracts." *American Economic Review* 93: 835–857.

Lin, Stephen F., Catherine Thomas, and Arturs Kalnins. 2011. "In-House and Arm's Length: Productivity Heterogeneity and Variation in Organizational Form." Mimeo, Columbia University, New York.

Lo, Desmond (Ho-Fu). 2008. "The Role and Extent of Economic Rent in Distribution Contracts." PhD dissertation, University of Michigan, Ann Arbor.

Lo, Desmond (Ho-Fu), Mrinal Ghosh, and Francine Lafontaine. 2011. "The Incentive and Selection Roles in Salesforce Compensation Contracts." *Journal of Marketing Research* 48: 781–798.

Lyons, Bruce R. 1994. "Contracts and Specific Investment: An Empirical Test of Transaction Cost Theory." *Journal of Economics and Management Strategy* 3: 257–278.

———. 2001. "Incomplete Contract Theory and Contracts between Firms: A Preliminary Empirical Study." Mimeo, University of East Anglia, Norwich, UK.

Macho-Stadler, Ines, Xavier Martinez-Giralt, and J. David Castrillo-Perez. 1996. "The Role of Information in Licensing Contract Design." *Research Policy* 25: 43–57.

MacLeod, W. Bentley. 2007. "Reputations, Relationships, and Contract Enforcement." *Journal of Economic Literature* 45: 595–628.

MacLeod, W. Bentley, and James M. Malcomson. 1989. "Implicit Contracts, Incentive Compatibility, and Involuntary Unemployment." *Econometrica* 57: 447–480.

Macneil, Ian R. 1978. "Contracts: Adjustment of Long-Term Economic Relations under Classical, Neoclassical, and Relational Contract Law." *Northwestern University Law Review* 72: 854–905.

Marvel, Howard P. 1982. "Exclusive Dealing." *Journal of Law and Economics* 25: 1–25.

Masten, Scott E., and Keith Crocker. 1985. "Efficient Adaptation in Long Term Contracts: Take-or-Pay Provisions for Natural Gas." *American Economic Review* 75: 1083–1093.

Mazzeo, Michael J. 2004. "Retail Contracting and Organizational Form: Alternatives to Chain Affiliation in the Motel Industry." *Journal of Economics and Management Strategy* 13: 599–615.

McAfee, R. Preston, and Marius Schwartz. 1994. "Opportunism in Multilateral Vertical Contracting: Nondiscrimination, Exclusivity, and Uniformity." *American Economic Review* 84: 210–230.

McDonald's Corporation. 2003. "Franchise Agreement" in *Franchise Offering Circular*. Oak Brook, IL: McDonald's, 100–112.

McMillan, John, and Christopher Woodruff. 1999a. "Interfirm Relationships and Informal Credit in Vietnam." *Quarterly Journal of Economics* 114: 1285–1320.

———. 1999b. "Dispute Prevention without Courts in Vietnam." *Journal of Law, Economics, and Organization* 15: 637–658.

Michael, Steven C. 2000. "The Effect of Organizational Form on Quality: The Case of Franchising." *Journal of Economic Behavior and Organization* 43: 295–318.

Michael, Steven C., and Holly J. Moore. 1995. "Returns to Franchising." *Journal of Corporate Finance* 2: 133–156.

Mortimer, Julie H. 2008. "Vertical Contracts in the Video Rental Industry." *Review of Economic Studies* 75: 165–199.

Mulherin, J. Harold. 1986. "Complexity in Long-Term Contracts: An Analysis of Natural Gas Contractual Provisions." *Journal of Law, Economics, and Organization* 2: 105–117.

Murrell, Peter, and Radu A. Paun. 2008. "*Caveat Venditor:* The Conditional Effect of Relationship–Specific Investment on Contractual Behavior." Mimeo, University of Maryland, College Park.

Okuno-Fujiwara, Masahiro, and Andrew Postlewaite. 1995. "Social Norms and Random Matching Games." *Games and Economic Behavior* 9: 79–109.

Palay, Thomas. 1984. "Comparative Institutional Economics: The Governance of Rail Freight Contracting." *Journal of Legal Studies* 13: 265–287.

Pinkse, Joris, and Margaret E. Slade. 1998. "Contracting in Space: An Application of Spatial Statistics to Discrete-Choice Models." *Journal of Econometrics* 85: 125–154.

———. 2010. "The Future of Spatial Econometrics." *Journal of Regional Science* 50: 103–117.

Pinkse, Joris, Margaret E. Slade, and Craig Brett. 2001. "Spatial Price Competition: A Semiparametric Approach." *Econometrica* 70: 1111–1155.

Pinkse, Joris, Margaret E. Slade, and Lihong Shen. 2006. "Dynamic Spatial Probit with Fixed Effects Using One-Step GMM: An Application to Mine Operating Decisions." *Spatial Economic Analysis* 1: 53–90.

Pirrong, S. Craig. 1993. "Contracting Practices in Bulk Shipping Markets: A Transactions Cost Explanation." *Journal of Law and Economics* 36: 937–976.

Prendergast, Canice. 2002. "The Tenuous Trade-Off between Risk and Incentives." *Journal of Political Economy* 110: 1071–1102.

Rao, Ram C., and Shubashri Srinivasan. 1995. "Why Are Royalty Rates Higher in Service-Type Franchises?" *Journal of Economics and Management Strategy* 4: 7–31.

Reid, Joseph D. 1977. "The Theory of Share Tenancy Revisited—Again." *Journal of Political Economy* 85: 403–407.

Robinson, David T., and Toby E. Stuart. 2007. "Network Effects in Governance of Strategic Alliances." *Journal of Law, Economics, and Organization* 23: 242–273.

Rubin, Paul. 1978. "The Theory of the Firm and the Structure of the Franchise Contract." *Journal of Law and Economics* 21: 223–233.

Ryall, Michael D., and Rachelle C. Sampson. 2009. "Formal Contracts in the Presence of Relational Enforcement Mechanisms: Evidence from Technology Development Projects." *Management Science* 55: 906–925.

Salop, Steven. (1986) "Practices That (Credibly) Facilitate Oligopoly Coordination," in Joseph E. Stiglitz and G. Franklin Mathewson (eds.), *New Developments in the Analysis of Market Structure*. Cambridge, MA: MIT Press, pp. 265–290.

Saussier, Stéphane. 2000. "Transaction Costs and Contractual Incompleteness: The Case of Électricité de France." *Journal of Economic Behavior and Organization* 42: 189–206.

Schneider, Henry. 2010. "Moral Hazard in Leasing Contracts: Evidence from the New York City Taxi Industry." *Journal of Law and Economics* 53: 783–805.

Scott, Frank A. 1995. "Franchising vs. Company Ownership as a Decision Variable of the Firm." *Review of Industrial Organization* 10: 69–81.

Shane, Scott A. 1996. "Hybrid Organizational Arrangements and Their Implications for Firm Growth and Survival: A Study of New Franchisors." *Academy of Management Journal* 39: 216–234.

Shearer, Bruce. 2004. "Piece Rates, Fixed Wages and Incentives: Evidence from a Field Experiment." *Review of Economic Studies* 71: 513–534.

Shelton, John. 1967. "Allocative Efficiency vs. 'X-Efficiency': Comment." *American Economic Review* 57: 1252–1258.

Shepard, Andrea. 1993. "Contractual Form, Retail Price, and Asset Characteristics." *RAND Journal of Economics* 24: 58–77.

Shi, Lan, and Anjana Susarla. 2011. "Relational Contracts, Reputation Capital and Formal Contracts: Evidence from Information Technology Outsourcing." Mimeo, University of Washington, Seattle.

Silvester, Trisha, John Stanworth, David Purdy, and Mark Hatcliffe. 1996. "Secrets of Success." Lloyds Bank Plc/IFRC Franchising in Britain Report 1(3), London.

Slade, Margaret E. 1991. "Market Structure, Marketing Method, and Price Instability." *Quarterly Journal of Economics* 106: 1309–1340.

———. 1996. "Multitask Agency and Contract Choice: An Empirical Assessment." *International Economic Review* 37: 465–486.

———. 1998a. "Beer and the Tie: Did Divestiture of Brewer-Owned Public Houses Lead to Higher Beer Prices?" *Economic Journal* 108: 1–38.

———. 1998b. "Strategic Motives for Vertical Separation: Evidence from Retail Gasoline." *Journal of Law, Economics, and Organization* 14: 84–113.

Smith II, Richard L. 1982. "Franchise Regulation: An Economic Analysis of State Restrictions on Automobile Distribution." *Journal of Law and Economics* 25: 125–157.

Stanworth, John. 1977. "A Study of Franchising in Britain: A Research Report." London: Social Science Research Council.

———. 1996. "Dispelling the Myths Surrounding Franchise Failure Rates—Some Recent Evidence from Britain." *Franchising Research: An International Journal* 1: 25–28.

Stiglitz, Joseph E. 1974. "Incentives and Risk Sharing in Sharecropping." *Review of Economic Studies* 41: 219–255.

Taylor, Charles T., and Z. A. Silberston. 1973. *The Economic Impact of the Patent System*. Cambridge: Cambridge University Press.

Telser, Lester G. 1960. "Why Should Manufacturers Want Fair Trade?" *Journal of Law and Economics* 3: 86–105.

———. 1980. "A Theory of Self-Enforcing Agreements." *Journal of Business* 53: 27–44.

Udell, Gerald G. 1972. "The Franchise Agreement." *Cornell Hotel and Restaurant Administration Quarterly* 13: 13–21.

Villas-Boas, Sofia Berto. 2007. "Vertical Relationships between Manufacturers and Retailers: Inference with Limited Data." *Review of Economic Studies* 74: 625–652.

Vita, Michael G. 2000. "Regulatory Restrictions on Vertical Integration and Control: The Competitive Impact of Gasoline Divorcement Policies." *Journal of Regulatory Economics* 18: 217–233.

Vukina, Tomislav, and Porametr Leegomonchai. 2006. "Oligopsony Power, Asset Specificity and Hold-Up: Evidence from the Broiler Industry." *American Journal of Agricultural Economics* 88: 589–605.

Wheaton, William C. 2000. "Percentage Rent in Retail Leases: The Alignment of Landlord-Tenant Interests." *Real Estate Economics* 28: 185–204.

Whinston, Michael D. 2001. "Exclusivity and Tying in *US v. Microsoft:* What We Know and Don't Know." *Journal of Economic Perspectives* 15: 63–80.

———. 2003. "On the Transaction Cost Determinants of Vertical Integration." *Journal of Law, Economics, and Organization* 19: 1–23.

Williams, Darrell L. 1999. "Why Do Entrepreneurs Become Franchisees? An Empirical Analysis of Organizational Choice." *Journal of Business Venturing* 14: 103–124.

Williamson, Oliver E. 1971. "The Vertical Integration of Production: Market Failure Considerations." *American Economic Review* 61: 112–123.

———. 1979. "Transaction-Cost Economics: The Governance of Contractual Relations." *Journal of Law and Economics* 22: 3–61.

———. 1983. "Credible Commitments: Using Hostages to Support Exchange." *American Economic Review* 73: 519–540.

———. 1985. *The Economic Institutions of Capitalism.* New York: Free Press.

———. 1991. "Comparative Economic Organization: The Analysis of Discrete Structural Alternatives." *Administrative Science Quarterly* 36: 269–296.

———. 1996. *The Mechanisms of Governance.* New York: Oxford University Press.

Wolak, Frank A. 1996. "Why Do Firms Simultaneously Purchase in Spot and Contract Markets? Evidence from the United States Steam Coal Market." in D. Martimort (ed.), *Agricultural Markets: Mechanisms, Failures, and Regulations.* Amsterdam: Elsevier, pp. 109–168.

Wooldridge, Jeffrey M. 2002. *Econometric Analysis of Cross Section and Panel Data.* Cambridge, MA: MIT Press.

Zanarone, Giorgio. 2009. "Vertical Restraints and the Law: Evidence from Automobile Franchising." *Journal of Law and Economics* 52: 691–700.

25

Relational Incentive Contracts

James M. Malcomson

1. Introduction

This chapter is about relational contracts, agreements for which the ongoing relationship between the parties plays an essential role in determining what happens. Its concern is with *relational incentive contracts*, those that involve incentives for taking actions, and not, for example, those involving only risk sharing, such as the relational contracts studied by Thomas and Worrall (1988) and surveyed in Malcomson (1999: 2300–2311). It focuses on supply relationships between firms, not purely financial contracts, sovereign debt (discussed in Obstfeld and Rogoff 1996: 349–428), or employment (surveyed in Malcomson 1999: 2337–2364). The same underlying principles apply to all these, though obviously details may differ, but because of the present focus the terminology of supply relationships between firms is used here even for results originally derived in other contexts. This chapter also focuses primarily on theory. Empirical evidence on interfirm contracts is surveyed in Lafontaine and Slade (this volume).

Some decades ago, Macaulay (1963) observed that many contractual relationships between firms in the United States were not tightly specified in legal terms. A striking example is the so-called battle of the forms. Orders for supply of goods are made on standard forms with, on the front, details of what is to be supplied and, on the reverse, the purchaser's standard terms of business. The supplier's acknowledgement of the order also has standard terms of business specified on the reverse. But the purchaser's and the supplier's terms differ, and no attempt is made to reconcile them. Such informality concerned lawyers interviewed for Macaulay (1963), some of them in-house lawyers for large firms employed to give legal advice on contracts who might thus be expected to influence the contracts used. Yet purchasing and supplying agents persisted in using loosely specified contracts with, seemingly, the view that there was so much business between the parties that they would work something out if either was dissatisfied. One

I thank the many people, too many to list individually, who have assisted me in writing this chapter. I am, however, particularly indebted to Robert Gibbons, Bentley MacLeod, John Roberts, Giancarlo Spagnolo, and Michael Whinston, who read and commented on complete drafts. I also thank Leverhulme Trust Major Research Fellowship F/08519/B for financial support of my research on relational contracts.

purchasing agent went so far as to say: "One doesn't run to lawyers if he wants to stay in business because one must behave decently" (Macaulay 1963: 61).

The literature on relational contracts is concerned with the impact of the ongoing nature of the relationship on trade between the parties, on their payoffs, on the nature of any legally enforceable contract used to supplement the relational contract, and on the design of organizations. Legal aspects of relational contracts have been explored by Macneil (1978). The underlying economic idea was explored early on by Telser (1980) and Klein and Leffler (1981). If a supplier does not deliver something acceptable, the purchaser can look elsewhere in future. Provided the supplier anticipates a profit from continuing to trade with the purchaser, that acts as an incentive to provide what the purchaser wants. So there is a tension between providing something less costly, but less acceptable, now and keeping business in the future. It is a tension widely recognized in the business world. But the future incentive applies only if the supplier anticipates a strictly positive profit in the future, so the relationship has to be one in which free entry does not compete away all profits, perhaps because there are relationship-specific investments, perhaps because the parties learn information about each other that is not available about other potential purchasers and suppliers, or perhaps just because other potential purchasers and suppliers are wary of dealing with those who have had trading relationships come to an end for no apparent good economic reason. Moreover, the supplier will not incur more in costs to keep the relationship going than the value of any future profits. That limits what can be sustained. Those agreements that can be sustained in this way are said to be "self-enforcing," because they do not need courts to enforce them.

There are a number of strands to the literature on the economics of relational incentive contracts. One strand builds on the traditional principal-agent literature. In the most basic version, there is a principal (purchaser) who uses a single agent (supplier) to provide something with characteristics for which there are no verifiable measures that can be used to write a formal contract. That is the starting point for Section 3 of this chapter. This starting point is extended to cases in which there is some verifiable measure, but it does not capture all the parties care about and in which there are multiple agents (suppliers), issues taken up in Sections 4–8. In this strand, the principal does not contribute to the relationship except to pay for, and make use of, what is provided. In a second strand, all parties take actions that contribute to what is produced, as in a partnership, team, or joint venture. This raises the issue, discussed in Section 9, of how each party is rewarded as a function of whatever measure of joint output is available. Yet another strand is concerned with organizational design—whether the purchaser and supplier remain separate firms or are vertically integrated to produce components in-house, and who has the right to make what decisions, issues taken up in Section 10. The chapter concludes with some other issues arising from relational contracts (Sections 11–13). But first, in Section 2, it discusses some classic applications of relational contracts and the issues they raise for theory.

2. Classic Applications of Relational Contracts

Although this chapter is primarily about theory, it is helpful to illustrate the issues that arise in relational contracts with two classic cases, the relationship between Fisher Body and General Motors (GM) in the period 1919–1926 studied in detail in Klein et al. (1978) and Klein (2000), and the relationships between large Japanese automobile and electrical goods manufacturers and their suppliers studied by Asanuma (1989).

Klein (2000) describes the GM–Fisher Body relationship as follows. In 1919, GM agreed a 10-year exclusive dealing contract with Fisher Body for the supply of bodies for its automobiles. This was a relational contract, supplemented by a cost-plus contract for each unit delivered specifying that GM would pay an amount equal to Fisher's variable cost plus 17.6%. The relationship worked well up to 1924 but then became problematic for two reasons given by Alfred Sloan, the chief executive of GM. First, the cost-plus contract became unduly burdensome with the increase in the volume of bodies required by GM. Second, Fisher Body became unwilling to put up large amounts of capital to establish body plants near GM assembly plants: especially "Fisher's refusal to make the investment in plant and equipment to move Fisher's production of Buick bodies from Detroit to a site near the GM Buick assembly plant in Flint" (Klein 2000: 116). The upshot was that GM took over Fisher Body. The interpretation Klein (2000) places on these reasons is that the "plus" element in the probably legally enforceable cost-plus contract became excessive in relation to capital and overhead costs, given higher than anticipated volume and given that the specific investments required to build body plants near GM assembly plants were too large to keep the arrangement within the zone of a self-enforcing relational contract.

Klein's interpretation of these events has been disputed—see, for example, the other papers in the issue of the *Journal of Law and Economics* in which Klein (2000) appears. But, whether or not correct, it raises interesting questions for theory. First, in what way might a larger specific investment make it more difficult to sustain a relational contract? Second, what is the role of an additional explicit contract, such as GM's problematic cost-plus contract with Fisher Body, within a relational contract? And third, what does theory have to tell us about when vertical integration, which brings the incentive issues within a single firm, is to be preferred to a relational contract between two firms? All these issues are discussed in this chapter.

Asanuma (1989) carried out a detailed investigation of the contractual relationships between large Japanese companies in automobile and electrical machinery manufacturing and their suppliers. As he describes it, these large purchasers typically each use a small number of associated companies. They normally have a basic contract lasting initially for 1 year but renewed unless there are objections by either party. The basic contract specifies general obligations. It also specifies that orders (or monthly schedules in the case of automobiles) are to be regarded as contracts once accepted by the supplier and the frequency at which prices are to be renegotiated (typically 6 months). There is a general expectation that suppliers will reduce prices over time as a production run lengthens and that less highly regarded suppliers will be used as capacity buffers.

Asanuma (1989) attaches considerable importance to the rating system purchasers use for suppliers. To explain this system, he considers suppliers in three categories. The first are those he terms "suppliers in general," those who supply off-the-shelf goods (purchased goods), for example, from catalogs. For these goods, a long-term relationship may not be important. The other two categories are for suppliers of ordered goods. Here suppliers are differentiated into "common subcontractors," who produce components to designs provided by the purchaser (drawings supplied) and "excellent subcontractors," who produce components to their own design that has been approved by the purchaser (drawings approved). The latter are subcontractors who have shown themselves to be responsible suppliers in the past and are given a more responsible role in production. Typically, any change in status is associated with a change in design of the part supplied (with, e.g., a new model of automobile), when the supplier would have to make new specific investments in any case. It is rare for a purchaser to switch supplier during the lifetime of a product model, so it is times at which a model changes that are most competitive.

The description provided by Asanuma (1989) raises some further questions for theory. When purchasers face, and want to find out more about, suppliers of potentially different types, what difference does it make to the relational contracts between the parties? And what does theory have to say about the process of dividing suppliers into different rating categories on the basis of past experience, giving more-highly rated ones additional responsibilities?

3. Two Basic Models

The role of relational contracts is isolated most clearly when a single purchaser buys from a single supplier and there is no measure of the supplier's performance that is verifiable in court. The purchaser's profit in period t from being supplied with quality $q_t \in \left[\underline{q}, \overline{q}\right]$ is $y_t\left(q_t\right) - P_t$, where P_t is the payment to the supplier. Quality can be multidimensional, with q_t a vector. It is essentially a short-hand term for anything under the control of the supplier that is of concern to the purchaser. Suppose that y_t is strictly increasing and concave (so when $y_t\left(q_t\right)$ is twice differentiable, $y_t'\left(q_t\right) > 0$, and $y_t''\left(q_t\right) \leq 0$ for all q_t), and that $y_t\left(\underline{q}\right) = 0$, so that the purchaser would not be prepared to pay for quality at the lowest level. The supplier incurs cost $c_t\left(q_t\right)$ from supplying quality q_t and so makes profit $P_t - c_t\left(q_t\right)$ in period t if paid P_t for doing so. Conventionally, c_t is continuous, strictly increasing, and strictly convex (so when $c_t\left(q_t\right)$ is twice differentiable, $c_t'\left(q_t\right) > 0$ and $c_t''\left(q_t\right) > 0$ for all q_t), $c_t\left(\underline{q}\right) = 0$, and $\lim_{q_t \to \overline{q}} c_t\left(q_t\right) = \overline{c}$ with $\overline{c}$ finite. If the parties choose not to trade with each other in period t, the purchaser receives payoff $\pi_t > 0$ (perhaps from producing the component in-house) and the supplier payoff $u_t > 0$ (from using the capacity to supply elsewhere). The parties have a common discount factor $\delta_t \in (0, 1)$. The purchaser checks the quality supplied with probability $\rho \in (0, 1]$.

When quality is unverifiable, it is not possible to write a legally enforceable contract that makes payment conditional on quality. However, as Bull (1987) and MacLeod and Malcomson (1989) observed, the parties can still use conditional payments provided the relationship is structured in such a way that it is worthwhile for the purchaser to make them. For that reason, it may be useful to have the payment P_t consist of two components, a legally enforceable component p_t that cannot be conditioned on quality and a voluntary bonus $b_t \geq 0$ that can. How these components relate to the types of payments actually made in practice is discussed later. Following Levin (2003), we can think of the purchaser and supplier agreeing informally a plan for q_t, p_t, and b_t for the duration of their relationship. This is their *relational incentive contract*.

3.1. Employment Model

In what has been termed the "employment model" in the literature, once the cost of supply has been incurred, the supplier cannot hold back supply until payment is made. The timing

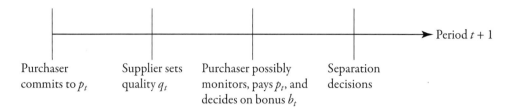

Figure 1. Timing of events for period t in the employment model.

of events for period t in this model is shown in Figure 1. At the beginning of each period, the purchaser commits to the legally enforceable payment p_t.[1] The supplier then decides what quality to deliver. The purchaser monitors the quality delivered with probability ρ, pays p_t, and decides whether to pay b_t. Finally in this period, the relationship may be terminated by either party, either because it is no longer even potentially mutually beneficial or because one or the other party decides to end it for some other reason.

The term "employment" should not be taken too literally. Although this model is clearly appropriate for employment, it also applies to the supply of many types of services. With this structure, no supply occurs if the relationship lasts for at most one period. With no future to be concerned about, the purchaser has no incentive to pay a positive bonus. Anticipating this, the supplier has no incentive to deliver quality above $\underline{q}$. When $q_t = \underline{q}$, the joint gains from the relationship, $y_t\left(\underline{q}\right) - c_t\left(\underline{q}\right) = 0$, are less than the joint payoffs $\pi_t + u_t$ the parties could get from making alternative arrangements, so there is no price p_t at which they would trade with each other. Thus, the possibility of trade depends on the relationship being at least potentially ongoing.

In a potentially ongoing relationship, the supplier's future payoff from t on for a relationship started at τ, if both parties stick to their agreement, consists of the payment $p_t + b_t$ less the cost of supply $c_t\left(q_t\right)$ in period t plus the expected payoff from the future. It can be written as

$$U_t = p_t + b_t - c_t\left(q_t\right) + \delta_t U_{t+1}, \quad \text{for all } t \geq \tau. \tag{1}$$

If, however, the supplier delivers quality in breach of the agreement, this is undetected with probability $1 - \rho$, and everything then continues as if no breach had occurred, with the supplier receiving payoff $p_t + b_t + \delta_t U_{t+1}$. The breach is detected with probability ρ, but the worst that can happen to the supplier is that the relationship comes to an end with payment of p_t, but without payment of the bonus b_t, because the supplier can always choose to quit at the end of period t. Let $\tilde{U}_{t+1}$ denote the supplier's payoff from $t + 1$ on in those circumstances. Thus, by setting $q_t = \underline{q}$, the supplier can obtain a payoff from t on of no less than

$$p_t + (1 - \rho)\left(b_t + \delta_t U_{t+1}\right) + \rho \delta_t \tilde{U}_{t+1}, \quad \text{for all } t \geq \tau. \tag{2}$$

---

1. In the employment model of Section 3.1, p_t could be paid at this stage, thus eliminating the need for it to be legally enforceable. But in models discussed later, p_t is conditioned on verifiable information not available until after the supplier has set q_t, and then the commitment is to a legally enforceable contract specifying these conditional payments.

From (1) and (2), it is certainly better for the supplier to set $q_t = \underline{q}$ than to stick to any agreement with $q_t > \underline{q}$, unless the following incentive compatibility condition holds:

$$\delta_t \{\text{future gain to supplier}\} \equiv \delta_t \left(U_{t+1} - \tilde{U}_{t+1} \right) \geq \frac{c_t \left(q_t \right)}{\rho} - b_t, \quad \text{for all } t \geq \tau. \quad (3)$$

The interpretation of this condition is most straightforward when $\rho = 1$: the future gains from having the relationship continue at the end of period t must then exceed the cost $c_t \left(q_t \right)$ of complying minus the current period incentive to supply provided by the bonus b_t. Moreover, for the supplier to continue in the relationship when there has been no breach, the following individual rationality condition must also hold:

$$U_t \geq \bar{U}_t, \quad \text{for all } t \geq \tau, \quad (4)$$

where $\bar{U}_t$ denotes the supplier's payoff from t on if the relationship ends for reasons unrelated to the performance of either party. In principle, $\bar{U}_t$ need not be the same as $\tilde{U}_t$.

If both parties stick to their agreement, the purchaser's future payoff from t on for a relationship started at τ consists of the value $y_t \left(q_t \right)$ derived from supply less the payment $p_t + b_t$ in period t plus the expected payoff from the future. It can be written as

$$\Pi_t = y_t \left(q_t \right) - p_t - b_t + \delta_t \Pi_{t+1}, \quad \text{for all } t \geq \tau. \quad (5)$$

If the purchaser does not pay the agreed bonus, the worst that can happen is that the relationship comes to an end, because the purchaser can always choose to quit at the end of period t. Let $\tilde{\Pi}_{t+1}$ denote the purchaser's payoff from $t + 1$ on in those circumstances. Thus, by setting $b_t = 0$, the purchaser can obtain a payoff from t on of no less than $y_t \left(q_t \right) - p_t + \delta_t \tilde{\Pi}_{t+1}$. Thus, it is certainly better for the purchaser to pay no bonus than to stick to any agreement with $b_t > 0$ unless the following incentive compatibility condition holds:

$$\delta_t \{\text{future gain to purchaser}\} \equiv \delta_t \left(\Pi_{t+1} - \tilde{\Pi}_{t+1} \right) \geq b_t, \quad \text{for all } t \geq \tau. \quad (6)$$

Moreover, for the purchaser to continue in the relationship when there has been no breach, the following individual rationality condition must clearly hold:

$$\Pi_t \geq \bar{\Pi}_t, \quad \text{for all } t \geq \tau, \quad (7)$$

where $\bar{\Pi}_t$ denotes the purchaser's payoff from t on if the relationship ends for reasons unrelated to the performance of either party. In principle, $\bar{\Pi}_t$ need not be the same as $\tilde{\Pi}_t$.

Let $S_{t+1} = U_{t+1} + \Pi_{t+1}$ denote the joint payoff (or *surplus*) the parties receive from $t + 1$ on if the relationship continues and $\tilde{S}_{t+1} = \tilde{U}_{t+1} + \tilde{\Pi}_{t+1}$. Then (3) and (6) can be added to give the pooled incentive compatibility condition

$$\delta_t \left(S_{t+1} - \tilde{S}_{t+1} \right) \equiv \delta_t \left(U_{t+1} - \tilde{U}_{t+1} + \Pi_{t+1} - \tilde{\Pi}_{t+1} \right) \geq \frac{c_t \left(q_t \right)}{\rho}, \quad \text{for all } t \geq \tau. \quad (8)$$

It is clear from the way they have been derived that (4), (7), and (8) are necessary conditions for the parties to stick to any agreement with $q_t > 0$, that is, for the agreement to be self-enforcing. Following the argument in MacLeod and Malcomson (1989), they are also sufficient. Formally, provided an agreement satisfies (4), (7), and (8), there exist strategies implementing the agreement that form a subgame perfect equilibrium. Hence, (4), (7), and (8) provide a complete characterization of subgame perfect equilibria with qualities strictly greater than q.[2]

The right-hand side of (8) is the cost of delivering quality q_t adjusted for the probability that cheating on the agreement is detected. That is sometimes referred to as the "reneging temptation." The left-hand side of (8) is the joint future gain to the parties from continuing the relationship at the end of period t. Thus, (8) requires that the joint future gain exceeds the reneging temptation. The joint future gain is independent of the payments made by the purchaser to the supplier—these cancel when U_{t+1} and Π_{t+1} are added—so the only element of the relational incentive contract that affects whether (8) is satisfied is the sequence of qualities $(q_t, q_{t+1}, \ldots)$ from t on. For any sequence of qualities that satisfies (8), it is always possible to find a sequence of bonuses $(b_t, b_{t+1}, \ldots)$ such that (3) and (6) are both satisfied for all t. Only the joint future gain, not its division between purchaser and supplier, enters (8), for the following reason. Future gain to the supplier affects the quality that can be delivered directly via the supplier's incentive compatibility condition (3). But future gain to the purchaser can do so too, because it can be used to induce the purchaser to pay a bonus via the purchaser's incentive compatibility condition (6) and that bonus affects the quality that can be delivered via (3).

As already explained, in a one-shot game the purchaser would never pay a positive bonus, so the supplier would always set quality at the lowest level. Thus, the one-shot game has a prisoner's dilemma type structure, and one can apply the intuition for the standard Folk Theorem in a repeated prisoner's dilemma game. Suppose δ_t is constant at δ for all t. The Folk Theorem tells us that, for a repeated prisoner's dilemma game, any individually rational cooperation can be sustained for a discount factor δ sufficiently close to 1 by strategies that revert to those of the one-shot equilibrium if either party deviates. Consider any sequence of quality $(q_t, q_{t+1}, \ldots)$ from t on for which the left-hand side of (8) is positive for all t. As $\delta \to 1$, that left-hand side goes to infinity, so any such sequence satisfies (8). Equality in (8) specifies the critical value of the discount factor for sustaining any particular sequence.[3] Provided supply of this sequence of qualities is mutually beneficial, there also exists a sequence $(p_t, p_{t+1}, \ldots)$ such that (4) and (7) are satisfied for all t. Then the ongoing nature of the relationship enables the purchaser to elicit quality above the minimum level from the supplier when that would not be possible in a one-period relationship.

Any sequences that satisfy (4), (7), and (8) can be sustained as equilibria. But some equilibria may be better than others. Let q_t^* denote efficient quality defined by

$$q_t^* = \arg \max_q y_t(q) - c_t(q), \quad \text{for all } t \geq \tau. \tag{9}$$

The purchaser and supplier can increase their joint payoff $U_\tau + \Pi_\tau$ at the start of the relationship (at τ) unless, for each $t \geq \tau$, either (a) $q_t < q_t^*$ and (8) holds with equality, or (b) $q_t = q_t^*$.

---

2. This result does not depend on payment of p_t being legally enforceable, for the reason given in note 1.

3. But see Blonski et al. (2011) on whether this value is actually critical for determining whether the parties sustain such a sequence.

To see why, note that the component of the joint payoff at date t', $U_{t'} + \Pi_{t'}$, arising at date $t \geq t'$ is just $y_t(q_t) - c_t(q_t)$, which q_t^* maximizes. Thus, the joint payoff $U_{t'} + \Pi_{t'}$ is always increased by having q_t move toward q_t^* for $t \geq t'$. So moving q_t toward q_t^* increases the left-hand side of (8) for all dates prior to t. Suppose $q_t > q_t^*$. Then the parties can always increase their joint payoff at τ, because reducing q_t increases the joint payoff for all dates up to t (thus relaxing the constraint (8) for all dates prior to t by increasing the left-hand side) and also relaxes the constraint (8) for t by reducing the right-hand side. Appropriate choice of p_t and b_t can ensure that neither U_t nor Π_t is reduced. Suppose now $q_t < q_t^*$. If (8) held with strict inequality at t, q_t could be increased without violating that constraint, which would also increase the left-hand side of (8) for all dates prior to t, thus relaxing the constraint for all dates prior to t. Thus, increasing q_t would increase the joint payoffs at all dates up to t without resulting in any of the constraints (4), (7), and (8) being violated.

The argument just given establishes that any constrained efficient self-enforcing equilibrium (ESE) has, for each $t \geq \tau$, either (a) $q_t < q_t^*$ and (8) holding with equality, or (b) $q_t = q_t^*$. In the model in Ray (2002), any ESE also maximizes the supplier's payoff from some finite $t' > \tau$ on as long as $q_t < q_t^*$ for all $t \geq \tau$. In that model, the purchaser is committed to the agreement at each t, which allows no scope for a discretionary bonus b_t. The result in Ray (2002) then follows from (3) with $b_t = 0$ for all $t \geq \tau$. For any $t \geq \tau$ with $q_t < q_t^*$, quality can be closer to the efficient level if $U_{t+1} - \tilde{U}_{t+1}$ is increased, which must therefore be maximized in any ESE. But that is not necessary if discretionary bonuses are included in the relational contract agreement.

Pooling of incentive compatibility conditions, as done to derive (8) from (3) and (6), is a standard feature in the literature that will recur in what follows. It is, though, important to recognize that it depends on the parties being risk-neutral. Also a standard feature in the literature is the limit on bonuses implied by (6), because the purchaser cannot receive a payoff from the future higher than is consistent with the supplier being prepared to continue the relationship. The result that conditions (4), (7), and (8) are necessary and sufficient does not depend on an environment, agreement, or payoffs that are stationary over time. But, as Levin (2003) shows, in a stationary environment the parties cannot do better than use a stationary agreement, one with q_t, p_t, and b_t the same for all t. Kranz and Ohlendorf (2009) consider the renegotiation proofness of relational contracts.

3.2. Outsourcing Model

In the employment model, once the cost of supply is incurred, the supplier cannot hold back supply until payment is made. But supply is sometimes of intermediate products produced on the supplier's own premises. That complicates the picture somewhat, because the supplier could then withhold the product and use it as a bargaining chip for payment. This scenario has been termed the "outsourcing model" in the literature. The timing of events for this model is shown in Figure 2. It differs from Figure 1 for the employment model, because at the third stage in period t the supplier, as well as the purchaser, can decide whether to stick to their agreement.

If both parties decide to stick to their agreement at this stage, the supplier delivers the already-produced quality to the purchaser, and the purchaser simultaneously pays the agreed bonus. If either decides to breach the agreement, the supplier retains the product and the purchaser pays no bonus. To complete the model, one must specify the alternative actions available to the parties

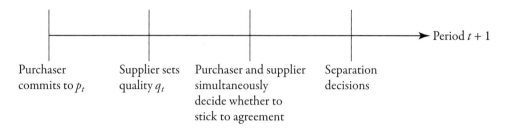

Figure 2. Timing of events for period t in the outsourcing model.

in the event of breach. A common assumption in the literature is that the outcome of those actions corresponds to a Nash bargain, but the precise formulation is unimportant here. For the present purpose, it suffices to denote by $z_t\left(q_t\right)$ the payment the supplier can get for quality q_t by withholding supply and bargaining. This payment will reflect not only what the product is worth to the purchaser but also what it can be sold for to some alternative purchaser. In this model, if the supplier were to decide not to provide the agreed quality and so risk breakdown of the relationship, it would not necessarily be optimal to set quality to $\underline{q}$, because the product could still be sold for some payment. It simplifies the exposition here without compromising later use to set $\rho = 1$, so that substandard quality is always detected by the purchaser. Then the optimal quality to deviate to is

$$\tilde{q}_t = \arg\max_{q \geq \underline{q}} z_t\left(q\right) - c_t\left(q\right). \tag{10}$$

This is precisely the quality the supplier would produce if there were no relational contract and all transactions were via a spot market. The payoff to deviating from the agreed-on quality corresponding to (2) with $\rho = 1$ is then

$$p_t - c_t\left(\tilde{q}_t\right) + z_t\left(\tilde{q}_t\right) + \delta_t \tilde{U}_{t+1}, \quad \text{for all } t \geq \tau, \tag{11}$$

and the incentive compatibility condition corresponding to (3) with $\rho = 1$ becomes

$$\delta_t\left\{\text{future gain to supplier}\right\} \equiv \delta_t\left(U_{t+1} - \tilde{U}_{t+1}\right)$$
$$\geq c_t\left(q_t\right) - c_t\left(\tilde{q}_t\right) + z_t\left(\tilde{q}_t\right) - b_t, \quad \text{for all } t \geq \tau. \tag{12}$$

In the outsourcing model, the supplier also has another decision to make, whether to supply the intermediate good once it has been produced. That will be worthwhile only if the bonus b_t combined with the benefit of having the relationship continue is more valuable than deviating by selling the good for $z_t\left(q_t\right)$ and having the relationship end. Formally, that requires

$$\delta_t\left(U_{t+1} - \tilde{U}_{t+1}\right) \geq z_t\left(q_t\right) - b_t, \quad \text{for all } t \geq \tau. \tag{13}$$

By the definition of $\tilde{q}_t$ in (10), the right-hand side of (12) is necessarily at least as large as the right-hand side of (13), so the former is always the critical incentive compatibility condition for the supplier.

The purchaser will pay the bonus for the agreed quality only if doing that and having the relationship continue is worth more than defaulting, paying $z_t(q_t)$ to get the supply despite defaulting, and having the relationship end. Thus, the incentive compatibility condition for the purchaser corresponding to (6) becomes

$$\delta_t \left\{\text{future gain to purchaser}\right\} \equiv \delta_t \left(\Pi_{t+1} - \tilde{\Pi}_{t+1}\right) \geq b_t - z_t(q_t), \quad \text{for all } t \geq \tau. \quad (14)$$

The overall incentive compatibility condition corresponding to (8) with $\rho = 1$ is obtained by adding (12) and (14):

$$\delta_t \left(S_{t+1} - \tilde{S}_{t+1}\right) \equiv \delta_t \left(U_{t+1} - \tilde{U}_{t+1} + \Pi_{t+1} - \tilde{\Pi}_{t+1}\right)$$
$$\geq c_t(q_t) - c_t(\tilde{q}_t) + z_t(\tilde{q}_t) - z_t(q_t), \quad \text{for all } t \geq \tau. \quad (15)$$

To see the incentive differences between the employment and the outsourcing structures, compare (15) with (8) when $\rho = 1$, so that the environments are otherwise identical. The incentive compatibility condition (8) for the employment structure depends only on the quality q_t specified by the relational contract. That for the outsourcing structure (15) also depends on the quality $\tilde{q}_t$ that the supplier would produce in the absence of a relational contract. Thus the structure of the relationship makes a difference to the quality that can be sustained. It is tempting to conclude that (15) is weaker than (8) when $z_t(q_t) \geq z_t(\tilde{q}_t)$. One must, however, be careful about this conclusion, because it may be that $\tilde{U}_t$ and $\tilde{\Pi}_t$ take different values in the outsourcing model than in the employment model. One obvious reason is that, in the outsourcing case, the supplier is willing to supply $\tilde{q}_t$ even in a spot market without a relational contract, because the product can always be sold for $z_t(\tilde{q}_t)$. In contrast, in the employment model, no supply would occur without a relational contract.

The argument used in Section 3.1 for the employment model to show that the purchaser and supplier can always increase their joint payoff if $q_t > q_t^*$ for any t does not work with the outsourcing model, because reducing q_t may increase the right-hand side of (15) if it reduces $z_t(q_t)$ more than it reduces $c_t(q_t)$. But it remains the case that the purchaser and supplier can increase their joint payoffs $U_\tau + \Pi_\tau$ at the start of the relationship (at τ) unless, for each $t \geq \tau$, either (15) holds with equality or $q_t = q_t^*$. Otherwise, moving q_t marginally in the direction of q_t^* would not violate (15) and would increase the joint payoffs for all dates up to t.

Because of its simpler structure, much of the discussion that follows is based on the employment model underlying (8) rather than on the outsourcing model underlying (15). But many of the arguments can be extended to the outsourcing model, and that model has been used in the literature to illustrate points that cannot be made using only the employment model.

4. Specific Investments

Basic as it is, the employment model of Section 3.1 can be used to address the first question arising from the interpretation Klein (2000) places on the relationship between GM and Fisher Body: in what way might a larger specific investment make it more difficult to sustain a relational contract? But first the model must be adapted to include a specific investment. A specific investment by the supplier of $I \geq 0$ at τ in general affects both the output from, and the cost of, delivering quality, so write these as $y_t\left(q_t, I\right)$ and $c_t\left(q_t, I\right)$, respectively, for $t \geq \tau$. It thus also affects the surplus from the relationship S_t. Furthermore, it may affect the ease of monitoring quality, which can be captured by writing the probability of monitoring $\rho\left(I\right)$. In addition, it may affect the supplier's payoff from breaching the relational contract. If, as in the GM–Fisher Body example, the specific investment involved moving the body plant, it may have reduced the payoff to trading with other potential purchasers. Denote that payoff by $\tilde{U}_{t+1}\left(I\right)$. Finally, if the supplier is to make the investment, the payoff in the period of investment τ must be large enough to make the investment worthwhile, that is, $U_\tau \geq \bar{U}_\tau + I$.

Consider a stationary environment and a stationary relational contract, for which t subscripts can be dropped. Then $S = \left[y\left(q, I\right) - c\left(q, I\right)\right] / \left(1 - \delta\right)$. Define $\tilde{u}\left(I\right)$ and $\tilde{\pi}$ by, respectively, $\tilde{U}\left(I\right) = \tilde{u}\left(I\right) / \left(1 - \delta\right)$ and $\tilde{\Pi} = \tilde{\pi} / \left(1 - \delta\right)$, so $\tilde{S} = \left[\tilde{u}\left(I\right) + \tilde{\pi}\right] / \left(1 - \delta\right)$. Then (8) becomes

$$\frac{\delta}{1 - \delta}\left[y\left(q, I\right) - c\left(q, I\right) - \tilde{u}\left(I\right) - \tilde{\pi}\right] \geq \frac{c\left(q, I\right)}{\rho\left(I\right)}. \tag{16}$$

It follows that a worthwhile specific investment that increases $y\left(q, I\right) - c\left(q, I\right)$ for a given q can make it harder to sustain the relationship only if it increases

$$\frac{c\left(q, I\right)}{\rho\left(I\right)} + \frac{\delta}{1 - \delta}\left[\tilde{u}\left(I\right) + \tilde{\pi}\right]. \tag{17}$$

The specific investment would thus have to do at least one of the following: (a) increase the variable cost of producing the given quality, with the benefits of the specific investment arising from an increase in $y\left(q, I\right)$ of more than the increase in $c\left(q, I\right)$; (b) make monitoring quality more difficult, corresponding to a decrease in $\rho\left(I\right)$; or (c) increase the payoff $\tilde{u}\left(I\right)$ the supplier receives from breaching the relational contract. This chapter focuses on theory and so does not consider in detail whether the higher specific investments that GM wanted Fisher Body to make could have operated in this way, but there are a number of straightforward considerations.

An obvious efficiency gain from siting a body plant close to an assembly plant would be a reduction in the cost of transporting bodies to the assembly plant. If that were all, it would be worthwhile only if it involved a net saving after taking into account the cost of transporting materials, that is, only if it reduced the cost $c\left(q, I\right)$ for given q of delivering bodies to the assembly plant. Also plausible is that it would reduce the payoff $\tilde{u}\left(I\right)$ the supplier could get from breaching the relational contract, because the plant would be farther from other potential purchasers. Moreover, it is not obvious why moving the body plant should increase the difficulty of monitoring quality. Thus, the reduction in transportation cost would seem to make it easier to sustain the relational contract. It may, of course, be that the specific investment increases the marginal benefit of quality $\partial y\left(q, I\right) / \partial q$ or decreases the marginal cost of quality $\partial c\left(q, I\right) / \partial q$, in which case it will change the efficient quality level defined by (9). Thus, it may be that, at a lower level of specific investment, efficient quality is attainable with a relational contract but not at a higher level of specific investment. But that does not, in itself, make it harder to sustain the relational contract.

The outsourcing model of Section 3.2 may, however, be more appropriate to describe the relationship between GM and Fisher Body, though the value of a Buick body to another automobile assembler is questionable. Then the relevant incentive compatibility condition is (15) instead of (8). In that case, the specific investment might affect the quality $\tilde{q}_t$ defined in (10) that the supplier would produce if planning to breach the relational contract. Then, in an obvious notation, (16) is replaced by

$$
\frac{\delta}{1-\delta} \left[y\left(q, I\right) - c\left(q, I\right) - \tilde{u}\left(I\right) - \tilde{\pi} \right]
$$

$$
\geq c\left(q, I\right) - c\left(\tilde{q}\left(I\right), I\right) + \left[z\left(\tilde{q}\left(I\right), I\right) - z\left(q, I\right) \right],
$$

(18)

and so (17) is replaced by

$$
c\left(q, I\right) - c\left(\tilde{q}\left(I\right), I\right) + \left[z\left(\tilde{q}\left(I\right), I\right) - z\left(q, I\right) \right] + \frac{\delta}{1-\delta} \left[\tilde{u}\left(I\right) + \tilde{\pi} \right].
$$

There is then the additional consideration of how the specific investment affects the difference in cost $c\left(q, I\right) - c\left(\tilde{q}\left(I\right), I\right)$ between producing q and producing $\tilde{q}\left(I\right)$, and how it affects the difference in the payment $z\left(\tilde{q}\left(I\right), I\right) - z\left(q, I\right)$ the supplier could get by withholding supply and bargaining.

These considerations apply to the continuation of the relational contract once the specific investment has been made. One of the issues arising between GM and Fisher Body, however, was the latter's unwillingness to make the specific investment in the first place. For a specific investment at τ to be worthwhile for the supplier, the supplier's payoff from τ on, U_τ, would have to increase by more than the cost of the investment. The previous section showed that, for any given sequence of qualities $\left(q_t, q_{t+1}, \ldots\right)$ that it is feasible to support in a continuation equilibrium, there exist continuation equilibria with any feasible U_t and Π_t that satisfy $U_t \geq \bar{U}_t$ and $\Pi_t \geq \bar{\Pi}_t$. So, as long as the specific investment is jointly worthwhile in the sense of increasing $U_\tau + \Pi_\tau$ by more than it costs, there exists a continuation equilibrium with the increase in the supplier's payoff sufficient to cover the cost of the investment without reducing the purchaser's payoff. But it is possible that Fisher Body's concern was with whether GM would in fact play such a continuation equilibrium. Predicting which equilibrium will be played in a multiple equilibrium context is problematic. But the usual assumption in the relational contract literature is that the parties will play a Pareto superior equilibrium, provided it is incentive compatible. Indeed, this assumption is implicit in Klein's (2000) view that, up to 1924, the relational contract arrangement between GM and Fisher Body was efficient.

Whether, of course, they actually do play a Pareto superior equilibrium is an empirical question that is not the subject of this chapter. But it is worth noting that there are many experimental studies indicating that participants cooperate even in the absence of third-party enforcement of agreements (for a survey, see Fehr and Falk 2002). Especially relevant here is Brown et al. (2004), in which the party acting in the role of purchaser could specify a payment corresponding to p_t and a performance level corresponding to q_t. In treatments in which these were a contract enforced by the experimenters, participants behaved very much in the way predicted by competitive market theory. But when they were not an enforceable contract, repeated interaction resulted in huge increases in the performance level over that in one-off interactions, though not to the level in the enforceable contract treatment. The possibility of choosing to terminate the relationship was important for this outcome. The experimental finding less consistent with the model used here is that, although each experiment lasted only a known finite number of periods, performance did not drop to the minimum level possible even in the final period. Indeed, performance in the final period increased with the generosity that the partner had shown in previous periods. The authors term this a "reciprocity effect." MacLeod (2007a) models this effect as arising from a small disutility of breaching an agreement. But, in an important sense, such an effect is complementary to the model here. It implies that cooperation does not necessarily unravel when the time horizon is actually finite, and the experimental findings emphasize that repetition increases performance beyond what the reciprocity effect alone delivers. What an experiment lasting just a few hours obviously cannot pick up is how long lived such reciprocity effects are likely to be in practice.

Ramey and Watson (1997) analyze an employment type model in which the specific investment is made by the purchaser, not the supplier, at a stage when the future environment is uncertain. There are just two possible levels of quality, $\underline{q}$ and $\overline{q}$. The purchaser can choose the level of specific investment I. Uncertainty about the future can be represented in the incentive compatibility condition (16) by reinterpreting ρ (independent of I in Ramey and Watson 1997) as a random variable taking one of two values, $\overline{\rho}$ and $\underline{\rho}$, with $1 > \overline{\rho} > \underline{\rho} > 0$, whose realization is unknown at the time the investment decision is made. For I sufficiently high, (16) is satisfied for quality $\overline{q}$ whether ρ takes the value $\overline{\rho}$ or $\underline{\rho}$, but for lower I it is satisfied only for $\overline{\rho}$. It is never satisfied for $\underline{q}$. When $\underline{\rho}$ is sufficiently unlikely, the purchaser's optimal level of I is such that (16) is not satisfied, and the relationship is not continued, if $\underline{\rho}$ occurs (termed a "fragile contract"). Ramey and Watson (1997) use this model to study the pattern of separations in a market equilibrium in which new trading partners cannot be immediately located and there are aggregate shocks. Improvements in the probability of rematching may result in greater use of fragile contracts. Ramey and Watson (2001) extend the model to the case in which both parties make specific investments and identify cases in which there is an optimal positive level of market friction that implements efficient investment.

5. Verifiable Performance Measures

The GM–Fisher Body relational contract contained a 10-year exclusive dealing arrangement supplemented by a cost-plus contract for each unit delivered. Klein (2000: 125) is of the view that a court would presumably have enforced the cost-plus contract. For it to be legally enforceable, the number of units delivered and the cost of provision would have to be verifiable. Of course, if everything the parties care about is verifiable, there would be no need for a relational contract. But there is an obvious question of when, if only some of the relevant information is verifiable, it is advantageous to use a supplementary legally enforceable contract using that information within a broader relational contract.

Outside one-shot simultaneous action games, it may, as Bernheim and Whinston (1998) show, be actively harmful to constrain the actions of the parties when there is verifiable information to do so. Although their formal results apply only to finite-horizon games, the essential point, as they show, carries over to infinite-horizon games. Indeed, it can be seen from the basic model set out above. In that model, provided payments are verifiable, it would be perfectly possible to fix by formal contract the bonus b_t that the purchaser pays to the supplier. But to do so would prevent the purchaser tailoring the payment to the unverifiable quality delivered by the seller.

Use of a supplementary formal contract can, nevertheless, enable a relational contract to work under a wider set of conditions, as Baker et al. (1994) show. This can be seen in the employment model of Section 3.1 with the addition of a verifiable outcome measure $x_t = \mu_t q_t$, where $\mu_t > 0$ is the realization of a random variable that is observed by the supplier before choosing q_t but is not observed by the purchaser. For simplicity, let $\rho = 1$, because this probability plays no role in the discussion. In a one-period relationship, basing payment on x_t alone distorts incentives but enables quality above the minimum level (see Baker 1992). Specifically, with legally enforceable payment $p_t(x_t)$ (assumed by Baker to have constant slope $p'_t(x_t) = \beta_t > 0$), actual quality depends on μ_t, even though efficient quality does not. With an ongoing relational contract, suppose the purchaser commits to the enforceable payment just described. (Baker et al. (1994) impose $b_t = 0$, but that is not essential to the argument.) Incentive compatibility for the purchaser is unchanged, because $p_t(x_t)$ has to be paid in any case. However, if the supplier is going to deliver substandard quality, it is optimal to do so in a way that maximizes the current period variable payoff $p_t(\mu_t q_t) - c(q_t)$. That is, the supplier will deliver quality $\tilde{q}_t(\beta_t \mu_t)$ defined by $c'_t[\tilde{q}_t(\beta_t \mu_t)] = \beta_t \mu_t$. Thus, the supplier's incentive compatibility condition (3) becomes

$$\delta\left(U_{t+1} - \tilde{U}_{t+1}\right) \geq c_t\left(q_t\right) - c_t\left[\tilde{q}_t\left(\beta_t \mu_t\right)\right] - \beta_t \mu_t\left[q_t - \tilde{q}_t\left(\beta_t \mu_t\right)\right] - b_t, \quad \text{for all } t \geq \tau.$$

Added to the purchaser's incentive compatibility condition (6), this inequality implies that the pooled incentive compatibility condition (8) is replaced by

$$\delta\left(S_{t+1} - \tilde{S}_{t+1}\right) \geq c_t\left(q_t\right) - c_t\left[\tilde{q}_t\left(\beta_t \mu_t\right)\right] - \beta_t \mu_t\left[q_t - \tilde{q}_t\left(\beta_t \mu_t\right)\right], \quad \text{for all } t \geq \tau. \quad (19)$$

For any $q_t > \tilde{q}_t(\beta_t \mu_t)$, the right-hand side of (19) is smaller than the right-hand side of (8), so higher quality at t is sustainable for any given future gain $S_{t+1} - \tilde{S}_{t+1}$, and this makes it feasible to sustain quality closer to the efficient level when that level is not sustainable without the formal contract. But β_t high enough to achieve efficient quality q_t^* when μ_t is low may result in $\tilde{q}_t(\beta_t \mu_t) > q_t^*$ when μ_t is high. Quality can still be kept to the efficient level, provided that level satisfies (19), by the purchaser not paying the bonus if quality is too high as well as if it is too low, but it may not be possible to choose β_t to sustain efficient quality for both high and low realizations of μ_t. Even so, appropriate choice of β_t enables the purchaser and supplier, at least on average, to come closer to the efficient level. It is thus optimal for the parties to use a formal contract to supplement their relational contract, even though it is based on imperfectly verifiable information.

The existence of such imperfectly verifiable measures is not, however, necessarily an unmixed blessing. It may increase the payoffs $\tilde{U}_{t+1}$ and $\tilde{\Pi}_{t+1}$ the purchaser and the supplier receive after breaching, because it may enable them to guarantee to other potential partners that an alternative match will be productive even if they are no longer trusted to stick to a relational contract. Baker et al. (1994) show that, for certain configurations, it may even destroy the incentive compatibility of the relational contract. Di Tella and MacCulloch (2002) provide a related application in which better outside alternatives can crowd out informal incentives. In their case, more generous state provision of unemployment benefit reduces informal intrafamily insurance more than one-for-one, so total transfers to the unemployed fall.

This model brings out a general point: a supplementary enforceable contract affects a relational contract through its impact on the payoffs the parties receive in the event one of them defaults on what they agree. In it, however, the verifiable outcome measure x_t is of no direct concern to the purchaser. It does not, therefore, actually capture the contractual arrangement between the Japanese manufacturers and their suppliers described by Asanuma (1989), and that between GM and Fisher Body, where the quantities ordered were treated as a formal contract and quantity was clearly of direct concern to the purchasers. That situation is captured by Schmidt and Schnitzer (1995), using the multitask agency approach of Holmström and Milgrom (1991). Suppose $q_t = \left(q_t^1, q_t^2 \right)$ has two components, q_t^1 measuring quantity that is verifiable and q_t^2 measuring quality that is not, with $c_t \left(q_t^1, q_t^2 \right)$ increasing in each argument. In the absence of a supplementary formal contract, the only difference to the analysis in Section 3.1 is that $\tilde{U}_{t+1}$ and $\tilde{\Pi}_{t+1}$, and hence $\tilde{S}_{t+1}$, need to reflect the possibility that the parties can trade without a relational contract using a legally enforceable contract on q_t^1 alone if that is worthwhile when q_t^2 is set at its lowest level $\underline{q}^2$. But this possibility applies whether or not the parties supplement their relational contract with an enforceable contract on q_t^1 and so does not affect whether, given the possibility of a supplementary enforceable contract, it is worthwhile using one. If the parties specify q_t^1 in a supplementary enforceable contract, it is optimal for the supplier, if defaulting, to deliver quality $q_t^2 = \underline{q}^2$ in quantity q_t^1. Thus, the incentive compatibility condition for the supplier (3) when $\rho = 1$ becomes

$$\delta \left(U_{t+1} - \tilde{U}_{t+1} \right) \geq c_t \left(q_t^1, q_t^2 \right) - c_t \left(q_t^1, \underline{q}^2 \right) - b_t, \quad \text{for all } t \geq \tau.$$

When added to the purchaser's incentive compatibility condition (6), it implies that the pooled incentive compatibility condition (8) is replaced by

$$\delta \left(S_{t+1} - \tilde{S}_{t+1} \right) \geq c_t \left(q_t^1, q_t^2 \right) - c_t \left(q_t^1, \underline{q}^2 \right), \quad \text{for all } t \geq \tau.$$

This condition is weaker than (8) with $\rho = 1$ and so enlarges the set of q_t that can be sustained as equilibria when the efficient level is otherwise unattainable. Thus, specifying quantity in an enforceable contract is certainly worthwhile. As in Baker et al. (1994), however, by improving the payoffs that can be attained without a relational contract, the possibility of specifying quantity in an enforceable contract may make it harder to sustain a relational one. Iossa and Spagnolo (2011) show that, even if q_t^1 is of no value to the purchaser (as a result of which delivery is not enforced in equilibrium), contracting on it can help sustain a relational contract by enabling an additional penalty to be imposed on a defaulting supplier. Daido (2006) analyzes a related model in which neither component of q_t is verifiable but y_t has two components, each randomly related to the corresponding component of q_t, and one of which is verifiable.

The model in Schmidt and Schnitzer (1995) does not fully capture the relationship between GM and Fisher Body, because the enforceability of the cost-plus contract would require that Fisher's cost was verifiable. In the model, that would remove the need for a relational contract altogether, so, to retain the role for a relational contract, it would need to be enriched further. But the model reemphasizes the result in Baker et al. (1994) that it may be valuable to supplement a relational contract with a legally enforceable one conditioned on verifiable information.

A different role for a legally enforceable contract to supplement a relational one arises when verifiable measures of performance are imprecise and the supplier is risk averse. Some individual suppliers are much smaller than such purchasers as GM and Toyota, and so they might be expected to be more risk averse. Asanuma and Kikutani (1992) show that the relations between the big Japanese automobile manufacturers and their satellite (as opposed to intermittent) subcontractors contain mechanisms through which the manufacturer absorbs the risks involved in their transactions to a substantial degree. Using a technique from Kawasaki and McMillan (1987), Asanuma and Kikutani estimate that four large Japanese auto manufacturers each bear close to 90% of the risk and estimate a corresponding degree of absolute risk aversion for the satellites.

Pearce and Stacchetti (1998) adapt the employment model to a risk-averse supplier in a relational contract. The purchaser remains risk neutral. The environment and the contractual arrangements are stationary. The outcome y in period t (from a finite set) is now a random variable with verifiable realization y_t that is independent and identically distributed (iid) conditional on the quality q_t (also from a finite set) delivered by the supplier in period t. The distribution of y can thus be written $F(y \mid q)$. Quality remains unverifiable but is observed by the purchaser. (In this respect, the model differs from the repeated principal-agent model in Radner (1985), in which the agent's effort is not observed by the principal.) With y_t verifiable, the parties can use a legally enforceable contract that specifies payment $p(y)$, required by Pearce and Stacchetti (1998) to be nonnegative. But they can improve on such a contract by adding a relational element with voluntary bonus $b(y)$ conditional on the agreed quality being delivered. The incentive compatibility condition for the purchaser to pay the bonus, corresponding to (6), then becomes

$$\delta \left[\Pi(y) - \tilde{\Pi} \right] \geq b(y), \quad \text{for all } y, \tag{20}$$

where $\Pi(y)$ is the future payoff to the purchaser in the continuation equilibrium when y occurs. Pearce and Stacchetti (1998) show that, if total compensation $P(y) = p(y) + b(y)$ is not independent of y (as it would be with efficient risk sharing), it is optimal to have (20) hold with equality for every y for which $p(y) > 0$. The intuition is that, if incentive compatibility for the purchaser were not a concern, lowering $p(y)$ and increasing $b(y)$ by the same amount would strengthen the supplier's incentive to deliver the agreed quality while leaving unchanged the overall payoffs to both parties when y occurs. This would provide scope for adjustment of payments to decrease the variation in total compensation to the risk-averse supplier and shift risk to the risk-neutral purchaser, a Pareto improvement that remains feasible until either $p(y) = 0$ or (20) holds with equality. Pearce and Stacchetti (1998) also show that a higher current total payment to the supplier $[P(y') > P(y'')]$ is associated with (a) a higher current legally enforceable payment $[p(y') > p(y'')]$; (b) a higher future payoff to the supplier $[U(y') > U(y'')]$; and (c) a lower current bonus $[b(y') < b(y'')]$. To see why, suppose it is desirable for incentive reasons to reward the agent more for outcome y' than for outcome y''. To smooth rewards intertemporally, it is then desirable to have both the present payoff to the supplier $P(y)$ and the future payoff $U(y)$ higher for y' than for y''. Because shocks are iid and hence the future joint surplus is independent of y, $U(y') > U(y'')$ implies $\Pi(y') < \Pi(y'')$. With

(20) as a binding constraint, that in turn implies $b\left(y'\right) < b\left(y''\right)$. But then $P\left(y'\right) > P\left(y''\right)$ only if $p\left(y'\right) > p\left(y''\right)$. This result yields the empirically testable prediction that a higher total payment at t' than at t'' consists of a higher fixed payment but a lower bonus payment.

The discussion so far in this section applies to the employment model. For the outsourcing model, a formal contract based on the verifiability of the quantity supplied can play a further role, as Itoh and Morita (2011) show. In the absence of a formal contract, the overall incentive compatibility condition is (15). Suppose the parties supplement their relational contract with a formal contract that the supplier will provide the intermediate product for the payment p_t and a court will enforce specific performance of the contract, so that, if the intermediate product is produced, it must be delivered to the purchaser and the purchaser must pay p_t. (Quality q_t cannot, of course, be the subject of a legally enforceable contract, because it is unverifiable.) Then the supplier cannot extract a payment other than p_t for delivery whatever quality is produced, and the situation is equivalent to the employment model with overall incentive compatibility constraint (8) and $\rho = 1$. Clearly, this condition is weaker than (15) for given q_t if $z_t\left(\tilde{q}_t\right) - c_t\left(\tilde{q}_t\right) > z_t\left(q_t\right)$, for which a necessary condition is obviously $z_t\left(\tilde{q}_t\right) > z_t\left(q_t\right)$. That might be the case when producing quality q_t instead of $\tilde{q}_t$ makes the intermediate product sufficiently more specific to the purchaser to reduce the payment the supplier could get for it by bargaining.

The results above that depend on verifiable delivery should not, however, be overplayed. With verifiable delivery, it may be possible to achieve efficient quality even without a relational contract. Suppose, in the spirit of the discussion of specific investments in Hart and Moore (1988), the parties were to contract on a fixed price $p_t = y_t\left(q_t^*\right)$ for delivery, where q_t^* is the efficient quality defined in (9), but the purchaser has the right to refuse to accept delivery. Then, even in a single-period model with no relational contract, it is optimal for the supplier to supply quality q_t^*, because the purchaser will not accept delivery of quality less than q_t^* at price p_t but will accept delivery of quality q_t^* at that price. An upfront payment by the supplier can be used to divide the gains from trade between the parties in any proportion. In Itoh and Morita (2011), a random variable, whose realization is not observed until after quality has been determined, also affects the value y_t to the purchaser, so it is not possible to determine the exact price in advance in the way just specified. But even then, provided delivery is verifiable, an alternative mechanism can still achieve efficient quality without a relational contract. Specifically, the parties can agree a legally enforceable contract giving the supplier the right to set any price at all for delivery after the uncertainty is resolved and the purchaser the right to choose whether to accept delivery at that price. Then it is optimal for the supplier to produce whatever quality is efficient, given the information available at the time the quality decision is made, and to set the price at the purchaser's valuation of that quality, given the realization of the random variable. Evans (2008) shows how powerful contracts of this type can be at achieving efficiency under quite general conditions.

The discussion thus far has taken as given what is verifiable and so can be made legally enforceable. But it may be possible for the parties to influence, at a cost, the extent to which an agreement is legally enforceable. In Kvaløy and Olsen (2009), the probability that a breach of the relational contract will be verifiable to the courts can be increased by incurring an enforcement cost. They use the employment model with either reliance or expectation damages. For spot market trading to be worthwhile, the parties must incur the enforcement cost. A relational contract reduces the benefit of incurring the enforcement cost, though, under appropriate conditions, it is still worth incurring some enforcement cost. However, the resulting equilibrium quality may be lower, despite the joint gains being higher because of the savings on the enforcement cost. Moreover, under a relational contract, higher δ (which Kvaløy and Olsen (2009) interpret as a proxy for greater trust between the parties) may actually result in lower quality.

Battigalli and Maggi (2002) develop a framework for analyzing when it is worth incurring the cost of describing contingencies to enable the parties to write a legally enforceable contract on them. Battigalli and Maggi (2008) extend that framework to repeated interactions with relational contracts. They consider an outsourcing model in which q_t is a vector of qualities, each of which is binary, with $c_t\left(q_t\right)$ additively separable in these qualities. All qualities are potentially verifiable at a cost, but efficient quality decisions may change over time because of exogenous events. The formal contracts the parties can write can contain a different type of clause for each element of q_t: a *contingent clause* specifying that element conditional on exogenous events, a *spot clause* specifying that element for period t only after the exogenous events for period t are known (formally this is a noncontingent clause that is modified after the events are observed and corresponds to settling for $z_t\left(q_t\right)$ in the outsourcing model), and an *enrichment clause* that starts off as a noncontingent clause but is changed to a contingent clause when a relevant contingency first occurs. Different types of clauses have different writing costs. The choice between clause type depends on the cost of describing contingencies relative to the cost of describing the quality to be delivered. For a contingent clause, both costs must be incurred, but only once. For a spot clause, the cost of describing contingencies is avoided, but the cost of describing the quality to be delivered must be incurred each period. An enrichment clause incurs the cost of describing the quality to be delivered at the start, postponing the cost of describing contingencies until an event occurs for which the noncontingent quality is inappropriate but then incurring the cost of describing quality a second time. Alternatively, the parties can allow an element of q_t to be enforced informally by a relational contract. Naturally, for δ high enough to satisfy a condition corresponding to (15) whatever exogenous events occur, it is optimal to rely on relational contracting, because it saves on writing costs. But for lower δ, it becomes optimal to specify those elements of q_t with high costs of supply in a formal contract. Contingent clauses have a single upfront cost and so do not affect incentive compatibility in the future, whereas spot and enrichment clauses have expected future costs that have to be deducted from the future gains to continuing the relationship, the left-hand side of (15). In this situation, an increase in writing costs or uncertainty leads to an increase in the number of elements of q_t enforced by the relational contract. For δ sufficiently low, a relational contract is ineffective, and all elements of q_t are optimally governed by a formal contract.

6. Private Information: Nonpersistent Types

It is clear from the discussion in Asanuma (1989) that Japanese auto and electrical machinery manufacturers are concerned to find out about the differences in characteristics of their suppliers and to treat them accordingly. From a theoretical perspective, we can think of suppliers being of different inherent types that the purchaser does not observe directly but that are important to the relationship. This is not captured by the models of Section 3 because there it is assumed that the purchaser knows everything about the supplier that is relevant, even though some things are not verifiable. In this section and the next, we consider a supplier with private information about type (the cost of supply) that is not known to the purchaser. We start in this section with the case in which type is not persistent, so that learning about the supplier's type in one period reveals no useful information about the supplier's type in the next period. The supplier's cost of maintaining quality may be higher in one period because of unusually high demand from other customers, because critical employees are off sick, or because quality control equipment is not working properly. That is not the situation Asanuma (1989) had in mind, but it is the case most fully discussed in the literature, notably by Levin (2003) and MacLeod (2003).

In Levin (2003), as in Pearce and Stacchetti (1998), the outcome y in period t in the employment model is a random variable that is iid conditional on q in period t and distributed $F(y \mid q)$, with corresponding density function f. Differences from Pearce and Stacchetti (1998) are that, as in the employment model of Section 3.1, the realization y_t is unverifiable, and the supplier is risk neutral. Moreover, before choosing q_t, the supplier observes a parameter of the cost function $\theta_t \in \left[\underline{\theta}, \overline{\theta} \right]$ that is an iid draw for period t. The cost of delivering quality q_t, now denoted $c\left(q_t, \theta_t\right)$, is differentiable and increasing in θ_t, and it satisfies the standard single-crossing property, corresponding to $\partial^2 c\left(q_t, \theta_t\right) / \partial q_t \partial \theta_t > 0$ when it is twice differentiable. Levin (2003) considers two cases. In one, the hidden information case, the purchaser observes q_t but not θ_t. In the other, the moral hazard case, the purchaser observes θ_t but not q_t. Both cases can be handled together by specifying the performance outcome as a subset $\phi_t \subseteq \left\{\theta_t, q_t, y_t\right\}$ that is observed by both purchaser and supplier and allowing the voluntary bonus to be conditioned on ϕ_t. In this stationary environment, there is no loss from restricting attention to stationary contracts in which total payment to the supplier can be written $P\left(\phi_t\right) = p + b\left(\phi_t\right)$, but it adds flexibility in this stochastic environment to no longer require that the bonus be non-negative.

The crucial difference from the models in previous sections is that it is now optimal to agree quality as a function $q(\theta)$ of type, with efficient quality $q^*(\theta)$ defined by

$$q^*(\theta) = \arg\max_q E_y\left[y \mid q\right] - c(q, \theta), \quad \text{for all } \theta \in \left[\underline{\theta}, \overline{\theta}\right],$$

where E_y is the expectations operator over the random variable y. But the purchaser observes only one of q_t and θ_t and so does not know whether the supplier actually delivered what was agreed. Thus, the supplier cannot be punished directly for breaching the agreement about quality, so the incentive compatibility condition for the supplier to deliver quality has to take the form familiar from one-period principal-agent models:

$$q(\theta) \in \arg\max_q E_y\left[P(\phi) \mid q\right] - c(q, \theta), \quad \text{for all } \theta \in \left[\underline{\theta}, \overline{\theta}\right]. \tag{21}$$

The incentive compatibility conditions for the parties not to breach the agreement on the bonus depend on whether both purchaser and supplier observe the outcome y_t or only the purchaser does. Start with the former, which Levin (2003) calls the case of an "objective performance measure." Because the agreed bonus can be either positive (in which case the purchaser pays the supplier) or negative (in which case the supplier pays the purchaser), we require incentive compatibility conditions for both. For the purchaser not to default on the largest positive bonus requires, analogous to (6),

$$\delta \left(\Pi - \tilde{\Pi} \right) \geq \sup_{\phi} b \left(\phi \right). \tag{22}$$

Similarly, for the supplier not to default on the largest negative bonus requires

$$\delta \left(U - \tilde{U} \right) \geq - \inf_{\phi} b \left(\phi \right). \tag{23}$$

These two conditions can be added to give a pooled condition that, like (8), is independent of the distribution of the gains from the relationship. Levin (2003) calls this pooled condition the "dynamic enforcement" constraint:

$$\delta \left(S - \tilde{S} \right) \equiv \delta \left(U + \Pi - \tilde{U} - \tilde{\Pi} \right) \geq \sup_{\phi} b \left(\phi \right) - \inf_{\phi} b \left(\phi \right). \tag{24}$$

This constraint imposes a restriction on the maximum difference in the bonuses that can be used and hence on the incentives that can be provided. This maximum difference is determined by the need to make payment of the bonus incentive compatible, given the limited future surplus that is available to induce the parties to pay it. Levin (2003) shows that a quality schedule $q\left(\theta\right)$ generating surplus S can be implemented if and only if (21) and (24) are satisfied. These replace (8) for the employment model of Section 3.1 which, in effect, combines the incentive compatibility constraint (21) and the dynamic enforcement constraint (24) for θ a fixed value known to the purchaser as well as the supplier. To see this, note that (3) corresponds to the constraint (21). With (3), the highest bonus required to induce the supplier to provide quality q_t is $c_t \left(q_t \right) / \rho$. The lowest bonus is zero. Thus the right-hand side of (8) corresponds to the difference between the highest and the lowest bonuses exactly like the right-hand side of (24), but with the supplier's incentive compatibility condition substituted for the highest bonus.

To understand the hidden information case (in which the purchaser observes q_t but not θ_t), suppose there were only the highest cost type $\overline{\theta}$. Then, with $\rho = 1$ as assumed in Levin (2003), the incentive compatibility condition (8) would be

$$\delta \left(S - \tilde{S} \right) \geq c \left(q \left(\overline{\theta} \right), \overline{\theta} \right).$$

With a continuum of types as in Levin (2003), type θ must not prefer the quality for some other type to $q\left(\theta\right)$. The conditions for that are familiar from standard, one-period adverse-selection models (see Baron 1989; Milgrom and Segal 2002): $q\left(\theta\right)$ must be nonincreasing, and type θ must receive the information rent over the highest cost type $\overline{\theta}$ of $\int_{\theta}^{\overline{\theta}} c_{\theta}(q(\tilde{\theta}), \tilde{\theta}) \, d\tilde{\theta}$. So the incentive compatibility constraint for type θ becomes

$$\delta \left(S - \tilde{S} \right) \geq c(q(\theta), \theta) + \int_{\theta}^{\overline{\theta}} c_{\theta}(q(\tilde{\theta}), \tilde{\theta}) \, d\tilde{\theta}. \tag{25}$$

With $q\left(\theta\right)$ nonincreasing, the right-hand side of (25) is nonincreasing in θ, so the constraint is tightest for $\theta=\underline{\theta}$. Levin (2003) shows that $q\left(\theta\right)$ nonincreasing and (25) satisfied for $\theta=\underline{\theta}$ are necessary and sufficient conditions for $q\left(\theta\right)$ to be implemented. He then shows that, for a concave cost distribution, if the efficient $q^{*}\left(\theta\right)$ does not satisfy (25) for $\theta=\underline{\theta}$, an optimal $q\left(\theta\right)$ satisfies one of the following:

1. *pooling:* $q\left(\theta\right)=\tilde{q}$ for some $\tilde{q}<q^{*}\left(\theta\right)$, for all θ; or
2. *partial pooling:* for some $\hat{\theta}\in\left(\underline{\theta},\overline{\theta}\right)$, $q\left(\theta\right)=\tilde{q}<q^{*}\left(\theta\right)$ for all $\theta\in\left[\underline{\theta},\hat{\theta}\right]$ and $q\left(\theta\right)<q^{*}\left(\theta\right)$ and is strictly decreasing for all $\theta\in\left(\hat{\theta},\overline{\theta}\right)$.

Thus, either quality is the same for all types, or it is the same for an interval of the lowest cost types and decreasing in type for higher cost types. As in the employment model of Section 3.1, quality is never above the efficient level $q^{*}\left(\theta\right)$ for any type.

The intuition for these results is as follows. If the relationship is sufficiently productive and the discount factor sufficiently close to 1, then (25) with $\theta=\underline{\theta}$ is not a binding constraint at efficient quality $q^{*}\left(\theta\right)$ for each θ. Because $q^{*}\left(\theta\right)$ is nonincreasing, it can then be implemented, and it is certainly optimal to do that. But when (25) with $\theta=\underline{\theta}$ is binding for $q\left(\theta\right)=q^{*}\left(\theta\right)$, it makes sense to reduce quality $q\left(\theta\right)$ below the efficient level $q^{*}\left(\theta\right)$ for all θ. It has to be below the efficient level for some θ, and reducing $q\left(\theta\right)$ marginally below $q^{*}\left(\theta\right)$ has only a second-order effect on joint surplus, whereas increasing $q\left(\theta\right)$ that is substantially below $q^{*}\left(\theta\right)$ has a first-order effect. Thus, rather than have $q\left(\theta'\right)=q^{*}\left(\theta'\right)$ and $q\left(\theta''\right)<q^{*}\left(\theta''\right)$ for some θ' and θ'', it is better to reduce $q\left(\theta'\right)$ marginally and increase $q\left(\theta''\right)$ marginally. Moreover, when (25) with $\theta=\underline{\theta}$ is binding, it must be the case that the requirement for $q\left(\theta\right)$ to be nonincreasing is also binding at $\theta=\underline{\theta}$. If that were not so, (25) with $\theta=\underline{\theta}$ would be relaxed by having $q\left(\theta\right)$ jump upward immediately above $\underline{\theta}$ to enable $c\left(q\left(\underline{\theta}\right),\underline{\theta}\right)$ to be reduced, and (because that would affect output for only one of a continuum of values of θ that has no probability mass) it would certainly be optimal. Thus, if efficient quality is not achieved for all θ, there must be pooling for θ sufficiently close to $\underline{\theta}$. If the constraint (25) with $\theta=\underline{\theta}$ is sufficiently tight, this pooling will apply to all θ. But when it is less tight, the intuition for not pooling higher cost types before lower cost types arises from the limit on incentives. Starting from the minimum quality level, the bonus does not need to be increased much to raise quality uniformly. But at higher quality levels, it requires increasingly high bonuses to raise the quality supplied by lower θ types. Thus, it is optimal to focus incentives on the higher θ types.

Payment in this model depends only on the quality delivered. So an implication is that, if either the discount factor δ or the total gain from cooperation $S-\tilde{S}$ is sufficiently low for full pooling of types to be optimal, quality and payment will be independent of day-to-day changes in the supplier's cost. For higher values of $\delta\left(S-\tilde{S}\right)$ such that partial pooling is optimal, there will be some variation in quality and payment, but only when day-to-day costs are particularly high. In practice, this might take the form of the purchaser paying less when delivered a batch of components with a particularly high proportion of defective items. Thus, one would expect to see quality more closely tailored to the supplier's cost conditions and greater payment variability in relationships in which the total gain from cooperation $S-\tilde{S}$ is greater and/or trade orders are more frequent, so that the discount factor δ relevant to the time between orders is higher.

Malcomson (2012b) analyzes the hidden information model in Levin (2003) with the additions that the value of quality to the purchaser changes from period to period without persistence and that the purchaser (but not the supplier) observes its value at the beginning of the period. There is thus private information about the purchaser's type, as well as about the supplier's, and efficient quality depends on both. The purchaser can signal her type to the supplier by making the payment p a function of that type and offering a bonus conditional on both it and the quality actually delivered. For those payments to be incentive compatible, the purchaser must expect an information rent when the value of quality is above its lowest level, which imposes restrictions on how p can vary with the purchaser's type. (It is an expected rent, because the purchaser does not know the supplier's type at the stage p is offered.) Pooling across both purchaser and supplier types is always an equilibrium (as is pooling across supplier types in Levin 2003). Efficient quality is increasing in the value of quality to the purchaser and decreasing in the cost of quality to the supplier but, as in Levin (2003), efficient quality may not be sustainable by a relational contract. When it is not, it turns out that if quality is increasing in its value to the purchaser for some purchaser types, it must actually be decreasing in its value to the purchaser for some other purchaser types. This property reinforces the advantages of pooling purchaser types and thus of making payment and quality independent of day-to-day changes in the purchaser's circumstances.

For the moral hazard case (the purchaser observes θ_t but not q_t), Levin (2003) uses two assumptions that also play a role in models discussed later.

Assumption 1 *(MLRP)   The probability density function f corresponding to F satisfies the monotone likelihood ratio property that*

$$\frac{\partial f\,(y\mid q)\,/\partial q}{f\,(y\mid q)} \tag{26}$$

is increasing in y.

Assumption 2 *(CDFC)   The distribution function F satisfies the convexity of the distribution function condition that $F\left(y \mid q = c^{-1}\,(x;\theta)\right)$ is convex in x for any θ.*

Levin (2003) shows that, for the moral hazard case under these assumptions,

1. an optimal contract implements $q\,(\theta) \le q^*\,(\theta)$ for all θ; and
2. payments $P\,(\theta,\,y)$ are one-step in the sense that $P\,(\theta,\,y) = \underline{P}$ for all $y < \hat{y}\,(\theta)$ and $\overline{P} = \underline{P} + \frac{\delta}{1-\delta}\left(S - \tilde{S}\right)$ for all $y \ge \hat{y}\,(\theta)$, where $\hat{y}\,(\theta)$ is the point at which the likelihood ratio $\left(f_q/f\right)\,(y \mid q\,(\theta))$ switches from negative to positive as a function of y.

The intuition is that, with a risk-neutral supplier, it makes sense to use the limited bonuses in the way that gives the strongest incentives, so the maximum incentive is given for outcomes that are more likely to arise with high quality. Thus, as in the employment model of Section 3.1, only one level of bonus is required.

Levin (2003) also considers the case in which the purchaser observes y_t but the supplier does not—the case of a subjective performance measure. This case adds a further complication to contracting. Now not only does the purchaser, not observing one of q_t and θ_t, not know whether the supplier has breached an agreement $q\,(\theta)$ on quality but also the supplier, not observing y_t, does not know whether the purchaser has breached any agreement about how the bonus is to vary with y_t. So if the bonus agreement specifies that the amount of the bonus is to depend on y_t, the purchaser can make a short-term gain by claiming that y_t is at the level corresponding to the lowest bonus payment. Formally, suppose after privately observing y_t, the purchaser delivers a message m_t to the supplier with a bonus $b_t\left(m_t\right)$ attached. Then the purchaser will make distinct reports m' and m'' in response to distinct outcomes y' and y'' only if the two reports yield the same payoffs. With a stationary contract, this requires $b\left(m'\right) = b\left(m''\right)$. But in a stationary environment with a stationary contract and hence a stationary future surplus S, this conflicts with providing incentives for the supplier, because the supplier's payoffs for outcomes y' and y'' will have to be the same. As an alternative to a stationary contract, Levin (2003) considers a termination contract with a cutoff threshold $\hat{y}$ such that, if $y_t < \hat{y}$, $P_t = p$ and the relationship terminates, whereas if $y_t \geq \hat{y}$, $P_t = p + b$ and the relationship continues. A termination contract is a special case of what Levin (2003) calls a "full review contract," defined as follows: given any history up to t and compensation offer at t, any two distinct outputs $y'_t \neq y''_t$ generate distinct reports $m'_t \neq m''_t$. The implication is that, in equilibrium, the purchaser maintains no private information from period to period. (This restriction can also be stated in terms of the equilibrium concept, namely, perfect public equilibria of the repeated game.) For the case in which q_t is not observed by the purchaser and θ is a fixed, known parameter, Levin (2003) shows that, if an optimal full review contract exists, a termination contract can achieve an optimum. Moreover, the termination contract preserves the property that there is just a single level of bonus, the one-step property. Because the stochastic term relating outcome to quality is iid, the gain from continuing the relationship at $t+1$ is independent of the outcome at t, so termination is always inefficient. It can nevertheless occur in equilibrium, because the stochastic shock will sometimes result in $y_t < \hat{y}$. When that happens, the parties are effectively "burning money." This is a price that has to be paid to induce the purchaser to report the outcome truthfully while still providing incentives for the supplier to deliver a better expected outcome.

It is natural to ask whether there might be some way in which the inefficiency resulting from termination might be reduced. One possibility arises because the inefficiency is the result of the purchaser and supplier having different information about the outcome. So, if it were possible to use a mediator to narrow the information gap, that might reduce the probability of the relationship being terminated. Another possibility is to adopt the procedure suggested in Abreu et al. (1991) of lengthening the period between performance reviews and using the average outcome over the longer period to determine whether termination is triggered. This procedure enables the threat of later punishments to provide incentives in earlier periods and reduces the probability that termination occurs at a review date. Fuchs (2007), in a model with two potential output levels and two potential quality levels, shows that a contract with the properties that the supplier receives a fixed payment until the relationship is terminated, with the purchaser providing no feedback on observed output in the meantime, is optimal. To see why, consider a T-period review contract in which the purchaser waits T periods before considering terminating the relationship, even if output is consistently low. Increasing T reduces the expected loss from termination along an equilibrium path. But increasing T beyond a certain point results in the limited penalty of termination providing insufficient incentives to the supplier in earlier periods. Fong and Li (2010b) consider the implications of the agent having limited liability in this setting. Fong and Li (2010a) show that garbling output signals intertemporally, with past outputs having an enduring effect on future signals, can increase the efficiency of contracting. Their model has two output levels. Incentive compatibility requires a bonus for the higher level. When higher output results in good outcome signals spread out over time, the same total reward for high output can be given with a lower bonus, thus relaxing the dynamic enforcement constraint (24).

MacLeod (2003) explores the case of a subjective performance measure when the supplier is risk averse, as in Pearce and Stacchetti (1998). While using a one-period employment model, and hence not formally a relational contract, he investigates limits on rewards similar to (24) that arise from a relational contract. In his model, as in the subjective information case in Levin (2003), the purchaser's information about performance is private and satisfies MLRP (Assumption 1). However, unlike in Levin (2003), the supplier receives a private signal about performance that is correlated with the purchaser's information. To allow for the possibility of "burning money" (which we know from Levin (2003) is essential when there is no objective performance measure) in the context of a single-period model, MacLeod (2003) introduces a third party to act as a budget breaker, that is, to enable the payment made by the purchaser to be different from that received by the supplier. He shows that, if the supplier's signal is perfectly correlated with the purchaser's, the optimal contract is the same as that if the purchaser's signal were verifiable. Moreover, the joint loss from imperfect correlation goes to zero as the correlation becomes perfect. In contrast, if the supplier's signal is uncorrelated with the purchaser's, the purchaser's payments are independent of his own signal but depend on the supplier's. Moreover, the supplier's compensation is the same for all signals of the purchaser except the worst, for which it is lower, because with MLRP (Assumption 1) the lowest signal is the most informative about whether effort is low. Thus, the one-step property applies not just to the risk-neutral supplier in the model in Levin (2003). Moreover, the supplier will normally (i.e., for most outcomes) receive the higher level and only occasionally, for the very worst performance, receive the lower. To get useful results for the case in which the supplier's signal is imperfectly correlated with the purchaser's, MacLeod (2003) uses the additional assumption that the supplier's signal is, with known probability, either the same as the purchaser's or completely uninformative. In that case, if the joint punishment to the purchaser and the supplier (i.e., the net payment to the third party) is bounded, the supplier's compensation increases with the signal up to a certain level but is the same for all signals above that level. There are also some results on the effect of the purchaser having biased perceptions of the supplier's performance. For further discussion of efficient contractual arrangements under these types of circumstances, see MacLeod (2007b).

Many of these models share a common characteristic. With relational contracts, the only thing that induces the parties not to breach their agreement is the potential gain from cooperation in the future. Because that potential gain is finite, the gap between the highest and the lowest future payoffs—and hence the maximum incentive that can be provided—is limited. When there is private information about nonpersistent types, and the potential gains from future cooperation are insufficient to sustain efficient quality for all types, more pooling across types typically results than when there is full information. This characteristic is encouraging for trying to understand supply relationships that, as documented by Carlton (1986), have relatively rigid prices over time despite apparent short-term changes in production conditions. But there remains research to be done to assess the extent to which those rigidities can genuinely be attributed to pooling across types that are private information.

7. Private Information: Persistent Types

The Japanese manufacturers studied by Asanuma (1989) used information about past performance of suppliers to determine the terms for future trades. There is no gain in productive efficiency from this practice when suppliers' types are, as in the models in Section 6, iid draws in each period, though there may be strategic reasons for it (to punish a supplier who has breached a relational contract). It is different when types are persistent over time and have to be discovered by the other party.

In Bull (1987), it is the purchaser's type that is persistent but unknown to the supplier, rather than the other way around. The issue there is how a relational contract can be sustained between an infinitely lived purchaser and a supplier who operates for only a finite period of time that is known in advance. In the basic model of Section 3.1, the purchaser would not pay a bonus in the final period of the relationship. With no future of concern, the supplier would then set quality at the lowest level in that period, and so the relationship would be terminated in the final period, because there is no possibility of mutually beneficial trade. Given this behavior, the same argument can be repeated successively for each previous period to show that the relational contract never gets off the ground in the first place. But, if there is a succession of short-lived suppliers who observe how their predecessors have been treated, the relationship can be sustained in the way described by Crémer (1986). In Bull (1987), there are two types of purchasers, those who never pay a bonus in the final period and those who do if the reputation so acquired is sufficiently valuable. The latter are induced to pay, because they do not wish to be thought to be the former. In Mukherjee (2008), the supplier has an unchanging type unknown to both parties in advance and only a finite (two-period) lifetime. The purchaser can choose whether to make information about performance available to other potential purchasers, in which case career concerns of the type discussed by Holmström (1999) provide incentives for effort, or to retain this information and rely on a voluntary bonus to provide incentives. Depending on the precise specification, career concerns can be either substitutes or complements for relational incentives. There is now a substantial game-theoretic literature on models in which one long-lived player faces a succession of short-lived players (see Mailath and Samuelson 2006).

The focus in this chapter is on long-lived suppliers. Hörner (2002), in a model in which purchasers are consumers, allows for both noise and privately known persistent types but simplifies by having just two potential outcomes and suppliers of just two types. Types are not specific to a particular purchaser, so any information revealed publicly affects what other potential purchasers are prepared to pay that supplier. Bad types always choose low quality. Good types choose between high and low quality. Whichever quality is chosen, the outcome y_t to consumers may be good or bad, though there is a higher probability it is good when quality is high. As a result, type is not fully revealed in the first period. Consumers are indistinguishable to suppliers, so it is never incentive compatible for them to pay a bonus, and all payment is thus via p_t. Hörner

(2002) focuses on nonrevealing equilibria in which consumers leave a supplier as soon as they experience a bad outcome, all suppliers who have been supplying for the same length of time have the same price, and newly entering good suppliers earn zero expected profits. In such an equilibrium, the probability that a supplier is good increases with the time that supplier has been in the market, and hence so also does price. For newly entering good suppliers to have zero expected profits, price must start out negative. Yang (2012) analyzes a similar setup with a single purchaser. Halac (2012) considers a model in which the purchaser's payoff π_t, if not trading with the supplier, is private information. When the purchaser receives all the gain from continuing the relationship, there is an incentive for the purchaser to behave as if π_t were low, even when it is high (to induce the supplier to believe that a higher bonus is incentive compatible and accordingly supply high quality) but then to renege by taking the high outside option π_t and not paying the bonus. Conversely, when the supplier receives all the gain, the purchaser has an incentive to behave as if π_t were high, even when it is low (to induce the supplier to believe that there is less gain to appropriate).

The alternative to two types analyzed in the literature is a continuum of types. In MacLeod and Malcomson (1988), as in Hörner (2002), types are not specific to a particular purchaser. Formal differences from the employment model of Section 3.1 are that the environment is stationary, the cost of quality is $c\,(q)\,/\theta$ (where θ is the supplier's type, which is known to the supplier but not the purchaser), the probability ρ that breach is detected is 1, and there are no bonuses (so that the only payment is the fixed payment). Suppose the purchaser were to group supplier types into a set of ranks r (1 being the lowest), assumed observable to potential purchasers, with the following properties:

- payment is $p^r > p^{r-1}$,
- a minimum quality performance $q^r > q^{r-1}$ is required to stay in r, and
- those in rank r who deliver quality below q^r are demoted to $r-1$ (or are dropped as a supplier and used by another purchaser in the equivalent of rank $r-1$).

The expected utility from staying in rank r forever is then

$$U^r\,(\theta) = p^r - \frac{c\,(q^r)}{\theta} + \delta U^r\,(\theta)\,, \quad \text{for all } r \geq 1, \;\; \text{all } \theta, \tag{27}$$

which corresponds to (1) in the employment model of Section 3.1 with the bonus set to zero. Because other potential purchasers observe a supplier's rank, the price for rank r is determined by the zero-profit condition $p^r = y\,(q^r)$, so (27) can be solved to give

$$U^r\,(\theta) = \left[y\,(q^r) - \frac{c\,(q^r)}{\theta} \right] / (1-\delta)\,, \quad \text{for all } r \geq 1, \;\; \text{all } \theta. \tag{28}$$

It is convenient to define $U^0\,(\theta)$ as the future payoff to type θ if dropped from the lowest rank (rank 1) permanently with payoff $U^0\,(\theta) = u/\,(1-\delta)$.

Consider which types θ will deliver quality high enough to stay in rank r if they reach it. The incentive compatibility condition for type θ to do this, corresponding to (3) with no bonus, is

$$\delta \left[U^r(\theta) - U^{r-1}(\theta) \right] \geq \frac{c(q^r)}{\theta}, \quad \text{for all } r \geq 1, \text{ all } \theta. \tag{29}$$

Define θ^r as the lowest value of θ that satisfies this condition. Substitution from (28), use of the convention that $q^0 = 0$ and $c(q^0) = -u$, and rearrangement gives

$$\theta^r = \frac{1}{y(q^r) - y(q^{r-1})} \left[\frac{c(q^r)}{\delta} - c(q^{r-1}) \right], \quad \text{for all } r \geq 1. \tag{30}$$

An *equilibrium hierarchy* is a triple (q^r, p^r, θ^r) that satisfies condition (30) and the zero-profit requirement that $p^r = y(q^r)$ for each r. Competition among purchasers ensures that all supplier types who can be profitably employed will be. In particular, θ^1 must be the lowest value that is incentive compatible, so q^1 is determined to minimize the right-hand side of (30) for $r = 1$, given the conventions $q^0 = 0$ and $c(q^0) = -u$. This determines q^1 and θ^1. Given q^1 and θ^1, q^2 is determined to minimize the right-hand side of (30) for $r = 2$. This determines q^2 and θ^2, and so on up to rank R such that $\theta^{R+1} > \bar{\theta}$, the highest type there is. This iterative process determines a unique equilibrium hierarchy.

In the description in Asanuma (1989: 14), purchasers "select a number of firms that have relatively good qualities from among those suppliers that have already been tried" for more responsible treatment. Suppose all supplier types start in rank 1 and are promoted to rank 2 if they deliver sufficiently high quality, then to rank 3 if they continue to perform sufficiently well, and so on. Can the purchaser set promotion criterion $\hat{q}^r$ from rank r to $r+1$ such that supplier types eventually sort themselves into equilibrium ranks? To sort properly, it must be that types $\theta \geq \theta^{r+1}$ deliver sufficiently high quality for promotion. They will do that only if meeting the quality criterion $\hat{q}^r$ to gain promotion to rank $r+1$ and then staying there has a higher payoff than staying in rank r; that is, only if

$$p^r - \frac{c(\hat{q}^r)}{\theta} + \delta U^{r+1}(\theta) \geq U^r(\theta), \quad \text{for } \theta \geq \theta^{r+1}, r \geq 1.$$

But for selection to occur, it must also be that those of type $\theta < \theta^{r+1}$ do not find it worthwhile to deliver sufficiently high quality for promotion, so

$$p^r - \frac{c(\hat{q}^r)}{\theta} + \delta U^{r+1}(\theta) < U^r(\theta), \quad \text{for } \theta < \theta^{r+1}, r \geq 1.$$

With θ continuous, these two conditions imply the sorting condition

$$p^r - \frac{c(\hat{q}^r)}{\theta^{r+1}} + \delta U^{r+1}(\theta^{r+1}) = U^r(\theta^{r+1}), \quad \text{for all } r \geq 1. \tag{31}$$

Substitution for $U^r\left(\theta^{r+1}\right)$ from (27) gives

$$\delta\left[U^{r+1}\left(\theta^{r+1}\right)-U^r\left(\theta^{r+1}\right)\right]=\frac{c\left(\hat{q}^r\right)}{\theta^{r+1}}-\frac{c\left(q^r\right)}{\theta^{r+1}},\quad\text{for all }r\geq 1. \tag{32}$$

Because θ^{r+1} is, by definition, the lowest θ for which the incentive compatibility condition for the supplier (29) is satisfied for rank $r+1$, it follows from (29) that

$$\delta\left[U^{r+1}\left(\theta^{r+1}\right)-U^r\left(\theta^{r+1}\right)\right]=\frac{c\left(q^{r+1}\right)}{\theta^{r+1}},\quad\text{for all }r\geq 1. \tag{33}$$

Equating the right-hand sides of (32) and (33) gives

$$c\left(\hat{q}^r\right)=c\left(q^{r+1}\right)+c\left(q^r\right),\quad\text{for all }r\geq 1,$$

which implies $\hat{q}^r>q^{r+1}$, for $r\geq 1$. So the quality required to be promoted from rank r to rank $r+1$ is higher than that required to stay in rank $r+1$ once there. This process, if implemented by the purchaser, eventually results in a supplier with θ between θ^r and θ^{r+1} being sorted into rank r. That is, all types reach the highest rank in which it is worthwhile for them to deliver the quality required to stay there. Moreover, implementing this promotion process is worthwhile for the purchaser. Those providing just sufficient quality to stay in a rank generate no profit for the purchaser. But those striving for promotion set quality higher while being paid the same, so it is clearly more profitable for the purchaser to set up the promotion system.

Malcomson (2012a) analyzes a development of the hidden information model in Levin (2003) in which the supplier's type is unknown to the purchaser, but instead of being iid, it is persistent over time. As in MacLeod and Malcomson (1988), there is a continuum of supplier types, with the outcome y_t a deterministic function of quality. But in contrast to MacLeod and Malcomson (1988), Malcomson (2012a) allows for bonuses. Moreover, the supplier's type is specific to the purchaser, which makes for a larger gain from continuing the relationship over alternative opportunities once information about type has been revealed. Provided the match is sufficiently productive, pooling of those supplier types who continue the relationship is always an equilibrium, as a result of which quality is not tailored to the supplier's type, and the purchaser does not learn about that type. When some separation of types is feasible, but efficient quality is not attainable, the parties can, however, do better in an equilibrium that initially partitions types into bands, followed by an optimal continuation equilibrium in which quality for those types in a band is at the highest level consistent with the commonly known information. That level is the highest that satisfies a condition corresponding to (16), with I (now an argument of only the supplier's cost function $c\left(q,I\right)$) denoting the highest cost type in the band. But with such a continuation equilibrium, separation may not be feasible, and full separation of types never is. These are also characteristics of the two-period ratchet effect model of Laffont and Tirole (1988) and thus seem robust in models with a continuum of privately known persistent types and the inability to commit to future contractual arrangements. Here, incentive compatibility for the purchaser restricts the spread of future rewards to different supplier types, which as in Levin (2003), limits the potential for separating them. But because here, unlike in Levin (2003), types are persistent, a supplier can obtain an information rent for the indefinite future, not just the current period, by pretending to be a higher cost type. In contrast, by revealing type, the supplier loses that information rent in an optimal continuation equilibrium. The implication is that quality must jump by a discrete amount between adjacent bands of types even though type is continuous. Thus, the characteristic of MacLeod and Malcomson (1988) that, as described in Asanuma (1989), suppliers of different types are grouped into categories is preserved, despite the use of bonuses and despite supplier types being specific to the purchaser. In this model, however, among supplier types for which efficient quality is not sustainable, quality in the first period is strictly lower than in the continuation equilibrium for all but the least productive for which the relationship can be sustained. Unlike in the model of Laffont and Tirole (1988), quality in the first period never exceeds the efficient level. Thus, the purchaser learns about the supplier by cautiously building up the relationship with levels of quality lower than can eventually be sustained.

Although types are banded in both MacLeod and Malcomson (1988) and Malcomson (2012a), the differences in what the bands provide are differences in quality, not fundamental differences in tasks that might correspond to the differences between the "drawings supplied" and the "drawings approved" subcontractors discussed by Asanuma (1989). If it is efficient for different types of supplier to do different tasks, there is an additional dimension on which incentive compatibility can operate, because there is a gain to the purchaser in having a supplier do the task for which it is efficient, given its type. Suppose, for example, the purchaser commits to a fixed payment p_t for drawings-approved work that is higher than that for drawings-supplied work by more than the difference in the cost of supply. Then a high-type supplier has an additional incentive to reveal its type, because, if promoted to drawings-approved work, future profits will be greater. Moreover, the purchaser has an incentive to promote sufficiently high types, because it is more efficient to have such types do drawings-approved work. Gietzmann and Larsen (1998) have a formal model of this idea based on the promotion model in Fairburn and Malcomson (1994) and developed further in Fairburn and Malcomson (2001). Though not an infinite-horizon model, the underlying mechanism would seem to apply to the relational contract approach. Prendergast (1993) develops a model based on a similar underlying idea, though again not formally in a relational contract.[4]

8. Multiple Suppliers

In the models discussed so far, the purchaser treats each supplier independently. New issues arise when there are multiple suppliers. They can, for a start, be rewarded according to their performance relative to other suppliers. Che and Yoo (2001) investigate this possibility. As in Pearce and Stacchetti (1998), the outcome y_t for each supplier, which depends on both quality and a random shock, is verifiable, so the principal (who makes a take-it-or-leave-it contract offer) can commit to a contract conditioned on y_t for each supplier. The outcome and the quality

---

4. Chassang (2010) explores a model in which private information takes the form of the supplier knowing which of many actions are potentially productive to the purchaser and which are not, whereas the purchaser does not know this. Because the model does not permit payments between the parties (which puts it in a different category from most of the literature discussed here), the possibility of noncooperation for a while is the only way for the purchaser to influence the supplier's incentive to take costly action.

delivered are each assumed to take one of just two values, with the probability of each outcome strictly positive whatever quality is chosen. Unlike in Pearce and Stacchetti (1998), quality is not observed by the purchaser, and because either outcome can occur whatever quality is chosen, quality cannot be directly inferred from the outcome. Moreover, the suppliers are risk neutral and have limited liability that is assumed to rule out payments from them to the purchaser. The important addition is that the shock is common to the two suppliers. Thus, even when the outcome for one supplier is independent of the quality provided by the other, their outcomes are positively correlated. When the relationship can last at most one period, the optimal contract takes the form that a supplier is paid only when her outcome is better than that of the other supplier. That is, payment corresponds to an extreme form of relative performance evaluation. The intuition is that, because the shock is common to both suppliers, a high outcome is a stronger signal of high quality when the other supplier's outcome is low than when it is high. Thus, this payment scheme gives the biggest incentive to deliver high quality. In a repeated relationship, the contract itself does not depend on whether a deviation has occurred in the past, because the principal, who determines the contract, cannot observe deviations in quality and all payments are legally enforceable. When each supplier observes the quality delivered by the other in the past, the optimal payment scheme for a discount factor sufficiently close to one is joint performance evaluation (a supplier is paid more the better the other supplier's outcome). The intuition is that, with a suitably chosen contract, it is an optimal response to joint performance evaluation for a supplier to deliver low quality in the future if the other supplier delivers low quality. That provides both suppliers with the strongest incentive not to deviate by delivering low quality. Che and Yoo (2001) also consider the case in which a single task can be allocated to either one supplier or two suppliers, but in the latter case the purchaser observes only a joint outcome.

Kvaløy and Olsen (2006) extend the model in Che and Yoo (2001) to the case in which the outcomes are not verifiable, but there are no common shocks. In that case, as in the employment model discussed in Section 3.1, payments by the purchaser that are conditional on outcomes have to be made incentive compatible. As in Che and Yoo (2001), an advantage of joint performance evaluation in a repeated relationship is that it can make use of suppliers' abilities to monitor each other. But with the outcome unverifiable, an advantage of relative performance evaluation is that it reduces the purchaser's incentive to breach the relational contract, because higher payments to one supplier correspond to lower payments to the other. Kvaløy and Olsen (2006) show that, for given differences between the high and low outcomes and between costs of high and low quality, a higher discount factor favors joint performance evaluation, because the higher value of the future when the discount factor is high relaxes the incentive compatibility constraint for the purchaser. Conversely, a lower discount factor favors relative performance evaluation. This result contrasts with that of Che and Yoo (2001), in which joint performance evaluation is always preferable in a relational contract with verifiable output.

Levin (2002) considers n risk-neutral suppliers and continuous quality, not just two suppliers and two possible levels of quality as in Che and Yoo (2001) and Kvaløy and Olsen (2006). As in the latter papers, the quality $q_t^i \in \left[\underline{q}, \overline{q} \right]$ chosen by supplier i in period t at cost $c^i \left(q_t^i \right)$ is unverifiable but is observed by the purchaser and the other suppliers. Otherwise, the assumptions are as for a stationary version of the employment model of Section 3.1 with $\rho = 1$. Suppose the outcome is additively separable across suppliers. In a bilateral relational contract in which each supplier ceases to perform only if individually cheated by the purchaser, the incentive compatibility constraint for each relationship i corresponding to (8) is then

$$\delta \left[S^i(q^i) - \tilde{S}^i \right] \geq c^i(q^i), \quad \text{for all } i, \tag{34}$$

where $\delta \left[S^i(q^i) - \tilde{S}^i \right]$ is the joint gain from continuing the relationship with supplier i. But with multiple agents, there can be a multilateral relational contract in which all suppliers cease to perform if the purchaser breaches on any one of them. Then the incentive constraints (34) can be pooled over suppliers to give the single constraint

$$\delta \left[S(q) - \tilde{S} \right] \geq \sum_{i=1}^{n} c^i(q^i), \tag{35}$$

where $\delta \left[S(q) - \tilde{S} \right]$ is the joint gain from continuing all n supplier relationships. The constraints (34) allow the gain from one relationship to be used to sustain only that relationship. Constraint (35) allows the gain from a relationship to be used in a cross-subsidizing way to sustain other relationships—in particular, those more productive at the margin. That can increase the total surplus sustainable. The mechanism is essentially the same as in the multimarket oligopoly model of Bernheim and Whinston (1990), where gains from collusion in one market can help sustain collusion in another. Levin (2002) also shows that if q_t^i is known only to i but generates an observable signal with error, an optimal multilateral contract is payment by relative performance (a tournament) with a fixed prize to at most one supplier. The underlying reason is the same as in Kvaløy and Olsen (2006).

There is, however, a potential downside to multilateral commitments: they are harder to back away from when outside circumstances change. Suppose production methods change in such a way that it is no longer efficient to use one of the suppliers. With bilateral relational contracting, the relationship with that supplier can be terminated without affecting the relationship with the other suppliers. With multilateral relational contracting, other suppliers may interpret termination with one supplier as the purchaser breaching the multilateral agreement. Suppose they do so with probability α. For concreteness, suppose there are just two suppliers, quality is a binary choice ($\underline{q}$ or $\overline{q}$), and supplier 2 becomes redundant with Poisson probability $1 - \gamma$. Then, with α chosen at the lowest level consistent with the purchaser's incentive compatibility, multilateral contracting improves on bilateral contracting if and only if

$$(1 - \delta) \left[S^2(\overline{q}) - \tilde{S}^2 \right] \geq \frac{1 - \gamma}{\gamma} c^2(\overline{q}).$$

The same idea extends to more than two suppliers in a way that fits the distinction in Asanuma (1989: 17–18) between suppliers kept operating more or less continuously and those used as a capacity buffer. Levin (2002) shows that, if there are two groups of suppliers all of whom are to be retained after a shock, the purchaser can always do at least as well by using a multilateral contract with them all. If there are two groups both containing suppliers to be dropped if requirements decrease, the purchaser will have to recontract with any suppliers in both groups who are to be retained in the event of an adverse shock. Again, the purchaser can do at least as well by combining the two groups. It follows that there will be an optimal arrangement with at most one group that includes suppliers to be released and (potentially, at least) another group that contains only suppliers to be retained. In this model (as in most models discussed in Section 7) there is, however, no reason for the two groups to be doing different tasks.

Other papers explore different avenues when there are multiple suppliers. Schöttner (2008) analyzes a model of task assignment with three tasks to be divided between two suppliers that is based on the formulation in Baker et al. (1994) and derives results on the characteristics that determine which tasks should be purchased from the same supplier. Board (2011) analyzes a model in which the purchaser must incur a specific investment each period to enable a supplier to produce, as a result of which the purchaser invests in at most one supplier in each period. The amount of specific investment required varies across time and across suppliers, so it is efficient to invest in different suppliers in different periods. There is, however, a benefit to having a set of preferred suppliers to whom the purchaser is loyal, in the sense of choosing only from this subset of possible suppliers. The underlying reason is that the higher the probability of future trades with a supplier, the weaker is the current period's incentive compatibility condition. Increasing that probability acts like increasing ρ in (8).

Finally, in Calzolari and Spagnolo (2010), as in Board (2011), the purchaser trades with only one supplier in each period. However, the fixed cost of each potential supplier is an iid random draw each period that is not observed by the purchaser. If quality were contractible, the purchaser could achieve efficient quality by inviting potential suppliers to bid in an auction. But with noncontractible quality, the purchaser has to induce the chosen supplier to deliver quality through the relational contract. In Calzolari and Spagnolo (2010), the purchaser holds auctions but may choose not to do so every period to avoid paying the fixed cost of organizing one and, when it does so, to restrict competition to a set of preferred suppliers for the same reason as in Board (2011). Reducing the number of competitors increases the expected informational rent to the winning supplier, so it reduces the purchaser's future gain from not cheating on the relational contract. Of course, it also increases the incumbent supplier's future gain by the same amount conditional on that supplier winning the next auction. So, conditional on the incumbent supplier winning the next auction, the joint future gains from not defaulting on the relational contract are unchanged. But reducing the number of competitors increases the probability that the incumbent supplier will win the next auction, so the net effect is to increase the joint gains from not defaulting, which is like increasing the left-hand side of (8) and so enabling higher quality to be sustained. Because the auction ensures that the purchaser gets the gains from increases in efficiency, there is a trade-off between increasing the number of competitors to obtain the lowest price and reducing it to increase quality. So if the number of potential competitors is sufficiently large, it is optimal to restrict the number entering the auction. Reducing the frequency of auctions can also increase sustainable quality. Calzolari and Spagnolo (2010) give conditions under which the purchaser actually does better by having suppliers collude in the auction process.

Underdeveloped in the relational contract context are the implications of the common agency situation in which multiple suppliers, each with private information about his own type, produce simultaneously. Martimort and Stole (2009) analyze common agency in the absence of relational contracts when the principal can choose which of a set of agents to contract with.

9. Partnerships

In all the models discussed so far, there are clearly identified suppliers whose decisions about quality affect the value of the output to a purchaser. In some contracts between firms, for example, joint ventures, the two parties are on a more symmetric footing in that the measurable output involves simultaneous inputs from both. In many models of such partnerships, the parties are, initially at least, entirely symmetric. To reflect the more neutral position, this section refers simply to "parties," $i = 1, 2$. It is concerned only with partnerships involving relational contracts. Section 10 on organizational design considers issues arising from the existence of assets and who should own them.

For a basic model of partnerships, let q_t^i denote the quality chosen by party i at time t, $y\left(q_t^1, q_t^2\right)$ the value of the joint output, $b_t^i\left(q_t^1, q_t^2\right)$ the amount received by party i conditional on performance as long as the relational contract has not been breached, and $z_t^i\left(q_t^1, q_t^2\right)$ the amount received by party i if the relational contract has been breached. The functions $b^i(.)$ are, like the voluntary bonuses in the models discussed in earlier sections, in general not legally enforceable. The sum over i of $b_t^i(.)$ equals the joint output, as does that of $z_t^i(.)$. There can also be fixed payments p_t^i made under the relational contract; the sum of these across i must be zero. Qualities are chosen simultaneously by both parties, with the choice of each subsequently observed by the other. A superscript i is attached to the previous notation to denote party i. If both parties stick to their relational contract, the payoff to party i, corresponding to that in (1) for the employment model, then becomes

$$U_t^i = p_t^i + b_t^i\left(q_t^1, q_t^2\right) - c^i\left(q_t^i\right) + \delta U_{t+1}^i, \ i = 1, 2; \quad \text{for all } t \geq \tau. \tag{36}$$

Because the quality chosen by party i affects the payoff $z_t^i\left(q_t^1, q_t^2\right)$ that party i receives from breaching the agreement, optimal breach behavior is similar to that for the outsourcing model in Section 3.2. Specifically, if i were planning to breach the agreement about quality, it would be optimal to deliver quality

$$\tilde{q}_t^i = \arg\max_{q_t^i \geq \underline{q}} z_t^i\left(q_t^1, q_t^2\right) - c^i\left(q_t^i\right), \ i = 1, 2; \quad \text{for all } t \geq \tau, \tag{37}$$

which corresponds to (10) for the outsourcing model. The payoff of party 1 from breaching, corresponding to (11) for the outsourcing model, would be no less than

$$p_t^1 + z_t^1\left(\tilde{q}_t^1, q_t^2\right) - c^1\left(\tilde{q}_t^1\right) + \delta \tilde{U}_{t+1}^1, \quad \text{for all } t \geq \tau. \tag{38}$$

The requirement that the payoff in (36) for party 1 exceed that in (38) gives the incentive compatibility condition corresponding to (12) for the outsourcing model:

$$\delta\left(U_{t+1}^1 - \tilde{U}_{t+1}^1\right) \geq \left[c^1\left(q_t^1\right) - c^1\left(\tilde{q}_t^1\right)\right] + z_t^1\left(\tilde{q}_t^1, q_t^2\right) - b_t^1\left(q_t^1, q_t^2\right), \quad \text{for all } t \geq \tau.$$ (39)

A corresponding condition holds for party 2:

$$\delta\left(U_{t+1}^2 - \tilde{U}_{t+1}^2\right) \geq \left[c^2\left(q_t^2\right) - c^2\left(\tilde{q}_t^2\right)\right] + z_t^2\left(q_t^1, \tilde{q}_t^2\right) - b_t^2\left(q_t^1, q_t^2\right), \quad \text{for all } t \geq \tau.$$ (40)

Recall that the sum over i of $b_t^i\left(q_t^1, q_t^2\right)$ equals $y\left(q_t^1, q_t^2\right)$. Thus, (39) and (40) can be added to give the pooled incentive compatibility condition

$$\delta\left(S_{t+1} - \tilde{S}_{t+1}\right) \geq \sum_{i=1}^{2}\left[c^i\left(q_t^i\right) - c^i\left(\tilde{q}_t^i\right)\right] - y\left(q_t^1, q_t^2\right) + z_t^1\left(\tilde{q}_t^1, q_t^2\right)$$
$$+ z_t^2\left(q_t^1, \tilde{q}_t^2\right), \quad \text{for all } t \geq \tau,$$ (41)

where $\delta\left(S_{t+1} - \tilde{S}_{t+1}\right)$ is, as before, the joint gain from continuing the relationship at the end of period t. To this condition must be added the individual rationality conditions corresponding to (4) and (7) and conditions to ensure that it is incentive compatible for each party i to pay any negative b_t^i (.).

The functions b_t^i (.) do not appear in (41). How the parties divide the joint output under the relational contract is important only for individual incentive compatibility via (39) and (40) and for satisfying the individual rationality conditions corresponding to (4) and (7). This property resurfaces later in the discussion of organizational design in Section 10. If the parties have a choice of the functions z_t^i (.), it is advantageous to choose them to make (41) as weak as possible when due account is taken of the effect on the $\tilde{q}_t^i$ through (37). In general, the z_t^i (.) functions that do this depend on the $\left(q_t^1, q_t^2\right)$ agreed under the relational contract, with a trade-off between increasing q_t^1 and increasing q_t^2. It has become conventional in the literature on relational contracts to use, for comparison purposes, the efficient qualities $\left(q^{1*}, q^{2*}\right)$ defined by

$$q^{i*} = \arg\max_{q^i} y\left(q_t^1, q_t^2\right) - c^i\left(q^i\right), \quad i = 1, 2.$$ (42)

Then, (41) with $q_t^i = q^{i*}$ for $i = 1, 2$ and all t becomes an incentive compatibility condition for achieving efficient qualities, and the value of the discount factor δ that makes it hold with equality is the lowest for which efficient qualities can be achieved for given z_t^i (.). The feasible z_t^i (.) that results in the lowest such δ is said to be relationally efficient.

Radner (1986) was concerned with how close the parties can get to a fully efficient outcome in a model of this type when (a) b_t^i (.) and z_t^i (.) are given exogenously, (b) there are no payments p_t^i, (c) there is no discounting ($\delta = 1$), and (d) stochastic terms that are imperfectly monitored enter the payoffs. Radner et al. (1986) give an example with discounting in which equilibria are bounded away from full efficiency even as the discount factor goes to one. Neither Radner (1986) nor Radner et al. (1986) considers a role for contracts to alter b_t^i (.) or z_t^i (.). Garvey (1995) does just that in a model with no stochastic elements by assuming joint output is verifiable, so that the parties can write a legally enforceable contract specifying z_t^i (.) as a function of $y\left(q_t^1, q_t^2\right)$. To simplify, he restricts contracts to constant shares of output and also imposes the restriction b_t^i (.) $= z_t^i$ (.). Because the b_t^i (.) then take only nonnegative values, (41) does not need to be supplemented by conditions that make it incentive compatible to pay negative ones. Garvey (1995) uses an example with (potentially different) quadratic cost of quality functions $c^i\left(q_t^i\right)$ and $y\left(q_t^1, q_t^2\right) = q_t^1 + q_t^2$ to show that the optimal shares are closer to one-half in a relational contract than in a spot market contract. Garvey relates these shares to ownership patterns, but that is not central to the analysis.

In McAdams (2011), the joint output at t is affected not only by the qualities $\left(q_t^1, q_t^2\right)$ but also by a partnership-specific state of the world that is stochastic. The state is persistent, depending positively (in a first-order stochastic dominance sense) on the state and qualities delivered in the previous period. In his general model, monetary payments are unrestricted except that it must be incentive compatible for the partners to pay them. This structure yields potentially rich patterns of partnership development that McAdams (2011) describes in terms of transitions between (a) "dating" partnerships that last just one period with zero quality, because they are immediately seen to be unpromising; (b) "honeymoon" partnerships that survive the dating stage, which have higher current payoffs, because they are better matches and, as a result, induce higher quality; (c) "hard time" partnerships that yield low current payoffs, because the state is less propitious but may, nevertheless, be kept going because of the probability of improvement; and (d) "golden years" partnerships, in which the state has become so favorable, and the quality delivered so high, that the partnership ends only with the "death" of one of the partners.

In Doornik (2006), one party's chosen quality is not observed by the other. Instead, there is for each i an observable (but not verifiable) stochastic individual performance measure x^i with iid probability density conditional on quality $f\left(x^i \mid q^i\right)$ that satisfies MLRP (Assumption 1). Party i receives return y_t^i, which is a deterministic function of both the realized performance measures $\left(x_t^1, x_t^2\right)$ but is not verifiable, so there cannot be a legally enforceable contract to share these. The parties can, however, agree a relational contract involving voluntary bonuses. Both parties are risk neutral. Doornik (2006) shows that, if a relationship is feasible, there is always an optimal relational contract that is invariant, in the sense of being the same every period apart from possibly calling for termination after some outcomes, even if continuation is feasible and efficient. When CDFC (Assumption 2) holds and the two parties are identical, an optimal invariant contract has the following properties: (a) the parties terminate the relationship with probability 1 when both performance levels are below some thresholds; (b) otherwise, the bonus payment takes one of two levels, depending essentially on the likelihood ratios of the observable performance measures in a way that corresponds to the party with lower relative performance paying the other. An optimal invariant contract does not necessarily require termination when continuation is feasible and efficient. An example is when each party's return is independent of the other's performance measure, so returns are separable. In that case, each party can act in the role of the purchaser in the moral hazard model in Levin (2003) with respect to the quality decision by the other. But, more generally, inefficient termination in some circumstances ("burning money") is required to keep the relationship incentive compatible, as in the moral hazard model in Levin (2003) with subjective performance measures. For some values of the discount factor, there is no fixed payment that is self-enforcing in the absence of bonuses, but efficient quality is implementable with an optimal relational contract. Thus, price (fixed payment plus bonus) varies with costs, as observed with Japanese automobile subcontracting. Price, however, varies less than if it were determined by period-by-period bargaining in the absence of a relational contract.

Rayo (2007) considers n risk-neutral parties choosing qualities $q_t = (q_t^1, \dots, q_t^n)$ whose joint output y is verifiable, as in Garvey (1995), but is a random variable with expected value $E[y \mid q]$. (There is also a party $n+1$, who plays no role in production and serves merely to balance the payments between the parties, but whose payments still have to be incentive compatible.) In addition, there is a signal x^i of party i's performance with density $f_i(x^i \mid q^i)$ that is independent across parties, is observed by all parties, but is not verifiable by outsiders. Denote by I the set of those who participate in a relational contract. Each participant receives a constant share $\alpha^i \geq 0$ of the realized output y_t, where the α^i are specified in a legally enforceable agreement and sum to one over all participants. Participants can also receive a legally enforceable fixed payment p_t^i and voluntary bonus payments $b_t^i(x_t)$ conditioned on the vector of realized signals x_t for all participants—by assumption, x_t is a sufficient statistic for (x_t, y_t). Rayo (2007) assumes that each participant i's net bonus plus discounted payoff in the continuation equilibrium at $t+1$ conditional on x_t is additively separable in her own performance signal x_t^i and the performance signals of the other participants, denoted x_t^{-i}. Thus, it can be written as $V^i(x_t^i) + W^i(x_t^{-i})$ for some functions V^i and W^i. (Without that assumption, the optimal contract would take the form of a winner-take-all tournament, which, it is argued, would have practical problems of implementation.) He then shows that the constraints for no party to default on the required bonus payments can, as in Levin (2003), be pooled into the single aggregate dynamic enforcement constraint

$$ \delta \left(S - \tilde{S} \right) \geq \sum_{i \in I} \left\{ \sup_{x_t^i} V^i \left(x_t^i \right) - \inf_{x_t^i} V^i \left(x_t^i \right) \right\}. \qquad (43) $$

Rayo (2007) calls the term in braces with superscript i in this i's "implicit incentive." It is the difference, under the relational contract and measured at the point bonuses are to be paid, between participant i's payoffs with the best and the worst possible values of x_t^i. These implicit incentives arise from the gain from having the relationship continue in the future, so their total over all participants cannot exceed the total gain, which is what (43) requires. That condition is effectively an extension of (24) to the case of many participants with the continuation equilibrium depending on the stochastic signals. If the continuation equilibrium did not depend on those signals, payoffs from $t + 1$ on would cancel on the right-hand side of (43), leaving only the bonus terms, as in (24).

Consider the implementation of some vector of qualities q with the vector of shares α. The share α^i provides an explicit incentive for participant i to deliver quality, but any additional incentive has to be provided by the implicit incentive, that is, by the term in braces with superscript i in (43). The minimum implicit incentive that will do this can be written $\Delta V^i \left(\alpha^i, q \right)$. Rayo (2007) first considers the case in which quality q_t^i is observed only by participant i and the $f_i (.)$ satisfy MLRP and CDFC (Assumptions 1 and 2). Then, for implementing any optimal vector of qualities $\hat{q}$ that is less than fully efficient, there exists an optimal allocation of shares $\hat{\alpha}$ such that one participant, call her l, has $\hat{\alpha}^l$ sufficiently high that $\Delta V^l \left(\hat{\alpha}^l, \hat{q} \right) = 0$. Participant l is the participant i for whom $-\partial \Delta V^i \left(\hat{\alpha}^i, \hat{q} \right) / \partial \alpha^i$ is largest. The intuition is as follows. Condition (43) constrains the total implicit incentives that can be provided to all participants. Because incentives are in short supply when efficient qualities cannot be attained, it is optimal to use the legally enforceable shares for that participant i for whom they are most effective at reducing the implicit incentive required, that is, for whom $-\partial \Delta V^i \left(\hat{\alpha}^i, \hat{q} \right) / \partial \alpha^i$ is largest. Intuitively, l is a relatively productive participant whose quality is hard to assess by means of x^l. Rayo (2007) shows that participant l can be interpreted as an endogenously chosen principal who, in the spirit of Alchian and Demsetz (1972), receives the total gain from continuation of the relationship but whose role as principal is just to make all the payments to other participants, not to monitor how they perform.

The other main case considered by Rayo (2007) is that in which all qualities are observable by all suppliers, that is, $x_t^i = q_t^i$. Then, provided some participants receive implicit incentives under an optimal contract, all do $(\Delta V^l \left(\hat{\alpha}^l, \hat{q} \right) > 0$ for all $i)$, and profit shares are dispersed $(\hat{\alpha}^i < 1$ for all $i)$. Rayo explains the intuition as follows. Suppose participant i receives no implicit incentive, so all her incentives come from $\hat{\alpha}^i > 0$. When q^i is chosen optimally, by the Envelope Theorem, the change in i's payoff from a small increase in q^i is of second order. Thus, the cost of inducing slightly higher quality from agent i with a small implicit incentive is essentially negligible and hence is always worthwhile. That $\hat{\alpha}^i < 1$ is shown by the following argument: if $\hat{\alpha}^i = 1$, i gets the full additional joint gain from additional quality and so would choose efficient quality without any implicit incentive. With an implicit incentive as well, i would choose quality above the efficient level, which cannot be optimal. Thus, given that there is some implicit incentive, it follows that $\hat{\alpha}^i < 1$.

The contrasting results for the two cases in Rayo (2007) illustrate the importance for incentive arrangements of the information quality of performance measures. When participants are able to monitor one another's performance only poorly, it is optimal to have one of them (one who is relatively productive but whose performance is particularly hard to assess) act as a principal who receives all the gain from continuation of the relationship and manages payments to all others. In contrast, when participants are able to monitor one another's performance well, a partnership in which they all receive shares of current output and also some of the gain from continuing the relationship in the future is optimal.[5]

---

5. Watson (1999, 2002) and Sobel (2006) consider partnerships in which partners contribute to a joint output but do not make direct payments to each other. From a modeling perspective, this means that the dynamic

10. Organizational Design

GM eventually took over Fisher Body, because, according to Klein (2000), efficiency requirements moved outside the zone of a self-enforcing relational contract. As the property rights
literature stemming from Grossman and Hart (1986) and Hart and Moore (1988, 1990) has
emphasized, however, a takeover does not remove the underlying incentive issues—it just moves
them inside the integrated firm. The basic models discussed in Section 3 can be used to throw
light on when it is more efficient to handle relational incentive issues within firms than between
firms, hence making vertical integration worthwhile.

In Baker et al. (2002), nonintegrated supply corresponds to the outsourcing model and
integrated supply to the employment model. The difference arises because ownership of the
assets used in supply is taken to confer ownership of the goods produced by those assets.
Then, when a supplier is taken over, its previous owner becomes a manager (as the Fisher
brothers became when GM took over Fisher Body). This manager still has to be induced to
provide appropriate quality but can no longer withhold supply for use as a bargaining chip for
payment, because the output belongs to the downstream firm. In the event one party breaches
a relational contract, the parties trade in the spot market thereafter (the so-called grim trigger
strategies), but they renegotiate ownership of the asset to provide the most efficient spot market
operation. In the basic models of Section 3, the implication is that $\tilde{U}_{t+1} + \tilde{\Pi}_{t+1}$ in (8) for the
employment model is the same as $\tilde{U}_{t+1} + \tilde{\Pi}_{t+1}$ in (15) for the outsourcing model, because,
whether or not the firms start out integrated, renegotiation leads to the same efficient spot
market trading. Then, (8) with $\rho = 1$ is a weaker constraint than (15) for given q_t if $z_t\left(\tilde{q}_t\right) -
c_t\left(\tilde{q}_t\right) > z_t\left(q_t\right)$, precisely the condition for use of a fixed-price contract to be advantageous
in the model of Itoh and Morita (2011) discussed in Section 5. Notice that every term in this
condition involves either the function $z_t\left(.\right)$ or the quality $\tilde{q}_t$, both of which apply only when
the relational contract is breached. It is only what happens in the event of breach that determines
efficient organizational design. Halonen (2002) considers another form of organization, joint
ownership, which is discussed further below.

Is this framework useful for discussing GM's takeover of Fisher Body? Suppose it were ini-
tially the case that $z_t\left(\tilde{q}_t\right) - c_t\left(\tilde{q}_t\right) < z_t\left(q_t\right)$, so that (15) is weaker than (8). Then a given
q_t is sustainable at a lower discount factor δ_t when the supplier is a separate company, so the
relationally efficient organization is outsourcing. For vertical integration to become efficient,

---

enforcement constraints of the partners cannot be pooled into a single constraint. From a practical perspective,
it makes the models less appropriate for studying contracts between firms. (In Sobel (2006), the probability that
cheating is detectable by the courts can, in addition, be increased by incurring an enforcement cost.) Thomas and
Worrall (2010) allow for transfers between agents via the equilibrium outcomes of a Nash demand game played
each period after output has been produced. This has the effect of imposing credit constraints that can result in
rewards to one party being postponed (backloaded) until a time at which the other party is unconstrained. The
formal structure of cooperation in repeated partnerships is related to that of collusion in repeated oligopoly, of
which there are recent models in Sannikov and Skrzypacz (2007) and Athey and Bagwell (2008). The former
makes the relationship explicit in an application of its result that collusion cannot be sustained when the parties'
actions are perfect substitutes, new noisy information arrives continuously, and the parties are able to respond to
that information quickly. But for reasons that are obvious in the context of illicit collusion, those models do not
allow direct payments between the parties.

that inequality would have to be reversed. Transferring Buick body production to Flint was presumably jointly advantageous to GM and Fisher Body, because the savings on the costs of transporting completed bodies outweighed any increased costs of inputs. It is not, however, obvious that a reduction in transportation cost alone would have changed the relationally efficient organization. Suppose, for concreteness, the cost $c_t(q_t)$ at the body plant gate was unaffected by the change in location, the advantage being measured by an increase in $y_t(q_t)$ resulting from the savings in transportation cost of k per body for each of q_t bodies delivered. Under the split-the-difference bargaining outcome assumed by Baker et al. (2002), z_t is determined by the parties sharing equally the gain from the purchasing firm receiving the output over it being sold to a third party. Formally, with v_t the value for which the output can be sold to a third party,

$$z_t(q_t) = v_t(q_t) + \frac{1}{2}\left[y_t(q_t) - v_t(q_t)\right] = \frac{1}{2}\left[y_t(q_t) + v_t(q_t)\right]. \tag{44}$$

So if the cost of transporting bodies to an alternative automobile manufacturer increased by the same amount k per body, $z_t(q_t)$ would remain unchanged, and the relocation to Flint would leave the relationally efficient ownership unchanged. This example is, of course, intended only to illustrate use of the theory, not to provide a full analysis of the situation faced by GM and Fisher Body. Some careful research is still needed to see whether the model can really be applied to that case and, if so, how.

Baker et al. (2002) show that there is another effect to consider. Suppose, as in Levin (2003), the outcome y is stochastic given q_t and so is z, with both iid given q_t, so that the expected future payoff to the relationship does not depend on the current realization. Also as in Levin (2003), suppose the purchaser observes neither q_t nor the realization of the stochastic terms but does observe the realizations y_t and z_t. Then, in the notation of Section 6, the jointly observed outcome is $\phi_t = \{y_t, z_t\}$. Because the purchaser does not observe q_t (and so cannot punish directly breach of an agreement about quality), the incentive compatibility condition for the supplier to deliver quality becomes (in a stationary environment)

$$q_t \in \arg\max_q E_y\left[P(\phi)\mid q\right] - c(q). \tag{45}$$

This condition is just like (21) for the model in Levin (2003) except that there is no argument θ, because the agent can be of only one type. In the employment model, the incentive compatibility constraints (22) and (23) for the purchaser and the supplier, respectively, to pay agreed bonuses apply just as in Levin (2003) and hence so does the dynamic enforcement constraint (24). In the outsourcing model, (45) continues to apply, but, in line with (13) and (14) for the outsourcing model, (22) and (23) become

$$\delta\left(\Pi - \tilde{\Pi}\right) \geq \sup_\phi\left[b(\phi) - z\right] \tag{46}$$

$$\delta\left(U - \tilde{U}\right) \geq \inf_\phi\left[z - b(\phi)\right]. \tag{47}$$

Hence, the interaction between the variation in bonuses and whether the firms are integrated affects the incentives to breach a relational contract, so the variation in payoffs, not just their expected values, can be important in the choice between organizational forms. Baker et al. (2002) make use of specific functional forms to show that the relationally efficient organization does indeed depend on the variation in output for given q_t and also to derive further results.

Several papers consider developments of the model in Baker et al. (2002). Baker et al. (2001) extend it to allow supply to have some verifiable characteristics, as in the models in Section 5. Then the contractual payment p can be conditioned on those verifiable characteristics. The main result is that it is not possible to replicate the payoffs of spot outsourcing with a relational employment contract. Kvaløy (2007) considers an alternative to grim trigger strategies, specifically, that the parties trade in the spot market for one period only and then revert to their relational contract. That affects $\tilde{U}$ and $\tilde{\Pi}$ and hence the relational contracts that are sustainable. Ruzzier (2009) adopts a different specification of how z_t (.) is determined. Instead of assuming split-the-difference bargaining as in (44), he assumes v_t is an outside option that can be taken up by the supplier only once bargaining with the purchaser has been broken off, giving the bargaining outcome

$$z_t = \begin{cases} \frac{1}{2}y_t, & \text{if } \frac{1}{2}y_t \geq v_t, \\ v_t, & \text{if } \frac{1}{2}y_t < v_t. \end{cases}$$

Then the distribution of v_t does not affect the choice between organizational forms if the top line applies (the case Ruzzier (2009) calls "high specificity") and the distribution of y_t does not affect it if the bottom line applies (low specificity).

The underlying framework has also been extended to the case in which both parties take actions that contribute to the value of their joint output (the partnership models of Section 9). In Halonen (2002), both parties make their quality decisions simultaneously, these are observed by the other party, and either or both can be applied to an asset. If both are applied to the asset, the joint output is $y(q^1, q^2) = q^1 + q^2$; if only party i's, party i's output is λq^i, with $\lambda \in [0, 1)$, and party j's output for $j \neq i$ is zero whatever q^j (λ is known, so there is no stochastic element). Neither quality nor output is verifiable, so no sharing contract is legally enforceable. In a one-period relationship, after one party has breached a relational contract, the parties still cooperate to apply both qualities to the asset, because doing so yields a higher total output. They share this output by bargaining that splits equally the difference between their joint output and what their individual outputs would be in the absence of cooperation. If the asset is owned by party i, these individual outputs are λq^i and 0. But the asset can also be owned jointly, in which case each party can prevent the other from using it, so both have individual outputs of zero. With ownership by party 1, the rewards in a one-period relationship that result from this bargaining are, in the notation of Section 9,

$$z^1\left(q^1, q^2\right) = \lambda q^1 + \frac{1}{2}\left[(1 - \lambda)\,q^1 + q^2\right] = \frac{1}{2}\left[(1 + \lambda)\,q^1 + q^2\right] \tag{48}$$

$$z^2\left(q^1, q^2\right) = \frac{1}{2}\left[(1 - \lambda)\,q^1 + q^2\right], \tag{49}$$

so the optimal qualities defined in (37) are

$$\tilde{q}^1 = \arg\max_{q^1 \geq \underline{q}} \frac{1}{2}\left[(1+\lambda)\, q^1 + q^2\right] - c\left(q^1\right) \tag{50}$$

$$\tilde{q}^2 = \arg\max_{q^2 \geq \underline{q}} \frac{1}{2}\left[(1-\lambda)\, q^1 + q^2\right] - c\left(q^2\right). \tag{51}$$

With joint ownership, both parties' individual outputs are zero, so the rewards in a one-period relationship are given by (48) and (49) with $\lambda = 0$. Thus, party 2 chooses the same quality $\tilde{q}^2$ under both forms of ownership and, provided $\lambda > 0$, party 1 chooses higher quality $\tilde{q}^1$ under single ownership (but it is still less than the efficient level, because $\lambda < 1$). Thus, in a one-period relationship, single ownership is better than joint ownership for $\lambda > 0$.

Under a relational contract, that is not necessarily the case. The formal analysis can be done by inserting the appropriate functional forms into (41). In contrast to Baker et al. (2002), Halonen (2002) considers primarily the assumption that ownership is not renegotiated in the event of breach by either party, which corresponds to making $\tilde{S}_{t+1}$ a function of λ. When $\lambda = 0$, single ownership and joint ownership are again equivalent. With joint ownership, nothing changes as λ changes (because λ is then irrelevant). However, with a single owner, $\tilde{S}_{t+1}$ is an increasing function of λ for $\lambda \in [0, 1)$, because from (50), $\tilde{q}^1$ is increasing in λ, and from (51), $\tilde{q}^2$ is independent of λ. So the long-term cost of breaching a relational contract for given (q^1, q^2) is decreasing in λ. The short-term gain from doing so is also decreasing in λ. Halonen (2002) shows that, for $c(q) = q^\gamma$ $(\gamma > 1)$ and an optimal payoff structure when efficient qualities are achievable, these two effects exactly balance when $\gamma = 2$. For $\gamma < 2$, single ownership is relationally efficient; for $\gamma > 2$, joint ownership is relationally efficient. Halonen (2002) also considers the assumption that ownership is renegotiated in the event of default (so that $\tilde{S}_{t+1}$ is independent of λ) but only for a specific numerical example.[6]

In Bragelien (2007) too, both parties make quality decisions, but—as in Baker et al. (2002) and unlike in Halonen (2002)—output is an iid random variable for given quality, and quality decisions are unobserved by the other party. Neither output nor quality is verifiable. The benefit to each party if they subsequently cooperate is their own quality plus an additive stochastic term; it is noncontractible but is observed by both. If, after observing the benefit, either decides not to cooperate, their benefits are lower and, in addition to depending on what the benefits would have been had they cooperated, also depend on the ownership structure. If they cooperate, they share the gains from doing so. The form payments take under an optimal relational contract consists of each party receiving the payoff it would receive in the absence of cooperation, together with a fixed payment independent of the benefits from cooperation and a payment depending on the realized values of those benefits that takes one of just two values (a one-step payment schedule). With sufficient symmetry, the last of these payments depends on which agent has the higher realized gain from cooperation and so resembles a tournament. This result extends results in Levin (2003) for the case in which just one party decides quality to the case in which both do.

---

6. Applied to the model in Baker et al. (2002), joint ownership might be interpreted as implying that the supplier cannot sell the supply to a third party without the agreement of the purchaser. Then, in the formulation in (44), $v_t(q_t) = 0$ for all q_t, and hence $z_t(q_t) = y_t(q_t)/2$.

The main focus of Bragelien (2007) concerns the choice of organizational structure. Noncooperation results in the parties operating as if in a spot market ever after. The paper considers both the case discussed by Halonen (2002), in which the parties are committed to the ownership structure forever once it has been determined, and that discussed by Baker et al. (2002), in which the parties can renegotiate their ownership structure if they move to a spot market relationship. For the first case, Bragelien (2007) gives conditions favoring an ownership structure that gives weaker (and, conversely, stronger) incentives in spot market interactions. They differ from those in Halonen (2002) because of the uncertainty. The generalization of Baker et al. (2002) is that the potential benefits are continuous, not just binary. For this case, the general result is that the ownership structure should never give worse incentives in the spot market for one party without giving better incentives for the other. ("Better" here may be stronger or weaker, depending on whether that party would otherwise choose quality below or above the efficient level.) There are also results for correlated performance measures. Bragelien (2007) illustrates the results with linear contracts, which may be optimal (if error terms are uniformly distributed and functions are linear) and for which explicit solutions can be derived.

Blonski and Spagnolo (2007) question whether, when modeled properly, there is actually a difference between the case in which ownership can be renegotiated following breach and the case in which it cannot. The essence of their argument, formalized in a model with both parties choosing quality but with no stochastic elements, is as follows. Trading in a spot market environment after one party breaches is inefficient, so the parties would gain by renegotiating back to continued cooperation. Doing so does not destroy incentive compatibility if the parties use restitution strategies, based on an idea in Farrell and Maskin (1989), in which the payoff to the breaching party in the continuation equilibrium played following breach is reduced to the level that party would have obtained by trading in the spot market ever after. (In the absence of wealth constraints, that can be achieved by a single monetary payment for restitution, but this is not the only possibility.) The reason restitution strategies do not upset incentive compatibility is that, if defaulting at t, the supplier still gets continuation payoff $\tilde{U}_{t+1}$, and if defaulting at t, the purchaser still gets continuation payoff $\tilde{\Pi}_{t+1}$—it is only the continuation payoff of the nonbreaching party that is affected by the restitution. But if the parties were using the relationally efficient organization before breach, they will have no reason to renegotiate the organizational structure after breach. Thus, it makes no difference whether they can renegotiate that structure.

Baker et al. (2011) consider a different issue of organizational design: how to allocate decision rights in an organization in order to adapt decisions to changing circumstances. To illustrate, consider two parties and a single decision about quality q_t that can, in principle, be made by either of them. Which has the right to do so has to be determined before all uncertainty, represented by a random state of the world s, is resolved. The party given that right makes the decision in its own interest, once the uncertain state of the world has been revealed.[7] So, in

---

7. Baker et al. (2011) contrast their approach with the incomplete contracts approach of Grossman-Hart-Moore in the following way. In the latter, a legally enforceable agreement about the decision to be made can always be negotiated between the parties after any uncertainty is resolved, no matter who has the formal right to make it. In the former, there is insufficient time to negotiate such an agreement, a situation referred to by Williamson (2000: 605) as "maladaptation in the contract execution interval."

a one-period relationship, it is optimal to give the decision right to whichever party's short-term self-interested decisions for each state s yield the highest expected joint payoff. But in an ongoing relationship in which actual decisions are observed by all parties, voluntary bonus payments and the payoffs in the continuation equilibrium can be conditioned on the state and on the decision made, so the decisionmaker can be induced to make decisions not solely in a short-term self-interested way. Then the party to whom the decision right is given becomes just like the supplier in the employment model of Section 3.1, except that there is uncertainty at the time the purchaser commits to p_t that is resolved by the time the supplier makes the decision q_t. (Baker et al. (2011) also allow for payments to be made between the state being revealed and the decision q_t being made.) Assume for simplicity that the state s is iid, and denote its realized value at t by s_t. Then in an obvious analogy with (1), we can write party 1's payoff conditional on being the decisionmaker in period t and on the relational contract continuing as

$$U_t^1\left(s_t\right) = p_t + b_t\left(q_t, s_t\right) - c_t^1\left(q_t, s_t\right) + \delta_t E_s\left[U_{t+1}^1\left(s\right)\right], \quad \text{for all } t \geq \tau, \quad (52)$$

where $c_t^1\left(q_t, s_t\right)$ is now to be interpreted as the net cost to party 1 of making decision q_t in state s_t instead of the decision that maximizes her short-term interest. One can make exactly the same notational changes to the purchaser's payoffs for the nondecisionmaking party 2 and so derive the incentive compatibility condition conditional on s_t, corresponding to (8) with $\rho = 1$:

$$\delta_t E_s\left[S_{t+1}\left(s\right) - \tilde{S}_{t+1}\left(s\right)\right] \equiv \delta_t E_s\left[U_{t+1}^1\left(s\right) - \tilde{U}_{t+1}^1\left(s\right) + \Pi_{t+1}^2\left(s\right) - \tilde{\Pi}_{t+1}^2\left(s\right)\right]$$

$$\geq c_t^1\left(q_t, s_t\right), \quad \text{for all } t \geq \tau.$$

Because the decision right could, in principle, be allocated to different parties in successive periods, the joint future gain $E_s\left[S_{t+1}\left(s\right) - \tilde{S}_{t+1}\left(s\right)\right]$ is independent of who has the decision right in period t, as well as of the decision made at t. The parties can thus implement the decision rule $q_t\left(s\right)$ for all s with the decision allocated to party 1 in period t only if

$$\delta_t E_s\left[S_{t+1}\left(s\right) - \tilde{S}_{t+1}\left(s\right)\right] \geq \max_s c_t^1\left(q_t\left(s\right), s\right).$$

One can derive a similar condition for when the decision is allocated to party 2. The incentive compatibility requirement is obviously weaker if the decision right is allocated to the party i for which $\max_s c_t^i\left(q_t\left(s\right), s\right)$ is smaller. The decision rule $q_t\left(s\right)$ can thus be implemented for all s by some allocation of the decision right only if

$$\delta_t E_s\left[S_{t+1}\left(s\right) - \tilde{S}_{t+1}\left(s\right)\right] \geq \min_{i \in \{1,2\}} \max_s c_t^i\left(q_t\left(s\right), s\right), \quad \text{for all } t \geq \tau.$$

This example illustrates the underlying idea. Baker et al. (2011) allow for richer structures with many parties and many decisions for which the right to decide can be allocated, not necessarily all to the same party. There are then many potential governance structures that specify who has the right to make which decision.

11. Rent and Relational Contracts

Crucial to sustaining a relational contract is that the sum of the future payoffs to the two parties from adhering to it is larger than the sum of their future payoffs from breaching it. If that is not the case, $S_{t+1} = \tilde{S}_{t+1}$ in (8), and no relational contract can be sustained. In other words, the parties must have a rent from continuing their relationship. The rent can go to either party— (8) is a condition on the total rent, not its distribution, and the payments p_t and b_t can be used to distribute that rent in any proportions. But that rent must exist. The same applies to all other models described in this chapter.

In much of the literature, the required rent comes from the assumption that, if one of the parties breaches the relational contract, they either trade in the spot market thereafter, or, if spot market trade cannot be sustained, they cease to trade completely. Even when, as in Blonski and Spagnolo (2007), they do not actually do that in the event of breach, the possibility of doing so is still important in ensuring that it is incentive compatible for the breaching party to pay restitution to the nonbreaching party. In practice, of course, each party may have other potential trading partners. This is not necessarily a problem if the potential partners observe which party has breached and treat the breaching party as a pariah, or even if other potential partners observe only that a relationship has come to an end and treat both parties to that relationship as pariahs (see MacLeod and Malcomson 1989). But in practice, there are many reasons other than breach for a relational contract to come to an end that third parties may not be able to distinguish from breach. As Bewley (1999: 298) emphasizes in the case of employment, many employers find it difficult to get information about potential employees from former employers. Dixit (2003) discusses market solutions, motivated by the Sicilian Mafia, in which intermediaries sell, at a profitable price, either information about the past behavior of potential partners or enforcement services. But a third party has no reason to pay that price unless it would reveal something inherent about the potential partner that is relevant to the productivity of a future relationship.

Without some way to generate the required rent despite outside markets, relational contracts will break down, as Bulow and Rogoff (1989) note in the case of sovereign debt. However, there are ways in which that rent can arise even if potential partners do not discriminate against those whose previous relationships have ended. Specific investments upfront are an obvious one. But in general, there is no reason why the efficient level of specific investment, even if positive, should be large enough to sustain a relational contract, let alone one that delivers efficient quality. An alternative widely discussed in the literature is the possibility that at least one party is not in a position to form another relationship straightaway. This may be because of exogenous market frictions due to search and matching, as in Kranton (1996b), Ramey and Watson (1997, 2001) and Sobel (2006). Or it may be generated endogenously through unemployment on one side of the market, as originally modeled in Shapiro and Stiglitz (1984) in the context of efficiency wages. In the latter case, it does not matter which party has difficulty rematching. It is an assumption of Shapiro and Stiglitz (1984) that the rent must go to employees in the form of efficiency wages, rather than to firms as the result of excess vacancies, as MacLeod and Malcomson (1989, 1998) show. But there must be a rent to one party or the other. For more on this issue in the context of employment, see Malcomson (1999).

Another possibility is explored by Kranton (1996a): starting the relationship with low quality, so that there is little to lose if the other party defaults, and having quality build up over time.

Recall that, in the basic employment model, (4), (7), and (8) are necessary and sufficient conditions for a quality sequence to be an equilibrium, and that these conditions are all inequalities. Moreover, only future gains (i.e., from the second period of the relationship $\tau + 1$ on) affect the left-hand side of (8), and lowering q_τ reduces the right-hand side. Thus, for any sequence of qualities $(q_\tau, q_{\tau+1}, \ldots)$ that can be sustained as an equilibrium, a sequence $(q'_\tau, q_{\tau+1}, \ldots)$ with $q'_\tau < q_\tau$ can also be sustained as an equilibrium, provided the individual rationality conditions (4) and (7) are still satisfied. As long as q_τ is not above the efficient level, it also yields less gain to starting a new relationship and hence less temptation to breach an existing one. Moreover, setting $q'_\tau < q_t$ creates some slack in (8) even if there were none before, so reducing $q_{\tau+1}$ (and hence the left-hand side of (8) for $t = \tau$) by a small amount will not upset incentive compatibility for period τ, creates some slack in the incentive compatibility constraint for $\tau + 1$, and does not affect incentive compatibility from $\tau + 2$ on. Thus, in the limit, one can always set $q_t = \underline{q}$ for as many periods after τ as needed to reduce U_τ to $\bar{U}_\tau$ and Π_τ to $\bar{\Pi}_\tau$, a way suggested by Murphy and Topel (1990) to remove the need for involuntary unemployment in the model of Shapiro and Stiglitz (1984). Watson (1999, 2002) and Sobel (2006) similarly explore starting relationships in a small or inefficient way.

Essentially, starting relationships small is a way of dissipating the potential gains from new relationships to make starting a new relationship less attractive than continuing an existing one. There are other ways this can be done. Klein and Leffler (1981) explore advertising. Carmichael and MacLeod (1997) explore gifts that cost the giver more than they are worth to the recipient. There are no doubt other possibilities.

12. Courts and Empirical Evidence

This chapter is primarily about theory. Empirical evidence on contracts between firms is discussed in Lafontaine and Slade (this volume), including the issues of rent and reputation that arise in relational contracts. But one issue of particular relevance to relational contracts is not covered there: the quality of the legal system.

Relational contracts are concerned with agreements that can be enforced without resort to courts. The spirit of much of the theory discussed here is that, although an effective legal system exists, important elements of the relationship cannot be enforced legally, because courts do not have the relevant information. However, relational contracts are also valuable for enforcing agreements that courts could in principle enforce but cannot in practice be relied on to do so. For example, the parties may be in different legal jurisdictions or courts may be too corrupt, cumbersome, or otherwise ineffective. Djankov et al. (2003) document how slow and ineffective courts can be, even in countries with highly developed legal systems, over such seemingly simple things as the collection of a check returned for nonpayment. Such circumstances provide good reason for parties to use relational contracts to avoid recourse to courts when they are effective substitutes, not just when crucial information is unverifiable (though the relational contracts may then not be able to rely on even noncontingent payments being legally enforceable). Greif (1994) documents the way in which eleventh-century Maghribi traders used reputations to enforce relational contracts when trading between countries. Fafchamps (1996) and Bigsten et al. (2000) document the widespread use of relational contracts among African businesses, and their less widespread use where legal institutions best support business. McMillan and Woodruff (1999) find that private sector firms in Vietnam provide customers with more credit when alternative suppliers are hard to locate and when customers are identified through business networks, both of which may provide sources of sanction for default. Banerjee and Duflo (2000) demonstrate the importance of reputational effects for Indian software. But even though relational contracts can clearly act as a substitute for well-functioning courts, better formal institutions can also foster contracting, as Johnson et al. (2002) find in post-communist countries.

13. Conclusion

This chapter does not cover anything like all the literature on relational contracts. As noted in Section 1, it focuses on theory as applied to supply relationships between firms and does not consider applications to purely financial contracts, employment, or relationships involving sovereign bodies. The inability to commit that underlies relational contracts is inherent to relationships involving sovereign bodies, because there is nobody to enforce a contract on such a body, even when the relevant information is publicly available. Thus, relational contracts have been applied to issues of sovereign debt, to treaties between sovereign states, and to the relationships between rulers and ruled within states. Acemoglu (2003), for example, develops incentive compatibility conditions similar to those used here when analyzing taxation under dictatorship and democracy.

This chapter has, moreover, not discussed relational contracts concerned only with risk sharing. Indeed, for tractability, most of the literature surveyed here assumes all parties are risk neutral, though there are notable exceptions, such as Pearce and Stacchetti (1998) and MacLeod (2003). Issues of risk aversion perhaps deserve greater attention. So (in addition to other issues noted above) do issues of which of the multiple equilibria will be played in practice and of the implications of nonstationary environments.

There are also foundational issues that deserve greater attention. The findings of Macaulay (1963) provided an important motivation for economic research on relational contracts. However, models of the type presented here certainly do not capture all those findings. One role for relational contracts discussed by Macaulay (1963) is as a substitute for planning exchange relationships completely, a framework within which the relationship can be adjusted in the face of either unforeseen contingencies or inconsistent perceptions by the parties about what should happen in certain eventualities. That role is not a feature of the models discussed above. Formally, equilibria in those models are in terms of strategies that specify what actions the parties are to take for every history that can occur, and thus for every possible contingency. Moreover, equilibrium strategies are consistent in the sense that each party's strategy is a best response to the other's. Relational contracts in these models are a substitute for enforcement by courts, not a substitute for careful planning. There is certainly no modeling of unforeseen contingencies. As in so much of economics, incorporating unforeseen contingencies remains a major challenge. Kreps (1996) reflects on these issues and on possible ways forward.

Some earlier writers about relational contracts, such as Dore (1983), contrasted them with standard economic analysis and, in particular, with economists' perceptions of allocative efficiency. As Dore (1983: 472) put it: "Any economist, at least any economist worth his neo-classical salt, would be likely to scoff at the idea. Just think, he would say, of the market imperfections, of the misallocation and loss of efficiency involved." That was, however, before most of the literature discussed in this chapter was written. It should be apparent from this survey that research by economists on relational contracts is precisely about how the parties may achieve more efficient outcomes by making use of relational contracts in circumstances in which courts cannot be relied on to enforce contractual agreements.

There remain important differences of interpretation, however, about the notion of trust. Trust is seen by many noneconomists as central to relational contracts. Some of the literature surveyed above interprets an equilibrium with quality above the level sustainable in a one-period relationship as involving trust, because at least one party leaves itself vulnerable to exploitation by the other. As MacLeod (2007b: 609) puts it: "in a relational contract, one party trusts the other when the value from future trade is greater than the one period gain from defection." In this spirit, Kvaløy and Olsen (2009) interpret an increase in the discount factor δ as an increase in trust, because it increases the stake that the parties are prepared to risk. That interpretation of trust is not, however, universally accepted. In the context of exchanges in which the gains from future dealings are sufficiently highly valued to induce cooperation, Sabel (1993: 1135) writes that "it would be wrong to associate cooperation with trust at all, because cooperation results from continuous calculation of self-interest rather than a mutually recognized suspension, however circumscribed, of such calculation." Sako (1992) develops different concepts of trust along these lines applicable to interfirm relations in Britain and Japan. These writers view relational contracts as being about more than self-interested cooperation.

Whether or not they capture all elements of relational contracts, however, the economic models discussed here have certainly been invaluable in illuminating important features of economic relationships. Further research will no doubt illuminate yet more.

REFERENCES

Abreu, D., P. Milgrom, and D. Pearce. 1991. "Information and Timing in Repeated Partnerships." *Econometrica* 59: 1713–1733.

Acemoglu, D. 2003. "Why Not a Political Coase Theorem? Social Conflict, Commitment, and Politics." *Journal of Comparative Economics* 31: 620–652.

Alchian, A. A., and H. Demsetz. 1972. "Production, Information Costs, and Economic Organization." *American Economic Review* 62: 777–795.

Asanuma, B. 1989. "Manufacturer-Supplier Relationships in Japan and the Concept of Relation-Specific Skill." *Journal of the Japanese and International Economies* 3: 1–30.

Asanuma, B., and T. Kikutani. 1992. "Risk Absorption in Japanese Subcontracting: A Microeconometric Study of the Automobile Industry." *Journal of the Japanese and International Economies* 6: 1–29.

Athey, S., and K. Bagwell. 2008. "Collusion with Persistent Cost Shocks." *Econometrica* 76: 493–540.

Baker, G. 1992. "Incentive Contracts and Performance Measurement." *Journal of Political Economy* 100: 598–614.

Baker, G., R. Gibbons, and K. J. Murphy. 1994. "Subjective Performance Measures in Optimal Incentive Contracts." *Quarterly Journal of Economics* 109: 1125–1156.

———. 2001. "Bringing the Market Inside the Firm?" *American Economic Review* 91: 212–218.

———. 2002. "Relational Contracts and the Theory of the Firm." *Quarterly Journal of Economics* 117: 39–84.

———. 2011. "Relational Adaptation." Massachusetts Institute of Technology, Department of Economics, Cambridge, MA.

Banerjee, A. V., and E. Duflo. 2000. "Reputation Effects and the Limits of Contracting: A Study of the Indian Software Industry." *Quarterly Journal of Economics* 115: 989–1017.

Baron, D. P. 1989. "Design of Regulatory Mechanisms and Institutions," in R. Schmalensee and R. D. Willig (eds.), *Handbook of Industrial Organization,* volume II. Elsevier Science: Amsterdam, pp. 1347–1447.

Battigalli, P., and G. Maggi. 2002. "Rigidity, Discretion, and the Costs of Writing Contracts." *American Economic Review* 92: 798–817.

———. 2008. "Costly Contracting in a Long-Term Relationship." *RAND Journal of Economics* 39: 352–377.

Bernheim, B. D., and M. D. Whinston. 1990. "Multimarket Contact and Collusive Behavior." *RAND Journal of Economics* 21: 1–26.

———. 1998. "Incomplete Contracts and Strategic Ambiguity." *American Economic Review* 88: 902–932.

Bewley, T. F. 1999. *Why Wages Don't Fall During a Recession.* Cambridge, MA: Harvard University Press.

Bigsten, A., P. Collier, S. Dercon, M. Fafchamps, B. Gauthier, J. W. Gunning, A. Oduro, R. Oostendorp, C. Patillo, M. Soderbom, F. Teal, and A. Zeufack. 2000. "Contract Flexibility and Dispute Resolution in African Countries." *Journal of Development Studies* 36: 1–37.

Blonski, M., and G. Spagnolo. 2007, "Relational Efficient Property Rights." J. W. Goethe University, Department of Economics, Frankfurt am Main, Germany.

Blonski, M., P. Ockenfels, and G. Spagnolo. 2011. "Equilibrium Selection in the Repeated Prisoner's Dilemma: Axiomatic Approach and Experimental Evidence." *American Economic Journal: Microeconomics* 3: 164–192.

Board, S. 2011. "Relational Contracts and the Value of Loyalty." *American Economic Review* 101: 3349–3367.

Bragelien, I. 2007. "Asset Ownership and Relational Contracts." Norwegian School of Economics and Business Administration, Bergen.

Brown, M., A. Falk, and E. Fehr. 2004. "Relational Contracts and the Nature of Market Interactions." *Econometrica* 72: 747–780.

Bull, C. 1987. "The Existence of Self-Enforcing Implicit Contracts." *Quarterly Journal of Economics* 102: 147–159.

Bulow, J., and K. Rogoff. 1989. "Sovereign Debt: Is to Forgive to Forget?" *American Economic Review* 79: 43–50.

Calzolari, G., and G. Spagnolo. 2010. "Relational Contracts and Competitive Screening." Discussion Paper 7434, Centre for Economic Policy Research, London.

Carlton, D. W. 1986. "The Rigidity of Prices." *American Economic Review* 76: 637–658.

Carmichael, H. L., and W. B. MacLeod. 1997. "Gift Giving and the Evolution of Cooperation." *International Economic Review* 38: 485–509.

Chassang, S. 2010. "Building Routines: Learning, Cooperation and the Dynamics of Incomplete Relational Contracts." *American Economic Review* 100: 448–465.

Che, Y.-K., and S.-W. Yoo. 2001. "Optimal Incentives for Teams." *American Economic Review* 91: 525–541.

Crémer, J. 1986. "Cooperation in Ongoing Organizations." *Quarterly Journal of Economics* 101: 33–49.

Daido, K. 2006. "Formal and Relational Incentives in a Multitask Model." *International Review of Law and Economics* 26: 380–394.

Di Tella, R., and R. MacCulloch. 2002. "Informal Family Insurance and the Design of the Welfare State." *Economic Journal* 112: 481–503.

Dixit, A. 2003. "On Modes of Economic Governance." *Econometrica* 71: 449–481.

Djankov, S., R. La Porta, F. Lopez-de-Silanes, and A. Shleifer. 2003. "Courts." *Quarterly Journal of Economics* 118: 453–517.

Doornik, K. 2006. "Relational Contracting in Partnerships." *Journal of Economics and Management Strategy* 15: 517–548.

Dore, R. 1983. "Goodwill and the Spirit of Market Capitalism." *British Journal of Sociology* 34: 459–482.

Evans, R. 2008. "Simple Efficient Contracts in Complex Environments." *Econometrica* 76: 459–491.

Fafchamps, M. 1996. "The Enforcement of Commercial Contracts in Ghana." *World Development* 24: 427–448.

Fairburn, J. A., and J. M. Malcomson. 1994. "Rewarding Performance by Promotion to a Different Job." *European Economic Review* 38: 683–690.

———. 2001. "Performance, Promotion, and the Peter Principle." *Review of Economic Studies* 68: 45–66.

Farrell, J., and E. Maskin. 1989. "Renegotiation in Repeated Games." *Games and Economic Behavior* 1: 327–360.

Fehr, E., and A. Falk. 2002. "Psychological Foundations of Incentives." *European Economic Review* 46: 687–724.

Fong, Y.-F., and J. Li. 2010a. "Information Revelation in Relational Contracts." Northwestern University, Kellogg School of Management, Evanston, IL.

———. 2010b. "Relational Contracts, Efficiency Wages, and Employment Dynamics." Northwestern University, Kellogg School of Management, Evanston, IL.

Fuchs, W. 2007. "Contracting with Repeated Moral Hazard and Private Evaluations." *American Economic Review* 97: 1432–1448.

Garvey, G. T. 1995. "Why Reputation Favors Joint Ventures over Vertical and Horizontal Integration: A Simple Model." *Journal of Economic Behavior and Organization* 28: 387–397.

Gietzmann, M. B., and J. G. Larsen. 1998. "Motivating Subcontractors to Perform Development and Design Tasks." *Management Accounting Research* 9: 285–309.

Greif, A. 1994. "Cultural Beliefs and the Organization of Society: A Historical and Theoretical Reflection on Collectivist and Individualist Societies." *Journal of Political Economy* 102: 912–950.

Grossman, S. J., and O. D. Hart. 1986. "The Costs and Benefits of Ownership: A Theory of Vertical and Lateral Integration." *Journal of Political Economy* 94: 691–719.

Halac, M. 2012. "Relational Contracts and the Value of Relationships." *American Economic Review* 102: 750–779.

Halonen, M. 2002. "Reputation and the Allocation of Ownership." *Economic Journal* 112: 539–558.

Hart, O. D., and J. Moore. 1988. "Incomplete Contracts and Renegotiation." *Econometrica* 56: 755–785.

———. 1990. "Property Rights and the Nature of the Firm." *Journal of Political Economy* 98: 1119–1158.

Holmström, B. 1999. "Managerial Incentive Problems: A Dynamic Perspective." *Review of Economic Studies* 66: 169–182.

Holmström, B., and P. Milgrom. 1991. "Multitask Principal-Agent Analyses: Incentive Contracts, Asset Ownership, and Job Design." *Journal of Law, Economics, and Organization* 7: 24–52.

Hörner, J. 2002. "Reputation and Competition." *American Economic Review* 92: 644–663.

Iossa, E., and G. Spagnolo. 2011. "Contracts as Threats: On a Rationale for Rewarding A While Hoping for B." Discussion Paper 8195, Centre for Economic Policy Research, London.

Itoh, H., and H. Morita. 2011. "Formal Contracts, Relational Contracts, and the Threat-Point Effect." Working Paper 3533, CESifo, Munich.

Johnson, S., J. McMillan, and C. Woodruff. 2002. "Courts and Relational Contracts." *Journal of Law, Economics, and Organzation* 18: 221–277.

Kawasaki, S., and J. McMillan. 1987. "The Design of Contracts: Evidence from Japanese Subcontracting." *Journal of the Japanese and International Economies* 1: 327–349.

Klein, B. 2000. "Fisher–General Motors and the Nature of the Firm." *Journal of Law and Economics* 43: 105–141.

Klein, B., and K. B. Leffler. 1981. "The Role of Market Forces in Assuring Contractual Performance." *Journal of Political Economy* 89: 615–641.

Klein, B., R. G. Crawford, and A. A. Alchian. 1978. "Vertical Integration, Appropriable Rents, and the Competitive Contracting Process." *Journal of Law and Economics* 21: 297–326.

Kranton, R. E. 1996a. "The Formation of Cooperative Relationships." *Journal of Law, Economcs, and Organization* 12: 214–233.

———. 1996b. "Reciprocal Exchange: A Self-Sustaining System." *American Economic Review* 86: 830–851.

Kranz, S., and S. Ohlendorf. 2009. "Renegotiation-Proof Relational Contracts with Side Payments." University of Bonn, Department of Economics, Bonn.

Kreps, D. M. 1996. "Markets and Hierarchies and (Mathematical) Economic Theory." *Industrial and Corporate Change* 5: 561–595.

Kvaløy, O. 2007. "Asset Specificity and Vertical Integration." *Scandinavian Journal of Economics* 109: 551–572.

Kvaløy, O., and T. E. Olsen. 2006. "Team Incentives in Relational Employment Contracts." *Journal of Labor Economics* 24: 139–169.

———. 2009. "Endogenous Verifiability and Relational Contracting." *American Economic Review* 99: 2193–2208.

Laffont, J.-J., and J. Tirole. 1988. "The Dynamics of Incentive Contracts." *Econometrica* 56: 1153–1175.

Levin, J. 2002. "Multilateral Contracting and the Employment Relationship." *Quarterly Journal of Economics* 117: 1075–1103.

———. 2003. "Relational Incentive Contracts." *American Economic Review* 93: 835–857.

Macaulay, S. 1963. "Non-Contractual Relations in Business: A Preliminary Study." *American Sociological Review* 28: 55–67.

MacLeod, W. B. 2003. "Optimal Contracting with Subjective Evaluation." *American Economic Review* 93: 216–240.

———. 2007a. "Can Contract Theory Explain Social Preferences?" *American Economic Review* 97: 187–192.

———. 2007b. "Reputations, Relationships, and Contract Enforcement." *Journal of Economic Literature* 45: 595–628.

MacLeod, W. B., and J. M. Malcomson. 1988. "Reputation and Hierarchy in Dynamic Models of Employment." *Journal of Political Economy* 96: 832–854.

———. 1989. "Implicit Contracts, Incentive Compatibility, and Involuntary Unemployment." *Econometrica* 57: 447–480.

———. 1998. "Motivation and Markets." *American Economic Review* 88: 388–411.

Macneil, I. R. 1978. "Contracts: Adjustment of Long-Term Economic Relations under Classical, Neoclassical, and Relational Contract Law." *Northwestern University Law Review* 72: 854–904.

Mailath, G. J., and L. Samuelson. 2006. *Repeated Games and Reputations: Long-Run Relationships.* Oxford: Oxford University Press.

Malcomson, J. M. 1999. "Individual Employment Contracts," in O. Ashenfelter and D. Card (eds.), *Handbook of Labor Economics,* volume 3B. Elsevier, Amsterdam, pp. 2291–2372.

Malcomson, J. M. 2012a. "Relational Incentive Contracts with Persistent Private Information." University of Oxford, Department of Economics, Oxford.

———. 2012b. "Relational Incentive Contracts with Private Information." University of Oxford, Department of Economics, Oxford.

Martimort, D., and L. Stole. 2009. "Market Participation in Delegated and Intrinsic Common-Agency Games." *RAND Journal of Economics* 40: 78–102.

McAdams, D. 2011. "Performance and Turnover in a Stochastic Partnership." *American Economic Journal: Microeconomics* 3: 107–142.

McMillan, J., and C. Woodruff. 1999. "Interfirm Relationships and Informal Credit in Vietnam." *Quarterly Journal of Economics* 114: 1285–1320.

Milgrom, P. R., and I. Segal. 2002, "Envelope Theorems for Arbitrary Choice Sets." *Econometrica* 70: 583–601.

Mukherjee, A. 2008. "Sustaining Implicit Contracts When Agents Have Career Concerns: The Role of Information Disclosure." *RAND Journal of Economics* 39: 469–490.

Murphy, K. M., and R. H Topel. 1990. "Efficiency Wages Reconsidered: Theory and Evidence." in Y. Weiss and G. Fishelson (eds.), *Advances in the Theory and Measurement of Unemployment.* Macmillan, London: pp. 204–240.

Obstfeld, M., and K. S. Rogoff. 1996. *Foundations of International Macroeconomics.* Cambridge, MA: MIT Press.

Pearce, D. G., and E. Stacchetti. 1998. "The Interaction of Implicit and Explicit Contracts in Repeated Agency." *Games and Economic Behavior* 23: 75–96.

Prendergast, C. 1993. "The Role of Promotion in Inducing Specific Human Capital Acquisition." *Quarterly Journal of Economics* 108: 523–534.

Radner, R. 1985. "Repeated Principal-Agent Games with Discounting." *Econometrica* 53: 1173–1198.

———. 1986. "Repeated Partnership Games with Imperfect Monitoring and No Discounting." *Review of Economic Studies* 53: 43–57.

Radner, R., R. Myerson, and E. Maskin. 1986. "An Example of a Repeated Partnership Game with Discounting and with Uniformly Inefficient Equilibria." *Review of Economic Studies* 53: 59–69.

Ramey, G., and J. Watson. 1997. "Contractual Fragility, Job Destruction, and Business Cycles." *Quarterly Journal of Economics* 112: 873–911.

———. 2001. "Bilateral Trade and Opportunism in a Matching Market." *Contributions to Theoretical Economics* 1: article 3. http://www.bepress.com/bejte/contributions/vol1/iss1/art3.

Ray, D. 2002. "The Time Structure of Self-Enforcing Agreements." *Econometrica* 70: 547–582.

Rayo, L. 2007. "Relational Incentives and Moral Hazard in Teams." *Review of Economic Studies* 74: 937–963.

Ruzzier, C. 2009. "Asset Specificity and Vertical Integration: Williamson's Hypothesis Reconsidered." Working Paper 09-119, Harvard Business School, Cambridge, MA.

Sabel, C. F. 1993. "Studied Trust: Building New Forms of Cooperation in a Volatile Economy." *Human Relations* 46: 1133–1170.

Sako, M. 1992. *Prices, Quality and Trust: Inter-Firm Relations in Britain and Japan.* Cambridge: Cambridge University Press.

Sannikov, Y., and A. Skrzypacz. 2007. "Impossibility of Collusion under Imperfect Monitoring with Flexible Production." *American Economic Review* 97: 1794–1823.

Schmidt, K. M., and M. Schnitzer. 1995. "The Interaction of Explicit and Implicit Contracts." *Economics Letters* 48: 193–199.

Schöttner, A. 2008. "Relational Contracts, Multitasking, and Job Design." *Journal of Law, Economics, and Organization* 24: 138–162.

Shapiro, C., and J. E. Stiglitz. 1984. "Equilibrium Unemployment as a Worker Discipline Device." *American Economic Review* 74: 433–444.

Sobel, J. 2006. "For Better or Forever: Formal versus Informal Enforcement." *Journal of Labor Economics* 24: 271–297.

Telser, L. G. 1980. "A Theory of Self-Enforcing Agreements." *Journal of Business* 53: 27–44.

Thomas, J., and T. Worrall. 1988. "Self-Enforcing Wage Contracts." *Review of Economic Studies* 55: 541–554.

Thomas, J., and T. Worrall. 2010. "Dynamic Relational Contracts with Credit Constraints." Economics Discussion Paper EDP-1009, University of Manchester, Manchester. Available at: http://ssrn.com/abstract=1599525.

Watson, J. 1999. "Starting Small and Renegotiation." *Journal of Economic Theory* 85: 52–90.

———. 2002. "Starting Small and Commitment." *Games and Economic Behavior* 38: 176–199.

Williamson, O. E. 2000. "The New Institutional Economics: Taking Stock, Looking Ahead." *Journal of Economic Literature* 38: 595–613.

Yang, H. 2012. "Nonstationary Relational Contracts with Adverse Selection." *International Economic Review,* forthcoming.

26

Hybrid Modes of Organization
Alliances, Joint Ventures, Networks, and Other Strange Animals
Claude Ménard

1. Introduction

The central message expressed throughout this chapter is that there is a whole class of economic organizations that contribute substantially to what Coase (1992: 713) called "the institutional structure of production." These arrangements fall neither under pure market relationships nor within "firm boundaries." They multiply because they are viewed as efficient in dealing with knowledge-based activities, solving hold-up problems, and reducing contractual hazards. They have properties of their own that deserve theoretical attention and empirical investigation.

Indeed, although the significance of these arrangements, hereafter identified as "hybrids," remains difficult to quantify, they play a major role in developed market economies. Joint ventures, strategic alliances, sports leagues, franchises, and consortia provide rich examples. In a first approximation, hybrids can be defined as arrangements in which two or more partners pool strategic decision rights as well as some property rights[1] while simultaneously keeping distinct ownership over key assets, so that they require specific devices to coordinate their joint activities and arbitrate the allocation of payoffs (Ménard 1997, 2004). Consequently, this chapter focuses on arrangements with joint mechanisms of governance.[2] It pays particular attention to multilateral agreements ($n > 2$), so as to build ideal types in which contracts are complemented by other means of coordination.

This chapter owes much to the participants in the National Bureau of Economic Research workshop on "Organizational Economics" as well as to participants in numerous seminars and conferences. I have also benefited from extensive exchanges with the volume editors, Robert Gibbons and John Roberts, and from fruitful questions raised by Claudine Desrieux, Anna Grandori, George Hendrikse, Geoffrey Hodgson, Chris Mantzavinos, Paolo Mariti, Mario Morroni, Joanne Oxley, Emmanuel Raynaud, Oliver Williamson, Josef Windsperger, and many others. The usual disclaimer applies.

1. This chapter follows Alchian (1987) in identifying property rights with the capacity to appropriate residual earnings.

2. Outsourcing illustrates the difficulty of delineating hybrids. Most outsourcing arrangements are of the arm's length type, with no specific mechanisms of governance besides contracts. However, there are also outsourcing arrangements with coordinating devices going far beyond what is contractible (e.g., the "Toyota system").

Efforts to capture the specificity of these arrangements within a coherent analytical framework remain underdeveloped. In economics, initial insights came from a coasian perspective, with hybrids viewed as challenging the boundaries of the firm. Richardson (1972) already emphasized the importance of modes of organization mixing cooperation and competition.[3] In his pioneering essay on franchising, Rubin (1978: 223) introduced the term "hybrid" as a catchword, extending the trade-off between market transactions and integration to situations in which decisions are jointly agreed on among firms. This view concurred with the analysis developed simultaneously by Klein et al. (1978). Williamson also pointed out early the significance of these nonstandard agreements, although he initially considered them as unstable and transitory before fully integrating hybrids in his model (Williamson 1975, 1991; Ménard 2009). Meanwhile, a significant literature developed in sociology and managerial sciences, mostly about networks and alliances.

Nevertheless, hybrids remain theoretical orphans, as already noted by Borys and Jemison (1989), and this deficiency translates into "a rather messy situation marked by a cacophony of heterogeneous concepts, theories, and research results" (Oliver and Ebers 1998: 549). A rich empirical material has accumulated, while theory has focused on relatively narrow issues. As rightly emphasized by Baker et al. (2002: 71), economists rarely paid attention to these arrangements, and when they did, "the focus has typically been on asset ownership and other formal aspects of organizational structure."

In this chapter I suggest that the time may have come for economic theory to harvest the abundant insights on hybrids. One obstacle is the diversity of arrangements, from forms close to market relationships to quasi-integrated organizations.[4] However, I shall argue that structural characteristics underlie this diversity. In doing so, I focus on determinants of existence and conditions of stability of hybrids, with a particular attention to the underlying modalities of governance. Section 2 illustrates distinctive features of hybrids with a stylized case, thereafter substantiated by a visit to the richness of these arrangements. Section 3 discusses forces pushing to go hybrid, in the hope of outperforming markets as well as hierarchies. Section 4 examines challenges hybrids face and strategic choices they can make to overcome opportunism. Section 5 explores the governance mechanisms on which hybrids rely to reach stability and remain sustainable. Section 6 proposes a typology of hybrids based on the combination of the elements thus pinpointed. Section 7 concludes with remarks on unsolved problems and policy issues.

2. What Do Hybrids Look Like?

The fluctuating terminology for hybrids signals conceptual difficulties. Three competing terms prevail in the literature: "hybrids," mostly used in economics, particularly in the Coase-Williamson tradition; "alliances," a favorite in management journals; and "networks," which dominates sociology.[5] "Symbiotic arrangements," "clans," and other terms can also be found,

---

3. Almost simultaneously, Blois (1972) pointed out the empirical significance of quasi-vertical integration, although with no reference to Coase.

4. Cheung (1983) argued that there is a continuum in organizations and that contract should be the sole focus of attention. In this chapter I try to show why this approach can be misleading.

5. The term here refers to networks of firms, not to network industries.

although more sporadically. "Hybrid" benefits from covering the variety of interfirm agreements while rooted in theory and models explicitly derived from Coase (1937).[6] I do not intend to emphasize definitional issues here. The fluttering terminology reflects the richness of relationships among businesses using means of coordination alternatives to the price mechanism without integrating. It also reflects the lack of a unified and satisfying theoretical explanation. To fix ideas, I start with an example that illustrates some key issues involved. The picture is then enriched by a visit to the variety of observable forms of hybrids.

2.1. A Stylized Example

In the late 1970s, faced with declining bread consumption and sharp competition from supermarkets using cheap flour and delivering mediocre products at low prices, a group of 35 French millers reacted by developing, successfully, high-quality products signaled by a brand name and supported by a complex organizational arrangement.[7] This arrangement defines (1) a formal structure, (2) an allocation of rights, and (3) governing modalities that differ markedly from the polar cases of markets and hierarchies.

First, the millers created a legal entity to develop high-quality products, market them, and guarantee compliance to their standards by all partners. This entity—let us call it the "strategic center"—is governed by a board of administration, of which each miller is a member. Decisions by the board are made according to a "one person, one vote" rule, notwithstanding the uneven distribution of capital: at one end of the spectrum, one miller holds 62 shares while at the other end, another miller has 391 shares. The center legally owns the brand name, delegating its use to the millers. The brand is marketed through a network of franchised bakers—nowadays more than 3,000 bakers are affiliated—who commit to sell exclusively products using inputs delivered by the millers or certified by the center. Each miller has an incentive to recruit bakers, whose affiliation is conditional on acceptance and monitoring by the center. Policies regarding the brand are implemented by an executive committee of twelve millers, elected by their peers for 6 years, and a marketing committee of three members. In addition, an ethics committee of three elected millers is in charge of solving conflicts. In sum, the millers own a franchisor to which they delegate the right to monitor and discipline them as well as to supervise the franchised bakers.

Second, this arrangement proceeds through a complex allocation of rights. Each miller keeps control over key assets, that is, mill(s) and the logistics needed to collect inputs and deliver flour. Partners can use these assets for activities beyond the control of the joint entity, for example, producing and delivering flour to industrial bakeries not affiliated to the brand. However, the legally distinct strategic center holds property rights over the brand name and owns several facilities to do research, manage quality control, and train bakers, and it also develops new products. The strategic center thus creates new assets that it formally owns.

Decision rights are allocated accordingly. The millers remain fully responsible for their own resources and their strategies. The strategic center makes decisions regarding the evolution of

---

6. According to the *Oxford English Dictionary,* the term "hybrid" goes back to 1601 and designates the offspring of two different species.

7. This subsection draws on Ménard and Raynaud (2010).

the brand name (new processes, new products, quality standards, and marketing strategies) and of the governance structure (status of shareholders, contracts with bakers, allocation of social capital, and acceptance of new entrants or exclusion of partners). When it comes to payoffs, each miller remains the sole residual claimant for profits generated by his or her own assets, including benefits from the spillover effects of the brand name. However, royalties paid by the bakers are shared with the strategic center, which also bills services to the millers (e.g., quality control). In principle, profits from the strategic center are redistributed according to the number of shares, although in practice they have been systematically reinvested in the development of the brand.

Third, the governance by the strategic center is framed by contracts and by the above-mentioned ethics committee that operates as a private court.

There are two sets of contracts: contracts linking bakers to the network, which are typical franchise contracts,[8] and contracts between the millers and the strategic center, which determine the core of the arrangement. Indeed, the millers, who are the shareholders, sign a contract with the strategic center that gives them the right to operate under the brand they formally own. The goal is to promote spillover effects by developing high-quality products, new techniques, and advertisement, while protecting parties against negative externalities, such as millers cheating on the quality of inputs delivered or adopting free-riding strategies to attract or capture franchisees (the bakers).[9] These goals are embedded in contractual clauses codifying (1) the production process (control over equipment, determination after each crop of the required quality of flour, etc.); (2) marketing conditions; (3) conditions under which the center can ban a shareholder from the arrangement; (4) the right of the center to authorize other millers to supply bakers previously affiliated to a noncompliant partner. These clauses by themselves confer significant power to the center. They are complemented by internal rules and the role of the ethics committee.

Internal rules facilitate upstream and downstream control. Upstream, major decisions—such as changes in statutes, changes in the contracts between millers and the center, or exclusion—require two-thirds of the votes on the board. Rules preventing any miller to hold more than 15% of the rights and prohibiting the sale of shares to outsiders without board approval reinforce this control. Downstream, strict internal rules regulate relationships between millers and franchisees (the bakers): entry is filtered by the center, which also keeps an eye on newly affiliated bakers through a probation of 6 months. Once affiliated, technical and commercial assistance provided by the center facilitates control over the relationships between a miller and the bakers in his pool.

Last, the so-called "ethics" committee operates as a private court regulating intrabrand competition. Indeed, the reputation premium of the brand name (remarkably stable at about 10%) as well as competition among millers to attract new bakers or capture affiliated ones fuel incentives to free ride. The elected ethics committee is there to thwart these strategies thanks to significant discretionary power, particularly the possibility to impose penalties or recommend exclusion of repeatedly noncompliant millers. On all these issues, the board operates as a court of appeal. With formal contracts binding partners, it would be technically possible to turn to

---

8. See Lafontaine and Slade (2007).

9. The affiliation of bakers determines volume sold and hence, profits. A typical free-riding behavior for a miller is to capture a baker who has been prospected and possibly initiated by another miller of the group by offering advantageous conditions—because the free rider did not invest in the search and training process.

the legal system. However, this approach is viewed as disruptive and risky, incompleteness of contracts making the issue highly uncertain. After 30 years of implementation, partners have never resorted to courts.

To sum up, this case illustrates a mode of organization in which co-owners, who compete in their joint activities as well as in activities independent of their arrangement, delegate to a specific entity the right to monitor and discipline them. They do so because the arrangement can create new assets that generate extra profits while simultaneously producing positive externalities[10] on their other activities. The complex allocation of rights that support the formal architecture involved as well as the mechanisms of governance needed for the success and durability of the arrangement is not specific to the millers' case.

2.2. A Brief Visit to the "Zoo"

Indeed, this stylized example captures only part of the richness of forms mixing cooperation and competition in interfirm relationships. From joint ventures to franchisee-owned franchisors, sports leagues, condominiums, consortia, or even cooperatives, "firms have invented far more ways to work together than organizational economics has so far expressed (not to mention evaluated)" (Baker et al. 2008: 146). In what follows, I focus on situations in which firms pass decision rights and even property rights across boundaries, so that some rights are no longer controlled by a single party. I illustrate the variety of solutions implemented by several different institutional structures dealing with shared control. This review is not intended to be exhaustive but rather points out properties analyzed thereafter.

In its usual form, *subcontracting* borders on standard market relationships, with parties sharing some decision rights while keeping assets and property rights distinct. For example, Toyota shares with its privileged subcontractors substantial decisions regarding the design of its cars. This arrangement often relies on the stability of the relationship. In a pioneering paper based on extensive interviews with 38 homebuilders in eastern Massachusetts, Eccles (1981: 339) discussed agreements between general contractors and subcontractors "over fairly long periods of time and only infrequently established through competitive bidding." Although most projects were short term, coordination requirements and the need for constant adaptation provided incentives to operate with the same partners. On average, relations persisted for more than 5 years (one persisted for 37 years), largely exceeding the duration of formal contracts. In more than 80% of the cases, subcontractors were selected through bilateral negotiations; less than 20% went through competitive bidding. This process does not discard the role of competition: the possibility of bidding maintains pressure. Other studies, particularly in the automobile industry, have shown the diversity of subcontracting, from arm's-length relationships to forms closer to supply-chain systems, up to quasi-integration (Helper and Levine 1992; Dyer 1997; Holmström and Roberts 1998). However, they all share at least two characteristics: key assets and decision rights remain distinct (as in the case of the millers), while one firm operates as the strategic center (which is distinct from the millers).

---

10. For example, the reputation gained through the brand has a positive impact on a miller's relationship with parties not dealing with the brand (e.g., industrial bakeries or restaurants).

Supplier parks, "a cluster of suppliers located adjacent to, or close to, a final assembly point" (Sako 2005: 3), share properties with subcontracting, although site interdependence usually imposes tighter coordination. The Volkswagen assembly line of trucks and buses in Resende, Brazil, is typical. Several firms operate under the same roof. They keep key property rights and decision rights distinct (several also supply competitors). However, specific assets and substantial decision rights are shared on the site (e.g., decisions regarding the physical distribution of equipment or the adjustments among partners along the assembly line imposed by the modular design of the subsystems). Supplier parks can also be partially virtual (e.g., Toshiba and its 200 direct partners and 600 "grandchild companies") or almost entirely so, as with Dell.[11] In all cases, the allocation of rights and payoffs as well as coordination devices remain an issue.

Whether physically located or virtual, supplier parks mostly operate under the control of one firm. However, there are cases in which shared activities are monitored through different forms of joint agreements, with partners in a more or less symmetrical position. *Strategic alliances* have attracted a lot of attention in managerial sciences. They can be characterized as "the relatively enduring interfirm cooperative arrangements, involving flows and linkages that utilize resources and/or governance structures from autonomous organizations, for the joint accomplishment of individual goals linked to the corporate mission of each sponsoring firm" (Parkhe 1993: 795). Partners maintain distinct core assets and keep control over related property rights, thus departing from mergers and acquisitions. However, they jointly plan and monitor substantial activities, as in the airline industry, using contracts to coordinate and build relational trust, which particularly matters when duration imposes continuing adjustments, making spot or short-term agreements of the market type inappropriate (Jorde and Teece 1989; Gulati 1995b). Using a database of 12,500 contracts between biotech and pharmaceutical firms from 1973 to 2001, Baker et al. (2008) showed that the twelve top biotech firms and the twelve top pharmaceutical firms were directly involved in more than 32% of the alliances in the sector. Hence, a few firms form many alliances, defining a dense network of ties mostly related to research and development (R&D) projects (55% of the contracts). However, other studies show that R&D alliances can also be a one-shot game (Ryall and Sampson 2006). Holmström (1989) suggested that R&D projects may be prone to alliances because they are: (1) risky, (2) unpredictable, (3) long-term and multistage, (4) labor intensive, and (5) idiosyncratic. The resulting problems of observability, with related risks of opportunism, push toward constraining contractual clauses and cautiously delineated rights. However, R&D projects are not the only engine of alliances. Strategic alliances exist in many other activities, from wholesaling in the American hardware industry (Dwyer and Oh 1988) to the airline industry (Holmström and Roberts 1998) to alliances between equipment and component suppliers (Artz and Brush 2000). In all these arrangements, the relative symmetry among partners give contracts a key role as a coordinating tool.

Supply chain systems also rely on contracts, but they differ from strategic alliances with respect to the density and extension of shared rights. Based on complementary activities and/or competencies among autonomous partners, they require tight coordination across stages, usually from production to distribution. In a pioneering paper, Brown (1984) pinpointed the tight

---

11. Some integrated firms attempt to replicate traits of these external networks, for example, ABB and its 1,200 autonomous entities and 4,500 profit centers (Achrol 1997).

organization of transactions among independent parties in the dairy milk industry through administered channels that monitored quantities, controlled assortment, and guaranteed quality. Ménard (1996) exhibited similar arrangements in the poultry industry, with a complex set of contracts linking growers, slaughterhouses, integrators, and distributors. The design varies, according to whether the arrangement is monitored by a leading firm or a specific governing entity. Supply-chain systems benefit from powerful market incentives while providing tight control over key transactions, without the burden of integration. The analysis of these forms is a booming industry, in the agrifood sector, logistic, and so on.[12]

Supply chains almost always involve production, while *franchises* concern primarily distribution. However, boundaries between these forms are blurred, many franchisors having developed tight vertical coordination to control inputs as well as output, as illustrated by McDonald's. What differentiates franchising from most supply chains is the large number of partners abandoning part of their decision rights while pooling property rights to benefit from brand names and joint actions. Franchise systems also share characteristics of subcontracting because of the central role of the franchisor, whether it is a unique entity or a group, as in the millers' relation to bakers. The now-abundant literature on franchising almost entirely focuses on agency problems and financial constraints as explanations of their existence, with little concern so far for the various forms they take and the problems of governance they raise beyond incentive issues (but see Lafontaine and Slade 2007, this volume).

Joint ventures exhibit important characteristics of hybrids in a relatively pure form. Joint ventures "are simultaneously contractual agreements between two or more organizations and a separate legal (and usually organizational) entity with its own purpose" (Borys and Jemison 1989: 245; see also Hennart 1988: 361–362). Parent companies transfer some assets and property rights as well as some decision rights to a child company monitored by a specific governing body, while parents remain autonomous and often compete on other activities. This mix of global sovereignty and local cooperation involves forms of hierarchy that complement contracts. The motivation comes from expected gains, either from knowledge-based activities requiring competences that exceed separate capabilities (as in R&D projects) or from economies of scale (as when competing automakers jointly produce transmissions). However, joint ventures confront issues of governance (e.g., about rights they can claim over parents' resources), of loss of control (e.g., the irreversibility of transfer of knowledge), and of rent allocation (e.g., measuring the value added of scientists involved in joint activities). Such problems may explain the short lifespan of many joint ventures (Hennart 1988).

There are many other ways to organize interfaces among partners. *Partnership* is another nonstandard mode of organization, taking various forms, from law firms to the collective organization of salmon fishermen of the Pacific Northwest (Farrell and Scotchmer 1988). These arrangements often develop to deal with common pool resources. *Cooperatives* define another important category, almost a class of its own. The variety of their forms makes their characterization difficult, because they are spread over a wide spectrum, from quasi-integrated firms to marketlike arrangements. However, numerous cooperatives share characteristics of hybrids with respect to the joint allocation of rights and their mode of governance, dominated by the "one person, one vote" principle (see Hansmann 1988; Ménard 2007b).

---

12. See such journals as *Supply Chain Management* and *Journal of Chain and Network Sciences*.

In sociology and managerial sciences, hybrids are often described as *networks*.[13] In a pioneering paper, Thorelli (1986: 37) characterized networks as long-term relationships between two or more organizations. Powell (1990) suggested a distinction between (1) networks structuring craft industries (e.g., construction or publishing), (2) networks shaping industrial districts (e.g., the Modena area or Silicon Valley), (3) networks framing vertical disaggregation (e.g., subcontracting in the automobile industry), and (4) networks organizing horizontal coordination (e.g., strategic alliances and partnership). The term then becomes a label more than a concept. A more specific approach, closer to Thorelli and to our concept of hybrids, identifies networks with durable collective action that requires specific governance. Early developments in the telephone industry illustrate the point (Barnett 1990; Barnett and Carroll 1993). The introduction of wire coils and new power technology at the beginning of the twentieth century allowed the expansion of long-distance calls, which required coordination among hundreds of companies (public and private), cooperatives, and "farmer lines" operated by groups of farmers.[14] Coordination imposed technological standardization, while parties maintained differentiated services and distinct rights. Similarly, the development of automated teller machines substantially increased the volume of transactions and the variety of services but also required costly coordination and control among banks, with ambiguous organizational effects between incentives to integrate and incentives to outsource (Clemons and Row 1992). The notion of network is also often used, particularly in sociology, to tag minisocieties "of interdependent, reciprocal exchange relationships" (Achrol 1997: 68), shaped by "the density, multiplexity, and reciprocity of ties and a shared value system defining *membership* roles and social responsibilities" (Achrol 1997: 59). Aoki (2001: 366–370) described venture capitalists of Silicon Valley accordingly.

All these arrangements as well as others (condominiums, consortia, etc.) differ from integrated solutions (the "firm"), which rely on a center that keeps control over decision rights and owns assets in the last resort, with residual claimants well identified. They also differ from markets, at least as defined in the neoclassical tradition, because markets preclude central coordination, so that assets and related payoffs remain with separate owners, parties interacting exclusively through prices or through contracts that respect their autonomy of decision. However, hybrids can lean toward one or the other of these polar cases, depending on the intensity of the coordination required and the density of rights shared (see Section 6).

To contrast hybrids with hierarchies or markets, let us boil their properties down to their simplest content. Let us consider two firms, 1 and 2, and four assets {A, a; B, b}, with A and B related to the core activity of 1 and 2, respectively, and remaining within their boundaries, while a and b are assets valuable only if used jointly. Each firm holds full decision rights, D_A and D_B, while rights d_a and d_b require coordination, because they are linked to the joint usage of a and b. The resulting payoffs are therefore Π_A, Π_B, π_a, and π_b, with the last two generated if and only if the corresponding assets are jointly used (profits are zero otherwise). Last, we identify the

13. The term "cluster" is also used, although less often.

14. During 1910–1930, 707 companies were operating in Pennsylvania. Interestingly, public authorities facilitated coordination. Between 1904 and 1919, 34 states adopted laws mandating interconnection among proximate systems. At the federal level, the Kingsbury agreement obliged large American firms to accept connection all over the United States.

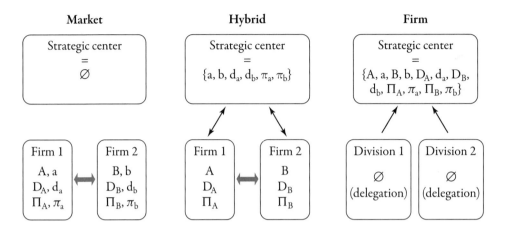

Figure 1. Modes of organization contrasted.

governing entity, if it exists and whatever form it takes, as the strategic center. Three resulting ideal types (markets, hierarchies, and hybrids) are summarized in Figure 1.

In markets, rights are allocated distinctly, and partners process transactions through the price system, without the interference of a joint strategic center. Cooperation that might be required to value some assets is monitored through contracts that do not encroach on the rights of the parties. In firms, divisions hold rights under delegation: in the last resort, they remain submitted to the control of the strategic center (the "headquarters"). In hybrids, key rights are in the hands of autonomous partners keeping title as residual claimants, while subsets of assets, rights, and associated payoffs are shared and monitored jointly. The following three sections explore further why parties prefer this last variety of arrangements, what makes them sustainable, and what governance mechanisms could allow them to outperform other modes of organization.

3. Why Go Hybrid?

Understanding why firms invest in projects that require loss of control over key rights raises important questions. Why do firms accept this loss of control? What forces push parties to go hybrid, rather than relying on pure market relationships or fully integrating?

As already noted by Rubin (1978: 223), these questions are very much in line with the problem raised by Coase (1937; see also Cheung 1983). Choosing alternatives to markets as well as to integration is motivated by expectations of improved allocation of resources: if hybrids exist and remain stable over time, it is likely because under certain conditions, they are better at handling transactions. However, the paucity of economic explanations of why hybrids develop is striking.[15] In what follows, I briefly review theories, embedded in models exposed in other

15. Other disciplines were faster in taking into account hybrids. Grandori and Soda (1995) already provided a stimulating survey of organization studies on hybrids, while Oliver and Ebers (1998) reviewed a large set of contributions already available in sociology and managerial sciences.

chapters of this book, assessing the existence of hybrids. I then turn to a highly relevant empirical literature that relates only partially to these models to better understand forces favoring hybrids.

3.1. Theoretical Explanations

Any satisfactory explanation of hybrids must shed light on what motivates parties to pool strategic assets and share rights without integrating. It must also exhibit how these distinctive arrangements can provide adequate safeguards against risks of free riding while keeping incentives superior to alternative solutions. The conception of the firm as a production function and of markets as a price-formation device do not even account for the existence of hybrids. Economies of specialization (as in the construction industry), of scale (as with shared trademarks), or of scope (as in joint R&D projects) likely play a role in the decision to pool resources, but they do not explain why the optimal solution would not be merger or acquisition.

Only recently has economic theory addressed hybrids, with transaction cost economics playing a pioneering role. Agency theory and relational contract theory have also taken into account some hybrid forms, while less-developed approaches, such as the resource-based view, have provided useful insights. Because leading theories are presented in other chapters of this book, here I report only elements relevant to the analysis of hybrids.

3.1.1. Transaction Cost Economics
Transaction cost economics (TCE) deserves priority. The idea that there are alternative ways to organize transactions goes back to Coase (1937), followed by Williamson (1975). Both focused on the trade-off between markets and firms. However, in *Markets and Hierarchies,* Williamson (1975: 109) noted the existence of "intermediate forms of contracting," but he expressed doubts about their stability and considered them as transitory. It is only in *The Economic Institutions of Capitalism* that he endorsed a more positive approach to arrangements later christened "hybrids," going as far as considering them potentially "dominant" (Williamson 1985: 83). In 1991, he explicitly modeled them as a governance structure that could be an efficient alternative to markets and hierarchies, from which they differ with respect to (1) contract law, (2) adaptability, and (3) incentives and control (Williamson 1991). Hybrids would fit transactions requiring assets of intermediate specificity and facing moderate uncertainty, thus providing a middle-of-the-road solution. The resulting concept remained a bit fuzzy, with its reference to "semi-strong" governance captured essentially through "contract law." This vagueness may explain why some Williamsonians questioned the possibility of a theory of hybrids (Masten 1996: 12), while critics challenged the idea that the attributes distinguishing hierarchies from markets (asset specificity, uncertainty, and frequency) provide adequate tools to understand the existence and properties of hybrids (Powell 1996; Hodgson 2002).[16]

Nevertheless, TCE has inspired a huge empirical literature (see Section 3.2), partly oriented toward enriching the heuristic model to substantiate the reasons that parties go hybrid. An illustration is provided by Artz and Brush (2000), who addressed the often rehearsed criticism,

---

16. From a different perspective, Holmström and Roberts (1998: 92) argue that "many of the hybrid organizations that are emerging are characterized by high degrees of uncertainty, frequency and asset specificity, yet they do not lead to integration."

going back to Granovetter (1985), that TCE does not capture the social dimension support-ing interfirm agreements. To include the role of interactions in the governance of hybrids, they introduced relational norms as a complementary attribute (see also Gulati et al. 2000).[17] Us-ing a different perspective, Ménard and Klein (2004) emphasized that the complexity of the transactions at stake might explain the decision to go hybrid, while Ménard (1996) noted that interdependent transactions may command such arrangements when parties want to avoid the drawbacks of integration, particularly bureaucratic costs and weak incentives. Notwithstand-ing their limits, these contributions and numerous others testify to the efforts of TCE to better capture the nature and strength of hybrids as alternatives to markets or hierarchies.

3.1.2. Relational Contracts

In partial continuity with TCE, the literature on *relational contracts* has shown a growing in-terest in hybrids (Klein et al. 1978; Klein and Murphy 1988; Baker et al. 2002; Malcomson, this volume). The initial inspiration comes from Macaulay (1963) and MacNeil (1974, 1978), who introduced the expression "relational" to emphasize the mix of contractible and noncon-tractible elements and the importance of the latter.[18] According to Goldberg (1980; also Baker et al. 2002), parties establish tight bonds to limit the impact of (1) imperfect and costly informa-tion, (2) opportunistic behavior, and (3) difficulties for outsiders to enforce agreements plagued with nonverifiable elements. Hence, "the parties will be willing to absorb a lot of apparent static inefficiency in pursuit of their relational goals" (Goldberg 1980: 339).

Formalizing this approach in a model initially developed to account for labor relations within firms, Baker, Gibbons, and Murphy combined TCE and the new property rights theory to ex-plain what forces push firms toward such solutions as joint ventures or strategic alliances (Baker et al. 2008). In this version, they differentiate governance structures according to how rights over assets and spillover payoffs are allocated. Even if relational contracts might help deal with non-contractibilities, they can also generate tensions and conflicts, and the magnitude of the resulting transaction costs depends on whether the coordinated use of assets complements or competes with the core activities of parties involved. The problem then becomes that of choosing a gov-ernance structure that allows parties to maximize their payoffs while facilitating adjustments. Hybrids provide alternative solutions, possibly optimal ones, when there are significant non-contractibilities.[19]

---

17. Using a survey of 400 firms specializing in industrial and machining equipment, electronic and electrical machinery, computer equipment, and transportation machinery, Artz and Brush (2000) approximated relational norms through three components (with associated proxies): collaboration, continuity in shared expectations, and communication strategy.

18. When referring to "relational contracts," economists emphasize the rational behavior of parties expecting future exchanges, while sociologists, who also refer to "relational governance," intend to capture norms and social ties emerging from prior exchanges (Poppo and Zenger 2002: 710). In the managerial literature, "relational" often refers to informal contracts as opposed to formal ones (Carson et al. 2006). In line with Goldberg (1980), Baker et al. (2002) or Malcomson (this volume) instead seek to incorporate noncontractible elements into the analysis.

19. This approach departs from the prevailing one in "the new property rights," which focuses on who of A or B owns assets; joint ownership may be feasible but most of the time is considered to be suboptimal (see Holmström 1999, who emphasized that in that approach it never pays to have joint ownership, because either side can veto the use of assets). Halonen (2002) extended the Grossman-Hart-Moore model (see Hart and Moore 1990) to cases in which it could be optimal to share some rights, but it is not clear if we end up with a different governance structure or simply a distinct sharing rule.

A major characteristic and a limitation of this explanation is that rights ultimately remain in the hands of separate entities, while noncontractibilities make agreements unenforceable by courts, so that the outcome depends on (relational) reputation. As Malcomson (this volume: Section 13) rightly emphasizes, "relational contracts in these models are a substitute for enforcement by courts, not a substitute for careful planning."

In contrast to TCE, this approach so far remains an exercise in theory. Some empirical analyses relate to "the spirit" of relational contracts in that they try to capture ex post adaptations when some decisions are noncontractible. For example, referring explicitly to MacNeil (1978) and Baker et al. (2002), Poppo and Zenger (2002) use 152 reliable responses (out of 181) from randomly selected senior corporate managers of information services to show that relational governance complements formal contracts. "Relational governance" is here understood as social processes emerging from repeated interactions that facilitate adaptation.[20] However, such tests have limited relevance to the theory because of conceptual differences (e.g., between relational governance and relational contract).

3.1.3. Agency Theory

There are alternative explanations to the existence of hybrids. *Agency theory* inspired numerous research papers on franchising (Brickley and Dark 1987; Lafontaine and Slade 1997, 2007), with incentives and financial motivation viewed as the main issues. For example, Maness (1996) and Holmström and Roberts (1998) suggest that franchise dominates fast food but not supermarkets because franchising provides better incentives to local managers having to monitor multiple inputs simultaneously, while costs in supermarkets mostly come from inventory and warehousing, which can be handled through specialized functions within an integrated structure. However, Lafontaine and Slade (1997, 2007) demonstrated that franchise contracts do not deliver tailored incentives, and that financial motivation has a weak explanatory power, contrary to what the theory predicts. More generally, Lafontaine and Slade (2007) have shown that TCE prevails over agency theory when it comes to predictability, and that the latter hardly explains the existence and variety of franchise systems.

3.1.4. Resource-Based View

The *resource-based view* is another influential approach, particularly in organization studies and management sciences. In essence, it conceives of networks and other hybrids as ways to deal with uncertainties and change by sharing essential inputs, particularly competencies (Wernerfelt 1984; Nooteboom 1999: 8–42). A positive contribution of this view is to have attracted attention on the key role of learning and capabilities. However, it hardly explains why integration is not preferred to hybrids and why there are so many ways to face uncertainty.

To sum up, we still need a convincing theory telling us why hybrids exist and prosper and how they differ from alternative modes of organization. However, and notwithstanding their limitations, the contributions summarized above help frame the partial explanations dispersed in the empirical literature.

---

20. Relational governance is captured through four dimensions: open communication and sharing information; trust; dependence; and cooperation, with associated indicators focusing on relations between vendors and buyers.

3.2. Empirical Evidence

A substantial part of this literature can be related to the unsettling question raised by Simon (1951) and reactivated by Cheung (1983): why do autonomous economic entities abandon substantial rights without certainties about the payoff? More specifically, why are there arrangements that purposely avoid relying primarily on prices to coordinate without going as far as integration, in the hope of outperforming markets as well as hierarchies? Three determinants emerge from an abundant literature only partially grounded on the theories above: improved capacity to face uncertainty, the creation of value through mutually accepted dependence, and expected spillovers if adequate sharing rules are implemented.

3.2.1. An Instrument to Deal with Uncertainty

A possible motivation to go hybrid is that sharing rights and pooling resources improve capacities to face uncertainty. I understand uncertainty as contingencies difficult or impossible to predict that generate adaptation problems (John and Weitz 1988). As already pointed out by Eccles (1981) in his study on the construction industry, interfirm connections respond to a combination of the specificity and high variability of each project, making adaptability a key issue.

Uncertainty has always been viewed by TCE as a key attribute conditioning organizational choices ex ante. TCE also shares with the relational contract approach the idea that ex post non-contractibilities impose adaptation, determining the fitness of these choices. However, there are few tests in economics of the role of uncertainty in the decision to go hybrid,[21] although uncertainty is viewed as a driving force in the sociological and managerial literature (Gulati and Gargiulo 1999). For example, Carson et al. (2006: 1059) proposed a distinction between volatility, defined as "the rate and unpredictability of change in an environment over time," stemming from exogenous shocks, and ambiguity, understood as "the degree of uncertainty inherent in perceptions of the environment state irrespective of its change over time." Using data from 125 informants on client-sponsored R&D relationships, they showed that formal contracts would be inefficient when volatility is high, while relational contracts fail when ambiguity is high.

This result suggests diversity in the types and sources of uncertainty, pushing parties to pool resources without integrating. It might partially explain the variety of hybrids. First, demand can be unstable or unpredictable. Using a survey of 183 responses collected in three Canadian industrial sectors (nonelectrical machinery, electrical and electronic machinery, and transportation equipment), Joshi and Stump (1999) showed that market turbulence plays a more significant role than competitive intensity in the decision to go hybrid. Second, technological change can promote hybrids as a mean to accelerate innovation or its adoption (Park 1996; Ghosh and John 1999; Powell 2003; Ryall and Sampson 2006). Superior technologies require a flexibility that the bureaucracy of integrated firms hardly provides, while hybrids would benefit from shared learning and resources (Anderson and Gatignon 2005). Third, variations in the quality of inputs and/or outputs may require tighter coordination than markets provide, as supply chain systems illustrate (Ménard and Valceschini 2005). Fourth, the risk of opportunism might encourage

---

21. There are some tests on the role of uncertainty in decisions to integrate, for example, Anderson (1985) and Saussier (2000), who estimated the role of uncertainty in the make-or-buy trade-off.

constraining agreements that mitigate hazards while preserving autonomy on key decisions. The role of opportunism in organizational choices (Williamson 1975: 26–30) underlies countless tests, starting with Anderson (1985).[22] It provoked strong reactions, particularly among sociologists, who defend trust as a more likely response to uncertainty. In both cases, there is room for hybrids. Finally, unsecured environments (e.g., property rights poorly defined or not backed by adequate institutions) generate "appropriability hazards," as in technology transfers, which hybrids could overcome without the disadvantages of full integration (Oxley 1999).

In developing joint strategies, sharing knowledge and risks, implementing common standards, and adopting adequate governance, hybrids might provide solutions not available to alternative arrangements (Robinson and Stuart 2007; Baker et al. 2008). This possibility could explain preferences for socially embedded relationships rather than arm's-length relationships when uncertainty is high (Khanna 1998; Gulati 1998), when high adaptability is required (Uzzi 1997; Podolny and Page 1998), or when it is difficult to differentiate between poor performance and bad luck (Park 1996: 803). However, the exact impact of uncertainty on the choice and performance of hybrids remains underexplored, likely because of difficulties in finding adequate proxies and collecting appropriate data.

3.2.2. Creating Value through Accepted Interdependence
Partners in hybrids share some rights and assets, although often remaining competitors and being uncertain about possible payoffs, as illustrated by the millers' case (see Section 2.1) or sports leagues. Why do they accept this mutual dependence on strategic segments of their activities, even when uncertainty is low?

An unambiguous answer is that they expect added value from their joint investments as well as from the spillover effects of these investments on assets and capabilities not pooled: they commit in the hope of creating value otherwise unattainable (Borys and Jemison 1989: 241). This strategic choice goes beyond cost minimization (Gulati 1998). As noted by Madhok and Tallman (1998: 336), "the flows of quasi-rents that stem from the dynamics among these relationships tend to hold the system together so long as the participant actors recognize that rents could well disappear with the alliance relationship, thus providing an economic incentive to avoid opportunistic actions."[23]

What are the sources of this added value?

Size is one possible determinant. When investments exceed the capacities of parties working solo (e.g., marketing products, promoting standards, and supporting R&D), firms might expect rents from bundled resources.[24] Joint assets might generate economies of scale and/or economies of scope (Park 1996). However, this explanation remains limited, notwithstanding advantages based on technology. First, if capital markets are efficient, why cannot firms find adequate support from banks or other lenders rather than taking the risk of pooling strategic

---

22. It is also a key argument used by Hansmann (this volume) to explain the existence of franchisee-owned franchisors.

23. See also Klein et al. (1978) and Klein (1996).

24. Powell (2003) argues the other way around: spin-offs would often be preferred to multidivisional structures by large corporations in order to benefit from financial advantages (e.g., obtaining federal grants, issuing stocks, and attracting new investors fascinated by the "new economy") as well as from legal ones (e.g., limited liability).

resources? Second, if size matters, why not integrate? In a survey of 225 independently owned companies in the human biotechnology sector during 1990–1994, Powell et al. (1996: 120) showed that it is from building "a sea of informal relations" rather than from size that firms expect gains.[25]

In that respect, complementarity might provide a powerful incentive to go hybrid. If it secures supply of existing resources, allows access to new resources, or facilitates diversification, mutual dependence becomes strategically valuable. In the same vein, separate firms may not have the resources to develop independent absorptive capacities (Cohen and Levinthal 1990), thus motivating strategic alliances, joint R&D projects, and the like. Complementarities between innovative firms and well-established ones when financial markets impose tight constraints may also encourage hybrid arrangements. Lerner et al. (2003) argue that the receptivity of financial markets to biotech is cyclical, so that when markets are cold, biotech firms turn to pharmaceutical and chemical firms. However, complementarities involve risk: innovation may fail, demand may change, and partners may behave opportunistically. Numerous studies emphasize the role of relational norms and social ties as buffers against these risks (e.g., Heide and John 1992; Artz and Brush 2000).

Learning effects provide another incentive to go hybrid, partially overlapping with complementarity. When markets cannot adequately bundle tacit knowledge and capabilities while firms need skills they cannot develop autonomously, incentives to join forces develop (Teece et al. 1997; Madhok and Tallman 1998; Ryall and Sampson 2006). Hybrids become portfolios of the skills they transfer and recombine, allowing novel syntheses (Powell et al. 1996; Stuart and Podolny 1996; Dyer and Singh 1998; Podolny and Page 1998; Powell 2003). However, joint learning effects remain difficult to capture and model, so that assessing their role is challenging.

These factors point out expected gains from pooled resources. However, sharing resources has drawbacks: it requires interfirm planning, which restricts individual decision rights and might generate costly negotiations and/or renegotiations. So why not prefer integration? Coase (1937) suggested limited managerial capacities as an explanation. Williamson (1996: 150) goes a step further, arguing that "selective intervention" that would allow integrated firms to replicate successful properties of alternative arrangements can hardly be achieved. Brickley and Dark (1987) argue that franchising develops because acquisitions may be too costly or too difficult to swallow, or resources needed to integrate may be too difficult to evaluate (see also Madhok and Tallman 1998; Brickley 1999). Baker et al. (2002) propose an alternative explanation. Upstream ownership decreases downstream parties' temptation to renege but creates temptation for the upstream party to renege. If the first consideration dominates, integration is optimal; otherwise, sharing rights through nonintegrative arrangements could offer the appropriate solution.

3.2.3. Sharing Rent while Checking Opportunism

Williamson (1991) argued that when markets do not provide adequate coordination, hybrids might be the first best, because they maintain higher incentives than do integrated firms. Incentives in hybrids are three dimensional: (1) each firm remains a residual claimant on payoffs provided by its own assets; (2) each partner can claim a share of the rent generated by jointly used assets; and (3) all partners may cash rents from activities unrelated to the arrangement,

---

25. "We argue that when knowledge is broadly distributed and brings a competitive advantage, the locus of innovation is found in a network of interorganizational relationships" (Powell et al. 1996: 119).

thanks to spillover effects of their joint reputation. In sum, parties accept mutual dependence because they expect increased ex post surplus, which improves ex ante incentives to join and invest.[26]

In that context, allocation of asset ownership becomes a key issue, because "[it] provides levers that influence bargaining outcomes and hence incentives" (Holmström and Roberts 1998: 79). However, this reasoning presumes the possibility of an unambiguous distribution of rights, while in many hybrids payoffs of types (2) and (3) are not contractible, or only partially so. Going hybrid and relying on relational contracts might then be an efficient solution when costs of integration would be too high and contributions from interdependent assets are difficult to assess. This approach is consistent with Hansmann (this volume), who emphasizes the trade-off between costs of ownership and those of contracting when choosing a mode of organization. Although there are cases of returns strictly proportional to equity shares, as in many joint ventures, most hybrids rely on incomplete agreements. This reliance comes about because standard contracts perform poorly or because of measurement problems, as in joint R&D, so that "organizing a satisfactory split of the gains becomes non trivial" (Ghosh and John 1999: 133).[27] Inadequate allocation of rents could challenge the comparative advantages of hybrids, with partners (1) scaling back investments, (2) adapting less, or (3) forgoing activities that raise hazardous measurement problems. This explains why hybrids are often considered suboptimal (Rey and Tirole 2001).

If we keep in mind this strategic significance of rent sharing rules in hybrids, we would expect an abundant literature on this issue. It is not so. Contributions remain scarce and focus essentially on two mechanisms, royalties and tournaments, which both presume well-defined rights. Royalty rules have been explored extensively for franchise systems. They typically have a linear form, such as

$$\text{Fees} = F + \beta y,$$

where F is a lump sum; y is the total sales; and β is the royalty rate, in most cases in the 4–8% range (Lafontaine 1993; Lafontaine and Slade 1997). This standardized rule challenges the idea that contracts vary incentives to match specific conditions across sectors, regions, or the like. Ménard (1996) reached a similar conclusion in his analysis of producers' groups in the certified agrifood sector, and Rubin (1978: 227) already wondered why franchisees accept such rigid rules.[28]

---

26. In the parlance of game theory, partners cooperate because they expect a net positive value. Parkhe (1993) compares strategic alliances to a stag hunt, with hunters pooling their skills in hope of capturing stags rather than free riding in hope for some of them to bag a rabbit. Cooperation then dominates alternative strategies.

27. Referring to 42 R&D alliance contracts, Ryall and Sampson (2006) noticed that in most cases property rights were allocated according to who the primary developer is. This approach does not solve problems that emerge when anteriority is unclear or when input contributions are difficult to identify, which is often the case with hybrids.

28. Rubin's answer was that parties prefer this arrangement rather than relying on capital markets because it would better motivate franchisors. "The most plausible explanation seems to be that the franchisee has some incentive to motivate the franchisor to be efficient—that is, just as the franchisor desires the franchisee to run the operation efficiently, so the franchisee desires to give the franchisor an incentive to be efficient in those aspects of the relationship which require an ongoing performance by the franchisor" (Rubin 1978: 227).

A variation of this rent sharing rule, and a more flexible one when factors determining contributions are difficult to assess, is to rank parties according to specific variables, with the possibility of integrating qualitative factors. Using data from contracts among growers and integrators in the poultry industry, Knoeber (1989) showed that ranking growers allows the parties to (1) adapt cheaply to changing productivity without renegotiating; (2) bind growers to integrators when the former provide their own assets; (3) induce self-selection of high-quality growers;[29] and (4) facilitate truthful revelation.[30]

However, tournaments depend on the capacity to rank contributions and match them with contributors, which is hardly the universal case in hybrids. As argued by Ménard (2004; see also Oudot and Ménard 2010), when transactions become complex and contributions are not verifiable, as in R&D projects, noncontractible rules, such as fairness (Grandori and Soda 1995: 196) or perceived equity (Fehr and Schmidt 1999) and ex post bargaining tend to prevail.

These insights remain limited. Many discussions on sharing rules in hybrids focus on specific devices based on the allocation of risks, for example, (1) fixed prices in chain systems in which suppliers support all risks, (2) target prices with shared risks, and (3) cost-plus formulas in which the buyers support all risks. These solutions apply to situations with rights unambiguously identified. When it comes to noncontractibles, the literature remains elusive. Because finding ways to share rents while preventing free riding is so crucial to hybrids, this paucity of analyses is striking. It may be due to the neglect of hybrids by economic theory but also to the difficulty of capturing how rents are allocated without well-defined, contractible rights.

4. How to Face Opportunism: Sustainability of Hybrids

The difficulties that hybrids face in finding appropriate sharing rules to cash positive externalities from their interaction while simultaneously confronting competitive pressure from partners as well as from outsiders are a source of tension and impose hard choices.[31] Solutions condition the possibility for hybrids to outperform markets as well as hierarchies. The survival and stability of hybrids depend on their capacity to find the right partners, to circumscribe risks of opportunistic strategies, and to implement procedures for arbitraging conflicts and reducing tensions among parties.

4.1. Challenges to Stability

Hybrids combine joint efforts and competing goals, which continuously create tensions among partners who intend to maintain a fruitful cooperation while valuing their own assets. Richardson (1972) already emphasized variations in tensions among partners to interfirm agreements,

---

29. Contracts can be canceled if a grower's performance is consistently below average.

30. Other references to tournament rules among partners in agrifood chains are Tsoulouhas and Vukina (2001) and Wu and Roe (2006). A reference to sports is Ehrenberg and Bognanno (1990), which deals with golf—a limited example, however, because performance can be easily associated with individual golfers.

31. Sako (2005) illustrates some of these dilemmas using the example of supplier parks. Should firms favor: (1) Modularity or outsourcing? (2) Voice (commitment) or exit (flexibility)? (3) Diversified employment governance or a unified one? (4) Suppliers' roles as assemblers or as partners?

depending on whether they share physical assets while competing or build joint resources to benefit from complementarities without competing.

First, there is the strategic decision about what resources to pool. Partners might (1) develop a subset of resources from which each one can draw, as in many R&D projects; (2) share resources sequentially, as with logistics in supply chain systems; or (3) build and maintain joint assets, as in collective trademarks. Pooling financial resources is a classical example: it is a leading explanation to the existence of franchising,[32] in that it allows expanding into markets otherwise hardly accessible (Brickley and Dark 1987; Oxley 1999). It also tightens bonds among partners in networks (Aoki 1988: 102).[33] Pooling physical assets might also support mixed strategies, as with laboratories jointly built and monitored by partners in the biotechnology industry (Powell 1996). Similarly, sharing human assets may allow spillover effects in competencies and know-how. However, pooling resources challenges the competitive advantage that each partner could expect from developing its own specific assets. Hence, partners confront the need to commit versus the risk of capture.

Second, the combination of separate and shared rights makes monitoring and disciplining parties particularly challenging and is used as an argument to qualify hybrids as second best (Rey and Tirole 2001; Baker et al. 2008). Mixing cooperation and competition, christened "coopetition" by Nalebuff and Brandenburger (1998), might not be exclusive to hybrids: employees or divisions compete within firms, notwithstanding the expectation of cooperation.[34] What distinguishes hybrids is the need to stabilize cooperation among otherwise competing partners without relying on hierarchy and with limited control over strategic rights.

On the one hand, accepted interdependence imposes constraints on the usage of pooled resources from which common returns as well as private benefits are expected (Gulati et al. 2000; Baker et al. 2008).[35] These benefits differ from those coming from the industry level (e.g., market structures or technological innovation) or from heterogeneity among firms (Dyer and Singh 1998). On the other hand, partners remain competitors. Hergert and Morris (1988) noticed that 71% of strategic alliances concern parties competing in the same market. Ménard (1996) exhibited similar results among networks in the poultry industry, and so did Park (1996) in a study of 204 equity-based interfirm linkages in the electronics industry and Robinson and Stuart (2007) in the biotechnology and pharmaceutical industries.

The challenge of stability versus autonomy that coopetition faces might help explain observable gaps between duration of formal contracts and duration of contractual relationships in hybrids. Hakansson (1989; see also Hakansson and Johansson 1993) documented the stability of networks among small and medium enterprises in Sweden, notwithstanding the short duration of formal contracts, with two-thirds of the partnerships lasting for more than 4 years and an average duration of 13 years. This confirms similar observations in the construction industry (Eccles 1981), among French small and medium manufacturing firms

32. This explanation has been seriously challenged (Lafontaine and Slade 1997, 2007).

33. Cross-financial participation among top shareholders may end up with control in the hands of the network, which raises the issue of its adequate governance, as pointed out by Aoki in the case of *keiretsu*.

34. Tirole (1986: 212) defined firms as a "network of coalitions and contracts that interplay."

35. Powell (1996: 211) noted the following about high-tech sectors: "membership in a common technological/intellectual community creates strong and visible mechanisms for peer-based governance."

(Paché and Paraponaris 1993), in the agrifood sector (Ménard 1996), and so on. However, tensions over usage of pooled resources or rent sharing also carry risks of instability, including the breach of contracts. For example, the mortality rate in horizontal alliances is higher than in vertical ones, stemming from competition (Bleeke and Ernst 1993). Sampson (2005) also found a high rate of dissatisfaction and alliance termination in 464 R&D alliances in the telecommunications industry during 1991–1993, while Khanna (1998) noted the risk that "racing" strategies among partners increases instability, particularly when mutual learning is at stake. Ambiguities about residual rights and difficulties in implementing clear sharing rules push hybrids to search for adequate mechanisms of governance (Park 1996; Ménard 2004). Finding stability without challenging the autonomy of partners remains a key issue for hybrids.

4.2. Finding the Right Partners

In that respect, selecting the right partners becomes crucial. Two dimensions of selection have particularly attracted attention. First, antecedents signal the reliability of potential partners and provide insights into the compatibility of management systems and decision processes (Lorenzoni and Baden-Fuller 1995). In a series of papers on strategic alliances and networks, Gulati (1995b), Gulati and Gargiulo (1999), and Gulati et al. (2000) showed that repeated interaction among parties is a key component in the selection process. Using data from 1980 to 1989 on 166 organizations located throughout the United States (54), Europe (46), and Japan (66) and operating in three industrial sectors (new materials, industrial automation, and automotive products), Gulati and Gargiulo (1999: 1447), quoting Granovetter (1985: 490), showed the importance of "trusted informants" and/or "information from one's own past dealings with this person" in choosing partners and reducing uncertainties when forming alliances. In line with Granovetter (1985; see also Dyer and Singh, 1998: 666 et seq.), they emphasized (1) past cooperation ("relational"), (2) indirect ties through third parties ("structural"), and (3) the role of potential partners in preexisting alliances ("positional") as factors framing selection. The analysis of the role of centrality and proximity in Robinson and Stuart (2007) supports this observation. However, Poppo and Zenger (2002) and Ryall and Sampson (2006) showed some puzzling effects of antecedents: prior alliances develop trust, signaling the high value of a relationship and encouraging informal governance, but repeated interactions also improve information and the capacity to write detailed contracts, making highly formal relationships easier to implement.

Second, the imposition of restrictions on potential partners operates as a screening device. Selection means barriers to entry. Hybrids have a more or less open architecture. Powell (1996) emphasized cross-traffic between universities and firms and among firms in the biotech industry as facilitating the development of co-specialized assets. However, Ménard (1996) displayed the tight restrictions imposed on partners in the French "label" system, and Baker et al. (2008) found a similar pattern in biotechnology and pharmaceutical alliances, dominated by a hard core of 12 firms. In addition, Grandori and Soda (1995: 196) argued that the broader the scope of cooperation, the stricter are the rules of access. According to Dyer and Singh (1998), variability in openness depends on (1) the level of ambiguities about sources of rents; (2) the degree of replicability of resources generating rents; (3) the degree of imitability of resources to be pooled;

(4) the availability of partners of the same type; (5) the accessibility to capabilities they offer; and (6) specificities of the institutional environment.

All in all, hybrids' permeability remains limited by provisions determining resources to be pooled, delineating decisions to be shared, and fixing rules of governance. The resulting contractual constraints—for example, nonlinear pricing, royalties, minimum prices, quotas, exclusive territories, exclusive distribution, and packages—and other commitments are integral components in selecting and monitoring partners. They also severely challenge competition policies (Rey and Tirole 1986; Ménard 1996, 2007a).

4.3. Straightening Ties to Reduce Opportunism

Beyond selection, the "willingness of trading partners to exert effort on behalf of the relationship" (Mohr and Spekman 1994: 137) is central to maintaining a stable arrangement while keeping opportunism in check. Shared goals and common expectations legitimize coordination, facilitate joint decisions, and prevent free riding. In an extensive analysis of 166 alliances, Gulati (1995b) showed that firms prefer to deal with partners already interacting with others, thus benefiting from informational advantages and mitigating control concerns. Among many others, Powell et al. (1996) or Robinson and Stuart (2007) on biotechnology, Baker et al. (2008) on alliances between biotech and pharmaceutical firms, and Aoki (2001: 347–375) on the role of venture capitalists in building networks in Silicon Valley confirm that "the social dimensions of interorganizational relationship play a crucial role in controlling and coordinating behavior in transactions" (Bradach 1997: 294).

This importance of informal relationships was already emphasized by Macaulay in 1963. In the 1980s, several contributions focused on the role of social ties in "nonstandard" modes of organization. Ouchi (1980) introduced the notion of clans as homogeneous networks minimizing goal incongruence while tolerating high ambiguity about outcomes, thanks to shared values. Ben-Porath (1980) pointed out the role of social ties in overcoming high uncertainty (e.g., about quality, or when obligations are spread over time). Granovetter (1985; see also Zucker 1986; Adler 2001) extended the idea to interfirm relations in an influential critique of standard economic assumptions as well as of Williamson's (1985) emphasis on opportunism. Social ties became a leading theme in the sociology of networks.

It also permeated managerial sciences, through the analysis of trust. Thorelli (1986: 40) defined trust as "an assumption or reliance on the part of A that if either A or B encounters a problem in the fulfillment of his implicit or explicit transactional obligations, B may be counted on to do what A would do if B's resources would be at A's disposal." Trust could emerge from prior history, from expectations of continuity, or from the interdependence of these two factors.[36] It would operate through (1) the convergence of expectations among partners with different goals; (2) the development of idiosyncratic language for carrying routines and

---

36. Sako and Helper (1998) identified three sources of trust: contractual (confidence that the other party will carry out the agreement); competence (confidence that the other party will be capable of doing what it promises to do); and goodwill (confidence that the other party will take initiatives mutually beneficial while restraining from taking unfair advantage). Their test, based on data collected from 3,000 suppliers in the automotive industry, exhibited that Japanese networks of suppliers are significantly more trusting than the competing U.S. suppliers.

information; (3) the transformation of tacit rules in common knowledge through shared norms; and (4) adaptation to unforeseen contingencies with reduced transaction costs (Jones et al. 1997: 929; Sako and Helper 1998: 388).

Williamson (1996: 250–275) challenged the role of trust, reducing it to calculative strategies. The resulting controversy, still going on, exhibited the complex role of trust in facilitating flexibility and solving conflicts (Achrol 1997: 65 et seq.). Using an example from Uzzi (1997: 55) about a manufacturer in the New York garment industry who moved his production to China after having notified his American partners ahead of time to let them adjust while he did not notify contractors with whom he had arm's-length relationships, Podolny and Page (1998: 61) concluded: "Cooperation does not arise as a route to future gains."

Economists and organization theorists interpret trust as a reputational issue (MacLeod 2007). *Reputation* relies on various supports (Farrell and Scotchmer 1988; Parkhe 1993; Gulati 1995b; Adler 2001; Poppo and Zenger 2002). It can grow out of (1) recurrent transactions among partners, a central explanation in game theory; (2) familiarity among partners sharing a common background, due to social similarities, geographic proximity, or devices purposely designed for that goal (e.g., training sessions, managerial seminars); (3) information about past agreements with third parties; or (4) institutional roots, as when partners belong to professional associations that implement behavioral norms or technical standards.

More generally, the density of ties likely plays an important role in the decision to go hybrid but also in the choice of a specific form. In their survey of more than 3,854 strategic alliances in biotechnology from 1976 to 1998, Robinson and Stuart (2007) showed that parties involved in a dense network (measured by the centrality and proximity of partners) are (1) less likely to rely on equity participation and (2) more likely to rely on extra contractual enforcement mechanisms to prevent hold-up. However, there might be "a potential dark side of overembedded ties," which could sustain relationships that are no longer fruitful (Poppo et al. 2008: 52; see also Anderson and Jap 2005).

4.4. Implementing Control

Ties help build a reputation that generates trust, facilitate selection of partners, influence the choice of the mode of governance, and smooth adaptation. However, hybrids often need more drastic means to control and discipline partners.[37] These "different safeguards are likely to have different set-up costs and result in different transaction costs over different time horizons" (Dyer 1997: 537).

The threat to expel underperforming partners or free riders is such a tool. Threat works if the expected losses from being ousted exceed the gains of free riding (Klein 1996) and if the mode of governance adopted allows such radical sanctions. The implementation of a private court to control and penalize noncompliant millers (see Section 2.1) illustrates the complex devices that

---

37. This could signal a difference between relational contracts among firms and within firms: in hybrids, reneging threatens the very existence of the agreement; within firms, hierarchy provides means for dealing with the situation. See the comparison between reneging temptations in outsourcing and in employment relationships in Baker et al. (2002).

may be needed to make threat effective.[38] Ostracism in the film industry or the destruction of traps of interlopers and noncompliants in the Maine lobster industry provide other examples (Jones et al. 1997). Greif (1993, 2005) similarly showed the power and complexity of threats that rely on collective sanctions in the network of the Maghribi traders.[39]

However, threat remains an ambiguous tool. First, it is often a one-shot game. Second, it signals conflicts and difficulties in solving problems, which might tarnish reputation and challenge future partnerships. Third, ousting noncompliants challenges hybrids, because they cannot rely on a central entrepreneur to do so.[40] Contracts may help discipline free riders (e.g., imposing penalties or defining conditions under which a concompliant can be expelled). However, they cannot control for all situations. In an extensive study of more than 1,500 alliances, Gulati (1998) demonstrated that when making decisions to cooperate, partners are less concerned by contractual hazards than by the expected costs of governing their relationships. Brickley and Dark (1987) and Bradach (1997) reached a similar conclusion about franchising and identified various control devices that (1) limit the discretion of agents, (2) reduce opportunistic temptation by restricting residual claims, (3) establish benchmarks through company-owned outlets, and (4) discipline franchisees through consultants in charge of persuading them to remedy violations of standards. Achrol (1997: 64 et seq.) suggested that control is exercised through expertise, reputation, and influence (which he calls "referential"), while Mohr and Spekman (1994) had already pinpointed several techniques implemented by hybrids to avoid relying on threat: joint problem-solving devices (e.g., a specific committee), persuasion, smoothing over differences, domination, harsh words, and arbitration.

The central lesson of these studies (and several others) is that checking free riders exceeds the capacity of contracts and pushes toward implementing specific control mechanisms, ultimately resulting in a governing body. In the long run, the search for stability and the need to fight opportunism might well drag hybrids away from quasi-market relationships and toward quasi-integration.

To sum up, the coexistence of pooled resources, autonomous rights, and distinct assets is a source of tensions that make devices to sustain hybrids both vulnerable and essential. Multitask models (Holmström and Milgrom 1991) might help frame the difficulty. Partners jointly owning some assets while keeping distinct rights on others must choose simultaneously joint actions and autonomous or even competing actions that can nevertheless benefit from spillover effects. How can parties limit the risks that some partners might divert their attention from joint actions or even endorse choices harmful to joint activities? In exploring answers to this question, the similarities with decisionmaking in teams and committees are limited. Economic theory does not yet have adequate models to capture

---

38. Raynaud (1997) emphasizes the limits to the threat of expulsion stemming from the internal conflicts that could result among remaining partners. In contrast, Bradach (1997), referring to the example of defranchising of restaurants in the United States, displays the limits coming out of a mix of institutional constraints and the risk of disrupting the network.

39. See also the role of "merchants' laws" (Milgrom et al. 1989).

40. This is precisely the raison d'être of entrepreneurs according to Alchian and Demsetz (1972).

how partially pooled resources and imperfectly contractible outcomes affect the decision process.[41]

5. Governance of Hybrids: A Variety of Answers

To monitor joint assets and create new ones, partners take the risk of exposing shared rights to opportunistic behavior, to the point of negative spillover effects.[42] The need to control and discipline partners to make hybrids sustainable encourages governance endowed with authority, the intensity of which varies according to the specificity of assets pooled, the allocation of rights, and the incentives at stake. The stability of a hybrid depends on its governance and on its ability to deal with the challenges it faces.

By governance, I mean devices that instill order in joint activities through the allocation of assets and rights, so as to mitigate conflicts while allowing benefits from mutual gains (Williamson 1996: 12). The specificity of governance in hybrids comes from the need for parties to coordinate while "partner sovereignty provides a constant strain" (Borys and Jemison 1989: 242).

As evidence from previous sections suggests, there are different ways of "encompassing the initiation, termination and ongoing relationship maintenance between a set of parties" (Heide 1994: 72). If autonomy characterizes parties operating on markets while administrative coordination prevails in hierarchies, hybrids mix autonomy and cooperation. This mix takes various forms, from tight coordination by a strategic center to looser ties relying on shared information. In what follows, I focus on three structural components of governance and the underlying role of relational contracts. Although these components are found in combination most of the time, I shall argue in Section 6 that the dominance of one of these components determines the type of hybrid.[43]

5.1. Coordinating through a Strategic Center

Ongoing competition among partners and the simultaneous quest for stability push toward tighter coordination when shared assets and rights become significant. Risks of opportunistic behavior need to be circumscribed when strategic decisions must be made jointly among otherwise sovereign partners. This might explain the key role of strong coordinators (strategic centers) in most stable hybrids.[44]

---

41. A stimulating approach to decisionmaking in complex organizations is proposed by Visser and Swank (2007). There are also similarities between decisionmaking in hybrids and choices in politics, with the key role of median voters. However, a nonnegligible difference is that in many hybrids, "voters" do not have the same weight. There are exceptions, though, as with the millers or in cooperatives using the "one person, one vote" rule, which is also a source of problems (Cook and Iliopoulos 2000; Hendrikse 2004; Ménard 2007b).

42. For example, in food franchising systems, spoiled food delivered by a single franchisee might spill destructive externalities over the entire network.

43. See also Hendrikse (2004). Bradach and Eccles (1989) argued early on that three basic control mechanisms govern transactions within and among firms: price, authority, and trust. The difference among modes of organization then depends on the prevalence of one mechanism over the others.

44. I retroactively discovered that Lorenzoni and Baden-Fuller (1995) also referred to "strategic centers" as coordinating devices.

Strategic centers can be understood as a shorthand expression for institutional entities under which transactions are initiated, negotiated, monitored, adopted, enforced, and terminated.[45] The specificity of hybrids is that such centers exert authority on a limited subset of rights. They can constrain partners by (1) adjusting collective action or joint decision rights, (2) designing enforcement mechanisms to discipline parties, (3) framing bargaining processes over quasi-rents, and (4) deciding dispute-resolution procedures. The millers' board, assemblies ruling condominiums (Klein et al. 1978), groups of producers (Sauvée 2002), and boards monitoring joint ventures provide examples.

First, strategic centers shape collective actions by monitoring joint decision rights. Thorelli (1986: 38) referred to "power," understood as "the ability to influence the decisions or actions of others." Ménard (1996, 1997, 2004) developed the concept of authority to capture the delegation of subsets of decision rights to an entity that is formally (and most of the time legally) distinct, with the power to discipline parties when it comes to joint actions. Authority differs from hierarchy in that it relies on consent rather than command, maintaining some symmetry among the holders of rights. In hybrids, authority is built through (1) control over the allocation of pooled resources, (2) development of shared competences, (3) provision of expertise, (4) creation of a sense of common purpose, and (5) legitimization through social acceptance.

Second, authority requires enforcement. Interpreting Williamson (1985), Park (1996) suggested that enforcement differs depending on whether it is operating in bilateral or trilateral arrangements. In the former, parties enforce decisions through negotiations, because in the last resort decisions remain in the hands of parent firms, as in joint ventures. When actions become more intertwined and/or the network becomes extensive, rendering internal transactions and joint decisions to monitor and enforce increasingly complex, coordination would require trilateral governance, with enforcement transferred to a well-defined entity (e.g., a professional staff or a central management that can select collective actions, evaluate performance, and penalize noncompliants).[46] Professional sports leagues or the millers discussed in Section 2.1 illustrate the point.

Third, authority allows strategic centers to frame the bargaining process. Ménard (1996) examined how a group of producers in the poultry industry implemented a central entity in charge of organizing negotiations among partners as well as regulating the bargaining process with distributors. Analyzing the success of Saveol, a network of producers of high-quality vegetables, Sauvée (2002) analyzed an arrangement in which small owners delegate substantial decision rights to two distinct cooperatives that themselves delegate rights to two joint ventures in charge of controlling inputs, developing products, and marketing them. However, delegation of rights over a limited subset of assets raises a difficult trade-off for hybrids: how to keep the arrangement adaptable through the transfer of adequate authority while keeping holders of this authority under control. This difficulty may explain why so many interfirm agreements place a "high premium on personnel with long memories, sound hearts, and a penchant for looking both ways before crossing the street" (Palay 1985: 164).

---

45. This definition is adapted from Palay (1984: 265).

46. "The central management has decision-making power over members and it monitors the members' cooperation activities and imposes sanctions, if necessary" (Park 1996: 812).

Fourth, the existence of multiple sources of tensions (see Section 4.1) encourages the adoption of formalized mechanisms to solve disputes within the strategic center or between the center and its constituencies. In their study of the U.S. hardware industry, Dwyer and Oh (1988) suggested that formal procedures might prevail over centralization and participation in differentiating modes of organization.[47] The development of routines that codify links among partners and serialize the decisionmaking process helps reduce disputes and/or facilitates their resolution. The implementation of transmission channels that facilitates control (e.g., automated management information systems) can similarly help formalize relationships. Detailed technical appendixes to contracts also frame disputes and renegotiations among partners. Policing devices, such as "mystery shoppers" in franchises or field audits and internal inspections in the millers' case, similarly ease identifying and redressing noncompliant behaviors. Enforcement procedures might go even further, implementing private courts to judge and discipline noncompliant partners (see Section 2.1 on the millers, or the now classical analysis of merchant laws in the Champagne fairs in Milgrom et al. 1989).

Numerous empirical studies (e.g., Brown 1984; Lorenzoni and Baden-Fuller 1995; Ménard 1996, 2004; Ménard and Raynaud 2010) confirm this role of authority delegated to and implemented by a strategic center.[48] They are in line with what TCE predicts: the more strategic the rights and assets shared, the more formal the governance becomes.

5.2. Third Parties as Ordering Forces

Strategic centers shape decisions from within, ideally making agreements self-sustainable. In the last resort they remain offshoots of parent companies. Because they get their authority from delegation, they depend on the commitment of their constituencies and remain directly exposed to risks of opportunism. To confront these difficulties, hybrids might turn to exogenous entities to facilitate coordination and discipline partners, either because shared rights are not sufficiently strategic to justify joint authority or because the impulse to cooperate comes from parties external to the relationship (e.g., public policies). These ordering forces can be public or private.

Public authorities can interfere directly in the development of hybrids through agencies, regulations, and the like. In the French poultry industry, a quality certification system initiated by small producers was later formalized, on their demand, with the legal creation of certifying organizations governed by representatives from the government, the sector, independent experts, and it was key to the success of "red label" products (Ménard 1996). Another example is R&D projects that depend on subsidies conditional on interfirm agreements, as with the European Galileo project, which intends to build a system that competes with the Global Positioning System. In addition, public authorities can provide indirect incentives to cooperate, as when they ease access to scientific centers or technology parks to firms willing to interact.

47. Formalization has become a standard variable differentiating arrangement in organization theory.

48. From a different perspective, Bradach (1997) noted that franchise systems also develop forms of strategic control to overcome agency problems, for example, combining a large monolithic hierarchy (company-owned units) and a federation of semi-autonomous hierarchies (e.g., KFC, in which 17 actors owned half of all franchises in 1989).

External monitoring of hybrids can also depend on private entities. Formal procedures can be embedded in the arrangement to facilitate adaptation, as when adjustments are delegated to identifiable arbitrators (often lawyers or experts) or to professional associations. In the French beef industry, networks privately initiated turned early on to professional unions for solving conflicts and enforcing agreements (Mazé and Ménard 2010). However, partners often prefer less-formal devices and refer to mediators for adapting their relationships (Rubin 2005). Ryall and Sampson (2006) go even further, showing how partners may plan penalties for those who become confrontational. One problem that researchers must deal with when identifying these devices is the difficulty of collecting information on private monitoring of adaptation and conflicts.[49]

In addition, numerous hybrids find support in mixed entities, in which private agents and public representatives jointly make decisions. Under pressure from the competition authorities of the European Union, who considered the initial arrangement as collusive, the certifying organizations mentioned above are now autonomous entities, in many cases with representatives from the private and public sectors, while others are entirely private (Ménard and Valceschini 2005; Raynaud et al. 2009).

However, monitoring hybrids through external agents faces severe limitations. It confronts problems of verifiability by third parties, a serious constraint in arrangements that reserve substantial rights for separate parties and/or organize complex transactions. Implementing decisions from exogenous entities might also have dissuasive costs, involve unacceptable delays, or require controls that are barely tolerable. Several studies suggest that these obstacles are better overcome through informal safeguards, which lower transaction costs and are hard for competitors to imitate (Gulati 1995a; Dyer and Singh 1998; Robinson and Stuart 2007).

5.3. Shared Information

Asymmetric information is a major source of opportunism in hybrids. Of course, information problems plague all modes of organization. They are amplified in hybrids, because existing assets and rights are partly shared, while new assets and rights are created that can hardly be attributed to specific contributions. Moreover, the autonomy of partners prevents hierarchical solutions, and overlapping assets and rights require more information than market prices can offer.

Relevant information might be collected through repeated transactions (Gulati 1995b); or through appropriate information systems, such as integrated logistics, shared transportation facilities, common buying procedures, and joint collection of data on customers (Clemons and Row 1992; Ménard 1996, 2003). Using their dataset from alliances between biotechnology and pharmaceutical firms, Robinson and Stuart (2007) refer to networks as platforms disseminating information, thus reducing uncertainty and benefiting from shared capabilities. New information technologies might help, although data are inconclusive about whether they favor interfirm agreements or integration (e.g., in the trucking industry). Following Arrow (1974), Heiman and

---

49. Lumineau and Oxley (2012) provide a rare analysis of private resolution of conflicts through arbitration, mediation, or negotiated settlement. They examined 102 contractual conflicts from 1991 to 2005 in which lawyers intervened, involving 178 firms operating in manufacturing and retail sectors. They showed that 41 conflicts were solved this way, while the remaining 61 ended up in courts.

Nickerson (2002) emphasize the role of physical channels linking partners. High-bandwidth channels (e.g., co-location) would allow rich interfaces among partners, facilitating coordination but also raising problems of delineation and enforcement of rights over tacit knowledge; low-bandwidth channels (e.g., e-mails or faxes) would reduce contractual hazards but restrict the transfer of information.

In all cases, information devices are intended to make partnership sustainable by reducing the risk of opportunism, facilitating mutual control, and lowering transaction costs. Shared information can help reach these goals through (1) modularity and replicability of know-how, which allows implementation of joint routines; (2) open standards, which make communication easier while increasing transparency of transactions; (3) implementation of devices that allow conversion and translation of protocols and interfaces at low cost; and (4) development of intuitive interfaces (Clemons and Row 1992; Paché and Paraponaris 1993; Langlois 2002; Anderson and Gatignon 2005).

The literature on the role of information in the governance of hybrids and how it might differentiate them from other modes of organization remains surprisingly sparse. Powell (1990; see also Powell et al. 1996), using data from the biotechnology sector, suggested that information in networks is "thicker" and "freer" than in hierarchies, while it requires reciprocity that does not fit arm's-length relationships of the market type. This remains an interesting intuition to be explored further.

5.4. Underlying It All: Contracts

In most hybrids, governance is at least partially framed by contracts. This framework provides a strong argument to examine hybrids through contractual lenses. Contracts are powerful tools, facilitating coordination as well as control. However, their role should not be overemphasized. Macaulay (1963) already noted that they primarily supply frameworks within which other devices prosper. Because the analysis of contracts plays an important role in this book, I hereafter focus solely on issues of particular relevance for the analysis of hybrids.[50]

Ideally, partners would rely on self-enforcing contracts embedded in formal safeguards that keep calculative parties within the range delineated by the agreement or in social norms pervasive enough to discipline them (Ouchi 1980; Artz and Brush 2000). As argued by Klein (1996; see also Baker et al. 2002: 40; Mazé and Ménard 2010), even when outcomes are not verifiable by a third party and are prohibitively costly to specify ex ante, no party may wish to renege if the expected value of the future relationship is sufficiently large.

However, theoretical insights on the importance of noncontractible elements as well as empirical studies on contractual flaws exhibit the limited role of contracts. The complex overlapping of autonomy and cooperation in hybrids typically makes contracts relational.[51] Changing

---

50. For a detailed review of contracts in interfirm relations, see Lafontaine and Slade (this volume) and Malcomson (this volume: Sections 8 and 9). Hansmann (this volume) also discusses related issues.

51. See Rey and Tirole (2001: 25–26):

There is little point writing a detailed contract that protects the partners by reducing potential externalities and specific covenants restricting the set of possible actions. Partners are already protected by their control rights; and such contractual features, which are pervasive under undivided control, only serve to reduce incentives

market conditions, uncertainties surrounding the outcome of joint projects, measurement problems, ill-defined property rights and/or weak institutions making enforcement dubious are factors motivating flexibility and the potentially positive effects of renegotiations.[52] These problems are not exclusive to hybrids. What make contracts in hybrids distinct are the amplitude of adjustments variables and the room left for relational adaptation, a point already noticed by Borys and Jemison (1989: 243) and emphasized by Robinson and Stuart (2007) in their examination of alliances in biotechnology. Ryall and Sampson (2006) exhibit how the resulting heterogeneity in contractual clauses coagulates in boilerplate terms motivated by the need to facilitate adjustments when hybrids face knowledge leakages or inefficiencies in dispute-resolution devices.[53]

Noncontractibilities translate into out-of-contract adjustments. Brown (1984: 266) already noted that in networks "the contract itself is more a formalization of an understanding than it is a legally-enforceable obligation. Breaches of contracts are rarely taken to court, even in the litigious US. This means that the contract can be renegotiated (or ignored) if need arises and the contingent claims problems are thereby avoided." Almost simultaneously, Palay (1984) showed in a detailed study of 51 transactions between rail freight carriers and shippers that if adhering to clauses or adjusting only at the margins prevailed in nonspecific transactions, adjustments exceeding the terms of contracts dominated idiosyncratic transactions. Similar observations have been made about franchises, in which contractual provisions define only a framework (Bradach 1997), or in strategic alliances, in which contracts operate primarily as facilitating devices. Grandori and Cacciatori (2006; see also Grandori and Furlotti 2006) showed in a survey of innovation-motivated alliances that contracts are typically simple and short (7–8 pages), with clauses focused on a few core issues, mainly the assignment of property rights, whereas decisions on tasks and process are left aside. In their study of 42 R&D alliances in the telecommunications equipment manufacturing and microelectronics industry, Ryall and Samson (2006) substantiate the role of contracts as blueprints helping to plan collaboration, define partner expectations, and reduce misunderstanding and costly missteps. Moreover, similar contracts might carry different meaning according to their environment. In a survey of carmaker suppliers in Japan and the United States, Sako and Helper (1998) show that American suppliers use long-term contracts as a protection against opportunism from their customers, whereas Japanese suppliers view long-term contracts as signaling opportunistic customers!

In sum, the governance of hybrids relies on a set of devices, of which contracts are only one element, although a very important one. The combination of these devices likely explains the variety of hybrids; the prevalence of one of them determines the subset to which a given empirical form belongs.

---

without improving efficiency. Joint ventures may also want to shut down the partners' otherwise desirable outside opportunities in order to foster their commitment to the joint venture.

52. The idea that contracts are deliberately left open goes back to Simon (1951), but still meets resistance (see Tirole 1999). For the potentially positive role of renegotiation, see Estache and Quesada (2002).

53. These regularities concern provisions on confidentiality; the right to terminate on bankruptcy or changes in key management; limitations of liability; and arbitration provisions. Numerous contracts explicitly waive firm rights to bring disputes before the courts or other administrative bodies (Ryall and Sampson 2006) or restrict the temptation to go to arbitration (e.g., clauses specifying that arbitration should be in the language and country of the partner not bringing the dispute).

6. Toward a Typology of Hybrids

Many economists are doubtful about the relevance of establishing a typology of organizations, although lessons from the history of science tell otherwise.[54] Having described hybrids as a class of their own, Rubin (1978: 232) nevertheless concluded that "the franchisee is in fact closer to being an employee of the franchisor than to being an independent entrepreneur." Cheung (1983: 1) went a step farther, arguing that firms and other arrangements are simply shorthand descriptions of ways to organize activities through contracts. Williamson (1975: 109) initially considered these intermediate forms as unstable and transitory, while as late as 1996, Masten (1996: 12) argued that "their form must be assessed on a case-by-case basis." True, the variety of observable forms suggests a continuum of arrangements between markets and hierarchies. However, when we examine, say, joint ventures, we are aware of looking at something different from franchising or supply chain systems. Is a classification of hybrids possible without flattening their characteristics?[55]

6.1. Alternative Approaches

Numerous studies have answered this question positively, using criteria derived from organization theory, with an emphasis on (1) the coordination mechanisms involved, (2) the degree of centralization, and (3) the formalization of decisionmaking. Other studies use the perspective of TCE to give a positive answer, with a key role for the specificity of investments involved and, to a lesser degree, the uncertainty surrounding transactions at stake.

Putting coordination at the forefront, Grandori and Soda (1995) classified interfirm networks as (1) social networks, relying on personalized relationships (e.g., industrial districts); (2) bureaucratic networks, obeying formal rules (e.g., franchises); and (3) proprietary networks, based on cross-holding property rights (e.g., joint ventures).[56] Sauvée (2002) categorized hybrids according to whether allocation of decision rights requires horizontal or vertical coordination. Park (1996) differentiated forms according to their degree of centralization, with alliances, and voluntary and mandatory trilateral agreements as the main categories. More recently, Carson et al. (2006) argued that uncertainty should be the key variable for classifying interfirm contracts as formal or relational.[57]

Endorsing a transaction cost perspective, Oxley (1997) identified three types of hybrid arrangements according to how they deal with contractual hazards and appropriability: *unilateral*

---

54. Developing appropriate classifications played a major role in, for example, the natural sciences (the Linnaen taxonomic system), chemistry (Mendeleev's periodic table), and medical sciences (nosology).

55. Biology provides a useful analogy here: the discovery that all living organisms share common characteristics (e.g., cells) did not destroy the usefulness of identifying distinct species. At the end of the day, what matters are losses and gains in reducing the spectrum of organizational forms to discrete "bands." In my view, the exercise plays a positive role in (1) boiling down properties of classes and subclasses to a small number of determinants and (2) helping identify flaws and black holes in our theories of organizations.

56. Their typology also differentiates subclasses depending on whether relationships are symmetric or asymmetric.

57. Ranging between markets adapted to weakly specific assets and hierarchies prevailing when specificity is high, arrangements would vary according to the type of uncertainty, with formal contracts more efficient when the ambiguity related to measurement problems is high, while relational contracts are more efficient when volatility is high.

contracts (e.g., licensing), close to markets although poorly adapted to high hazards; *bilateral contracts* (e.g., technology sharing agreements), with more committed parties who are nevertheless exposed to ex post haggling or third-party adjudicative costs in solving conflicts; and quasi-integrated *equity-based alliances,* in which partners share resources, organizational routines, and communication methods but must deal with costly monitoring and control. Gulati and Singh (1998) argued that anticipated coordination costs—not appropriation—determine organizational choices, because they delineate the authority acceptable by autonomous partners and the role of trust in alleviating costs.[58] Using a dataset on alliances, they differentiated (1) *contractual alliances,* with no shared ownership but joint activities coordinated through negotiations (e.g., distribution agreements); (2) *minority alliances,* in which one or several partners take minority equity, so that (weak) hierarchical relationships develop (e.g., participation in a board); and (3) *joint ventures,* with an independent command structure that internalizes pricing, operating procedures, and dispute resolution. More recently, Baker et al. (2008) characterized the variety of governance structures according to the allocation of asset ownership, decision rights, and payoffs. Their typology runs from mergers and acquisitions to total divestitures, with intermediate agreements (e.g., licensing, alliances, franchising) when some decision rights and/or payoffs rights are contracted and parties abandon part of their autonomy in exchange for expected spillovers.

6.2. A Governance Perspective

Building on these contributions and based on the variables examined in the previous sections, I propose a typology that encapsulates these variables as instruments shaping the outcome of hybrid form, that is, the prevailing mode of governance. The underlying logic is that forces pushing to "go hybrid" on the one hand and strategic choices commanding the degree of centralization needed to provide sustainability on the other hand result in various governance structures.

If we contrast hybrids with the two standard polar cases of pure markets (with autonomy of strategic resources and rights and decentralized coordination as key characteristics) and pure hierarchy (with strategic assets and rights unified under a centralized entity in charge of their allocation and control in the last resort), we can substantiate our simplified Figure 1.

Facing uncertainty and complexity through arrangements that allow the creation of extra value requires sharing rules that maintain cohesiveness. The intensity of these forces that push to endorse specific modes of governance translates to the variable density of pooled strategic rights and resources (horizontal axis in Figure 2). In contrast, the sustainability of an arrangement requires instruments for checking on partners eager to preserve their autonomy, with various solutions determining the degree of control or coordination needed (vertical axis in Figure 2). The outcome is the variety of arrangements summarized in Figure 2, in which the outer frontier along the two axes captures what would be termed "pure" modes of governance.

58. "By coordination costs, we mean the anticipated organizational complexity of decomposing tasks among partners along with ongoing coordination of activities to be completed jointly or individually across organizational boundaries and the related extent of communication and decisions that would be necessary" (Gulati and Singh 1998: 782). They tested their hypothesis with a multinomial logistic regression on a sample of 1,570 alliances involving U.S., European, and Japanese firms from 1970 to 1989 in three sectors (biopharmaceuticals, new materials, and automobile manufacturing).

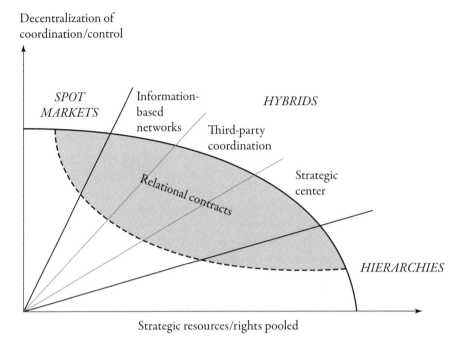

Figure 2. Typology of hybrids. The lens-shaped shaded area delineates the tolerance or acceptance zone.

The perspective adopted builds on the Coase-Williamson tradition, with hybrids located between spot markets (in which autonomous parties cash benefits from their own actions, so that deliberate coordination is at a low) and hierarchies (which capitalize on coordination and control over common resources and rights, considerably reducing the autonomy of insiders and their capacity to privately appropriate surplus). In the hybrid zone, we find the variety of answers to governance issues, according to the prevalence of one of the devices identified in Section 5. The more partners expect from pooling resources, the more autonomy they will be ready to sacrifice with respect to their decision and property rights, up to the point where rights are fully integrated. Likewise, the more coordination is needed to maintain the stability of an arrangement, the more centralized will be the monitoring and control of that arrangement.

On the left of the spectrum, close to spot markets, *information-based networks* rely essentially on information platforms to coordinate; ownership over assets and decision rights remain distinct, so that payoffs are closely linked to the actions of separate parties. Porous frontiers and continuous exchanges among biotech firms in the Boston area or among information technology firms in Silicon Valley, as well as forms of consumers' associations, provide illustrations.[59] At the other end of the spectrum, partners rely on tight coordination by means of strategic centers empowered with formal authority and contractual clauses constraining members who pool

59. Recent studies suggest that networks can be more formal than expected. In their study on the biotechnology sector, Robinson and Stuart (2007) show that centrality in the web and proximity to potential partners give powerful means to some firms, facilitating control and reducing the need to hold property rights.

significant rights; appropriation of residual gains becomes a key issue. Joint ventures in R&D projects or the millers' case (see Section 2) illustrate the point. In between we find arrangements in which partners keep control over the hard core of their assets, although they develop non-negligible relationship-specific investments. Such arrangements tend to rely on third parties to monitor tensions and coordinate efforts, whether the third party is a public entity (e.g., agencies monitoring part of the label system in the French agribusiness) or a private arbitraging entity jointly agreed upon and in charge of filling blanks in contracts (as in many strategic alliances).

However, as argued in this chapter, we are rarely on the optimal frontier. Because noncontractible rights are so significant most of the time, while the autonomy of parties and their rights impose constraints on the arrangement, relational contracts are at the core of hybrids. The lens-shaped area in Figure 2 captures the idea of a tolerance or acceptance zone that allows adjustment and adaptation among partners. The lower bound delineates the inferior limit of what is acceptable to parties. Hence, the shaded area is where modes of governance operate most of the time

Most hybrids fall into one of the three types identified in the figure, according to the governing device that prevails. However, devices often overlap, thus mixing pure types. The light rays radiating from the origin and separating types of hybrids suggest this permeability. Indeed, one advantage of this typology is to help understand why and how arrangements often grouped under the same umbrella (e.g., franchises or cooperatives) actually take many different forms according to the activities they coordinate or the strategies they pursue, notwithstanding similarities in the transactions they organize. This richness results from (1) the complex forces that explain the existence of hybrids and delineate the acceptance zone within which they operate and (2) the trade-offs hybrids continuously face in organizing transactions along nonstandard procedures intended to maintain cohesion and stability in the partnership.

7. Conclusion

The central lesson of this chapter is that "there is an increasing sense that the networks of relationship in which particular exchanges are embedded have properties that are greater than the sum of its parts and outcomes that cannot be explained by studying its parts alone" (Achrol 1997: 63). Hybrids are institutional structures with characteristics of their own. They resort to specific governing devices developed to deal with (1) property rights that ultimately remain distinct, although significant assets are pooled; (2) decision rights that keep partners independent, although shared rights restrict their autonomy; and (3) the need to design adequate incentives in a context in which frontiers among residual claimants are blurred. Hybrids proliferate because they can take advantage of coordination and cooperation that overcome gains associated with market competition, while partners remain autonomous, thus providing more flexibility and better incentives than what an integrated structure could offer.

The existence and characteristics of hybrids are substantiated by an abundant empirical literature. However, explanatory theories remain underdeveloped. Models are needed that would capture the role and richness of these arrangements in market economies. We also lack adequate data for estimating the weight and dynamics of these forms in modern capitalism. Five unsolved problems deserve a particular attention in my view. First, we need to understand why hybrids often co-exist with integrated firms. Second, we still remain in the dark with respect to the exact significance of these arrangements in the production and distribution of goods and services.

Third, we do not clearly understand the role of technological changes (e.g., information and communication technologies) in the evolution of their governance. Fourth, the interaction of hybrids with their institutional environment (e.g., rules governing property rights) requires in-depth studies. Finally, several characteristics of hybrids challenge competition policies, which remain largely grounded in theories built on the simplistic trade-off between markets and firms, so that substantial revision of these policies is likely required.

These issues only define part of the rich research agenda opened by the acknowledgment that in modern market economies, hybrid arrangements may be the normal and prevailing way of doing business.

REFERENCES

Achrol, Ravi S. 1997. "Changes in the Theory of Interorganizational Relations in Marketing: Toward a Network Paradigm." *Journal of the Academy of Marketing Science* 25: 56–71.

Adler, Paul S. 2001. "Market, Hierarchy, and Trust: The Knowledge Economy and the Future of Capitalism." *Organization Science* 12: 214–234.

Alchian, Armen A. 1987. "Property Rights," in John Eatwell, Murrell Milgate, and Peter Newman (eds.), *The New Palgrave*, volume 3. London: MacMillan, pp. 1031–1034.

Alchian, Armen A., and Harold Demsetz. 1972. "Production, Information Costs, and Economic Organization." *American Economic Review* 62: 777–795.

Anderson, Erin. 1985. "The Salesperson as Outside Agent or Employee? A Transaction Cost Analysis." *Marketing Science* 4: 234–254.

Anderson, Erin, and Hubert Gatignon. 2005. "Firms and the Creation of New Markets," in Claude Ménard and Mary Shirley (eds.), *Handbook of New Institutional Economics*. Berlin: Springer, pp. 401–431.

Anderson, Erin, and Sandy D. Jap. 2005. "The Dark Side of Close Relationship." *Sloan Management Review* 46(3): 75–82.

Aoki, Masahiko. 1988. *Information, Incentives, and Bargaining in the Japanese Economy*. Cambridge: Cambridge University Press.

———. 2001. *Toward a Comparative Institutional Analysis*. Cambridge, MA: MIT Press.

Arrow, Kenneth. 1974. *The Limits of Organization*. New York: Norton.

Artz, Kendall W., and Thomas S. Brush. 2000. "Asset Specificity, Uncertainty and Relational Norms: An Examination of Coordination Costs in Collaborative Strategic Alliances." *Journal of Economic Behavior and Organization* 41: 337–362.

Baker, George P., Robert Gibbons, and Kevin J. Murphy. 2002. "Relational Contracts and the Theory of the Firm." *Quarterly Journal of Economics* 117: 39–84.

———. 2008. "Strategic Alliances: Bridges between 'Islands of Conscious Power.'" *Journal of the Japanese and International Economies* 22: 146–163.

Barnett, William P. 1990. "The Organizational Ecology of Technological Systems." *Administrative Science Quarterly* 35: 31–60.

Barnett, William P., and Glenn Carroll. 1993. "How Institutional Constraints Affected the Organization of the Early American Telephone Industry." *Journal of Law, Economics, and Organization* 9: 98–127.

Ben-Porath, Yoram. 1980. "The F-Connection: Families, Friends, and Firms and the Organization of Exchange." *Population and Development Review* 6(1): 1–30.

Bleeke, Joel, and David Ernst (eds.). 1993. *Collaborating to Compete: Using Strategic Alliances and Acquisitions in the Global Marketplace*. New York: John Wiley and Sons.

Blois, Keith J. 1972. "Vertical Quasi-Integration." *Journal of Industrial Economics* 20: 253–272.

Borys, Bryan, and David B. Jemison. 1989. "Hybrid Arrangements as Strategic Alliances: Theoretical Issues in Organizational Combinations." *Academy of Management Review* 14: 234–249.

Bradach, Jeffrey. L. 1997. "Using the Plural Form in the Management of Restaurant Chains." *Administrative Science Quarterly* 42: 276–303.

Bradach, Jeffrey L., and Robert G. Eccles. 1989. "Price, Authority, and Trust: From Ideal Types to Plural Forms." *Annual Review of Sociology* 15: 97–118.

Brickley, James A. 1999. "Incentive Conflicts and Contractual Restraints: Evidence from Franchising." *Journal of Law and Economics* 42: 745–774.

Brickley, James A., and Frederick H. Dark. 1987. "The Choice of Organizational Form: The Case of Franchising." *Journal of Financial Economics* 18: 401–420.

Brown, Wilson B. 1984. "Firm-Like Behavior in Markets. The Administered Channel." *International Journal of Industrial Organization* 2: 263–276.

Carson, Stephen J., Anoop Madhok, and Tao Wu. 2006. "Uncertainty, Opportunism, and Governance: The Effects of Volatility and Ambiguity on Formal and Relational Contracts." *Academy of Management Journal* 40: 1058–1077.

Cheung, Steven N. S. 1983. "The Contractual Nature of the Firm." *Journal of Law and Economics* 26: 1–22.

Clemons, Eric K., and Michael C. Row. 1992. "Information Technology and Industrial Cooperation: The Changing Economics of Coordination and Ownership." *Journal of Management Information Systems* 9(2): 9–28.

Coase, Ronald H. 1937. "The Nature of the Firm." *Economica* 2: 386–405.

———. 1992. "The Institutional Structure of Production." *American Economic Review* 82: 713–719.

Cohen, Wesley M., and Daniel A. Levinthal. 1990. "Absorptive Capacity: A New Perspective on Learning and Innovation." *Administrative Science Quarterly* 35: 128–152.

Cook, Michael L., and Constantine Iliopoulos. 2000. "Ill-Defined Property Rights in Collective Action: The Case of US Agricultural Cooperatives," in Claude Ménard (ed.), *Institutions, Contracts and Organizations. Perspectives from New Institutional Economics.* Cheltenham, UK: Edward Elgar, pp. 335–348.

Dwyer, F. Robert, and Sajo Oh. 1988. "A Transaction Cost Perspective on Vertical Contractual Structure and Interchannel Competitive Strategies." *Journal of Marketing* 52: 21–34.

Dyer, Jeffrey H. 1997. "Effective Interfirm Collaboration: How Firms Minimize Transaction Costs and Maximize Transaction Value." *Strategic Management Journal* 18: 535–556.

Dyer, Jeffrey H., and Habir Singh. 1998. "The Relational View: Cooperative Strategy and Sources of Interorganizational Competitive Advantage." *Academy of Management Review* 23: 660–679.

Eccles, Robert G. 1981. "The Quasifirm in the Construction Industry." *Journal of Economic Behavior and Organization* 2: 335–357.

Ehrenberg, Ronald G., and Michael Bognanno. 1990. "The Incentive Effects of Tournaments Revisited: Evidence from the PGA Tour." *Industrial and Labor Relations Review* 43(3): 74–88.

Estache, Antonio, and Lucia Quesada. 2002. "Concession Contract Renegotiations: Some Efficiency vs. Equity Dilemmas." World Bank Policy Research WP 2705, World Bank, Washington, DC.

Farrell, Joseph, and Susan Scotchmer. 1988. "Partnerships." *Quarterly Journal of Economics* 103: 279–297.

Fehr, Ernst, and Karl M. Schmidt. 1999. "A Theory of Fairness, Competition and Cooperation." *Quarterly Journal of Economics* 114: 817–868.

Ghosh, Mrinal, and George John. 1999. "Governance Value Analysis and Marketing Strategy." *Journal of Marketing* 63: 131–145.

Goldberg, Victor P. 1980. "Relational Exchange: Economics and Complex Contracts." *American Behavioral Scientist* 23: 337–352.

Grandori, Anna, and Eugenia Cacciatori. 2006. "From Relational to Constitutional Contracting: The Case of Project-Based Strategic Alliances." Working paper, Bocconi University, Milan.

Grandori, Anna, and Mario Furlotti. 2006. "The Bearable Lightness of Interfirm Strategic Alliances: Associational and Procedural Contracts," in Africa Arino and Jeffrey J. Reuer (eds.), *Strategic Alliances: Governance and Contracts*. London: Palgrave Macmillan, pp. 31–41.

Grandori, Anna, and Giuseppe Soda. 1995. "Inter-Firm Networks: Antecedents, Mechanisms and Forms." *Organization Studies* 16: 183–214.

Granovetter, Mark. 1985. "Economic Action and Social Structure: The Problem of Embeddedness." *American Journal of Sociology* 91: 481–510.

Greif, Avner. 1993. "Contract Enforceability and Economic Institutions in Early Trade: The Maghribi Traders." *American Economic Review* 83: 525–547.

———. 2005. "Commitment, Coercion and Markets: The Nature and Dynamics of Institutions Supporting Exchanges," in Claude Ménard and Mary Shirley (eds.), *Handbook of New Institutional Economics*. Berlin: Springer, pp. 727–786.

Gulati, Ranjay. 1995a. "Does Familiarity Breeds Trust? The Implication of Repeated Ties for Contractual Choice in Alliances." *Academy of Management Journal* 38: 85–112.

———. 1995b. "Social Structure and Alliance Formation Patterns: A Longitudinal Analysis." *Administrative Science Quarterly* 40: 619–652.

———. 1998. "Alliances and Networks." *Strategic Management Journal* 19: 293–317.

Gulati, Ranjay, and Martin Gargiulo. 1999. "Where Do Interorganizational Networks Come From?" *American Journal of Sociology* 104: 1439–1493.

Gulati, Ranjay, and Harber Singh. 1998. "The Architecture of Cooperation: Managing Coordination Costs and Appropriation Concerns in Strategic Alliances." *Administrative Science Quarterly* 43: 781–814.

Gulati, Ranjay, Nitin Nohria, and Akbar Zaheir. 2000. "Strategic Networks." *Strategic Management Journal* 21: 203–215.

Hakansson, Hakan. 1989. *Corporate Technological Behavior. Cooperation and Networks.* London: Routledge.

Hakansson, Hakan, and Jan Johansson. 1993. "The Network as a Governance Structure: Interfirm Cooperation beyond Markets and Hierarchies," in Gernot Grabher (ed.), *The Embedded Firm: On the Socioeconomics of Industrial Networks*. London: Routledge, pp. 35–51.

Halonen, Maija. 2002. "Reputation and the Allocation of Ownership." *Economic Journal* 112: 539–558.

Hansmann, Henry. 1988. "The Ownership of the Firm." *Journal of Law, Economics, and Organization* 4: 267–304.

Hart, Oliver, and John Moore. 1990. "Property Rights and the Nature of the Firm." *Journal of Political Economy* 98: 1119–1158.

Heide, Jan B. 1994. "Interorganizational Governance in Marketing Channels." *Journal of Marketing* 58(1): 71–85.

Heide, Jan B., and George John. 1992. "Do Norms Matter in Marketing Relationships?" *Journal of Marketing* 56(2): 32–44.

Heiman, Bruce, and Jack A. Nickerson. 2002. "Towards Reconciling Transaction Cost Economics and the Knowledge-Based View of the Firm: The Context of Interfirm Collaboration." *International Journal of the Economics of Business* 9: 97–116.

Helper, Susan, and David I. Levine. 1992. "Long-Term Supplier Relations and Product Market Structure." *Journal of Law, Economics, and Organization* 8: 561–581.

Hendrikse, George. 2004. "Governance in Chains and Networks," in Theo Camps, Pieter J. M. Dierderen, Geert J. Hofstede, and Bert Vos (eds.), *The Emerging World of Chains and Networks.* Amsterdam: Reed Business, pp. 189–204.

Hennart, Jean François. 1988. "A Transaction Cost Theory of Equity Joint Ventures." *Strategic Management Journal* 9: 361–374.

Hergert, Michael, and Deigan Morris. 1988. "Trends in International Collaborative Agreements," in Farok K. Contractor and Peter Lorange (eds.), *Cooperative Strategies in International Business.* Lexington, MA: Lexington Books, pp. 99–110.

Hodgson, G. 2002. "The Legal Nature of the Firm and the Myth of the Firm-Market Hybrid." *International Journal of the Economics of Business* 9: 37–60.

Holmström, Bengt. 1989. "Agency Costs and Innovation." *Journal of Economic Behavior and Organization* 12: 305–327.

———. 1999. "The Firm as a Subeconomy." *Journal of Law, Economics, and Organization* 15: 74–102.

Holmström, Bengt, and Paul Milgrom. 1991. "Multi-Task Principal-Agent Analysis." *Journal of Law, Economics, and Organization* 7(special issue): 24–52.

Holmström, Bengt, and John Roberts. 1998. "The Boundaries of the Firm Revisited." *Journal of Economic Perspectives* 12(4): 73–94.

John, George, and Barton A. Weitz. 1988. "Forward Integration into Distribution: An Empirical Test of Transaction Cost Analysis." *Journal of Law, Economics, and Organization* 4: 337–355.

Jones, Candace, William S. Hesterly, and Stephen P. Borgatti. 1997. "A General Theory of Network Governance: Exchange Conditions and Social Mechanisms." *Academy of Management Review* 22: 911–945.

Jorde, Thomas M., and David J. Teece. 1989. "Competition and Cooperation: Striking the Right Balance." *California Management Review* 31(3): 25–37.

Joshi, Ashwin, and Rodney L. Stump. 1999. "Transaction Cost Analysis: Integration of Recent Refinements and an Empirical Test." *Journal of Business-to-Business Marketing* 5(4): 33–71.

Khanna, Tarun. 1998. "The Scope of Alliances." *Organization Science* 93: 340–355.

Klein, Benjamin. 1996. "Why Do Hold-Ups Occur? The Self-Enforcing Range of Contractual Relationships." *Economic Inquiry* 34: 444–463.

Klein, Benjamin, and Kevin Murphy. 1988. "Vertical Restraints as Contract Enforcement Mechanisms." *Journal of Law and Economics* 31: 265–297.

Klein, Benjamin, Robert G. Crawford, and Armen A. Alchian. 1978. "Vertical Integration, Appropriable Rents, and the Competitive Contracting Process." *Journal of Law and Economics* 21: 297–326.

Knoeber, Charles R. 1989. "A Real Game of Chicken: Contracts, Tournaments, and the Production of Broilers." *Journal of Law, Economics, and Organization* 5: 271–292.

Lafontaine, Francine. 1993. "Contractual Arrangements as Signaling Devices: Evidence from Franchising." *Journal of Law, Economics, and Organization* 9: 256–289.

Lafontaine, Francine, and Margaret Slade. 1997. "Retail Contracting: Theory and Practice." *Journal of Industrial Economics* 45: 1–25.

———. 2007. "Vertical Integration and Firm Boundaries: The Evidence." *Journal of Economic Literature* 45: 629–685.

Langlois, Richard N. 2002. "Modularity in Technology and Organization." *Journal of Economic Behavior and Organization* 49: 19–37.

Lerner, Josh, Hilary Shane, and Alexander Tsai. 2003. "Do Equity Financing Cycles Matter? Evidence from Biotechnology Alliances." *Journal of Financial Economics* 67: 411–446.

Lorenzoni, Gianni, and Charles Baden-Fuller. 1995. "Creating a Strategic Center to Manage a Web of Partners." *California Management Review* 37(3): 146–163.

Lumineau, Fabrice, and Joanne E. Oxley. 2012. "Let's Work It Out (or We'll See You in Court . . .)—Litigation and Private Dispute Resolution in Vertical Exchange Relationships." *Organization Science,* forthcoming.

Macaulay, Stewart. 1963. "Non-Contractual Relations in Business: A Preliminary Study." *American Sociological Review* 28: 55–67.

MacLeod, W. Bentley. 2007. "Reputations, Relationships, and Contract Enforcement." *Journal of Economic Literature* 45: 595–628.

MacNeil, Ian R. 1974. "The Many Futures of Contracts." *Southern California Law Review* 47: 691–816.

———. 1978. "Contracts: Adjustments of a Long Term Economic Relation under Classical, Neoclassical, and Relational Contract Law." *Northwestern University Law Review* 72: 854–906.

Madhok, Anoop, and Stephen B. Tallman. 1998. "Resources, Transactions and Rents: Managing Value through Interfirm Collaborative Relationships." *Organization Science* 9: 326–339.

Maness, Robert. 1996. "Incomplete Contracts and the Choice between Vertical Integration and Franchising." *Journal of Economic Behavior and Organization* 32: 101–115.

Masten, Scott E. (ed.). 1996. *Case Studies in Contracting and Organization.* London and New York: Oxford University Press.

Mazé, Armelle, and Claude Ménard. 2010. "Private Ordering, Collective Action, and the Self-Enforcing Range of Contracts. The Case of French Livestock Industry." *European Journal of Law and Economics* 29: 131–153.

Ménard, Claude. 1996. "On Clusters, Hybrids and Other Strange Forms. The Case of the French Poultry Industry." *Journal of Institutional and Theoretical Economics* 152: 154–183.

———. 1997. "Le Pilotage des formes organisationnelles hybrides." *Revue Economique* 48(3): 741–750. [The English version can be found in "The Governance of Hybrid Organizational Forms," in C. Ménard (ed.). 2004. *International Library of New Institutional Economics,* volume IV. Cheltenham, U.K.: Edward Elgar, pp. 105–113.]

———. 2003. "Nouvelle économie institutionnelle et politique de la concurrence: le cas des formes organisationnelles hybrides." *Economie Rurale* 277–278: 3–18.

———. 2004. "The Economics of Hybrid Organizations." *Journal of Institutional and Theoretical Economics* 160: 345–376.

———. 2007a. "The Inadequacy of Competition Policies: A New Institutional Approach," in Nicholas Mercuro (ed.), *Law and Economics,* volume 3. London: Routledge, pp. 345–376.

———. 2007b. "Cooperatives: Hierarchies or Hybrids?" in Jerker Nilsson and Kostas Karantininis (eds.), *Vertical Markets and Cooperative Hierarchies.* Berlin, Boston, Dordrecht, and New York: Springer, pp. 7–27.

———. 2009. "Oliver Williamson and the Economics of Hybrid Organizations," in Mario Morroni (ed.), *Corporate Governance, Organization Design and the Firm. Cooperation and Outsourcing in the Global Economy.* Cheltenham, UK: Edward Elgar, pp. 87–103.

Ménard, Claude, and Peter Klein. 2004. "Organizational Issues in the Agri-Food Sector: Toward a Comparative Approach." *American Journal of Agricultural Economics* 86: 746–751.

Ménard, Claude, and Emmanuel Raynaud. 2010. "Ulysses and the Sirens: Hands-Tying Governance in Hybrid Forms." Working paper, Centre d'Economie de la Sorbonne, Paris.

Ménard, Claude, and Mary Shirley (eds.). 2005. *Handbook of New Institutional Economics.* Berlin: Springer.

Ménard, Claude, and Egizio Valceschini. 2005. "New Institutions for Governing the Agri-Food Industry." *European Review of Agricultural Economics* 32: 421–440.

Milgrom, Paul, Douglass C. North, and Barry Weingast. 1989. "The Role of Institutions in the Revival of Trade: The Law Merchant, Private Judges, and the Champagne Fairs." *Economics and Politics* 2: 1–23.

Mohr, J., and R. Spekman. 1994. "Characteristics of Partnership Success: Partnership Attributes, Communication Behavior, and Conflict Resolution Techniques." *Strategic Management Journal* 15: 135–152.

Nalebuff, Barry, and Adam Brandenburger. 1998. *Co-opetition.* New York: Currency and Doubleday.

Nooteboom, Bart. 1999. *Inter-Firm Alliances. Analysis and Design.* London and New York: Routledge.

Oliver, Amalya L., and Mark Ebers. 1998. "Networking Network Studies: An Analysis of Conceptual Configurations in the Study of Inter-Organizational Relationships." *Organization Studies* 19: 549–583.

Ouchi, William G. 1980. "Markets, Bureaucracies, and Clans." *Administrative Science Quarterly* 25: 129–141.

Oudot, Jean-Michel, and Claude Ménard. 2010. "Opportunisme ou équité? Le cas des contrats d'approvisionnement de défense." *Revue Française d'Economie* 24(3): 196–226.

Oxley, Joanne. 1997. "Appropriability Hazards and Governance in Strategic Alliances: A Transaction Cost Approach." *Journal of Law, Economics, and Organization* 13: 387–409.

———. 1999. "Institutional Environment and the Mechanism of Governance: The Impact of Intellectual Property Protection on the Structure of Inter-Firm Alliances." *Journal of Economic Behavior and Organization* 38: 283–309.

Paché, Gilles, and Claude Paraponaris. 1993. *L'entreprise en réseau.* Paris: Presses Universitaires de France.

Palay, Thomas M. 1984. "Comparative Institutional Economics: The Governance of the Rail Freight Contract." *Journal of Legal Studies* 13: 265–288.

———. 1985. "Avoiding Regulatory Constraints: Contracting Safeguards and the Role of Informal Agreements." *Journal of Law, Economics, and Organization* 1: 155–175.

Park, Seung Ho. 1996. "Managing an Interorganizational Network: A Framework of the Institutional Mechanism for Network Control." *Organization Studies* 17: 795–824.

Parkhe, Arvind. 1993. "Strategic Alliance Structuring: A Game Theoretic and Transaction Cost Examination of Interfirm Cooperation." *Academy of Management Journal* 36: 794–829.

Podolny, Joel, and Karen Page. 1998. "Network Forms of Organizations." *Annual Review of Sociology* 24: 57–76.

Poppo, Laura, and Todd Zenger. 2002. "Do Formal Contracts and Relational Governance Function as Substitutes or Complements?" *Strategic Management Journal* 23: 707–725.

Poppo, Laura, Kevin Zheng Zhou, and Sungmin Ryu. 2008. "Alternative Origins to Interorganizational Trust: An Interdependence Perspective on the Shadow of the Past and the Shadow of the Future." *Organization Science* 19: 39–55.

Powell, Walter W. 1990. "Neither Market nor Hierarchy: Network Forms of Organization," in L. L. Cummpings and B. Staw (eds.), *Readings in Organizational Behavior.* Greenwich, CT: JAI Press, pp. 295–336.

———. 1996. "Inter-Organizational Collaboration in the Biotechnology Industry." *Journal of Institutional and Theoretical Economics* 152: 197–215.

———. 2003. "The Capitalist Firm in the 21st Century. Emerging Patterns," in Paul J. DiMaggio (ed.), *The Twenty-First Century Firm: Changing Economic Organization in International Perspective.* Princeton, NJ: Princeton University Press.

Powell, Walter W., Kenneth W. Koput, and Laurel Smith-Doerr. 1996. "Interorganizational Collaboration and the Locus of Innovation: Networks of Learning in Biotechnology." *Administrative Science Quarterly* 41: 116–145.

Raynaud, Emmanuel. 1997. *Propriété et exploitation partagée d'une marque commerciale: aléas contractuels et ordre privé.* PhD thesis, Université de Paris (Panthéon-Sorbonne), Paris.

Raynaud, Emmanuel, Loïc Sauvée, and Egizio Valceschini. 2009. "Aligning Branding Strategies and Governance of Vertical Transactions in Agri-Food Chains." *Industrial and Corporate Change* 18: 869–899.

Rey, Patrick, and Jean Tirole. 1986. "The Logic of Vertical Restraints." *American Economic Review* 76: 921–939.

———. 2001. "Alignment of Interest and the Governance of Joint Ventures." Institut d'Economie Industrielle Working Paper 441, University of Toulouse, France.

Richardson, George B. 1972. "The Organization of Industry." *Economic Journal* 82: 383–396.

Robinson, David T., and Toby Stuart. 2007. "Network Effects in the Governance of Strategic Alliances." *Journal of Law, Economics, and Organization* 25: 242–273.

Rubin, Paul H. 1978. "The Theory of the Firm and the Structure of the Franchise Contract." *Journal of Law and Economics* 21: 223–233.

———. 2005. "Legal Systems as Frameworks for Market Exchanges," in Claude Ménard and Mary Shirley (eds.), *Handbook of New Institutional Economics.* Berlin: Springer, pp. 205–228.

Ryall, Michael D., and Rachelle C. Sampson. 2006. "Do Prior Alliances Influence Contract Structure?" in Africa Arino and Jeffrey J. Reuer (eds.), *Strategic Alliances: Governance and Contracts.* London: Palgrave Macmillan, pp. 206–216.

Sako, Mari. 2005. "Governing Automotive Supplier Parks: Leveraging the Benefits of Outsourcing and Co-Location?" Working paper, Said Business School, University of Oxford, Oxford.

Sako, Mari, and Susan Helper. 1998. "Determinants of Trust in Supplier Relations: Evidence from the Automotive Industry in Japan and the United States." *Journal of Economic Behavior and Organization* 34: 387–417.

Sampson, Rachelle C. 2005. "Experience Effects and Collaborative Returns in R&D Alliances." *Strategic Management Journal* 26: 1009–1031.

Saussier, Stéphane. 2000. "Contractrual Completeness and Transaction Costs." *Journal of Economic Behavior and Organization* 42: 189–206.

Sauvée, Loic. 2002. "Effectiveness, Efficiency, and the Design of Network Governance," in *Chain and Network Management in Agribusiness and the Food Industry.* Conference Proceedings. Noordwijk-aan-Zee, the Netherlands: 673–684.

Simon, Herbert A. 1951. "A Formal Theory of the Employment Relationship." *Econometrica* 19: 293–305.

Stuart, Toby E., and Joel Podolny. 1996. "Local Search and the Evolution of Technological Capabilities." *Strategic Management Journal* 17: 21–38.

Teece, David E., Gary P. Pisano, and Ann Shuen. 1997. "Dynamic Capabilities and Strategic Management." *Strategic Management Journal* 18: 509–533.

Thorelli, Henry B. 1986. "Networks: Between Markets and Hierarchies." *Strategic Management Journal* 7: 37–51.

Tirole, Jean. 1986. "Hierarchies and Bureaucracies: On the Role of Collusion in Organizations." *Journal of Law, Economics, and Organization* 2: 181–214.

———. 1999. "Incomplete Contracts: Where Do We Stand?" *Econometrica* 67: 741–782.

Tsoulouhas, Theofanis, and Tomislav Vukina. 2001. "Regulating Broilers Contracts: Tournaments versus Fixed Performance Standards." *American Journal of Agricultural Economics* 83: 1062–1073.

Uzzi, Brian. 1997. "Social Structure and Competition in Interfirm Networks: The Paradox of Embeddedness." *Administrative Science Quarterly* 42: 35–67.

Visser, Bauke, and Otto H. Swank. 2007. "On Committees of Experts." *Quarterly Journal of Economics* 122: 337–372.

Wernerfelt, Birner. 1984. "A Resource-Based View of the Firm." *Strategic Management Journal* 5: 171–180.

Williamson, Oliver E. 1975. *Markets and Hierarchies: Analysis and Antitrust Implications.* New York: Free Press.

———. 1985. *The Economic Institutions of Capitalism.* New York: Free Press and Macmillan.

———. 1991. "Comparative Economic Organization: The Analysis of Discrete Structural Alternatives." *Administrative Science Quarterly* 36: 269–296.

———. 1996. *The Mechanisms of Governance.* New York and Oxford: Oxford University Press.

Wu, Steven, and Brian Roe. 2006. "Tournaments, Fairness, and Risks." *American Journal of Agricultural Economics* 88: 561–573.

Zucker, Lynne G. 1986. "Production of Trust: Institutional Sources of Economic Structure, 1840–1920," in *Research in Organizational Behavior,* volume 8. Greenwich, CT: JAI Press, pp. 53–111.

PART VI

Beyond Firms

27

Corruption

Abhijit Banerjee, Rema Hanna, and Sendhil Mullainathan

1. Introduction

Corruption is rampant in many poor countries. As such, anticorruption policies continue to be a central component of development strategies. For example, since 1996, the World Bank alone has supported more than 600 anticorruption programs.

Unfortunately, this is one area where research has lagged policy. Research on corruption faces two important obstacles—one empirical and one theoretical. On the empirical side, the primary challenge is measurement. Corruption, by its very nature, is illicit and secretive. How does one study something that is defined in part by the fact that individuals go to great lengths to hide it? How does one deal with the fact that attempts to measure corruption may cause the actors involved to either reduce their illicit behaviors during the periods of measurement or find new ways to obscure their behavior? If we cannot accurately measure corruption, how can we test among different theories, measure its impacts, or even produce suggestive correlations?

In recent years, some progress has been made to deal with these challenges. In particular, while the previous generation of corruption measures were mainly based on the perception of corruption by participants (with various assorted problems in interpreting these measures), the current generation of studies have focused on collecting and reporting objective information, obtained either from direct measurement or from other information.

The theoretical challenge comes in part from the need to go beyond thinking of corruption as a generic form of moral hazard in organizations to the point where we can map different manifestations of corruption to different underlying environments. Here the word "environment" is interpreted to cover both the usual focus of the corruption literature (the nature of the monitoring and the punishments) as well as the intrinsic motivation of the bureaucrats (e.g., how corruption fits into their moral compass)—and what is less emphasized, the nature of the particular economic decision that the bureaucrats are participating in. This expansion is important for two reasons. First, from the point of view of empirical research, differences in the nature of corruption in different economic settings is an important source of testable predictions. Second, for policy design, it is vital that we are able to think of how changing the environment might be an effective substitute for simply adjusting the punishment (which may not be feasible).

An example might clarify the second point. Bandiera et al. (2009) study waste in government procurement in Italy, a country that is often rated as one of the most corrupt in Europe. Using detailed data, they show that different branches of government pay very different prices for the same product (down to the brand and color). These price discrepancies can differ by 50% or more. In fact, they estimate that the government could save up to 2% of GDP if most purchase officers paid the same price as that obtained by the most frugal officers.

They also show, however, that the price differences are a function of where the purchase officers buy. They can either obtain their supplies from the market or from an approved supplier, Consip. Consip charges a publicly announced price, which leaves no scope for kickbacks. Going to the market, in contrast, potentially allows the buyer to negotiate his own deal, which might include something extra for himself. If buyers go to the market to get kickbacks, we would expect the least-corrupt officers (i.e., those who were previously paying the lowest prices) to be the ones who switch to the Consip option when it becomes available. In fact, the data suggest the opposite. When a new item is added to Consip's list of available items, the bureaucrats paying the highest prices turn to Consip. Moreover, these purchasing officers are also the ones that were, by all accounts, the best monitored—members of the centralized bureaucracies rather than the more autonomous hospitals and universities. These observations suggest a different narrative. These officers pay much higher prices than others not only because of kickbacks. The issue is also one of justifiability. Buying from the official supplier requires no justification—and no effort. Bandiera et al. (2009) argue that a major source of the waste here is the fear of being prosecuted for corruption. Bureaucrats pay high prices to avoid any taint of corruption. Notice that under this logic, changing the bureaucratic rules to give the bureaucrat a fixed procurement budget but full discretion—so that she can even pocket any money she saves, may generate both less waste and less corruption. She might even pocket more money, but that would be perfectly legal, and being free to keep the money may give her a strong reason to avoid waste.

This argument does not imply that full discretion is always a good idea. Think of the allocation of hospital beds. If need is not related to ability to pay, giving a bureaucrat full discretion about how to allocate beds may lead to a large proportion of them going to those who do not really need them. Making stringent rules about how the bureaucrat is supposed to allocate the beds will generate corruption, as the greediest bureacrats will bend the rules to make more money, but also, potentially, a better allocation, because the more honest bureaucrats will adhere to the rules.

The more general point is that corruption is the result of the task that the bureaucrat is assigned to carry out. We can usually get rid of it by setting the appropriate task (giving discretion), but that is not always desirable from society's point of view. The optimal response to the possibility of corruption may often be to change the nature of the task. Note that the change in the task may not always reduce corruption: it might just address the misallocation or degradation of services that corruption often causes (e.g., that hospital beds were going to the rich or that the wait for a bed was unacceptably long).

Starting from the premise that the corruption we observe may be the result of the task assigned to the bureaucrat gives us a way to generate testable implications. In particular, we will then be able to map the specific problem the government is trying to solve into a vector of outcomes (e.g., bribes, lines, or misallocation of beds). The questions we seek to answer are of the form: Are the waits likely to be longer when the government is trying to target hospital beds to the very poor rather than to the less poor? Are bribes likely to be greater when trying to target hospital beds to the very poor?

This repositioning of the corruption literature away from a purely crime-and-punishment approach toward a more task-focused approach connects it more closely to the literature on the internal economics of organizations that has emerged over the past two decades. This literature explicitly recognizes that most organizations use bureaucratic mechanisms similar to the ones associated with government bureaucrats for many of their internal decisions, which creates scope for corruption (Tirole 1986). However, there is much to be gained from focusing on the specific characteristics of the kinds of settings in which governments work. For example, one source of corruption in government is that governments are expected to deliver goods and services to those who cannot pay for their full value. This issue is less important in for-profit organizations. We return to the relationship between corruption in government and similar issues in private firms in Section 3.5.

This chapter highlights the progress made in the corruption literature over the past decade or so, with a focus on the doors this progress opens for future research. In this way it aims to be more forward than backward looking, less of a comprehensive review of corruption research and more of a guide to where it appears to be headed.[1] It provides a theoretical framework to illustrate the tasks approach and an overview of the tools now available for empirically analyzing corruption. It then lays out the open questions we think are both interesting and within reach.

We start with a discussion of what we mean by "corruption" in Section 2. The key point is that corruption involves breaking rules, not just doing something that is unethical or against the collective interest. This approach leads us naturally to think of the task that the bureaucrat has been assigned (which includes the rules). This is the subject of Section 3, where we develop a simple theoretical framework for thinking about corruption and its many manifestations. We then discuss strategies for measuring corruption in Section 4. Section 5 discusses a recent empirical study that provides a clear test of the model, and Section 6 reviews the growing literature on how to combat corruption. We conclude with a discussion of the main areas we think important for future research (Section 7).

2. Defining Corruption

We define corruption as the breaking of a rule by a bureaucrat (or an elected official) for private gain. This definition includes the most obvious type of corruption—a bureaucrat taking an overt monetary bribe to bend a rule, thereby providing a service to someone that he was not supposed to. However, it would also encompass more nuanced forms of bureaucratic corruption. For example, it would include nepotism, such as if a bureaucrat provided a government contract to a firm owned by her nephew rather than to a firm that ought to win a competitive, open

1. Summarizing a literature as large and multidisciplinary as corruption poses unique challenges. In this chapter, we have erred on the side of being forward looking, trying to paint a picture of where this literature is headed. Though we have aimed to cover all important existing literature, some gaps are an unfortunate necessity to keep this chapter manageable in length: our apologies to authors whose work we could not cover in much detail.

procurement process. This definition would also cover the case of a bureaucrat who "steals time": she may, for example, not show up to work, but still collect her paycheck.[2]

Under this definition, the rules define what is corrupt. As a result, the same act can be classified as corruption in one setting but not in another. For example, in many countries (the United States, India, etc.) a citizen can obtain passport services more quickly if he pays a fee. While this act would not be considered corruption in these countries, it would be in others, where no such provision in the law exists. In contrast, many important political economy issues may not necessarily be considered corruption under this definition. For example, a government official providing patronage to supporters may have important ethical and allocative implications, but this act would not necessarily be corruption if no formal rule is technically broken.[3]

The definition of corruption used in this chapter is similar to those used by others in the literature, but there are important distinctions. For example, our definition is quite similar to that discussed by Svensson (2005: 20)—"the misuse of public office for private gain"— and to Shleifer and Vishny (1993: 599), who define corruption "as the sale by government officials of government property for personal gain." All three definitions imply that the official gains personally from her particular position. Moreover, as Shleifer and Vishny (1993) define property quite loosely to include both physical assets (e.g., land) and assets that have an option value (e.g., a business license), their definition encompasses many of the same acts of corruption discussed in this chapter and in Svensson (2005). However, there are slight differences in what qualifies as corruption across the definitions. For example, suppose we assume that a government official has the final say over whom to allocate a government contract to. He may choose to sell it to his nephew, and gain great personal happiness from doing so. Thus, this may be considered corruption under Svensson (2005) and Shleifer and Vishny (1993). However, if the official has the final say, and has not broken any official rules, this would not be considered corruption under our definition, despite being morally questionable.

We have chosen to use this definition for a combination of pragmatic and conceptual reasons. Pragmatically, the emphasis on breaking formal rules (as opposed to moral or ethical ones) sidesteps the need to make subjective ethical judgments and thereby avoids the need to have a deeper discussion of cultural differences.[4] The emphasis on all kinds of gain rather than just monetary sidesteps a measurement problem: bribes by their very nature are hard to measure, whereas rule breaking is easier to measure. Conceptually, these distinctions are also in line with the framework we describe in the next section.

3. A Formal Framework for Understanding Corruption

The challenge of modeling corruption comes from the very definition of corruption. As stated in Section 2, corruption is when the bureaucrat (or elected official) breaks a rule for private gain. This immediately raises some questions, because the rules themselves are chosen by the

---

2. Quite often, we see the same forms of corruption in the nonprofit sector, where a social good is being provided, and the private and social value may not necessarily coincide. The models presented in this chapter would naturally extend to the nonprofit sector.

3. For a deeper discussion of political corruption, see Pande (2007).

4. Of course, culture is discussed explaining corruption, simply not when defining it.

government. Specifically, why have these rules, which we know are going to be violated, been put in place? Why not change the rules so that there is no incentive to violate them? This idea leads to an ancillary question: can you change the rules costlessly and eliminate corruption without affecting anything else that you care about?

To understand these issues, we begin by thinking about the underlying task. Our model of tasks is simple, and yet it captures many of the tasks bureaucrats (and also those in the private sector) typically carry out. We focus on an assignment problem. A bureaucrat must assign a limited number of slots to applicants. The applicants differ in their social valuation of a slot, their private valuation of it, and also their capacity to pay for it. This simple setup captures many important cases. Consider a profit-maximizing firm selling a good. In this case, the slot is the good, and private and social values coincide perfectly. Next, consider the case of a credit officer assigning loans at a government bank. Here, the private ability to pay may be the lowest precisely among those who have the highest social returns from the loan. This potential for divergence between private and social returns is not incidental—it may be the reason the government was involved in providing the loans in the first place. However, it is also the reason there is corruption.

The bureaucrat's task here goes beyond just allocating the slots: she may also face rules about what prices she can charge for them and whether she can engage in "testing" to determine an agent's type. The government sets both these rules and the incentives facing the bureaucrat.

Although this framework does encompass many models of bureaucratic misbehavior in the literature, we make no claims of generality for it. We make a large number of modeling choices that are pointed out as we develop the model. These are made mostly in the interests of simplicity and clarity, but many of them can also have substantive implications.

3.1. Setup

We analyze the problem of a government allocating slots through a bureaucrat who implements the allocation process. There is a continuum of slots of size 1 that need to be allocated to a population of size $N > 1$. Agents (i.e., citizens) have differing private and social values for slots. Specifically, there are two types of agents: H and L with mass N_H and N_L, such that $N_H + N_L > 1$. The social value of giving a slot to type H is H and L for type L. We assume that $H > L$. Private benefits can be different, with each group valuing their slots at h and l. Agents' types are private information and unknown by either the government or the bureaucrat, though the bureaucrat has a technology for learning about type that is called "testing," which we describe below. Agents also differ in their ability to pay for a slot, which we denote by y_h and y_l: because of credit constraints, agents may not be able to pay full private value, so $y_h \leq h$ and $y_l \leq l$.

There is a generic testing technology to detect agent types that the bureaucrat can use. If used on someone of type L (who is trying to pass the test) for a period of time t, the probability that he will fail the test (i.e., get an outcome F) is $\phi_L(t)$, $\phi'_L(t) \geq 0$. The corresponding probability for a type H who wants to pass is 0; he always passes if he wants to (i.e., gets the outcome S). Either type can always opt to deliberately fail. The cost of testing for t hours is νt for the bureaucrat. The cost of being tested for the person for t hours is δt. A simple example of testing would be a driving exam to verify that one can drive.

Testing is the only costly action taken by the bureaucrat in our model. We assume that the bureaucrat does not put in any effort to give out the slots. We capture much of what is relevant about bureaucrat shirking through this device, but there are no doubt some nuances that the model misses.

3.1.1. Possible Mechanisms

The basic problem for the bureaucrat is the choice of a mechanism. The bureaucrat announces a direct mechanism that she can commit to ex ante.[5] Each mechanism constitutes a vector $R = (t_x, p_{xr}, \pi_{xr})$, where t_x is the amount of testing for each announced type $x = H, L$; π_{xr} is the probability that someone acquires a slot conditional on announcing type $x = H, L$ and achieving result $r = F, S$; and p_{xr} is the price this individual will pay in the corresponding condition. We restrict this discussion to winner-pay mechanisms here (mechanisms where the applicant does not pay when he does not receive a slot). For analysis of the more general case where a nonrefundable fee is required to enter the bidding, see, for example, Banerjee (1997).

Because the bureaucrat only chooses direct mechanisms, any R is supposed to satisfy the incentive constraints:

$$\pi_{HS}(h - p_{HS}) - \delta t_H \geq \pi_{LS}(h - p_{LS}) - \delta t_L$$

and

$$\pi_{LS}(l - p_{LS})(1 - \phi_L(t_L)) + \pi_{LF}(l - p_{LF})\phi_L(t_L) - \delta t_L$$
$$\geq \pi_{HS}(l - p_{HS})(1 - \phi_H(t_H)) + \pi_{HF}(l - p_{HF})\phi_H(t_H) - \delta t_H$$

Moreover, the clients are allowed to walk away. This is captured by the participation constraints:

$$\pi_{HS}(h - p_{HS}) - \delta t_H \geq 0$$
$$\pi_{LS}(l - p_{LS})(1 - \phi_L(t_L)) + \pi_{LF}(l - p_{LF})\phi_L(t_L) - \delta t_L \geq 0.$$

There is also a total slot constraint:

$$N_H \pi_{HS} + N_L \pi_{LS}(1 - \phi_L(t_L)) + N_L \pi_{LF}\phi_L(t_L) \leq 1.$$

Finally, there is affordability: agents cannot pay more than they have:

$$p_{Hr} \leq y_H, r = F, P$$
$$p_{Lr} \leq y_L, r = F, P.$$

Define **R** to be the set of values of R that satisfy these conditions.

3.1.2. Rules

The government chooses a set of rules for the bureaucrat that take the form $\mathcal{R} = (T_x, P_{xr}, \Pi_{xr})$, where T_x is the set of permitted values for amount of testing (t_x), P_{xr} is the set of permitted

---

5. We recognize that the actual mechanism used will often be very different from the direct mechanism. We discuss some of the issues this raises in Section 3.6.

prices, and Π_{xr} is the set of permitted values for the probability that someone acquires a slot (π_{xr}) for $x = H$, L and $r = F$, S. Although we assume that the government does not observe every individual's type, we do allow P_{xr} and Π_{xr} to depend on the buyer's type. The idea is that if there is a gross misallocation of slots or large-scale bribery by one type, there may be some way for the government to find out (the press might publish a story stating that the hospital beds were all being occupied by cosmetic surgery patients who are paying high prices, or the government might sample a few people who received slots). However, we do not assume that being able to observe violations of P_{xr} automatically implies being able to observe violations of Π_{xr}: it may be easy to find out that some people are being charged more than the permitted prices without learning anything more generally about how the slots are being allocated.

We assume that $\mathcal{R}$ is feasible in the sense that there exists at least one $R = (t_x, p_{xr}, \pi_{xr}) \in \mathbf{R}$ such that $t_x \in T_x$, $p_{xr} \in P_{xr}$, and $\pi_{xr} \in \Pi_{xr}$. If $\mathcal{R}$ is not a singleton, then the bureaucrat has discretion.

The government also chooses p, which is the price that the bureaucrat has to pay to the government for each slot he gives out. Assume that this is strictly enforced, so that the price is always paid. This assumption can be relaxed easily, but the result offers no new insights.

In specific examples, we make specific assumptions about what the government can contract on, which will give structure to $\mathcal{R}$. For example, if t_x is not contractible, then the rules will not address it—in other words, T_x will be $[0, \infty] \times [0, \infty]$.

3.1.3. The Bureaucrat's Choice
For each mechanism $R \in \mathbf{R} \cap \mathcal{R}$, the bureaucrat's payoff is

$$N_H \pi_{HS}(p_{HS} - p) + N_L \pi_{LS}(p_{LS} - p)(1 - \phi_L(t_L))$$
$$+ N_L \pi_{LF}(p_{LF} - p)\phi_L(t_L) - \nu N_H t_H - \nu N_L t_L.$$

However, if R is in $\mathbf{R} \cap \mathcal{R}^c$, we assume that a bureaucrat pays a cost for breaking the rules, which is γ. Hence, the bureaucrat's payoff for any R in $\mathbf{R} \cap \mathcal{R}^c$ is

$$N_H \pi_{HS}(p_{HS} - p) + N_L \pi_{LS}(p_{LS} - p)(1 - \phi_L(t_L))$$
$$+ N_L \pi_{LF}(p_{LF} - p)\phi_L(t_L) - \nu N_H t_H - \nu N_L t_L - \gamma. \tag{1}$$

We assume that the cost γ is unknown to the government when setting rules, though it knows that it is drawn from a distribution $G(\gamma)$. A corruptible bureaucrat is one for whom γ is finite.[6] As a result, we write $R(\mathcal{R}, \gamma)$ as the mechanism chosen by a bureaucrat with cost of corruption γ when the rule is $\mathcal{R}$.[7]

3.1.4. The Government's Choice
We assume that the bureaucrat is the agent of what we call the "government" (but what others have called the "constitution maker"), a principal whose preference is to maximize the social welfare generated by the allocation of the slots. This assumption is partly an artifact of the way

---

6. This formulation is quite specific, and the cost of violating the rules is independent of the extent of violation.
7. We assume that when indifferent, the bureaucrat chooses what the government wants.

we model things. What is key is that the bureaucrat has a boss whose objectives are different from hers and who is in a position to punish her. Otherwise, she would never have to break any rules, because she, in effect, would make her own rules. The assumption that her boss cares only about social welfare is convenient but not necessary. Much of what we have to say would pertain if the principal cares less about the bureaucrat's welfare and more about that of the other beneficiaries, which may be true even if one thinks of the principal as the standard issue, partly venal, politician. After all, the politician cares about staying in power, and making the bureaucrat happy may not be the best way to do so. Of course, it is possible that the bureaucrat is the one who cares about beneficiaries and is trying to protect them from her boss. This is an interesting and perhaps important possibility that we do not investigate here. More generally, a setup like ours deliberately rules out the more interesting strategic possibilities that arise in models of political economy, to focus on the implementation issues that arise even without them.[8] The government therefore maximizes

$$\int [N_H \pi_{HS}(R(\mathcal{R}, \gamma))H + N_L \pi_{LS}(R(\mathcal{R}, \gamma))(1 - \phi_L(t_L(R(\mathcal{R}, \gamma))))L$$

$$+ N_L \pi_{LF} \phi_L(t_L(R(\mathcal{R}, \gamma)))L - (v + \delta)N_H t_H(R(\mathcal{R}, \gamma)) - (v + \delta)N_L t_L(v)] \, dG(\gamma)$$

by choosing $\mathcal{R}$.

3.1.5. Interpretation

We intend for this model to be the simplest one that can illustrate all features of interest. Specifically, it allows the bureaucrat to have multiple dimensions of malfeasance:

- *Corruption.* The bureaucrat breaks the rules.
- *Bribe taking.* The bureaucrat charges higher prices than those mandated.
- *Shirking.* The bureaucrat fails to implement mandated testing.
- *Red tape.* The bureaucrat implements more than the mandated amount of testing.
- *Allocative inefficiency.* The wrong people obtain the slots (according to the rules), or some slots remain unallocated when the rules require that all slots be given out.

There is corruption in equilibrium because the government does not observe the cost γ. If the government knew the particular bureaucrat's γ, it would know what the bureaucrat would choose, given the rules that are set; hence, the government would be able to set rules that would not be broken. However, when γ can take different values, the government has to choose between rules that give the bureaucrat a great deal of discretion (so that they will almost never be broken) and rules that are more rigid (to induce the bureaucrat to act in the social interest) and therefore will be broken by some bureaucrats (precisely because they are more stringent).

---

8. It is also worth making clear that the assumption of welfare maximization, although standard, is quite particular. The government could care, for example, about the distribution of welfare between the bureaucrats and the potential beneficiaries. In this case the government may prefer an inefficient outcome, because it achieves distributional outcomes better and may therefore create a more complex set of trade-offs than are permitted here. We return to this issue in Section 3.6.

This straightforward problem goes beyond the standard resource allocation problem under asymmetric information in two important ways. First, we do not assume that the private benefit to the person who obtains the slot is necessarily the social benefit. Such a divergence is characteristic of many situations involving the government. For example, society wants to give licenses to good drivers ($H > 0$) and not to bad ones ($L < 0$), but the private benefits of getting a license are probably positive for both types. Or suppose the slot is avoiding a jail sentence. H types are innocent. L types are not. $H > 0$ is the social benefit of not sending an innocent to jail. $L < 0$ is the social benefit of not sending a criminal to jail. However, the private benefits are positive for both types: $h \lessgtr l$ but $h, l > 0$. Second, we allow the potential beneficiaries to have an ability to pay that is less than their private benefits (or willingness to pay) ($l > y_L$ or $h > y_H$). This condition is conventionally treated as being equivalent to the beneficiary being credit constrained, but it is worth emphasizing that it covers a range of situations (including the credit-constraint case). For example, consider the person who wants to take his child to the hospital to be treated, but his permanent income does not cover the cost. He would, however, be willing to pay his entire income (less survival needs, say) to save his child's life and also would be willing to additionally stand in line for 4 hours a day every morning. In this case, his total willingness to pay (in money and time) is clearly greater than his ability to pay. Clearly, if he could freely buy and sell labor, this case would reduce to the standard credit-constraint case, but given the many institutional features that govern labor markets, this would be an extreme assumption.[9]

However, the formulation embodies a number of important simplifying assumptions. We impose, for example, that rule breaking of any type has the same cost, which obviously need not be the case. For example, when a bureaucrat and an agent collude in such a way that the agent is better off than under the official rules, there will probably be less chance of being caught than when the bureaucrat attempts to make the agent worse off. We also do not deal with distributional issues: the government is indifferent to who—between the bureaucrat and his various types of clients—gets to keep how much money. We return to why this issue may be important later in the chapter.

3.2. A Useful Typology

Before jumping into the analysis of this model, it is helpful to underline some of the different possibilities that can arise in our framework (Table 1). The following typology will prove to be particularly handy. The labels of the cases should be self-explanatory, but more explanation emerges as we analyze each case.[10]

---

9. Another example that exploits a different rigidity in labor markets is the following. There is a woman who is not allowed by her family to work, but she is willing to walk 3 miles every day to make sure that her child gets an education. Her ability to pay (assume that the rest of the family does not care about education) is clearly less than her willingness to pay.

10. That we have only four cases is an artifact of the assumption that all H types are identical in their willingness and ability to pay and likewise for L types. However, the basic distinction we are trying to make here is between the case where H types are willing and/or able to pay more and the case where they may not be (captured by $h \leq l$ and $y_H \leq y_L$). The situation where a large fraction of L types are willing and/or able to pay more than a large fraction of H types is qualitatively very similar to the case where all L types are able/willing to pay more than all H types.

Table 1. Possibilities arising from the corruption model

Agent's valuation of slot	Agent's relative ability to pay	
	$y_H > y_L$	$y_H \leq y_L$
$h > l$	Case I: alignment	Case III: inability to pay
$h \leq l$	Case II: unwillingness to pay	Case IV: misalignment

3.2.1. Examples of Case I: Bids Aligned with Value

In this case, social and private value rankings align. Although the pure market case, $H = h = y_H$, $L = l = y_L$, belongs to this category, this case is ultimately broader than that, because even though the rankings may align, the actual ability to pay may not match social value. Some other examples that fall into this case include:

1. *Choosing efficient contractors for road construction.* Type H are the more efficient contractors. For the same contract, they make more money ($h > l$): Within our framework, contractors asking a lower price for their work is the same thing as them paying more up front to secure a contract that will eventually pay them a fixed amount. Because the contractors will be paid for their work, the price that they pay to obtain the contract can be seen as just a discount on how much they will eventually be paid rather than viewed as an out-of-pocket expense. It is plausible therefore that $y_H = h$ and $y_L = l$.

2. *Allocating licenses to import goods to those who will make the socially optimal use of them.* In an otherwise undistorted economy, the private benefits should be the same as the social benefits, as in the road construction example, but in this example, there may be credit constraints, because the license is first paid for and the profits come later. However, it is plausible that type H agents should be able to raise more money than type L agents. Thus, $y_H < h = H > L = l > y_L$, and $y_L < y_H$.

3.2.2. Examples of Case II: Unwillingness to Pay

This case is the least likely of the four cases, and so we do not spend much time on it. However, one possible example is a merit good, such as subsidized condoms for protection against HIV infection: H are high-risk types. They like taking risks. Hence, $h < l$. However, they may also be richer than type L (e.g., because they can afford to buy sex): $y_H > y_L$.

3.2.3. Examples of Case III: Inability to Pay

In this case, there is alignment of values: the high type values the good more than does the low type, but there is an inability to pay.

1. How to allocate hospital beds? The H types more urgently need the hospital beds (e.g., compared to those who just want cosmetic surgery). The social valuation probably should be the private valuation in this case: $H = h > L = l > 0$. However, there is no reason to assume that the H types can afford to pay more. We capture this situation by assuming $y_H = y_L = y$.

2. How to allocate subsidized foodgrains targeted to the poor? Presumably, the H types are the poor who benefit more from subsidized foodgrains, and the social benefit is plausibly

just the private benefit ($H = h > L = l > 0$). However, the poor may not be able to pay as much for the grain as can the nonpoor: $y_H < y_L$.

3. How to allocate government jobs to the best candidates? The private gains from landing the job may be higher for the H types (because the jobs offer so much more rents than the next-best alternative, and the better candidate may get more out of the job). However, everyone is constrained by how much they can pay for the job up front ($y_H = y_L = y$).

3.2.4. Examples of Case IV: Values Misaligned

In this case, there is simple misalignment between social and private valuation: those to whom the government would like to give the slot value it the least:

1. *Law enforcement.* We have already mentioned this example, where the slot is avoiding jail time: $H > 0 > L$, $y_H = y_L = y$, $h = l > 0$.

2. *Driver's licenses.* We discussed the setup of this example previously. However, this example would fall under Case IV if bad drivers value the license more, because they are more likely to be picked up by the police: $H > 0 > L$, $y_H = y_L = y$, $h < l$.

3. *Procurement.* The government wants to procure a fixed number of widgets and has a fixed budget for them (e.g., Bandiera et al. 2009). Suppose there are high-quality firms and low-quality firms. It is socially efficient to procure widgets from the high-quality firm, even though these firms have higher costs. In this case the slot is the contract, which needs to be allocated among firms. The gains from getting the contract are obviously higher for the low-quality firm, which has lower costs. So $l > h$. As long as these firms are not credit constrained, that would also mean that $y_H = h$ and $y_L = l$.

3.3. Analyzing the Model

This very simple model nevertheless allows for a rich variety of possibilities and situations. Here we confine ourselves to some illustrative examples of the kind of incentive issues that can arise in this framework, the corresponding patterns of rules chosen, and the violations of the rules. Specifically, we focus on a set of special instances of Cases I, III, and IV, which yield many of the insights we are looking for. We then briefly discuss the other cases.

3.3.1. Analysis of Case I

In this case, private and social rankings are aligned. Assume in addition that $N_H < 1$, but $L > 0$, so that it is optimal to give the leftover slots to L types. To solve the government's problem, we start with the mechanism design problem. Consider the following candidate solution (we drop the success or failure subscripts when a particular type is not being tested):

$$p_H = y_L + \epsilon, \quad p_L = y_L$$

$$\pi_H = 1, \quad \pi_L = \frac{1 - N_H}{N_L}$$

$$t_H = t_L = 0.$$

Notice that the low types would not want to pretend to be high types. They cannot pay p_H. What about the high types? If they pretend to be the low types, they could pay ϵ less, but they would receive the slot with probability less than 1. As long as

$$h - (y_L + \epsilon) \geq \frac{1 - N_H}{N_L}(h - y_L),$$

the high types would prefer to pay the price and be guaranteed a slot. We can always set ϵ low enough to ensure that this is the case. Therefore, the mechanism is incentive compatible for small enough ϵ. Because both types receive positive expected benefits, the participation constraints are also satisfied. The solution is feasible, because the ratio $\frac{1-N_H}{N_L}$ was chosen precisely to exhaust the total number of slots. Finally, it is affordable, as long as ϵ is small enough, because $y_H > y_L$ in this case. Define E to be the set of ϵ such that this mechanism is in $\mathcal{R}$.

This solution is also social-welfare maximizing, because every H type receives a slot, every slot is taken, and no one is tested. The key question is whether the bureaucrat will want to choose this mechanism for some $\epsilon \in E$: if he will choose it, then the government's problem is solved. However, it is possible that he might prefer an alternative mechanism.

Given our assumption that there is a fixed cost of breaking the rules, if the bureaucrat is corruptible and chooses to break the rules, he will choose the mechanism that maximizes his payoff given by (1). Therefore, he will want to maximize the amount of revenue he can extract. The mechanism already allows him to extract all possible revenues from type L. To maximize his payoff (in this class of mechanisms), he will set ϵ to its maximal value in E. That is, he will set

$$p_H = p_H^* = \min\left\{y_H, y_L + (h - y_L)\frac{N-1}{N_L}\right\}.$$

Let us, with some abuse of terms, call the following the "auction mechanism":

$$p_H = p_H^*, \quad p_L = y_L$$

$$\pi_H = 1, \quad \pi_L = \frac{1 - N_H}{N_L}$$

$$t_H = t_L = 0.$$

However, in this scenario, he is not extracting all the rents from type H, because p_H might be lower than y_H. What are the other mechanisms that could potentially give him higher payoffs? One is the class of monopoly mechanisms. Set

$$p_H = \widetilde{p_H} \leq y_H, \quad p_L = y_L$$

$$\pi_H = 1, \quad \pi_L = \min\left\{\frac{(h - \widetilde{p_H})}{(h - y_L)}, \frac{1 - N_H}{N_L}\right\}$$

$$t_H = t_L = 0.$$

These mechanisms are constructed so that the probability of getting the slot as an L type is low enough that no H type will want to pretend to be an L type. No L type can afford the slot at the *H* type's price, so that incentive constraint also does not bind. By construction, these mechanisms also satisfy the slot constraint, as well as the participation and affordability constraints. However, they generate an inefficient outcome, as some slots are wasted.

Obviously, this class of mechanisms will only interest the bureaucrat if $(h - y_L)\frac{N-1}{N_L} + y_L < \widetilde{p_H} \leq y_H$. The condition that it makes more money than the auction mechanism is that the expression

$$N_H(\widetilde{p_H} - p) + N_L\frac{(h - \widetilde{p_H})}{(h - y_L)}(y_L - p)$$

is increasing in $\widetilde{p_H}$, because for $\widetilde{p_H} = (h - y_L)\frac{N-1}{N_L} + y_L$, this is exactly the payoff from the auction mechanism. The relevant condition is therefore

$$N_H > N_L\frac{(y_L - p)}{(h - y_L)}.$$

If this condition holds, the monopoly mechanism that maximizes the bureaucrat's earnings will have $\widetilde{p_H} = y_H$. Otherwise, the auction mechanism dominates.

Finally, the last alternative we consider is the testing mechanism:

$$p_H = \min\left\{y_H, h - (h - l)\frac{1 - N_H}{N_L}\right\}, \quad p_{LS} = p_{LF} = y_L$$

$$\pi_H = 1, \quad \pi_{LS} = \pi_{LF} = \frac{1 - N_H}{N_L}$$

$$t_H = 0, \quad t_L = \max\left\{0, \frac{1}{\delta}\min\left\{(h - y_L)\frac{1 - N_H}{N_L} - (h - y_H), (l - y_L)\frac{1 - N_H}{N_L}\right\}\right\}.$$

The exact construction of this mechanism is less obvious, so let us look at it in a bit more detail. The idea of this mechanism is to use testing just to reduce the rents of the self-declared *L* types, so that *H* types would not want to pretend to be *L* types. It is inefficient, because testing is wasteful. Because *H* types are more likely to pass a test than *L* types are, it would be counterproductive to reward "passing": the goal is to discourage *H* types from pretending to be *L* types. To reward failing the test also does not work: *H* types can always fail on purpose. Therefore, there is no advantage to conditioning on test outcomes.

To see that testing relaxes type *H*'s incentive constraint, note that now it becomes

$$(h - p_H) \geq (h - y_L)\frac{1 - N_H}{N_L} - \delta t_L.$$

Clearly, p_H can go up when t_L increases, which is why the bureaucrat might want it to. However, there is obviously no point in driving t_L past the point where $p_H = y_H$. This defines one limit on how large t_L should be:

$$(h - y_H) - (h - y_L)\frac{1 - N_H}{N_L} \geq \delta t_L.$$

Another limit comes from the fact that, by imposing testing, the L type is made worse off. So t_L must satisfy IR_L:

$$(l - y_L)\frac{1 - N_H}{N_L} \geq \delta t_L.$$

As long as IR_L is not binding, raising t_L always pays off in terms of allowing p_H to be raised. Once it binds, it is possible to continue to increase t_L by reducing p_L below y_L. However, this will never pay off, because reducing p_L also forces the bureaucrat to reduce p_H. Setting $\delta t_L = (l - y_L)\frac{1-N_H}{N_L}$ and plugging this into type H's incentive constraint gives us the limit on how high we can drive p_H by testing L types:

$$p_H \leq h - (h - l)\frac{1 - N_H}{N_L}.$$

Putting these observations together explains why we construct the testing mechanism in this way.

It is also worth observing that $t_L = 0$ when $y_L = l$. This result occurs because when IR_L is binding, red tape will never be used. Thus, the fact that the bureaucrat's clients are unable to pay the full value of what they are getting is key for the result that there is red tape (that is why they pay in "testing" rather than money).

These three mechanisms do not exhaust the class of feasible mechanisms. For example, it may be possible to combine the testing and monopoly mechanisms. However, it is easy to think of situations where each of them may be chosen by some bureaucrats, depending on the rules that the government sets and other parameters. The trade-offs that this model generates are mainly what we need to understand.

Scenario 1   *Suppose that $(h - y_L)\frac{N-1}{N_L} + y_L \geq y_H$. Then, the auction mechanism extracts as much rent as possible. The government can give the bureaucrat full discretion (no rules) and expect the optimal outcome. It can then set p to appropriately divide the surplus between itself and the bureaucrat. The bureaucrat chooses the auction mechanism.*

Scenario 2   *Suppose that $(h - y_L)\frac{N-1}{N_L} + y_L < y_H$. Assume that π_{xr}, p_{xr}, and t_x are contractible. The rules do not impose any restrictions on the choice of t_x. Also, assume that the bureaucrat has no cost of testing ($v = 0$) and that it is possible to extract maximal rents from type H by testing the type L, which will be true when[11]*

$$y_H \leq h - (h - l)\frac{1 - N_H}{N_L}.$$

Suppose first that the government sets no rules. Because the bureaucrat pays no cost for testing and testing allows her to extract maximal rents, she will choose the testing mechanism described above as a way to create artificial scarcity.

11. As long as $y_L < l$, this condition is consistent with the condition $(h - y_L)\frac{N-1}{N_L} + y_L < y_H$ imposed above.

One alternative for the government is to set the rules so that the maximum price the bureaucrat can charge is $(h - y_L)\frac{N-1}{N_L} + y_L$, and all testing is forbidden. For those bureaucrats not prepared to break the rules, the optimal mechanism in this case will be the auction mechanism (because they were deviating from it precisely to charge the H type a higher price, which is now not allowed).

However, those bureaucrats who have a low cost of breaking the rules (low γ) will deviate from the auction mechanism and choose the testing or the monopoly mechanism.[12] The testing mechanism tends to extract less money from each L type (because they also pay the cost of being tested), but more L types get slots. Which of the two will be chosen depends on the parameter values. For example, an increase in $y_H - y_L$, keeping $l - y_L$ fixed, makes the monopoly mechanism relatively more attractive (intuitively, when the H type can pay relatively more, the cost of including the L type increases). If the monopoly mechanism is chosen, there will be no red tape, but large bribes (price above the maximum allowed price) will occur. If the testing mechanism is chosen, we will observe both bribery (price above the maximum allowed price) and red tape. Nevertheless, from the social welfare point of view, this outcome is strictly better than the no-rules outcome, because a fraction of the bureaucrats (those with high γ) choose the auction mechanism. What is particularly interesting here, though, is that the rules themselves are now affected by the potential for corruption. A different set of rules make sense when the bureaucrats are more corruptible.

Scenario 3   *Suppose that $(h - y_L)\frac{N-1}{N_L} + y_L < y_H$. Assume p_{xr} and t_x are contractible, but π_{xr} is not.[13] However, let v be very high, so that the bureaucrat is not prepared to use red tape.*

In the absence of any rules, the bureaucrat will either choose the auction or the monopoly mechanism. We already generated the condition under which the monopoly mechanism makes more money:

$$N_H > N_L \frac{(y_L - p)}{(h - y_L)}.$$

Interestingly, this condition is less likely to hold if p is lower—the government may be better off not charging the bureaucrats for the slots. However, even with $p = 0$, it is possible that the above condition holds (especially if y_L is very low), and the bureaucrat, unconstrained, would choose the monopoly mechanism. Suppose that this is the case. Then the no-rules outcome will leave many slots unallocated.

The government may prefer to set a rule where the prices that can be charged are capped by $(h - y_L)\frac{N-1}{N_L} + y_L$. Then the bureaucrats who have high γ will choose the auction mechanism, while the low-γ bureaucrats will choose the monopoly mechanism. There will be bribery, because the monopoly price is higher than the price cap.

12. It is true that in our model we would get the same result with either a rule on testing or a cap on the price, but this reflects our extreme assumption that breaking one rule is the same as breaking them all. An epsilon extra cost of breaking two rules instead of one would make it strictly optimal to have both rules.

13. In our model, because the bureaucrat always pays the government for the slots, the government actually knows how many slots he has used and therefore should able to contract on π_x. However, it is easy to think of an extension of the model to a state of the world where the demand for slots is lower and the government does not observe this state.

3.3.2. Analysis of Case III

Let us focus on one special case: $L > 0$, $N_H < 1$, $h > l$, $y_H = y_L$ (which are the assumptions under which this case is analyzed in Banerjee 1997). To limit the number of cases, let $y_H = y_L = y < l$ and $\phi_L(t) = 0$; that is, no one ever fails the test. In this case, once again there is an auction mechanism:

$$p_H = y, \quad p_L = p_L^*$$

$$\pi_H = 1, \quad \pi_L = \frac{1 - N_H}{N_L}$$

$$t_H = t_L = 0,$$

where p_L^* is such that[14]

$$l - y = \frac{(1 - N_H)}{N_L}(l - p_L^*).$$

This mechanism implements the efficient outcome, because the high types, though they cannot pay more, value the slot more ($h > l$) and hence would rather pay the high price (all they can afford) and ensure a slot rather than risk not getting one at the low price. The logic of auctions still works.

However, now consider an alternative testing mechanism:

$$p_H = y, \quad p_L = y$$

$$\pi_H = 1, \quad \pi_L = \frac{1 - N_H}{N_L}$$

$$t_H = t_H^*, \quad t_L = 0,$$

where t_H^* is given by

$$l - y - \delta t_H^* = \frac{1 - N_H}{N_L}(y - l).$$

As in Scenario 2, testing only happens when $l - y > 0$.

A third is a lottery mechanism, given by

$$p_H = y, \quad p_L = y$$

$$\pi_H = \pi_L = \frac{1}{N}$$

$$t_H = 0, \quad t_L = 0.$$

The bureaucrat charges everyone y and simply holds a lottery to allocate the slots.

---

14. This only works if y is high enough. Otherwise, p_L might have to be negative.

Scenario 4   *Suppose that π_{xr}, p_{xr}, and t_x are all contractible, and $v = 0$.*

What would happen if the government set no rules? The bureaucrat would always prefer the lottery, with a very significant misallocation of slots.

Now, suppose the government sets the rules so that the bureaucrat is required to choose

$$\pi_H = 1, \quad \pi_L = \frac{1 - N_H}{N_L},$$

but there is no rule for what prices he can charge or the amount of testing. Every bureaucrat will choose the testing mechanism, because it gives them the same payoff as the lottery without breaking any rules.

Suppose the government wants to stop this unnecessary testing. Then it can set rules so that the bureaucrat is required to set the auction mechanism:

$$p_H = y, \quad p_L = p_L^*$$

$$\pi_H = 1, \quad \pi_L = \frac{1 - N_H}{N_L}$$

$$t_H = t_L = 0.$$

This mechanism will be chosen by those bureaucrats who have high enough γ. However, the low-γ bureaucrats will choose the testing mechanism, and there will be both bribery and red tape.[15]

Alternatively, the government could choose the lottery as the rule. All bureaucrats would then choose it and there would be no corruption and no red tape, but the outcome that everyone chooses would involve misallocation. However, because there is no testing, this outcome might be better than that from testing, if the cost of being tested, δ, is high enough. Moreover, the testing mechanism is only better because it makes the high-γ bureaucrats choose the optimal mechanism. Therefore, if most bureaucrats face a low value of γ, representing a government that cannot enforce the rules very well, then the lottery mechanism is likely to dominate.

3.3.3. Analysis of Case IV

Let us restrict our attention to the specific situation $N_H > 1$, $y_L = l > h = y_H$, and $L < 0$. The goods are scarce, but the private valuation of the high types is lower than that of low types. The low types should ideally not obtain the slots.[16] The analysis in this section draws on Guriev (2004). Consider the following testing + auction mechanism:

$$p_{HS} = p_H^*, \quad p_{HF} = p_L = l$$

$$\pi_{HS} = 1/N_H, \quad \pi_{HF} = \pi_L = 0$$

$$t_H = t_H^*, \quad t_L = 0,$$

---

15. Once again we assume that the bureaucrat (at least weakly) prefers to break one rule rather than two.

16. For examples, see Laffont and Tirole (1993).

where t_H^* and p_H^* solve the two equations[17]

$$h - \delta t_H^* - p_H^* = 0 \tag{2}$$

$$(1 - \phi_L(t_H))(l - p_H^*) - \delta t_H^* = 0. \tag{3}$$

It is easy to check that this mechanism satisfies all the constraints. Of particular interest are type L's truth-telling constraint:

$$(1 - \phi_L(t_H))(l - p_H^*) - \delta t_H^* \leq 0,$$

which states that type L individual voters weakly prefer not getting the slot to pretending to be a type H and getting it with some probability. It is clear that for this condition to hold, $t_H^* > 0$, because without testing, the L types always want the slot if the H types do. Testing is necessary in this case.

This mechanism also implements the optimal allocation (only H types get the slots) with the least amount of testing.

However, the bureaucrat may consider other mechanisms. One possibility is a straight auction:

$$p_H = p_L = l$$

$$\pi_H = 0, \quad \pi_L = 1/N_L$$

$$t_H = 0, \quad t_L = 0.$$

Another is a lottery. No one is tested, but the allocation is all wrong—only L types receive the slots:

$$p_H = p_L = h$$

$$\pi_H = 1/N, \quad \pi_L = 1/N$$

$$t_H = 0, \quad t_L = 0.$$

Scenario 5   *Suppose that π_{xr}, p_{xr}, and t_x are contractible, and $v > 0$. Consider what would happen without any rules. The auction mechanism maximizes the bureaucrat's earnings without any testing and will be chosen. Now suppose the government sets rules about t_x, π_{xr}, and p_{xr} exactly at the level given by the testing + auction mechanism. Bureaucrats who do not want to break the rules will then choose the testing + auction mechanism. The ones who are prepared to break the rules will choose the auction mechanism. There is bribe taking, shirking, and misallocation of resources (similar to Bandiera et al. 2009).*

However, the government could also give up on trying to implement the ideal testing + auction mechanism. It could set the rules corresponding to the lottery mechanism. The advantage of this mechanism is that the bureaucrats are making more money from the slots, because $h > p_H^*$, and spending less effort on testing; hence, the gains from deviating are smaller. The disadvantage is that some slots go to the L types, even if the bureaucrat is not corrupt. However, fewer of them deviate from the rules and give all slots to the L types.

---

17. We assume that a solution with $p_H^* \geq 0$ exists, which is true when $l - h$ is not too large.

3.4. Interpretation of Results

The above analysis makes clear the essence of our approach. Governments are interested in setting rules when the laissez-faire outcome does not maximize social welfare. Put simply: in this model, governments only interfere to improve an inefficient situation. Corruption, however, results when these rules do not extract maximum surplus for the bureaucrat. Sometimes the rules allow the bureaucrat to extract surplus exactly as she wants (e.g., Case I in Section 3.3.1), but in many other cases they may not. The task assigned to the bureaucrat and the rules are chosen by a government cognizant of the possibility for corruption. In several of the cases, it is clear that the presence of corruptible bureaucrats changes the rules and tasks. The government chooses those rules, and the task is assigned to the bureaucrat, recognizing that the rules will sometimes be broken. The overall outcome is still improved by setting those rules. This is the essence of the tasks approach.

However, the model also offers other, more specific, insights. The first observation is that red tape goes hand in hand with bribery. Given that testing is costly, there is no reason to overuse it, unless there is extra money to be made. However, there are two distinct reasons for using it. When the willingness to pay is aligned with ability to pay and social valuation (Case I; specifically, Scenario 2), red tape is faced by L types, that is, those who have a low probability of obtaining the good, and is designed to create some artificial scarcity and extract more rents for the bureaucrat (along the lines suggested by Shleifer and Vishny 1994). In other words, the purpose of the red tape is to screen in the types with a high willingness to pay. When ability to pay is not related to the willingness to pay (Case 3, Scenario 4), then red tape emerges, because even corrupt bureaucrats prefer to generate as efficient an allocation as possible, conditional on not making less money. The red tape is then placed on the H type, and the purpose is to screen out the types with a low willingness to pay.

The second point is that red tape only emerges when $y_L < l$. Moreover, it is easy to check that in both cases, red tape increases in the gap between the willingness to pay and the ability to pay. The intuition is simple. It is precisely because this gap exists that it is possible to impose red tape. If there were no such gap, the client would simply walk away if faced with a great deal of red tape. This reasoning makes it clear why people do not have to endure red tape when they try to buy most marketed goods (i.e., goods for which $l = y_L$). Governments are associated with red tape, in this view, because governments often supply goods to people whose ability to pay is less than their willingness to pay. For that reason, this problem is particularly acute for governments serving the poor.

A third point, which is related to the first, is that red tape does not have to result from scarcity. Scarcity may have a positive or a negative effect on red tape, depending on whether we are trying to discourage the H type from pretending to be an L type (Scenario 2, where scarcity reduces red tape) or the opposite (Scenario 4, where scarcity increases red tape).

A fourth point comes from thinking about the correlation between red tape and bribery. This correlation is emphasized by La Porta et al. (1999), who, looking at cross-country data, argue that the positive correlation of testing with bribery is evidence that much testing is unnecessary and hence is red tape. As already observed, red tape only occurs when there is bribery. However, we cannot assume that there is always more red tape when there is more bribery—that depends on what is the underlying source of variation as well as the underlying economic problem. For example, both in Scenarios 2 and 4, the incentive to move away from the auction outcome toward the testing outcome is always stronger when $l - y_L$ is larger. Therefore, there will be more red tape and corruption when y_L is lower, as long as the government sets rules that correspond to the socially efficient mechanism. In contrast, when $y_H - y_L$ goes up, keeping $l - y_L$ fixed, corrupt bureaucrats will switch from testing to monopoly (see Scenario 2). There is an increase in the size of bribes and a fall in red tape.[18]

A fifth point follows from Scenario 5. Bribery can be associated with red tape, but it is also associated with shirking, which, in a sense, is the opposite of red tape.

A sixth point follows from the observation in Scenario 4 that a rightward shift in the distribution of γ will lead the government to switch from rules that correspond to the lottery mechanism to those that correspond to the testing mechanism. This switch leads to greater bribery and more red tape but to less misallocation and is therefore worthwhile. In other words, greater state capacity might be associated with more red tape and bribery. Conversely, a lack of bribery cannot be interpreted as evidence that all is well.

A seventh observation is that corruption might force the government to give up on trying to maximize its revenues from the sale of slots. In Scenarios 1 and 3, we saw that the government should set the price of the slots to the bureaucrat as low as possible to reduce corruption.

Finally, it is clear that the government often faces a choice between more desirable mechanisms that are more subject to corruption and less desirable ones that are less so. This is exactly the choice in Scenario 4 but also in Scenario 5. Corruption is therefore an outcome of this choice.

3.5. Firms and Governments: A Digression

The broad framework developed above would apply, mutatis mutandis, to any situation where the principal cares about the assignment of slots to the right people but not how much money he makes from the slots, but the slot allocation is implemented by an agent who does not care about who gets the slots but is concerned about how much money she makes. The first assumption comes directly from our framework.

However, much of what is interesting here also relies on two additional assumptions. First, the private valuation of those who receive the slots is not necessarily equal to the value the principal puts on giving them the slots. Second, the private valuation may not be the same as the ability to pay.

These assumptions are quite natural in the context of thinking about governments and similar organizations, such as nonprofit organizations. However, in the conventional way of

---

18. A negative correlation would also result if we were prepared to go outside the world of the model and assume that the government has other unmodeled reasons for setting a price cap that do not have to do with promoting efficiency. For example, the government may be sensitive to distributional or ideological concerns—government bureaucrats should not be seen as becoming too rich, even if that is what efficiency demands. Or there may be some political or symbolic argument for making all public goods free or very cheap. This might lead the government to set the price cap below y_L. Take the extreme case where the good is supposed to be free (the cap is zero). In this case, the government would actually want the bureaucrat to test those who apply for the slots (because the price mechanism will not do any screening). Here a bureaucrat who is corrupt might actually do some good: all he needs to do is to raise the price for the H types to $y_H + \varepsilon$ and scrap the red tape, and social welfare would unambiguously go up. In such cases, bribe taking would be an antidote to red tape, and they would move in opposite directions. This is the old idea that corruption greases the wheels and increases efficiency (Huntington 1968), but note that it can only happen when the government is not using its choice of rules to maximize welfare.

looking at market transactions (think of the principal as the manufacturer, the agent as the retailer, and the clients as buyers), none of these *three* defining assumptions probably apply. We now recognize that there are many transactions involving firms where the firm is not seeking to maximize short-run profits, because of multitasking, reputation, or signaling, for example, or because the transaction is internal to the firm (e.g., who should be promoted). In such cases, our first two assumptions are likely to be satisfied. However, the third key assumption (about the divergence between the willingness and the ability to pay) is less obviously applicable.

Thus, Cases I and IV probably fit the private sector best (see Sections 3.3.1 and 3.3.3). We know that there can be corruption in both these cases (Scenario 2 or Scenario 5), even if the ability and the willingness to pay are the same ($y_L = l$, $y_H = h$). However, as already observed, there will not be red tape in such cases, though shirking may occur.

Other potential sources of corruption that do not arise in our model may occur in private firms. There may be conflicts over the division of the surplus with a profit-maximizing principal—for a variety of reasons (e.g., the agents may be credit constrained), the firm may want to share enough of its realized revenues with its agents to align their incentives. This may be even more of an issue for private firms than for governments, though as discussed in Section 3.6, it is central to some things that governments do, such as tax collection.

Many reasons not in our model account for why the government may have more corruption than private firms do. One big difference between firms and the government is that even when many of the transactions take place within the firm, there is still an ultimate principal (or principals) whose business is maximizing profits. This could place a limit on the level of rents that could possibly be captured. Consider corruption in promotion decisions. This context offers opportunities for corruption in both sectors. In the government context, there are jobs that one would like to capture because they offer rents in terms of bribes from customers (e.g., the job of a policeman). Thus, both the capacity to engage in corruption and a willingness to do so exist (there are big rents). The firm context allows room for corruption, because promotions are also not allocated through a market mechanism. However, the upside gains from capturing the job are far more limited: the customers are paying market prices, and hence, there are no rents to be had from them. At best, one gets the rents from a higher paying job and, in most cases, these are nowhere near the rents to be had from having access to customers who are willing to pay a bribe.

A related point is that governments and firms are held accountable through different mechanisms. Governments have to convince voters to reelect them, but the welfare of the voters depends on a combination of many outcomes. As a result, the electorate cannot simply use single metrics, such as revenues or taxes collected, to evaluate performance. Firms, however, are (much more easily) evaluated along a single dimension—profitability. This difference generates opportunity for corruption in government that does not exist in firms. For example, consider procurement procedures. In firms, a clear mapping connects from corruption in procurement to lower profitability, which the boss typically does not like. Whereas in the government, the resultant rise in costs is probably submerged somewhere in the general budget, and while the loss of quality might be noticed by some voters, they would most likely place small weight on it in their decision of whom to vote for. Indeed, we might speculate that those who are in favor of corruption in government have a stake in arguing against any single metric of performance.

In summary, firms have less slack at the edges than governments. This lack of slack limits the room for corruption within the organization. Of course, it does not completely eliminate corruption. Nor does it mean that all firms face little slack. For instance, poorly governed firms or those with monopoly power or other factors generates slack. We are merely speculating that qualitatively, governments experience much more slack when dealing with clients, and this slack translates into more opportunity for corruption in the organization.

3.6. Limitations of the Framework

3.6.1. Monitoring

A clear limitation of our framework is made clear from the discussion in Section 3.5 about the differences between external incentives faced by governments and private firms. It tells us very little about monitoring structures, other than the obvious point that better monitoring would reduce corruption. The emphasis on monitoring in theorizing corruption goes back, of course, to the classic paper by Becker and Stigler (1974). Although the insights from this paper remain fundamental, we see it more as a paper on agency problems generally and not particularly about corruption.

There is also now a literature that emphasizes the institutional aspects of monitoring. Clearly, a choice exists for who monitors (the superior bureaucrats, the community, the voters?) and how intensively (should there be pro-active public disclosures of public accounts, of the performance of individual bureaucrats, etc.?). Even though the Bardhan and Mookherjee (2006) model captures the important and basic idea that communities may have an informational advantage in monitoring (and therefore in controlling) corruption, the theoretical literature on this subject has not advanced very much beyond this point, though there is a lot of interesting empirical material available.

An important theoretical literature emphasizes the endogeneity of the effectiveness of monitoring. Lui (1986) makes the point that corruption may be harder to detect when everyone else is corrupt. Tirole (1996) shows that in a model where experimentation is costly, when enough bureaucrats are corrupt, everyone acts as if all of them were corrupt, which removes the incentive to be honest. There is also the idea that people feel less bad about being corrupt when everyone else is corrupt. To our knowledge, little rigorous empirical research has been done based on these ideas, though they are obviously important.

3.6.2. Reintroducing Distributional Concerns: Understanding Extortion

Another limitation of our framework is that it assumes that the government maximizes total social welfare. However, ignoring the distribution of welfare between the beneficiaries and the bureaucrats is clearly wrong in many instances. One obvious example is tax collection. Tax collection is all about who pays. In such cases, the government might prefer an inefficient outcome, because it achieves the distributional outcome better and may therefore create a more complex set of trade-offs than are otherwise permitted.

Similarly, the fact that the outside option in our model allows people to withdraw from obtaining a slot is also potentially problematic, especially because this outside option does not vary by type. Consider a tax collection example. Suppose you are trying to get a tax-exempt certificate, because you have no money. An undeserving taxpayer (a type L), who actually can afford to pay the taxes, does have the option to walk away: if she does not have the certificate, she can always pay the taxes and be done with it. In contrast, the deserving taxpayer (type H) cannot pay the taxes. As a result, if he withdraws from trying to get the certificate, he risks prison. His outside option is worse than that of the type L.

More generally, our assumption about outside options limits the possibility of extortion. However, it has long been recognized that one reason many government functions cannot be privatized is because of the potential for extortion. We need a framework that helps explore these issues.

3.6.3. Screening on Multiple Dimensions

In our framework, the assumption that there is only one dimension of asymmetric information is very restrictive. The bureaucrat may want to know about both the beneficiary's type (because misallocation is punished) and his ability to pay (because the bureaucrat wants to make the most money), and the two traits may not be perfectly correlated. A simple example of what can happen in such situations is worked out in Banerjee (1997), but the general multidimensional screening case is not well understood.

3.6.4. Modeling Corruption

Our framework also embodies one specific view of why there is corruption in equilibrium. Corruption occurs because the cost of violating rules varies across bureaucrats. However, as discussed at some length in Tirole (1986), there are other reasons. For example, the government may recognize that in some states of the world, the bureaucrat and his clients are in position to cut a profitable private deal that the government would like to prevent but lacks the information to do so.

Why not then simply recognize that this deal will happen and make it legal? One possible answer is that there are many other states of the world where the same deal would be available, but in these other states of the world, the government is in a position to detect such behavior, prosecute the bureaucrat, and thereby prevent the transactions. However, if the courts cannot distinguish between those states of the world where such private transactions are proscribed and other states of the world where they are not, the bureaucrat could always claim that the transaction was allowed and get away with it. By banning all transactions between the bureaucrat and his client, the government is creating the possibility that the rules will be violated from time to time, but it gains in terms of being able to prosecute the bureaucrat if he goes too far.

4. Measuring Corruption

Measuring corruption is the primary challenge in the empirical literature. Without robust measures, the theories cannot be tested, the magnitudes of corruption cannot be quantified, anticorruption policies cannot be assessed, and so forth. However, measuring corruption is challenging, and even today, relatively few studies are able to credibly describe the extent of the problem. As Bardhan (1997: 1320) notes in his review of corruption, "our approach in this paper is primarily analytical and speculative, given the inherent difficulties of collecting (and hence nonexistence of) good empirical data on the subject of corruption."

The measurement challenges are driven by several problems. First, the very fact that corruption is illegal makes people reluctant to talk about it for fear of getting into trouble and, possibly, for shame. Second, the existing literature—because of the theory it draws on and how it defines corruption—takes a transactional view of corruption. Measurement means finding out who bribed whom and by how much, which is inherently harder to quantify. Third, the traditional narrow focus on monetary transactions also makes it more difficult.[19] When a government official benefits by stealing "time"—she decides not to show up for work—random spot checks can be very revealing (e.g., see Chaudhuri et al. 2006). Finally, measurement systems will evoke responses that make the measurement system less reliable. If the government has a monitoring system in place, people adjust to it and find ways around it. As a result, these measurement systems will underestimate corruption.

Despite these difficulties, many early attempts at measuring corruption relied on rich qualitative data and were occasionally backed up by numbers. These studies gave the first real evidence about the channels through which corruption occurred and possible methods to eliminate it. Wade (1982) in particular provides a detailed description of how irrigation engineers reap revenue from the distribution of water and contracts in a village in South India. The most fascinating aspect of this study was the documentation of a fairly formal system in which the engineers redistributed revenue to superior officers and politicians. To obtain transfers to lucrative posts, the junior officers paid bribes based on expectations about the amount of bribe money that can be collected from the post. Thus, the value of the bribe payment in the transfer process was higher for jobs that had greater potential for bribe extraction. In essence, the ability to take bribes in a job induces bureaucrats to bribe others to get it. This highly detailed study gives a glimpse into the pervasiveness of corruption in this area and the mechanics of how it operates. It also illustrates how corruption is interconnected throughout the entire organization and raises the possibility that rather than trying to remove one aspect of corruption, it may be necessary to invoke coordinated policies to stamp it out throughout the system. However, like all case studies, the study raises questions of generalizability. Is there as much corruption in other contexts? Under what set of circumstances do these systems come into being?

Other early studies focused on anticorruption policies. For example, Klitgaard (1988) provides several case studies of successful elimination of corruption, such as in the Hong Kong Police Force, Singapore Excise Department, and the Bureau of Internal Revenue of the Philippines. In all these cases, the levers used are intuitive from the perspective of agency theory—more intense or better monitoring, replacing individual actors, and so forth. They also all seem to involve a person at the top of each institution who was eager to implement these changes. On the one hand, these cases represent a vindication of an agency theory of corruption. On the other hand, they raise the more fundamental question: if these levers for eliminating corruption are in the choice sets of governments, why are they not implemented? Although they spark hope that corruption can be fought, these examples leave lingering questions about why conditions were ripe for these interventions but not for those elsewhere. Is what we observe due to particular institutional factors in these settings or to more generalizable features of how governments function? What particular combinations of institutions, policies, or conditions would lead to similar steps being taken elsewhere? Should we expect the same consequences of similar anticorruption policies in different settings?

---

19. There are exceptions. For example, Tran (2008) gathers a comprehensive set of internal bribery records from a firm in Asia to document the cost of bribe payments over time.

To address these inherent problems of case studies, the next attempts to measure corruption tried to provide consistent measures of corruption across countries. However, given the difficulty of inducing people to talk about corruption, these measures focus on collecting perceptions of corruption rather than on the actual bribes paid or the actual theft of resources. This perception-based approach has been carried out at quite a large scale, generating interesting cross-country and cross-time datasets. The Economist Intelligence Unit created one of the first such datasets.[20] The data collection effort consisted of factor assessment reports that were filled in by the Unit's network of correspondents and analysts. The reports were then aggregated into risk factors for about 70 countries. The factor assessment reports included, for example, a question where the respondents rated "the degree to which business transactions (in that country) involve corruption or questionable payments" on a scale of 1–10, where a high value implies good institutions (Mauro 1995: 684). Other cross-country measures on subjective perceptions of corruption followed, including the Control of Corruption measures in the World Bank Governance Indicators (a description of the measures can be found in Kaufmann et al. 2004), and measures by Transparency International (2008).[21] Each of these indicators uses a different methodology with its own advantages and disadvantages, which we do not discuss here due to space constraints.[22] The real advantage of such data is their breadth, which allows one to run large correlational studies. Mauro (1995) is an often-cited example of this kind of study. He uses the Economist Intelligence Unit measures in a cross-country growth regression equation to study the relationships among economic growth, corruption, and red tape.

While these perception-based measures of corruption provided evidence on which countries tend to report more or less corruption, many have pointed out their limitations. First, as Rose-Ackerman (1999) noted, it is unclear what the corruption indices actually mean and what a particular rank implies about the type and level of corruption in a country. For example, in the Transparency International Corruption Perceptions Index for 2008, Brazil, Burkina Faso, Morocco, Saudi Arabia, and Thailand all have the same index value. However, the value does not tell us what the form of corruption in these countries entails, nor does it indicate whether the types of corruption observed in these very different countries have different efficiency implications. For example, in the theoretical framework developed in this chapter, bribe taking can actually promote efficiency, if the problem is that the government is committed, for political or ideological reasons, to set the price cap below what it should be. Moreover, corruption often emerges as a result of government interventions designed to deal with some other distortion (see Section 3). These countries may have very different problems—why would the gap between l and y_L or between h and y_H be the same in Saudi Arabia and Burkina Faso, given their very different levels of per capita wealth? Or corruption may be a result of the government's attempt to fight some other form of misbehavior by its bureaucrats—for example, in Case I (Section 3.3.1), absent a price cap, the bureaucrat might choose the monopoly outcome, and

20. These datasets are also called the "Business International Indicators."

21. Papers that use perception-based measures of corruption in cross-country regressions include Mauro (1995), Knack and Keefer (1995), LaPorta et al. (1999), Treisman (2000), Adsera et al. (2003), Fisman and Gatti (2002), Fredriksson and Svensson (2003), Rauch and Evans (2000), and Persson et al. (2003).

22. Svensson (2005) provides a thorough description of the differences among the most common cross-country indicators of corruption.

many slots may be wasted. A price cap might move the outcome to more visible malfeasance by the bureaucrats (red tape and bribe taking) but less misallocation and less inefficiency overall. Greater corruption in one country could simply be a reflection of a greater willingness to fight corruption in that country. Because they do not supply information about the sources of corruption, these corruption indices actually tell us little about what types of governance interventions would help deal with the problems or even whether we should reward or praise governments that have less corruption by these measures.

Second, perceptions may indicate little about the actual reality of situations, because they are influenced by the way we see everything else. For example, perhaps when the economy is good, we perceive less corruption, because we are more satisfied with the government. Olken (2009), for example, compares the perception of corruption in a roads project with actual missing expenditures. He finds that although there is real information in perceptions, reported corruption is not particularly responsive to actual corruption. For example, "increasing the missing expenditures measure by 10 percent is associated with just a 0.8 percent increase in the probability a villager believes that there is any corruption in the project" (Olken 2009: 951). He also finds that the bias in perceptions is correlated with demographic characteristics, implying that perceptions of a nonrandom sample of the population may not adequately reflect real corruption levels. This bias is particularly problematic, as many perception measures are not necessarily based on random samples. For example, the measures from the Economist Intelligence Unit are based on the perceptions of foreign analysts, who may have different perceptions of corruption than the average citizen of the country. Finally, and perhaps probably most importantly for our purposes, these data are most useful for cross-country or cross-geography analysis. They are less useful for testing microtheories of corruption.

New methods for measuring corruption have been developed that solve the small-sample problem and move to more concrete measures of corruption. The first such method focuses on refining survey and data collection techniques to improve the ability to assemble data on self-reported bribes and service delivery quality. For example, Svensson (2003) analyzes a dataset that provides information on bribes paid by firms in Uganda. To encourage truth telling in the survey, it was conducted by a trusted employers' association; it also asked carefully worded, hypothetical questions to measure corruption.[23] Hunt (2007) uses the International Crime Victims Surveys and Peruvian Household surveys, both of which contain information on bribes to public officials if the individual has been the victim of a crime.[24] Other studies collect prices paid for services that should be free. For example, Banerjee et al. (2004) collects data on fees paid at government health centers in India (that should mostly be free), Atanassova et al. (2008) collect data on prices paid and quantities received from the public distribution system in India and compare them to the official prices for these commodities. The main benefit of these methods is a move to measures that have actual meanings. For example, using the measure in Banerjee et al. (2004), we can estimate the bribe amounts paid at the health centers and use this information to understand

---

23. For example, "Many business people have told us that firms are often required to make informal payments to public officials to deal with customs, taxes, licenses, regulations, and services, etc. Can you estimate what a firm in your line of business and similar size and characteristics typically pays each year?" (Svensson 2003: 213).

24. Mocan (2008) also uses the International Crime Victims Surveys to determine what characteristics were associated with greater corruption.

how the bribes affect the allocation of health services. We can also use it as an outcome measure to study the effectiveness of anticorruption policies in government health centers. However, these types of measures are limited if individuals are underreporting bribes, and particularly if this underreporting is biased by corruption levels. Moreover, most of the time, these measures are often limited to petty corruption, because it is difficult to ask individuals about the larger bribes that they may have paid. Indeed, in many of these cases, the reports are assumed to be reliable precisely because the agents do not know how much they should have paid, and therefore do not see themselves as paying bribes. It is also clear that people might be more willing to reveal bribes that they paid in settings where the good they receive is abundant (so that they are not displacing anyone else by paying the bribe).

The second method is the use of physical audits of governmental processes. For example, Chaudhury et al. (2006) conducted a multicountry study of teacher and health worker absence, where they performed spot checks to determine whether bureaucrats were showing up for work.[25] Similarly, Bertrand et al. (2007) followed individuals through the process of obtaining a driver's license in India and recorded all extra-legal payments made and the rules that were broken in exchange for these payments. Barron and Olken (2007) designed a study in which surveyors accompanied truck drivers on 304 trips along their regular routes in two Indonesian provinces. The surveyors observed the illegal payments the truck drivers made to the traffic police, military officers, and attendants at weighing stations.

One of the key challenges to the audit studies is whether the observed outcomes actually reflect corruption rather than some less intentional form of bureaucratic ineffectiveness, because often there is no smoking gun (bribe overtly paid, job left entirely unattended, etc.). For example, Bertrand et al. (2007) find that there is a misallocation of licenses—people who cannot drive are able to obtain them. Could this be due to an overworked bureaucrat who does not have time to screen license candidates or due to an incompetent one who cannot distinguish between good and bad drivers? To understand this issue, Bertrand et al. collect detailed quantitative and qualitative data on how the bureaucrats behave during the licensing process. They document extreme behaviors (e.g., simply never administering a driving test), which would be hard to label as "incompetence." Similarly, Duflo et al. (2012) measure teacher absenteeism in rural India using audit methods. Does the fact that teachers often do not come to school imply that they are consciously breaking the rules for private gain? Or are lives of these teachers so difficult that they just cannot make it to school often enough, despite trying as hard as they can? The research design provides information that allows the authors to answer these questions. Specifically, they evaluate a program that monitors the teachers and provides incentives to them based on their attendance. They find that teachers are very responsive to the incentives. That teachers respond to the incentives so strongly implies that the teachers were previously ignoring the rules and were not incapable of attending.

We refer to the third technique as "cross-checking." The idea behind it is to compare official records of some outcome with an independently collected measure of the same outcome. One example of cross-checking is to compare how much money was released to the bureaucrat with how much the ultimate beneficiaries of the funding report have received. For example, Reinikka

---

25. Other such studies include Duflo et al. (2012), who measure teacher absence, and Banerjee et al. (2008a), who measure absenteeism among medical providers.

and Svensson (2005) compare data from records on central government disbursements and a public expenditure tracking survey to measure dissipation in a school capitation grant in Uganda. They find that the average school received only about 20% of central government spending on the program. Fisman and Wei (2004) compare Hong Kong's reported exports to China at the product level with China's reported imports from Hong Kong to understand the extent of tax evasion. Another way to conduct a cross-check would be to collect records from the bureaucrat documenting how the government resources were spent in achieving a task and then compare them with an objective measure of how much it should have cost to conduct the task. The difference between the two measures is, then, the estimate of how much was stolen. Olken (2007) uses this method. He calculates corruption in the context of road projects by comparing the actual expenditures reported with an independent measure of what it should have cost to build a road of that particular quality. To obtain the independent measure, he sampled each road to determine the materials and labor used, and then used local prices to cost these elements. He finds that, on average, about 24% of expenditures across the project villages were missing.[26]

As with any other method, this one has both strengths and limitations. Its innovation lies in the fact that it creatively allows the measurement of dissipated government resources without asking the actors involved if they have paid or received an actual bribe, reducing the chance of under- or misreporting. Thus, it often allows us to move past petty corruption and perhaps look at larger scale corruption. However, it is difficult to understand whether the dissipated recourses are actually corruption or simply mismeasurement in the indicators or even just a sign of bureaucrat incompetence. For example, in Olken (2007), it remains possible (though unlikely) that road quality is mismeasured or that the bureaucrats are not good at building roads. It is possible (though again unlikely) that the missing resources indicate that the bureaucrats are trying to reallocate funds to better uses. For example, in Reinikka and Svensson (2005), it is possible (although again unlikely) that the resources that should have gone to the school capitation program were actually spent on services that the community deemed more important and did not end up in the pockets of government officials. Would this result have necessarily been bad?

One way to get around these concerns is to look for correlations (motivated by theory) between the extent of dissipation and some other variable. For example, to show that the differences in reported shipments is corruption and not just mismeasurement in the shipments, Fisman and Wei (2004: 471) document that the differences are "negatively correlated with tax rates on closely related products, suggesting that evasion takes place partly through misclassification of imports from higher-taxed categories to lower-taxed ones, in addition to underreporting the value of imports."[27]

---

26. Other examples of cross-checking in the developing world include the Hsieh and Moretti (2006) estimate of bribes in Iraq's Food for Oil Program; Olken (2006) and Atanassova et al. (2008) measure theft in food distribution programs using the same method, and Di Tella and Schargrodsky (2003) use it to measure corruption in hospital procurements.

27. Duggan and Levitt (2002) provide an interesting example of cross-checking in sumo wrestling. They basically show that a wrestler has a higher probability of winning than expected when the match is key to his rank. To distinguish match throwing from effort, they use theory as a guide: the effect goes away when there is

In addition to these methods recently used in the literature, there are several innovative methods being explored in current studies. Although some of the work is not yet published, such methods will surely contribute to the tools available for studying corruption. For example, Banerjee and Pande (2009) attempt to use second-hand data on which politicians have gotten rich since they entered politics to identify those who have profited from corruption.[28] They find that this measure correlates strongly with other, more direct (perceptual), measures of corruption (e.g., the answer to the question "do you think the politician used his office for private gain?"). Cai et al. (2009) use predictions from auction theory to argue that certain types of land auctions in China are used to promote collusion between the auctioneer and the participants, for their mutual benefit.

All these methods pick up the direct correlates of corruption, such as bribes and absence from work, rather than its more indirect ramifications. In some cases, such as teacher absenteeism, the direct consequence may be the most important. However, the point of our framework is to argue that in many situations, the bribe may just be the tip of the iceberg, with the more serious repercussions showing up in terms of misallocation and red tape. The next section discusses an example of empirical research that tries to capture the bureaucrat's entire decision process and its various ramifications.

5. Understanding the Structure of Corruption

Most empirical research has been based on measuring the extent of bribery or shirking and on how incentives affect these behaviors. Bertrand et al. (2007) differs from much of the empirical research by focusing on the entire resource allocation problem faced by the bureaucrat and therefore looking beyond bribe taking as the measure of welfare. The basic strategy of the paper is to experimentally vary the underlying types a bureaucrat faces and use the bureaucrat's responses to infer their chosen allocative mechanism.

Specifically, Bertrand et al. (2007) compare three randomly chosen groups of license candidates. The first group was told to obtain a license as usual, the second group was given a large incentive to obtain the license in the minimum legal time allowed (30 days), and a third group was offered free driving lessons. In our model, the second group represents a situation where h and l have both increased by the same amount. The third group represents a situation where some of those who were low types become high types.

The driver's license case corresponds to Case IV (see Section 3.3.3). To reduce the number of possible cases, assume that $y_H = h < l = y_L$ (which, as always, is interpreted as the case where

---

greater media scrutiny, suggesting that it is not effort. Moreover, the next time the same two wrestlers meet, the opponent is more likely to win, suggesting that throwing future matches is a form of the bribe paid for winning a key match. Similarly, Antanassova et al. (2008) cross-check receipt of a BPL card (which in India identifies someone to be poor and allows them access to a set of redistributive programs) against actual income levels. They correlate the error rate with such features as the caste of the recipient and his or her place in certain social networks, and they argue that the correlations are what a simple theory of corruption would predict.

28. Di Tella and Weinschelbaum (2008) provide a theoretical framework for thinking about unexplained wealth as an indicator for corruption.

a substantial fraction of L types are willing and able to pay more than a large fraction of H types are). Moreover, assume $N < 1$ but $L < 0$.

We assume that the bureaucrat faces people drawn from this altered distribution of types. However, because he does not know the environment has changed, both he and the government use mechanisms that match the prior type distribution. Of course, consumers can change their behavior as a result of the treatment: subjects who are more desirous of a license can offer higher bribes, for example. In principle, this change may allow the bureaucrat to learn of the experiment and adjust his overall strategy. In practice, we assume that the samples involved are too small for the bureaucrat to change his behavior. In effect, in interpreting this experiment, we assume that it changes people's types rather than modifying the bureaucrat's anticipated type distribution.

It is easy to check that in Case IV, an equal increase in h and l, without any change in the rules, will have several different effects. L types will now want to apply even if they are assigned to a bureaucrat who is being honest (i.e., a bureaucrat whose cost of breaking the rules is too high compared to the benefit from breaking the rules). Therefore, the fraction of those who apply to an honest bureaucrat and end up getting a license should decrease. However, just because many more L types apply, many more will (just by chance) end up passing, and the average quality of those who obtain a license would decline. However, the gains from being corrupt would also be higher, which will reduce the fraction of bureaucrats who choose to be honest.

The corrupt bureaucrats (i.e., the ones who opt to break the rules), of whom there are now more, will raise their prices. The fraction of L types getting through, conditional on being allocated to a corrupt bureaucrat, should not change, but because there are now more corrupt bureaucrats, the average quality of driving among those who get a license should decline. Moreover, because there are now more corrupt bureaucrats, the average amount of testing should also decrease.

In contrast, converting some of the high types in the population (the second treatment group) to low types should improve the fraction of drivers who obtain a license when they are allocated to an honest bureaucrat, as well as the average quality of licensed drivers. Those who are allocated to a corrupt person should receive more or less the same treatment, with the licenses going to the highest bidders and perhaps some red tape experienced by those who want to pay less (H types) to discourage those who are willing to pay more from claiming otherwise.

Empirically, individuals who were offered the incentive were 42 percentage points more likely to obtain it in 32 days or fewer. However, they paid about 50% more to obtain their licenses, and they were more likely to break a rule during the process (e.g., they were 13% more likely to not take a driving test). In the end, these extra payments translated to a greater number of bad drivers on the road: those offered the incentive were 18% more likely to obtain a license despite not knowing how to operate a car. These results are entirely consistent with theoretical predictions discussed above, as long as there are enough bureaucrats around who have a relatively low cost of breaking the rules. In particular, although the decline in the quality of driving among those who have a license would happen both with honest and corrupt bureaucrats, the reduction in testing can only occur in our model if the bureaucrat is corrupt.

It is worth pointing out that one would not observe the same pattern if the bureaucrats did know that the distribution of h and l has shifted. In this case, if h and l go up by the same amount, both types would now want to be tested when they encountered an honest bureaucrat. If they instead deal with a corrupt person, both types just pay and get the license without being tested.

The average price would not change, and the fraction being tested would go up. However, the quality of driving among those who get a license would decline, because the L types who deal with the honest bureaucrat now want to be tested. This clearly does not fit the facts about price and testing.[29]

The results of the driving-lessons treatment are also broadly consistent with the theory. Those in this group are tested more often and are more likely to have obtained a license based on passing the test. This last fact, in particular, suggests that there are some honest bureaucrats. They also pay less for the license, though much more than they should have legally. This is a prediction of our model, but only because we assumed (for convenience) that all H types have a lower willingness to pay than all L types. A more plausible argument is that the H types actually have an incentive to shop around (i.e., go to multiple bureaucrats until they find one who is honest). In fact, Bertrand et al. (2007) did observe shopping around in the data, and it is therefore a plausible explanation for why the increase in the fraction of H types reduces the average amount paid.

Betrand et al. (2007) also provide evidence that there is a lot of red tape (i.e., pointless testing). They show that of those experiment participants, who, at least initially, tried to follow the rules (i.e., get tested, not pay bribes, etc.), there is a higher success rate among those individuals found to be unqualified to drive based on the independent test (74% compared with 62%). In other words, the probability of obtaining a license is less than 1 even for those who can drive, and it is not any higher for them than for those who cannot drive. Thus, passing the test is uncorrelated (at best) with driving ability. The testing serves no direct screening purpose.

Both these features—a probability of winning less than 1 and pointless testing—are consistent with Case IV in the scenario where slots are abundant. However, to induce pointless testing, it is important that $y_H < h$; otherwise, the price might just as well be raised up to h. This divergence between the ability to pay and the willingness to pay seems implausible in this context. The amount of money involved (about $25) is not large for the poor in Delhi, which is where the experiment was carried out.

A more plausible story might be that the applicants do not fully understand the rules of the game and therefore think that it is easier to use the official channel than it actually is, while the bureaucrat is not in a position to directly explain to them how things really work; therefore she uses the fruitless testing to signal to the applicants that they need to readjust their expectations. This story would be consistent with the fact that no one directly pays a bribe to the bureaucrat. Those who want to use bribery go to an agent who facilitates the transaction. When someone

---

29. However, our assumption that bureaucrats are randomly assigned to applicants plays a very important role here. One alternative assumption would be that applicants can either chooose to go through the official system knowing that an honest bureaucrat will be assigned to them with some probability, but otherwise they end up dealing with a corrupt individual who will always fail the applicant (because in the official channel there are no bribes, the corrupt bureaucrats find it at least weakly optimal to fail everyone who comes through the system). Or applicants can choose to go through the unofficial channel, which guarantees that they pay a bribe and obtain the license. In the original equilibrium of this game, it is likely that all H types will try the official channel, while the L types will choose the other way. In this scenario, only H types ever take the test and fail.

In this case, during the experiment, H types will shift toward the corrupt route and therefore end up paying more, testing less, and having an increased probability of receiving a license. However, counterfactually, average licensed driver quality will increase, because the fraction of H types who fail declines.

directly approaches a corrupt bureaucrat through the official route, the bureaucrat does not ask for a bribe and instead goes through the motions of what she is supposed to do, while presumably trying to make sure that the applicant subsequently deals through an agent.

These type of empirical results are an intriguing complement to the theoretical framework we have laid out. They focus attention on the allocative outcomes and not just on the bribes. They focus on the details of testing and not only on the transfers made. In short, they illustrate the broader view on corruption that we advocate in this chapter.

6. Combating Corruption

There is a large and growing empirical literature that studies the effect of efforts to fight corruption. For example, Fisman and Miguel (2007) find that an increase in punishments for parking violations in New York City reduced the violations among the set of diplomats most likely to violate the rules. Using experimental techniques, Olken (2007) finds that theft in road projects is greatly reduced by raising the probability of being caught. Banerjee et al. (2008a) and Duflo et al. (2012) find that strengthening incentives reduces absenteeism. Using a natural experiment in Buenos Aires hospitals, Di Tella and Schargrodsky (2003) find effects of both more stringent monitoring and higher wages on procurement prices.

Several more recent papers on this topic have also tried to go a step further and understand whether a reduction in corruption through monitoring and incentives improves the final allocation of services. In the case of the Di Tella and Schargrodsky (2003) study, less bribe taking means better procurement prices, which is the outcome of interest. Olken (2007) looks at the effect of auditing not only on theft but also on the quality of the roads that were built. Duflo et al. (2012) study whether incentives can create distortions stemming from multitasking. In other words, they are concerned that to complete the task as specified by the incentives, the agent reduces his effort along other dimensions. Specifically, they ask whether providing incentives for teachers to attend school will cause the teachers to compensate by teaching less. To answer this question, they measure not only teacher attendance as the final outcome but also the learning levels of the children. They find that the multitasking problem is certainly not large enough to outweigh the benefits of better incentives.

6.1. Institutional Structures for Monitoring

Corruption exists because there are not enough monitoring and incentives to eliminate it. What then determines the extent of monitoring and incentives?

One challenge of looking at this issue empirically is essentially methodological. What should we assume about the extent to which these rules are the product of optimization by the government? Governments may make rules to combat malfeasance by government officials, but how well do they understand the consequences of these rules for corruption?

There are two possible approaches to answering these questions. One is what might be called the "political economy approach." This approach is taken in the theory section here (Section 3). We assume some preferences for the government and figure out how the rules and the nature and extent of corruption should vary as a function of the underlying economic environment if the government were optimizing based on those preferences. We could then look for evidence for the comparative static implications of that model and jointly test the model and our assumption about what is being optimized.

The alternative is to assume that the forces of political economy, although important, leave a significant amount undetermined, and as a result, changes in rules can often arise as pure organizational innovations, without changes in the fundamentals. This approach leads naturally to an experimental approach to studying the effects of the rules.

Banerjee et al. (2001) implement a version of the first approach in the context of the governance of localized sugar cooperatives. They assume that the cooperative maximizes a weighted average of the profits of the various principals of these cooperatives—the different types of member farmers who grow the cane that the cooperative turns into sugar—taking into account the desire of the management of the cooperative to siphon off as much of the profits as possible. Banerjee et al. (2001) then generate a set of comparative statics predictions that map the pricing of cane and the productivity of the cooperative onto the underlying mix of farmers in the cooperative. These implications are then tested and seem to be broadly confirmed.

However, corruption in these cooperatives is essentially private sector corruption, embodied primarily by the underpricing of cane. We have yet to come across a paper that combines this political economy approach with the more complex manifestations of corruption identified in Section 3.

More importantly, in many instances, theories of political economy are simply too incomplete to be useful guides to what rules are actually chosen. The objective of a specific government at a specific point in time is some complex product of its long-term goals and its short-term compulsions. Moreover, the way it chooses rules must take into account the compulsions of all future governments. Although there is an interesting and growing literature on this subject, it is not clear that it is ready to be taken to the data.

It is also not clear how much governments understand about the consequences of the various policy choices they make or about the policy options available to them. A more evolutionary approach to policy change, where changes happen because political actors are trying to solve some local problem but the solutions often have unanticipated and often global consequences, may be more descriptively accurate. Certainly this approach fits better with the kinds of stories that one hears about how change came to China.

An advantage of this second approach is that it permits us to think of policy changes as organizational innovations that are therefore at least initially exogenous in a way that technological innovations are usually thought of as being exogenous. That is, the assumption is that the need to solve problems is a product of various forces of society, but the adoption of a particular solution at a particular point in time is less so.[30] The approach also makes it clear that governments might choose bad rules (rules that go against its own objectives), because it does not understand the consequences of its choices.

Several recent empirical exercises start from this point of view. For example, Besley et al. (2005) find that, in South India, there exists a relationship between holding village meetings (i.e., more community participation in the process) and better allocations of Below Poverty Line cards, which provide privileged access to subsidies and government services. Bjorkman and Svensson (2009) study decentralization in an experimental context. Rather than imposing all

---

30. Banerjee (2002) discusses many of these methodological issues in greater detail.

centralized rules on health centers, community meetings are held to decide the most important rules that health centers should follow and the mechanisms for the community to monitor the health centers. They find huge impacts: infant mortality rates were cut by one-third. However, Banerjee et al. (2008b) evaluate a similar decentralization program in India and find that it performs no better than the civil service–based system of monitoring teachers.

It is difficult to make anything of these vastly different empirical findings, given that we do not have a particularly good theory of how decentralization affects corruption and the distortions associated with corruption.[31] How does decentralization change the kinds of rules that are optimal and the way in which they are violated? How does the exact nature of decentralization factor into all this?

As it is, the presumption behind the empirical literature is that decentralization is a shift of control rights into the hands of those who have more local information. The basic notion is that the community now has more information and therefore can limit the extent of malfeasance by the bureaucrat. We do see some evidence that the easy availability of information matters. In the driver's license experiment, Bertrand et al. (2007) report that there are two obstacles that bribes cannot get around: one is the requirement of showing some proof of address and the other is the requirement of waiting at least 30 days after making the initial application for a learner's permit. Neither of these seems as important as being able to drive, especially in India, where the driver's license is not always accepted as an identification. However, violations of these rules are easy to observe, whereas the inability to drive properly is something that requires another test to verify. Therefore, these are the rules that are enforced.

However, the answer to the question of what rules are violated in what way must also depend on who exercises which type of control rights and what information reaches whom, which all turns on the exact model of decentralization adopted. More generally, theoretical work mapping the effects of alternative organizational forms on the choice of rules and corruption outcomes must be a high priority if this literature is to make progress.

7. Conclusion

Where should the literature go next? We have already discussed a number of the gaps in the literature. In Section 6, we discussed the need to more tightly model learning about the system. Here, we discuss other important gaps.

7.1. Corruption and Competition

Thinking about organizational forms naturally leads to the role of competition in reducing corruption, as emphasized by Rose-Ackerman (1978). The way we modeled corruption takes as given the idea that the assignment of the applicants to the bureaucrats is random. This effectively places the applicants and the bureaucrat in a bilateral monopoly setting. However, the nature of competition among bureaucrats ought to be a policy choice governed by the nature of the underlying incentive problems. This area of study needs further exploration.

---

31. Bardhan and Mookherjee (2006) provide a rare exception.

In particular, competition is not always a plus. As pointed out by Shleifer and Vishny (1994), competition among corrupt distinct and uncoordinated authorities, each of whom has the power to block the application, might be worse than a single monopolistic rent seeker. Barron and Olken (2007) document this phenomenon using a unique dataset that they collected in Indonesia of the bribes paid by truck drivers at road blocks. Reduction in the number of checkpoints along the road reduces the total amount of bribes collected from them. Credible evidence on the salutary effects of competition has so far been hard to find, though no doubt the right setting to look for them will emerge soon.

7.2. Implications of Illegality and Nontransparency

One reason that corrupt bureaucrats find it hard to coordinate with one another is that corruption is illegal. This essential nontransparency has several important implications that deserve further study. First, if the applicants for the slots differ in their ability to make illegal deals for either intrinsic or extrinsic reasons, then the playing field is no longer level, which introduces important distortions. This concern is not merely theoretical. Many countries have laws that forbid their firms to pay bribes in foreign countries, which could potentially act as a constraint on foreign investment in countries with high levels of corruption (see Hines 1995).

Another fallout of this nontransparency that we already noted is the reliance on agents who facilitate bribe taking (see Roseen 1984; Bertrand et al. 2007, 2008). The theory on how the use of agents alters the nature of corruption is yet to be developed. Barron and Olken (2007) provide an interesting insight into this relationship. They observe that in Indonesia, truckers can either pay a bribe at every checkpost or pay a single bribe to an agent at the starting city. However, the contract with the agent tends to be very simple—the amount of the single bribe does not depend on the load carried by the truck—probably because of the same lack of transparency. Thus, only the most overloaded trucks pay the fixed bribe, and the shape of the total bribe paid as a function of the truck's load is concave, whereas theory suggests that the optimal penalty function ought to be convex.

A third issue is that many drivers who try to get a license without paying an agent probably do not know the rules of the game. This happens because corruption is meant to be secret. In other words, understanding the process by which the real rules of the game become (or fail to become) common knowledge between the bureaucrat and the applicants should be an integral part of the study of corruption.

Bertrand et al. (2007) actually gather data about what individuals who are trying to obtain a driver's license know about the licensing process. They find that not much is known, and more surprisingly, many applicants believe that the official process is more onerous than it actually is. They also found in their qualitative work that discovering the actual rules was surprisingly difficult, given that they change periodically.

These observations lead Bertrand et al. (2007) to speculate on whether the bureaucrats deliberately try to make the rules more complicated than they should be to extract more in rents. Atanassova et al. (2008) find that individuals who are supposed to receive subsidized allocations of foodgrains in India are misinformed about their exact entitlements, and the qualitative evidence in this case suggests that the shopkeeper often manufactures "rules" that increase the scope for his corruption, such as that all grain must be bought on one of two days.

Thinking about this issue leads us to an interesting theoretical possibility. Is it possible that the government's attempts to change the rules, perhaps to fight corruption, generate so much confusion among the citizens that corruption actually increases?

7.3. Learning among Bureaucrats

The emphasis on learning brings up another important issue. Although much of the work in the field has focused on innovations in fighting corruption, there has been little focus on the innovations in corruption. A change in policy and/or institutions may reduce the prevalence of corruption to start with, but over time, the bureaucrat may learn how to adapt to the new policy or institutions. For example, Camacho and Conover (2011) provide evidence that individuals were better able to game the eligibility rules for social welfare programs in Colombia as rules for eligibility became better known over time. More generally, how much of the knowledge regarding how to conduct corruption is general knowledge, versus knowledge about a specific institution?

7.4. Norms of Corruption

The idea that the rules may be important for establishing a simple norm that the courts can easily interpret suggests a further line of inquiry. Perhaps the rules that the government makes for bureaucrats have a signaling role. The bureaucrat or the citizen uses them to infer the society's preferences and therefore to decide what they should and should not do. If the government formally allows its bureaucrats to extort money from its citizens, the citizens might take this as a signal that the moral standards of society are low, and therefore citizens feel comfortable about extorting others. This idea could explain why governments continue to have rules on their books that are violated all the time.

However, a government that has rules on the books but does not manage to enforce them is also signaling something about its view of rules and rule-governed behavior that might spill over into other walks of life. For this reason and others, corruption may have a direct social cost, which is something our model does not take into account.

7.5. The Social Psychology of Corruption

To fully understand how corruption (or lack of corruption) becomes the norm, there is a need to try to understand the psychology of when and where people feel more or less comfortable about engaging in corruption. For example, a tendency to try to legitimize corruption is often observed. It could take the form of "excuse making" (i.e., the bureaucrat not directly asking for a bribe but instead discussing the costs of her time in providing a service to a citizen). Or alternatively, the citizen may suggest making a payment in kind, rather than a monetary bribe, to make the bureaucrat feel as if she were simply accepting a gift from a happy citizen rather than engaging in an illegal act.

The concept of legitimization may be a powerful part of our understanding why there is not as much corruption in the world as there could be. For instance, even in the most corrupt countries, empirical antidotes suggest that bureaucrats will often ask for a bribe to break a rule that impedes a given citizen but will not threaten to punish him for no reason. For example, traffic policemen often ask for a bribe if a citizen has committed a violation. However, they will not necessarily ask for a bribe if the person has done nothing wrong, and yet it is not clear that the enforcement in these two cases is very different. Locating the study of corruption in the broader context of how people relate to one another and to the state may be important in getting a handle on why corruption exists in some settings but not in others.

REFERENCES

Adsera, Alicia, Carles Boix, and Mark Payne. 2003. "Are You Being Served? Political Accountability and the Quality of Government." *Journal of Law, Economics, and Organization* 19: 445–490.

Atanassova, Antonia, Marianne Bertrand, and Sendhil Mullainathan. 2008. "Misclassification in Targeted Programs: A Study of the Targeted Public Distribution System in Karnataka, India." Mimeo. Harvard University, Cambridge, MA.

Bandiera, Oriana, Andrea Prat, and Tommaso Valletti. 2009. "Active and Passive Waste in Government Spending: Evidence from a Policy Experiment." *American Economic Review* 99: 1278–1308.

Banerjee, Abhijit. 1997. "A Theory of Mis-Governance." *Quarterly Journal of Economics* 112: 1289–1332.

———. 2002. "The Uses of Economic Theory: Against a Purely Positive Interpretation of Game Theoretic Results." Mimeo, Massachusetts Institute of Technology, Cambridge, MA.

Banerjee, Abhijit, and Rohini Pande. 2009. "Parochial Politics: Ethnic Preferences and Politician Corruption." Working paper. Available at: http://economics.mit.edu/files/3872.

Banerjee, Abhijit, Dilip Mookherjee, Kaivan Munshi, and Debraj Ray. 2001. "Inequality, Control Rights and Rent-Seeking: Sugar Cooperatives in Maharashtra." *Journal of Political Economy* 109: 138–190.

Banerjee, Abhijit, Angus Deaton, and Esther Duflo. 2004. "Health Care Delivery in Rural Rajasthan." *Economic and Political Weekly* 39: 944–949.

Banerjee, Abhijit, Esther Duflo, and Rachel Glennerster. 2008a. "Putting a Band-Aid on a Corpse: Incentives for Nurses in the Indian Public Health Care System." *Journal of the European Economic Association* 6: 487–500.

Banerjee, Abhijit, Rukmini Banerjee, Esther Duflo, Rachel Glennerster, and Stuti Khemani. 2008b. "Pitfalls of Participatory Programs: Evidence from a Randomized Evaluation in India." Mimeo, Massachusetts Institute of Technology, Cambridge, MA.

Bardhan, Pranab. 1997. "Corruption and Development: A Review of Issues." *Journal of Economic Literature* 35: 1320–1346.

Bardhan, Pranab, and Dilip Mookherjee. 2006. "Corruption and Decentralization of Infrastructure Delivery in Developing Countries." *Economic Journal* 116: 107–133.

Barron, Patrick, and Benjamin A. Olken. 2007. "The Simple Economics of Extortion: Evidence from Trucking in Aceh." NBER Working Paper 13145, National Bureau of Economic Research, Cambridge, MA.

Becker, Gary S., and George J. Stigler. 1974. "Law Enforcement, Malfeasance, and Compensation of Enforcers." *Journal of Legal Studies* 3: 1.

Bertrand, Marianne, Simeon Djankov, Rema Hanna, and Sendhil Mullainathan. 2007. "Obtaining a Driving License in India: An Experimental Approach to Studying Corruption." *Quarterly Journal of Economics* 122: 1639–1676.

———. 2008. "Corruption in the Driving Licensing Process in Delhi." *Economic and Political Weekly* 43(5): 71–76.

Besley, Timothy, Rohini Pande, and Vijayendra Rao. 2005. "Participatory Democracy in Action: Survey Evidence from India." *Journal of the European Economics Association* 3: 648–657.

Bjorkman, Martina, and Jakob Svensson. 2009. "Power to the People: Evidence from a Randomized Field Experiment of Community-Based Monitoring in Uganda." *Quarterly Journal of Economics* 124: 735–769.

Cai, Hongbin, J. Vernon Henderson, and Qinghua Zhang. 2009. "China's Land Market Auctions: Evidence of Corruption." NBER Working Paper 15067, National Bureau of Economic Research, Cambridge, MA.

Camacho, Adriana, and Emily Conover. 2011. "Manipulation of Social Program Eligibility." *American Economic Journal: Economic Policy* 3(2): 41–65.

Chaudhury, Nazmul, Jeffrey Hammer, Michael Kremer, Karthik Muralidharan, and F. Halsey Rogers. 2006. "Missing in Action: Teacher and Health Worker Absence in Developing Countries." *Journal of Economic Perspectives* 20(1): 91–116.

Di Tella, Rafael, and Ernesto Schargrodsky. 2003. "The Role of Wages and Auditing During a Crackdown on Corruption in the City of Buenos Aires." *Journal of Law and Economics* 46: 269–300.

Di Tella, Rafael, and Federico Weinschelbaum. 2008. "Choosing Agents and Monitoring Consumption: A Note on Wealth as a Corruption-Controlling Device." *Economic Journal* 118: 1552–1571.

Duflo, Esther, Rema Hanna, and Stephen Ryan. 2012. "Incentives Work: Getting Teachers to Come to School." *American Economic Review* 102(4): 1241–1278.

Duggan, Mark, and Steven D. Levitt. 2002. "Winning Isn't Everything: Corruption in Sumo Wrestling." *American Economic Review* 92: 1594–1605.

Fisman, Raymond, and Roberta Gatti. 2002. "Decentralization and Corruption: Evidence across Countries." *Journal of Public Economics* 83: 325–345.

Fisman, Raymond, and Edward Miguel. 2007. "Corruption, Norms, and Legal Enforcement: Evidence from Diplomatic Parking Tickets." *Journal of Political Economy* 115: 1020–1048.

Fisman, Raymond, and Shang-Jin Wei. 2004. "Tax Rates and Tax Evasion: Imports in China." *Journal of Political Economy* 112: 471–496.

Fredriksson, Per G., and Jakob Svensson. 2003. "Political Instability, Corruption and Policy Form." *Journal of Public Economics* 87: 1383–1405.

Guriev, Sergei. 2004. "Red-Tape and Corruption." *Journal of Development Economics* 73: 489–504.

Hines, James. 1995. "Forbidden Payment: Foreign Bribery and American Business after 1977." NBER Working Paper 5266, National Bureau of Economic Research, Cambridge, MA.

Hsieh, Chang-Tai, and Enrico Moretti. 2006. "Did Iraq Cheat the United Nations? Under-Pricing, Bribes, and the Oil for Food Program." *Quarterly Journal of Economics* 121: 1211–1248.

Hunt, Jennifer. 2007. "How Corruption Hits People When They Are Down." *Journal of Development Economics* 84: 574–589.

Huntington, Samuel P. 1968. *Political Order in Changing Societies.* New Haven, CT: Yale University Press.

Kaufmann, Daniel, Aart Kraay, and Massimo Mastruzzi. 2004. "Governance Matters III: Governance Indicators for 1996, 1998, 2000, and 2002." *World Bank Economic Review* 18: 253–287.

Klitgaard, Robert. 1988. *Controlling Corruption.* Berkeley: University of California Press.

Knack, Stephen, and Philip Keefer. 1995. "Institutions and Economic Performance: Cross-Country Tests Using Alternative Institutional Measures." *Economics and Politics* 7: 207–227.

Laffont, Jean-Jacques, and Jean Tirole. 1993. *A Theory of Incentives in Procurement and Regulation.* Cambridge, MA: MIT Press.

LaPorta, Raphael, Florencio Lopez-de-Silanes, Andrei Shleifer, and Robert Vishny. 1999. "The Quality of Government." *Journal of Law, Economics, and Organization* 15: 222–279.

Lui, Francis T. 1986. "A Dynamic Model of Corruption Deterrence." *Journal of Public Economics* 31: 215–236.

Mauro, Paolo. 1998. "Corruption and Growth." *Quarterly Journal of Economics* 110: 681–712.

Mocan, Naci. 2008. "What Determines Corruption? International Evidence from Micro Data." *Economic Inquiry* 46: 493–510.

Olken, Benjamin. 2006. "Corruption and the Costs of Redistribution: Micro Evidence from Indonesia." *Journal of Public Economics* 90: 853–870.

———. 2007. "Monitoring Corruption: Evidence from a Field Experiment in Indonesia." *Journal of Political Economy* 115: 200–249.

———. 2009. "Corruption Perceptions vs. Corruption Reality." *Journal of Public Economics* 93: 950–964.

Pande, Rohini. 2007. "Understanding Political Corruption in Low Income Countries," in Paul Schultz and John A. Strauss (eds.), *Handbook of Development Economics* 4. Amsterdam: North-Holland, pp. 3155–3184.

Persson, Torsten, Guido Tabellini, and Francesco Trebbi. 2003. "Electoral Rules and Corruption." *Journal of the European Economic Association* 1: 958–989.

Rauch, James E., and Peter B. Evans. 2000. "Bureaucratic Structure and Bureaucratic Performance in Less Developed Countries." *Journal of Public Economics* 75: 49–71.

Reinikka, Ritva, and Jakob Svensson. 2005. "The Power of Information: Evidence from a Newspaper Campaign in Uganda." *Journal of the European Economic Association* 3: 259–267.

Rose-Ackerman, Susan. 1978. *Corruption: A Study in Political Economy.* New York: Academic Press.

———. 1999. *Corruption and Government.* Cambridge: Cambridge University Press.

Roseen, Keith. 1984. "Brazil's Legal Culture: The Jieto Revisited." *Florida International Law Journal* 1: 1–43.

Shleifer, Andrei, and Robert W. Vishny. 1993. "Corruption." *Quarterly Journal of Economics* 108: 599–617.

———. 1994. "Politicians and Firms." *Quarterly Journal of Economics* 109: 995–1025.

Svensson, Jakob. 2003. "Who Must Pay Bribes and How Much? Evidence from a Cross-Section of Firms." *Quarterly Journal of Economics* 118: 207–230.

———. 2005. "Eight Questions about Corruption." *Journal of Economic Perspectives* 19(3): 19–42.

Tirole, Jean. 1986. "Hierarchies and Bureaucracies." *Journal of Law, Economics, and Organization* 2: 181–214.

———. 1996. "A Theory of Collective Reputations (with Applications to the Persistence of Corruption and to Firm Quality)." *Review of Economic Studies* 63: 1–22.

Tran, Anh. 2008. "Can Procurement Auctions Reduce Corruption? Evidence from the Internal Records of a Bribe Paying Firm." Mimeo.

Transparency International. 2008. *Corruption Perceptions Index.* Available at: http://www.transparency.org/policy_research/surveys_indices/cpi.

Treisman, Daniel. 2000. "The Causes of Corruption." *Journal of Public Economics* 76: 399–457.

Wade, Robert. 1982. "The System of Administrative and Political Corruption: Canal Irrigation in South India." *Journal of Development Studies* 18: 287–327.

28

Delegation, Control, and the Study of Public Bureaucracy
Terry M. Moe

1. Introduction

For most of the past century, the study of public bureaucracy was a theoretical backwater in political science. Public administration, its home field until recently, was heavily focused on good management and the nuts and bolts of government operation, and these concerns tended to drive out theoretical thinking. Moreover, unlike the more advanced fields of political science—legislatures, elections, public opinion—bureaucracy did not provide scholars with raw materials that were readily quantified. Legislators vote, for instance, and bureaucrats do not. This single fact had much to do with putting the study of legislatures on the fast track and that of bureaucracy on the slow track.

Theory was also impeded by a conceptual blind spot. Early studies rightly saw public agencies as strategic players in the political process, seeking out relationships with legislative committees and interest groups, nurturing their own constituencies, and otherwise engaging in bureaucratic politics (e.g., Long 1949). But scholars failed to see that the underlying *organization* of bureaucracy is thoroughly political too—for organization affects performance, and powerful actors have incentives to design and shape it to their own advantage. In the scholarship of the time, bureaucratic behavior was understood in political terms. But bureaucratic organization was not.

This nonpolitical approach to organization had deep roots. During the early decades of the twentieth century, reactions against political corruption and party machines led scholars to see bureaucracy as the savior of good government and as properly nonpolitical. They embraced the "separation of politics from administration": the notion that, although policy is inevitably a product of politics, it should be implemented by impartial experts in the bureaucracy, which in turn should be organized for effective performance (Knott and Miller 1987).

As scholarship became more scientific, and thus more concerned with explaining the actual features of public agencies, this nonpolitical take on bureaucracy was not overcome. In fact, it was reinforced by the emerging organization theories of the era—which took their orientations from sociology, social psychology, and psychology and offered only nonpolitical explanations for why bureaucracies became organized as they did (Perrow 1986). Even the groundbreaking contributions of Herbert Simon and James March, both political scientists, did nothing to make the theory more political. Simon and March developed an elaborate theoretical tradition—the dominant perspective on organization among political scientists from the 1950s through the 1970s—that explained formal organization by reference to the cognitive limitations of human beings, and it had almost nothing to say about how public organizations arise out of politics (Simon 1947; March and Simon 1957).

The turning point came during the 1970s, when economists began developing a new set of theories and analytical tools—transaction cost economics, agency theory, theories of repeated games—for explaining economic organization. Fairly quickly, political scientists began applying the same theories and tools to the study of government organization, and the long-stagnant theory of public bureaucracy was soon transformed (Moe 1984; Williamson 1985; Milgrom and Roberts 1992).

At the heart of the new theory is a unifying focus on the problems that politicians face when delegating to bureaucrats and on the control mechanisms they can employ in trying to ensure that bureaucrats faithfully implement public policy. Some of these control mechanisms operate ex post, with the authorities monitoring and reacting to what bureaucrats do in the performance of their jobs. But much of the emphasis has been on controls that operate ex ante, with the authorities taking action through politics to strategically organize the bureaucracy in such a way that bureaucrats are constrained to pursue the right policies. A theory of political control and delegation, therefore, is ultimately a *political theory of bureaucratic organization:* one that shows how the structural details of bureaucracy arise out of the political process and how they are connected to the strategies and motivations of those who exercise (or influence) public authority.

Today's theory has developed well beyond this simple core and addresses a wide range of contiguous topics. Most important, it sheds light on the struggle among legislatures, executives, and the courts for control of the bureaucracy in systems based on separation of powers, and it has begun to explore the delegation dynamics of parliamentary systems. This is a theory that is growing rapidly, and is increasingly best thought of as a theory of the institutional system more generally, in which the various branches of government are all integrally connected (Strøm et al. 2003; de Figueiredo et al. 2006).

My focus here is on the political theory of bureaucratic organization, and thus on delegation, control, and their implications for the structure of government. My aim is to highlight the major ideas and approaches that have oriented this literature over time, giving special attention to the light they shed—or fail to shed—on the major substantive issues they attempt to explore and explain. Along the way, I argue that there are basic analytic problems that remain to be overcome: problems that arise, in part, because the normal science that now governs the theory—a standardization that testifies to its very success—has been limiting and even misleading in important respects. All told, the progress from the early days has been astonishing. But some rethinking is in order.

The review I am providing, then, puts a spotlight on the basic analytics of the theory, while at the same time keeping it close to the reality of government—and understanding and evaluating it accordingly. For readers interested in more detailed attention to the technical details of delegation models, excellent treatments can be found in Bendor and Meirowitz (2004) and Bendor et al. (2001). My own view is that, as this literature has developed and matured, technical issues have come to the fore and essentially have come to dominate the attention of the people who are prime movers in this field—to the point that very basic analytical and substantive concerns are no longer regarded as very interesting or important. But the tail should not be wagging the dog here. In the end, the purpose of these models is to explain government.[1]

I should add that even with the more substantive themes I am pursuing here, many theoretical contributions to the larger study of public bureaucracy and its politics must go undiscussed to keep the job manageable. This applies to the literature on ex post control, which is not really about issues of delegation or organization (Hammond and Miller 1987; Ferejohn and Shipan 1990; Eskridge and Ferejohn 1992; Hammond and Knott 1996). It also applies to work on the internal dynamics of bureaucracy, which is mainly about supervisory and employee issues rather than the politics of delegation and control (Hammond and Miller 1985; Miller 1992; Brehm and Gates 1999). All this work is relevant, but the line has to be drawn somewhere.

2. Early Theories of Public Bureaucracy

Rational choice first made its mark on bureaucratic theory during the mid-1960s with the appearance of two innovative books, Tullock's *The Politics of Bureaucracy* (1965) and Downs's *Inside Bureaucracy* (1967). Both were attempts to show that much can be understood about bureaucracy, and a powerful theory someday constructed, by assuming that bureaucrats are rational actors largely motivated by self-interest.

This approach was a sharp departure from existing scholarship. It was also a quantum change in the way rational choice was then being applied to organizations generally. At the time, the work of Simon and March was the only theory of bureaucracy grounded in rational choice, and theirs was an unconventional version of it to be sure. They relaxed all its key assumptions (about rationality, information, goals), shifted the terrain from economics to psychology, and developed a theoretical tradition centered on the cognitive limitations of individuals and on how, as individuals seek to solve the problems that arise in organizational settings, these limitations ultimately give rise to organizational structure. Along the way, self-interest and its correlates—strategy, conflict, opportunism—were mostly ignored, as were their profound consequences for organization. Tullock and Downs brought these core components of rational behavior to center stage and, for the first time, argued for a full-blown rational choice theory of bureaucracy.

Although both were especially interested in government, they cast their nets widely to address a full gamut of topics on public and private organization. Tullock's is a theory of authority relationships in general. Downs's is a theory of all large organizations whose outputs are not evaluated in external markets. In each case, the analysis is informal but is still based on clear assumptions about actors and their contexts, with the spotlight on motivation. Tullock's perspective is built on the assumption that bureaucrats are motivated by career advancement. Downs creates five motivational types—conservers, climbers, zealots, advocates, and statesmen—and shows how the changing mix of these types shapes the growth and operation of bureaucracy. Even though these analyses are very different in content, their bottom lines are much the same. The

---

1. For a related (and highly recommended) review that also puts substance ahead of the technicalities of modeling, see Miller (2005), which is about principal-agent models and their implications for various aspects of politics.

rational foundations of bureaucratic behavior, they argue, promote excessive growth, capture, weak accountability, and related problems that work against effective government.

With these two books, rational choice made a stunning entrée into the world of bureaucratic theory, upsetting the good-government vision of public administration and charting a bold new path for analysis. Downs, especially, was widely read by political scientists and cited for what he had to say about agency life cycles, control problems, communication foul-ups, and other central issues. His typology of bureaucratic motivation, which he put to insightful use, became broadly popular.

Future work in rational choice, however, was not destined to build explicitly on either of these contributions. Their sweeping approach to bureaucracy did not provide a clear focus for constructing new theories, nor did it suggest any productive strategies of formal modeling. Many found these books exciting but also complicated and multifaceted. No one really knew what to do with them.

3. The Niskanen Tradition

What the movement needed was some sort of catalyst, a new and promising analytic basis for cumulative work. And it came in the form of Niskanen's *Bureaucracy and Representative Government* (1971), which was hailed as a pathbreaking contribution and quickly generated a cottage industry of new theoretical work.

The key to Niskanen's success was that, unlike his predecessors, he restricts his focus and simplifies with a vengeance. Although he too is interested in grand issues—the size and efficiency of government—his analysis centers much more narrowly on public agencies and their budgets, and his model is starkly simple. He assumes that bureaucrats are budget maximizers, thus endowing them for the first time with a simple utility function amenable to formal analysis. And he strips away the daunting complexities of budgetary politics by building his model around just two actors, the bureau and its legislative sponsor.

Their relationship is one of bilateral monopoly, with the bureau holding two pivotal advantages. First, its position as sole supplier gives it a monopoly over information about the true costs of production. Second, the bureau knows how much the legislature values every level of output, and it uses this information to present a take-it-or-leave-it offer (of a given output for a given budget) that it knows the legislature will accept. It has information power, and it has agenda power. These powers enable the bureau to act as a perfectly discriminating monopolist, forcing the legislature to accept an oversized budget it barely prefers to no budget at all, with any surplus kept and spent by the bureau. The upshot is that government is too big and grossly inefficient.

Niskanen's earliest critics focused on his assumption of budget maximization, arguing that bureaucrats actually maximize something else (Migue and Balanger 1974; Blais and Dion 1991). But the most telling critiques have centered on control issues. As I have suggested, bureaus dominate in his model for two reasons: they control information and they control the agenda. Yet Niskanen is not at all clear about this, and tends to merge the two factors under the general heading of information—as though it is the agency's control over information that allows it to present the legislature with take-it-or-leave-it budgetary offers, thus giving the agency agenda control. Which is not the case (Bendor 1988).

Efforts to clarify matters soon revealed that agenda control is the big chink in Niskanen's armor. The first indication came from Romer and Rosenthal (1978, 1979), who show that the power of agenda control depends on the "reversion level": the budget that would prevail if the bureau's take-it-or-leave-it offer were rejected by the legislature. Niskanen assumes the reversion level is zero, and thus that legislators must choose between the bureau's offer and no budget at all, which gives the bureau far greater power than it otherwise would have. A more reasonable assumption, more in line with the real-world budgetary process (where legislatures routinely fall back on status quo budgets in times of impasse), would have produced less gloomy conclusions about the size and efficiency of government.

The larger question, however, is why bureaus have agenda power at all. As Gary Miller and I pointed out (Miller and Moe 1983), Niskanen's model is curiously one-sided: bureaus are strategic actors, but the legislature is passive and sits by idly while the treasury is looted. An adequate model, we argued, should treat the legislature as a strategic actor too—and recognize that it has authority over the bureau and can structure the bargaining in any way it wants. Their relationship is not simply one of bilateral monopoly. It is an authority relationship, a hierarchical one, in which the legislature has the legal right to tell the bureau what to do. The legislature is the principal, the bureau the agent.

It follows that the legislature need not put up with the kind of agenda control Niskanen grants the bureau. It might force the bureau to submit a complete schedule of budget-output combinations for legislative choice rather than a take-it-or-leave-it offer, for example. It might engage in monitoring to gain information. It might impose sanctions when the bureau is caught lying. And so on (see also Breton and Wintrobe 1975, 1982). The fact is, the bureau must play the budget game according to rules set by the legislature. And in this crucial sense, it is the legislature that sets the bureau's agenda, not the other way around. A model that incorporates these new elements, we showed, leads to a more variegated—and more moderate—view of bureaucracy and government.

From this point on, Niskanen's approach to bureaucracy gave way to the new economics of organization. Much of the new work paid little or no attention to Niskanen. But some of it did, at least early on, creating what amounted to a bridge between the two—one that highlighted Niskanen's attention to budgets but understood the relationship between the bureau and the legislature in game-theoretic or principal-agent terms. Take-it-or-leave-it agenda control was out as a basis of bureaucratic power. The focus was now on asymmetric information, especially the bureau's private information about costs (its expertise); on the legislature's authority to set the rules; and on basic mechanisms of political control, such as auditing and sanctions (Bendor et al. 1985, 1987a,b; Banks 1989; Banks and Weingast 1992).

Although no longer a distinctive research program, the Niskanen tradition has clearly had a lasting impact on bureaucratic theory. Pre-Niskanen, the natural inclination among scholars was to see bureaucracy as a complex organization subject to a tangled array of authorities, constituencies, and pressures. Niskanen brought simplicity, clarity, and structure to an otherwise messy field, and in the literature to follow his distinctive stamp would be difficult to miss: bureaucracy would routinely be modeled as a unitary actor driven by a single goal, the focus would be on its relationship with the legislature, and attention would center on the key role of information—expertise—and the leverage it gives bureaucrats in pursuing their own interests.

4. Legislative Control and Congressional Dominance

During the early 1980s, political science was swept by the new institutionalism. Until then, despite the provocative work of Niskanen, most rational choice theorists were little interested in bureaucracy. For them, the rationale for studying institutions arose out of a voting puzzle: the social choice theory of voting predicted endless cycling, whereas voting processes in the real world tended to be highly stable. Why so much stability? Their answer was that institutions impose structure on the voting process, bringing order out of chaos (McKelvey 1976; Shepsle 1979; Shepsle and Weingast 1981).

As the theory of political institutions got underway, then, the natural focus was on legislatures—whose members do their work by voting, and who are elected through the votes of constituents. The theory that emerged, therefore, was a decidedly legislative theory, and the rest of the political world came to be viewed through legislative lenses. Bureaucracy nonetheless attracted great interest: for the policies that legislators adopt are empty abstractions until they are implemented, and they can be implemented in many ways depending on who controls the bureaucracy, how well, and what they want it to do. This being so, scholars quickly put the spotlight on political control of the bureaucracy—which meant, in almost all cases, congressional control of the bureaucracy.

Barry Weingast stands out as the most influential figure in the early theory of congressional control. Of his several articles on the subject, one co-written with Mark Moran on congressional control of the Federal Trade Commission is widely cited as seminal (Weingast and Moran 1983; see also Weingast 1981, 1984). The theory begins with a social choice model of legislative decision, in which a committee uses its agenda powers to engineer voting outcomes on the floor. Having thus shaped legislative policy, the committee then becomes a principal trying to ensure faithful implementation by its bureaucratic agent: wielding an array of (ex post) control mechanisms—oversight, the budget, threats of new legislation—so formidable that the bureau has overwhelming incentives to go along. The theme is one of congressional dominance.

This theme was also driven home in an influential article by McCubbins and Schwartz (1984) on the nature and potency of oversight. They argue that reelection-minded legislators, as principals, have little incentive to engage in the broadly based "police patrol" oversight of bureaucracy that the traditional literature presumed. Legislators are better off simply responding to the "fire alarms" set off by constituency groups when something goes wrong. Doing so makes the groups happy, gets them to bear the costs of monitoring, and focuses oversight on problems with electoral salience. It also produces tight control: for when the fire alarms go off, Congress's weapons are so powerful that the bureaucracy will toe the line. Indeed, bureaus will anticipate as much and comply from the outset.

These articles, together with others arguing similar ideas (e.g., Fiorina 1981; Barke and Riker 1982), heightened scholarly interest in political control. Yet their claims of congressional dominance also provoked controversy, and for good reason. As I pointed out at the time (Moe 1987), they do not really develop a theory of control. For they never attempt to model the goals, strategies, or resources of the bureaucracy, and thus cannot shed light on its motivation or capacity to shirk. The profound importance of private information (expertise), which so empowered Niskanen's bureau, is given short shrift here, along with the entire bureaucratic side of the control relationship. Their focus is entirely on the legislature.

Their presumption, moreover, is that budgets, oversight, and other mechanisms nicely translate into tight control for the legislative principal—when the whole thrust of the economic theory of agency is that control is costly and likely to entail substantial slippage. The theme of a well developed theory of political control, it is reasonable to suggest, should be that Congress has a very difficult time controlling the bureaucracy, and that the latter probably has considerable autonomy. This is precisely what mainstream empirical work by political scientists had long maintained (Wilson 1989).

In some sense, the problem in this early literature on political control was just the reverse of what we found with Niskanen. Niskanen overstated bureaucratic power by assuming a strategic bureau and a passive legislature. The congressional dominance theorists flipped it around, overstating legislative power by assuming a strategic legislature and a passive bureau.

5. Ex Ante Control and the Politics of Structure

The early theory of congressional dominance was a theory of ex post control, asking how legislators could prevent runaway bureaucracy by monitoring the behavior, rewarding the compliance, and punishing the noncompliance of existing agencies. Yet legislators (and presidents) also have the authority to exercise control ex ante: by imposing structures and personnel systems that promote agency compliance from the outset. Through strategic choices about *organization,* in other words, they can design bureaucracy to do their bidding.

Rational choice theorists quickly recognized as much and moved to incorporate ex ante control into their analyses. This simple step, although obvious in retrospect, may represent the most important single development in the modern theory of bureaucracy, as it paved the way for an explanation of how bureaucracy emerges out of politics and why it takes the organizational forms it does.

The study of ex ante control is rooted in issues of delegation. Several influential studies carried out early on—by Aranson et al. (1982), Fiorina (1982a,b, 1986), and McCubbins (1985)—proposed formal approaches to delegation and focused attention on some of the key questions that needed addressing. Why does Congress delegate authority to an agency rather than writing detailed laws itself that are enforceable in the courts? When it delegates, does it prefer vague mandates that give agencies great discretion or highly specific mandates that severely limit what agencies can do? And when agencies have discretion, how can Congress design their structures so as to channel bureaucratic behavior toward legislative ends?

Soon thereafter came two articles by McCubbins, Noll, and Weingast (1987, 1989) that gained widespread attention, provoked controversy, and established ex ante control as a growth industry. Their big splash was due in part to their audience. McNollgast (as they are sometimes collectively known) addressed themselves to the law-and-economics community, arguing that administrative procedures—this audience's main organizational focus—are explained not by the traditional normative concerns for fairness, due process, or equity, but rather by the self-interested control strategies of legislative actors. Such an argument grew naturally out of rational choice thinking, but it challenged convention, and it demanded and got a spirited response (e.g., Mashaw 1990).

McNollgast see the relationship between Congress and the bureaucracy as a principal-agent problem, in which an "enacting coalition" within the legislature seeks to minimize bureaucratic "drift" (shirking). The problem arises because the typical agency has its own policy preferences, often different from those of Congress, and because it may be able to use the information asymmetry built into their relationship—owing to its greater expertise—to go its own way in policy. What can Congress do to keep the bureaucracy in line? The authors argue that, while the prior literature had emphasized ex post control, such efforts to monitor, reward, and sanction agencies are costly to employ and, at any rate, do not work very well. This is an implicit way of saying that the earlier work on congressional dominance—their own work—did indeed have it wrong. Their new claim is that, precisely because ex post control is highly problematic, Congress places great emphasis on ex ante control, which works much better. Ex ante control emerges as the key to understanding how Congress gets its way—which it continues to do, on their account—and why bureaucracy looks and performs as it does.

Properly chosen procedures, McNollgast argue, can mitigate problems of asymmetric information by forcing agencies to take certain kinds of technical or constituency information into account or to publicize their policy aims well in advance of formal promulgation—creating an early-warning system for politicians and ruling out faits accomplis. The Administrative Procedures Act, they argue, is a prime example of how Congress uses procedures to open up agency decisionmaking and make private information public.

Procedures also enfranchise favored constituencies by selectively granting them access and participation rights, thus injecting special interests directly into the informational and early-warning system, as well as shaping decisionmaking according to the balance of group power. In these ways, legislators stack the deck in favor of groups in the enacting coalition and ensure that changes in the interests and relative powers of groups over time are mirrored in agency process and policy. If well designed, the agency should be on autopilot: programmed to do Congress's bidding.

In a series of articles that appeared shortly thereafter, I developed an analysis of the "politics of structure" that shares central themes with the McNollgast work—regarding the problems of information, for example, and the role of procedures in stacking the deck (Moe 1989, 1990a,b; Moe and Caldwell 1994; Moe and Wilson 1994). Yet the approach is also different in key respects and attempted to take the theory in new (at the time) directions, the most fundamental of which are discussed below. The arguments I made on their behalf are the arguments I made then and still make. As subsequent sections of this chapter show, some of these new directions have since been pursued in various ways. But some, even after all these years, remain virtually unexplored.

5.1. Multiple Principals

The McNollgast analysis submerges presidents in the enacting coalition and pays no special attention to them. But the fact is, presidents *are* special. Their powers and leadership are the driving forces of modern American government—and they are absolutely fundamental, as well, to the politics of structure. It would be odd if they were not.

Clearly, presidents have distinctive roles to play. They have the power to veto legislation, which allows them to pressure Congress for concessions that produce bureaucratic structures more conducive to their own goals and interests: structures that give them more discretion and control. They also have powers of unilateral action—due in part to their position as chief executive—that allow them to move on their own to create favorable administrative arrangements (see, e.g., Howell and Lewis 2002; Lewis 2003). Through it all, moreover, they are operating on preferences and following strategies that make them very different from legislators, for they respond to broader constituencies, seek central control over the bureaucracy—and indeed, are threats that many legislators must worry about and guard against.

A theory with presidents, then, points to aspects of bureaucracy that bear a distinctly presidential stamp—some of them structures that presidents themselves create, on their own, to try to gain control. Regulatory review is an obvious example. So is much of the institutional presidency, a defining feature of modern American government that rational choice theorists largely ignore. A theory with presidents also emphasizes that many bureaucratic structures are designed by legislators to insulate parochial interests from presidential influence, and that presidents counter by adding structures of their own. These structures and dynamics are fundamental to American bureaucracy, and they are missed when presidents are lumped into the enacting coalition.

Much the same is true of the courts. They are not active players in the legislative process, as legislators and presidents are. But they have the authority to impose their own structures on the bureaucracy—as they have done with a vengeance, for example, in school desegregation disputes. And the expected outcomes of delegation decisions are clearly very different, and thus the politics of delegation is very different, depending on whether the courts can be counted on to backstop Congress—pushing wayward agencies back where Congress wants them—or can be expected instead to act on their own political preferences.

The more general theoretical point here is that the organization of American bureaucracy arises out the politics of a separation of powers system. In such a system, the legislature is not the only principal that counts. There are typically multiple principals competing for control—the legislature, the president, and the courts—and they use structure not only to impose constraints on the bureaucracy, but also to insulate it from the influence of their competitors. A simple focus on the enacting coalition misses all this.[2]

5.2. Forward-Looking Actors

McNollgast's political actors are rational and strategic, but they do not do a serious job of looking ahead. In particular, they fail to take account of the "political uncertainty" inherent in democratic politics. If they did, their incentives and behavior would look very different than McNollgast claims. In American democracy (and in most democracies), today's power holders cannot count on maintaining their hold on public authority forever. Their future power is uncertain. As a result, they cannot commit tomorrow's authorities—who may turn out to be their opponents—to respect whatever deals are arranged, and whatever structures and policies are created, in the current period. They face a commitment problem: they want to provide a stream of benefits into the future for their own constituents, and in return receive those constituents' votes—but they cannot guarantee that the future benefits will actually be provided. Constituents, then, have good reason not to believe their promises. And not to support them or make deals with them. So what can today's power holders do? How can they commit?

---

2. For pioneering efforts (at about this time) to model multiple principals and their struggle to control the bureaucracy, see Calvert et al. (1989), Hammond and Miller (1987), and Hammond and Knott (1996—although earlier versions were floating about years before).

The answer is that the policies and structures being created today must be protected from future authorities and thus insulated from democratic control. The best way to do this is through ex ante control mechanisms—decision procedures, civil service rules, independent forms of organization, formal timetables—that not only stack the deck, but also lock in the bias to protect against future changes in power and authority. Today's enacting coalition, in other words, wants to ensure that *tomorrow's* legislature—perhaps led by an opposing coalition—*cannot* control the bureaucracy.[3]

Obviously, this logic puts a different spin on things. McNollgast's enacting coalition fixes its gaze on the bureau, which threatens to drift away. On their account, the coalition relies not only on deck stacking but also on procedures that force the bureau to *reveal* information, *open* its internal processes, and suffer outside *intervention* to keep it in check. In a world of political uncertainty, however, the enacting coalition must also cast a wary eye *on the legislature itself*, indeed on all future authorities and group opponents, and use structure to insulate against their control. Because of political uncertainty, the coalition often *does not want* openness or intervention, and it favors structures that shut out most opportunities for control by others.

Because of political uncertainty, then, the shortcomings of ex post control should prove more severe than McNollgast suggest, and they should arise from more than just the usual slippage in the principal-agent relationship. Basic obstacles to control should purposely be *created by Congress itself*, which should often have incentives to build bureaucracies with considerable autonomy that pursue the original intent of the law—and that resist Congress's own efforts at ex post control. Ex ante control, then, emerges as a two-edged sword: it promotes the control of today's Congress by rendering tomorrow's Congress weak.

5.3. Institutional Context

The McNollgast theory is Congress-centered and peculiar to the American political system. Yet there is good reason to think that different institutional systems have their own distinctive politics of structure and thus their own distinctive bureaucracies. The logic of politics in the United States should be different from the logic of politics in Britain and elsewhere. A focus on political uncertainty—which scholars usually ignore—makes the case very clearly (see especially Moe and Caldwell 1994).

Consider the American system of separation of powers. It fragments power among institutions, and its multiple veto points ensure that new laws are difficult to enact. Whatever does get enacted, however, tends to endure because separation of powers then works to its advantage, setting up obstacles that prevent opponents from changing it. This feature makes the lock-in of current interests possible: whatever protective structures are imposed to insulate today's creations from change probably cannot be lifted by opponents in the future, even if they are powerful—because supporters can likely find a way to block change. The agencies and policies they seek to protect, then, will remain protected. And the flow of benefits to constituents will endure.

In such a system, all actors therefore have incentives to rely heavily on formal structure to insulate their creations, solve their commitment problems, and solidify their political deals.

---

3. The importance of forward-looking rationality is emphasized throughout my own work, but it is also recognized in early work by Horn and Shepsle (1989) and in a full-length book by Horn (1995). Interestingly, Horn does not pursue the differences between presidential and parliamentary systems (see below).

Formal structure protects them against political uncertainty, ensuring that whatever is created today will endure tomorrow. And because all players have strong incentives to formalize, the bureaucracy in such a system will tend to be buried in formal rules.

Now consider a pure Westminster-like parliamentary system. In such a system, power is entirely concentrated in the majority coalition, and there are no veto points in the policy process. As a result, political uncertainty is dramatically heightened. Passing laws is relatively easy, but so is overturning them: for if the opposing coalition comes to power, it too will have concentrated power, and it will be able to subvert everything the first coalition has put in place. *Formal structure therefore has little strategic value* as a protector of interests or solution to commitment problems—and the incentives to formalize are therefore much reduced. This should tend to produce a bureaucracy that, by comparison to its counterpart in the American system, is granted more discretion and is much less burdened by formal constraints. The logic of politics is very different in the two systems, and their bureaucracies should be very different as well.[4]

Most parliamentary systems are not at the Westminster end of the continuum, of course. Some divide institutional authority in various ways (e.g., through bicameral legislatures), and some have electoral systems that often give rise to minority or coalition governments, yielding institutions whose veto points place them somewhere between the American and the Westminster extremes. For these contexts, the incentives to formalize should also tend to be somewhere between, as would the nature of their bureaucracies. The argument here is not that presidential and parliamentary systems represent dichotomous system types, but rather that the basic features of political systems generally—such as divided authority and veto points—tell us a lot about the politics of structure and about bureaucracy. The American system is not necessarily very representative. A more broadly based, more fully comparative theory is surely preferable.

5.4. Effectiveness

The McNollgast theory is about what Congress can do to prevent runaway bureaucracy, which is an important issue. The question that has traditionally been at the heart of public administration, however—the effectiveness of the bureaucracy—is given no serious attention. The presumption seems to be that, as long as agencies are under control and prevented from drifting, they will perform effectively and constituents will get their benefits.

The theory needs to deal with effectiveness head-on. Actually, the control relationship itself points immediately to potential problems for effectiveness: for when the legislature imposes structures to stack the deck and otherwise constrain agency behavior, it interferes with the agency's best applications of its own expertise and undermines its ability to perform. Moreover, particularly in the American system, political uncertainty gives the winning coalition incentives to load agencies up with burdensome formal constraints to insulate them from unwanted future influences; and, especially for agencies in complex policy areas or changing technological environments, these constraints may impede performance. Similarly, the American system's many veto points often require that the winning coalition compromise with the losing coalition in the design of agencies; but the losers often have incentives to impose formal restrictions that purposely undermine agency performance—they have incentives, in other words, to create agencies

---

4. The evidence suggests as much. See Moe and Caldwell (1994).

that are *designed to fail.* Still more problems arise because of competition among principals: for attempts by Congress to insulate against presidential influence will create additional layers of formalism and restriction, whose purpose is political and is likely to get in the way of effective performance.

Effectiveness should also vary with institutional context. In a classic Westminster system, burying agencies in formal rules does not work as a strategy for insulating them from political enemies—so such rules should tend not to be imposed, and agencies should be less burdened with ineffective structures. Moreover, the losers in these systems need not be granted a role in designing public agencies, and there are no competing principals to insulate against one another's influence. These features, too, suggest that bureaucracies should tend to be less burdened with structures that, in the American system, make it difficult for agencies to do their jobs.

The discussion as I have developed it actually begs a deeper question, which is: effective for what? The meaning of effectiveness turns on the specific goals that are to be achieved; and much of the politics of structure, and thus many of the formal structures that are heaped on bureaucracy to insulate and control it, are driven by the fact that different principals—today's legislative coalition, the president, the legislative losers, the future holders of power—have different political goals. Any given principal surely wants the bureaucracy to use its expertise effectively in pursuing that principal's own goals. But if other goals threaten to take priority, expertise and effective performance can become bad things, and restricting them becomes a rational strategy. Bureaucratic effectiveness is in the eye of the beholder. What is effective for principal A is not effective for principal B: it depends on whose goals are being pursued and whose ox is being gored.

6. Formal Models of Delegation

Some of the early work on political control was formal (e.g., Bendor et al. 1985, 1987a,b; McCubbins, 1985; Banks 1989; Banks and Weingast 1992; Calvert et al. 1989). But many of the basic ideas—in McNollgast's work, for example, as well as my own—were set out in arguments that, while firmly rooted in the new economics of organization, were developed informally rather than through modeling. There were advantages to doing so, as it allowed for analyses that were more wide ranging and able to shed light on aspects of political control that would likely have been difficult to explore—and doubtless would have gone unexplored and undiscussed, at least for some time—if the focus had been narrowed from the start by the technical constraints of formal models. Modeling is deductively powerful, if done right. But it can also be conceptually limiting, and there is much value in having a division of labor in which formal and informal analyses work together, with each doing what it does best.

Since the early 1990s, the literature on political control has grown considerably, and it has become much more formal. This newer work incorporates and explores some of the key foundational ideas—but not all of them—and extends the theory in a variety of ways. One stream focuses on ex ante control, most often the legislative decision to delegate. The other is about ex post control, taking the agency and its mandate as given and exploring how legislatures and other political actors can shape the behavior of existing agencies.

Models of delegation have shed light on the foundations of bureaucratic organization, and they are the focus here. As in the early work on ex ante control, the legislature is naturally at center stage in these models, because it makes the laws and is in the position of creating, designing, and empowering administrative agencies. But what the newer models do, in effect, is to whittle away at the theoretical arguments of the earlier literature, reducing them to bare-bones formal representations. (They also, of course, introduce new arguments of their own.) In the process, some of these arguments are more powerfully explored—but for reasons I discuss below, some are dealt with in stilted and unsatisfying ways, and others are not really pursued at all.

One contribution is clear: these models put the earlier claims of congressional dominance firmly to rest. A central theme running throughout these newer models is that the legislature faces a trade-off between expertise and political control. All else being equal, the legislature ben-efits when it imposes structural restrictions, limits administrative discretion, and gains control over the agency's policy choices: maneuvers that are intended to get the agency to target the "right" goals. But these very restrictions render it difficult for the agency to adapt to changing circumstances—new technologies, new problems—and thus to use its expertise effectively, even if it does pursue those goals.

This is essentially a variation on the effectiveness dilemma we discussed in the prior section. The legislature fears that the agency will use its expertise to effectively pursue the "wrong" goals—but by imposing restrictions to get it to pursue the "right" goals, it undermines the agency's ability to pursue *those* goals effectively. The legislature's challenge, of course, is to strike the right balance between control and expertise. It is clear, however, that total political control is an extreme solution that is usually not desirable (were it possible) and would be irrational to pursue. An optimal balance would lead, in most cases, to conscious limitations on political control and thus to situations in which agencies are designed to have a measure of autonomy. Congress would not even try to "dominate."

An early formalization of this balancing act was carried out by Bawn (1995), who, as it happens, did not highlight its implications for congressional dominance. Her model contains two actors, the legislative coalition and a bureaucratic agency. The agency is assumed to have greater expertise than the coalition, and its expertise is defined by reference to a distinction between policies and outcomes—a modeling strategy that was gaining prominence at the time in the larger literature on political institutions (see, e.g., Gilligan and Krehbiel 1990) and would eventually become quite fundamental to the theory of delegation. The agency implements its congressional mandate by choosing a specific policy, located somewhere on a unidimensional continuum, and this choice of policy then generates an outcome (in terms of solutions to social problems or effects on constituents, say) that may be located somewhere else on the continuum. Mathematically, the realized outcome of agency action is assumed to be a function of the agency's implemented policy and a random error term—and it is the agency's knowledge about the distribution of the error term, and thus, more generally, its knowledge of what outcomes are most likely when it chooses a particular policy, that constitutes (and within the model, defines) its expertise.

Bawn's legislative coalition exercises control by using "procedures" to choose the level of agency "independence," where the latter is broadly defined as the agency's freedom to make its own decisions without legislative constraint. Her model shows that independence has two contradictory effects. On the one hand, the agency is better able to apply its expertise (opera-tionalized as a smaller error variance in its estimation of outcomes) the more independence it is granted. This effect is beneficial to the coalition. On the other hand, the agency is more likely to have policy preferences that diverge from those of the legislature (operationalized as a larger variance of agency preferences around a legislatively induced mean) the more independence it is granted. This effect threatens greater bureaucratic drift and is costly to the coalition. The coalition's optimal solution is to choose the level of independence that gives it the greatest net gains, and this level varies, depending on conditions specified in the model. When policy is especially salient to powerful interest groups, for example, bureaucratic drift threatens to be especially costly, and the optimal level of independence will be lower. In complex policy areas, the value of agency expertise to the legislature will tend to be higher, and the optimal level of independence higher. Sometimes the legislature will exercise substantial control, then, and sometimes it will not.

Although the themes of Bawn's analysis have become central to the literature, the model itself has not. Its assumptions, which express how independence is dealt with operationally, were particularly complicated and difficult to work with mathematically, and (for that reason) the model was actually set up as an exercise in decision theory, with the legislature as sole decisionmaker, rather than as an exercise in game theory that explored the interdependent decisions of the legislature and the agency.

Writing at about the same time, Epstein and O'Halloran (1994, 1996) developed a much more straightforward approach to the modeling of delegation and control. Instead of dealing with procedures and independence, and indeed, instead of dealing with aspects of agency organization in any explicit way, they collapsed all these considerations into one simple concept that became the foundation of the entire analysis: the level of discretion that the legislature delegates to the agency. They also operationalized it in an exceedingly simple way. Their approach was a conceptual breakthrough, and it blazed a path that the rest of the formal literature on delegation would ultimately follow.

Specifically, Epstein and O'Halloran assume that the legislature sets a baseline policy, p, and a level of discretion, d. (The story line is that the legislature crafts d by writing statutes that are more or less detailed in their structural constraints—but these elements are not modeled.) The agency is required to implement a policy of its own, p_A, that is within plus or minus d of the baseline policy. If the legislature has done its job right in delegating, the agency will use its expertise—its superior knowledge about the connection between policy and outcomes—to choose a policy within its discretionary range that, once an outcome is realized, proves to be better for the legislature than the baseline policy is and thus better than the legislature could have done by giving the agency no discretion at all.

Epstein and O'Halloran's *Delegating Powers* (1999) is their most comprehensive statement on the subject and is a tour de force of social science analysis: combining grand theory, an elaborate formal model, and wide-ranging empirical tests based on original data. They develop what they call a "transaction cost theory of delegation," arguing that the legislature's decision to delegate is analogous to the make or buy decision that firms confront in the private sector and is subject to the same hold-up problem. The make or buy component arises because the legislature can either make policy itself, relying on its own specialized committees to specify all aspects of policy in excruciating detail, or it can buy the policies externally by delegating to agencies and giving them the discretion to determine what those details should be. Both options come with their own costs. If policy is made by committee, there are costs of information, delay, collective decisionmaking, and the like. However, buying policy from the agency—delegating—threatens the legislature with a hold-up problem (as they characterize it), because the agency has incentives to shirk. The legislature must therefore determine when delegation is more efficient than internal production, as judged by reference to their own political goals.

The logic at work here is a bit strained. In a typical economic analysis, the hold-up problem arises when two firms, A and B, stand to gain from cooperating—B is going to buy its inputs from A, let's say—but the deal involves investments by A that are specific to the relationship; and once A's investments are made, B has an incentive to hold-up A by threatening to renege on the deal and demanding lower prices. Because A can anticipate this problem from the outset, it may refuse to enter into the deal at all, leaving both worse off. The classic solution is vertical integration: firm B purchases firm A, overcoming the cooperation problem by bringing the latter under its own authority and control—and giving it the capacity to make the goods it previously wanted to buy.

The situation that Epstein and O'Halloran are analyzing—a situation rooted in government—is actually different. The bureaucratic agency and the legislature are *already* vertically integrated: the legislature is the superior authority, the agency is the subordinate, and the latter is not free to make its own independent decisions. The legislature might be said to have a make or buy decision, in the sense that one potential producer (the committee) is inside the legislature and one (the agency) is outside. But both producers are under the legislature's own authority from the outset and are subject to its control. It may have a hard time getting the agency to do exactly what it wants, and presumably a harder time than with the committee; but this is the case for any superior in any organization and is simply a version of the shirking problem that frustrates top-down control efforts. There is no hold-up problem in the usual sense.

More generally, the transaction cost framework, which is presented as the analytic foundation for the book, is not put to very productive use. Indeed, after devoting a good deal of attention to the transaction costs involved in producing policy—the haggling, the collective action problems, the delays, and so on—they ultimately construct a formal model that leaves almost all of these costs out and is not different or better in any distinctive way because it is "derived" from the logic of transaction costs.

That said, the make or buy framing itself, properly interpreted, is helpful. There is value in recognizing that the legislature always has the option of producing policy itself and that its delegation decisions are calculated with reference to the baseline of internal production—its costs and benefits, its problems and advantages. This may seem obvious on reflection, and indeed it was central to the way delegation was approached in the earliest attempts to model it (e.g., Fiorina 1982a,b, 1986). But when the new economics of organization took hold in the 1980s and spawned interest in political control, serious interest in the baseline of internal production fell by the wayside. The focus was simply on how the legislature could delegate to an agency and still maintain control. Epstein and O'Halloran deserve credit for reasserting the importance of the baseline and for trying to build a theory that explores it more fully.[5]

---

5. Their effort to do so, however, led to a game-theoretic model (described below) that is far more complicated than the simple discretionary-window component I discussed earlier, for it has a signaling model—in which the committee (as agent) makes proposals to the full legislature (the principal)—nested within it. I suspect it is for this

In the Epstein-O'Halloran model, there are three players: the legislative floor, the committee, and the agency. And there are three stages to the game: in the first, the committee gains (incomplete) information about the link between policy and outcomes, designs a bill, and sends it to the floor; in the second, the floor either enacts legislation or delegates to the agency with some discretion, *d*; and in the third, the agency—which is perfectly informed about the link between policy and outcomes—chooses a final policy within the discretionary limit set by the legislature. The legislature can gain from delegating to the agency and allowing it (via *d*) to use its perfect information in choosing a "good" policy; but the agency has its own policy preferences and may stray from what would be best for the legislature. Rather than put up with the dangers of agency shirking, the legislature could rely on in-house production of policy through its committee; but the committee has preferences that may also differ from the floor's, and it is not as well informed as the agency, so there are problems on this end as well. Both options are imperfect, and the floor chooses delegation when it is the better option.

This model leads Epstein and O'Halloran to two basic conclusions, which then become the focus of their extensive empirical tests.[6] They show that, all else being equal, the legislature is more likely to delegate and grant discretion to an agency (1) the more uncertain and complex the policy area, and (2) the closer the agency's policy preferences are to those of the legislative floor. The first is often referred to in this literature as the uncertainty principle. The second is often referred to as the ally principle. In moving from model to reality, they relate the ally principle to divided government: arguing that the president plays the key role in determining agency preferences, and thus that, when the president and the Congress are controlled by different parties, there is likely to be greater policy conflict (divergence of preferences) between the agency and the legislature, and less delegation and discretion. This assertion about divided government is the best-known and most influential substantive claim to come out of their research program.

In focusing scholarly attention on the simple concept of discretion and in demonstrating how discretion can be modeled and empirically studied, Epstein and O'Halloran have put an indelible stamp on this literature and contributed greatly to its progress. As is perhaps inevitable at this stage, however, their approach fails to incorporate certain aspects of delegation that are quite important and that ultimately need to be taken into account. One of these arises from a key assumption about how the agency responds to political control: they assume that, once the legislature sets the level of discretion, *d*, the agency chooses a policy in its own best interests—but that it also stays *within* the discretionary window. In this crucial respect, then, the agency is assumed to be *perfectly compliant*. This assumption would seem to be out of place in a model of delegation and control, for compliance should be regarded as problematic and worth explaining. A whole realm of agency choice gets assumed away, and power is attributed to the legislature that it may not have in reality.

---

reason that other researchers have embraced the discretionary-window framing of the Epstein-O'Halloran model but dropped the make or buy component. The lesson: the internal production baseline is clearly important to the logic of delegation, but no one has yet figured out how to model it in a manageable way, given all the other things that demand inclusion in a theory of legislative delegation.

6. Another basic conclusion has to do with the internal baseline: Congress is less likely to delegate to an agency the closer the committee's ideal point is to its own (and vice versa). But the empirical tests focus on delegation to agencies, and that is the focus of the book as well, so this aspect of the analysis is not highlighted in their empirics.

The other limitations of the Epstein-O'Halloran model have to do with its failure to move in the new directions discussed earlier:

- The president is essentially ignored, aside from their assumption—now standard—that he sets the agency's policy ideal point (always setting it equal to his own). Epstein and O'Halloran say that omitting the president is not a problem, because it does not affect the comparative statics of their model. But this is just a way of saying that their model is limited. Yes, the directional effects of policy uncertainty (the uncertainty principle) and policy conflict (the ally principle)—the two effects they focus on—would be the same, president or no. But the reality of American politics is that the president has an obvious stake in getting as much discretion for executive agencies as possible and thus in opposing (perhaps by vetoing) legislative attempts to restrict it. And any model that adds the president would certainly lead us to expect more discretion for agencies overall—a very important conclusion—as well as variations in discretion, depending on how particular agencies bear on his agenda and leadership. In general, it is difficult to see how, with the president such a powerful and central player who places enormous value on bureaucratic discretion, an adequate theory of delegation can be built by leaving him out.

- Epstein and O'Halloran's actors are not forward looking and thus are completely unconcerned about the political uncertainty associated with future shifts in political power. A new president could take office and radically change agency ideal points. A new party could take control of the legislature itself and begin redirecting public agencies. New legislators could take control of key committees and assert control over the agencies in their jurisdictions. Today's decisionmakers obviously need to recognize these possibilities and shape their delegations accordingly. To do otherwise would simply be a mistake.[7]

- Their model is legislature centered and peculiar to the American system of separation of powers. Yet it does not have a president, and it does not contain any of the veto points that make the American system what it is. (The model does contain an internal committee, but the latter is not a veto player.) It is also not designed to explore the dynamics of a parliamentary system, nor of other forms of government. So in general, what it has to say about the effects of institutional context is limited.

- The model speaks to the trade-off between control and expertise but otherwise does not explore the various ways in which political control can undermine agency effectiveness. Questions of whether agencies can actually do their jobs well and how their capacity for effective performance is affected by the control activities of politicians need to be brought more fully into the theory.

Subsequent work has helped to address these issues. Volden (2002), for instance, focuses specifically on Epstein and O'Halloran's omission of the president. Using their agency discretion framework, he develops a more general model that incorporates the president and allows agencies to have their own policy preferences that are not presidentially imposed. He also

---

7. Epstein and O'Halloran (1994) actually did devote a small portion of an early article to questions of political uncertainty, but the subject never became part of their research agenda and was not incorporated into their 1999 book.

departs from Epstein and O'Halloran in another significant way. He notes that, although they essentially allow Congress to start from scratch in dealing with agencies—as though the latter were brand new—the typical situation, empirically, is that Congress is dealing with existing agencies that already have policy positions and levels of discretion. Thus, Volden assumes that each agency comes with a status quo policy and a status quo level of discretion, which then serve as reversion levels should Congress decide not to act or be unable to.

Volden's analysis clearly shows that, when presidents are taken into account, agencies do indeed get more discretion. He shows, in addition, that there is an important asymmetry inherent in the dynamics of delegation. This occurs because, when an agency has a low status quo level of discretion, the president will tend to go along with any legislative attempts to increase it—but when an agency has a high status quo level of discretion, he will tend to veto any legislative attempts to decrease it. Thus, over time, increases in agency discretion tend to be difficult to reverse: they can move up much more easily than they can move down.

That such a ratcheting effect might arise out of the politics of delegation is a thought-provoking result and potentially important. And it would never have been discovered, needless to say, in a model that simply ignores the president. It is worth adding, however, that Volden's model—in a feature that embraces, rather than departs from, its lineage—assumes that actors are not forward looking. A legislature capable of looking down the road (or engaged in a long-running repeat-play delegation game)[8] would surely recognize that today's delegation of discretion would become tomorrow's status quo level of discretion and be difficult to reverse. It would see the status quo level of discretion (and policy) as endogenous, not simply as fixed and given, and it would recognize Volden's ratcheting effect. This would affect its decisions today, probably inducing it to choose less discretion. A more complete picture awaits a model of forward-looking decisionmakers.[9]

The most ambitious attempt to build on the Epstein-O'Halloran base is *Deliberate Discretion?* by Huber and Shipan (2002). Like Volden, Huber and Shipan include presidents in their model of the American system of separation of powers. But their larger purpose is to move beyond the traditional Americanist focus of the literature to develop a comparative theory of delegation: one that explains delegation decisions across a range of institutional contexts. Like Epstein and O'Halloran's *Delegating Powers,* this analysis is a legitimate tour de force, an exercise in theory and empirics that stands as one of the landmarks in the field.

8. The delegation models common to this literature assume that the superior makes one delegation decision. For an attempt to understand delegation as a repeated game (but focused, substantively, on the relationship between the legislature and its committees, not the bureaucracy), see Diermeier (1995).

9. I should note that Volden's analysis contains an ambiguity that reflects a confusion of sorts in the larger literature. He begins his model by fully embracing the Epstein-O'Halloran agency discretion framework, but he describes it as one in which the agency is required to choose a final outcome that is within d of the baseline policy, and he constructs his own model accordingly. This is not the Epstein-O'Halloran set-up. In their model, the agency must choose its own policy position so that it falls within the discretionary region—but because the final outcome is a function of agency policy and random error, the final outcome could well fall outside that region. In Volden's model, the outcome must be inside the region, but the policy may be outside of it. The two models are very different, then, in how they define the discretionary region, but they are presented as being the same. Their differences, moreover, cannot help but lead to different conclusions about delegation, making comparison difficult.

Using an agency discretion framework, Huber and Shipan give due regard to the two main concerns at the heart of the modern literature: policy conflict between the agency and the legislature (which leads to the ally principle) and policy uncertainty (which leads to the uncertainty principle). But these factors are insufficient, they say, for understanding how statutory controls—and thus discretion—vary across institutional systems, and they highlight three additional sets of factors that need to be taken into account.

The first is the capacity of the legislature to write specific statutes, as this determines how costly it is for the legislature to restrict agency discretion; legislatures with part-time members who meet every year or two, for example, would find it very difficult to write finely tuned, well-researched statutes to control agency behavior in just the right ways, whereas professional, full-time legislatures would be much more capable of it.[10] The second is whether delegation decisions involve veto players, which may be presidents but may also be a second house of the legislature. And the third consists of "nonstatutory factors"—the courts, legislative oversight and vetoes, corporatist arrangements—that can intervene after the delegation decision is made and can affect its outcomes.

Embedded in this third component is another expansion of the theory, and a particularly important one: the agency may decide to choose a policy outside its discretionary region, and thus not to comply with legislative directives. If it does go this route, there is some probability that nonstatutory factors may intervene to catch and sanction it—as might occur, for example, if its noncompliance is overturned by the courts. This probability may be large or small, depending on how well any given institutional system is set up to detect and respond to agency noncompliance.[11]

In formalizing a broader array of influences on the delegation decision, Huber and Shipan (2002) generalize the theory. But at least as important—certainly in explaining its reception among students of government—the authors also provide insightful discussions of how the various formal components should be thought about and empirically operationalized in different institutional contexts. In a separation of powers system, for example, policy conflict is understood in terms of the contrasting preferences of the legislature and the agency, with the latter assumed to be in line with the president; but this obviously does not work in a parliamentary system, where there is no separation between the legislature and the executive. In a parliamentary system, they argue, policy conflict arises when the parliamentary majority is made up of more than one party, as it is in coalition and minority governments. In these cases, the parties will have different preferences, and those that do not control the relevant ministry (with jurisdiction over the agency) will have incentives to use statutory controls to restrict discretion. A divided majority, then, is the parliamentary analogue to divided government. Similar differences in operational meaning apply to the other key variables. It is this empirical maneuver, more than

---

10. Note that this is an indirect and very simple way of taking into account Epstein and O'Halloran's internal production baseline, as it allows the legislative floor to make its delegation decisions based on a recognition of how costly it would be to make all policy decisions in house.

11. See also Gailmard's (2002) analysis of bureaucratic subversion. His model allows bureaucrats to move beyond the discretionary bounds at a cost and arrives at interesting and provocative conclusions. Among them: that the legislature is actually better off when subversion is relatively cheap (because it often benefits when agencies are able to use their expertise in choosing policies better than the uninformed legislature had asked for), and agencies are better off when subversion is made more expensive (because if it is easy to subvert, the legislature tends to constrain discretion).

anything else, that makes their analysis comparative: the same theoretical concepts are given different empirical referents in different systems, and these differences are primarily what account for expected differences in delegation and discretion across institutional contexts.

The downside is that the formal models themselves are not doing enough of the work here, and are disappointing in certain respects. One problem has to do with the way nonstatutory factors are handled. Huber and Shipan lump all these factors (the courts, legislative oversight, etc.) together, assume there is a fixed probability they intervene to correct agency policy choice—and further assume that, if such intervention occurs, *policy automatically moves to the legislature's ideal point.* But why should the legislature be able to count on being perfectly backstopped (with some probability) by the courts? Why shouldn't it worry that the courts might have their own preferences and move policy to their own ideal points (Segal and Spaeth 2002)? Simplification is one thing, but Huber and Shipan's assumption creates a best-of-all-possible-worlds scenario for the legislature and ensures that it will write more discretionary laws when the probability of intervention is high. *Outside intervention is always good.* More realistic, less benign assumptions about the political environment would obviously lead to very different conclusions about delegation and discretion.[12]

These are not the only assumptions that should raise eyebrows. Huber and Shipan also assume, for example, that the probability the agency is caught and punished for noncompliance is exactly equal to the probability that nonstatutory factors will intervene, and that this probability is fixed. Fixing the probability, however, ensures that the agency's risk from engaging in noncompliant behavior has nothing to do with how "bad" its policy choices are—how far outside the discretionary range it chooses to go. This assumption is obviously quite unrealistic, and it distorts the agency's true incentives for noncompliance.

Their formal models are also disappointing for a more fundamental reason. Huber and Shipan build three distinct (but overlapping) models that can be compared and contrasted: a parliamentary model, a veto model, and a bicameral model. As a strategy for providing a comparative analysis of institutional systems, this multiple-models approach makes good sense. But there is less here than meets the eye. The parliamentary model is nothing more than a simple game between the legislature and the agency—and, shorn of peripheral assumptions, is essentially the *same* as Epstein and O'Halloran's model of legislative delegation in the United States: which, of course, is not supposed to be about parliamentary systems at all. What exactly is parliamentary about the Huber-Shipan model? Only that it lacks a veto player (namely, a president). Otherwise, it does nothing to incorporate any other distinguishing features of parliamentary government. This model is then contrasted with the veto model, which adds an executive veto, and to the bicameral model, which adds a second house of the legislature—features that are found in separation of powers systems (and, ironically, are entirely missing from the Epstein-O'Halloran model of the United States).[13]

---

12. Bendor and Mierowitz (2004: 301) agree that this perfect-backstopping assumption by Huber and Shipan is a problem for their analysis, essentially for the reasons I have stated—adding that it gives superiors "a perverse incentive to induce agents to shirk," so that the outsiders can catch them and bring them back to the superiors' ideal policies.

13. Note that the veto model is supposed to represent a (unicameral) presidential system, and the bicameral model is structured in such a way as to represent a separation of powers system, not a bicameral parliamentary system.

There is, at least, institutional variation to explore here, and the focus on veto points (none, one, or two) is basic and important. Still, the institutional set-up is overly spare for gaining insight into parliamentary government—particularly given that, in all three models, actors are thinking only of the here and now. They are not thinking about how power alignments might change in the future, nor are they thinking about the long-term durability of what they are creating—and so the fact that political uncertainty is especially severe in parliamentary systems (and durability a much more difficult problem less amenable to solution through formal structure) plays no role whatever. The rest of the literature is guilty of this same omission, of course. But for Huber and Shipan, the omission is more critical, for their analysis is much celebrated precisely because it aims to construct a comparative theory of delegation—and what they leave out is quite fundamental to an understanding of why delegation should differ across parliamentary and presidential systems, and why bureaucracies should differ as well.

This is an opportunity missed, and it promotes conclusions that are likely to be misleading. Indeed, their formal analysis indicates that the effects of their key variables—policy conflict, legislative capacity, the probability of intervention by outside forces—are the *same* for presidential and parliamentary systems. Empirically, differences arise because the measured levels of conflict, capacity, and intervention vary from system to system. But the underlying analytic relationships are the same, as is the basic logic of delegation. The only fundamental contrast is that, in their models, the level of discretion is always at least as great in a presidential system (all else being equal), because presidents want more of it and use their veto power to get it. As discussed earlier, however, the logic of delegation should be distinctively *different* in presidential and parliamentary systems once actors are allowed to be forward looking and take political uncertainty into account. And the implications run in precisely the *opposite* direction of the Huber and Shipan model: pointing to much less discretion in a presidential system (all else being equal).[14] The empirical evidence, moreover, suggests that American bureaucracy is, in fact, far more constrained by statutory restrictions than bureaucracies in parliamentary systems are (e.g., Moe and Caldwell 1994).

Epstein and O'Halloran (1999) and Huber and Shipan (2002) are the keystones of the modern literature on political control of the bureaucracy. Both have their drawbacks, but that is to be expected in work that strives to push the envelope. There is simply too much that needs to be done, and it cannot be done all at once. The important thing is that both have clearly succeeded in generalizing the theory and framing the way political control is thought about and studied. In the years since their publications, they have stimulated a spate of new work that builds on their analytic base and elaborates the theory still further. I do not have the luxury of discussing all of these developments, but I want to spotlight several that, because of the substantive topics they address, are especially promising avenues of inquiry.

6.1. Appointments

This is a legislature-oriented literature that only minimally explores the powers and impacts of presidents. Huber and Shipan (2002) and Volden (2002) include the president as a veto player in

---

14. To be clear: presidents use their leverage *within* a separation of powers system to push for bureaucratic discretion—but bureaus should still tend to have far *less* discretion in a separation of powers system than in a parliamentary system.

the legislative process, but the president's power of appointment—which is obviously relevant here—has received little attention. Typically, appointments come into play only indirectly in delegation models: bureaucratic agencies are assumed to have ideal points identical to the sitting president's (or this "result" is derived from assumptions that readily guarantee it). Little is learned, therefore, about the strategic use of appointments by presidents, its impact on the legislative delegation, and the consequences for agency behavior—all of which ought to be integral components of the theory.

McCarty (2004) attempts to do something about this shortcoming, developing a model of political control in which the president and the legislature are essentially co-equal actors. For reasons that are unclear, however, he does not adopt the agency discretion framework and crafts his model instead along quite different lines. The three actors are familiar: the legislature, the president, and the agency. But the set-up is not, for it is built around budgets. The legislature has the power to make budgetary proposals for funding the agency, and it also has a role in confirming presidential appointments. The president makes appointments and can veto legislative budgetary proposals. And the agency makes policy choices under the constraint that any departure from the status quo is costly and requires budgetary funds provided by the legislature. The upshot of this last assumption is that, when the legislature grants the agency a budget, it is essentially placing bounds on how far in either direction the agency can move from the status quo. In this sense, it retains one of the trappings of the agency discretion framework, with the budget determining how much discretion the agency has.

The thrust of McCarty's argument is that there is a dilemma inherent in the ongoing struggle between the legislature and the president to control the agency. The nub of the problem is that the president cannot commit to the appointments he makes—because once the legislature decides on a budget, the president can remove his initial appointees and replace them with others whose views on policy are closer to his own. Realizing this ex ante, however, the legislature may decide to give the agency a smaller budget, and thus less discretion, than it would actually like to. Both the president and the legislature are likely to be worse off as a result. The dilemma could be resolved if appointment and budgetary powers could somehow be centralized in the same hands, as in a parliamentary system. But more practically, the problem can be mitigated through independent commissions, civil service, and other devices whose statutory restrictions essentially allow the president to commit. Once he is able to do so, he can effectively obtain higher levels of discretion (budgets) for the agency by trading off appointments more to the liking of the legislature.

This analysis is interesting, but it is also problematic. One reason is that the idiosyncrasies that set it apart from the rest of the literature—creating an awkward fit, and making comparison and cumulative work more difficult—are also hard to justify. A key driver of this model's results is the assumption that any agency shift away from the status quo in either direction is costly, but this does not square well with reality. A regulatory agency might find it enormously expensive to launch waves of new inspections and enforcement actions, for example, whereas cutting back on inspections and enforcement would cost it nothing—indeed, it might save tons of money. So even when agencies make important shifts away from the status quo, these shifts are not necessarily costly at all. This is especially true when the shift involves doing less work—which is precisely the way many agencies do in fact change their policies. The model's basic assumption about agencies—which, in turn, determines how legislatures and presidents deal with them, and with one another—seems off the mark.

More fundamental still, this is an article about a commitment dilemma, but whether it really captures something empirically central to the struggle for political control is debatable. Presidents certainly do not have a history—even at the margins—of making initial appointments, waiting for the legislature to make key policy choices, then firing the appointees and making new, more extreme appointments. The legislature could punish any president who behaved in this way, not only by refusing to confirm the new appointees (regardless of the latter's policy views) but also by undermining his policy agenda, launching investigations, and in myriad ways making his life miserable. And perhaps most importantly, there are heavy costs to presidents if they continually appoint and fire bureaucrats—for it creates disorganization, discontinuity, lack of expertise, and weak leadership within the agencies, and it takes time and attention from the president's own staff. Removing appointees is something presidents do not want to do.

Thus, the commitment problem at the heart of McCarty's model would seem to be a non-problem in practice and not the place to start in understanding the role of presidential appointments. Even so, this is a useful contribution, because it puts the focus squarely on appointments, argues the need for modeling their dynamics, and encourages future work along these lines. Presidential appointments need to be an integral part of the political logic of delegation.

6.2. Development of Agency Expertise

At the heart of these delegation models is the agency's advantage in expertise. How or why the agency develops its expertise, however, is left unexplored. Typically, the agency is simply assumed to have perfect knowledge of the connection between policy choices and policy outcomes, the legislature is assumed to be uninformed on this count, and the models go on to show why it is beneficial for the legislature to delegate discretion to take advantage of what the agency knows. With expertise so crucial to an understanding of delegation, though, there is good reason to explore its role in greater depth by making it endogenous to the theory, and thus a product of decisions by key actors.[15]

A provocative step in this direction has recently been taken by Gailmard and Patty (2007). Using an agency discretion framework, they build their model around two types of bureaucrats: the zealot who is purely motivated by policy and the slacker who is purely motivated by material gain. They use these types to shed light not only on the legislature's decision to delegate discretion but also on the bureaucrats' decisions about whether to invest in expertise and whether to continue their jobs with the agency (or leave for the private sector).

The model reveals that only the zealots have incentives to invest in expertise and stay with the government long term—and that the legislature, to take advantage of agency expertise, essentially pays for it by giving discretion to bureaucrats (the zealots) who have their own policy preferences and can be expected to depart from the legislature's ideal. Moreover, the legislature has incentives to provide these zealots with tenure in their jobs, for otherwise they would not make investments in expertise—which can only pay off with continued service to the agency over time.

---

15. Incentives to specialize have been explored, however, in models of legislative organization, where the question is whether and to what extent committees will choose to pay the costs of becoming experts in their substantive jurisdictions. See, for example, Gilligan and Krehbiel (1990). See also Bendor and Mierowitz (2004) for applications to delegation.

There are a few questionable assumptions here that shape the analysis. Gailmard and Patty assume, for instance, that expertise has value to the bureaucrat only within government, and that its value is zero in the private sector. For many government jobs, this is clearly not true. Indeed, the well-known "revolving door" phenomenon, in which governments lose employees to the private sector, is largely driven by the expertise these employees gain from their public service.[16] The authors also assume that the private sector wage is always greater than the agency wage—which gives *all* slackers incentives to *leave* the agency very quickly (with zealots staying on), a cataclysmic result that influences the entire analysis. Yet such a blanket (and radically consequential) assumption is unwarranted; for the private sector wage advantage is more myth than reality, especially when benefits (e.g., health and retirement) are taken into account.[17] It also ignores attitudes toward risk, as well as the likelihood that government jobs may selectively attract many people (including slackers) who are risk averse and willing to accept a lower government wage in return for greater job security (Brehm and Gates 1999).

These are serious problems that raise red flags about this particular model. But as a general avenue of inquiry, the Gailmard and Patty (2007) analysis is among the most innovative in the literature. It helps point the way toward a better understanding of how bureaucratic expertise may develop as an integral part of the nexus of decisions involved in delegation. And it goes further, suggesting how key components of the civil service system—such as tenure—might arise from the politics of delegation, be rational and productive for the players involved, and contribute to an explanation of bureaucratic expertise. Although the specifics of their model can be questioned, then, it encourages new work that connects delegation to the internal organization of the bureaucracy. And it gets back to the kinds of issues that were central to the control literature years ago, before formalization shifted the focus to discretion.

6.3. Bureaucratic Capacity

The usual delegation model is built around the information problem and thus around the legislature's reliance on an expert bureaucracy to carry out policy. It is the bureaucracy's expertise that makes it distinctive and drives much of the analysis. But Huber and McCarty (2004) rightly argue that there is another aspect of the bureaucracy—its capacity for effective performance—that deserves central attention as well. Implicitly, the delegation literature has assumed that capacity is not an issue and that all bureaucracies are highly capable. Yet even though agencies may have considerable expertise about their policy environments, they may also be quite incapable— due to mismanagement, corruption, or patronage, among other things—of carrying out policy effectively. Expertise and capacity are simply different dimensions, and both are likely to be important for understanding delegation.

The model Huber and McCarty develop is similar to the others in basic respects. The authors use the agency discretion framework, treat bureaucratic expertise in the usual way (with policy

16. Accounts are legion. See, for example, Katzmann (1981) on how young attorneys flocked to the Federal Trade Commission to gain experience in anti-trust and consumer cases so that they could move into lucrative positions in private law firms after a short time.

17. Compensation across sectors, although bundled differently, is sufficiently comparable in total value that there is considerable debate over which sector has the advantage. See, for example, Federal Reserve Bank of Chicago (2009).

outcomes partly determined by random shocks that the agency knows with certainty), and—following Huber and Shipan (2002)—assume that the agency is caught and punished with some probability if its implemented policy falls outside the discretionary region. The difference here is that the agency's implemented policy consists of two parts: an action a chosen by the agency and a random adjustment w that reflects its capacity for effective performance. Unlike the random shocks associated with expertise, the agency does not know w. But it does know the variance of w's distribution. The larger the variance, the lower the agency's capacity for effectiveness, and the farther the implemented policy is likely to depart from the agency's chosen action a.

Given the literature's implicit focus on high-capacity agencies, Huber and McCarty center their analysis on those that have low capacity. They begin by showing that low-capacity agencies, because their own actions have so little impact on implemented policy (stemming from the high variance of w), actually have little control over their own fates—and this reduces their incentive to even try to comply with legislative policy directives, making them harder to control. This implication is interesting, but they go on to derive conclusions that are even more instructive. For instance, they show that the ally principle, long at the theoretical core of the delegation literature, tends to fall apart once capacity is taken into account. The legislature can often obtain better policy outcomes by delegating to competent agencies with distant political preferences than to low-capacity agencies that are closer by.

They also derive much more general implications for institutional reform. They show that, although politicians always benefit from reforms that enhance bureaucratic capacity, their incentives to engage in such reforms are weakest in systems populated by low-capacity agencies. In these environments—which appear in some areas of the United States but are quite common in Latin America and other developing regions (Geddes 1994)—politicians have reduced incentive to develop their own policy expertise, reduced incentive to bolster institutions (such as courts) that would improve bureaucratic compliance, and enhanced incentive to politicize the bureaucracy: all of which create a drag on reform and tend to keep the system in an incompetency trap.

Overall, this is a remarkable analysis. Bureaucratic agencies are the government's means of carrying out public policy, and their capacity for effective performance is clearly central to how any rational politician, interest group, or citizen would go about understanding them or assessing their value. Yet the delegation literature has focused all its attention on the information problem and brushed capacity aside. Huber and McCarty have now put a spotlight on it and shown that it does indeed have far-reaching theoretical consequences. In so doing, they have taken a key step toward moving the theory away from its American origins and making it truly comparative in scope, because low-capacity bureaucracies are a serious problem throughout the world. This analysis not only sheds new light on these non-American contexts, but it also shows that the logic of delegation—and reform—may work quite differently in such settings than scholars had previously thought.

7. Discussion

The theory of public bureaucracy has made dramatic progress over the past few decades. From the pioneering work of Downs and Tullock to Niskanen's theory of the budget-maximizing bureau to the more recent theories of political control and delegation, the field has put together a sophisticated analytic base for understanding how the organization and performance of bureaucracy arise out of politics. The modern literature is defined by work that is formal and game-theoretic, and its trajectory has propelled it from the realm of early breakthroughs into the realm of normal science. Modelers in the field now see themselves as building incrementally on a common analytic foundation, and they agree on what good work looks like.

The most influential achievement is the analytic foundation itself, whose rigor has allowed this literature to move beyond informal argument to deductively powerful theories with testable implications. The most basic of these implications—the ally principle, the uncertainty principle—are the cornerstones of the modern field and central to how the dynamics of delegation are understood.[18] But the literature has also expanded its horizons over time, as scholars have sought to incorporate a range of actors and topics—presidents, courts, appointments, bureaucratic capacity, legislative capacity, bicameralism, the endogenous development of agency expertise—that are clearly relevant to the politics of delegation and demanding of attention. Today's theory, as a result, is a less legislature-centered and more broadly institutional approach that explores key features of the American separation of powers system and extends to parliamentary governments as well. Along the way, the legacy of congressional dominance has weakened, as formal models have clearly shown that legislators face a trade-off between control and expertise, that it is rational for them to accept imperfect control, and that agencies should often have substantial autonomy.

All literatures have their problems, and this one is no exception. Despite the expansion of the theory, the legislature is still the center of its political universe, and other institutional actors—the president, the courts, even the bureaucracy—are given far less serious attention than they deserve. Consider the president. It is not unusual for delegation models to ignore his veto power—even though the president clearly benefits from agency discretion and can reject legislation that does not provide enough of it. These same models typically assume that the agency has policy preferences identical to the president's, implicitly claiming that he has no problem getting the agency to do his bidding—which is far from accurate and diverts attention from the fact that, as chief executive, the president has his own problems controlling the bureaucracy. Some of these problems arise because Congress is trying to control it too. But many arise simply because top-down control is highly imperfect in any hierarchy, including the executive branch.

---

18. Bendor and Meirowitz (2004) explore the robustness of the theory of delegation by examining how well its better known implications stand up as fundamental assumptions are varied. They show that the ally principle stands up quite well, but that (not surprisingly) it does not hold under all conditions. For example, when information varies across bureaucrats—which can happen when bureaucrats are not perfectly informed, information is costly, and some specialize more than others—then political superiors may pass up an incompetent ally for a competent agent whose ideal point is farther away. To take another example, they show that, if agents can precommit to particular policies—which is precisely the point, for instance, of setting up an independent central bank (a bureaucratic institution) for monetary policy—then superiors may find it advantageous in some cases to delegate discretion to bureaucrats whose ideal points are not close to their own. See also Bendor et al. (2001). As for the uncertainty principle, Bendor and Meirowitz show that it is a robust conclusion and that the value political superiors place on (bureaucratic) expertise has little to do with attitudes toward risk—the superiors do not, in particular, have to be risk averse for the principle to hold. The decision to delegate is mainly driven by their desire to achieve policies close to their ideal, and by other factors (e.g., the variance of the random shock) that are separate from attitudes toward risk.

Both give presidents strong reasons to use his powers—of the veto, of appointments, of unilateral action—to impose structures that enhance his own control. Indeed, much of the organization of the federal bureaucracy was created by presidents or their appointees, not Congress (Howell and Lewis 2002; Lewis 2003). A theory that aims to explain the organization of public bureaucracy, then, needs to treat presidents as the pivotal actors they are, not as a planet orbiting the legislative sun.[19]

The courts have also been marginalized. If they are incorporated at all, they tend to be treated as faithful backstoppers of the legislature, beefing up its power.[20] But judges clearly have preferences of their own, they act on them, and there is a large empirical literature on judicial behavior that documents as much (e.g., Segal and Spaeth 2002). Like presidents they can take unilateral action, without legislation, to impose their own structures on the agencies. And like presidents they have serious control problems to worry about and address: for they cannot count on having agencies faithfully obey their written orders, or indeed obey them at all. Ultimately, then, this literature needs to incorporate all the major institutional actors as (roughly) co-equal players and model the dynamics of their interactions. The legislature, the president, and the courts all have authority over the bureaucracy; they all have problems controlling it; and they all are involved in imposing structures to engineer more desirable behavior and policy outcomes. This is what the theory ought to be about, not just delegation by legislatures.

Even though the legislature is the star player in this literature, it has actually been explored in surprisingly little depth. Congress is a complex institution with two houses, two parties, huge numbers of committees (several of which may be relevant to any given decision), and hundreds of members driven by parochial interests; and it is plagued by severe transaction costs when it attempts to take action. As such, it is not an actor in the same sense that the president is. Yet despite the centrality of transaction costs to the new economics of organization, and notwithstanding Epstein and O'Halloran's claim to have developed a transaction costs theory of delegation, Congress is modeled as a coherent actor that instantaneously, smoothly, and flawlessly makes optimal decisions in pursuit of its well-defined policy objectives.[21] By uncritically going down this modeling path, the formal literature fails to recognize Congress's nature as an institution and is out of sync with what are supposed to be its own theoretical origins. Theorists ought to be trying to model the very ponderousness and decisional difficulty that make Congress what it is—and that cannot help but shape the larger struggle for control.

19. For a recent attempt to explore explicitly presidential effects on the politics of delegation, see Wiseman (2009). Wiseman argues that, when the president can engage in review and adjustment of agency decisions subsequent to delegation—notably, through the regulatory review activities of the Office of Information and Regulatory Affairs (OIRA)—both the president and Congress can actually be better off. According to Wiseman, this reasoning helps explain why OIRA continues to survive.

20. This is true of the delegation literature (Huber and Shipan 2002), but it is also true of the work on ex post control. The courts are portrayed as Congress's helpers. See Ferejohn and Shipan (1990) and Eskridge and Ferejohn (1992).

21. Epstein and O'Halloran (1999) begin to get at these internal decision problems in their make or buy framework, and Huber and Shipan (2002) do too by recognizing variations in legislative capabilities, but these are not attempts to model the truly burdensome transaction costs that afflict Congress, and they only scratch the surface. I should add that legislatures in parliamentary systems are much less burdened in this respect—a variation of theoretical consequence that ought to be central to this literature.

And then there is the bureaucracy itself, which, despite its universal role as the agent in these analyses, has actually received very little attention. The early work on ex ante control—by Mc-Cubbins, Noll, and Weingast, Moe, and others—was explicitly about bureaucratic organization. It argued that legislatures (and presidents) used various aspects of organization—the location of the agency, its decision criteria, its decision processes, appointments, personnel rules, rules for appeals, interest group participation, reporting requirements, and more—to gain control over agency behavior. My own work, moreover, also put the focus on bureaucratic effectiveness and how it tends to be undermined by politically imposed structures. But these organizational concerns are less central today. With the recent formalization of the theory, the focus is on how much discretion the bureaucracy is delegated. Various aspects of bureaucratic organization are still discussed—informally—as the means by which discretion is restricted. But they are not explicitly modeled, and they are not explored in terms of the different effects they might have on bureaucratic behavior. They are essentially lumped together into one homogeneous mass, as the structural means by which discretion is restricted. This characterization does not tell us much about why agencies are organized as they are, nor about how their politically imposed structures affect their capacity for effective performance. For now, the organizational aspects of bureaucracy have gotten organized out of the formal theory.[22]

It seems clear that, with the focus and momentum that normal science imparts to a research community, the theory will naturally be expanded and improved over time along most of the dimensions I have just discussed. So in this sense, progress is inevitable. Yet normal science is constraining as well as empowering, because its consensus on analytics inherently produces a research dynamic that pushes the theory in "normal" directions—and pushes it away from other avenues that, even if potentially productive, are not compatible with the accepted way of thinking about things. Over time, as the field is guided by this framing, a kind of path dependence sets in that makes certain kinds of progress more difficult to achieve. An obvious example is the one I just discussed: precisely because this literature is now built around the concept of discretion, all aspects of bureaucratic organization get telescoped into this one concept, propelling inquiry in directions that are less about organization than they might otherwise be.

Another troubling constraint built into the normal framing, an exceedingly consequential one, is that actors are not forward looking. It has long been part of the working knowledge of the field that, because tomorrow's power holders may be very different from today's—different policy agendas, different ideologies—rational actors in a position to design bureaucratic agencies have incentives to look ahead and take this political uncertainty into account. The greater the likelihood their enemies may gain power in the future, the more they will have incentives today to adopt restrictive structures that shield "their" agencies from unwanted influences. But even though this forward-looking logic could not be more basic to rational behavior and is often discussed, it is simply omitted from formal models of delegation and control. Among those doing the modeling, this omission is not regarded as a problem, or even an issue worth pointing out. It is normal.

---

22. Some of Ting's (2002, 2003) work, however, links delegation to issues that are explicitly organizational—exploring, for example, how superiors might try to use redundant bureaucratic agents (multiple agents doing the same tasks) to obtain better outcomes and increase effectiveness (Ting 2003), and how superiors might be able to obtain better outcomes by assigning different jurisdictions to different agencies (Ting 2002).

In essence, then, existing models assume that their actors behave in rather stupid ways. They are fixated on the present, as though politics is never going to change.[23] When the legislature makes its delegation decisions with an eye to the president—assuming, for instance, that he alone determines the agency's policy preferences—it is looking only at the current president and ignoring the fact that he will soon be out of office, replaced by another person. And another and another. If legislators want to maximize the long-term benefits to themselves and their constituents, it is obviously a big mistake for them to base their entire calculation on the sitting president alone. Would it have made sense, in 2007 and 2008, for the Democratic Congress to make its delegation decisions under the assumption that the only president of relevance was George W. Bush, when they knew for certain he would be gone by January 2009? Of course not. *But this is just what the existing models of delegation assume.* And because it is normal, no one thinks twice about it.[24]

This problem is pervasive and carries over to the literature's attempt to build a comparative theory of delegation. Parliamentary governments are not all alike. But it is surely the case that, in most of them, there are far fewer veto points than in the American system; it is much easier for the government to pass new laws; and because of this, the current government needs to be very concerned that its creations will be undermined or destroyed when the opposition

---

23. To be more accurate: legislators do think ahead, in the sense that they need to ponder what agencies are likely to do with whatever discretion they are granted. But legislators do not think ahead in other basic respects, for example, by recognizing that the sitting president and the agency's presidential appointee are temporary and will be replaced by others with perhaps very different policy preferences. Also, legislators do not think ahead with regard to themselves: today's legislators need to be concerned about what will happen down the road if opposing legislators grab the reins of power and take control of the agencies being created today. In short, existing models allow the players to be forward looking about agency compliance and shirking, but not about the structure of power and control.

24. The most notable exception—outside of one attempt by Epstein and O'Halloran (1994) to model political uncertainty—is the formal treatment given to the concept by de Figueiredo (2002). His analysis is not about delegation per se but about whether interest groups will favor overturning one another's policies when their party gains power, and whether they will insulate their agencies (and suffer the inefficiencies that might go along with it) in separation-of-power systems that allow such restrictions to endure. He argues that insulation is pursued by weak groups, not strong ones, in separation of powers systems and that groups often respond to political uncertainty in parliamentary systems by cooperating and thus agreeing not to overturn one another's policies. He also argues that, in general, political uncertainty works somewhat differently than I have suggested in my own work and is less likely to produce insulation and bureaucratic inefficiency. This is not the place for me to write out a response, needless to say. I do think that there is much to agree with in de Figueiredo's basic conclusions about the effects of political uncertainty, although he has a tendency to couch them in more extreme terms than is warranted. Despite his categorical claims about the model's clear-cut implications, there is actually no clear, definitive way to translate some of his mathematical results into statements about the empirical world—because it involves, for example, interpreting what it means for a given parameter to be "sufficiently high." My own view is that softer versions of his stated conclusions are more likely on the mark: that weak groups have greater incentives to insulate than do strong groups, and that groups in parliamentary systems are sometimes able to cooperate in not overturning one another's policies. These conclusions are entirely compatible with my own logic (e.g., Moe and Caldwell 1994). More generally, however, the main point to drive home here is that de Figueiredo's model is just one of many ways that political uncertainty might be modeled—and other reasonable approaches would surely lead to different conclusions. The bottom line is that more scholarly work is needed on political uncertainty. It is a concept that—unless we want our actors to behave stupidly—should be taken seriously, integrated into our models, and debated.

comes to power. Simply burying agencies in formal restrictions does not work very well, as such restrictions can be lifted by the next government. American lawmakers need not be nearly as worried, because they are protected by all the checks and balances built into their system: whatever they create and embed in formal structures will tend to endure. Thus, when actors look forward, the logic of delegation is clearly very different across these political systems. Yet the existing literature does not allow them to look forward, and it entirely ignores this fundamental source of cross-system difference. The same is true, interestingly enough, of recent parliamentary analyses that are entirely informal, and thus are not constrained by the need to simplify and mathematize their key ideas. They are very informative in describing how delegation operates in these systems, how linear and hierarchical it is compared to the American case, the key role of parties, and the like—but they pay no attention to political uncertainty and its crucial implications, staying very much within the normal science bounds (Strøm et al. 2003).

Finally, I want to mention one more aspect of the normal framing that I find especially important but have not discussed at all to this point—because it is completely missing from this literature. The normal assumption is that bureaucrats are *subordinates* in the hierarchy of government, pure and simple. In terms of public authority, of course, this is accurate and makes perfect sense. But it systematically diverts attention from a feature of democratic politics that has clear relevance to control and delegation. In a democracy, political superiors are elected; and this means that, if ordinary bureaucrats can get organized to take collective action in politics—through public sector unions, for example—*they can exert political power over their own superiors.* When this happens—and it regularly does, in the United States and throughout the developed world (Blais et al. 1997)—they can play major roles in determining who gets elected and what policies the latter pursue once in office. This being so, the kind of "control" that political superiors want to exercise may often—depending on the specific group and the power it wields—tend to favor bureaucratic interests: by favoring policies and structures, say, that promote job security, enhance autonomy, protect established programs, and lead to higher spending and taxing. In contrast, the normal way of thinking about bureaucrats assumes that they have no *political* power at all: bureaucrats are difficult to control, and have a measure of power, because they have *informational* leverage over their superiors. They are experts. The idea that they may also have political power and that, in some realms of behavior, politicians may actually be agents of the bureaucrats—and acting as such in their delegation decisions—is entirely foreign and never seriously considered. As a result, an important part of the delegation story is missed, and theorists tend to underestimate what bureaucrats can do to get their way (see Moe 2006).

8. Conclusion

There is reason, then, for both enthusiasm and concern in assessing the contributions of formal models to the study of public bureaucracy. Tremendous progress has been made, and along the way one of the most traditional and underdeveloped fields in all of political science has been transformed into a juggernaut of cutting-edge work. In important respects, the trajectory continues to look promising, and will likely take the theory further beyond its legislature-centered origins to capture some of the distinctive dynamics of separation of powers and parliamentary systems. But just as formal models are powerful tools in the development of theory, so they are also powerful means of constraining it. As their influence has taken hold, they have generated a normal science that inherently mobilizes research around certain sets of ideas—and discourages the pursuit of others, including some that are quite important to an understanding of control, delegation, and bureaucracy.

The real challenge for scholars in the years ahead, therefore, is not simply to push for incremental progress along the same trajectory. It is to push against the constraints, to be open to abnormal ideas, and to think actively about shifting the theory onto new paths that might be more productive.

REFERENCES

Aranson, Peter, Ernest Gelhorn, and George Robinson. 1982. "A Theory of Legislative Delegation." *Cornell Law Review* 68: 777–795.

Banks, Jeffrey. 1989. "Agency Budgets, Cost Information, and Auditing." *American Journal of Political Science* 33: 670–699.

Banks, Jeffrey, and Barry R. Weingast. 1992. "The Political Control of Bureaucracies under Asymmetric Information." *American Journal of Political Science* 36: 509–524.

Barke, Richard P., and William H. Riker. 1982. "A Political Theory of Regulation with Some Observations on Railway Abandonments." *Public Choice* 39: 73–106.

Bawn, Kathleen. 1995. "Political Control versus Expertise: Congressional Choices about Administrative Procedures." *American Political Science Review* 89: 62–73.

Bendor, Jonathan. 1988. "Formal Models of Bureaucracy: A Review." *British Journal of Political Science* 18: 353–395.

Bendor, Jonathan, and Adam Meirowitz. 2004. "Spatial Models of Delegation." *American Political Science Review* 98: 293–310.

Bendor, Jonathan, Serge Taylor, and Roland van Gaalen. 1985. "Bureaucratic Expertise versus Legislative Authority: A Model of Deception and Monitoring in Budgeting." *American Political Science Review* 79: 1041–1060.

———. 1987a. "Stacking the Deck: Bureaucratic Missions and the Search for Alternatives." *American Political Science Review* 81: 873–896.

———. 1987b. "Politicians, Bureaucrats, and Asymmetric Information." *American Political Science Review* 81: 796–828.

Bendor, Jonathan, A. Glazer, and Thomas Hammond. 2001. "Theories of Delegation." *Annual Review of Political Science* 4: 235–269.

Blais, Andre, and Stephane Dion. 1991. *The Budget-Maximizing Bureaucrat: Appraisals and Evidence.* Pittsburgh, PA: University of Pittsburgh Press.

Blais, Andre, Donald E. Blake, and Stephane Dion. 1997. *Governments, Parties, and Public Sector Employees.* Pittsburgh, PA: University of Pittsburgh Press.

Brehm, John O., and Scott Gates. 1999. *Working, Shirking, and Sabotage.* Ann Arbor: University of Michigan Press.

Breton, Albert, and Ronald Wintrobe. 1975. "The Equilibrium Size of a Budget-Maximizing Bureau: A Note on Niskanen's Theory of Bureaucracy." *Journal of Political Economy* 82: 195–207.

———. 1982. *The Logic of Bureaucratic Conduct.* Cambridge: Cambridge University Press.

Calvert, Randall, Mathew D. McCubbins, and Barry R. Weingast. 1989. "A Theory of Political Control and Agency Discretion." *American Journal of Political Science* 33: 588–611.

de Figueiredo, Rui. 2002. "Electoral Competition, Political Uncertainty, and Policy Insulation." *American Political Science Review* 96: 321–333.

de Figueiredo, Rui, Tanya Jacobi, and Barry Weingast. 2006. "The New Separation of Powers Approach to American Politics," in Barry R. Weingast and Donald Wittman (eds.), *The Handbook of Political Economy.* New York: Oxford University Press, pp. 199–221.

Diermeier, Daniel. 1995. "Commitment, Deference, and Legislative Institutions." *American Political Science Review* 89: 344–355.

Downs, Anthony. 1967. *Inside Bureaucracy.* Boston: Little, Brown.

Epstein, David, and Sharyn O'Halloran. 1994. "Administrative Procedures, Information, and Agency Discretion." *American Journal of Political Science* 38: 697–722.

———. 1996. "Divided Government and the Design of Administrative Procedures: A Formal Model and Empirical Test." *Journal of Politics* 58: 379–397.

———. 1999. *Delegating Powers.* New York: Cambridge University Press.

Eskridge, William N., and John Ferejohn. 1992. "Making the Deal Stick: Enforcing the Original Constitutional Structure of Lawmaking in the Modern Regulatory State." *Journal of Law, Economics, and Organization* 8: 165–189.

Federal Reserve Bank of Chicago. 2009. "Public and Private Sector Compensation: What Is Affordable in This Recession and Beyond?—A Conference Summary." Chicago Fed Letter 262a (May). Chicago.

Ferejohn, John, and Charles Shipan. 1990. "Congressional Influence on Bureaucracy." *Journal of Law, Economics, and Organization* 6: 1–20.

Fiorina, Morris P. 1981. "Congressional Control of the Bureaucracy: A Mismatch of Capabilities and Incentives," in Lawrence Dodd and Bruce Oppenheimer (eds.), *Congress Reconsidered,* second edition. Washington, DC: Congressional Quarterly Press, pp. 332–348.

———. 1982a. "Legislative Choice of Regulatory Forms: Legal Process or Administrative Process?" *Public Choice* 39: 33–66.

———. 1982b. "Group Concentration and the Delegation of Legislative Authority," in Roger G. Noll (ed.), *Regulatory Policy and the Social Sciences.* Berkeley: University of California Press.

———. 1986. "Legislative Uncertainty, Legislative Control, and the Delegation of Legislative Power." *Journal of Law, Economics, and Organization* 2: 33–50.

Gailmard, Sean. 2002. "Expertise, Subversion, and Bureaucratic Discretion." *Journal of Law, Economics, and Organization* 18: 536–555.

Gailmard, Sean, and John W. Patty. 2007. "Slackers and Zealots: Civil Service, Policy Discretion, and Bureaucratic Expertise." *American Journal of Political Science* 51: 873–889.

Geddes, Barbara. 1994. *Politician's Dilemma: Building State Capacity in Latin America.* Berkeley: University of California Press.

Gilligan, Thomas W., and Keith Krehbiel. 1990. "Organization of Informative Committees by a Rational Legislature." *American Journal of Political Science* 34: 531–564.

Hammond, Thomas, and Jack Knott. 1996. "Who Controls the Bureaucracy? Presidential Power, Congressional Dominance, and Bureaucratic Autonomy in a Model of Multi-Institutional Policymaking." *Journal of Law, Economics, and Organization* 12: 119–166.

Hammond, Thomas, and Gary J. Miller. 1985. "A Social Choice Perspective on Authority and Expertise in Bureaucracy." *American Journal of Political Science* 29: 1–28.

———. 1987. "The Core of the Constitution." *American Political Science Review* 81: 1155–1174.

Horn, Murray J. 1995. *The Political Economy of Public Administration.* New York: Cambridge University Press.

Horn, Murray J., and Kenneth Shepsle. 1989. "Commentary on 'Administrative Arrangements and the Political Control of Agencies': Administrative Process and Organizational Form as Responses to Agency Costs." *Virginia Law Review* 75(2): 499–508.

Howell, William G., and David E. Lewis. 2002. "Agencies by Presidential Design." *Journal of Politics* 64: 1095–1114.

Huber, John D., and Nolan McCarty. 2004. "Bureaucratic Capacity, Delegation, and Political Reform." *American Political Science Review* 98: 481–494.

Huber, John D., and Charles R. Shipan. 2002. *Deliberate Discretion?* New York: Cambridge University Press.

Katzmann, Robert. 1981. *Regulatory Bureaucracy: The Federal Trade Commission and Anti-Trust Policy.* Cambridge, MA: MIT Press.

Knott, Jack, and Gary J. Miller. 1987. *Reforming Bureaucracy.* Englewood Cliffs, NJ: Prentice-Hall.

Lewis, David E. 2003. *Presidents and the Politics of Agency Design.* Stanford, CA: Stanford University Press.

Long, Norton. 1949. "Power and Administration." *Public Administration Review* 9(4): 257–264.

March, James G., and Herbert A. Simon. 1957. *Organizations.* New York: Wiley.

Mashaw, Jerry. 1990. "Explaining Administrative Process: Normative, Positive, and Critical Studies of Legal Development." *Journal of Law, Economics, and Organization* 6: 267–298.

McCarty, Nolan. 2004. "The Appointments Dilemma." *American Journal of Political Science* 48: 413–428.

McCubbins, Mathew D. 1985. "The Legislative Design of Regulatory Structure." *American Journal of Political Science* 29: 721–748.

McCubbins, Mathew D., and Thomas Schwartz. 1984. "Congressional Oversight Overlooked: Police Patrols versus Fire Alarms." *American Journal of Political Science* 28: 165–179.

McCubbins, Mathew D., Roger G. Noll, and Barry R. Weingast. 1987. "Administrative Procedures as Instruments of Political Control." *Journal of Law, Economics, and Organization* 3: 243–277.

———. 1989. "Structure and Process, Politics and Policy: Administrative Arrangements and the Political Control of Agencies." *Virginia Law Review* 75: 431–482.

McKelvey, Richard D. 1976. "Intransitivities in Multidimensional Voting: Models and Some Implications for Agenda Control." *Journal of Economic Theory* 12: 472–482.

Migue, Jean-Luc, and Gerard Balanger. 1974. "Towards a General Theory of Managerial Discretion." *Public Choice* 17: 27–43.

Milgrom, Paul, and John Roberts. 1992. *Economics, Organization, and Management.* New York: Prentice-Hall.

Miller, Gary J. 1992. *Managerial Dilemmas.* New York: Cambridge University Press.

———. 2005. "The Political Evolution of Principal-Agent Models." *Annual Review of Political Science* 8: 203–225.

Miller, Gary J., and Terry M. Moe. 1983. "Bureaucrats, Legislators, and the Size of Government." *American Political Science Review* 77: 297–322.

Moe, Terry M. 1984. "The New Economics of Organization." *American Journal of Political Science* 28: 739–777.

———. 1987. "An Assessment of the Positive Theory of 'Congressional Dominance.'" *Legislative Studies Quarterly* 12: 475–520.

———. 1989. "The Politics of Bureaucratic Structure," in John E. Chubb and Paul E. Peterson (eds.), *Can the Government Govern?* Washington, DC: Brookings Institution, pp. 267–329.

———. 1990a. "The Politics of Structural Choice: Toward a Theory of Public Bureaucracy," in Oliver E. Williamson (ed.), *Organization Theory: From Chester Barnard to the Present and Beyond.* New York: Oxford University Press.

———. 1990b. "Political Institutions: The Neglected Side of the Story." *Journal of Law, Economics, and Organization* 6: 213–253.

———. 2006. "Political Control and the Power of the Agent." *Journal of Law, Economics, and Organization* 22: 1–29.

Moe, Terry M., and Michael Caldwell. 1994. "The Institutional Foundations of Democratic Government: A Comparison of Presidential and Parliamentary Systems." *Journal of Institutional and Theoretical Economics* 150: 171–195.

Moe, Terry M., and Scott Wilson. 1994. "Presidents and the Politics of Structure." *Law and Contemporary Problems* 57(Spring): 1–44.

Niskanen, William A. 1971. *Bureaucracy and Representative Government.* New York: Aldine-Atherton.

Perrow, Charles. 1986. *Complex Organizations.* New York: Random House.

Romer, Thomas, and Howard Rosenthal. 1978. "Political Resource Allocation, Controlled Agendas, and the Status Quo." *Public Choice* 33: 27–43.

———. 1979. "Bureaucrats versus Voters: On the Political Economy of Resource Allocation in Direct Democracy." *Quarterly Journal of Economics* 93: 563–587.

Segal, Jeffrey, and Harold Spaeth. 2002. *The Supreme Court and the Attitudinal Model Revisited.* New York: Cambridge University Press.

Shepsle, Kenneth A. 1979. "Institutional Arrangements and Equilibrium in Multidimensional Voting Models." *American Journal of Political Science* 23: 27–59.

Shepsle, Kenneth A., and Barry R. Weingast. 1981. "Structure-Induced Equilibrium and Legislative Choice." *Public Choice* 37: 503–519.

Simon, Herbert A. 1947. *Administrative Behavior.* New York: Macmillan.

Strøm, Kaare, Wolfgang C. Muller, and Torbjorn Bergman. 2003. *Delegation and Accountability in Parliamentary Democracies.* New York: Oxford University Press.

Ting, Michael M. 2002. "A Theory of Jurisdictional Assignments in Bureaucracies." *American Journal of Political Science* 46: 364–378.

———. 2003. "A Strategic Theory of Bureaucratic Redundancy." *American Journal of Political Science* 47: 274–292.

Tullock, Gordon. 1965. *The Politics of Bureaucracy.* Washington, DC: Public Affairs Press.

Volden, Craig. 2002. "A Formal Model of the Politics of Delegation in a Separation of Powers System." *American Journal of Political Science* 46: 111–133.

Weingast, Barry R. 1981. "Regulation, Reregulation, and Deregulation: The Political Foundations of Agency Clientele Relationships." *Law and Contemporary Problems* 44: 147–177.

———. 1984. "The Congressional-Bureaucratic System: A Principal-Agent Perspective." *Public Choice* 44: 147–192.

Weingast, Barry R., and Mark Moran. 1983. "Bureaucratic Discretion or Congressional Control: Regulatory Policymaking by the Federal Trade Commission." *Journal of Political Economy* 91: 765–800.

Williamson, Oliver E. 1985. *The Economic Institutions of Capitalism.* New York: Free Press.

Wilson, James Q. 1989. *Bureaucracy: What Government Agencies Do and Why They Do It.* New York: Basic Books.

Wiseman, Alan E. 2009. "Delegation and Positive-Sum Bureaucracies." *Journal of Politics* 71: 998–1014.

NAME INDEX

Page numbers for entries occurring in figures are followed by an *f;* those for entries in notes, by an *n;* and those for entries in tables, by a *t.*

SUBJECT INDEX

Page numbers for entries occurring in figures are followed by an *f;* those for entries in notes, by an *n;* and those for entries in tables, by a *t.*

tournament models, 83–84, 219–23, 220t, 221t, 223t, 484–86

See also performance measures

incentive systems

commissions, 494

competition and, 823–24

distortions, 488

fiscal years and, 490

group-based, 507–8, 508n39, 546–47, 547n41, 549, 551

innovation and, 353–54, 578–80, 583, 883

multiple devices, 77–78

in multiproduct firms, 829–30

productivity effects, 488–90

relational contracts and, 699

self-selection, 219

signaling function, 494–95

variable pay, 219

vertical integration and, 860–61

See also piece rates

incomplete contracts

commitment problems, 787–89

decisionmaking and, 374

definition, 944

delegation and, 768, 786–89

employment contracts, 315, 316

enforcement, 928, 951

fact finding, 941–42

innovation and, 587–90

interpretation, 942, 944–47

models, 344, 787

moral hazard, 226–27

reasons for incompleteness, 945–46

relational, 718

research on, 952

responses, 856

transactions, 164–65, 171

unwanted terms, 947

See also contracts

independent contractors. *See* contractors

in-depth clinical papers. *See* clinical studies

India

business groups, 670–71

corruption, 1132, 1134, 1135, 1141–42, 1143–44

lean manufacturing, 292n24

teachers, 278–79

textile plants, 279–80

industrial organization

clinical studies, 199–200

double marginalization model, 859–60

insider econometric studies, 280n17

market structure, 873–74, 876, 877

multiproduct firms, 828

topics, 4

vertical integration, 853, 854, 855, 873–74

industry evolution, 874–75

inequality, 765

influence activities, 89–90, 375, 378, 397–98, 399, 483, 483n6, 828–29

influence costs, 89, 104n7, 181, 397, 399, 829

informal contracts. *See* relational contracts

information

acquisition, 86–87, 392–93, 394–95, 419–20

of employees, 405–7

endogenous flow, 407–8

hard and soft, 673

hidden, 1032, 1033, 1035, 1041–42

horizontal dispersion, 408–9

public, 382–83, 713

sharing, 1091–92

transmission, 862, 869–70

verifiable, 381–82, 389, 390

vertical dispersion, 407–8

See also asymmetric information; knowledge; private information

information-based networks, 1096–97

information intermediaries, 781–82

information processing

constraints, 607

coordination and, 607

costs, 343

decentralized, 606, 607, 630–34

delays, 632–35

by managers, 766

parallel computation, 634, 634f

real-time decentralized, 634–40

information technology (IT)

adoption effects, 294, 294n27

CAD/CAM, 26n6, 619, 875

empowerment, 619

enterprise resource planning, 27

human capital and, 28

industry structure, 881–82

innovation, 584

organizational change and, 820

returns to, 28–30, 28n8, 33–34, 34t

wages, 1171
See also government agencies
pure cash rights, 110, 111
pure control rights, 110, 111

quasi–integration, 1067, 1070, 1095
quiet-life hypothesis, 748n35
quotas, 205–6, 489, 490

R&D. *See* research and development
ratchet effect, 70, 206, 482, 546
rational choice perspective on public bureaucracy, 1150–51, 1154
reciprocity
    moral hazard and, 227
    norm, 92
    positive and negative, 235
    strong and weak, 233–34
    voluntary effort and, 226–28, 232–36, 238–39
    See also gift exchange
recruitment, 459, 489, 541, 550, 693, 776
red tape, 1116, 1122, 1123, 1125, 1127–28
reference points, 224
referral markets, 611–13
referrals, 362, 404
regulation
    antitrust, 182, 593, 911, 967
    banking, 347, 667
    of corporate governance, 735
    environmental, 735
    health and safety, 735
    of markets, 911
    of monopolies, 421–22
    transaction-cost economics and, 182–83, 183n37
relational contracts
    advantages, 1058–59
    authority, 369
    in blue-collar settings, 699–701, 700t, 701t
    clarity problem, 705, 714–22, 723
    competition and, 709n15
    costs, 708–10
    credibility problem, 683, 705, 714
    definition, 681, 969
    employment as, 316–18, 369
    enforcement, 928, 929–31, 969, 1093
    future research directions, 723
    games, 73, 930
    hybrid organizations, 1076–77, 1092–93

    imperfectly shared understandings, 715–18
    implementation problem, 703–5, 710–11
    incentives and, 72–75
    incomplete, 718
    job design and, 507
    managerial practices and, 696–97
    models, 697–99, 704–5, 708–10
    optimal, 74–75
    path dependence, 710, 712, 722–23
    private information and, 709–10, 1038–42
    reputations and, 1000
    self-enforcing, 72–73
    shared understandings, 719–22
    trust, 1060
    in white-collar settings, 701–3
relational incentive contracts
    classic applications, 1015–17
    definition, 1014
    employment model, 1017–21, 1018f, 1023–24, 1026
    enforcement, 1025–26, 1058
    future research directions, 1059–60
    incentives, 74
    multiple suppliers, 1042–46
    organizational design, 1051–56
    outsourcing model, 1021–23, 1022f, 1024–25
    partnerships, 1046–50
    performance measures, 1026–31
    private information, 1031–42
    rents, 1057–58
    research on, 1015
    specific investments, 1023–26, 1057
relational knowledge, 715
relative performance evaluation (RPE), 67, 77–78, 79, 484–86, 503
rents
    in interfirm contracts, 998–99
    quasi-, 65, 194, 966, 979, 1079
    in relational contracts, 1057–58
    sharing, 1080–82, 1084
rent seeking, 395–96, 661, 669–70
repeated games
    collusion, 697
    coordination, 720
    delegation, 419
    equilibria, 930
    formal authority, 352
    leadership, 443–44
    in networks, 709

schooling. *See* education

scientific research. *See* academia; pharmaceutical industry; research and development

scope economies
  joint production, 827
  of research and development, 869–70
  vertical integration, 853, 854

screening, 493, 541, 550, 821–22

seemingly similar enterprises (SSEs). *See* persistent performance differences

self-enforcing contracts, 72–73, 927–28, 969–70, 1015, 1092

self-investments, 124–25, 129, 131, 133, 138–39

semiconductors, 689

seniority, 483, 497

separation of powers, 1156, 1157–58, 1165, 1166

share contracts, 960, 964, 982, 983–85t, 986–90

shared beliefs, 469, 808, 813

shareholders
  blockholders, 752
  control, 755–56
  decisionmaking, 903–4
  dispersed, 751–53, 897
  dominant, 732, 734, 736, 752–54
  minority, 736
  protection of interests, 732, 734
  rights, 897, 904, 913
  self-dealing, 736, 752
  takeover bids and, 751–52
  threats to, 732, 736–38
  See also corporate governance; ownership; stock

shipping, 866, 879, 976, 978

signaling
  in decisionmaking models, 380–81
  by incentive systems, 494–95
  matching, 494
  by promotions, 521, 529–30, 531–35, 534n17, 539, 555

signaling games, 380–81, 440n22

signaling model of leadership, 81, 248, 380

signal jamming, 378–80, 399

Silicon Valley, 581–82, 596, 861, 1085, 1096

Singapore Airlines, 817–18

Skil, 824

skill development
  costs, 504
  employer-paid programs, 504–6
  in high-performance work systems, 691
  on-the-job training, 493n21, 552

multiskilling, 552, 554–55
  specialization, 608

skills
  firm-specific, 83–85, 552, 554
  technical, 28

Sloan, Alfred, 415–16, 841

small companies, 811, 988

social capital. *See* social networks

social comparison, 328–30

socialism, 606–7, 620, 791

social mobility, 765

social networks
  closed, 584
  of employees, 317n1
  of employers, 327
  experiments, 255
  knowledge spillovers and, 580–81
  of managers, 670
  productivity and, 273–74, 275, 286t
  of research teams, 583–84
  See also networks

social psychology
  corruption, 1144–45
  employment relationship, 315, 319
  experiments, 216
  fundamental attribution bias, 456–58, 722
  social comparison, 328

social relationships
  employment as, 315, 336–39
  norms, 335
  welfare internalization, 324–27

social structures. *See* social networks

sociology
  economic, 4
  employment relationship, 315, 319
  organizational, 4
  organizational ecology, 810n10
  social network characteristics, 584

soft authority, 364–67, 368

Sony, 825

source-of-strength doctrine, 667

Southwest Airlines, 691, 817, 818

spaghetti organization. *See* Oticon

span of control
  of CEOs, 619, 822, 823, 835
  increasing, 351n7, 613, 821, 822, 823, 835
  limits, 769

specialization
  international, 649–50

symmetric learning and insurance model, 525–27

turnover decisions, 539–40

See also internal labor markets; promotions

wages

decreases, 522

efficiency, 65, 321, 322, 486

fairness, 224, 236

in gift-exchange markets, 227–28, 232, 233

inequality, 500n33, 553, 649, 650

labor supply and, 223–24

monitoring and, 486–87

in public sector, 1171

reducing, 404–5

supervision and, 771–72

temporary increases, 223–24

See also compensation; incentives; piece rates

Walmart, 14, 668

weak-link coordination games, 240–43, 240t, 244–45, 251–53

welfare internalization, 324–27

Western Electric Company, Hawthorne Works, 205

white-collar settings, 694–96, 701–3

Williamson model of hierarchy, 769, 770, 794

worker collectives, 318

workers. *See* employment relationships; wages

workplace organization. *See* hierarchies; job design; organizational structure; teams

World Bank, 1109, 1133

Xerox Palo Alto Research Center, 816

yardstick competition, 793–94

yes men, 390

Zimmer, George, 322–23